David Wozniak
116 West Valley St.
Endicott, N.Y.

$1595

MOTIVATION: THEORY AND RESEARCH

MOTIVATION:
THEORY AND RESEARCH

C. N. Cofer
Professor of Psychology, Pennsylvania State University

M. H. Appley
Professor of Psychology, York University

JOHN WILEY & SONS, INC.
NEW YORK   LONDON   SYDNEY

To *the theorists and investigators whose work, both good and bad, we have used and perhaps abused, we gratefully dedicate this book.*

Preface

This book had its beginnings when we were, respectively, at the University of Maryland and Connecticut College. We had each separately undertaken writing efforts in attempts to clarify and understand the concept of motivation. At the time we began, there were no up-to-date treatments of either motivation theory or research, and we found the sources of relevant work varied, scattered, and extensive. As we each became more deeply involved in the project, and its scope became more evident, the idea of a collaboration turned from an inviting possibility to a sheer necessity, and our efforts were joined in the Fall of 1957. We must frankly confess, however, that the six years which this joint venture has required have not been as much due to the exigeant nature of the task itself as to the exigent nature of other duties incumbent on us as members of academic faculties. The book has remained a relentless task-master through the journeys of CNC, from Maryland through New York University and the University of California at Berkeley to Pennsylvania State University; and of MHA, from Connecticut through Southern Illinois University to York University. To the colleagues, students, libraries, and facilities of these institutions we record our indebtedness. One of us (MHA) is also indebted to the National Science Foundation whose award of a Science Faculty Fellowship took him to the Universities of Southern California and Montreal during the tenure of this writing.

We have looked at the literature extensively and in depth and report it in our chapters in length and in some detail. Such clarification as we have achieved is recorded in the numerous sectional summaries and in Chapter 16. This final chapter must be regarded only as a progress report, rather than a final solution, however, since neither of us feels completely comfortable with the resolution we have achieved there.

Insofar as possible, we have attempted to keep our material up to date, but the desire to do so has vastly exceeded the possibility. In

1960–1961, having gone beyond our first reasonable deadline, we revised and updated the approximately 400 pages completed to that time, so as to retain a comparable contemporaneity throughout the book. Despite our best continuing efforts to take account of new publications, undoubtedly some authors will feel that their recent contributions have not been given the attention they deserve. Our coverage is good through 1961, less adequate for 1962, and spotty for 1963. Before the critic whose just complaint is the one of incompleteness, we bow our heads; but prepotent over the response of *mea culpa* is the one of *let him try it*. Of two things we can be certain: our own conscientiousness in attempting to be fair and sympathetic (to the extent that our own biases permitted us an objective view of the field) to the various theorists whose views we have treated; and that the coverage and its attendant extensive bibliography can serve the student as a bridge to the vast primary literature. Our chapters should, we believe, make the writing of their sequels considerably easier than they themselves were to produce.

A work taking so long to accomplish, covering so wide a range of fields, and filling so many pages has many silent contributors in addition to the authors in whose words the final product appears. Parts of this book have been read by colleagues and students too numerous to list by name. Many have made comments which have influenced and improved our treatment of one topic or another. We acknowledge a special indebtedness to Robert R. Holt for his very extensive comments on Chapter 12, and we express appreciation for the encouraging and generally constructive commentary to Gordon Allport, Harry F. Harlow, Ernest R. Hilgard, Ross R. Stagner, and Elliot Stellar. Needless to say, we did not always follow the advice we received, and the responsibility for the content of the chapters which follow must remain ours alone.

Since we have both traveled and changed our institutional affiliations since the beginning of this project, a more than usual number of secretaries have had a hand in the typing of manuscripts and compiling of references. They share in their anonymity the credit and the blame for accuracy and errors alike. We shall probably never know the full toll of amanuentic license which has crept in to modify quotations and dates, for example, as the manuscript went through successive revisions. Mrs. Marilyn Moske and Mrs. Clara Bornemisa were the most recent secretaries participating in the final drafts and we owe them a debt of gratitude, as we do to Miss Julie Kranhold, whose blue pencil culled most, if not all, of the grammatical and stylistic errors the manuscript contained.

Finally, we acknowledge that permission to quote or reproduce materials has been received from many individuals and publishers. Specific acknowledgments are made in the text by reference to the full citations in the bibliography.

C.N.C.
M.H.A.

University Park, Pennsylvania
Toronto, Ontario
December, 1963

Contents

Chapter 1

The Concept of Motivation

No matter where we begin the study of psychological processes or phenomena, we must sooner or later deal with the problem of motivation. The literature of experimental psychology—whether of learning or of perceptual processes, of animal or human behavior—is replete with assumptions and hypotheses about underlying motivational principles. Likewise in the various attempts to develop integrative personological or behavioral theories, key roles are assigned to motivational concepts.

The reason for this central location of motivational constructs in psychological systems is quite simple. It helps to account for behavior more easily. The very wide variations amongst existing behavior theories do not contradict this basic truth. They simply attest to the fact that when explanatory systems are constructed to deal with so complex an area as organismic behavior, the particular types of concepts used and the relative weights assigned to each may differ widely from system to system.

Our purpose in this volume is to examine some of the main forms which motivational concepts have assumed in the major theoretical systems current in psychology today. In order to realize this purpose, we have first attempted to assemble some of the historic background of the problem both generally and in relation to each of the more-or-less systematic positions. For each of the systems discussed, we have tried to show how the need for one or more motivational constructs developed and how the system attempts to account for the motivational phenomena with which it deals.

MOTIVATION AND BEHAVIOR

Scientific psychology, as currently defined, studies *behavior*. When we ask questions about the "why" of behavior we are seeking information about processes *not* directly observable in an individual's overt actions, or even from his verbalizations about his covert actions. The processes we must study are only indirectly inferable, painstakingly and tentatively, from the events available to direct observation or assessment.

To complicate matters further, inferable processes are not all of the same order. Any set of events or phenomena can be studied from many points of view and at different levels of complexity. Thus animal (including human) behavior can be studied as a function of its physical, chemical, or biological substrata, as an aspect of a man-environment system; or as an integral component of a social complex. Changes in behavior may be considered a result, either temporary or permanent, of structural modifications of cells in the nervous system, of the unfolding of an invariate sequence of precoded events in a living computer, or as the happenstantial effect of environmental events external to (and independent of) any particular organism under study.

MOTIVATION AND PSYCHOLOGY

Because the field of behavior study is so enormous, and the possibilities of subdivision so many, numbers of groupings, subgroupings, and regroupings have been tried since the beginnings of scientific psychology. The problems to be treated in this book have at various times been (1) incorporated as subordinate parts of larger areas, such as the study of personality or of learning processes; (2) ignored, as in structuralism and early experimental psychophysics; or (3) treated as a separate set of problems worthy of independent focus, as in many current approaches. In 1952, Wolfle et al. assigned an independent role to motivation in the psychology curriculum as both a theoretical area and an investigative field. A series of symposia on motivation theory, started in 1953 (Brown et al., 1953; Jones, 1954–on), proved so successful that annual volumes of papers from successive symposia have been issued since. And within the past decade, at least a dozen new volumes have been devoted exclusively to treatments of the motivation field (Atkinson, 1958a; Bindra, 1959; Brown, 1961; Hall, 1961; Leeper & Madison, 1959; Lindzey, 1958; Madsen, 1959; McClelland, 1955a; Maslow, 1954; Olds, 1956; Peters, 1958; Stacey and DeMartino, 1958; Toman, 1960; Woodworth, 1958; and Young, 1961).

This recent growth of interest in motivation has come about in several ways. Theories and research in perceptual and learning processes have led to the need for more information about underlying differences in response-likelihoods not attributable apparently to sensory processes or to habits. Studies of personality organization, predictive efficiency of psychometrics, group dynamics, and clinical and abnormal behavior have again and again produced a need for concepts dealing with intervening processes presumably of a motivational character.

A scientific study of behavior must either stem from or arrive at a set of principles (or a system) in the context of which individual events are predictable.[1] Both behavior theory and personality theory are replete with assumptions and hypotheses about underlying motivational principles. It is our impression that these principles were developed to account for variability which was left unexplained by the concepts of perception, habit, and personality structure.

NATURE OF THIS BOOK

In this present book we intend to examine the major views, currently extant, in terms of their significance both to the contexts from which they derive and to general psychological science. In view of the scope of the problem areas which these theoretical systems attempt to encompass, it is not unexpected that many of their concepts will appear to be both sweeping and vague. There is little doubt that each system has some postdictive value and that all are serious attempts to provide comprehensive accounts of phenomena within their scope. The sophisticated reader will have familiarity with one or more of these systematic approaches, and may use this knowledge to compare systems. We would offer the caution, however, that both the language and the applications of any one point of view derive from a setting which must be taken into account, if the *systematic* value of the approach is to be appreciated. Our treatment attempts to provide this contextual framework, at the same time offering a basis for comparison of the different views on certain critical questions.

To increase the comprehensiveness of our own efforts, critical reviews are presented not only of the major theoretical systems of motivation, but also of fundamental research in the field which is not part of any one systematic outlook. Throughout this book, as has been earlier implied, we are concerned primarily with concepts and evidence pertinent to motivational constructs themselves, rather than motivational concepts secondary to principles of learning, perception, or personality organization. To be sure, we could not ignore the relevance of these latter contexts in dealing with our subject, but we have made a deliberate attempt to focus on the motivational principles

---

[1] It is too soon to presume to answer the question of whether psychology will eventuate as a nomothetic or ideographic discipline—whether general principles will be found applicable to specific instances or whether we will have to evolve highly individualized personological concepts from which to make our predictions.

independent of the value, completeness, or adequacy they may have in the behavior or personality system which they serve.

SOME GENERAL OBSERVATIONS

In preparing this book, we have been impressed with a number of very evident facts. First, that *all* psychological theories use motivation-like variables. Some theories give them more importance in their particular system than others. Some identify them with real or inferred events, while others treat them only as convenient fictions. Second, the type of motivational construct used is likely to be consistent with the philosophical origins of the larger theory, even if it becomes necessary to extend the motivational concept by assigning a quite new meaning(s) to it. Third, the use of the same concept-name by more than one theorist is no guarantee that he seeks common ground with a second user, or, more specifically, that he means the same thing when he uses the same term. And fourth, it is clear that evidence in support of a theory is more often gathered for just that purpose—from instances and settings and in ways likely to prove congenial to the view in question—rather than in a manner likely to provide a critical test of the theoretical system which gave rise to it.

A notable omission here, because it would have extended the scope beyond reasonable bounds, and because it is outside the limits of our intentions in producing this book, is any extensive treatment of motivation as it affects particular kinds of behavior. As a specific example, the so-called new look in perception (cf. Bruner, 1958) has given rise to considerable research and some speculation on the role of motivational variables in perceptual distortion. Where relevant, such studies are mentioned, but an inclusive treatment of such data is more appropriate to a study of perception than it is to us here. Likewise, effects of motivation on learning have been widely studied for many years (cf. Hilgard, 1956). We have extensively sampled this voluminous literature and extracted from it that which seemed of use to our treatment of motivation theory—namely, such assumptions, principles, and relevant data regarding motivation as were to be found in studies of learning (e.g., related to concepts of drive, incentive, reinforcement). Any extensive treatment of the precise role (or adequacy) of these concepts in explaining habit, expectancy, or response acquisition has been excluded here.

Finally, the reader will recognize some similarity between the motivation theories treated here and some of the better known personality theories (e.g., those examined by Hall and Lindzey [1957] in their survey). As in the case of learning and perception theories, motivational assumptions and principles have been identified in the contexts of personality theories but examined in their own right.

SOME COMMON TERMS AND COMMON PROBLEMS

Before proceeding to a review of the history of motivation theories and the examination of current models and research data, we may profit from a preliminary discussion of some common terms and common problems. When the hypothetical man on the street asks, "What motivates behavior?" he is asking to have identified one or a combination of three kinds of things: (1) an *environmental determinant* which precipitated the behavior in question—the application of some irresistible force which of necessity led to this action; (2) the internal *urge, wish, feeling, emotion, drive, instinct, want, desire, demand, purpose, interest, aspiration, plan, need,* or *motive* which gave rise to the action; or (3) the *incentive, goal,* or *object value* which attracted or repelled the organism.

In the case of the first of these alternatives, the *why* question is addressed to causation probably independent of the organism, whereas in the second and third instances, a hypothetical internal state is posited. In other words, wherever no clearly identifiable relationship is found between an environmental and a behavioral event, some hypothesized intervening event(s) is (are) postulated to account for the behavior (see p. 9). Some of these intervening events themselves are capable of being specified, others not. Thus, an endocrine discharge into the bloodstream, a change in the electrical potential of a nerve, a heightening of muscle tonus, or a peristaltic movement of the intestines can be identified, isolated, and measured. Less obvious are inferred changes in the organization of the memory system, the intensity of a wish or drive, the valence of a goal. We can specify certain antecedent events and measure extensity of resultant behaviors. The discrepancies between antecedents and consequents leave room for considerable speculation as to the nature of the mediating systems, processes, or mechanisms. It is into this void that men have poured their ideas about motivation, offering one or another model to fill the gap of knowledge.

With this framework in mind, let us look at some of the terms we have mentioned. They would seem to divide themselves into three categories: those having *biological* import (emotion, force, drive, instinct, need), those having *"mental"* import (urge, wish, feeling, impulse, want, striving, desire, demand), and those having reference to *objects or states in the environment* (purpose, interest, intention, attitude, aspiration, plan, motive, incentive, goal, value). These are neither mutually exclusive nor even necessarily correct classifications. On the other hand, the terms represent spectra of meaning on one or more of biosocial, push-pull, innate-acquired, body-mind, present-future continua. The terms have in common only the fact that they are used to represent, more or less and in different ways, states or conditions of the organism having to do with the vigor, persistence or direction of behavior. The subtleties of the differences among the terms could never be examined exhaustively, because they are used in different ways at different times, even by the same writers. We would not be foolish enough, at the outset of a work intended to permit comparison of theories, to try to legislate this matter of language usage. At best, we shall try in each instance, where a term is to be used in a new setting for the first time, to give as clearly as possible the precise meaning and referents intended by its user.

The models used to describe motivational processes vary considerably. They range from purely biogenic hypotheses, in which behavior unfolds from a series of innate drives or instincts, following willy-nilly the course prescribed by the set of built-in determinants forcing action upon the environment, to highly sociogenic theories which suggest the almost complete docility of behavior and its moldability into patterns determined by cultural forces. Motives may be seen to be conscious or unconscious, pushed inexorably by urges, drives, and instincts or pulled inevitably by incentives, goals, purposes, and values.

One view may hold that man is a biological beast—the slave of his bodily needs and active only when these needs require him to provide means to their reduction. The fabric of society, such a position would maintain, is built upon this biological base. Or, equally plausibly, perhaps, an opposing view would hold that man is a creative, self-actualizing organism—freeing himself from his bodily tensions incidentally as part of an unfolding god-like nature.

Man's needs, it may be agreed, are body-bound. But man's wants, some would argue, soar beyond these needs. Motives may be seen as energy arising from unfulfillment and directed toward gratification. Learning, for most theories, plays an important directing role, although the inevitability of certain need-gratifier relations may be claimed to determine some of the direction, if the organism is to survive.

With what, then, are we dealing? First, an organism capable of stimulation and of response. It is possessed of an energy system—a system able to respond differentially to stimulation and thus able to store and to convert energy at least partly independently of outside forces. The animal system is metabolic—constantly expending energy in the process of self-maintenance and thus constantly in need of replenishing its energy sources. At a minimum level, then, it engages in responses effective in maintaining itself. Where the environment is permissive or plentiful, minimum survival level is assured even with a limited response repertory. Such a situation can be observed in lower species and in defective members of higher species. A rather primitive theory of motivation may be sufficient to account for this simple order of behavior. On the other hand, the apparently long-range, complex, goal-directed behavior of higher species and especially of man—the delayed, involved, and sometimes seemingly self-defeating behaviors—seems less likely accountable for on the basis of biological need-dominated responding.

What we might expect to find is that theories dealing primarily with simple behaviors in simple organisms studied under relatively straightforward situations would put forth clear and somewhat unsophisticated hypotheses. Those theories attempting to account for complex social behavior in man should be pressed to develop complicated models involving multiple variables. What the reader will find, however, is that the complexities and subtleties of the theoretical models proposed bear little relation to the behavior samples studied, but are often presented as having universal application.

SOME DEFINITIONS OF MOTIVATION

It is traditional for authors to define their topic in the preface or first chapter of a book. In this book, however, certain difficulties present themselves in the definitions of terms, as the reader is already aware. What is motivation? It is a field of psychological investigation concerned with certain types of phenomena and events. What are these? Unfortunately, the answer to this question will differ somewhat with the orientation of the tradition from which it derives. We shall have more to say about some of these traditions later in this chapter. The best way for us to handle this question here might be to cite some of the varied definitions which have been given. The scope of the subject will then reveal itself.

P. T. Young has stated the matter well in his recently revised and expanded *Motivation and Emotion* (1961), offering at the same time his own definition of the concept:

The concept of motivation is exceedingly broad—so broad, in fact, that psychologists have attempted to narrow it. . . . [singling] out one aspect or another of the complex processes of determination. The two most important aspects are the *energetic* aspect and . . . *regulation and direction.* [We may] . . . define the study of motivation broadly as *a search for determinants (all determinants) of human and animal activity* (p. 24).

He sees motivation more specifically as ". . . *the process of arousing action, sustaining the activity in progress, and regulating the pattern of activity*" (p. 24). Gardner Murphy (1947) considers motivation as the "*General name for the fact that an organism's acts are partly determined by its own nature or internal structure*" (p. 991). On the other hand, N. R. F. Maier (1949) used the term motivation to "characterize the process by which the expression of behavior is determined or its future expression is influenced by consequences to which such behavior leads" (p. 93).

In 1949, D. O. Hebb wrote that ". . . the chief problem that the psychologist is concerned with, when he speaks of motivation, is not arousal of activity but its patterning and direction" (p. 172). Further, in his own terms, he wrote:

The term motivation then refers (1) to the existence of an organized phase sequence, (2) to its direction or content, and (3) to its persistence in a given direction, or stability of content.

This definition means that "motivation" is not a distinctive process, but a reference in another context to the same processes to which "insight" refers; it also means that the waking, normal adult animal always has some motivation . . . (p. 181).

Hebb later re-examined the question, and in an excellent example of self-correction on the basis of further evidence and analysis, reversed himself, separating cue and arousal aspects of sensory events. Only the latter are motivational concepts: "Without a foundation of arousal, the cue function cannot exist . . . arousal . . . is synonymous with a general drive state . . . the drive is an energizer, but not a guide . . ." (1955, p. 249). And, again, drive is ". . . some process [which] provides the energy of movement but . . . like the engine of an automobile, does not determine what the movement will be" (1958, p. 157).

Atkinson (1958*a*) also incorporates the vigilance or arousal function, but ties it closely to the cue functions of situations, thus: "The term motivation refers to the arousal of a tendency to act to produce one or more effects. The term motivation points to the final strength of the action tendency which is experienced by the person as an 'I want to . . .' The particular aim of the momentary state of motivation is situationally defined" (p. 602). And Maslow (1954) writes: "Sound motivational theory should . . . assume that motivation is constant, never ending, fluctuating, and complex, and that it is an almost universal characteristic of practically every organismic state of affairs" (p. 69). Brown (1961) considers a specific variable motivational: "(1) if it tends to facilitate or energize several different responses, (2) if its termination or removal following a new response leads to the learning of that response, (3) if sudden increases in the strength of the variable leads to the abandonment of responses, and (4) if its effects on behavior cannot be attributed to other processes such as learning, sensation, innate capacities, and sets" (p. 55).

Having cited some of the differences in emphases, let us turn now to a discussion of some of the bases on which a comparison of theories can be made.

COMPARISONS OF VIEWPOINTS

We have stressed that there is no one set of phenomena, or conditions under which behavioral phenomena occur, with which all motivational theorists are concerned. Some writers focus attention on one thing and others on another. The kind of evidence sought in relation to and integrated by the several theories, therefore, tends to vary. Comparative evaluation of theories and of the adequacy with which they encompass available data is made difficult by this diversity of interest. Nevertheless, comparative evaluation is, we think, desirable; and in this section we outline a number of issues and questions concerning motivation which may guide the reader in his examination of the theories and the evidence. In addition, we point to traditions from which inquiry has emerged as an important reason that the interests of investigators vary as much as they do.

Why Is the Motivation Construct Used?

The subject matter of the behavioral sciences is, of course, the behavior of the living organism. Yet these disciplines use terms and concepts which appear to involve processes that are not apparent in this behavior. A man runs—slow or fast; he runs one way rather than another; he runs under some conditions but not under others. The behavioral fact is that he runs and does so at a given speed, at a given time, in a given place, and in a given direction. In this raw behavior and its properties we do not directly see perception, habit, motivation, attitude, values, or thought. Yet these terms, and many others like them (such as those listed on page 5), form a large part of the lexicon of the behavioral sciences; behaviors such as running do not. What are such terms and why are they used instead of the direct behavioral descriptions?

The answer to the first of these questions is that these terms refer to concepts or constructs which are postulated to account for the behavior observed. Why are they used? To this question we must answer that behavior is too varied, complex, and intertwined a phenomenon to be spoken of without analysis. And these terms provide an analytic framework of processes in terms of which behavior may be classified or ordered and conceptualized. There is, to be sure, a danger in concepts which go beyond behavior itself and the conditions with which it is associated; much of the confusion and argument in the behavioral sciences arises from the failure to delimit concepts precisely to specific behaviors and their associated conditions. We can only maintain an alert vigilance over the use of such concepts by constantly restating their behavioral and circumstantial referents.

So far, it is clear that the motivation construct must have been developed to correspond to certain properties of behavior—properties for which other constructs are presumed not to be sufficient. In general, this is historically true. However, as we shall see throughout this book, there is still a question about the necessity of the motivation construct as such. We are required to ask whether there are any properties of behavior which uniquely require it, and whether other concepts of demonstrated usefulness are sufficient without it.

First let us look at some general *conceptions* of the nature of behavior which require the motivation construct to have a central role. Such conceptions involve a commitment to the motivation concept, without concern for identifying those specific characteristics of behavior that are uniquely motivational. After we have examined the nature of such conceptual commitments to motivation, we will turn to the specific aspects of behavior which have been used to identify motivational variables in behavior.

Conceptual Commitment to Motivation. It is often said that *all* behavior is motivated and that behavior serves the organism's needs. Without motivation an organism would not behave; it would be an inert lump, doing virtually nothing. Galvanized into action by a need, it would engage in actions motivated by that need, and its actions would continue until the need was satisfied. The actions *serve* the need; the behavior is the instrument by which the need is satisfied. Behavior is a means, not an end.

We shall see, in the next chapter, that these notions concerning motivation arose from the influence of evolutionary theory and physicalistic biology on comparative psychology, on the study of learning, and on the psychoanalytic study of mental illness. Animals were thought to be moved by internal sources or drives; organisms seemed to learn if drive satisfactions occurred; and abnormal behaviors were believed to stem from urges and wishes which were largely unconscious. From observations such as these, it was easy to generalize that all behavior is motivated and that behavior serves as a device of adjustment in the presence of needs.]

These conclusions marked a major step forward in the study of behavior. They permitted a deterministic view to be taken of behavior, which earlier had often been attributed to such agencies as the soul or free will. Motivational concepts, in this context, appeared to be primary causative factors. But it is not necessarily true that all the causative factors for behavior are motivational ones.

Behavior can occur under an externally applied force—such as a shove—and this is not a motivational cause, though it is a cause. More importantly, we can speak of the physical structure of the organism, its sensory and perceptual capacities, its motor abilities, and the like, as factors causative in its behavior. Further, habits, after they have been formed, can certainly be seen as psychologically causative in subsequent behavior. There are many causes of behavior, and motivation is only one of them.

In dynamic and purposive psychologies, however, there is a tendency to think of motivation as a more basic or root cause than many of the others. Perhaps this is because restless activity seems to be a primary consequence of states of need, and because conflicts and frustrations seem to focus around activities with high affective significance.

But activity or behavior is a fact of life; that is, by its very nature activity is a property of living organisms. It does not add much to assert that all behavior is motivated, unless the assertion leads to attempts to identify motivational properties in specific behavioral events (see next section). Further, if to be alive is to be active, it may be that behavior is an end in itself, rather than serving only as an instrument of need satisfaction. Conflicts and frustrations involve complex experiences in a social environment; they probably do not represent unalloyed motivational variables.

Another facet of the general commitment to motivation is that functional biology and functional psychology tended to think in homeostatic terms. Behavior was conceived as adjustment—a means to rectify the imbalance caused by tissue needs or deficits. When hunger arose, for example, behavior occurred which led to finding and eating food, thus restoring the depleted tissue. Behavior is here instrumental, but it is seen as part of an overall system, with balance or equilibrium of the system as the sign that needs are at rest. Behavior is a response to disequilibrium. Some writers have gone even further to define psychological health as a continuing ability to satisfy certain needs.

Specific Motivational Properties of Behavior. Many more specific characteristics of behavior are utilized by other writers in defining motivation or identifying motivational variables. In some instances, these aspects are related to the general considerations just outlined. For example, energization is related to the proposition that all behavior is motivated and direction to the proposition that behavior serves the organism's needs. We turn now to five specific properties of behavior.

1. *Energization or facilitation of a variety of responses.* Notions of general drive or arousal states which interact with innate or habitual response tendencies to produce behavior have been advanced by Hull (1943), Brown (1953, 1961), Spence (1956), and Farber (1954, 1955), among others. Their point is that motivational processes as such do not control or guide *specific* forms of behavior but influence behavior by energizing innate or associative tendencies. The specificity, direction, appropriateness, persistence, goal-directedness, or apparent purposiveness of behavior are attributed to nonmotivational factors like habit, albeit that some of the stimuli which control such habits may have a remote motivational origin.

2. *Behavioral vigor and efficiency.* Weak stimuli may sometimes be the occasion for vigorous responses, whereas sometimes weak responses may occur in the presence of strong stimulation. Or, despite unvarying stimulation, responses may vary in vigor, or conversely, response vigor may remain constant despite varying stimulation. The energy expended in behavior, as revealed in its vigor, is often said to indicate the need for motivational concepts, especially when energy variations do not accord with the levels of environmental stimulation (Brown, 1961; Underwood, 1949). Activation theorists, such as Duffy, Malmo, Lindsley, Schlosberg, and Hebb (see Chapter 8), tend to concentrate on the efficiency or adequacy with which behavioral events occur as evidence of an underlying arousal, that is, motivated, state. Arousal has many parallels to the general drive of drive theory (see Chapter 10), but the relation of arousal to specific acts of behavior is not so explicitly suggested in activation theory as it is in drive theory.

3. *The direction of behavior.* Behavior is often described as guided, directed, goal-oriented, persistent, or purposive. Such a characterization may describe its occurrence in a short sequence or over extended periods of time, or may describe facts of choice, preference, or decision. This selective, directed character of behavior is, for writers like Young (1961), McClelland, et al. (1953), Hebb (1949), Bindra (1959), and Irwin (1958), the critical property of behavior which leads to postulation of a motivational process. It should be remembered that the directional aspect of behavior is attributed to associative, not moti-

vational, processes by others.) Muenzinger (1942) saw as the proper unit for behavioral investigation a sequence of specific acts initiated and directed by a motivating state and ending when the motivating state was ended. McGeoch (1942) and Melton (1941) also suggested the completion of a specific response sequence as one evidence that a motivating process had ended.

4. *Reinforcement.* A response sequence is often terminated by commerce with a goal object. Such an encounter, with or without the actual consumption of the goal object, frequently strengthens the behavior which has led up to it. When such strengthening occurs, it is called reinforcement. Miller (1951a), Brown (1953, 1961), and Farber (1954, 1955) have indicated that the occurrence of reinforcement permits the inference that a motivational variable must have been active in the behavior sequence.

5. *Weakening of behavior.* Brown (1961) has suggested that the weakening or cessation of behavior, when aversive stimulation (punishment) is a consequence of it, may qualify as evidence for asserting that the aversive stimulation has motivational status.

In summary, there are both conceptual reasons and specific behavioral properties which have suggested to theorists that motivation is an essential construct. Some of these conceptual commitments involve the assertions that all behavior is motivated and that behavior serves the needs of the organism. Reasons for these ideas and problems they raise were outlined. There are a number of more specific aspects of behavior which have seemed to theorists to be uniquely motivational. However, theorists do not agree as to which ones are crucial, and these differences will be further analyzed in this book. At the moment we must be content with the statement that any one or any combination of the following points about behavior may lead to the postulation of a motivational process: that behavior occurs at all, that a variety of responses is facilitated by some operation (like deprivation of food), that responses vary in vigor, that behavior has direction, that certain kinds of subsequent event may strengthen (and other kinds may weaken) a behavioral sequence. The reader may ask of each theory whether it purports to deal with these points, whether it is adequate to do so, and whether the evidence concerning these issues permits a choice in favor of or against a viewpoint as compared with others.

SOME PERVADING ISSUES

In addition to the reasons that the motivation construct is advanced, there are a number of general issues on which viewpoints can be compared. Such issues are relevant to the problem of motivation, but are not specific to it, as they arise concerning many other aspects of the study of behavior as well. We define these issues briefly.

1. *Emphasis on innate or acquired processes in behavior.* A controversy of long standing pertains to the extent that features of behavior may be attributed to the experiences of an organism after birth or to characteristics which are present at birth or, being present in potential, unfold in the course of maturation and development. This nature-nurture issue arises in the case of specific behaviors, such as mating and maternal activities. It is also present in the overall judgment as to whether nature or nurture is the most important determiner of the aggregate of characteristics of the human or infrahuman animal. Research of recent years, if it has indicated nothing else, has shown that the nature-nurture problem is a complex one and that there are intricate interrelations between environmental stimulation and the unfolding of behavioral potentialities. We will examine the evidence carefully as to the role of these factors in specific behaviors. We think, however, that it is a sterile enterprise to attempt to estimate the relative contributions of nature and nurture to the sum of any animal's characteristics.

2. *Conscious and unconscious factors in behavior.* Great argument has raged over the place of processes of which we are aware and of processes of which we are unaware in determining what we feel, do, and think. Part of this controversy results from inadequate definition of terms and from a ready hypostatization of conscious and unconscious tendencies; the latter is illustrated by such phrases as "the unconscious" or "the conscious." It is clear to us that behavioral processes may be described as conscious or as unconscious or more appropriately in terms of degree of availability to consciousness or conscious recall; but that the entities of "consciousness" or of "the unconscious" are not useful. Even more important is the point that most of what is meant by the word "conscious" is more legitimately indicated by the phrase "verbally reported," and much of what is meant by the word "unconscious" is made clearer by the phrase "unreported verbally." Actually, the terms "reportable" and "unreportable" reflect dimensions of the above distinctions which have even greater significance to the problem involved. In other words, the real problem of consciousness is the degree to (or conditions under) which material is reportable, rather than whether it is (or how much of it is) reported or not.

3. *Is behavior primary or is it instrumental?* We have alluded to this issue before. When we take behavior as primary, we describe it and attempt to discover the conditions of which it is a function and

perhaps what consequences it has. But we need not look for what functions the behavior has, so far as the welfare and the economy of the organism are concerned. When we do the latter we tend to look at behavior less as it is and more as how it serves the organism, that is, what is its instrumental value?

This issue is one which, unlike the two preceding, is not in principle capable of decision either through careful definition of terms or careful study of behavior itself and of the conditions under which it occurs. It is more like an attitude or an orientation in terms of which a phenomenon is examined. We try to look at behavior from both sides of this issue, attempting to point out at least some of the consequences of holding either point of view.

4. *Is organismic functioning conservative or growth-oriented?* This issue is closely related both to the one above and the one that follows. Does the organism's behavior serve primarily to maintain a steady state or equilibrium, that is, is it homeostatically organized and conservative? Or, alternatively, does the organism's behavior serve to take it to new levels of development, unfolding potentialities that a conservative principle could not encompass? Growth, or as it is sometimes called, actualization of potential, is often regarded as opposed to homeostatic balance or equilibrium maintenance.

Again we have the impression that these are essentially attitudinal differences. It is difficult to find evidential criteria by which these differences may be resolved.

5. *The nature of human nature.* This is a central question in the minds of many who are interested in motivation. Is man—unfettered and untarnished by the experiences and constraints of society—essentially good, altruistic, brotherly, creative, peace-loving? Or, alternatively, is he essentially bad, egocentric, aggressive, competitive, warlike, requiring the constraints of society in order to keep him from destroying his fellows and himself?

We think that one should make no prior assumptions on this issue. Instead, we should look to the circumstances of past and present life as the sources of man's "human nature." In doing so it is apparent that we are aligning ourselves with an emphasis on nurture rather than on original nature.

Caveat lector!

TRADITIONS

The study of behavior has, as we have seen, many facets and is carried out for many reasons. One reason that an observer investigates behavior, and selects the aspects of it which he examines, may lie in the tradition of inquiry to which he owes allegiance. There are various such traditions and their presuppositions often determine, in important ways, what an investigator will do, what he deems to be important, how he will regard the work of others, and, perhaps, how he will interpret his findings. Although the lines of separation among the traditions are not sharply defined, and although theorists cannot easily be classified as belonging to one tradition or another, there is yet enough disparity in the attitudes, goals, and commitments of the traditions to justify concern with what they are. Three traditions have especial pertinence to motivation.

1. *Philosophic-theological tradition.* Persons interested in philosophical and theological problems frequently have concern for certain issues already described, especially the one dealing with human nature. Such concern arises from philosophical interest in moral conduct and ethical principle, from concern about freedom of choice, from the theory of political association, the nature of historical causation, esthetics, religion, and the like. An investigator from this tradition will display interest in matters motivational with which other investigators may be impatient. The impatience is likely to be reciprocated.

2. *Biological tradition.* The scientific tradition is chiefly represented in the study of motivation by the general field of biology, as seen in the heritage of evolutionary theory and in the physicalistic approach to biological phenomena. Ethologists, medical investigators, physiologists, comparative psychologists, and experimental psychologists (particularly the learning theorists) are generally in this tradition. The emphases tend to be on adaptation to the environment in the interests of survival, an objective, quantitative approach to problems, and, where possible, an experimental analysis of the behavior in question. Investigators of this stamp have usually confined themselves to relatively limited classes of phenomena to the study of which they devote intensive work. As a rule (although the rule has many exceptions), this kind of investigator would have relatively little concern for issues such as those involving consciousness and the nature of human nature. He would probably tend to emphasize some type of homeostatic model in his thinking. Medical investigators, including many psychiatrists and psychoanalysts dealing with clinical problems, stem from this tradition. Their interest in the *ab*normal presumes a normal from which the behavior they observe varies, and their concern for human neurosis and psychosis in the individual patient often limits the generality of their findings. The clinical nature

of so much of their work makes it difficult for them to subject their hypotheses to experimental analysis.

√ 3. *Cultural tradition.* Interest in the behavior of social classes, societies, and cultures and their variations often leads to a concern with motivational problems. It is not surprising, then, that social psychologists, anthropologists, and sociologists develop hypotheses concerning motivation. Their hypotheses generally tend to relate motivational processes to the experiences of individuals in their particular cultures. Investigators in this tradition, while often aware of biological factors and responsive to them, are likely to emphasize cultural determination through experience rather than universal biological characteristics or biological predeterminism.

The three sets of traditions we have outlined encompass most of those to which the viewpoints and the research covered in this book may be ordered. There are many others, such as those which stress individual differences and those which are highly empirical and utilize very few concepts. From time to time reflections of these and of still other traditions will be seen in the chapters of this book.

PLAN OF THIS BOOK

As we have already indicated, the term "motivation" applies to many problems. The specific aspects of behavior, which in one view or another have been taken as its hallmarks, obviously spread its scope to a very wide range of phenomena. Some writers have narrowed the definition of motivation and therefore have reduced the span of their coverage. We have chosen otherwise. We attempt to represent most of the viewpoints and many of the data collected under a wide variety of definitions or conceptions of motivation.

We begin (Chapter 2) by portraying the historical development of motivational concepts in psychology, trying to understand why these concepts have in the past several decades come to have such central importance in thought about behavior. In the centuries before, they did not. We then treat biological aspects of motivation, such as instinct as used in ethology (Chapter 3), specific instinctive behaviors and drives (Chapter 4), bodily drives such as hunger and thirst (Chapter 5), activity and exploration (Chapter 6), and homeostasis (Chapter 7). These come first, because we believe the origins of the motivational concept lie in biology, and much of the thinking about motivation has been molded by this biological heritage. The homeostatic model represents a synthesis of much biological knowledge, and it has been extended to include social processes. Next, we turn to emotion and hedonic theories (Chapter 8), which have a long history and have lately been conceived to have major motivational significance. Conflict, frustration, and stress represent areas of related empirical study of great interest (Chapter 9). The concept of drive has been used synonymously with motivation (Chapter 10), and the study of learning has been closely linked to drive-like notions (Chapter 11). In its treatment, we extend the range of our coverage somewhat to deal with the effects of motivation on behavior, since this is the major interest of learning or behavior theorists in motivation, as it is of students of personality. Psychoanalysis has been called the most complete theory of motivation (Chapter 12), and it has been extended to cover a wide range of phenomena. Self-actualization, in which psychological health seems to be the major interest of theorists as far as motivation is concerned, is discussed in Chapter 13. Problems of motivation in human beings are dealt with in Chapter 14. And in Chapter 15, we speak of motivation developed in social contexts.

Finally, in Chapter 16, we bring together some common assumptions of the different motivation theories and offer a set of integrating concepts upon which we feel a sound psychology of motivation can be developed.

for our purposes, in his doctrine of the souls. There were three
of souls: the *vegetative*, involved in propagation and other basic
ns and found in all living things; the *sensitive* soul, which was
ed by animals and men and which had (in addition to sensing)
wer of locomotion as well as appetite; and the *rational* soul,
on, possessed only by man. In his rationality, man partakes of
divine and immortal.

cannot, within the limits of our space and purposes, enter into
ccount of dualism. The brief discussion of the classical Greeks
at least the point at which it entered philosophy, its contrast
onism, and something of its nature. The contrast of body with
mind has remained a constant issue in Western philosophy,
ristotle through the Church philosophers like Augustine and
to Descartes and beyond. Mind and soul, being immaterial,
ually seen as being beyond investigation except by rational
hat is, by speculative inquiry. And to pretend to investigate
tters by other methods led one to the risk of being charged
elief in the prevailing religious doctrine.

s more significant for our understanding of the background
ation are certain other issues, often related to the dualistic
on but relating more specifically to issues concerning conduct,
nd ethics. These we can conveniently discuss under the fol-
eading.

INANTS OF CONDUCT

history of thought, the problem of how conduct (or be-
may be understood has had its full share of attention, and
xplanations were advanced. The problem was conceived in
ways, and this is reflected in the kinds of explanations pro-
ny explanations had, or, from our vantage point, have moti-
mplications, and we discuss several of them here, including
e, instinct, will and free will, active unconscious factors,
and *conceptions of human nature and its motives.*

e

the central issues which interested Socrates, Plato, and Aris-
he determination of how it is that *virtue* or *right conduct*
hieved. This issue was the major one with which Socrates
himself, and his thoughts on the subject influenced both
Aristotle.

arch for truth, Socrates appears to have been guided by the
knowledge and virtue are identical and that right knowing

Chapter 2

Motivation in Historical Perspective

It is our impression that overriding concern with motivation is a relatively recent preoccupation of the behavioral sciences, and this impression is shared by other observers. MacLeod (1957) dates the current interest in motivational phenomena to Darwin and Freud. It is
probably true that the particular form in which the dominant motivational questions have been asked in the last century does stem largely
from the concepts of Darwinian evolution. Freud, along with other
psychologists of his time and ours, was influenced by these concepts.
But it is probably *not* true that all motivational questions of this period readily fall into this framework. Nor is it true that there were
no motivational concepts prior to Darwin. Although the terminology
was different, the problems differently cast, and the concepts and
methods for the solution of the problems quite dissimilar to those
we use today, there seems to have been a considerable concern with
problems we would now call motivational ones. In fact, most of the
notions we find in current use indeed have a pre-Darwinian ancestry.
This includes the notion of evolution, itself, as well as instinct, hedonism, rationality, irrationality, unconscious processes, active mental
forces, mechanism, and determinism.

We shall begin our treatment of the history of ideas concerning
motivation by briefly discussing the broader area of controversy
known as dualism. Then we shall consider concepts which are more
specifically motivational in nature and which appeared in Western
thought in the centuries prior to Darwin. In greater detail, and finally,
we shall review the course which concern for motivation took from
Darwin's day into the twentieth century.

DUALISM

Primitive man, if he compared himself and his characteristics to the
objects in his surroundings, must have been impressed by at least two
differences. One is the fact that he, and, of course, animals as well,

had the property of self-induced motion. Stones, earth, leaves, and the like remain motionless unless motion is imparted to them by some external agency. Man could and did move without the agency of such external goads. That animals do so as well must have led early man to an understanding of the great division between animate and inanimate matter. Included as animate may have been objects, the external causes of whose motions he did not perceive, like clouds, perhaps, or planets, but the division between the self-moving and the non-self-moving classes must have been an important one to him (Russell, 1945, p. 537).

The other distinction which he must have made at some early stage is that between animals and himself, although according to Werner (1948, p. 427), this distinction is not always found when primitive peoples are investigated. But certainly he must have observed, after the development of language, the use of tools, some degree of foresight, and perhaps some rudimentary moral or ethical principles, that in these respects he differed from animals. The differences from animals and the problem of self-induced motion would seem to be reasonable hypotheses, at least, to account for the development of ideas concerning man's unique nature.

Murphy (1950, p. 5) has suggested the importance of dreams in laying a foundation for man's conception of himself. In dreams, one may appear to go elsewhere and do many things, while the body remains presumably immobile and at rest. Further, in dreams one can meet the dead, who once again are moving, talking, living. Here we have motion and activity despite the evidence of immobility in sleep and in death. It is not hard to see how a postulate of some other agency—independent of the body—could be made from such observations and have the form of a spirit or a soul, different from the body and incorporeal. Murphy suggests that from this kind of experience came the germ of *dualism,* a notion, one form of which is that there is a spirit or soul which inhabits the body but which is not dependent on it. Such a dualism is often involved in early conceptions of the difference between animate and inanimate matter and of the difference between man and animal.

It is beyond the scope of our task here to enter into a discussion of primitive religions and related beliefs, including, as they do, much that we now call superstition, magic, totemism, and related notions. It may suffice to indicate that the tendency to animism was pronounced in them, as it often is among young children in our present-day culture. Animism, as a term in the behavioral sciences, refers to the tendency of people to think of animals and aspects of inanimate

nature, like clouds and the wind, for exam as being moved by purposes, wishes, and those which people see in themselves.

The dualism of soul or mind and body e ern thought, being widely accepted in tl fifth century B.C. The assertion of a *m* that there is only matter, was advocate parently had little influence. Epicurus figure affected by it.

Dualism is found in Empedocles and A century B.C.). The latter thought that the distinguished living from dead matter, r Socrates, Plato,[2] and Aristotle that dualis tion in Greek philosophy, a formulation and science for many, many centuries.

Fundamental is the notion that there not sensible to bodily perception but or contemplation. We perceive things festations—shadows even—of the ultim the thing is at best a poor sample or re are the objects of reason, are forms in material and are the objects of percept perceptions of many concrete instance one from another in many ways; no This essence, the idea, is supposed to ence and can only be realized throu 1945) in the soul.

The thought of Aristotle was to s world conception of his teacher, Plat lem, at a speculative level, probably His doctrine of universals, but more *form* from the *matter* of a thing, so this dualistic conception. Aristotle as entities different from the body

[1] Materialistic monism was suggested by ritus, about 420 B.C., in the form of the i which are in motion and whose actions a Their view, then, is a determinism as well laws, rather than purpose, were emphasi

[2] It is unnecessary for us here to attemp those of Plato (cf. Taylor, 1933; Wind in many respects, to represent a develop thought.

cated, grades functic possess the po or reas what is

We a full a shows with m soul or from A Aquinas were us means, these ma with dis

Perhap of motiv concepti morals, a lowing h

DETERM

In the havior) various e different posed. M vational i *knowledg hedonism,*

Knowledg

Among totle was may be ac concerned Plato and

In his s belief that

leads always of itself to right acting (Windelband, 1956, p. 131). The purpose of inquiry was for Socrates largely the discovery of knowledge of the Good, since he believed such knowledge would necessarily lead to virtuous action. Plato, too, was concerned with the notion of the Good which could be reached by an approach to the ideas through contemplation. He suggested that the Soul has three parts, one a *reasoning* part and two which are passionate parts. Of the latter, one is concerned with *willing* and the other with *sensual appetites*. The three parts of the soul are located, respectively, in the head, above the midriff, and below it, and there are virtues corresponding to each: wisdom, will power, and self control; a fourth virtue is a suitable arrangement of all these parts. It is clear from these virtues, as well as from Plato's general concern with the achievement of the Good through wisdom, that in general Plato equated the Good with knowledge, the beautiful, and the control of the passions. Notions similar to these are found in other places. For example, Werner (1948, p. 431) cites a primitive people who "distinguish between feelings of sensual lust and nobler feelings; the former arise in the belly, the latter in the chest."

Aristotle believed that the highest goal of human life is happiness, to be achieved through the activity that is unique to man, that is, reason. But a prerequisite to the full use of reason was virtue. In order to achieve ethical virtue, the desires had to be subjected to control of the practical reason; this led, when all went well, to the choice of the mean or midpoint between extremes to which the unchecked desires themselves would go. An example of this would be courage, seen as the midpoint lying between fear and daring; or mildness, the mean between irascibility and indifference. Moderation in these matters was seen as apparently essential to the achievement of the use of reason, the development of which reached its highest peak among philosophers. Philosophers were, therefore, the happiest people (Windelband, 1956; Taylor, 1919).

These considerations point, in this phase of Greek philosophy, to a heavy emphasis on virtue through knowledge and reason and to the control of passion by knowledge and rationality. A large part of Western thought has been influenced by these conceptions, and the conventional notions of the sinfulness of what is bodily or is due to the flesh and of the superiority of the spiritual or mental aspect of life owe a good deal to these Greek conceptions. Somewhat similar ideas may be found in the Stoic school and in the philosophy of the Christian Church, as in St. Augustine, who was much influenced by Plato, and in St. Thomas Aquinas, who interpreted Aristotelian thought. In general, however, the Christian emphasis has been less on the value of knowledge in the control of the body and the achievement of salvation and more on purity of heart. As Troland (1928) has observed, a catalogue of important human motives could be made up from the wishes and actions regarded as sins in the various religions. These sins usually were attributed to the flesh (or sometimes to possession by evil spirits), whereas desirable actions or virtues were attributed to the soul. Freedom of choice, or of the will, was usually believed to be possessed by normal men, so that they could be held accountable for the wrong actions they undertook under the impulse of fleshly desire or, even, the spell of an evil dream.

Instinct

The preceding section brought out the importance of knowledge in contributing to control of the passions and hence to right conduct through an act of will. But these processes were often reserved to man, and lower animals were often believed not to possess them. The denial of rational souls to animals, by both Plato and Aristotle, nevertheless left them with lower level souls capable of monitoring basic organic functions. The Stoic school is generally credited with the invention of the instinct concept, at least in a fairly full form, and the assignment of instinct as a major factor in the conduct of animals. Wilm (1925, p. 40) summarizes their view as follows: "The natural promptings called instincts are purposive activities implanted in the animal by nature or by the world reason or creator for the guidance of the creature in the attainment of ends useful to it, in its own preservation or the preservation of the species, and the avoidance of the contrary." Wilm states the Stoics to have seen as characteristics of instincts their independence of experience, their adaptive utility, and their uniformity.

St. Thomas Aquinas, of course, continued the separation of animals and man by equipping the former with a sensitive soul alone and the latter, in addition, with a rational soul. "The animal is impelled by sense impulse, directed toward the pleasurable. Man's activity, though impulse plays a part, is motivated by rational insight into the relation between the act and its end, which is the realization of the good" (Wilm, 1925, p. 64).

René Descartes' (1596–1650) assignment of instinct to animals was not novel, in the light of the above, but Descartes stands at the beginning of the modern period in philosophy and science, and his conception of animal behavior was entirely mechanistic. Descartes conceived the nerves as tubes through which "animal spirits" moved. Their movement caused the muscles to move. For animals, no further conception was necessary, as their actions were entirely determined by the mechanical forces or pressures imparted to the muscles by the spirits. Descartes suggested that in the human being a similar mechanism existed, but in this case he also provided for a non-mechanical influence on the movement of the spirits. This was the soul. The soul had its point of contact with the body at the pineal gland and could influence the movement of the spirits in the nerves. Cartesian dualism, then, is an interactionism; that is, the incorporeal soul influences the body in the case of man. It must not be forgotten, of course, that Descartes' conception of animal behavior was mechanistic and monistic, and it is perhaps his emphasis on mechanism, rather than his interactional dualism, which gives him his importance. Descartes stood at the beginning of the modern scientific era, when physics and astronomy were making major discoveries. For this reason, in all probability, his mechanism was attractive to others. La Mettrie (1709–1751) adopted it but abandoned the soul in the case of men. His view, then, was a mechanistic monism.

We shall return to the notion of instinct in the discussion of the post-Darwinian period. It is sufficient to observe that instinct managed to satisfy the necessity of accounting for the behavior of animals without giving them reason or a soul (see, also, Beach, 1955); nothing much more than that was done with the concept in its early history.

Will and Free Will

There are a number of words pertinent to the area of our heading, but the major phenomena they designate appear to be described by the terms *choice* and *striving*. We shall concern ourselves here primarily with choice and striving.

In Aristotelian ethics, the concern, as it is in Ethics generally, is with the suitable direction of desire and action. Aristotle did not think reason sufficient for right action, though it was important to it. Needed in addition was strength of will, developed through practice; he believed the will to choose freely that which knowledge indicated to be good—that is, the midpoint between extremes to which the desires, if left to themselves, would go. But we must be compelled, at least at first, to perform good or just acts; if done often enough, they will become pleasurable and habitual.

To St. Augustine the will was the most important aspect of life, and will was separate from knowledge. Will ruled the body, and Augustine was especially concerned about bodily activities, like the sexual act, which seem to overthrow the monarchy of the will. The will was free to choose the path of Christian virtue, knowledge of which was probably most readily obtained through authority, to whom it had been revealed. Belief leads to understanding.

In the centuries that followed, will seems to be a sort of faculty, whose tendency, when it is effective, is to control the animal or passionate side of man in the interests of right virtue and salvation. Although often closely linked to knowledge and feeling, it is separate from both, though its nature and laws remain largely unspecified. This is well expressed in Immanuel Kant, who suggested that "the ultimate moral and religious reality lies not in the field of knowledge but in the process of will. His adoption of a 'faculty psychology' made feeling and willing each quite separable from knowledge" (Murphy, 1950, p. 45). Kant seemed to regard good actions as arising from duty or from consideration of moral law; the will is impelled to choose such courses of action because "the thought of the universal law itself excites in us a feeling of esteem and veneration" (Höffding, 1955, Vol. II, pp. 86–87). Use, experience, example, authority, and pleasure do not determine the goodness of an action. The will must choose in the light of moral law, which asserts "that the principle which I follow in my action must be such that it can form the basis of a general legislation . . . it must be valid for all rational beings who find themselves in a similar case to my own" (Höffding, 1955, Vol. II, p. 85).

We shall not follow further this aspect of the treatment of the will, which, as a concept relating to choice and the issue of freedom of choice, persists in psychological systems following Kant. We can recapitulate, however, by indicating that will was invoked as an agency in the control of passions or the animal nature of man and that it seems to have had a status independent of knowledge, although the will, especially in Kant's treatment, had many rationalistic features. At any rate, knowledge and will as determinants of conduct seem to have been set against instinct and passion in many treatments.

Will in the sense of a basic force or striving was characteristic of the thought of Arthur Schopenhauer (1788–1860), and he seems to have regarded the intellect, consciousness, and the knowledge it develops as servants of the will. We shall find this doctrine more completely developed in evolutionary theory, functionalism, and in psychoanalysis. Schopenhauer's philosophy is largely pessimistic, the will —the prime matter of the world as well as of the individual—being bad and evil, its impulses never bringing pleasure, only pain; and their gratification leading only to satiety, not happiness. Schopenhauer finds a temporary solution in esthetics. More permanent is the solution from India, called Nirvana, which is a turning of the will away from life or extinction, as Schopenhauer seems to interpret it (Russell, 1945; Höffding, 1955, Vol. II).

As Höffding observes (1955, Vol. II) much in Schopenhauer seems to anticipate evolution and other latterday doctrine. Perhaps this can be summarized by saying that Schopenhauer asserted the primacy of the nonintellectual factors in human conduct and thus opposed a purely rationalistic interpretation of human behavior (see also Peters, 1953, pp. 548–552).

Active Unconscious Factors

Over the whole history of Western thought, it has been said, from time to time, that factors which are not available to awareness may influence behavior, and that reason may not be sufficient to action. Boring (1950) has suggested that Leibnitz's active *monads,* which existed in various degrees of clearness, are an expression of these ideas and a forerunner of recent notions. Herbart, too, emphasized the point that ideas must compete for space in consciousness and that, in this competition or conflict, some would lose out, thus becoming unconscious; in this state, however, they did not cease to agitate for readmission to awareness. Schopenhauer's will, also, would seem to be unconscious, since consciousness and knowledge are its servants.

Perhaps the fullest systematic expression of an emphasis on unconscious factors was achieved by Eduard von Hartmann in 1869 and subsequent years. Brett (Peters, 1953, p. 553) has put it this way: No one can deny that Hartmann

powerfully influenced the development of nineteenth-century thought. Whatever Hartmann said always came back to the one and only essential conclusion—the Unconscious must be accepted. And it has been accepted. Some writers almost apologize for using the term "rational." The old habit of putting "clear ideas" in the foreground is almost obsolete. We are told that men live by impulses; that actions express the efforts of a vital energy which moves darkly on the wings of heredity through the generations of men; that we do not act from conscious reasons, but rather construct reasons to explain what has been done in and through us. The soberest psychology of the twentieth century is leavened by these ideas.

It is probably not due to Hartmann alone that all of these developments took place, but his point of view does reflect a considerable deviation from the intellectualism and rationalism of an earlier day as well as from the notion that the mind is more or less passive in its relation to external forces. This view seemed to be a logical consequence of English associationism and empiricism, which held sway from the time of Locke (1632–1704) both in England and in France into the nineteenth century.

We should mention that the study of hypnotism and of psychoneurosis probably helped pave the way for the acceptance of the idea of unconscious factors. Hypnotic phenomena came to have great popular and some scientific interest from about 1766 when Anton Mesmer began to publish and demonstrate it. Hypnotism is a phenomenon in which rational control and control by one's own will would seem to be given up in deference to those of the hypnotist. In the later nineteenth century, hypnosis was a method widely used in conjunction with neurotic disorders, especially hysteria. When neurotic disorders came to be treated humanely, during the nineteenth century, they could hardly be explained in terms of the rational processes postulated in the contemporary philosophical systems (Zilboorg & Henry, 1941). While unconscious processes were not systematically considered factors in hypnosis and neurosis until Freud's work, the very existence of these phenomena probably prepared the way for the admission of unconscious factors as objects of study and as concepts.

Hedonism

Common experience suggests that pleasure and pain are potent determiners of conduct and that we seek to find pleasure and avoid pain. This conception, generally known as hedonism, has in various forms a long history, and we turn now to a brief sketch of it.

Aristippus of Cyrene, whose life was partly contemporaneous with that of Socrates, is usually regarded as the originator of hedonism in philosophy. He believed that pleasure is the only thing worthy of striving for and that pleasure is the good and happiness. Pleasure to Aristippus and his group meant pleasure of the moment (Windelband, 1956, p. 148), and virtue was "identical with the ability to enjoy." Self-control, however, was advocated, and the Cyrenaic conception of the wise man was "that of the perfected man of the world. He is susceptible to the enjoyment of life, he knows what animal satisfactions are, and how to prize spiritual joy, riches, and honor" (Windelband, 1956, p. 149).

The doctrines of Aristippus persist, but in modified form, in the teachings of Epicurus, who held the goal of life to be happiness or pleasure; the pleasures he advocated were those yielding mild and tranquil states, like the absence of pain or the moderate satisfaction of a desire like hunger. (He disapproved of sexual intercourse.) Friendship was the best and safest of social pleasures (Russell, 1945). Epicurus opposed religion because he thought the fear of the life hereafter was a deterrent to happiness. His hedonism was one of present life, unlike that of many religions which promise future pleasure to the elect in the next world.

The emphasis on hedonism languished from the time of the Epicureans (Epicurus died in 270 B.C.) and the early Christian era until it became a chief principle of the British associationists and of the French associationists and empiricists. It is found with some degree of emphasis in viewpoints from those of Thomas Hobbes (born 1588) to John Stuart Mill (died 1873) and Herbert Spencer (1820–1903), and it still has a significant place in conceptions of motivation (see especially, Chapter 8).

Perhaps its fullest development and advocacy, especially in relation to political behavior and the State, comes in Jeremy Bentham (1748–1832), who argued that the conduct of practical affairs must accord with what is good, and he defined good as pleasure or happiness. He believed that each person works toward his own happiness and that legislation must harmonize these private interests and those of the public at large. The principle, "the greatest good for the greatest number," comes from Bentham's point of view. This is also the notion of utility, which means here the tendency to produce happiness (hence the name Utilitarians for Bentham and his supporters).

Troland (1928) has suggested that there are actually three hedonisms—one which emphasizes the present, as in the view of Aristippus; one which stresses the future, applying to the Utilitarians and the promise of happiness in an after-life; and a hedonism of the past. Boring asserts that Freud advocated a hedonism of the future, whereas learning theory, in its emphasis on the law of effect, has used the hedonism of the past (Boring, 1950, p. 706). We thus see that hedonism figures widely in contemporary motivation theory. It is expressly adopted in the views of D. C. McClelland and P. T. Young (see Chapter 8).

Nature and Motives of Men

Implicit in what we have said already are two points which should receive direct stress. One concerns a general evaluation of human nature: it is sometimes conceived as intrinsically good, with evil arising from a weak will, evil spirits, ignorance, or the ill effects of society; or it may be conceived as essentially evil, with law or the social order required to keep it in check. Sometimes the evil part is associated with the flesh or the body, the good part with soul or spirit. McDougall

(1908) argued that many theologians and philosophers have been puzzled by aberrant and evil acts because they view man as essentially
rational or good. On the other hand, he felt that the surprising thing
is that man ever does act rationally or decently, impelled, as Mc-
Dougall thought he was, by powerful instincts.

The second point that should be made is that, in the past, theorists
have often based their conceptions of man on a few dominant motives
or have seen him handicapped by some primary factor. Briefly, now,
we mention the views of four writers to show the range and variety
of such conceptions. It should be understood that these views were
reached by these writers on the basis of their own observations and
their own experience, and they came to rather different conclusions.
Indeed many contemporary notions have much similarity to those of
the four men we mention: Machiavelli, Hobbes, Shaftesbury, and
Rousseau.

Machiavelli (1469–1527). This writer of the fifteenth and early sixteenth centuries described what he observed during the course of many
years in the government of Florence. He felt Florentine politics to
be much inferior to those of ancient times and he attributed these
political defects to bad education and to religion. Leaders (or princes)
were apparently motivated to gain power by egoism, Machiavelli
thought, and the major motives they could manipulate in dealing with
and controlling the populace were fear and love, the former being
stronger and more dependable than the latter.

Hobbes (1588–1679). This British philosopher felt that people are
equal, but that their desires (like hunger, thirst, sex, fear, for pleasure
and the avoidance of pain, and for honor) would lead to conflicts
among them. Since he viewed man as being innately competitive,
Hobbes thought man would be constantly at war with his fellows in
the natural state, in the interest of his desires. Hobbes conceived that
men, realizing their conflicts, would contract to give over control to
a sovereign; the state, in other words, is created to protect the individual from attack and to permit him to gain some gratification of his
desires. Fear, Hobbes thought, is the strongest motive.

Shaftesbury (1671–1713). He was the grandson of the patron of
John Locke, and he believed that there is an instinct which holds the
individual to his race, so that it is natural for man to exist in society;
hence societies are not formed by contract, as Hobbes and Rousseau
thought. He also postulated a moral sense, which is inborn because
it arises out of the instincts when we reflect concerning the internal
impulses we have. This moral sense consists in a "sense of order and

harmony" (Höffding, 1955, Vol. I, p. 395) among our internal impulses, a state reached apparently through thought and introspection. There is a strong religious note in this doctrine, and God is said to be the ideal example of the harmony which should reign within us.

Rousseau (1712–1778). Feelings were stressed, by Rousseau, as the aspect of experience having the greatest value, and he thought this aspect of experience most realizable in a state of nature (i.e., among noble savages). Because it was not realized by most of the civilized people of his time, Rousseau condemned society and its influences on the developing individual. Society generates egoism, and then one's needs and capacities do not correspond with one another; frustration, doubt, suicide, and the like appear. Rousseau advocated correctives in a new system of education, a new attitude toward religion, and a full recognition of the rights of man by the State.

We see in these four writers two views of men and, in parallel, two views of the role of society. Machiavelli and Hobbes do not have a very high opinion of human nature and its motives. Machiavelli sees how the prince can control the populace to serve his own ends. Hobbes believes people to have arranged for a sovereign so that their competitive strife can be controlled. Shaftesbury thinks men come together in society naturally, and the innate moral sense reflects a favorable view of man's nature. Rousseau sees evil arising from social organization. Man is good, and is spoiled in a bad society.

THE IMPACT OF EVOLUTION

The nineteenth century was a period of tremendous advance in scientific inquiry and in understanding of the phenomena of nature. Earlier centuries had, of course, yielded major studies in physics and astronomy, and these fields continued their development unabated, or even at an accelerated pace. But the nineteenth century also saw major growth in physiology; observations and concepts concerning nerve conduction, reflex action, cerebral function, and sensory process can be numbered among the physiological advances most significant to the behavioral sciences. They strongly influenced psychology through Wilhelm Wundt, whom Boring (1950) calls the first "professional psychologist." Wundt called much of his psychology "physiological," and this term referred primarily to the use of *experimental* methods for the study of psychological problems, in contrast to the "armchair" psychology of the time. A little later we shall see something of the kind of psychology to which this view led and some of its implications for motivation. First, we must deal with evolutionary theory, which, in its widespread impact on all the behavioral sciences, is the greatest single biological event of the nineteenth century.

We associate the theory of evolution with the name of Charles Darwin, in whose book, *The Origin of Species* (1859), the notion was put forward in full form, together with a mass of supporting evidence. However, although it in no way demeans Darwin's achievement, the idea of development, even of the emergence of one species from others, is a very old one. It is present in Anaximander (611–545 B.C.), who is said by Windelband (1956, p. 42) to have observed "that animals appeared when the primitive liquid earth dried up, and were originally fish in form. Then some of them, adapting themselves to their new environment, became land animals," including man. Empedocles (500–430 B.C.) believed that life emerged from inert matter, first in the form of plants and, from them, in the form of animals. He suggested that parts of animals, like heads and arms, appeared first and that these parts were merged through forces of attraction and repulsion to form various kinds of combinations. Many odd or unusual combinations would, of course, result, and those combinations which were able to survive in the environment and reproduce themselves would persist.

More proximal to the time of Darwin were the views of men who can be regarded as actual predecessors of his development. Charles Lyell (1797–1875) founded historical geology, thus helping to provide a conception that the earth has existed for a very long period of time, necessary for evolutionary processes to work (Eiseley, 1959b). The prevailing view had put earth's creation in 4004 B.C. (Daniel, 1959). Darlington (1959) has stressed, among others, the views of Erasmus Darwin (the grandfather of Charles), Thomas Malthus (1766–1834), and Lamarck (1744–1829); and Boring (1950), the views of Goethe (1749–1832), as being anticipatory to Darwin's views. Herbert Spencer (1820–1903) likewise anticipated some of Darwin's ideas. None of these men, however, reached the particular synthesis, especially in relation to a mass of evidence, which Darwin achieved. The nearest approach, without the evidence, was made by Alfred Russell Wallace, Darwin's friend, whose paper on the subject Darwin published simultaneously with his own in 1858 (Eiseley, 1959a).

The most significant features of the theory of evolution for the study of behavior lie, first, in its conception that there is continuity in development, from the lowest form of life to the highest; and second, in its emphasis on the point that survival requires adaptation to the prevailing environment. Study of the mechanisms and processes of this adaptation, therefore, assumes the highest priority. We shall elaborate these ideas shortly. What was Darwin's theory and how did he arrive at it? [3]

Darwin's Theory

Two chief factors seem specifically instrumental in Darwin's development of his theory. One is the extensive observations he made as a young man when, for several years, he voyaged on the *Beagle*, visiting various parts of the world. The other was his reading of Thomas Malthus' essay on population (published 1798). Darwin's observations concerned the dissemination of many species over wide geographic areas and the changes which had occurred in them as a result of continued separation and isolation. This led him to the notion of variability in the members of a species and to the idea that the specific environmental factors to which some members of the species were exposed were associated with the modifications observed when separation or isolation had persisted over many generations. Further, Darwin was aware of several other points: the fact that animal breeders were able to develop desired characteristics through selective breeding; the relationships between characteristics of species now extinct and those of similar species which still survive; and the fact that there are similarities in the embryonic development of a wide variety of quite different species.

Malthus emphasized that animals and men tend to increase their numbers beyond the earth's capacity of food and maintenance. From this, Darwin took the notion of struggle and conflict in the process of survival. Epitomized, his theory reduces to the following: The members of a species vary in their characteristics. There is competition among species and members of the same species for use of the earth's limited resources (in a particular environmental setting). In the competition some organisms will survive, others will not.

If the characteristics of the survivors are transmitted to their offspring (and of course those of the nonsurvivors cannot be transmitted) there will be modification of the species over time. Further, environmental change will also lead to differential survival of those best and those least able to adapt themselves to the change, with consequent variation in species. These points are covered in the phrase, "survival of the fittest." The phrase "multiply, vary, and let the fittest survive" expresses, briefly, much of Darwin's theory, but it should be under-

---

[3] We can here deal but briefly with the theory and its implication. For more extended treatments see Simpson (1953) and Roe and Simpson (1958) and the references cited therein.

stood that environmental characteristics and changes and transmission of characteristics to offspring are essential features of it.

Significance of Evolution to Psychology

Almost all historians agree that Darwin's contribution resulted in an intellectual revolution, with wide consequences for the social and biological sciences, as well as for social thought, philosophy, theology and cultural enterprises in general (see, e.g., Hofstadter, 1959; Lerner, 1957; and Bury, 1932). For psychology there were several compelling implications. One was that man is not unique among creatures, because the difference between man and animal is one of degree rather than of kind. Man is not a being specially created. In short, there is continuity between man and animal, rather than separation. This view raises two questions: "How is man like the other animals?"; and "How are the other animals like man?" We shall have more to say about these questions shortly.

Another significant implication arises from the emphasis in Darwinian theory on survival and on the characteristics of animals which promote or defeat it. A thorough investigation of this implication involves the study of the characteristics of many animals and consideration of the role of these characteristics in survival. Further, adaptation to environmental change is significant to survival, so investigation of processes of adaptation assumes significance following this implication of evolutionary theory.

A third implication from evolutionary theory is that, in the views of many workers, psychology came to be regarded as a biological science. This is probably implicit in the first two points already mentioned, but it deserves separate emphasis. Heretofore psychology had been seen as derivative primarily from philosophical questions having to do with the mind. Kant had said it could never be a science. Herbart had asserted its scientific potentiality but believed experimentation was impossible. Fechner and Wundt had shown that experimentation was possible, but their experimentation was largely concerned with describing and, perhaps, measuring the contents of consciousness (cf. Littman, 1958, pp. 137–138). That psychology could be a biological science concerned with the psychological characteristics of men and animals essential to adaptation and survival provided a new direction to psychological inquiry.

The Development of Comparative Psychology

A specific consequence of these implications of Darwinism was to foster the development of a comparative psychology. The study of animals, especially their behavior, had not progressed much prior to Darwin's time, but the period after Darwin saw a major surge in this kind of activity. Some of this activity sought to find evidences of human characteristics, like reason and intelligence, in animals; likewise, the emphases on instinct in man, and on the study of primitive peoples and children as "bridges" between animal and man were further expressions of the evolutionary point of continuity between man and animal. Peters (1953, p. 661) has succinctly stated this consequence as "a developing tendency both to humanize animals and to brutalize men." He further observes, "the development of theories of 'instinct' in psychology and the great stress placed by Freud and McDougall on the irrational determinants of behavior exemplifies the latter aspect of this tendency: the studies of learning and intelligence in animals and the interest in herd phenomena or the social groupings of animals exemplifies the former aspect . . ." Darwin, of course, had led the way to the study of emotions in relation to evolutionary theory in his book, *Expression of the Emotions in Man and Animal* (1872).

The genetic and comparative trend which evolutionary theory gave to psychology was important; it led to the emergence of research interests that might otherwise have been delayed in appearance. However, the emphasis on instinctual and irrational sources of conduct is perhaps even more significant for the study of motivation, since this topic is usually not considered as including intelligence, reason, and skill. Evolutionary theory thus reinforced trends which we have already noted, for example, in Schopenhauer and Hartmann.

Still another effect, already mentioned in our discussion of psychology as a biological science, may be stressed. This is the role of psychological processes in adjustment or adaptation to, or survival in, an environment. Consciousness, reason, memory, learning, skill, affect, and the like were seen from the vantage point of evolution as having *utility* to the organism in its or its species' struggle to survive; this is a dynamic conception as opposed to the descriptive analysis of the contents of consciousness or of their relations to stimulus variables which characterized Wundt's psychology. And it was a fundamental thesis of the functionalist psychology which emerged in the United States at the beginning of the twentieth century. The theory of evolution, then, had something to do with the very conception of the nature of psychology and the functions which it is to serve. Motivation, as a concept, was central to the functionalist school and its derivatives. That it is basic also to psychoanalysis perhaps allows us to understand why it has figured so centrally in this century in the behavioral sciences. Evolution has played an important role in this development.

We shall not follow the many developments in the study of "animal intelligence" as it was reflected in the work of Romanes, Lloyd Morgan, Lubbock, Hobhouse, Yerkes, and many others (see Warden, Jenkins, & Warner, Vol. I, 1935; Boring, 1950). Our task requires, instead, that we turn to other topics, namely, the instinct and anti-instinct controversy, teleology and vitalism, and the concepts of mechanistic biology.

Instinct: Pro and Con

The term *instinct* has never been a very precise one, and we have already seen something of its use in pre-Darwinian times. Troland (1928, pp. 41–42) has indicated the problem of definition very well in the following statement, which pertains to the usage of the term in the decades preceding 1928:

it seems impossible on the basis of contemporary discussions to formulate an exact definition of the term, instinct, which will apply satisfactorily to all the uses to which the word is put. In a general way, it is agreed that an instinct is an inherited tendency to action of a specific kind, usually set off by a limited range of stimuli, and having definite survival or biological value —in the struggle for existence. As a rule, an instinct is conceived as a purely physiological mechanism, although the term may be used loosely as if it stood for a psychical force having a teleological or purposive form. The most mechanistic conception of an instinct regards it as being comprised of a group of reflexes or processes of a fixed type, energizing the muscles via the out-going nerves. Perhaps the least mechanical conception is that of McDougall . . . according to which an instinct is a purposive force, the motor expressions of which are very plastic or variable.

The early post-Darwinian period saw considerable study of instincts or innate behavior tendencies in a variety of animal forms. Among them we may mention birds, ants, wasps, spiders, and various mammals. There was a good deal of controversy concerning the innateness of specific acts and some attempt to determine by experiment whether some specific behaviors are or are not innately determined. A case in point is the song patterns of birds. However, there seems to have been wide agreement, in this period, that instinctive patterns were present.

The textbooks of the period (from the 1880's to the early twentieth century) characteristically give extensive lists of animal instincts. Likewise, they also usually show lists of human instincts. The case for the instinctiveness of many human actions was frequently anecdotal, argumentative, or logical. Thus, James, in a chapter on instincts, gives examples from the behavior of his own children on occasion, argues from analogy with the behavior of lower animals on others, and points out the evolutionary advantage to organisms of certain instincts (like destructiveness) in still others (James, 1890, Vol. II, p. 412). All of these points were used to justify the assumption of the instinctive character of one or another human action tendency. Admitting that instincts could be transitory (a sort of critical period hypothesis sometimes involving a process like imprinting, see Chapter 3), and that they were subject to modification through experience, James nevertheless held that the human being has many instincts, or instinctive tendencies, in fact more than any other species. Instincts, to James, involved purposive actions, though awareness of purpose was not essential. (McDougall, who will be discussed shortly, was apparently influenced by these thoughts of James.) Among the tendencies James listed as human instincts were locomotion, vocalization, imitation, rivalry, pugnacity, sympathy, hurting, fear, acquisitiveness, constructiveness, play, curiosity, sociability, secretiveness, cleanliness, modesty, love, jealousy, and parental love.

We need not elaborate the discussion of lists of instincts further. Suffice it to say that the postulation of instincts became almost a vocation among writers dealing with human capacities, and the promiscuity with which action tendencies were assigned to the instinct category was one of the reasons that the concept fell into disrepute. L. L. Bernard (1924) summarized the views of a number of such writers and found, altogether, that several thousand human actions were designated as instinctive, by one writer or another (see Chapter 3).

We turn now to other aspects of the post-Darwinian concern with instincts, dealing first with vitalism and teleology and then with mechanistic biology. Our discussion of instinct as such, in this chapter, will be concluded with considerations of the anti-instinct movement, which took two forms: that they do not exist; and the notion that there is a considerable variety in organismic behavior, even though inner states may determine that the behavior occur.

Vitalism and Teleology. These terms designate approaches to the study of life, both of which can be found in Greek thought and, very likely, earlier. We shall discuss vitalism first, although the more important viewpoint, perhaps, is that of teleology.

Vitalism, as Warden, Jenkins, and Warner (1935, Chap. 2) have described it, consists in the assertions that living things have characteristics which cannot be reduced to physicochemical terms and which indicate the existence of some force or entity which transcends the physical or material. One such viewpoint is "neovitalism," as espoused by Hans Driesch (1867–1941). Driesch experimented with the eggs and early stages of sea urchins. In some of his studies, he found that cells and partially developed organisms, if divided, would regenerate entire, normal organisms. This suggested to Driesch that the cell contained some principle, or *entelechy*, which was responsible for the developments observed. He believed this vital principle to be beyond the province of physics and chemistry and to lie essentially beyond scientific, material, or mechanistic explanation: memory and the evaluative use of past experience he saw, also, as requiring nonmechanical principles for explanation (Müller-Freienfels, 1935).

Later investigations have suggested that at least some of the phenomena that Driesch observed, and others like them, can be explained or understood on the basis of physicochemical principles, and that there is hope that all such phenomena can be so explained.

Teleology implies that knowledge of purpose or ends determines the course of actions or of developments. It is a belief which the beginning student of evolution can easily embrace, because it is so easy to rephrase evolutionary doctrine in the form that variation and natural selection occur *in order that* a species, or some characteristic of a species, develop and survive. The fullest representation of teleological thinking, in connection with the evolutionary viewpoint, relates to the instinct concept. The outstanding system based on a teleological view of instinct was developed by William McDougall, to a brief treatment of whose views we now turn. Teleological considerations are neither a necessary nor a characteristic feature of evolutionary theory or instinct theory, however.

William McDougall (1871–1938) insisted that the most important determiners of conduct were instincts and their associated emotions. McDougall may thus be classified as an activity psychologist (see Boring, 1950, p. 466), as well as an instinct theorist and purposivist. He also stressed the role of irrational forces in conduct, rejecting the essentially rationalistic assumptions of certain philosophers, like the British Associationists. He went so far as to say (McDougall, 1908) that those who denied that man is essentially an irrational, impulse-driven being must be persons in whom the instincts are unusually weak. His problem, as he saw it, was to explain why organisms *ever* behave rationally and socially, rather than why they also, on occasion, behave irrationally.

The prime movers of conduct, in McDougall's view, are the instincts and their associated emotions. Without them, the organism would not act in any significant way. There were a number of instincts, McDougall thought (he later called them "propensities"), and he conceived of each "instinct as an inherited or innate psychophysical disposition which determines its possessor to perceive, and to pay attention to, objects of a certain class, to experience an emotional excitement of a particular quality upon perceiving such an object, and to act in regard to it in a particular manner, or, at least, to experience an impulse to such action" (McDougall, 1908, p. 30). One would apparently be aware, McDougall seemed to think, during his conduct, of features of purpose, direction, and striving. McDougall thought the essential feature of animal behavior was orientation to goals. This led him to reject the notion that instincts might be reflexes or combinations thereof.

The list of major instincts, which McDougall postulated in 1908, included those of flight, repulsion, curiosity, pugnacity, self-abasement, self-assertion, reproduction, gregariousness, acquisition, and construction. Each of the first seven of these instincts was accompanied by a distinctive and specific emotion. The emotion is said to be "associated" with its instinct, but this does not imply that the relationship is a learned one; the association is an innate one. The emotions which correspond, respectively, to the first seven instincts are fear, disgust, wonder, anger, negative self-feeling or subjection, positive self-feeling or elation, and the tender emotion. The remaining three instincts had no such specific emotional accompaniment. McDougall later modified his list, but we need not follow this aspect of his conception further here. Many emotional experiences represented compounds of the seven primary emotions, and feelings of pleasure and pain as well as of excitement and depression (all apparently independent of the instincts) could enter into such compounds.

Although learning could modify the expression of instincts in bodily movements and the kinds of situations in which the instincts could be aroused, it did not apparently affect the underlying instinct itself or the emotional experience to which it gave rise.[4]

As we have indicated, the instincts are, to McDougall, the main-

---

[4] The instincts were only the building blocks out of which McDougall constructed the human personality, and learning was an essential feature in the combinations and organizations of instincts achieved in the course of human development. Among these organizations is the *sentiment*, which consisted of a cluster of instincts and associated emotions around the idea of an object or class of objects. The control of the instincts, which, as we saw, was a central problem to McDougall, was accomplished through the sentiments, including especially the sentiment of self-regard. McDougall's discussion of this sentiment has a modern, although usually unacknowledged, ring and resembles several theories in which notions about the self play a central role (cf. Chapters 12 and 13). Our purpose here, however, is to deal with McDougall's instinct-motivation theory, so that we shall speak no further of the sentiments, their development, and vicissitudes.

springs of action. No action can take place without the participation of an instinct, and behavior serves the end or the purpose of the instinct, which, of course, is the teleological aspect of his viewpoint. Every instance of instinctive behavior "involves a knowing of some thing or object, a feeling in regard to it, and a striving towards or away from that object" (McDougall, 1908, p. 27). Boring (1950, p. 467) feels that McDougall, in addition to purposiveness, permitted some freedom or indeterminateness in behavior, as against a strict determinism.

Perhaps the single most important aspect of McDougall's viewpoint, at any rate for motivation, is his continued insistence on the purposive and striving, or impulse-driven, character of behavior. He later referred to his viewpoint as a "hormic psychology," from the Greek word *hormē*, meaning impulse or striving. Peters (1953, pp. 665–666, 674) indicates that this aspect of McDougall's theory led later writers to emphasize the concept of *drive* (see Chapter 10) in their theories. Hull and Tolman, Peters observes (Peters, 1953, pp. 665–666), "make great use of the concept of 'drive,' which turned out to be the objectively testable component of McDougall's more metaphysical concept of 'instinct' . . ." Although he spoke of fewer instincts, Freud's emphasis on striving parallels McDougall's.

Another way of emphasizing this aspect of McDougall's theory is conveyed by Woodworth (1918). Woodworth points out that the James-Lange theory of emotion (see Chapter 8) does not emphasize the impulsive aspect of emotion, or its tendency to some sort of consummation. McDougall recognized this aspect of emotion, Woodworth suggests, in his association of the primary emotions with the instincts. While agreeing that instincts are important, and listing even more of them than McDougall did, Woodworth did not believe that all conduct is ultimately derivative from a few instincts. He elaborated a notion that mechanisms can act as drives (see Chapters 11, 14), thus emphasizing the motivated character of behavior, which, as we have seen, was a central thesis in McDougall's system.

In summary, we may observe that vitalistic and teleological views have stressed the idea that form [5] or purpose determines evolutionary development and conduct. In this emphasis, they have kept alive and made of central importance the viewpoint that organisms are active rather than passive participants in their interactions with the environment. This active participation is due to innate, impulsive forces which figure significantly in survival and development. The concept of instinct, as used by such a writer as McDougall, is a more specific, de-

[5] This is a notion we have seen in Plato and in Aristotle.

notable concept representing these features than is the concept of entelechy as proposed by Driesch.

Mechanistic Biology. This is another viewpoint, in many respects almost the direct opposite of teleology and vitalism, which arose in the late nineteenth and early twentieth century. It was probably an expression of the great strides made during the nineteenth century in physics and chemistry. An early and significant indication of it occurred in 1845 (Boring, 1950, p. 708) when four young physiologists, all of them students of Johannes Müller, agreed to fight vitalism. The four were Hermann von Helmholtz, Emil du Bois-Reymond, Carl Ludwig, and Ernst Brücke. All of them achieved great distinction and influence in physiology, and the principle of the conservation of energy, which Helmholtz announced in 1847, was one with which all were in sympathy. As Hall (1954, pp. 5–6) points out, Brücke in 1874 "set forth the radical view that the living organism is a dynamic system to which the laws of chemistry and physics apply." Brücke was the physiologist by whom Freud was much influenced (see Chapter 12).

A more specific expression of mechanistic biology in relation to behavior is the *tropistic school*, whose major advocate was Jacques Loeb. This view, which has a strong resemblance to Cartesian mechanism, is summarized by Troland (1928, p. 52) as follows:

. . . animals are provided with response systems which are balanced around certain axes of symmetry in their organisms. A condition of equilibrium with regard to the exciting stimulus is produced when the animal orients itself so that the portions of the response mechanisms on either side of the axis are equally stimulated. Thus, an animal will swim towards the light because, firstly, the light rays excite movements of forward propulsion in the swimming apparatus, and secondly, because these movements become of equal intensity on the two sides of the body only when the illumination of both sides is equal. This mechanism necessitates that under light stimulation, the animal shall not only move toward the source of the light, but in doing so shall turn until it faces the luminous point. Simultaneously operative tropisms, based upon different kinds of stimuli, may also resolve themselves in this way, to yield resultants which have as complex a mechanistic foundation as may be required. Loeb developed his views even to the point of explaining advanced instinctive behavior in accordance with tropistic- or at least mechanistic-conceptions.

Loeb did, however, allow for a "psychic life" in animals capable of associative memory.

This radical mechanism, then, insists on the sufficiency of physicochemical forces for explanation of animal conduct and suggests a relative rigidity of animal behavior. It has little or no place for internal sources of behavior, like drives or more mentalistic or vitalistic concepts, and stresses the role of external stimuli (cf. Harlow, 1953a). The conception was most easily applied to lower animals, although some efforts were made to apply it to infant rats (cf. Crozier & Hoagland, 1934). Loeb has said, "Our wishes and hopes, disappointments and sufferings, have their source in instincts which are comparable to the light instinct of the heliotropic animals" (quoted by Müller-Freienfels, 1935, p. 187).

Even though special motivation concepts were in a sense replaced by tropisms in the view of Loeb and his followers, the physicalistic conception of forced movement and the nonpurposive, nonmentalistic conception of animal behavior, which they developed, have probably had an influence on motivation theory. Objective psychology owes something to this movement (Boring, 1950). The very fact of its existence has probably had a modulating effect on those who see animal behavior as more variable and flexible than the tropistic view would imply. Variability and flexibility were espoused by H. S. Jennings, who, like Loeb, was a student of Max Verworn, and we shall describe it further in the next section, after first discussing the anti-instinct movement.

The Anti-Instinct Controversy. We have already seen that the uncritical and widespread use of the instinct concept, as illustrated in Bernard's (1924) summary of the situation, was a factor in the disrepute into which the concept fell. There were other reasons. One was the growing awareness of considerable variation in behavior among cultural groups. Such anthropologists as Franz Boas contributed early to this awareness. What was involved was the realization that many characteristics, values, beliefs, and behavior patterns typical of Western culture were not shared by groups living in other cultures. This variation made it difficult to continue to adhere to the notion that such manifestations were instinctive.

Within psychology, there were a number of negative reactions to the concept of instinct and of innate emotional patterns. Watson and Morgan (1917) observed infants under various kinds of stimulation and concluded that there were but three innate emotional reactions (fear, rage, and love) and that these reactions could be elicited by only a small variety of stimuli. All other emotional reactions, they thought, were learned. Ultimately, Watson, who founded the school known as behaviorism, took the position that there are no human instincts, and that so-called instinctive behavior can be explained by the individual's body structure and his early training (Watson, 1930,

p. 94). Dunlap (1919), F. H. Allport (1924), and Kuo (1921) joined in the attack on instincts, and the decade of the 1920's saw a great deal of controversy over the instinct issue.[6]

The result was that instinct, as a concept, seemed to have disappeared by the next decade. It has been revived recently, in conjunction with various specific behaviors, like hoarding, and in the ethological movement (see Beach, et al., 1947; and Chapters 3 and 4). However, one of its meanings was never really eliminated, and its revival in ethology and in specific behaviors is considerably different from its earlier one. We will comment briefly on these two points.

The term *drive* preserved in psychology some aspects of what was connoted by the word *instinct*. As we have seen, instinct had come to be associated with the notion of purpose. It also implied an urge or impulse, as well as a pattern of behavior that was relatively fixed or invariant. The purposive implication of the term was not acceptable to many behavioral scientists, who felt that the purposive character of behavior (where it can be said to exist) is a problem to be explained, rather than being itself an explanation for the behavior. The cultural evidence suggested that many of the urges and behavior patterns were not innate, because of variation in different cultures, and experimental analysis in many cases revealed that experience is an important determiner of a number of "instincts" of animals. Yet, there are a number of behaviors, like those of eating, drinking, mating, sleeping, which are present in virtually all members of the higher species. Such behaviors provide the means whereby individual and species survival is accomplished. Dunlap (1922) stressed the point that desire resides in tissues, and Dashiell (1928) emphasized tissue needs as sources of drives. So drive, a term apparently introduced by Woodworth (1918) [7] in another context, as a tissue need came to replace the term instinct in many of the places where, in the earlier literature, the term instinct was used. It should be emphasized that this was not a mere substitution of one word for another. While there are, as we shall see later, difficulties with the notion of tissue needs as the sources of drives, this conception, together with operations (such as fasting) for inducing tissue needs, provided a concreteness of meaning and the possibility for investigation that instinct did not

[6] The nature-nurture controversy, which reached its peak in the 1930's, was focused upon the role of experience and innate factors in the determination of intelligence. We shall not pursue it here (see Anastasi & Foley, 1948).

[7] The term *drive* is not listed in Baldwin's comprehensive dictionary of psychological and philosophical terms (Baldwin, 1911). Nor, for that matter, is *motivation* listed there.

have. In this sense, then, drive continued the urge meaning of instinct; it may be added, however, that relatively few drives were thought to be native, and that most of the human motives were believed to be learned (cf. Woodworth, 1918; Miller & Dollard, 1941; Allport, 1954; Murphy, 1954; also, Chapter 11).

The recent revival of the instinct concept has been concerned with the demonstration of the development or the existence of behavior without the role of training or experience and with study of the factors which control such behavior. Such patterns as hoarding, maternal, and mating behavior are believed by some students not to require experience or practice for their appearance, at least in some species of animals. Beach (1955) has observed, in this connection, that the more we know about the factors that control such behaviors the less need there is to talk about instincts. This means, quite clearly, that the term has little or no explanatory value and serves mainly as a means of classifying certain behavior patterns as primarily determined by innate factors. We shall review the evidence concerning a number of such patterns in Chapters 3 and 4. The use of instinct by the ethologists is rather different from what we have just said, but as they are dealt with fully in Chapter 3, we shall not discuss them further here.

Variability of Behavior. The idea that animal behavior was rigidly fixed by purely mechanical forces, implied in a strict interpretation of the tropism, was opposed by H. S. Jennings (1868–1947). Jennings was neither a vitalist nor a teleologist, and was as much a mechanist as was Loeb, but his studies of the behavior of lower organisms convinced him that even the protozoa do not react automatically and immediately to the forces provided by external stimulation. He found variable or approximative behavior in their reactions, as if the organism were adjusting its movements to the stimuli by "trial and error." The reactions were modifiable as well. Schneirla (1947) has credited Jennings with pointing out the varied stimuli to which protozoa will react, the fact that their behavior shows variability, and the significance of the internal conditions of the individual for the kind of reaction it will show. Jennings' doctrines of trial and error and of the resolving through behavior of the animal's physiological (internal) states provide an orientation to the study of adaptive behavior, which is consistent with and probably significant to the development of the drive concept just mentioned. Indeed, Harlow (1953a, pp. 23–24) has deplored the influence of Jennings in the following statement: "Jennings' . . . demonstration that 'physiological state' played a role in determining the behavior of the lower animal was given exaggerated importance and emphasis, thereby relegating the role of external stimulation to a secondary position as a force in motivation."

Wallace Craig (1918) developed a somewhat similar interpretation based on his experiments with doves. Craig believed that a physiological state, like hunger, induces restless "search," which may lead to the discovery of a stimulus, like food, toward which a consummatory response can be made, thus quieting the physiological state and the restlessness. Tolman (1932, pp. 272–274), who has made significant contributions to the study of learning (Chapter 10), has acknowledged the influence on his views of Craig's scheme, and this kind of model is well represented in conceptions of the operation of drive as a tissue need (Dashiell, 1928), so important in drive theory as described in Chapter 10. This model shades imperceptibly into the homeostatic conception, which sees behavior as a regulatory process that enables the organism to rectify internal imbalances by commerce with the environment. Its significance for motivation theory is fully developed in Chapter 7.

Summary

The theory of evolution is significant to the study of behavior both for its denial of any qualitative difference between man and animal and for its emphasis on the functional utility of various behavioral processes, like instinct, intelligence, learning, and motivation, for the adaptation of organisms to the environment in the interest of survival. Behavior is thus seen to *serve* the organism's needs—a functional conception which probably has no clear or highly influential precedent in the history of Western thought. While evolution has had numerous repercussions in the form of emphasis on and controversy about instincts, of stress on purposiveness and goal directedness of behavior, and of attempted mechanical accounts of behavior, it is our impression that its greatest significance lies in the functional or utility model to which it has given rise. The range of investigation of animal behavior following evolutionary principles has been enormous. One of its main consequences has been the notion of drive, a term used to describe internal states whose consequence is restless activity to be terminated only when the internal state is quieted by consummatory activity or death. Motivation has tended to be identified with these internal states, and the thought of the last half-century has come to be increasingly dominated by motivational ideas. We shall see in later chapters that this way of thinking is coming to be challenged, and it is our impression that the renewed stress on activation and external sources of "motivation" (Chapters 6 and 8), on cognitive processes which are independent of motivation (Chapter 12), and on self-actualization (Chapter 13) will, in the long run, if it continues, lead to a reconsideration of the importance which the last few decades have placed on motivation. At the present time, however, it is difficult to predict the ultimate outcome of this kind of thinking.

OTHER POST-DARWINIAN DEVELOPMENTS

There are certain other trends of which any historical sketch of the development of motivational ideas must take account. We follow Boring (1950, Chap. 26) here in dealing with three such trends. These are, first, *activity psychology* (or as we call it here, *intentionality*); second, the study of hypnosis and neurosis and the emergence of *psychoanalysis;* and third, the expression of hedonism in the *law of effect.* We will indicate, as appropriate, where evolutionary theory had its impact on these trends, but we have placed them in a section by themselves because they represent more specific influences on the development of motivation in psychology rather than some of the matters we dealt with in discussing evolution. Psychoanalysis and the law of effect were certainly influenced by evolutionary thought, but their initial interest lay in rather specific problems—the nature of neurosis and of learning, respectively. The influence of evolution on intentionality is less clear. There are interrelations among these three trends, also, which we shall attempt to delineate.

Intentionality

It is probably true in general, though wrong in detail, that one of the major inheritances from the British empiricist-associationistic tradition of philosophy is the notion that the mind is passive. John Locke saw the mind as a blank tablet at birth, with contents—its ideas—coming from experiences with the outer world. He also said that the mind could generate ideas through the process of reflection (he meant something related to thought), and this is the detail in which our generalization is erroneous. But the influential formulation, the one which characterizes the empiricists as against the nativists, is that the mind's ideas come from the sensations whose source is the external world. There is little emphasis in British empiricist psychology, from Locke's time to that of James Mill, on the mind's activities. It is true that faculties of the mind were stressed in the Scottish school, but faculty psychologies seldom have led to stress on intentionality as such.

When psychology came into separate existence in Wundt's laboratory at Leipzig, the influences of this conception of the mind as being passive are apparent. A major enterprise of Wundt's and of his more or less faithful followers was to describe and classify the basic elements of mental life. These elements were to be identified through introspection concerning the conscious consequences of controlled stimulation. We do not demean here the purpose or the execution of this work. Physics and chemistry were showing the value, in their fields, of analysis, and the data obtained by the psychological laboratories were at least data—empirically obtained under controlled and denotable conditions—as opposed to the speculations of philosophers and moralists. But the content was restricted, and it had no place for motivational concepts or notions that the mind was active in itself. Association was the mechanism whereby the mental elements were put together.[8]

We have already seen that alternative views had long been in existence. Nativism is an old concept, and Leibnitz, Herbart, and Schopenhauer had, in various ways, indicated that activity is a primary fact of mind. In the concepts of evolution and instinct, impulse and purpose assumed importance, and we shall see more of this orientation in the study of psychoanalysis. A somewhat similar idea arose in systematic psychology and, as well, in the experimental laboratory in the late nineteenth and early twentieth century. Peters (1953, p. 669) indicates this when he states that attitude and determining tendencies are introspectional concepts which arose because of the realization of "the inadequacy of the traditional picture of the mind as a passive container of sensations and images. . . ."

Franz Brentano (1838–1917), more a philosopher than an experimental psychologist, held that the important aspects of the mind are *acts,* not *contents* as Wundt averred. The act is intentional; that is, it is directed to the content which will be its object, but the content as such is not in the act, though it is *immanently* so. To Brentano (Boring, 1950, p. 360), "When one sees a color, the color itself is not mental. It is the seeing, the act, that is mental. There is, however, no meaning to *seeing* unless something is seen. The act always implies an object, refers to a content." Flugel (1951, p. 146) indicates Brentano's contribution to be "the emphasis he laid upon activity," while, at the same time, uniting this emphasis with the importance of experience.

A number of systematic writers were influenced by, or developed,

[8] This description is again erroneous in detail. Both Fechner and Wundt accepted the notion of degrees of consciousness, and Wundt spoke of apperception and of creative synthesis (Wundt, 1897) as important operations of the mind. Titchener (1908) was aware of the importance of attention and action. Yet the burden of the work of these men on those who followed them was the analysis into elements of an essentially inert mind (cf. Littman, 1958, pp. 137–139).

views similar to those of Brentano. Among them we may mention
Oswald Külpe and the Würzburg school, the Austrian school and its
emphasis on the Gestalt-qualität, and James Ward (by whom Mc-
Dougall was influenced) and G. F. Stout in England. William James
and John Dewey developed viewpoints in the United States which
have many points of similarity with Brentano's.

Brentano also seems to have influenced Freud (Boring, 1950; Merlan,
1945, 1949), and it is possible to read his formulation of the intentionality of acts as foreshadowing the essentially purposive conception
with which Freud viewed mental phenomena and which underlay his
methodology. Clearer, perhaps, is his influence on Külpe, transmitted
at least in part by his student, Edmund Husserl. At any rate, the experimentation which Külpe led and for which the Würzburg school
became famous is usually seen more as supporting Brentano than
Wundt.

The Würzburgers attacked the problem of thinking.[9] Little experimental work had informed this topic, but the prevailing notion had
been that thinking was made up of images and associative processes.
The Würzburg group studied thinking by means of introspection.
They found that thought could and did occur without images and,
more important to our discussion, that thoughts contained directions,
determining tendencies, task orientations, and Einstellungen, which
controlled the course of thinking but which they could not consider
associative. It is possible to regard these factors as "intentional," that is,
instrumental to the selection of associations in accordance with the ends
which the task or the experimental task required the process of thinking
to achieve. But the directional or selective agencies were not considered
associative in themselves,[10] and their action may be taken as representative of the activity of the mind rather than as indicative of its passivity.
Lewin (1917, 1922) also stressed the importance of motives in the activation of associations.

We shall not follow the Würzburg doctrine further, as its main
importance to our discussion is its revival of and demonstration of the
notion of the active character of mind; some of the reports from
Würzburg also implied that these directional activities of mind could
be outside awareness. To this extent, like instinct, drive, and related
conceptions, the Würzburg contribution is responsible for the heavy

[9] For a full account of the work of the Würzburg school on thought, see Humphrey (1951).

[10] While directional characteristics of thought are well established (Humphrey,
1951), it is not necessarily true that directionality is inexplicable on associative
principles (see Judson & Cofer, 1956; Judson, Cofer & Gelfand, 1956; Cofer, 1957).

emphasis on motivation, which, as we have said, seems to characterize the twentieth century.

Hypnosis, Psychoneurosis, and Psychoanalysis

These three topics are inextricably linked, and we shall deal with them together briefly, indicating their significance for the topic of motivation.

Hypnotism and psychoneurosis are treated historically in several sources as well as in the usual histories of psychology.[11] We shall provide only a sketch here.

It is likely that hypnotic phenomena were known long before the time of Anton Mesmer (1734–1815), but this Viennese physician, who later moved to Paris, was the first to demonstrate the phenomena on a wide scale. (It was known for several decades as mesmerism.) Mesmer attributed the phenomenon to "animal magnetism," a force which he presumably possessed and by which he was able to affect others. He used it chiefly as a therapeutic for various kinds of ills—ailments today we would probably consider hysterical in character. The chief controversy around Mesmer's work lay in the process by which he produced his cures. Apparently the fact of his cures was more or less accepted in a qualified way by the scientific commissions in Paris, which investigated his work, but that the cures had anything to do with animal magnetism was a claim which was rejected. Mesmer was offered a large sum of money to divulge his "secret"; not knowing what it was, apparently, he found it impossible to comply with this request. Although mesmerism continued to be practiced, it fell, generally, into disrepute.

The next period of interest arose in England, where John Elliotson (1791–1868), who made several valuable, if radical, innovations in the practice of medicine, began treating hospital patients by means of mesmerism. He had some results, but the disrepute in which mesmerism by then was held caused his medical colleagues to reject his findings. Elliotson carried his fight onward, however, founding a journal of his own, continuing the practice, but unfortunately confounding mesmerism with certain aspects of spiritualism and clairvoyance. This did not help mesmerism.

James Esdaile (1808–1859), at about the same time, had used mesmerism successfully in India as a means of anesthetizing patients requiring surgery, and it is quite likely that the story of hypnotism and

[11] See Bramwell (1921) Janet (1925), Boring (1950), Flugel (1951), Müller-Freienfels (1935), Murphy (1950), and Zilboorg and Henry (1941). See also Dorcus (1956).

perhaps of psychology itself would have been different had not the anesthetic effect of drugs, like nitrous oxide, ether, and chloroform, been discovered in the 1840's. Interest in them caused a decline in the interest of mesmerism.

James Braid (1795–1860), meanwhile, became convinced of the reality of the phenomenon and proceeded to do research on it. He convinced himself that, while the phenomenon is real, it arises from a sort of sleep, or a modification of attention. From this, he developed the name hypnotism. Interestingly enough, this new name and the observations and hypotheses underlying it made the whole matter more acceptable to medicine and less so to the mesmerists. Braid's work became known in France, where the next episode in hypnotism's history took place.

The first worker in the Nancy School was A. A. Liébeault (1823–1904), who found hypnosis useful in the treatment of various ills he encountered in his practice. His experience influenced H. Bernheim (1837–1919), whom Liébeault convinced of the value of his methods, and who joined with Liébeault in their utilization and study. The Nancy School was a fairly direct descendant of Braidism, and its conception of the hypnotic process involved suggestion and a sleep-like state. Further, Bernheim believed that almost everyone has some capacity to be hypnotized; that is, everyone is to some extent suggestible; he thus denied that suggestion is in any way a symptom or a characteristic of neurosis. In this, as Zilboorg observes, he made "the first (known) attempt to evolve a general understanding of human behavior and its motivation on the basis of the study of psychopathology rather than on the basis of philosophical systems" (Zilboorg & Henry, 1941, p. 368).

J. M. Charcot's (1825–1893) view was different. As a neurologist, he viewed hysteria as a disease entity which he treated and studied by means of hypnotism. But he concluded that the characteristic states of hypnosis "could be induced and observed only in those people who suffer from hysteria" (Zilboorg & Henry, 1941, p. 362). The ability to be hypnotized is thus a symptom or sign of a disease process. Modern views of hypnotism are more akin to those of the Nancy School than they are to the ideas of Charcot.

It is worthwhile noting, of course, that even in Charcot's view, hysteria was regarded as a disease. The important thing about this is that it was *not* regarded as a sign of demoniacal possession or of inadequate will power. Charcot's school, as well as that of Nancy, had advanced beyond such notions, and this had indeed been the trend of thought since sometime at least in the eighteenth century.

Current theories of drive are embedded in general theories of behavior which also stress the role and nature of learning in behavioral problems. In general, as Chapter 10 shows, drive theories stress either the energizing functions of the drive states on behavior or the goal-determining functions of the drive states. In these points we can see reflected both the notion of the urge and that of purpose, as we described them in our discussion of instinct. In some learning theories reinforcement (law of effect) is a significant topic, and we have already mentioned the relation of hedonism to this concept. Most learning theories postulate only a few bodily drives and suggest that many important motives are learned.

Psychoanalysis (Chapter 12), in its classical form, depended on instinctive urges, whose goal was satisfaction or pleasure. It, too, was strongly influenced by evolutionary and physicalistic thinking, and the end state involved the restoration of homeostatic equilibrium. The relations of psychoanalysis to hypnotism, neurosis, and the psychology of intentionality have already been mentioned.

Contemporary interest in emotion (Chapter 8) shows two major facets. One is that emotion activates behavior, and this probably reflects, at least indirectly, the urge concept of instinct. The other facet is the emphasis on affective enjoyment or pleasure in setting up motivational forces. The derivation from hedonism here is evident.

Theories in social psychology have tended to be concerned with the motives for social behavior and with the social control of conduct. Hedonistic and homeostatic conceptions are currently popular, replacing, in a large measure, the earlier attempts to rely on one or just a few motives or instincts as basic to social behavior and its control.

This brief summary of models shows that they are heavily indebted to instinct, homeostasis, evolution, and hedonism for their origins; active unconscious factors are also strongly implicated in some of them. In some models only a few motives are assumed, in others many, though usually in the latter case only a few have innate status. All these models try to explain conduct or behavior—what its causes are and the factors which control it. In general, behavior is seen as serving the needs of the organism in some sense. Problems of dualism, will and free will are seldom discussed in this context, but these models in general can be characterized as monistic and as seeing problems of choice and striving as derivative from the needs of the organism in interaction with its environment. Rationality and knowledge tend to be regarded as unreliable reflections of more basic determiners.

Very recently, there has been a tendency to reject as adequate the general kind of model we have just described. Still stressing homeo-

But when hypnotism and psychoneurosis came to be regarded as natural phenomena, involving neither magnetic, spiritual nor willful aspects, they yet remained phenomena requiring explanation. The great systems of philosophy, in general, and in their psychological principles, had almost always been constructed by and with a view to normal, rational men. Their principles, even the motivational ones like hedonism, the urge for power, the social contract, the will, and the like, could not easily accommodate the phenomena of mental disorder and hypnotism. Equally difficult, as a matter of fact, were phenomena of crowd behavior, sometimes referred to as "mass hysteria." The phenomena of abnormal behavior, individual and social, and of hypnotism pointed to a need for concepts which had not been emphasized much in the systems of the past. Efforts were made among the forerunners of social psychology to rely on suggestion, imitation, sympathy (Allport, 1954), and similar single concepts; dissociation, suggestibility, and various physical disorders were mentioned as explanatory bases for abnormal individual behavior. But it was Sigmund Freud (1856–1939) who developed the most influential and wide-reaching theories of the nature of neurosis, hypnotism, and certain crowd phenomena. His theories were and are essentially motivational in nature.

Freud studied with Charcot and at Nancy. In Vienna his teachers had included Brentano and Brücke, names with which we are already familiar. As a neurologist, his medical practice included many hysterical patients and, at the example of Josef Breuer, he used hypnosis to treat such cases. His method ultimately went beyond hypnosis, which he later abandoned, and his cases included many kinds of disorder aside from hysteria. Nevertheless, we can see that in Freud the study and use of hypnosis and the study and treatment of neurosis converged. Out of this convergence developed a very general theory of human motivation, one which emphasized the notions of unconscious instinctual energy, conflict, and a hedonistic principle. A detailed exposition of Freud's views of motivation is presented in Chapter 12, and so we shall not follow his ideas and career further here.

The period from Mesmer to Freud is over a century long, and, in the present context, it was marked by the emergence of hypnosis and mental abnormality as natural phenomena requiring explanation. We have then another problem to add to our list. So far it has included the influence of evolution, instinct, and purpose (and their controversies), the general problem of adaptation, and intentionality as sources from which the twentieth century concern with motivational problems has, we think, emerged. One last trend remains to be mentioned, the expression of hedonism in the law of effect.

Hedonism and the Law of Effect

We saw earlier the long history and the important place which the hedonistic principle has held in the thoughts of philosophers concerning man's conduct. We also discussed the emergence of the study of animal behavior following the development of the theory of evolution. An important merging of these two historical trends took place at the very end of the nineteenth century when E. L. Thorndike (1874–1949) formulated his well-known *Law of Effect*. Thorndike had started, with James at Harvard, some studies of the intelligence of young chickens, but his famous investigations of the behavior of animals in the puzzle-box were carried out at Columbia, where he received his doctorate in 1898. In these studies, hungry animals, such as cats, were confined in boxes with food located out of reach outside the boxes. If the animal operated a latch, or pulled a string, a door would open, thus permitting the subject to reach food; Thorndike observed that progress in this task seemed to depend on success in reaching the food. He suggested that the "pleasure" arising from the success and from obtaining the food somehow operated to "stamp in" the associations between the stimuli of the situation and the successful movements, and also that when an animal's reactions led to discomfort (punishment) they would tend to be eliminated. Thorndike later modified his formulation greatly, redefining the processes of success, pleasure, and discomfort in more objective ways, and altering his views of the effects of punishment. He devoted many experiments to these problems (cf. Postman, 1947), and many other workers have sought also to understand them. While Thorndike's laws had antecedents in such writers as Herbert Spencer and Alexander Bain (and, indeed, in Aristotle), their emergence from experimental work gave them both an empirical base and provided means for their further study. The law of effect has had a central place in learning theories, and it is one of the reasons that such theories have laid much stress on drive, reinforcement, amount and delay of reinforcement, and a host of problems which have a heavy motivational loading (see Chapters 10 and 11).

Before leaving this point, one dissimilarity between Thorndike's hedonism and that found in the earlier use of the hedonistic principle should be mentioned. Mowrer (1952, p. 419) has stated it as follows:

Hedonism . . . held that we are "propelled by pleasure and repelled by pain." And it is possible to find traces of this thinking in the works of both Freud . . . and Thorndike . . . But the notable difference is that, with the latter two investigators, pleasure ceased to be a drive in and of itself and was

conceived as the experience which occurs when a drive, or motive, terminates, i.e., is satisfied, relieved, or fulfilled.

This distinction can still be seen in the later chapters which deal with tension or drive reduction viewpoints (Chapters 10 and 11) on the one hand and the one which stresses affective enjoyment or pleasantness on the other (Chapter 8).

CURRENT MODELS AND THE HISTORY OF MOTIVATION

A glance at the table of contents for this volume will reveal that, as we have organized the field, there are several major views toward motivation which are prominent in the present scene. We may briefly characterize them here and quickly indicate some of their relations to the topics we have just reviewed in our historical sketch.

Contemporary interest in *instinct* resides in the work of the ethologists and in the study of certain patterns of behavior, like hoarding, migration, sex, parental, and filial behavior. The ethologists find relatively fixed kinds of behavior, which they call instinctive, and attempt to understand the factors which release energy for the performance of these and other acts. They thus combine the two major meanings of instinct, that is, unlearned behavior and energy (urge, impulse). They regard their work as generally falling into an evolutionary framework. Students of the other kinds of behavior just mentioned, hoarding, for example, seem primarily concerned with the discovery of the factors which control such behaviors. Instinct, for them, only as a very general classificatory rubric and has no explanatory value; explanation is to be sought in the understanding of the factors which control the pertinent behaviors. Small-scale theories of one or the other of these behaviors are beginning to emerge. Chapter 3 deals with the work of the ethologists, while Chapter 4 presents material concerning several of these behaviors and their theories.

As a concept homeostasis has wide usage. There are models in cybernetics, which depend largely on homeostatic and related notions for their account of the systems of variables with which they deal. This use of homeostasis has a relatively short history, deriving from evolutionary thought and from the work of physiologists like Cannon and his followers (Chapter 7). The homeostatic conception of drive as an end state toward which other behavioral processes move, or which they have as a goal, has a widespread use. We will find it in treatments of instinct, psychoanalysis, learning theory, physiological emotion, and some theories deriving from social behavior. Homeostasis, then, is a model with widespread implications.

static and evolutionary conceptions, the group of whom we speak in the chapter on self-actualization has seemed to emphasize reason and knowledge, the fundamental goodness of human nature, and the idea that, in the explanation of behavior, behavior can be viewed as an end in itself rather than necessarily serving other organismic needs. This view would seem consonant with the early stress we found in such writers as Socrates, Plato, Aristotle, some of the Church Fathers, and Rousseau.

We would conclude this chapter with a warning (cf. Asch, 1952, pp. 3–39). The foregoing models represent only certain ways of looking at the problem of the motivational aspects of behavior. There are undoubtedly many others. The student who finds the models presented in this book unconvincing, unsatisfactory, or wanting, in some respect, need not conclude that satisfactory models cannot be built. What he should conclude is that new models are needed. Perhaps he himself will try to construct one.

Chapter 3

The Concept of Instinct: Ethological Position

Beach (1955) has traced the history of the instinct concept from its origin in antiquity to its continued use in modern-day motivation theory. As was seen in Chapter 2, many forms of instinct theory were prevalent in psychological thinking at the turn of the century, and it was not until the early 1920's that the use of this concept as an explanatory motivational principle began to wane. Under the onslaught of the environmentalism of the rising new behaviorism, and as a result of the overextended claims of some of the instinctivists themselves, the concept gradually came to be replaced by other explanatory notions like drive, reflex, habit, and native response. Withering attacks were directed at the instinct concept from an experimentalist viewpoint (Dunlap, 1919; and Kuo, 1924), and it was criticized as being logically and experimentally useless (Eggan, 1926; E. B. Holt, 1931; P. T. Young, 1936). From another view, Bernard (1924) pointed up the meaninglessness of the widely used concept by tracing, in the literature, the assignment of the designation "instinctive" to some several *thousand* different classifications of behavior. He showed the inconsistent and often contradictory ways in which the concept was applied.[1] More recently, Beach (1955) and Ginsberg (1952) have reanalyzed the concept to show why, as it has been employed, it has had both limited usefulness and has been actually limiting of research hypotheses instead of being productive of them. We shall return to this point later in the chapter.

We might expect, as a result of such wide criticism from so many varied points of view, that the concept would have disappeared, and

---

[1] Two examples from the large list of varied uses compiled by Bernard will make his point clear: ". . . with a glance of the eye we estimate instinctively the age of a 'passerby,'" and ". . . the instinctive morality developed by personal groups" (Bernard, 1924, pp. 132–134).

56

that the likelihood of its reappearance in psychological writing, if similar to its earlier form(s), would be slim indeed. Surprisingly enough, this has not been the case at all. The term has, of course, continued in use in literary works, and to a large extent in the writings of social scientists and some biologists and medically oriented psychologists. This has stemmed primarily from the psychoanalytic concept of instinct, rather than the more classical concepts of McDougall (1923, 1926, 1933), James (1890), and others in the mainstream of psychology.

The continued use of the term in social scientific writing, despite sociologist Bernard's devastating criticisms, may possibly be explained, although probably not justified, on other grounds. For a social scientist dealing with institutional (social, economic, or political) man, rather than with individual man, the exact origin or nature of an assumed urge, drive, or instinct (e.g., aggression) is not vital to the level of thinking involved. Under these circumstances, use of such "convenient" concepts as instinct may go unchallenged. Perhaps it is analogous to the psychologist's use of hypothetical neurological or physiological constructs as assumptions of convenience for his psychological theorizing (see Hempel, 1952).

By and large, the term *drive* has come to replace instinct in the language of American behavior theorists. Most current textbooks of general psychology use terms like drive or motive when referring to motivational variables and their sources. There are some notable exceptions (e.g., Morgan, 1956), but on the whole we find little acceptance of the concept of instinct today.

However, despite the focusing of American psychological writing and research on the mechanisms of drive and habit as organizing forces in behavior, a small group of European (and some American) zoologists and psychologists has continued a series of systematic studies on what they call the innate mechanisms of behavior, namely, instincts. In the past decade or so, an increasing number of books and papers have appeared in the English language describing the work of these ethologists [2] and presenting the theoretical framework they have developed for their investigations. The first general survey of the ethological position was offered by Tinbergen (1951). A briefer and recent summary is that of Hess (1962).

The work of the ethologists has attracted a large (and largely sympathetic) audience among psychologists as well as biologists. We

[2] Fletcher (1957) reminds us that the term *ethology* was originally employed by J. S. Mill to designate "The Science of Character." As used here it will always mean "The Scientific Study of Animal Behavior," the use ascribed to it by Tinbergen (1951).

therefore think it desirable to present the ethological view as a "case study" of the development and application of a behavior theory built upon instinct as its motivational core.

BACKGROUND OF ETHOLOGICAL POSITION

A recent glossary description for objective behavioral science describes an ethologist as ". . . a behaviorist who, typically, has been trained in zoology, usually studies the behavior of insects, fishes, and birds more often than that of mammals and other groups . . . a student of comparative behavior . . . a behaviorist who likes his animals" (Verplanck, 1957, p. 14). A behaviorist, according to this same source, is ". . . a scientist who investigates the behavior of animals objectively and who attempts to relate his observations together in a theoretical system that does not include concepts borrowed from introspection and mental philosophy" (Verplanck, 1957, p. 6).

The student of American psychology will be familiar with this last definition. American behaviorists, particularly, have sought to stress the objectivity of their work and to dissociate themselves from subjectivist and vitalist positions of earlier (and some contemporary) psychologists. Verbal reports of subjective experiences have been used by some recent neobehaviorists, not as subjective data, however, but only as units of response which could be treated in the same way as any other response units, namely, counted, classified, or correlated.[3]

What, then, are the differences between ethologists and comparative psychologists of American behaviorist orientation? If we return to the glossary description of an ethologist, some of the differences become clearer. First, an ethologist is usually a zoologist by training. Because of this, and the specific traditions and associations it implies, one might expect close liaison between the language and the theories of ethology and the thinking of morphologists, geneticists, evolutionists, taxonomists, ecologists, and other biologists. In fact, this is both claimed and found in the ethological literature. Second, the systematic observation of ". . . insects, fishes, and birds more often than . . . mammals" might be expected to lead to theoretical concepts less dependent on learning ability and on intelligence of the organism under study than those of psychologists who have, by and large, restricted their studies to a few mammalian species. Third, the emphasis on "comparative" study and on "liking his animals" suggests a naturalist approach as contrasted with the more restricted (some would say more rigorous)

[3] See, for example, Miller & Dollard, *Social Learning and Imitation* (1941), or Skinner's treatment of *Verbal Behavior* (1957).

laboratory method(s) of American behaviorists. Actually, the term *neonaturalist* has been applied to the ethologists in at least one case (Nissen & Semmes, 1952).

One further difference might be mentioned, before quitting this comparison. The ethological movement, as we have noted, had its origin largely in Europe. Most of the early publications, as well as many of the current reports of ethological research, are in German. Thus, until fairly recently, the major literature of this movement was not broadly available to American psychologists. Obviously, the geographic and language separations of ethologists and psychologists have limited the amount of interaction which might otherwise have led to earlier and greater cross-fertilization. Examination of the reference lists in the writings of each group shows only peripheral reference to either the investigations or the thinking of the other. It is possible that such separateness resulted from a positive rejection of the work of the other group, but, as we shall see, it would appear to have been a lack of familiarity with this work that kept it from being included.

This appearance of the ethological writing in the German (and Scandinavian) tongue, and in journals not readily available to Americans, is certainly partly responsible for the delayed response to ethology in this country. On the other hand, the very time-consuming nature of the ethological field studies, as well as their own prolific literature (and the biological research with which they appear to keep abreast), have probably kept the ethologists from becoming more closely acquainted with current American psychological thinking. To take one main example, Tinbergen, one of the main spokesmen of the ethological movement, in his *Study of Instinct* (1951), refers to Tolman's *Purposive Behavior in Animals and Men* (1932) as if this early work could be said to be representative of present-day American behaviorist thinking.

We have not meant, in the above discussion, to demean the thinking or research of either the European ethologists or the modern American behaviorists. These remarks are intended to show how the two positions, developing out of separate traditions, have evolved patterns of thinking which call upon different conceptual language. That neither dealt precisely with the data or the theories of the other appears to have been a matter of geography, language, and origin of discipline. We should note, however, that these barriers are no longer serious ones. The two positions have now come into close enough contact to warrant a more direct comparison of their theories, and, indeed, several comparisons have already been made. We shall return to the results of such comparisons after we have had a chance to examine the ethological position itself.

THE ETHOLOGICAL CONCEPT OF INSTINCTIVE BEHAVIOR

In setting forth the ethological theory of instinctive behavior, two facts must be kept in mind. First, the position conceives instinctive behavior as a complex of several levels and stages involving a number of particular concepts, only one of which (albeit an important one) is the instinct proper. We will here be primarily concerned with assessing the role of the motivated behavior of the organism. Only secondarily, will we deal with the question of whether or not the ethologists have made a sufficiently good case for the existence of instincts. We should also take account of the fact that ethological studies (those so identified at least) first began to appear in the early 1930's, and formal statements of ethological theory have but recently and tentatively been put forth. As Konrad Lorenz, one of the acknowledged prime movers of ethology, has explained (1950), the ethologists have proceeded inductively, from careful and detailed descriptions based upon natural observations, to tentative systematization, and only slowly *toward* causal analysis. Tinbergen (1951) likewise presents many of his conclusions tentatively and repeatedly mentions the possibility that the conceptual framework he has arrived at is subject to revision. This acknowledged willingness to modify the details, and even the nature of the central concepts of the theory, can be found throughout the papers of other ethologists (e.g., Thorpe, 1950, 1956; Armstrong, 1947, 1950), as well as those of Lorenz and Tinbergen.

Instinct and Instinctive Behavior

Instinctive activity involves the arousing, ordering, and sustaining of behavior in particular direction and intensity until an appropriate environment is found in which the instinctive energy can be discharged. In all instinctive behavior, according to Lorenz,

. . . there is a hard core of absolutely fixed, more or less complex automatism—an inborn movement form. This restricted concept is the *instinct* (*erbkoordination*) . . . such instincts, or movement forms are items of behaviour in every way as constant as anatomical structures and potentially just as valuable for systematic and phylogenetic studies (Thorpe, 1948, p. 3).

The *instinct*, then, is an inherited, specific, stereotyped pattern of behavior. It is further said to have its own energy and is *released*, rather than guided, by particular environmental stimuli. The distinction between instinctive behavior and instinct is an important one for the proper evaluation of the ethological view. Unfortunately, different writers have used the terms in contradictory and overlapping ways. Tinbergen (1951, pp. 110–111), although recognizing this fact, nevertheless insists that the term *instinctive* be used descriptively for several levels of behavior, since, in his opinion, it is appropriate not only to one but to many phases of a motivated act.

In general, the term *instinct* will usually refer to the consummatory (terminal) phase of a motivated act, in which the ongoing behavior is finally ended, whereas *instinctive behavior* will be used to describe one or more sequences of motivated acts, including appetitive (seeking) as well as terminal (energy discharge) phases.[4] Since much of the earlier writing has slurred over this distinction,[5] criticism of instinctivist writers has been in part a result of the confusion (both in the writing itself and in interpretations) as to what exactly the limits of an instinct were to be. For Lorenz (and for the other ethologists as well) the instinct is only a fraction of the instinctive behavior, and it is the instinct alone which, as the "hard core" of the system, is described as absolutely fixed and inborn. (Hess [1962] has recently used the phrase "fixed action pattern" as a substitute for instinct in this narrow sense.)

The specificity of the instinctive action and its independence of "receptor-steering" or stimulus control is illustrated in an experiment of Lorenz and Tinbergen (1938). This example may also serve to indicate to the reader what is meant fundamentally by the ethologists when they speak of instinctive behavior. They sought to differentiate taxic[6] and instinctive components in the egg-retrieving behavior of the greylag goose. In their view, retrieving an egg that has rolled from the nest is an instance of instinctive behavior, but only certain of the motor acts involved are "true instincts." A portion of their conclusion will illustrate what is meant:

A directed outstretching of the neck, as the initial orienting reaction, creates the stimulus situation in which the instinctive action is released and, at the same time, the spatial relationships required for its biologically effective discharge. . . . The instinctive action which it activates is a breastward flexion of the neck and head, which pulls the egg, resting against the undersurface of the bill, toward the nest. From beginning to end, an additional orienting reaction accompanies this motor pattern which runs in the sagittal

[4] In fact, the ethologists' use of the term instinctive behavior could be equated to others' use of motivated behavior.

[5] See Bernard (1924) and Lashley (1938a) for reviews of such multiple uses of the term instinct.

[6] The term *taxis* refers to a broad class of behaviors specifiable in terms of the responses (locomotor and orientative) and of the stimuli (most often visual) controlling them (Verplanck, 1957).

plane throughout. [Stimulus] controlled lateral motions hold the egg in balance and in its proper direction on the undersurface of the bill (Lorenz & Tinbergen, 1938, pp. 207–208).

Lorenz and Tinbergen found that if they removed the egg, once the striving action had been started, the sagittal plane movements continued but were now unmodified by the side-to-side balancing head movements. These taxic lateral elements could also be eliminated by substituting a round tube for the egg, again leaving the fixed pattern component of the retrieving response unaffected. They thus concluded that the undisturbed direct bill movements were the hard-core instinct, and the lateral movements a part of the instinctive behavior but not of the instinct proper.[7]

Instinct and Reaction Specific Energy

Ethological theory can immediately be seen as a form of motivation theory when we consider that each of the specific instincts is assigned its own *reaction specific energy*. This motivational energy is said to accumulate in specific centers in the central nervous system and to be released, usually,[8] only in the performance of the specific instinctive act.

Lorenz writes:

. . . the appetitive behaviors resulting from the accumulation of action specific energy all tend to bring about, by *variable* movements, an *invariable* end or goal, and they go on until this goal is reached or the animal as a whole is exhausted (1950, p. 248).

The organism, thus, is driven not to *seek* a goal, in a finalistic teleological sense, but nevertheless acts purposely, as Tolman (1932) has used this term.

The neural centers in which the energy accumulates form an ordered hierarchy. Each center in turn contributes to the inhibition or release of energy from a lower center governing more specific aspects of instinctive behavior (or a more specific instinct). Figures

---

[7] Without disparaging the ingenuity of their demonstration, we may here question whether, had Lorenz and Tinbergen distorted the horizontal plane on which the egg-rolling occurred, or used a nonconcentric object which would roll off sideways each time, they might not have found the lateral elements remaining and the sagittal movements modified.

[8] Despite the insistence that energy is reaction specific, there are a number of instances in which ethologists have allowed that other behaviors (e.g., appetitive behaviors) draw upon these restricted energy supplies. This matter is discussed in several places in the chapter. To our knowledge it has never been fully clarified by the ethologists.

3–1 and 3–2 present Tinbergen's schematic diagrams of this hypothesized hierarchical relationship of neural centers. According to Tinbergen, the regulatory mechanisms are not simple correlates of stimuli, but involve elaborate braking and releasing features. Thus, energy stored in a particular center (e.g., Center 1, Fig. 3–2) is subject to influence from (1) hormones, (2) external motivational impulses (sensory factors), and (3) intrinsic motivational impulses, these last from the same level (e.g., neural impulses from activities in progress) and from superordinate levels (e.g., energy released from a prior step

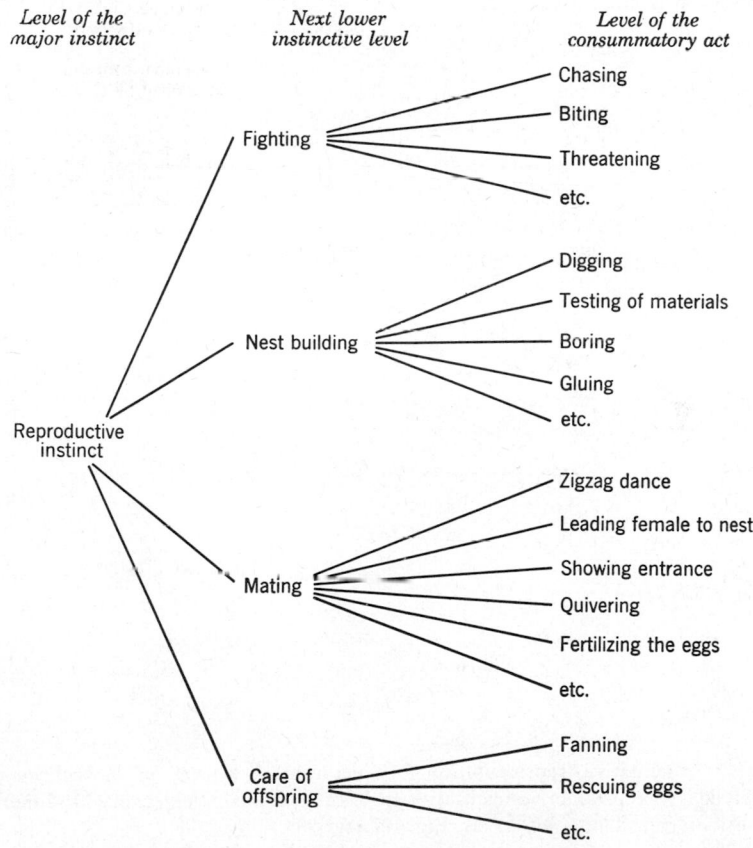

Figure 3–1. The principle of hierarchical organization of instincts illustrated by the reproductive instinct of the male three spined stickleback. Reproduced by permission from Tinbergen (1951, Fig. 89, p. 104).

in the sequence). The energy can be discharged usually only after release of the blocking mechanism through activation of an innate releasing mechanism by an appropriate external stimulus (see below).

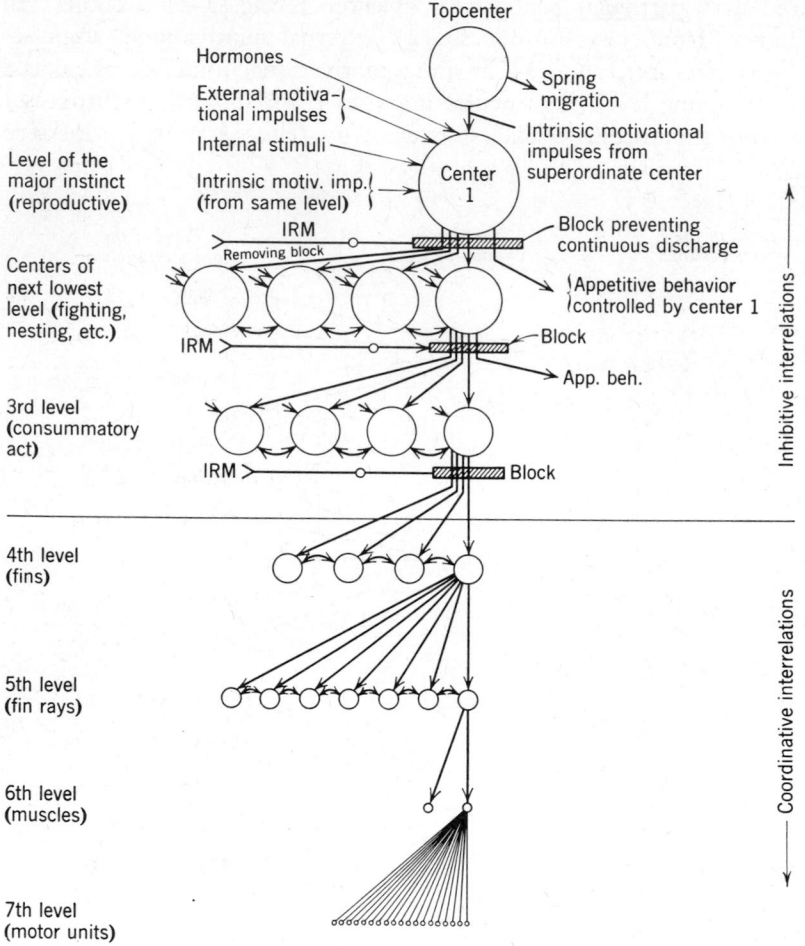

Figure 3–2. Tentative representation of hierarchical system of neural centers underlying the reproductive instinct of male three-spined stickleback. Modified by permission from Tinbergen (1951, Figs. 97 and 98).

Figure 3–1 schematically illustrates how a major instinct, in this case the reproductive instinct, is in turn divided into a series of sub-instincts, each representing a particular behavior pattern (e.g., fighting, nesting, etc.), and each in turn controlling specific motor responses (of muscle groups, etc.).[9] Tinbergen was aware of, and incorporated, aspects of earlier theories of neural patterning (Weiss, 1941; Beach, 1942*a*) into the hierarchical neural structure he described, but it was primarily on the basis of the ethological observations that he adopted this system. In other words, observations of the orderliness of the sequence of behaviors constituting eating, reproductive, and other activities led to the hypothesis of a neural hierarchy rather than a single neural center, which was earlier held to be the case. This reliance on an empirical base for ethology is emphasized by Lorenz as distinct from the hypostatization of the purposivists: "We have not gone out from finalistically considering what the animal *ought* to do, in order to sustain itself and its species [referring here specifically to Tinbergen's work on the reproductive instinct], but from what it actually *does*" (Lorenz, 1950, p. 262).

Appetitive Behavior and Goal Behavior

The building up of reaction specific energy, or drive, leads to a type of behavior which is not itself an instinct. The drive aspect of instinct serves as a forcer of noninstinctive *appetitive behavior*. This behavior, in turn, bridges the gap between the energized organism and the particular environment in which its energy can be released. Figure 3–3 (Thorpe, 1948) shows the relationship of instinct, appetitive behavior, and goal behavior. The link between instinct-energizer and appetitive behavior is accounted for neurally (see Fig. 3–2).

Once activated, the appetitive behavior must persist, its energy activating further and more specific appetitive behavior, until finally "released" by the performance of the instinct (consummatory act) itself. It is never fully clear, however, what the source of energy for the appetitive behavior is. The most likely inference is that the energy is derived from the instinct proper (i.e., the reaction specific energy). This is suggested by Tinbergen's description of the operation of the innate releasing mechanisms and by Thorpe (see Fig. 3–3). If so, it is conceivable that the energy would be exhausted in appetitive be-

[9] It would be useful if the term *instinct* were restricted to the consummatory acts, consistent with Lorenz' and Thorpe's use (see p. 74). In that sense, Fig. 3–1 describes an instinctive behavior sequence, rather than an instinct. A more serious difficulty with Tinbergen's schema is pointed out by Hess (1962), namely, that the schema ignores the fact that some of the consummatory level acts (e.g., locomotive behaviors) may be involved in more than one hierarchical organization. We may add that this would inordinately complicate the matter of sequential control, although this would not rule it out as a possible model of neurophysiological function.

havior long before the proper environmental key is found to release the consummatory act (to which the energy is presumably quite specific). If this is the case, the variety of behaviors thus motivated would give the energy much more flexible range than seems implied in its very specificity. However, it is possible that a separate source of appetitive energy exists. If it does, it would have to be accounted for in terms which would explain its force, its duration, and, perhaps, its own specificity, much as the instincts proper are specific.

Goal behavior refers to the performance of the consummatory act (i.e., instinct, or fixed action pattern) in the environment containing its appropriate releaser. The "receptory correlate" referred to by Thorpe (see Fig. 3–3) is an innate (though modifiable) central neural

A	B	C
Drive	Appetitive Behavior	Goal Behavior
(state of the organism leading to B)	(directed action terminated by C)	(specific act terminating A)
The as yet unreleased *instinct* (i.e., stereotyped behavior pattern) differentiates and accumulates round itself a store of *reaction-specific energy*. This process may be associated with or preceded by a *physiological* need or a *psychological* state (conative urge, emotion, or both).	The expression of a conative urge or appetite for a particular direction or kind of activity. This may be: (*a*) Random locomotion (*Kineses* *) or (*b*) Directed locomotion (simpler types) (Kineses plus *Taxes*) or (*c*) Directed locomotion (more complex types) consisting of specific taxes interlaced with subsidiary instincts.	*Instinct* released by the environmental *releaser* acting via the *receptory correlate* and minutely adjusted to the environment by the "coat of reflexes" (von Holst).† The release of the instinct results in the dissipation of the tension due to the accumulation of reaction specific energy and in the satisfaction of the need.

Figure 3–3. Diagram of instinctive behavior. Modified by permission from Thorpe (1948, p. 6).

* Kineses are movements of body members resulting from muscular contractions (Warren, 1934). Taxes have already been defined (see footnote 6).

† The "coat of reflexes" describes the regular responses of the organism to specific features of the environment. Such mechanisms are ". . . interposed between the rigid automatisms [of the organism] and the equally hard conditions of the environment . . . as a blanket of snow softens the outline [without changing the shape] of a roof" (Lorenz, 1939, p. 249).

process which is responsible for the selective release of instincts when the appropriate environmental cues are perceived. It is a part of the innate releasing mechanism, which we shall turn to next.

Environmental Releasers and the Innate Releasing Mechanism (IRM)

What kinds of stimuli can act as releasers of instincts, and how do they effect the discharge of energy in the instinctive act? That this is not a simple matter is well illustrated by Tinbergen:

From a study of sensory capacity we can infer what changes in the environment can or can*not* be perceived by the animals, but a positive answer about what *does* release the observed reaction is impossible. This turns upon the peculiar fact that an animal does not react to all the changes in the environment which its sense organs can receive, but only a small part of them. This is a basic property of instinctive behavior, the importance of which cannot be stressed too much (Tinbergen, 1951, p. 25).

Tinbergen cites the behavior of the carnivorous water beetle, *Dytiscus marginalis,* as an example. Although elsewhere determined to be entirely capable of visual discriminations, this organism apparently utilizes chemical and tactile rather than visual stimulation in its hunting and feeding responses. A tadpole presented in a glass tube is ignored, whereas a meat extract solution leads to searching and grasping behaviors (Tinbergen, 1936). He points out that the use of visual stimuli might actually be more appropriate to the satisfaction of the pressing motivational need (hunger). "The occurrence of such 'errors' or 'mistakes,'" he observes, "is one of the most conspicuous characteristics of innate behavior" (1951, p. 27).

Tinbergen's studies of stickleback responses to experimental models yield further evidence on this point. In these experiments, dummy fish were presented, with only one aspect of the natural stimulus retained. Thus shape *or* color *or* size, etc., was the same as in the real fish, while the remainder of the "proper" stimuli were markedly distorted. The releasing "potency" of different models was then able to be determined with great precision (Tinbergen, 1951).

It is on the basis of this distinction between capacity to be stimulated, or receptor sensitivity, and the selectivity shown in responses to particular stimuli, that ethologists arrived at the concept of the *innate releasing mechanism (IRM).* Presumably, the particular pattern(s) of stimuli which effects the release of the instinctive response is itself unlearned, but somehow directly correlated with a central neural mechanism that "recognizes" and responds exclusively to these stimuli, regardless of the presence or not of other stimulation. The *specificity* of the relationship between natural releaser and instinct is emphasized in the phrase "as a lock fits the key" (Thorpe, 1948, p. 10).[10] The role of the innate releasing mechanism is described by Tinbergen, as follows:

Outgoing impulses are blocked as long as the IRM is not stimulated. When the adequate sign stimuli impinge upon the reflex-like IRM, the block is removed. The impulses can now flow along a number of paths. All but one lead to subordinate centres of the next lower level [see Fig. 3–2]. However, most of these centres are prevented from action by their own blocks, and most of the impulses therefore flow to the nervous structures controlling appetitive behavior. The appetitive behavior . . . is carried on until one of the IRMs of the lower level removes a block, [. . . and so on] (Tinbergen, 1951, pp. 124–125).

This system, then, seeks to account for two facts of observation, namely, that instincts are not discharged continuously, and that related instincts (and associated appetitive behavior) occur in predictable sequences. The successive blocking mechanisms provide time for the accumulation of reaction specific energy, and, as lower-order blocks are released by their respective IRMs, they "drain away the impulses" (Tinbergen, 1951) from higher appetitive centers to those lower in the system. This suggestion of a hydraulic model is made explicit by Lorenz (1950) and will be discussed later in this chapter.

The schematic neural program of the ethologists further attempts to take account of the various known factors affecting motivated behavior: for example, the influence of hormone level, activities in progress at the moment, sensory processes, etc. However, it is not intended as a neuroanatomical model, but a functional schema only.

Tinbergen (1951) and Hess (1962) present considerable evidence from their studies of fish, birds, insects, and bees, to support the hypothesis that there are optimal stimulus situations which apparently release particular reactions. That these situations are innate perceptual patterns is inferred from the fact that animals reared in isolation from others of their species appear to respond predictably to specific aspects of experimentally manipulated environments, even when opportunities for learning do not seem to be present. Some examples of releasers are "red male intruding into the territory," which releases fighting behavior in the male stickleback (Tinbergen, 1951); sight of flying bird of prey (or reasonable facsimile), which releases escape behavior in

[10] This descriptive phrase appears in the writings of Lorenz, Tinbergen, and others, as well as in Thorpe's work.

gallinaceous chicks (Tinbergen & Keunen, 1939), and moving legs in small mammals, which releases predatory responses in the tawny owl (Räber, 1949). As we shall note later, in considering some of the criticisms of the ethological approach (see p. 98), isolation experiments unfortunately do not provide learning-proof situations, and the possibility that such stimulus-response links are not innate cannot be dismissed. That this is not a closed matter even for the ethologists can be inferred from Tinbergen's writings. In explaining how he and Lorenz (1937) came to posit the IRM concept, he writes: "The strict dependence of an innate reaction on a certain set of sign stimuli leads to the conclusion that there must be a special neurosensory mechanism that releases the reaction and is responsible for its selective susceptibility to such a very special combination of sign stimuli" (Tinbergen, 1951, pp. 41–42). However, he then quickly points out that apparently the dependence isn't so strict.

There is some evidence [Lack, 1943, and his own observations on sticklebacks] which tends to show that there is no absolute distinction between effective sign stimuli and the non-effective properties of an object. . . . These observations suggest that dependence on a sharply limited number of sign stimuli might represent an extreme case and is, perhaps, a specialization. Another possibility is that conditioning is responsible for the effectiveness of additional stimuli (Tinbergen, 1951, p. 42).

We might extend this last speculation to ask, then, if conditioning (in either the physiological sense of hormonal and other determinants of readiness, or the psychological sense of learning) might not be responsible for the observed specific relationships as well. Hess (1962) has recently re-examined the issue, concluding that deprivation or isolation experiments, as well as brain stimulation work, *do* provide evidence for an innate releasing mechanism. We will turn to these considerations later.

Before completing this discussion of environmental releasers, special mention should be made of the fact that an important class of releasers is composed of those which are associated with other living organisms, including other members of one's own species. These *social releasers* play a significant role in sexual behavior, parent-young interaction, and group behavior (e.g., distress calls, warning calls, etc.).

Threshold Change and Vacuum Activity

In the previous discussion it was assumed that the animal was in a sufficiently free and abundant environment for its appetitive behavior to lead it to the proper situation for the release of the action-specific energy. However, this is not always so, and ethological theory takes account of this possibility. If, by virtue of its own inadequacy, or the paucity of the environment, the animal is unable to reach the goal situation, accumulation of action-specific energy continues. This somehow effects a lowering of the appropriate sensory threshold to a point where a less-than-optimal stimulus will suffice to release the IRM. Observations have been reported (Lorenz, 1950) where complete or near-complete instinctive acts have apparently been performed in the absence of any observable releasing stimuli. This has been termed *vacuum activity* (Leerlaufreaktion). However, Thorpe (1948) has suggested that in this last case it is probable that some minimal stimulation is present and simply not recognized by the observer; Armstrong (1950) goes even further to deny the likelihood that true vacuum activity ever occurs.

Thus, the not infrequent observation that an action, which ought to be withheld until an adequate releaser is found, is given anyway, is accounted for within the same general framework of theory. As Lorenz makes clear, the likelihood of a response is a function not only of the releaser, but of the quantity of accumulated energy in combination with the environmental context. The greater the accumulation of energy, the less adequate the releasing stimulus need be. Conversely, when only a small amount of energy is present (as in the case of a recently performed instinct), it may be released only under optimal stimulus conditions.[11] He further points out that certain endogenous activities (instinctive acts) ". . . have a rather quick generation of action-specific energy, but [referring to the hydromechanical model which he had been using to explain the dynamics of energy relationships] . . . a narrow reservoir in which to hold it" (Lorenz, 1950, p. 258).

We find, then, a complicated interdependency among (1) the amount of available action-specific energy, (2) the rate at which such energy has accumulated, (3) the degree of adequacy (i.e., number and quality) of the releasing stimuli present, and (4) the frequency with which the act has been elicited. The "lock and key" notion, with its appealing simplicity, has to be modified to take account of these other simultaneously operating factors. The automatic release of in-

[11] Hess (1962) makes the point that in certain of the ethological experiments, releasers are artificially enhanced (e.g., Koehler and Zagarus [1937] found that ringed plover egg recognition, released by normally dark brown spots on light brown eggs, was exaggerated when a black spotted white egg was substituted). Such *superoptimal* stimuli release responses stronger than normal.

stincts in given stimulus settings is not quite so straightforward as it may sound.

The positing of a threshold change suggests a means at least of testing the hypotheses put forth. As a result of frequency of elicitation, a heightening of the threshold may be expected. The longer the time from last elicitation, the lower the threshold ought to be. In the absence of elicitation, there should be an eventual "overflowing" of response in "energy accumulation activity" (Armstrong, 1947) or vacuum activity, suggesting that the threshold has been lowered to a functional zero level, perhaps.

Both the threshold change and vacuum activity hypotheses are derived from reports of observations (see Lorenz, 1950; Tinbergen, 1951), and in turn are used to explain what would otherwise appear to be exceptions to the straightforward "lock and key" relationship of releasers and instinctive acts.

Displacement Activities and Social Releasers

Many observers have noted the appearance of behavior patterns that are inappropriate to the situations in which they occur or are "out of order" in the sequence to which they belong. Such "irrelevant" responses occur in situations of conflict, where two or more sources of energy are present. The intruding instinctual pattern may appear ". . . in an incomplete, eccentric, or imperfectly orientated form . . ." (Armstrong, 1950, p. 361), as if the energy which supplied it were not its own.

Such responses, called *displacement activity*, rather than being erratic and unpredictable, are seen by the ethologists to be in fact orderly and systematic, and to occur only when the drive for expression of primary behavior patterns is thwarted or in conflict with an incompatible drive (Armstrong, 1950; Tinbergen, 1952). Armstrong compares the concept of displacement activity in animals with certain types of substitute behaviors in man (e.g., the exaggerated physical activity of school children during recess) and suggests the possible parallel with Freud's description of symptom development in conversion hysteria (see Chapter 12).[12]

Displacement activities may play the role of social releasers; that is, inappropriate responses (instincts performed out of context or sequence) appear to become ritualized, and in their expression in this

---

[12] Fletcher (1957) goes even further in drawing parallels between certain of the ethological and psychoanalytic concepts, but we shall deal with these later.

"wrong" context take on sign significance for other members of the species, eliciting instinctive responses from these others (Armstrong, 1950; Tinbergen, 1951, 1952). Thus Tinbergen (1951) cites the example of male stickleback display behavior serving (when displaced rather than when part of the reproductive instinct pattern) as a warning to other male sticklebacks to keep clear of the territory of the displaying fish. Actual morphological changes may indeed coincide with (result from?) the secondary gains of certain displacement activities. The use of color displays as social releasers in fish and in birds has suggested the likelihood of such changes playing a selective evolutionary role (Tinbergen, 1951), and Armstrong concludes that ". . . a displacement-prone species will be more adaptable, and consequently more successful, than a species not so equipped" (1950, p. 378). The species-survival value of such social releasers is seen in sexual interplay between males and females of the same species (leading to successive steps in courtship), between males and males of a species (protecting privacy of territory and thus undisturbed mating and increased likelihood of survival of young), and as warnings of imminence of danger to the flock.

In a paper devoted to displacement (derived) activities, Tinbergen (1952) spells out the circumstances under which they might be expected to occur, and their nature when they do occur. He agrees with Armstrong that they result from a conflict of antagonistic and incompatible instincts (drives?) aroused simultaneously. The mutual thwarting prevents a discharge of energy in either of the instinctive acts. The energy then overflows into an activity which is available to be performed for reasons of hormonal readiness, postural convenience, or just by chance.[13] Thus "pure reactions" (e.g., wing-drying in fowl, a response which requires a particular local noxious stimulus in order to be elicited) are never used as displacement activities, but activities which are not so uniquely tied to specific stimuli may be so used. Some of these would be foraging activities in birds, nest-building movements, sexual movements, movements of care of the body surface, food-begging movements, false brooding, and sleep.

[13] Displacement activities differ from vacuum activities in that an adequate stimulus is available for the former, the response being interfered with by an incompatible reaction, which is thwarted in turn. Vacuum activity, on the other hand, occurs in the absence of an appropriate releaser. The simultaneous arousal of two mutually exclusive instincts may lead to partial, abortive, or compromise responses, whereas vacuum activity is more likely to be "pure" in nature. Despite these differences, the two types of responses may nevertheless be considered aberrations of a similar sort. (See also discussion of frustration and conflict in Chapter 9.)

Tinbergen suggests that displacement activities occur mainly in hostile and purely sexual situations, in both of which approach-avoidance conflict behavior is demonstrable. It may be noted here that at least one of these activities is commonly found by American behaviorists in laboratory rats under shock-avoidance conditioning circumstances. Here the rat displays excessive washing behavior (i.e., movements of care of the body surface) following early shock experiences. The usual interpretation of this behavior has been to associate it with fear or anxiety, rather than with hostility or purely sexual situations, at least in the instance cited. But perhaps this laboratory observation does not sufficiently duplicate a natural setting for the animal. However, the appearance of this activity would suggest that a broader base may exist for displacement activities than the two types of situations cited by Tinbergen. Hess (1962) has also expressed this view.

Tinbergen (1952) notes (as had Armstrong, 1950) the fact that these derived responses are usually more superficial and less complete than the "examples" from which they derive.[14] He considers this all the more odd because these responses usually occur in situations of great tension (conflict) and might on this basis be expected to have greater rather than lesser strength. He concludes that there must be an inner resistance (neural block of some sort) which prevents the full discharge of energy in the motor centers of these responses. He draws support for this conclusion from the observation that on occasions when the "true" instincts break through they are performed with greater vigor than usual. Consistent with this hypothesis is the notion that the inhibition of mutually antagonistic drives "ties up" a portion of the energy, an idea not dissimilar to Freud's concept of energy binding (see Chapter 12).

The form which displacement activities take appears to be influenced by the body position of the organism at the moment of conflict, the presence of adequate (though secondary) stimuli in the environment, and the availability of the response in the repertory of the animal (e.g., preening and grooming activities, low-energy responses with a high frequency of occurrence often appear as displacement activities).

Instinctive Behavior and the Role of Learning

Lorenz (1952a) makes it perfectly clear that the instinct is something different from other forms of innate reactions. Kineses, tropisms, taxes, and reflexes all represent innate response mechanisms but are devoid of the spontaneity and the energizing attributes of the instincts and certain endogenous automatic movements (e.g., stimulus-producing

---

[14] See previous footnote.

centers of the heart, in the respiratory mechanism, etc.). Starting with this motivating core (the endogenous energy of the instinct proper) a complex and modifiable program of appetitive behavior may be developed. We have already shown the intimate relationship hypothesized between the instinct proper and the reflex-like kineses and taxes which are part of the appetitive behavior (see Fig. 3–3). The wide range of permissibility allowed to appetitive behavior permits learned responses to play a role here (see Thorpe, 1956). In the actual performance of the instinctive act itself, we may once again see the role played by learning.

The fixed action pattern, or instinct proper, is "finely adjusted to the exact details of the environment" (Thorpe, 1948, p. 10) by the "coat of reflexes" (von Holst, 1936) [15] in which it is embedded. Exteroceptive and proprioceptive stimuli play a role in governing these adjustive processes, and improvement in coordination—making optimal the circumstances of instinct discharge—is definitely attributed to skill acquisition and conditioning (Thorpe, 1948).

Lorenz (1958, 1960) and Hess (1962) have recently re-emphasized the ethologists' acceptance of the fact that there is an "interlacing of innate and learned elements of behavior" (Hess, 1962, p. 248). They maintain, nevertheless, that certain inborn behavioral structures (e.g., the instincts proper, IRMs) are phylogenetically evolved and correspond to real physiological mechanisms. In fact, Lorenz (1961) goes even further in suggesting that learning *capacity* itself represents a form of survival adaptation and is a result of phylogenetic selection.

We are reminded here of the phrase of two American learning theorists when clarifying an earlier ambiguity with respect to the innateness or acquired status of aggression (Dollard et al., 1939). Assigning responsibility largely to learning in determining the role of aggression in the response hierarchy, they comment: "In emphasizing learning we do not wish to deny the role of innate factors" (Dollard & Miller, 1950). In fact, Dollard and Miller make the distinction between *learned* and *learnable* drives, the latter referring to such responses as fear which, they suggest, ". . . may occupy different positions in the innate hierarchy of responses to different cues" (1950, p. 69), although fear can be attached, through conditioning, to other stimuli. We are led to observe that the ethologists likewise acknowledge the shaping effects of learning in many aspects of instinctive behavior (except, of course, in modifying the instincts proper). We might then paraphrase the above and, in behalf of the ethologists, say: "In em-

[15] See footnote, Figure 3–3 (p. 66).

phasizing the innateness of instincts we do not wish to deny the role of learned factors."

Finally, lest the differences obscure them, the parallel between the work of the ethologists and the learning theorists should be seen. Whereas the ethologists focus their attention on the invariable instinctive core of adaptive behavior and seek to enumerate and classify the instincts, they have paid somewhat less attention, for the time being, to the possibly significant effects of stimulus direction or environmental control in the development or shaping of the instincts. This is not to say that they have ignored the use of environmental manipulations as a technique of exploring their subject matter. The "model" experiments of the ethologists are themselves model experiments. However, they have sought the constant, invariate responses in the masses of behavior sequences they have observed.

On the other hand, the behaviorists have tended to emphasize the variations that could be produced in behavior as a direct result of environmental manipulation. However, in much of their work if not all of it, an innate core of "unconditioned response" or an assumed initial "habit family hierarchy" of responses or, at least, an acknowledgment of the concept of response repertory has been the point of departure for their research. Further, both groups have begun to explore quite systematically the neurophysiological processes underlying behavior. There is little question that the continuing investigations of both groups will narrow down the bases of difference between them. The common acknowledgment of the importance of not dissimilar "drive" concepts and the denial of subjective, vitalistic, and teleological concepts should be a starting ground for a closer liaison between the two "schools" of behavior study.

SUMMARY OF THE ETHOLOGICAL POSITION

Actually, the ethological position can best be understood in its own context. The very interesting and prolific examples of complex behavior sequences which are used as illustrations in ethological writings cannot be included here, much to the limitation of this treatment. The reader is urged to become acquainted with some of the original sources. A recent authoritative summary of the position is given by Hess (1962). Other fairly extensive treatments can be found in Tinbergen (1951), Thorpe (1956), Fletcher (1957), and in three collections of papers by ethologists and others (*Society for Experimental Biology*, 1950; Schiller, 1957; Grassé, 1956). A most delightful source, somewhat less technical than the above, is Lorenz's *King Solomon's*

Ring (1952b), where the full flavor of the naturalist animal lover, as well as the patient investigator and shrewd theorist, can be found.

The ethological theory of instinct is a motivational theory in every sense of that term. To account for the arousal of behavior, the ethologists call upon the action-specific energy (more recently called "drive-specific energy" and "specific action potential" [Tinbergen, 1952]) of innate fixed behavior sequences, that is, instincts. This energy accumulates in groups of centers in the central nervous system until released by specific, though often complex, environmental stimuli. An hierarchy of coordinating neural centers is postulated to account for the orderly sequences of related instinctual behaviors and to permit of influences from hormonal and other factors which can either facilitate or inhibit the performance of responses.

To bridge the gap between arousal and release of instinctual energy, a sequence of appetitive behaviors is described, involving both learned and unlearned reflexes, kineses, tropisms, and taxes. Instinctual energy is inhibited until discharged through the activation of innate releasing mechanisms (IRMs) which are attuned to their own unique environmental stimulus complexes (releasers). Each of the IRMs is like a lock or valve in a hydraulic system, which, when released by operation of the special releaser key in the environment, permits the flow of energy to the next stage of the neural sequence or, behaviorally, produces the instinctive response. ". . . once the act is released (i.e., elicited) its performance occurs in complete form, coordinated by impulses from the center and without any chain-reflex character. The function of the stimulus is to release or elicit the act. Once released, the act no longer depends for its form on anything outside the central nervous system" (Lehrman, 1953, pp. 338–339). As we have noted, however, during the performance of sequences of appetitive behavior, and, again, even in the performance of the instinctive act itself, a "coat of reflexes" serves to adapt the response to the particular nature of the environment.

Variations in intensity and frequency of response are accounted for by hypothesizing (1) threshold lowering directly as energy accumulates; (2) the additive nature of releaser stimulus elements in the environment; and (3) vacuum or overflow response when the amount of energy reaches some maximum point and the appetitive behavior fails to produce appropriate environmental cues for the release of the instinct. The increased difficulty in producing instinctive responses with repeated elicitation is attributed to depletion of the reserve of action-specific energy.

Displacement activity is described as the occurrence of the instinctive act, in abortive form, out of its proper context, and, instead, in the context of an apparently unrelated instinctual sequence. This last phenomenon is shown to be related to drive conflict or thwarting, in much the same way as symptom formation is thought to occur as a function of energy overflow and rechanneling in conversion hysteria. The secondary elaboration of displacement activities as social releasers for other members of the species, and a similar analysis of intension movements (incomplete or early phases of instinctive acts) suggests the species-survival value of such behavior in an evolutionary sense. It also gives evidence for the growing extension of ethological analysis from individual behavior of species members to considerations of social behavior of animal groups (e.g., see Tinbergen, 1953a; Lorenz, 1952b, 1955).

In the ethological literature there are repeated warnings to the reader that the hypotheses put forward are only tentative formulations and that ethological concepts are being evolved from data inductively, rather than being imposed on data deductively. Whether such a separation is indeed possible at all has been a problem that has troubled philosophers of science for some time (see Feigl & Brodbeck, 1953; Feigl & Sellars, 1949). However, in the progressive changes in theoretical structure that have been observed in the ethological writing (e.g., broadening of notion of specificity of reaction-specific energy [see Tinbergen, 1953a; Lorenz, 1952a]), in the acknowledgment of a greater role for learning than originally conceived (see Thorpe, 1956; Hess, 1962), and in the elaboration of the basis and meaning of displacement responses (see Armstrong, 1950; Tinbergen, 1952; Lorenz, 1952a), the ethologists would appear to be perfectly willing to be self-correcting, and, in being so, they differ from antecedent instinct theorists.

Three major areas of work in which the ethologists have pioneered remain to be discussed more fully: the phylogenesis of behavior, the neurophysiological substrata of specific behaviors, and the phenomena of critical period impressionability, or imprinting.

TYPES OF SUPPORTING EVIDENCE

Three types of observational studies form the basis for the ethological conceptual system:

1. field studies, in which the observer, without intruding directly, stations himself in such a way as to observe the "natural" behavior of members or colonies of insect or animal groups in their usual habitat.

2. transplanting of colonies to specially constructed vivaria, which,

though resembling natural habitats in most ways, permit more convenient observation and a degree of environmental control (e.g., of
lighting, temperature, number and type of species members, timing
of contacts between species members, etc.) not possible in natural
field conditions. (Lorenz [1952b] most amusingly describes the problems of "reverse-caging" in which the human members of a house-
hold containing such a colony were protected by screening from the
free-roaming birds.)

3. laboratory-type conditions, where no attempt is made to replicate
natural conditions, but rather specific environmental factors are systematically varied in order that their effects might be assessed. The use
of models, previously discussed, illustrates this type of investigation.

Natural Field Observation. The first of these types of study is
probably the most widely familiar. This includes the bird-walking
and bird-watching types of expeditions in relatively undisturbed
wooded areas that ornithologists have long made popular among ama-
teurs. Such observations of birds and insects (see Allee et al., 1953) are
used by ethologists to catalogue behavior (acts, movements, responses,
and their eliciting stimuli where observable) as it occurs, with or without intrusive stimulation, in the self-selected habitat of the organism
under surveillance. From these observations, ethologists can construct
general (Type 2) and special (Type 3) environments for specific
identification of releaser-instinct mechanisms. *Ethograms,* or complete and detailed descriptions of the "natural" behavior of a species
or subspecies, are the ideal sorts of data desired of these field investigations.

Recreated Environments. It was from studies of the transplanted
colonies that Tinbergen (1951) evolved his conception of the hierarchical system of reproductive instincts and subinstincts in the stickleback (see Figs. 3–1 and 3–2). Schiller's study of innate behavior in
chimpanzees (1949) is still another example of the many studies of
this type. He observed the types of reactions given by chimpanzees
in restricted environments to different kinds of stimuli (sticks, boxes,
strings) without in any way seeking to exploit the limits of their
capacities to deal with these objects, as might be done in a similar
situation by an American learning theorist.

The Use of Models. The identification of specific releaser-instinct
mechanisms has been accomplished in series of "model" experiments
by Tinbergen and by others (see Tinbergen, 1951). Examples include
Lorenz and Tinbergen's (1938) studies of the egg-retrieving response
of the greylag goose through use of artificial eggs of various shapes,
sizes, and textures and Tinbergen and Kuenen's (1939) studies of the

gaping responses of young thrushes (part of the food-begging reaction) to a variety of artificial stimuli substituted for the natural stimulus of the food-bearing parent bird. In these studies an experimental model is constructed to resemble one or more dimensions of the environment in which an instinctive response occurs. By systematic variation of the form or content of the model, identification of the particular stimulus dimension to which the response is given is then possible. With this procedure, Tinbergen (1951) reports the isolation of "innate alarm and escape" responses in young nestling birds, of response-produced and mate-produced stimuli to specific subinstincts of the reproductive instinct in male sticklebacks, and of the egg-rolling instinct component of egg-retrieving behavior of the greylag goose (described earlier). These are but a few examples of the application of this experimental technique. We shall have occasion to return to some of them as we examine the criticisms of ethology later.

The Isolation Study. Evidence for the innateness of behavior components is taken largely from isolation studies. In these, single members of a species are reared in complete isolation from others of their own species, either by "foster-parents" of another species, or by human observers. In both instances, catalogues of behavior are constructed and compared with behavior of other young which are reared by their own parents or by foster-parents of the same species. Behaviors found common to a species (i.e., species-specific) under these conditions are considered innate.

Somewhat comparable are the studies of releaser mechanisms in controlled environments where opportunity to learn is minimized or, ostensibly, absent. Carmichael's study (1926) of the development of the swimming response in *Amblystoma* embryos is cited by Tinbergen, for example, as evidence for innate movement responses (instincts). It will be recalled that Carmichael raised his subjects from fertilized eggs in a chloretone solution, thus inhibiting movement but not growth. At the end of a period where normally reared control organisms were swimming freely, the chemically isolated group were then "freed" and, in a short while, could not be distinguished in their swimming performance skill from the untreated controls. This appearance of the swimming response in the absence of opportunity to practice was taken as "proof" that the response is innate.[16]

Hess (1962) discusses the difficulties associated with drawing con-

---

[16] Tinbergen did not cite Fromme's (1941) carefully controlled repetition and elaboration of Carmichael's research, however. Fromme reported a quantitative decrement in efficiency of swimming due to the retarding effect of immobilization on functional development in the state of partial movements, rather than the premotile stage.

clusions from isolation or deprivation experiments from the ethologists' point of view.[17] Intended primarily to deprive the young of any
opportunity to learn, the effects of such isolation (e.g., rearing young
birds in the dark or in severely restricted cages to prevent wing
movements) on the general health of the organism involved cannot
be controlled or, for that matter, properly assessed. Thus the demonstration that a behavior does *not* appear is not necessarily proof that
its absence is due to lack of opportunity to learn or experience. On
the contrary, Lorenz (1958) considers the likely interference with
bodily health a sufficient reason to predict serious direct disturbance
of unlearned behavior patterns. Hess argues further that behavior
patterns, like muscles, may atrophy with disuse. Needless to say, this
last suggestion is considerably less tenable than the debility argument.
Finally, it is held, the conditions of testing the effects of isolation must
be carefully examined to be sure that they provide a reasonable opportunity for the display of the behavior in question. This argument
reduces to the statement that proper controls must be exercised in
experimental procedures, and there can be no disagreement in general
with this position.

Phylogenesis of Behavior. Finally, the ethologists draw upon inferential evidence in demonstrating the consistency of their findings
with morphological data and with evolutionary theory. Thus Tinbergen (1951) observes that courtship preening movements in mallard
ducks, as one example, make a more prominent display of gaudily
colored structures (in this case the metallic speculum of the wing)
that are species-specific. This correlation of morphological characteristic and specific behavior, which maximizes display of such characteristics, is taken as evidence for the innate basis of the behavior.
The further use of instinctive acts as intimate parts of the courting
sequence serves to isolate species from each other and thus to preserve
their special identities and their survival. This intraspecies consistency
and interspecies difference in instincts serve an evolutionary purpose
and must, by inference, reflect their innate character.

Having established, then, to their own satisfaction at least, the existence of instincts as highly reliable characteristics of the species studied,
the ethologists have gone on to show how this high degree of consistency of instinctive acts can lead to a taxonomic use of behavior
for species-link identification. Examples of such use are Lorenz's
(1937) study of pigeons, in which he was able to show a behavior
similarity (sucking motions in drinking, unlike other birds) among
species in one family (Columbidae), although no group of morpho-

---

[17] For further critical discussion of this type of experiment see p. 98.

logical characteristics was distinctive to all species in the family; and Adriaanse's (1947) differentiation of two species of digger wasps, previously undifferentiated, on the basis of behavioral differences (cited by Tinbergen, 1951).

The ethological position clearly holds that the unlearned, species-specific fixed action patterns are based on bodily structures and physiological mechanisms (Hess, 1962). Just as comparative morphologists use structural criteria to identify species similarities, so, it is argued, can *homologous* behavioral structures be used in the same way. Homologies are based on similarities in (1) movement form, (2) internal causal factors, (3) releasing situations, (4) order of occurrence and nature of linkage of sequential movements, also called *homonomies* (Remane, 1956). Homologies must be distinguished from analogies; that is, instances in which similar behavioral structures may evolve as adaptations are made to a same environment. Thus animals inhabiting a same area or using a similar terrain might store food in a same way. But this would be analogous rather than homologous because of its relation to function and not to common history (Hess, 1962). On the other hand, Hess cites several examples of the use of such *ritualized* behaviors in courting as simple head movements, grooming, display, or drinking movements that occur within behavior sequences in which they have no apparent utility. By examining parallel responses in related species, it is possible to identify an earlier or symbolic meaning in these actions. This is particularly true for behaviors which express *mood* or *affect*. Abortive features of such actions as symbolic greeting or threat movements may appear as *intention movements* and constitute a form of communication of incipient approach, attack, or flight. The same motion, in different species, may signify something else (Hess, 1962, gives the example of tail wagging in dogs and cats here). Only in relation to its phylogenetic significance can the meaning of specific response patterns, or aspects of these response patterns, be understood.

The analysis of homologous behaviors—particularly of ritualized, symbolic intention movements in courtship, territorial defense, and other social behaviors—has led to the conclusion that in the evolution of behavior patterns certain instincts may become linked with others to form fixed sequences. In many of these instances, a fixed pattern ". . . may become motivationally autonomous of the situation that originally aroused it, or dependent on another motivation" (Hess, 1962, p. 177). Although we have found no extensive discussion of this point anywhere in the ethological literature, it is a point of great interest. We could interpret such a state of affairs as being a direct contradiction of the basic ethological theory of specific-action energy. As we noted earlier in discussing displacement activity, the source of drive for the displaced activity, namely as a kind of overflow from the conflicting or frustrated drive(s), must also be re-examined alongside the otherwise highly specific drive concepts generally presumed by the ethologists. Hinde (1959b, p. 586) suggests that the ethologists may be required to adopt a "general drive" theory to deal with such phenomena.

HUMAN ETHOLOGY

Following our discussion of the evidential basis of ethological theory, it should be noted that the ethologists do a considerable amount of arguing by analogy. They fully recognize the need for substantial evidential support, but nevertheless seem prone to intersperse the citation of experimental and observational evidence with such analogous references (e.g., see Tinbergen, 1951, 1953a, 1953b; Lorenz, 1950, 1952b). In a carefully written and documented section on "releasing and directing stimuli," for example, Tinbergen (1951, p. 88) follows his citation of experiments on egg retrieving in the greylag goose and gaping in the nestling thrush with an illustration of orienting behavior in the frog. Describing such behavior, he differentiates between aiming (moving head in direction of fly in motion) and subsequent "shooting" of the frog's tongue at the fly. Without comment, he includes a parallel figure showing what appears to be an American Indian aiming and shooting a bow and arrow in two separate operations. If we are not to infer that a similar analysis is applicable to both, their inclusion in this manner is clearly misleading. Similarly, in the section of his text devoted to the "Ethological Study of Man," Tinbergen points out both that little is known of complex human behavior and that instinct has not been much studied in man. He then describes Lorenz's (1943) analogue to the model experiments in man. He cites three types of evidence that, he says, have "about the same value as such experiments." These are (1) that dolls are adapted to meet the demands of the IRM; (2) the optimal baby developed by the film industry "to meet man on an instinctual level"; and (3) pets selected as substitutes for babies by childless women. Common features in these three examples lead him to conclude that the human parental instinct is responsive to the following sign stimuli: ". . . a short face in relation to a large forehead, protruding cheeks, maladjusted limb movements" (p. 209). An illustration, after Lorenz, is given of these "morphological releasers" in human, rabbit, dog, and bird young (Tinbergen, 1951, p. 209).

Since, as we are reminded repeatedly, the ethological study of man is in its infancy, there is a paucity of evidence which can be cited for the existence of instincts in man. Tinbergen, in addition to the above description of what is called the parental instinct, refers to an instinct of comfort (care of the skin), which is shown as displacement activity in situations of conflict. Thus, women "adjust nonexisting disorder of the coiffure" while men stroke their beards and mustaches, even in this "clean-shaven" era. The occurrence of sleep under tension of combat stress and of displacement sperm-ejaculation "as a consequence of a blocked escape drive at examinations" (Bilz, 1941) are likewise cited by Tinbergen (1951) as evidence of instinctive behavior in man.

Despite the limited evidence available, it is clear that Tinbergen considers motivation in man to have an important instinctual base. He makes very explicit his feeling that an objective study of the instinctual basis of motivation in man, along the lines of ethological study thus far described in this chapter, must proceed independently of the psychological study of subjective motivational experiences. Thus the subjective experience of hunger would not be a datum of the ethologist. Tinbergen seems to equate psychology with the study of subjective phenomena, although he acknowledges that this would be "Psychology only in the restricted sense" (pp. 205–206). It is, in fact, introspection which Tinbergen rejects as a method of investigation of motivation on the dual basis (1) of its acknowledged unreliability ("we have learnt from Freud that non-conscious phenomena of a quite different nature are at work as well" [p. 208]); and (2) that motivation is basically dependent on hormones and external stimuli.[18]

On the basis of analogy with animal behavior and his own experiences in life he would accept patterns of locomotion, sexual behavior, food-seeking, sleep, and care of the body surface, at least, as instinctual. Some of these behaviors are presumed to be innate on the basis of experimental and systematic observational evidence, others on the basis of analogy, and others as inferences from life.[19] The following example of one of the aspects of the sexual pattern of motivation will illustrate this last point: "Criminologists teach us that the number of crimes, even of serious ones like murder, committed in obedience to the instinctive urge to show off before a female is astonishingly high" (Tinbergen, 1951, p. 208). On the other hand, Tinbergen rejects the likelihood of the existence of either a "social instinct" or a single "aggres-

---

[18] This view is not shared by other ethologists, nor is it consistent with the basic hypothesis of action specific energy.

[19] Fletcher (1957) offers an interesting discussion and has made some similar criticisms of the ethological views of human instincts.

sive instinct" in man on the basis that there is no likely underlying neurological center for such behavior and, perhaps more important, that social aspects of other instincts and particular aggressive behaviors (subinstincts, e.g., fighting, threatening) are better understood in the ethological contexts of the larger fixed action patterns of which they may form parts. Fighting, for example, which is typically used as an example of the aggressive instinct, appears in animals to take place for biologically advantageous purposes of territorial protection and sexual rivalry. Further it rarely involves physical combat, but consists mainly of threatening types of movements. Tinbergen argues that the evolutionary appropriateness (for species survival) of such "aggression" does not warrant the positing of a separate aggressive instinct. Nor does he appear to find sufficient reason for presuming such an instinct to exist in man.

Lorenz, on the other hand, as Fletcher points out, ". . . is full of allusions to human experience and behavior." Concerned about man ". . . with atomic bombs in its hands and with the endogenous aggressive drives of an irascible ape in its central nervous system . . . ," Lorenz feels, ". . . it is high time that the collective human intellect got some control on the necessary outlets for . . . endogenously generated drives . . . [like] . . . 'aggression,' and some knowledge of human innate releasing mechanisms, especially those activating aggression" (Lorenz, 1950, pp. 266–267).

Unlike Tinbergen, Lorenz does not hesitate to assume in man all of the instincts attributable to animals, nor is he, like Tinbergen, unwilling to accept introspective evidence for the existence of instincts in man. In agreement with McDougall and with Darwin, Lorenz accepts the usefulness of "qualitatively distinguishable emotions" as clues to the number and nature of human instincts. That he is arguing by analogy, as well as by appeal to consensual observation and introspection, is illustrated in his comparison of human ritualistic dancing in the Far East with ritualistic "dancing" in courting fish, and his observations on the "human" nature of a jackdaw learning from its elders how to recognize an enemy.

Finally, both Tinbergen and Lorenz reason by analogy for instinctive *inhibition* of aggression in man. The wide occurrence in animal societies of gestures of submission, which serve as social releasers of the inhibition of aggression in their attackers, is noted. Comparison is made with the observations in man of such submissive gestures as bowing, removal of the hat, presentation of arms, and the relative difficulty soldiers experience in killing other men who are defenseless, when such killing is on a face-to-face basis as contrasted to long-distance bombing or shelling. Lorenz offers a most fascinating description of combative behavior in timber wolves to show how a defeated wolf, within seconds after the height of violent contact, will expose to its victor the most vulnerable part of its body (its jugular vein) and, upon presenting this stimulus, can cause immediate cessation of hostility in its opponent. We shall let Lorenz describe the sequence from this point in his own words:

Both wolves are growling angrily, the older [victor] in a deep bass, the younger in higher tones, suggestive of the fear that underlies his threat. But notice carefully the position of the two opponents; the older wolf has his muzzle close, very close against the neck of the younger, and the latter holds away his head, offering unprotected to his enemy the bend of his neck, the most vulnerable part of his whole body! Less than an inch from the tensed neck muscles, where the jugular vein lies immediately beneath the skin, gleam the fangs of his antagonist from beneath the wickedly retracted lips. Whereas, during the thick of the fight, both wolves were intent on keeping only their teeth, the one invulnerable part of the body, in position to each other, it now appears that the discomfited fighter proffers intentionally that part of his anatomy to which a bite must assuredly prove fatal. . . . Every second you expect violence and await with bated breath the moment when the winner's teeth will rip the jugular vein of the loser. But your fears are groundless, for it will not happen (1952*b*, pp. 186–188).

Lorenz gives many other examples of instinctive inhibition, responding to social releasers, and preventing the consummation of aggressive behaviors. It is argued that these must be innate patterns, developed as a result of selective evolution, or species would have long since annihilated themselves. Unhappily, Lorenz points out, however, man's capacity to develop weapons of destruction has far outstripped the slow, evolutionary development of instinctual patterns of inhibition. Since " we did not receive our weapons from nature" we ought not to expect that we can defend ourselves against these weapons by depending on innate inhibiting mechanisms. It will then, he feels, be necessary for man to "build up these inhibitions purposefully . . . to engender the feeling of responsibility . . . the inhibitions without which our race must perish by virtue of its own creations" (Lorenz, 1952*b*, p. 198).

Thus we see that the ethologists, as represented by two of their leading exponents, are by no means in agreement on a specific list of human instincts, nor can they muster a great deal of evidence of the experimental study of instinct in man. However, they do agree that (1) the study of fixed action patterns in man is an important and urgently needed thing; (2) man, consistent with evolutionary theory, is a biological organism like all other animals and therefore ought to be possessed of instincts (albeit species-specific); (3) analogical reasoning from animals to man is fruitful; and (4) the study of instincts in man will provide an objective, scientific basis for a sound theory of human motivation.

Before turning to a consideration of some of the criticisms of ethological theory, we will describe some recent ethological research on neurophysiological correlates of instinctive behavior and imprinting.

NEUROPHYSIOLOGICAL CORRELATES OF INSTINCTIVE BEHAVIOR

Ethologists hold that instinctive behaviors are governed by central nervous system, rather than peripheral, mechanisms. The energy for specific behaviors accumulates centrally, being kept from running off into activity by a hierarchical system of inhibitory blocking and releasing mechanisms that permit energy storage and discharge, respectively, in accordance with adaptation needs. We have already discussed the ethologists' view that evolutionary changes should have produced such survival-relevant behavioral structures, as well as anatomical structures; and we have examined their arguments and the supporting evidence for behavioral homologies as natural events within an evolutionary sequence. Now let us look at the evidence from neurophysiology.

Neural System Interference. Von Holst and his associates [20] have, for a number of years, explored the neural bases of locomotor activities in a number of lower species. They were particularly interested in segregating the roles of central factors and of receptory determinants in coordinating movement. In studies of worms and fish, in which sequential section responding had suggested a chain-reflex theory, von Holst was able to show, through selective severing of neural links, that the coordination of responses responsible for rhythmic locomotion could not be due to peripheral, unit-to-unit stimulation (E. H. Hess, 1962). Lorenz (1950) has drawn upon this research of von Holst and others on neural system interference to support the ethological theories of central coordination and of energy storage and release.

[20] Von Holst's works, as well as those of W. R. Hess and many others related to this area, have appeared mostly in German biological publications. The recent paper by von Holst and von St. Paul (1962) is an exception. Reviews and summaries of this work can be found in Hinde (1959b), Schiller (1957), and, most fully, in E. H. Hess (1962).

Brain Stimulation. More recently, von Holst and his collaborators (1962; Hess, 1962) have undertaken direct electrical stimulation studies of animal brains to elicit specific action patterns. They found that they could reliably produce fixed, sequential complex patterns that always followed the same order, regardless of the length or strength of stimulation. This order, paralleling the "natural" sequence in survival-relevant fixed action patterns, led Hess to conclude that they had successfully stimulated instinct-releasing centers, thus strongly supporting ethological claims of a hierarchical central structural organization paralleling the lawfulness of observed behavior (Hess, 1962, pp. 214–215).

Von Holst and von St. Paul (1962) have been able, according to their own and Hess' (1962) reports, to elicit, at will, parts or all of instinctive acts, depending on the locus of stimulation. Sleeping, food or water seeking and consuming, fight, flight, and disgust behaviors have been aroused, some requiring real objects with which to interact, whereas others gave the appearance of "hallucinations."

When two or more areas are stimulated simultaneously, von Holst and von St. Paul report a series of types of interactions: *superposition,* where both activities occur; *overlapping,* where superposition occurs but the two acts are changed in intensity; *oscillation,* where equally motivated acts alternate in appearance; *cancellation,* where equal but opposite acts result in the performance of neither; *transformation,* where apparently opposing acts produce a completely new behavior; and *suppression,* where one of two opposing drives [21] is dominant, the second act appearing only as an *afterdischarge.* By manipulating amounts and duration of stimulation of each of the separate loci, von Holst and von St. Paul hoped to be able carefully to quantify the nature of the dominance patterns among the acts. They note that "freezing," for example, even when elicited at a low intensity, can suppress most other acts.

Hess points up the fact that there is an emphasis on study of coordination in this research, as contrasted with "the usual reflexology." He enthusiastically concludes that these researches have "far-reaching implications," and have already ". . . confirmed the ethological propositions on the nature of appetitive behavior and fixed action patterns, particularly the hierarchical organization of behavior" (Hess, 1962, p. 218).

[21] The use of drive here need not confuse the reader, if he keeps in mind the ethological concept of action-specific energy.

IMPRINTING

One of the most interesting of the phenomena studied by the etholo-gists is that of *imprinting*. In the life of a young duck in its natural habitat, its first social encounter will normally be with its mother. The duckling will follow its mother immediately and will thereafter persist in approach behavior in the presence of the mother. If, in an artificial setting, another animal or object is substituted at the first experience, the duckling will become strongly attached to it.

Lorenz, who named this phenomenon, although he was not the first to observe it, has imprinted geese on humans (1935, 1952b); and Ramsay (1951) has imprinted fowl on such diverse objects as a football and a green box. Hess (1962, p. 226) reports that imprinting has been shown to occur in a variety of birds, insects, and fish, and in some mammals—mammals in which the young are mobile shortly after birth —and suggests that it probably exists in all social species in which parents and young interact.

The strong social attachment is said to be imprinted because it is formed in a very brief encounter, and yet appears significantly and permanently to affect the later social behavior of the individual or-ganism, determining, in particular, the type of sex object which will be chosen. This social identification process thus normally permits a member of a species to recognize and to prefer "one of its own kind." However, the Heinroths, Lorenz, and others (see Hess, 1959) have shown that strong preferences can be had for human caretakers or other "foster parents" over members of the same species, depend-ing on early imprinting experience. Freedman, King, and Elliott (1961) report that if dogs are not socialized with humans between the ages of three-and-one-half to thirteen weeks they cannot be made into pets; and Hess (1962) interprets some of the data on child rearing and aso-cial development to suggest that orphans who grow up "incurably unsocialized" do so for having missed contact with people during an early critical period.

Lorenz called attention to this matter of the *critical period* for im-printing experience, a fact which distinguishes imprinting from ordi-nary learning, which presumably has no such optimal time. E. H. Hess (1957, 1959) has extensively studied the factors associated with the critical period and imprinting, and arrived at the following conclusions:

1. The strength of imprinting is a function of the *effort* expended by the organism in following the imprinting model (he states this precisely as $Is = \log E$).

2. *Primacy* governs the establishment of imprinting. That is, if two

or more imprinting objects are exposed, the first object exposed will be preferred in the largest number of cases.

3. The effect of *punishment* during imprinting is to *enhance* the effectiveness of the imprinting experience.

Hess (1962) reports that the time of appearance and the duration of the critical period are governed by *the onset of locomotor ability and the appearance of the fear response,* respectively. Thus, a plot of the frequency of effective imprinting against age would turn out to be a bell-shaped curve, the parameters being determined by the onset of necessary locomotion at one end and the onset of inhibiting fear at the other (see Fig. 3–4).

Hess has formalized his conclusions regarding the role of effort in imprinting into a Law of Effort (Hess, 1959). He and his associates further support this role by experiments using muscle relaxants (meprobamate and carisoprodol). The drugs are administered both during imprinting and later testing for effects of imprinting (Hess, 1960; Hess, Pott, & Goodwin, 1959). They found that only the *process* of imprinting was affected by the drug administration. Thus the onset of the critical period for effective imprinting is determined by the maturation of the locomotor ability, which, Hess (1962) claims, is necessary to the expenditure of effort (in following). The role of effort posited here as a requisite correlate of imprinting is not unlike

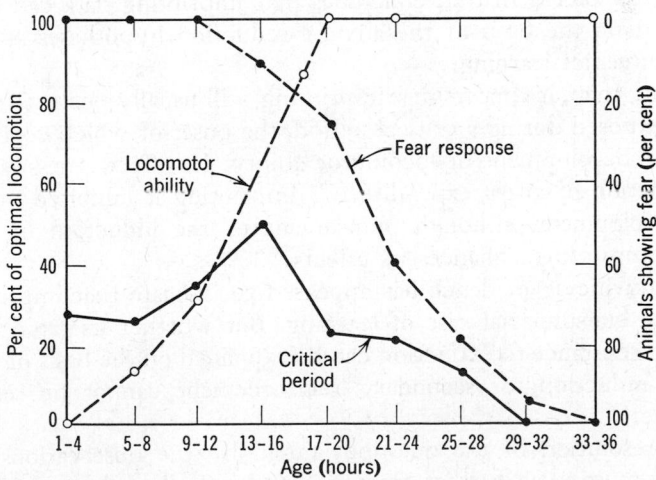

Figure 3–4. Hypothetical and empirical curves of the critical period in chicks (White Rock stock) and mallard ducklings. Reproduced by permission from Hess (1959, Fig. 12).

a similar relationship known to hold for effort and the acquisition of an instrumental conditioned response (Applezweig, 1951). Hess' claim that imprinting is not the same as learning would not be supported on this score.

As to the inhibition of imprinting by the arousal of fear, the matter is far from clear. Moltz, Rosenblum, and Halikas (1959) found that the following response in ducklings was significantly increased when paired with an anxiety situation produced by electric shock. Kovach (reported by Hess, 1962, pp. 235–236) showed that shocks administered to ducklings during imprinting enhanced following in the critical period and interfered with imprintability afterward. These data might likewise be examined in the light of a possible alternate anxiety-reduction hypothesis, if the other behaviors of the ducklings before, during, and after imprinting were known. Pilz and Ross (1961), showing that a sudden, intense auditory stimulus presented whenever a young chick approached the stimulus object enhanced following, conclude, with Hess, against a drive reduction hypothesis and in favor of an *arousal* explanation.

Moltz and Rosenblum (1958) have challenged the claim of the ethologists that imprinting is irreversible on the basis of their experimental findings. They took especial care to remove any secondary reward associated with the imprinting object. Under these conditions they report that imprinting is a highly unstable phenomenon. Moltz (1960), in a review of the matter, concludes that imprinting data can be reinterpreted on the basis of the anxiety-reduction hypotheses as a form of instrumental learning.

In sum, then, it appears that imprinting will usually occur to the first object exposed during a critical period, the onset of which corresponds with the development of locomotor ability. Its effectiveness is a positive function of effort expenditure.[22] Imprinting is inhibited by innate fear development, although punishment or the induction of anxiety *during* imprinting enhances its effects.

No convincing evidence has appeared to indicate that imprinting is anything but a special case of learning. But whether its rapid acquisition and resistance to extinction can be explained on the basis of arousal, anxiety-reduction, or secondary reinforcement cannot be settled at this time.

The resolution of the questions raised by the observations in imprinting must await further empirical study of all of the variables con-

[22] Baer and Gray (1960), however, have established imprinting in chickens without overt following. They suggest that visual discrimination, rather than effort, is involved.

tributing to this phenomenon. The matter will not be resolved by choosing up sides or by fiat, nor in terms of the ". . . barren issue of 'native' or 'acquired'" functions (Schneirla, 1959*b*, p. 79). The importance of imprinting to later development and behavior is not to be denied. On the other hand, further study of early approach-following behavior may provide clues as to the variables which influence its occurrence and determine its impact. It is related to our concern as a unique behavior sequence whose arousal, long maintenance, and specific directionality may need to be explained in motivational terms.

CRITICISMS OF THE ETHOLOGICAL THEORY OF INSTINCTS

The criticisms which have been directed at ethological theory can be divided into two main groupings. First, there are the constructively critical papers from the ethological group itself, in which experimental or observational evidence is presented or reinterpreted in attempts to show that one or another of the earlier ethological formulations needs revision, to be discarded, or to be further substantiated. A number of these criticisms can be found in Fletcher's review and critique of ethology (1957), in papers appearing in *Animal Behaviour* and *Behaviour*, in Thorpe (1956), and in a recent international symposium (Grassé, 1956).

The second, and by far the more serious attack, has come from American comparative psychologists. This criticism is the more significant because it challenges the very essence of the ethological postulate system, namely, the primacy assigned to innate behavior mechanisms and the innateness of instincts. Actually, these criticisms are also directed, point by point, at the ethological evidence as well. We shall deal first with the intra-ethology papers.

Criticisms from Within Ethology

It is not unusual, as a formal position develops in scientific theory, for a certain amount of disagreement about particulars to occur among the supporters of the general point of view. The ethological school is no exception. Accepting the basic position with regard to the innateness and importance of instincts, specific dissensions have been recorded with regard to other aspects of the theoretical framework. Gray (1950), on the basis of a careful experimental analysis, was able to show that peripheral (proprioceptive) sensory control was sufficiently in evidence in controlling locomotion (in the toad) to warrant ". . . the main conclusion . . . that the existence of centrally controlled patterns of locomotion should be regarded as nonproven" (p. 124). At the same time, Rudolf Brun was critical of the neurological hypothesizing about central control mechanisms not on the basis of behavior analysis but because of what he considered contradictory neurophysiological evidence (Brun, 1951, discussed by Fletcher [1957] in some detail). Simultaneous with these criticisms (1950, 1951) both Lorenz and Tinbergen were elaborating their neurological hydro-mechanical and hierarchical models.

We may note here two major current developments which have been supportive of ethological claims of innate mechanisms and a central hierarchical neural structure. The first is the discovery of biological pacemakers and the exploration of the whole concept of endogenous rhythmicity (see Harker, 1958; Pittendrigh & Bruce, 1957, 1959). And second is the important current brain stimulation research of von Holst and von St. Paul (1962), discussed in this chapter. Thorpe (1961) and Hess (1962) consider this work a landmark for etholo-gists. It is clear evidence of the vitality of the ethological movement and will provide independent means of assessing hypotheses on central hierarchical arrangements, threshold operation, specificity of energy (drive), and the significance of vacuum and displacement activities.

Armstrong (1950), as we have already noted (see pp. 71 ff.), criti-cized the minor role assigned to displacement [23] activities in ethological theory. He felt that recognition of the greater significance and wide-spread occurrence of displacement activities would require a broad-ening of the specificity limitation of action-specific energy. In other words, if displacement activities occur frequently, and he (and later Tinbergen) acknowledged that they did, such activities must be elicited (if at all) by stimuli other than their traditional or optimal environ-mental releasers. The revised conception was expressed by Lorenz (1952a) as follows:

. . . certain facts have come to light which clearly indicate that the way in which the accumulated "something" is specific for a certain instinctive action is not based on the specificity of an excitational substance. What is action-specific is apparently not that which is accumulated, but the "reser-voir" in which it is accumulated. In certain circumstances a reaction differ-ent from the one normally correlated can be fed from this "pot." At any rate, this is how we would today like to interpret the fact of displacement activities . . . (Lorenz, 1952a, p. 295).

We should note that whereas this interpretation takes full account of the import of the additional evidence, it does so by a relatively minor shift in emphasis in the theoretical structure. Thorpe (1948, 1956) has

[23] Tinbergen (1952) expanded this role considerably (see discussion of displace-ment activity on pp. 71 ff.).

likewise noted the nonspecificity of reaction-specific energy on a basis similar to Armstrong's. The implications of these criticisms, together with Armstrong's (1950) previously cited attack on the concept of vacuum activity and the implied threshold changes (see Fletcher, 1957), removes some of the certainty of the observational base for the theory's motivational system. Intensity, persistence, and direction of behavior were all initially related to the specificity of the drive (instinct) aroused. If there are circumstances in which varied reactions can be "fed from the same pot" the formerly posited simple correlative relationship, between an instinctive performance and its specific instinctual motivational base, breaks down.

A continually active research field is subject to constant revisions in thinking. We shall call attention to two additional re-emphases (or revisions) in ethological theory before concluding this section, but it is apparent that further revisions continue to be made all the time. Bastock, Morris, and Moynihan (1954) have re-examined the concept of displacement activities in a paper on conflict and thwarting in animals. They first point out that the term "displacement" has been used to include (1) ambivalent movements and postures, (2) displacement activities, (3) animal "neuroses," (4) "overflow activities," and what they call (5) redirection activities. That these five groups may be different in both form and etiology has led, they believe, to some of the confusion in description and causal explanation which exists. They then proceed to analyze some instances of displacement activity in which they feel that Lorenz's "water tank analogy—that the 'energy' of an instinctive centre 'discharges' through the appropriate motor centres when the consummatory act is performed"—is unable to account for the facts. They propose an alternate *feed-back* hypothesis, in which the instinctive energy is consumed in "the perception of the 'right' feed back stimuli rather than the performance of the 'right' act." The new hypothesis is explicitly an expectancy hypothesis, shifting the drive discharge mechanism from the consummatory act to the perception of an expected consummatory stimulus.

Finally, Thorpe's extensive treatment of the interrelationships between instincts and learning (1956) should be noted. In a discussion of "drive and the theory of instinct," Thorpe calls for the recognition ". . . that there is within the drive itself some inherent directiveness, some extremely restricted purposive influence, perhaps, identical with . . . expectancy and insight . . . , which is in some degree independent of any pre-existing channels" (1956, p. 44). At the same time he supports Lorenz's idea of action-specific energy ". . . being generated, through some feed-back or other mechanism, by the later or lower elements in the hierarchy of behavior." Thorpe is careful not to carry his purposivism to the point of "supposing that the animal is aware of the biological final cause of its activities." Actually, his conclusion is very similar to the hypothesis suggested by Bastock, Morris, and Moynihan just discussed. Thorpe further greatly extends the range of significance of learning in instinctive behavior, particularly in determining the nature and direction of appetitive behavior. He draws upon a vast array of current studies by American behaviorists to support the necessity of such extension of ethological study.

Hinde (1954, 1956) criticized the hydraulic neural models of Lorenz and Tinbergen, and especially their vague use of the drive concept (e.g., such notions as a "reservoir" of energy or of "motivational impulses" which flow from "nervous centres" and the replenishment of which occurs from uncertain sources). He considered these descriptions as oversimplifications and as leading to misconceptions of the underlying neural mechanisms.

In a later paper (1959a), Hinde also took Thorpe to task for equating internal drive and neural patterning, and assigning both directionality and energizing functions to this unitary drive concept. He maintains that the two aspects need not—in fact, cannot—be handled within a unitary drive concept. Hinde concludes that if one assumes a continuously active nervous system, no *energizing* drive concept is required. On the other hand, he grants that an energy-storage drive concept is not inconsistent with the known evidence.

In another context, Hinde (1959c) more broadly criticizes the multiple use of the drive concept by ethologists, noting that his own suggestion of a concept of specific action potential (SAP), as a direct measure of responsiveness to a given stimulus (originally offered as a substitute for Lorenz's reaction-specific energy), was also probably multiply determined and thus did not improve the precision of language. Perhaps the new research of von Holst and associates will help clarify this matter, too.

Criticisms from Outside Ethology

As the ethological position became more widely known outside the group identifying itself with the new ethology, both the theories and research were to receive careful critical appraisal from animal behaviorists not committed to the Lorenz-Tinbergen orientation. Hebb (1953), in an address to the ethologists, urged that they abandon the term "instinct" entirely, since the term was a reflection of a false heredity-environment dichotomy and implied misleadingly a mechanism of neural process independent of environmental factors and uninfluenced by learning. As he pointed out, and as others have indicated, the environment in which development occurs quite directly influences the structure as well as the behavioral direction of the growing organism. Thus the temperature of the environment of the fruit-fly larvae, as one example, is directly related to the number of legs which will develop, and thus to the subsequent behavior patterns. Citing an experiment by Nissen, Chow, and Semmes (1951), in which young chimpanzees were reared in such a way as to prevent certain somesthetic experiences, Hebb indicates the importance of early learning, as well as prenatal conditions, for the subsequent development of "instinctive" behaviors.

Kennedy (1954), a British zoologist though not an ethologist, attacks Lorenz's distinction between endogenous and reflexive neurophysiological processes as based on an untenable dualistic notion and as being subjective. He compared (as does Fletcher, 1957) the Lorenzian and Freudian energy models and concluded that the two instinct concepts are fundamentally the same. The ethologists are endangering their own progress, Kennedy feels, ". . . because of their tendency to force into the portmanteau of instinct as much of the variation of behavior as they possibly can. This tendency is the inevitable result of subjectivist separation of a motivating core from a reflex coat in the causation of behavior" (1954, p. 15). He then goes on to criticize Tinbergen (1951), who claimed that ethologists must study instincts *first* and *then* learning. Kennedy agrees with Hebb that this cannot be done. Tinbergen's extensive experimental work with sticklebacks, Kennedy feels, will all have to be redone because of this bias which entered into the observational program itself.

Fletcher (1957), a sociologist, on the other hand, takes issue with both Lorenz (1950) and Tinbergen (1951) for so distinguishing the ethological approach from what they claim to be the subjectivism of psychology. Tinbergen, particularly, goes to great lengths to divorce ethology from the subjective and irrelevant hypothesizing of psychology (see Kennedy, 1954). This has not prevented Tinbergen, as we have noted earlier, from utilizing psychological hypotheses where they seemed convenient. Lorenz, however, does acknowledge the usefulness of emotion, and other psychological categories as a meaningful basis for hypothesizing in human ethology. Fletcher makes the interesting point that whereas Tinbergen draws heavily on evolution theory to show why instinct theory, if valid for animals, should be applicable to man, he fails to recognize his own inconsistency when he rejects the relevance of "psychological" variables to animal behavior other than man's!

Lorenz & T-berg distinguish Eth from subjectivism of psych yet they use the theories when convenient

In the period from 1949 to 1957, a series of criticisms of ethology were made by two American comparative psychologists, Lehrman (1953, 1956a, b) and Schneirla (1949, 1952, 1956, 1957). Both psychologists, although willing to acknowledge the existence of innate behavior patterns, and even willing to designate them as instincts (Schneirla, 1956), emphasized the need for careful ontogenetic study of experience in relation to innateness.

Lehrman (1953) argued that the preconceived notions of the instinctivists tended to restrict artificially what was looked for and to limit what was found. Rather than opening avenues for fruitful investigation, as the ethologists claimed, Lehrman saw their system as short-circuiting ". . . investigation of intraorganic and organism-environment developmental relationships which underlie the development of 'instinctive' behavior" (Lehrman, 1953, p. 359).

Schneirla (1956) and Hebb (1953), as well as Lehrman (1953, 1956b), cited two experiments they believed provided evidence that behavior which appeared for the first time need not be preformed or innate. These studies have now both been questioned, and we shall mention them here only to indicate the *nature* of the argument. Both nest building and pup retrieving are considered aspects of an innate maternal instinct. Lehrman and the others suggested that certain preparturitional developmental factors, themselves not directly related to maternal behavior, might nevertheless contribute to nest building and to retrieving and licking of the young. Riess (1950) reared female rats on pulverized food and with no access to their own feces or any other objects with which they could gain "handling experience." When later made pregnant and given nesting materials, these rats showed little or no nest-building behavior, and when they littered, there was a 75 per cent loss of young due to absence of pup-retrieving and nursing behavior. In a second (unpublished) study, Birch (1956) reared rats with special collars that prevented them from licking their own genitalia up to parturition. In 13 of 14 observed births, all of the young were lost through cannibalism or neglect (Schneirla, 1956). A control group, wearing equally weighted but noninterfering collars, showed "normal" maternal responses.

These experiments were interpreted to mean that previous experiences, though in themselves irrelevant to the maternal behavior in question, contributed (along with temperature [Kinder, 1927] and perhaps other independent hormonal and environmental conditions) to the performance of the complex sequence attributed to an inborn maternal instinct.

Eibl-Eibesfeldt (1955, 1956) repeated Riess' study, correcting for a design limitation,[24] obtaining both nest-building and normal retrieving behavior. Eibl-Eibesfeldt (1958) also reported an unpublished study by Coomans, which failed to confirm the Birch experiment.[25]

Lehrman (1961), reviewing these experiments, accepts that his earlier conclusion about the practice effects in these experiments was incorrect, and expresses the hope that ". . . further work on this problem will provide data that will allow a more confident interpretation" (1961, p. 1338). Hess (1962, p. 223), in discussing Eibl-Eibesfeldt's findings in some detail, suggests that experience *is* used by the rats to integrate their motor responses more adaptively, but concludes that the behavior patterns themselves "were immediately available to the animals like ready-made tools."

In another example, Lehrman analyzes predisposing prenatal and early postnatal conditioning factors (citing Kuo's developmental studies [1932] and Coghill [1929]) to suggest a possible experiential basis for the development of instinctual pecking behavior in chicks. From Kuo's step-by-step analysis of prenatal development of the chick embryo, Lehrman derives a quite reasonable set of relationships between parts of the pecking sequence and earlier developmental precursors: head lunging, for example, is seen as arising out of "the passive head-bending which occurs contiguously with tactual stimulation of the head while the nervous control of the muscles is being established" (Lehrman, 1953, p. 342). Bill-opening and swallowing are likewise connected with prenatal conditioning determiners.[26]

The experimental study of Thorpe and Jones (1937) is also used by Lehrman as reasonable evidence for predisposing factors in the environment which lead to instinct-like behaviors. In this study, Thorpe and Jones found that flies choose a particular flour moth larvae as food when adult. By careful observation, they were able to determine that the choice corresponded to the moth larvae on which the fly larvae fed. By substituting other food for the fly larvae, Thorpe and Jones found that they were able to predetermine the choice of food in adult flies.

Taking the ethological concepts one by one, Lehrman is critical of their limitations. For example, about innateness he says: "The use of

[24] Riess had removed his rats to a special parturition cage which was both new to the rats and undifferentiated. Eibl-Eibesfeldt tested his animals in their own home cages, and partly partitioned the cages.
[25] A master's thesis completed by Friedlich (1962) under one of the present writer's direction (MHA) likewise failed to confirm Birch.
[26] In answer to Kuo and Lehrman, Lorenz (1958) has pointed out that whereas all birds have similar ontogenetic experience in the egg, some peck, others gape, and still others shove bills into the parents' mouths.

'explanatory' categories such as 'innate' and 'genetically fixed' obscures the necessity of investigating developmental *processes* in order to gain insight into the actual mechanisms of behavior and their interrelations . . . within the organism and its internal environment, and between the organism and its outer environment" (1953, p. 345). Both Lehrman (1953, 1956*b*) and Schneirla (1956, 1957) criticize the isolation or deprivation experiment (see pp. 79 ff.) on which so much of ethological evidence is based. Schneirla writes: "In simple logic, the 'isolated' animal is not shut off from itself; it is obviously no less a member of its own species, and thus may present to itself, through the processes of its own development and self-stimulative associations, at least some of the influences which normally affect later species associations, as in mating" (1956, p. 413). Specifically, Schneirla and Lehrman point to visual, tactual, olfactory, and auditory cues which organisms can and probably do produce in isolation from others of their species. These cues in turn lead to what has been called instinctive "recognition of own kind," as reported by Howells and Vine (1940) and by Schooland (1942).

Lehrman has recently undertaken a series of studies on the ring dove (1955, 1956*b*, 1958*a, b*) to explore some of the developmental and experiential factors which he has claimed should significantly influence so-called instinctive behavior. He has so far been able to demonstrate social interaction, physiological condition, and hormonal factors as contributing to certain types of behavior in the ring dove (e.g., nest building, incubation, parental feeding behavior).

It should be clear that not all the work of Lorenz and his associates is rejected by these comparative psychologists. Both Schneirla and Lehrman, in parallel contributions to a symposium on instinctive behavior (Grassé, 1956), acknowledge the research-stimulation value of the ethological group:

Lorenz has provided a framework for the study of taxonomic distribution of behavior patterns which has proved to be most stimulating. The insistence of all of the ethological school that problems of research must arise from the lives of the animals studied is a much-needed corrective for the tendency of many psychologists to restrict "comparative" work to the use of a few mammals to study problems essentially arising out of theoretical considerations of human behavior. . . . Lorenz's attempts to provide an orderly organization of many facts which had hitherto appeared unavailable to analysis must command our respect" (Lehrman, 1956*b*, p. 502).

One final specific criticism of an item of ethological research should be mentioned here, since the experiment which is brought in question has already entered American psychological literature (Miller, 1951*a*).

Here we refer to the studies cited by Tinbergen (1948) of fear reactions in inexperienced birds to a silhouette shaped in such a fashion as to resemble a hawk if moved in one direction and a long-necked goose if the direction of movement is reversed (see Fig. 3–5). According to the ethological interpretation, movements of the suspended model toward the short-neck side, providing a "bird of prey" silhouette, release innate escape (flight) reactions in young gallinaceous birds, ducks, or geese, whereas movements of the model toward the long-neck side, resembling a nonthreatening adult, have no releasing function (see Eibl-Eibesfeldt and Kramer, 1958).

Schneirla (1956, 1959a, and earlier cited by Ginsberg, 1952) offers an alternate, more parsimonious explanation to the instinctive one given by Tinbergen. Criticizing what he calls ". . . a diagnosis dependent upon apparent adaptive significance," Schneirla (1956, p. 412) suggests the simpler explanation of a "shock effect" of the suddenness of stimulus intrusion on the visual field to account for the differential reaction to the two stimulus conditions. He then proposes a simple test of his hypothesis. "The corresponding opposite behavioral effects should then be produced by triangles drawn across the visual field base or apex first, sounds breaking suddenly or gradually, and the like" (1959a, p. 16). Size, or brusque movements, rather than "enemy" quality, may govern initial flight-provocation. Schneirla then warns: "The artifact method requires careful control against subjective impressions of what common external object or situation the test model may represent to the animal. 'Short-neckedness' . . . is a cue to the human observer, a

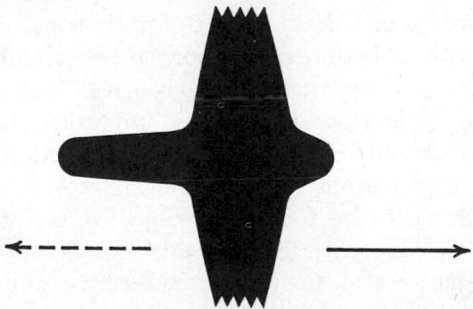

Figure 3–5. This model, moved to the right, releases flight or escape reactions in certain birds, ducks, and geese, presumably because it resembles a short-necked bird of prey. Moved in the other direction (broken arrow), it does not elicit such reactions. Shape in relation to direction of movement thus constitutes a sign or releasing stimulus. Reproduced by permission from Tinbergen (1948, p. 34).

perceptual 'sign' indicating an innate escape reaction to him but not necessarily to the bird" (Schneirla, 1956, p. 412). McNiven (1954), and Hirsch, Lindley, and Tolman (1955) have since repeated Tinbergen's studies, though with different species of birds (domesticated White Leghorn chickens), and have failed to confirm Tinbergen and Lorenz's findings (see also Rockett, 1955). Lorenz (1961) has scornfully rejected these failures at replication as inappropriate because of the species-specific character of the response involved.[27] The validity of Lorenz's criticism probably hinges more on the fact that Hirsch, Lindley, and Tolman used domesticated fowl than that they used a different species, since the original study was based on turkeys, pheasants, and greylag geese.

These are but a few of the analyses and studies of so-called instinctive and innate behavior patterns which Schneirla, Lehrman, and other psychologists have made in attempts to challenge the ethological hypotheses. Such criticism is the most direct, since it specifically takes account of the ethological concepts and directs both research and analyses to the particulars of this theory. Notice should also be taken of such general anti-instinct positions as that recently stated by Beach (1955) and Beach and Jaynes (1954), who take a position not dissimilar to those just noted. Beach has pointed out that instinct has remained in psychology because those who fought it, as well as those who accepted it, started from the premise that "all behavior is either acquired or inherited." He rejects such a dichotomous classification as arbitrary, naive, and meaningless, suggesting that premature classification of behaviors be avoided until *systematic* analysis of their nature and grouping is undertaken. This analysis must include study of gene-behavior relationships and *development* of various behavior patterns in the individual, with attention to the normal behavior control factors. Beach concludes: "When these methods have been applied to the various types of behavior which today are called 'instinctive,' the concept of instinct will disappear, to be replaced by scientifically valid and useful explanations" (1955, p. 409).

Whereas Beach has called for greater objective study, Kubie (1956) and Fletcher (1957) are critical of the ethological-type analysis partly because of its purposeful neglect of subjective and psychological variables as causal factors in the expression of instinctive behavior (see p. 95). Thus, Kubie, citing both pathological and normal examples of sexual behavior in man, argues that it is impossible to conceive the measurement of the strength of innate sexual instincts in any specific aspect of the consummatory act. That social and "psy-

[27] Hess (1962) adds that even breed differences must be taken into account.

chic" factors contribute to the whole complex of sexual and other forms of instinctive behavior in man, he points out, would be difficult to doubt. Fletcher, as we have noted, showing that the ethologists themselves have utilized psychological concepts in at least certain of their analyses (e.g., of appetitive behavior), seeks to extend the logic of this use to require consideration of psychological phenomena (e.g., dreams and other "psychic" experiences) in at least higher vertebrate levels.

COMMENTARY

The comments which have appeared in the *Annual Review of Psychology* (1950–1962) make a worthwhile addendum to this chapter. Hebb (1950), in the opening review of this series, directs the attention of American psychologists to the work of the ethologists in a brief paragraph, expressing the belief that this independent group's views may open "new avenues to behavioral experiment and [provide] a corrective against concentration on the study of too few species or . . . [too narrow] . . . theory" (1950, pp. 175–176).

The review of the next year, by Deese and Morgan (1951), completely ignores the ethological group. In 1952, however, Nissen and Semmes devote approximately one-fifth of their review to a non-critical presentation of the papers of the 1950 symposium (*Society for Experimental Biology*, 1950), describing the relevant ethological concepts of instinct (Erbkoordinationen, Instinktbewegungen, endogenous movements), social releasers, displacement activities (sparking over), the recommended method of "keeping" animals in a relatively free "pet" environment (Lorenz), and the systematic model experiments of Tinbergen and his colleagues. By 1953, Hess intrudes a value judgment as follows: "Although the term 'instinct' has certainly fallen into ill repute as far as present-day psychology is concerned, it yet remains as the central problem in comparative psychology" (1953a, p. 242). He then proceeds to make instinct the major topic of his review. Typical of the studies he reports is one by Peiper (1951) in which evidence for vacuum endogenous sucking responses was reported. We should recall Lehrman's caution here (retrospectively) that the vacuum activity hypothesis may have led the investigator to identify the behavior as such and kept him from looking further for either suboptimal stimuli present or developmental factors within the organism.

By 1954, Russell by and large ignored the ethological group's activity with the comment: "No radical new principles or techniques have been suggested in the publications of the comparative ethologists

. . . It would seem that we are now in a stage where this approach is undergoing careful and detailed scrutiny . . ." (1954, p. 244). This scrutiny was not long delayed. By the next year Meyer took the ethologists severely to task for substituting a new definition of instinct for the one previously rejected by "psychological schools of behavior study." He notes that both old and new definitions refer to ". . . behavior that is relatively complex, constant, and presumably inherited, and related to a situation rather than a stimulus" (pp. 260–261). Chiding the ethologists for their claimed intention to clarify the concept, he asks: "But where is the increased precision? Perhaps it is thought that making instinct a mechanism and giving it a neural reference lends respectability to the term, but maneuvers of this kind have been tried long ago. Again, it may be the stress on the hierarchical feature that is regarded as increasing the precision; if so, clarification could be a simple matter" (1955, p. 261). Meyer goes on to point out that the criterion of innateness was a major reason for the decline in use of the concept instinct, and commends familiarity with such discussions as Hebb's (1953, see p. 94) clarification of heredity-environment language to the ethologists. Meyer finally takes note of the similarity of the hydraulic energy model and the Freudian libidinal energy model and the objections raised to this by Kennedy (1954) and Lehrman (1953), which we have discussed earlier.

By 1956, the reviewer comes, at least partially, to the defense of the ethologists. E. H. Hess writes that the last previous review (by Meyer) contained

. . . some unfortunate implications. The first of these was that ethologists have produced only theoretical papers in which they speculate on vague constructs. It would seem that almost the exact opposite is true. A tremendous body of accurate data has been published, albeit along with some, perhaps unfortunate, theoretical material. The American answer to this work has not been consistent with the scientific attitude. No research has been done to test any of the hypotheses advanced by Lorenz and others. Instead, polemic articles have been written, the crowning example being Lehrman's [1953] critique of Lorenz (1956, p. 305).

He goes on to acknowledge that Lehrman (1955) did then proceed to some of this very research, but he fails to note that the Lehrman critique of Lorenz, to which he refers, did cite a quantity of experimental data as the basis for the criticisms offered.[28]

---

[28] As we have discussed (see pp. 96 ff.), some of these data (specifically, the Riess and Birch studies) have now been rejected on the basis of new evidence. Nevertheless, they did represent evidence against the ethological position at the time of Lehrman's article.

Bindra's review of 1957 would appear to be an attempt to reconcile the two extremes: "If American comparative psychologists have a fixation on the rat, the European ethologists are spreading their libido too thinly on too many species. In the extreme, both approaches can be unhealthy" (1957, p. 399). He goes on to point out, with Scott (1955), that both laboratory and naturalistic study are essential to sound scientific (particularly biological) research, and that they effectively supplement each other. Bindra distinguishes between primarily descriptive ethological studies (the Ethograms) which report (usually in great detail) the observations of a particular species and its behavior in a particular environmental setting, on the one hand, and the analytic and theoretical papers of the ethologists, on the other. The latter are devoted to hypothesizing mechanisms underlying observed instinctive behavior and proposing theoretical systems as frameworks for such mechanisms. It is the first type of descriptive study which he especially considers to be of great potential use to psychologists as background for their intensive studies of particular behaviors. With regard to the more formal theoretical aspects of ethology, he takes note of the criticisms we have earlier discussed and the renewed psychological emphasis on developmental studies as alternatives to instinct hypothesizing. He lists Hebb's (1953, 1954) five suggested variables to be investigated: (1) genetic, (2) chemical characteristics of the uterine environment of the embryo, (3) postnatal chemical environment of the nervous system, (4) species-common learning through sense organ stimulation, and (5) individually variable sense organ learning. His conclusion should by now strike a familiar chord: "The facts and theories that now appear under the rubric of 'instinctive behavior' would then find their place in discussions of the role of these developmental factors in determining behavior" (Bindra, 1957, pp. 403–404).

Verplanck's review of 1958 is a sharp departure from the previous reviews of the series in a number of ways. First, the author spent considerable time during the previous year visiting the laboratories of, and talking at length with, the leading ethologists. By virtue of this intimate contact with their then latest thinking, he believed himself in a position to go beyond the literature accounts of ethology, and took full advantage of this unique position. Referring to the earlier reviews as having "misleadingly emphasized some now obsolete part of ethological theorizing," he went on to say that as a result of close recent contact with experimental psychologists,

. . . most ethologists have radically changed their viewpoint on the interrelationships between genetic structure and behavior; instinct is once again dead. Unlearned, or innate, means now to ethologists pretty much the same as it means to psychologists: what the animal brings with him to a set of observations that he doesn't seem to have had a chance to learn. That is to say, it merely sets a problem (1958, pp. 100–101).

In the remainder of his review, Verplanck documents this change in outlook of the ethologists by citing studies in which experimental situational variables are manipulated, and in which analyses take fuller account of possible learning and interactive influences on behavior.

The 1959 review gave no space to ethological work, nor was there discussion of ethological theory in the 1960 volume, with the exception of one brief reference to Thorpe's concept of habituation (Drever, 1960, p. 137). On the other hand, this volume saw the introduction, for the first time in the series, of a review of *behavior genetics* (Fuller, 1960), which covered a closely related (largely American) literature.

By 1961, the review of comparative psychology was written by an ethologist who, after discussing the similarities of the fields and the differences in attitudes of psychologically and zoologically trained investigators (see beginning of this chapter), concludes that ethology is the broader of the two and should henceforward incorporate comparative psychological material (Thorpe, 1961, p. 28). He argues for the acceptance of a case or clinical approach to animal study as a necessary means of obtaining information pending more precise methodology.

Thorpe acknowledges the effects of criticism from comparative psychologists in the "increasing sophistication" of recent analyses of instinctive behavior by ethologists. Referring to Verplanck's statement, "instinct is once again dead," Thorpe writes, "all one can say is that if it was true then, there has been, within two years, a remarkable resurrection" (1961, pp. 30–31). Significantly, he goes on to say, in agreement with Hinde (1959a, b, c), and as a tribute to the comparative psychologists: "It is now almost universally recognized among ethologists that the more complex action patterns which would previously have been labelled instinctive almost invariably include important learned components" (1961, p. 33).

Thorpe then goes on to review the growing work on the interaction of hormonal, genetically coded inborn behavior patterns and external stimuli (e.g., see Lehrman, 1961), and the new developments in the neurophysiology of drive and behavior, and innate and conditioned rhythmicity (e.g., see our earlier discussion, pp. 86 ff.). The review leaves little reason to doubt the vitality of this "resurrected" field.

As an addendum to Thorpe's review, it may be noted that by 1962 the editors of the series had adopted his suggestion, and the first review of ethological literature under that title appeared (Lindauer, 1962). Although restricted to work on the social life and communication among animals, it dealt with some 290 papers, covering a variety of species, and showed the influence of evolution on the development of social communities (largely in lower species).

CONCLUSIONS

We have here presented what amounts to a case history of an instinctive theory of motivation. The ethologists started with behavior observations. These led to the formation of hypotheses to account for the behaviors they observed. The hypotheses in turn were elaborated to meet the requirements of internal consistency in the theoretical system they formed. Having developed a framework of concepts, further ethological observations were guided by the language of the concept system, and "facts" recorded consistent with the ordering theoretical (and perceptual) framework. That such perceptual ordering can occur is an established principle of general psychology, and a repeated observation in the history of science. The ethologists, as we have shown, have modified an earlier extreme position to take account of criticisms from workers in a parallel field who have approached similar subject matter in a different way. At the same time, the ingenuity of many of their procedures and the fullness of their naturalistic observations have had a salutary influence on others to the point where a common field may now be said to exist.

We have seen a reaffirmation of the Lorenz-Tinbergen hypotheses of a central hierarchical neural control of energy release through innate, though modifiable channels. A very large amount of empirical research is now underway to isolate and identify gene-controlled behavior characteristics, neurophysiological bases of specific fixed-action patterns, and the questions of drive specificity as these can be understood from the study of displacement and vacuum behavior.

At the moment, ethological theory would appear to support a variant of need-reduction theory, the energy being related to the frequency and fullness of discharge of hereditary units of consummatory behavior. These fixed action patterns, or instincts, are considered to be different from taxes, kineses, tropisms, and reflexes, on the one hand, and from conditioned or learned responses or habits, on the other, although as motives they have been both forcers and reinforcers of learned (appetitive) behavior. Instincts are said to lie somewhere between the two extremes—larger than the reflex, smaller than the habit—as preformed response patterns evolved in much the same manner as morphological characteristics and likewise serving survival value for the individual and the species.

The ethologists have used the concept of instinct as the explanatory motivational principle of their system. Arousal, persistence and direction of behavior are all implied in its definition and description. That they have chosen an old theme should not prevent our careful examination of the evidence they have amassed in its behalf. Certainly the facts of a biological organism, genetic inheritance, evolution, similarity of behaviors across species, apparent stereotypy in behavior (particularly in lower species), and common neurophysiological mechanisms underlying similar behaviors in many different species, to mention but a few, attest to the inviting nature of the ethologists' particularization. That caution in generalization is necessary—particularly to the human species—is now acknowledged by even the strongest adherents of ethology. In any case, instinct is very much with us (once again)!

Chapter 4

Bodily Conditions: I

The heritage of the instinct concept, as we suggested in Chapter 2, is twofold: the drive concept and the notion that there are relatively unmodifiable, essentially innate patterns of behavior. Both features of this heritage are biologically conceived; that is, anatomical structures and physiological mechanisms are involved, and they interact with environmental circumstances. Ethology, reviewed in the last chapter, represents this heritage. However, there are other representatives of it and in this and the next chapter we concern ourselves with the empirical study and small-scale theorizing that have been the work of these other representatives.

We have called both of these chapters by the name "Bodily Conditions," but we have placed the topics in one or the other of the chapters for a reason. The present chapter stresses those kinds of bodily conditions which are thought usually to express themselves in relatively consistent behavior patterns. It is the behavior patterns themselves, apparently organized around some physiological condition or end state, which is the primary focus of interest. The factors which control the pattern are the concern of investigation and theory. Thus, we now bring together such activities as maternal, nesting, sucking, and contact behaviors, hoarding, homing and migration, and sexual behavior. Temperature regulation, respiration, elimination, sleep, inhibition, and fatigue are included also. Much, though by no means all, of the work to be surveyed has involved mammals, as contrasted to the emphasis by the ethologists on submammalian forms. It has been directed to activities which tend to be adaptive, cyclic, and apparently difficult of interpretation on the basis of experience. These activities seldom depend on manipulations involving deprivation, as is the case with hunger and thirst. Seldom, also, do their goal objects or states enter into the laboratory as reinforcement for behaviors other than those intrinsic to the activity itself. One is tempted to call them innate or instinctive patterns, although such a designation, in our view, is not a particularly valuable way of classifying them. At any rate they reflect that aspect of the biological heritage which deals with relatively unmodifiable patterns of behavior.

In Chapter 5 the activities with which we are concerned also reflect bodily processes, but interest is focused much less on patterned behavior than it is on the conditions and the mechanisms of the sheer occurrence of the behavior. Little attention is directed, for example, to how a rat eats or drinks (as opposed to how it builds nests or mates). But interest is devoted to the fact of eating, and how the amount eaten and the rate of eating, for example, are related to such variables as deprivation. Goal objects and states in these instances are often used as reinforcers for other behaviors.

As a generalization, perhaps we could say that in these chapters, given the final consummatory behaviors of the conditions, Chapter 4 is concerned primarily with the relatively stable behavior pattern by which this consummatory point is reached, whereas in the behaviors treated in Chapter 5 the approach to the consummatory response is known to be variable and possibly subject to instrumental learning. These activities include the drive aspect of the biological heritage.

We think the distinctions we have just drawn are real ones, but we recognize that they are neither sharp nor highly compelling. They do provide us, however, with a basis for putting together in one chapter activities whose traditions of investigation show a certain similarity.

MATERNAL, NESTING, SUCKING, AND CONTACT ACTIVITIES

Depending on the particular species and/or the habitat, the maternal behavior of animals is said to contain four essential activities: nest-building, behavior during birth, retrieving the young, and suckling the young. Not all of these activities, however, occur in all species of animals. Responses of the young to their parents include sucking in mammalian species and the factor of contact. Recent thought has suggested that these two matters may reflect primary motivation, independent of feeding, etc. We include them here because they are, of course, so closely tied up with animal infancy as to be linked to maternal activities. We will treat these various aspects of maternal behavior, sucking, and contact separately, recognizing that in a natural situation they would often be found in an integrated pattern.

Our discussion here will be restricted to a small number of species, including mammals and birds, although there are many interesting aspects of these problems in insects, fish, and amphibia. Beach (1951) has reviewed much of the literature that pertains to these forms. Types of "family" that exist among various species of mammals have been described by Crawford (1939) and by Smith and Ross (1952). Gilliard (1958) provides information on many species of birds, as do Eisner (1960) and Lehrman (1956*b*, 1961).

Nesting

Nesting behavior has been studied in several species, but a great amount of information, especially in quantitative form, concerns the rat. In a number of studies, strips of paper were provided the rat, and the amount of nesting behavior was measured by the number of strips employed.

The nests made by rats consist of piles of nesting material, usually pushed into a corner, and sometimes shredded into small pieces. The rat sits on the nest, thus giving it a hollow or depressed place in the center. There are many individual differences in the nests constructed and in the extent of nest-building activity. Most of our comments refer to what is more or less typical of this species.

Both male and female rats build nests, and rats of either sex will do so from ages as young as 20 days (Kinder, 1927). There is little evidence that experience makes much difference to nest-building, although Ross, Denenberg, Sawin, and Meyer (1956) found that the quality of nests made by rabbits improved from the first to the third litter.

Three major factors, which are probably interrelated, seem to control the amount of nest-building in the rat. These factors are the external temperature, pregnancy, and the care of the young. Kinder (1927) showed a marked relation of nest-building to the external temperature, nest-building being reduced or ceasing under high temperature (within the range 50 to 90° F), and increasing within limits at low temperatures. She also found nest-building to parallel food intake, the two variables increasing or decreasing together. Kinder believed that nest-building is essentially a heat-regulating process. This notion is supported by Richter (1937), who found that nest-building increases after extirpation of the thyroids, adrenals, gonads, or pituitary (Lehrman, 1961, p. 1346). These glands are involved in the regulation of the rate of metabolism, a factor in heat regulation.

Kinder (1927), as well as Sturman-Hulbe and Stone (1929), observed that pregnant rats, a few days before parturition, showed a very high level of nest-building behavior, which continued through the postpartum period but declined from 10 to 20 days after parturition. Temperature variations did not affect nest-building in the parturient female (Sturman-Hulbe & Stone, 1929). Morgan (1943, p. 408) has suggested that disturbances in temperature regulation during pregnancy may underlie this increased nest-building in the parturient female rat.

Such a rat will move her nest and her young if a fan is arranged to blow air on the nest in its previous location (Sturman-Hulbe & Stone, 1929).

Nest-building, as well as other maternal activities, survives the loss of one sensory avenue, like vision or smell (Beach, 1951, p. 418). Cortical lesions delay the onset of nest-building in the pregnant female and, if they are widespread, can eliminate it (Beach, 1937).

Nest-building, then, appears to be a complexly controlled activity, mainly concerned with temperature regulation. It would be of great interest if this form of behavior were to be studied in relation to modifications in the temperature-regulating centers in the hypothalamus and other parts of the nervous system.[1]

Behavior During Birth

In general, a given species of lower animals displays a pattern during and immediately after the birth of young which is relatively constant and stereotyped, and is much the same in the animal having her first offspring (primiparous female) as it is in the animal which is multiparous. Infrahuman mammals, however, show wide differences in their behavior during birth, when a variety of species are considered (Lehrman, 1961, pp. 1310–1312). Munn (1950) has summarized the observations of Wiesner and Sheard (1933) and Sturman-Hulbe and Stone (1929) concerning the female rat as follows:

Onset of labor is evidenced by peristalsis passing along the uterine horns some 45 minutes prior to delivery, by stretching . . . , and by descent of the abdominal mass. As soon as a fetus passes into the vagina, most rats take a "head between heels position" and lick the vaginal orifice and fetus. A few stay on all fours and drag the fetus. When a pup is delivered, the rat takes it in her paws and deftly removes the fetal membranes. The mother severs the cord with her teeth. She may pull the placenta out with her mouth . . . mothers devour the placenta . . . often before cleaning the young. A pup is cleaned by moving the tongue rapidly over its body. It is held in forepaws and turned into various positions while being licked. The pup's genital region comes in for most attention. Quite frequently the mother stops and washes herself (Munn, 1950, pp. 31–32).

Cleaning behavior does not appear in nulliparous females to whom newborn are offered.

Nissen (1951) indicates that in captive chimpanzees parturition occurs easily, even without prior experience. The reaction of the primiparous chimpanzee mother to the offspring is variable; occasionally

---

[1] For further information on the control of nest-building in mammals, especially for work with species other than the rat, see Lehrman, 1961, pp. 1305–1310.

some will be apparently terrified by it and run away from it. Most chimpanzee mothers, however, are interested in and solicitous for the infant and are skillful in caring for it (Nissen, 1951, p. 437). The many books about child care and the controversies about methods of child-birth suggest that in humans these matters depend a great deal on experience and learning.

The licking of fetuses and the increased licking of the mothers own genital area at the time of birth may be related to salt lacks in pregnant animals; irritability of the genital region may also be a factor. The hormonal condition of the mother is involved, as licking and related behaviors were not found in hypophysectomized cats (Allan & Wiles, 1932) and hypophysectomized rhesus monkeys (Smith, 1954).

Retrieving the Young

Many animals will carry their young about and, if the young are removed from the nest, will often retrieve them. Virgin mice or rats do not usually retrieve pups, if offered to them. Some will do so, as will some males, after having been caged with pups. Nonpregnant multiparous females will, however, retrieve pups (Wiesner & Sheard, 1933; Leblond & Nelson, 1937; Leblond, 1940). Some mammalian mothers can discriminate their own offspring from others, and conversely, but this is not a universal situation; some rats will retrieve baby rabbits as well as steal rat pups which belong to another mother. There are marked individual differences.

Interest in and retrieving of the young usually endure so long as the mother nurses the offspring; Wiesner and Sheard (1933), however, prolonged the period of retrieving by offering the mother rat new sets of pups after her own had been weaned. If a chimpanzee child is removed immediately after birth, the mother may not seem to miss it, but if removal follows a longer period of being together the mother is often distressed for some time (Nissen, 1951, p. 437). The macaque monkey and the chimpanzee, at birth, have grasping reflexes which enable them to take hold of the mother (Tinklepaugh, 1942, p. 381); this not only prevents their falling out of trees but makes retrieving less necessary in these forms. For several months, clinging to the mother is common among these primates.

Various characteristics of the pups have been found to influence retrieving in the rat. Among them are temperature (Beach & Jaynes, 1956) and size, which, of course, is highly related to age (Wiesner & Sheard, 1933). A variety of stimuli from the young are capable of eliciting retrieving behavior (Lehrman, 1961).

Strength of retrieving has been measured with the obstruction method. Nissen (1930) put the litter and the mother rat in the two compartments of the apparatus; among other findings, he reported that the strength of the drive to retrieve, as measured by number of crossings, was as great or greater than the maxima reached by hunger, thirst, and sex, and that it decreased as the age of the pups increased. Seward and Seward (1940a) showed that the willingness of a guinea pig mother to overcome a barrier between herself and her young declined as the age of the young increased; a similar decline in retrieving in rats was noted by Wiesner and Sheard (1933). Seward (1940) also found that infant guinea pigs would surmount a barrier to get to the mother. Simmons (1924) showed that female rats would learn a maze for the reward of finding their litters in the goal box.

Nursing and Sucking

The nursing behavior of the female rat consists largely of crouching over the pups and remaining motionless for some time. It is up to the pups to find the nipples and to suck. That the mother will remain quiet is perhaps associated with the general reduction in activity, which appears early in the postpartum period. Lehrman (1956b) has suggested that this tendency to remain still is influenced subsequent to the first (and accidental) feeding by the fact that the suckling of the young, since it reduces pressure in the mammary glands, is rewarding.

According to Tinklepaugh (1942, p. 382), the monkey (macaque) mother after cleaning her infant "holds the baby either over one arm or against her breast. But she does nothing to determine the orientation of the infant relative to herself. By its grasping reaction, the baby turns itself so that its ventral surface is toward the mother's breast, and in this position it discovers the nipple unaided. If the baby . . . is too weak thus to orient itself in relation to its mother, the latter does nothing to facilitate its receiving nourishment, and it perishes."

Sucking behavior, that is, the activity of the offspring in the nursing situation, has received a great deal of attention in the last several decades, largely because it is often taken as an expression of the erogenous character of the oral zone in classical psychoanalytic theory (see Chapter 12). The problem of breast feeding in the human being has received a great deal of emphasis, especially in relation to the effects on adult personality of too little or too much gratification at the breast in infancy. In large part, insofar as our concern with this chapter goes, this issue reduces to the question whether there is or is not a need or drive to suck, which is independent of the intake of food. A second issue, pertinent here, is whether the act of sucking is one which requires little or no experience for it to appear in final form very soon after birth. We shall discuss the second of these issues first. Reviews of the literature on sucking behavior have been supplied by Ross, Fisher, and King (1957), Lehrman (1961), and McKee and Honzik (1962).

There seems to be little question that the sucking act, in animals where it occurs (including the human infant), is usually present at birth, although some changes, especially in its vigor, may occur as experience and age increase. The response is initially elicitable by tactile stimulation in the lip and cheek areas, and components of the response, at least, have been observed in fetuses delivered prior to their full term.

As to the question of an independent sucking need or drive, there appear to be three alternate hypotheses: (1) there is a sucking need or drive which will show itself in non-nutritive sucking behavior unless the drive is satisfied during feeding; (2) the sucking that occurs aside from the feeding situation is due to some degree of hunger; (3) sucking activity aside from feeding is a learned activity which persists because it has learned reward value. The major critical and well-controlled experiments (see Ross, Fisher, & King, 1957; McKee & Honzik, 1962), pertinent to these issues, have been carried out with dogs and with human infants.

Levy (1934) worked with collie puppies. Starting on the tenth day of life, two were fed by means of bottles with fast nipples, two by means of bottles with slow nipples, and two were left with the mother. The fast nipples were used to satisfy the dogs' hunger quickly and with relatively little sucking effort; much sucking was required with the slow nipple. The slow-nipple group, then, should have obtained satisfaction for both hunger and sucking, whereas the group fed with the fast nipples should be satisfied for food but not for sucking. After-meal, non-nutritive sucking developed in the fast feeders (fast nipples); that is, they "developed sucking movements for several minutes after meals, sucking noises during sleep, sucking of their own bodies, and sucking or licking objects in the kennel . . . [and] . . . sucked the inserted finger of the examiner in various tests throughout the experimental period (of 20 days) more vigorously and frequently" (Levy, 1934, p. 221) than the other groups. Ross (1951*a*, *b*) confirmed these results in cocker spaniel puppies. He used mother-fed, bottle-fed, and dropper-fed groups during the first two weeks of life; he also separated puppies from their mothers at 2, 3, 4, or 5 weeks of age for a 2-week period and confirmed Levy's observations in this study. James (1957, 1959), studying hybrid pups, injected enough milk directly into the stomachs to fill them prior to sucking tests. The pups sucked as much as the controls, indicating to James that sucking is independent of food need (cf., also, James & Gilbert, 1957). These several studies with dogs suggest a primary oral or sucking need or drive.

Kunst (1948) studied nonfeeding sucking over the first year of life in 143 orphanage children. In general, she found instances of sucking to be related to the time since last feeding. She interprets this and other findings as supportive of an interpretation in favor of hunger as the factor responsible for non-nutritive sucking but admits that her study is not critical to this point. At least superficially, her data do not fit well with those reported by James.

Davis, Sears, Miller, and Brodbeck (1948) studied 60 newborn human infants in a hospital nursery for the first 10 days of life. One group was fed throughout by cup, one group by bottle, and one group by the mother's breast. Various behavioral measures were studied, but the major difference was that the breast-fed group showed more responsiveness on a finger-sucking test. The cup-fed group showed *no* evidence, in this case, of oral deprivation; Freeden's (1948) results confirm these findings. Brodbeck (1950) found that infants who were switched from bottle to cup-feeding at four days of age showed an immediate decline in non-nutritive sucking, whereas a control group, continuing on the bottle, did not.

It is quite clear that these results with human infants are at variance with those for dogs. The latter show support for a sucking need or drive, independent of nutritional intake, whereas the former do not show that absence of sucking, as in the cup-fed subjects, is associated with an overflow of sucking activity to non-nutritional conditions. As a matter of fact, there is evidence that obtaining food by means of sucking in the human infant is associated with non-nutritive sucking, and the implication is that non-nutritive sucking obtains its value from its association with food intake. Sears and Wise (1950) reported data tending to support the idea that degree of frustration at weaning (to a cup) is related not to frustration but to amount of sucking, that is, to a strong, learned sucking drive. Yarrow's (1954) and Bernstein's (1955) data may be given a similar interpretation.

It is possible that sucking in dogs does represent a non-nutritional pertinent drive and that in humans it is, when it occurs, a learned drive or reward. McKee and Honzik (1962), however, offer the interpretation that sucking may be inherently pleasurable and regard sucking as therefore having comforting and reward values. Further work is required before these issues can be regarded as settled, and other species should be studied.

Contact

Another factor probably involved in maternal-filial behavior and in the development of offspring has been stressed by Harlow (1958) and by Harlow and Zimmerman (1959). He and his associates have carried out a number of experiments with infant macaque monkeys in which substitute mothers have been used. One was made of a block of wood (with a head and painted face), covered with sponge rubber which, in turn, was covered with terry cloth. The other was made in much the same shape, but it was made of wire and offered no soft surfaces (see Fig. 4–1). In some cases, both "mothers" were heated by means of an electric light bulb, and both were arranged so that the infant was free to spend as much time as he wished with either "mother"; most of the infant's time was spent with the cloth mother, even for those for whom feeding was carried out on the wire mother. (A nursing bottle was installed on the wire mother.) Harlow indicates that the general behaviors exhibited by the infant toward the cloth

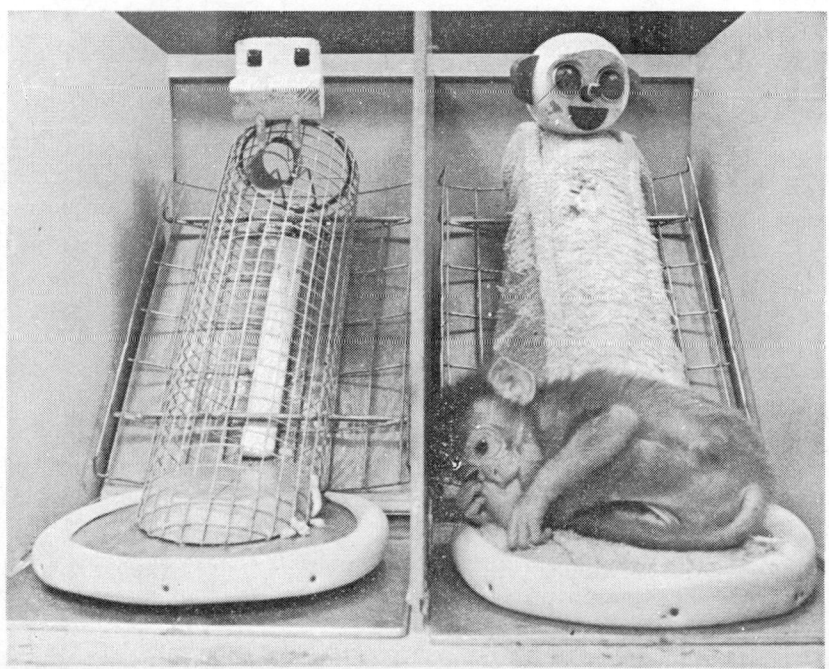

Figure 4–1. Wire and cloth-covered "mothers" used in experiments by Harlow. Reproduced by permission from Harlow (1958, Fig. 4).

mother are very similar to those which infants display toward real mothers, and he has presented evidence that the infant obtained emotional security from the cloth mother. The infant was also more adventurous and exploratory of the environment when he had had contact with a cloth rather than a wire mother. Various other tests have suggested that the infant develops a close affectional bond to the cloth mother and that this bond is persistent over considerable periods of time, even in isolation from the cloth mother.

Harlow believes he has discovered an important need or drive in these experiments and that this drive is independent of the feeding relation to the mother and that its satisfaction is important to proper development.

Later experiments have indicated that satisfaction of the contact need by means of the cloth mother is not sufficient to normal social development of monkeys (Harlow, 1962; Harlow & Harlow, 1962). Aberrant sexual behavior, play, and defensive behavior appeared in individual animals reared alone, reared with wire mothers, with cloth mothers, or even with a real mother. Such animals, in varying degrees, seemed interested in sexual activity but were unable to carry out the mating pattern successfully. They seldom paid much attention to other monkeys and spent much of their time staring into space and pacing their cages. They did not play with other monkeys and often reacted with extreme aggression to advances, sexual or otherwise, from their peers. They inflicted wounds on themselves by biting and would often engage in stereotyped, ritual acts. Efforts to overcome these deficiencies, by the use of interactions with normal monkeys, have been unsuccessful, and it appears that the disordered behaviors are irreversible.

On the other hand, infant monkeys raised without mothers, but with opportunities for interactions with other infants, have developed relatively normally following initial retardation. It is suggested (Harlow & Harlow, 1962) that peer relations among infants may be substitutable for mothering and that, even with normal mothering, it is essential to satisfactory social development. There is some reason to believe that there is a critical period during development in which social relations must occur if development is to be normal. Monkeys isolated for their first 80 days seem to recover from the effects of the isolation, whereas animals isolated for 6 months seem to be permanently damaged. This would place the critical period at from 3 to 6 months as far as these monkeys are concerned.

These findings place a somewhat different light on the original results concerning the importance of contact. While the data from the cloth-covered mothers certainly suggest that contact with a soft surface is rewarding and comforting to the infant monkey, the monkeys do not develop normally later on. Rather, it seems that experience with live monkeys—mothers and, especially, peers—is necessary to normal development. Whether this experience creates motives or rewards related to social behavior, or whether it creates habits and skills relative to social behavior, or both, is very difficult to say on the basis of present evidence. Certain parallel findings with human children are reviewed in Chapters 12 and 13 (see, also, Chapter 14, pp. 765–766).

Factors Involved in Maternal Behavior

It has often been supposed that an important factor in the occurrence of maternal activities is discomfort in the mammary glands of the parturient female (Young, 1936, p. 122). However, Wiesner and Sheard (1933) cauterized the nipples of female rats, thus destroying them and, also, in a number of cases, preventing swelling in the region of the mammary glands. They found, however, that mothers so treated showed normal nesting and retrieving behavior and also crouched over the young as does a normal mother in the suckling process. Hence the role of the mammary glands seems not to be that of a necessary condition for the appearance of various maternal behaviors, although other evidence exists which both supports and negates a role for these glands (Lehrman, 1961, pp. 1330–1331).

We have already indicated, in reference to details of maternal and filial behavior, that external stimuli, including those from the young, are important factors. Others which have been studied are hormonal and neural factors. We consider each of them briefly.

Hormones. Various aspects of maternal behavior may be induced in nonpregnant females and in males by the injection of prolactin (Riddle, Lahr, & Bates, 1942), and, in general, the administration of substances that inhibit the production of sex hormones tends to be associated with the appearance of maternal behavior. Estrogen, which is associated with the period of heat, depresses maternal behavior when it is administered (Beach, 1951, p. 422). Other pituitary hormones are also involved in maternal behaviors, in various indirect ways. Bindra (1959, p. 284) has suggested that some of the effects of hormonal factors on maternal behavior may arise from changes in bodily temperature regulation.

Neural Factors. We have already remarked that nest-building is adversely affected by sufficient cortical damage. Beach (1937, 1938) observed a general deficiency in most of the maternal activities of the rat when more than 20% of the cortex was damaged, and, when the extent of the damage was great enough, severe deficits in maternal behavior were displayed.

Our review of the complex of behaviors which surround nesting, parturition, maternal activities, sucking, and contact should suggest that the "maternal drive" is probably not a simple, unitary one, and that its component features are complexly and variously controlled. We should stress, in addition, that many of these activities are found to some degree in the nonparturient female and in the male, and that some of them are not manifest in the parturient female. Even where a pattern does occur, its form may vary from individual to individual and in the same individual at different times; many circumstances are important to what the animal does. Some of the components may appear but not others.

Bindra (1959, p. 48) summarizes the state of knowledge. Listing these points, he suggests that "These facts point to the inadequacy of any simple interpretation of what for convenience is called 'maternal behavior' in terms of a single 'maternal drive' . . . [a] . . . one-factor hypothesis cannot account for the various distinct activities. . . . We must look separately for the specific factors that are responsible for each of nest building, cleaning, retrieving, and nursing."

Parental Behavior in the Ringdove

As a further example of the complex control of behaviors relative to progeny, we turn next to a discussion of an integrated series of experiments conducted with the ringdove by Lehrman. This bird is similar in many respects to the common pigeon but is smaller in size (Lehrman, 1959a).

Lehrman's work has involved the study of the roles of hormones, experience, and stimulation from the mate and nesting materials chiefly in incubation and feeding behavior in the ringdove. These birds feed their young by regurgitation of "crop milk," which consists of cells sloughed off the epithelial layer of the crop wall. The young (squabs) place their bills into the parent's throat, and the parent then regurgitates crop milk into the squab's bill. The crop itself is an extension of the esophageal wall, and during incubation its walls thicken, thus providing the cells that slough off into the lumen of the crop.

The hormone, prolactin, is thought to be involved in the development of this feeding behavior. In one of his experiments, Lehrman (1955) compared the responses of experienced and inexperienced birds to administration of prolactin. The experienced birds had bred twice. The experimental doves were injected with prolactin; the controls, with distilled water. A squab was then placed in a nest in the cage with each adult dove, and the occurrence of feeding behavior was noted. Ten of the twelve experienced, prolactin-injected birds fed the squabs, whereas none of the controls or the inexperienced, prolactin-injected birds did so. Prolactin, thus, does not seem to induce the feeding activity in the absence of breeding experience. Anesthetization of the crop, in experienced birds, led to a reduction in frequency of feeding squabs (as compared to suitable controls), suggesting that when prolactin does induce feeding behavior it does so by acting on the crop.

Lehrman (1955) also suggests a role for experience in making certain stimuli adequate to elicit feeding behavior. In an inexperienced adult, the first occurrences of feeding are apparently elicited by tactual stimulation provided by the movement of the squab's head against the adult's breast. In forty-one cases of birds breeding for the first time, such tactual stimulation was always the instigator of feeding. In forty-nine experienced birds, however, tactual stimulation was involved only twelve times. Apparently, breeding experience permits other stimuli (visual, auditory) to become conditioned to the feeding responses.

Lehrman (1958a) has studied incubation behavior and factors involved in it. Adult birds were placed in a cage containing a nest with eggs in it. Birds tested singly did not incubate the eggs, but a pair of male and female birds, placed in the cage together, did so in five to seven days. If the pair had been in the cage together for seven days prior to the introduction of nest and eggs, they incubated the eggs one day after they were introduced, and if the pair had nesting material during the period before the eggs were introduced, they incubated the eggs at once, when the eggs were placed in the nest (Fig. 4–2). From these findings, it appears that stimulation from the mate and from nesting material facilitates the onset of incubation.

Lehrman, Brody, and Wortis (1961), using experienced birds, again found that the presence of a mate induced incubation behavior in both males and females and that nesting material accelerated the appearance of incubation. Parallel studies of the females were made to determine the occurrence of ovulation and oviduct growth. Curves describing these two measures closely parallel those for the occurrence of incubation behavior in the female birds (Fig. 4–3). It is suggested that ovulation and oviduct growth, like incubation behavior, occur under the stimulation arising from the presence of the mate and the nesting material, very likely because production of relevant hormones is stimulated by the mate and the nesting material (see, also, Lehrman,

Wortis, & Brody, 1961). Lehrman (1958*b*) suggests that courtship behavior stimulates the secretion of estrogen and that this hormone, in turn, stimulates nest-building. The nest-building activity, he believes, stimulates the secretion of progesterone, which leads to incubation (Lehrman & Wortis, 1960; Lehrman & Brody, 1957, 1961).

Lehrman's work provides a good illustration of the complex control

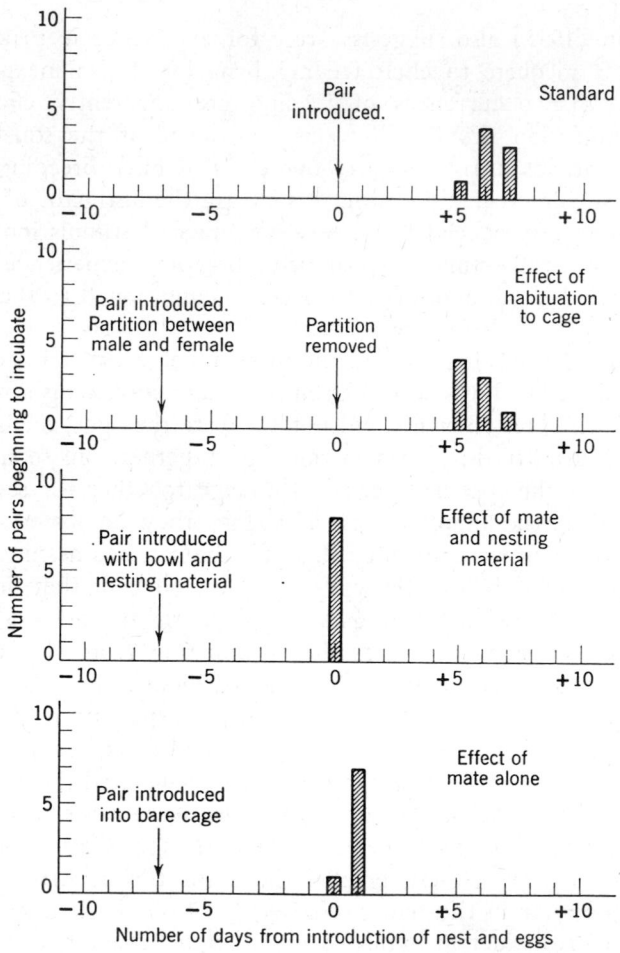

Figure 4–2. Time taken for incubation behavior to begin in doves following several conditions of association with mate and availability of nesting material. Reproduced by permission from Lehrman (1958*a*, Fig. 1).

of various aspects of parental behavior and of the role of external stimulation in inducing physiological changes which are essential links in the process. To what extent similar effects of stimulation are in-

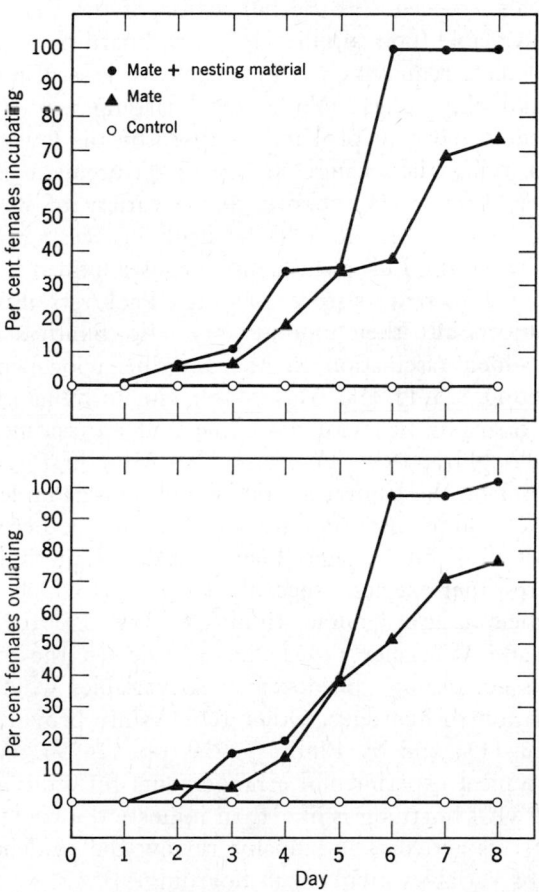

Figure 4–3. Per cent of females incubating (upper panel) or ovulating (lower panel) after a given number of days spent with a mate *and* nesting material, with a mate alone, or alone in a cage (control). Each point represents independent groups of 20 birds each and the proportion responding to placement in the cage of a nest bowl containing a nest and two eggs. Modified by permission from Lehrman, Brody, and Wortis (1961, Figs. 1 and 3).

volved in other species remains largely to be determined (but, see Lehrman, 1959*b*). Lehrman has also pointed to the important roles which experience and learning may have in various aspects of complex patterns of behavior that, considered globally without detailed analysis, might be dismissed as innate or instinctive.

HOARDING

Many animals, especially as the fall season of the year foretokens a reduction in available food supplies, begin to hoard or to store food in excess of immediate requirements. This behavior is seen in such rodents as squirrels and chipmunks. While this hoarding may appear to be foresightful, the behavior is probably released by the lowered temperatures accompanying the change in season (Morgan & Stellar, 1950, p. 409). Stone (1951, p. 55) reports that a variety of woodpecker in California stores acorns in the holes he drills in trees and that the extensive hoarding of the European hamster causes human beings, during periods of famine, to raid its stores of grain. Pack rats also accumulate varieties of objects into their mounds (see, also, Smith & Ross, 1953). There is an added fascination in hoarding behavior because of the parallel collecting, saving, and storing behavior in human beings.

Since 1939 hoarding behavior has come under experimental analysis (Hunt & Willoughby, 1939; Wolfe, 1939). Most of the research has been carried out on the laboratory rat, which hoards under some conditions, although some attention has been paid to other species, like mice, hamsters, and guinea pigs. There would be merit in extending these studies to other species, especially to animals which do extensive hoarding in their natural habitats (Smith & Ross, 1953; Beach, 1950). Ross, Smith, and Woessner (1955) have reviewed the many experimental reports concerning the dozen or so variables which have been studied in relation to hoarding. Other reviews are provided by Munn (1950, pp. 103–113) and by Bindra (1959, pp. 72–79). We shall first describe the typical experimental arrangements for studying hoarding in the rat and what hoarding is like, then indicate the views concerning the nature of this activity, and finally review the evidence pertinent to a number of variables involved in hoarding.

Experimental Situation for Studying Hoarding

Wolfe (1939) placed a runway, 36 inches in length, between the rat's cage and a bin of food pellets. J. McV. Hunt (1941) modified this apparatus slightly, constructing a set of alleys. At one end of each alley was the animal's living cage, at the other end, 39 inches from the door to the living cage, was a food cup. A treadle in the alley recorded the animal's progression to the food cup during 30-minute hoarding tests. Pellets hoarded were also counted. Other investigators have modified this apparatus further, sometimes to introduce experimental variables, but the basic plan has been largely preserved.

In hoarding, the animal traverses the alley from the cage to the food cup and carries the pellet back to the cage, where it is "stored." Then he goes for another one. At least some animals do this. To qualify as a hoarder, convention has it, the animal must accumulate at least five pellets (in excess of any eaten) during a test period (Ross, Smith, & Woessner, 1955, p. 307). In addition to food pellets, the hoarding of water "pellets" has also been studied (Bindra, 1947). In this case the pellets were cotton rolls soaked in water.

Views Concerning the Nature of Hoarding

Ross, Smith, and Woessner (1955, pp. 307–308) find three main hypotheses regarding hoarding. Morgan (1947) has held that it is an instinct—that is, that the behavior is a native response of particular species to conditions of bodily need—relatively little influenced by learning. A second hypothesis holds that learning processes are important to the hoarding behavior (J. McV. Hunt, 1941; Marx, 1950; Bindra, 1959). The third view emphasizes the role of stress, induced by environmental factors or by deprivation, as important. This third view would be compatible with either or both of the others. Much of the experimentation on hoarding has been motivated by a desire to resolve these views.

Major Variables Studied in Relation to Hoarding

The studies of hoarding have involved two major classes of variables. One, composed of variables like temperature, illumination, properties of the objects to be hoarded, familarity and other characteristics of the apparatus, and social factors, is essentially external in character. The other class involves changes or variations in the animal itself, like those induced or represented by deprivation, experience, age, sex, temperament, genetic inheritance, and neural insults. We shall mention most of these briefly in the discussion which follows.

1. *Deprivation.* There are two kinds of studies here. One of them involves general food or water deprivation. The other is concerned with more specialized aspects of the diet. It was initially thought that food-deprivation was an essential condition for the appearance of food-pellet hoarding. Morgan, Stellar, and Johnson (1943) found substantial hoarding in 20 of their 36 animals which were maintained on a 24-hour deprivation cycle. However, the onset of hoarding did not occur immediately but only after several days of food deprivation, presumably indicating the building up of an accumulative tissue deficit;

many rats continued to hoard at high levels for a few days after un-limited access to food before hoarding subsided. Again, hunger was presumably not involved in this carry-over of hoarding.

Bindra (1948a) found that rats would hoard saccharin-flavored foods, even when they were not food-deprived, and Ross and Smith (1953) discovered that moderate deprivation reduced hoarding in mice; the mice ate, rather than hoarded. So deprivation is not an essential pre-cursor of hoarding, although it is probably a factor (Licklider & Lick-lider, 1950). Hoarding of water-soaked cotton pellets is similarly in-fluenced by deprivation of water (Bindra, 1947).

Introduction of dietary supplements, like lettuce and cod liver oil (Wolfe, 1939; Ross & Smith, 1953), reduces hoarding. It may be that some of the hoarding shown by nondeprived animals may reflect the insufficiency of laboratory diets (cf. the discussion of specific hungers in the next chapter). However, studies of various aspects of body metabolism and specific dietary deficiencies have not yielded con-sistent results (Ross, Smith, & Woessner, 1955, p. 312).

2. *Frustration.* McCord (1941) permitted his hungry rats to see and smell food pellets but not to eat them; hoarding was significantly increased by this procedure. J. McV. Hunt (1941) produced feeding frustration in infant rats (24 and 32 days of age) over a period of several days. Five months later, these animals and matched controls were given hoarding tests under both deprivation and nondeprivation conditions. The group frustrated at 24 days of age hoarded (during adult depri-vation) much more than its control group, although there was no effect of the frustration at 32 days of age or under nondeprivation conditions. Hunt et al. (1947) confirmed these findings, as have Albino and Long (1951). McKelvey and Marx (1951) failed to obtain con-firming results, however. Hunt's experiment, of course, is important not only in showing that frustration influences hoarding but in sug-gesting the carry-over from infancy of the effects of frustration. Marx (1952) found that rats deprived in infancy ate at a faster rate than the controls and suggests that the faster eating rate could account for increased hoarding in these animals, as they would have more time in which to hoard (after eating) than would the controls.

3. *Experience.* The experiments by both Hunt and his associates and by Marx represent studies of the effects of experience (frustra-tion) on later hoarding. Other types of studies of experience have been carried out. Wolfe (1939) found that animals which had been fed powdered food were inferior hoarders compared to those which were fed food pellets. On the other hand, Stellar and Morgan (1943) found a great deal of hoarding in animals deprived on a 24-hour

schedule over 18 days when they were given the opportunity to hoard later. A group given opportunities to hoard over the 18 days while satiated and another group which for the 18 days could hoard under conditions of deprivation showed no more hoarding on the test trials than the inexperienced first group. Stellar and Morgan believe deprivation to be a much more important determinant of hoarding than experience.

More recent experiments have given further conflicting results. Holland (1954) gave 20 days of hoarding experience to one group of animals and permitted another group only to explore the alleys during this period. In hoarding tests following deprivation, the experienced group hoarded more pellets than the inexperienced group. Smith and Ross (1953) found no difference in hoarding in mice reared on food pellets or on a liquid diet. Bevan and Grodsky (1958) varied rearing experiences of golden hamsters but their hoarding results do not seem to support the role of an experience factor.

Marx (1950) has indicated that the acts of which the hoarding activity is composed are present in the animal's repertoire long before he enters the hoarding situation. The integration of these acts and their occurrence in the hoarding situation might, he thought, be influenced by learning. Marx (1951) trained two groups of animals in the following way to test this idea. Under food deprivation each animal was allowed to take 10 pellets to his cage. The pellets were taken away from one group immediately, whereas the other group was allowed to eat or retain its pellets (only a few were eaten). Hoarding, in a later test under conditions of satiation, was much greater in the animals which had eaten the pellets than in those that had not. This suggests that terminal reinforcement is significant to the development of the hoarding tendency. Under other conditions, however (Marx, 1957; Marx & Brownstein, 1957), terminal reinforcement has not been found to be crucial to hoarding.

While a good deal of effort has gone into the study of experience and hoarding, the results, as this review suggests, are still inconclusive.

4. *Other variables.* Deprivation, frustration, and experience have received the largest share of the research attention that has focused on hoarding. Among other variables that have been studied are the following. Smith and Powell (1955) found a relation between hoarding and emotionality in mice, but Stamm (1955) found no relation between aggressiveness and hoarding in rats. Hess (1953b) showed in the rat that shyness (time to leave the home cage to explore) was related to hoarding. In an open alley, the shy rats hoarded little but became the most frequent hoarders in a walled alley. These variations may

represent genetic differences. Stamm (1954b) showed differences in the hoarding behavior of three strains of rats and (Stamm, 1956) that hoarding patterns in hybrid animals are consistent with a single gene difference among the strains. Zubek (1951) found that hoarding is increased by lesions almost anywhere in the cortex. Lesions of the median cerebral cortex, however, significantly *reduced* the amount of hoarding (Stamm, 1954a). Age is significantly related to hoarding (Porter, Webster, & Licklider, 1951), the amount hoarded increasing with age in a negatively accelerated way. It is probable, further, that there are sex differences in hoarding and even different mechanisms for hoarding in males and females (Ross, Smith, & Woessner, 1955, p. 315).

A number of external variables have been found to influence hoarding. McCleary and Morgan (1946) induced hoarding in satiated rats by reducing the temperature to 13°C. The number of pellets hoarded decreased with temperature from 12 to 30°. Ross and Smith (1953), with mice, found more hoarding with higher than with lower temperatures. Varying the illumination of the situation affects hoarding. Lighting the home cage tends to reduce hoarding but lighting the alleys or the food source increases it (Morgan, 1947; Ross, Smith, & Woessner, 1955, p. 322). This is not true in all strains of rats, however (Marx, Iwahara, & Brownstein, 1957). The familiarity of the situation also is important. Viek and Miller (1944) got rats to hoard more pellets into a familiar rather than an unfamiliar cage; this difference is apparently based on the odor of the familiar cage (Miller & Viek, 1944). Bindra (1948b) found that rats which would not hoard in closed alleys would do so in the less "secure" unwalled alley. Familiarity with the hoarding alley increases hoarding in both rats and hamsters (Miller & Viek, 1944; Smith & Ross, 1950). Wooden blocks are not hoarded by rats when the blocks are mixed in with food (Miller & Viek, 1944), but rats tended to prefer foil-wrapped to unwrapped food pellets for hoarding (Licklider & Licklider, 1950). Miller and Postman (1946) allowed animals from several cages to hoard simultaneously from the same food bin. In the group situation, some animals hoarded from other cages, rather than from the bin. Ross, Smith, and Denenberg (1950) found that dominance was a factor in the amount an animal would hoard in a social situation.

We have not exhausted all the studies of hoarding, but it may be seen from what we have discussed that this simple, "foresightful" behavior is affected by a complex set of variables, at least in the laboratory situation. The role of experience in hoarding and the crucial factors which set off hoarding are by no means clear, even yet.

HOMING AND MIGRATION

Among the behaviors of lower organisms which have aroused the interest of many investigators is that called homing and migration. This behavior may involve short distances over land or in the air or water or journeys of thousands of miles. Interest in it has some practical and commercial value, as in the spawning migrations of fish, the migrations of game birds, or the homing of pigeons. However, much of the interest in these phenomena arises from general curiosity as to the manner in which apparently tremendously difficult feats of navigation and travel may be accomplished.

Travel, seeming to naive observation to be directed or purposeful, appears in a large variety of animals (Carthy, 1956). Sensitivity to chemicals in the air or water apparently controls patterns of locomotion in such organisms as flatworms, whelks, bees, ants, and termites, involving sensory modalities which human beings would liken to smell or taste. Auditory cues, in the range above human hearing, are important to the flight of bats (Griffin, 1958), and visual cues seem to be significant to wasps in learning locations of landmarks which enable them to return to their nests (Carthy, 1956); bees, and other similar forms, also use visual cues. Various fish, like salmon, apparently return to the river of their birth to spawn. Homing and migratory journeys have been found in species of eels, seals, whales, mice, dogs, and horses, and a variety of factors has been suggested as involved in these skills.

While the description and analysis of these activities in various species illustrate the fascinating problem of unraveling the complex set of factors involved in these "mysterious instincts," our space does not permit an account of most of the work that has been done (see Carthy, 1956, for an overall review). We shall confine our discussion to the migration and homing of birds, seeking by this discussion to illustrate the nature of the problem and the kinds of factors found to be involved in it.

Facts of Migration. There is little question that some birds make extensive seasonal migrations. The Arctic tern nests in northern Canada but it migrates to the Antarctic pack ice and back in a year's time. In some species of birds the same individual may spend winter in the same area or return in summer to the nest it had previously occupied (Carthy, 1956; Matthews, 1955). Shorter migrations than those of the Arctic tern are of course prevalent, and migrations generally occur in the spring and fall. Often the younger birds migrate separately from the older birds; thus the older birds cannot guide the younger. Cuckoos are often raised by parents of another species; yet such cuckoos migrate successfully, even though they cannot have learned to do so from their foster parents. Various experiments are cited by Matthews (1955) as indicating that innate factors probably govern the direction or bearing as well as the distance of the flight that is undertaken. (Features of the terrain, like coastlines, also are significant.) Migration appears to be instigated by the effects of light and temperature (cf. Kendeigh, West, & Cox, 1960). In some species the increasing duration of light in the spring activates the pituitary gland, which in turn stimulates growth in the gonads (cf. Lehrman, 1959*b;* Farner, 1961); in the fall the decrement in light has the reverse gonadal effect, and these changes are associated with migrations. However, the role of this factor may be indirect through the effects it has on food supplies; duration of light during the day also controls the amount of time birds can forage for food (Carthy, 1956). The full picture of the factors that instigate migration is not entirely clear, and migrations occurring in the spring may be controlled differently from those occurring in the fall.

Facts of Homing. The pigeon is, of course, the best known of the homing birds, but many other species of wild birds also have this capacity. Perhaps the most dramatic instance of homing is reported by Matthews (1955, p. 28). A Manx Shearwater was taken from Wales to Boston and released there. It had returned to its home area in Wales in twelve-and-a-half days, actually arriving there ahead of a letter from Boston telling of its release. Homing usually refers to the following sequence of events: a bird is taken from its home area by train, car, or whatever, to some other place where it is released. The question is, will it return to its home base? Migration, of course, refers to movements of large groups of birds, seasonal in character, and related to the weather and to reproduction.

Pigeons have been used for centuries as message carriers as well as for racing. They are usually carefully trained by releasing them successively a little farther from the place to which they are to return, and such training is essential to effective homing in most birds. This might suggest that pigeons must learn landmarks and the general nature of the terrain in order to home successfully. While they undoubtedly do make use of such cues, they also have been known to home successfully from strange places where familiar landmarks were not available. They have also homed successfully along routes different in direction from those in which they were trained (Matthews, 1955).

Factors in Migration and Homing. It is clear that these phenomena are real, and the problem has been to uncover the bases on which birds do apparently navigate. Investigators have been unwilling just to accept the facts of behavior and account for them by speaking of migratory or homing instincts. Rather, they have tried to discover the cues on which the birds depend. We shall briefly review the chief cues suggested, although this aspect of the problem is less a motivational question than is the initial instigation to migration and homing.

Several hypotheses that have been advanced as to cues by which birds navigate do not seem to fit well with the results of the few experimental and theoretical investigations that have been designed to test them (Matthews, 1955). These include the suggestions that birds can perceive and use polarized light, the magnetic field of the earth, the earth's Coriolis force and the earth's wind patterns. The two major hypotheses currently being favored refer, for daytime navigation, to the use of the sun, and, for nighttime navigation, to the use of the stellar constellations (Thorpe, 1961). It should be mentioned here that such navigation may be based on several factors, which may vary with the species. Such factors probably have to provide cues as to general direction only, with details of routes arising either from accident or from features of the general terrain or from memory of familiar landmarks.

Experiments made by G. Kramer (cf. Matthews, 1955, pp. 61–64 for summary) clearly showed that Starlings orient themselves by the sun's position and that they are able to take account, also, of the time of day. This was especially true during the period of the birds' migratory restlessness but could be demonstrated at other times as well. The technique was to confine a bird in a cage placed inside a pavilion with six windows giving views of the outside. The bird's orientation could be observed from beneath the cage. On very cloudy days there was no orientation but when the sky cleared the bird was strongly orientated to windows in one quadrant of the pavilion. Using mirrors, the investigator altered the apparent position of the sun, and the orientation of the bird was modified accordingly. It was the sun, or an area of sky near to it, which the bird had to see in order to be orientated. Starlings were also fed in one direction at a specific time of day, but were tested at other times. The birds oriented themselves in the tests according to the direction of the sun, as they had in the experiment just mentioned. These findings are interpreted as suggesting that the birds can "measure" the lapse of time, and other experiments also suggest that these birds possess an "internal chronometer."

These experiments, together with others which they cite, have convinced Matthews (1955) and Carthy (1956) that the sun is an essential element in navigational activity in birds and may operate through memory on migrations at night. But how is the sun used? Matthews has proposed a theory, which he states as follows:

The essential feature is the *sun-arc*. This is inclined at an angle from the horizontal which is constant for a given place and is a measure of the latitude of that place. Farther north the arc is inclined at a lesser angle, farther south at a greater, so that the highest point on the arc is, respectively, lower and higher than at home. This highest point is due south of the observer in the northern hemisphere and so gives a reference point in space by which the "grid" is related to the surroundings. It is also reached at local noon, and so gives a reference point in time. The speed at which the sun moves round its arc is, for practical purposes, constant, at 15° an hour. When it has reached a particular point on its arc at home, it will have advanced further to an observer in the east, and less far to one in the west, the differences in arc angle (the angle round the arc from the noon position) being directly proportional to the change in longitude. At home the bird will become familiar with the features of the sun-arc, and the sun's position on it at different (local) times. These will be related to the internal "chronometer" which is also an essential part of the hypothesis. In unfamiliar surroundings the bird will have to construct the sun-arc from observation . . . it observes the sun's movement over a small part of its arc and extrapolates to obtain the highest point. Measurement of the altitude of this point, the angle from the horizontal, and comparison with the remembered value for home . . . will give the latitude change. The arc angle from the observed sun to this highest point when compared with that obtaining at home for the same chronometer time will give the longitude change (Matthews, 1955, pp. 92–94).

Despite its complexity, this hypothesis is regarded as plausible by such other writers as Carthy (1956), Griffin (1958), and Sauer (1958) for daytime navigation. Matthews has summarized evidence which suggests that homing and migratory birds have the visual and other capacities requisite to a performance like this; and the calculational activities suggested in the quotation might well be reduced, in actuality, to a simpler form, like the restoration by flight of a normal sun-arc for the home conditions (Matthews, 1955, p. 117). We should add that natural features of the terrain and remembered landmarks, together with random search in flight, would all, perhaps, operate with the sun-arc basis in migratory and homing activities (see Lehrman, 1956a, pp. 532–537; Kramer, 1959).

Sauer (1958) has been concerned with nocturnally migrating birds, to which the sun-arc hypothesis would be much less applicable. His birds have shown evidence of restlessness during the period of seasonal migration, even when they were hatched and raised in chambers where the conditions were those of "eternal summer." When these birds were allowed to view the night sky full of stars, they orientated in the direction of the ordinary migration route of their species, but showed no orientation on cloudy nights. Further tests were made in a planetarium with birds that had been reared in cages from birth and had never traveled under natural conditions. The results were confirmatory of the observations already made. ". . . the warblers have a remarkable hereditary mechanism for orienting themselves by the stars—a detailed image of the starry configuration of the sky coupled with a precise time sense which relates the heavenly canopy to the geography of the earth at every time and season. At their very first glimpse of the sky the birds automatically know the right direction" (Sauer, 1958, p. 46).

Summary

Directional travel, as in migration and homing, is a well-established phenomenon in many animals and birds and is a good illustration of what is usually called an instinctive behavior pattern. Migration, at least, is seasonal, and it appears to be set off in birds by complex hormonal changes instigated by changes in the duration of daylight. Numerous hypotheses have been proposed to account for the migratory and homing behavior of birds, but at the present time it appears that daytime navigation is dependent on reaction to the sun's position relative to an innate or learned norm, and the bird must fly to its home location to achieve this. Migration at night, on the other hand, seems to be guided by innate reactions to stellar constellations, and to be instigated, apparently, by the glandular changes underlying the tendency to migrate seasonally.

TEMPERATURE

The human body, not to mention the bodies of many other animals, must maintain its temperature within a rather narrow range. It accomplishes this adjustment by means of a large number of processes, among them sweating, vasodilation and vasoconstriction, shivering, respiratory adjustments, variations in activity, etc. In addition, temperature regulation is further accomplished by use of clothing, central heating, air cooling or conditioning, migrations to better climates (as in winter and summer vacations), etc. Clearly, temperature regulation is one source of a good deal of behavior, although much of it serves comfort rather than dire, physical emergency, at least in the temperate zones.

We need not enter into a detailed discussion of the effects of temperature extremes, since we are all aware of the enervation arising from a prolonged heat wave (especially when the humidity is high) and of our vigorous efforts to stay warm when subjected to prolonged exposure to the cold. Actually, except for studies under extreme conditions, as in desert or Arctic climates, and for the study of performance under different temperatures, not a great deal of effort has been devoted to the study of temperature as a motivational variable. We discuss here, very briefly, neural mechanisms in temperature regulation and some of the behavioral reflections of temperature which have received experimental inquiry. Temperature is a prominent factor in a number of other topics related to bodily conditions, among which are nesting, activity, eating, drinking, and hoarding.

Neural Mechanisms

It has been known for about thirty years that hypothalamic lesions disturb temperature regulation. There are apparently two areas of the hypothalamus involved: the one in the anterior hypothalamus when damaged permits hyperthermia to develop, whereas if the one in the posterior hypothalamus is damaged, it causes both animals and men to become poikilothermic—that is, their bodies assume the temperature of the external air, rather than remaining constant.

Brobeck indicates that peripheral mechanisms operating reflexly contribute a good deal to thermal regulation. The hypothalamic role, he states (Brobeck, 1955a, p. 1119), is that of "an integrator of all of the information available to the nervous system relative to temperature, and . . . [also] . . . a sensory element capable of supplying a specific type of information, namely the central or deep body temperature."

Some Behavioral Effects of Temperature

Yoakum (1909) found that his rats could learn to discriminate between tunnels having temperatures of 40 and 24°C, respectively. Nicholls (1922) found that the spontaneous activity of guinea pigs varied with the external temperature, increasing at the lower ones. Browman (1942, 1943) found similar results for blinded rats and for female rats. Wever (1932) measured the swimming speed of rats in water of various temperatures. The animals swam most slowly at water temperatures approximating that of their bodies; at lower temperatures swimming speed was much greater and was also faster at higher temperatures (hot to human touch). Escape from ice water was used by Moss (1924), but the study employed too few animals for the results to mean much. Ruch (1930), however, found that rats would learn a water maze for the reward of escape from the water, which was at room temperature. Moore (1944) found that the number of crossings of the grid in the Columbia obstruction box was inversely related to room temperature. Munn (1950, p. 465) observes that rats will huddle together when the temperature is low, a finding also true for mice and bobwhite quail (Collias, 1951, p. 396). Salmon and trout apparently prefer some water temperatures more than others (Fisher, 1950) and would congregate at the points in an aquarium where their respectively preferred temperatures were present. Salmon may also use temperature as a cue to migration.

Limited though these findings are, they give some empirical support to the notion that temperature can affect behavior in definite ways. Changes in temperature can also be reinforcing. Weiss (Weiss & Danford, 1956; Weiss, 1957, 1958) and Carlton and Marks (1957) have shown that when a rat is in a cold environment raising the temperature can reinforce a response. In Weiss' experiments, a heat lamp was turned on briefly on lever depression. Satisfactory response rates can be maintained in this manner, and Weiss and Danford (1956, p. 1) indicate that significant differences arise in the rates generated under different temperatures.

RESPIRATION AND ELIMINATION

There are a number of bodily conditions which, in certain circumstances, have considerable motivational potential but which do not figure very importantly in everyday life. Included here for brief treatment are the needs to breathe and to eliminate waste substances from the body. Our discussions of these matters will be brief, because of their relative insignificance as ordinary sources of motivation. We shall therefore omit the discussion of their physiology and of the history of their investigation.

Respiration

The act of breathing is complexly controlled by neural centers and by afferent stimuli and chemical conditions which influence them (Carlson & Johnson, 1953; Fulton, 1955). Of these conditions the concentration of carbon dioxide in the blood is important in generating a drive to breathe. If one rebreathes from a closed air chamber long enough, the carbon dioxide will accumulate in the chamber and in the blood with resultant discomfort and accelerated breathing. Oxygen deficiency alone, on the other hand, does not seem to produce these effects.

For obvious reasons, it has not been easily possible to use the induction of a drive to breathe in experimentation. The only case we are aware of, in which variations of this drive were used, was reported by Broadhurst (1957). He required rats to make a discrimination in a Y-shaped apparatus, with the reward being escape from water to air. While in the water, the animal had to swim under water, and his swimming to the choice point could be delayed. Hence, several levels of air deprivation could be induced, and the speed of swimming was measured relative to air-deprivation levels. Speed of swimming increased up to air deprivations of about 20 seconds, presumably indicating the energization of swimming by the drive induced by air deprivation.

Elimination

When introspective reports of excretory needs and functions are obtained, the primary characterization of these conditions is of a pattern of pressure, with pain sometimes present as well (Boring, 1915). These factors can occasionally lead to powerful needs to urinate or to evacuate, but relatively little use of these drives is represented in the behavioral literature. They tend to be periodic in the rat (Richter, 1922). Evidence was obtained by Berg (1944) that the typical patterns of urination in male and female dogs are controlled, in part, by sex hormones. Freeman (1938a, b) showed that widespread postural and reactivity changes occurred in his male human subjects in the effort to inhibit urination when the desire to do so was great.

In one respect, the behavioral literature has been much concerned with urination and defecation. This is the area of toilet training, impetus for the study of which came from psychoanalysis (see Chapter 12). There are wide cultural differences in the age and the extent to which these patterns are brought under control and in the extent to which shame and other negative feelings are associated with them. However, experimental studies in which the strength and effects of these drives have been varied and investigated seem limited to those we have just reviewed. The psychoanalytic and cultural aspects of these drives are treated elsewhere in this book. Urination and defecation are also sometimes used, especially in animals, as measures of anxiety, fear, other emotional states, or of "emotionality."

FATIGUE

The repeated observation of impaired output with continued performance of an activity and reports of tiredness following strenuous work led to the assumption that a bodily condition must exist to account for this loss and change. Fatigue has been given this role. Since rest periods usually reduce both the deleterious effect on performance and the felt fatigue, it appeared reasonable to assume further that the underlying mechanism was a restorable factor, at work either in the member(s) [i.e., muscle(s)] involved in the activity or in the organism in general. Such a mechanism would permit either an accumulated undesirable substance to be eliminated, or a depleted desirable or needed substance to be restored. We shall turn to the evidence on this question shortly. But first it would be well to consider some of the alternative ways in which the concept of fatigue has been used. This will not avoid confusion, unfortunately, but it will at least forewarn the reader that we are dealing with several concepts rather than one, and perhaps provide some order for what is to follow.

Uses of the Concept

The term fatigue is variously used to denote a motivational state of the organism associated with a need for rest (physiological fatigue), a negative feeling tone (subjective fatigue), or any decrement in a response following upon its prolonged or repeated exercise (objective fatigue). A fourth category denoting long-term, chronic or clinical fatigue is also widely employed. In addition, the term is often coupled with adjectives descriptive of types of functions or situations, such as mental fatigue, operational fatigue, combat fatigue, pilot fatigue, driver fatigue, etc.[2] Fatigue-like states are also found as secondary effects of anxiety, stress, and other conditions of affective or bodily upset (cf. Bartley & Chute, 1947; Bartley, 1957; McFarland, 1953; Tidwell & Sutton, 1954).

Not only has fatigue been defined and studied in this great variety of ways and situations, but where criteria have been compared they are found to be poorly correlated. The explanation for this lies not only in the likelihood that these are not identical conditions, but also in the fact that fatigue (however defined) is subject to influence by (1) state-of-the-organism factors, such as the condition of the muscles, recency of sleep, rest, or activity, and state of health and other bodily needs; (2) psychological factors, such as morale, interest in the task at hand or its purpose, boredom, self-instruction, worry, or threats of punishment; and (3) environmental or situational factors, such as levels of illumination, noise, oxygen and carbon dioxide, temperature, humidity, etc. Thus, although fatigue states seem pretty clearly to have motivational implications, simple assessment of their intensities or their effect(s) cannot be made.

[2] Such terms as auditory fatigue and visual fatigue are also used to describe phenomena related to performance decrement and/or loss of sensitivity in specific sensory members. These will not be treated here.

Biochemical and Physiological Factors

In general, fatigue is seen by most physiologists as a symptom of the temporary breakdown of bodily metabolism. However, there is little agreement as to whether this failure is due to the exhaustion of energy reserves or the accumulation of toxic substances in the blood. Accompanying muscle contraction, there is an increased flow of blood, bringing oxygen from the lungs and glycogen from the liver to replace that being converted in the process of liberating energy. The increased blood flow likewise removes excess lactic acid and carbon dioxide— the end products of glycogen conversion. In normal, moderate response, anabolic and catabolic processes appear to keep pace with each other. However, under prolonged, rapidly repeated, or highly effortful responding, there may be an insufficiency of oxygen, a depletion of the ready supply of glycogen, or a failure to remove the conversion end products (Bartley & Chute, 1947; Tidwell & Sutton, 1954). Thus Dill et al. (1936) were able to show that the lactic acid concentration in the blood was a useful index of accumulating fatigue in normal subjects. However, studies of miners who work at high altitudes, marathon runners, and others in athletically fit condition indicate that lactate is not the only factor. On the other side, Christensen et al. (1934) showed that a low blood-sugar level would give rise to complete exhaustion, and McFarland (1953) reports that the administration of carbohydrates (e.g., glucose) during such strenuous activities as marathon racing helps to maintain energy and stave off fatigue. By the same token McFarland points out that glucose ingestion by pilots in flight (who, he notes, do *not* work strenuously) is also helpful in reducing fatigue. He attributes this to the fact that the "metabolism of the central nervous system is dependent on glucose" (p. 337).

There seems to be some uncertainty as to whether the same metabolic processes occur in the presence and absence of an adequate oxygen supply (cf. Bartley & Chute, 1947). However, there is general agreement that an insufficiency of oxygen is a contributing factor to fatigue onset (Hemingway, 1953; Noltie, 1953). One of the difficulties in using oxygen consumption as a measure of fatigue, however, is the fact that the organism may contract a short-term "oxygen debt" during strenuous effort, which is then repaid during the subsequent rest period (see Noltie, 1953; Ryan, 1947).

The biochemical and physiological mechanisms of fatigue are by no means limited to muscle metabolism. The failure of function in a muscle or group of muscles involved in an activity may occur as a result of a failure of the muscle fibers themselves to develop tension, or it may reflect a failure of conduction in nerve fibers, across synapses, or in the muscle end plates (Hemingway, 1953). Evidence exists for the separate fatigability of both nerve and muscle fibers. It has been shown that muscle tension, in the gastrocnemius muscle of the cat, lost after continued stimulation through its nerve, would be immediately regained and sustained by electrically stimulating the muscle directly (Brown & Burns, 1949). Hemingway (1953, p. 70) interprets these findings to mean that a partial block is developed at the nerve endings, "limiting the number of impulses that can pass from the nerve to the muscle rather than by reducing in any way the intensity of stimulation." Continued direct muscle stimulation, on the other hand, leads to reduced muscle tension. Muscle fatigue has been shown to influence the local production of acetylcholine, in turn inhibiting neuromuscular action (see Bartley & Chute, 1947, pp. 139 ff.).

The intake of food substances and both the timing of intake in relation to work and the availability of quickly convertible food products play a significant role in fatigue. Likewise, the timing of impulse flow and the synchronization in the various steps of metabolism during work are determinants of the appearance of fatigue. Apparently fatigue can result from the failure of one or more mechanisms involved in the maintenance of metabolism in any of the parts of the neuromuscular response systems. This may involve the failure of supply of oxygen or glucose to the system involved, the absence of "potentiator" substances, or the presence of "depressor" substances (substances which may reduce or actually be a function of a failure at intermediate metabolism), or a breakdown in either removal or resynthesis of end products of nerve or muscle metabolism.

The intricacy of the relations of facilitating and inhibiting mechanisms to each other suggests that the main controlling mechanism of fatigue lies in the central nervous system rather than peripherally in the muscles. Metabolic changes in the muscles and muscle end plates may in turn provide information feedback to such a central nervous control center. A number of investigators have emphasized nervous regularity (cf. Otani, 1953; Merton & Pampiglione, 1950; Schwab, 1949; Kozlowski, 1952), but no specific mechanism or central locale has been identified. Independent of neurophysiological evidence, the persistent reports of voluntary induction or postponement of fatigue and the occurrence of fatigue as a symptom of emotional stress would be consistent with a central rather than peripheral mechanism.

Objective Fatigue

Studies of work and efficiency have generally relied on measures of work decrement as an index of fatigue. Reduction of output is at best a rather inconsistent criterion, however. Prior to an actual reduction in performance level there may occur a variation in behavior, reflected in errors, accidents, or in erratic rhythm of activity (depending on the task involved), which may itself be attributed to an increasing fatigue condition. Likewise, the requirement of continued activity may lead to an increase in effort expenditure, resulting either in no change in performance quality or level, or an actual improvement in performance, even though at marked "cost" to the organism involved. This masking effect of effort increase on performance makes assessment of fatigue from performance measures alone exceedingly difficult.

H. D. Darcus (see Ross, 1952) enumerates the following main effects of repeated exertion: (1) a same or lesser output, with greater activity; (2) a longer rest requirement after given amounts of work; (3) the involvement of muscles other than those directly used in the task; (4) a change in the pattern of activity; (5) a greater effect on newly acquired habits as contrasted with older ones; (6) greater difficulty in maintaining unusual movements, as contrasted with regular movements; and (7) the occurrence, even after an activity ends, of such effects as tremor, muscle hypersensitivity, soreness, etc.

Fatigue and Psychomotor Performance

Most motor skills involve responses to changing stimulus displays. Bartlett and his associates at Cambridge (cf. 1943, 1953) have extensively studied psychomotor tasks under a variety of conditions. They report the main effect of fatigue to be a "splitting" of the display field, outlying elements either being ignored (forgotten) or overemphasized. Lapses of behavior and/or unexpected (unpredicted) behaviors follow. Continued performance leads to a disruption of self-pacing and a resulting increasing irregularity of the internal timing of performance. Bartlett (1953) concludes that the three main characteristics of fatigue in such psychomotor tasks are (1) this irregular internal timing, (2) the disintegration of the display field [3] (see also Broadbent, 1953), resulting in inappropriate actions or omissions, and (3) an acute stage of (subjective) discomfort.

[3] Hauty and Payne (1956) tested this hypothesis and failed to confirm it. They compared the relative impairment of proficiency of control of marginally located instruments with those centrally located on a simulated aircraft control panel over a 7-hour work period. No difference in rate of decrement was found.

Because of its industrial and military importance, there is a voluminous amount of literature on the effects of prolonged and repeated activities and of conflicting task requirements as inducers of fatigue. Typical of the findings is a study by Aiken (1957) in which subjects were trained in a fatigue-inducing procedure to acquire two successive incompatible tasks. The results showed an increase in "psychological blocking" (see Bills, 1943) and a decrease in both speed and accuracy of performance. Carmichael, Kennedy, and Mead (1949), using a persistence test, reported an inability (or unwillingness) of their subjects to maintain an initial level of performance over time. They conclude that ". . . the pattern of human fatigue . . . is one of periodic blocks or interruptions of performance of varying frequency and duration, rather than the continuous decrements as shown in work curves secured in the study of isolated muscle groups" (p. 695). Similar conclusions regarding the erratic nature of work-decrement curves, drawn from studies of fast work under pressure, were reached by Bornemann (1952) and by Davis and Josselyn (1953).

Broadbent (1953) attributes such disruption of coordination to a drift in the focus of attention, allowing irrelevant elements to enter the field of perception. That it is the general organization of behavior rather than energy output per se which is affected by prolonged work is further suggested by Broadbent in the observation that when individuals tire of monotonous work they often turn to strenuous physical activity for relief. The role of subjective factors in such activity shift is also to be noted, however.

Subjective Fatigue

The concept of fatigue described in the preceding section is one that can be inferred from changes in the quality or quantity of performance over time. In contrast to this, the reader himself may have experienced what is called felt or subjective fatigue. Feelings of tiredness, weariness, or exhaustion may be specific (to the responding limb or part) or general throughout the body. Such feelings can apparently precede, accompany, and/or follow upon performance or effort change.

Bartley and Chute (1947; Bartley, 1951, 1957) are leading exponents of the view that *only* subjective fatigue qualifies as a motivational construct. Traditional studies of work and efficiency, they claim, do not provide information about fatigue, only about performance decrement. The lack of correlation between objective and subjective indices (cf. Poffenberger, 1942), and the long-known fact that even in simple ergographic performance individuals will report fatigue and cease responding well before actual neuromuscular exhaustion occurs (see

Woodworth and Schlosberg, 1954, p. 802), lend support to their contention.[4]

After an extensive analysis of fatigue experiments, Bartley and Chute (1947) conclude that fatigue is not a function of any part but of the whole individual. Fatigue, for them, "always involves the individual's evaluation of himself and his abilities" (p. 398). It thus has a self-preservative or self-protective character. In addition, they note eleven other characteristics of (subjective) fatigue: (1) it is cumulative (via increased susceptibility to thwarting); (2) it is distinguishable from both feelings of effortfulness and (3) actual energy expenditure—in other words, it is not energetic in character; (4) it is a function of interest or (5) of conflict rather than amount of physical activity; (6) it does not follow a simple growth or decay function, but may be suddenly increased or decreased as a function of other factors; (7) it is a central nervous function, subject to repatterning and reorganization; (8) it may occur at the mere anticipation or contemplation of activity—that is, it can be aroused by thoughts or by situational cues; (9) it is reciprocally related to feelings of enthusiasm; (10) it can be overcome or indefinitely postponed in an emergency and in periods of carefree goal pursuit; and (11) it is not directly related to either sleep or recovery periods as such.

In short, Bartley and Chute use the term *fatigue* to describe a negative feeling state related to the state of emotional well-being of the individual as a whole. Although the aversive nature of fatigue is emphasized, not all feelings of fatigue or tiredness are action-inhibiting or unpleasant. Bartley and Chute themselves have observed that a "good" day of sport may produce a desire to go dancing in the evening; and Wenger, Jones, and Jones (1956) similarly observe that the kind of "psychological fatigue" that follows a game of tennis or a hike may be an enjoyable tiredness.[5]

The emphasis given by Bartley and Chute to fatigue as an organizational variable in the central nervous system receives support from others (e.g., Bornemann, 1952; von Bracken, 1952; Davis, 1953; Gugen-

[4] Shands and Finesinger (1952) and Schwab and Prichard (1951) argue that fatigue is a warning to the individual to cease activity before he damages himself. The fact that the voluntary fatigue curve is shorter than that of the nerve muscle preparation is taken as supportive of this view of fatigue as a protective mechanism. Merton and Pampiglione (1950) have demonstrated that voluntary activation of muscles *can* reach limits paralleling electrical stimulation, however. The fact that they ordinarily do not reach these limits suggests a role of learning.

[5] This raises the question (which exists for most so-called aversive conditions) of the positive motivational value of small degrees of arousal. This matter will be discussed in greater detail in Chapter 8.

heim, 1953) and is similar to the conclusion drawn with regard to objective fatigue from entirely different kinds of data. "Fatigue," writes Bornemann, results "from disturbances in the interplay of internal functions and systems. Recovery is brought about by the reorganization of these mechanisms."

Mental Fatigue

It is general knowledge that persons engaging in intellectual work, although often remaining physically sedentary, may nevertheless show deteriorated performance over time, and experience increasingly intense weariness. However, the actual metabolic cost of such mental work is slight (McFarland has cited Benedict's reported finding that the brain in several hours of sustained mental work utilizes the calories contained in one-half a peanut!). McFarland (1953) suggests that the exhaustive nature of mental work may not be attributed to the involvement of the nervous system alone, but that musculature and other parts of the body may be held tense and thus lead to an increased oxygen consumption. He points out that attention, associated with mental work, leads to an increased muscular tonus throughout the body, and thus may produce fatigue in this way.

Actually, what has been called mental fatigue does not produce identical symptoms to those of physical exhaustion. Prolonged mental activity as well as motor activity (see p. 138) leads to an increase in errors and accidents, a greater variability in performance, and increased irritability and loss of self-control (Darrow & Henry, 1949; Tidwell & Sutton, 1954). These symptoms, although labeled fatigue, may in fact reflect boredom, satiation of attention, or a conflict of interest with other activities. Supporting the idea that this is not the same phenomenon as muscular fatigue is Browne's (1953) observation that there is an *inverse* relationship between the mental effort demanded by a task and performance deterioration. Likewise, in a series of classic studies of work and efficiency, Bills (e.g., 1931, 1937) showed that in especially monotonous work an increased number of "transient mental blocks" of inactivity occur, with continuous performance leading to an increase in errors, etc. In a review of mental fatigue, Bills (1943) suggests that it results from a combination of four factors: (1) a specific factor associated with the depletion of the particular mechanisms involved in the task, plus supporting tension and reinforcement processes; (2) a general fatigue factor where the work is complex and involves a series of different specific functions; (3) a general fatigue factor associated with attention and control dimensions; and (4) a general debility or exhaustion factor, associated with long mental exertion.

That mental fatigue is probably a different class of events from physical fatigue is further supported by the finding that there is no transfer between the two. Further, the recovery rate in mental work is closely associated with shifts in attention and organization of the problem or work strategy, processes not likely to be directly attributable to muscular fatigue products. On the other hand, prolonged mental effort, when accompanied by restrictions of either the physical or psychological environment, may give rise to performance decrement or subjective fatigue symptoms indistinguishable from those arising from prolonged general motor activity.

Operational and Chronic Fatigue

So far we have been discussing fatigue in terms of relatively short-term continuous and/or repeated exercise or activity. However, fatigue is also experienced under circumstances of restricted or attention-restraining activities, even when excessive amounts of energy are not rapidly expended. A variety of industrial as well as military situations involve requirements of vigilance over time. Long-distance drivers, radar operators, and pilots have been most systematically studied. The appearance of fatigue in such groups is so frequent, in fact, that special terms—driver-fatigue, pilot-fatigue, as well as the more generic term operational fatigue—have been employed to denote the situation-related nature of the response patterns.

McFarland (1953) summarizes the findings of his own and others' studies of operational fatigue in airline pilots and in drivers. Effects of continuous performance include a deterioration in steadiness, vigilance, reaction time, and coordination, and an increase in errors and accidents. But these performance decrements could not be reliably related to changes in blood or urine content or to rate of heart or blood pressure. Studies of military pilots (e.g., Fraser, 1956) support a conclusion which McFarland comes to, namely, that operational fatigue is the result not only of direct stresses of performance requirements, but is attributable to "emotional tensions arising from personal and social maladjustments" of the men involved. This role of emotions in producing and prolonging fatigue symptoms is often emphasized by those who have studied men in restricted environments. Likewise, the interaction of physical stresses and work requirements as producers of fatigue is well known (cf. Darrow & Henry, 1949; Ellis, 1953; Mc-Farland, 1946, 1953). In other words, disturbances of metabolism and/or neuroendocrine balance, of which sluggishness and general fatigue are symptoms, may be produced by disruptions of homeostasis as a result of anxiety or stress, independently of any local breakdown in neuromuscular oxidation resulting from activity.

When the conditions producing fatigue are long continuing—as in the case of combat infantrymen or men under the duress of extreme cold or heat over extended periods—the more severe symptoms of chronic fatigue occur. Unlike acute fatigue states, these chronic types of reactions are not relieved by normal rest. Clinical descriptions of cases of chronic operational fatigue usually include a general malaise or apathy (although this is sometimes a vague restlessness), accompanied by feelings of exhaustion and some sensory disorientation. But as von Bracken (1952) has pointed out, the severe symptoms resulting from combat fatigue are in fact cases of *over*fatigue, which is not the same as an ordinary need for rest. What was said a few paragraphs ago about the role of anxiety and stress in operational fatigue is particularly true for—and perhaps really demarks—chronic fatigue.

Measurement of Fatigue

Having briefly examined at least four distinguishable aspects of fatigue—objective, subjective, physiological, and chronic or clinical— we can readily agree with the statement that there is no one fatigue entity! (Browne, 1953; Cloche, 1951). As might be expected to follow from the diversity of types and of factors influencing fatigue, there is little correlation of measures across criterion conditions, or even within them.

Performance decrement, noting the limitations we have already discussed, is a crude index of objective fatigue, provided that one is interested in output as such. The complications we have noted would make it a rather poor measure of fatigue as drive, however. Errors, accidents, and disruptions in timing or organization would seem more accurately to reflect the disintegrative nature of fatigue than would speed or gross productivity indices. These too suffer the limitations noted, however. There is some suggestion that a combination of speed, accuracy, and organizational measures might provide a useful index of fatigue, but no formulae for the weighting of contributions of each have yet come forth.

A number of physiological and neuroendocrine indicators have been proposed as measures of fatigue, but they do not check out consistently across different criteria, or even reliably against the same criteria. Among these are basal metabolic rate (BMR) and pulse rate (Fortuin, 1958), critical flicker fusion frequency (CFF) (Davis, 1955; Ross, Hussman, & Andrews, 1954; Ishizuka, 1951), auditory flutter (Davis, 1955), 17-ketosteroid excretion (Gomberg, 1947), muscle action potential (MAP) (von Bracken, 1952), heart-rate recovery curves

(Brouha, 1954; Monjauze et al., 1953), eye-blink rate and EEG (Carmichael & Dearborn, 1947; Monjauze et al., 1953), body temperature (Brouha, 1954), pupillary reactions to light (Lowenstein & Lowenfeld, 1951, 1952), and galvanic skin response (GSR) (Burch & Greiner, 1958).

Other measures which have been used include tests of perceptual organization (Lybrand, Andrews, & Ross, 1954), duration of negative after-images (Haider, 1957), steadiness, body sway, tapping rate (Ross, Hussman, & Andrews, 1954), and even handwriting (Voigt, 1956). A number of these measures, particularly those involving indices of organization and coordination, have yielded positive correlations with some type of fatigue. However, Bujas (1957) has probably summarized the matter as well as it can be stated at this time: "Changes in the function of isolated mechanisms cannot serve as a test of fatigue, as they do not occur in all subjects in the same direction, nor are they qualitatively the same in the same subject if the test is repeated" (Bujas, 1957).

Drugs and Fatigue

Having indicated the increasing likelihood that fatigue is a central nervous system phenomenon, it would appear likely that it could be affected by those drugs which modify central nervous system metabolism. This indeed seems to be the case.

Two main groups of drugs—the so-called tranquilizers and energizers—have been studied quite extensively in the past decade, primarily in regard to their treatment potential in mental illness. As a side effect of these treatment programs, some information is available on the effects of these drugs on normal function and on fatigue.

The *tranquilizers* include three main groups: the phenothiazine derivatives (of which chlorpromazine is perhaps the best known), the alkaloids of Rauwolfia serpentia (of which reserpine is best known), and a mixed group (of which meprobamate is most widely known). These have generally been found to have a sedating effect on behavior, to decrease ability to perform complex, rapid movements, and to reduce hyperactivity (Felix, 1958; Leake, 1956).

The *energizers*, or antidepressant drugs (e.g., amphetamine, methylphenidylacetate, pipradrol, iproniazid), have been shown to clearly have antifatigue effects (Felix, 1958). In fact, by varying doses of either tranquilizers or energizing drugs, the entire range of activation —from death or coma to psychotic excitement—can be produced. Highly unique individual side-reactions sometimes occur with these drugs, but, in general, moderate doses have the indicated effects.

Davis (1947) found that amphetamine increased speed of performance and seemed to counteract pilot fatigue, although it had no effect on performance accuracy. Nash (1962) administered both amphetamines and barbiturates to a large sample of normal men, measuring the effects of the drugs on a variety of psychological tasks, including perceptual organization. He found that moderate doses of amphetamine enhanced motor functions, elevated indices of visual functioning (CFF, visual acuity, perceptual speed), and improved performance in a series of reasoning and mental arithmetic tasks. Similar findings of improvement in performance, under amphetamine influence, have been reported by others as well (e.g., Barmack, 1938; Nowlis & Nowlis, 1956; Andrews, 1940; Turner & Carl, 1939). The improvement has been attributed to increased focusing of attention, heightened subjective feelings of pleasure and allayed feelings of fatigue. Barmack (1938, 1940) had earlier suggested that amphetamine acts on a central process concerned with alertness, a hypothesis which was confirmed by Bradley and Key (1958) who showed that amphetamine lowered the behavioral and EEG-arousal threshold to direct stimulation of the reticular formation. It is this alerting action of amphetamines which, Nash concludes, is responsible for both the capacity changes and the mood and antifatigue effects.

With the barbiturates, Nash, as well as Kornetsky (1958) and Cranston et al. (1952), observed no significant changes in behavior under sedative doses of phenobarbital. Under hypnotic doses, however, impairment of visual functioning and motor control were obtained (Goodnow et al., 1951; Kornetsky et al., 1957, 1958; Landis & Zubin, 1951; Lehmann & Csank, 1957; von Felsinger et al., 1953). Reitan (1957) tested the effects of extremely heavy vs. clinical doses of meprobamate on the Halstead battery of tests of psychological function, finding no effect with clinical doses but significant impairment of alertness, coordination, motor speed, and precision with excessive doses.

Tyler (1947) compared the effects of benzedrine and amytal on a variety of fatigue tests after periods of athletic activity of up to 112 hours. Benzedrine at 36–48 hours postponed later performance deterioration, whereas barbiturate administration had little effect. Seashore and Ivy (1953) compared the effectiveness of caffeine, benzedrine, and an ephedrine compound in combating fatigue in actual work situations. They found benzedrine most effective overall. Caffeine relieved subjective fatigue, but produced little sensorimotor improvement. Desoxyephedrine had the reverse effect. Using different measures, Nash (1962) reported the subjective effects of caffeine to be milder than its performance effects. Pieron (1952) found that caffeine ingestion would maintain the CFF threshold under physical or mental effort expenditure.

These experiments represent only a sampling of the many studies of the effects of drugs on fatigue, but it serves to indicate the significance of central nervous control in fatigue, as the drugs described appear to attenuate or to inhibit the actions of central-neural control of activity. After a searching analysis of current knowledge of brain monoamines, Brodie and Costa (1962) conclude: "These results give food for thought since they indicate that chlorpromazine acts on central mechanisms that are oriented towards patterns of behavior which utilize oxidative metabolism and require energy; while in contrast reserpine stimulates pathways which provide for protection and promote restorative processes" (p. 23). Thus it would seem that "central fatigue" (a term used by Burch & Greiner, 1958), which may perhaps underlie the types of fatigue here discussed, may be no more than a descriptive aspect of central arousal-inhibitory processes.

Summary

Fatigue is a term applied to a variety of conditions, from a decrement in the work curve of a single muscle to a state of total collapse of the organism. There is evidence for a series of interlocking cyclic metabolic processes, from central neurochemical activator-depressor mechanisms to local neuromuscular activity. Inadequate or excessive input or performance requirement disturbs the balance, and either endogenous control (via compensatory hormonal changes, at least in part a function of affective state) or exogenous control (via drugs that attenuate arousal or depressive tendencies, or manipulations of the psychological or physical environment which modify input to the central arousal mechanism) will affect fatigue symptoms.

Periodic rest permits the restoration of balance of energy components to or in the responding member or to or in its control center(s). Fatigue as a condition of the whole organism may apparently be induced through muscular overexertion, response requirement at a rate so rapid as to disturb neuromuscular homeostasis, or under conditions involving prolonged attention and concomitant bodily tension.

Fatigue is a motivational phenomenon to the extent that its accumulation leads to behavior change. Individuals appear to use kinesthetic feedback to withdraw from activities, the continuation of which could be damaging to them. This withdrawal seems to occur before the limits of physiological capacity to respond are reached. Thus the underlying neuromuscular fatigue or exhaustion is only an indirect contributor to "rest-seeking" behavior. It appears to be an aversive condition which the individual learns to anticipate and avoid.

This role of learning may in part account for the discrepancies between criteria of objective and subjective fatigue. Also, as fatigue appears to be a result of metabolic disturbance, it is both a cause of systemic stress (via feedback presumably to the reticular formation) and a by-product at least of those physiological and physical factors which generally affect homeostasis (see Chapters 7 and 9). Under the circumstances, it is difficult to treat fatigue as a separate (i.e., independent) motivational state. The reasons for this will become clearer, we believe, from our next discussions of inhibition and sleep.

INHIBITION

Pilkington and McKellar (1960) point out that the term *inhibition*, in its present dictionary meaning of "an action of preventing, hindering, or checking," derives from a definition by Brunton (1883) which referred to the "arrest of the functions of a structure or organ by the actions upon it of another, while its power to execute these functions is still retained and can be manifested as soon as the restraining power is removed." [6]

In the previous section we suggested that the concepts of fatigue and inhibition were closely related. In fact we alluded to the central processes associated with fatigue as neurochemical inhibitory processes. Yet Brunton's definition suggests that an inhibited function is restrained but intact, whereas fatigue of a function implies its diminution or exhaustion, at least temporarily. Two important links exist between the processes, however. First, in both instances, there is an interruption of response. In both instances, therefore, any potential damage to the responding member from continuation of the response would be prevented. It would thus appear that both fatigue and inhibition may subserve the same end of protection from injury, or survival. A second link, which may become clearer as this section develops, is the possibility that information feedback from a responding member could somehow induce an inhibitory process before the member had completely exhausted its response capacity. What we are saying here is that it is possible that both inhibition and fatigue form part of a single response system subserving a restorative function.

A second aspect of Brunton's definition is its reference to the source

---

[6] See discussion by Diamond, Balvin, and Diamond (1963) of the early history of the concept.

of inhibition as lying outside the blocked structure. In fatigue we found that the source was for the most part inside the system under consideration. In examining inhibition, we shall have reason to refer to both external and internal sources.

Our particular reasons for including a discussion of inhibition in this chapter arise from its widespread use in connection with conditioning phenomena (Pavlov, 1927, 1928; Hilgard & Marquis, 1940), and its use particularly to describe a negative drive state resulting from effortful responding (Hull, 1943). Here again we find a close link with fatigue. At least it seems to us, as we examine the literature on response-produced inhibition, that little more than a fatigue-like process is ever implied. Indeed, references to the accumulation of fatigue products in the blood (see Chapter 10) suggest that this may be the physiological model assumed.

But before turning to this discussion, we should make note of the increasing attention paid to inhibitory processes in current neurobehavioral research. Briefly, then, we shall look at inhibition as a neurophysiological concept.

Inhibition as a Central Neural Process

Used in its neurophysiological sense, inhibition does not refer to an occasionally operative need of the organism, superimposed on its action systems and leading to a temporary action decrement. Rather, it is in itself an integral mode of nervous functioning, equally important as excitation in determining behavior outcome. Sherrington's *Integrative Action of the Nervous System* (1906) is perhaps the best known work to make this emphasis, but it was by no means the first time the thought had been voiced. Both the logical necessity of central inhibitory processes and experimental research demonstrating inhibition existed long before Sherrington's classic demonstrations and clarifying lectures on synaptic function, and so did, especially, the emphasis on the crucial role which inhibition must play in influencing choice of neural pathways. A very considerable amount of experimental evidence on central inhibitory processes has been reported since (cf. Eccles, 1953, 1959; Grundfest, 1960; Diamond, Balvin, & Diamond, 1963).

Adaptation requires inhibition as well as excitation. Therefore both must have developed fairly early in the evolution of organismic control systems. "A purely excitatory nervous system," argue Diamond, Balvin, and Diamond (1963, p. 394), "could not have evolved beyond a very rudimentary stage without introducing unsupportable new difficulties into the life of the organism." Two major difficulties would of course be that such an organism, with no inhibitory mechanism, could neither protect itself from excessive environmental stimulation nor reduce or stop its own actions once these had begun. Even primitive organisms are capable of both withdrawing from stimulation and of ceasing activity, however (Schneirla, 1959*a*).

Clinically, extreme instances of manic and of depressive behaviors suggest the range of possibility from unbridled excitement to almost complete inhibition displayed by human adults. A range almost as wide is observable in the behavior of normal children, and a developmental comparison suggests the gradual ascendancy of inhibitory processes over "natural" excitement. In pathological extremes there is often a history of injury- or disease-produced brain damage, with the resultant failure to develop (or the loss of) a balance between excitatory and inhibitory processes.

Experimental studies using drugs, ablation techniques in animals, and brain stimulation have provided dramatic evidence of "runaway" behavior, resulting from the interruption or destruction of inhibitory control functions.[7]

Even cursory acquaintance with the current Soviet research on conditioning (cf. Brožek, 1962) makes apparent the primary role assigned to inhibition by those following in the Sechenov and Pavlovian traditions. And research in a number of countries in neurophysiology, psychopharmacology, and particularly in the neurochemistry of behavior further points to the finely integrated excitatory-inhibitory matrix underlying behavior. The model of an inert nervous system, activated by stimulation and then returned to quiescence upon removal of reduction of stimulation, clearly no longer fits the facts. Diamond, Balvin, and Diamond (1963, p. 374) rather poetically sum up the emerging nature of neural integration: "The essential processes of the organism," they write, "each with its own systole and diastole, form a contrapuntal harmony, in which inhibition and counter-inhibition are in constant interplay with excitation and counter-excitation."

It would be irrelevant to the purposes of this chapter for us here to further examine the nature of neural (or more properly neurochemical) inhibition and its role in neural organization. On the other hand, it would have unduly minimized our recognition of the importance of inhibition as a fundamental and all-pervading neurobehavioral event [8]

[7] For examples and further discussion of neural control see Chapter 8. See, also, Brazier (1959, 1960), Diamond, Balvin, and Diamond (1963, Chaps. 14 and 15).

[8] We are convinced that before the end of the present decade the highly significant current research in the neurobehavioral disciplines—and particularly neurochemistry—will have provided entirely new models for our understanding of behavior. Our knowledge of *all* the bodily conditions affecting motivation, dis-

were we to have failed to introduce this broader concept in its proper context before turning to the far narrower matter of inhibition as a negative drive state.

Inhibition and the Coordination of Behavior

Response systems, whether neurochemical or motor, involve both action and opposition to action. Extending a limb is an obvious example. Here the extensor muscles contract, but the limb will not be extended unless the flexor muscles are simultaneously relaxed, or their contraction is inhibited. On first glance, this would appear to be an opposition of two action tendencies. However, closer examination reveals that *within* each muscle group, both action *and* inhibition of counter-action must take place. To relax the flexor, its rigidity must be overcome—to contract the extensor, the forces which keep it relaxed must be overcome. Let us go back a step. The very position of the limb, and the condition of the muscles supporting this position, prior to the initiation of change, must be seen as the resultant of a balance of activating and inhibiting tendencies. Overt response (limb movement, in this case) can occur only when, within each unit, both an excitatory and an inhibitory change take place and when simultaneous reverse adjustments occur in the opposing set of muscles. (Obviously, the latency and the vigor of the resultant movement will be a function of the nature of the internal changes—perhaps its algebraic sum.)

The point of this detailed description has been to emphasize that if smoothly coordinated behavior is to be effected, a rather subtle signal system must exist—one capable of giving rise quite rapidly to action and prevention of action (inhibition) simultaneously in separate loci and in carefully measured amounts. It seems unlikely that the inhibitory processes which play a role in the coordination of such rapid changes could be dependent on the transport of fatigue-substances from the musculature, except perhaps in the regulation of the length of any particular behavior sequence. Immediate regulation would necessarily fall to a central excitatory-inhibitory control system.

Pavlov's Theories of Inhibition

In order to try to explain the phenomena he and his associates were observing in their study of conditioned salivary reflexes in dogs, Pavlov

cussed in this and the following chapter, should be remarkably improved in the process. The interested reader may turn with profit to any of the following recent collections: Abramson (1957), Bass (1959), Brazier (1959, 1960), Delafresnaye (1954, 1961), Fields (1957), Florey (1961), Jasper (1958), Magoun (1959–1960), Roberts (1960), Sheer (1961), Uhr and Miller (1960).

developed a rather elaborate theory of cortical functioning.[9] The two fundamental concepts in his theory were excitation and inhibition. Afferent stimulation, suggests the theory, creates an area of excitation in the cortex, which then "irradiates" throughout the cortical "analyzer" system. Excitation created by the conditioned stimulus is thereby attracted to the stronger excitation area produced by the unconditioned stimulus, forming a link between the two.[10] However, the repeated stimulation of the cortex in the absence of reinforcement (i.e., of the unconditioned stimulus) would lead to inhibition, which likewise irradiates through the cortex, weakening other bonds inversely with distance from the point of origin.

Following its irradiation, the excitation or inhibition would regress to (or be reconcentrated in) the area of stimulation, and in the process would induce the opposite effect (i.e., either inhibition or excitation) in the area surrounding the focus of stimulation. As stimulation subsided, the induced opposite condition might then become dominant.

Pavlov at first believed that the extent of the irradiation of either excitation or inhibition was a simple positive function of the intensity of the conditioned stimulus (Pavlov, 1930). However, certain phenomena could not be explained on this basis. For example, weak stimuli sometimes elicited a stronger response than strong stimuli, and positive stimuli sometimes gave rise to inhibitions. Pavlov therefore accepted the possibility that cortical cells might differ in their degree of excitability, and further that there might be a maximum capability for excitement—a kind of load factor—for each cell, influenced by such factors as age, fatigue, etc. (cf. Konorski, 1948, p. 27; Kimble, 1961, p. 34). With the addition of these variables, Pavlov could account for several perplexing phenomena which his earlier notion could not explain. One was that exceedingly strong stimuli, rather than elicit-

[9] Pavlov's theory of cortical functioning was based on inferences from the conditioning research he and his associates were conducting, and not on direct physiological investigation. Pavlov himself made no pretenses about what he was doing (cf. Pavlov, 1927), which was inventing a system which *might* fit the cortex but *did* fit his data. The fact that his physiological hypotheses have been severely criticized—and in large part discredited as physiological facts—in no way decreases the fruitfulness of his postulations as explanatory concepts (i.e., hypothetical constructs) for conditioning phenomena. The interested reader can find more detailed descriptions of Pavlov's theories than we will here present and details of the experimental evidence on which they were based in Pavlov (1927, 1928, 1930, 1941) and Konorski (1948). Evaluations of this work can be found in Kimble (1961) and in Diamond, Balvin, and Diamond (1963).

[10] Note that the association is between CS and UCS, not between S and R (Reid, 1960).

ing strong responses, tended to have a disrupting effect. Pavlov then suggested that the positive relation between stimulus intensity and response magnitude would hold up to the load limit, after which a protective inhibition would be induced, limiting the spread of excitation and thus preventing damage to the cortex. In succession, as the load limit was lowered an increasing amount, the following phenomena would occur: (1) a *phase of equalization*, in which strong stimulation would produce effects no greater than weak stimuli; (2) a *paradoxical phase*, where the effects of strong stimulation are weaker than those of weak stimuli; and (3) an *ultraparadoxical phase*, resulting from excessive fatigue or other factors causing a severe lowering of cell capacity, in which the apparently completely inhibited cell would respond to excitatory stimulation with inhibition (i.e., show no effect), while inhibitory stimuli would produce a positive effect. Pavlov attributed this last to the effects of induction (see p. 151).

Inhibition and Extinction. What has thus far been described as inhibition is what Pavlov called internal inhibition, that is, inhibition intrinsic to the processes of stimulation. It was invoked to explain the following conditioning phenomena: (1) The continued presentation of a conditioned stimulus in the absence of reinforcement [11] leads to the gradual weakening and finally the elimination of the response. This process was called extinction.[12] (2) That this process results in a suppression and not an abolition of the response is indicated by the spontaneous reappearance of the response, without reintroduction of reinforcement, after a rest period following extinction. (3) The stimulus to which a response is extinguished in turn becomes a *conditioned inhibitor*, which is evidenced by its capacity to weaken the effects of other conditioned stimuli with which it is paired. (4) If the extinction process is carried on even after the response no longer appears (below zero, as it were), the negative effects of pairing the stimulus with a new one are further accentuated, and the spontaneous recovery of the extinguished response is delayed (Woodworth & Schlosberg, 1954; Kimble, 1961).

A fifth type of evidence for active inhibition during extinction comes from studies of what Pavlov called *external inhibition*. This refers to the interference of one activity with another (in the sense of Brunton's definition). Pavlov and his associates frequently observed, in the non-sound-conditioned laboratories in which they worked, that

[11] When used to describe Pavlovian conditioning, the term *reinforcement* always refers to the presentation of the unconditioned stimulus.

[12] Extinction was an unfortunate choice of term, since the response is not lost but merely held in check, as the next point indicates.

distractions during conditioning would invoke orienting or defensive reactions in their animals. These reactions, in competition with the responses being conditioned, would have the effect of inhibiting or weakening them. (It could be equally argued that this was stimulus competition rather than response competition, but that is irrelevant here.)

If the external inhibition or distraction occurred during an extinction series rather than during conditioning, its effect would be to inhibit the inhibition, serving in this case to restore or increase the response. Pavlov called this process *disinhibition*, explaining that external inhibition acted on the process which was dominant at the time of its occurrence.

Two additional phenomena give evidence of an active inhibition process, and we shall mention them briefly. First, extinction effects, like conditioning effects, have been shown to generalize to stimuli other than the ones which were extinguished (Pavlov, 1927; Bass & Hull, 1934).[13] And, second, in delayed- and trace-conditioning studies, the animal gradually learns to withhold the response until shortly before the appearance of the unconditioned stimulus. During this interval, called the *inhibition of delay*, external inhibition (disinhibition) can be demonstrated (see Kimble, 1961, p. 85).

Inhibition of Reinforcement. Except in the inhibition of delay, all other indications of inhibition occurred in the absence of reinforcement. However, Pavlov had reported that inhibition could be observed even in a regular conditioning series (Pavlov, 1927, p. 234). Hovland (1936) demonstrated that such "inhibition of reinforcement" resulted from the massing of trials, was temporary, and would be dissipated with rest. By running two groups of subjects under massed and distributed practice trials and then extinguishing the (GSR) response immediately, Hovland showed an initial rise in the extinction curve for those subjects given massed reinforcements and no opportunity to rest. A second group, permitted two rest periods during the acquisition trials, showed no such rise. Hovland explained that the rest periods allowed the dissipation of inhibition accumulated during the conditioning trials, whereas no dissipation of inhibition was possible for the massed-practice group. Thus, under the changed stimulus conditions attending the onset of extinction, disinhibition took place, its effects being visible in the group that had accumulated inhibition during conditioning.

For the first time in our discussion of inhibition in relation to con-

[13] Woodworth and Schlosberg (1954, p. 579) summarize criticisms of these studies, challenging whether they demonstrate Pavlov's irradiation hypothesis.

ditioning mention has been made of a temporary accumulation of inhibition and its dissipation with time or rest. Yet implicit in the explanation of such phenomena as spontaneous recovery, for example, is the assumption that inhibition is temporary and that its dissipation is what accounts for the recovery of the response "spontaneously." We will turn next to the concept of *reactive inhibition* (Hull, 1943), in which the concept of internal inhibition is developed as a negative drive state, the dissipation of which may itself serve as a reinforcement. But before doing so, one further aspect of Pavlov's inhibition theories should be mentioned.

Sleep as Protective Inhibition. Although our presentation of Pavlov's theories of inhibition has been exceedingly brief and sketchy, the scope of these theories would not be indicated unless mention was made of his concept of sleep as generalized internal inhibition. His observations that experimental animals, sometimes in the midst of a conditioning sequence involving strong stimulation, would suddenly fall to sleep, led him to conclude that sleep was "nothing but internal inhibition which is widely irradiated." Hypnosis was seen as a form of local sleep, and catalepsy and other forms of similar withdrawal were also perceived as disturbances of the balance between excitation and inhibition in the nervous system (see Pavlov, 1941). In essence, some form of generalized inhibition was invoked under conditions of intense stimulation, conflict, or exhaustion as a protective inhibition against damage to the nervous system. The paradoxical conditioning phenomena, earlier described, were milder forms of such protective inhibition. (For further discussion of sleep theories, see next Section.)

Hull's Concept of Reactive Inhibition (I_R)

Clark Hull (1943, 1952), as part of his attempt to develop a comprehensive behavior theory, dealt with the phenomena of extinction and spontaneous recovery, at least in part, in much the way that Pavlov had. Hull postulated a response-produced *reactive inhibition*, as follows: "Whenever a reaction (R) is evoked from an organism there is left an increment of primary negative drive (I_R) which inhibits to a degree according to its magnitude the reaction potential (sE_R) to that response" (Hull, 1952, p. 9). Reactive inhibition developed as a result of *each* response (whether during reinforcement or extinction) as an increasing function of the rate of response elicitation and the effortfulness of the response. It had, as Hull indicates, the characteristics of a negative drive state, not unlike fatigue, leading to the cessation of the response which produced it. As a drive, its effects would dissipate with rest (or cessation of response), and, in terms of

Hull's theory, would thus be capable of reinforcing the association between any stimulus and response present at the time of its reduction. On this basis Hull postulated *conditioned inhibition* (sIr), a concept in this case not so similar to the one of the same name offered by Pavlov. We shall turn to a consideration of conditioned inhibition in a moment.

Reactive Inhibition as a Drive. Despite the fact that a fairly significant number of experiments and theoretical papers have been addressed to Hull's inhibition concepts (cf. Jones, 1958; Jensen, 1961), the nature of reactive inhibition *as a drive* remains unclear. Kimble (1949), along with Hull (1943), suggested that in respect of its relation to effortfulness of response and to rest it resembles fatigue. However, he added the following explanatory footnote: ". . . As used in this paper, resting is thought of as active, motivated behavior which is a goal response and reduces the drive Ir. In this sense, the resting response must be distinguished from the cessation of activity which results from neuromuscular impairment. The physiological accompaniments of Ir and of the response of resting are not known" (p. 15). Hull himself used Ir in the sense of a hypothetical construct, and although he described it in the manner of fatigue, as used in his theory it did not need to be referred to either muscle or to brain. Kendrick (1960), however, has suggested that it is now regarded by most research workers as being centrally generated.

There has been experimental confirmation of the relation of Ir to rate of response elicitation (e.g., Spence & Norris, 1950), and to effortfulness of response (e.g., Mowrer & Jones, 1943; Applezweig, 1951). However, reactive inhibition alone has been insufficient by itself to explain some of the parameters of learning phenomena (Kimble, 1961). Findings which are not predictable from simple inhibition theory are (1) that partial reinforcement produces greater resistance to extinction than continuous reinforcement, (2) massed extinction trials produce slower extinction than do widely spaced extinction trials, and (3) spontaneous recovery is rarely complete (Kimble, 1961, p. 325).

The fact that Hull's Ir is "effector-localized" (Kimble, 1961, p. 294) and produces distinctive kinesthetic feedback (Solomon, 1948) has led to a suggestion of a generalization-decrement hypothesis. This would help to explain in part why altered spacing of extinction trials, through producing differential stimulus components, would result in different rates of extinction for massed vs. spaced extinction trials. We cannot further pursue this hypothesis or the attempts to explain these learning phenomena by other extensions of inhibition theory. Suffice it to say that inhibition theory appears to provide a partial explanation of a number of phenomena, but not a complete explanation. We shall briefly consider some of the more serious criticisms of inhibition theory, but turn first to the second half of Hull's inhibition theory.

Reactive Inhibition and Conditioned Inhibition. As was earlier noted, the reduction of reactive inhibition satisfied the condition of a reinforcer in Hull's system. Since the "response" most closely associated with this drive reduction was that of response cessation, Hull proposed that a new habit was formed on the first occasion of such a conjunction and that it was strengthened on each succeeding sequence of response, reactive inhibition, reduction of reactive inhibition, reinforcement of the resting response. He called this new response *conditioned inhibition* (sIR). In combination with the temporary reactive inhibition (IR), a new *aggregate inhibitory potential* (IR) would effect a reduction in response strength. This additional concept served to broaden Hull's theory to one of inhibition plus interference, since the effect of sIR was to compete with the habit (sHR) for expression. See Chapter 10 for further discussion of Hull's theories.)

By moving to a two-factor theory of inhibition, Hull was able, more effectively than Pavlov, to account for the permanence of extinction and the incompleteness of spontaneous recovery, since he now had a temporary (drive) and a permanent (habit) form of inhibition, each having characteristics of its own class of phenomena, but both being able to contribute to (active) response inhibition. (See Kimble, 1961, for further discussion of the implications for learning.)

Shortcomings of Inhibition Theory

Both Pavlov and Hull have been attacked on a number of grounds, including the types of phenomena which their theories of inhibition are unable to explain (Koch, 1954; Reid, 1960; Kimble, 1961; and see Chapter 6). Kimble (1961, p. 306) summarizes some of the inadequacies of inhibition theory: (1) It would be difficult for an inhibition concept related to effortfulness of response to explain extinction of so relatively effort-free a response as the GSR; (2) the theory does not account for the failure of extinction of certain effortful responses, as jumping a hurdle to escape shock; (3) extinction at a rate of one trial a day could not be handled by the theory; (4) the apparent possibility of extinction without overt response could not be handled by the theory; (5) the implication of a "resting" subject during extinction is contradicted by observation in most animal studies; and (6) the effects of varying schedules of reinforcement on extinction do not fit the explanation based exclusively on inhibition.

In partial defense of the theory, it might be noted that the criticisms all relate, to a greater or lesser extent, to the description of reaction inhibition in terms of the effector model of fatigue. Were inhibition to be referred to a central process, some of the significance of these criticisms would be lost.

A Re-examination of Inhibition as a Central Phenomenon

Increasing dissatisfaction has been expressed in the past few years with the adequacy of the available inhibition models, while at the same time increasing acceptance is being given to the existence of an inhibitory concept (cf. Stretch, 1960; Walker, 1958; Kimble, 1961; Diamond, Balvin, & Diamond, 1963; Thompson, 1960). A number of converging researches and concepts (some of which are discussed in later sections of this book and some of which have been mentioned briefly already) suggest the necessity for a concentrated program of research directed toward the clarification of the relation among inhibition, fatigue, and related concepts. Thus, for example, the concepts of habituation (Sharpless & Jasper, 1956), stimulus satiation (Glanzer, 1953), reactive inhibition (Hull, 1943, 1952), action decrement (Walker, 1958), internal inhibition (Pavlov, 1927), reciprocal inhibition (Sherrington, 1924; Wolpe, 1958), and learned inhibition (Harlow, 1959), among others, appear to be addressing the same or similar problems, although attacking them in somewhat different ways.

It would be our prediction that a central inhibitory process, supported by feedback from peripheral receptors, will emerge as a significant unifying concept to account for the numerous phenomena which have been discussed in this section. We would suspect further, somewhat in agreement with Stretch (1960) and Diamond, Balvin, and Diamond (1963), that the concept will not only be related to effort and intense stimulation at one end, but that it will be curvilinear in shape, capable of being invoked by low arousal conditions at the other. (Further discussion of related topics will be found in Chapters 8, 9, 10, and 11.)

The discussion of inhibition would not be complete unless sleep were included. And yet sleep has some status as a motivational state in its own right. Let us turn, then, to a somewhat fuller consideration of this unique inhibitory phenomenon.

SLEEP

If we use the amount of time spent in consummatory behavior as our criterion, sleep is by far the most important of man's activities. The human infant spends as much as *two-thirds* of his time asleep. As an adult he can never do better than reverse this ratio, paying the price on the average, of one hour of sleep for every two hours of wakefulness (Kleitman, 1957). And yet, despite "the absolute necessity for us to spend a considerable portion of our lives in abject mental annihilation," as Sir John Eccles put it in opening an international symposium on sleep, "it is remarkable how little we know about it, how little we can say to account for the necessity of sleep" (Eccles, 1960, p. 1). Actually, sleep has been studied quite extensively, and something is known about it as a process and as a motivating condition. It is in respect of its biological *function* that we remain so completely in the dark.

Characteristics of the Sleep State

What is the nature of sleep? It is generally characterized as a state of lowered alertness and lowered responsiveness. But on closer examination we find that there are no absolute criteria by which we can be sure it is present. "Are you asleep?", we may ask someone who is lying down with his eyes closed. The fact that he is lying down, has his eyes closed, and is perhaps breathing in a quite regular rhythm, gives rise to our question, and a failure to reply may be accepted as confirming our guess. The *eyes-closed-prone-position* and lack of responsiveness are likely correlates of sleep, but they are not assurance of its presence. Else our question would be unnecessary. And, on occasion, the answer "no, just resting," or "just thinking," may be given. In this example, however, is a second, more general characteristic of sleep, namely, a *lowered state of alertness*. In such a state, stimuli normally capable of arousing response fail to do so. That this is a common expectation is confirmed in our everyday experience by our typical behavior of increasing the intensity of the stimulus if we wish to awaken the sleeper. Thus we will call louder, shake harder, raise the blinds to let in more light, etc.

However, it is equally well known that stimuli of considerably lesser intensity will serve to arouse the sleeper if they have some special "meaning" for him. Thus the cry of a baby will awaken its mother, the soft-spoken name of the sleeper will be distinguished from a list of other names spoken with equal loudness (Oswald et al., 1960), etc., whereas loud sounds (as of traffic) will not usually disturb sleep. These observations make us aware that even in the state of lowered awareness of sleep, the cortex is still capable of making rather subtle distinctions among stimuli on bases other than intensity.

Other characteristics of the sleep state likewise have their exceptions. In addition to lowered alertness, *lowered activity level* is a characteristic generally associated with sleep. And yet states of quiet wakefulness may be far less active than a restless, perhaps dream-filled, sleep. The rapid eye movements reported during dreaming and the occasional "jerky" movements which, despite their intensity, do not waken the sleeper (Kleitman, 1960*a*) are examples of "active" sleep, while the interested audience at a lecture, concert, or drama, or the soldier on guard duty may display little or no overt activity.

Loss of consciousness is a fourth characteristic of sleep. However, Kleitman (1957) has argued that certain borderline states of wakefulness-sleep produce confusing evidence with respect to consciousness. States of wakefulness, defined in terms of bioelectric level, can exist without consciousness (a certain example being the case of very young infants), and dreaming-in-sleep states suggests that consciousness can be present in sleep (see also Oswald, 1962, pp. 19 ff.) [14] More significant is the fact that loss of consciousness is also associated with certain comatose states induced by injury to the brain or by the application of drugs affecting brain function. These states differ from sleep in their electrophysiological patterns, as well as in respect to "arousability" (Morgan & Stellar, 1950).

A fifth means of identifying the sleep state is found in the *characteristic brain-wave pattern* associated with it (see Kleitman, 1939; Oswald, 1962). The typical electroencephalogram (EEG) of sleep shows high voltage, slow frequency waves, with brief bursts or "spindles" of medium-voltage waves of intermediate frequency. Wakefulness records, on the other hand, usually show low-voltage, fast frequency waves (see Fig. 4–4). Although experienced electroencephalographers can read these records with considerable reliability, there are difficulties in determining whether the subject is asleep or awake in borderline states. Furthermore, depending on the location of the electrodes, sleep may be recorded in some areas and not in others.[15] When compared with behavioral criteria, EEG evidence of sleep is not always accurate. Some responsivity to stimulation—for example, a kind of "second-degree" vigilance (Fischgold & Schwartz, 1960)—can be demonstrated during EEG signs of light to medium sleep.[16]

[14] There is not always agreement on the meaning of consciousness, of course. See Chapter 12 for discussion of the psychoanalytic use of this concept. (See, also, J. G. Miller, 1942.)

[15] The phenomenon of "paradoxical sleep" refers to a situation of sleep in one part of the brain and not another. Its explanation is related to the fact that sleep states reflect more than one inhibitory mechanism, and not all such mechanisms are active at the same time. (See Jouvet, 1960; Dement, 1958; Dell et al., 1960.)

[16] Sleep researchers generally agree that five stages of sleep can be determined from EEG records. They are designated, after Loomis et al. (1937), as *A*-drowsiness, *B*-light sleep, *C*-medium-depth sleep, *D*- and *E*-deep sleep. (For identifying characteristics of EEG at each level, see Oswald, 1962, pp. 35 ff.)

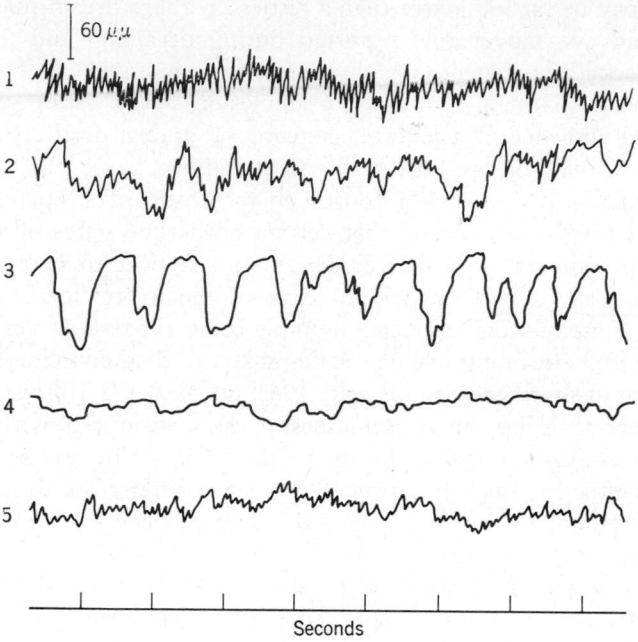

Figure 4–4. Characteristic brain waves at various levels of sleep-wakefulness: (1) Alpha rhythm of wakefulness, (2) alpha and delta waves of light sleep, (3) delta rhythm of deep sleep early in the night, (4) "null" rhythm which later replaces the delta rhythm, (5) alpha rhythm on awakening. Reproduced by permission from Kleitman (1939, p. 45).

In sum, it appears that the simple question of when the individual is actually asleep can only be answered by comparison of a series of indices with the waking state. This may explain some of the difficulty which has attended the study of sleep.

Species-Specific Patterns in Sleep. Postural relaxation seems to be one characteristic of human sleep which is not found in all other species. Birds, for example, will sleep while standing on one leg; ruminants (cows, goats, sheep) may "become recumbent but keep their heads erect and eyes open" (Oswald, 1962, p. 22); horses will lie down when in their own stalls but not elsewhere; and seals are said to sleep for snatches of minutes at a time between surfacings for air (Oswald, 1962). These differences suggest that different functions may be served by sleep in different species. The upright position of ruminants is conducive to continuing digestive processes, which would be upset otherwise. Man, on the other hand, may need to rest both his musculature,

associated with maintaining his erect position, and the neural structures, which coordinate such muscular effort (Elithorn, 1960, p. 385).
Alternatively, the prone posture assumed in sleep, or the drooping of
the head, at least, may be associated with changes in baroreception
(blood pressure) in the carotid sinus, known to be related to sleep
induction (cf. Oswald, 1962, p. 28). An evolutionary theory (cf. Kleitman, 1939) might hold that man's more relaxed position reflects his
relative immunity from predatory attacks, for which lowered alertness
and the poorly defensive sleeping posture would leave him ill prepared.

The Sleep-Wakefulness Pattern

Developmental Changes. In the beginning of this discussion of sleep
we noted Kleitman's observations on the change in sleep-wakefulness
ratio with development. Kleitman and Engelmann (1953) compared
infants of less than one month with those of six months of age and
found a reduction in only one hour, on the average, in the total of 12
to 17 hours of sleep taken by infants. The overall pattern, however
(as any parent can gratefully testify), has already begun to shift.

From the beginning, the infant shows a two- to four-hour cycle,
which is not diurnal but rather directly associated with its food and
water needs (Kleitman has called this the "wakefulness of necessity").
Even within this cycle, a 50 to 90 minute cycle is discernible in the
restlessness of sleeping infants. Kleitman summarizes the changes with
age as follows:

> Grafted on the innate sleep-wakefulness periodicity, as a result of onto-
> genetic development of the cerebral cortex and of individual experience
> of the infant, is a new sleep-wakefulness rhythm, whose characteristics are:
> (*a*) a consolidation of the sleep and wakefulness phases, with a fixed adjust-
> ment to the astronomical alternations of night and day and a social ac-
> culturation to the family and community pattern of living, long unbroken
> sleep occurring at night and (*b*) a lengthening of the wakefulness phase,
> which gradually achieves temporal dominance, with a sleep-wakefulness
> ratio in man, reversed, becoming 1:2 (Kleitman, 1957, p. 357).

The underlying cycle of 50 to 90 minutes persists and can be detected in adult EEG records in both sleep and wakeful periods (Kleitman, 1960*b*). No clear explanation of the mechanism of this transition
exists, although it is attributed to a combination of conditioning and
the development of both neural feedback circuits between the cortex
and the mid-brain and endocrine factors associated with the pituitary-
adrenocortical system (Kleitman, 1957).

Kleitman (1939, 1957) distinguishes the social "wakefulness of
choice," developed as a function of the above-described changes from

the "wakefulness of necessity"; the two combine to produce the adult sleep pattern. Whereas the "wakefulness of choice" is in some degree an arbitrary imposition,[17] the ultimate ratio of sleep to wakefulness apparently is not (see p. 163). Figure 4–5 shows the changes in depth and pattern of sleep with age.

How Much Sleep Is Needed? In order to answer the question as to how much sleep is needed by the human adult, we would have to know something of the purpose(s) served by sleep, which we do not. However, one can approach an answer to the question in two ways: (1) by sleep deprivation studies (see p. 172), and (2) by observing how much sleep the human adult generally takes, and inferring from this

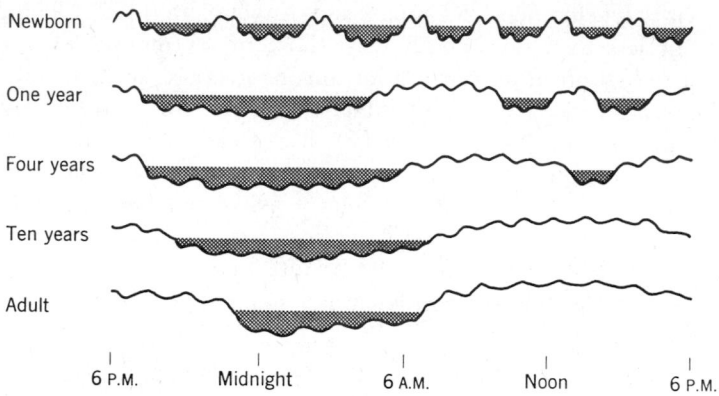

Figure 4–5. Diagram illustrating the cycles of sleep at different ages. Reproduced by permission from Kleitman (1963, Fig. 36–1, p. 367).

something about the amount needed. On the basis of extensive studies of the latter kind, Kleitman has concluded that approximately 8 hours of sleep are taken every 24 hours, as we have already noted. This ratio appears to be independent of cultural influence, although the lengths of periods of uninterrupted sleep seem to vary with diurnal factors and with cultural factors (which in turn usually co-vary). Lewis (1960) studied men in the relatively culture-free environments of five different polar expeditions. Sleep records were kept by the men, who

[17] Halberg (1961, 1962) refers to combined "socio-ecologic" and "physico-chemical" (e.g., light and food) environmental rhythmicities as forcing a synchronization of innate rhythms, including sleep-wakefulness, to a circadian (approximately 24-hour) cycle.

were free to sleep whenever and generally as much as they pleased. He found that under the different circumstances of the five expeditions,[18] in nonorganized communities, and in all-light or all-dark conditions, "times of going to sleep and getting up varied greatly." The differences were not attributable to season, to cold, or to the amount of physical activity taken (although there was slightly more sleep taken per 24-hour period when it was all dark *or* all light). Over the one to two years which the different expeditions lasted, however, Lewis found that: "Though men were at liberty to sleep almost as long as they wished, the mean duration of sleep was approximately eight hours" (1960, p. 328). Kleitman has confirmed these observations in studies of polar expeditions and of artificial environments in caves and in submarines (Kleitman, 1949, 1960*b*, 1961). Kleitman and Kleitman (1953) set up 18-, 24-, and 28-hour "days" with some success, although there were marked individual differences. They found that age was a factor in adaptability (presumably because cultural patterns were less firmly established), with younger persons adapting better. The ratio of sleep to wakefulness, regardless of cycle, was retained at 1:2. Lewis and Lobban (1954) set watches of men in polar isolation to run 10½ or 13½ hours per each 12 hours of clock time. On the 21- and 27-hour days which resulted, the amount of sleep was proportionately decreased or increased respectively, so that a 1:2 sleep-wakefulness ratio continued to obtain. (See Halberg, 1961; Aschoff, 1962; Lehmann, 1962; Ray, Martin, & Alluisi, 1961, for further discussion of cyclic phenomena.)

The Course of Sleep. During a night's sleep one does not go from light sleep through deeper layers and gradually up again to wakefulness in a systematic, unicyclic course, although the sleeper may remember it this way. EEG studies have now clearly established that this is not the case (cf. Aserinsky and Kleitman, 1955). Figure 4–6 illustrates the fluctuations in depth of sleep during a single night. Here we see the subcycles noted earlier by Kleitman, light sleep recurring approximately every 90 minutes in this case. Rapid eye movements, associated with dreaming (see below), occur in the light-sleep stages. If, as is suspected, the so-called restorative effects of sleep take place primarily during deep sleep periods, it is evident that these will be accomplished in the early (first four) hours of sleep. This hypothesis has led to attempts at experimental modification of work-rest schedules

---

[18] The expeditions varied considerably in location, nature of terrain, amount of light or darkness, temperature ranges, type and schedule of activities, and relative duration. However, all were isolated communities and set their own patterns of life.

for possible use in the prolonged confinements expected in space flight and in other isolated environments in which men may be placed.

Relatively little research has been conducted on the effects of artificially manipulated sleep-wakefulness cycles upon sleep itself, although such studies have reported effects on various types of performance. Lilly (1962, p. 93) found that under severe sensory isolation (immersion in water) two hours of sleep made him feel "about as rested and refreshed as eight or nine hours' sleep." It is possible that the complete exclusion of external stimulation would provide a continuous deep sleep, with omission of intervening light sleep patterns (as in Fig. 4–6), but we know of no EEG-monitored sleep records in such situations.

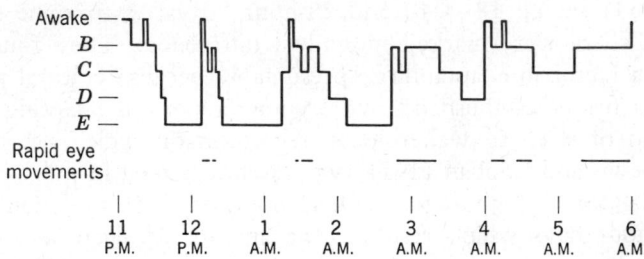

Figure 4–6. An illustration of the fluctuations in the depth of sleep throughout one night (based on an actual recording). Depth of sleep is shown in terms of Loomis EEG stages. Presence of rapid eye movements is also shown. Reproduced by permission from Oswald (1962, p. 125).

Kleitman (1949) has reported successful use of modified work-rest schedules aboard submarines over a several week period with no evidence of sleep loss, although Utterback and Ludwig (1949), in a similar study, found that those sailors shifted to sleep during "normal daytime" reported they had had difficulty sleeping. It is not possible to isolate this report from noise and other conditions which may have contributed to sleeplessness, however. Reports on some of the polar stations show marked variation in pattern from base to base, with some suspicion of a "social contagion" affecting reports if not behavior (Rasmussen, 1963).

Adams and Chiles (1960) varied work-rest schedules for aircrews confined in small groups (5 or 6 men) for two weeks, with findings similar to those of Kleitman. Reports of sustained morale in these and similar experiments suggest that sleep may have been adequate, but direct evidence on its course is lacking. Lewis' studies suggest that a "free environment" leads to a modification in the course of sleep from the consecutive eight-hour pattern common to men living in normal social environments.

Physiological Basis of Sleep

The last two decades have provided considerable information about the functioning of nervous structures in both sleep and wakefulness. Continuing investigation has inevitably led away from simple one-factor theories, such as Pavlov's conception of sleep as a spread of cortical inhibition (see p. 154), or the idea of a controlling "sleep center" in the mid-brain (von Economo, 1930) which is activated after an accumulation of noxious chemical substances reaches a critical stage (see Morgan & Stellar, 1950; Kleitman, 1939).

W. R. Hess (1954, 1957), whose earlier experimental work had supported the "sleep center" theory, has more recently described both waking (ergotrophic) and sleeping (tropotrophic) functions as interacting in determining the momentary level of alertness. This has followed from results of explorations by Moruzzi and Magoun (1949) and others (see Magoun, 1958) of the mid-brain reticular formation.[19] It is now clear that the reticular formation plays the central role in regulating sleep-wakefulness, and also that it is not an autonomous center (nor do any of its functions appear to be autonomous).

Reticular Deactivation. In our discussion of inhibition (see p. 149) we indicated the growing knowledge we are gaining of inhibitory activities of the subcortical centers. Dell, Bonvallet, and Hugelin (1960) suggest that the current evidence points to *reticular deactivation* as the physiological basis for sleep, a view with which there is little disagreement (see Wolstenholme & O'Connor, 1960). Two possible sets of mechanisms are proposed to account for the deactivation and hence for sleep: one of *active* and one of *passive* processes.

The central reticular structures are normally "energized" as a result of combined peripheral sensory stimulation (via sensory collaterals) and autochthonous physical, biochemical, and hormonal changes in the *milieu intérieur*. When these are blocked or missing, reticular deactivation occurs. Such deactivation may result from either or both a reduction in outside stimulation and diurnal biochemical and hormonal variations in combination with conditioned humoral changes. Normal sleep-preparatory behavior would lead to a reduction in both types of

---

[19] The reticular formation is made up of diffuse groupings of several different types of cells and numerous fibers that extend from the medulla to the dorsal hypothalamus, subthalamus, and thalamus. (See Chapter 8, p. 399 and Fig. 8-4.)

stimulation. A postactivation neuronal depression might likewise contribute to temporary deactivation.

These processes are what Dell et al. have called *passive reticular deactivation*. Bremer (1954) has described such deactivation as a "cumulative defacilitation" and considers that it is a sufficient condition to account for sleep (see, also, Bremer, 1960). However, Dell et al. believe that there is evidence for *active* deactivating processes as well. They describe two types of active influences on the reticular system: those *ascending* from bulbar structures and those *descending* from the cortex. The *ascending* inhibitory effects are in turn ascribed to two factors: a cumulative overload of vegetative centers (e.g., circulatory strain, tension of a full stomach), acting either through the thalamus or through somatic sensory collaterals at the bulbar level (or both), and a negative feedback loop from the reticular formation to the lower centers, whereby "activating reticular effects are dampened by ascending bulbar effects which they have themselves initiated" (Dell et al., 1960, p. 96).

Descending inhibitory influences from the cortex are in turn ascribed to a reticulo-cortico-reticular negative feedback loop. A descending tonic influence, itself a by-product of reticular activation of the cortex, exerts a dampening effect in proportion to the amount of activation present. Thus the greater the cortical arousal, the greater the "corticofugal effects acting back on the reticular formation and inhibiting its activity." Timing is then quite important to these processes. Cortical arousal can be sustained only when there is continuing activation *and* at least temporary interruption of this negative feedback loop. Cortical control, they believe, is lost momentarily in the process of arousal, but a recovery phase, "characterized by powerful downstream cortical inhibitory effects" (p. 99), always follows. If the reader has followed this intricate pattern, he can properly infer that emotional excitement and rapid response elicitation would both be followed by strong inhibition, leading to drowsiness and sleep, in a manner consonant with the observations of Pavlov and others.

Cortical inhibition in this explanation, however, serves to deactivate the reticular formation, and sleep is a product of reticular deactivation, not cortical inhibition, itself, as Pavlov thought. Dell, Bonvallet, and Hugelin recognize that what they are describing as the sleep mechanisms involve an "interplay of numerous cerebral structures," but they consider it a more adequate representation of the actual processes involved than the earlier notions of two antagonistic centers (for sleep and waking). In their view, the *same* structures are involved in *both* activation and inhibition. The behavior of these structures is, however, more analogous to "the mathematics of games and decisions," they feel, "than to simple arithmetic" (p. 101). Figure 4–7 is a diagrammatic representation of the processes discussed by Dell, Bonvallet, and Hugelin, as well as some others which will be dealt with in later portions of this section.

Before concluding this treatment, however, it might be well to point out the alternative possibility that there are two distinct sleep mechanisms (included in the description just given) and also two distinct sleep phenomena. Thus Jouvet (1960) has reviewed the EEG data to suggest that passive and active sleep patterns may represent separate processes—bodily and cerebral sleep, or sleep of vital need and sleep of disinterest (see Kleitman's categories, p. 161). Such a two-factor theory of sleep might help explain some of the anomalies seen in EEG

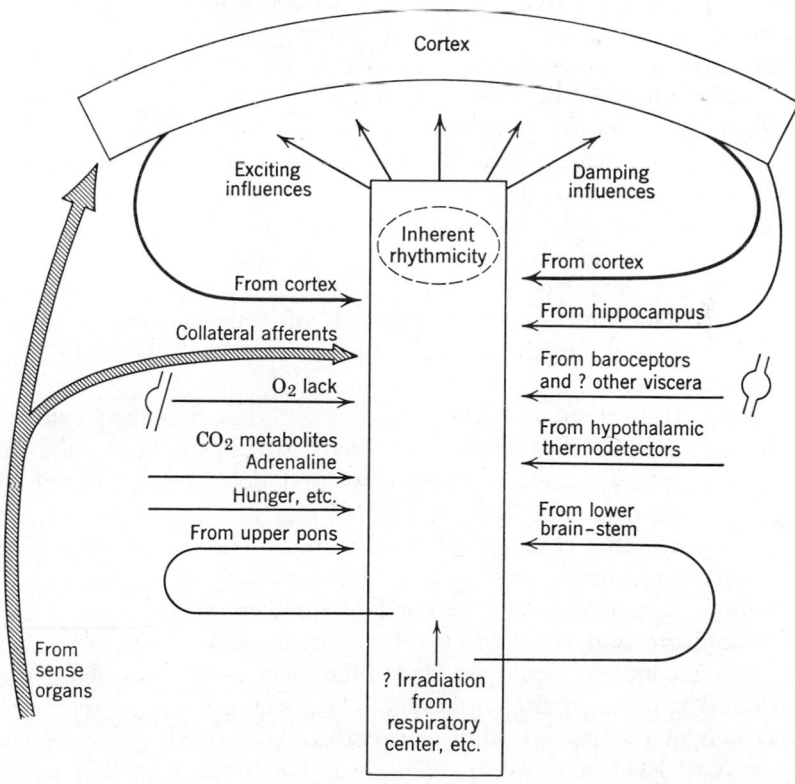

Figure 4–7. The factors that maintain the dynamic equilibrium of the upper reticular formation and the consequent level of sleepiness-wakefulness. Reproduced by permission from Oswald (1962, p. 15).

records, where rapid cortical activity phases occur in "deep sleep" records (see Dement, 1958). It might account for the difficulties we observed in trying to describe consistent sleep characteristics. It would as well be consistent with the differentiations drawn by Dell, Bonvallet, and Hugelin as between vegetative and cortical influences on the reticular formation. And, finally, it might also provide a basis for understanding the highly varied subjective differences in satisfaction reported after sleep. This two-factor hypothesis is not to be confused with the two-centers theory noted earlier. It is put forward as a purely speculative notion, but to our knowledge is entirely consistent with the behavioral, as well as the neurophysiological, evidence on sleep to date.

Neurological Activity in Sleep. Kleitman (1957) has argued that it is necessary to retain the distinction between waking and wakefulness and between going to sleep and sleeping. This is an important distinction insofar as the activity of the brain is concerned. There is, in the transition from one state to another, a temporary increase in energy consumption and an increase in quantity of activity in the brain. However, although *overt* behavior is reduced *during* sleep, it is becoming increasingly clear that there is no reduction in the amount of neural activity during sleep. Creutzfeld and Jung (1960) have shown that in the motor cortex of the cat, for example, there is no change in the average discharge rate between sleep and wakefulness, but rather "a different pattern of discharge." This is coordinate with findings of Evarts (1960) and Kety (1960). Adrian (1960) has suggested that there may be a more even distribution of activity throughout the brain during sleep, but there are not enough data available yet to know if this is the case.

Energy Metabolism in Sleep. Kety (1960) has presented evidence to discredit three earlier biochemical theories of sleep. These held that sleep is due to a cerebral ischaemia (blood deficiency), arterial anoxaemia (insufficient aeration of the blood), and a "sleep-substance" accumulated during brain-energy expenditure. In studies of oxygen and glucose utilization in the brain, he has shown, first, that there is actually a slight *increase* in cerebral blood flow during sleep, rather than the decrease that would have been predicted by the first of these theories. Second, he could find no differences in oxygen content of the blood as between sleeping and wakeful states, contrary to the expectations of the second of these theories. And, third, he found that the activity level of the sleeping brain is *not* lower than that during wakefulness, thus contradicting the theory that sleep is induced in order to provide a period of inactivity to permit the removal of a sleep substance. This last may of course be present, but cannot be removed in periods of inactivity, if they do not occur.

He did find some evidence for a differential energy distribution, however, between sleep and wakefulness, confirming the findings of Creutzfeld and Jung. It should not be inferred from these findings that sleep does not serve a restorative function, of course, as it is entirely possible that the redistribution of function which occurs permits precisely such restoration for *both* excitatory *and* inhibitory cells. In light of the new recognition of active excitatory and inhibitory processes in both wakefulness and sleep, it should not be surprising to find that these one-sided theories would fail to be substantiated.

Relation of Sleep to Other Bodily Processes

The sleep-wakefulness cycle is only one of the circadian (approximately 24-hour) rhythms of the body, all of which show considerable synchrony with each other and with geophysical rhythms of the environment as well (see Brown, 1962). It is not possible to ascertain direction of synchrony—that is, whether the sleep-wakefulness rhythm dominates and "sets" other rhythms (e.g., temperature), vice versa, or whether all of these rhythms (including sleep-wakefulness) are synchronized by extrinsic (environmental) rhythmic factors (such as geomagnetic forces, as has been suggested by some). Aschoff (1962) tried to "drive" activity cycles by artificial light-dark manipulations. He could not exceed 21- to 27-hour cycles, however, without having his subjects (mice) abandon the light-dark cues and revert to apparently spontaneous circadian rhythms. (See the study by Lewis and Lobban [1954] cited earlier.)

Gooddy (1958) and Wiener (1958) have independently suggested that the alpha rhythm (10 per second) of the EEG, which appears in normal resting, disappearing in both activity and sleep, reflects the synchronous period of the many body-clock systems. We can at this time merely note some of the correlates of sleep-wakefulness rhythms, fully expecting the current research on "biological clocks" to elucidate further these intriguing relationships in the next several years.[20]

Temperature. A drop in body temperature is associated both with inactivity and with sleep (Kleitman, 1961). Although there is a mean difference of only a little more than one degree (Fahrenheit) between waking and sleeping temperatures, Kleitman has found a significant negative correlation between temperature and activity level. Dell (1960)

[20] References to cyclic phenomena were given on page 163. Interesting discussions of related timing factors can be found in Whitrow (1961) and Fraisse (1963).

has suggested that the relation of body temperature to sleep may be mediated by vasodilation. We have already noted that body temperature can be shifted with work-rest cycles and even to artificial "diurnal" cycles (Kleitman, 1961; Halberg, 1961). "Feeling sleepy," performance level, and sense of well-being tend to follow an adaptation curve associated with temperature adjustment to the new cycle in these cases.

Respiration and Other Bodily Functions. Although there is no change in cerebral oxygen consumption during sleep (Kety, 1960; Mangold et al., 1955), there is a shift to slower and shallower breathing during sleep, with a slight rise in carbon-dioxide tension.[21] This last is reduced by a brief period of hyperventilation on arising (Oswald, 1962). Systolic blood pressure falls in sleep (Kleitman, 1939), heart rate slows, pupils become constricted, and palmar skin resistance increases significantly in deep sleep (Levy et al., 1958). Basal metabolism drops, and there is a general reduction of muscle tonus (Oswald, 1962). The relation of baroreceptor changes to sleep is a most important one. Factors affecting blood pressure are associated with eating, body position, temperature, and excitement, all of which are related to sleepiness. An interesting relationship between atmospheric pressure and sleep is apparently mediated by baroreception (Roboutet et al., cited by Oswald, 1962). A drop in atmospheric pressure is detected by baroreceptors in the carotid sinus and the aortic arch, leading to a damping effect on the upper reticular formation and hence to sleep. Likewise, excitement leads to an increase in blood pressure and thence to reticular damping and sleep, as would any increase in blood temperature (Oswald, 1962).

Urinary, salivary, gastric, and biliary discharges all decrease in sleep (Kleitman, 1939). Lacrimal discharge is likewise decreased, perhaps serving as the basis for eye-rubbing behavior when one arises, and perhaps also the basis of the "sandman" myth so widely used with children. Internally, there is an increase in both water content of the blood and of antidiuretic hormone (ADH). Actually, sleep can be induced by giving water in combination with ADH injections (Schütz, 1944; Dell, 1960). However, the mechanism of sleep induction is not known.

Psychological Functions During Sleep

Discrimination and Memory. We have already cited evidence that cortical function as seen in discrimination does occur during light to

---

[21] An early chemical theory of sleep attributed falling asleep to this increase in carbon dioxide. However, the increase follows rather than precedes sleep, and sleep-deprived subjects show no buildup of carbon dioxide (Morgan and Stellar, 1950, p. 361).

medium sleep (EEG stages *A* and *B;* see footnote 16, p. 159). *Habituation* occurs rapidly to repetitive stimulation, and the response disappears. But, like *extinction,* habituation would appear to be a response inhibition rather than a raising of the stimulus threshold leading to a failure to receive stimulation. A slight change in the quality of a tone to which the subject has become habituated will reinstate the response (Sharpless & Jasper, 1956). There is no evidence of discrimination in deeper levels of sleep, however (below Stage *B*), and therefore it is highly doubtful that learning could take place, as has sometimes been claimed, during deep sleep. Emmons and Simon (1956), using EEG monitoring to determine sleep level, could find no evidence of registration of experience (in memory tests) [22] at medium to deep-sleep levels (see, also, Simon & Emmons, 1955; Oswald, 1962).

Performance. Cyclic performance curves in a variety of tasks have been shown to be related to sleep-wakefulness level, but it is difficult to know if they are a function of temperature changes, attention factors associated with interest rather than alertness level, or other factors. (Some of these studies were mentioned before and others will be treated in a later section on sleep deprivation.) The mental blocks discussed in relation to fatigue (see p. 141) are very likely short episodes of sleep (cf. Oswald, 1962; Bjerner, 1949), which may explain why they affect performance in the particular way they do (see Williams et al., 1959).

Miscellaneous Sleep Phenomena

Borderline Experiences. In the processes of falling asleep and awakening, a variety of subjective experiences are reported. There is some similarity between the hallucinatory, and sometimes bizarre, experiences reported in these states and psychotic experience. The "disordered" sensory and affective experiences would appear to be related to changeover processes between cortical and subcortical control. Distortions in temporal orientation, for example, are extremely common during these periods, as are hypnagogic hallucinations (both visual and auditory). These seem to be related to momentary oscillations between sleeping and waking states. Subjects queried at these times will often deny that they have been asleep, or that the experiences are real. A not unrelated phenomenon is the reported panoramic review of one's life that occurs in near-drownings.

Sleep and Hypnosis. Although there is an outward appearance of similarity between sleep and hypnotic states and brief sleep is used

[22] Oswald (1962) considers the recall conditions used to elicit memory too different from the sleep condition to provide a proper test. He suggests use of hypnosis as a more appropriate recall medium.

to obtain and dispel the hypnotic trance, Oswald (1962) points out that the two are at opposite ends of a continuum of *suggestibility*. Sleeping subjects (in deep sleep, at least) are not influenced by suggestion, whereas suggestibility epitomizes the hypnotized subject.

Dreaming. Kleitman (1960a) and his associates have studied dreaming by monitoring EEG and REM's. They find that 100 per cent of their subjects report dreaming 100 per cent of the time if awakened during that stage of sleep which shows an emergent stage I [*A* or *B*] EEG pattern and when rapid eye movements are present. From this they conclude that *all persons dream* (an average of approximately two hours per night), and that dreaming is a "regular, repetitive concomitant of natural sleep" (p. 359). Persons awakened when these signs are not present, on the other hand, rarely report that they had been dreaming. Kleitman attributes the failure of many people to report that they have dreamed to forgetting or repression.

Dement (1960) suggests that there may be a "need" for dreaming. He interrupted dreams each time dream-signs appeared, finding that his interruptions had to occur more and more rapidly, as compared with control groups interrupted an equal number of times but only when dream-signs were absent. In addition, the dream-interrupted group spent 27 per cent of a "recovery" night in dreaming (112 minutes) as compared with 20 per cent (82 minutes) for the controls. Thus, both the increased tendency to dream within a single night and the "accruing dream deficit during successive dream-deprivation nights" (Kleitman, 1960a, p. 362) suggest to Dement and to Kleitman that dreaming as such, although a rather uncritical cortical activity, may serve some necessary function. They offer no comment with respect to dream content, however.

Sleep Deprivation

Effects of sleep deprivation on arousal level appear to depend on the situation. Wilkinson (1960) found that the effects of 30 to 60 hours of sleep deprivation "can vary from almost complete inability to perform a task [e.g., watch-keeping duties] to no impairment at all if the situation is a complex and challenging one" (p. 331). This is partly attributable to effort-input on the part of the sleep-deprived person. Wilkinson found muscle tension (in the arm not used in the task—a simple motor performance) higher than normal in those subjects whose task performance did *not* suffer with increased deprivation. In another study he reports that he was able to counteract performance loss by providing knowledge of results to his subjects, thereby presumably increasing effortfulness of participation. However, the overwhelming evidence shows performance decrement with increase in sleep deprivation (Kleitman, 1960*b*, p. 337).

Williams et al. (1959) used an experimenter-paced vs. a self-paced task to test the hypothesis that loss of skill with increased sleep deprivation is a function of the intrusion of an increasing number of brief episodes of light sleep. They confirmed their expectation. Lapses in rate but few errors occurred in self-paced activities, whereas an increase in errors was found when rate was set by the experimenter. Presumably these subjects "missed" stimuli presented during periods of light sleep. In some self-regulating tasks which permitted correction, subjects tended to make more errors but also made more corrections, again supporting their hypothesis.

Performance decrement under conditions of increasing sleep deprivation is not linear. It tends to follow diurnal variations, associated with body temperature. Thus a subject will do better on a third afternoon of a continuing sleep-deprived period than during the night period preceding it (Kleitman, 1960*b*, p. 337). Kleitman observes that after approximately 48 hours without sleep there is no increase in sleepiness, but the individual is increasingly sleepbound and requires increasing amounts (and variety) of stimulation to keep him from falling asleep.

Oswald (1962, pp. 178 ff.) reports a general deterioration of cortical control with increasing sleeplessness. Speech becomes slurred and rambling, repetitions and mispronunciations increase, there is an impairment of handwriting, an increase in irrelevant acts and speech, an increase in perceptual illusions, and an increasing sense of detachment, with loss of temporal, spatial, and body-image orientation.

Recovery. Interestingly enough, when subjects are sleep-deprived for several days, and then allowed unlimited "access" to sleep, they do not take an absolute amount of sleep equal to that lost. About 11 or 12 hours of sleep seem to be all that are taken (and presumably needed). Under wartime and similar emergency conditions, persons are known to have gone for weeks at a time with no more than "catnaps" now and then. However, there are no systematic reports of residual effects, if any, of such experiences.

Sleep as a Drive

Malmo and Surwillo (1960) studied EEG, EMG, respiration, palmar conductance, and heart rate as arousal indices, finding increased *activation* with up to 60 hours of sleep deprivation. This was interpreted as supporting a drive theory of sleep. However, as Wilkinson (1960) has noted, possible painful (thermal) stimulation was occasionally used to mark errors in the ongoing tracking task, raising question as to whether their arousal indices were reflecting sleep phenomena only. Furthermore, there would be great difficulty controlling compensatory effort increase and self-stimulation (as a test of stamina by the individual) in human subjects.

Webb (1956) studied sleep deprivation in rats, using a "wakefulness-enforcer" activity wheel partially immersed in water, which required the animal to maintain a modest amount of movement to stay above water level. He found a significant negative relationship between hours of sleep deprivation (0 to 30) and latency of falling asleep immediately afterward. However, a mean latency difference of only five minutes was obtained between extremes, and Webb noted that even rats which appeared "exhausted" took time to groom and explore, sleep appearing to "overwhelm them as they were in this process of adjustment, [some] going to sleep leaning against the wall or in the midst of some activity" (p. 9). He suggests that a "need to keep awake" may have been induced by time on the wheel, which must be extinguished before sleep can occur. Throughout a series of studies he found highly consistent individual sleep patterns, regardless of imposed activity, sleeplessness, or an irrelevant (hunger) drive. He concludes that sleep behavior has a strong overlay of habit—and both wakefulness *and* sleep tendencies contribute to sleep behavior.

In human subjects there is no doubt that sleep deprivation increases feelings of sleepiness and efforts toward gratification. EEG sleep signs increase and body temperature decreases with deprivation (Murray et al., 1958; Armington & Mitnick, 1959). There is some biochemical evidence that sleep loss acts as a stressor (Luby et al., 1960).

Summary

Sleep, like fatigue, is a bodily condition intimately associated with neural inhibition. The mechanisms of sleep are seen to be a set of complex interactions of excitation and inhibition of brain-stem reticular formation activity, involving feedback circuits from the cortex and the medulla. Like fatigue, sleep can be induced or delayed by drugs affecting reticular formation-activation level.

The ratio of sleep to wakefulness seems clearly established at approximately 1:2, although the sleep-wakefulness pattern is strongly influenced by social and diurnal conditioning. What bodily needs are satisfied by sleep are not yet clear, although it is suspected that neural cell-restorative functions are served. Sleep is an active state, neurally and neurochemically, although the sleeping organism may be less active overtly. Dreaming is a regular concomitant of sleep, and the quantity of dreaming appears to increase when interfered with.

Although there are individual differences in the amount of sleep required, sleep deprivation leads to increased performance degradation as a result of an increase in the frequency of automatic periods of light sleep during forced wakefulness, and a heightening of the threshold of stimulation required to keep the individual from falling into sleep.

Sleep behavior appears to be a function not only of a sleep drive (which can be partially ignored but never completely denied by the individual), but perhaps of a wakefulness tendency, as well. The overlay of habitual wakefulness and sleep tendencies, as shown in highly consistent individual sleep patterns and in socio-ecologic sleep patterns, needs also to be taken into account in studies of sleep as a motivation phenomenon.

SEX

Many writers and theorists seem to hold that sexual motivation is perhaps the most powerful factor in energizing and directing behavior (see Chapter 12). Yet extensive experimental work on the sex "drive" itself has been limited to relatively few species, and the use of sexual motivation in the laboratory in studies of learning and other aspects of behavior has been substantially less frequent than the employment of hunger, thirst, and fear. It is interesting to note that in six books on motivation published since 1959, the topic of sex is accorded very little space, only two of them devoting more than one or two pages to it. There is, however, an extensive literature on sexual functions. Much of it has to do with sexual patterns in a variety of species and with the physiology of reproductive activities. Our treatment of this literature is a selective one.[23]

In considerations of motivation, it is common for authors to list sex as a primary drive along with, mainly, hunger and thirst (as well as others). Because hunger and thirst seem to be taken so often as providing general models for all of motivation, it is important to note major differences between them and sexual motivation. Beach (1956) has questioned the classification of sex with hunger and thirst. He has suggested, in the first place, that sex is perhaps more of an "appetite" than a drive for reasons that will be clear when his theories of sexual mechanisms are described later in the section. Beach further observes,

---

[23] There are several excellent reviews of the work on sexual mechanisms and behavior. In particular, we may cite those by Beach (1948, 1951), Ford and Beach (1951), and the two-volume work edited by W. C. Young (1961a). In what follows, the reader will note our extensive references to the work of F. A. Beach. We have depended a great deal in this discussion on Beach's work, both because his research on sexual behavior has been extensive and because his reviews of the topic have been thorough, well organized and thoughtful.

as a second point, that sexual activity is not essential to the life of any individual, whereas eating and drinking are: sexual abstinence does not cause death. For a *species* to survive, of course, sexual relations among at least some of its members are required. A third difference is that deprivation of food or water results in depletion of bodily tissues, but this is not true of sexual deprivation. On the contrary, it is the performance of sexual activity which may be exhausting, and sexual abstinence permits recovery. Put another way, one can say that starvation is catabolic and eating anabolic. Sexual deprivation is anabolic and sexual activity catabolic. And, in the fourth place, Beach observes, external stimuli are important to sexual behavior, more so, he thinks, than they are to eating and drinking. We will return to this fourth point a little later.

A review of the other conditions treated in this chapter will also reveal differences between them and hunger and thirst as well as some similarities. Most of Beach's points would be applicable to maternal, nesting, and parturitional activities, as well as to sex, and perhaps, also, to homing, migration, and hoarding. Temperature regulation, respiration, and sucking show several similarities with hunger but contact activities perhaps do not. Fatigue is catabolic; sleep and rest are anabolic. Stimuli are important to the alertness—sleep continuum. The point is that no one "drive" state can provide a model that will be satisfactory for all motivational conditions. In Chapter 16, however, we will try to determine whether there are some mechanisms common to the *motivational* aspects of all of these conditions.

Mechanisms in Sexual Behavior

Local Factors. The control of sexual behavior is complex, as we shall see, but it is often proposed that tension in specific organs is the basis for sexual activity. Various organs have been mentioned. In the male frog, J. R. Tarchanoff in 1887 proposed that sexual behavior arose when the vesicles were full, and, for mammals, J. T. Carpenter in 1900 offered impulses arising from the testes as the source (Beach, 1948). Nissen (1929) hypothesized, for the rat, that sensations of tension in the penis, in the male, and in the uterine and vaginal epithelium, in the female, were the basis of sexual activity. Similar suggestions have been made for other species.

There can be little question that stimulation arising from organs such as these plays a role in both sexual arousal and sexual behavior in all of its aspects. However, whether such stimulation is necessary is open to question.

M. E. G. Schrader in 1897 removed the prostate gland and seminal vesicles of male frogs and found that sexual behavior survived, thus refuting Tarchanoff's suggestion (Beach, 1948). Many castrates (animals with testes or ovaries removed) can perform sexual acts when gonadal hormones are administered (and sometimes without such hormones). This fact appears to remove the gonads from consideration as sources of necessary tension or stimuli critical to mating. Riddle (1924–1925) reported a number of pigeons in which apparently normal (but infertile) mating behavior occurred despite the congenital absence of gonadal tissue. Beach (1945) was able to induce normal mating behavior in a female rat which had no ovarian tissue and whose vagina and uterus had grown only to an infantile, postnatal level (see, also, Ball, 1934).

Sensitivity of the vagina, vulva, and the surrounding skin was abolished in rabbits by removal of the sacral portions of the spinal cord (Brooks, 1937) with no apparent inadequacy of sexual behavior. Root and Bard (1947) deafferented the pelvic viscera, external genitalia, and the nearby skin without eliminating sexual behavior in either the male or the female cat (Bard, 1935). Beach and Holz (1946) found that male rats would continue to try to mate even though their penes had been damaged by surgical removal of part of the bone. Complete copulation was, however, reduced in frequency, and ejaculation disappeared. Money (1961) has reported continued sexual arousal and orgasm in humans in whom the clitoris or penis has been removed, and in one patient who had had a vulvectomy. He also cites cases of arousal in paraplegic patients in whom there are no intact neural connections remaining between the genital tactile receptors and the brain.

This information suggests that sexual behavior, or at least major components of it, need not be dependent on tensions in genital organs. Unfortunately, in most of the studies reviewed, prior normal sexual experience preceded the tests after genital damage or deafferentation. It is possible that the role of these structures is important in the development of sexual behavior in *in*experienced organisms (cf. Rosenblatt & Aronson, 1958, for evidence in prepuberally castrated cats).

Hormonal Factors. Even a cursory inspection of the literature on sex behavior will reveal that this form of activity is markedly dependent on hormonal control. While the degree of this dependence varies considerably among species and is perhaps never complete (Beach, 1948, p. 28), the relationship is so strong as to lead W. C. Young (1961*b*, p. 1174) to say that, in most of the vertebrates on which there are adequate data, the full display of mating behavior occurs only when gonadal hormones are present.

The *gonads*, of course, are the testis in the male and the ovary in the female. These organs show little activity in early life but, as puberty approaches, are acted upon by certain hormones of the anterior pituitary gland, called gonadotrophins. Under the influence of these hormones, the testis and the ovary begin to secrete their own hormones and, a little later, to produce germ cells—sperm and eggs. Secondary sex characteristics also develop. The hormone secreted by the testis is called *testosterone* and those by the ovary *estrogen* and *progesterone.*[24] The role of these hormones in sexual behavior can best be described by illustrative investigations organized around the stages of immaturity and adulthood and involving the effects of administration of hormones and of castration.

1. *Immature animals.* It has been observed in many species of animals that some of the reflexes, as well as other features, of mature mating behavior are present prior to puberty. Among reflexes, genital erection has been seen on the natal day. Orgasm, or sexual climax,[25] has been observed in the human male infant, along with pelvic thrusts, when the genitals are manipulated (Kinsey, Pomeroy, & Martin, 1948). And there is abundant evidence in human societies of autosexual, homosexual, and heterosexual behaviors, such as genital stimulation and simulation of copulation, from early ages to puberty (Kinsey, et al., 1948, 1953; Ford & Beach, 1951).

Similar statements may be made as to sexual behavior patterns in lower animals prior to puberty. This is especially true among chimpanzees and monkeys and of *males* in subprimate mammalian species. Females of the latter groups of animals seldom show feminine sexual behavior patterns before puberty (Ford & Beach, 1951, p. 193).

a. Administration of hormones. Gonadal hormones in immature animals are supposed to have two distinguishable, though interrelated, effects (Young, 1961*b*). One is to energize the neuromuscular structures essential for the mature mating pattern to appear. The other is to play a role in the development and organization of these structures themselves. The evidence which we now summarize is germane to these functions.

Sexual behavior can be displayed in many prepuberal animals after

[24] Testosterone is also secreted by the cortex of the adrenal gland and by the ovary (Ford & Beach, 1951). The generic name for testosterone or male sex hormone is *androgen*. Other hormones are secreted by the ovary, especially in relation to pregnancy and lactation. We do not consider them here. A suitable *balance* in hormonal secretion is very important. Thus, if there is too much androgen, male characteristics will appear in females.

[25] In the adult male, orgasm and ejaculation usually occur together. However, such mutual dependency is not invariant.

administration of either pituitary or gonadal hormones (Beach, 1951; Ford & Beach, 1951; Young, 1961*b*). The anterior pituitary extracts probably act on sexual behavior indirectly by stimulating the gonads to secrete their hormones. The evidence that either anterior pituitary or gonadal hormones can give rise to premature sexual behavior comes from studies of such organisms as male guppies, male toads, female and male chameleons, domestic fowl of both sexes, rats, mice, dogs, and monkeys (Beach, 1951; Ford & Beach, 1951). Similar effects are seen in boys with undescended testes who are treated with pituitary extracts. In such cases, an excess of gonadotrophic hormone will lead to accelerated development of the sex organs and the secondary sex characteristics (Ford & Beach, 1951, p. 169).

A representative investigation by Beach and Holz (1946) on male rats supports these findings in another way. They castrated their animals at ages ranging from 1 to 350 days. Three months following this operation, the animals were treated with androgen and tested with receptive females. All animals showed complete copulation after this treatment, and most of them copulated to ejaculation. The major exceptions, so far as ejaculation was concerned, were the animals castrated when they were one day old. These animals did not show normal penis growth, and this deficiency was probably responsible for their failure to ejaculate. The important conclusion from this study, however, is that the normal copulation pattern appeared on administration of androgen despite the absence of gonadal secretions (following castration) from as early as one day of age. This suggests that the neuromuscular structures essential to copulation are present long before puberty and do not require gonadal secretions for their organization and development. Young (1961*b*), however, thinks that, perhaps prenatally, gonadal hormones may have a role in organizing the structures mediating sexual behavior and cites some supporting evidence. Beach (1942*d*) has induced sexual behavior in female rats a month before it would normally appear by injecting them with estrogen.[26]

In summary, it seems clear that, at least in many animals, precocious sexual behavior will arise on administration of appropriate pituitary or gonadal hormones. The implication is evident that the neuromuscular structures involved in sex behavior are available long before maturity.

---

[26] Beach (1942*f*) also injected male rats with estrogen at maturity, after they had been castrated at 21 days of age. Response to the female was augmented by the estrogen, in comparison to tests made before administration of estrogen, and there were some instances of complete copulation though without ejaculation. Evidently, estrogen can lead to an increment in sexual excitability in male rats, though not as much as androgen.

This is especially true in organisms in which little experience is required for mature mating patterns to appear.

b. Removal of endocrine glands. Removal of the pituitary gland or failure of it to function normally prevents the development of the gonads and other evidence of sexual development (Ford & Beach, 1951, p. 168). This is true in human beings as well as in lower animals. Prepuberal castration likewise prevents sexual maturation and the appearance of mature mating patterns (Beach, 1951), although there are some reports of sexual behavior in prepuberally castrated human males (Ford & Beach, 1951, p. 231). However, the sex play of immature male rats is not affected even when they are castrated at birth (Beach, 1942*f*). This may mean that such sex play (briefly mentioned earlier) does not arise from effects of gonadal hormones, although the gonads are known to display some activity before puberty.

In passing, it should be noted that sexual behavior may also be affected by removal or deficiency of function of other endocrine glands, such as the thyroids. This effect, however, appears to be due largely to impaired health and vigor, rather than to specific influences on sexual behavior (Beach, 1951, p. 403). It may also arise from the interactions of endocrine secretions, some of which are trophic for other glands, as, for example, those of the pituitary and the hypothalamic neurosecretions. There may be effects on sexual arousal but not on specific sexual behaviors.

2. Adult animals. The sexual behavior of some animals, such as many birds, fish, amphibians, and reptiles, is seasonal, and this is true in both the female and the male. In many higher species, however, breeding is not seasonal but is controlled by regular periods of receptivity ("heat" or oestrus) in the females. In such species, the male is usually able to mate at any time, given a receptive female. There is a much less pronounced dependence of sexual behavior on oestrus in the female among higher primates, like the chimpanzee, and it is virtually absent in the human species. One way of describing these variations is to say that there are varying degrees of hormonal control over sexual behavior, the control being at a minimum in man. Another way of speaking about the variations is to say that experiential, social, and cultural factors increase their role in controlling sexual behavior as we move from lower animals to man. Sexual behavior in subprimate females is more dependent on hormones than is true in males, but the difference decreases in primates and is least in man.

It is possible to interpret the decreased hormonal control over sexual behavior from lower animal to man as an instance of the overriding of biological factors by experience and social conditioning. Perhaps habit and expectation can negate hormonal control. Unfortunately, there is no evidence that clearly supports this interpretation. At least there is no way to reject the alternative that diminished hormonal control makes possible the ascendancy of experiential, social, and cultural factors.

 a. Administration of hormones. Sexual behavior may be aroused out of season (in species which normally breed seasonally) by administration of either pituitary or gonadal hormones. Beach (1951) indicates, for example, that this effect has been obtained in goldfish, male and female frogs and toads, lizards, ferrets, and the opossum. Female mammals can be brought into heat by appropriate administration of ovarian hormones, and this procedure is widely used by students of sexual behavior. Naturally impotent male rats showed sexual behavior following administration of testosterone propionate (Stone, 1938), and sexual behavior was reactivated in senile rats by similar injections and by administration of pituitary extracts (Minnick, Warden, & Arieti, 1946). Administration of testosterone in males and of estrogen (or of both estrogen and progesterone) in females has usually restored sexual behavior in castrated male and female animals, respectively, in the species which have been studied.

 Hormonal administration in humans is usually reported to have less substantial effects, and this may be because of the lessened hormonal control of sexual behavior in man or because the factors responsible for the conditions for which hormone therapy was instituted override the biological factors. Ford and Beach (1951) indicate that cases of impotence in human males do not typically respond much to androgen, and neither male nor female homosexuals typically respond to hormones by shifting to sexual behavior patterns considered normal for their sexes. Human male homosexuals to whom large amounts of androgen have been given do show augmented sexual arousal, but the manner of its expression does not change to the typical male heterosexual pattern (Ford & Beach, 1951, p. 236). These findings with humans indicate that the effects of hormonal administration in animals are not paralleled and suggest that hormonal imbalances are rarely responsible for human homosexuality or for male impotence.

 Beach (1941b) induced female sexual responses in some male rats by administration of testosterone, and several investigators (see Beach, 1948) have induced feminine responses in male rats by giving them estrogen. (Estrogen, under some circumstances, will also induce male copulation patterns in some males.) Spayed females, treated with androgen, will show many features of masculine sexual behavior (Beach, 1942e; Beach & Rasquin, 1942), and Ball (1940) found male-copulatory behavior in female rats which had been injected with testosterone for several weeks, a result confirmed in prepuberally castrated females by Beach (1942e) and Koster (1943). These results, together with the finding of occasional "opposite-sex" behavior manifested normally by both male and female rats, suggest that mechanisms for either male or female sex behavior are possessed by both sexes. This is probably true in a great many species other than the rat.

Evidences of hormonal control of mating behavior in adult animals are very clearly indicated by the effects of castration.

b. Castration. After removal of the testes or of the ovary, sexual behavior in many species disappears, even when the castration occurs in adulthood. The decline in sexual behavior, when it occurs, is typically more rapid in the female than in the male. Restoration of sexual functions after castration can usually, however, be accomplished by suitable gonadal hormone therapy. Ovariectomy has been shown to eliminate sexual behavior in such organisms as jewel fish, Siamese fighting fish, lizards, domestic and wild birds, rats, guinea pigs, mice (Beach, 1951), rabbits, cats, dogs, horses, and cows (Ford & Beach, 1951, pp. 221–223). Sexual responsiveness is reduced but not entirely eliminated by ovariectomy in monkeys (Klüver & Bucy, 1939) and chimpanzees (Ford & Beach, 1951, p. 222). In the human female, sexual desire often survives either ovariectomy or the natural decline in ovarian function which occurs during the menopause. Some women report no change in sexual desire after these events, whereas others report loss of it. This is a further indication that many other factors, aside from hormonal control, are involved in the sexual behavior in the human female, and it is evident that loss in sexual desire, after ovarian function ceases, need not be attributed to lack of hormones (Ford & Beach, 1951, p. 223). Custom, attitudes, and enjoyment of sexual relations are probably as important in continuation of sexual activity in women following the menopause as they are to sexual behavior prior to the menopause.

Breeding behavior is eliminated by castration in male amphibians, lizards, pigeons, and other domestic and wild birds, rats, rabbits, hamsters, and guinea pigs (Beach, 1951; Ford & Beach, 1951). However, the disappearance of sexual behavior need not be immediate. In experienced male rats, for example, Stone (1927) found that two-thirds were still able to copulate a month after castration and one-fifth were still doing so at the end of the fifth month following the operation. Beach (1951, p. 405) points out that the ejaculation response disappears first, followed by erection and intromission. Incomplete mating responses, however, endure almost indefinitely in rats. The picture here, then, is one of declining sexual responsiveness, rather than abrupt cessation. Some male dogs continue to show sexual behavior for as long as two years after castration (Ford & Beach, 1951, p. 230).

Among the primates, evidence concerning the castration of males in adulthood suggests that sexual behavior may continue for some time after castration in monkeys (Hamilton, 1914), and an adult chimpanzee, castrated in infancy, is reported to mate normally except for the absence of ejaculation (Ford & Beach, 1951, p. 231). Castration of adult human males produces variable effects. Some such persons report a loss of sexual desire and capacity, others report desire but no potency, and still others report continuation of desire and potency for as long as 30 years following castration (Ford & Beach, 1951, pp. 231–232). These findings parallel those for women without ovarian function. Presumably, experiential factors are responsible for the continued sexual activity in human male castrates in whom it occurs. By the same token, this suggests the much reduced importance to sexual behavior of gonadal hormones in man as compared to lower animals.

Summary. The evidence reviewed indicates that sexual behavior in many animals is dependent on the presence of gonadal hormones and that such manipulations as hormone administration or castration may have marked effects in stimulating or suppressing sexual behavior. In general, it can be said that hormonal control is greater in lower animals than it is in higher animals and that it tends to be greater in males than in females in most species. Among the higher primates, however, hormonal control seems to be considerably diminished, and other factors, such as experience and social and cultural variables, may play a dominant role. Some evidence as to these factors will be summarized later in this section.

In conclusion, it is worth noting that Beach (1948, p. 28), speaking of vertebrates, indicates that in no such animal is overt sexual behavior rigidly or completely controlled by somatic (including hormonal) factors.

Neural Factors. From studies of operated animals or injured people, there is evidence that some aspects of sexual behavior can occur under control of the spinal cord alone. Thus erection and ejaculation can occur at the spinal level in male rodents, rabbits, dogs, and the human (Beach, 1951, p. 400), and female cats and dogs continue to show some features of oestrus behavior following transsection of the spinal cord. Normally, of course, these reflex aspects of sexual behavior would be under cortical control in an integrated mating pattern. Many partial sexual responses can also be elicited by stimulation in a variety of places in the brain (Olds, 1962).

More attention has been paid to higher structures of the central nervous system than to spinal-cord functions. A number of experiments with several mammalian species suggest that sexual behavior is less dependent on cortical structures in the female than it is in the male. Sexual activity survives surgical insults to the cortex, hippocampus, and corpus striatum in female guinea pigs, rabbits, cats, and rats (Beach, 1951, p. 401). The anterior hypothalamus, as might be expected, because of its intimate association with the pituitary and thus with the control of secretion of sex hormones, is important to sexual behavior in several of these species, and destruction of this area results in a cessation or substantial decline in sexual responsiveness (Beach, 1951, p. 401). It is interesting to note that male sexual reactions shown by normal female rats in the presence of another female in heat are abolished by substantial cortical lesions. In the same animals, however, female mating responses persist (Beach, 1943). This suggests the greater dependence of male sexual behavior on the cortex as compared with female sexual reactions, a point noted already. There is some disturbance in the feminine mating behavior of female rats after decortication, but it is primarily in the organization and synchronization of the behavior, rather than a reduction of it (Beach, 1944a).

Although male rabbits deprived of the neocortex continue to mate more or less normally, this is not true in rats, cats, and dogs (Ford & Beach, 1951, p. 241). This finding for rats, cats, and dogs is consistent with the loss of male sexual behavior in largely decorticated female rats; evidently the male pattern, whether it occurs in males or in females, requires some intact cortex for its occurrence. Beach (1940) examined mating behavior in male rats after varying amounts of cortical injury. In the vast majority of the animals, mating behavior was not affected when 19 per cent or less of the cortex was removed, but this behavior was lost to almost all of the animals when from 50 to 59 per cent of the cortex was eliminated. Ablations involving more than 60 per cent of the cortex eliminated sexual behavior altogether. Thus, in the male, sexual behavior appears to require that there be substantial integrity of the highest parts of the brain. Rather similar results were obtained when the male rats that were operated on were inexperienced and had been reared in isolation from 21 days of age (Beach, 1941a).

Another experiment by Beach (1944b) with male rats throws further light on the role of the cortex in mating behavior. These rats were castrated and subjected to various cortical lesions. Mating behavior was tested with and without injections of testosterone propionate. Animals with lesions smaller than total decortication, in whom mating behavior had been eliminated by the cortical insult, could still mate after injections. Complete decorticates, however, did not mate even after injections of over 20 times as much testosterone as is required for castrated rats with normal brains to copulate.

Beach (1951) thinks that these various results show, for the male rat, the importance of the cortex in maintaining excitability in lower centers so that they will be responsive to external stimuli. He believes that the components of sexual behavior are controlled by lower centers in the brain but that cortical facilitation is essential to their integrated activity. The cortex, Beach observes, is perhaps even more important to sexual behavior in higher animals, such as cats (Beach, 1951, p. 402).

From these experiments we can see that neural control of sexual behavior becomes more "cortical" as we move from lower to higher species, so far as males are concerned. In the females of species which have been studied, however, cortical integrity seems less necessary to copulatory behavior than it is to males. The cortical role, where it is important, seems to be that of contributing to arousal. It also provides for experience to play an important role in sexual behavior. In the human, this perhaps leads to the large influence which social and experiential factors can have on sexual behavior.

Variables Related to Sexual Behavior

Sexual behavior is a complex affair, and there are many factors to be considered, aside from the genitals, hormones, and the nervous system. Among these factors are deprivation and satiation, stimulation from several sources, social relations, age, experience, and diet. Before discussing these variables, however, we turn briefly to the measurement of sexual behavior.

Description and Measurement of Sexual Behavior.[27] Sexual behavior may be measured in several ways. The occurrence of the total consummatory behavior pattern may be noted and perhaps rated for adequacy, and its frequency may be related to other variables. Or instrumental behavior may be required for an animal to reach a sexual incentive (perhaps under the influence of different antecedent conditions), and characteristics of the instrumental behavior may be studied.

---

[27] In the space available, we cannot provide descriptions of mating behavior of many species. For references descriptive of mating patterns in fish, amphibians, birds, small mammals, pigs, ewes, and infrahuman primates, see Young (1961b, fn. 3, p. 1174) and the references listed in the papers he cites. A convenient source of descriptions of mating behavior in rats is afforded by Munn (1950, p. 17 and p. 28). Ford and Beach (1951) provide many details of human coitus in a variety of human societies and offer descriptions and comparisons of sexual behavior in a variety of animals. See, also, Kinsey, Pomeroy, and Martin (1948) and Kinsey, Pomeroy, Martin, and Gebhard (1953).

Finally, various components of sexual behavior may be separated for analysis. (The general methods for measuring motivation are outlined in Table 5–1, p. 237.)

1. *Occurrence of total mating response.* In this method, an animal is placed with one of the opposite sex, and copulatory behavior is observed and its frequency recorded (e.g., Anderson, 1938). In studies of rats, for example, a male will be placed in an enclosure (with which he has been familiarized) with a receptive female. The occurrence of copulation and ejaculation (or not) will be noted. This may complete the test, for this occasion, or the animals may be left together for a period of time and additional copulations and ejaculations may be observed. In the female, of course, no ejaculation occurs, so that the number of times she accepts a given male or the number of males with which she copulates in a given time period is the index used. It should be clear already that the occurrence of the total mating response is a gross measure and that components of it may yield valuable information.

Somewhat similar observational procedures are used for other animals. In the human, a questionnaire or an interview report has usually been substituted for direct observation. The well-known studies by Kinsey et al. (1948, 1953), for example, asked for estimates of the frequency, on a weekly basis, with which sexual "outlets" (defined as orgasms) were achieved and by what means (intercourse, masturbation, etc.).

Another variation in measuring sexual behavior by observing overall copulatory behavior is to provide a variety of stimuli and determine to how many the animal responds. Beach (1942*b*) and Beach and Holz-Tucker (1949) used this method. In one experiment, castrated male rats were given different amounts of androgen. Then they were tested with receptive females, nonreceptive females, males, and other "inadequate" stimuli. A measure of sexual motivation can be the number or the degree of inadequacy of objects as sexual incentives toward which the male exhibits copulatory behavior. Beach and Holz-Tucker (1949) found that the higher the androgen level the less adequate a stimulus had to be to evoke mating responses.[28]

2. *Instrumental behavior.* A number of instrumental performances have been used to assess sexual motivation.[29] Among the earliest to be employed was the Columbia Obstruction Box, in which what is

---

[28] The reader will recall (Chapter 3) that similar methods have been used by the ethologists.

[29] General activity (see Chapter 6) has also been employed as a means of studying sexual motivation, especially in the female rat.

measured is the number of times in an observation period than an animal will cross an electrified grid to get to the incentive object (Warner, 1927). Other methods include learning a task with a sexual incentive as a reward (Kagan, 1955), bar-pressing to get a female (Schwartz, 1956), or a male (Bermant, 1961), speed of running a runway to a sexual incentive (Beach & Jordan, 1956a; Beach, 1956, p. 13; Seward & Seward, 1940b). Anderson (1938) employed various obstruction tests to measure sexual motivation—for example, digging through sand to get to the sexual incentive.

3. *Components of the mating response.* As an illustration of what is meant here, we may use the male rat (Beach, 1956; Munn, 1950). When placed with a receptive female, this animal typically engages in investigatory responses, such as nuzzling the female. It mounts her and palpates her sides. Then it will achieve intromission and engage in a number of copulatory thrusts. Mounting, intromission, and copulation may occur a number of times before this sequence of acts results in ejaculation. Thus (Beach, 1956), one may assess the latency of the first mount or the first intromission or copulation, the number of copulations in a given series, the number of repeated intromissions and copulations to ejaculation, the intercopulatory intervals, the total time from mounting to ejaculation, the time after ejaculation to the next mount and copulation (Beach & Jordan, 1956b), etc. Durations of individual events can be measured. The sexual act, in this species and many others, can be fractionated into a number of part-processes, which can be separately gauged. As we shall see later, such analytic measurement has value to the development of theoretical accounts of sexual mechanisms.

4. *Relationships among measures.* Anderson (1938) gave 8 sex tests to 55 albino male rats. The first test was given at 148 days of age and the last at 314 days. In his typical procedure, Anderson preceded each test session by permitting copulation with a receptive female in the home cage. This was done to keep arousal and recent sexual activity constant across tests. Anderson used copulation tests (twice), ejaculations (twice), time spent near a barrier separating the male from the receptive female, speed of running to a sexual lure, digging through sand to get to the female, and the Columbia Obstruction Box. The intercorrelations of these tests ranged from .153 (time near barrier vs. Columbia Obstruction Box) to .677 (copulation retest vs. sand-digging test). Of the 21 intercorrelations reported (Anderson, 1938, p. 62, Table 25), all are positive; eleven are .50 or above. These intercorrelations are considerably higher than are the correlations between the sex tests and tests for other drives. The direct sex tests (copulation, copula-

tion retest, and ejaculations) are negatively correlated (.4 to .5) with emotionality as independently measured by defecation in a separate situation.

There is, then, a certain homogeneity in the evaluation of sexual motivation by these tests, but the relationships, nevertheless, are not high enough to permit one test to be regarded as a substitute or as an equivalent for another. Wood-Gush (1960) has pointed out, for two strains of cockerels, that a strain of infrequent copulators more often ejaculated and yielded more semen than a group of frequent copulators. Depending on whether one used frequency of copulation or a ratio of ejaculations to copulations, one would assess the relative sexual motivation of these strains quite differently. In the male guinea pig, Jakway (1959) has observed that ejaculation frequency and rate of intromission do not depend on the same factors as other features of mating behavior (see, also, Whalen, Beach, & Kuehn, 1961).

As a further problem with respect to the equivalence of measures of sexual motivation, it is also true that over a series of sexual tests

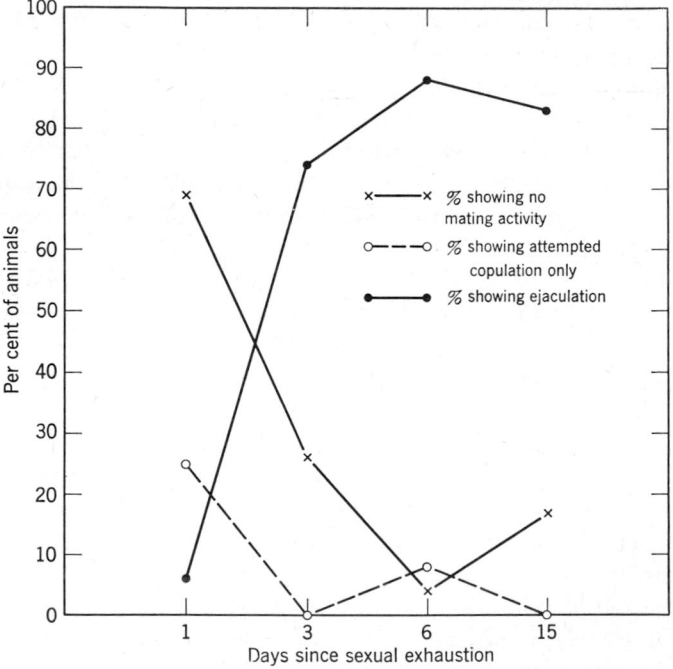

Figure 4–8. Course of sexual performance in male rats after copulation to exhaustion. Plotted from data shown in Beach and Jordan (1956b, Table II, p. 126).

some components of the sexual act change in different directions. Thus, latency of copulation may increase over several tests, whereas number of intromissions before ejaculation may decrease (Beach, 1956).

Deprivation and Satiation. A study of deprivation of sexual behavior in the male rat was made by Warner (1927) by means of the Columbia Obstruction Box. Warner permitted his animals two hours of free copulation, and then they were segregated into deprivation groups. No copulation was permitted to occur in the test situation. The measure used was number of grid crossings to an incentive female in a 20-minute period. This value increased sharply from 6-hours' deprivation (about 4 crossings) to 24-hours' deprivation (about 14 crossings). From 1 to 25 days of deprivation, the number of crossings did not increase; in fact, it actually showed a slight decline. Sexually potent animals (as determined by direct copulation tests) make more crossings than same-aged impotent rats (Stone, Barker, & Tomilin, 1935), a result confirmed by Anderson (1937).

After recovery from the effects of immediate copulation, it is probable that sexual motivation in the male rat does not vary much with duration of sexual deprivation. Beach and Jordan (1956b) have provided data for recovery of sexual performance in male rats after copulation to exhaustion; Figure 4–8 shows their findings.

Ejaculation is an important factor from which the male must recover. As mentioned before, a male chimpanzee, castrated in infancy, could copulate and would do so as many as ten times in an hour but there was no ejaculation. Under androgen administration, however, orgasm recurred, and his limit then was two or three coitions in an hour (Ford & Beach, 1951, p. 234).

In female mammals, it is the oestrus cycle [30] (except in women and perhaps chimpanzees), rather than deprivation, which determines their sexual performance. There is some evidence that copulation will not decrease sexual activity during a session while the female is in oestrus. Bermant (1961) trained oestrus female rats to press a bar in order to obtain a male. After one male had copulated, he was removed and replaced by another, when the female pressed the bar. Over five copulations in a session, the latency of the female's bar-press declined toward the middle of the series, presumably indicating that copulation had not decreased motivation. Many females will accept a succession of males

---

[30] Sex behavior in animals which mate seasonally, whether male or female, would not show any particular relation to deprivation, either. Rating scales for the evaluation of sexual receptivity of certain female animals have been developed by Ball (1937) and Young, Boling, and Blandau (1941) and for males, by Goy and Young (1957).

during oestrus, with no apparent decline in interest, and will actively stimulate a male whose activity lags after he has copulated several times.

Using the obstruction box, Warner (1927) found that female rats would cross the grid to a male most often at the time of oestrus. At other points in the sex cycle, considerably fewer crossings would be made. For female chimpanzees, Yerkes and Elder (1936) found copulation to occur most frequently at the time of genital swelling, which corresponds with the time of ovulation. However, instances of copulation are found in this animal at all times in the female sex cycle. Women report maximal sexual desire either pre- or postmenstrually (Davis, 1929; Terman, 1938), neither time being associated with ovulation (Ford & Beach, 1951, p. 208). Sexual activity, however, is not restricted to these periods. The evidence is not great, but in societies other than that of the United States, on which Davis' and Terman's data are based, there are some findings which parallel those for American women. According to Ford and Beach (1951, p. 210), the Aranda, Lepcha, and Masai believe women's desire is low premenstrually and high postmenstrually. The Hopi believe female desires to be greatest at both times. Ford and Beach point out that sexual relations during menstruation are frowned on or actually prohibited in many societies and that this may concentrate the woman's desire in the pre- and postmenstrual periods. However, they do not regard this as a completely satisfactory explanation for the fact that the desire of women, unlike the coital behavior of female chimpanzees, is greatest during nonovulatory periods. Whatever the factors involved, it is clear for the human female that they are nonhormonal and probably are associated with custom. (For a summary of sexual cycles in a variety of species, see Ford & Beach, 1951, Chapter 11.)

One may conclude from these investigations that deprivation is not a particularly significant contributor to sexual activity, except in the male who must recover following copulation, especially when copulation has occurred to satiation or exhaustion. We speak here, of course, of healthy animals under conditions relatively ideal for sexual behavior. Poor health and other circumstances may obscure such predictive significance as deprivation does have for the occurrence of sexual behavior.

Stimulation. Two types of external stimulation play a role in arousing sexual behavior: those arising from the environment generally and those emanating from the partner. Studies of animals with sensory deficiencies throw some light on the role of stimulation in sexual behavior.

1. *General environment.* In connection with the discussion of sleep,

we mentioned the existence of bodily rhythms. Many of these rhythms are correlated with light-dark cycles and with temperature variations, and the correlations are probably mediated through activity of the pituitary gland and other structures involved in general regulatory processes in the body, such as the hypothalamus and the reticular formation. Some of the effects of the general environment on sexual behavior are probably mediated in the same way, although the details of such mediation have not, for the greater part, been worked out. At any rate, it is known in some animals (Beach, 1951) that illumination and temperature seem to prepare the organism to exhibit sexual behavior; these factors do not *elicit* sexual behavior but are instrumental in making the animal physiologically ready for it. The seasonal character of sexual behavior in many varieties of fish, birds, and mammals is related to the amount of daylight in the 24-hour day. Typically, as the days get longer in the spring of the year, courtship and sexual behaviors appear. Changes in the pituitary gland apparently occur in response to alterations in the amount of daylight, and these changes probably affect the gonads (Beach, 1948, 1951). Artificial modification of illumination can alter the occurrence of breeding, for example, to make it occur out of season or to prolong it beyond the usual time of cessation. Many animals sleep at night, but others are active in the dark. The rat, a nocturnal animal, mainly active in the dark, tends to mate at night (Beach, 1951), whereas other animals, active during the day, sleep at night and mate during the daylight hours. Human beings tend to prefer to mate at night; this preference may arise from the desire for privacy (Ford & Beach, 1951), but the fact that work occupies the daylight hours is no doubt a factor. Human sexual activity can and does occur at almost any time. Kinsey and his colleagues report that American women prefer that sexual activity be conducted in darkness to an extent greater than is true among men, but this sex difference does not exist in many societies (Ford & Beach, 1951).

Temperature is involved in the breeding behavior of many species of animals, especially invertebrates (Beach, 1951). This fact probably reflects the interaction of external temperature with bodily rhythms and perhaps with dark-light cycles.

Association with other animals is also a condition for readying the individual for sexual behavior. When African mouthbreeders can see others of their species, they make nests and lay (infertile) eggs; without such stimulation these activities are infrequent (Beach, 1951). Female pigeons require visual stimulation for egg-laying; even that provided by mirrors in the bird's home cage has some effect (Matthews, 1939). Large colonies of herring gulls seem to be more effective breeding units than small colonies (Beach, 1951). Pelc (1959) found changes in the seminal vesicles of male mice kept with females that did not appear in those of isolated males. However, copulation may have been responsible, rather than simple social stimulation alone. Various other findings of these kinds could be cited to show the importance to breeding of stimulation from other animals (see, also, Lehrman's experiments with the ringdove, discussed earlier in this chapter).

The specific environmental setting is important to breeding in many animals. Presence of water is necessary to mating in some amphibians and aquatic birds. Other features may include rocks and plants, as in the catfish, or a particular kind of nest in various birds and fish. Some animals establish a breeding area and mate only within this territory (Beach, 1951). A familiar environment, such as the home cage, is often found to be more conducive to rapid mating by male rats and cats. In strange surroundings, exploratory activity is apt to supervene (this is also true for going to sleep, eating, and other activities). Oestrus females of these species, however, are not as distracted from sexual behavior by strange surroundings as are the males. Males may also be conditioned to sexual behavior when it has taken place frequently in a given setting (see p. 196).

The foregoing brief account at least indicates the range of stimuli which may be involved in sexual behavior. Many details of the time and place for sexual behavior in human societies and several species of animals are provided by Ford and Beach (1951).

2. *Stimuli arising from the partner.* Beach (1951, pp. 391–396) has reviewed the contribution of chemical, tactile, auditory, and visual stimulation to sexual attraction and mating behavior in insects, fish, amphibians, reptiles, and birds, and many examples can be found in his presentation. Suffice it to say here that stimuli of all of these types provided by the partner are often critical to the occurrence of attraction and to the execution of mating behavior (see Chapter 3). In many instances, the sequence of movements in actual courtship or mating is dependent on the occurrence of stimuli from the mate. Without this stimulation, the pattern does not occur or is interrupted (and perhaps started over).

In higher animals, too, stimulation contributes to sexual arousal and to the initiation and continuation of the mating pattern. The oestrus female rat, cat, or dog can arouse a male's interest in her, very probably through chemical as well as other stimulation. In the rat, various features of a female's behavior, such as running and hopping, increase the male's arousal. Oral stimulation of the male's genitals may occur. The male, too, stimulates the female, by oral and tactile stimulation of her genitalia, by palpating, mounting, and biting her, etc. Ford and Beach (1951) have provided an account of sexual stimulation in a number of animal species as well as in a variety of human societies. The Kinsey reports (Kinsey et al., 1948, 1953) afford descriptions of stimulative practices in the United States and indicate variations with socio-economic class. For example, stimulation such as kissing, manipulation of the breast and genitals, and oral stimulation of the genitals occurs much more commonly in the higher socio-economic classes than it does in the lower ones.

Genital stimulation is very common in animals. As just noted, it occurs frequently in humans, too, but two other types of human stimulation, kissing and manipulation of the female breast, hardly ever occur in animals, nor do there seem to be equivalents or analogues in animals. There are also some human societies in which neither kissing nor breast stimulation takes place. Grooming behavior occurs frequently in primates and in preliterate human societies. No doubt fancy and revealing dress, perfumes, and other sorts of self-grooming, and all sorts of self-adornment and efforts at physical development, serve the same functions of stimulation in literate and more highly technological societies.

In summary, stimulation afforded to one another by the sexual partners occurs in many, perhaps all, species of animals and, perhaps, in the vast majority of human beings. It seems to initiate and augment sexual arousal, and to guide the sequence of courting and mating activities, especially when the role of experience in sexual behavior is limited.

There is some evidence, also, that reduction in sexuality after ejaculation by the male may be overcome by substituting for the previous mate a new one. This finding has been reported for the rooster (Skard, 1936), guinea pig (Grunt & Young, 1952), monkey (Carpenter, 1942), rat (Fisher, 1962, Fowler & Whalen, 1961, but see Larsson, 1956), and bull (Almquist & Hale, 1956). It is tempting to entertain a stimulus satiation or habituation explanation for this fact and to argue that a fresh stimulus can overcome reduced sexual interest. It may be, however, that unresponsiveness on the part of the female immediately after copulation with a given male is the reason. This is suggested by data reported by Peirce and Nuttal (1961). In their apparatus there was an escape box which the males had been conditioned to avoid but which the female could enter. They found that, after a male had ejaculated with her, the female rat would spend more time in the escape box than otherwise. The mechanisms involved in this finding, however, are not known.

3. Reduction of sensory stimulation. From what has just been said, it follows that reduction in stimulation should impair sexual behavior to some degree. Beach (1942*b*) reared male rats in isolation from the age of 21 days until testing, so that they were sexually inexperienced. At about three months of age, sensory deficits were imposed by destroying the olfactory bulbs, removing the eyes, sectioning sensory nerves serving the snout, lips and lower jaw, or frequent clipping of the vibrissae. Multiple operations were performed in some of these animals, that is, some were made both blind and anosmic, or blind and insensitive in the mouth region, or anosmic and orally insensitive, and some were made blind, anosmic, and insensitive in the mouth region. Copulation frequency in these inexperienced males was somewhat reduced by one sensory deficit, and they did not attempt copulation if they had two or more sensory deficits. Sexually experienced males, on the other hand, continued to copulate with either one or two sensory deficits but not when three senses were eliminated. These results suggest that stimulation is important to sexual arousal but that experience can compensate, to some extent, for inadequate sensory input. Comparable investigations do not seem to have been made with higher species.

Other Drives and Diet. The presence of other drives, such as hunger and thirst, may interfere with sexual behavior due to debility (see Chapter 5, section on drive interaction). Beach (1956, p. 3, fn.) suggests that drives important to individual survival may take precedence over such a species-relevant drive as sex, when they conflict. This statement is supported by experiments reported by Tsai (1925) and by Stone and Ferguson (1938). They studied choices made by male rats over a series of tests (extending for a number of days) in a T-maze. One choice led to food, the other to a sex object. In both experiments, the food turn was chosen more often than the sex turn. In the Stone and Ferguson experiment, this was especially true in the early trials but less so later on. Further study is perhaps required before a definitive statement can be made.

Stone (1924*a*, *b*, 1925) found that age of initial copulation was influenced by diet. A poor or inadequate diet delayed the appearance of copulation, a very good one accelerated it. More analytic information on the character of the items in the diets responsible for retardation and acceleration would be desirable. However, we have already observed that good general health and adequate hormonal functioning in the case of extragonadal endocrines are essential to normal sexual behavior, even though they have no specific role in relation to sexual behavior.

Dominance Relations. Social relations, especially dominance, are found to interact with sexual behavior. This is true in two ways. A dominant male may, where appropriate conditions prevail, arrogate to himself alone sexual privileges with the females available, even when other males are present. The other aspect is that nondominant animals will often assume sexual postures with respect to the dominant one. The former case is not especially typical of animals, but it does occur. Baboons provide one instance. The dominant members of a group of baboons may possess all the females, and other, nondominant males, none. Females, however, may solicit the nondominant males when the dominant male is otherwise preoccupied (Ford & Beach, 1951).

Female sexual postures may be assumed by nondominant males apparently in order to prevent aggression by dominant males. Females, also, are likely to mate with dominant males when they are not in oestrus, if, by mating, they can forestall attack or, perhaps, obtain food (Ford & Beach, 1951; Crawford, 1939). These statements apply primarily to primates, although they are not unknown in infraprimate animals. Parallels can be found in humans, too, as in the submission of a wife (without desire) to the sexual advances of her husband, *droit du seigneur*, etc.

Age. We have already seen that sex play is common in prepuberal males of subprimate mammalians and is found in both sexes among the primates. Full sex behavior does not occur until puberty, and there is evidently a period of adolescent sterility (Ford & Beach, 1951), during which adult copulation can occur but with a limited probability of fertilization.

There are relatively few data on older animals other than man (Ford & Beach, 1951). Although there are wide individual differences at any age, Kinsey et al. (1948) report that erectile potency, frequency of orgasms, and other measures of sexual performance among American men decline steadily from adolescence to old age. Husbands who are less than 20 years of age report orgasms at a frequency of almost five a week, whereas in men in their sixties the average drops to 1.3 a week. In women, however, there is no comparable decline (Kinsey, et al., 1953) for several decades from the age of thirty.

Experience. Two generalizations are commonly made about the role of experience in the performance of mating activities (Ford & Beach, 1951, p. 195). One is that as one moves from lower to higher species the role of experience increases in importance. The other is that experience is more important to male behavior than to that of the female. Experience has been studied in relation to the performance of the copulatory pattern, the association of sexual behavior with particular places, inhibition of sexual activity, and the development of preferences for particular mates.

Beach (1951, p. 407) summarizes evidence that experience is at least necessary for the male to limit his activity to a receptive female in cichlid fish, blackbirds, doves, and bulls. Neither selection of appropriate sex object nor practice in copulation is necessary to adequate sexual performance by rats of either sex (Stone, 1922, 1926; Beach, 1942c, 1958) or of dogs (Beach, 1951, p. 407). Zimbardo (1958), however, has reported findings in disagreement with those of Beach as to the role of experience in rats, and Young and his collaborators (Valenstein, Riss, & Young, 1955) find that experience is important to adequate mating in the guinea pig. M. Jenkins (1928) has reported that, depending on its duration, segregation of male and female rats reduced the tendency of the segregated animals to cross an electrified grid to an incentive object of the opposite sex.

In higher animals, observations, especially of primates, indicate that experience is essential to adequate mating behavior in the male (cf. Bingham, 1928; Yerkes & Elder, 1936). This is to a somewhat lesser extent true of female primates (Beach, 1951). The occurrence of sex instruction in many societies (and the wealth of books and other materials on sexual behavior in the United States, for example) is evidence that, in the human, experience is very important to adequate mating, in both sexes. Some sex instruction is devoted to attitudes toward sex, rather than to details of performance, and this may be especially true in restrictive societies, like that of the United States.

Male animals often will not breed in unfamiliar places (Beach, 1951), but this is not so true of females. Familiarity of the situation is, of course, important to many other activities as well, such as sleeping and eating. Punishment, frustration, and pain associated with sexual experience may lead to suppression of sexual behavior in animals (Beach, 1951), and anxiety, shame, and guilt undoubtedly suppress sexual behavior in human societies which regard sexual behavior as sinful. As noted earlier, if copulation has occurred repeatedly in a particular place, male rats, when placed there again, will attempt to copulate with males or with nonreceptive females, indicating that sexual arousal has been conditioned to that location (Beach, 1942b). Similar findings have been reported for other species.

For a number of species, there is evidence of conditioning of sexual behavior to specific partners, or, at least, to partners which resemble a past one or ones (Beach, 1951). This is reported more often for males than for females.

In summary, it can be seen that experience can contribute to sexual behavior in a variety of ways. Beach (1951, p. 410) has cautioned that broad generalizations as to the role of experience are dangerous, because of species variations. Nevertheless, for the human, he very clearly indicates the enormous role of learning, and speaks, for the human and perhaps for other species, not of sexual *drive* but rather sexual *appetite* (Beach, 1956). The use of the word appetite, as we noted earlier, suggests the role of experience in making sexual arousal occur in particular places and under the influence of external stimuli. It is to be contrasted here with the word drive, which implies major and inevitable determination by internal factors, set into operation mainly by duration of deprivation.

Theoretical Sexual Mechanisms. The most complete statement we have encountered which attempts a theoretical integration of sexual behavior is the one made by Beach (1956) for sexual behavior in the male rat. Beach suggests that copulatory behavior in this species requires the successive activation of two excitatory mechanisms, the *sexual arousal mechanism* (SAM), and the *intromission and ejaculatory mechanism* (IEM).[31] The argument is that in sexual behavior there is first the necessity for sexual arousal. When this occurs, intromission can be achieved and copulation can begin. These processes are the functions of SAM. Intromission and copulation then provide new or additional sources of stimulation so that the animal passes the ejaculation threshold and ejaculates.

Beach points out that the inexperienced male, on being placed with a receptive female, first engages in investigation of the female, especially of her anogenital region, her head, and her ears. The female's response to this is a pseudo-retreat, which is usually followed by prompt pursuit and further investigation on the part of the male. If, however, the male does not follow, the female approaches the male and may investigate his genitalia. If the male shows interest, the pseudo-retreat then occurs again. A further part of the female's behavior, usually elicited by the male's mounting her, is the lordosis response. In this, the female's back is bent concavely, elevating the hind parts. The tail moves aside, exposing the genitalia. This may be followed by intromission and pelvic thrusts on the part of the male.

Beach sees these events as increasing the male's excitement so that he can begin to copulate. The investigation of the female's body, her response, her stimulation of the male all contribute to this process. Not

[31] Division of sexual behavior into two stages, or two drives, has been proposed before. See Beach (1956, p. 19) and Young (1961*b*, p. 1178) for references. This division has been suggested for species other than the rat, and including the human.

all inexperienced males take long to begin copulation, but some do. Beach implies that in experienced males some of these stimulational phases can be short-circuited, probably because of the association between arousal responses and stimuli from the female or from the (familiar) situation. It should be emphasized that these processes are seen to *bring about* sexual arousal. While the male may be rested and physiologically ready for sexual behavior, Beach does not consider the animal, without stimulation of the kinds already described, to be sexually "driven" (there is a certain parallel between this account and the ethologists' notion of releasing mechanisms). Sexual drive (or "appetite") is a result of appropriate *stimulation* in the rested, normal animal. Beach (1956, p. 27) thinks the same analysis to be applicable to the human male. However, in this case, the role of symbolic stimuli in arousal is pronounced, and arousal can occur from thinking about sex. In the human, also, the SAM, itself, may be more labile in respect to the effects of experience on it than is the case with the rodent.

When the male rat is placed with a receptive female, copulation is unlikely to occur at all unless it takes place within five to ten minutes of the beginning of the interaction. This suggests that SAM is subject to habituation in the situation over time.

After ejaculation, there is a refractory period, during which sexual responsiveness is not present. Whether this refractory period should be conceived in terms of changes in SAM or in some other mechanism cannot be decided at present (Beach, 1956, p. 23).

The IEM is suggested because, in the rat, a number of intromissions are necessary before ejaculation. The typical sequence is for the male rat to mount the female, execute a few copulatory thrusts, dismount (with a backward lunge), engage in genital licking, remount, and repeat the process. During one of these sequences, ejaculation occurs (and the backward lunge does not take place). The intromissions, Beach points out, may serve to increase excitement, or, alternatively, to maintain it for the *time* required for ejaculation to occur. There is evidence that time is the critical factor (Beach, 1956, p. 25).

The intromissions are necessary to ejaculation, as males do not ejaculate, although they attempt copulation, with females whose vaginas are closed (Kaufman, 1953). However, if mating is interrupted after each intromission, fewer copulations are required for ejaculation than otherwise (Beach & Jordan, 1956b). This is consistent with time of excitement, rather than number of intromissions, as the important variable in leading to ejaculation. There is evidence (Beach, 1956, p. 26) that the excitatory effect of a single intromission may last, in the rat, for as long as five minutes but not so long as ten minutes.

As we indicated, ejaculation temporarily reduces sexual responsiveness. However, when the animal starts mating again, fewer intromissions and less time are needed to achieve ejaculation than were required before (Beach & Jordan, 1956*b*). Repeated ejaculations progressively increase the sexual refractory period. That is to say, as noted before, that copulatory latency (SAM) increases whereas ejaculation time (IEM) decreases with successive ejaculations. No explanation for this difference is at hand.

Beach proposes these mechanisms quite tentatively for the male rat and suggests that other species may require additional processes. Beach's analysis can plausibly be extended to other species, as, for example, to the human male, however, until alternative or better accounts are developed. Very important, in our opinion, is the emphasis Beach's formulation places on stimulation. This permits the inference that learned sources of sexual arousal can be significant in many species, especially the higher ones.

We have not encountered a parallel formulation for females. In lower animals, however, it appears to be true that sexual behavior occurs primarily when ovarian hormones are active, and an interpretation in terms of sensitization to certain stimuli is not out of the way. However, a detailed account of mechanisms involved in the sexual behavior of females must await further investigation.[32]

Summary of Sexual Behavior. Sex is commonly listed as a primary drive, but there are major differences between the circumstances and factors involved in sexual behavior and those responsible for hunger and thirst. Sexual behavior is catabolic, for example, whereas eating and drinking are anabolic.

A variety of factors are involved in the initiation and performance of sexual behavior. Among them, local stimulation or tension arising in the genitals has been found to be unnecessary for arousal and maintenance of sexual behavior, at least in sexually experienced organisms. Hormones of the anterior pituitary are significant to the development and activation of the gonads, and there is much evidence of the importance of the hormones of the testis (testosterone or androgen) and of the ovary (estrogen and progesterone) to the occurrence of sexual behavior in male and female animals, respectively, of many species. Administration of the pituitary or gonadal hormones is often followed by precocious sexual behavior in immature organisms, and it appears that the neuromuscular structures involved in mature sexual

---

[32] Other aspects of sexual behavior are noted in Chapter 3, and, as a drive, it is discussed briefly in Chapters 6 and 11. Psychoanalytic considerations of sex are treated in Chapter 12.

behavior are available and ready for energization by the appropriate gonadal hormones long before puberty. Removal of the pituitary or of the gonads, or their failure to function, prevents sexual development to a large extent, in most animals, including man. Sexual behavior may be evoked, out of season, and oestrus may be achieved in females, by hormone administration, and castrated adult and senile animals exhibit restoration of sexual function following hormone therapy. Castration reduces sexual behavior in adult animals, the effects being more rapid and complete in females than in males. The effects of hormonal administration and of castration are less pronounced in higher than in lower animals, and the differences between the sexes in respect to hormonal control of sexual behavior are reduced in the primates, especially in man.

The evidence suggests that the cerebral cortex is important to sexual behavior, especially in males of many species. The cortex is generally less important to mating behavior in the female, and cortical involvement increases as we move from lower to higher species. This greater cortical involvement permits experience and social factors to play important roles in the sexual behavior of higher species and perhaps replaces, to some degree, the hormonal control so dominant in lower species.

The measurement of sexual behavior can be achieved in a number of ways, which, however, are not entirely equivalent. Deprivation of sexual activity does not affect sexual activity much, at least after the immediate effects of copulation have passed (in the male). In seasonally mating species and in females with sex cycles, deprivation is not a factor.

General environmental stimulation is important to the physiological preparation of many animals for sexual behavior, and stimuli from the mate play a very significant part in the initiation and execution of the copulatory pattern. There is evidence that, through experience, sexual arousal may be conditioned to places and partners, and maximal stimulation may be less important to the experienced than to the inexperienced organism. The presence of other drives, adequacy of diet, and age are all influential to sexual behavior. In general experience assumes a greater place in the sexual behavior of males than of females, and of higher species than of lower species.

The theory of sexual mechanisms is not far advanced, but Beach has proposed that, in the male rat, two mechanisms are involved, the sexual arousal mechanism, which leads to copulation, and the intromission and ejaculatory mechanism, which leads to ejaculation. Stimulation is important to the activation of these mechanisms, and they have some independence of each other. In a general way, Beach's account may be appropriate to males of other species, but theoretical analyses of mechanisms in female sex behavior have not come to our attention.

GENERAL SUMMARY

In this chapter, various bodily conditions relevant to motivation were considered. Several of these conditions are sometimes classified as "instinctive"; they have seldom been studied in the laboratory in relation to the general energization of behavior or to reinforcement.

Maternal activities include nest building, behavior during birth, retrieving and suckling the young, and the factor of maternal contact with the young. Nesting behavior, where it occurs, is not restricted to animals which are to bear young, but it appears prominently in such animals. Heat regulation seems to be the major basis for the instigation of this activity, and experience does not seem to affect it much, in the species which have been studied. Behavior during parturition occurs without training or experience in infrahuman animals but, in the human, many aspects of it are responsive to attitudes and training. A number of animals retrieve their young, and this behavior is apparently influenced by the hormonal condition of the mother, as well as by characteristics of the objects provided for her to retrieve. Sucking behavior has been investigated chiefly with respect to the question whether there is a sucking need or drive in the young which is independent of nutritional intake. Present evidence suggests that there is an independent sucking need in dogs but that in the human sucking derives its impetus from associations with feeding behavior. There is evidence that contact with the mother, such as is provided by tactile and other stimulation, is important to infant monkeys but, also, that it is not sufficient, in itself alone, to permit the appearance of normal social and sexual relationships in later life. Contact with peers, however, is followed by normal social and sexual behavior.

Maternal behavior in lower animals seems primarily to occur under hormonal control, but it is subject to influence by neural defects and stimulus variables. The maternal "drive" is not a simple, unitary affair. Work with the ringdove has brought out the importance of social stimulation to maternal or parental behavior.

Hoarding is an activity which occurs in a number of animals. There is question as to its instinctive status, whether it is learned, or whether it arises in response to stress. Hoarding has been studied in relation to such variables as food deprivation, infantile frustration, experience, and others, but the available literature provides no clear answers to most of the questions that have been asked about hoarding.

Homing and migration are activities which may be or are set off by motivational variables. This is especially true of migration. The occurrence of migratory excursions seems to be related to activity in the gonads, themselves under the control of the anterior pituitary. Temperature and amount of daylight contribute to changes in the pituitary which ultimately result in migrations. The navigational aspect of homing and migration has received a good deal of study. Training is often involved in homing, but it is not sufficient, alone, to account for all instances. Navigation in migrations, according to present notions, makes use of the position of the sun during the day and of information from stellar constellations at night. Learning does not seem to be a factor in the navigational feats of migration.

Temperature regulation, respiration, and elimination are often seen as motivated activities, but the available literature on their behavioral effects is limited.

Fatigue is a term with many meanings, and there is little agreement as to the meaning it should have or how it should be measured. Involved in it are factors ranging from central neurochemical activating and depressing mechanisms to local neuromuscular conditions. These evidently are normally in balance, and disturbance of the balance leads to symptoms of fatigue. Fatigue is an aversive condition, which individuals learn to anticipate and to avoid.

Inhibition is discussed because of its importance in the conditioned response literature and because Hull's notion of reactive inhibition was conceived as a negative motive. It is clear that inhibitory processes are essential to coordinated and integrated behavior. Pavlov's theories of inhibition were advanced to explain extinction and related phenomena and were extended to a theory of sleep. Hull's notions of reactive inhibition and conditioned inhibition were likewise tied closely to such topics as extinction and spontaneous recovery. Neither of these theories seems satisfactory any longer, and it is likely that a central inhibitory process will emerge from current and future neurobehavioral research.

Sleep is often mentioned as a drive, but attempts to find a sleep "substance," or a characteristic blood deficiency, or sleep centers in the brain have not been successful. Rather, sleep seems to be related to interactions of excitation and inhibition in the reticular formation, involving feedback circuits from both the cortex and the medulla. The ratio of sleep to waking time is about 1:2 in the adult, this ratio emerging during development. Sleep is an active, restorative state, but its exact functions cannot be specified. Deprivation of sleep leads to degradation of performance and difficulty in staying awake. Many factors govern sleep, such as habituation and sociocultural factors, so that while it may be a drive the relationship between sleep deprivation and the behavior it is said to motivate is neither clear nor simple.

Sexual behavior is often regarded as arising from a primary drive, but there is reason to question its classification as comparable to hunger or thirst. Stimulation from local sources, such as the genital organs, does not seem essential to the maintenance of sexual behavior in experienced organisms, but, especially in lower animals, hormonal control is highly significant. Gonadal hormones appear to be essential to sexual behavior in many animals, but their importance is much reduced in higher animals, such as the chimpanzee. In man, gonadal hormone control is limited if it exists at all, at least in the adult. In general, hormonal control is more definite in the female than in the male, though this sex difference appears to be reduced in the highest animals. The hormones of the anterior pituitary, often implicated in sexual behavior, seem to have their effects through the stimulation of the gonads; the hormones of the gonads energize the neuromuscular structures of sexual behavior, these structures being ready for action long before puberty. Females of many species can mate satisfactorily in the absence of the cerebral cortex, but most males require some intact cortical tissue for arousal to sexual activity.

Sexual behavior can be measured in a number of ways, but the methods do not seem to be mutually equivalent. While sexual activity requires a period for recovery, deprivation as such does not seem to be related to sexual motivation in the male. In animals that mate seasonally or in females that display oestrus cycles deprivation is perhaps not related to sexual activity at all. Stimulation, arising both from the general environment and from the sexual partner, is of great importance to the arousal and execution of sexual behavior, but experienced animals require somewhat less stimulation than do naive ones. Other drives, diet, social relations, age, and past experience have, in one species or another, been found to influence sexual behavior.

The theory of sexual behavior is not far advanced, but, in the male at least, it may involve two mechanisms. One, the sexual arousal mechanism, must be engaged in order for copulation to be initiated. The other, the intromission and ejaculation mechanism, is responsible for ejaculation and seems to require a certain time of excitation before it can pass the ejaculation threshold.

Chapter 5

Bodily Conditions: II

Although the drive concept is often used in relation to maternal and sexual behavior and the other bodily conditions described in the last chapter, it has been employed most frequently in conjunction with hunger and thirst. Hunger and thirst are the states most commonly induced in the laboratory in studies of learning, and the study of motivation in animals has usually been directed to hunger and thirst. Much of our thought about motivation has been based on models of hunger and thirst, especially hunger.

This chapter is devoted to a review of hunger and thirst. It considers histories, theories, and the many factors which, aside from deprivation itself, influence food and water intake. We have also included here a section on pain avoidance. This has been done because drive theorists have predicated much of their treatment of acquired motivation on pain avoidance. The studies of acquired drive will be reviewed in Chapter 11, and the material in this chapter concerns some of the basic facts about pain itself.

HUNGER

In hunger, as with thirst, there is some confusion as to what the word "hunger" denotes. There are at least three possibilities. One is to consider hunger as a sensation; that is, when people say they are hungry they are, in effect, reporting that they have an experience (a "pang," for example) in the abdominal region. Such an experience is often described as unpleasant. A second meaning is indicated by the word "appetite." This means that one wishes to eat and has a positive anticipation of enjoying food. The experience of appetite is usually described as pleasant, and it may exist, for example, with reference to the dessert which is to follow an ample meal. These two meanings usually refer to the experience of human beings, although food ingestion and preference based on palatability factors may allow the inference of appetite in animals. However, we also speak of hunger in a

204

third sense, that is, the fact that animals (and humans) eat and engage in activities leading to eating after food has not been taken for some time. The hunger "drive," for example, is usually indexed by duration of food deprivation, and, of course, there is a general relationship between the duration of deprivation and the amount and rate of eating. Human subjects also will eat on a basis of deprivation (as in eating three meals a day), even in the absence of reported hunger or appetite. Habituation factors, as well as deprivation, are involved, but it is fair to say that experienced hunger and appetite are not essential to eating. In no case can we legitimately say, for animals, that eating occurs on the basis of experienced hunger and appetite, since verbal reports are necessary evidence for the identification of such experiences.

Hunger, appetite, and eating (especially after deprivation) are words which may denote the same or different processes. It is well to keep the distinctions just described in mind, in order to avoid unnecessary confusions (see Rosenzweig, 1962, pp. 76–77).

Early Theories and Observations

Hunger in all of its meanings has probably been known since the dawn of human experience—Plato, Aristotle, and Galen wrote about it and offered specific hypotheses as to the nature of experienced hunger. Serious considerations of hunger, however, by physiologists began with Albrecht von Haller who wrote, 200 years ago, that hunger arises from "the grinding or rubbing of the delicate and villoid folds of the gastric mucosa against each other . . ." and that "the naked villi of the nerves on the one side (of the stomach) grate against those of the other, after a manner almost intolerable" (quoted by Boring, 1942, pp. 553–554). This vivid description obviously applies to experienced hunger; it is a *local* and *peripheral* theory, ascribing to the stomach itself the processes which underlie experienced hunger. Carlson (1916) distinguishes six and Boring (1942) five such peripheral theories of the origin of hunger which differ in the specific nature of the local processes in the stomach postulated to account for it.[1]

Magendie offered an alternative view in 1817, holding (Boring, 1942, p. 552; Carlson, 1916, p. 20) that hunger arises from a general depletion of tissues that affects the nervous system and the brain. This view is usually known as one of the theories of the *central origin* of hunger, and it de-emphasizes the role of stomach contractions. A third type of theory, similar to the central origin theory, stresses the role of afferent stimulation from all the organs of the body. This stimulation indirectly affects a hunger center in the brain on which, in addition,

[1] Cf., also, Cannon (1929, 1934) and Rosenzweig (1962).

some change in the blood exerts a direct influence. This third class (Carlson, 1916, p. 21) is known as the view that hunger is "a *general sensation.*" Boring has indicated that experienced hunger seems to correspond to the ideas of the peripheral theories, whereas appetite and drive meanings of hunger are perhaps more consistent with emphasis on central origins.

Empirical work with gastric processes was initially concerned mainly with the effects of severing the vagus and the splanchnic nerves, which innervate the stomach. In 1829 Sedillat (Boring, 1942, p. 552) severed the vagi in animals without eliminating eating, and other investigators thereafter confirmed these findings for section of the vagi as well as for section of the splanchnics and the taste nerves (Carlson, 1916, pp. 22–23). Sectioning of these nerves changes the activity of the stomach to some extent and also prevents the afferent consequences of stomach action from reaching higher neural centers. Hunger, however, persists. This would seem to rule out stomach activity (local or peripheral theory) as an important factor, and such cases as that reported in 1858 by Busch seem to contradict this theory further. Busch studied a woman who had a fistula just below the duodenum, thus preventing entry of food to the intestine from the stomach (unless Busch connected them with a rubber tube). Even though her stomach was full of food, she experienced an intense desire for food, but there were no hunger "pangs" (Boring, 1942, p. 552).

Stomach Contractions and Hunger

That hunger arises "from strong contractions of the entirely empty stomach" (E. H. Weber, 1846, as quoted by Boring, 1942, p. 555) is a view, however, which persisted. The contractions were first studied extensively by Boldireff in 1905, in dogs, but it remained for Cannon and Washburn (1912) apparently to establish the relationship between the contractions and experienced hunger pangs.[2] As early as 1905, Cannon had observed, by listening with a stethoscope to his own abdominal sounds, that there were rhythmic noises associated with the pangs of hunger. Shortly thereafter, one of his associates, Washburn, trained himself to swallow a balloon that, located in the stomach, could be inflated; the contractions of the stomach, in compressing the balloon, forced air or water up a tube through the esophagus, and on relaxation of the stomach the balloon would fill again. A recording system enabled these oscillations of the pressure to be registered, thus making a record of the contractions of the stomach. Simultaneously,

[2] Rosenzweig (1962) has treated the history of theories and investigations of hunger and thirst more thoroughly than can be attempted here.

Washburn, who could not see the record of his stomach contractions, registered his hunger pangs by pressing a key, causing a mark to be made on the record with that of the stomach contractions. It was noted that a hunger pang was usually recorded after contraction took place (Cannon and Washburn, 1912).

These observations were extended and confirmed by other workers (cf. Carlson, 1916; Cannon, 1929, p. 293), so that Cannon (1929, 1934, 1939) felt quite confident that the stomach contraction was the basis of the experienced pang of hunger. This led him to think of hunger as a spur or drive to action. In characterizing both hunger and thirst, he argued: "If the requirements of the body are not met . . . hunger pangs and thirst arise as powerful, persistent and tormenting stimuli which imperiously demand the ingestion of food and water before they will cease their goading" (Cannon, 1939, p. 76). Cannon admitted that the explanation of how the stomach contractions were initiated, regulated, and terminated was not known, but he was sure that the pangs of hunger arose from the contractions and that this was a satisfactory conception of the hunger state.

Carlson, in a long series of experiments (see Carlson, 1916), fully confirmed these observations by Cannon and Washburn, both by studies on himself and his associates, on a case with a stomach fistula, in animals, and on newborn human infants. Carlson, however, was aware that there are aspects of the hunger experience which transcend the pang itself and that food-seeking may not depend on the contractions.[3] We shall not follow further the extensive literature on the characteristics and conditions of contractions of the stomach, except to point out that Carlson (1916, pp. 40–41) reported full-blown stomach contractions by means of the balloon method in newborn human infants before they had nursed. Carlson stated that these contractions are like those found in adults, except for a greater frequency of occurrence in the infants than in older people. The sleeping infant would sometimes be awakened by very vigorous contractions, and the waking infant often responded to strong contractions by restlessness and crying.

There can be little question that contractions of the stomach provide a basis for the report of hunger and probably for the "drive" of hunger.

---

[3] For a further review of investigations concerning gastric contractions, see Patterson (1933) and Quigley (1955). That duodenal motility is also involved in the experience of hunger is stressed by Quigley (1955, pp. 10–17). It has been argued that with a balloon inserted in it, the stomach is not empty. Davis, Garafalo, & Kveim (1959) recorded gastric activity electrically. They found that the empty stomach was quiescent and that activity increased while a balloon was located in the "empty" stomach.

Prevailing opinion, however, as well as many observations from the past, would insist that the gastric contractions by no means provide an adequate basis for hunger experiences. There are several lines of evidence to which we shall now turn.

Evidence Contrary to the Dependence of Hunger on Gastric Contractions [4]

There are certain general observations which do not fit well into the local theory of hunger as being dependent on gastric contractions. Some of these we mentioned earlier. Others that come to mind are provided by animals which go for extended intervals without eating, as in hibernation. Certain salmon go without food for long periods during their spawning migrations (Carlson, 1916), and the bull seal does not eat during his prolonged period of sexual excitement (Hoelzel, 1927). A number of birds are known not to eat while incubating their young. Among penguins, for example, the incubating Emperor male penguin fasts for about two months, and the male Adelie penguin about six weeks (Gilliard, 1958). Gilliard further observes that ". . . there are records of penguins going without food for nearly four months . . ." (Gilliard, 1958, p. 17). It is true that all these fasts occur in association with other activities, but it would seem reasonable to assume that, in such cases, gastric motility, if it occurs, is unable to dominate the organism's behavior. Carlson, too, has pointed out that many insects never eat after their final metamorphosis despite doing a great deal of work (Carlson, 1916); he also observes that herbivorous and ruminating animals eat, even though their stomachs are never empty. In general, we can conclude that duration of food deprivation is not a perfect predictor of food-seeking and consuming activities. Further, stomach contractions often cease with the sight of food, with swallowing, or when the first bite reaches the stomach (Carlson, 1916), yet eating and hunger continue.

Tsang (1938) successfully removed 90 to 95 per cent of the stomachs of seven rats and, after recovery, tested them on maze learning to a food reward and on activity as measured by a revolving cage. He found them to learn and to be active in relation to hunger, more or less, as are normal rats. However, Tsang did find hunger motivation in his animals to be reduced by very small amounts of food, and he did not consider his results to be inconsistent with the local theory. Bash (1939a) de-afferented the stomachs of his male rat subjects, so that gastric activity could not stimulate other parts of the nervous

[4] Findings concerning specific hunger, often considered to contraindicate the local theory of hunger, will be reviewed in a later section of this chapter.

system. He tested his animals for activity, for going to food by gnaw-ing through a cardboard obstruction, and for maze learning. The rats continued to eat, and their obstruction box and maze scores were equal to those of the unoperated control animals. Bash did find one differ-ence. The operated animals showed a decline in the frequency with which activity increases preceded feeding time, whereas the control group continued to show maximal activity at this time. Bash believed his results showed that food-getting responses were *learned* "on pri-mary basis of reflex response to gustatory and random responses to visceral stimuli" (Bash, 1939*b*, p. 157); Cannon and Washburn (1912, p. 443) had offered a similar interpretation for the persistence of food-related behavior following elimination of the effects of gastric stimula-tion.

Morgan and Morgan (1940) vagotomized their rats and then in-jected them with insulin, which normally induces food-taking. The vagotomized animals showed this effect; that is, insulin injection caused their food intake to increase, although, because of the vagotomy, this increase could not have been due to the effects of increase in gastric activity. Similar results were obtained with dogs by Grossman, Cum-mins, and Ivy (1947).

Two observations may be made here. The experiments by Tsang and Bash certainly indicate that food-related activities will *continue* without the gastric stimulation. It must be remembered, however, that the animals in these experiments were experienced in eating: it is possible that because of experience cues other than gastric ones were able to take over the role of regulating food-related behavior (a dis-cussion of consummatory behavior follows). On the other hand, the experiments by the Morgans and by Grossman et al. clearly point to fac-tors other than gastric activity in the regulation of food intake. What such factors may be is suggested by a study made with human subjects, who had been vagotomized for peptic ulcer (Grossman & Stein, 1948).

Insulin was administered to these patients postoperatively, and after a fifteen hour fast, the patients answered the question, "How do you feel?"

Most of the patients reported hunger after insulin, though there were no gastric contractions (due to the vagotomy). Hunger con-sisted of a sensation of emptiness in the abdomen, or "all-over," and of weakness and desire for food. Grossman and Stein (1948, p. 265) make this interesting observation: "Most of the patients did not recognize any alteration in the character of their hunger sensations as a result of vagotomy." They further suggest that the kinds of hunger phenomena just mentioned are perhaps more common than the epigastric pang that is associated with the contractions and which was emphasized by Cannon. Carlson (1916) referred to these phenomena of emptiness as being accessory, but they may be what led to the notion of hunger as "a general sensation."

Chemical, Mechanical, and Oral Factors in Hunger

The control of the hunger mechanism, whatever the functional significance of the stomach contractions, is a problem which has engaged the attention of workers for many years. Several possibilities have been explored; among them are suggested hormones, blood-sugar level (as regulated by fasting and eating or by insulin), the bulk, and caloric value of foods. Stimulation of the mouth and throat also seems important. Neural factors have recently received much stress, and their importance is such as to lead us to devote the next major section to them and to the recent theories of hunger, which have largely developed through their study.

Hunger Hormone

Many years ago, Luckhardt and Carlson (1914) transfused blood from dogs that had been starved for several days, or from dogs with pancreatic diabetes, into normal dogs. They found that, if at the time of transfusion the stomach of the recipient animal was showing some tonus and some contractions, these contractions were much augmented to the point of virtual tonus by the transfusion. This effect lasted from 10 to 30 minutes. However, there was "practically" no effect if at the time of transfusion the recipient dog's stomach was atonic and if contractions were absent. "Starved blood," then, appeared to augment though not to initiate stomach contractions, and Luckhardt and Carlson suggested that a "hunger hormone" might be involved. Bash (1939b) cited an experiment by Tschukitscheff in which the reverse effect was observed; that is, "satisfied blood" was found to quiet the stomach contractions in a hungry dog.[5]

[5] These results have been questioned by Siegel, on the basis of two more recent experiments. Siegel and Taub (1952) injected rats intraperitoneally with blood serum from either normal (not hungry) or from hungry (24 hours' deprivation) donor rats. In the second experiment (Siegel & Dorman, 1954), essentially the same procedure was used save that the recipient animals drank the serum of the hungry or normal donor rats. In the first experiment the recipient rats were food-deprived for 4 hours before the injections and in the second experiment the animals were deprived of food and water for 24 hours prior to drinking the donors' serum. Shortly after the injections or the drinking, a record was made of eating over a 2-hour interval. No differences were observed in the food intake of the differently

A number of experiments have been conducted in which a part of the stomach has been transplanted to another part of the body, with blood supply intact but with nerves severed (see Quigley, 1955, p. 11, for summary). Such pouches show motility in relatively close correspondence with that of the remaining main stomach. These experiments suggest that a blood factor can initiate the stomach contractions, but nothing is yet known of the nature of this factor. A hormone, enterogastrone, secreted by the mucosa of the upper small intestine when this region is stimulated by quantities of fat or sugar from the stomach, is apparently capable of inhibiting contractions of the stomach (Quigley, 1955, p. 13; Grossman, 1950). Janowitz and Grossman (1951) suggest that enterogastrone does not contribute to satiety directly but delays gastric emptying, thus postponing the onset of hunger.

Blood Sugar

Another variable which is a logical candidate for the role of the blood factor involved in hunger is the concentration of sugar in the blood. This factor has been studied in three ways: by measurement of blood sugar levels during fasting and in association with reports of hunger or recording of stomach contractions; by inducing hypoglycemia through the administration of insulin and observing effects on reported hunger, stomach contractions, or food intake; and by setting up a hyperglycemic condition and studying similar effects.

In normal fasting men the blood-sugar level does not vary much, if any, from prefasting levels, at least over the durations of fasts studied, and there are no relationships between manifest variations and the occurrence either of stomach contractions or of reported hunger (Scott, Scott, and Luckhardt, 1938; Quigley, 1955, p. 12). On the other hand, injections of insulin, which produce a reduction in blood sugar (hypoglycemia), will lead apparently to reported hunger, increased food consumption, and gastric-motility (cf. Quigley, 1955, pp. 12–13; Grossman, 1955, pp. 82–88). We have already seen that this effect of insulin

treated animals in either experiment, so the existence of a hunger hormone is questioned by the authors.

The detailed description of the procedure used by Siegel and his coworkers indicates that there were many procedural variations between these experiments and the one by Luckhardt and Carlson. It is therefore not possible to conclude that their experiment invalidates the findings of Luckhardt and Carlson. In addition, one may question whether their techniques of injecting blood serum intraperitoneally or of having it drunk by the recipient animals is a satisfactory method of testing for the existence of a hormone.

on manifestations of hunger is not dependent on gastric activity [6] (pp. 209–211).

The administration of sugar, either to restore the blood-sugar level in the blood following the induction of insulin hypoglycemia or to establish a hyperglycemic condition, has yielded conflicting results (Grossman, 1955, pp. 80–82). Some experimenters have shown that reduced hunger, reduced food intake, or diminished gastric contractions follow this procedure; others show the procedure does not affect these measures.

It is not possible to reach a satisfactory conclusion as to the role of blood-sugar in the phenomena of hunger on the basis of the present evidence. Except for the effects of insulin injection, the results conflict. We shall encounter this problem again later, in the context of the glucostatic theory of hunger.

Drugs

Various drugs have been studied in relation to measures of hunger, in addition to insulin. Phlorhizin reduces blood-sugar level, but it depresses stomach contractions and reduces the desire for food (Quigley & Lindquist, 1930). The amphetamines (S. C. Harris, 1955) seem to reduce food intake, probably by suppressing appetite, but the mechanism of the action of this drug group is not clear. However, central mechanisms have been suggested (see section on neural factors, following). Sangster, Grossman, and Ivy (1948) found that the motility in a denervated pouch was not affected by d-amphetamine sulfate, whereas activity in the stomach proper was diminished. This suggests that the drug's effects are mediated neurally.

The major inference we can draw from these drug studies is that local factors are insufficient to account for the effects seen in hunger phenomena.

Caloric Intake

When food is ingested, the contractions of the stomach cease (Carlson, 1916), and this is true at least briefly even when the food passes out of the animal's body through an esophageal fistula and tube rather than entering the stomach (Larber, Komarov, & Shay, 1950). It is of considerable interest to know the extent to which animals can regulate their food intake on the basis of their caloric need. This factor probably is not mediated by stomach contractions, which, as we have just seen, may cease with the first swallow. In normal dogs, Janowitz

[6] Bachrach (1953) has reviewed the effects of insulin hypoglycemia on motility and secretory activies of the gastric tract.

and Grossman (1949*a*) found that subsequent food intake was reduced appropriately if the animals were prefed a substantial part of their regular diet. This effect may, however, arise from the satisfaction of caloric need; from the distension in the stomach, which the food would produce; or from the factors of chewing, tasting, and swallowing. For

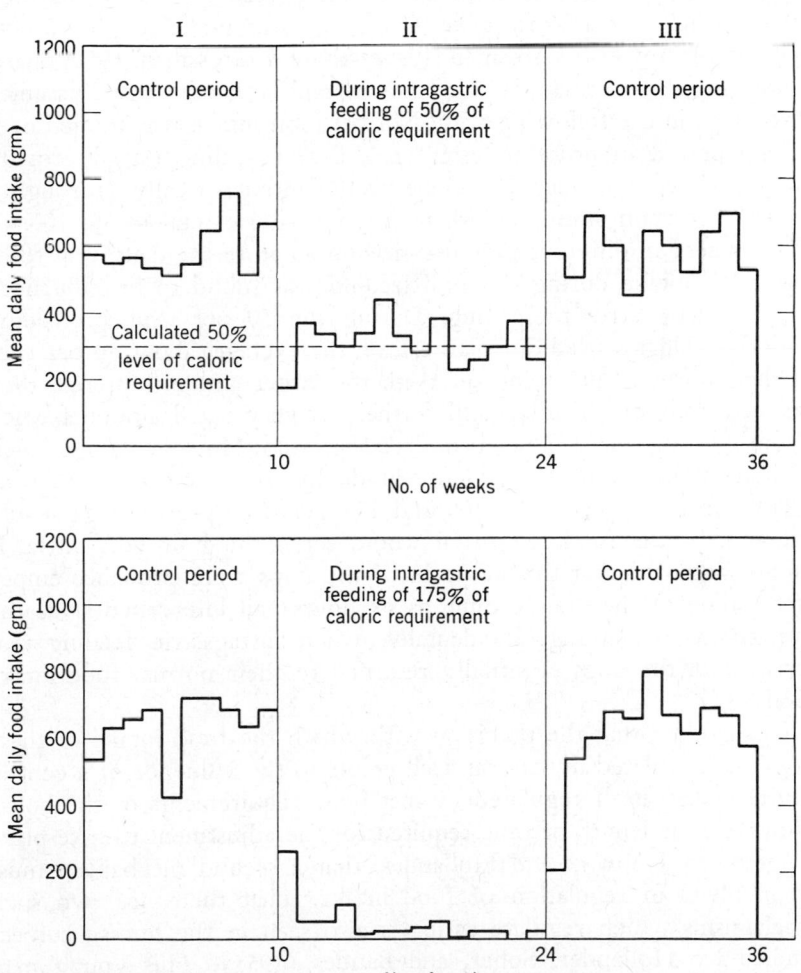

Figure 5–1. Oral food-intake in a dog during periods of intragastric feeding of either 50% or 175% of normal caloric intake. Note that some time is required for adjustment of oral feeding to intragastric feeding and to its cessation. Modified by permission from Janowitz and Hollander (1955, Figs. 1 and 3).

the moment, we shall limit ourselves to the first of these three effects.

Animals will increase the amount of food they take in when the food eaten has been diluted by the inclusion of calorically inert bulk, at least within limits (Janowitz & Grossman, 1949b). However, adjustment of food intake to caloric need is not made rapidly. Thus, when food is administered directly into the stomach, or otherwise into the body, it may take several weeks for the animal to reduce his food intake sufficiently so as to make his total caloric intake roughly a normal one (Janowitz & Grossman, 1949c; Share & Grossman, 1950; Share, Martyniuk, & Grossman, 1952). Janowitz and Hollander (1955) studied three dogs in the following way. Normal food intake was studied over a long period in order to establish a firm base line (steady for 10 weeks). Then the dogs would be prefed intragastrically (through a fistula) a certain amount of their average caloric intake—50, 100, or 175 per cent in different periods—six hours before the daily oral feeding. Food intake during this oral feeding was found to be influenced by the intragastric prefeeding. During the 50 per cent prefeeding period the dogs settled down to eat, on the average, about 50 per cent of their normal caloric intake. With the larger amounts prefed, they reduced their oral feeding still further, to very small amounts when the prefeeding was 175 per cent (see Fig. 5–1). However, these levels of oral intake were reached only gradually, requiring an average of 4.4 weeks to achieve. The 100 and 175 per cent prefed dogs would still sniff at the food but often would eat nothing or very little. It should be noted that the stomachs of the dogs were probably empty at the time of the oral feeding, as six hours had intervened since the intragastric prefeeding. Incidentally, when intragastric feeding was terminated, the dogs eventually returned to their normal food-intake levels.

It is evident that the precision with which the food intake of these dogs was regulated by caloric need points to the influence of a central neural factor, itself regulated by metabolic requirements of the body. However, the length of time required for the adjustment to take place suggests, to Janowitz and Hollander, that a second mechanism must be involved in regulation of food intake. That there are two such mechanisms which regulate eating is also seen in the human subject studied by Hollander, Sober, and Bandes (1955). This young man was fed through a jejunostomy (an opening in the middle section of the small intestine), because, while he could eat normally, he could not retain food. For a part of the period during which he was under observation, the oral intake of food seemed to vary with the caloric need left over from the jejunostomal feedings. Later, however, emotional disturbance, which was reflected in bulimia (excessive eating), upset this suggested relationship. This emotional disturbance perhaps reflects the second mechanism. A similar interpretation may, perhaps, be made of certain experiments by Miller and his co-workers.

Gastric Distension

In the normal organism, there are probably cues arising in the stomach which indicate that food has been eaten. We have already mentioned one such cue—the cessation of stomach contractions at the beginning of the processes involved in ingestion of food. Another cue that has been studied is gastric distension. Paintal (1954) has found fibers in the vagus nerve that are apparently activated by stimulation of stretch receptors in the smooth muscle of the stomach by distension of the stomach. He believes the normal role of these fibers is "to signal the state of the distension of the stomach" (Paintal, 1954, p. 268), and that such signals eventually reach hypothalamic nuclei.

Several studies have shown that gastric distension tends to depress food intake, though not to eliminate it. Such studies have achieved distension of the stomach by directly introducing into the stomach calorically inert material, like gum arabic, celluflour, or water-filled balloons. Share, Martyniuk, and Grossman (1952); Janowitz and Grossman (1949*a*); Miller (1957); and Smith and Duffy (1957*b*) have all reported some cessation of food intake in short-term experiments involving gastric distension. Regulation of food intake under these conditions, however, is not at all accurately adjusted to the amount of bulk introduced, and, as animals with denervated gastro-intestinal tracts regulate food intake adequately, the gastric distension stimulus cannot alone be the cue for satiety. The experiment of Janowitz and Hollander (1955) further supports this point, since the stomachs of their pre-fed dogs were presumably empty by the time oral feeding was permitted.

Oral Factors

Stimulation of the mouth and lip regions and the acts of chewing and swallowing will often temporarily, at least, inhibit stomach contractions (Carlson, 1916). Recently, the role of mouth factors in regulating food intake and reinforcement over short periods of time has been studied by Miller and his associates.

These experiments have compared, in rats, the effects of introducing an enriched milk solution directly into the stomach by means of a fistula with those produced by drinking the same quantity of milk in the normal way. Kohn (1951) found that, while the milk introduced into the stomach reduced the number of instrumental responses the animal would make to obtain food as compared to a control condition in which saline was introduced directly into the stomach, this "stomach milk" procedure did not reduce the occurrence of the panel pushing response as much as did the ingestion of the same quantity of milk by mouth. Berkun, Kessen, and Miller (1952) repeated this experiment but omitted the panel pushing response and directly measured the amount of milk drunk following the experimental treatments. They found, as would be expected from Kohn's results, that "mouth milk" reduced the tendency to further drinking more than did the same quantity of milk introduced directly into the stomach. Similar findings were obtained for dogs by Janowitz and Grossman (1949a).

Miller and Kessen (1952) also found, comparing animals in a learning task, that the rewarding effect of food by mouth was greater than that of food introduced directly into the stomach. Another experiment by Miller and his associates (Miller, 1957, p. 1273; 1955, pp. 142–143) compared the effects of prefeeding with saccharin, a non-nutritive but sweet-tasting substance, to those of nutritive substances. Prefeeding with saccharin did reduce subsequent intake of saccharin and nutritive foods but not as much as did prefeeding with a dextrose solution of equal preference value. Further, direct injection through a fistula of saccharin into the stomach did not reduce the subsequent drinking of a saccharin solution, whereas saccharin drunk by mouth did reduce the later intake of saccharin (Miller, 1957, Fig. 3).

These results certainly indicate that oral stimulation, arising from the contact of foods with mouth receptors and from the acts of lapping, chewing, and swallowing, have the effect of controlling subsequent food intake. The effectiveness of these oral factors may be short-lived, however. Hull and his associates (1951) permitted a dog to eat to satiation, but the food passed outside his body through a fistula in his throat. This was done on eight successive evenings. During the first evening he ate 80 per cent of his body weight, but his food intake decreased on subsequent evenings, reaching zero on the eighth session. Apparently, this "extinction" of eating was restricted to the specific situation, as the animal after extinction would eat in another room, even though this was also sham feeding.[7]

We have seen that the theory of hunger arising primarily from the contractions of the stomach has had a long history and achieved a position of considerable acceptance under the advocacy of Walter Cannon and abetted by the extensive experimental work of A. J. Carlson. However, there is a good deal of difficulty with this conception in view

[7] It has been pointed out by Rosenzweig (1962, p. 132) that these results are at variance with those from somewhat similar experiments reported by Pavlov.

of the persistence of phenomena of hunger, despite gastrectomy and gastric denervation. Unfortunately, naive organisms have not been used in these experiments, so that the persistence of hunger may possibly depend on associated factors, which originally received their hunger-inducing impetus from their relations with stomach contractions. This is to say that alternative cues may be available and can be utilized when one set—gastric stimulation—is no longer available (see Appley, 1961*b*, p. 153).

It is quite clear that there are many factors contributing to food intake and other phenomena of hunger. Some of those which have been implicated are possible hormones, blood-sugar concentration, the caloric value of food ingested, distension of the stomach, and the sensory stimulation of the oral cavity, together with the acts of chewing and swallowing. Such factors must be accounted for in any theory of the food-ingestion-satiety mechanism, and we shall later review additional factors that appear to influence it. Before doing so, however, we turn to the recently obtained evidence that neural centers are involved in these processes of hunger, together with the theories which have arisen as a result of these findings. These theories may be called *central theories* of hunger, since they do not involve local matters, like stomach contractions or gastric distension, as primary explanatory processes. Rather, they attempt to explain the occurrence of the local factors while sometimes using them as a source of feed-back into neural centers.

Neural Factors in Hunger

That central neural mechanisms may be involved in hunger has long been suggested (cf. Carlson, 1916; Brobeck, 1955*b*, p. 44; Morgan & Stellar, 1950, p. 394). However, techniques for the precise investigations required to get at these mechanisms have become available only in relatively recent years. Techniques of stimulating points in the hypothalamus, electrically or chemically, have been utilized in uncovering the role of this area of the brain in hunger.

Hetherington and Ranson (1940) demonstrated that obesity could be produced in animals by causing hypothalamic lesions. Prior to their work such lesions had not been successfully established independently of damage to the pituitary, so that the controlling factor in the obesity was uncertain. Brobeck, Tepperman, and Long (1943) showed that this obesity arose because of overeating (hyperphagia), and then Anand and Brobeck (1951) made electrolytic lesions in various hypothalamic regions of rats and cats and found that cessation of eating, even in hyperphagic animals, was produced by bilateral lesions in the lateral

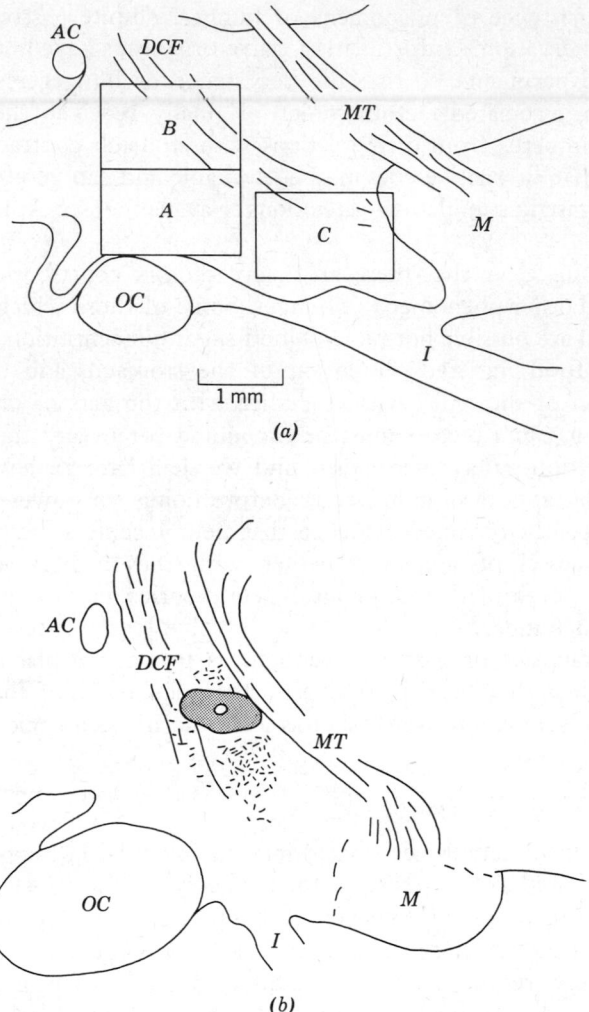

Figure 5-2. Diagram of hypothalamic areas involved in eating and drinking. Modified by permission from Rosenzweig (1962, Figs. 14, p. 121, and 15, p. 127).

The area marked *C* in the upper panel (*a*) includes hunger centers, but areas *A* and *B* do not. The upper panel represents a section cut through the rat hypothalamus parallel to the midline. The lower panel (*b*) represents a similar section through the hypothalamus of the goat. The black area represents the region where electrical stimulation elicits drinking, the central white area yielding the most pronounced effect. The dotted area indicates where drinking is elicited by microinjections of hypertonic salt solution.

AC represents the anterior commissure; *DCF*, the descending column of the fornix; *MT*, the mammillothalamic tract (tract of Vicq d'Azyr); *OC*, the optic chiasma; *I*, the infundibulum; and *M*, the mammillary body.

regions of the hypothalamus. Anand, Dua, and Schoenberg (1955) verified this finding in monkeys and cats. Hyperphagia, as shown in various experiments, results from lesions in a different part of the hypothalamus, the ventromedial nuclei. While these regions are not far apart, the differential results arising from their respective destruction suggest that two mechanisms are involved in the control of hunger at the hypothalamic level [8] (Fig. 5–2).

One of these centers appears to be instrumental in causing eating. This is the one in the lateral areas of the hypothalamus, since aphagia results from its destruction. While some writers have suggested that animals with lesions in this area will never eat again, Teitelbaum and Stellar (1954) have shown that eating behavior will recover if the animals are maintained long enough by means of stomach-tube feedings. Without this support, however, some of their animals did in fact starve to death. Delgado and Anand (1953) and O. A. Smith (1956) electrically stimulated this lateral region and found that food intake was thereby increased.

Teitelbaum and Epstein (1962) have confirmed earlier observations (Teitelbaum & Stellar, 1954; Montemurro & Stevenson, 1957) that destruction of lateral hypothalamic areas in rats produces not only aphagia but also a refusal to drink water (adipsia). They have carefully analyzed the course of recovery in animals subjected to large lateral hypothalamic lesions, maintaining them by means of a liquid diet through gastric intubation (Fig. 5–3). In the immediate period following hypothalamic destruction (stage I), the animal will neither eat nor drink and seems to have an aversion toward food or water. In the second stage of recovery, the animal will take only wet and palatable food and rejects dry food; it does not drink at all, nor does it eat enough to maintain itself without supplemental tube feedings. It does not seem to have a hunger "drive," only a slight interest in highly palatable foods. This period (stage II) seems to end suddenly, for "one day, it eats a large quantity of food"; after this happens the animal will properly regulate its intake of wet and palatable foods, but it still does not drink water. It develops into a normal eater, accepting dry food, for example, only if it is provided with fluids which have a sweet taste (if nutritive fluids are not provided). Hydration of the animals by means of a stomach tube also permits them to eat normally. In this stage (III), then, the aphagia appears to arise because of dehydration, and if only dry foods were offered, the animals would not eat. (Hydration, however, does not induce normal eating in stages I and II.)

[8] See Brobeck (1946) for a review of factors involved in the development and characteristics of hypothalamic obesity.

Eventually many animals drink water again (stage IV) but not in a normal pattern. This is to say, they drink only when eating and do not drink in response to dehydration or water deprivation. They seem to drink to wet their mouths, rather than to maintain water balance, and they reject water flavored with quinine, which normal rats would accept, even to the point of death. This rejection of unpalatable water in stage IV carries over to foods; that is, the animals are finicky eaters. Eventually, however, at least in some animals, eating and drinking appear to return to normal, but full recovery may take months. The duration of the four stages varies, and the effects are related to the extent of the lateral hypothalamic lesions.

Teitelbaum and Epstein suggest that their evidence is consistent with the idea that the lateral hypothalamus contains both drinking and eating centers and that they overlap. However, the overlap is probably not complete, as electrical stimulation has successfully yielded drinking without eating and eating without drinking. It is clear that the act of eating recovers before that of drinking and that before either recovers (if it does) to a near normal state, it passes through a period of finicky consummatory behavior, which is nonregulatory and is apparently highly responsive to peripheral aspects (such as taste) of food or water.

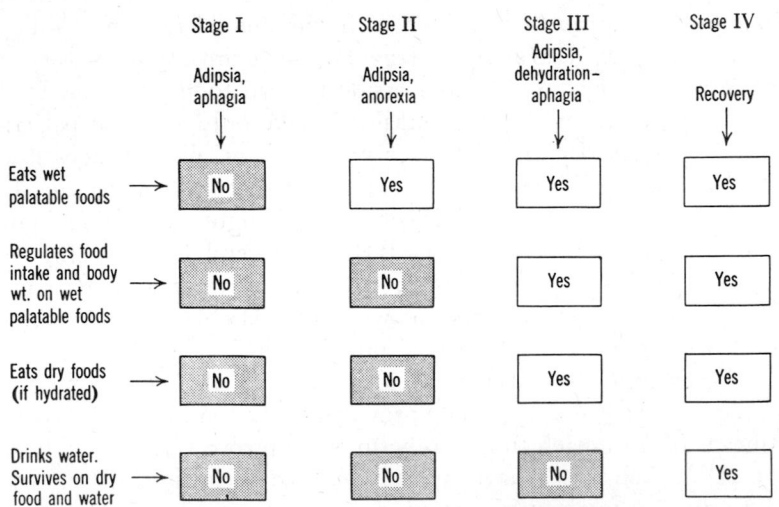

Figure 5–3. Stages of recovery seen in the lateral hypothalamic syndrome. (The critical behavioral events which define the stages are listed on the left.) Reproduced by permission from Teitelbaum and Epstein (1962, Fig. 3).

The other center, the one in the ventromedial nuclei whose destruction leads to hyperphagia, is perhaps plausibly called a "satiety center"; that is, its activity suppresses eating. This suggestion is supported in the work of Brobeck, Larsson, and Reyes (1956), who recorded electrical activity from the hypothalamus of anesthetized cats. The cats were given amphetamine derivatives which normally depress food intake. The electrical activity of the medial hypothalamus was augmented in frequency and amplitude by the amphetamine, suggesting that the drug excites activity in the inhibitory or satiety center.[9] That this center does not activate eating is suggested by the aphagia which arises when, with this center intact, the lateral region of the hypothalamus is destroyed. Further, Miller, Bailey, and Stevenson (1950) have shown that hypothalamic hyperphagic animals will eat excessively only when food is readily available. They are not, on the other hand, strongly motivated to work to obtain food—for example, pressing a bar or raising a weighted lid to get food, approaching food by running or overcoming a restraint, or tolerating shock to get to food. Neither would the hyperphagic animals accept food adulterated with quinine as readily as would controls deprived of food for the same length of time.

It would seem, then, that the hyperphagia resulting from lesions of the satiety center does not reflect a strong motive for food. Instead, it perhaps reflects a failure to cut off feeding behavior once started. These animals were particularly inclined to overeat when the diet offered them was high in fat content. They were not as hyperphagic when low fat diets were available. Kennedy (1950) has also stressed dietary selectivity in hyperphagic rats. Similar findings have been reported by Teitelbaum (1955, 1957). Brobeck (1955b, pp. 47–48) has summarized evidence which shows that general activity has no clear relation to hyperphagia (or to aphagia, either, for that matter).

On the other hand, Miller (1958, pp. 102–103) has shown that eating responses, elicited electrically, do seem to function as if they were motivated by hunger. Thus, after food satisfaction, a thirsty rat would leave the water spout and push a panel to get food when stimulated electrically in the appropriate area. Similarly, such stimulation activated a food-satiated rat to make bar-pressing responses, which were rewarded with food, and to drink milk (though not water). Termination of such central stimulation also served as a reward in a learning situation. Presumably, these findings involve the eating center rather than

[9] Epstein (1959) has been able to show that certain sympathomimetic amines, which depress normal appetite, decrease eating in hyperphagic animals. Presumably, this effect is due to direct suppression of the eating center.

the satiety center. Thus, the properties usually associated with drive would seem to have their locus, so far as these experiments go, in the eating center. However, Morgane (1961) found that drive effects (such as crossing an electric grid to get to a bar whose depression yielded food) were found only with lesions in the far lateral hypothalamus. Lesions in the mid-lateral hypothalamus produced eating, but not grid-crossing.

Despite the emphasis in the work we have just surveyed on the hypothalamus, it is well to keep in mind that other regions of the brain, from the cortex down, have often been implicated in hunger phenomena (Stellar, 1954; Morgan, 1957). Larsson (1954) has obtained hyperphagia in sheep and goats not only from electrical stimulation of the hypothalamus but also of the medulla; and earlier investigations (cf. Morgan, 1943, p. 456; Morgan & Stellar, 1950, p. 394) have produced hunger, gastric contractions, and cessation of contractions from various manipulations of the frontal cortex.

It is worth noting, in passing, that techniques other than electrical stimulation and electrical ablation of hypothalamic centers have yielded similar results. Some of these will be mentioned below in connection with theories of how these neural mechanisms work. We may note here that Larsson (1954) introduced small amounts of hypertonic saline solution and hypertonic saccharose into the lateral hypothalamus of goats and obtained hyperphagia. In the lateral hypothalamus, Grossman (1960) found eating to follow insertion of adrenergic and drinking insertion of cholinergic chemicals. Forssberg and Larsson (1954) have further suggested by studying the hypothalamus with radioactive phosphorus that hunger affects the extent of capillary dilatation and rate of activity in hypothalamic eating centers.

Recent Theories of the Hunger Mechanism [10]

The evidence that hypothalamic mechanisms play a central role in food intake and satiety has led to two main hypotheses as to the mechanisms which influence these centers and which operate to mediate their control: the glucostatic hypothesis and the thermal regulation hypothesis. We shall turn now to a brief consideration of these views, together with related ideas and such evidence as is available. Both

---

[10] The extensive literature which has concerned hypothalamic regulation of eating and drinking and the theoretical interpretations of the mechanisms involved has been brought together in the following reviews: Anand (1961), Andersson & Larsson (1961a), Brobeck (1960a, b), Hightower (1962), Janowitz (1961), Van Itallie (1959).

would be classified as central theories and they are concerned with the factors to which hypothalamic centers respond by initiating or terminating eating behavior.

The Glucostatic Hypothesis. In a number of publications, Mayer has set forth the hypothesis that receptors in the hypothalamic centers which regulate eating are sensitive to and respond to variations in blood glucose insofar as they can utilize it (Mayer, 1953*a, b,* 1955). Mayer recognized that the regulation of food intake has both a short-term and a long-term aspect. He suggests the glucostatic mechanism to account for short-term regulation but seems to favor the lipostatic hypothesis suggested by Kennedy (1952–1953) as the basis for long-term regulation (Mayer, 1955). Mayer would also recognize that other factors, probably including stomach contractions and stomach distension, must be regarded as contributing to the regulation. We shall consider the glucostatic and lipostatic mechanisms here.

Mayer's argument for the glucostatic hypothesis is as follows (Mayer, 1953*b*): Eating occurs in frequent episodes; hence, the hypothalamic centers must be sensitive to changes in bodily stores of substances that can change quickly. Such a substance is the carbohydrate (starches and sugars), little of which exists in storage in the body. Protein and fat stores of the body do not normally decline rapidly, so that carbohydrate supplies would seem to show the greatest rapid variability. This leads Mayer to suggest the notion "that the central nervous system, dependent exclusively on a continued supply of glucose in the blood, should maintain 'glucoreceptors' sensitive to fluctuations of available blood glucose" (1953*b*, p. 474).

Mayer is fully aware that blood glucose levels have been extensively investigated in relation to aspects of hunger and that the evidence has, if anything, led to negative conclusions concerning the relationship (see previous section on blood sugar). However, Mayer feels that these studies have been concerned with the absolute levels of blood sugar, not with "the actual degree of availability and utilization of carbohydrates" (1955, p. 34). Availability and utilization of these substances, Mayer proposes, are more appropriately measured by peripheral arteriovenous blood-glucose differences. If there is a substantially larger concentration of glucose in peripheral arterial or capillary blood (as found, for example, in a finger) than there is in the peripheral veins, then there is glucose available for utilization or storage as fat, and hunger will not exist. When this arteriovenous blood-glucose difference drops to zero, however, hunger supervenes. A diagram may help to make this proposition clear. Figure 5–4 shows two curves. The solid one represents the concentration of arterial blood sugar, the dashed one of venous blood sugar. Cross-hatching at the bottom of the chart indicates hunger. It can be seen that when the two curves are very close together, indicating little or no difference in arteriovenous blood-sugar concentration, hunger occurs. When the arterial curve is substantially higher than the venous curve, however, there is no hunger.

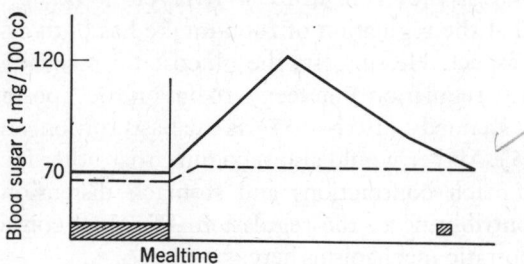

Figure 5-4. Peripheral arteriovenous differences and hunger. Reproduced by permission from Mayer (1955, Fig. 10).

Mayer's hypothesis was developed in terms of the arguments which we have already summarized as well as from various kinds of indirect evidence (Mayer, 1953*b*). Somewhat more direct approaches have also been used. One such evidence comes from the demonstration that obesity can be produced in mice by injecting them with goldthioglucose (Brecher & Waxler, 1949; Waxler & Brecher, 1950). Overeating seemed to result from this drug, and led to the obesity. Marshall, Barrnett, and Mayer (1955) looked for hypothalamic lesions within three days of the injection of goldthioglucose and other substances into mice, since the obesity arising from hypothalamic lesions appears to be similar to that occurring after the administration of goldthioglucose. They always found damage in the ventromedial hypothalamic areas of the goldthioglucose-injected mice, and apparently the damage was more or less restricted to this area. Control injections of a similar substance (goldthalomate) did not produce these lesions. The suggestion made is that the glucose component of the goldthioglucose "makes this limited hypothalamic portion of the brain barrier much more permeable to this compound than to compounds not containing glucose" (Marshall et al., 1955, p. 244). To Mayer this suggests support for the notion that the area contains glucoreceptors (see, also, Anliker & Mayer, 1957). Some evidence presented by Duner (1953) seems to support at least the fact of the sensitivity of hypothalamic regions to glucose. The injection of a glucose solution into the hypothalamus of cats resulted in changes in secretion of the adrenal glands, an effect not found with injection of glucose into other brain areas or attributable to peripheral blood-sugar level.

Other experimental tests of the glucostatic hypothesis have yielded supporting results. Stunkard, Van Itallie, and Reis (1955) made intravenous injections of glucagon into human subjects. (Glucagon is a hormone which raises blood-sugar levels.) They found that stomach contractions and reported hunger were quickly abolished by this procedure and that the capillary-venous glucose difference increased rapidly following the injection, as it should according to Mayer's theory. Stunkard (1957) extensively studied a young man who was unconscious for a long period of time as a result of brain injury, and who was clinically a "decorticate." Stomach contractions were recorded, and he was fed by a stomach tube or by intravenous administration of various substances. Stunkard found that IV glucagon abolished stomach contraction, whereas intravenously administered fat, amino acids, or glucose did not affect them. The IV glucagon increased the capillary-venous difference, whereas the glucose did not, supporting Mayer's theory. The failure of the contractions to cease on injection of amino acids would seem to oppose Brobeck's theory (see below), since they presumably raised heat production and did cause peripheral vasodilatation. Anand (1961, pp. 687–688) summarizes studies showing that hyperglycemia increases electrical activity from the satiety centers and that hypoglycemia decreases it. The feeding center was less affected.

On the other hand, Bernstein and Grossman (1956) found no differences in food intake or reported appetite from human subjects in association with variations in the peripheral arteriovenous glucose differences. Fryer, Moore, Williams, and Young (1955) also failed to support the relation between arteriovenous differences and reported hunger or appetite. We should note that these two experiments utilized rather gross measures of hunger in relation to more-or-less normal conditions of eating. Mayer (1955, p. 40) has indicated that his theory has "never claimed to be able to interpret the initiation of eating at a given time because habits, learned behavior, taste . . ." and other factors are involved.

Kennedy (1952–1953), as mentioned before, has suggested that fat stores in the body probably regulate long-term food-taking behavior. His experiments show adaptation on the part of his animals to environmental temperature and suggest that the long-term regulation of food intake is somehow due to lipostatic effects on the hypothalamic centers. Both he and Mayer feel that this view can be integrated with the glucostatic hypothesis.

The Thermal Hypothesis. In a number of papers (cf. Brobeck, 1955*a*, *b*, 1957, 1960*a*), Brobeck has suggested that the regulation of food intake is due to cells in the hypothalamus which are sensitive to temperature changes. Food "is a thermal stress that acts upon the hypothalamus to bring about cutaneous vasodilatation" (Brobeck, 1957, p. 571). ". . . feeding is inhibited when heat content of the body is rising, and facilitated when heat content is falling" (p. 572). The relations of eating to external temperature and to bodily temperature changes, together with known temperature regulating mechanisms in the hypothalamus, form the basis for this hypothesis. Rats stop eating at temperatures beyond which they could not further maintain a normal body temperature. Further, there is a relation between satiety and the specific dynamic action (heat production) of foods, such that protein yields satiety more readily than other foods. Heat production following eating increases, and feeding is followed by a slight rise in central and a larger rise in peripheral temperatures (Brobeck, 1957). Such findings are consistent with the notion that animals eat to keep warm and stop eating to avoid hyperthermia. On the other hand, Mellinkoff (1957, p. 196) has suggested that the desire for food is influenced by the amino acid patterns of the extracellular fluids, a hypothesis which does not attribute the value of protein to heat production.

A direct test of the thermal hypothesis was made by Andersson and Larsson (1961*b*) with two goats. A "thermode" was devised, consisting essentially of a partially insulated cannula in which warm or cold (ice) water could be circulated. The thermode was implanted into hypothalamic regions having to do with temperature regulation (preoptic and rostral hypothalamus). Local cooling in these areas caused the animals to shiver and they would start eating hay "with good appetite" within two or three minutes after cooling was initiated. Cooling induced rumination when hay was not available. Although goats do not normally eat when their rectal temperatures are at or above 40° C, central cooling induced eating at these temperatures. Under 48 to 72 hours of water deprivation, the goats would not eat hay, but they would do so, despite the dehydration, under central cooling.

The opposite effects were observed from warming these brain areas. Warming caused a cessation of eating within a minute of its onset, even when the goat had just received his ration and was eating well. Drinking was instigated. The short latencies of the responses to both cooling and warming make a chemical basis for these effects unlikely and suggest that they are mediated by neural impulses to the feeding and satiety centers. The centers themselves were probably not directly warmed or cooled by these maneuvers.

Some evidence contrary to the Brobeck hypothesis has been mentioned earlier (Kennedy, 1952–1953; Stunkard, 1957). [Mayer and Greenberg (1953) found higher body temperatures in hypothalamic hyperphagic rats than in controls or in nonhyperphagic-operated rats. They feel that this association of hyperphagia with elevated body temperature does not support the thermal hypothesis.]

It is only fair to indicate that Brobeck (1955*b*, 1957) is fully aware of the complex set of factors which may, and probably do, influence feeding and satiety. He mentions and summarizes evidence concerning the following (in addition to thermal and glucostatic hypotheses): water concentration in various parts of the body, sensations from the upper digestive tract, osmoreceptors in the hypothalamus (see later section on thirst), intermediary metabolism, and the like. The importance of some kind of feed-back arising from eating is shown in an experiment by Hervey (1959). Parabiotic rats, that is, animals whose circulations are connected, were used, and one was made hyperphagic by means of hypothalamic lesions. It gained weight and became obese, but its partner decreased its food intake and became thin. Evidently some kind of feed-back, arising from the overeating of the one animal, acted to reduce the eating activity of the other.

Summary: Recent Neural Discoveries and Theories

The evidence reviewed concerning the role of neural factors in hunger rather strikingly suggests that there are two hypothalamic centers important in the control of hunger. One, in the lateral hypothalamus, appears to be an eating center, since its stimulation induces eating and other drive-like aspects of behavior, and since its destruction renders animals aphagic (the role of dehydration in this aphagia may be important). The other center, located in the ventromedial hypothalamus, may be an inhibitory or satiety center, since appetite-depressing drugs increase its activity, and since its destruction is associated with the development of hyperphagia and obesity. While stress has been mainly placed on these hypothalamic areas, other parts of the brain no doubt figure in the control of hunger-related behavior.

Recent theory would suggest that these hypothalamic centers are probably responsive either to changes in the blood constituents or to changes in body temperature, or to both, and several authors (e.g., Janowitz, 1961) stress multiple controlling factors. The hypothalamus has a rich blood supply, and various experiments have long made it clear that blood factors are probably involved in hunger. Both the onset and the termination of stomach contractions and of other peripheral factors of hunger may well be controlled by impulses arising in the hypothalamic centers, and these centers may also be controlled in their activity by impulses arising from contractions, distension, smelling and tasting food, as well as chewing and swallowing it. The role of learning in welding together the complex of factors which seem to control the onset, occurrence, and termination of hunger-related behavior is yet to be adequately and fully evaluated (see Stellar, 1954; Grossman, 1955; and Janowitz, 1958, for integrations).

SPECIFIC HUNGERS

It is a common observation that the choice of specific foods or classes of foods may shift from time to time, and that sometimes the interest in a particular food or food class may be so strong as to suggest a "craving" for it. Thus we are all familiar with stories concerning trips made by animals to "salt-licks" or the eating by various animals of bones or other mineral-bearing objects. Strange tales are recounted as to the food preferences of pregnant women, and children have been known to scratch walls and to eat the calcium dislodged. There is a tremendous variety in human cravings for and aversions to foodstuffs (see Snapper, 1955), many of which have a cultural or social basis, others of which may have an emotional or neurotic basis, and some of which probably have a nutritional basis.

A good deal of attention has been paid, in recent years, to the adequacy of self-selected diets to support health and nutritional status and to the ability of animals to make up, in their diets, deficiencies which have been developed through experimental means. The result of this work has been the concept of specific hungers, that is, that deficiencies in certain kinds of dietary elements will lead to the selective ingestion of the deficient kinds of foodstuffs. Specific hungers are not the full explanation of dietary selection and change, as suggested already, but they provide an interesting illustration of the regulation of behavior by bodily conditions. We shall now turn to a description of some of the facts of the self-selection of diets, the effects on food selection of deficiencies experimentally introduced, the conditions which control these phenomena, and hypotheses as to the mechanisms which underlie them.

In passing, it may be noted that the existence of specific hungers is usually taken as disproof of a local theory of hunger, at least one based on stomach contractions. This is because it is not evident how gastric motility could provide for differential selection of the kinds of food objects relevant to the specific hunger. This is to say that stomach contractions would not differ from one specific hunger to another.

Self-Selection of Diet

It has been known for many years that, given free choice of various dietary components, various animals, including swine, mice, and rats, will select a diet which adequately maintains health and promotes growth. Two experiments may be cited, one with rats and one with human children, which illustrate this kind of work. Richter, Holt, and Barclare (1938) provided rats with eleven pure-food elements, three in solid form and eight in liquid form. The foods were casein, olive oil, sucrose, sodium chloride (3 per cent solution), sodium phosphate, calcium lactate, potassium chloride, baker's yeast, cod-liver oil, wheat-germ oil, and water. Measurements were made each day of the quantities of these elements that were ingested, and records of growth were also obtained. The dietary selections on a day-to-day basis showed consistency and were appropriate in terms of nutritional requirements, and the growth records of these animals were somewhat better than those of animals maintained on a standard laboratory diet. Davis (1928) provided newly weaned, human infants with all the required components of an adequate diet but permitted them a daily cafeteria-like choice of their foods over a period of several months. On any given day, an infant might eat disproportionate amounts of some foods, and such disproportions continued, in some cases, over substantial periods of time. On the average, however, over the entire experimental period, the infants selected a satisfactory diet, and their health and growth were normal. It should be noted that, in both these experiments, choices of inadequate food substances were not available (see, also, Young, 1961, p. 129).

A number of experimental reports, together with field observations, could be cited to illustrate the adequacy of diets selected in this cafeteria fashion (cf. Young, 1941, 1948b, 1961; Morgan & Stellar, 1950, pp. 394–401). Indeed, as Young (1941, p. 130) observed, "It is obvious, of course, that before standard synthetic diets were even heard of, wild animals somehow managed to locate foods, select, and so far as possible balance their diets from the edibilia of forest and plain." However, the experimental studies already cited have, to some extent, aided the selection of proper diets by providing only suitable foods. There is evidence that self-selection of foods does not lead inevitably to a healthy diet. Hausman (1932) provided alcohol in addition to regular diets and water. Consumption of alcohol was compensated for by a drop in intake of other food components, total caloric intake remaining constant. Wilder (1937) made rats develop rickets by maintaining them on an inadequate diet and then gave them a choice of foodstuffs yielding an adequate or an inadequate diet. The animals did not choose the antirachitogenic diet; they tended to select the unfamiliar food of the two offered. Other evidence (cf. Young, 1941, p. 132; Pilgrim & Patton, 1947) also suggests that dietary choices by rats are not always nutritionally wise. In some instances, however, this arises because the needed dietary component does not yield a taste discrimination for a particular animal. Scott and Verney (1949; cf. also, Harris et al., 1933) found that rats do not prefer pantothenic acid ordinarily. However, when it was flavored with anise they could select it accurately, even though anise is not an ordinarily preferred substance.

The evidence we have reviewed, even though it has shown numerous instances in which dietary self-selection is fallible, indicates that self-selection of food may often lead to a satisfactory diet. We turn now to studies in which needs for dietary components have been manipulated experimentally. These studies, together with those already reviewed, have led to the identification of a number of specific hungers, displayed, at least, by rats.

Experimental Manipulation of Nutritional Needs

We may review, summarily, some of the outstanding findings which have been uncovered in a variety of studies. These studies have used several methods to induce specific needs, like removing a component from the diet for an extended period or surgically removing a gland (like the parathyroids or the adrenals, which are involved in the use of such foodstuffs as calcium or salt). Reviews of the extensive literature of this type have been provided by Young (1941, 1948a, 1961) and by Morgan and Stellar (1950). When the parathyroid glands are removed, rats will take large quantities of calcium if available and reject phosphorus, thus preventing the onset of the symptoms of calcium deficiency. Pancreatectomized rats will reduce their sugar intake and thus avoid diabetes. Deprivations of parts of the vitamin-B complex, fat, protein, carbohydrate, water, and of other substances often lead to compensatory changes in food intake.

There are other effects even more complex than those just cited. Rats deficient in thiamin (vitamin B_1) not only have a specific hunger for this substance but also show a reduced intake of sugar and increase their intake of fats. These two changes presumably reflect the disturbance in metabolism of carbohydrates, arising from the thiamin deficiency.

The foregoing results are typical of those reported for the approximately one dozen specific hungers which have been reported and generally reflect the influence of such specific hungers as measured in terms of gross food intake. Preference testing of foodstuffs also reflects the influence of specific hunger. For example, Bare (1949) permitted his adrenalectomized rats to drink from either one of two bottles. In one bottle there was tap water and, in the other, a salt solution which varied on different occasions in its concentration of salt. He showed that the adrenalectomized animals strongly preferred salt solutions in concentrations over a range much wider than that for which normal animals showed a preference (Fig. 5–5).

Conditions Controlling Selection of Foods

When animals do select satisfactory diets from the available foods and modify their dietary choices when special dietary needs are set up, as by deprivation, surgical manipulation, or such bodily processes as pregnancy and lactation, what are some of the factors that influence these adjustments? One, of course, must be the state of bodily need itself, as already indicated. Another is that the needed dietary component be discriminable so far as the animal is concerned. We have already seen that pantothenic acid (a B vitamin) will not be chosen

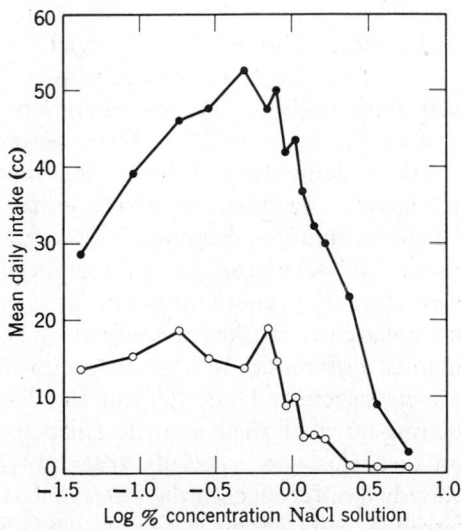

Figure 5–5. Salt preference curves (as measured by intake) in normal (open circles) and adrenalectomized (filled circles) white rats. Modified by permission from Bare (1949, Fig. 4).

despite a bodily need for it, unless it is distinctively flavored. Vitamins A and D, also, are not apparently recognized in foods, as rats deficient in these substances do not evidence compensatory diets.[11]

Other factors involved include habit; individual and species differences, such as age and those genetically determined; intactness of taste nerves; and properties of the foodstuffs themselves. We give brief illustrations for several of these variables.

That habit may play a role is illustrated in everyone's experience and by an experiment reported by Young and Chaplin (1945). They maintained animals on a self-selected diet and determined initially that the subjects preferred sucrose to casein, a protein. Then casein was removed from the diet, and a protein-free diet was maintained for 32 days, generating a condition of marked protein starvation. Preference tests between sugar and casein, run during this period of protein deficiency, however, continued to show a strong preference for sugar, despite the need for casein. These tests were run on an apparatus in which the preference for sugar had been manifest prior to the onset of the protein deficiency. Only when another method of testing was used, involving a different apparatus, did the rats shift their preference from sugar to casein, and even then, when tested again, five minutes later in the original situation, the preference would shift back to sugar. Thus the preferential habit was evidently strong enough in the original apparatus to overrule the condition of bodily need for protein. Young generalizes these results in the following principle: "Habits tend to form in agreement with bodily need but established habits tend to persist regardless of need" (1955, p. 227). That this may be true, even to the point of death, is demonstrated in an experiment by Harriman (1955b). Some of Harriman's animals learned to prefer a sugar solution to a salt solution prior to an adrenalectomy. This sugar preference persisted postoperatively, and several of the animals died and all suffered severe weight loss from the continuing salt deficiency. Again the learned preference apparently masked the effects of bodily need.

There are individual differences in a given group of animals in the adequacy of the diets selected. Thus, Pilgrim and Patton (1947) observed that about one-third of their animals failed to grow normally on a self-selection diet; this was especially true for young adult rats. There are also individual differences in the *kinds* of fats, carbohydrates, or proteins preferred by rats (Scott & Quint, 1946; Scott & Verney, 1947, 1948). Dove (1935) has attributed individual differences in the ability of chicks to select an adequately balanced diet to gene differ-

[11] Harriman (1955b), however, has shown the development of a preference for provitamin A.

ences. Pfaffman (1955) recorded nerve impulses in the cat, rabbit, and rat on stimulation of the tongue with several substances. He found that there are species differences in neural reactions for several substances. Carpenter (1956) conducted taste-preference tests in several species and also found differences. For example, cats did not discriminate sucrose solutions and tended to avoid saccharin solutions, whereas these two substances were both preferred to water by hamsters and rabbits. It is clear that responses to taste solutions vary among species, as measured both electrophysiologically and by behavioral preferences. It would seem likely that the phenomena of specific hungers would perhaps also vary among species, though there is little direct evidence on this point.

It would seem obvious that intact taste nerves would be necessary to the phenomenon of specific hungers, but this is not necessarily so. Richter (1941) found that adrenalectomized rats give up their high salt intake if their taste nerves are severed and, as a consequence, die. Evidently, stimulation from the receptors must be communicated centrally in order for this specific hunger to be reflected in behavior.

We have already seen that animals vary their intake of food as a function of its properties. Bare (1949) found salt solutions at about 0.9 per cent concentration to be preferred by rats to other concentrations; and Beebe-Center, Black, Hoffman, and Wade (1948) found that intermediate concentrations of saccharin were preferred to water, whereas water was preferred to high concentrations. Guttman (1953) [12] found in rats that rate of responding under periodic reinforcement (one sip every minute) was a positive function of concentration of the solution up to the highest concentration used (32 per cent). Guttman (1954) has shown that response rate is always greater for sucrose than for glucose solutions of equal concentration, a finding which is paralleled by the report of greater sweetness for sucrose by human subjects. Young and Greene (1953) showed that rats would take greater quantities in an hour of a 9 per cent solution of sucrose than of a 36 per cent solution, but when offered both solutions simultaneously they would take more of the stronger concentration. Apparently, there is more than one factor at work here. There is a preference for the sweeter solution *but a more rapid satiation for it* than for the weaker solution; this would account for the increased intake of the 9 per cent solution when it was offered alone.

These illustrations are perhaps sufficient to indicate that dietary

[12] The results Guttman (1953) reports for continuous reinforcement which showed the highest rate for a 16 per cent solution he now regards as an artifact (Young, 1955, p. 222).

preferences and intake are influenced by characteristics of the food-stuffs. Not all of these facts pertain to specific hungers but they do point to one of the important factors requiring explanation in any theory of food acceptability, including the fact of specific hungers. It should be clear from this entire discussion that the determination of food intake is quite com lex.

Explanations of Specific Hungers

Generally, explanations of specific hungers fall into several types. The first hypothesis, espoused by Richter (1939), was based on the evidence that adrenalectomized rats preferred solutions in which the salt concentration was so low as to do them little good and too low to be preferred by normal rats. He suggested that the receptor threshold for the salt taste after adrenalectomy might be lowered to account for this fact and suggested, further, that changes in receptor thresholds might underlie the preferential behavior of the specific hungers in general. Three experiments, however, have failed to verify this hypothesis. Pfaffman and Bare (1950) measured the thresholds for salt by means of electrical discharge in nerve and found no difference between normal and adrenalectomized rats. Carr (1952) and Harriman and MacLeod (1953) also found identical thresholds in adrenalectomized and normal animals when the animals' choice was motivated by electric shock. Although it is not impossible for some peripheral changes to occur in specific hungers (Morgan, 1959, p. 655), the evidence to date does not support Richter's hypothesis.

Another interpretation is that the preferential behavior in specific hungers is learned. This interpretation is favored by Bindra (1959, pp. 87–88) and appears to be viewed at least as an important one by Young (1941, 1949b, 1955, 1959). Young regards the affective enjoyment attendant upon the ingestion of needed substances as perhaps the basis for the development of preferences for the substances and high ingestion rates of them. A number of studies have shown that preferences related to specific hungers develop gradually (Harriman, 1955a; Epstein & Stellar, 1955, p. 168), and this finding is consistent with a learning viewpoint. Such studies also have tended to use a two (or more) choice preference situation, so that the animal has to learn to discriminate which bottle or container holds the needed substance.

Gradual development of a preference, of course, could also reflect the gradual increase in bodily need for the preferred substance, after an operation or deprivation. Epstein and Stellar (1955) appear to favor this alternative. They performed an experiment in which rats were adrenalectomized. One group of them was immediately put in a two-bottle preference situation, one containing a salt solution, the other water; a gradual increase in the amount of salt solution taken by these animals over a ten-day postoperative period was shown. The rest of the operated animals were maintained on a salt-free diet for the ten postoperative days (several died) and then, in a condition of severe salt need, were permitted to drink a salt solution. It is noteworthy here that no choice was involved, as only *one bottle* was presented. The amount of salt ingested by these deprived animals per day started at a high level and continued high. Epstein and Stellar argue that since experience was not provided this group the high rate is attributable to the need for salt developed over the ten postoperative days. They are probably right, but it must be remembered that these animals were not in a preference situation; they had little to learn, having only to continue drinking from the one bottle. It seems to us, as it seems to Bindra (1959, p. 88), that rapid learning to drink a lot *could* have occurred in this single-bottle situation. We think a better comparison could have been provided by placing both groups of animals in a two-choice situation.

[Learning as an important factor in the manifestation of specific hungers, especially in actual *choice* situations, has not been ruled out on the basis of present evidence. As a matter of fact, it is likely that important information could be contributed to our understanding of reinforcement by further study of the nature of specific hungers.]

Some work has been directed to the physiological factors involved in specific hungers, usually under the interpretation that, in the case of salt preference, this preference is a reaction "to a gradually increasing physiological need for the sodium ion" (Epstein & Stellar, 1955, p. 169). This interpretation of specific hungers has led to a number of experiments which have been directed to the identification of the physiological processes involved in specific hungers. Illustrative is another experiment reported by Epstein and Stellar (1955), and one reported by McCleary (1953). Epstein and Stellar allowed adrenalectomized rats to drink (and therefore taste) a 3 per cent solution but diluted their food with a resin whose action internally permitted the absorption of only about half the salt concentration. The animals' behavior showed a substantial increase in intake of the 3 per cent salt solution during the period of resin intake, suggesting that the salt intake was governed by internal need rather than by the saltiness of the liquid ingested. McCleary (1953) interpreted the results of his studies of stomach loading with sugars and salt as showing that the control of some of the behaviors in specific hungers is due to intracellular dehydration. The drawing of fluids into the stomach as hyper-

tonic fluids are ingested would cause the dehydration. If this interpretation should have generality, it would permit an interpretation of
the nature of the internal need alternative to those usually given which
emphasize the specific nature of the deficits in basic food elements. We
are not now in a position to determine, however, whether McCleary's
hypothesis is indeed valid as a general one.

In summary of specific hungers, we may indicate that the selective
or exaggerated intake of some substance which is lacking in an organism's diet, or for which there is an extreme need due to surgery, as well
as the selection of a nutritive diet by normal animals, is a well authenticated fact. A number of factors, however, control these phenomena;
among them are habit, individual and species differences, and properties of the foodstuffs. Most of the interpretations of specific hungers
emphasize receptor changes, learning, and changes in the organism's
internal environment. Some evidence places doubt on receptor changes
as a sufficient condition, but the roles of learning and the internal environment, if they are in fact different or incompatible, have not
been resolved.

Factors Regulating Food Intake

We have now sketched the history of investigation of hunger, with
especial reference to theoretical conceptions of hunger and the nature
of specific hungers. However, there are a number of additional factors
important to food intake which will be reviewed briefly, and it must
be remembered that hunger is often supposed to have drive properties
which enable it to contribute to features of behavior more general
than food intake. We shall complete the account of hunger by identifying factors known to govern food intake and related variables. Later,
in Chapters 6 and 11, we shall consider hunger, as well as other drives,
in relation to less specifically food-related categories of behavior, such
as reinforcement, activity, and the like. This division of the roles of
hunger in relation to behavior (which is also appropriate to other
drives as well) will be clearer if we digress at this point in order to
outline the general problem of the measurement of influence of biological conditions, like hunger, on behavior.

Measurement of Motivation Due to Bodily Conditions

A number of techniques have been and are employed to measure
bodily motivations and to establish variations in their strength. In
general, measurement techniques may be classified into those which
do not and those which do involve incentives as a part of the testing
procedure.

Table 5–1. Outline of methods for establishing and measuring motivation based on bodily conditions.

Antecedent *	Response Class	Incentive Present or Not

Deprivation	(1) Activity
	   (*a*) running
	   (*b*) restless
		No

Deprivation	(2) Crossing an electrified grid	Yes
Either deprivation or no deprivation	(3) Latency, rate, amount of consummatory activity	Yes
Deprivation	(4) Acquisition or performance of a learned instrumental response	Yes, if response is reinforced No, if extinction is used
Either deprivation or no deprivation	(5) Latency, speed, or rate of approach to incentive objects	Yes
Either deprivation or no deprivation	(6) Selection or choice of one of two or more incentive objects	Yes
Electric shock	(7) Latency, speed, rate, force of escape responses	Yes, if shock is "negative" incentive or if escape is to nonshock area

* Conditions equivalent to deprivation, in general, or deprivation of specific substances can sometimes be achieved by drugs or surgical manipulations. "Satiety" is sometimes similarly induced.

Table 5–1 presents an outline of the chief methods which have been used in the case of such bodily conditions as hunger, thirst, pain, sex, and the like. Doing without food, water, and sexual behavior for periods of time illustrates what is meant by the term "deprivation" and the table indicates that deprivation (which may vary in duration) is a condition commonly used as an antecedent factor in measurements of motivation. Electric shock (or other noxious stimuli) is usually considered as an analogue of deprivation in studies of motivation, since it arouses or activates behavior.

In certain kinds of studies, however, deprivation is not always used. These investigations are usually concerned with features of incentive objects. Thus, the latency, rate, or amount of consummatory behavior (response class 3) might be measured for different foodstuffs or one might determine the latency or speed of approach to these objects (response class 5), or the preference for one over the others (response class 6) in nondeprived animals. In other experiments, however, these response classes might be studied in deprived animals.

Turning to the third column of Table 5–1, we find with only certain response-class measures that incentives are *not* employed in the measurement of motivation. These response classes are activity (number 1) and the performance of a previously learned response (class 4). Special features of these measures, as well as of the acquisition of a performance, require their separate consideration, and we treat measures of activity in Chapter 6 and of response class 4 in Chapter 11.

So far as the other response classes identified in Table 5–1 are concerned, the acquisition of instrumental responses is not emphasized, although instrumental responses are involved. Thus, in the Columbia Obstruction Box (Warden, 1931; Munn, 1950, pp. 85–87; Young, 1936, pp. 93–96), the animal must cross an electrified grid between the starting box and the incentive (food, sex object, etc.). The number of crossings he makes in a fixed period of time (response class 2) is measured. Approach, escape, and choice responses (classes 5, 6, and 7) may involve instrumental acts, but it is the latency, speed, or rate of the approach or escape, or the proportion of choices of one incentive that is of interest. To study consummatory behavior directly, the animal is usually provided with food, water, or a sexual object, and characteristics of his behavior toward the incentive (response class 3) are measured.

Response classes 2, 3, 5, 6, and 7 have been used in the studies of motivation reviewed in this chapter, and reference to Table 5–1 will help the reader to have a clear picture of just what is being done in some of the investigations. Before going on to the factors that regulate food intake, however, we may ask: Do all these measures assess the same thing?

Relationships among Measures

Ideally, it would make no difference whether we used the obstruction method or measured the amount consumed of the incentive object; the measure of the drive or of the incentive value should be the same for both methods. Unfortunately, this ideal is seldom realized. Anderson (1938) found that several measures of the hunger drive did not agree well with one another, a result consistent with the more recent findings (Fig. 5–6) of Miller (1956, pp. 319–320). While results with other drives show greater agreement among measures than is the case with hunger, we must be constantly alert to the possibility that the results of investigations may hold with one method of inquiry but not with another. With this cautionary note in mind, we can turn to brief considerations of factors controlling food intake.

1. *Deprivation.* When animals are deprived of food, it is reasonable to expect that their tendency to take food is thereby influenced. Such an expectation is supported by observations made by Skinner (1938, pp. 343–351), who showed that after a rat is deprived of food for 22 or 23 hours and then is permitted to eat, he will start eating rapidly and then gradually slow down his rate of intake until he is satiated (i.e., eats no more in that session). Bousfield (1933, 1934) has found similarly regular curves following substantial fasts in cats and chickens, but Horenstein (1951) reported a rather complex function relating duration of deprivation to eating over short intervals. Fasts of shorter intervals have been studied, but the conditions differed considerably from those used by Skinner, Bousfield, and Horenstein. These experiments will be discussed in connection with the energization of habit by drive in Chapter 11.

The Columbia obstruction method has also been used to study hun-

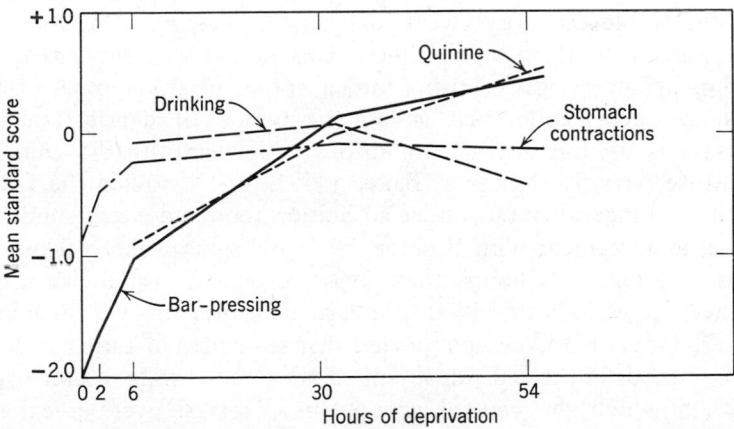

Figure 5-6. Values given by four measures of hunger after equal periods of food deprivation. Standard scores are plotted. "Drinking" refers to amount of enriched milk the rats took before satiation. "Quinine" refers to amount of quinine added to the milk before the animals stopped drinking. "Bar-pressing" is the rate of bar-pressing for food on a variable-interval schedule. "Stomach contractions" are measured by means of a balloon implanted on the end of a plastic fistula. Reproduced by permission from Miller (1956, Fig. 1).

ger. The fasts involved have ranged from zero to 192 hours, the actual intervals being 0, 2, 3, 4, 6, and 8 days (Warner, 1928a). The number of crossings of the grid increased from zero to two days' deprivation in female rats and to four days' deprivation in males, following which respective periods there was a decline in both sexes. This decline has usually been interpreted as an effect of weakness arising from inanition; certainly, the animal's need for food cannot have been reduced.

These observations show that deprivation is one of the conditions which controls eating and that duration of deprivation, within limits, is associated with increasing frequency of food-incentive related behavior (see, also, the discussion of Activity, Chapter 6). Animals satiated on food will often refuse to eat any further, except under certain conditions (described later). For example, James and Gilbert (1957) injected the stomachs of puppies with food until food ran out of the mouth; given an opportunity, then, to eat the puppies did not do so. However, satiation on some foods does not always preclude further ingestion of other foods, as is seen later in the discussion of properties of foods.

2. *Rhythms.* Another aspect of food intake which may be mentioned here is whether there is a rhythm or cycle of eating episodes. Animals do not eat continuously, even when food is present all the time and easy to obtain. Many years ago, Richter (1927) observed that rats would eat every two hours, on the average, even when food was available to them at all times. This periodicity, suggestive of a rhythm or an eating cycle, fits into a notion of the control of food intake by deprivation, that is, a brief period of deprivation (two hours) sets up the internal conditions which activate the animal to eat. More recently, however, Baker (1953, 1955) studied the feeding activities of individual rats under ad libitum food and water conditions. While, in agreement with Richter, he found a mean interval between meals of about two hours, there was tremendous variability around this average as indicated by a standard deviation of over 90 minutes (Baker, 1953). He likewise reported that sequences of eating and noneating periods in the individual animal were random. In a later experiment, in which the control group was observed over an extended period, there was again an absence of eating cycles (Baker, 1955). Evidently, then, the periodicity which Richter reported is not a fact that we can consider well established.[13]

3. *Experience.* A number of experiments suggest that aspects of

[13] There are other rhythms in animal behavior, including feeding behavior. We shall mention some of them later. However, they are associated, at least in the case of feeding, with external cues, which are constant in Baker's experiment.

food intake are affected by experience. This point was demonstrated by Bousfield and Elliott (1934), who found that rats required several days for readjustment following disruptions of their feeding regimes. Baker (1955), Lawrence and Mason (1955a, b), and Reid and Finger (1955, 1957) have all indicated that the rat requires a considerable period of time to adjust his food intake to a new schedule. The experiments go something as follows: Rats are placed for the first time on a restricted feeding schedule, for example, food is provided for one hour of the 24, and food intake and weight are recorded during this schedule for a number of days. The amount of food taken during the feeding periods is usually found gradually to increase with experience on the restricted schedule, despite the fact that there may be weight loss during the days immediately following the initiation of the schedule. Following a return to an ad libitum feeding regimen (Lawrence & Mason, 1955a), there may be a period of overeating before the animals compensate their intake in accordance with food supplies.[14] Lawrence and Mason (1955b) have also indicated that the amount of food taken following a given deprivation will be greater if the feeding period comes at a time when the animals are accustomed to eating rather than at some unfamiliar time. In experiments which measured details of the rat's behavior shown in eating periods following first being placed on restricted feeding schedules, Ghent (1951, 1957) has similarly shown that it takes repeated experiences of 23-hour deprivation of food for rats to take full advantage of the limited period of time in which they must eat. Over several days' experience, they begin eating more quickly and use a greater part of the feeding period for eating than is true at the beginning.

There can be no question that experience of deprivation or of feeding schedules affects food intake. Whether this may be attributed to gradual building up of a food deficit or whether learning is involved is not clear from these experiments.

It is, of course, obvious that experience is involved in food intake in the case of human beings. We eat periodically whether hungry or not, and the types of food we eat and prefer are determined by many kinds of cultural and similar factors (see Lee, 1957, and later discussions in this chapter). Recently some attention has been paid to experiential factors governing human food intake. Siegel (1957a) showed that male college students have a marked tendency to eat the entire amount of any food item served them rather than to leave portions

---

[14] It will be recalled that adjustments of food intake by dogs to various direct stomach feedings also required an extended period of time (Janowitz & Hollander, 1955).

242 MOTIVATION: THEORY AND RESEARCH

unfinished. He has also shown (1957*b*) that a highly monotonous though ample diet decreases the amount of food eaten. Smith, Powell, and Ross (1955) have summarized evidence that food aversions are related to neurosis and other correlates of personality. Food intake will also be greater for one food rather than another. We turn now to factors of this type. The experiments reviewed in the section just concluded involved a measure of overall intake.

4. *Properties and amounts of food.* In discussing specific hungers, we have already, in effect, indicated that food intake is affected by the make-up of the particular substances offered. However, in that case, there is a condition of specific need so that the intake of a particular food is a joint function of both need and the properties of the foods themselves. Are there preferences for foods aside from conditions of need?

Human experience, both adult and child, would certainly lead to an affirmative answer to this question, and the affirmation is supported by work with animals.[15] In discussing specific hungers, we pointed out that there are concentrations of salt and sugar solutions which seem to be preferred to others. Further, the concentrations offered an animal are an important determiner of the amount it will ingest. In many animals, there are apparently preferences for sugar and saccharin rather than for substances which (to the human at least) taste bitter, sour, or salty.

The amount of food offered will sometimes make a difference in the intake. Bayer (1929; cf., also, Katz, 1937) showed that the size of the pile of grain offered to hens determined the amount they would eat, within limits; that is, they would eat more from a large than a small heap. They would eat more whole than cracked grain and would eat much more if they pecked on a soft rather than a hard surface.

This summary of factors relating to food itself that are involved in intake is not exhaustive, but it illustrates the kinds of factors that may often be involved.

5. *External cues and factors.* We have already observed, in discussing specific hungers, that factors like habit will often determine food selection and intake. Here we can mention others. Rats eat less in warm temperatures than in cold (Donhoffer & Vonotzky, 1947; Weiss, 1958; Brobeck, 1955*b*). Rats tend to eat more in the dark than

---

[15] Additional relevant evidence will be considered in a discussion of the roles of incentives and variations in their quality and amount in relation to behavior (see Chapter 11).

in the light (see, e.g., Gilbert & James, 1956), and time of day continues to affect food intake, despite conditions of deprivation (Bare, 1959). Young (1948a, p. 300) has stressed that such factors as position of food, size of food particles, accessibility of food, and "distraction, humidity, odor, etc.," doubtless have a measurable effect upon the process of feeding.

6. *Social factors.* Bayer (1929) observed that a hen, fed in isolation to apparent satiety, would eat again in large amounts if another hen or hens were introduced and started eating. Social facilitation of feeding has similarly been reported in fish (Welty, 1934), rats (Harlow, 1932), puppies (Ross & Ross, 1949a, b; James, 1953), in the case of a less preferred food in rhesus monkeys (Harlow & Yuden, 1933), and chimpanzees (Yerkes, 1934). Thus, it is abundantly clear that, over a wide range of species, food intake may be affected by social factors.

Dominance relations, too, may affect food intake, and food-getting has often been used as a measure of the dominance hierarchy in animals (cf. Nissen, 1951, p. 448). If one animal is dominant over another, it is likely to get the most food, and this is true even if the subordinate chimpanzee is hungry; if the latter is starved, however, and the dominant animal has eaten well, the starved animal is likely to get more food despite the presence of the dominant animal (Nowlis, 1941).

At the human level, it is often true that food intake is affected by food taboos, social habits and customs, social facilitation, and so on. Duncker (1938), among others, has shown that food preferences of children may be modified by social suggestion, and a good deal of information is available which suggests that total food intake may be affected, at least temporarily, by dietary fads and weight-control schemes.

Summary Concerning Factors Governing Food Intake. While the primary factor governing food intake is probably deprivation, the operation of this factor has been shown to be modified by such factors as experience, properties of foodstuffs, external factors, and social factors. The prediction of food intake is therefore not a simple matter, since all of these factors may enter into it at once. Some caution should be observed, however, in overestimating these factors since, if deprivation is severe enough (before weakness sets in), it may well override them all. Nevertheless, it is important to note that the regulation of food ingestion is not through drive alone.

Summary of Hunger

The nature of hunger has long been of interest as a subject of investigation, and many theories have been advanced to explain it. Included are local and central theories and the idea that hunger arises from the depletion of a variety of bodily organs. The major local theory, dominant for much of this century, held that hunger arose from gastric contractions.

A variety of factors has been investigated in the attempt to discover the mechanisms of hunger. The theory of gastric contractions seems to have been largely discredited. Hunger is complexly controlled, as is seen in findings suggestive that there may be a hunger hormone and that such matters as gastric distension, blood-sugar level, caloric intake, and stimulation of the oral cavity are involved. Current thinking, however, based on developments in neurophysiology, indicates that there are neural "centers" in the hypothalamus (and probably elsewhere) that control eating and satiety. These centers themselves are seen to monitor eating as a result of their being affected by level of utilizable blood sugar or by bodily temperature. While neural centers are important, it should be noted that they could be sensitive to information from gastric distension and oral stimulation, for example.

In addition to general hunger, there are also "specific hungers," and these hungers relate to differential intake of foods in relation to dietary lacks and imbalance. While specific hungers exist, dietary self-selection is certainly not always perfect and is itself subject to many influences aside from bodily need. The mechanisms of specific hungers remain to be worked out.

There are a number of factors which regulate general food intake. While deprivation is perhaps chief among them, it is not a perfect predictor of what, when, and how much an animal will eat. Experience, food characteristics, external cues and circumstances, and the social situation have all been found, under at least some conditions, to play a role in the intake of food.

THIRST

Early Theories and Observations

While thirst and drinking behavior have not received the attention in psychological investigation that has been accorded to hunger and eating, the theories of thirst have a remarkable similarity, in their general nature and in their development, to those suggested for hunger. Albrecht von Haller in 1747 (Boring, 1942) suggested a local origin for thirst, just as he had for hunger. In this case, dryness of the structure of the mouth region and of the pathway to and including the stomach was said to be the cause of thirst.

Although Magendie, early in the nineteenth century, held thirst to be an instinctive sentiment and inexplicable, Beaumont emphasized dryness in the mouth and throat area, arising from the viscidity of the blood due to insufficient water. Beaumont's position was similar to that proposed by Dumas in 1803, who held that thickening of the blood, arising because of insufficient water, was the cause of thirst; elements of the blood, concentrated due to the lack of water, irritated nervous tissue. Theories stressing that thirst is a general sensation, arising from water deficit throughout the body, and stressing that there is a central neural locus for thirst have also been advocated (Rosenzweig, 1962; Wolf, 1958, p. 42).

Experiments in the early nineteenth century showed that intravenous administration of water resulted in cessation of the tendency to drink in thirsty dogs (Boring, 1942, pp. 558–559), and Claude Bernard's experiments in 1856 showed that sham drinking in a dog and a horse continued until exhaustion rather than ceasing when the mouth area was wet. Schiff in 1867 argued that thirst is a general sensation (Wolf, 1958, p. 47) and could cite in support of his view the fact that in cats and dogs severing of pertinent nerves (thus desensitizing the mouth-throat area) did not eliminate drinking. Bernard did not stress the notion of thirst as a general sensation but instead its origin in a general need for water in the body: "Ce sentiment est bien l'expression du besoin général causé par la diminution de quantité des liquides du corps" (quoted by Wolf, 1958, p. 66). As early as 1900, Mayer (Wolf, 1958; Boring, 1942; Rosenzweig, 1962) suggested that neural centers regulate drinking behavior and are activated by impulses arising from the blood vessels; these impulses, he thought, arise from changes in the osmotic pressure of the blood.

Observations which seemed to support the role of dryness in the throat continued to be made, however. Tying off the salivary glands in dogs resulted in readiness to drink, and reports were also made that the anesthetization of the throat by drugs, like cocaine, resulted in cessation of drinking in both a child and dogs. Neither result, however, was regularly confirmed in other experiments (Wolf, 1958, pp. 45–48). Nevertheless, Cannon (1918) convinced himself, on the basis of his own experiments and his interpretations of the experiments by others, that thirst arises because of dryness in the mouth and throat, due to decreased salivary flow. He addressed himself vigorously to the advocacy of this local theory of thirst, just as he had to the local theory of hunger. We will consider his theory and the experiments pertinent to it in the section immediately following.

First, however, it should be made clear that in thirst, as in hunger, there are at least two processes operative. Deneufbourg in 1813 (Wolf, 1958, p. 38) had discriminated the seat of thirst from its cause; he thought it occurs in the throat but is caused by generally insufficient bodily water. Various observations have shown that thirst can be distinguished from dryness in the mouth and throat. Wettendorff in 1901 and Winsor in 1930 (Wolf, 1958, p. 53; Boring, 1942) distinguished "true thirst," arising from dehydration of the tissues, from "false thirst," arising from a dry mouth and throat. We said in the case of hunger that some of its features, notably the pang, are probably due to stomach contractions, but that other features are not; it is still possible to speak of hunger in the absence of pangs. So it also seems to be with thirst. A "parched throat" no doubt is an important component of thirst and arises from local dryness; but thirst has other existence and aspects independent of the local dryness.

The Local Theory and Its Vicissitudes. Cannon presented his theory in 1918 (Cannon, 1918), as follows:

The theory of thirst . . . is that the salivary glands have, among their functions, that of keeping moist the ancient water-course; that they, like other tissues, suffer when water is lacking in the body—a lack especially important to them, however, because their secretion is almost wholly water, and that, when these glands fail to provide sufficient fluid to moisten the mouth and throat, the local discomfort and unpleasantness which result constitute the feeling of thirst (p. 295).

Cannon observed that salivary flow diminishes after profuse sweating and deprivation of fluids, and that thirst accompanies the decreased flow. Thirst also was instigated when atropine, which reduces salivary flow, was administered. This thirst continued with little abatement if the mouth was merely washed out with water, but it was diminished with novocaine. Drinking, of course, eliminated the thirst. Emotional states, also, Cannon pointed out, disrupt salivary flow and, correspondingly, induce thirst. The "torment of the sensations" arising from inadequate salivary flow, Cannon indicated, is the reason we take steps to restore our bodily water supplies. The survival value of such steps is evident.

The evidence pertinent to Cannon's theory is of several kinds: (1) experimental interruption of salivary flow by either drugs or surgical removal; (2) experiments in which anesthetization of the throat by means of drugs or by denervation has been used; (3) experiments in which sham-drinking and direct stomach-loading have been carried out; and (4) general subjective reports of the coexistence of thirst and local dryness. We turn now to brief consideration of the results of these types of investigations.

Evidence of continued thirst, arising from a variation in salivary flow induced by drugs, is conflicting. Pack (1923) and Gregerson and Cannon (1932) found that pilocarpine, which stimulates salivation, reduced the tendency to drink in rabbits. In patients with diabetes insipidus, however, some reports show that pilocarpine induces salivation and reduces thirst and others that it does not reduce thirst (Wolf, 1958, p. 49). Adolph et al. (1947) found pilocarpine to have little effect on water intake, despite increased salivation, in dehydrated men who had been exposed to desert conditions. In rats, on the other hand, Adolph (1948) found no difference in amount of salivation after injections of quantities of pilocarpine which both did and did not suppress drinking. Montgomery (1931*b*), using dogs with and without salivary glands, found little difference in their water ingestion after injection of pilocarpine or atropine in small doses. Schmidt et al. (1958) found that atropine increased water intake but not to the extent they believe Cannon's theory requires. Other experiments could be cited, but the foregoing evidence is representative.

Montgomery (1931*a*) extirpated the salivary glands in dogs but observed no rise in water intake per day—results which at least seem to conflict with those reported by Gregerson and Cannon (1932). These results, however, depended on the fact that the dogs were panting, which would dry their mouths. It may be that Montgomery's findings do not invalidate Cannon's theories, as the mouths in the dogs in her experiment may have remained moist (Wolf, 1958, p. 52).[16] Total water intake of these animals without salivary glands did not differ from that of normal animals (Montgomery, 1931*a*; Gregerson, 1932*b*).

The severing of sensory nerves serving the mouth region was accomplished by Bellows and Van Wagenen (1939), who, in different dogs, cut the trigeminal nerves, glossopharyngeals and chorda tympanae bilaterally, and the olfactory tracts. No effect was observed on water-drinking either in normal dogs or in animals with diabetes insipidus (which drink abnormally large amounts). We have already observed that anesthetization of the back of the mouth by drugs sometimes leads to cessation of drinking, sometimes not.

The sham-drinking experiments permit the animal to drink through

---

[16] Salivary glands are, of course, not present in many species of animals, among them many water animals and birds (Wolf, 1958, p. 52).

the mouth, and thus the mouth and throat areas are moistened, but the water passes from the body through a fistula before it reaches the stomach. In stomach water-loading experiments, amounts of water are introduced directly into the stomach by fistula, and the effects are observed on drinking behavior (which can be either normal or sham drinking). Bellows (1939) concluded that, in his experiments with sham drinking, as in Bernard's, the local dryness must have been overcome, yet the animals continued to drink (cf. also, Adolph, 1941; Bruce, 1935). Towbin (1949), however, observed satiation from sham drinking, although it was short-lived. Both of these investigators, as well as Solarz (1958), have found that introduction of water directly into the stomach will, after a period of time, reduce the drinking behavior of animals; it is possible, of course, in this last type of experiment, that salivary secretion was restored following water absorption. If so, this would hardly be critical evidence against the local theory, but it seems unlikely in view of the short periods of time involved.

Much of the foregoing evidence is really not decisively clear one way or another, so far as the local theory is concerned. Results have conflicted, factors that may be important have not been controlled, and methods and species have varied. Perhaps more convincing are the following kinds of evidence.

It was said before that thirst and dryness in the throat can be distinguished. Wolf (1958, p. 53) summarizes a number of reports in which human subjects speak of having dry mouths but not of being thirsty. On the other hand, Winsor (1930) found that while gum-chewing caused a continuation of salivary flow it did not prevent thirst under dehydration. King (reprinted in Wolf, 1958, pp. 375–380) described the reactions to water of men suffering from severe desert thirst: "Although water was imbibed again and again, even to repletion of the stomach, it did not assuage their insatiable thirst, thus demonstrating that the sense of thirst is, like the sense of hunger, located in the general system, and that it could not be relieved until the remote tissues were supplied" (Wolf, 1958, p. 379). Presumably, their mouths were wet, but their thirst continued. We need not cite other evidence, but there is a good deal of it. These reports lead to two related conclusions: One can have a dry mouth but not be thirsty; one can have a wet mouth (from salivation or from drinking) and still be thirsty.

Cannon's theory of thirst is no longer considered sound (Stellar, 1954; Wolf, 1958), but we would remark that the evidence we have reviewed is not absolutely critical against it. (Nor, we would add, is the evidence very convincing for it, as Cannon thought.) Like his theory of hunger, Cannon's theory of thirst is mainly pertinent to but one aspect of the total phenomenon: the reported "sensation." Perhaps the chief problem for his theory is that, as with hunger, there is a variety of facts to which it is largely irrelevant. To say this in another way, the variety of factors which control drinking behavior is great and the whole set of thirst and drinking phenomena suggests that the mechanism is complex. Let us look at some of these factors.

Some Internal Variables Affecting Thirst

Hormonal Factors. The possibility has been suggested that hormones which regulate thirst are secreted by the kidney (Wolf, 1958, p. 205, fn.) and the subcommissural area in rats (Gilbert, 1956). More commonly implicated, however, is the posterior pituitary (neurohypophysis) (Barker, Adolph, & Keller, 1953). This area has been especially stressed in relation to the condition of excessive urination (polyuria) and excessive thirst (polydipsia) known as diabetes insipidus (Morgan & Stellar, 1950, pp. 387–388; Wolf, 1958, pp. 97–103). Verney (1947) has emphasized the role of the antidiuretic hormone secreted by the posterior pituitary in the regulation of the body's water balance. Wolf (1958, pp. 189–190) has summarized Verney's theory succinctly as follows:

According to this theory, there exist in the central nervous system, in the bed of the internal carotid artery, osmoreceptors which are possibly tiny vesicular bodies—or even neurons—capable of swelling or shrinking with changes in the effective osmotic pressure of their ambient fluid. When water is taken in positive load, these osmoreceptors, behaving as osmometers, respond to the resulting dilution of body fluids by swelling. They may then act as stretch receptors for afferent nerves, impulses along which reflexly cause the neurohypophysis to reduce below normal its rate of secretion of antidiuretic hormone. Following a latent period during which already circulating hormone disappears from the plasma, there results a decreased reabsorption of water by the renal tubules and a consequent diuresis. As the kidney excretes this urine which is more dilute osmotically than body fluids, the osmotic pressure of the remaining body fluids rises toward normal and again stimulates (or perhaps fails to stimulate) osmoreceptors as before. Antidiuretic hormone reappears, reducing the diuresis to normal (homoluric) flow.[17]

[17] In the discussion which follows, we shall encounter such terms as tonic, hypertonic, isotonic, and hypotonic applied to various fluids. We may illustrate what these terms mean, for our purposes, by an example. Suppose we have a salt solution which is isotonic to some other solution, with a semipermeable membrane between them. In this instance, since the two solutions are isotonic for salt, the concentration of salt will not change in either. However, if one is hypertonic

This theory, which Wolf (1958, p. 190) finds has some limitations but which is also compatible with many other features of recent work in thirst, is essentially one that deals with water conservation, that is, through the operation of the antidiuretic hormone water excretion is reduced. With water intake in excess of requirements, excretion can occur. While Verney emphasized the role of salt concentration in the blood as stimulus for the osmoreceptors (Verney, 1947), he also suggests that emotional stress can release the antidiuretic hormone (cf., also, Gaunt, Birnie, & Eversole, 1949).

Characteristics and Distribution of Body Fluids. Generally speaking, there is a relation between deficit in body water and thirst and drinking behavior. However, as we shall see, it is possible to induce drinking or thirst without actual water deprivation. This evidence suggests that the critical factor in thirst and drinking lies in the characteristics and distribution of body fluids and that water deprivation or deficit, in themselves, have their effects via these factors.

We have already seen that changes in the viscosity of the blood and in its osmotic pressure were proposed very early as factors inducing thirst (cf., also, Gregerson, 1932a; Gregerson & Bullock, 1933). Wettendorff (1901) found a rise of the osmotic pressures in the blood of dogs after water deprivation, but it did not occur immediately. This led him to think that it is general dehydration of body tissue that is the source of thirst, rather than a localized change.

A number of studies have examined the role of salt solutions introduced into the body. Putting 30 to 100 cc of a saturated saline solution into the stomachs of adult human subjects reduced salivation in some subjects but increased it in others (Smith, 1935). When sodium chloride was injected under the skin of rats, drinking occurred within ten minutes of the injection (Young, Heyer, & Richey, 1952). O'Kelley (1954) preloaded the stomachs of rats with an amount of one of several concentrations of sodium chloride solutions and found that the amount of water subsequently taken in was related to the concentration of the salt solution; bar-pressing for water reward showed a similar relationship (O'Kelley & Falk, 1958). Wayner and Reimanis (1958), using the subcutaneous injection method, also found a relation between latency and amount of drinking and the concentration of solution injected. They report additional experiments, however, which suggest

(i.e., with a high concentration of salt), fluid will pass into it from the other across the membrane, tending to bring them into isotonic equilibrium. Osmosis and osmotic pressure are related to these terms, and the term *osmoreceptor* is used to indicate structures which may be sensitive to changes in tonicity.

that it is the absolute amount of salt injected, rather than the concentration, which is the factor important to drinking.

When hypertonic salt solutions are given intravenously into human subjects, there is a decrement in salivation and marked thirst (Holmes & Gregerson, 1947). If the injections were preceded, however, by injection of substantial quantities of water, thirst was not reported if 20 to 30 minutes intervened between the opportunity to drink and the salt injection. Several experiments have shown that the effects of introduction of salt solutions into the body are not necessarily a consequence of the sodium and chloride, themselves. Potassium salts taken in water did not increase thirst, whereas sodium chloride and sodium bicarbonate taken in water did (Arden, 1934). However, Holmes and Gregerson (1950) showed that sorbitol (a carbohydrate) aroused thirst as much as salt does, even though sorbitol depressed the concentrations of sodium and of chloride in blood plasma. Holmes and Gregerson (1950) induced drinking in dogs by administering glucose, sucrose, sorbitol, urea, and the like.

Administration of these various substances in solution probably causes water to leave various tissues of the body so that dilution is achieved (O'Kelley, Falk, & Flint, 1958). Wolf (1958, p. 71) points out that "thirst is characteristic not simply of water loss alone but also of water excesses, provided salt excess is relatively greater . . ." and ". . . the totality of body cells behave . . . as an osmometer such that fluid moves in or out of cells in response to gradients of osmotic pressure." Gilman (1937), using dogs, injected either solutions of salt or urea in concentrations such that they effected equal rises in the osmotic pressure in the blood. Drinking occurred much more quickly after the salt injection than after the urea injection, this apparently being due to the fact that water leaves the body cells very rapidly to dilute the salt, whereas this does not happen with urea. This suggests that cellular dehydration is the factor responsible for the onset of thirst and drinking. As supporting evidence, we may mention the experiment of Darrow and Yannet (1935). They found that dogs did not drink even though they had been deprived of water, and their mouths were very dry. This effect was accomplished by introducing a 5 per cent glucose solution intraperitoneally, which caused the body cells to become hydrated (i.e., water enters them). So drinking was absent in the presence of cellular hydration. Cizek et al. (1951) used a similar technique to cause overhydration of the body cells and observed that their dogs, nevertheless, drank (cf., also, Holmes & Cizek, 1951). Wolf (1958, pp. 106–107) does not think these latter experiments rule out the role of cellular dehydration in drinking and suggests that other factors may be operative in drinking under conditions of cellular hydration (cf., also, Wolf, 1958, pp. 203–205).

Gastric Distension and the Regulation of Drinking. Overall water intake in at least some species, especially dogs, is rather precisely gauged to water deficit. Since absorption of water requires some time after it has been imbibed, there is interest in the factors which lead to cessation of drinking prior to absorption. Gastric distension is a source of possible cues for the stopping of water intake. Bellows (1939), however, as we have already indicated, observed that introduction of water directly into the stomach did not inhibit drinking in dogs unless 10 or 15 minutes elapsed before the dog was allowed to drink. While this period of time is too short, in all probability, to allow for complete absorption of the water (which has been estimated to require over a half hour), the fact that the dogs drank immediately after a preloading and did not drink a short time later suggests that gastric distension may have little to do with the process of satiation.

However, there is evidence suggesting that gastric factors do play some role, though perhaps not a precise or invariant regulatory function. Towbin (1949), in experiments beyond those already cited, first used sham-drinking to determine how much a thirsty dog would drink before temporary satiation. Having determined this quantity, he then introduced this amount directly into the stomach, allowed time for its absorption, and then allowed the dog to drink. Preloading of the stomach with as little as 40 per cent of the water which the dog had sham-drunk was enough to inhibit drinking. Obviously the dog had grossly over-estimated its need in terms of the amount it had sham-drunk. Towbin also reduced the amount the dog would drink by placing a water- or air-filled balloon in the dog's stomach; in order to gain a marked suppression of drinking, however, he had to inflate the balloon to a size considerably greater than that of the control sham-drink. These experiments seem to suggest a role for stomach distension in the control of drinking, but perhaps it works only when distension is extreme. Adolph (1950), however, found that induced stomach distension inhibited immediate drinking in the rat, hamster, guinea pig, and adult rabbit, in which drinking occurs in distinct episodes, whereas immediate drinking was not affected (unless distension was excessive) in dogs and young rabbits. The latter two animals tend to drink water in continuous drafts. Vagotomy led to an increase in the amount of water taken by dogs per drink; this overdrinking is apparently due to the lack of feedback to the central nervous system from afferent nerves serving the stomach. Sympathectomy had the opposite results

(Towbin, 1955). Applying cocaine to the gastric mucosa (Montgomery & Holmes, 1951, 1955; Holmes & Montgomery, 1953) eliminated the inhibition of drinking arising from gastric distension.

Although the foregoing account supports the notion that gastric distension may be a factor in inhibition of drinking, it seems likely (Wolf, 1958, p. 161) that in man, who customarily drinks small quantities of water, the gastric factor is not very important. Wolf suggests "pharyngeal metering" and other factors as alternatives.

Oral Factors and the Regulation of Drinking. The mouth, throat, and esophagus, of course, constitute another possible source of signals of water intake that might be a part of a satiety mechanism. Bellows (1939) thought that satisfaction might arise from the act of swallowing. Wolf (1958, p. 59) reports some evidence that water placed directly into the stomach does not satisfy thirst as well in man as it does when it passes first through the mouth. Epstein (1960.) studied water intake in the rat through a chronic gastric tube. The animal regulated the amount of water he received through the tube by bar-pressing. Normal, everyday water intake was similar to that obtained in the control period, suggesting that oropharyngeal stimulation and consummatory responses are not factors in ordinary water regulation. However, when the water injected for bar-presses was increased, the animals took in an excess amount of water (though making fewer responses), suggesting that "The loss of precise 'metering' of water intake by feedback from licking and swallowing . . ." may be important (Epstein, 1960, p. 498).

The most thorough evaluation of oral factors in drinking behavior was made by Miller, Sampliner, and Woodrow (1957). They compared water consumption and bar-pressing for water after 14 cc of water had been given their rats by fistula directly into the stomach, or had been drunk by mouth, or (in controls) no water had been given. On an 18-minute test, the controls drank 21 cc of water; the stomach-watered animals, 16; and the mouth-watered animals, 6.7. All differences were significant, indicating that water by fistula reduces thirst but that water by mouth reduces it more. Oral factors thus can, at least in the experienced organism, play a role in the regulation of water intake. Similar findings were reported, in the section on hunger, as to the role of oral factors in regulating food intake.

Summary. We have reviewed evidence which points to the possible role of hormonal mechanisms in body-water conservation, the role of various substances, like salt, in inducing bodily changes (probably cellular dehydration) involved in thirst, and the role of gastric and oral factors (along with actual absorption of water) in satiety. We go next to studies of the central nervous system, where events of further significance to thirst and drinking take place.

Neural Factors

In our discussion of hunger the discovery of areas in the hypothalamus that are important to the regulation of food-taking behavior was seen as an important advance in understanding. A similar situation exists for water intake.

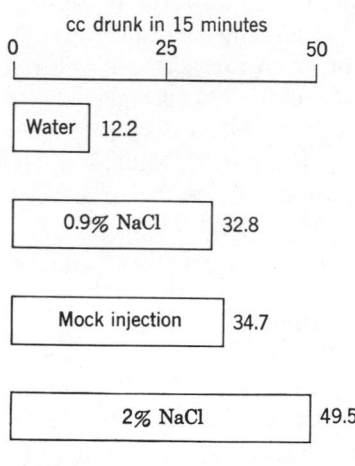

Figure 5–7. Effects on water-intake of minute injections into the rat's brain. Injection of water (0.15 milliliters) reduces drinking but injection of the same amount of 2% saline increases it. Effects of control injections (0.9% NaCl and a mock injection) are also shown. Reproduced by permission from Miller (1957, Fig. 11).

In a series of experimental reports (Andersson, 1953; Andersson & McCann, 1955*a*), direct injections of small amounts of sodium chloride into the hypothalamus evoked, in many instances, drinking responses in goats. Andersson and McCann (1955*a*) made very small injections, so that the area stimulated could be precisely delimited as residing in the medial hypothalamus proximal to the third ventricle. Stimulation not only causes drinking of water but also acceptance and drinking of urine. Miller (1957, p. 1274, Fig. 11), using cats, found no effect on drinking of very small amounts of isotonic saline but an increase in drinking with the injection of hypertonic saline into the same area (see Fig. 5–7). On the other hand, a tiny injection of distilled water decreased water intake. Electrical stimulation of the hypothalamic area concerned also caused drinking in goats (Andersson and McCann, 1955*a*) and in the rat (Greer, 1955). Andersson and McCann (1955*b*) also made lesions in the hypothalamus of dogs by means of electrical coagulation and found reduced water intake in animals in which the lesion was made in the area corresponding to the one involved in the prior experiments. The three best cases refused water for 9 to 14 days, although they would readily drink milk or broth. Wolf cites the case (1958, p. 93) of a girl whose thirst was relieved when a cyst which had been pressing the hypothalamic area from the base of the brain was opened.

It seems likely that there are two excitatory drinking areas (see Fig. 5-2) in the hypothalamus (Rosenzweig, 1962, p. 130), one in lateral (cf. Teitelbaum & Epstein, 1962) and one in ventromedial areas (Stevenson, Welt, & Orloff, 1950). A possible inhibitory center was suggested by Bellows and Van Wagenen (1938).

Theory of Thirst

We can be quite brief as to the present status of the theory of thirst. Everything seems to point to the existence of cells in the hypothalamic region which are sensitive to changes in the tonicity or osmotic pressure of the fluids which bathe them. Changes in the characteristics and distribution of bodily fluids, very probably involving cellular dehydration, may be the factors which throw these cells into excitatory activity. We may note that Verney (1947) had hypothesized that similar kinds of receptors might be involved in the regulation of water excretion through the antidiuretic hormone.

Factors Controlling Water Intake

Measures and their relationships. Much the same measures have been used to assay thirst as have been employed in the case of hunger. In one of his experiments, Anderson (1937) compared results for three measures of thirst. One employed the obstruction procedure, and the other two were a test and retest of the influence of 24 hours' thirst on activity as measured in a wheel. The latter two measures, taken 10 days apart, were highly intercorrelated (r of .917). However, the obstruction method yielded a correlation of only .331 with the first activity test. In a later experiment, Anderson (1938) used 10 measures for thirst, including obstruction tests, measures of drinking, speed, etc. The two highest intercorrelations were .83 and .633, between two drinking tests and two obstruction tests, respectively, and there were moderately high correlations among other measures of drinking (up to .631). In general, however, the correlations, especially among different methods of measuring thirst, like obstruction vs. drinking, were low and insignificant. Miller (1956) has also shown that different measures give quite different results for the measurement of given durations of water deprivation (see Fig. 5-8). As was true of hunger, then, the measures of thirst do not seem to be highly interrelated, and

our comments concerning the facts of thirst must always be restricted
to the particular methods employed to measure it.

Deprivation. The most commonly used method for establishing
a water deficit is to deprive animals of water for a period of time, the
continuing loss of water through perspiration and respiration leading
to a deficit. Drinking can be instigated by spending time in a hot, dry
room (or in a desert), by food ingestion, or by salt injection.

Many investigators (e.g., Adolph, 1943) have been impressed with
the sensitivity of men and animals, especially dogs, to water loss. Dogs
will begin to drink when their water loss is half of one per cent of their
body weight. Wolf (1958, p. 159) says that the dog is unusual in his
ability to make up a water deficit (and no more) by drinking and that
many animals, including man, are not as precise in making up deficits
(Wolf, 1958, p. 9). Drinking, he says, "may fail completely as an index
of need."

Warner (1928b) ran rats on the obstruction box under durations of
deprivation of 1 to 6 days. There were negligible sex differences, and
he found the maximum number of grid-crossings at one day's deprivation, the curve trailing off for durations longer than one day. There
were sex differences for hunger, and the peak of crossings occurred

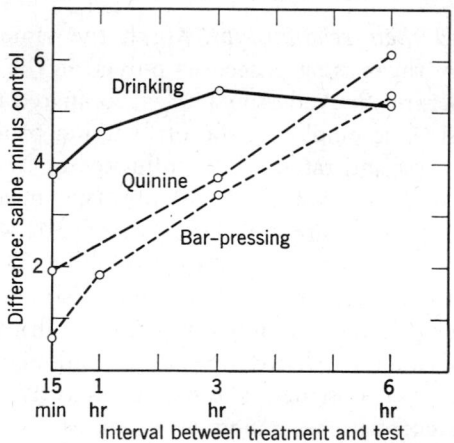

Figure 5–8. Values given by three measures of thirst at given intervals following
stomach intubation of 5 cc of 2-molar NaCl solution. Differences are plotted between these test scores and control scores. Water was used in all tests, that is, the
rats drank it, bar-pressed for it, or drank it when it was adulterated with quinine.
For further explanation, see caption to Figure 5–6. Reproduced by permission from
Miller (1956, Fig. 2).

at a later day. Young and Richey (1952) studied the drinking of rats as a function of time of day. They found little drinking between the hours of 6 A.M. and 6 P.M. and that most of the rats' water intake occurred during the night, the results corresponding to those of Siegel and Stuckey (1947*a*). Water intake was measured by Siegel (1947), who found a sigmoid function for amount of water taken in a 5-minute drinking period after deprivations of up to 48 hours. This does not agree with Warner's findings. Siegel and Stuckey (1947*b*) had found a relation between water intake and food intake. Stellar and Hill (1952) also found that, with deprivations up to 168 hours, the curve relating deprivation to drinking is negatively accelerated.

Skinner (1936), using an instrumental response, found drinking curves which, while more irregular, were like those reported for hunger, that is, the rate of response is rapid at first and slowly declines. Smith and Smith (1939), using cats in a Skinner box, found curves for drinking to satiety that differed a good deal from those reported by Skinner. Whether this is due to the species difference or to other factors is not known.

Experience. According to Adolph (1957) newly born puppies and rats will drink milk but not water, even in the presence of a water deficit. It takes 10 days for water-drinking to appear. Adolph, Barker, and Hoy (1954) showed, however, that weanling rats were better able to restore a water deficit than they were at later ages. Whether these findings indicate a role of experience or of other factors is uncertain. Ghent (1957), using young adult rats which had not previously been deprived of water, found that the latency of the drinking response decreased sharply and that the amount of drinking increased over the first seven experiences of 23 hours of water deprivation. She concludes that ". . . experience of deprivation increases the ease of arousal and amount of drinking behavior" (Ghent, 1957, p. 174). Zimbardo and Montgomery (1957*b*) also found delays prior to the initial drinking response after water deprivation but observed the longer the deprivation period (24 to 72 hours) the shorter were the delays. They interpreted the delays as due to the exploratory behavior in which their rats engaged, rather than to experience (see Chapter 6 for further work on exploration).

Wolf (1958, pp. 94–97) has suggested that there is a conditioned thirst reflex. It is probable, he asserts, that stimulation from dryness or other conditions in the mouth or throat comes, through learning, to be a conditioned stimulus for drinking behavior. We think this is a reasonable postulate and that a number of the phenomena of drinking behavior, as well as of eating (like the cessation of drinking before absorption can have occurred or the role of gastric distension in terminating drinking), may be explicable on the basis of a well-developed account of this mechanism.

Characteristics of water and other cues. Although water does not vary as much in its characteristics as does food, there is evidence that variations occur and affect drinking. Young (1955) reports that rats prefer tap water to distilled water, and rats and men often prefer slightly salty water to distilled water (Wolf, 1958, pp. 121, 123, 162). Various liquids like salt water, brackish water, foul water, blood, and urine are not ordinarily drinkable; but under extreme need men and animals may drink them. Rheingold and Hess (1957) studied the attractiveness for three- and seven-day-old chicks of various visual properties of water. They found that preferences were not affected by experience and that water itself was not as attractive as mercury, a plastic that looked like water, and blue-colored water. They consider that the brightness and movement in the stimulus perhaps govern attractiveness.

Social factors. Some evidence has been reported for social facilitation of drinking in chicks (Breed, 1911), but Craig (1912) did not find this true for doves. E. W. Rasmussen (cited by Munn, 1950, p. 466) and Bruce (1941) found that drinking by rats was socially facilitated. There has been little interest, however, in using thirst and drinking in relation to problems of social behavior in animals (Crawford, 1939; Smith & Ross, 1952).

Summary of Thirst

As with hunger, the local theory of thirst (local dryness in the mouth and throat) seems to have been superseded by findings emphasizing control by central hypothalamic structures. It appears that these structures must be sensitive to change in the distribution of body fluids and that a critical factor in thirst is cellular dehydration. Oral and gastric factors, no doubt, contribute to the control of drinking, perhaps because of learning, and there are hormonal regulations as well. Drinking occurs primarily to deprivation of water, but it is also influenced by experience, characteristics of fluids offered, and, perhaps, by social factors.

PAIN AVOIDANCE

One of the commonly postulated primary drives is the avoidance of pain. Many of the stimulus conditions which the human being reports as painful possess the characteristic of producing injury to the bodily tissues if they continue long enough, and others, especially those which arise from sources inside the body, are often associated with disease and other states whose continuation is prejudicial to the health and well-being of the person. Pain is often regarded as a warning signal, and a prompt response to it may have considerable biological value. That is, doing something which eliminates the painful stimulus protects the body from further injury, and correcting the internal condition which is responsible for pain may lead to eliminating the disease or other factor which is not conducive to health or continued survival.

Pain has further significance to the field of motivation. In a sense, almost all of the primary drives have, at one time or another, been regarded as having their effects through the intense, unpleasant, disrupting, powerful stimuli which they are capable of producing. The pangs of hunger, the parched mouth and throat of thirst, the painful swelling of the mammary glands as a stimulus to nursing, the stress of extreme cold or extreme heat, and the imperious demands of the sexual drive are cases in point. E. B. Holt (1931) once said that we are scourged through life by such stimuli. We have seen already that Walter Cannon spoke of the goading of hunger and thirst. Such views imply the idea that much of our activity has the relief of pain or pain-avoidance as its goal. This, in general, is the view that behavior serves to reduce stimulation or tension and reflects the assumption that tension reduction usually has survival value. This kind of goal or motivation—that is, to eliminate motives because they are painful—is sometimes described as a negative view of motivation and is contrasted with views that see motivation as arising also from positive enjoyment, even, on occasion, involving an increase in stimulation.

Pain which arises from tissue injury or disease, however, is not the lot of a substantial proportion of the population [18] in any chronic or continued sense. We quickly remove ourselves from painful stimulation, and our tissues heal. We often use analgesics immediately after the injury and during the healing. We seek quick relief from internal conditions which give us pain—the aching back, the recurrent headache, the painful abdomen. While it lasts, pain, especially severe pain, may be the dominant fact of one's existence, but its primary direct motivating effect is to lead to corrective or ameliorative action. It is an indirect effect of pain that, both in life and in theory, has the greatest significance for motivation.

[18] In this discussion we say little about "psychosomatic" pain. Such pain arises from very complex factors and probably involves a great deal of learning. It seems often to serve less as a motive to escape or avoid pain than as a way to achieve other goals.

This effect of pain motivates us *to avoid it*. Having experienced pain, we take steps to make sure that we will not experience that source of pain again. We need only cite the many analgesics that are available, the safety devices for the prevention of injury, the constant abjurations to take care of oneself, or the occasional suicide because of severe, chronic pain to remind ourselves that much of life is or may be organized to avoid pain or to lessen its effects when it comes. Of course, avoidance of injury and disease has other values as well, but we can hardly doubt that pain-avoidance is one of the major factors in the emphasis on protection from injury and disease.

We shall see in Chapter 11 that pain-avoidance has figured largely in the theory of acquired or learned drives or motives. It does not exaggerate the matter to say that, in the view of many, pain-avoidance or discomfort-avoidance, is the major basis of learned motivation. This is perhaps the most noteworthy feature of pain in systematic considerations of motivation, and our concern in this chapter is limited to topics relevant to it.

Some Features of Pain

Pain has been extensively investigated. Much of this work, however, has concerned itself with the description of kinds of pain, the search for its adequate stimulus and for its receptors, for neural and chemical mechanisms in pain, and for methods for relief of chronic pain by drugs or surgical procedures.[19] We shall not attempt to deal with these problems here, as they are not immediately concerned with pain as a drive factor. Instead, we shall direct our attention to (1) individual differences in sensitivity to pain stimulation; (2) the problem of the reaction to pain; (3) the role of social and experiential factors in response to pain; and (4) the effects of varying intensities of noxious stimulation, including arousal.

Individual differences in sensitivity to pain stimulation. That there are differences in the sensitivity shown by people and animals is evident in everyday experience. Some persons respond to the slightest painful stimulation; others stoically tolerate such stimulation. The majority of reports in the literature amply support this observation. Lanier (1943) studied the reaction of 15 college women to electric shock and

---

[19] The history of early pain research is briefly reviewed by Boring (1942, pp. 467–475). Other valuable reviews and discussions have been provided by Dallenbach (1939), Morgan and Stellar (1950, pp. 243–254), Jenkins (1951, pp. 1178–1179), Stone and Jenkins (1940), Edwards (1950), Geldard (1953), Hardy, Wolf, and Goodell (1952), White and Sweet (1955), Wolff and Wolf (1958), and Barber (1959).

found a wide range of reaction around the group mean. The application of radiant heat is another commonly used measure for inducing cutaneous pain. Chapman and Jones (1944), using this technique with 200 normal subjects, and Hall and Stride (1954) with several hundred psychiatric patients of several types found wide variations in pain threshold. Beecher (1957) has also found much variation with this technique. Clark and Bindra (1956) studied 46 subjects with several kinds of painful stimuli and also reported variations in pain thresholds. The variability among people, then, of the pain threshold is well documented in the research literature. Unfortunately, it cannot be ascertained from the studies reviewed how much of this variation arises from basic sensitivity differences, uncontaminated by the many factors which are known to influence the report of pain, and there is evidence (Schumacher et al., 1940) for uniform pain threshold among people.

There are, however, a number of cases reported in the literature in which the person involved is apparently insensitive to pain stimulation and in which this condition has existed from birth (McMurray, 1950, 1955; Cohen et al., 1955). Extensive study of several of these cases clearly indicates that pain has not been a factor in the lives of these people. They often bear numerous scars reminiscent of burns and cuts and other injuries; their insensitivity to pain has prevented their avoiding potentially injurious situations (especially in childhood) or in escaping quickly enough from a noxious stimulus once in contact with it. We mention these findings again in Chapter 11, because the absence of pain in such people has interesting implications for the theory of acquired drive.

There is some evidence of variation in pain sensitivity in animals. Muenzinger and Mize (1933) used a method for shocking rats which held skin resistance roughly constant and determined thresholds for reaction to electric shock. They found differences among their rats.

The reaction to pain. Pain can be reported before it reaches intensities that cause a person to wince or to withdraw. Pain can exist in presumably similar degrees but with considerably different effects at different times, even in the same individual. A number of reports (summarized by Barber, 1959, pp. 438–440) indicate that with prefrontal leucotomy for the relief of pain, the pain itself is still present postoperatively, but the patient is less responsive to it than he was before. If his attention is brought to the pain, he experiences discomfort. Opiates may have a similar effect. This suggests the important role of emotional reactions to pain and to the fearful anticipation of future pain in the significance of pain to motivation. Hypnosis can also obviate the pain experience in some subjects to at least some noxious stimuli (Barber, 1959, pp. 445 ff.). Placebos will alleviate pain in at least some patients. Important here is the conviction that the placebo (usually a fake drug) will actually work. What these studies suggest is that the individual's emotional reaction to pain is an important aspect of his tolerance for pain and of its significance to his behavior. We are not clear, however, as to how widely this particular conclusion may be generalized.

Experiential and social factors. The discussion just concluded suggests that the reaction to pain is subject to many influences. From ordinary experience we would expect that the social situation would make a difference in the readiness to tolerate given levels of painful stimulation. Stoicism in the face of pain is a virtue in many cultures, and children, especially boys, are urged in our culture to tolerate some degree of pain. Seidman et al. (1957) found that their human subjects would tolerate a higher level of self-administered shock when it was presumably shared by a partner than when they were by themselves. Jenkins (1951, p. 1178) has observed that some pain is apparently pleasurable, at least in a context of other social and stimulational factors: "Some people derive pleasure from the consumption of hot spices, horseradish, etc., which appear to obtain their distinctive effects by the stimulation of pain receptors." [20]

That experience or learning can influence either the reaction to pain or the fact of pain experience itself is suggested by several experiments. Pavlov (1927) used various noxious stimuli, like shock, as conditioned stimuli for food. The noxious stimuli were at first mild, but were gradually increased in intensity. After training the dogs, Pavlov reported he could discover no reaction to the noxious stimuli in these dogs comparable to the normal reactions to them; even pulse and respiratory changes were absent in response to these stimuli. Somewhat similar experiments with cats, also successful, have been reported by Masserman (1943). Melzack and Scott (1957) reared dogs from an early age to maturity in special cages which limited their sensory experience and isolated them socially. Noxious stimulation was probably experienced very little by these dogs, if at all. As compared to normally reared dogs, the animals with restricted experience did not seem to adapt themselves readily to avoid a pin-prick, an electric shock, or a burn on the nose. Ordinary emotional reactions to such stimuli also were lacking in some of these animals, suggesting that perception of

[20] The phenomenon of masochism may be relevant here, although the factors which develop and control it are probably quite complex.

the stimuli was abnormal. Response to the stimulation did occur but it was so different from that of the controls as to make one wonder if the restricted animals could "feel" the pain. There is, of course, no way to answer this query. K. R. L. Hall (1955) has suggested a conditioning interpretation for the reduction in the pain threshold which occurs in human subjects with a rise in skin temperature.

The limited evidence available does support the general observation that social and experiential factors may at least affect the *response* to pain stimulation.

The effects of varying intensities of noxious stimulation: arousal. In general, the more intense a noxious stimulus the greater the response to it. In response to minimal stimulation by a von Frey hair, the human subject will merely report quietly whether he feels pain. From this point on, as stimulus intensity grows, the subject shows greater reluctance to accept the stimulation and gives more wincing and withdrawal reactions. At a high level of stimulation (not ordinarily used in experimentation), one may be "wild with pain," that is, highly aroused or activated. Pain stimulation is certainly one way for bringing about an arousal reaction. Excited behavior, electrical changes in the skin, muscle tension, blood pressure, EEG, respiration, locomotor behavior—these are some of the indices that can be affected by intense painful stimulation. Barber (1959) indicates that pain has its arousal effects via the reticular formation (see Chapter 8) and that anesthetics have their effects (other than local) at this point. Miller and Lawrence (1950) developed a fear drive on the basis of electric shock (see Chapter 11). The strength of this fear drive was related to the strength of the shock on which it was developed. Other indices of behavior also show some relation, within limits, to the strength or intensity of the noxious stimulus employed.

Summary of Pain. We have not treated pain extensively because it is the reaction to pain, rather than the pain itself or its mechanisms, that has major significance to motivation. There are marked individual differences in the reaction to pain, many of which relate to social and cultural upbringing but some of which may arise from basic sensitivity differences (as in congenital insensitivity to painful stimuli). Present social attitudes may modify reactions to pain, and there is some evidence that pain reactions, or even sensitivity to pain, are altered in animals reared in a "pain-free" environment. Arousal appears to be an important effect of pain, and its degree is probably partly a function of the intensity of the painful stimulation.

DRIVE INTERACTIONS

A problem in the use of more than one motive or drive in the control of behavior arises because drive states are not independent of one another. This has long been known and remarked upon, but its significance to some of the experiments arising in the context of learning theory became fully recognized only in the 1950's. The experiment by Verplanck and Hayes (1953) crystallized this recognition.

Warner (1928b) had observed that rats did not eat as much, despite an abundance of food in their cages, when they were under prolonged water deprivation. Verplanck and Hayes (1953) found that food-deprived rats drank only about 40 per cent as much water as rats that had a continuous food supply available, and water-deprived rats ate only about 60 per cent of the food eaten by animals not deprived of water. After termination of food or water deprivation, the previously deprived animals would drink or eat quantities approximating those they would drink or eat after corresponding periods of direct water or food deprivation. They could hardly, therefore, have been satiated. Somewhat less striking findings were reported by Calvin and Behan (1954). In Manning's (1956) results, however, it is clear that there are strong effects. Very few choices leading to water were made by water-deprived animals if they also were 35 hours hungry. A 35-hour water deprivation period reduced food route choices markedly for animals under 11 or 23 hours of food deprivation.

Food depletion is commonly reported to reduce sex drive (Moss, 1924; Miles, 1919; Keys et al., 1950). Food intake varies, in the female rat, inversely with the oestrus cycle (Wang, 1923), as does nest-building (Kinder, 1927). It is probable, thus, that in various ways the effects of different deprivation operations do interact. Little is known, however, of the mechanisms of such interactions (cf. Young, 1936, pp. 145–148).[21]

DRIVE DISCRIMINATION

As we shall see in a later chapter, it is a question of some interest whether drive stimuli can be discriminated from one another, or whether stimuli corresponding to different intensities of the same drive can be differentiated. If different drives can be discriminated and if

---

[21] There are a number of experiments in the older literature, which employed the Columbia obstruction apparatus, that were designed to compare the strength of different drives in rats. We have not reviewed this work here because it seems to have little systematic significance and because generalization to other species and situations would seem inappropriate.

intensities of the same drive can also be discriminated, then it is possible for the underlying stimuli to enter into the discriminative control of behavior. Several investigations have been carried out to study these questions, with positive answers to both.

A number of experiments have demonstrated that stimulation of internal organs can serve as the conditioned stimuli for conditioned reflexes (Airapetyantz & Bykov, 1945; Razran, 1961). Hull (1933) used a two-choice maze, with the choice of one side leading to food and the other to water. The animals learned to choose the appropriate side when they were hungry and the other side when they were thirsty. Leeper (1935) confirmed these findings and, by changes in technique, obtained the discrimination much more rapidly than had Hull (cf. Seeman & Williams, 1952; Bolles & Petrinovich, 1954). Heron (1949) also obtained a discrimination between hunger and thirst in his rats, as did Bailey and Porter (1955) with cats. Heron suggested that rather than discriminating hunger from thirst the animals were discriminating a full from an empty stomach. However, Jenkins and Hanratty (1949) found that their rats could learn one response under 11½ hours' food deprivation and another one under 47½ hours' food deprivation; Bloomberg and Webb (1949) obtained a discrimination between 3 and 22 hours of food deprivation. These findings do not fit well with Heron's interpretation. Festinger (1943) found that rats would develop a preference for a route which led to more food than another route. The difference was more marked under higher drive than under less drive.

Other findings suggestive that drive discrimination can be accomplished are provided by Amsel's (1949) experiment. He used escape from electric shock in a T-maze; when hungry the animal could escape by turning one way, but when thirsty he could escape only by turning the other way. Levine (1953; see, also, Winnick, 1950) did a similar experiment in which the rat could turn off a very bright light by pushing one panel, if hungry, and another panel, if thirsty. Both experiments were successful in obtaining evidence of discriminations. Amsel and McDonnell (1951) had some success in training rats to go one way in a T-maze to escape shock and the other way to escape stimuli associated with shock. Bailey (1955) demonstrated that rats could discriminate hunger from thirst, hunger from satiation and thirst from satiation and found such discriminations to be about as effective as those made by other rats on the basis of an external shock-associated stimulus such as a tone.

There can be little doubt that drive states and intensities of drive states can be discriminated, though the evidence so far pertains pri-

Reread this top paragraph.

. marily to hunger and thirst in the rat. Manning (1956), after training rats in such a drive discrimination (11 hours of hunger or thirst), tested choices under several levels of each drive. With thirst at zero hours, choice of the food-leading turn was virtually constant (at 100 per cent) for 11 through 35 hours' food deprivation, and the reverse condition (zero hunger, different levels of thirst) yielded almost identical results. However, other, especially high, degrees of hunger tended to be associated with preferences for the food-turn, despite strong thirst. The interpretation of this is not entirely clear, but factors of drive-interaction may be involved.

Kendler's (1946) experiment added a new dimension to the problem. He trained rats in a T-maze, in which one arm contained water and the other food, while the animal was simultaneously hungry and thirsty. Subsequent tests were run under either hunger or thirst, and the animals chose the side on which the goal object appropriate to their deprivation state would be found. A good deal of work has followed this and similar experiments directed to discover the mechanisms underlying this performance. At present, it appears that an explanation involving the fractional anticipatory goal-response mechanism may work, although the final word on this issue has not been said.[22]

A GENERAL TRAIT OF MOTIVATION? A CENTRAL MOTIVE STATE?

Morgan (1943) suggested the notion of a central motive state to designate the role of the central nervous system in motivated behavior. It was Morgan's recognition that a stimulus (local) interpretation of motivation was no longer adequate that led him to this conception, together with findings indicating that humoral and chemical factors are significant to motivation. Stellar (1954) brought together the then available evidence concerning the importance of the hypothalamus in mediating various motivated behaviors and pointed out the relevance of these facts to Morgan's conception. Morgan (1959) has also reviewed recent work which supports his general conception. Our reviews of the evidence in the preceding two chapters have, as the reader will have recognized, given much documentation to the notion that areas in the brain are of focal importance to the regulation of motivated behavior. Chemical and hormonal variables, external stimuli, and, no doubt in some instances, local "drive stimuli" contribute inputs

[22] Much of this work involved the latent learning controversy. For a review of this issue, see Thistlethwaite (1951) and Hilgard (1956). Webb (1955) and Hall (1961) have focused on the aspect of the discriminative functions of drive stimuli.

to these centers, which in turn activate or inactivate behaviors relative to given drives. As a general, integrating notion, the central motive state has considerable support.]

A possible parallel conclusion would be to speak of a trait of motivation—that is, to speak of a given animal as being characteristically more motivated than another. Certainly this is often done informally. We speak of people as well motivated or highly industrious. But there is at present little more that we can say. While strain and breed differences exist and may be genetically determined in the main (Hall, 1941; Fuller & Thompson, 1960), differences within a strain have not been consistently found (Anderson, 1937, 1938). Perhaps more sensitive instruments and better environmental control than we have had in the past studies will permit the development of a general trait of motivation for a given strain or breed of animals, but, on present evidence, the prospects do not look bright.

SUMMARY

This chapter has been devoted to consideration of hunger, thirst, and pain avoidance. Much of general motivational theorizing has been predicated in the past on these three problems.

Hunger has been studied for many years, and, while a variety of theories has been advanced in its explanation, the notion that stomach contractions are the basis of hunger—a local theory—has had preeminence during most of the present century. Evidence reviewed here indicates, however, that gastric contractions are not an adequate basis for a general account of hunger, although they do play a role in some of its manifestations. Other factors which have been proposed include a hunger hormone, gastric distension (in the case of satiety), blood-sugar levels, caloric intake, and oral stimulation. Hunger is undoubtedly controlled by many variables.

The most recent developments in hunger have been the identification of "centers" in the hypothalamus which control eating and satiety. That these areas exist seems to be well established, but how the state of tissue need controls their activity is uncertain. Several theories have been advanced, one holding that these centers are sensitive to the level of blood glucose available for utilization, the other that they respond to temperature variations arising from eating and from fasting. Most investigators agree, however, on multiple control of the hunger-related centers.

Food intake is basically a response to deprivation—in general or in relation to some specific deficiency, such as specific "hungers." Aside from deprivation, however, food intake is influenced by such variables as habit, food characteristics, external cues, and the social situation.

Thirst has been investigated less extensively than hunger, but it, too, for many years, was thought to arise from local stimulation, that is, dryness in the mouth and throat. Again, however, centers have been found in the hypothalamus, which, as in the case of hunger, seem to control drinking. These centers appear to respond to changes in the distribution of bodily fluids and may act as osmoreceptors. Cellular dehydration is perhaps the key condition for their activation. Other variables involved in drinking include gastric distension, oral stimulation, and hormonal regulation. Deprivation provides the major impetus for drinking, but drinking is affected, to some extent, by experience, characteristics of fluids, and perhaps by situational and social variables.

Pain is discussed briefly in this chapter, because the major use of it in motivation has been as a source of avoidance or escape behavior. Much attention is paid to pain as a basis for the development of acquired motives (Chapter 11). Summarized here is evidence that there are marked individual differences in the response to pain (including some persons who are congenitally insensitive to it), and social and cultural training probably contributes to this variability. The response to pain is modifiable and can be altered by experience and social environments. One of the major effects of pain is emotional arousal.

The chapter concludes with brief mention of certain other topics. It is clear that at least some drives interact, so that, for example, if one is hungry he does not drink water normally. Such interactions have importance in the control of motivation for various theoretical and experimental purposes.

Evidence is reviewed that deprivation states, like hunger and thirst, can provide distinctive stimuli and that animals can learn to make one response when hungry and another when thirsty. They can also discriminate between intensities of at least some deprivation states.

Much of the work reviewed in this chapter is germane to a notion that there may be a central motive state. This is an idea that there are many sources which contribute, in the central nervous system, to an overall motivational level. On the other hand, when responses under varying conditions of motivation are considered, there is little evidence that lower animals, at least, display a "trait" of motivation.

Chapter 6

Activity and Exploration

In Chapters 4 and 5, we discussed the behaviors traditionally conceived as largely innate or as stemming from certain biological drives. In most of the instances we described, an essential factor in the instigation of the behavior is said to be an internal state, a specific hormonal condition, or a deficit of specific substances in bodily tissues. And, again in most of the instances, relatively circumscribed behaviors seem to arise from the internal states—sexual behavior, for example, or eating.

The list of drives or motives offered by various writers has often included others additional to those described in Chapters 4 and 5. Among them are an activity drive (independent of other motivations) and such various motivations as curiosity, exploration, manipulation, and the like, also regarded as motives in their own right, independent of other drives. This chapter is devoted to the consideration of these motives.

ACTIVITY

"Spontaneous" or general activity in animals is a phenomenon which has received very wide study in the biological and behavioral disciplines. One of the early interests was concern with the factors that control it, that is, to the question whether it is "really spontaneous" or whether it is subject to the control of denotable variables. In the early work it seemed that one set of variables related to activity was motivational in character, and general activity came into use as a measure of motivated states. Activity often seemed to increase in connection with deprivation states or with other evidence of the existence of a motive. This finding was consistent with the idea that if an animal in a state of need became active, he would increase his chances of encountering the required goal object. This would be because he was moving about rather than remaining still. We saw, especially in Chapter 2 and in Chapter 5, in the discussion of hunger and thirst, that the notion that restless activity is a response to need has made sense in the functionalist interpretation of behavior arising to serve the organism's needs. In many respects, this idea, together with the compatible concept of homeostasis (Chapter 7), has been the systematic root of a large part of thinking about motivation.

In what follows, we shall not review everything that is known about activity or about the factors which control it. Rather, after briefly sketching the variables of which activity is a function, we will discuss its status as an independent drive and then turn to its relationship to other drive and motive states. In doing so, we will raise the questions whether activity is an automatic expression of need states and whether its occurrence can have a significant learned component. First, however, we discuss the kinds of activity that may be identified.

Kinds of Activity

The methods used to study activity provide the chief classes into which activity has been divided for experimental purposes. It is obvious that such classes are not the only ones which could be devised, and that many classes might ensue were one to study very specific kinds of activity (Bindra, 1961). However, the literature identifies three methods for studying activity.

Running Activity. Everyone is familiar with the "squirrel cage," which is a circular cage that rotates freely around its axis. This type of instrument, referred to as an activity wheel, has been much employed in studies of activity. A typical apparatus contains a small living cage, from which there is ready access to the wheel. A counter is arranged so that the revolutions of the wheel may be recorded, as the animal runs in it.

It is also possible to study running in other situations and to measure its speed. Cotton (1953) used a straight runway to measure running and the responses the animal made in the runway other than running. This is, perhaps, not the same kind of "running" as running in the wheel, a point to which we will return later.

Restless Activity (Stabilimeter or Stationary Cage). Activity which involves moving around the environment, jumping, sitting, pawing, sniffing, chewing, and the like is not readily recorded on a wheel, and the stabilimeter cage is designed to record at least some of these movements. Such a cage may be an ordinary one, mounted in such a way that if the animal moves from one position to another the cage tilts. By tambours, microswitches, or other devices such cage movements are registered. An alternative is to pass beams of light through the cage and to measure activity by the interruptions of the light beams caused by the animal's movements. Stabilimeter arrangements can be made for many kinds of organisms, including human infants.

Restless Activity (Relatively Unrestricted Situations). Animals can be observed for activity in a pasture if they are equipped with a pedometer (Liddell, 1925), and observations of free-moving animals can be made in the open field, mazes, runways, and so on (Hall, 1936; Dashiell, 1925). Cotton's procedures, just mentioned, could be classified here.

Relations Among Measures. Anderson (1937) correlated scores made by rats on the activity wheel with scores they made on the Dashiell checkerboard maze (the closest measure to restless activity Anderson used). The correlations, though positive, were less than .2 and insignificant. Eayrs (1954) reported an *r* of .18 between wheel activity and a kind of stabilimeter activity. It has been widely reported that amounts of running activity differ from amounts of restless activity and that the two kinds of activity do not respond in the same way to a number of variables. From this evidence, it seems likely that these two kinds of activity are fundamentally different from one another. Woodworth (1958) has suggested that, in the wheel, running provides a stimulus for further running, that is, the movement of the wheel, caused by running, leads to further running.

Factors Governing Activity [1]

Among mammalian forms, at least, information concerning activity is most abundant for the rat, although other animals have been studied. The rat is a nocturnal animal, and, when its activity is recorded continuously, the bulk of it is shown to occur in the dark. This cycle can be shifted by arrangements of external illumination. Thus, if a light is kept on all night and the room is dark during the day, the rat's activity will be greatest during the daytime hours. Activity is or may be affected by age, sex, genetic factors, some drugs, diet, lesions of the nervous system, temperature, and the functioning of various endocrine glands. Individual differences in amount of activity are often pronounced.

Is There an Activity Drive? Various writers have suggested that there may be a drive for activity, so that animals whose activity has been restrained by some means should manifest heightened activity when the restraint is removed. Shirley (1928b) confined her rats in cages so small that even to turn around was difficult, and varied the

[1] Reviews of this literature and of apparatus for studying activity may be found in the following sources: Fuller and Thompson (1960), Hall (1961), Harker (1958), Morgan (1943), Morgan and Stellar (1950), Munn (1950), Reed (1947), Shirley (1929).

amount of time the animals were so restricted. Short periods of restriction, such as one or two days, were followed by increased (nonsignificant) running activity, but following longer periods of restriction activity was found to decline. Siegel (1946a) found only slight changes following periods of restriction up to one day in a stationary cage situation. Montgomery (1953b) found that restriction of activity for several days led to reductions in later wheel running. Thompson and Heron (1954) restricted activity in dogs for several months and found the restricted dogs to be more active in an open room than were the controls. Hill (1956, 1958a) examined activity in both a wheel and in a stabilimeter cage. He found that wheel activity did increase as a function of activity deprivation up to about 2 days and obtained increased activity in the stabilimeter cage after 2, 4, or 40 days of confinement. In another experiment, Hill (1958b) studied wheel activity after 36 or more days of confinement. The findings here were like Montgomery's, that is, a suppression of activity in the confined animals, a suppression that tended to be overcome over a 4-day period.

Short periods of activity deprivation, then, can apparently increase both wheel and stabilimeter cage activity, but long periods of confinement reduce wheel activity but continue to increase, albeit relatively slightly, restless activity. Hill (1958b, p. 772) suggests that the reduction of running after long confinement may be due to the "canalization" (cf. Murphy, 1947) of activity into small movements. Such movements can be made despite confinement, whereas running is not possible. Hill seems to think that the effects of short periods of activity deprivation may justify the postulation of an activity drive. Access to wheel running has been shown to reinforce bar pressing (Kagan & Berkun, 1954), a finding that might support a drive interpretation of activity.

It appears to us, however, as it does to Hall (1961), that a drive for activity is somewhat difficult to conceive. This is for several reasons. One is that both general and spontaneous activity refer to a variety of responses which may have their own stimuli and which may have little to do with one another. Secondly, at least some of these responses are taken as evidence, by various investigators, for other drives, such as curiosity or exploration, for example, not to mention hunger, thirst, and sex. A third reason is the complex of factors known to control activity, to which we gave brief attention at the beginning of this section. If other drives, hormones, the nervous system, age, illumination, and the like are important to activity, it may not contribute much to confer drive status on it. We also show, later, that learning can affect amount of activity.

It is possible to breed animals and develop active and inactive strains (Rundquist, 1933), as well as relatively emotional and unemotional animals (Hall, 1941). Timid or fearful rats tend to be more active in a wheel (after adjustment to it) than fearless rats (Billingslea, 1940). Perhaps activity indexes less a specific drive than a general condition of excitability or responsiveness. Unfortunately, as we indicate elsewhere, there is not much support in the literature for such a broad trait as this.

Activity as a Mechanism of Adaptation to Needs

We are familiar by now with the idea that internal stimuli, arising from deprivation states, goad or "drive" the organism into activity. Such activity is seen as instrumental to obtaining whatever is needed to requite the need. Studies of spontaneous or general activity as a function of duration of deprivation have seemed to support this conception, but later work has thrown some doubt on it. We summarize first the experiments relating activity to hunger, thirst, and sex and then go on to the investigations which have raised the interpretative questions.

Early work from Richter's laboratory (Richter, 1922, 1927) suggested a relation between gastric contractions and periodic bursts of activity (see, also, Wada, 1922). Using two connected, tambour-mounted cages, one of which was the food cage, Richter found with rats that most episodes of entering the food cage were associated with increases in general activity. Activity tended to occur first, and then eating, a finding often paralleled in comparison of stomach contractions and restless movements during sleep in humans (Wada, 1922) and in observations in the rat of stomach contractions and muscular movements (Powelson, 1925). Richter also plotted 24-hour activity for rats, which were fed one time a day always at the same hour. Tambour-cage activity was greatest in the hour before mealtime; it decreased after feeding, remained low over several hours, and began to rise as the time for next feeding approached. Irwin (1932) reported similar findings for human infants. Measures made during continued deprivation show increased activity in stationary cages, up to the point at which weakness sets in (Richter, 1922; Siegel & Steinberg, 1949; Teitelbaum, 1957), and also in open-field or exploration situations (Dashiell, 1925; Fehrer, 1956a).

Other experiments also show that after rats are placed on a restricted feeding schedule their activity patterns change. In such experiments, usually the animal is allowed access to food for only one hour out of the 24. When wheel activity is recorded it typically increases over a period of 2 to 5 weeks, especially during the hour just before feeding (Reid & Finger, 1955, 1957; Hall & Cannon, 1957; Hall & Hanford, 1954; Hall et al., 1953). Hall (1955) also found wheel activity to rise during the 21 days of a restricted drinking schedule. However, the rise was not marked and was very substantially less than it is for a restricted feeding schedule.

Wang (1923) studied wheel activity in female rats. After puberty these animals exhibited activity cycles, apparently correlated with the oestrus cycle. Wang found activity to vary over a 4-day period, with a rise to a peak, followed by a decline and then a repetition of the pattern. The period of greatest activity corresponds to the period of sexual receptivity, the periods of relatively less activity with unreceptive periods. Pregnancy, the menopause, and ovariectomy abolish these rhythms, which are not, of course, found in the male rat. Finger (1961a) ran female rats in stationary cages (in which movement interrupted a light beam) as well as in wheels. He found activity cycles, like those described by Wang, in stationary-cage activity as well as in the wheel, but the cycles were much more pronounced in the wheel than in the former apparatus.

We have not reviewed all the evidence relating hunger, thirst, and sexual drives to activity, but perhaps we have said enough to show that, under various circumstances, activity is related to these deprivation states. How does one interpret this relationship?

The interpretation has been made that drives push or goad the

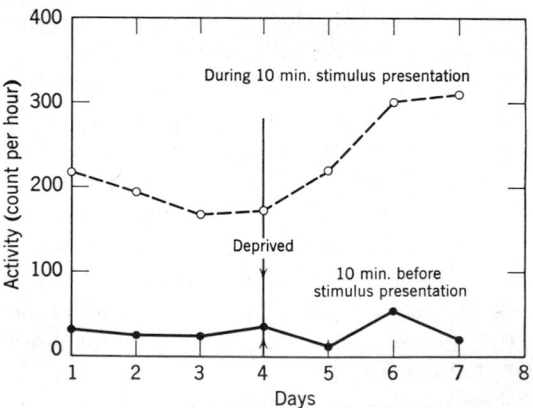

Figure 6–1. Activity records (stabilimeter) during ad libitum and deprived days with and without external stimulus presentation. Reproduced and modified by permission from Campbell and Sheffield (1953, Fig. 1).

organism into activity. The evidence we have cited supports this interpretation, insofar as a *correlation*, such as that between deprivation time and activity, can be conclusive.

Campbell and Sheffield (1953) questioned this relationship, offering as an alternative the notion that drive states may lead to increased sensitivity to stimulation but not directly to the elicitation of behavior. On this argument, deprivation would not automatically lead to correspondingly increased activity in a relatively unstimulating environment.

To test this, Campbell and Sheffield placed rats in stabilimeter cages for seven days in the dark, in a sound-proofed room in which a ventilating fan provided a masking noise. Four days of ad-lib feeding were provided and then three days of starvation. Total daily activity was recorded as well as activity in a ten-minute period just before stimulation and for another ten-minute period just after stimulation. The stimulation occurred daily and consisted of turning on the lights and turning off the fan.

There was little change in activity through the deprivation days as compared with the ad-lib days for the ten-minute observation period before stimulation, and total daily activity showed only a small, though significant, rise during the deprivation interval. However, marked rises in activity were associated with stimulation in both the satiated and the starvation conditions, the rise being larger during starvation than during satiation and increasing over the starvation interval (Fig. 6–1). This seemed to confirm the sensitivity to stimulation interpretation, and Campbell and Sheffield argued that the slight rise during starvation in total daily activity might also be due to heightened sensitivity to available cues. Strong (1957), using a more sensitive stabilimeter cage, found an actual decline in activity with starvation up to 72 hours, and Weasner, Finger, and Reid (1960) found much less change in activity during deprivation as measured by interruptions of a light beam than by the wheel. Hall (1956) essentially repeated the Campbell-Sheffield experiment using, however, the wheel. He found increments of activity during starvation despite the absence of special stimulation. However, deprivation did not change activity on a Dashiell maze (Hall, Hanford, & Low, 1960).[2]

These findings suggest, then, that for adult rats restless activity does not increase with food deprivation in circumstances of external stimulus control. Wheel activity, however, does so. A somewhat different picture was obtained by Campbell, Teghtsoonian, and Williams (1961) when rats of different ages were studied. They used tilt cages in a

[2] Cf., also, Moskowitz (1959).

controlled environment and recorded activity during starvation to death in groups of rats in which deprivation was initiated at 23, 38, 54, or 100 days of age. For the 100-day old animals they found essentially no change in activity as a result of deprivation but for each of the younger groups activity increased, its peak shifting to a later deprivation day as the age of the animals shifted from 23 to 54 days. Finger (1962) studied activity in response to 48-hour food deprivation in animals that were 30–31 days of age. He used the interruption of a light beam as his measure. Activity scores increased over the food-deprivation interval; observations made 10 days later during water deprivation, however, produced decrements in activity. It is not entirely clear what these age differences mean, or what factors control them, but they represent, at present, an important limitation to the generalization that restless activity, in the absence of external stimulation, does not respond to deprivation states.

Wheel activity does respond to deprivation states more consistently and dramatically, as we have seen. An aspect of this, which may be discussed, is that wheel activity may be unrepresentative of the kind of activity which animals display in natural environments. Running in a wheel is perhaps not paralleled anywhere in nature, and it seems likely that running in the wheel is a stimulus to more running. Perhaps restless activity is a more adequate representative of the kind of spontaneous activity an animal would display in its natural habitat. We would observe, also, that running would tend to deplete still further the energy reserves already reduced by deprivation. From the standpoint of adaptation, it makes some sense to think of a deprived animal as conserving his resources through inactivity, responding by means of restless activity mainly to stimuli to which his sensitivity has been increased, rather than running wildly around his environment without stimulation.

Another complication with activity, both restless and running, is that it is susceptible to learning. Slonaker (1912), Richter (1922), Shirley (1928a), and Skinner (1933)[3] all suggested that activity might be susceptible to modification by the fact that feeding occurs at a given time. The fact that activity tends to build up in the last hour before feeding is due supports this notion. Sheffield and Campbell (1954) studied rats in stabilimeter cages under the following conditions. After adaptation, all groups were starved for three days. Then in the next days food delivery was associated with a stimulus change in experimental animals but was not so associated in control animals. It was found that activity tended to increase in the experimental ani-

[3] See, also, Seward and Pereboom (1955a, b).

mals in response to the stimulus change, but not in the controls (see, also, Amsel & Work, 1961). Sheffield and Campbell interpret this rise in activity as occurring because of the frustration of anticipatory consummatory responses previously conditioned to the stimulus change in the experimental animals. Finger, Reid, and Weasner (1957) fed experimental animals immediately after wheel running but delayed feeding in controls. They found greater and longer lasting rises in activity for the experimental group under a restricted feeding schedule than in the control group. Similar results were obtained by Hall (1958). Finger (1961b) has shown that activity can be reduced by making reinforcement after an instrumental response be contingent on inactivity prior to the instrumental response.

In sum, then, activity turns out to be a complicated matter. Restless and running activity are probably evidence of different things. They respond differently to several variables. Running seems more responsive to deprivation under controlled stimulation than restless activity, but the latter does increase in young animals under deprivation. There is some evidence consistent with the notion of an activity drive or drives. Experience affects both kinds of activity and can either increase or decrease it. It is not at all clear whether drive instigation or stimulus sensitization is the better interpretation of activity, but it would seem that either has some merit as an interpretation so far as adaptation is concerned.

EXPLORATION AND RELATED PHENOMENA

In the decade of the 1950's, doubt was increasingly expressed as to the adequacy of internal states, such as those reviewed in Chapters 4 and 5, to account for many of the behaviors in which organisms engage. One important facet of this doubt has arisen with regard to behavior that explores or manipulates the environment or which appears to raise the stimulation level to which the organism is subjected. Terms like curiosity, exploratory drive, manipulation motive, stimulus hunger, or the need for stimulation have come into vogue, and there has been a clear implication that the phenomena designated by these concepts cannot be explained in terms of, or reduced to, or derived from, internal processes like those described in the last two chapters. On the other hand, these phenomena are not seen as learned but would probably be postulated as representing basic, unlearned characteristics of organisms (see White, 1959; Hunt, 1960).

Broadly, we may distinguish between phenomena perhaps indicative of a *need for* stimulation and phenomena which can be characterized as being *released by* stimulation. The first kind has been studied in experiments, the major manipulation of which has been to reduce for some length of time the degree of stimulation to which the subject is exposed. Then the effects of such stimulus "deprivation" or isolation are observed either during the period of stimulus reduction or after it is over. The second kind of phenomena has been observed under conditions which have *provided* stimuli with various known characteristics so that the effects of these stimuli on some aspect of behavior can be assessed. The two kinds of phenomena, then, are the consequence of very different operations. Many writers, however, would regard them as intimately related, as are the two sides of a coin.

These experiments, of both kinds, have an important relation to the topic of arousal (Berlyne, 1960), which we will discuss in the context of the activation theory of emotions. We have chosen to place our discussion of these experiments in the present chapter because the experimenters and theorists chiefly responsible for them have viewed them as controverting the exclusive emphasis on internal states of bodily need in motivation.

In what follows, we discuss first the experiments on so-called sensory deprivation, turning next to the studies in which specific types of stimulation have been provided. The latter will be divided, following Berlyne (1960, pp. 79–80), into studies which have stressed (1) orienting responses, (2) locomotor exploration, and (3) investigative responses. Brief attention will also be paid to experiments in which the acquisition of information has been studied; Berlyne (1960) refers to these as dealing with "epistemic curiosity." Finally, theoretical implications and interpretations of the findings from these diverse experiments will be summarized and discussed.

Reduction of External Stimulation (Stimulus Deprivation, Isolation)

Boredom arising from a monotonous environment, or from stereotyped, repetitive tasks, is a phenomenon with which most of us have some experience; it is usually a condition which we attempt to prevent or avoid unless we are trying to go to sleep or to rest and relax. Boredom, leading, as it often does, to inattention, is an important problem in tasks requiring vigilance, as in automobile driving, routine work processes, guard duty of various kinds. Much of the literature on the problem has been concerned with overcoming boredom in practical situations (cf. Holland, 1958; Rohrer, 1959), but several experiments have been designed to study directly the effects of reduced variety of stimulation or, simply, reduced stimulation (cf. Solomon et al., 1957, 1961). The effects have suggested to some writers that the organism "needs" stimulation to some degree, and physiological hypotheses have been advanced to explain this need.

Karsten (1928) asked her subjects to perform tasks for as long a time as they wanted to, the tasks being mechanical and repetitive, like drawing vertical lines, drawing the same thing repeatedly, placing thimbles into holes. While Karsten told her subjects to work only so long as they wanted to, she implied that they should work as long as possible. The subjects did go on for considerable periods, but the quality of their work deteriorated over time, and, simultaneously, they attempted to introduce variety into the situation by varying the way they did the tasks. They became increasingly dissatisfied with what they were doing, felt angry toward the experimenter, and thought fondly of other things they would like to do. Eventually, they refused to continue, not, presumably, because of muscular "fatigue" (they could and did make other responses with the same muscles) but, as Karsten put it, because of a mental saturation or satiation with the task.

The later experiments concerning the general problem have employed the procedure of reducing the total amount of external stimulation. Bexton, Heron, and Scott (1954) provided the first report and, although other experimenters have established somewhat different conditions and have studied the resulting phenomena in a variety of ways, the general outlines described in this first report have been followed. Bexton, Heron, and Scott employed college students at twenty dollars a day in their first study. The subjects were to remain 24 hours a day (with time out for meals and toilet needs) lying on a cot in a lighted, partially sound-deadened room (Fig. 6-2). The subjects wore translucent goggles, which did not permit pattern vision, and gloves and cardboard cuffs, which minimized tactile stimulation. A masking noise was provided by the air-conditioner, and the subjects rested their heads in a U-shaped foam rubber pillow. After a period, usually filled with sleeping, the subjects eventually found this situation a difficult one to tolerate, and, despite the high wage, they terminated the experiment (which they were free to do), seldom enduring it for as long as two or three days. Heron, Doane, and Scott (1956) used themselves as subjects and remained in isolation for six days. Lilly (1956) suspended himself and another subject (separately) in a tank of tepid water and wore a black-out breathing mask. There was thus little visual, auditory or tactual stimulation.

In the various other experiments that have been reported, the period of isolation has varied from as little as a half-hour to several days. In some of the other experiments the room was unlighted, and arrangements were made for the subject to have his meals and to use toilet facilities without leaving the chamber. In addition to boredom, a desire to terminate the isolation, restlessness, irritability, and emotional lability (all of which suggest that continued reduction of sensory input is an aversive condition), a number of more specific effects have been reported. Among them was the fact that the subjects used by Bexton, Heron, and Scott seemed to relish hearing an old stock-market report and a talk for young children on the dangers of alcohol. They looked forward to being tested, although the tests gave them difficulty, and used various kinds of devices to stimulate themselves; Lilly (1956) noted the same thing—that a hunger for stimulation and action de-

Figure 6–2. A diagram of a sensory deprivation chamber showing the subject lying on a cot with cuffs over his forearms and hands and goggles over his eyes. Above the subject's head there is an exhaust fan and above his feet an air-conditioner. A microphone and speaker are also shown. Redrawn by permission from Fig. 2–1 of a paper by W. Heron published in P. Solomon et al. (eds.) (1961, p. 9).

veloped, leading to such responses as touching the fingers together and twitching the muscles. Perhaps the unbearable, aversive feature of reduction of stimulation is its most important one for motivation. But other phenomena offer some clues as to the nature of the effects being caused.

Sensory and Perceptual Effects. Bexton, Heron, and Scott (1954) reported that some of their subjects had hallucinatory experiences during sensory deprivation, and Heron, Doane, and Scott (1956) verified this finding on themselves. They reported that after the first day each of them had hallucinatory activity.

At first this tended to be "simple" in form (rows of dots, geometrical patterns, mosaics, etc.); later it became more "complex" (scenery, people, bizarre architecture, etc.). There was a considerable amount of movement in the hallucinations: landscapes might appear divided into strips which moved in opposite directions; parts of a scene, or entire scenes, might become inverted, and pivot slowly from side to side. At times this type of movement was unpleasant, and caused the observer to feel nausea . . . (the) eyes became tired from trying to "focus" on the hallucinations (Heron, Doane, & Scott, 1956, p. 14).

Lilly (1956), Solomon (1958), and Goldberger and Holt (1958) have reported somewhat similar effects. However, there are a number of reports which do not mention the hallucinatory effect or explicitly deny that it occurred (cf. Vernon, McGill, & Schiffman, 1958). Since the reports vary in other findings as well, we shall defer discussing possible reasons for the differences until other results have been reviewed.

While the hallucinatory experiences are the most dramatic of the phenomena arising in conjunction with sensory isolation, other sensory and perceptual effects have been reported both during and following the deprivation experience. Isolated subjects do less well after four days than do controls on a test of perceptual ability (canceling numbers) and continue to do less well through the remaining isolation period (Zubek, Sansom, & Prysiazniuk, 1960), but there was no difference after isolation. The bulk of the reports have compared pre- and post-isolation-test performance and changes in perceptual experience. Heron, Doane, and Scott (1956) found, among other things, after removing themselves from the isolation chamber, that the visual world seemed to move or swirl around, that objects seemed to move when the observer turned his eyes or head, that straight lines tended to appear curved, that they had strong negative afterimages, and that color and brightness contrasts were enhanced.

Vernon, McGill, Gulick, and Candland (1959) found some difficulty with a color-perception test when the subjects had been isolated for 48 or more hours but not for a 24-hour isolation period. No significant differences between the isolated subjects and the controls appeared, after these intervals, on a test for depth perception. Held and White (1959) found that the speed of moving objects was underestimated by subjects following sensory isolation; they reasoned that the absence of pattern vision in the isolated subjects (who wore translucent goggles in a lighted room) permits the nervous system to engage in spontaneous, patternless activity. This may reduce apparent speed. On this argument, exposure of a subject to a field of randomly changing dots should increase visual lag whereas exposure to a very stable, patterned environment should cause an increase in apparent visual speed. These effects were, in fact, obtained when observations were made under suitable conditions. A further experiment (Freedman & Held, 1960) permitted the measurement of the subject's perception of visual speed at intervals over a three-hour period; during this time the subjects either saw random light flashes or diffuse (nonpatterned) light, or he was in the dark with black goggles over his eyes. The random flash condition reduced the apparent speed of objects to a significantly greater degree than did either of the other conditions, although they too reduced it.

There appear, then, to be a number of sensory and perceptual effects of sensory isolation, some of which, at least, persist beyond the isolation period itself.

Cognitive and Motor Effects. Bexton, Heron, and Scott (1954) tested their subjects prior to, during, and following isolation by means of number, arithmetic, and word tests. The isolated subjects did more poorly than the controls on these tests, but only on an anagrams test was the difference significant. A block-design test and a digit-symbol test, given to other isolated subjects, revealed performances significantly inferior to the controls. Vernon, McGill, Gulick, and Candland (1959) found some impairment on a pursuit-rotor task, a mirror-tracing task, and a rail-walking test after isolation lasting more than 24 hours. Zubek et al. (1960) found no difference between isolated and control subjects before, during, or after isolation on such abilities as verbal reasoning, rote learning, abstract reasoning, spatial relations, verbal fluency, and number facility. However, the isolated subjects developed inferiority to the controls during isolation on dexterity, recall, and recognition. Vernon and Hoffman (1956) and Vernon and McGill (1957) compared control and isolated subjects on rote-learning tasks. Such differences as were found tended to favor those subjected to isolation. On the other hand, Goldberger and Holt (1958) found subjects to suffer impairment on a paper-and-pencil complex-reasoning task following isolation. Heron, Doane, and Scott (1956) had reported difficulties with concentration during and after isolation: both they and Zubek, et al. (1960) have reported that abnormalities (large, slow waves) appear in the EEGs during isolation, persisting for a while after isolation.

Aside from the variable of duration of isolation, there are four major differences in the ways the various sensory deprivation experiments have been conducted. One is the presence of illumination or its absence. A second is whether constant auditory stimulation was supplied or whether it was not. A third is the kinds of functions assessed and the methods used to assess them in the several experiments. And the fourth is that subject samples probably varied, and there is evidence for strong individual differences in reaction to sensory isolation (Solomon, 1958; Goldberger & Holt, 1961).

It is fair to say that the most dramatic effects—that is, the hallucinatory experiences—arising from sensory isolation have appeared under conditions of diffuse, nonpatterned visual stimulation. It is also under these conditions that most of the reports of disturbed visual perception have been made. Held and his associates have shown that certain visual defects are maximized when random visual stimulation is given. It may be argued, therefore, that it is not *absolute* deprivation of visual stimulation that is involved but rather a *change* from the ordinary, patterned character that visual stimulation usually has. Brief intervals of nonpatterned stimulation also may have disruptive effects (Rosenbaum, Dobie, & Cohen, 1959; Hochberg, Triebel, & Seaman, 1951).

Only certain of the cognitive functions seem to be disturbed by the isolation experience. The more general cognitive disturbances are associated with the presence of diffused light and constant auditory stimulation. After time in the dark and with no auditory stimulation, recall and recognition are impaired; some of the other impairments reported in variously named cognitive functions could be due to this particular kind of impairment. This is especially true in cases in which the material was presented orally rather than visually. Memory would typically be involved in oral presentation to a greater extent than in visual presentation. It is difficult, on these findings, to generalize about the perceptual, motor, and cognitive effects of sensory isolation.

There are also differences in the emotional-motivational effects. The subjects used by Zubek, et al. (1960) apparently, on the average, did not suffer as greatly from isolation (darkness and no sound) as did subjects in many other experiments. Some of Zubek's subjects actually reported a subjective sharpening of their intellectual abilities. We are unable to define the reasons for these differences or for the comparable findings to those of Zubek reported by Vernon and associates. Goldberger and Holt (1961) emphasize that some of their subjects tolerated isolation fairly well, whereas others did not; and they suggest that personality variables are responsible. We do not have evidence, of course, as to the personality factors involved in the experiments of Zubek and of Vernon.

In sum, then, perceptual or sensory isolation has been found to have profound motivational, affective, perceptual, cognitive, and motor effects in some people, whereas others are not so adversely affected under the same conditions. It is still too early to say, however, just what variables are responsible for the effects which have been reported. There may be some conditions of isolation in which relatively few people arc affected.[4]

Reduction of Stimulation and Reinforcement from Stimulation

We could infer that in sensory deprivation experiments with human subjects there would, after a period of deprivation, be an increased interest in stimulation, and some of the reports we have reviewed have in fact found an increment in such interests. A more precise attack on this problem, however, has been made with monkeys in a series of experiments by Butler. The reinforcing value of stimulation following deprivation has been the dependent variable in these experiments.

Butler (1953) confined rhesus monkeys individually in wire cages, each of which was covered with an opaque box. There were two windows in one wall of the box, and the windows could be covered by different-colored cards. The windows either were locked or could be opened by slight pressure. After a time in this dimly illuminated box, the monkey might respond to one window and finding it unlocked open it. The other window he would find locked. The experimenter switched the colors on the windows in a random order so that one color always covered the window which, on a given trial, was unlocked. The reinforcement for a correct response was a peek for thirty seconds through the window at the laboratory environment in which the box was situated. Learning of the discrimination occurred under this reinforcement, and the response was quite persistent (Fig. 6–3), showing no tendency to satiation over ten 4-hour testing sessions (Butler & Harlow, 1954; Harlow, 1953*b*). Butler and Alexander (1955)

[4] Schachter (1959) isolated subjects from people, though not from stimulation, for from 2 to 8 days. Of 5 subjects run, only 2 seemed much affected by the experience. Schachter concludes that "we were unable to produce a state of social need or even of mild suffering with any consistency . . ." (p. 10).

found that rhesus monkeys would spend, in a 10-hour test period, about 40 per cent of their time in visual exploratory activity. Butler (1957a) showed that the rate of this activity increased as a function of time spent in the box without visual exploration. Thus the subject would make more responses following two, four, and eight hours of deprivation than after no deprivation, with the major increase occurring for visual deprivation up to four hours.

Butler (1957b) has also found that isolation from sounds will lead to a preference for the one of two levers whose depression yielded fifteen seconds of noise from the monkey colony (as feeding time neared). This response did not seem to be readily satiable, either. Butler (1958) compared several kinds of visual and auditory incentives as reinforcers. Monkeys opened a window frequently when they could see another monkey through the window, but did so much less when the opened window permitted a view of an empty cage. The monkeys would open the window hardly at all when they could see a large, active dog through it. (Presumably, fear was involved in this last condition.) In the auditory incentive conditions, the barking of a dog and rage sounds of a monkey led to fewer lever presses than the sounds of the monkey colony at feeding time, the sounds of a single monkey, or a white noise. Clearly, incentives vary in their ability to reinforce and maintain the behavior involved in seeking environmental stimulation or in exploration. Fear seems to suppress this behavior, but the variation otherwise is largely unaccounted for.

These experiments, together with those which have reduced external sources of stimulation for periods of time, suggest that stimulation is a state which organisms seek and which will reward them.

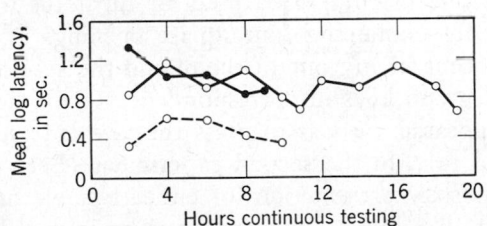

Figure 6–3. Persistence of behavior in three normal monkeys reinforced by 30-second peeks through a window at the laboratory environment. Mean log latencies of response show little change but, if anything, decline over the periods indicated. Reproduced from Butler and Harlow (1954, part of Fig. 6).

Provision of External Stimulation

Orienting Responses. We shall limit our discussion of orientation to what Berlyne (1960, p. 95) classifies as orienting responses, recognizing that a much larger class of responses, the orientation reaction, could be dealt with. The orienting response refers to "processes that focus, direct, or sensitize receptor organs and thus have an unmistakable exploratory function" (Berlyne, 1960, p. 95).

This definition has much in common with what at one time was usually referred to as *attention*. Treatments of attention (cf. Woodworth & Schlosberg, 1954, pp. 74 ff.) usually stress two classes of variables as determining attention. One consists of properties of the organism, like interest and set, and the other, properties of stimuli. Among the properties of stimuli mentioned by Woodworth and Schlosberg (1954, pp. 74–76) and Woodworth and Marquis (1947, pp. 405–406) as determiners of attention are size, intensity, color, motion, position, repetition, change, contrast, and novelty. Berlyne's (1960, pp. 96–103) list of factors determining the occurrence of selective orienting responses includes several of these, and, in addition, *indicating* stimuli, surprisingness, complexity, uncertainty, incongruity, conflict. It will be sufficient to indicate the kind of work involved with orienting responses if we deal with certain of Berlyne's experiments on novelty and complexity, uncertainty, and incongruity.

Two major dependent variables have been used in these experiments. One is the choices that subjects will make between stimuli. The other is the amount and direction of fixation on one, rather than another, stimulus. The latter measure is perhaps the more direct indication of an orienting response, although the former can be inferred to reflect orientation. Berlyne (1951, 1957a) used an apparatus which consisted of a vertical board containing four square openings in a line. A spot of light could occur in any one of them, and the subject was to press one of four telegraph keys in correspondence to the lighted opening. If two lights appeared, he was to press the key corresponding to the light he noticed first. In the second experiment (Berlyne, 1957a) the subject first saw sixty presentations of either a single or a pair of red or white lights distributed over the four positions. Following this habituation phase, he saw both red and white stimuli. The subject tended to respond to the novel color—that is, the one he had not seen during the habituation phase. A similar finding occurred in the earlier experiment (Berlyne, 1951) in which novelty was associated with changes in the shape as well as the color of the stimuli. Hence, change or novelty is a factor in attention or orienting responses to stimuli.

In several experiments, Berlyne noted to which stimulus a subject looked first. In human infants aged three to nine months it was the figure with the greater amount of contour which captured the infant's gaze (Berlyne, 1958b). Thus, a checkerboard pattern was more compelling than simpler patterns. Fantz (1958a, b) reported similar findings for human infants and infant chimpanzees. With human adults, Berlyne (1958a) found that more complex or incongruous pictures were fixated longer than were congruous or less complex pictures. Complexity was introduced by irregularity in arrangements of the parts of figures, by increasing the number of parts of figures, by making the parts heterogeneous, or making their shapes irregular (Fig. 6–4). Incongruity was provided by unlikely combinations of parts of animals, such as an elephant's head on a lion's body. In this experiment the pair of figures was only briefly exposed (10 seconds) but a longer exposure

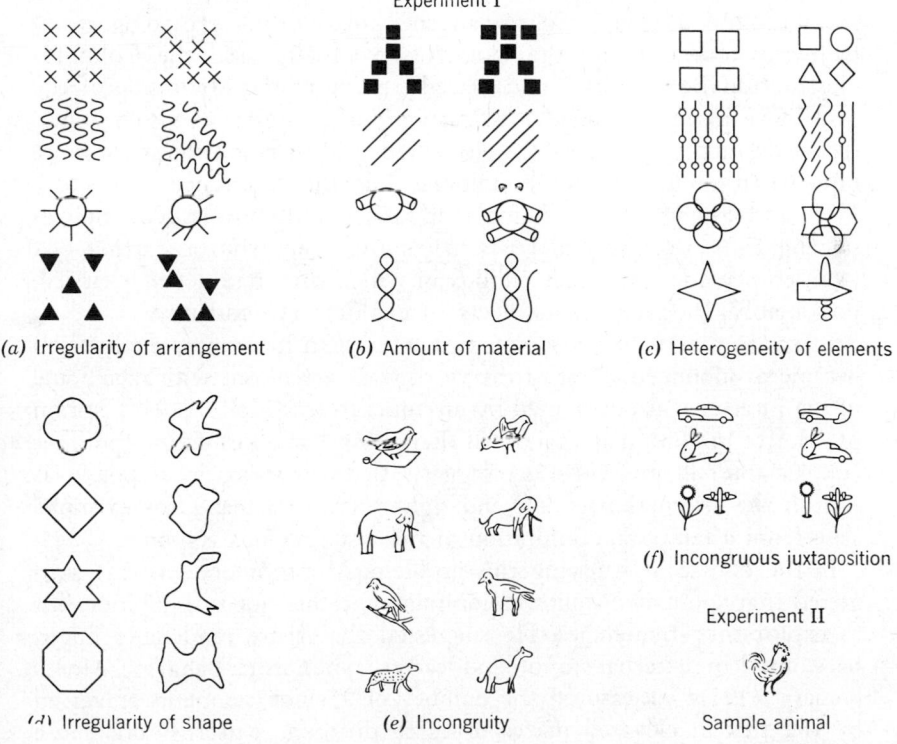

Experiment I

(a) Irregularity of arrangement

(b) Amount of material

(c) Heterogeneity of elements

(f) Incongruous juxtaposition

Experiment II

Sample animal

(d) Irregularity of shape

(e) Incongruity

Figure 6 4. Arrangements of visual material designed to produce stimulus complexity. Reproduced by permission from Berlyne (1958a, Fig. 1).

time (two minutes, Berlyne, 1958c) did not alter the results.

These experiments are representative of the finding that subjects orient themselves to stimuli in accordance with such properties of the stimuli as may be called novel, incongruous, or complex.

Locomotor Exploration. One of the major ways of studying exploration behavior involves the requirement that an animal traverse space to get to the object of exploration or make a choice between pathways for his locomotion. While locomotion cannot be considered always, or even usually, to be instigated by exploratory tendencies, experimenters have contrived environmental circumstances that, when present, often permit the inference of exploration. Sometimes observations of such behavior as sniffing, manipulation, and the like, will also support the inference that the locomotor behavior, at least in part, had an exploratory basis.

The first systematic observations in an experimental situation, which we can cite concerning exploration, were made by Dashiell (1925). He found that rats, even though neither hungry nor thirsty, would roam around a checkerboard-patterned maze, thus providing many pathways, corners, and the like. Nissen (1930) used the Columbia Obstruction Box method, and placed a maze at the other side of the grid. The maze contained sawdust and other objects. Nissen found that male rats would cross the electrified grid to reach the maze more often than under control conditions, but the difference was small. Mote and Finger (1942) found that rats would show a reduction in starting time, over several trials, when they ran from a starting box to an empty and unfamiliar endbox in which they had never been fed. Presumably, their running reflects an exploratory tendency.

It was in the 1950's, however, that interest in locomotor exploration became pronounced. Most of the work was carried out with rats. Some of the interest was occasioned by attempts to test Hull's (1943) notion of reactive inhibition as a factor in alternation behavior. This hypothesis (cf., Chapter 4, pp. 154–156) suggests that variations in response, as seen in the alternation of left and right turns in a maze, for example, arise from a temporary inhibition of the last previous response.

In the course of studying this problem, Montgomery (1951a) suggested that spontaneous alternation might be due not to inhibition but to exploratory tendencies. He suggested that these tendencies might be aroused by external stimuli and lead to exploratory behavior. Montgomery (1951b) measured the number of 15-inch segments traversed by the rats in elevated mazes of three different patterns: one maze section, two sections in the form of an "L," and three sections in a "T." The animals were experimentally naive and were not under deprivation conditions. The largest number of segments entered was for the T-maze, next for the L-maze, and least for the straight single section, but the distance traversed into the segments entered per maze section did not differ. This suggested that exploratory behavior in that situation is a function of the *area* that can be explored. All of the animals were equally active during the first 100 seconds of observation, the difference between groups occurring during the next 500 seconds of the 10-minute exploratory period. Analysis of the animals' behavior suggested that novelty of stimulation was evoking their behavior, or, put another way, they tended to avoid places they had recently visited (Montgomery, 1952*a*).

Montgomery (1952*b*) and Glanzer (1953) used a cross (+) maze pattern (Fig. 6–5) in further efforts to determine whether alternation arises from avoidance of the last response made or the last stimulus situation encountered. The experiments were run as follows: On one trial the animal would run a T-maze (the opposite leg of the cross being blocked off), and he would make a left or right turn. On the next trial he would be started in the alley on the opposite side of the maze and would be forced to turn right or left (as now the previous starting leg was blocked off). If his turn on the second trial was the reverse of that on the first trial, it would appear that he was avoiding response repetition but not stimulus repetition; on the other hand, the same turn on the second as on the first trial would indicate avoidance of stimulus repetition and not of response repetition. Both Glanzer and Montgomery found that their animals tended to avoid the prior stimulus situation rather than the prior turn. In this their results agree with

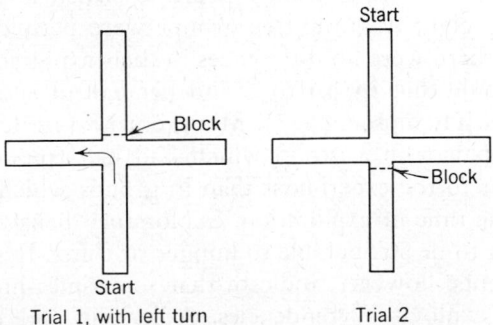

Figure 6–5. A schematic diagram of a cross maze. On trial one, the animal turns left. On trial two, started from the opposite side, if he again turns left, he will repeat the prior *response* but encounter a *new arm* of the maze; if he turns *right*, he will *avoid* the former response but will encounter the *old arm* of the maze.

those of earlier students (Dennis & Henneman, 1932; Dennis & Sollenberger, 1934; Dennis, 1935, 1939).

Berlyne (1950) provided his rats two opportunities to explore objects (cubes or cardboard cylinders). Two 5-minute exploration periods were separated by ten minutes, and at the second exploration one of the original objects had been replaced. This novel object received more exploratory attention than the other familiar ones. Schoenfeld, Antonitis, and Bersh (1950) found that rats confined in a Skinner box would approach and depress the bar with some frequency, even though no food or other reward was forthcoming.

Exploratory behavior has been observed in the cockroach (Darchen, 1952, 1954) and in the primates (cf. Yerkes & Yerkes, 1929). As we shall see, some experimental attention has been given to such behavior in children and human adults.

Factors in Exploration

Much of the work which has appeared in connection with locomotor exploration has been concerned with two general problems: (1) does exploration arise as a consequence of other drives or is it an independent drive itself? (2) what are the characteristics of exploratory behavior, and what conditions and factors influence its occurrence and characteristics?

Is Exploration Due to Other Drives? The role of activity, hunger, thirst, and fear drives in exploratory behavior has been studied. Montgomery (1953b) confined one group of rats to small living cages and another group to similar cages from which activity wheels could be entered 22 hours a day. The former group was an activity deprivation group (and the results from it were discussed in the section on activity). After eight days the two groups were permitted to explore a Y-maze, and there were no differences in their exploratory behaviors. Exploration would thus appear to be independent of activity need (cf. Charlesworth & Thompson, 1957). Montgomery (1953c) found more exploratory behavior in a group which had had free access to food and water prior to the experiment than in groups which were hungry or thirsty at the time of exploration. Exploratory behavior would not, therefore, seem to be attributable to hunger or thirst. Results of several other experiments, however, indicate that sometimes hunger or thirst may facilitate exploratory tendencies. Adlerstein and Fehrer (1955) used a complex maze and found that hungry rats explored in it more than satiated rats. However, they ran their animals, apparently, at the usual feeding time, which might account for this finding (Zimbardo & Montgomery, 1957b; Sheffield & Campbell, 1954). Thompson (1953) found little difference in exploration as a function of drive from zero to 48 hours of deprivation. Zimbardo and Montgomery (1957b) point out that his animals may have been fearful, as Thompson used an elevated maze, and they showed, in a complex maze, that exploration was adversely affected by hunger. Conflict between exploratory tendencies and incipient consummatory responses in hungry or thirsty animals may explain why such animals explore less than satiated ones (Zimbardo & Montgomery, 1957b).

Fehrer (1956a) found that after spending 24 hours in one box, hungry rats would spend more time in another exploration box than sated ones, whereas there was no difference in entrances of the two boxes of hungry and satiated animals when both boxes were novel. Zimbardo and Miller (1958) measured the speed with which animals left one compartment for a novel one. The animals were either hungry or satiated and either detained or not detained in the first compartment. The satiated animals left the first compartment faster than the hungry animals when departure was delayed. This implies that it takes longer for a hungry animal to finish exploring an environment than it does a sated animal, an explanation consistent with Fehrer's results but differing from her interpretation.

It is evident that there is a complex relation between hunger or thirst and exploration, whose exact nature can only be further explicated by more investigation.

Fear induced by shock or by a buzzer *during* exploration appears to reduce exploration, but subjecting animals to fear-inducing stimuli *prior* to maze exploration had no effect on exploration (Montgomery & Monkman, 1955). Montgomery (1955) showed that elevated alleys induce more fear in rats than enclosed alleys, a result consistent with the interpretation of Thompson's results as just given. Over time, the animals, given a choice between an elevated and a closed alley, spend more time in the elevated alley, presumably indicating that exploration appeared as fear was reduced. There is a good deal of evidence suggesting that novel stimulation elicits not only exploration but also fear, and that the amount of exploration may be inversely related to the amount of fear present (Welker, 1957, 1959; Bindra & Spinner, 1958; Barnett, 1958; Hayes, 1960; Williams & Kuchta, 1957).

Features of Exploration. A major feature of locomotor exploration that has received attention is its time course. Montgomery (1951b, 1952a) observed a decline in the amount of exploratory behavior shown over the 10-minute test interval on any given test day, but he reported that 24 hours later the exploratory behavior had fully recovered. Berlyne (1955), using a different kind of situation, verified the decrement in exploratory behavior over the test interval, but he did not find complete recovery after 24 hours when the animal was placed again in the exploration situation. Zimbardo and Montgomery (1957a) also failed to find recovery of exploration, even when four days separated the test runs. Within-session reductions in exploration thus seem to be well established, but the subsequent recovery of exploration must remain in doubt. The duration of the test periods may be an important variable. Danziger and Mainland (1954) exposed rats to a circular enclosure for a total of 40 minutes. One group had a continuous exposure to the enclosure in one session 40 minutes in length; the other had one 2-minute exposure a day for 20 days. Those in the single, 40-minute-session showed a decline in movements around the enclosure over the interval, but those in the 2-minute-sessions traversed as much of the enclosure on the 20th day as they had at the beginning.

Much more attention has been paid to other variables of which locomotor exploration is perhaps a function. Receiving considerable attention has been the stimulus to exploration, and Berlyne (1960), as we have seen, has suggested that novelty and complexity are contributing determinants.

Stimulus Factors. So far as novelty is concerned, Montgomery (1953a) studied the effect of similarity of successive test situations on exploratory behavior. He used three mazes, identical in pattern but varying in brightness. One was white, one gray, one black. He tested each animal for exploration twice and measured the amount of exploration in the second test as a function of its similarity to the first one. The least exploration of the second maze occurred when its brightness was identical to that of the first maze, and the greatest exploration of the second maze was found when the difference between the two mazes was maximal (i.e., black to white or white to black). The amount of second maze exploration was intermediate when the difference between it and the first maze was intermediate (i.e., black to gray, white to gray, etc.). Presumably, the novelty of the second maze varied as it differed increasingly from the first maze. We have already mentioned Berlyne's experiment (1950) in which he found that the rats, at a second testing, spent more time with a newly introduced object than with objects encountered before. Berlyne and Slater (1957) used a T-maze with two goal boxes which were empty, save that figures were placed on the rear walls. In one goal box the figure was the same, trial after trial, whereas in the other it was changed each time. The chief difference that emerged in this experiment was that exploration of the novel figure endured much longer when that goal box was entered than did exploration of the familiar figure when its goal box was entered. Thompson and Solomon (1954) placed their animals in a box containing a pattern of black and white vertical stripes. They were returned to the box after having been removed for two minutes. Animals which, on return, found a new, triangular pattern there spent more time exploring it than animals returned to the same vertical pattern. Havelka (1956) found that rats would develop a preference for going over a route to a goal box where the food location was varied randomly from occasion to occasion rather than to a goal box in which food was always found in the same place. Sutherland (1957) used two mazes, each with two pathways. In one maze, the two pathways led to but one goal box, whereas in the other the two pathways led to two distinctively different goal boxes. There were no blind alleys in either maze, and food was present in all the goal boxes. The group run in the maze with distinctive goal boxes alternated the paths it took more often than the group with a single goal box. If an animal from the group which ran to the distinctive goal boxes was prefed in one of them, it tended to choose the pathway leading to the other goal box on the subsequent trial.

There are other experiments we could cite that indicate that novel stimuli, at least under some circumstances, seem to be preferred or to be explored more than familiar stimuli. The point, however, has probably been adequately demonstrated by the studies already reviewed.

It is somewhat difficult to separate complexity of stimuli from their novelty, but the experiment by Dember, Earl, and Paradise (1957) attempted to do so. They used a maze in the shape of the figure 8. In one loop of this figure the walls were painted with horizontal black and white stripes and in the other with vertical stripes, there being more stripes in the latter than in the former case. Over a three-day period in this apparatus, most of the animals were observed to spend more and more of their time in the more complex section, that is, the one with more stripes per unit. Other experiments have studied complexity somewhat differently. Thus Williams and Kuchta (1957) found that rats tended to enter more frequently the arm of a Y-maze which contained black-colored objects than the other arm painted with black stripes of area equal to the objects. Welker (1957) had his rats explore an enclosed area which had five irregularly shaped objects and five cubes attached to the walls. The animals tended more often to approach the irregularly shaped objects than the cubes. In both Welker's results and those of Williams and Kuchta the preference for the more complex object tended to increase with time.

Stimulus variables, then, such as novelty and complexity, are associated with locomotor exploration. Such stimuli need not be visual. Glickman (1958) blinded his rats peripherally and tested them and normal controls for locomotor exploration in an open field and in a Y-maze. In both situations, the blind animals explored more than the sighted ones, suggesting to Glickman that the blind animals, in order to maintain an optimal level of stimulation, had to move about more.

Other Factors. Aside from stimulus variables, other factors have been studied. Carr and Williams (1957) found hooded rats to explore more in the same situation than either albino or black rats. These differences could implicate genetic strain differences in exploratory behavior. Several experiments have attempted to rule out certain kinds of experience as factors in exploration, though their aim was not to bring out the genetic contribution. Charlesworth and Thompson (1957) found no differences in exploratory behavior among animals which had been confined for from three to nine days in boxes with opaque walls. The boxes had nothing in them and some were lighted and some dark. These groups did not differ, either, from a control group kept in ordinary cages. Montgomery and Zimbardo (1957), using rats, also found no differences in exploration as compared to controls after periods of sensory deprivation or activity restriction of up to 100 days. These experiments would suggest that exploration does not depend on an internal factor, which builds up under deprivation, but rather on external stimulation. Conflicting results, however, have been obtained for dogs by Thompson and Heron (1954) and by Zimbardo and Montgomery (1957a). It may be that contradictory results can be accounted for by the complexity of the testing situations, however (Berlyne, 1960, p. 117; Dember & Earl, 1957).

Exploration as a Reward. As a last aspect of locomotor exploratory behavior, we mention evidence that animals will learn a response if the response is followed by an opportunity to explore. Montgomery (1954) found that rats would learn a preference for that side of a Y-maze which terminated in a Dashiell checkerboard maze rather than that which led to a blind alley. Montgomery and Segall (1955), in a similar experiment, found that rats would learn a black-white discrimination for the same reward. In these experiments, unfortunately, the Dashiell maze was roomier than the blind alley, and spaciousness may have been the critical factor. However, Chapman and Levy (1957) controlled for spaciousness, as did Berlyne and Slater (1957), in one of their experiments. Chapman and Levy introduced novelty by modifications of color and surface texture of the walls in the goal box, and Berlyne and Slater by putting objects in one goal box and leaving the other one empty. Both experiments found evidence of learning to go to the novel stimulus. Miles (1958) found that kittens would learn a position habit, learn also to reverse it, and learn a brightness discrimination problem when the reward involved was exploration of objects in a goal box or exploration in the experimental room. Denny's findings (1957) suggest that over a series of trials rats will learn to choose, in a T-maze, the side that, at the time of choice, they have visited less often.

Figure 6–6. Monkeys working to "disassemble" a mechanical puzzle. Reproduced by permission from Young (1961, Fig. 10, p. 51) and from H. F. Harlow.

Novelty or complexity of stimulation seems, then, to be suitable as reinforcement for learning. We turn next to another kind of externally related behavior—investigative responses.

Investigative Responses. In Berlyne's classification (1960), investigative responses differ from orientation and locomotor exploration mainly in the fact that investigation involves action directed to the object of investigation itself, usually through manipulation of it. Thus, investigative responses are limited mainly to the primates, in which manipulation is more readily accomplished than it is in other species.[5] Work

[5] Berlyne (1960) includes, in his discussion of investigation, responses in lower forms which have sensory consequences, such as raising the level of illumination. We discuss this topic under reinforcement (Chapter 11), as this is the main outcome of such sensory changes.

on investigative responses in primates began mainly in the 1950's, although the manipulatory behavior of monkeys has long been described (see Dennis, 1955, who cites earlier sources).

The most widely known experiments on manipulatory behavior in monkeys are those from Harlow's laboratory. Harlow, Harlow, and Meyer (1950) provided rhesus monkeys with an assembled mechanical puzzle (see Fig. 6–6) over a 12-day period. Disassembling the puzzle led to no reward other than manipulating it, as food and water and other rewards presumably were never associated with these actions. Other (control) monkeys were provided disassembled puzzles over the same period. Then both groups were tested with assembled puzzles in the next two days of the experiments. The monkeys given assembled puzzles had been observed to disassemble them, whereas those given disassembled puzzles had not assembled them.[6] The effects of this practice on the test days was that the experimental animals were more adept at disassembling puzzles than were the controls. Similar results were obtained by Harlow (1950) and Harlow and McClearn (1954). Harlow has argued that the rewarding effects of manipulation and the persistence over a number of days shown by his monkeys in working the puzzles must indicate that there is a drive for manipulation independent of other drives and of primary or secondary reinforcement based on other drives. Manipulatory behavior is apparent in monkeys by 20 to 30 days of age and shows increasing strength over the next month (Harlow, Blazek, & McClearn, 1956; Mason, Harlow, & Rueping, 1959). Cho and Davis (1957) measured preferences in rhesus monkeys, offering two objects at a time and observing responsiveness to them. The monkeys responded at a high rate to all twelve objects but did show relative preferences for solid objects as compared to elongated objects. There can be no question that monkeys behave manipulatively to puzzles and other kinds of objects, thus showing "interest" or "curiosity" about them.

Welker (1956a), working with young chimpanzees, observed playful manipulation of various objects he inserted into the cages, although there was a within-session decrement of such behavior and a decrement from session to session. Welker (1956b) showed further that, with blocks, heterogeneity of color and shape led to more manipulative behavior than homogeneity of color and shape. These findings

---

[6] Behavior of the monkeys toward the disassembled puzzles was not stressed, and a stronger case for a manipulation motive could be made if the unassembled puzzles were actually played with. Failure to assemble them, however, might mean only that the monkeys did not possess the requisite skills.

presumably implicate the variable of stimulus complexity in such manipulative behavior.

Some study, although of rather limited scope, has been made of investigative and manipulative behavior with human subjects. It is reasonably evident to observation that healthy children, from infancy on, respond by inspecting and manipulating objects in their environment (Piaget, 1936). Berlyne's experiment (1958*b*) on the orienting reactions in infants is a case in point. With adults, Berlyne (1957*b*) arranged a set-up in which the subject sat alone in a darkened room. He could, by pressing a key, expose pictures, which were presented in a tachistoscope for 0.14 seconds on each key press. With each subject, Berlyne ran four experiments designed to study various stimulus factors relative to this kind of investigative behavior. The subject could expose a picture as many times as he wished, and the picture would be replaced only when the subject indicated he was finished with it. Some of the pictures were *incongruous*, for example an elephant's head attached to the body of a dog, and more responses were given for incongruous animal pictures than for normal pictures. *Complexity* was varied in a series from a picture of a circle to that of a teddybear. Between these two extremes there were four other pictures showing various additions to the circle in the process of making it a teddybear. The most complex pictures elicited more key presses than the less complex pictures. Complexity was also studied with geometric figures. In one series, for example, there were four pictures of five vertical lines. In the least complex figure, all the lines were identical, but in the most complex figure, only one line was straight and solid, one was dotted, one was wavy, and so on. Again the more complex figures elicited more responding than the less complex figures. The last variable studied was *surprisingness*. One series was composed of 12 figures; the first 6 were red triangles, then there were 5 green circles, and, finally, a violet square. Berlyne says that surprisingness is a feature of figure 7 (the first green circle) and figure 12 (the violet square) since they differ from the immediately preceding figures in highly prominent features. More responses were elicited by figures 7 and 12 than by the other figures. Rather higher rates of responding were found for these pictures in five-year-old children than in adults (Berlyne, 1960, p. 162).

Our review of the literature in this section has indicated that orienting responses, locomotor exploration, and investigative responses have led some writers to postulate special drives underlying these behaviors. We will deal with the drive status and the systematic significance of these findings shortly. It does seem clear, however, that animals and men will respond to stimulus novelty, complexity, and similar stimulus attributes by orientation, exploration, or investigation, at least under some conditions. Hunger, thirst, and fear seem to limit these behaviors, and responses which are followed by or which involve orientation, exploration, or investigation may be learned without further reward. Before turning to the discussion of the theoretical implications of this work, we will briefly treat Berlyne's notion of epistemic curiosity.

Epistemic Curiosity

Behaviors that augment knowledge can be called epistemic, from the Greek word for knowledge, *episteme*. There are a number of kinds of knowledge-augmenting behaviors in Berlyne's classification (Berlyne, 1960, p. 265), but relatively little experimentation has been devoted to them. Hence, we restrict ourselves to epistemic curiosity. Berlyne has suggested that seeking of knowledge arises because of conceptual conflicts or incongruities (cf. the discussion of dissonance theory in Chapter 15). He carried out an experiment to test this proposition.

Berlyne (1954) gave, to an experimental group, a questionnaire which contained 48 questions about animals; each question had two alternative answers between which the subject was to choose. The control group did not have this questionnaire. All subjects then received a set of 72 statements concerning animals, including the answers to the questions of the previously administered questionnaire. Finally, the subjects of both groups were given the questionnaire again (the questions were in a new random order), and they had to answer the questions (no answers were provided).

The experimental group supplied significantly more correct answers on the post-questionnaire than the control group and, when asked to do so, expressed an interest (in writing) in knowing more about more animals than the control group. Berlyne interprets this as indicating that the first administration of the questionnaire aroused epistemic curiosity in the experimental group and that it carried over to the other parts of the experiment. Greatest interest was expressed, further, in knowing answers to the questions which had surprised them rather than in knowing answers to questions which had occasioned no surprise. These results fit with Berlyne's notions about conceptual conflict and incongruity as the factors responsible for epistemic curiosity, but unfortunately this experiment can be interpreted in other ways. Familiarity with the critical materials was greater in the experimental group, for one thing, and this could explain at least their superior retention. However, the experiment does serve as a reference for the meaning of epistemic curiosity, and perhaps more study can further clarify it.

Systematic and Theoretical Significance

When we began the discussion of external factors in motivation, we observed that the demonstrations to be reviewed have been taken as evidence contra-indicating the proposition that internal, bodily drives form the sole motivational basis of behavior and reinforcement. We agree that the effects of impoverished stimulation, on the one hand, and of the provision of stimulation, on the other, probably would not have emerged readily from conceptions of motivation based largely on hunger, thirst, and the like. We turn now to an evaluation of the work on external motivation in terms of other aspects of its theoretical significance.

There has been, first of all, a tendency on the part of workers on external motivation to add to the list of drives. Montgomery has spoken of exploratory drive, Berlyne of curiosity, Harlow of manipulation motives, and workers on sensory deprivation have implied a motive for stimulation. In these views, the *source* of the drive is not internally or homeostatically conceived, although it might still be possible to interpret the effects of the drive on the organism or on its behavior homeostatically. Hall (1961) has pointed out that exploration, as studied by Montgomery, could be called *activity*, as well as exploration.[7] We have pointed out, also, that the factors controlling *attention* have much in common with those controlling exploration and investigative responses (Dember & Earl, 1957; Cofer, 1959). On the response side, then, the hallmarks of exploration and certain investigative responses could easily be used as indicators of constructs other than exploratory or curiosity drives. This is not so true of manipulation, however.

On the stimulus side, the situation is not much better. Certain stimuli are provided or withdrawn, and, if the animal behaves in a certain way, he is said to be exploring, manipulating, or investigating. There is no other antecedent condition that defines these drives other than the presentation or withdrawal of stimuli. However, it may be possible to identify general characteristics of stimuli that, whatever the particular stimulus, would evoke responses in the absence of other drives or reinforce

---

[7] Activity deprivation was defined by Montgomery (1953b) as preventing access to an activity wheel. Exploratory behavior appears to be much closer to restless activity than to running activity. (See the section on activity, earlier in this chapter.)

them. This would avoid circularity and, at least, provide some degree of predictability of behavior under certain stimulus (or stimulus change) conditions. It is not clear, however, that the drive concept has any advantage in this context over the use of such terms as attention or orientation responses.

The "insatiability" of manipulative responses has been taken as evidence of the drive character of the manipulation motive. We should clarify, however, that in the situation in which this persistence of manipulation was observed, there was little else for the monkey to do. It would be of interest to study the persistence of manipulation under conditions in which other responses, such as generalized activity, were more likely. Perhaps the monkey manipulates a puzzle as the human may play a game of solitaire—until something better comes along.

Returning to the problem of the stimuli involved in these studies, there are possibilities in many experiments of interpretations not involving new "drives." As Brown (1961) has pointed out, in some instances the objects explored may resemble the animal's food, and this may lead to exploration. Little has been done to control factors such as these in experiments so far reported; in some instances, the animal may "explore" because, in a variety of situations, moving about has been rewarded in his past by food, water, or sexual contacts.

There are other possibilities. Brown (1961) suggested that anxiety may have underlain the tendency of Butler's monkeys to move about the box, and during this time they just happened to push open a window, permitting them a peek at the laboratory room. Harlow (1953b) has argued that no signs of anxiety were present, but more direct and specific evidence would be desirable. Similarly, Berlyne (1960), while not speaking of anxiety as such, has proposed that a kind of emotional arousal is established by novel stimuli and, over time, by sensory isolation or deprivation. Davis (1959) found increased muscular and circulatory activity and decreased respiration in subjects submitted to reduced stimulation for 40 minutes. He characterized this pattern as "anticipation." Exploration, manipulation, and the seeking of stimulation, then, would have a "drive-reduction" value (cf. Lana, 1960, 1962), in that the arousal occasioned by novelty or boredom would be reduced by exploratory or manipulative behavior or by "seeking" stimulation. One could also fit exploratory, manipulative or stimulus-seeking behavior into a framework established by adaptation-level theory (see Chapters 7 and 8). According to this view, as represented by Hebb and by McClelland, for example, relatively small deviations from a prevailing adaptation level would be pleasurable and therefore sought after. This might involve, so far as Hebb is concerned, the maintenance or the establishment of an optimal level of arousal, necessary to optimal cortical functioning, deviations in either direction from which are distinctly unpleasurable.

In sum, the major conclusion of the work on exploration, sensory isolation, orientation reactions, and investigative responses is that external stimuli (and their absence) probably have the capacity, in themselves, so long as they have certain characteristics, to arouse behavior. The theoretical significance of this fact is not entirely clear, but there are enough alternative explanations available to obviate the immediate conclusion that there are special drives for exploration, manipulation, and the like, or that some drive or tension-reduction interpretation of the data is implausible. Only further investigation can solve these problems.

SUMMARY

In this chapter, we have reviewed the status of activity and of external stimulus conditions as sources of drive.

Activity is not a unitary matter, seeming to consist of at least two kinds (restless and running activity), which are little correlated and which respond differently to a number of variables. A number of physiological variables contribute to the presence of activity, and there is some evidence consistent with the notion of activity drive or drives. However, there is also evidence that external stimulation is often important in eliciting activity and that many features of activity reflect learned associations of activity with external and internal stimuli, acquired under reinforcement.

Considerable work has been devoted to orientation, curiosity, exploration, manipulation, sensory deprivation, and the like, and interpretations have been made that behaviors arising in relation to these terms do not arise from internal states. Rather, external stimuli have been implicated as the motivational sources of such behaviors. A review of the characteristics and conditions of these "motives" suggests, however, that alternative interpretations can be made and leads to uncertainty as to their systematic status.

Chapter 7

Homeostatic Concepts and Motivation

In Chapter 1 we suggested that motivation theories could be divided into two camps: those which posit essentially conservative principles and those which hold that growth is the overriding behavioral orientation. Of fundamental import to the former, and in fact assumed as a part of many growth theories as well, is some form of equilibrium concept. We have seen it already in our brief discussion of early motivation theories (Chapter 2), in the ethological instinct position (Chapter 3), and in the minor theories relating bodily condition to behavior (Chapters 4 and 5). As the reader later examines the basic assumptions of theories of emotion as motivation (Chapter 8), of conflict and stress theories (Chapter 9), of the drive concepts held by learning theorists (Chapter 10), of psychoanalysis (Chapter 12), and of socially derived motivation (in Chapters 11, 14, and 15), he will again and again rediscover an underlying assumption of equilibrium maintenance or homeostasis, though not always so identified.

The late R. C. Davis, remarking on this increasing use of the principle as a model for behavior, wrote that it "presents itself in rivalry with the time-honored formula of stimulus-response" (1958, p. 8). The prospect of such wide use in fact alarmed Davis, and he urged careful evaluation of the concept as an all-around model for behavior. In the present chapter we will attempt such an evaluation, dealing in order with its origin and use in physiology, its extension into psychology, first in the service of physiological equilibrium maintenance and then as a principle of psychological homeostasis. Here our attention will be given to the attempts to develop homeostasis as *the* unifying explanatory motivational concept. And finally, we will present and briefly examine in turn four different existing models of fundamentally homeostatic theories.

THE CONCEPT OF HOMEOSTASIS

The term *homeostasis* was coined by Walter Cannon, the Harvard physiologist, to describe the steady states attained at any particular moment by the physiological processes at work in living organisms. This term, although of relatively recent origin (1932), has had wide currency. However, the idea of a natural balancing tendency or "equilibrium-seeking" had been noted and described considerably earlier. In one form or another, it had appeared in the writings of philosophers and of physical, biological, and social scientists. Cannon himself traces the idea to Hippocrates (460–377 B.C.), and others have noted its similarity to Spinoza's *conatus se conservandi* [1] (1675), Herbert Spencer's idea of equilibrium as an evolutionary goal (1855, 1862; see Flugel, 1955), Fechner's concepts of stability (1873), and other ideas (e.g., see Raup, 1925; Child, 1924). We shall have occasion to return to some of these views as we examine the implications of the concept of homeostasis later in this chapter.

Let us turn first to a consideration of the ideas of equilibrium as presented by Claude Bernard (1859), Child (1924), and Cannon (1932, 1939, 1941, 1945) in physiology, since it is on the basis of these particular conceptualizations that the motivation principle in psychology, utilizing the name of homeostasis, has been developed.

The particular starting point for Cannon's dramatic description of *The Wisdom of the Body* (1932) was the work of Claude Bernard, the distinguished French physiologist, about 100 years ago. It was Bernard who drew attention to the importance of the constancy of the fluid matrix of the body in which all living tissue exists. Each cell can maintain itself only to the extent that it draws upon this fluid matrix for needed substances and discharges into it such excesses of waste products as cannot be utilized or stored.

It is the fixity of the "milieu intérieur" which is the condition of free and independent life . . . All the vital mechanisms, however varied they may be, have only one object, that of preserving constant the conditions of life in the internal environment (1859, as quoted in Cannon, 1939, p. 38).

Constant, as used here, should by no means be confused with the ideas of static, fixed, or unchanging. It was because of this possible confusion that Cannon chose to introduce his new term to describe these constant states. As Cannon (1939) explained it:

Organisms, composed of material which is characterized by the utmost inconstancy and unsteadiness, have somehow learned the methods of maintaining constancy and keeping steady in the presence of conditions which might reasonably be expected to prove profoundly disturbing (pp. 21–22).

The constant conditions which are maintained in the body might be

---

[1] Spinoza, *Ethics*, P. III, Prop. VI. "Each thing, in so far as it is in itself, endeavors to persevere in its being" (p. 135).

termed *equilibria*. That word, however, has come to have fairly exact meaning as applied to relatively simple physiochemical states, in closed systems, where known forces are balanced. The coordinated physiological processes which maintain most of the steady states in the organism are so complex and so peculiar to living beings—involving, as they may, the brain and the nervous system, the heart, lungs, kidneys and spleen, all working cooperatively—that I have suggested a special designation for these states, *homeostasis*. The word does not imply something set and immobile, a stagnation. It means a condition—a condition which may vary, but which is relatively constant (p. 24).

Child (1924) earlier made a similar distinction in his analogy between the living organism and a stream: "The stream like the organism is always approaching equilibrium, but if it attains equilibrium it ceases to flow and is 'dead' " (p. 237). In a very close parallel to Cannon's later description, Child wrote:

We reach the conclusion that the organism does not, strictly speaking, represent the maintenance of a certain equilibrium, in spite of external disturbance, but rather a continuous alternation and equilibration in reaction to external factors. It is not a "closed system" maintaining itself against the rest of the world, but a system open at every point and in continuous and necessary relation to the environment and the same is true for its parts in their relations with each other (p. 238).

We shall return in a later section of this chapter to a consideration of various types of stability or equilibrium which open systems can attain (see pp. 344–346), and even to a further refinement of the homeostatic concept as "dynamic homeostasis" (see p. 317). Here let us take a closer look at the mechanisms of physiological homeostasis.

PHYSIOLOGICAL HOMEOSTASIS

The Physiological Homeostatic Apparatus

The fluid matrix to which Bernard and Cannon refer is the combined circulatory and lymphatic systems. It is the relative constancy maintained in these systems, on which all living parts of the organism feed, that constitutes homeostasis.[2] The greater part of Cannon's significant volume (1932, rev. 1939) is devoted to detailed descriptions of the ways in which specific constancies are maintained. Thus the maintenance of the constancy of the water content of the blood, the con-

[2] We may note that whereas Cannon proposed the term *homeostasis* to refer to the constant *states,* it is also sometimes applied to the *process* of maintaining constancies. To maintain the distinction clearly we shall use *homeostatic process* when referring to the latter.

stancy of the salt content of the blood, the homeostasis of blood sugar, blood proteins, blood fat, blood calcium, acid-alkaline neutrality, the constancy of body temperature, and the maintenance of an adequate oxygen supply are all described and supported with experimental data (largely from Cannon's own laboratories).[3]

The majority of the "hard" evidence presented by Cannon describes compensatory mechanisms which preserve the types of constancies just noted. These mechanisms are shown to involve most of the internal organs, the nervous systems (particularly the sympathetic portion of the autonomic nervous system), the endocrine system, and chemical factors in the fluids themselves. Cannon's conception of the wisdom of the body goes far beyond these data, however. He describes protective reflexes, for example, as serving to maintain the integrity of the organism. An illustrative example may be seen in the case of a foreign body entering the nasal passage. In such an instance it will be sneezed out or, failing this, it will produce a cough. This latter will occur usually only if it penetrates beyond the sneeze defense line or if, of infectious origin, the foreign object enters from below.

Other adjustive processes are also described by Cannon as homeostatic in nature. Some of these are fairly slow processes as, for instance, the development of callosity of the skin, serving ". . . both as a cushion and a shield." Others are more rapid, as the clotting of the blood and the formation of scar tissue over cuts, and the even more rapid healing of internal injuries. Other quite slow processes seen as essentially homeostatic in nature are the adjustive responses to climatic changes, fur growing, feather moulting, and so on. Bacterial infections are also defended against in such a manner as to maintain the essential integrity of the living organism.

Of interest to us here is the fact that Cannon has perceived (or conceived) a principle of organization which seemed to him to describe *all* of these varied activities of parts of the body system. His own work on the circulatory mechanisms gave him courage to expect that, since mechanisms could be observed (or inferred) to be operating for these subsystems, more than likely further research would yield the mechanisms determining the maintenance of other aspects of organismic integrity as well.

Cannon saw the nervous system, and particularly the sympathetic part of the autonomic nervous system, as playing an important role in the preparation of the organism for what he called emergency ac-

[3] These cannot be described here, but the interested reader should examine these descriptions for himself (cf. Cannon, 1939; Dempsey, 1951; Morgan & Stellar, 1950; Young, 1961).

tion (see Chapter 8, p. 391). He pointed to hunger and thirst and to a parallel mechanism of salt craving as extensions into behavior of the internal homeostatic system. These mechanisms are prompted by peripheral cues directly resulting from such internal processes (e.g., dryness of the throat resulting from water shortage in the body and the resultant lowered salivation). They serve the same major aim of maintaining constant the internal environment. In this, as we shall see, he anticipated the experimental work of Richter and his associates (1942–1943, 1947; see also our previous discussions in Chapter 5).

Homeostasis and Evolution

If an individual organism requires water in order to survive, it must have available a continuous supply of water. Where there is no mechanism for maintaining an internal supply, the organism must restrict its habitat to localities where water is available. Organisms capable of maintaining their own water reserves and drawing upon them as needed are that much less immediately dependent on their external environment. This dependence on water and other sources of supply can be said to be inversely related to the degree of development of mechanisms of self-regulation. Spencer (1855), Child (1924), and others (e.g., Howells, 1947; Pick, 1954) have suggested such a relationship. Pick goes even further to trace the development of neural (particularly autonomic) regulators through the evolution of higher species. He suggests that the dependence of the organism on its environment for continuous supply of needed substances was progressively reduced with the development of such self-contained regulatory mechanisms. These mechanisms developed usually, he believes, out of structures already in existence and functioning, although he acknowledges that this evolutionary interpretation has been challenged. For example, he points to the air bladder of the fish, originally serving to raise or lower the fish in the water, as perhaps becoming the rudimentary lung, the existing structure permitting further functional development. With such development new freedom existed.

Reptiles were no longer restricted to a water environment, as were amphibia, and mammals were even freer, etc. Pick points to the evolution of the autonomic nervous system from a role in the conservation of energy exclusively to an eventual role in the expenditure of energy as well. This could come about because of the greater economy of function in energy storage. With this change, the parasympathetic (the remaining old function) and the sympathetic nervous systems (utilizing some of the energy of the system in the preparation for action and for defense) were thus functionally differentiated. Dempsey

(1951) offers a somewhat similar theory of the role of homeostasis in the evolutionary development of animal species, and this position seems to be generally held by animal ecologists (see Allee et al., 1949).

Actually, the very process of evolution, implying increased adaptation as it does, would point to improved development of mechanisms of homeostasis. As Child said some forty years ago: "Evolution is a process of standardization of the potentialities of behavior, of regulation, and of its mechanisms, and through this means, of the environmental conditions to which the individual is likely to be subjected" (1924, p. 238). This standardization [4] or adaptation through stabilization, as Howells (1947, p. 31) has pointed out, ". . . is achieved only by incorporating and stabilizing the outer environment in the inner environment." In other words, homeostasis and the mechanisms which support it are the very essence of evolutionary development.

The General Features of Physiological Homeostasis

Cannon (1939, pp. 286–287) reminds us of the essential frailty of the living being:

Only a brief lapse in the coordinating functions of the circulatory apparatus, and a part of the organic fabric may break down so completely as to endanger the existence of the entire bodily edifice. . . . [However] . . . as a rule, whenever conditions are such as to affect the organism harmfully, factors appear within the organism itself that protect it or restore its disturbed balance.

How is this protection accomplished? First, we must recognize that the fluid matrix, the constancy of which constitutes homeostasis, is isolated from the outside environment by the skin (Bernard, 1859). The stability, within certain limits, of this internal environment is maintained by an intricate set of checks and balances (we shall later come to call these processes feed-back mechanisms). Cannon (1939, p. 288) described some of them as follows:

A noteworthy prime assurance against extensive shifts in the status of the fluid matrix is the provision of sensitive automatic indicators or sentinels, the function of which is to set corrective processes in motion at the very beginning of a disturbance. If water is needed, the mechanism of thirst warns us before any change in the blood has occurred, and we respond by drinking. If the blood pressure falls and the necessary oxygen supply is

---

[4] To say that evolution leads to standardization is to state the matter in a deceivingly simple fashion. In fact evolution first accentuates variation, following which new norms are established on the basis of their efficiency in maintaining homeostasis. Ineffective norms would by definition be eliminated.

jeopardized, delicate nerve endings in the carotid sinus send messages to the vasomotor center and the pressure is raised. If by vigorous muscular movements blood is returned to the heart in great volume, so that cardiac action might be embarrassed and the circulation checked, again delicate nerve endings are affected and a call goes from the right auricle that results in speeding up the heart rate and thereby hastening the blood flow. If the hydrogen-ion concentration in the blood is altered ever so slightly towards the acid direction, the especially sensitized part of the nervous system which controls breathing is at once made more active and by increased ventilation of the lungs carbonic acid is pumped out until the normal state is restored.

Cannon pointed to other regulatory mechanisms not then clearly understood, such as the operation of the sympathico-adrenal apparatus to increase blood sugar when the glycemic percentage begins to fall below the critical level, and so on. As we have now come to know, through the extensive research of Selye (1937, 1946, 1950 on) and others (cf. Christman, 1950), many of the regulatory functions are mediated by chemical (hormonal) substances in the blood itself, with neural factors sometimes precipitating, sometimes following, sometimes coordinate with hormonal changes.

An important additional factor in permitting the successful maintenance of homeostasis is what Cannon has called "the margin of safety." By this he refers to the fact that our bodies contain a duplicity of organs (e.g., an extra kidney, extra lung) and in most organs and tissues a "surplus" of substance, or "allowance for contingencies." Further evidence for such a safety margin is the fact that higher-than-needed "normal" levels are maintained in such processes as blood pressure, etc.[5]

Independence of the external environment is facilitated by homeostatic regulation of both materials and processes. The homeostasis of materials is accomplished through storage in body organs and cells and through elimination of excesses and waste materials. Storage for immediate accommodation and use, as Cannon saw it, occurs through a simple process of "inundation" of tissue spaces, while more permanent storage "for later and lasting service" appears to be accomplished by segregation in certain parts of cells, subject to release only through particular neural or neurohumoral action. Storage is complemented

---

[5] Although emphasized by Cannon in relation to physiological processes, some relevance of this "contingency allowance" observation can be seen to such psychological processes as those involved in effort expenditure (see Robinson, 1934) and in setting of levels of aspiration (see p. 316). Sensory processes similarly utilize only a fraction of the available "information" and limited portions of the receptor mechanisms. The existence of two cerebral hemispheres and a surplus of neural tissue may also be noted in this connection.

by "overflow" as a means of maintaining the constancy of the fluid matrix. The kidneys contribute to the regulation of the amounts of useful substances retained by the blood, keeping down the concentrations of useful as well as waste materials.

By homeostasis of process, Cannon referred to the regulation of rate of heart action, oxygenation, respiration, temperature change, etc. to accommodate changing needs in the system. Usually, as he points out, storage and process mechanisms operate in combination (as in assuring uniformity of oxygen tension).

In *summary*, then, the concept of physiological homeostasis conceives of the organism as an open biological system, in contact with its external environment, but maintaining relatively stable states of material and process within its own internal environment. Such states can be maintained through the complex cooperation of most of the internal organs, the nervous system, and the endocrine system. The constancy of the fluid matrix (which *is* the environment of living cells within the organism) is maintained within a "normal" range, rather than at a fixed level, by virtue of a series of mechanisms capable of operating in such a way as to increase or decrease the intake, exchange, or loss of specific substances in the blood and lymph. The "self-regulatory" apparatus is considered to operate automatically and in response to a specific signal (or signals) within the system being regulated, and is not considered to be under direct cortical control.[6] "If a state remains steady it does so because any tendency towards change is automatically met by increased effectiveness of the factor or factors which resist the change" (Cannon, 1939, p. 299). The optimal levels or homeostatic states maintained within the organism's internal environment at any moment may be modified in relation to the demands made on the organism by its external milieu. These changes may be slow (as in climatic adjustments) or quite rapid (as in blood coagulation when the skin is punctured), but they would appear to be consistent with the continuance of life in the organism.

Now, what has all this to do with behavior?

[6] Although the idea of self-contained, subcortical regulatory mechanisms was emphasized by Cannon, some ambiguity remains as to the role played by neural receptors in triggering adjustive responses. Prof. Ross Stagner has reminded the authors (pers. comm.) that such changes as vitamin deficiencies would affect the receptors physiologically, perhaps leading to modification of threshold values and thus to response. This matter, discussed again later in the chapter, is by no means resolved.

Physiological Homeostasis and Behavior

Thus far we have dealt with the concept of homeostasis almost exclusively as it involves intra-organismic variables. Regulation, by neural and hormonal factors, of constancies within the fluid matrix will be successful only in a fairly constant external environment, however. Where intake of needed substances (such as air, food, and water) are automatic, or where supplies are readily obtainable at the surfaces of the body (as in the case of air, or the fetus in utero), the concept of physiological homeostasis would probably suffice to explain the functioning of the living organism. However, as is obvious, this is not often the case. Even with apparently available "air," its content may be so unusual in regard to quantities of oxygen or carbon dioxide as to require major homeostatic adjustments.

Cannon, of course, recognized this. As we have already noted (p. 305), his conception of homeostasis extended beyond the internal regulation to include hunger, thirst, and adaptive "emergency" reactions. The stomach contraction and the dry throat were natural results of food and water deficit, he believed, and cued the behavior which would restore the imbalance (but see Chapter 5). Also, unexpected or intense stimuli produced autonomic responses, which prepared the individual for "fight or flight" (see Chapter 8).[7]

It was the psychobiologist C. P. Richter who extended Cannon's experimental approach to the study of behavioral effects of physiological homeostasis. Richter described what he called "behavior or total organismic regulators" as supplements to Bernard and Cannon's physiological and chemical regulators. In a series of experiments on operated rats, Richter[8] and his associates showed that when the physiological regulators were surgically eliminated ". . . the animals themselves made an effort to maintain a constant environment or homeostasis" (Richter, 1942–1943, p. 64).

The evidence, like that of Cannon's, is quite dramatic. For example, rats given a choice between tap water and a 3 per cent sodium chloride solution, tended to drink approximately 22 cc of water to 2 cc of

---

[7] Actually, Cannon thought that the homeostatic concept could include the whole of social organization as a means of providing individuals with environments stable enough to assure their organic homeostasis. He recognized that such a theoretical extension was entirely speculative on his part, and offered no conceptual bridge from physiological to social homeostasis. His remarks are included at the end of the "Wisdom" volume, assigned to an "Epilogue" to emphasize further the discontinuity of these speculations from the earlier evidence-supported sections of his book.

[8] Some of this work has already been discussed (see Chapter 5).

the salt solution. Following adrenalectomy, however, where the operation "eliminates their physiological control of sodium metabolism . . ." Richter reported a shift in preference to 13 cc of the sodium chloride solution. At the same time, tests for preference of other minerals were negative. Needless to say, animals not receiving a sodium chloride supplement in this or some other way would die.

Similarly, Richter (1942–1943, p. 66) reports that parathyroidectomized rats ". . . which on a regular diet develop tetany and usually die within a few days will, when given access to a calcium solution, take sufficiently large amounts to keep themselves alive and free from tetany." The shift in consumption was from 3 cc to 17 cc of calcium solution. After a parathyroid implant to the anterior chamber of the eye, calcium appetite apparently returned to normal at once. Richter further reported a reduced appetite for phosphorous solutions following parathyroidectomy.

In still another illustration of his thesis, Richter (1942–1943, p. 68) reports that ". . . pancreatectomized rats, which have lost their physiological means of regulating carbohydrate metabolism, ingest large amounts of water, presumably to assist in eliminating the unoxidized glucose." These rats seemed also to vary their diets considerably after removal of the pancreas, as though "searching for" needed substances. In another experiment, Richter and his associates removed the posterior lobe of the pituitary gland, thereby eliminating ". . . one of the chief physiological regulators of water metabolism. Without anti-diuretic hormone from this gland animals excrete large amounts of urine and as a result become dehydrated and soon die" (p. 68). Given free access to water, however, such animals increased their intake of water drastically (to as much as two times body weight for some) and appeared to remain in good health.

Finally, Richter described experiments on behavioral adjustments to temperature imbalance. In these studies a means was devised to provide caged rats with measurable amounts of paper for nest building. Richter reported a markedly increased paper use in hypophysectomized and thyroidectomized rats. Such increased nest building behavior (increase in paper use from 700 to 3500 cm per day) was shown to be related to surgically produced breakdown of the physiological heat-regulating mechanisms. When given thyroid extract, the amount of nest building was reduced not only in thyroidectomized rats but, when given in excess, in normal rats as well (see Kinder, 1927; Richter, 1937). Although most of the evidence noted here has been based on studies of "insulted" organisms, data like the effect of thyroid extract on nest building in normal rats supported Richter's belief that his findings were applicable to intact organisms.

At the beginning of this section we called attention to the fact that physiological homeostasis may break down either because of (1) an interruption in functioning of some phase of the bodily regulatory mechanisms, or (2) a lack of necessary material(s) in the environment. Richter and his associates have clearly supported the case of "self-regulatory" behavior in the former instance. That behavior may be invoked similarly in the latter case is also strongly implied. Richter cites evidence for self-selecting diets in intact organisms experimentally deprived of certain required food substances and given the opportunity to provide for this deficiency in food choice. He further calls attention (1942–1943, p. 92) to ". . . the possibility that various phenomena, ordinarily spoken of as perverted appetites, such as coprophagy (feces eating), infantophagia, autophagia, placenta eating, and bone eating, may be regarded as instances of self-regulatory activities." Feces-eating rats lived longer when on single food-dextrose diets than feces-deprived rats (54 vs. 34 days). Urine-drinking (ourondypsia), salt-craving in humans with Addison's disease (destruction of the adrenal cortex), and eating of chalk, plaster, and other substances with high calcium content in parathyroid-deficiency are all seen as consistent with Richter's hypothesis of self-regulation. Richter suggested that physical activity of children and the withdrawn behavior of certain depressed patients were further instances of behavior serving to accomplish physiological homeostasis, in this case general energy balance (see later discussion of Freeman).

In answer to critics who cite instances of apparent failure of self-regulation, Richter points to confusions of tastes in many food mixtures, chemically impure food preparations (including actual lacks of essentials in some modern refined foods), and the likelihood of sensory[9] defects in those failing to display appropriate self-regulatory responses.

Richter, as the previous discussion suggests, places emphasis on taste as the means by which bodily deficiencies are translated into appetitive preferences. He had conducted several experiments which would seem to support the likelihood that taste thresholds are modified by dietary factors, and that interference with taste nerves disrupts ability to make beneficial dietary selections (e.g., adrenalectomized rats whose taste mechanisms have been interfered with fail to increase their salt intake and thus die). However, more recent work on taste thresholds (e.g., Pfaffmann & Bare, 1950; see earlier discussion on p. 234) has indicated

---

[9] We may note here the key role assigned to sensory input of some type.

that relationships between dietary factors and taste are probably somewhat more complicated than Richter believed them to be.

Summary

So far we have seen that a number of intra-organismic mechanisms may become active when an imbalance exists in the internal environment. Such activity seems to persist until the old balance is restored, a new balance achieved, or exhaustion or death intervenes. Where the "automatic" physiological mechanisms fail, or perhaps in conjunction with them, behavior may be evoked that results in a change in the condition of the environment, making it possible for physiological homeostasis to be restored once more. Thus an organism may remove itself to a place where some needed substance can be taken in, or it can "choose" the one of two or more substances which will help restore inner equilibrium. In all instances dealt with so far, behavior is in the service of bodily need. The evidence seems clear enough for us to agree with Richter's conclusion that ". . . in human beings and animals the effort to maintain a constant internal environment or homeostasis constitutes one of the most universal and powerful of all behavior urges or drives" (1942–1943, p. 101).[10]

However, at least two important questions remain. First, *what are* the various components of physiological homeostasis and *how* are they served by behaviors of different sorts? To attempt a real answer to this double-headed first question would not only go beyond the scope of this book but would go beyond the state of current knowledge in the field as well.

The principle itself has general acceptance in biology, and can be said to be the starting point for a tremendous amount of research. Besides Cannon, Richter, and their associates, there have been major programmatic efforts by Selye (1937, 1950 on), and others (cf., Hoagland, 1945 on) on physiological homeostatic systems and their behavior under stress. Related studies are being conducted on the influences in behavior of autonomic and endocrine factors and on the intricate interrelationships of neural, hormonal, and behavioral factors as influenced by drugs and other stress phenomena (e.g., Dempsey, 1951; Fortier, 1951; Solomon & Wynne, 1950; Mason, 1958, 1959; Miller, Mirsky, & Stein, 1953; Appley, 1957, 1961*b*; Miller, 1957; Morgan, 1957; Brady, 1958; Appley & Moeller, 1962; Miller & Ogawa, 1962).

Needless to say, research in physiology, following up Cannon's

---

[10] We should note that Richter has not made homeostasis *the one* key principle of motivation. This may be contrasted with the more extreme positions of Freeman, Stagner, and others (later in this chapter).

sweeping hypotheses, has come up with a certain amount of discon-- firmation. Details of both the theory and the facts are constantly being modified. So, for example, Richards (1953) has asked if a converse principle, *hyperexis* (having too much), wasn't needed to account for unhomeostatic excess responses. R. C. Davis (1958) has similarly suggested *heterostasis* to deal with the same problem of imbalance of one system in the process of regulating another (e.g., sweating increases to reduce temperature excess). Vogt (1954) and Rogoff (1945) have critically re-examined some of the aspects of the autonomic and adrenal responses, and Arnold (1945) has questioned Cannon's description of how counteraction was set in motion (see Chapter 8).

The second and for present considerations the more significant question remaining is whether the homeostatic model is applicable to events not directly and innately associated with the physiological constancy of the fluid matrix of the body. We have seen that Cannon had envisioned the principle of homeostasis as operating at a level far beyond the physiology of the individual. A number of other biologists and psychologists—both before and after Cannon introduced his new term —had observed equilibrium-seeking or equilibrium-finding tendencies in the behavior of living organisms (Fechner, 1873; Freud, 1915*a;* Herrick, 1922; Child, 1924; Raup, 1925; Warden et al., 1935; Guthrie, 1938; Poffenberger, 1938; Lindner, 1945; and others previously mentioned). Within the past two decades attention has been focused more systematically on the possibility of a theory of behavior based on homeostasis as the underlying motivational principle. Let us turn now to some of the attempts to expand the concept to encompass psychological events.

PSYCHOLOGICAL HOMEOSTASIS

Fletcher (1938, 1942) is credited by some as being the first psychologist to ask directly if psychology couldn't take over the principle of homeostasis as its own (cf. Toch & Hastorf, 1955). Fletcher considered that Cannon's demonstrations of the wisdom of the body could be taken as examples of organic intelligence at *one* level of organization. Since the personality may itself be conceived as a level of organization of the organic whole (Fechner, 1873; Allport, 1937), might we not look for the equivalent of "normal body states" here as well? Fletcher realized that certain new problems would arise, but he was convinced that a principle of psychological homeostasis could be demonstrated, and that it was an entirely reasonable one for psychology: ". . . the facts are that acquired action tendencies, or habits, the drives of cultivated interests, ideational preservative tendencies, developed personality traits, not to mention acquired drug addictions, all may without doing violence to either logic or facts be subsumed under the category of homeostasis" (Fletcher, 1942, p. 83).

Now we must point out some of the problems raised by Fletcher's conclusions, before we can agree or disagree with his confident assertion. To begin with, we must recognize that two distinct ideas are involved: (1) that physiological steady states can be protected by complex, higher order processes, such as cognition and reasoning; and (2) that subjective states (or habit systems) can become valued steady states, themselves to be protected. Earlier, we were able to go, with Cannon and Richter, from intra-organic systems into behavior (by a simple extension of logic and with fairly clear empirical support), from behaving part-systems or organs to the behaving whole-system or organism. The homeostatic states to be preserved in both cases *were precisely the same*. Whether the adjustment involved a kidney response or a more complex higher order response of the whole individual, such as "searching" or "choosing," the end state was the reduction of a physiological tension and the restoration of physiological homeostasis.

However, if we wish to speak of psychological or behavioral homeostasis in the second sense just noted, it is necessary (satisfactorily) to account for several things.

First, the "habits, drives of cultivated interests, ideational preservative tendencies," and so on, of which Fletcher wrote, are clearly *acquired* conditions. It would therefore have to be determined *how* acquired states could become the "normal states," the balance of which is homeostatic. What is the nature of the equilibrium? What cues signal its disturbance? its re-establishment? How, if at all, are such equilibria related to body-fluid homeostasis?

A second though related problem is that of the *timing* of the corrective or adaptive responses. Cannon, it will be recalled, described corrective action in physiological homeostatic systems as being set in motion by the *occurrence* of a disturbance. With regard to emotional states, at least, Arnold (1945) has emphasized the *reactive* nature of adaptive responses, showing that corrective actions are induced by the *effects* of disturbance (see Chapter 8). Thus physiological equilibrium is maintained by the continual *counteracting* of disturbances. At the behavioral level, however, adjustments often appear to begin *before* disturbances occur, and sometimes seem to prevent the occurrence of the disturbance completely. It would therefore have to be determined how the organism *anticipates* disruptive stimuli, and even successfully forestalls them.[11]

Although these matters have by no means been resolved, there is a considerable body of evidence, from a variety of sources and of a number of types, suggesting the existence of equilibrating (i.e., balance-seeking, stabilizing, or constancy-seeking) processes in behavior. The existence of such constancies may be interpreted as illustrating (and/or supporting) a homeostatic theory. These studies were not conducted as tests of such a theory, but the consistency of their findings is perhaps sufficient to warrant further consideration of the principle of homeostasis in relation to behavior motivation. We turn to this evidence now.

Types of Supporting Evidence for Psychological Homeostasis

Four types of data appear to be consistent with the operation of psychological homeostasis:

1. *Psychophysical data.* The phenomena of brightness, color, form, and size constancy are routinely demonstrable in psychological laboratories and readily observable in everyday life. These and other instances of the maintenance of stable percepts and the organizing of perceptual fields (e.g., into figure and ground, "good Gestalts" appear to represent equilibrating tendencies [12] (Fechner, 1873; Fletcher, 1942; Stagner, 1951; Stagner & Karwoski, 1952; Helson, 1947, 1953).

2. *Studies of work and efficiency.* It is an often-repeated observation in laboratory and industrial studies of performance that fairly constant work levels are maintained under conditions of distraction and of tension, effort modulation being used to keep performance within given limits (Robinson, 1934; Bartley & Chute, 1947; Freeman, 1948; Seashore, 1951).

3. *Studies of "level of aspiration."* Lewin and his students have frequently demonstrated the steadying effect on performance in a variety of tasks of self-set goals, determined in part by the results of past experience (Lewin et al., 1944; Murphy, 1947). The demonstration

---

[11] The reader will recognize this as *avoidance* learning, for which an intervening conditionable anxiety state has been postulated. This problem is discussed in several places in the book (cf., Chapters 10, 11, 14).

[12] Although the nativism-empiricism argument still continues with regard to perceptual organization (cf. Hochberg, 1962), it should be recognized that the constancy phenomena are the result of experience and that in many dimensions familiar or preferred patterns and levels of stimulation may become valued steady states to be protected and maintained. This will be explored more fully a little later.

of the Zeigarnik effect (Zeigarnik, 1927; Atkinson, 1953), that incompleted (interrupted) or unsuccessful tasks serve to motivate resumption and success, provides further evidence for a type of psychological homeostasis (see later discussion and criticism of the work of Lewin and his associates).

4. *Clinical data.* A considerable clinical literature describes the operation of compulsions, and the so-called mechanisms of defense in personality organization and in psychosomatics, pointing to the equilibrating nature of these response systems (Freud, 1920; A. Freud, 1937; Fenichel, 1945; Masserman, 1946; Nuttin, 1953; Menninger, 1954; and see Chapter 12).

Common to all instances of psychological homeostasis, if these examples are indeed illustrative of this principle, is the assumption that the "steady state" incorporates the effects of experience, thus representing a new equilibrium point on successive occasions. In treating of physiological homeostasis, Cannon (1939) also provided for a shifting base line as a function of aging (pp. 202 ff.), experience (e.g., athletes vs. untrained "hypodynamic heart," cf. p. 212), and long-term environmental shifts (as in climatic changes, cf. p. 221).

Stagner (1951, 1952, 1954) suggests that this "dynamic homeostasis" evolves out of physiological homeostasis as a result of learning. Thus, after any first exposure to new stimulation,

(1) The organism perceives minimal physiological changes as *cues* and *anticipates* the disturbance. Forestalling action therefore becomes possible. . . . We suggest that energy mobilization for forestalling tactics must be explained in terms of a *cortical tension* which reflects the visceral-proprioceptive pattern of the original biological disequilibration. (2) The organism perceives environmental objects as potential sources of equilibrium-restoration and behaves differently toward them (hoarding food, building houses or nests, etc.). Thus repeated disequilibration results in continuous modification of the organism and its perception of the external world. *Dynamic homeostasis* involves the maintenance of tissue constancies by establishing a constant physical environment—by reducing the variability and disturbing effects of external stimulation. Thus the organism does not simply restore to prior equilibrium. A new, more complex and more comprehensive equilibrium is established (Stagner, 1951, pp. 5–6).

For Stagner, as for Freeman, the stability remains that of the fluid matrix, incorporating, however, a much wider range of musculature and behavior as part of the mechanisms of stability maintenance. Thus, perceptual *cues and* perceptual (and motor) *responses* of the whole individual become part of the homeostatic system and are involved both in turning on and in turning off motivated behavior. By shifting the locus of energy mobilization to the nervous system (his "cortical tension" hypothesis),[13] Stagner leaves the way open for an explanation of "anticipation" in terms of conditioning and learning principles (see Freeman, p. 330, and Mowrer, Chapter 10). Fletcher had thought that consciousness played a mediating role in the anticipation of disturbance. However, as Fletcher is not a dualist, this may simply be a way of speaking of cortical tension. Stagner, like Fletcher, relies on the extensive data on perceptual constancy to support his concept of dynamic homeostasis. He cites the researches of Ames (1946), Helson (1947), Hebb (1949), and Hastorf (1950) as evidence for the importance and nature of the development of perceptual constancies out of learning (ontogenetically). From a developmental point of view, as well as from an evolutionary one (see earlier), the maintenance of constancies in the external environment is seen to arise on the basis of the need to maintain internal constancy.

Perceptual constancies play an important role in maintaining the individual's orientation and in reducing uncertainty and the resultant discomforting anxiety. These constancies may have arisen as a result of experiences, but they serve also to contribute to the shaping of experiences. In this regard, Stagner agrees with Fletcher that habits (including the perceptual constancies), drives, developed personality traits, etc., may in time seem to become the basis for their own perpetuation.[14]

We shall turn shortly to the role of homeostatic motivation in personality organization at the highest levels, but first let us briefly examine some of the criticisms of what has so far been said.

Some Criticism of Homeostatic Theory of Motivation

Homeostatic motivation theory has been criticized for failing to explain enough, on the one hand, and attempting to explain too much, on the other.

Weber (1949), for example, accepts homeostasis as accounting for the "routines" of life but feels that many activities (as in the classic example of the creative, driven scientist) deliberately break down

[13] Freud had early proposed a central nervous mechanism for "abolishing stimulation," but did not pursue the matter very far (see p. 600).

[14] This position is not unlike Allport's notion of the "functional autonomy" of motives or habits (1937). However, as McClelland (1942) and others have pointed out, an explanation for the perpetuation of these responses may be found in more fundamental laws of reinforcement or, as is here suggested, because their effects are equilibrating.

homeostasis. Placing oneself in the path of danger, working or playing to exhaustion, self-sacrificial acts (including suicide), and other apparently disequilibrating behaviors might also be cited as illustrating the limitation of homeostatic motivation theory.[15] P. T. Young (1949*b*) has sought to demonstrate that organisms may be motivated to more vigorous action by preference (appetite, choice, desire) rather than by homeostatic need. In free-choice experiments, Young has shown that rats will prefer a non-nutritive (*ergo* nonequilibrating) saccharin solution, and Carper (1953) confirmed earlier findings of Sheffield and Roby (1950) that saccharin had reward value in both hungry and satiated rats. Carper reported equal resistance to extinction for rats reinforced with glucose or saccharin. Young (1961) cites these studies, as well as his own, in support of his thesis.

Stagner rejects these criticisms. He believes that a much wider range of motivated behavior can be incorporated within the framework of the homeostatic concept than its narrower construction as physiological homeostasis would seem to permit. Nevertheless, homeostatic theory does not allow for pleasure-seeking, wishing, desiring, deliberate self-excitation, etc., except as these may be seen to serve delayed homeostatic ends. Taking Young's example, Stagner proposes that the saccharin preference may be the result of an error in perception—preference for a warm sweet substance being based on the learned constancy of mother-milk. Citing some of Young's other extensive research (e.g., Young & Chaplin, 1945), Stagner writes:

Young's own experiments show conclusively that preferences can be built upon a homeostatic need. It thus appears far more defensible to hold that homeostasis is the primary motivational principle involved, and that preference (palatability, affectivity) is simply a derivative based upon (1) inherent sensitivity thresholds of homeostatic significance, or (2) non-discriminable differences from signs of homeostatic goal-objects (Stagner, 1951, p. 10).

Stagner goes on to point out that the failure of man to detect X-rays, gamma rays, and certain other destructive stimuli is not a criticism of homeostatic theory, ". . . but only a recognition of the fact that some new sources of tissue disequilibrium have been invented" (Stagner, 1951, p. 9). Indeed, as radiation sources multiply and hazards increase,

[15] Although Weber implies that *most* activities are of this sort, it is perhaps unnecessary for him to deny the preponderant conservatism of most human activities (e.g., see W. J. Newman's *The Futilitarian Society* [1961]). If Weber can establish that *some* activities are exceptions to homeostatic theory, the burden of proof shifts to its supporters to explain such nonhomeostatic behaviors within their conceptual framework.

it might not be unreasonable to anticipate the eventual evolution of some type of sensory or biological detection system for these sources of danger (if man survives, that is!).

Errors due to sensory limitations, and errors due to misidentifications based on learned constancies, may well occur, but, if they are themselves lawfully predictable, do not destroy the soundness of the homeostatic principle.[16]

As for other objections, Stagner acknowledges that acquired tensions (resulting from intensive or extensive particular series of experiences) may lead to short-run disequilibrating responses. But motivation continues (if the organism itself continues) and results in long-term equilibrium. It is possible that social needs, when coupled with unlearned responses, may lead to an apparent breakdown of one or more homeostatic response systems. If we take Weber's example of the driven scientist, or Allport's (1955) example of the explorer who leaves the comforts and pleasures of home for the discomforts and possible pains of his explorations, Stagner (1961a, p. 63) suggests that ". . . the explorer has built up, over a period of time, the percept of himself as the kind of person who goes adventuring. Failure to act in this manner is disturbing . . . he can restore equilibrium only by engaging in the activity he perceives as appropriate to himself." Stagner conceives of a hierarchy of steady states, such that when one of these is upset, restoration to equilibrium may be achieved at the cost of disturbing one lower in the scale, but never at the cost of one higher in the scale. Thus, the stable self-percept of the explorer qua explorer may be retained or regained only through apparently unhomeostatic (Davis' [1958] heterostatic) behaviors.[17]

The maintenance of a constant self-percept appears then to be a pivotal factor in the argument for psychological homeostasis. Let us examine this concept in the contexts of social perception and personality theory, where some exploration of the notion has been made.

[16] This might be crudely analogous to pointing out that the demonstration that heavier-than-air airships may be made to rise from the ground does not invalidate the general principle of gravity.

[17] Stagner (1961a) cites body water regulation as a simpler illustration of the same pattern: high temperature → sweating (homeostatic) → water deficit (heterostatic) → drinking (homeostatic). Obviously, a careful analysis of such patterns of interaction of interlocking systems—or patterns of energy distribution to part systems (as suggested by Freeman and others, see later discussion)—is needed to resolve this issue.

Social Perception and Self-Consistency

Persons are important objects in the perceptual world of the developing child. Social perceptual constancies (e.g., "mother image," social stereotypes, "halo" effects, role perceptions) may therefore be expected to develop as "stable states" of perception. At the apex of the hierarchy of such states to be balanced, Stagner and Karwoski (1952) propose an evolving "self-picture," the consistency of which is homeostatic.

Recurring needs, such as hunger, and need satisfactions contribute to one's developing picture of himself. Habits are acted out often and the child perceives himself as a person who has these kinds of habits. People often struggle to carry out certain habitual acts, even though there is no longer any goal for the habit. Interference with the habit is treated as interference with an important constant state.

One's social status is another significant aspect of the self. I expect to be treated in a certain way by my friends, by strangers, by students, and so on. If a friend seems colder than usual, I am disturbed; if a stranger tries to be excessively familiar, I may also find this annoying. People in positions of authority demand certain forms of behavior as assurance of their status; deviations from these prescribed acts may be seen as threats to status and punished accordingly. Thus the principle of homeostasis appears to function on the social as well as the biological level.

The self can therefore be thought of as an elaborate pattern of desired constant states, which are protected if anything threatens them (Stagner & Karwoski, 1952, p. 18).

This last idea, that the integrity of the self-picture is defended against threat, is very similar to Prescott Lecky's theory of self-consistency (1945; Hall & Lindzey, 1957) and forms the basis for many descriptions of personality organization. Lecky, whose premature death prevented the full development of his ideas, saw unity and integrity as the main values in life. Motivation was synonymous for him with striving for a sense of unification. Like Stagner, Lecky stressed both the influence of experience on the formation of the self-picture—through socialization and acculturation—and the influence of the value system associated with the self-structure on successive experiences.

Thus the evolving yet constant self-percept is of focal significance to personality structure in these views. Because the self participates in all of life's experiences, the strength (consistency) of the pervading self-percept is seen as the most important (generalized) source of motivation for social behavior.

Homeostasis and Personality

The term *personality* is used, sometimes interchangeably with *ego* and *self*, to describe the highest (and most complex) level of organism-environment integration (Allport, 1937; Novikoff, 1945; McClelland, 1951; Nuttin, 1953; Menninger, 1954; Teitelbaum, 1956). In a hierarchy of homeostatic systems, such as proposed by Stagner, the personality may be conceived as the largest and most inclusive of these systems, incorporating intra-organic, organic, and organism-environment adjustment mechanisms in such a manner as to provide consistency and continuity to the organism's individuality. In this view no distinction is drawn between physical and mental, biological and cultural. The organism is regarded as an action-system, receiving, organizing, and distributing energy in the ". . . patterned interaction of the personality and its environment" (Martin, 1945, p. 341).

We have earlier described simple homeostatic systems as involving the mobilization of energy within a part system as a result of any disequilibrating stimulation introduced into that part system, whether by excess or failure of input. As personality may itself be conceived as a system composed of lower-order systems, it is to be expected that imbalance could occur here through any disequilibration of one or more of its part systems. Since such part-system disequilibration is met initially by part-system reaction, it becomes important to distinguish between equilibrating responses occurring at the *same* level of organization and those invoking responses at a *higher* level. Teitelbaum (1956) suggests the use of the terms *mobilization* and *motivation* to mark these two aspects of adjustment.

Mobilization describes corrective actions to preserve homeostasis within a *particular level* of organization, whereas motivation occurs only when such processes fail and a higher or larger system becomes involved. ". . . when lower order mobilization functions fail to maintain the end-processes of the various systems within their optimal range of fluctuation . . . the higher-order motivation processes become clearly evident" (Teitelbaum, 1956, p. 318). Especially at the highest (personality) level of organization does Teitelbaum consider motivation the result of a failure of mobilization of counteractive processes. Motivation is described as involving ". . . highly complex neurone integrative processes that are experienced as emotional feeling, motor expression, and thought. In mature personalities the effect is behavior that tends to limit the excessive fluctuation of the homeostatic end-processes with the successful attainment of real environmental goals" (Teitelbaum, 1956, p. 319). This view is similar to those held by Stagner and Fletcher, and is perhaps generally descriptive of the theory of motivated behavior held by most homeostatic theorists.[18] It extends physiological homeostasis of the part-systems to psychological homeostasis of the personality level of organization through some type of neural mediation (e.g., Stagner's cortical tension, or his more recent endorsement of Morgan's [1943] central motive state; Breuer and Freud's "tendency of the organism to preserve a constant level of tonic cerebral excitement" [see Chapter 12]; or Freeman's neuromuscular homeostasis [see later discussion]). The particular links in the chain from lower to higher levels of organization are yet to be worked out in detail.

Nevertheless, an increasing number of writers have recently been using the concept of homeostasis in one form or another to describe the organization of the personality. Thus, Menninger (1954, p. 704) has defined the ego as ". . . the integrated operation of all homeostatic partial systems—physiological and psychological—which comprise the total personality." Aldrich has coined the term "emotional homeostasis" to describe the condition of the personality in well-adjusted individuals (Aldrich, 1955), and Stagner (1951, 1961*b*) and Emerson (1954) have separately written of "dynamic homeostasis," Emerson preferring this term to some twenty similar concepts he examined.

From applications to personality it is a short step to psychopathology and to social behavior, and as illustrations of the breadth of the concept's applications, let us briefly turn to these areas.

Homeostasis and Psychopathology

Psychopathic Personality. Lindner (1945, p. 521) has clinically described the behavior of psychopathic personalities in terms of (psychological) homeostasis. He saw the psychopath's ". . . apparently maladjustive behavior not as an end-result in itself but as an automatic striving for the recovery of balance, as homeostatically initiated and sustained." And Van Vorst (1947), agreeing with Lindner, felt that homeostasis helped explain the intense emotional outpouring of energy in "violent, predatory, consistently rebellious" behavior as a kind of overflow of excess,[19] thereby re-establishing the emotional equilibrium of the personality. Lindner wrote of prisoners, anticipating emotional

---

[18] Stagner and Karwoski (1952) made a somewhat similar distinction in their emphasis on "static" and "dynamic" homeostasis; cf., also, Poffenberger, 1938; Martin, 1945; Masserman, 1946; Richter, 1947; Freeman, 1948; Nuttin, 1953; Menninger, 1954; Aldrich, 1955.

[19] Neither Lindner nor Van Vorst makes clear what is meant by this term, though they are obviously using a hydraulic model.

"blowoffs," asking for protection from their own excesses. He also noted the high suicide rate in psychopaths as further evidence for the operation of gross equilibrating mechanisms at the level of the personality.

Anxiety and Psychosomatics. Anxiety is thought by some to arise when homeostasis is threatened. Holmes and Ripley (1955), in a set of clinical studies, have observed that anxiety, "a feeling of apprehension in response to danger which threatens the integrity of the individual . . . accompanied by alterations in . . . physiological variables . . ." (p. 921), can both induce and aggravate symptoms of physical illness. "The evidence . . . indicates that threats of danger due to stressful life situations may become important in the genesis of illness. Often the discomfort and tissue damage evoked by symbols is indistinguishable from that produced by physical and chemical agents or infectious micro-organisms" (p. 923). Not only do these authors show the relation of anxiety to disease symptoms, but they also give clinical evidence for their belief that early conditioning experiences are part of the genesis of anxiety. Their findings lend support to Stagner's and Fletcher's contentions that learned tendencies may play a role in homeostatic equilibration. Holmes and Ripley come to the rather interesting conclusion from their case studies that since homeostasis is "inherent in man's biological endowment," any threats to his physical and emotional integrity automatically elicit adaptive responses.

Such reactions . . . usually are manifested as alterations in behavior which may vary widely in degree, content, duration, and effectiveness. When sustained, these reactions may be productive of discomfort and impairment of tissue integrity. Many of the illnesses experienced by man . . . may occur in large part as a byproduct of his attempts at adaptation (p. 928).

We shall return to the implications of this conclusion in at least two other places in this book (Selye's concept of the "diseases of adaptation" in Chapter 9 and Freud's treatment of the role of anxiety in symptom formation in Chapter 12).

Anxiety, as a set of physiological symptoms, and as a state of discomfort, may thus be perceived as a concomitant of homeostatic imbalance and a mediator of adaptive responses. As Stagner and others have implied, and as Holmes and Ripley show, the adaptive responses may themselves become excessive and require counteradaptive measures.

Homeostasis and Schizophrenia. Rosenzweig (1955) has analyzed the disturbances of association and disharmony of affect in schizophrenic disorders and concludes that schizophrenia is a disturbance in the homeostasis of ideational-affective units. He takes note of the recent neuropsychological discoveries of the "centrencephalic" integrating systems (Penfield & Rasmussen, 1950; Magoun, 1952) in the reticular and limbic areas of the midbrain (see Chapter 8). Both phylogenetic and ontogenetic development have given rise to a coordinating center in the old "smell brain," or rhinencephalon, where sensory input and "affective" responses are integrated. If they are synchronized (i.e., equilibrated), action follows, but if they are not coordinate, anxiety results.

Anxiety may arise whenever there is an extreme shift of the homeostatic equilibrium resulting from a stress which has not been offset. . . . In the ordinary course of events, emotionally determined behavior patterns are developed by the organism which serve as more or less automatic behavioral or "mental" mechanisms of defense against anxiety. These mechanisms depend on effective operation of the centrencephalic and limbic systems for their success (ego strength). . . . In schizophrenia we postulate a disturbance to be present within the centrencephalic system. The disorder of the comparatively delicately balanced and vulnerable system results in an interference with the feedback circuits [the "traffic jam" of Wiener—see below]. The functions of selective conation and emotional associations break down, giving rise to the primary symptoms (Rosenzweig, 1955, p. 553).

Rosenzweig sees the effects of breakdown as "snowballing," secondary defenses being elaborated on a less real basis, delusional systems, etc., resulting, and schizophrenia being the product of the failure of homeostasis. Supporting evidence can be found for the presence in schizophrenics of multiple homeostatic disturbances (Bowman et al., 1950; Hill et al., 1951; Sackler et al., 1951; Pincus & Hoagland, 1950; Hoskins, 1946).

Homeostasis, Values, and Society

C. A. Mace (1953), in his presidential address to the British Psychological Society, argued that homeostasis, if it were properly extended, offered a basis for a psychology of values. Values (in the long run) must be consistent with the nature of the individual adjustment matrix. Psychologists acknowledge this implicitly, he feels, when they describe goals of behavior as being "adjusted," "integrated," "coordinated," etc. Mace proposed three extensions of the homeostatic concept, some of which we have already dealt with:

1. . . . what is maintained or restored is not so much an internal state of the organism as some relation of the organism to its environment (p. 204). [Adaptation, adjustment.]
2. the . . . goal, end or norm [may be] . . . some state or relation which has never previously been experienced (p. 205). [Maturation, learning.]

3. to . . . cover second and higher order needs . . . [thus at the personality level] . . . it is the state in which the greatest satisfaction would be given to the total system of original and acquired needs (p. 206). [Values.]

Mace would make homeostasis, in the broadened sense he has proposed, the basis for all motivation. In all three suggested extensions he seems to be calling for a concept somewhat like Stagner's dynamic homeostasis, including as his second point a continuing integration of change, and subsuming in his third a hierarchical structure. The establishing of new equilibria, incorporating aspects of change, subsumes both maturation and learning under the homeostatic rubric. With change, balance could better be established in a new way—as a new form of the old— than in the predisturbance way. Thus Mace would see problem solving as an instance of tension reduction, and sensory (and motor) activities as containing intrinsic need-reward patterns, including learned goals.

Kurtz (1956) comes to a similar conclusion that what is valuable is that which contributes to the ". . . dynamic homeostatic continuance and expansion . . ." of the field of life.

Both Mace and Kurtz, avoiding a "ghost" teleology, consider natural law the only sound basis for a theory of value. Homeostasis provides the major principle on which they support this hypothesis. Kurtz draws not only on psychology and biology for evidence of the operation of the homeostatic principle but on sociology, cultural anthropology, and economics as well. He points to the balance of social institutions (Merton, 1949; Parsons, 1949), the mutual dependence of cultures and their cultural surrounds (Malinowski, 1939; Benedict, 1946), and the economic theories of "dynamic equilibrium" of supply and demand as illustrations of the general validity of the homeostatic principle.[20]

SOCIAL HOMEOSTASIS

When we moved from intra-organic to organic levels of organization, we cautioned that a gap in logic would have to be bridged. The extension of homeostasis to the social unit requires an even larger jump. We saw earlier that the theories of dynamic homeostasis developed sometimes elaborate but nevertheless direct paths from physiological to psychological equilibration. Via neural and/or hormonal

[20] We should recall that Cannon also perceived in society a large network of devices suitable to the maintenance of homeostatic balance in individual members of these societies. The complex systems of specialization, transportation, and communication were seen by him as analogous to the processes within individual organisms assuring the maintenance of internal equilibria.

links, anxiety, or physiological tensions and their psychological con-comitants, it was possible to conceive of psychological homeostasis as consistent with the maintenance of the integrity of the biological or-ganism. When the individual responded to external stimulation in such a way as to improve the likelihood that the environment would favor its continued homeostatic adjustments, we were still dealing with a single action system.

However, when the concept of social homeostasis is introduced, we are faced with the necessity of considering simultaneously the action systems of two or more individuals working in concert. If we now shift focus to the larger system (e.g., the family, colony, community, na-tion, etc.) the relationships between parts (individuals) must be recon-ceived in terms of their contributions to the welfare of that larger system, even at the expense of their own temporary or permanent disequilibration.

At the animal level, the ecologists (Allee, Emerson, Park, Park & Schmidt [1949]) make a most convincing case for such a shift of focus. Ecology is the study of the "interrelation between living organisms and their environment." Allee et al. (1949, p. 6) write: "The tendency towards homeostacy extends through the diverse phases of ecology. . . . Such tendencies are found under primarily physical relations within nonliving environments and also when all the relations are primarily biotic." Describing how groups of insects may "sacrifice themselves apparently for the good of the colony," they continue (p. 426):

Division of labor and integration are associated principles. Integration has no function unless there are differentiated parts that must act in relation to the whole. Specialization of function cannot occur unless the specialized parts are coordinated. Efficient homeostasis follows an increase in the special functions of integrated parts. These principles apply to every organismic level from the cell to the cosystem. . . .

These authors consider homeostasis as ". . . clearly the result of adaptive evolution" (p. 631), and carry their concept to the level of the supra-organism, or population unit. They cite examples of beaver dam-building, insect colony nest-building, and man's vast reshaping of his physical and social environment as illustrations of social be-haviors serving homeostatic needs. "Homeostasis is not only character-istic of the cell environment in the multicellular organism and the individual environment in the aggregated species population, but to a certain extent it is also characteristic of the evolving ecological com-munity" (p. 672). One further important point made by these ecologists should be noted here, although it would be impossible to do justice to their major volume in these few remarks. They develop elaborate concepts of intraspecies and interspecies relationships, leading up to ecosystems (interacting environmental and biotic systems) and a biosphere of ecosystems, etc. The following quotation from their description of the supra-organism illustrates their concept of social homeostasis:

It may be concluded . . . that the community maintains a certain balance, establishes a biotic border, and has a certain unity paralleling the dynamic equilibrium and organization of other living systems. Natural selection operates upon the whole interspecies system, resulting in a slow evolution of adaptive integration and balance. Division of labor, integration, and homeostasis characterize the organism and the supra-organismic intraspecies population. The interspecies system has also evolved these characteristics of the organism and may thus be called an ecological supra-organism (Emerson, 1946; cited by Allee et al., 1949, p. 728).

The concept of the supra-organism is not itself a new one (see Kroeber, 1917), but the paralleling of concepts at intraorganic, organic, and superorganic levels suggested by the ecologists would seem to provide fruitful hypotheses for further ecological (perhaps including human) study.[21]

Henry (1955) has criticized the application of homeostatic principles to society on the basis of some careful analyses of societies wherein markedly different and sometimes destructive "adjustment" modes are clearly in evidence. Since there are societies which show a high degree of social instability, Henry does not see how *stability* could be the basis of their social organization. He sees a conflict between individual homeostasis and social homeostasis—for example, the interruption of the infant's homeostatic processes as a result of the mother's anxiety about hospital rules, eating schedules, etc. In this and other instances, where social controls do exist, he questions whether they actually serve to maintain "optimal" homeostatic social environments. He concludes that ". . . man evolves physically in terms of a perpetually unstable social life" (1955, p. 308), citing stress and anxiety as the basis for his conclusions, and psychosomatics as his evidence.

It is clear that a good deal of systematic evidence will have to be gathered and examined before any final conclusions can be drawn with

[21] It has been suggested, for example, that the mother and the infant form a homeostatic unit. This refers not only to the fact that the infant cannot protect equilibria without the cooperation of the mother, but some observations by clinicians suggest that the baby also plays a role in restoring equilibria in the mother.

regard to the feasibility of the hypothesis of social homeostasis. The extensive data of Allee et al. and the observations of anthropologists, sociologists, psychologists, ecologists, and social scientists, in many areas, would suggest processes analogous to intra-organismic homeostasis at work in society. As we have earlier seen, apparently heterostatic phenomena, such as stress, anxiety, and psychosomatic evidence, need not be interpreted as negating the homeostatic principle.

Comment

Before concluding our review of the general concept and turning to specific models, it is well to note that there has not been universal agreement, even among homeostatic theorists, on the breadth of applicability of the concept, particularly with regard to personality and behavior organization. Cannon, with whom the term began in physiology, drew a line somewhere in the vicinity of mind. Although he speculated quite freely on homeostasis at the level of society and political organization, he was unable to foresee the more direct extension of the concept of equilibration as a principle of motivation at the level of personality organization. Others (e.g., Allport, 1953; Young, 1949b, 1961; Henry, 1955; Maze, 1953; Murphy, 1947) have recorded objections to the homeostatic principle as being either too limited to explain the many instances of disequilibrating behaviors observed clinically and in everyday experience, or as requiring unwarranted assumptions. Many of these criticisms have been discussed, where appropriate; others will be considered toward the end of the chapter.

FOUR HOMEOSTATIC MOTIVATION MODELS

The remainder of the present chapter will describe four programmatic approaches to motivation in terms of homeostatic-like principles. The first, G. L. Freeman's, is based primarily on his own extensive research in physiological psychology, drawing particularly from his work with the physiological indices of response to stress stimulation and the study of behavior energetics. The second model, Helson's "adaptation-level" (AL), is derived from psychophysical studies of the factors influencing judgment, drawing on social as well as on classical experimental psychology. The third model, Wiener's cybernetics, comes initially from communications research, and meets psychology on the mutual ground of speculation as to how behaviors may be produced in different types of theoretical brain mechanisms. The particular model described by the cyberneticists, based on the feedback principle, is, avowedly and in fact, a homeostatic model. And, finally, Lewin's field-theory model, which, while not explicitly identified with the conceptual language of homeostatic theories, has sufficient formal similarity to be treated as an example of the equilibrational idea central to this point of view.

FREEMAN'S "NEUROMUSCULAR HOMEOSTASIS"

G. L. Freeman, in a carefully reasoned and systematic analysis of *"the energetics of human behavior"* (1948), offers a behavior model based squarely on the thesis ". . . *that all behavior is an attempt to preserve organismic integrity by 'homeostatic' restorations of equilibrium"* (1948, p. 1). Rejecting dualism ("We want no monster, half-mind, half-body . . ."), Freeman argues strictly from objective analyses of psychophysiological research—a field in which he himself has been a significant contributor. He sets forth a series of "principles of homeostatic behavior," beginning with the idea of *adjustment levels:*

In maintaining essential constant states and preserving its identity, the organismic energy system has several lines of defense, or levels of adjustive response. The organ or cell is the primary immunological level of defense. A higher and more complicated level is found in the generalized emergency reactions of the total organism, integrated via the autonomic nervous system. The highest level involves cerebrally controlled total behavior, including response that is specifically adaptive to external stimulation and the so-called "ego defenses" that guard the inviolacy of the personality from psychological insult (1948, p. 98).

Like most homeostatic theories, Freeman's is frankly evolutionary, and his reference to "ego defenses" does not imply a discontinuity between physiological and psychological processes. Although he does employ the idea of "subjective" disturbances of equilibrium, he explicitly rejects the notion of psychic energy. Behaviors, even at the highest levels of adjustment, are instances of neuromuscular homeostasis ". . . related in all essential respects to the limited organ reactions which keep the body alive and maintain its identity" (p. 63).

Freeman believes that a shortcoming of earlier studies of behavior energetics was their attention to the quantity of energy output only, and their neglect of the all-important *patterns* of energy distribution in the part-systems of the organism. He draws an important distinction between basal metabolic rate and basic energy level. The latter represents "the metabolic demands of the persistent internal conditions of alert rest" (p. 110) and is somewhat higher than the BMR. By precise measurement of these basic energy levels and assessments of continuing input as well as distribution of energy in reaction, Freeman feels that much otherwise conflicting data could be understood as fundamentally homeostatic.

In the analysis of neuromuscular homeostasis (his term for total behavior), Freeman proposes the physiological constructs, *Arousal Index* (AI), *Discharge Index* (DI), and *Recovery Quotient* (RQ), as indices of the three aspects of homeostatic response, the last being ". . . the integrative measure of homeostatic response, a term used to describe the relationship between the arousal and discharge features of behavior (total or part). It is a construct dealing with the degree of balance or unbalance in neuromuscular homeostasis" (1948, p. 102). Figure 7–1, taken from Freeman, shows three hypothetical homeostatic response curves representing, from left to right, respectively, a high degree of energy mobilization and a low degree of energy discharge (hence low recovery), an equivalent degree of mobilization and discharge, and a supernormal recovery, wherein the organism discharges a portion of the prestimulus excitation and thus lowers the basic energy level. In Figure 7–1, *A* represents the basic energy level (alert rest), *B* the peak of energy mobilization (measured one-half minute after stimulation), and *C* the level reached five minutes after peak mobilization (*B*). The Recovery Quotient is, then:

$$RQ = \frac{B - C}{B - A}$$

Freeman elaborates considerably more fully on the advantages and limitations of such a quantitative approach to energetics. For our purposes it may suffice to indicate that this approach derives from measurement of skin conductance, blood pressure, muscular tension, calorime-

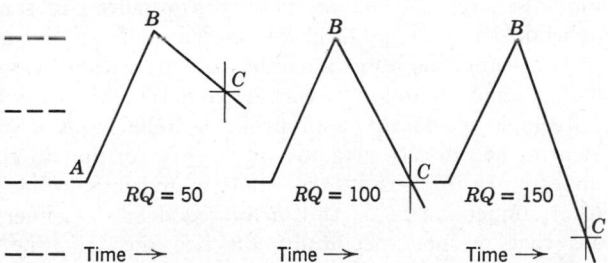

Figure 7–1. The homeostatic response curve. Recovery in neuromuscular homeostasis may be greater or less than 100%. Reproduced by permission from Freeman (1948, p. 82).

try, and other metabolic indices of reactivity. As Freeman points out, these techniques offer a most useful way of inferring the motivational state of the individual from peripheral measurement.[22]

In addition to the ideas of adjustment levels and the indices of neuromuscular homeostasis, Freeman's principles include:

1. *compensatory energy mobilization*—a recognition of the widely observed fact that distraction or interference with ongoing motivated behavior calls forth extra energy, so that performance rate is kept constant (cf. Courts, 1942; Bartley & Chute, 1947);

2. *principle of backlash action*—every overt response that is made has re-excitatory (neural and chemical) effects on the energy system. Stimuli set up either excitatory (catabolic) or relaxing (anabolic) organic processes. Equilibratory motor discharge must not only dispel the catabolic effects of initial stimulation but "rid the system of more excitation than it puts back in" (p. 104) through backlash action. To explain why "some overt responses bring relaxation and quietude, whereas others only increase internal excitement and raise the general energy level" (p. 106; see below), Freeman suggests that this depends on whether or not the re-excitatory effect of backlash stimulation is specific to the centers generating the action or diffuse, and further that the effectiveness of the action in reducing the stimulation will be inversely related to the total backlash stimulation;

3. *focal background (FB) response ratio*—points up the importance of considering the portion of energy expended in direct as against indirect action—as in Luria's measurements of muscle action in the hand used in response (signaling) and in the unused hand during conflict (Luria, 1932). How this and the preceding backlash principle operate is indicated in the following quotation:

All behavioral discharge appears to excite the organism in some degree, because of chemical effects and backlash excitation from the muscles involved. . . . The stimulus arouses a number of interacting part-systems to increased activity, and all follow a course from arousal to discharge. But when a discharge is specifically appropriate in relieving the stimulus induced excitement, i.e., in changing the organism's relation to the original irritant, it appears not to re-excite the whole system but to backlash upon its own central connection . . . , and in limited degree. Conversely, those part-reactions that do not specifically alleviate the irritating condition

─────────

[22] Although not essential to his logic, it has been suggested that a number of technical problems are ignored by Freeman (cf. Ax, 1953). He has also been accused of overgeneralizing his results on the basis of an overestimation of the reliability and validity of his experimental findings, which are based on very few subjects and situations.

would backlash more diffusely and so help maintain the total system in a state of mobilization until a more equilibratory part-reaction was made (pp. 80–81).

Freeman does allow for circumstances in which nonspecifically adaptive motor responses (e.g., wiggling, nervous movements, and the like) may be homeostatic-regulatory, removing more excitation than they put back in the system. This notion is similar to the role assigned by the ethologists to displacement responses in conflict situations (see Chapter 3), and has some similarity as well to treatments of anxiety responses (cf. Chapters 12, 14).

A number of other principles deal with:

4. *the establishment of habitual or characteristic energy base lines* (a function of patterns of work or stimulation and determinant of amount of available energy at any given time). Freeman here takes account of both individual differences in basic energy levels and the effects of shifts in living regimen and such factors as cumulative fatigue, real or artificial "pressures," etc., on energy level;

5. *an optimal reaction range* (midway between sleep and high excitement, allowing a maximal operation of neuromuscular homeostatic mechanisms);

6. *residual load*[23] (. . . "the unexpressed excitation effects left in the system after an attempted adjustment to stimulus displacement" (p. 115); and

7. possible *tension discharge types* (individuals having characteristic discharge patterns through skeletal, verbal, ideational, or somatic channels).

Finally, Freeman offers a set of "principles of response discharge," through which effective homeostatic behavior may occur. These are: (1) *Diversification*—the larger the number of possible energy discharge outlets available, the greater the RQ (neurosis may be a result of highly restricted situations). (2) *Specificity*—the quantity of discharge does not alone produce equilibration. As already indicated, RQ will be higher when discharge is through the part-reaction(s) " . . . most specifically appropriate to the irritating condition" (p. 123). (3) *Supplementation*—when direct outlet cannot discharge all of the energy aroused, accessory (background) outlets help increase RQ,

---

[23] This is an important concept in Freeman's theory, and offers a quantitative index of "frustration tolerance" or "adjustive capacity." Its strength can be inferred from the degree of lowering of the RQ and the resultant rise in basic energy level. It is the accumulation of residual load that leads to emotional collapse.

provided they do not become competing channels of focal discharge. (4) *Reactivation*—unlike the first three principles, which deal with channeling of equilibrating energy, this principle governs ". . . discharging of residual load by a return to situations originally producing the unbalance between arousal and discharge . . . conversion of excitation residuals, due to blocked or ineffective reaction, into stimuli that get the organism started back into the originally exciting condition" (p. 126). (5) *Moderation*—". . . Overt reaction has to be set in relation to the amount of arousal; underreaction or overreaction makes for ineffective homeostatic adjustment" (p. 127). There is a "golden mean," or optimal middle reaction range.

Applications to Motivation

Freeman makes the flat assumption that ". . . all the complicated adjustments to external stimuli as well as all creative efforts of man are fundamentally associated with the maintenance of essential steady states of the fluid matrix of the body" (p. 140). This includes not only physiological processes but ". . . conditioned reactions far in advance of . . . immediate internal needs" (p. 141). In addition, where normal equilibratory processes fail, the organism ". . . will initiate a most extravagant series of behaviors in an attempt to restore internal equilibrium" (p. 141).

Such behaviors may take a variety of forms, depending on the conditioning circumstances, from direct and appropriate action to apparently irrelevant creative behaviors to highly bizarre symptom formation. The behavior may even have the appearance of being disequilibrating in the extreme. Thus, in the case of martyrdom, Freeman suggests that ". . . only because his internal processes are abnormally displaced does the martyr willingly die at the stake rather than retract his heresy; physical death is here more homeostating than is continued existence under the tension (residual load) of the hypocrite" (pp. 142–143). Acquired needs develop and perpetuate more stable external surrounds. The stabilities of social milieu are protective defenses for the more vital internal milieu, and threats to these acquired stabilities are perceived as disequilibrating and reacted to homeostatically. *All* behavior, from "functionally autonomous" habits to compulsions to creative acts, and including "the so-called altruistic acts," evolves in relation to these acquired stabilities or their underlying biological needs: "Altruistic actions seem to flower most readily in those individuals whose essential needs are neither so completely satisfied as to render them complacent and unresponsive to the potentialities of unique modes of adjustment, or so completely unsatiated that all their energies must go into the low-order 'dog-eat-dog' struggle for existence" (pp. 148–149).[24]

Phobias and other "bad" responses are seen by Freeman as developing on the same basis as the "good" (survival-supporting) behaviors, both being "maintained by homeostatic regulatory action." The theory likewise accounts for reactions to frustration in terms of energy mobilization. The classic instances of apparent preference for the more difficult of two alternatives (e.g., the girl who is hard to get, the sales prospect who is hard to sell) illustrate that ". . . greater pleasure is derived from reducing tensions artificially raised by the additional frustration" (p. 161). Although Freeman does not make clear how the choice of initially disequilibrating responses gets started, his distinction between short- and long-term goals and his emphasis on the role of conditioning would presumably be the basis of his explanation of this type of seemingly self-disequilibrating choice.

Space does not permit a detailed consideration of the many other applications of Freeman's theory to behavior, nor a fair description of his research on energy distribution, from which his principles were derived. We may summarize, in Freeman's words, his purpose in proposing his theory: "We have in neuromuscular homeostasis a basic principle that puts a biological floor under much of current psychological thinking. [And in the principles here suggested] . . . gap-bridging physiological constructs . . . as substitutes for the psychic energy constructs that have beset dynamic psychology since the time of Freud" (p. 128).

Comment on the Freeman Model

Freeman's "energetics" model has been presented here as a kind of "tour-de-force" of a strongly held equilibration theory. His system, as Young (1961) has pointed out, deals with physical energy derived from food intake, being concerned not with the source but with the distribution of energy and with the regulation of energy release. He has extended the concept of homeostasis to the neuromuscular system; he suggests some quite precise means of assessing energy level change; and he puts forward a series of hypotheses or principles to account for energy discharge in homeostatic regulation. His position is tightly argued and set out in some detail. Supportive evidence is offered largely from his own research (see Freeman, 1948), although generally sup-

[24] It is interesting to compare this statement of Freeman's with Maslow's description of self-actualized motivation (see pp. 668 ff.).

portive studies (e.g., in neurophysiology) exist outside of this work (cf. Chapter 8). As we have noted, Freeman tries to account for the widest range of human reactions through his proposed principles. However, now, more than a decade later, we find that little new research has been stimulated by Freeman's treatise, nor have there been any serious attempts to adopt, extend, or even properly test the theoretical concepts he put forth.

HELSON'S "ADAPTATION-LEVEL" THEORY

Harry Helson, in a series of papers (1947, 1948, 1951, 1953, 1959), has offered the concept of *adaptation-level* (AL) as a means of understanding perceptual activities in the larger context of behavioral homeostasis. Such activities play a significant role, he believes, not only in initiating and regulating equilibrational mechanisms, but more particularly in providing the feed-back from action by which the organism can determine the effectiveness of its adjustive responses. AL defines the range of stimulation within which adaptive responding is not required.

Thus, stimuli perceived to be white, gray, or black are chromatically neutral, and so must be regarded as leaving the *color* receptors in equilibrium. Similarly, a verbal statement with which one neither agrees nor disagrees may represent his point of equilibrium with respect to the meaning universe represented by the statement, and propositions may be formulated which lie above (agree) or below (disagree) the level represented by this statement (Helson, 1953, p. 36).

Helson points out that "momentary adjustment" is a function of the combination of such series, of background stimuli, and of "past experiences with similar stimuli" (p. 36). He expresses AL quantitatively as follows:

$$\log \text{AL} = \frac{(k_1 \, \Sigma \log X_i)/(N + k_2 \log B + k_3 \log R)}{k_1 + k_2 + k_3}$$

where k_1, k_2, and k_3 are constants to be evaluated, and X_i, B, and R represent series, background, and residual stimuli, respectively.

In order to understand the AL and how it is applied, four important facts of adjustive behavior are stressed by Helson. First is the *bipolarity of responses*. There is a tendency to order stimuli by means of graded dichotomies (e.g., good-bad, hot-cold, beautiful-ugly). In arranging stimuli on any one such continuum, ". . . there is a stimulus or group of stimuli which is neutral or indifferent. The stimuli in this neutral, transitional zone represent the stimuli to which the organism is adapted [25] so far as the quality or attribute in question is concerned" (Helson, 1953, p. 35). AL is thus a level or range with respect to a particular stimulus dimension at a particular time. But an object is judged in relation to its surrounds, the frame of reference in which it is seen, and this may change. AL may be expected to change in relation to changes in background: "If the level of stimulation is raised or lowered by changing all the stimuli, or by introducing an extreme stimulus into the field, or by changing the background against which stimuli are perceived, the adjustment of the organism changes correspondingly . . . the level of adjustment . . . more or less matches the level of stimulation" (Helson, 1953, p. 35). Helson next notes that the judged center of a series is rarely at the actual arithmetic center, but usually below the geometric mean of any series.

This phenomenon of decentering to establish the balance point of the behavioral field seems at first sight to argue against adaptation or adjustment as the basic mechanism by which the organism responds . . . however, the very fact of decentering is a strong argument for its adaptive nature, for by establishing its equilibrium point as *low* as possible, the organism does less work and is under less strain than if it neutralized extreme stimuli (1953, pp. 35–36).

Helson fails to explain why the arithmetic mean would be a less desirable subjective center in most situations. His argument derives from psychophysical studies of weight-lifting, where it may well be valid, but it is obviously not literally applicable to other forms of judgment situations (e.g., judgments of hot are no more or less effortful than judgments of cold). However, when conceived in terms of energy requirement to *shift* the AL, as in adopting a new attitude different from the old, his description of decentering as analogous to "social lag" as a general conserving tendency at work in the organism is perhaps more tenable. Helson points to Gesell's developmental principle of "functional asymmetry," which describes the greater frequency of one-sided functioning in the bilaterally symmetrical organism (Gesell, 1946) as an instance of decentering.

As his fourth point, Helson notes the frequent occurrence in perceptual fields of "anchoring stimuli," which, for some reason of intensity, novelty, emotional connotation, location, or other, may have a preponderant influence on the AL. These four factors, then, (1) the bipolarity of responses, (2) the adjustment to changing level, (3) the

---

[25] It may be worth recalling here the fact that such levels need not be "native" to an organism, but become preferred levels of stimulation as a result of cumulative experience, etc.

decentered position of the neutral category, and (4) the influence of preponderant stimuli, may act to determine the location of the AL in any particular instance of perceptual response or decision-making.

Helson (1953, 1959) draws on a large number of extant studies of perception and learning to demonstrate the usefulness of the AL concept in ordering the data. In addition, he and his associates have been conducting an increasing series of experiments in which systematic manipulation of variables permits a precise evaluation of the particular influences of the three types of determinants his equation specifies (e.g., Helson, 1938, 1947; Michels & Helson, 1949; Nash, 1950; Philip, 1951; Johnson, 1949; and see later discussion). Helson considers AL theory applicable not only to judgments in a single sense modality continuum, but to interactions of sense modalities, emotional and cognitive factors, and in general ". . . to higher-level types of behavior in which social, personality, and meaning factors are the important determinants of behavior" (1953, p. 38).[26] He also extends the concept to deal with social and cultural levels, ". . . in view of the fact that there are indices of group behavior no less than of individual behavior" (1953, p. 41). Not in itself a complete theory, AL provides a frame of reference and a means of quantification (prediction) of behavior. The AL is a function of the *pooled* effects of present and past experience, both direct and mediated. It thus simultaneously takes account of both situational and inner (motivational and "state-of-the-organism") determinants—what the organism finds as well as what it brings to a situation. Knowledge of the AL then permits determination of the degree to which change is required to reach a state of equilibrium incorporating a new stimulus and/or the direction of action (and its intensity) most likely to be expected.

To show the operation of the AL, a few examples may be cited. Helson (1947) has shown that when weights are judged within a 200 to 400 gram range, an AL of 250 grams is established. The addition of a 900-gram weight to the series shifts the AL to 313 grams. But having the 900-gram weight hefted before each judgment as a background stimulus raises the AL to about 350 grams, ". . . with resultant changes in judgments of all the series stimuli" (1951, p. 384). Helson doubts that explanations of these shifts in judgments of how stimuli actually feel could be made in terms of the subject having gained "insight" or "understanding" from his experiences. He thus argues for the automatic operation of AL as an equilibrating mechanism. Similar findings

---

[26] Cf. Osgood's congruity principle and Festinger's theory of consonance and dissonance (see Chapters 14 and 15).

of the effects of residual and background factors on succeeding judgments of physical stimuli were found by Johnson (1949) for pitch, and by Nash (1950) for weights. Johnson's findings of a quantitative effect of practice at one level on shift in AL at a different level in a subsequent judgment series is consistent with Helson's formulations, and shows their applicability to analyses of learning phenomena (Helson, 1953).

Individual value systems, or frames of reference, are long-term or "pooled" AL's. Helson (1953) cites two studies with similar findings of the effects of frames of reference (AL) on social perceptions. In one, Marks (1943) asked colored students to rate skin color of people they knew. In another, Hinckley and Rethlingshafer (1951) had tall and short students rate heights. In the first instance, Marks found that darker subjects rated their subjects as lighter than did the lighter subjects: "Each judge established his own reference scale . . . this scale is independent of the subjects rated but not of the rater's past experience . . . each judge's rating scale tends to be egocentric, i.e., a subject is seen as darker or lighter than the rater and judgments are made accordingly" (Marks, 1943, pp. 374–375, as quoted in Helson, 1953). Similarly, in the study involving height ratings, tall men judged heights as significantly shorter than did short men, the latter consistently overestimating height while the former underestimated it. In both these instances, Helson points out that the subject's own position (with respect to the variable under consideration) is taken as the neutral point (AL) from which judgments are made. However, where the subject is at one end of the continuum (as Marks found with very dark raters) a compromise is effected in setting the AL somewhere between objective and subjective reality. The settings of subjective neutrality (AL) at "egocenter" is consistent with AL theory and with homeostatic personality theories in general.

Helson considers these studies to illustrate AL theory, and he rejects the possibility that the ratings result from a fundamental personality trait. In fact, his position would argue against the very existence of such fundamental traits, except as this concept might refer to the effects of highly consistent experience or limiting physical-physiological condition in producing a heavy weighting on the residual factor.

Blake (1958) has recently reviewed a series of experimental applications of AL theory to social perception. Working closely with Helson and others at the University of Texas, Blake focuses on the influence of "the other person in the situation." His restatement of Helson's general formulation of AL theory in terms of the social context is quoted below. Although it does not change Helson's concept, it nicely illustrates an important particular application and a comparison with Helson's earlier statement (1953, p. 36) is instructive.

In any given social situation, a specific response is the product of the inter-action of . . . (a) the central stimulus in the immediate focus of attention that defines the *type* of response for that situation; (b) the background or context, consisting of all other stimuli present, but in these studies repre-sented only by reactions of *others;* and (c) personality factors including individual differences in past experiences and physiological states. Each produces a force of varying strength that influences the response. Predic-tion of behavior is possible only in terms of a resultant, the product of the interaction of all influences present (Blake, 1958, p. 229).

Blake describes a series of studies in which artificial social environ-ments are constructed and manipulation of the role of the other used as a means of producing change in AL and in resultant behavior. In one study (Blake, Mouton, & Hain, 1956) college students were asked to sign a petition on a relatively neutral matter. Two independent variables were manipulated: (1) the strength of the request to sign, and (2) the presence of a positive or negative social influence (i.e., another person signing or refusing to sign, a short or long list of names already on the petition). As anticipated, the best prediction was yielded by combining factors of stimulus and background influences. In a separate but similar study, Helson, Blake, Mouton, and Olmstead (1956) were able to show that residual factors (personal conformity tendencies) also combined with the others to determine the adjustment that occurs.

Other studies cited by Blake (1958) cover a range of social actions, including disobeying rules (Freed, Chandler, Blake, & Mouton, 1955; Lefkowitz, Blake, & Mouton, 1955; Kimbrell & Blake, 1958), volun-teering (Rosenbaum, 1956; Rosenbaum & Blake, 1955), contributing or gift-giving (Blake, Rosenbaum, & Duryea, 1955). In all of these experiments, as in petition-signing just described, systematic study of the three types of factors affecting AL consistently confirmed the efficacy of applying AL theory to social behavior. Blake emphasizes the notion of adaptation in showing how the several factors interact,

. . . for whether a central stimulus or a social background is positive or negative for any particular person is a function of his present adjustment level. . . . It is when the subject is close to his equilibrium or adjustment level . . . that additional stimulation referable to perceived qualities of the social situation has its maximum impact in influencing behavior (Blake, 1958, p. 241).

The role of norms as "stabilizing influences" is seen by Blake as a basis for a model of social order. The establishment of norms, in turn, may be perceived as a general case of stabilizing or equilibrating the external environment, a concept central to homeostatic motivation theory.

As it was necessary for Blake to spell out the nature of the variables composing AL in social situations in order to apply AL theory there, so do George and Bonney (1956; Bonney & George, 1958) impose certain modifications on the AL model in applying it to personality studies. These investigators have generally confirmed the usefulness of AL theory in clinical studies, but in the process suggest a refinement of the residual concept in terms of several levels of influence. First-order residuals derive from "the ethnofamilial complex in which the individual is born and matures." These are thought to be of a "generalized and persistent nature." In step order are second-level residuals (derived from certain psychoanalytic concepts), and "third order residuals derived from . . . more immediate events in the *S's* life which are sufficiently dramatic to alter his *AL*" (1956, p. 21). Each level of residual in turn influences the next.

Bonney and George suggest that the effective AL at any moment in fact represents several AL's and to stress still further the interactive nature of the different types of factors, they write: "Background varies as a function of the situation out of which behavior arises, or as a function of the test situation in which behavior is measured. The nature of the background will determine which residuals are activated" (1956, p. 21).

Comment

In developing the main themes of this chapter we have repeatedly pointed to the need for bridging formulations that would permit us to move from physiological to psychological and even social homeostasis by more measured means than a leap of faith. Helson's concept of Adaptation Level and the proposed means of quantifying the relative contributions of its various determinants appear to be steps in the direction of a more firmly based homeostatic motivation theory. As an inferred variable, AL is not attributed to any particular neurophysiological mechanism, and so would not be incompatible with either a central motive state idea or a neuromuscular tension notion such as Freeman's. Its empirical referents, however, are in judgmental situations rather than in physiological measures. It would be interesting to apply the types of criteria used by both Freeman and Helson in the same experiment.

CYBERNETICS AND THE FEEDBACK PRINCIPLE

The third homeostatic model to be considered in this chapter is that of the self-regulating machine presented by cybernetics.[27]

The reader of Mark Twain's delightful descriptions of *Life on the Mississippi* will remember the important depth measurements taken from time to time by men standing in the bows of the Mississippi steamers as they cautiously treaded their ways through the shifting channels of that river. These soundings, shouted back to the pilot, were essential to the proper control of the vessel. The helmsman would set his wheel, and then the effect of the course would be determined by what new reports were called back from the bow. If the channel were deepening, the steersman would maintain his course, while a shallow channel would require corrective steering until a safe mark was heard.

What we have here described is a somewhat complex system consisting of a steamer, its crew, and its environment—the river of swift current and treacherous channels. The systems which Cannon and Bernard described, while not literally the same as this, are functionally similar, and the maintenance of an "even keel," or the avoidance of upset, would appear to be the goal of both.

The principle of control demonstrated in the case of the steamboat example (and, as we shall see, in the case of homeostasis as well) is what the cyberneticians call *feedback*. This principle, operating nowadays quite a bit less crudely than in Mark Twain's time, with radar, sonar, and other electronic devices, forms the basis of automation in rocketry and space exploration, military fire-control, aircraft traffic regulation, and infinite varieties of industrial and home gadgetry and appliances.

A whole new science is devoted to the study of control mechanisms and communication based on information feedback. Appropriately enough, the science is called *cybernetics*, a term derived from the Greek word for helms- or steersman. The name was coined for this

[27] Cybernetics is an interdisciplinary science which is far more extensive in scope than the narrow frame within which some of its concepts will here be treated. Contributors to the field include communications and electronics engineers, mathematicians, philosophers, physicists, physiologists, and psychologists, and its ramifications are widespread. For more extended treatments of the subject, the reader may refer to any one of an excellent series of clearly written works by Ashby (1952, 1956), Walter (1953), Wiener (1954), Sluckin (1954), or Wisdom (1951). More technical materials will be found in Wiener (1948), Quastler (1953), and in the series of *Josiah Macy, Jr. Foundation Symposia*, edited by von Foerster (1951).

purpose by Norbert Wiener, the distinguished mathematician, for much the same reason that Cannon introduced the word homeostasis: the want of a term free from ambiguity or specific other reference.

Actually, the concept of feedback mechanisms, on which cybernetics is based, was described by Clerk Maxwell in 1868, in an analysis of the functioning of Watt's *governor* (a term, incidentally, having the same origin as cybernetics). Wiener considers Maxwell's paper to be the first significant scientific treatment of the subject (see Wiener, 1948).

Self-Regulation and Feedback. The difference between a regulated and a self-regulating machine can almost be summarized in the one word: feedback. Regulated machines, once "turned on," perform their function until they are "turned off" or break. The energy allotted to them is utilized to perform the function for which they were constructed. Changes in the environment within which they function—unless such changes were anticipated by the machine's designer—simply do not enter into the machine's operation. The well known example of the Sorcerer's Apprentice may come to mind here. This enterprising young man managed, by imitating his master, to cause his broom to fetch water for him. The broom obeyed, bringing bucket after bucket. But the young apprentice hadn't learned all the tricks of his master's trade. When the task should have been finished, the obedient broom kept right on faithfully bringing additional bucket after bucket after bucket until the Sorcerer himself appeared to save the situation from disaster. Were the broom a servomechanism, on the other hand, it would have automatically stopped when the appropriate amount of water had accumulated.

Self-regulating machines, or servomechanisms—machines with feedback, that is—*monitor* their own performances. They utilize some of the energy they receive or generate to control their energy output. When action-in-progress is enhanced, we speak of *positive* feedback, while the inhibition of such action is referred to as *negative* feedback. It is this latter type of feedback which is postulated to be of greatest importance to the action of the nervous system, although both types are thought to occur.

The most commonly used example of a self-regulating system is the thermostatically controlled room. Here the heat of the room regulates the metal elements of a thermostat, which in turn regulates the heat of the room. The thermostat is a simple switching device connected to the furnace motor. It contains two sensitive metal elements which expand or contract in accordance with their temperature, and which can thus be caused to contact each other at any particular temperature, depending on how far apart they may be set. Contact serves to break a circuit, cutting off the input of heat to the system and permitting cooling to occur. When the room has cooled to the point where the elements separate again, the switch is thus "made" again and the heat source reactivated, etc. The thermostat differs from a simple machine which turns on the heat source for a fixed period of time in that the thermostat functions on the basis of *actual* rather than *expected* performance. That is, the simple machine would shut off at the end of its set period, whether or not the temperature had reached the desired level, whereas the thermostat would continue to operate until (and *only* until) the actual desired level was reached. And this is the key to the feedback principle. As Wiener has summarized it, self-regulation is possible whenever a system has some form of sensory members actuated by its own motor members, which in turn regulates its output.

Control and the Nervous System. Of particular interest to us here are the hypotheses of the cyberneticians about the operation of the nervous system. The basic contention of cybernetics in this regard, as Wisdom (1951) has pointed out, is that the chief mechanism of the central nervous system is one of negative feedback. And, as we shall see, they consider this mechanism sufficient to explain purposive or adaptive (i.e., motivated) behavior.

Attempts to develop machine models of the nervous system—or even to conceive of animal behavior control mechanistically—have always fallen short, in the past, of one major accomplishment: an adequate accounting for adaptive or apparently purposive behavior. It was always possible for vitalistic or teleological theorists to point to the failure of such models to account for apparently goal-oriented, planned, adaptive, or purposive behavior as showing the necessity for a "life-principle" or "purposiveness-in-nature" type of explanation. Cyberneticians feel that their new type of machine model—the machine with feedback—shows promise of resolving the question in favor of a non-vitalistic explanation.

The Concept of System. Now to appreciate the ideas of cybernetics, it will be useful to look once again at the concept of *system*. We earlier described the views of Cannon, Child, and others (see pp. 303 ff.) on biological systems as necessarily open, and continually interacting with their environments. Von Bertalanffy (1950, 1951), Krech (1950), and Ashby (1940, 1952) similarly stress the importance of distinguishing between the dynamics of open and closed systems. For instance, the physicochemical laws governing energy conservation, particularly the second law of thermodynamics (entropy), would require that any *closed* system eventually reduces to a static equilibrium—a state of minimum energy exchange. Such a static system could neither receive nor discharge energy—would perform no work, as it were.

That biological systems seem (at least temporarily) to "disobey" this natural law has been a main argument in behalf of the vitalist and teleological positions.[28] As von Bertalanffy points out, however, there is no contradiction, if it is recognized, that *open* systems, by definition, draw upon the free energy of their environments. Thus an open system may actually display *negative* entropy—utilize *more* energy in its operation and in its effect(s) on the environment than exists in its own system. Open systems may attain steady states (i.e., remain constant or stable) while at the same time maintaining a continuous flow and interchange of energy and component materials. And, as Krech has shown, a dynamic system may even move toward states of greater heterogeneity and complexity rather than simplicity, for the same reasons. In other words, no vitalistic or teleological explanation is required, in this view, to account for either the maintenance of a dynamic equilibrium or the sometimes complex searching behavior displayed by living organisms. But more of this later.

Another aspect of system must also be kept clear. We ordinarily envision actual objects in space when machines are discussed. The cybernetic concept of machine goes beyond such a simple physical model and includes *any* set of variables which affect each other, whether physically connected or not. Thus the Mississippi steamer *and* its crew, when functioning together, may constitute one integral system and be considered a "machine" in this larger sense. The only requirement for a machine, according to Ashby, is that its behavior be ". . . sufficiently law-abiding or repetitive for us to be able to make some prediction about what it will do" (1952, p. 225). And this is *all* that is required.

Still a third aspect of system, that of level of organization, will be considered more extensively below.

Biological Systems and Stable Equilibrium. Biological systems maintain stable equilibria. When displaced from a "neutral" position, they tend to remain active until the disturbed equilibrium is restored, or, in combination with other part-systems, a new equilibrium is reached. Ashby (1940, 1956) uses the analogy of a cube resting on its side to describe a system in stable equilibrium. When a force is applied to the cube, it results in resistance, and a tendency on the part of the cube

---

[28] See Brillouin (1949) for an interesting discussion of this problem, and Sommerhoff (1950) for a more extended treatment. An early exposition of the cybernetic view on this question can be found in Rosenblueth, Wiener, and Bigelow (1943).

to return to its prior state of rest. This is in contrast to a system in *un*stable equilibrium, such as a cone balanced on its nose. The cone, when disturbed, falls with greater energy than was attributable to the strength of the applied force alone. Actually, the cone system may be said to be stable within extremely narrow limits,[29] whereas the cube and its environment form a system of much greater range of stability. However, this system has its limits as well. Within its range, the greater the displacement, the greater the resistance. But if the limits of the range are reached—if an excessive force were applied to the cube—it would topple to a new surface and, like the cone, become in effect a new system, with a new neutral point, and so forth. A wedge placed under its resting surface would also alter both the neutral point and the range of permissible fluctuations within which the cube system could effectively retain its equilibrium.

Stability characterizes a system, then, when its parts are arranged in such a manner as to counteract or resist disturbance. But a system can operate stably only within a given range, and deviations beyond the limits of this range would, when the limits are reached or surpassed, either temporarily or permanently destroy the system. The thermostat, to use one of Ashby's examples, may effectively regulate the heat (i.e., maintain the stability) of the system of which it is a part only when it is functioning within its defined limits of temperature. When these limits are exceeded, as when freezing or melting temperatures intrude upon the system, the metal parts of the thermostat fail to function and the system breaks down. Likewise, when the limits of any life-maintaining homeostatic system are reached, a new state (coma, death) quickly follows (cf. Selye, 1950).

But how is a system maintained in stable equilibrium? It should be clear by now that the answer of cybernetics is feedback.

The operation of feedback in relation to behavior might be summarized as follows: Reacting to disturbance (i.e., stimulation), the system (or any subsystem) responds. Its response affects the environment in some particular way, at the same time "reporting back" what has been done. The central regulatory apparatus then computes the discrepancy between performed and intended action and the succeeding response is "corrected for error." Such a sequence is repeated until the residual error is so small as to lie within the range of the target—or, in other words, until a stable equilibrium has been secured.

[29] In this and the ensuing discussion, the notion of limits implies a threshold or series of thresholds in the psychophysical sense, and the further implication of a sensing member or mechanism.

Two everyday examples from Wiener may illustrate what is meant more prosaically:

If I pick up my cigar, I do not will to move any specific muscles. Indeed in many cases, I do not know what those muscles are. What I do is to turn into action a certain feedback mechanism; namely, a reflex in which the amount by which I have yet failed to pick up the cigar is turned into a new and increased order to the lagging muscles, whichever they may be. In this way, a fairly uniform voluntary command will enable the same task to be performed from widely varying initial positions, and irrespective of the decrease of contractions due to fatigue of the muscles. Similarly, when I drive a car, I do not follow out a series of commands dependent simply on a mental image of the road and the task I am doing. If I find the car swerving too much to the right, that causes me to pull to the left. This depends on the actual performance of the car, and not simply on the road; and it allows me to drive with nearly equal efficiency a light Austin or a heavy truck, without having formed separate habits for the driving of the two (1954, p. 26).

This is, of course, an oversimplified presentation of what occurs. Nevertheless, it can be seen that the concept of feedback, even without knowledge of the specific mechanisms through which it operates, is consistent with the hypothesis of homeostasis, and provides a conceptual continuum for the extension of this concept to the analysis of behavior of total organisms and organismic systems. Actually, supportive evidence for the type of schematic organization here presented can be offered from two sources: neuropsychology and machine analogy. We will turn to this evidence as soon as we have examined some of the important concepts and implications of Ashby's *Design for a Brain* (1952; revised edition 1960).

Adaptiveness, Goal-Seeking, and Stable Equilibria. In his highly interesting and carefully reasoned *Design for a Brain* (1952), W. R. Ashby shows how the organism and its environment form an "absolute" system, such that changes in the one affect the other, and vice versa.[30] This is true not only for innate but for learned patterns of behavior as well. Thus the courtship pattern in sticklebacks and the maze learning behavior of cats both serve to illustrate this mutual dependence. Survival may be seen as the result of successful adaptations of organisms to the variable environments with which they interact, both in an historic, evolutionary sense and in a day-to-day sense as well.

[30] A similar notion is found in Angyal's *Foundation for a Science of Personality* (1941).

Now one might ordinarily be inclined to describe adaptive behavior in living organisms as "intelligent" and impute intention or purpose to the organism. Ashby considers this an unnecessary metaphysical complication. He points out the similarity between adaptive behavior in organisms and in stable systems in general. Both appear to adapt their behavior in such a way as to maximize the perpetuation of stability—that is, survival. Both adjust their behavior on the basis of performance-actuated feedback. Thus an organism seeking a particular goal would be akin to a radar-controlled searchlight or anti-aircraft gun seeking its target, a thermostat seeking its set temperature, or a pendulum seeking the center of its arc. In all of these instances, the behavior of the system is what Ashby terms "error-controlled." The system corrects its own behavior on the basis of the discrepancy between actual and optimal performance, and continues such corrective responding until it "reaches its goal." Ashby concludes: "Once it is appreciated that feedback can be used to correct any deviation we like, it is easy to understand that there is no limit to the complexity of goal-seeking behavior which may occur in machines quite devoid of any 'vital' or 'intelligent' factor" (1952, p. 54).

Essential Variables and Critical States. It can be said that the goal of all stable systems, living or not, is survival. And survival, as we have seen, is synonymous with the maintenance or achievement of stability. But stability can be achieved in a system only to the extent that the variables active in the system are kept within their normal range. Ashby makes it clear, however, that not *all* of the variables operating in a dynamic system are necessary to the survival of that system. He designates *essential variables* as those only in which excessive change would be incompatible with the system's survival. Adaptive behavior can now be seen as any behavior serving to retain the essential variables within their "safe" limits.[31] What these limits are—as well as which variables are essential in a system—can be determined for any particular system empirically. Thus, for example, the *physiological limits* of variation permitted to living organisms vary from species to species and variable to variable. A change in length of hair on a man's head from 4 inches to 1 inch would be trivial, as Ashby puts it, whereas

---

[31] Ashby here anticipated the type of criticism raised by Davis (see p. 314) that some part of a system must disequilibrate in order that other parts may remain—or become—stable. This is precisely the purpose of Ashby's distinction, the activity of nonessential variables having importance only insofar as they maintain the constancy of the essential variables and, thereby, the stability of the system. For stability, in Ashby's view, is an attribute of the system rather than any of its component parts.

a change in his systolic blood pressure from 120 mm of mercury to 30 would be critical. We would then consider systolic blood pressure, and those variables directly linked with it, to be essential. And we observe that a homeostatic system *does* react adaptively (i.e., with negative feedback) when these variables threaten to reach their physiological limit. When such adaptive measures fail, the system ceases to be.[32]

Now it is clear that systems could not long survive if efforts to maintain their stability were activated only *after* essential variables had reached the limits of their ranges. Ashby therefore proposes that there must be *critical states* (i.e., series of thresholds) for these variables, lying somewhere along their behavior "lines" between the "safe" range and the "breaking" point. When a behavior line reaches such a critical state, it leads to a reorganization of the field of the variables in such a way as to prevent a "runaway" condition. Thus the bicyclist, endeavoring to retain his balance, may at the last moment, before he falls, violently throw his shoulders in an opposite direction, touch the ground briefly with his foot, or turn his wheel sharply, etc. to "reorganize" the relationship of the variables in this particular man-machine system, the stability of which is found in balanced motion.

The Step-Function and Ultrastability. The reorganization of the field just mentioned comes about because some variables display what Ashby calls a *step-function*. That is, they remain relatively constant up to a point, and then they change value drastically and/or suddenly. Examples of variables which characteristically operate in this way are abundant in nature. The light switch which floods a dark room with electric light, the nerve net which responds in "none or all" fashion, the pain stimulus of a shock applied suddenly, etc. Depending on what time scale is used, such other significant value changes as accompany puberty or mark a mutation might also be described as step-functions.

Not all variables in a system show step-functions. Some do not change at all—at least during any particular period of observation— and these are referred to as *null-functions*. Others show constant variation (*full-functions*) and still others show characteristic periods of quiescence and change (the *part-functions*). The variables active at

[32] Although Ashby seems here to imply a strict dichotomy between essential and nonessential variables, it is worth noting that even essential variables probably form a hierarchy with respect to urgency, some leading to quick system destruction, while others demand consideration after short or long intervals (e.g., oxygen deficit has priority over water deficit, which in turn has priority over food deficit). In such a hierarchical system one steady state (even of an essential variable) could be deliberately upset if needed to restore one of more urgent standing. Time and intensity variables need also to be taken into account.

any particular time are called the *main* variables of the system.

Since the behavior of any part of a system is affected by the behavior of all other parts, Ashby is able to show that step-function changes are precipitated by changes in the main variables of the system. Following from what was said earlier, step-functions would be induced whenever main variables reached a critical stage, thus in effect forcing a change in the interconnections of all of the variables in the system. If the step-function has led to a change such that the system moves toward stability, no further step-functions will be precipitated and the system will come to rest. If, however, the step-function leaves the main variable(s) in a critical stage, or pushes other main variables toward the limits of their ranges, further step-functions will be led to, and so forth, until the system either destroys itself (i.e., fails to stabilize) or becomes stable.

Ashby formalized this pattern of successive step-function changes in what he calls the *principle of ultrastability:* ". . . an ultrastable system acts selectively towards the fields of the main variables, rejecting those that lead . . . to a critical state but retaining those that do not" (1952, p. 91). Important to recognize in the position taken by Ashby is the fact that goals are reached by a process of trial, error, and change. Adaptation is accomplished by a process of *aimless* change, since the principle calls only for rejection or nonrejection of fields produced as a result of step-functions, and cannot give rise to a particular next value for the variable that changes in step-function fashion. Ashby considers the principle of ultrastability capable of accounting for unlearned and learned behavior alike, and for the action of the nervous system in adapting to either drastic changes in its external environment or surgically or biochemically induced changes in its own structure. He further proposes an intimate connection between gene patterns and ultrastable living systems, in effect arguing that natural selection could produce an organism having step-function variables, and that successive mutations would then be rejected or not in accordance with the principle of ultrastability.

We are unable here to go into the many further ramifications and qualifications of Ashby's *Design*. Suffice it to say that he attempts to deal with the complexity of human behavior by showing that an ultrastable system *could* perform all of the types of behavior found in humans without an excessive number of separate variables being posited. This is possible when it is recognized that variables displaying step-functions will give rise to a number of different organizations of system fields far in excess of the number of variables composing these possible fields. Carrying out some simple mental arithmetic on the possible combinations of two, three, four, etc., variables will at once make clear what is meant here. By further assuming that the nervous system does not engage in *all* of its possible behaviors at the same time,[33] Ashby is able to increase the scope of his few essential principles to account for such important factors as the effects of repetition and the phenomena of habituation and memory.

The Multistable System. Finally, Ashby introduces the concept of the *multistable system*. This is an ultrastable system composed of subsystems, each of which is also ultrastable. The multistable system is Ashby's model of the human nervous system. With this concept he feels it is possible to account for the adaptations of systems within the nervous system to each other as well as to factors lying outside the organism. This may be illustrated by use of an example Ashby considers very simple but nevertheless typical of the multiple (in this case serial) adaptations of which a multistable system is capable. He offers the case of an animal that must secure its own food in an environment containing obstacles which the animal must avoid if it is not to be injured. For convenience these are referred to as the "feeding" and "avoidance" systems. The feeding system contains the brain and food supply as variables and is ". . . stable so as to hold the blood-glucose concentration within normal limits." Likewise, the avoiding system consists of eyes, muscles, skin receptors, parts of the brain, and hard external objects. Once established, this system ". . . always acts so as to keep within limits the mechanical stresses and pressures caused by objects in contact with the skin receptors" (Ashby, 1952, p. 187). Each system is acquired by processes of ultrastability, but additionally, each system responds to an environment *including the other*. Thus the terminal product will be a multistable system adapted with regard to both acquiring food and avoiding injury.

Ashby assumes that one system (avoiding) is probably established before the other (feeding), though this assumption is not necessary. In Figure 7–2, he diagrams the integration of the two systems (note the multiple feedback circuits and the common pathways).

Clearly this pattern of multiple adaptations can be extended to include other motivational conditions and adaptations to new environmental circumstances, and this is how Ashby believes the nervous system may well perform.

---

[33] The fact that neural nets may utilize final common pathways, thus automatically involving the inhibition of otherwise probable action, further increases the alternative possibilities.

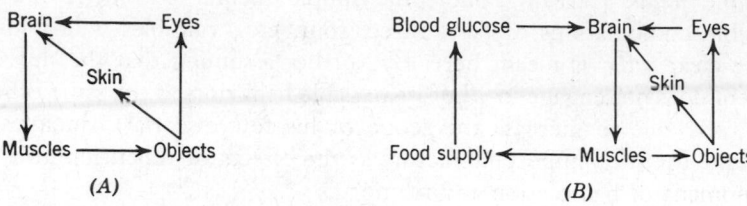

Figure 7–2. Diagram of immediate effects of (*A*) the avoiding system and (*B*) the combined feeding and avoiding systems. Each word represents many variables. Reproduced by permission from Ashby (1960, p. 202, Figs. 15/10/1 and 15/10/2).

Types of Supporting Evidence

A Model of the Model: the Homeostat. Ashby devotes an impressive appendix of his *Design for a Brain* to a set of mathematical proofs of his model. But the proof that a model is logically consistent falls short of demonstrating the main thesis, namely, that this is the nature of nervous action. A further step in the direction of proof is offered, however, by the development of working models—physical machines— built in accordance with cybernetic principles and able to perform functions analogous to (if not identical with) those of animal nervous systems. One such machine is Ashby's *homeostat.* This ingenious device was designed to duplicate not an actual object in nature (it has no natural prototype) but an ultrastable system in action.

It consists of a series of identical box-like units, wired together so as to permit a maximum number of feedback circuits (see Figure 7–3). Input to each unit can be made by environmental manipulations of the experimenter, by all of the other units, and by its own response. The amount and direction of displacement of a pointer in each unit from its neutral center position is "reported" precisely as input to all four units. Depending on its value, such input will either go to a magnet maintaining the pointer at its appropriate position, or, if its value is excessive (or insufficient) so as to reach a critical value, a step-function change (via a stepping-switch arrangement) will occur, the value being either reduced (or increased) to an "acceptable" level, or continuing to provoke step-function changes until the ultrastable system reaches its optimal condition of equilibrium. Incidentally, as with the nervous system, Ashby's apparatus may show considerable "normal oscillation" within its neutral range.

The entire system is freely supplied with (electrical) energy. By feeding the apparatus random variations in current, Ashby can show graphically the pattern of adaptation the homeostat will follow. Interestingly enough, the pattern is *not* predictable, as on successive occasions the homeostat may "choose" any one of 300,000 combinations of values (resulting from the step-switch changes), successively changing these until zero adjustments are required and all of the pointers reach their homeostatically neutral ranges. Ashby stresses this aspect of its organization—that random variation *can* lead to a desired goal, provided the principle of ultrastability is maintained.[34] Unlike machines with more prescribed (programmed) modes of operation, the homeostat is quite flexible, from an observer's point of view, in the way it goes about its goal-seeking. As Grey Walter (1953) has pointed

Figure 7-3. The homeostat. Reproduced by permission from Ashby (1960, Fig. 8/2/1, p. 101).

[34] To complete his argument, Ashby has done such things as tying two of the pointers together so that the excursions of one were no longer independent of its neighbor, and even more dramatically he deliberately crossed wires, initially leading to "run-away" results but in turn continuing self-correcting adjustments until the "goal" of stability was reached. This last demonstration of adapting to a new and opposite goal is used by Ashby to show the independence of the homeostat from its designer, since the design could not have taken into account one mode of operation and its converse as well.

out, it would be necessary to "kill" the homeostat and "dissect" its wiring system to know at any moment the behavior route it is following, although its goal is common knowledge.

Other Machine Models. Sluckin (1954) and Walter (1953) describe other machines which are capable of quite varied behavior. Most of these were constructed as model learning organisms. Walter's "machina speculatrix" and its successor, "machina docilis," combine mobility, problem-solving capacity, and conditionability. This tortoise-like apparatus, composed entirely of simple circuits and parts, wanders about exploring its environment, moves toward moderate light, avoids obstacles, appears "attracted" by its mirror image and by its own kind, but will break off its wandering and return to its "hutch" when it is in need of recharging (moderation giving way to appetite, as Walter puts it). It re-enters its brightly lit hutch long enough to "feed," immediately thereafter rushing forth to resume its explorations. The machina docilis can "learn" to come to a whistle, much as a dog is taught, by simple Pavlovian pairing of stimuli! [35]

In many of their aspects (space has permitted us merely to touch on a few) these creatures of the workbench and the laboratory would appear to behave like motivated organisms, showing evidence of arousal, sustained, purposive, goal-directed, yet highly variable and adaptive behavior. Such demonstrations provide only indirect evidence, to be sure, but they perhaps permit the inference that if animals had analogous feedback circuitry, the cybernetic model would be sufficient to account for their apparently purposive, motivated behavior. That there is some reason to believe in the existence of such neural circuitry will be shown in this next section.

Neurophysiological Findings. Evidence of feedback circuitry in the nervous system has been in existence for some time now. Brazier (1950) reviews the dynamic role of neural nets in the integration of behavior. In cuttlefish (Sanders & Young, 1940), spinal dogfish (Flynn, cited by Brazier, 1950), cats (Bailey & Davis, 1942), monkeys (Ruch & Shenkin, 1943), and rats (see Sperry, 1958), it has been shown that select surgical interference with higher centers can disrupt the balance between excitation and inhibition by removing the latter. Insulted organisms were apparently unable to "shut off" activity, walking or swimming continuously, or otherwise showing unrestrainable activity. Bailey and Davis reported quite dramatic findings in one such operation (cauteriz-

---

[35] Still other machines can run mazes, profit from experience by eliminating errors on subsequent runs, and show what we normally call insightfulness by taking advantage of short-cuts, choosing between goals, etc. See Shannon (1951); von Foerster (1951); and J. A. Deutsch (1954).

ing of the interpeduncular nucleus in cats). The damage apparently ". . . develops in these animals an obstinate progressive movement in which they walk continuously forward until they die. If they meet an obstacle such as the wall of the cage they press ceaselessly forward until all the hair is rubbed off and the scalp macerated" (Brazier, 1950, pp. 36–37).

In the 1930's, Lorente de Nò posited his now famous theory of "self-re-exciting chains" in the central nervous system, and ample histological and anatomical evidence exists for the validity of this view of an active nervous system consisting of reverberating circuits or feedback loops (see Brazier, 1950; Ashby, 1950). It is not clear what percentage, if any, of these reverberating chains results from development as a function of use. That circuits *can* be organized as a result of experience (or learning) would be generally agreed. The capacity of the organism to adapt to changes in the environment with changed neural organization has also been demonstrated in the retraining and functional recovery of aphasic and ataxic patients. Ashby (1950) cites the experiments of Marina (1915) with apes and of Sperry (1947) with spider monkeys as further evidence for the operation of the principle of ultrastability in nervous organization. Marina crossed the internal and external recti muscles of the eyeball of the ape, which should have reversed the controls for binocular vision. He found, however, that after operative recovery the animal was able to re-establish apparently "normal" binocular vision. Similarly, Sperry reversed the flexors and extensors in the arm of the spider monkey and found that initial malcoordination was progressively replaced with coordination approximating the normal mode. These studies are compared by Ashby with the adaptation shown by his homeostat to having its wires crossed as further support for the validity of his model. (However, see Sperry, 1958, for discussion of limitations of these plasticity experiments.)

What these demonstrations provide, it seems to us, is an indication of the fact that neural factors are not immutable elements upon which motivational variables operate, but are themselves a changing (or changeable) part of a complex behaving system subserving the motivational objective of stable self-maintenance.

Comment and Evaluation of the Cybernetic Position

The cybernetic model has attracted a good deal of excitement in the past several decades. The advances in electronic know-how, primed in the United States, Great Britain, and the Soviet Union by the practical needs of the Second World War and its aftermaths for rapid automatic methods of destruction and detection, have, as a certainly most laudable by-product, provided the means for more precise exploration and understanding of nervous organization. Increasing numbers of laboratories and neurosurgical operating rooms are electrically stimulating and recording from previously inaccessible centers deep in the brain. We have had to recast our model of brain-behavior relation from a static to a dynamic one, at the same time recognizing that a dynamic model can be consistent with natural law and mathematical formulation. Cybernetics has directly attacked the vitalist argument for discontinuity between animal and environment and with increasingly impressive demonstration has been narrowing the gap between the physical and biological universes of understanding.

Obviously, more than a feedback principle is needed to explain all of the activities of the nervous system. The cyberneticians have recognized this and—as in Ashby's principle of ultrastability—are providing testable hypotheses about the ways organisms perceive and learn, as well. Craik in England and McCulloch in the United States have independently proposed processes akin to the operation of the radar and TV scanning devices as a way in which organisms can focus upon objects in the environment and recognize them. That machines may someday be capable of evolving "symbolic models" and planning purposive action consistent with these "values" has already been considered—an extrapolation of cybernetic thinking quite consistent with strides already taken. That electroencephalograms provide clues to the normal oscillating function of the central nervous system would appear to be confirmed by the studies relating alpha-activity to ongoing behaviors. Wiener (1954) has proposed that psychoses in organisms may well be analogous to a "traffic jam" in telephone circuitry, where insufficient pathways are available for the number of messages needing to be transmitted simultaneously. The cures so far found effective —electric shock, lobectomy and lobotomy, and the dramatic drug effects on brain function so widely being explored lately—would tend to confirm the belief that blocking or cutting of certain wires will relieve the traffic bottlenecks and permit normal, if more limited, flow. Recent research in depth electroencephalography (e.g., Sem-Jacobsen, 1958) has begun to make more specific the pathways involved, as has. of course the impressive work on the reticular and other mid-brain areas (cf. Jasper et al., 1958; Magoun, 1958; Brazier, 1959).

Finally, it must be recognized that the models so far presented by the cyberneticians have been purposefully simplified to show the possibility of *types* of functions being performed, rather than actual duplicates of nervous systems, even in miniature. To go from such simplified models, even by analogy, to the complex behavior of human adults may, as W. R. Garner (1954) has suggested, require some considerable step-functions of step-functions.

LEWIN'S PSYCHOLOGICAL FIELD THEORY

A fourth and final model which is based on homeostatic or equilibrating principles is that of Kurt Lewin (1898–1947). Variously designated as "neo-Gestalt," "topological," "vector," "dynamic," and "field" theory, Lewin's work has had significant influence on broad areas of experimental, educational, developmental, and social psychology and the study of personality. In some ways like Freud (see Chapter 12), Lewin was wont to be all-encompassing in his conceptualizing —to paint on a large canvas, as it were—and, like Freud, he attracted an extremely loyal following and strong criticism. Unlike the psychoanalytic group, however, Lewin and his associates generated many testable experimental hypotheses and contributed a wide range of meaningful and provocative data to the experimental literature.

Lewin's major systematic writings are spread over five books: *A Dynamic Theory of Personality* (1935), *Principles of Topological Psychology* (1936), *The Conceptual Representation and the Measurement of Psychological Forces* (1938), *Resolving Social Conflicts* (1948), and *Field Theory in Social Science* (1951), the last two issued posthumously. Four review articles (Leeper, 1943; M. Deutsch, 1954; Escalona, 1954; Cartwright, 1959) summarize the contributions of field theory and should be referred to, along with the original sources noted, for a more complete study of the systematic position and the many experimental studies that were done in its context. Here we will examine only the outlines of some of Lewin's work to show how it exemplifies the equilibrational model as it relates to psychological phenomena.

The Overall Point of View. Lewin was critical of much of traditional psychological theorizing on the grounds that it artificially abstracted limited aspects of complex situations and then dealt only with its own abstractions. In his writings and lectures, he repeatedly emphasized the need for observational data as well as conceptual schemata. Scientific psychology must be "two-faced," he claimed, orienting simultaneously to the concrete phenomena of life and to explanatory concepts, but faithful primarily to the actual events in a contemporaneous "here and now." He argued persuasively for a *dynamic* psychology, with stress on the interdependence of factors, considered in their totality, as they were present in an immediate actual situation. Most psychological theories, he claimed, followed the mislead of the Aristotelian tradition by ascribing psychological events to such reified intra-individual concepts as instincts, habits, needs, personality, etc. Concepts such as these were artificial abstractions, he felt, neither true to details of the observational data from which they were presumably derived nor useful in describing events in the changing psychological world of the individual whose behavior is to be predicted.

Cartwright (1959) summarizes four directing principles in Lewinian theory: First, "only what is *concrete* can have effects"; second, *all* (concrete) aspects of a situation must be taken into proper account; third, there is an *"interdependence"* of events in any given field, so that dimensionalization obscures significant relationships; [36] and fourth, *only* that which is *present* in a situation can influence its outcome. Thus, field theory stands squarely for contemporaneity and for the contextual analysis of factors influencing behavior. It is the *net* effect (or the resultant) of simultaneous forces operating in the psychological field of the individual that serves to reorganize this field and thus affect behavior.

The Life Space. The key construct in Lewin's theory—the psychological field in which behavior occurs—is the *life space.* It represents the totality of "the person and his environment . . . as *one* constellation of interdependent factors" (Lewin, 1951, p. 240). Behavior is a function of the person and the (psychological) environment, and thus of the constellation of the life space. The formula is thus: $B = F(P, E) = F(LSp)$. By environment Lewin refers to one's "psychological" rather than physical surrounds, including both internal and external factors, but only as they affect the life space. This important distinction between the psychological and physical fields is illustrated schematically in Figure 7–4, taken from Cartwright. Here the solid lines connect the parts of the Life Space: person (P), psychological environment (E), and the sensorium (S) and motorium (M), the two parts of the boundary zone of the Life Space which receive stimulation from and act upon the physical-social world, respectively. S and M are thus windows or screens to the Life Space— and therefore interacting parts of same. The hull (H) and alien facts (A) lie outside the Life Space, and "together make up the 'objective' world of physical and social facts" (Cartwright, 1959, p. 71).

The lines of connection and points of contact between S and H and

---

[36] This can be recognized as similar to the Gestalt view that "the whole is greater than the sum of its parts." Lewin was, of course, much influenced by the Gestalt position, with which he personally and his early work are closely identified.

M and *H* represent the complex two-way filtering processes involved in perception and action. The broken line between *A* and *H* designates the area in which "nonpsychological laws" operate, that is, the extra-individual determinants of what is made available to the sensorium and what follows upon the individual's actions but lies beyond his control.

The interconnecting lines among *P*, *E*, *S*, and *M* in fact represent multiple and complex directional influences (both ways), and Cartwright makes it clear that no one variable or link between variables is seen as anything less than a part of a dynamic and interdependent system. If we further suggest that such a diagram must add "layers" to represent degrees of reality-irreality and panels to represent previous and successive time slices ("psychological past" and "psychological future"), the true complexity of what is being proposed becomes clearer (see MacKinnon, 1954).

Such an apparently gross emphasis on the relatedness of everything to everything else would have little value as a scientific theory, and it would be unfair to suggest that this was Lewin's intention. A statement of this sort does indicate, however, both the dynamic nature and the scope of what Lewin saw as the task of psychology. He tried both to set a broad enough conceptual framework for the problems he saw, and, having set a suitable framework, he and his students devoted their energies to the specific tasks of determining the ways in which the varied dimensions they proposed related to each other empirically. In order to characterize the complex relations he saw, Lewin used the language and some of the methods of a branch of mathematics called topology. He felt that this form of geometry could express the qualitative relations of position and connection of parts of a field undergoing transformation, which is what the Life Space appeared to be.

What he sought to describe was *locomotion* in the psychological

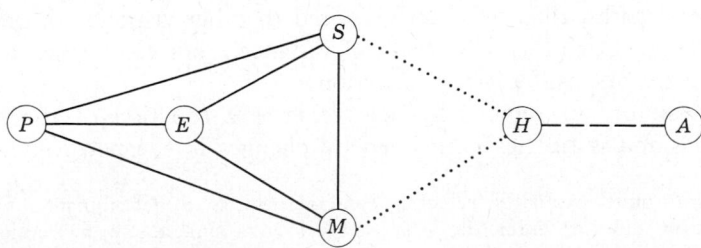

Figure 7–4. A schematic diagram of the facts and relations involved in the life space, the boundary zone, and the physical and social world. Reproduced by permission from Cartwright (1959, Fig. 3, p. 71).

environment. By this he did not mean actual movement in space, but change in "psychological space." Actually, in field theory, the term *behavior* is used primarily to describe change in structure of this environment, rather than overt action in the outside world (although in some instances these could be identical). Thus a change in behavior could be an overt act, an attitude shift, a change in the perceived [37] value of an object, a newly established connection between two events, etc. To deal with these matters in an orderly fashion, Lewin conceived of the Life Space as a *structural* entity composed of *regions* separated by *boundaries*. Regions connote such things as specific activities (watching television, making a decision, mailing a letter), passive states of being (being admired, being rewarded), group and class memberships (family, urbanite), roles and statuses (teacher, community leader), self-percept(s) (handsome, bright), and even objects, events, and other people (doll, date, Aunt Suzy) as they are perceived or functionally meaningful to the person.

The arrangement and condition of regions (the cognitive structure) determines the degree to which "movement" can take place. Where clear *paths* exist, sequential behavior patterns may occur. Where regions are not linked so as to permit locomotion in the direction of a desired goal, restructuring of the environment must occur. Development, regression, and learning are periods particularly characterized by such restructuring of the psychological environment. The newborn has a relatively undifferentiated cognitive structure. As development and learning occur, increasing differentiation (discriminations) of regions and subregions takes place. Regions become not only more differentiated, but ordered (structured) in terms of "centrality" (core concepts, permeating or basic roles, or percepts would be more central than transitory phenomena, e.g., "being a father" would probably be more central than "playing golf"). Relations among regions would vary in degree along lines of communication (a region may be a part of several paths, thus differently related to other regions with which it has contact) and as a function of distance from each other (again, along paths of possible communication).

Accessibility of regions to each other is a function of the above variables and is further controlled by changes in the permeability of

---

[37] Lewin quite explicitly rejected consciousness as a determinant of what entered or did not enter the psychological environment. By perception we simply mean functionally effective or value-to-the-person in contradistinction to "real" value. A kind word properly placed, a souvenir, a bit of string when needed would exemplify this notion, even if the person had no "awareness" of conscious goal-seeking.

their respective interfaces or boundaries. This last variable, as well as the structural stability, is affected by such *dynamic* qualities as *tensions* and *psychological forces*—the motivational constructs (if such can be distinguished) in Lewin's theory.

Inner-Personal Tension Systems. Activation of a psychological need

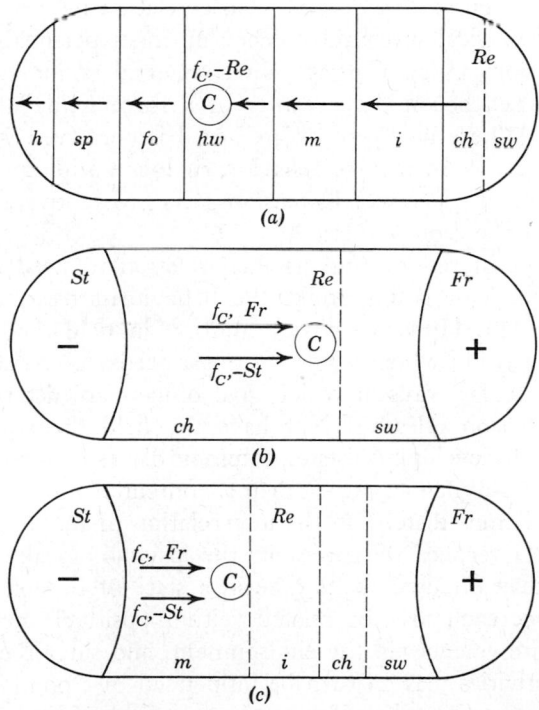

Figure 7-5. The representation of the life space, a finitely structured force field consisting of macroscopic regions.

(*a*) Eating situation in case of disliked food. C, child; *Re*, real eating; *h*, putting hand on table; *sp*, taking spoon; *fo*, putting food on spoon; *hw*, bringing spoon halfway to mouth; *m*, bringing spoon to mouth; *i*, taking food into mouth; *ch*, chewing; *sw*, swallowing; eating has a negative valence $[Va(Re) < O]$; the force away from real eating, $f_{c, -Re}$, increases stepwise with the decrease of distance between C and *Re*.

(*b*) Change of direction of forces after the child has started real eating. *St*, struggle with adults; *Fr*, freedom; $f_{c, Fr}$, force in the direction to freedom; $f_{c', -St}$, force away from the struggle. Other symbols as above.

(*c*) In a later stage of "learning" to eat the disagreeable food, the situation might be restructured so that bringing spoon to mouth (*m*) is now seen as a subpart of the region of real eating (*Re*). Adapted by permission from Lewin (1938, p. 117).

or intention (quasi-need) gives rise to tension in one or more inner-personal regions. The magnitude of the tension is related to the strength of the need. Fulfillment of the need reduces the tension. According to M. Deutsch (1954, p. 200), tension has these conceptual properties: "(a) it is a state of a region or system S which tries to change itself in such a way that it becomes equal to the state of its surrounding regions S^1, S^2 . . . S^6, and (b) it involves forces at the boundary of the region S in tension." There is a close relation between the person and his psychological surround. "When an inner-personal region is in a state of tension, an 'appropriate' environmental region acquires positive valence (i.e., becomes the center of a force field)" (Cartwright, 1959, p. 32). Where no "appropriate" goal is perceived, the existence of tension gives rise to restless behavior, or locomotion away from the present region. In other words, tension serves to motivate behavior in the direction of tension-reduction.

The concept of tension and its dual relation to need and to consummatory behavior is not unlike the behaviorist treatment of drive (see Chapter 11). However, little attention in field theory has been given to the ways in which needs (or quasi-needs) give rise to tensions or to the particular ways in which goal objects are determined to be appropriate tension releasers. Nor have the field theorists concerned themselves with developing lists of common drives or tensions. Lewin's was a structural-dynamic, rather than a content theory. The emphasis has been more immediately on the interrelation of tension systems and the resultant interplay of forces in the psychological environment. Since more than one system may be in a state of tension at the same time, and since each may be related (either positively or negatively) to one or more valences in the environment, and since the valences of objects or activities may in turn be influenced by "nonpsychological" or "alien" factors as well as by tensions, a field of forces is created. Behavior occurs as a result in the direction and with the intensity of the resultant of the force field. Figure 7–5 illustrates how these forces might interact in the life space of a child (Lewin, 1938, p. 117; M. Deutsch, 1954, p. 191).

Experimental Evidence

Field theory has given rise to several groups of significant experiments as "tests" of its predicted relations.[38] Zeigarnik (1927), for example, demonstrated that subjects who were interrupted on some tasks and permitted to finish others tended to recall the interrupted tasks

---

[38] Some of this work is also reviewed in Chapters 14 and 15.

with a much greater frequency than they recalled completed tasks. Ovsiankina (1928) similarly showed that subjects given the opportunity to resume interrupted tasks did so overwhelmingly. Although these experimental tasks have been subsequently shown to be more complicated than originally thought (see Alper, 1948*b;* Zeller, 1950*a, b,* 1951), they nevertheless support the conception of tension systems and psychological forces put forth by Lewin.

In an experimental analysis of the phenomena of satiation (see Lewin, 1951), some indication was obtained for the assumption that ". . . continued performance of a task leads to a lowering of the tension level in the system corresponding to the task. . . . This [leads] the person to turn away from the repeated task to other activities" (M. Deutsch, 1954, p. 203). The direction of choice or locomotion is determined by the relative strengths of tension systems and their relatedness (i.e., their ability to substitute for one another). Ultimately, the person would turn to completely unrelated activity areas.

In studies of activity substitution (see Henle, 1942), substitute value (measured by decrease in recall or resumption of an original activity after completion of a substitute activity) was inferred to be related to tension-reduction. And finally, in studies of frustration (see Chapter 9), Lewin and his associates were able to use the concept of tension and tension spreading to explain the apparent regression of their subjects (Barker, Dembo, & Lewin, 1941) as a de-differentiation of regions of the person resulting from a kind of tension "overflow."

Tension, Force, and Equilibration. The concept of tension in the intrapersonal system and the concept of force in the psychological environment both represent analogues to the physical concepts from which their names were borrowed. Lewin was not attempting, by this use of physical terms, to suggest that psychological phenomena could be explained by physical laws. On the contrary, he made a strong case for the desirability of dealing at the level of psychological events. This is not to be taken to mean that Lewin was a phenomenologist, as Spence (1944) once suggested, however. Lewin used verbal reports as data, but did not restrict himself to them. In addition, Lewin was well aware of the existence of an "alien" world and the impact of nonpsychological determinants on the life space (the field of "psychological ecology"). By using tension and force, Lewin sought to portray a dynamic, fluid psychological world, ordered in terms of the multiple relationships of its interdependent parts. The motivational model Lewin has used is an equilibrating model. Tension in one region or subregion of the person continues to motivate behavior until it is released, overflows, or is somehow reduced. The direction of flow in this system is from regions of high tension to regions of low tension, until all tension differences between regions are (hypothetically, at least) eliminated. Similarly, in the psychological field, locomotion occurs as a function of any imbalance of forces and in the direction of equilibration of field forces. In a field in which the person is in a region equidistant from regions of equal positive or negative valence, no locomotion is to be expected. In other words, tensional imbalance in the inner-personal system or an imbalance of forces in the psychological field, whether induced initially through biological need or through frustration or quasi-needs aroused via instruction, threat, or manipulation of the real environment, sets the condition for regulatory, adjustive behaviors (overt or covert) leading to a re-establishment of a balanced state.[39]

Like some of the other equilibrating models discussed in this chapter, field theory does not conceive of its system as closed. Generous allowance is made for structural change on the one hand (an integral part of the point of view) and ecological influence on the other. The key concept of tension reduction does not start with a static organism aroused to action and returning to a static quiescent state, but rather suggests a continual energy exchange following the principle of equal energy distribution rather than energy dissipation.

Further discussion of some aspects of Lewinian theory appears elsewhere in this book (with particular experiments stemming from this approach treated in Chapters 14 and 15).

GENERAL SUMMARY AND COMMENT

The theory of homeostasis can be traced far back into the history of biopsychology. It has, in one way or another, been deeply woven into the fabric of explanation of biological science. The usual starting point is taken from Bernard's now classic work in physiology in the middle of the nineteenth century, and from Cannon, whose systematization and christening of the concept have, more than anything else, helped to formalize its lawfulness.

The position taken is, in general, that the organism (and each of its subsystems) tends to resist changes in its environment that are of a magnitude large enough to upset its equilibrium or threaten its survival

---

[39] It is worth noting here that the tension and force concepts serve two purposes. They determine that behavior will occur—its duration on the one hand and the particular direction it will take on the other. Initially, tension would suggest arousal, and force direction, but no clear separation is made. It is perhaps in the very nature of the interrelatedness of systems to each other in field theory that this difficulty arises.

as a stable system. Natural selection and homeostasis are considered as two aspects of the evolutionary process. Systems which survive do so because they have developed—both in species and in individuals—mechanisms which ensure their safety; systems which fail to have this type of development—unstable systems—cannot survive.

Although so criticized, the theory does *not* require that a disturbed system return to its *prior* state of equilibrium (perhaps a logically impossible thing to do anyway), but it allows for a variety of means and states through which and at which stability can be reached. This is possible by assuming that biological systems are *open*, having continuous energy exchange with the environment, and that equilibrium can be achieved even though there be a continuous supplanting of specific materials in both.

Adaptation—acquiring stability in the face of disturbance—is achieved automatically. There is no fixed and immutable system, either under cortical dominance or otherwise, but a continually changing set of systems maintaining a balance of relationships within the environments created by all the other systems and part-systems and the environment at large. Genetically determined optima set the limits within which variability may be consistent with survival, but ample evidence is available to show that adaptation can take place to drastic disturbances of system integrity.

In a free science in a free society, it is unfortunately obligatory on no one to systematize the findings in a field, and since Cannon's attempt, based largely on his own work, no more extensive integration has been offered. However, it is possible to trace through the related writings, as we have tried to do in this chapter, a quite consistent thread which ties together—albeit loosely—the speculations and the findings at physiological and behavioral levels. The extensions of homeostatic hypotheses to social groups, tentative at best, are nevertheless able to be dramatically illustrated in the ecological surveys of insect and animal societies. Recent studies (Bonney & George, 1958; Berrien, 1962; McFarland et al., 1958) would suggest that there is some promise in the extension of these applications to human social behavior as well.

The four models which we have used to illustrate equilibratory motivation theory have, each from a somewhat different orientation than the others, attempted to provide an experimental and/or logical base for the investigation of conceivable mechanisms of operation of homeostatic-like processes. These are admittedly programmatic rather than complete models, but each has proved fruitful and, so far as they have been carried forward, none has had to be abandoned because of contrary evidence. (Of course, the very nature of the viewpoint is such that critical contrary evidence is difficult to obtain if stasis can in turn be found or shown somewhere else in a system.)

There seems little doubt that much of the behavior of organisms and of organ systems is consistent with homeostatic theory. The main objections have been that the theory doesn't account for enough or for all behavior. The concept is thought to be necessary but not sufficient, so to speak, as a theory of motivation.

Three major criticisms are leveled at homeostasis as *the* theory of animal—and especially of human—motivation. First, it is essentially negative in nature—that is, it nowhere appears to allow for spontaneous action, but conceives of systems only in terms of their response to disturbance. Second, its critics maintain that equilibration cannot adequately account for altruistic and creative behaviors. Third, and conversely, it is not thought able to explain satisfactorily behaviors apparently directed at destruction of the very system(s) of which they are presumed to be a function. (This last argument is answered by the counterclaim that it arises from misperceptions of the relative importance of subsystems [or subgoals].)

These are not, of course, distinct and separate criticisms, as they all revolve around the thesis that the richness of experience and the complex structure of particularly human strivings cannot be so simply explained as avoidance of disequilibrating stimulation.

The philosophic and teleological implications of some of these criticisms have already been discussed, along with attempted answers from the homeostatic point of view. It is clear that each side has oversimplified the case presented by the other, and that the evidence is far from approaching the point where a choice can be made. However, there is little doubt that current homeostatic theories, and cybernetics in particular, have not only aroused once again the perennial problems of mind-body, vitalism-mechanism, free will–determinism, but their advocates feel that they have also provided a satisfactory means of accounting for motivated acts without resort to untestable teleological or phenomenological explanations.

Finally, we should note that the homeostatic viewpoint does not represent a unified scientific "school" in any sense of the word. If we but recall that Cannon conceived of physiological homeostasis as serving to free the organism for higher activities, and contrast this view with that of Wiener and Ashby for whom *all* activity could be described as "mechanistic," or with Lewin's rejection of mechanism in favor of a dynamic, organismic model, we can begin to see the range of differences surrounding the common equilibratory core.

Chapter 8

Hedonic and Activation Theories of Emotion

To the average person it would perhaps be of no importance to attempt a distinction between motivation and emotional states or feelings. The everyday language of emotion and feeling is replete with expressions indicative also of motivational implications. One may act in a "passion," or his response may arise from "emotional disturbance," or he might "cry from joy." Having failed to carry out an expected task or having done less well at some performance than expected, one may excuse himself by saying he had not *felt* like doing the task, or performing, or that he was determined to do better next time.

Words indicating emotional and feeling states are widely used in the popular vocabulary, then, to describe processes of motivation. The very word *emotion* itself has much in common with the word *motivation*. Young (1943, p. 25) discusses its origin as follows:

The word emotion is derived from the Latin *e* (out) and *movere* (to move). Originally the word meant a moving out of one place into another, in the sense of a migration. Thus: "The divers emotions of that people (the Turks)" (1603). "Some accidental emotion . . . of the Center of Gravity" (1695). The word came to mean a moving, stirring, agitation, perturbation, and was so used in a strictly physical sense. Thus: "Thunder . . . caused so great an Emotion in the air" (1708). "The waters continuing in the caverns . . . caused the emotion or earthquake" (1758). This physical meaning was transferred to political and social agitation, the word coming to mean *tumult*, popular disturbance. Thus: "There were . . . great stirres and emocions in Lombardye" (1579). "Accounts of public Emotions, occasioned by the Want of Corn" (1709). Finally the word came to be used to designate any agitated, vehement, or excited mental state of the individual. Thus: "The joy of gratification is properly called an emotion" (1762).

We have previously observed (Chapter 2) that *hedonism*, a widely influential doctrine persisting from the time of the ancient Greeks to the present day, has held that behavior is regulated by the pleasantness or the unpleasantness of its expected or actual outcomes. These terms, *pleasantness* and *unpleasantness*, are instances of that group of affective states called feelings, which are often regarded as less intense than, but closely related to, the other group of affective states, the emotions. The feelings in hedonistic doctrine, at least, have a role in motivation.

In more precise and technical usage, however, motivation has often been held to be a term denoting processes distinct from affect. There are many reasons for this. At an earlier time, when the division of mental processes into knowing, willing, and feeling was made, affect or feeling was not given the status of an impulse to action; rather action was a result of acts of will (volition) or of striving (conation) (cf. Gardiner, Metcalf, & Beebe-Center, 1937; Ruckmick, 1936). Furthermore, affective states were often regarded mainly as transitory conscious contents, to be described introspectively or to be analyzed in terms of physiological correlates, but without reference to their connection with action. When motivational concepts came to be introduced explicitly, they consisted of animal instincts and drives often related to conditions of deprivation by which they could be defined. The drive model (see Chapter 10), while not incompatible with emotion, did not stress it, nor did the instinct model, for example, in the hands of the ethologists (Chapter 3) or of Freud (Chapter 12), even though emotional words form an important part of the psychoanalytic idiom, and though McDougall (1908), in his own instinct theory, suggested that each instinct was accompanied by a characteristic emotion.

Aspects of Emotion

There has been recognition that emotions and feelings are closely related to motivation, and most of the introductory textbooks in psychology take this view, frequently defining emotion as a process which disorganizes behavior. There has also been doubt concerning the usefulness of the affective category as a separate rubric for the classification of behavior. Bentley (1928) suggested that there are no distinguishing characteristics of emotion and that emotion is usually identified in terms of bodily reactions to the situation. Meyer (1933) argued that none of the behaviors involved in emotion—visceral, endocrine, skeletal, or nervous—was unique to it and that it was difficult, if not impossible, to draw a line between emotional and nonemotional instances of these behaviors. Duffy (1934) examined definitions of emotion and concluded that only two criteria were at all sound, and even these were most inexact: (1) type of stimulus situation [1] and (2)

[1] Duffy's emphasis on situational aspects receives confirmation from experiments reported by Schachter and Singer (1962). Indeed it can be argued from

intensity of reaction. She believed it appropriate to discard the concept (Duffy, 1941*a*), together with a number of others (Duffy, 1941*b*, 1949), and to replace it by more fundamental and measurable dimensions along which behavior can be shown to vary. Her characterization of emotion suggests the categories she would substitute for many of the concepts of psychology:

[Emotion is] . . . an adjustment made to a stimulating condition of such a kind that the adjustment involves a marked change in energy level. It involves, like other behavior, interpretation of the situation, or response to relationships. And from the goal-direction of overt behavior, or of the set for response, are derived the classificatory divisions into the particular "emotions," such as "fear" or "rage" (Duffy, 1941*a*, p. 292).

Leeper (1948) also examined the problem of the definition of emotion. Objecting to the commonly accepted textbook definition of emotion as a state of disorganization of behavior, he offered a motivational conception of emotions, one perhaps anticipated by Cannon (1927) and Jastrow (1928) and having certain features in common with Duffy's earlier considerations. Leeper's view is that:

. . . emotional processes are one of the fundamental means of motivation in the higher animals—a kind of motivation which rests on relatively complex neural activities rather than primarily on definite chemical states or definite receptor states, as in the case of bodily drives or physiological motives such as hunger, thirst, toothache, and craving for salt (Leeper, 1948, p. 19).

Leeper's argument was the occasion for a number of commentaries. Duffy (1948) pointed out that Leeper had not gone far enough in his attack, and that the important points indicated by the word emotion are the energy-arousal dimension and directionality. These dimensions characterize all behavior. Webb (1948) agreed with Leeper that emotion is a motivational term, but argued that its continued use would be justified only if some unique operations flow from it or have consequences for behavior. Waters and Blackwood (1949) examined behavioral and physiological criteria of motivation and found that emotion could fit them, although further research is needed to verify this judgment. Young (1949*a*), on the other hand, defended the notion that, at least under some conditions, emotion disorganizes behavior.

Feeling and emotion may legitimately be regarded as having something to do with motivation, but the detailed factual and theoretical

their results that the identical physiological arousal (from adrenalin) can be interpreted, depending on the person's perception of the situation, either as elation or anger.

relationships are perhaps not matters of definition, as the Leeper controversy implies,[2] but rather are dependent on the development and specification of the roles of both kinds of concepts in mediating behavior. Recent use of affective concepts has followed this course, and it is the description of these developments with which we shall be concerned in most of the rest of this chapter. In turn we shall describe hedonic theories of motivation and activation theories of emotion. Various aspects of the subjects of frustration and conflict, which words suggest an emotional implication, will be treated in Chapter 9.

HEDONIC THEORIES OF MOTIVATION

The contributions of at least three investigators and their associates may be summarized here: P. T. Young; D. C. McClelland; and Helen Peak. All of them use *affect* in some way as an important aspect of a theory of motivation, usually stressing its hedonic dimension—that of pleasantness and unpleasantness. Some features of his earlier treatment of motivation suggest that Hebb (1949) might be included here; later modifications of his viewpoint (1955, 1958) have led us to treat it as an activation theory.

Paul Thomas Young

Young has been a student of affective processes for 40 years, in both human and animal subjects. Since 1927, food preferences in rats have been the major concern of his experimentation, and the development of his hedonic theory of motivation has arisen from this work. Reviews of his extensive experimental work, as well as that of others, are presented by Young (1941, 1948a), and his theoretical considerations have been worked out in additional articles and a book (Young, 1949b, 1952, 1954, 1955, 1959, 1961). Our present concern is largely with the theoretical position Young has developed. His research is considered in Chapter 5.

Young's central thesis is that positive and negative affective states must be postulated in order to account for the various aspects of motivation—that is, the arousal, maintenance, and direction of behavior. Young (1949b, pp. 101–103) suggests eight sets of facts which indicate that food preferences are controlled by factors other than bodily need alone: (1) preferences for test foods are observed in normal, healthy rats when metabolic needs are absent. (2) Such substances as saccharin are accepted "avidly" by rats, even though such substances have no food value. (3) Characteristics of food, like the concentra-

---

[2] The paper by Brown and Farber (1951), discussed in Chapter 9, makes this point. It was the final paper in this controversy.

tion in a solution, temperature, and texture, affect the amount that will be ingested. (4) Animals may ingest foods to excess, with harmful bodily effects, when the foods are presented under optimal conditions. (5) Food selection by rats does not always reflect known bodily needs or deficiencies. (6) Toxic substances are sometimes accepted and eaten. (7) Foul odors may lead to rejection of needed medicine. (8) Habitual factors may determine choice of foodstuff and cause choice to be incompatible with bodily need.

Evidence such as this has led Young to suggest that two factors, additional to the biochemical or need state of the organism, participate in food selection: habit and the characteristics of the food itself, or its "palatability" (Young, 1949*b*, pp. 100–101).

Palatability and Affect. It is the factor of palatability which, perhaps more than anything else, has determined Young's emphasis on affective processes. Ultimately, he believes that both habit (in which would presumably be integrated another factor, the environmental surroundings of the food) and actual bodily need are closely interlinked with hedonic factors, but the palatability variable would seem to offer the prime reason for stressing hedonism. Young states it this way: ". . . the writer is basing a theory of food acceptance upon the assumption that contact between the head receptors and a food object produces an immediate affective arousal . . . there is an immediate liking or disliking, an enjoyment or disgust, with a certain degree of affective intensity" (Young, 1949*b*, p. 103). It is suggested that *needed* foods are also, ordinarily, *enjoyed* foods, so that there is a correlation, albeit an imperfect one, between bodily need and affective enjoyment.

A brief description of rat behavior, as presented by Young, may perhaps clarify what is involved in the assertion that affective processes underlie the development of food preferences. The animals in question are well nourished, free from hunger and other known metabolic need during the experiment.

In the experiment under consideration there are two groups of rats. The animals in one group are rewarded on each daily run with a nibble of sugar; those in the other group, with casein. At the start all rats spend considerable time exploring the apparatus and some of them seem to find the food quite accidentally. With practice the animals run more and more directly to the food. Occasionally a practiced rat may be seen poised at the door of the starting-box and oriented toward the food (especially with sugar). After a few days of practice there is this difference between the two groups. The animals running to sugar accept this food almost at once; they do not pause to explore . . . Their speed of locomotion in approaching the sugar steadily increases from day to day and their day-to-day variance of performance is relatively low. In contrast, the rats running to casein are slower; they delay longer before accepting the food and sometimes pause to explore before accepting it. Their performance shows less change with practice and the day-to-day variance of performance is definitely greater than that of the sugar-incentive rats. Since all experimental conditions are the same for the two groups, except the kind of food, we may conclude that the observed differences in behavior are dependent upon the kind of food offered as a reward or incentive (Young, 1949b, pp. 106–107).

In addition to the factor of food acceptance, preference, or palatability, Young points to the fact of specific hungers (see Chapter 5) as making difficulty for a theory of general hunger drive (Young, 1949b, p. 104). These findings—that animals will select a diet that meets general nutritional requirements among available foodstuffs, and, more significantly, that they will tend to select diets that make up for experimentally imposed nutritional deficiencies—are, Young thinks, not accountable for in terms of the idea of a general hunger state that affects behavior as a stimulus. Presumably, however, the affective enjoyment conception could accommodate these findings.

Young's Theory of Motivation. These phenomena of food preference and specific hunger suggest to Young the following formulation as a theory of motivation.

[When] a practiced rat is placed on the apparatus there is redintegrated a preparatory set. Along with this there is a proprioceptive tension associated with the preparation to run to food. The proprioceptive tension . . . is a persistent motivation within the food oriented rat. Persistent drive stimulation comes from the muscles, tendons, and perhaps the joints, when a specific foodseeking determination has been activated by the environmental situation. This proprioceptive tension, we assume, is greater in the running-to-sugar drive than in the running-to-casein drive (Young, 1949b, p. 107).

Underlying this proprioceptive tension is an "acquired neural organization," based on the affective experiences, which carries over temporally within the animal and can redintegrate the set to run for food in a particular situation; the neural organization is "organized to continue enjoyment and to relieve distress" (Young, 1949b, p. 111).

Although relief from distress is perhaps similar to the drive or tension-reduction conception of reinforcement, Young (1954) insists that such relief is only half the picture and that a positive enjoyment, perhaps sometimes involving tension increment, can be "rewarding." However, he would tend to emphasize the role of enjoyment and relief from distress only in terms of "organizing and disorganizing of patterns of response" (1949b, p. 112), that is, the acquired neural or neural-muscular set or determination, and he would not include this kind of change in his concept of learning. He regards learning as "the fixation of organized *response patterns* through exercise" (1949*b*, p. 112, italics added). For him "the laws of learning are entirely laws of exercise, practice or training. . . . Affective arousal is related primarily to the organizing and disorganizing of psychological processes. If an organized response is made, to prolong enjoyment or relieve distress, this organized response leaves after it some neural trace. This neural trace is fixated by exercise rather than by affective processes" (1949*b*, p. 116). Affective intensity and degree of practice regulate the strength of instigation toward a particular food and regulate food preferences.

Young's formulations derive primarily from the work on food preference and selection carried out by himself and others, but he has reinterpreted Miller's work on "fear" (Young, 1955) in affective terms and has shown a considerable interest in the work of Olds (1955) on reward centers in the brain as perhaps related to the affective processes he has postulated.

Comment. It seems clear that the empirical work on which Young predicates his theory is an important body of fact that must be dealt with by any theory of motivation. (We reviewed some of this work in Chapter 5.) However, the fundamental theoretical difficulty lies in the identification of affective processes. Young himself (1952, p. 253) admits that there is no independent means of assessing affective reaction, but he believes that this can be done through the study of temporal organizing of behavior patterns. Even here, however, there is no compelling reason to postulate an affective process; that is, there is no independent evidence of affective process, only the behavior which affective process is postulated to explain. It is clear that food selection and preference are closely linked to past learning experiences. It is not impossible that some theory of secondary reinforcement or even of differential primary reinforcement based on need or characteristics of foodstuffs could be developed to deal with these phenomena. Admittedly, such a theory has not been developed to date (however, see Spence, 1956, 1960, and Chapter 10). The existence of potential alternative explanations, however, detracts from the cogency of the affective process formulation.[3]

---

[3] Relevant to these points are the experiments reported by Miller and his associates on the role of oral factors in food intake (Chapter 5). There is at least some evidence that experience may be involved in the reinforcing effects of oral stimulation and specific hunger.

David C. McClelland and Associates

A point of view in motivation, quite similar to the one presented by Young but arising in a different context, has been developed by McClelland and his co-workers. This group has been concerned mainly with the study of the need for achievement and other needs in human beings—their arousal, measurement, and effects. In this work they have followed Freud and, more specifically, H. A. Murray in using fantasy as their measure of motivation, and the logic of the study of animal drive in attempting experimentally to arouse and to satiate motives. In the course of this research attention has, of course, been directed to the problem of a theory of motivation. The theory McClelland and his co-workers have developed is neither compelled by nor directly derived from their data, but it is presumably consistent with the data. We shall here be concerned only with the theory as presented by McClelland (1951, pp. 466–475; reprinted in McClelland, 1955a, pp. 226–234) and his associates (McClelland et al., 1953, pp. 27–96), leaving until later a discussion of the techniques for measurement, the correlates of need achievement and its relationships to other behaviors (Chapter 14). In this chapter we will examine, however, evidence related to basic theoretical assumptions.

Nature of Motives. In this theory, all motives are considered to be learned. A motive is defined (McClelland et al., 1953, p. 28) as *"the redintegration by a cue of a change in an affective situation."* An earlier, perhaps more understandable definition (McClelland, 1951, p. 466) is that a motive is *"a strong affective association, characterized by an anticipatory goal reaction and based on past association of certain cues with pleasure or pain."* What these definitions appear to mean may be indicated as follows. Let us suppose that a man is experiencing a very pleasant affect or emotion. While this experience is occurring, he is also receiving various stimuli or cues from his environment, his body, his thoughts, and his emotional state itself. Through this contiguous occurrence with the emotion, any one or more of these stimuli or cues may become associated with the emotional state; that is, they can, on later occasions, reactivate some part of it.[4] This fractional reactivation of the emotional state is apparently motivating; that is, the man will now engage in instrumental activities which will

[4] McClelland is very careful to indicate that the cues cannot reactivate the entire emotional state. If they did, of course, there would presumably be no motivation, since the cues would arouse the goal state. Also, it is evident from conditioning literature that the conditioned response does not usually duplicate the unconditioned reaction (cf. Hilgard & Marquis, 1940).

bring him to approach the circumstance under which he experienced the pleasant affect or emotion. If the emotion had been unpleasant, cues likewise could redintegrate some of this state leading him away from commerce with the situation which would fully reproduce it (avoidance). One further essential point is that the redintegrated affect must represent a *change* from present affect; a person is presumably not motivated to approach or avoid a situation in which he is already present or which would not produce or have the potential for producing a positive or a negative affective change.

While the foregoing example has implied the redintegration of affective change by means of an external cue, it is not necessary, or perhaps even typical, that solely external cues be involved. Cues arising in one's own behavior—his thought processes, for example, or in an affective state itself—may be sufficient. For example, thinking of some past event, remembering an occasion on which one secured pleasure from reading, for instance, would perhaps partly reinstate the affect and possibly lead to the search for something to read with the anticipation that reading will restore the original pleasant state, or one similar to it. We should point out that since revivifying the entire original affective state would not lead to action, reliving pleasure in fantasy alone would presumably not be a motivated state. In a state of some negative affect, fear (the redintegrated portion of negative affect) may be aroused and lead to avoidance responses; these will prevent the further full development of negative affect, say, by causing the individual to leave the situation.[5]

From the foregoing discussion it follows that motivated behavior is that behavior which falls on the dimension of approach-avoidance or appetite-anxiety. This is stated by McClelland et al. (1953, p. 39) as follows, ". . . only when the succession (of responses) becomes a sequence which results in approach to or avoidance of a situation can we argue that there is evidence for the existence of a motive." In many instances, behavior may not *apparently* show approach or avoidance characteristics, but at base it must reflect these tendencies in order to indicate the existence of a motive. Another way of saying this is that approach or avoidance must be involved, *genotypically*, no matter what the behavior may appear to be, phenotypically speaking.

Why Affective Process? The McClelland group was led to choose affective processes as fundamental to motivation for a number of reasons. One was negative. They found the drive model, especially in view of its stimulus or tension-reduction implication, inconsistent with

[5] There is a striking relationship between this formulation and the one presented by Mowrer (see Chapter 10), which emphasizes hope and fear.

motivation to obtain (and to be rewarded from receiving) moderate increases in stimulation. Otherwise, they felt that affective processes are "obviously" quite important to motivation, a point reflected by the long history of the hedonistic principle. Also they believe that affect as the basis for "motivational associations" would permit a distinction between motivational and *other* associations. The McClelland group holds direction, not arousal, of behavior to be the proper function of motivation, and permits unmotivated associations—that is, those with no affective element. Further, it seems that they wished to accord to external stimuli or cues a role in motivation greater than that usually suggested in a drive model. In this desire they parallel Young's emphasis on palatability as a characteristic of food and Tinbergen's (1951, see Chapter 3) emphasis on the releasing function of stimuli. This last point is indicated in their statement that perhaps man's reactions to "releasing" stimuli are attenuated and occur ". . . as diffuse reactions of the autonomic nervous system signifying . . . affect" (McClelland et al., 1953, p. 31).

Indicators of Affective Process. How may affective processes be identified? Are there signs suggested by these authors which would permit the identification of affective states independently of the kinds of behavior they are postulated to explain? (Cf. p. 373.) On the response side, they suggest that indicators of activity in the autonomic nervous system (respiratory changes, blood pressure, skin resistance, etc.) may identify the *presence* of affect though not whether it is pleasant or unpleasant. In this they agree with activation theorists and the traditional ways of studying emotions. However, expressive movements, verbal statements of liking or disliking, certain innate response and reflex patterns (e.g., purring, tail wagging, sucking, grasping), and *learned* approach and avoidance responses are additional sources of evidence permitting the inference of positive or negative affect.

Admittedly, none of these indicators is a completely satisfactory means of identifying positive or negative affect. However, an attempt is also made to offer suggestions on the conditions antecedent to affective arousal, which conditions are similar to those suggested by Hebb (1949; also Troland, 1928). It is postulated that primary, unlearned affect arises from "discrepancies between expectation (adaptation level) and perception . . ." (McClelland et al., 1953, p. 28). What this suggests is that if the events that happen to you are what you expect—for example, if the sights and sounds stimulating you do not deviate appreciably from the sights and sounds you are accustomed to —you will not react affectively or emotionally. However, if these stimuli deviate by some magnitude from expectation, you will react with affect; then the cues associated with the occurrence of this affect may at some later time redintegrate some of it, and a motive will be in action.

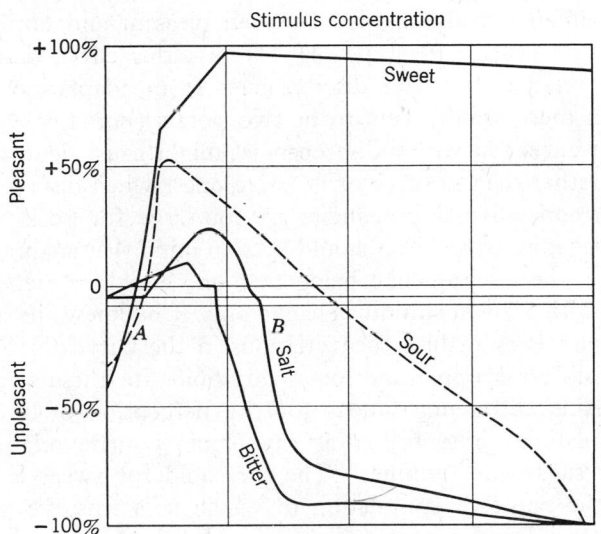

Figure 8–1. Judgments of pleasantness and unpleasantness in relation to concentrations in solution of cane sugar, tartaric acid (sour), salt, and quinine sulfate (bitter). The ordinate gives per cent of "pleasant" judgments minus per cent of "unpleasant" judgments. The data are from Engel (1928) and are reproduced by permission as shown in Woodworth (1938, p. 498).

Whether the affect arising from discrepancies will be positive or negative is a function of the *size* of the discrepancy. Relatively small discrepancies from expectation or adaptation level (AL) [6] yield positive affect, whereas large discrepancies give rise to negative affect or unpleasantness. This argument applies to all instances of expectations and perceptions, although it is easiest to illustrate and to understand in a relatively simple sensory example, such as preferences for salt solutions of varying concentrations (see Fig. 8–1).

In this figure, the curve for judgments of the varying concentrations of the salt solution is illustrative of the postulated relation between discrepancies from adaptation level and positive and negative affect.

[6] See treatment of Helson's theory of adaptation level in Chapter 7. McClelland and his co-workers acknowledge the influence of Helson's work.

A solution with a very slight concentration of salt is affectively neutral, but as the concentration increases the preponderance of the judgments is pleasant. With further increases of concentration, however, the judgments pass from a preponderance of pleasant to a preponderance of unpleasant, passing through a zone of "neutrality" where the judgments are about equally divided between pleasant and unpleasant. If, as McClelland et al. (1953, pp. 43–44) say, this curve describes the postulated relation between discrepancies from adaptation level and affect, then there would seem to be two points (noted as A and B on Engel's salt curve) at which discrepancies might cause neutral affective reactions, rather than positive or negative ones: when discrepancies are very slight and when discrepancies are too large for positive but too small for negative affect. We should keep in mind that adaptation levels can change, the consequence being that one could predict the affect associated with a given stimulus change only if he knew the adaptation level as well.[7] Presumably, the variations in the curves in Figure 8–1 arise from differing upper and lower thresholds for these solutions and from differing difference limens for the perception of a change in these stimulations. The following comment is made relative to the curves for sugar and quinine: "The threshold for sweet is relatively high and the range of stimulation to which it is sensitive sufficiently narrow so that large discrepancies from AL which probably lies near the threshold are impossible. With bitter the threshold is so low that small fractions of the maximum concentration . . . still represent fairly large discrepancies from an AL near the threshold" (McClelland et al., 1953, pp. 44–45).

The AL sensory-event discrepancy must persist for a time to produce a hedonic reaction, and the size of the discrepancy required to produce a hedonic response may be considerably larger than the size required to produce a just-noticeable difference in sensory discrimination. The AL, also, "must be built up to a certain minimum level of stability through successive experiences . . . before discrepancies from it will produce affect" (1953, p. 48). Further, in instances in which events can differ from AL in more than one way, discrepancies in either direction from the adaptation level will generate, as a function of size, a positive-negative affect continuum. Somatic processes (e.g., salt hunger) and experience can produce changes in the AL. There are presumably many dimensions, especially in adult human beings, on which events can

[7] Thus sheer stimulus intensity is not a good indicator of affective level nor could it be definitive of motivation. This is an important difference from Dollard and Miller (1950, see Chapter 10), who define a motive or drive in terms of (apparently) the absolute physical strength of stimuli.

vary from expectation; the sensory examples we have used do not begin to exhaust the possibilities. It is believed, for example, that even in rats some of the variability in their performances arises *in order to* introduce "uncertainty" relative to expectation (McClelland et al., 1953, p. 62). The thesis here is that continued confirmation of highly probable expectations is boring, whereas some uncertainty concerning an expectation permits, on confirmation, a sufficient affective change to qualify as pleasure. Unpleasantness should follow confirmation of a highly improbable expectation or, presumably, failure to confirm a highly certain expectation. On their face, by the way, these last two cases seem improbable. If one's Irish Sweepstakes ticket is the winning one, there is the confirmation of a highly unlikely expectation, which should presumably make one unhappy because of the marked disconfirmation of an expectancy. Similarly, though conversely, the condemned man who receives a last-minute reprieve also has the widest change in his expectancies of the events of the immediate future. Yet his reaction is probably not an unpleasant one.

The notion that the *certainty* or *uncertainty* of the confirmation of an expectation may be closely tied to affective states is especially prominent in the treatment of conflict and frustration and of need for achievement. Brown and Farber (1951; see Chapter 9) consider frustration as a drive state arising from competition of response tendencies. McClelland et al. (1953, p. 63) would regard frustration as a negative affective state but would agree with Brown and Farber in many respects:

". . . we too would argue that the more nearly equal in strength two response tendencies are, the more they would give rise to negative affect (F); because such competition means that if either response is made, the expectation based on the other is not confirmed; or that if neither is made, both are unconfirmed. Similarly, the effects of nonconfirmation should be greater, the greater the strength of the response tendency."

However, unlike Brown and Farber they would expect "that when the size of the discrepancy between the stronger and weaker response tendencies is large, there should be a stage when the competition of the weaker response tendency should give rise not to frustration but to pleasure, if the stronger tendency is confirmed." This would require a change in Brown and Farber's formula for frustration (see Chapter 9).

As to achievement, one "must continually work with more and more complex objects or situations permitting mastery, since, if he works long enough at any particular level of mastery, his expectations and their confirmation will become certain and he will get bored" (Mc-Clelland et al., 1953, p. 64). Level of intelligence is obviously related to this point, and there is also a danger of producing negative affect from attempting achievement on tasks which are beyond the person's ability to perform; achievement situations, on the basis of this kind of experience, could be avoided rather than approached.

It is believed that the dimensions on which adaptation levels and confirmation or disconfirmation of expectancies can be attained at the human level are so numerous and complex as to provide for high level and highly individual motives, the expression of some of which could involve "taking" pain at one level in order to experience pleasure at another.

Learning of Motives. The factors responsible for the learning of motives are the "laws of learning," that is, presumably, contiguity and frequency of occurrence of cues with the affective state they will redintegrate. (The law of effect is not involved, in this view.) Three dimensions are suggested for the strength of motives: their dependability, intensity, and extensity. Dependability is indicated by the probability that a motive will arise in reference to a cue, and it derives from the frequency of association of cue with affect, the degree of their continuity, and the rate of affective change. Intensity arises from the magnitude or extent of the affective change, and it is indicated by features of the choice response such as response magnitude, rate, latency, or speed. Extensity means essentially the variety of cues that can arouse the motive or the degree of resistance to extinction of the appropriate choice response, and it derives from the variety of cues acting at the time of affective change and therefore connected with it.

The reader may have wondered earlier at the bold assertion of this group that all motives are learned, when it is quite clear that biological conditions, arising from deprivation, are closely associated with motivation. "Biological drives" *are* learned, on this theory, and they are highly dependable motives. In "hunger," for example, there is no motive until the cues of hunger (and other related cues) are associated with the pleasure derived from eating and obtaining visceral relief. These associations are formed very early in life and occur quite regularly in any individual who survives for long, since one must eat in order to live. So both external and internal cues are capable of arousing the hunger motive with great dependability. Longer periods of food deprivation elicit stronger and stronger hunger motivation either because with greater hunger there is a higher probability of very pleasurable affective change or because the increasing insistence of the cues arising from continuing deprivation elicits hunger with greater certainty, regularity, and dominance.] McClelland and his associates believe this kind of thinking to be applicable also to the other biological "motive" states and that such phenomena in hunger as the value of prefeeding an animal before a maze run or the "salted nut phenomenon" can be understood as the release by cues of anticipations of further affective enjoyment.[8] There is then no distinction between primary and secondary (learned) motives or drives.

The occurrence of a primary reward eventually, if not at once, disrupts the motive; this is because reward changes either the hedonic adaptation level or the cues that release affective change. "Secondary rewards" are simply cues that evoke an anticipated change in affect and thus arouse a motive; they are not different from other cues which have the same property and are not substitutes for actual primary reward. In fact, they do not seem to be regarded in this theory as rewards at all. The phenomena in learning which are regarded as requiring the postulation of the "empirical law of effect" are dealt with on the assumption that if the anticipated affective change (the motive) is itself pleasurable, then "the animal will learn to perform those acts which cue off the affective change state most dependably" (McClelland et al., 1953, p. 92). Responses close to the goal, of course, are those most dependably related to the positive affect resulting from commerce with the goal; hence such responses should be most readily and rapidly learned, producing a sort of goal gradient effect. This argument is, essentially, that while contiguity governs the formation of associations, "the anticipation of affective change . . . somehow *weights* or gives precedence to [one] associative chain so that it tends to continue and grow stronger until it erupts into action" (McClelland et al., 1953, p. 94). This is not a two-factor theory of learning, although associations mediated by the central nervous system are seen as perhaps more often instrumental in character, whereas those involving the autonomic nervous system are considered motivational in nature.

Motives are defined and classified in the McClelland system primarily in terms of the expectations, and secondarily in terms of the results of action. Motives common to a species will develop in the case and "to the extent that conditions can be identified which will give rise regularly to affective change either through biological or cultural arrangements" (McClelland et al., 1953, p. 77). Our analysis of hunger, just presented, illustrates how biological conditions foster the development of a common motive for those who survive. If a culture provides

[8] The discussion of incentive motivation (Chapter 10) contains parallels to these notions.

common expectations and standards of evaluation of performance which are widely applied by parents to their offspring, then a common motive is likely to develop, even in the absence of a strictly biological basis. The need for achievement is an illustration for our culture as it probably involves affective reaction to evaluation of performance. It is perfectly clear, of course, as it is for any theory that stresses the idea that motives are learned by individuals in their interactions with the environment, that there could be highly unique motives in individuals as well as unique elements in the shared motives.

Comment. A viewpoint which breaks with the traditional nature of drive theory must command attention, because, as we indicate in Chapters 5, 10, and 11, there are a number of problems with the drive viewpoint. Further, the emphasis on affective processes is significant, since the stress in acquired drive theory has shifted to emotional responses (see Chapter 11). Similarly, stress on the elicitation by cues of an anticipation of an affective change leading to approach or avoidance seems similar, in outline, at any rate, to the developing emphasis on the incentive value of stimuli—an emphasis present in recent developments in the motivational aspects of learning and behavior theory (see Chapter 10). The resemblance of the McClelland conceptions to those of Young, Peak, and Hebb assures us that the notion is not a wild shot in the dark, unsupported by congruence with other views.

It remains to be seen, however, whether McClelland and his co-workers have found a solution to the problem of independent identification of pleasantness and unpleasantness, a problem which Young, another hedonic theorist, has not solved. That pleasantness and unpleasantness correspond to deviations by particular amounts from the adaptation level has not figured prominently in past theories of these affective reactions (Beebe-Center, 1932; Gardiner, Metcalf, & Beebe-Center, 1937; W. A. Hunt, 1939, 1941; Peters, 1942; Woodworth, 1938). On the other hand, some relation between pleasantness and unpleasantness and stimulus intensity (but without apparent reference to adaptation level) was suggested by Wundt (1902, pp. 311–312; cf. Beebe-Center, 1932, p. 166; Ruckmick, 1936, p. 46). Wundt presented a schematic diagram which showed the intensity of sensation to be a negatively accelerated increasing function of stimulus intensity; on the same schematic graph he showed affective reaction to be indifferent at the absolute threshold for stimulus intensity, to shift quickly to a maximum of pleasantness as stimulus intensity increases and then, as stimulus intensity increases still further, to pass from the maximum of pleasantness through another zone of indifference to degrees of unpleasantness.

Beebe-Center (1932, pp. 166–177) reviews four experiments which pertain to this suggested function. All of them show results that agree, in a general way, with Wundt's scheme. However, there is no unequivocal support for the second point of indifference, that is, the area of transition between stimulus intensities that yield judgments of pleasantness and those higher intensities that are judged unpleasant. Beebe-Center suggests "the possibility that the function relating hedonic tone to intensity of stimulation is discontinuous . . ." (Beebe-Center, 1932, pp. 176–177).

In none of these experiments (which include the one by Engel, 1928, some of the results of which are shown in Fig. 8–1),[9] however, has there apparently been a direct test of the critical feature of the McClelland hypothesis: that pleasantness and unpleasantness correspond to deviations *from the adaptation level*. In Engel's experiment, for example, the judgments of all concentrations of the four sapid substances were presumably made from the same "zero point" or adaptation level. Apparently no systematic control was exerted over the AL's with which the observers began their judgments; the AL at the beginning was established by whatever experiences of everyday life the observer had encountered before starting the experimental session.

A recent investigation by Haber (1958) was explicitly designed to study affective judgments as a function of the deviation of temperature stimuli from the prevailing AL. Haber presents a hypothetical graph of the expected relationship between affect and AL, shown in Figure 8–2. He tested for this hypothetical relationship by having eight subjects first adapt both hands in water of a given temperature (it was assumed that AL was reached when the subject said the water felt neutral or yielded no temperature sensation). Then the subjects placed both hands

---

[9] The plot of Fig. 8–1 represents the number of judgments of pleasant minus the number of unpleasant judgments. Where the frequency of these two classes of judgments is about equal, the resulting sum approximates zero, and our prior discussion has implied that such values represent "indifference." This may be justified statistically, but in fact the indifference points so generated do not correspond well to the points where *actual judgments* of indifference predominate. For example, when judging the pleasantness and unpleasantness of concentrations of tartaric acid (sour), judgments of indifference and of doubt were made. At the point of concentration at which about as many pleasant judgments as unpleasant judgments were made (the point of statistical indifference since pleasant and unpleasant judgments cancel out), *there were no actual judgments of indifference.* Almost all of the actual judgments of indifference were made for low concentrations (Engel, 1928, Figs. 4, 11, and 12.) Such evidence may mean, for the individual observer, that affective judgment above minimal concentrations is either pleasant or unpleasant. It also points to marked individual differences in affective judgments, a finding stressed by Beebe-Center (1932) throughout his review.

simultaneously in different buckets which contained water of other temperatures (both temperatures deviating, if at all, in the same direction from AL). No indifferent reports were allowed, and the subject "reported" by removing his hand from the water that felt less pleasant. A set of preference "judgments" was thus obtained, for stimuli deviating in steps from AL compared with each other as well as with stimuli at AL.

Haber's data seem to verify the hypothetical relationship (the "butterfly" curve) of Figure 8–2. Plots of judgments for the stimuli for five subjects showed a preference for thermal stimuli which deviated +1 degree from AL and showed for three a preference for a +3 degree discrepancy, when the stimuli to be judged were warmer than the AL; all subjects tested preferred a −1 degree discrepancy when the deviations were colder than the AL. The preference curves fell regularly for stimulus values on either side of these maxima. These findings pertained to an AL set near skin temperature. Observations were also made on three subjects in whom AL's were established at several temperatures above skin temperature. In these cases the raising of AL from 33 degrees C. (skin temperature) to 35 degrees C. caused no change in the discrepancy preferred, but at higher AL the preferred "discrepancy" changed and finally reached the zero discrepancy value. With still further increases in AL temperature "the affect curve decreased in a linear fashion as discrepancy from AL increased further" (Haber, 1958, p. 374).

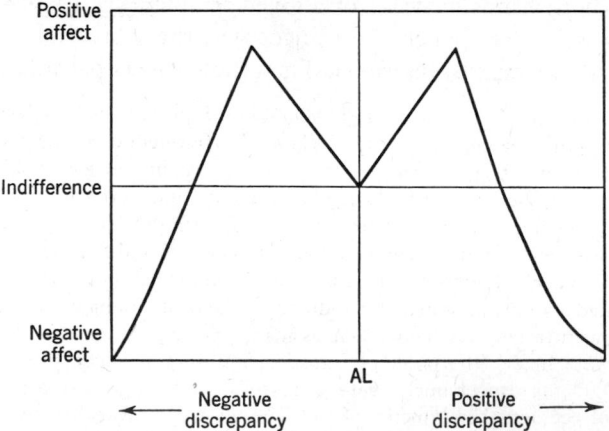

Figure 8–2. Hypothetical relations between judgments of "pleasant," "neutral," and "unpleasant" affect to deviations of stimulation from the Adaptation Level (AL). Reproduced by permission from Haber (1958, p. 371).

Haber's results are an encouraging verification of the supposition that pleasant and unpleasant judgments relate to deviations from adaptation level. It may be observed that hedonic judgment has been shown to vary in relation to many characteristics of stimuli and observers. Whether all such variations can be ordered by the McClelland hypothesis yet remains to be seen. Some of these other dimensions on which hedonic tone has been shown to vary (Beebe-Center, 1932) are saturation of colors, hue, contrast of colors, area of the stimulus, and sequence of stimuli (time-error).

A further point on this whole matter troubles the authors, although its validity must somehow be subjected to empirical scrutiny. This concerns the fact that most of the experiments on hedonic tone involve very mild affective reactions which have a large "cognitive" component. This problem can only be registered at the present time, rather than settled, but elsewhere we have treated viewpoints whose motives are regarded as powerful, turbulent emotions and drives rather than as mild affective reactions. Can the latter serve as a basis for the former?

Experimental results which at least superficially seem not to fit well into the McClelland model are those which deal with a change in incentive (see Chapter 11). Zeaman's (1949) study may serve as an example. Zeaman ran rats in a three-foot runway and measured starting time or latency. One group of animals was run to a 0.05-gram food reward and the other to a 2.4 gram food reward. Runs to these rewards continued until performance in each group was stable (asymptotic). Then the reward was shifted in both groups, from 0.05 to 2.4 grams in one group and from 2.4 to 0.05 grams in the other group. Presumably, both groups had reached an AL, though different ones, and the size of the change from AL in both was 1.9 grams. Performance, however, was affected in opposite ways. The group whose food reward was increased speeded up markedly, while the group whose reward was decreased slowed down markedly. If running speed can be taken as an indicator of "pleasure," this result seems to mean that only the first group was "pleased" by the change from AL. Yet both groups had a change identical in magnitude from their respective AL's.

There are many things obviously wrong with this interpretation of Zeaman's experiment. The groups must have had different initial AL's, but we do not know that the equal changes in reward magnitudes are equal psychologically in any sense, let alone when they occur from different initial AL's. So the analysis just made may be inappropriate and irrelevant. It illustrates, however, the difficulty of applying McClelland's interpretation to existing data, and, in some ways, considering this experiment gives the whole hypothesis some degree of implausibility. Can we ever conceive, for a hungry rat, that decrease in food reward (from AL) would be pleasurable? Such a conception might not, of course, actually derive from the theory, but specific and limited assumptions would probably have to be invoked in order to invalidate it. It may be that disappointment is psychologically very different from surprise at good luck. If so, the symmetry of the "butterfly" curve would be invalidated.

Similar kinds of reservations arise from study of results of experiments that have employed the level of aspiration (see Chapter 15; Lewin et al., 1944). The affective reactions in the level of aspiration situation, which perhaps parallel pleasantness and unpleasantness, are feelings of success and failure. These feelings do depend on standards derived from one's own performance or from that of others, about which one has been told or which one has seen. However, we have the impression that, for most people, any achievement which exceeds expectation, no matter what its amount, is accompanied by feelings of success (and by a raising of the level of aspiration), whereas any failure to perform up to expectation is regarded (by most people) as failure and is accompanied by a lowering of the level of aspiration. A "butterfly" curve is not an obvious outcome here. While it is not impossible, perhaps, to use McClelland's theory to account for such findings, such an account must probably and necessarily involve at present complex and *ad hoc* assumptions. Only further development and application of the theory to such complex cases as these and evaluation by various empirical tests can indicate whether the foundation assumption of the McClelland theory—that pleasant and unpleasant affect relate to size of deviation from expectation—is a valid and useful one.

Helen Peak

A point of view emphasizing affective processes, but in a way different from the use of Young and McClelland, has been outlined by Helen Peak (1955).[10] Although primarily concerned with attitudes she felt the need to outline a conception of motivation, because of the intimate connections of these concepts.

Peak dispenses with the notion of motive as a push or drive (1955, p. 160) and suggests that persistence of behavior to a goal and the direction of behavior (discrimination and choice) are the chief properties or functions of motivation.

[10] For other aspects of her formulation, see Peak (1958a, b). McReynolds (1956) has offered a theory of motives that seems to have similarities to Peak's, as well as to McClelland's and Festinger's (see, for the latter, Chapter 15).

Nature of Motives. The persistence and intensity of behavior appear to arise "when disparity exists between two or more psychological events or states which are associated and therefore mutually activating" (Peak, 1955, p. 162). The two events out of which a motive structure arises must be "seen at once as disparate and as similar in some way . . . the resultant uncertainty of coding and of reacting may be thought of as a source of persistence and intensity of the resulting behavior" (Peak, 1955, p. 163). Disparity may arise in nonaffective situations, as when the intensity of a sound differs from the adaptation-level, and hence "commands" attention. If the stimulus cannot readily be categorized or compared with the AL, "attention will tend to continue until it is so categorized" (Peak, 1955, p. 164). Disparity may exist in many dimensions and will lead to (i.e., motivate) searching and exploring. In such instances, affect is not the cause of, though it may result from, the disparity.

More often, however, a differential in affect also occurs in the motive system. ". . . the terms of the disparity itself involve affective loading. Thus Harry's feeling about his present job is less positive than his feeling for the ideal job he imagines. This involves disparity in affect" (Peak, 1955, p. 166). Two attitudes, involving different affective loading, may be set in relation to each other and produce a motive structure. One is motivated away from present conditions if, relative to some other conditions, he has "some expectation with a different affective loading from the one prevailing . . ." (Peak, 1955, p. 166). When positive and negative attitudes exist toward the same object, there is conflict and tension (by definition, attitudes involve affective reactions to their referents).

In Peak's conception, it is the discrepancy, not the affect (as in the theories of Young and McClelland), that is the source of persistence and intensity of behavior. Affect, however, determines the direction of behavior. In addition to discrepancy, other features are required in a motive structure. One is that the two or more terms or processes must be associated, that is, be in psychological contact. This apparently means that they must be seen as related or as belonging in the same framework, as, for example, to the "self." Thus, "when disparity occurs between perceptions and attitudes about the self, motivation is likely to be set up" (Peak, 1955, p. 169),[11] but if the subject, let us say, sees no relevance to him in some remark made by another person, he will not be motivated by it.[12]

[11] This appears to be somewhat similar to the affective-motivational role that Sherif and Cantril (1947) gave to "ego attitudes."

[12] Cf., also, Lewin's (1935) concept of "Psychological Environment."

These disparate but related processes will contribute to motivation only so long as there is a balance between forces to keep them together and forces to isolate them. If Harry's ideal job is a dream, which he isolates completely from the reality of his present situation, he will presumably not be motivated to change; on the other hand, if, through time, the ideal job is modified to resemble the present one, he will not be motivated either. This example illustrates what we take Peak to mean when she says (1955, p. 170) that the two states will mutually activate each other "only so long as there is a certain balance between the pressures to maintain contact (assimilation) and to break contact (isolation)" and that "motivation should be maximal when the pressures to assimilation and isolation are equal . . ." [13]

Peak seems to feel that activity and anxiety will be produced as a function of degree of disparity of two psychological states; sometimes they are good indices of the state of motivation, that is, when the motive persists through failure of satisfaction.

Role of Affect. Peak suggests that the direction of behavior—that is, what responses will occur—will be determined on "the history and present state of the relations between the motive structure and the possible alternative responses . . . a frequency-contiguity principle in some form and at least an 'empirical law of effect' must be involved in determining the direction which action takes" (Peak, 1955, p. 176). The subject's attitude, that is, his affective loading toward acts, will also enter in determining what acts will take place; affect, especially positive affect (or attitude), "has the effect of emphasizing [acts or objects] . . . with the result that their probability of activation and of choice and selection is increased" (Peak, 1955, p. 178). However, Peak does not believe that all acts serve the ends of positive and negative affect; reflexes and highly practiced acts are cases in point. Most often, however, "we act toward positive ends, even though we may on occasion reduce our motives by accepting the less positive of two states in a disparity relation. . . . motivation persists until the motive system is disrupted. This is tension reduction. At the same time, acts and goals are chosen and *direction* taken as a function of affective consequences" (Peak, 1955, p. 179).

Comment. Peak's formulation is not very full or complete and fails to deal with many details essential to the understanding and evaluation of her theory. It is of interest, though, that she has chosen disparity in psychological processes as the basic aspect of motivation and has used affect primarily as the basis of the direction of behavior. In these

[13] Relevant here would appear to be much of the work on level of aspiration. See Lewin et al. (1944).

formulations, especially in the former one, she has considerably altered the usual way in which we have thought of motivation—in a manner similar to Festinger's notion of cognitive dissonance (Chapter 15). Unfortunately, as she herself indicates, her viewpoint is not an easy one to translate into terms concrete enough to permit investigation. If this deficiency can be remedied, and if a fuller statement of her viewpoint is developed (for example, she says nothing about hunger and thirst), her theory would merit serious consideration. This is because, as indicated in several footnotes, many of the things she has said suggest an integration of certain concepts of Lewin (1935) and of Sherif and Cantril (1947), as well as the extensive data on the level of aspiration (Lewin et al., 1944). Also, there are relations between her ideas and the conflict model described in our next chapter.

Summary of Hedonic Theories

The role of emotion and feeling as factors in motivation languished when these terms were taken largely to denote conscious states, but in contemporary theorizing these concepts are being integrated into motivational theory. In the next section of this chapter we will deal with emotion. So far we have dealt mainly with affect. Young has argued that affective factors underlie food preferences, which are manifested in animals that are not hungry. From this evidence he suggests that affective enjoyment (and probably its converse) is a general process which may organize, direct, and energize a variety of other behaviors. Unfortunately, he offers no way to identify and assess affective factors independently of the behaviors they are proposed to explain.

McClelland regards all motives as learned approach-avoidance tendencies. Approach is undertaken when a cue triggers off an anticipation that positive affect will be experienced in the situation, which the cue signifies; avoidance will occur when the cue arouses an anticipation of unpleasantness from further commerce with the situation. Positive affect arises from small while negative affect results from large deviations from AL. While this formulation, as does Young's, faces formidable problems in its further development and testing, it represents an intriguing departure from some of the theoretical ideas long prevalent concerning motivation.

Peak has suggested that a disparity relation between two related psychological events is the source of motivation. The behavior so activated persists until the desparity is resolved. Peak makes use of affect, but, unlike its role in the theories of Young and of McClelland, her role for affect is not a motivational one. Rather, affect determines the direction of behavior, that is, what responses will occur. It is the likely affective consequences of actions that select what ones will occur.

There are perhaps three major things that should be emphasized in these treatments. One, of course, is their use of affect and another is their emphasis on disparity. The third is not so obvious. It is that motivation is largely seen as a cue-related or as an event-related affair, rather than as a factor arising from drive. We will expand this comment in our final chapter. It is noteworthy that disparity figures in other motivational theories, for example, Festinger's (see Chapter 15) and that something akin to cue-released affect is assuming increasing importance in theories of incentives. Incentives, rather than drives, may well be the chief content of the field of motivation in the future. In Chapters 9 and 10, as well as in 16, these points are elaborated in the discussions of the work of Amsel, Spence, Mowrer, Seward, and others.

ACTIVATION THEORY OF EMOTIONS

While *feelings* like pleasantness and unpleasantness have long been linked to motivation in the hedonistic principle, *emotions* as such have, until recently, received little emphasis in relation to motivation.[14] As mentioned earlier, McDougall (1908) linked a characteristic emotional state with each of the instincts he postulated, but the instinct itself was regarded as the "prime mover." As was pointed out elsewhere, words denotative of emotions figure importantly in the lexicon of psychoanalysis and in the treatments of secondary motives in the drive model. Yet it would seem that perhaps both psychoanalysis and the drive model place such emotions in a status secondary to instinct and drive, respectively, with the possible exception of fear or anxiety which receives major emphasis in both viewpoints; however, even fear or anxiety has a somewhat secondary role, in that it is derived from painful experiences and serves as a sort of control factor (especially in classical psychoanalysis) over the expression of other motivational processes. In his chapter on the antecedents of dynamic psychology, Boring (1950) gives little stress to emotion as such, although he does point out the role of hedonism in dynamic formulations and, of course, indicates McDougall's usage of emotion and a few other instances. Troland (1928), in his review of earlier doctrines of motivation, gives little attention to specific concern with emotions as such as motivational processes, except for hedonism and McDougall's formulations.

Early Theories of Emotion. Until the last few years, the two dominant theories of emotional processes have been the James-Lange theory

[14] See Mandler (1962).

and Cannon's thalamic or emergency theory.[15] The James-Lange theory concerns the *experience* of emotion and stresses the idea that emotion is an *effect* of bodily processes aroused by a situation. Thus, having experienced a situation to which running is a response, we run. And running, together with other skeletal and visceral responses, causes the conscious experience of fear, as weeping causes sorrow. While this provocative doctrine has served as a stimulus to much research, it has generally been found wanting in full verification.[16] More importantly, to us, it is clear that emotion is conceived largely as a conscious experience and as an effect of responses that are aroused or released by other factors. Emotion, as such, on this theory, can have little to do with motivation; it is an effect of behavior aroused in a situation.

Cannon's theory was elaborated as a result of dissatisfaction with the James-Lange conception and as a result of research which appeared after the formulation of this viewpoint. In Cannon's view the "seat" of emotions lies in the thalamus. It is the discharge of a pattern of excitation in the thalamus that, when communicated to the cortex, gives rise to the experience of emotion; this pattern is not dependent on reaction in muscles and glands, though ordinarily such reaction will give rise to kinesthetic stimulation, which will support or supplement it. Lashley (1938b) reviewed evidence on which he questioned the assignment of the function of emotion to the thalamus, and, as Lindsley (1951, p. 503) has stated, this was the "final shot" in a series of volleys concerning this phase of Cannon's theory.

An aspect of Cannon's viewpoint, somewhat more pertinent to motivation than his emphasis on the thalamus, was his suggestion that certain emotions, like fear and rage, serve an emergency function by preparing the organism for action; or as Morgan (1943) has summarized it, "emotion serves the purpose of mobilizing the resources of the organism to meet a situation that might endanger it" (p. 363). In rage and fear, the kinds of changes in the body, on which Cannon based his notion of the preparation for action, are these: inhibition of salivation, gastric motility, secretion of gastric juices and peristalsis, thus stopping or retarding digestive processes; acceleration of heartbeat, redistribution of the blood to the musculature and brain from the

[15] These viewpoints cannot be described fully here, but many adequate accounts are available (cf. Arnold, 1960; Cannon, 1927; Gardiner, Metcalf, and Beebe-Center, 1937; James, 1884; Lange, 1885; Mandler, 1962; Ruckmick, 1936; Young, 1943, 1961).

[16] It is fairer to say that physiological response patterns do not differentiate the various emotional states. As a theory of the conscious experience of emotion, the James-Lange theory has probably not been adequately tested, and perhaps it cannot be (cf. Schachter and Singer, 1962).

viscera, increase in blood pressure, all of which presumably prepare the body for vigorous muscular activity (cf. Morgan, 1943, p. 364). Other changes could be mentioned but they are consistent with the interpretation of the foregoing changes.

Arnold (1945) has criticized Cannon's formulation for fear, arguing that the physiological changes he reported in fear in response to adrenalin and to sympathetic activity are both capable of alternative interpretations. She also holds, psychologically speaking, that fear is "enervating rather than energizing. Fear may be useful to the organism, indeed, not because it prepares us for action but because it forces us to caution" (Arnold, 1945, p. 40), and she would paraphrase the James-Lange theory in these terms:

". . . we run *before* we are really afraid: but as we run we begin to realize our danger and become more and more afraid, until we collapse with shaking knees and pounding heart, far more exhausted than we should be from the muscular effort alone . . . the emergency theory of emotion does not seem to hold good for the emotion of fear. Neither can the effects of fear be explained as an adaptive reaction by which the organism restores its internal equilibrium (homeostasis)" (Arnold, 1945, p. 40).

Fear, Arnold would assert, brings too much excitation to the sympathetic nervous system for it to have an emergency function. Hence she would conclude that the emergency aspect of Cannon's theory is invalid (cf. Rogoff, 1945; Mandler, 1962).

However this may be, and a full evaluation of this phase of Cannon's theory of emotions is beyond the scope of our concern, Cannon's theory did suggest a role for emotion somewhat akin to one that has been advocated recently in the activation theory of emotion (see Duffy, 1951, p. 31). Actually, as far as we can see, activation theory is less a theory of emotion than it is the assertion that a useful, measureable, and influential dimension is provided by variations in activation, or, in Duffy's earlier (1951) phrase, "energy mobilization." Emotional states presumably fall at points on such an activation dimension, and perhaps drive states do so as well.

The Emphasis on Activation

As we see it, activation theory has arisen in relation to two main bodies of fact (and activation theorists have, we think, not speculated much beyond what their data show). These are, first, that behavioral efficiency varies as a function of energy mobilization and muscular involvement; and, second, that recent neurophysiological discoveries have suggested that cortical function is related to activity in an arousal system of the brain stem. The notion that these facts are related to emotion and motivation arises from two further points: first, that emotion and motivation are concepts designed partly for the purpose of dealing with variations in behavioral vigor or arousal; and, second, some of the physiological indicators of arousal have figured, also, historically, as methods of expression in the study of emotion, stress, and conflict (see Chapter 9).

Laboratory studies of the relationship between effort (tension) and efficiency have been carried out at least since 1906 (Robinson, 1934, p. 641) and striking evidence was presented by Bills (1927), who showed that tension arising from grasping a hand dynamometer facilitated such performances as memorization, solving addition problems, and naming letters. Later investigators, however, found that not all degrees of tension were equally facilitative of performance and that functional relationships between behavioral efficiency and tension level could be established (Courts, 1942, pp. 347–349). While several functions between these measures were described, one of especial interest, in view of the recent suggestions by activation theorists, was an inverted U-shaped relationship (see Fig. 8–3). This showed behavioral efficiency to increase to a maximum as tension rose from a minimum to an intermediate level and then to decline as tension rose still further (Stauffacher, 1937; Courts, 1939; Freeman, 1933, 1938c). This inverted U-

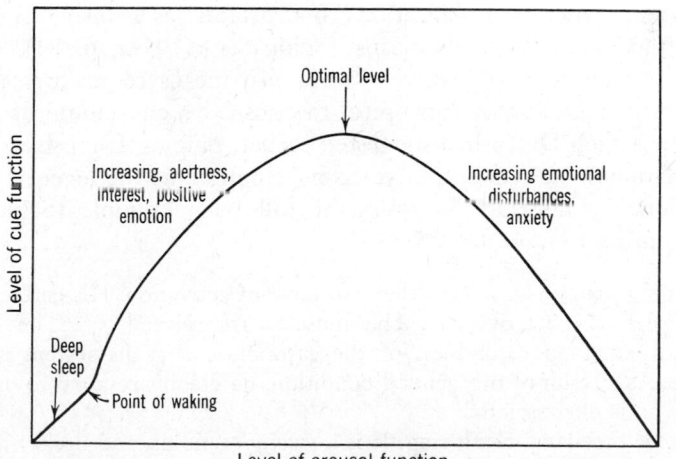

Figure 8–3. Hypothetical "inverted U-shaped" relationship between behavioral efficiency or level of cue function and level of arousal. Reproduced by permission from Hebb (1955, Fig. 2).

shaped function had been previously noted by Duffy (1932), as well as by Freeman (1931, 1933), and Robinson (1934) had suggested that stimulation or excitement in the cortex might be the basis for the facilitative aspect of tension.

We have already mentioned that for years Duffy (1934, 1941a, 1951) has argued that one of the two meaningful aspects of the word emotion is its reference to energy mobilization. She has stressed that arousal or energy mobilization may be measured by electrical phenomena of the skin (PGR, GSR), the electroencephalogram (EEG), and skeletal muscle tension, all of which in one way or another have been used in the study of emotional "expression" (Duffy, 1951, 1957; see also Arnold, 1950). While Duffy's point of view is certainly a precursor of current activation theory, she had not, from 1932 until 1957 (Duffy, 1957, p. 268), emphasized the inverted U-shaped relationship between activation and performance. This appears to be a distinctive feature of activation theory as it is reflected in the writings of Hebb (1955, 1958), Lindsley (1951, 1957), Malmo (1957, 1958), and Schlosberg (1954a, b), as well as in Freeman (1948, pp. 15, 70, 113). As Freeman's views were discussed in Chapter 7, we shall now turn specifically to the theoretical contributions of the other four writers, citing some of the appropriate evidence pertinent to their viewpoints.

Harold Schlosberg

This writer acknowledges the priority of Elizabeth Duffy and her concept of "energy mobilization" but prefers, as a term, Lindsley's word, "activation," which means (Schlosberg, 1954a, p. 82) ". . . a bit more than to make active . . . it also means to make reactive." Schlosberg suggests that it is useful to consider a continuum of activation, one which Duffy had suggested earlier, ranging from sleep, at the level of minimum activation, to strong emotion, at the level of strong activation. To illustrate, he gives the following example (Schlosberg, 1954a, pp. 82–83).

[A sleeping man] . . . is near the zero level of activation. His cerebral cortex is relatively inactive . . . The muscles are relaxed . . . The sympathetic, or emergency, division of the autonomic nervous system is fairly inactive. As a result of this general condition, he doesn't respond to ordinary stimuli; he is unconscious.

Now let the alarm clock ring. It is a strong stimulus, and breaks through the high threshold. Gross muscular responses occur, and feed back impulses into the central nervous system. There is also autonomic discharge, and the resulting responses of muscle and gland lead to more feedback, probably through some interwoven pathways, the reticular substance. These impulses reach the hypothalamus, increasing its level of activity, and this center activates the cerebral cortex . . . the individual is awake and responsive to stimulation . . .

Let us assume that our hero has reached an optimum level of activation by 10:00 A.M. He is alert, and responds efficiently to his environment. But now he finds that a book he needs is missing from his shelf. This frustration produces an increment in level of activation, perhaps not high enough at first to be dignified by the name of anger. But as he continues to search for the book the level of activation builds up until he is "blind with rage" . . . he probably wouldn't find the book now if it were under his nose.

Blind rage is, of course, a strong emotion, which represents high activation and behavioral disorganization; milder emotions would also fall on this activation continuum, although at lower (and perhaps facilitative) levels, and we must not forget that minimal activation, continuous with these emotional states, corresponds to sleep. Emotion, then, becomes simply one way of designating activation level; the important problems, however, are to measure activation level and relate its measures to other aspects of behavior.

Schlosberg realizes that the activation dimension does not represent all of the aspects of emotion, and he has attempted to get at these other aspects by studies designed to identify dimensions other than activation on which judgments of facial expressions of emotion, for example, may be described. We will not follow this line of inquiry, since the main relevance of emotion to motivation, at present, lies in the activation dimension. The problem of other dimensions of emotion is, as Schlosberg sees it (1954a, p. 86), ". . . quite analogous to that in the closely related field of motivation. Both hunger and thirst will raise the general level of drive, as measured by an activity wheel, but each will also act selectively on an appropriate family of S-R units. Unfortunately, the analogy isn't complete, for we haven't yet found differentiated emotional patterns as clean-cut as are eating and drinking."

We have already mentioned some of the earlier work which related muscular tension to various aspects of performance. Most of this work dealt with *induced* muscle tension, which would ordinarily escape the designation "emotional." There is also, however, considerable evidence that bears on the relations between other indicators of noninduced as well as induced arousal and performance. Many of these indicators are also used as indicators of emotion; we have already mentioned the three which figure most prominently in relation to activation theory: skin resistance, EEG, and muscular tension.

Schlosberg has stressed electrical skin resistance as a measure of arousal, emphasizing, however, the slow drifts in absolute level of conductance as the appropriate indicator, rather than transitory changes. Increases in skin conductance are associated with arousal. Changes in conductance were recorded by Duffy and Lacey (1946) for subjects who were working through several cycles of the task of judging tones. As the first series began, conductance rose sharply, falling as the subject progressed through the cycle and the rest period which followed, only to rise again at the start of the next phase of the task with a subsequent drop-off. A sort of sawtooth pattern appeared for the conductance measure, with the high points corresponding to starting a cycle of the task and the declines presumably corresponding to the subject's relaxation as he went through the cycle. Similar results were found by Schlosberg and Stanley (1953).

There is also evidence that behavioral efficiency varies with arousal as measured by conductance. Freeman (1940) took reaction times and skin conductances simultaneously at various points during a day and found an inverted U-shaped function which showed the shortest reaction times to correspond with intermediate levels of conductance. Schlosberg (1954a, p. 85) has also reported an inverted U-shaped relationship between skin conductance and hand steadiness and between skin conductance and simple auditory reaction time. For the former, eta was .81, and for the latter .77. Schlosberg expresses the opinion, however, that neither his data nor those reported by Freeman are yet sufficient to give conclusive support to the inverted U-shaped function.[17]

These findings, together with the general acceptance of the idea that electrical resistance of the skin is related to processes controlled by the autonomic nervous system and of this measure as indicative of emotional responsiveness, are representative of the basis which Schlosberg advances in support of the arousal or activation theory of emotion and of skin conductance as a measure of arousal.

Robert B. Malmo

As an activation theorist, Malmo's ideas are essentially similar to those of the other writers discussed in this section, and he has been among the most productive investigators of problems related to activation theory. Recently, he has urged the close correspondence between the arousal concept and the notion of generalized or nondirective drive (Malmo, 1958; see Chapter 10).

Malmo's argument is that generalized drive, as usually considered, is akin to arousal, that there are difficulties in the use of deprivation

[17] In a later report, Schlosberg's findings did not verify the relationship previously observed (Schlosberg & Kling, 1959).

indices or the properties of stimuli in assessing general drive level, and that these difficulties may be circumvented by using indicators of physiological arousal. Two major points stand in the way of this unification of generalized drive with arousal. One concerns the extent to which the measures advocated by activation theorists do in fact reflect changes due to drive as established by deprivation or other drive-inducing operations. The other is that drive theorists have usually assumed a monotonic relationship between deprivation (or other drive-inducing operations) and drive level, and this suggests that behavior would be a monotonic function of drive level (excluding such factors as inanition), rather than be related to drive level by the inverted U-shaped function stressed so much by the activation theorists.

Malmo cited a study of the relationship between 60 hours of sleep-deprivation and skin conductance for three human subjects (1958, pp. 236–240). Skin (palmar) conductance rose during the vigil (especially from the middle to the end), substantiating the notion that arousal indicates the effects of deprivation; respiration rate also fits into this pattern. Malmo (1959, p. 371), Bélanger and Tetreau (1961), and Ducharme and Bélanger (1961) have reported data that heart rate, a measure of arousal, increases with intensity of electrical shock and length of deprivation of water (up to 72 hours), and food (up to 60 hours). Bar-pressing rate, however, is a nonlinear, inverted U-shaped function of these shock and deprivation levels. Thus, there appears to be some evidence meeting these two points.

There is much more evidence pertinent to activation theory than we have summarized so far, and it seems wise to indicate something of its scope here, before going on to discuss Lindsley and Hebb. Rather full accounts of this evidence are provided by Courts (1942), Duffy (1951, 1957), and Malmo (1957, 1958, 1959), and we shall give only illustrative material here.

Malmo and his associates have shown that there are tension gradients during the performance of a task. Thus, when electrical records of muscle activity were made during mirror drawing, a size discrimination task, listening to a story, or visual tracking there was a gradient of increasing tension from the start of the task to a point before completion when tension dropped off (Bartoshuk, 1955; Bélanger, 1957; Wallerstein, 1954; Surwillo, 1956). The steepness of the gradients was also shown to be related to adequacy of actual performance; this measure is assumed to reflect arousal, as does skin conductance. Observations made on psychiatric patients lead Malmo to think that the activation concept may bear relations to psychopathology: ". . . under 'stress,' psychoneurotic patients appeared to show a higher level of physiological reaction than controls . . . level of reaction seemed to be particularly high in patients suffering mainly from pathological anxiety" (Malmo, 1957, p. 279). Duffy (1951) has summarized evidence indicating that muscle tension varies in an expected fashion from sleep through the normal waking state to startle and that tension increases as task difficulty and attentiveness increase.

Stennett (1957) studied skin conductance and muscle tension while his subjects performed a tracking task under several degrees of motivation, induced by variations in instructions. These degrees of motivation yielded varying degrees of activation, and there was evidence, further, that intermediate levels of arousal were associated with better tracking performances than were the more extreme arousal levels. These are the kinds of relationships that activation theory anticipates, and the evidence suggests that they can be found. Such relationships, however, must always be limited by the facts of individual differences (cf. Lacey & Lacey, 1958) and by the imperfect correlations among the several measures of arousal (cf. Duffy, 1951, pp. 38–39; 1957, p. 266).[18]

Donald B. Lindsley

While there is a certain plausibility and reasonableness in activation theory, it is, as we have already indicated, hardly appropriate to call it a theory. As we see it, its major tenet, aside from the assertion that emotion means arousal, is that there is a curvilinear relationship between behavioral efficiency and measures of physiological arousal—a tenet of high theoretical neutrality. The redefinition of emotion is also hardly theoretical. In short, we doubt that activation theory would have a great deal of appeal, were it not for certain recent neurophysiological discoveries with which Lindsley has been associated and with the psychological significance of which he has been concerned.

Lindsley coined the phrase, "activation theory of emotions" (Lindsley, 1951, p. 505; see also 1950, 1952). He began with the fact that the effect of emotion on the electroencephalogram (EEG) is to produce an " 'activation' pattern, characterized by reduction or abolition of synchronized (alpha) rhythms and the induction of low amplitude fast activity" (Lindsley, 1951, p. 505). This pattern is similar to that

---

[18] It is worth pointing out that these findings are relevant to the Leeper controversy, summarized earlier in this chapter. That intermediate levels of emotional arousal facilitate performance is consistent with Leeper's view that emotion motivates and organizes behavior. Extreme levels of arousal are associated with disruption of behavior, and this finding is perhaps consistent with the view that emotions disorganize behavior.

produced by sensory stimulation and problem-solving, which are presumably activation states. Lindsley stressed that the extremes of emotion, that is, strong and weak emotions, could be conceived mainly as arousing varying activation patterns, and he suggested a complex neural mechanism as underlying emotional reactions (Lindsley, 1951, Fig. 9, p. 507).

Lindsley's major interest in this neural mechanism concerns a part of it, the brain-stem reticular formation, and much of the interest in activation theory has centered upon this structure, concerning which a number of interesting neurophysiological discoveries have been made. As we see it, emotion is less important in this aspect of activation theory than the mechanisms of activation themselves, and we shall now be mainly concerned with these mechanisms.

Although the reticular formation of the brain stem has been known for a long time, anatomically, its functions have not been well understood until recently. This formation (Fig. 8–4) "consists of a rather dense network of neurones which form a central core extending from the medulla of the lower brain stem to the thalamus in the diencephalon. It extends through the region of the pons and the midbrain tegmentum upward through the caudal portions of the hypothalamus and subthalamus" (Lindsley, 1958, p. 57). Fibers descend from it, providing means for impulses from it to influence the bodily musculature and the autonomic nervous system, and fibers also go from the formation upward, probably through the thalamus (connecting with the diffuse thalamic projection system) and through extrathalamic routes (Lindsley, 1958, p. 58). This formation has, as suggested already, effects on spinal motor activity, providing balance or regulation for it. These effects indicate a system over and beyond the traditional means of efferent control, the pyramidal and extrapyramidal tracts.

The most dramatic influences of the reticular formation came to light with the discovery by Moruzzi and Magoun (1949) that electrical stimulation of the reticular formation leads to the appearance of an "activation pattern" in the EEG. Thus, if, prior to such stimulation, the animal's brain showed an EEG characteristic of sleep, the stimulation changed the pattern at once to one corresponding to arousal or activation. Lindsley, Bowden, and Magoun (1949), also working with the cat's brain, observed the opposite effect. Working with an unanesthetized, isolated brain (isolated by severing the spinal cord at the first cervical level) they found that

. . . the EEG picture was that of a normal, unoperated cat, showing low amplitude fast waves of relatively desynchronized pattern, characteristic of the waking state. Progressively higher transections of the brain stem were (then) made with increasingly more synchronized slow waves and spindle formations appearing as more and more of the reticular formation and its collaterals from the classical afferent pathways were eliminated. With lesions of the central reticular core in the rostral midbrain region, but with lateral afferent pathways intact, or with lesions in the hypothalamus in the region of the projections of the reticular formation, the EEG of the cat showed an electrocortical picture characteristic of deep sleep or somnolence (Lindsley, 1958, pp. 62–63).

Lesions in the specific sensory pathways, however, did not abolish the wakefulness pattern of the EEG, so long as the reticular formation remained intact.

We see from these experiments, which have been paralleled by simi-

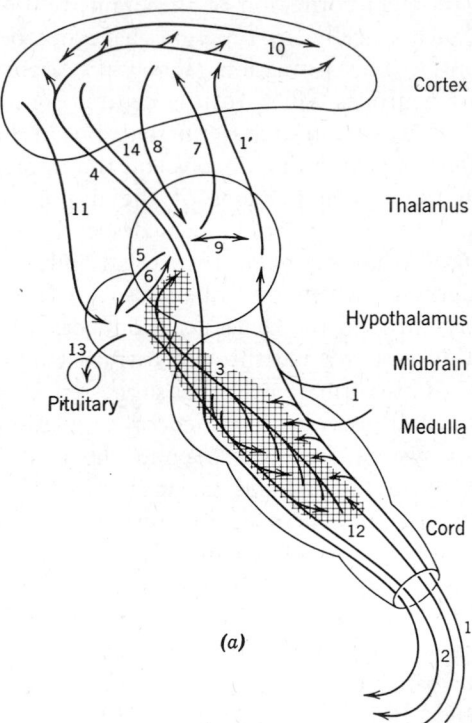

(a)

Figure 8–4. The reticular formation and some of its relationships. (*a*) General demarcation and location of the formation. Reproduced by permission from Lindsley (1951, Fig. 9). (*b*) Ascending reticular activating system (ARAS). Reproduced by permission from Lindsley (1957, Fig. 4). (*c*) Corticoreticular influence upon reticular formation and ARAS. Reproduced by permission from Lindsley (1957, Fig. 6).

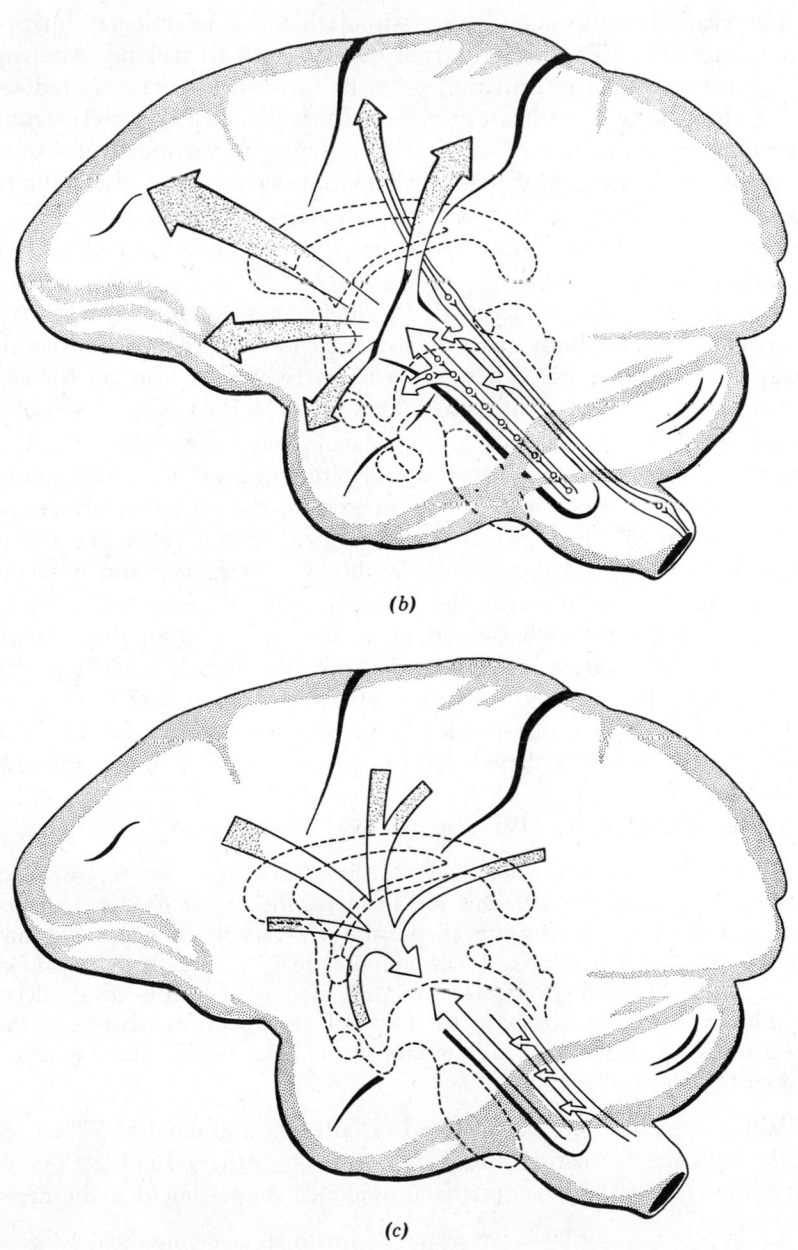

(b)

(c)

lar observations on monkeys, that stimulation of the reticular formation changes the EEG pattern from one of sleep to waking, whereas lesions in the reticular formation or in its upward projections (reducing or eliminating its influence) changed a waking EEG pattern from one of activation to one of sleep. The reticular formation would thus appear to be involved in the dimension sleep-waking (see, also, Ellingson, 1956), a dimension we have already seen emphasized by activation theorists; as pointed out before, its functional effects on the EEG parallel those of emotion.

How does the reticular formation itself become active so that it may contribute impulses both upward, toward the cortex, and downward, toward the musculature? There seem to be two major sources for activation of the reticular formation. One arises as the result of sensory stimulation. The classical afferent pathways, on their ways from the sensory receptors to their cortical termini, give off collateral nerve fibers in the region of the lower brain stem to the reticular formation. Action in any of these pathways, therefore, arising from peripheral stimulation from somatic, visual, auditory, olfactory, and visceral sources, feeds impulses into the reticular system. Apparently these impulses can act somewhat interchangeably in activating the system. In addition, however, it is also true that the cortex itself sends impulses into the reticular formation. French, Hernandez-Peon, and Livingston (1955) stimulated various cortical areas electrically and found, in a monkey, that these stimulations led to electrical activity in the reticular formation.

As Lindsley observes (1957, pp. 68–69):

Thus the perceptual discriminations of the present, or those of the past stored as memories, the ideations and imagery, the higher level symbolizations and thinking of man, are all presumably capable of generating impulses in the cortical matrix. These impulses may . . . result in excitation of the ARAS (ascending reticular activating system), which in turn reflects its influence upon the cortex in the form of electrocortical change in the direction of "activation." . . . The end result behaviorally may be action or suppression of action.[19]

While stress has here been placed on afferent and cortical influences on the reticular formation, there are, no doubt, others. Lindsley (1956, pp. 330–331; 1960) has summarized evidence suggesting that the cere-

[19] In the scope of this book, we cannot deal with all of the neurophysiological developments related to psychological problems. However, see Adrian, Bremer, and Jasper (1954), Fields (1957), Magoun (1958), and Sheer (1957), in addition to references cited in the text. Lindsley (1960) has provided a thorough review of reticular formation functions. See, also, Zanchetti (1962, pp. 308–316).

bellum and the amygdaloid nucleus of the rhinencephalon can affect this system and indicates (Bonvallet et al., 1954) that cortical activity is related to activity in the sympathetic nervous system. For example,

. . . visceral and nociceptive stimuli produce marked activation of the cortex and parallel sympathetic changes. [And] . . . two mechanisms are involved, one a direct influx of such stimuli into the bulbar reticular formation with immediate cortical activation, and two, a delayed "humoral" process which acts not upon the cortex directly but instead upon the ponto-mesencephalic reticular activating system and then the cortex. This "humoral" activation permits cortical adjustment to peripheral sympathetic activity then in effect (Lindsley, 1956, p. 330).

Bonvallet and associates have also shown that it is possible to prevent or inhibit reticular formation activation of the cortex by distension of the carotid sinus. "These findings . . . imply that certain conditions of emotional and sympathetic tone, particularly with sudden reduction of such tone, or possibly under fatigue which differentially affects certain components of the interlocking nervous and humoral control of activation and homeostasis, will permit a 'damping' or inhibition of the ascending reticular formation in such a way as to induce sleep rather than to prevent it" (Lindsley, 1956, p. 331).

From what we have said, it is apparent that the reticular formation operates under diverse and complex influences and that under some of them its activation influence may be inhibited. We have spoken of this system as if it is a unitary one, all parts of which are equally liable to stimulation by just any impulse, from whatever source, that happens to gain entrance to it. This is probably not true. With recording from single neuronal units, it is found "that a given cellular unit might be fired by one type of sensory stimulus and not another but that in all probability many units capable of being fired by more than one sensory modality also exist" (Lindsley, 1956, p. 328). Sharpless and Jasper (1956) have suggested that the ascending reticular formation has different functions in its upper and lower parts. The upper part is sensitive to small qualitative variations in stimuli and can lead to quick and short changes in reactivity.

[The lower, or caudal, formation] . . . is capable only of crude differentiation between stimuli and produces long-lasting, persistent changes in the level of reactivity. The properties of the lower brain-stem reticular system, therefore, are well-suited to the maintenance of wakefulness over long periods of time, but are ill-adapted to the sudden and brief changes in reactivity that must occur in response to highly specific stimuli, if the animal is to meet the demands of its waking environment (p. 675). . . . The unspecific thalamic system is strategically situated for subserving attentive processes in the conscious animal (p. 676) . . . and has physiological properties distinct from those of the lower reticular activating system (p. 675).

What we have said concerning the reticular formation indicates that present knowledge of cortical and subcortical interrelations suggests that they are very complex. We cannot go into these matters further, although they are quite significant to our understanding of learning, memory, thought, waking, vigilance, attention, and so on. We will confine ourselves here to summarizing certain observations relative to the reticular formation and behavior and to the role of cortical activation in behavior. Most of what we have said so far has discussed electrocortical activation by the reticular formation. As Stellar (1957) has suggested, if this work with reticular activation is to be related to behavior, it is essential that behavioral reflections other than the EEG be examined with respect to the significance of the reticular activation system.

Perceptual Phenomena. It is argued by most activation theorists that cortical "registration" of afferent stimulation can occur by way of the afferent pathways in the absence of reticular formation activation of the cortex. However, such registration seems to go no further under these conditions (Lindsley, 1957, 1958; Hebb, 1955, 1958). Lindsley has summarized this matter as follows:

Under deep anesthesia . . . , the ARAS and its electrocortical activating role is reduced or abolished. Under these conditions, however, evoked potentials may be elicited as well as before. Therefore, . . . the elimination of the ARAS (has) not prevented the transmission of sensory messages over the classical sensory pathways and via the specific relay nuclei of the thalamus and their topographical projections to the primary receiving areas. However, behaviorally (and subjectively, in the case of humans), the animal does not respond to these messages in a discriminative way. Thus one may draw the inference that elaboration and integration of messages received at the cortex in order for perception to occur is dependent upon the ARAS, and probably also the diffuse projection nuclei of the thalamus (1957, pp. 72–73).

Direct stimulation of the reticular formation during performance of a perceptual task has resulted in facilitation of performance. This represents the opposite condition from that just described. Fuster (1958) trained rhesus monkeys to discriminate between paired objects, by placing food under one of them. Then the objects, in a subsequent series, were illuminated for brief intervals of time, following which the monkey was to select one object. The number of correct choices and the reaction time were facilitated if the brief exposure of the objects was made while the reticular formation was being stimulated through implanted electrodes at moderate intensities. Lindsley (1957, pp. 85–86) has reported that the visual cortex responds, as shown through electrical recordings, differentially to two brief light flashes presented close together during reticular stimulation, but that without reticular stimulation it does not respond differentially to the two flashes, responding to them as to one flash.

Another role of the reticular formation is suggested in an experiment reported by Hernandez-Peon, Scherrer, and Jouvet (1956). They recorded responses from the cochlear nucleus in a cat while click stimuli were being presented. The recording showed responses of the nucleus to the click when the cat was relaxed. But when a mouse (in a glass jar), or the odor of fish, or a shock was introduced the response to the click disappeared, while the cat was apparently orientated to these stimuli. Direct electrical stimulation of the reticular formation will depress the response of the cochlear nucleus to stimuli, and this perhaps justifies the inference that it was the reticular formation that, during the presence of mouse, odor, or shock stimuli, suppressed the response to the click. Suggested here is a role of the formation in the selectivity of attention.

Cortical Rhythms as Excitability Cycles. Lindsley (1957, 1958) has elaborated a hypothesis that the alpha rhythm of the EEG represents an excitability cycle. The hypothesis is that if impulses arrive at the cortex during the excitable portion of the cycle, further excitation is possible; further excitation would not occur if the time in the cycle at which the impulse arrives is unfavorable. The argument, further, is that in resting and relaxed states, the excitability cycles of many cells are in phase with one another; this would lead to the resting alpha picture (and to the larger, slower waves of even less-active states), and the possibility of excitation by incoming stimuli would be reduced, since the many neurons would be excitable (simultaneously) only a part of the time. In desynchronized ("activated") cortical activity, however, the excitability cycles of these same cells would be out of phase, so that excitation would have a greater likelihood of arriving at a time of excitability in at least some cells. Further excitation in the cortex would then have increased likelihood. This hypothesis, in effect, makes cortical activity an index of excitation cycles. Presumably, the cortical activity reflects reticular formation activity, so that, indirectly, degree of "phasedness" (synchrony in cell activity) of excitation cycles is inversely related to amount of reticular activation.

Lindsley and his students have tested the hypothesis that cortical rhythms represent excitability cycles. Lansing (1957) studied the reaction time to a light of a finger response. Recording occipital and motor area EEG's simultaneously, he was able to determine at what part of the alpha cycle the stimulus had been presented. He found, as Lindsley (1957, p. 82), has summarized it, "That in the case of the greatest speed or efficiency of response, the stimulus message arrived in the cortex at an optimal excitability period in a certain phase of the occipital alpha wave, and the motor discharge originated in the motor area in a similar optimal phase of the motor alpha wave." Lansing, Schwartz, and Lindsley (1959) studied reaction times and alpha rhythms under conditions in which the subject had been or had not been adequately alerted for the impending occurrence of the visual stimulus. In part, the alerting was varied through the duration of the foreperiod between warning and occurrence of the stimulus to be reacted to. When the alerted reaction-time curve and the alpha-rhythm-blocking curve were both plotted as a function of duration of foreperiod (Lindsley, 1957, p. 83, Fig. 9), the curves were almost exactly parallel. This would seem to confirm the notion that desynchronization of the EEG is a condition favorable to efficient behavior. (Presumably the favorable alerting conditions provided time for EEG desynchronization via reticular formation activation.) [20]

It is clear that, as Lindsley now views it, activation theory has become almost totally concerned with the complex interrelations of the reticular activating system to the rest of the nervous system and to behavior. In his hands, then, activation theory has turned to the neural structures involved in activation, although Lindsley remains concerned with the psychological phenomena that need explanation. His orientation appears to be different from that of Duffy, Schlosberg, and Malmo, most of whose attention has gone into the study of the essentially correlative relation between measured arousal and behavioral efficiency. From the standpoint of a student of behavior, of course, the behavioral aspects of activation have the greatest interest.

A report by Sprague, Chambers, and Stellar (1961) offers evidence apparently contrary to much of what Lindsley has said about the reticular arousal system. They severed, in cats, the classical sensory pathways, and while some damage was done to the reticular formation, it remained largely intact and continued to be innervated below the site of the lesion. The animals were maintained for up to two-and-one-half years and given a variety of behavioral tests, from reflex function to adaptive behavior. Marked deficits and other changes were found

[20] Other experiments related to these are reported by Gengerelli and Cullen (1955) and by Shaw (1956).

in these animals. Sensory deficits (including visual and olfactory defects not attributable to direct lesions), inappropriate behavior in many situations (heat, cold, sexual, food stimuli), lack of affect, and hyperactivity akin to exploratory behavior were some of the changes observed.

Sprague and associates attribute these changes to the sensory deprivation arising from lesions in the sensory pathways and do not believe they are due to reticular involvement. Their report implies that reticular activation is not sufficient to maintain normal, integrated behavior. At this writing, it is difficult to evaluate these results. The problem of reticular-formation lesions, or deficits of input to the system from sensory pathways, may be important. In addition, the cats were maintained by Sprague et al. for a long time, and it is not clear just when the various tests, which form the basis of the behavioral reports, were made. It is unlikely that time periods this long were involved in the experiments summarized by Lindsley.

It is also worth noting, however, that the behavioral testing in the work of Sprague et al. appears to have been much more extensive than it was in other experiments involving the reticular formation.

Donald O. Hebb

In his book *Organization of Behavior*, Hebb (1949) suggested that since the central nervous system and most of the muscles are continually active, the problem of motivation is not that of activation or arousal of behavior but rather the patterning and direction that behavior takes. Persistence and direction are always present in the normal adult animal, so that there is always motivation; but motivation, as such, although conferring persistence and direction on behavior, was conceived as only one of a number of concepts whose functions include persistence and direction. The term motivation was thought to be "a reference in another context to the same processes to which 'insight' refers . . ." (Hebb, 1949, p. 181).

The theory presented in 1949 was essentially the argument that nerve cells in the brain when more or less simultaneously excited constitute assemblies of mutually facilitating, and to some extent stimulating, elements; a series of such cell assemblages acting one after another constitute a "phase sequence." This sequence gives rise, generally, to the direction and persistence in behavior and provides for central regulation of behavior in some independence of external stimuli. The variables which control motivational states (like deprivation) are presumably ways of activating particular cell assemblies and phase sequences, but are not logically or significantly different from non-motivational variables. Hebb seemed to stress goal expectancy as a feature of phase sequences relevant to motivation, and this involves a great deal of learning in motivation, even in hunger. He also argued that constant repetition of the same phase sequences would lead to boredom and monotony (arising from changed relations in the members of a phase sequence) and implied that some degree of failure to confirm expectancies, especially perceptual ones, could confer interest and pleasure on the organism, although discrepancies which were too great would produce unpleasantness. (The similarity of McClelland's and Peak's notions to these of Hebb's should be apparent.) "The totally unfamiliar does not arouse a phase sequence so 'interest' and 'motivation' are likely to be preoccupied by whatever is new in the combination of familiar events, and by events that produce *some* frustration and *some* fear (which tend to break up the phase sequence . . .)" (Hebb, 1949, p. 230). Pleasure is a state "in which a conflict is being reduced, an incipient disorganization being dissipated, or a new synthesis in assembly action being achieved" (p. 232).

In later discussions, however, Hebb (1955, 1958) reviewed evidence which requires, in his view, a major modification of the orientation briefly sketched above. One kind of evidence is that while the brain is always active, the activity is not the kind which is transmitted and leads to behavior; further, there is now evidence of true inhibition and fatigue in nerve function. More emphasized, however, is the evidence pertaining to the kind of activation systems and processes emphasized by Lindsley. That the cortex requires activation by stimulation seems a necessary conclusion from the results of sensory deprivation experiments (see Bexton, Heron, & Scott, 1954, and Chapter 6). These experiments indicate that in the sensorily deprived human subject there is, after several hours, a state of great discomfort, together with visual hallucinations and other evidences of cortical dysfunction, like poor intellectual performance. These findings suggest that some degree of stimulation from the environment is necessary to maintain the timing and integrity of cortical function.

Sensory events have two functions, Hebb points out, a cue function and an arousal, activation, or vigilance function, the latter probably being mediated by the reticular activating system. And Hebb suggests that this arousal "is synonymous with a general drive state," one that "is an energizer, but not a guide; an engine but not a steering gear" (Hebb, 1955, p. 249). Hebb suggests that there may be a level of activation which is optimal for efficient functioning, as did Schlosberg (see Fig. 8–3). Thus low levels and very high levels of activation would not be conducive to efficiency, but intermediate levels would be. Hebb adds "that the same stimulation in mild degree may attract (by prolonging the pattern of response that leads to this stimulation) and in strong degree repel (by disrupting the pattern and facilitating conflicting or alternative responses)" (1955, p. 250). This would presumably permit mild stimulation to be sought, enjoyed, and rewarding, whereas strong stimulation might have none of these features.

Hebb suggests, quite tentatively, that there may be but one general drive or arousal state, which can be established by a number of mechanisms, as by hunger, pain, thirst, and sex "drives"; the feedback from cognitive processes themselves might possibly function to arouse the vigilance or activation mechanism. Hebb later recognized (1958, pp. 159–160) that there may be specialization within the reticular arousal system, as brought out in our discussion of Lindsley. Further, learned motivation may be involved (including the heavy learned component which Hebb believes hunger, thirst, and pain reactions to possess), as well as those fears which appear not through learning but through maturation.

It is important to recognize that Hebb's acceptance of a general activating or drive state provides that stimulation and cognitive activity may be important in inducing and maintaining an optimal activation level, even in the absence of "primary drive." Further, some degree of such stimulation and cognitive activity would, no doubt, have reward value. In these respects his viewpoint still differs from that of Hull's drive theory, which emphasizes stimulus reduction.

General Summary of and Comment Concerning
Activation Theory

Activation theory seems to have begun in Cannon's emergency theory of emotions and in Duffy's and Freeman's insistence that a major meaning of emotion is arousal or energy mobilization. It was perhaps furthered by Leeper's contention that it is wrong to define emotion as a state of behavioral disorganization, when, on the other hand, emotion often organizes and strengthens behavior. Activation theorists such as Duffy, Schlosberg, and Malmo have mainly stressed that behavioral arousal can be indicated by a variety of measures and that arousal is a continuum, varying from sleep to excited states. They also urge that behavioral efficiency is a curvilinear function of arousal, being at its peak when arousal has reached intermediate magnitudes. Much evidence in the literature, recent as well as past, supports these general contentions. Lindsley and, to a large extent, Hebb have stressed the role of cortical arousal by means of the nonspecific projection system, a system whose complex neurophysiological story is beginning to emerge from the laboratory. The implication is that stimulation (which affects arousal) is essential for efficient performance and, probably, that moderate levels of stimulation are preferred by organisms to either very much or very little stimulation. Drive, as Hebb and Malmo would see it, is identical with arousal; it is still an unanswered question how different drives contribute to arousal and, further, just how their qualitative features contribute to the control of behavior from the activation viewpoint.

Some years ago, Elliott and Bousfield (1936) integrated the concepts of emotion and drive by means of the mechanisms of proprioception and the sympathetic-adrenal complex. Their integration was not followed up. It is to be hoped that a similar fate does not await the current attempt to integrate motivation and emotion in the activation concept.

Recent work has stressed individual differences in emotionality (Mahut, 1958; Broadhurst, 1958) and in ways of expressing emotion (Lacey & Lacey, 1958). Individual differences have not been stressed in drive theory, although they are undoubtedly present. It is probable that the individual difference factor can be an advantage to, and may be an important factor in, the further development of activation theory as a general theory of motivation.[21]

GENERAL SUMMARY

Feeling and emotion have long been important psychological concepts but have, historically, mainly referred to conscious mental experiences or states. In this chapter, however, it was seen that, in some contemporary theories, they are being given central roles in theories of motivation.

One kind of theory emphasizes affect, more particularly pleasantness and unpleasantness. Young argues that affective enjoyment is an important factor in the organization, direction, and energization of behavior, and he thinks of affective enjoyment as not explicable (in all its forms, anyway) on the basis of learning. McClelland also uses pleasantness and unpleasantness in his motivational theory. Deviations from an adaptation level define these states; small deviations yield pleasantness, large ones unpleasantness. Cues associated with pleasant and unpleasant experiences can evoke anticipations of pleasantness or unpleasantness and therefore approach or avoidance of the situations

---

[21] We have not reviewed here the application of activation theory to the problem of vigilance made by Deese (1955). Alternative interpretations are available (see Holland, 1958).

the cues signify. In this function of energizing approach or avoidance, the affective states play a motivational role. For McClelland, all motives are learned.

While Helen Peak uses affect, it is rather a direction-giving factor for behavior rather than a motivating agent. Motivation, in her theory, arises when mutually relevant psychological events are in a relation of discrepancy.

So far as emotion is concerned, its use as a motivational concept is associated with the redefinition of emotion in terms of activation level (it also has directional aspects). Activation varies from a minimum (in sleep or coma) to a maximum (as in wild excitement). The various emotions (and perhaps drives, too) are thought to be correlated with points on this continuum of arousal. Various physiological measures (e.g., GSR, MAP, EEG) are taken as indicating levels of arousal, and these measures are then compared with other measures of behavioral efficiency. The general proposition held by many of those who treat emotion as arousal or activation is that behavioral efficiency increases from a low point, when arousal is low, to a high point at an intermediate level of arousal, only to decline again as arousal increases still further. Some evidence is available which supports this inverted U-shaped relation of behavioral efficiency to arousal. Neurophysiological discoveries have indicated that activation of the brain, supplied by the reticular formation, is necessary (in intermediate amounts) for optimal brain functioning.

The names associated with activation theory, in one or another of its aspects, include W. B. Cannon, Elizabeth Duffy, G. L. Freeman, Harold Schlosberg, Robert Malmo, Donald Lindsley, and D. O. Hebb.

Chapter 9

Frustration, Conflict, and Stress

We turn now to a consideration of the effects of extreme conditions on behavior and to a search for common principles in the vast quantity of physiological, psychological, social, and related literatures on frustration, conflict, and stress.

These titles are perhaps no more than modal terms in an array of interrelated concepts, including privation, emotionality, emotional instability, anxiety, tension, threat, distress, breakdown, disaster effects, environmental extremes, ego-involvement, and others. That there has been no standardization of language usage will come as no great surprise to the reader who has persevered thus far. That these are significant areas of concern to motivational psychology is perhaps self-evident.

In this chapter we will examine some of the conditions of the environment (including the organism) which give rise to or are concomitant with extreme motivational states.

Frustration implies that a course of action has not been carried through to its goal or conclusion, or that an end state of some sort has not been reached, or that an expected outcome or consequence has failed to materialize. This may describe a single set of events on a particular occasion, or it may refer to repeated instances so as to become characteristic of an individual's relationship to his environment (e.g., as in the descriptive phrases "low frustration tolerance," "chronic frustration," "frustration prone," etc.).

Conflict usually refers to the simultaneous or immediately successive existence of two incompatible response or action tendencies. Thus, one cannot, at the same time, both extend and bend one's elbow; if both movements are equally and simultaneously instigated, neither movement should occur, but rather there should be a freezing at, or movement to, an intermediate position where the arm would remain under considerable tension until the conflict is resolved or some other process supervenes. (See related discussion of inhibition, in Chapter 4.)

Conflict is often conceived as occurring not only between action tendencies, but also between motives or drives and between goals or end states of action. One may speak, for example, of a conflict between desire and fear, on the motivational side, or between anticipated pleasure and pain, on the side of the end state resulting from action. Conflict may produce frustration, as persistence of a conflict without resolution must, almost by definition, preclude the satisfaction of either motive, the execution of either action tendency, or the attainment of either goal state. As with frustration, conflict may presumably be a transitory, situational matter or a chronic condition; a chronic conflict may be supposed to underlie, as a matter of fact, states of chronic frustration.

Both of these terms, and to a considerable extent the interest in them, have arisen from descriptions and considerations of psychopathology, in which conflict and the resulting frustration have been seen to figure prominently and basically (cf. Dollard & Miller, 1950). It is also true, however, that the term *conflict*, at least, arose independently in the early work of experimental laboratories on reaction processes, which followed the discovery of the "personal equation" in recording the time sequences of astronomical events.[1] Studies of animal behavior and of young children in nonpathological investigations have likewise employed such procedures as introducing barriers to goal attainment, interrupting activities in progress, and presenting insoluble problems —conditions generally identified with the concept of frustration.

Decision processes, generally, and many learning and problem-solving situations as well, may usefully be regarded from the standpoint of conflict and frustration, and the study of frustration and conflict in the wider spectrum provided by decision, learning, and problem-solving situations may illuminate them so far as psychopathology is concerned, as well as the converse.

Implied here is perhaps the same point that underlies the activation

---

[1] This interesting historic footnote to early experimental psychology is probably familiar to most readers (Boring, 1950). Maskelyne, the Astronomer Royal at Greenwich Observatory in 1796, dismissed his assistant, Kinnebrook, because the latter reported the times of stellar transits with an "error" consistently almost a second beyond Maskelyne's observation times. The matter seemed closed until Bessel, the astronomer at Königsberg, came upon a report of the incident in 1816. He made a systematic study of observational reports, finding consistent differences between highly skilled observers. This led him to conclude that a "personal equation" exists in so-called objective observing. The discovery of both constant and variable individual differences led to changes in the methods of astronomical observation, but, more important for us, it opened the way for psychophysiological and psychophysical studies of reaction time and its determinants.

theory of emotions. In our earlier discussion of that position (see Chapter 8), it was seen that the main notion is the activation dimension, to points on which various emotional states may be ordered. In the present instance too, perhaps, the effects of conflict and frustration, whatever they may be, may provide a dimension at certain points on which the phenomena known to psychopathology would appear. This would constitute essentially a quantitative rather than a qualitative conception of psychopathological conflict and frustration, and attention should be directed to this possible orientation as these topics are treated in the pages which follow.

Stress is perhaps the most difficult of the three concepts of this chapter to define. At the moment, let us attempt only to convey its meaning by a rather general formulation: The concept of stress is associated with a disturbance of sensory input, sensory here being regarded as composed of afferent stimulation from both external and internal sources. This concept, as we shall see, has much to do with such internal states as activation level, emotion, frustration, and conflict, but external factors (e.g., stimulus change, disaster, threatening conditions) must also be included, as well as more general organismic states as "fatigue," "health," and the like. We turn now to a more detailed discussion of each of the three concepts with which the chapter is concerned, and to the relations among them.

FRUSTRATION — *many connotations*

No reader will have avoided in his own life some one or more experiences to which he would give the name frustration. And yet if we were to compare any group of these experiences we would find that they cover a large variety of situations and a wide range of reactions. Why, then, do they earn the same label? What is frustration?

Unfortunately, the term is a loose one, having many meanings (Lawson & Marx, 1958). Part of the difficulty arises because the term frustration is sometimes used in place of motivation—referring to conditions of simple deprivation, or to the delay in reinforcement. Hall (1961) has described the use of the term frustration as involving a "process-product confusion," and Britt and Janus (1940) earlier noted that the term is used in at least three main ways, describing (1) a frustrating situation or instigating condition, (2) the effects of such instigation on the person (e.g., "change in tension, disturbance of homeostasis, and maladaptation"), and (3) the effects on the person's reaction system (e.g., anger, aggression, withdrawal, regression). In the present treatment we shall follow the distinctions drawn by Britt and Janus wherever possible.

Conditions Which Give Rise to Frustration

There are *two* necessary preconditions to frustration: (1) the presence of a previously aroused and unrequited drive or motive, and (2) some form of interference with or thwarting of its means of gratification.

1. *Privation.* If only the first of these conditions is met we may speak of privation or deprivation, but not of frustration. Privation refers to the condition in which an existing need or tension increases in intensity in the absence of means of its reduction. Privation, or deprivation, as Maslow (1943) has observed, implies "much less" than is implied by frustration. Marx (1956) makes a similar point, specifically noting that deprivation does not involve "prior instrumental or consummatory behavior."

Rosenzweig (1944) has also emphasized the difference between privation and frustration. He attempted to indicate the priority of the two conditions by calling them *primary* and *secondary* frustration, respectively. However, we feel that the distinction is better maintained if the term privation alone is used to identify the first condition and the term frustration is reserved for instances which meet both conditions.

2. *Thwarting.* Frustration arises, according to Dollard et al. (1939), "when a goal-response suffers interference to its occurrence" or "if the organism could have been expected to perform certain acts and if these acts have been prevented from occurring." Thwarting is another name for response interference. Both privation and thwarting are necessary preconditions to frustration.

Brown (1961) describes three methods of producing thwarting: (1) via physical barriers, (2) via removal of maintaining stimuli, and (3) via elicitation of incompatible responses. Physical barriers may vary from involving the total restraint of the organism involved to a specific withholding of a reinforcement (e.g., as in locking the door to a food dish to which an animal has been trained to go for its food). The second type of thwarting described by Brown involves the removal of some stimulus or stimuli necessary to the goal-attaining behavior, even though the individual may remain unrestrained. Thus, for example, the lever used to produce food may be removed from a Skinner box in which an animal is feeding itself, or the food may be removed. An analogous example in human experience to these two thwarting methods might be that of a hungry visitor in a foreign land who, in the first case, finds that the restaurant he has learned to go to is closed, whereas, in the second instance, he might find the directional signs removed and thus be unable to locate the restaurant. Brown's third method of thwarting will be discussed later in this chapter (see *Conflict*).

Rosenzweig (1944) makes an interesting distinction between passive and active barriers. Thus a locked door may effectively thwart need gratification (a passive barrier) without itself being threatening. On the other hand, a policeman or soldier barring the same door (an active barrier) serves to frustrate the initiating need (e.g., hunger), while at the same time leading to aversive (conflict) behavior with respect to further approaches to the door.

Brown (1961) suggests that one can never be sure that a response which is presumably thwarted will lead to frustration unless there is evidence that the response would have continued (toward goal-attainment) in the absence of the thwarting agent. He thus proposes several criteria of thwarting. Although no one is an absolute indication that thwarting has taken place, they do provide some independent check on the thwarting operation. The criteria are: (1) efforts on the part of the thwarted individual to continue an interrupted behavior (e.g., a restrained dog continues to lunge against its restraining collar, even though the lunges are incomplete and unsuccessful), (2) the resumption of the response upon removal of the thwarting agent (however, the failure to resume the response may not be taken as a negative indicator), and (3) the omission of previously regularly given responses even though cues sufficient to elicit them are present. This last criterion would be most appropriate to the measurement of conflict-induced frustration.

In sum, it has been suggested that both privation and thwarting are necessary preconditions to frustration. However, this does not mean that they are sufficient conditions as well. The effect of depriving an organism of some needed or desired substance or object is normally to lead to instrumental or coping behavior until its need is satisfied or the instigation removed. This may involve the repetition of an act or the performance of varied acts which make up the individual's response repertory. We ordinarily speak of such behavior as drive-instigated (rather than frustration-instigated), although it has been suggested (Melton, 1941) that all learning situations involve frustration. We would think it preferable to reserve the term frustration, however, for a more limited class of events, namely, that point in a response-shifting series which follows the failure (or anticipated failure) of available responses to attain the desired goal. In other words, only when normal coping behavior fails (or its likelihood of failure is anticipated) does the new process come into play.

In light of highly varied precedents, this is an admittedly arbitrary limitation on the use of the term frustration, but we feel that such a restriction on its meaning may prove useful. We shall return to this point later in the chapter.

Sources of Frustration

An Inner-Outer Distinction. Frustration is sometimes said to arise because of an inadequacy on the part of the individual to satisfy his needs in the face of ordinary environmental requirements. At other times, frustration may result from an overwhelming environmental demand or requirement, or perhaps because of an unusually impoverished environment. In other words, the demands of the environment may not be excessive, as measured by some independent scale, and yet the capacities of the individual may be unequal to them; on the other hand, ordinarily adequate capacities may be insufficient in an environment that has no resources or one which requires extraordinary capacities.

This inner-outer distinction has useful implications for the psychotherapist or the social engineer, who may be called upon to modify one or the other in order to reduce the likelihood of frustration. But for our present considerations, the identification of the shortcoming as belonging to the individual or to the environment is a matter of choice, as between two sides of the same coin. Whether the individual demands more than his environment can provide or the environment provides less than the individual demands or needs, or whether the goals are within normal reach and the reach is subnormal, or the goals are beyond normal reach although the reach is normal, the essential conditions for frustration are still the existence of the unrequited need and the failure (or anticipated failure) of available coping behaviors to attain the requisite goal.

Developmental Crises and Frustration. The "human situation" has built in to it a number of crisis situations which may serve as instigators to frustration. Symonds (1946; see, also, P. T. Young, 1961) lists a series of events throughout the normal life cycle which almost of necessity leads to frustration. These include the restriction of infant activity, thwarting of autoerotic expression, loss of attention and care, unsatisfactory nursing experiences, weaning, toilet training, loss of love or security and support, forced independence in adolescence, and adult economic hardships and other losses, including those due to death of loved ones or anticipation of one's own death.

Most, if not all, of these situations contain an assumed underlying prior need, and either fancied or real loss (or threat of loss) of satisfaction. In each instance a means of satisfaction is removed, and/or a previously adequate mode of coping with the deprivation or threat of privation is made ineffective (see related discussion in Chapter 12).

Relation to Underlying Drive. It should be clear by now that frustration is not identical with the unrequited need which is one of its necessary preconditions. On the contrary, most definitions suggest that frustration is a *new* process, tension, or need state, perhaps related to the intensity of the underlying need, but unrelated to its nature. Alternatively, it has been suggested that frustration arises as a negative function of the anticipated likelihood of goal attainment or need satisfaction.

But frustration is not an automatic consequence of the interruption of *any* goal-seeking behavior. Zander (1944), for example, after reviewing studies in the field, concluded that frustration will occur only when the goal in question is "believed important and attainable." Others (e.g., Sherman, 1941; Maslow, 1943; Rosenzweig, 1944; Sargent, 1948) have also stressed the fact that the drive involved must be important to the individual. Maslow and Rosenzweig have each proposed a division between states akin to deprivation and those representing threats to the personality. The terms "ego-defensive," "ego-threatening," and "ego-involving" (see Iverson & Reuder, 1956; Hall, 1961) have come into use to describe these more intense motivational states, the interference with which may lead to frustration. (In Chapter 7, it will be recalled, we use these terms in connection with psychological homeostasis.)

Procedures intended to ego-involve a subject are those which pose a threat to his self-esteem or his integrity as a person. Thus, for example, a group of college students can become "involved" by instructing them that they are about to take an intelligence test, the results of which would be made a part of their permanent records. Such instructions arouse an important motive, and information that they are failing or have failed constitutes a thwarting of the aroused ego-protective behavior.

In sum, then, frustration is a consequence of interruption of motivated behavior only when such behavior is important. Importance, in turn, is determined by the centrality of the privation (or contrived privation—that is, deprivation operation) to the ego- or self-maintenance of the individual involved. (See Iverson & Reuder [1956] and Chapters 7, 14, and 15 in this book for further discussion of ego-involvement as an experimental variable.)

The Nature of Frustration

We earlier suggested, along with Britt and Janus (1940), that the frustration concept has been applied to instigating conditions, to a state of the organism, and to forms of reaction. Unfortunately, it is difficult to define the borderlines among these three aspects of the concept. If we turn now to a consideration of the frustration state, we find that it has been characterized as an unpleasant emotional state (Sargent, 1948), "against which the affected individual's energies are more or less strongly mobilized" (Mowrer, 1938). However, except for the implication that the organism is aroused, there have been no reliable correlations demonstrated between particular arousal conditions and state variables, or between state variables and forms of reaction (cf. Thetford, 1951; Child & Waterhouse, 1953; Marx, 1956).

We are left, then, with only one alternative for the time being, namely, to consider frustration as an intervening construct of a vaguely emotional or motivational character. This leads us to ask, if the operations intended to produce frustration are invoked: Does the state which follows display motivational characteristics?

Frustration as a Drive

The Brown-Farber Theory. Brown and Farber (1951) have offered a two-factor explanation of how frustration arises and of its effects, based on the principles of Hull's (1943) general behavior theory (see Chapters 10 and 11). The two factors they invoke are drive (D) and habit (H). Frustration (F), which they treat as a hypothetical variable (see Brown, 1961, p. 203), results from the interference with an ongoing motivated (excitatory) behavior sequence (E_o) by either an inhibitory tendency (I) (produced by blocking, nonreinforcement [extinction], or a function of work) or a competing excitatory tendency (E_c) [2] (see Fig. 9–1).

Frustration is usually a *temporary* process, which is resolved ultimately as a function of the relative strengths of the competing tendencies (including those evoked by the frustration itself) and in a direction which is the resultant of the separate excitatory and inhibitory tendencies. Frustration, then, according to this formulation, is both energizing and directional. It produces an increment to general drive (ΔD), which is a truly motivational effect. This drive increase energizes

[2] Amsel (1958) has pointed out that this represents a conflict between two opposing tendencies $(E_o$ vs I or E_o vs $E_c)$, and is therefore a conflict theory of frustration (see p. 429).

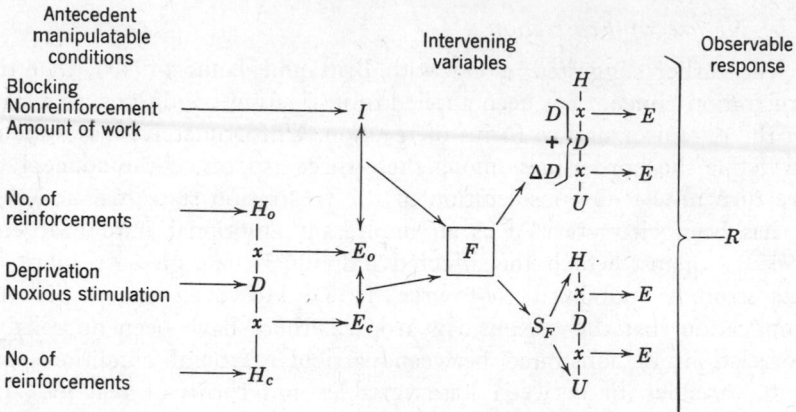

Figure 9–1. This diagram summarizes the antecedent conditions and hypothetical variables of the frustration theory of Brown and Farber (1951). The state of frustration (*F*) is assumed to be produced by competition (indicated by arrows) between an ongoing excitatory tendency (*E_o*) and either an inhibitory tendency (*I*) or a competitive excitatory tendency (*E_c*). These interacting tendencies are shown to depend upon their respective habit strengths (*H_o* and *H_c*), drive (*D*), and upon the indicated antecedent conditions. The consequences of frustration are shown as either an increment in general drive (*ΔD*) or frustration-specific stimuli (*S_F*), or both. These factors are assumed to have, respectively, the same kinds of motivational and associative functions assigned to them in Hull's behavior theory. Reproduced by permission from Brown (1961, p. 203).

both the ongoing and competing tendencies (indiscriminately). The directional effect, on the other hand, is a result of frustration-specific stimuli (S_F). Such stimuli elicit response tendencies, either unlearned (U_F) or previously learned (H_F) in connection with frustrating states of affairs. Brown and Farber thus make no plea for frustration as introducing any special motivational or directional principles, but rather explain it in terms of the drive and habit concepts of general behavior theory.

The Amsel Theory. Whereas the Brown-Farber explanation sought to include a wide range of thwarting experiences, Amsel (1951, 1958, 1962) has concentrated on nonreward following the development of reward expectation ("frustrative nonreward") as his model frustration-inducing operation. Amsel (1958, p. 104) agrees with Brown and Farber that frustration is "a motivational condition contributing to *D* and providing directive cues (S_D)." However, in addition, Amsel proposes a *third* factor, namely, "a secondary (learned) form of this primary aversive conditioned [frustration], termed *fractional anticipatory frustration* $(r_F - s_F)$," which, he claims, "develops through classical conditioning and is the inhibitory mechanism in nonreward" (p. 103).

Amsel and his associates have conducted an impressive series of experiments designed to support this three-factor explanation of frustration effects. In most of their studies they have used a two-part straight runway containing two goal boxes, one in the middle and one at the end of the alley. Their subjects have been rats. In the first of a series of defining studies, Amsel and Roussel (1952) ran food-deprived rats (to food rewards in both goal-boxes) for a series of 28 days (84 trials), until stable running speeds were achieved. On half of the next 36 trials (randomly spaced) food was omitted from the first goal box, the effects of this frustration operation being measured (against the remaining 18 control trials) in the latency of responses in the alleyway between the goal boxes (food being present in the second goal box in all trials). Latencies decreased further on frustration trials, but not on control trials, leading the authors to conclude that a drive increment had indeed been demonstrated as a result of the frustrative procedure.[3]

Wagner (1959) has more recently confirmed these findings and the conclusions of Amsel and Roussel in an experiment controlling against an alternative explanation [4] in terms of a response depression hypothesized for the rewarded trials as a function of eating. (Wagner ran a control group in which his animals were not fed in the first goal box at all.)

Amsel and Ward (1954) next reported a series of experiments which gave further support to the conclusions of Amsel and Roussel and furnished evidence for the second factor in Amsel's (and Brown and Farber's) frustration theory, namely, the cue function of frustrative procedures. Instead of the alleyway continuing in a straight line following the first goal box in the apparatus just described, Amsel and Ward provided a single-choice T-maze following this first box. Animals were then required to turn in one direction if they had been rewarded in the first goal box and the other direction if their experience had been frustrative. They conducted five experiments in all, employing various control procedures to eliminate differential cues other than the effects of frustration. The findings (of discrimination learning, and of more rapid response following nonreward) are interpreted to support the

---

[3] Evidence in support of a drive-increment function of frustration has been offered by Finch (1942) and Sheffield and Campbell (1954), but see Marx (1956) and Brown (1961) for critical discussions of these and other studies relevant to this point.

[4] See earlier criticism by Seward et al. (1957) and reply by Amsel (1958); see, also, discussion by Marx (1956) and Seward (1956b).

hypothesis that "frustration provides drive stimulation which gives it directive properties" (p. 46) and "that frustration reduction is reinforcing," a conclusion which supports the frustration-drive hypothesis just discussed.

Amsel's third factor, *fractional anticipatory frustration* ($r_F — s_F$) is modeled on Hull's (1943) postulated fractional anticipatory goal response mechanism ($r_g — s_g$) (see Chapter 10). Amsel posits that after a series of frustrative nonreward experiences in a goal box, conditioned *anticipatory* frustration responses (r_F) will begin to appear in the alley leading to the goal box. On the assumption that frustration (F) is an aversive motivational condition, Amsel argues that frustration-produced stimuli (s_F) will become associated with avoidant response tendencies which will compete with (and thus inhibit) goal approach behaviors. However, as approach tendencies are usually stronger, the later trials show increased running speeds, as a function of the attachment of approach responses to frustration stimuli. It is Amsel's belief that the findings of both partial-reinforcement and discrimination-learning studies can be explained in terms of the competition between reward and frustrative factors. Support for the notion of conditionability of frustration is offered by studies of Holder et al. (1957, and see Marx, 1956). A somewhat similar view was offered by Seward (1951; see, also, Seward, 1956*b*).

Whereas Brown and Farber had posited response competition as a precondition to frustration, Amsel in fact proposes the reverse. Nonreward following reward is the necessary precondition for frustration, and the $r_F — s_F$ mechanism in turn produces response competition. However, since Amsel has not tried to deal with a situation involving more than one initial incompatible response tendency, the two theories are not necessarily in disagreement. On the other hand, Brown (1961), while accepting Amsel's assumptions that frustration is both motivational and aversive, believes that the Brown-Farber formulation could account for the appearance of anticipatory frustration "without the added assumption that frustration is directly conditionable" (p. 207). He suggests an alternate explanation in terms of the competitive interaction of conditioned and generalized excitatory tendencies *already present* prior to reaching the goal.

Reactions to Frustration

If the distinction which has been drawn between privation and frustration is valid, and if we further accept the evidence for frustration as a drive, we may well ask whether this drive, as others, has any particular patterns of behavior associated with it (e.g., as food-seeking and food-consumption are associated with hunger, water with thirst, etc.). The answer is not a simple one, in part, at least, because frustration is not a simple (primary) drive state, arising from a bodily need and reduced through removal of that need. Frustration is an emotional state, as we have seen, arising again and again in the natural course of life's events, and leading to patterns of resolution as a function of the contexts of its arousal and the consequences of the responses which occur to it. Four major hypotheses have been proposed with regard to frustration outcome. We will briefly discuss each in turn.[5]

1. *Frustration-Aggression*. Dollard et al. (1939) defined frustration, as we noted earlier (and see Chapter 14), in terms of "goal-response interference," a natural consequence of which, they proposed, was anger and attacking behavior. The intensity of the aggression will be related to (1) the strength of the instigation, (2) the degree of interference with the frustrated response,[6] and (3) the frequency with which response sequences are interrupted. Its occurrence might also be expected to be an *inverse* function of the amount of anticipated punishment for the aggressive act(s). It follows from this that although young children may express their aggression overtly and directly, experience (of punishment or threat of punishment for aggression) will modify the response (i.e., from physical to verbal aggression, from immediate to delayed expression, and from direct to displaced aggression).

Aggression may be directed toward the frustrating agent or turned against some other object or person, including the self.[7] Freud (1924), in dealing with aggression as an aspect of the "death instinct," emphasized the consequences of this latter form of displacement of aggression (see Chapter 12). The Yale group (Dollard et al., 1939) analyzed the lynching of Negroes in some of the southern United States in terms of a "scapegoat" theory of displacement as a stimulus-generalization phenomenon (see, also, Miller, 1948*b*; Bush & Whiting, 1953). The nature of the aggressive response and of the choice of the object of aggression may both be understood as resultants of (1) instigating conditions, (2) habitual modes of action, and (3) anticipated outcome

[5] More extensive discussions of these alternatives can be found in Rosenzweig (1944) and in Lawson and Marx (1958).

[6] Arbitrariness as well as degree of interference are also factors (Pastore, 1952), as is source of interference (or nature of interfering agent). Thus Cohen (1955) has shown that frustration-instigated aggression is greater when a peer is involved than when the source is a figure of authority, and Stagner (1961*b*) has suggested that this would be further aggravated if the source is a perceived inferior.

[7] The terms "extrapunitive" and "intropunitive" (Rosenzweig, 1944) have now come into general use to describe aggression directed outward and inward, respectively.

(e.g., amount of counteraggression) (Stagner, 1961*b*).

Finally, we may note that although the early suggestion was that aggression *always* results from frustration and that frustration *always* leads to aggression, the Yale group soon modified the second half of this hypothesis (Miller, 1941) to acknowledge that a number of other reactions to frustration, in addition to aggression, were possible. Considerable evidence that the relationship is by no means invariate has accumulated since (see Berkowitz, 1962).

2. *Frustration-Regression.* Both the life-history oriented psychoanalysts and the ahistoric field theorists have proposed that regression is a likely consequence of frustration. Freud (1920) placed emphasis on the inevitability of frustrative events in the psychosexual development of civilized humans, with the combined physical and social pressures to change requiring the successive establishment and abandonment of levels of psychosexual adjustment. Where limited development occurs there would be little distance along which to regress. But where the individual has moved progressively through the developmental stages to a relatively mature psychosexual level, the occurrence of traumatic events (insurmountable obstacles) results in a regression to earlier modes of coping where success was achieved. Freud refers to these relatively successful earlier stages of development as *fixated* periods or, as Mowrer (1940) has suggested, strongly reinforced habits.

In addition to the clinical and anecdotal support for this hypothesis, there has been a large number of animal demonstrations of habit regression which have been interpreted within the Freudian view. Mowrer (1940), for example, trained rats to minimize shock by "freezing." He then forced the acquisition of a new pedal-pressing response to terminate shock, after which the pedal was made aversive (it produced a shock itself when touched). Animals which had learned the "freezing" response previously regressed to this earlier response. Control animals, on the other hand, continued to perform the now punishing pedal-pressing. (See, also, studies by Hamilton & Krechevsky, 1933; O'Kelly, 1940; Perkins & Tilton, 1954; and discussion by Hall, 1961, pp. 238 ff.)

Barker, Dembo, and Lewin (1941), in a now classic study, gave 30 nursery school children an opportunity to play with ordinary toys, followed by a play period with new and more highly attractive toys in another part of the room. When the children became involved in play with these new toys, they were then returned to the less desirable play materials, with a mesh screen separating them from the more attractive toys. The authors then rated constructiveness of play during this "frustrating" period where the nicer toys could still be seen but not played with. Comparing ratings before and after, they reported that 22 of the 30 children regressed to less constructive play, 3 showed no change, while 5 showed increased constructiveness. In addition, there was a change in emotional expression (less happiness) and an increase in ratings of motor restlessness and hypertension. Barker, Dembo, and Lewin concluded that strong frustration causes tension, leading to emotionality and restlessness and to a *dedifferentiation* of the personality. (The Lewinian concept of regression differs from the Freudian in that it does not imply a literal return to a habit form previously acquired by a particular individual, but rather a "primitivization" or less differentiated [less structured] level of organization [see Chapter 7]).

Child and Waterhouse (1952, 1953) have offered an alternative interpretation of the Barker, Dembo, and Lewin data in terms of response competition. They suggested that constructiveness of play decreased in proportion to the arousal of responses which interfered with play (e.g., incompatible aggressive responses as a result of the frustration itself). Waterhouse and Child (1953), using college students, then demonstrated their point by showing that criticism of performance on a variety of tasks (intended to produce frustration) produced either a decrement *or an increment* in performance as a function of the frustration-produced response interference.

3. *Frustration-Repression.* We earlier spoke of ego-involvement as a determinant of the importance of events to the individual and thereby their likelihood of frustration-instigation. By the same token, events which are ego-involving or ego-threatening and which occur nevertheless can be responded to retroactively only by "motivated forgetting" or repression. Thus Rosenzweig (1943) had college students solve a series of jig-saw puzzles, only half of which he permitted them to complete. He made half of his subjects "ego-defensive" by informing them that *they* were being tested (for intelligence) while the other half ("need-persistive" group) was told the *tasks* were being tested. Both groups were then asked to recall the tasks. Significantly more of the need-persistive or task-oriented group recalled the *un*finished tasks, whereas the relation was reversed for the involved group. The failure of the latter group to recall unfinished tasks is interpreted in terms of protection of self-integrity via repression of ego-threatening material (see related discussions in Chapters 7, 12, and 14).

4. *Frustration-Fixation.* N. R. F. Maier (1949, 1956) has presented a frustration-response theory which differs from those of others in its main import: namely, Maier claims, that frustration-instigated behavior

is not motivational, not goal-oriented, and not adaptive. He thus sets up a dichotomy between motivated (or directed) behavior and frustrated behavior which is fixated or stereotyped, abnormally resistant to modification, and without a goal.

Although he has attempted to explain delinquent and clinically disturbed human behavior in terms of his motivation-frustration dichotomy, Maier's theory is based on studies in a quite restricted type of animal experiment, which he and his students have nevertheless explored extensively. They have used rats (largely hooded) in a Lashley jumping-stand, the frustration being produced by a requirement to respond in a no-solution situation. The Lashley apparatus consists of a small, elevated platform from which the animal is taught to jump over a distance of about one foot of open space to one of two windows a few inches from each other, which are covered by differentially identifiable stimulus cards. If the animal makes a correct choice, its weight causes the card to swing back, and the (hungry) rat lands on a platform on which it finds food. If an incorrect choice is made, the animal bumps its nose on the locked door (set in a smooth wall) and drops into a trough several feet down.

After initial discrimination training, the problem is changed to become insoluble (the cards are reinforced at random). The animal may then continue to jump for a varying number of trials, but it soon refuses to jump completely. Maier then introduces electric shock, noxious air blasts, or prodding to force jumping, with the result that the response assumes a stereotyped form showing a marked position preference (although by definition such responding leads to punishment 50 per cent of the time) and persisting in essentially the same form over hundreds of trials. It is clear from observation of behavior at this time (and Maier has preserved excellent samples of such behavior on slow-motion film) that the response has nothing to do with its original function. Maier has shown that once the fixated behavior is established he can make the problem completely soluble (using one open window) and still the animal will jump in such a way as to be unable to enter the opening.

Maier contrasts motivated (which to him means directed, or goal-oriented) and frustration-instigated behavior (behavior without a goal) in a number of ways. The latter is rigid and invariant, the former adaptive, variable, plastic. A well-learned motivated behavior can be manipulated by changes in rewards and punishments, whereas frustration fixates responses which are in progress even when they are non-adaptive, and these then resist change. (Punishment may indeed serve

as a frustration-instigator, changing motivated to fixated response.)
Fixated responses are apparently ends in themselves, rather than instrumental behaviors, and show little indication of the influence of
anticipation of consequences. They are performed compulsively with
apparent lack of interest or excitement, in contrast to motivated responding. Motivated behavior leads to learning and an increase in differentiation and discrimination. In contrast, frustrated behavior is a
form of dedifferentiated behavior, and in some instances apparently
uncontrollable convulsive responding occurs (see earlier discussion on
frustration-regression).

Aggression is, for Maier, a form of nondiscriminating (and non-
instrumental) behavior which may result from frustration but is not
directed at problem solution. Maier believes that delinquent acts can
be analyzed as motivated or frustration-instigated on the basis of their
responsiveness to an awareness of consequences. Irrational, unresponsive
behavior is frustration-instigated and, following from his position,
would be relatively immune to rewards or punishments. On the other
hand, guidance (which in the case of the rat means literal hand-direc-
tion of movement) may ultimately modify fixations, having little effect
on motivated behavior.

In sum, Maier's basic position is that frustration-instigated behavior
is not more *highly* motivated, as most others generally believe. It is,
on the contrary, not motivated at all, but, as the subtitle of Maier's
book suggests, "behavior without a goal."

Needless to say, Maier's theory has been challenged by a number
of motivational and learning theorists who do not accept his dichotomy
(see discussion by Mowrer, 1960). Eglash (1951), Mowrer (1950*b*), and
McClelland (1950, 1951) each attacked the basic assumption made by
Maier that the behavior following frustration was no longer motivated.
They point out that the goal has been *shifted* from food-seeking to
pain avoidance, and the behavior in turn undergoes an *adaptive* change
in form. Mowrer (1960) has suggested that the reversion to a position
habit "is *realistically justified* and does not at all imply a loss of normal flexibility and intelligence" (p. 413). Mowrer further suggests
that fear generated by punishment of the position response, might
generalize back (see earlier discussion of Amsel's $r_F - s_F$ mechanism)
to the jumping stand and so perpetuate the fixated response. However,
it seems to us that the air blast or other means of response-forcing on
the jumping stand itself is a sufficient motivator of the now adaptive
avoidance (escape) responses. The stereotypy of avoidance responses
in general (see McClelland, 1951) is perhaps a function of some other

principle (e.g., least effort [Mowrer, 1960, p. 416]) but does not in itself warrant the conclusion that the stereotyped behavior is not motivated.

Farber (1948) and Wilcoxon (1952) have presented evidence in support of more traditional learning-theory interpretations of the type of data on which Maier's theory is based. Farber argued that perseverative, apparently nonadaptive responses in shock situations, after shock had been removed, could be explained on the basis of *anxiety reduction*. To demonstrate this he compared the resistance to extinction of two groups of rats trained in a T-maze to a food reward. Both groups received shock immediately after the choice point and both developed position habits as a result. Farber then fed one group (for two ten-minute periods) at the place in the maze where shock had been given and then extinguished both groups. He had hypothesized that the shock would have induced anxiety in association with alley cues and that feedings in the same locations in the maze would eliminate or reduce the anxiety, thus preventing the perseveration of the position responses in the fed group. His results confirmed his prediction. The fed group extinguished significantly faster than did the group in which shock-induced anxiety was still presumed to be operative. (Two nonshock control groups also extinguished more rapidly than this anxiety group.)

Maier and Ellen (1951) re-examined Farber's data to observe that only a few animals (5 of 24) contributing extreme scores accounted for his findings. They argued from this that anxiety-reduction theory could not account for such a bimodal response distribution, whereas Maier's frustration theory would have predicted that some animals would be frustrated and others not. In his reply, Farber (1954) noted that his differences would be significant even if these extreme rats were eliminated, and that perhaps strain differences (his animals had been drawn from several sources) might account for the Maier-Ellen criticisms without challenging the meaning of his data.

Wilcoxon (1952) challenged Maier's explanation of fixation in an insoluble problem situation on the hypothesis that the procedures here constitute a form of *partial reinforcement*, and are explainable in those terms. By introducing a partially reinforced group he was able to show a 92 per cent fixation, as compared with 58 per cent under Maier's usual conditions and 38 per cent under continuous reinforcement.

Maier (1956), however, has not conceded that either Farber's or Wilcoxon's studies (see, also, Maier & Ellen, 1954; Ellen, 1956) obviate his fundamental dichotomy between motivated and fixated behaviors. We may conclude, with Maier, that "systematic evaluation of the facts" is the only way this matter can ultimately be resolved.

Maier (1956, pp. 381 ff.) raises a point of further interest to us in discussing the physiological basis for a frustration mechanism. He suggests the possibility of a threshold mechanism operative at the transition points between anger and rage, fear and terror, and choice and compulsion. "Frustration theory would demand some kind of sharp transition, either in the form of a dropping out of voluntary control mechanisms or a sheer dominance of autonomic processes as provocation exceeded a certain point" (p. 382). This type of thinking is highly consistent with views expressed in other contexts (see related discussions in Chapters 7 and 8) and will be dealt with at greater length in a later discussion of stress. However, the validity of a frustration threshold, if established, would not necessarily support Maier's contention that frustration is a nonadaptive process. On the contrary, it is our belief that the ultimate clarification of mechanism may show that extreme as well as moderate reactions are aspects of a complex self-regulating apparatus which is in essence adaptive.

Summary

Frustration refers to the state of a motivated organism when its goal behavior is thwarted. Such thwarting may result from the intrusion of physical barriers between organism and goal, the removal of directional cues, or a conflict of action tendencies, goals, or motives. Barriers may be active or passive, external or internal. Normal development contains a number of crisis situations which may serve as instigations to frustration. Frustration appears to be related to the intensity and the centrality to ego-maintenance of the underlying motive, but frustration is "more than" the drive whose thwarting gives rise to it.

Frustration is an emotional state which has both drive and cue properties and may, through a fractional anticipatory mechanism, be conditionable. Four main reaction patterns are discussed: aggression, regression, repression, and fixation. The evidence seems to support each as a possible reaction to frustration, but none as a necessary consequence of instigation to frustration. Learning seems to play a major role in determining frustration-instigated responses, which, in the main, appear to be motivational in nature.

CONFLICT

Conflict is the result of two or more equal but incompatible response tendencies. In a sense it is the equivalent of a condition of double or multiple frustration, each of the competing action tendencies serving as the barrier to the completion of the other(s). As in the case of other frustrations, conflict is a state of increased tension, but by its very nature it is characterized by vacillation, hesitancy, fatigue, and often complete blocking (Miller, 1944).

Like frustration, conflict is a common occurrence in all lives. Each choice and each action implies the overcoming of alternatives and thus the resolving of conflicts (see earlier discussion of inhibition, p. 147). Freud (see Chapter 12) emphasized the role played by conflicts in psychopathological behavior, and conflict resolution is one of the primary aims of psychotherapy. From another context, Pavlov (see Chapter 4) showed how extremely difficult choices—between discriminanda made increasingly similar—could lead to conflict and thence to conflict-resolving rather than problem-solving behavior. In both clinical observations and experimental studies, conflict has been shown to be an emotional response to a situation requiring incompatible responses and to invoke responses which themselves serve a motivational function (i.e., of an aversive character motivating escape behavior).

But not all situations involving competing response tendencies produce conflict. When the antagonistic tendencies are of unequal strength, when they occur in temporal sequence rather than simultaneously, when they represent underlying motives of unequal importance, or when their goals or end-states are not equally available, one response may occur before or to the exclusion of the other. Similarly, if two incompatible response tendencies exist in a situation where a third response is possible (e.g., escape), the individual may respond in a direction which is neutral with respect to the conflicting tendencies. Or where a third goal may incorporate aspects of the mutually frustrating goal actions, the resultant response is likely to be in the direction of this new goal.

Sources of Conflict

We said earlier that conflict may arise not only from action incompatibilities but between motives and goals as well. It should be clear, however, that motives or end-states of action must at some time involve response tendencies, if not responses, and that the conflict arises because of the incompatibilities between the action tendencies and not the motives or goals themselves. Theoretically, motives and goals may be incompatible and yet not produce conflict. That is, one may live with incongruities between facts and fancies, present and future, realities and aspirations, etc., without the contradictions producing conflict. It is only when the satisfaction of one motive (or striving behavior in the direction of one goal) *via invoked action tendencies* precludes the satisfaction of the other (either real or fancied) by preventing the performance of instrumental acts which would serve the competing motive that a conflict will come into existence.

Types of Incompatibilities

Our care in distinguishing action or response tendencies from actions to this point has been intentional. Not all competitions involve overt or muscular responses. Miller (1944, pp. 456 ff.) suggests that there are at least five types (or levels) of incompatibilities. These can occur between competing mechanical, neural, chemical, perceptual, or acquired processes.

Mechanical (or motor) conflicts refer to the mutual inhibition of incompatible muscular or overt motor responses. (This form of conflict has been the most widely studied in psychological research dealing with complex reaction time and choice behaviors [cf. Hovland and Sears, 1938; Sears and Hovland, 1941; Andreas, 1958].) *Neural* incompatibilities refer to conflicts between those central processes which accompany or sometimes precede or short-circuit motor choices. (See earlier discussion of central inhibitory processes, particularly Sherrington's notion of reciprocal inhibition, p. 148.) Smith and Guthrie (1921), in describing instances of what they call *un*stable equilibria in conflict behavior, note Sherrington's example of a dog simultaneously tickled on both sides. The dog fails to give the scratch reflex on either side, although if one or the other is somehow started, it will continue to completion. The conflict here is between neural response tendencies. (Smith and Guthrie use this illustration to show that an opposition of equal positive choices will, once a resolution is begun, quickly disappear. This is in contrast to situations of *stable* equilibrium, as we shall see in discussing various types of conflict later in this section.)

Chemical incompatibilities refer to those instances of hormonal or biochemical antagonism (as between the stimulating and inhibiting effects, respectively, of acetylcholine and epinephrine on intestinal peristalsis) which may occur in emotional experiences during eating. Although Miller (in 1944) did not give too much emphasis to this type of conflict, more recent evidence on the importance (and conditionability) of subtle biochemical changes in relation to behavior suggests that biochemical conflicts may play a significant role in both response perpetuation and response change (see Bykov, 1957; Miller, 1960).

By *perceptual* incompatibilities, Miller refers to the fact that certain forms of perceptual response (as occur in resolving reversible illusions or ambiguous figures) tend to remove the stimulus to the alternative response (at least temporarily). Alternations in fixation and shifts in attention and in eye movements show evidence of conflict by the vacillation in response.

Finally, *acquired* incompatibilities are those which result from differential conditioning procedures or cultural training, in which initially (and intrinsically) compatible responses become incompatible by virtue of selective association with rewards and punishments. Many examples of this can of course be drawn from everyday life. Social *faux pas* are classic instances where the "natural" and "social" or acquired ways of responding may lead to conflict, especially during the acquisition of the social graces. In similar fashion, habit acquisition provides a number of opportunities for conflicts at all levels of response during the period in which earlier and later habits are of approximately equal strength.

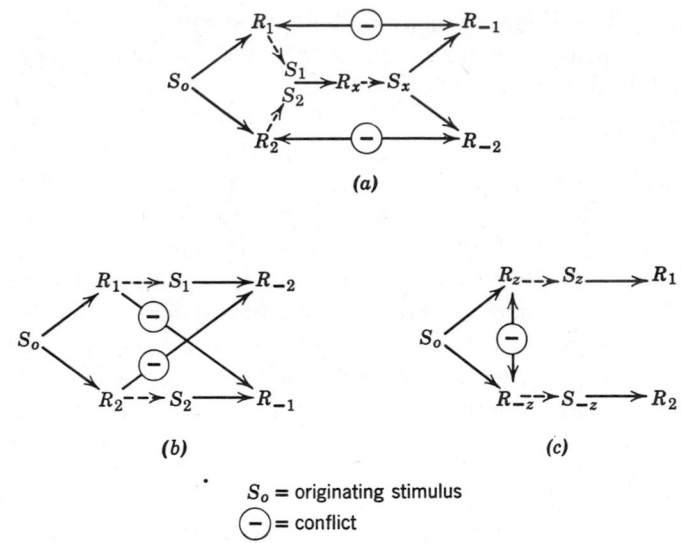

S_o = originating stimulus

$\ominus$ = conflict

Figure 9–2. S_o is any stimulus situation eliciting two responses, R_1 and R_2, which originally were compatible. These responses produce the proprioceptive stimuli S_1 and S_2. In (*a*) the pattern of S_1 and S_2 appearing together elicits the anxiety response R_x, producing the anxiety stimulus S_x. This stimulus elicits the responses R_{-1} and R_{-2} incompatible with R_1 and R_2, respectively. In (*b*) the responses inhibiting R_1 and R_2, are attached directly to the stimuli produced by R_1 and R_2, respectively, whereas in (*c*) the two original compatible responses R_1 and R_2 are dependent on mutually incompatible cue-producing responses, R_z and R_{-z}. To the extent that these mediating responses are themselves mutually exclusive, R_1 and R_2 will not appear simultaneously. Reproduced by permission from Miller (1944, p. 458).

In sum, *any* type of response which can be isolated from any other response can be or can become incompatible with any other response at either a covert or overt level. Miller (1944, p. 458) shows three ways, schematically, in which responses can acquire incompatibility, through the mediation of anxiety and other cue-producing responses. If we allow the S and R symbols of his diagram (see Fig. 9–2) to represent either internal (e.g., chemical, neural, symbolic) or external events, the models can be seen to be quite general.[8]

Types of Conflict

Lewin (1931, 1935, 1938; see, also, Leeper, 1943) has analyzed types of conflicts in terms of his field theoretical system (see p. 357). Considered on the basis of movements in space in relation to goals (although Lewin's vector and force analysis is admittedly more complex than this), response tendencies can be divided into two groups: those involving *approach to* and those involving *avoidance of* a goal or goal region. Using only two goals (or motives), four types of conflict can be derived from these two basic response patterns: approach-approach, avoidance-avoidance, approach-avoidance, and double approach-avoidance. Lewin (1935, pp. 88 ff.) describes the first three of these patterns diagrammatically in terms of forces acting upon a young child. The fourth is described by Miller (1944, pp. 446 ff.). Figure 9–3 shows all four conflict paradigms. Each will be described briefly.

Approach-Approach. The simplest form of conflict is one between two goals of positive valence or between two approach tendencies. The proverbial ass which is supposed to have starved to death because it found itself equidistant from two equally attractive bales of hay exemplifies this type of conflict. However, it would be most unusual for a conflict of this type to produce consequences so dire as these. As noted earlier, this is an *un*stable situation which is quickly resolved in one direction or the other. Vacillation in this case would lead to choice, since no forces increase against a choice once it is made.

Avoidance-Avoidance. The opposite of approach-approach situations, double avoidance problems, involves a choice between equally *un*desirable goals ("between the devil and the deep blue sea," as it were). Unless there is a barrier enclosing the field, most avoidance-avoidance problems are resolved by compromise solutions which avoid both negative goals. When a barrier is present—or where there are latent alternative tendencies involved—the conflict produces what

[8] For purposes of explication, the further discussion of conflict in this chapter will be in terms of response tendencies or responses, but these should always be understood to be applicable to any level of incompatibility.

Smith and Guthrie (see p. 431) described as a *stable* equilibrium. Movement away from one undesirable goal brings the individual closer to the opposite goal, which is also undesirable and thus gives rise to countermovement. Thus where possibilities of escape are limited, vacillation and response blocking may be expected to go on indefinitely.

Approach-Avoidance. No external barrier is needed in an approach-avoidance situation to keep the individual from escaping the field, since he is trapped there by his own desire to attain the goal. At the same

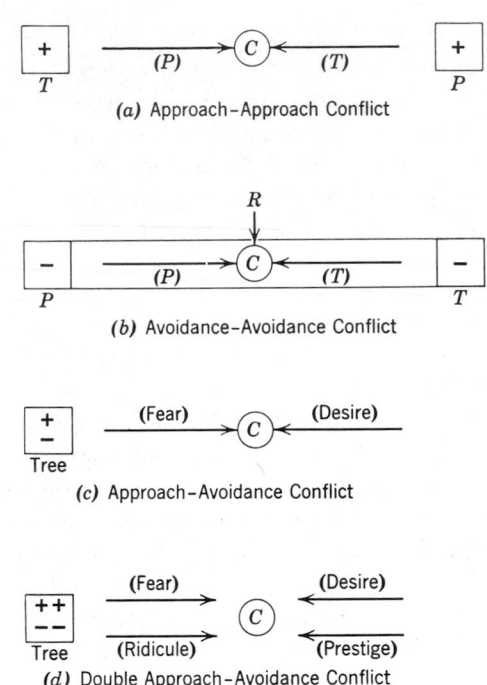

Figure 9-3. Four types of conflict. (Plus and minus signs represent positive and negative valences of goals and goal regions, respectively. Arrows represent direction of forces acting upon child.) (*a*) A child (*C*) must choose between the equally attractive (+) alternatives of playing with a new toy (*T*) and going to watch a parade (*P*). (*b*) A child (*C*) is forced to perform an undesirable task (*T*) on threat of punishment (*P*). The choices are equally unattractive (−). Barriers are shown surrounding the field to indicate that escape (shown as resultant force [*R*]) is not possible. (*c*) A child (*C*) wishes (+) to climb a tree. He is fearful (−) of being hurt. The tree is thus an object he both wishes to approach and avoid. (*d*) A child (*C*) wishes (+) to climb a tree. He is fearful (−) of being hurt. His friends are watching. He will gain prestige (+) if he succeeds, be ridiculed (−) if he tries and fails.

time he is kept from his objective by fear or some other negative incentive associated with the goal state or goal region. Under these circumstances, even more than in an avoidance-avoidance conflict, vacillation would be expected, the individual both approaching and retreating from the goal, movement occurring at a distance and within a range determined by the relative strengths of the two tendencies.

Double Approach-Avoidance. Finally, a number of combinations of approach and avoidance tendencies may produce a double (or multiple) approach-avoidance conflict. Two or more goals may be involved, each of which has both approach and avoidance tendencies associated with it. In some instances, the strength of both approach and avoidance tendencies to a single goal region may be the result of a summation of several separate tendencies (Miller, 1944, p. 446).

The latter situation is illustrated in Figure 9–3*d*, where a child may wish to climb a tree (approach) but is fearful of injury (avoidance). At the same time climbing the tree (approach) will gain social prestige for him and failing to do so (avoidance) will lead to ridicule by his peers. A variety of additional factors could be posited on the side of approach (e.g., gain a view, build a tree house) or avoidance (e.g., parental punishment, broken tree limb).

A two-goal situation might be any combination of approach-approach and avoidance-avoidance situations, where the two goals are in opposition and each elicits avoidance as well as approach tendencies. Thus the new toy of Figure 9–3*a* may be a fragile one, eliciting play behavior but also fear (the child having been previously punished for breaking toys), while the parade watching elicits desire *and* fear in the case of a child frightened by crowds. Movement toward one goal and away from the other would be expected to summate, as would the opposing pair of action tendencies, frustrating goal approach in either direction. In either the case of the toy or that of the parade the approach tendencies might be stronger than the avoidance tendencies. However, the summation of factors would serve to increase the ambivalence and thus the conflict. A child in this circumstance, trapped by the equal and opposite forces as it were, may burst out in tears or display some other form of emotionality.

In all these forms of conflict, it should be recognized that conflict will occur only in the absence of alternatives other than the equal and opposing tendencies. Thus the individual may be kept in the field of conflict by his own desires, by fears of consequences (i.e., real or imagined punishments) associated with abortive or escape reactions, or by physical barriers preventing escape. The crucial role assigned to conflict as a basis for neurosis and to conflict resolution in therapy, particularly by the psychoanalysts, makes it important to recognize the importance of unconscious factors not only in the conflict proper but in keeping the individual in the conflict field. The role of anxiety in this respect is of particular significance (see discussions of anxiety and defense in Chapters 12 and 14).

Miller's Conflict Model

Neal Miller (1944, 1951c; Dollard & Miller, 1950) has presented and elaborated a stimulus-response analysis of conflict from which a number of predictions (of conflict behavior, displacement, effects of drugs, and psychotherapeutic outcome) have been made (see Miller, 1958, 1959). His theoretical model contains the following five basic assumptions (1951c, p. 90): (1) There are *gradients* of approach and (2) of avoidance. The tendency to approach a goal (and to avoid a feared stimulus) is stronger the nearer the subject is to it; (3) the avoidance gradient is *steeper* than that of approach, increasing more rapidly with nearness; (4) both approach and avoidance tendencies vary directly with the strength of their respective underlying drives; (5) when two incompatible responses are in conflict, the stronger one will occur.[9]

Applying his theory to an approach-avoidance conflict, Miller and others have been able to show the effects of the relative heights of gradients upon the distance from the goal at which conflict behavior will occur. The assumptions, although stated in terms of a spatial model, are not intended to be restricted to spatial conflict.[10] However, support for the model is drawn from a study by Brown (1948) and one by Kagan (1958) which do equate nearness to goal with spatial distance, response tendency with directional physical strength of pull, etc.

Brown (1948) trained rats to run down a short alley either to a food reward or to avoid a shock. Each rat was fitted with a harness so that strength of pull could be measured. Brown was able to confirm a series of deductions from Miller's theory, finding that: rats pulled harder when nearer the goal than when farther away under either approach or avoidance motivation; the strength of avoidance-motivated response tendencies increased more rapidly with nearness to the goal than did that for approach-motivated responses (later confirmed by Kagan,

[9] In terms of the definition of conflict put forward in the past several pages, we would have to note that when two incompatible responses are in conflict, neither *could* be stronger.

[10] Brown (1957) points out that conflicts may be of three varieties: spatial, temporal, and discrimination-induced. Although there are some important distinctions, especially as regards the last of these, we believe the description of the spatial paradigm is appropriate to conflict in general. Some comments about the other two will be made a little later.

1958); increases in drive (via either increase in shock strength or hours of food deprivation) led to an increase in harness-straining.

Figure 9–4 shows the hypothetical interactions which can be expected, on the basis of Miller's theory, between approach and avoidance tendencies of different strengths. Areas of conflict would occur at the points of intersection of any two competing tendencies (i.e., at the points of equal opposition). Any factors which either increase the strength of approach tendencies or decrease the strength of avoidance tendencies, other things being equal, would move the loci of conflict closer to the goal. Conversely, increasing avoidant tendencies or decreasing approach motivation would serve to produce conflict at a distance farther from the goal.

Applications. Miller's model is an attempt to quantify the relationships between approach and avoidance tendencies and the prediction of distance from the goal at which conflict behavior (i.e., vacillation, hesitancy, tension, blocking) will occur. The model has been extended

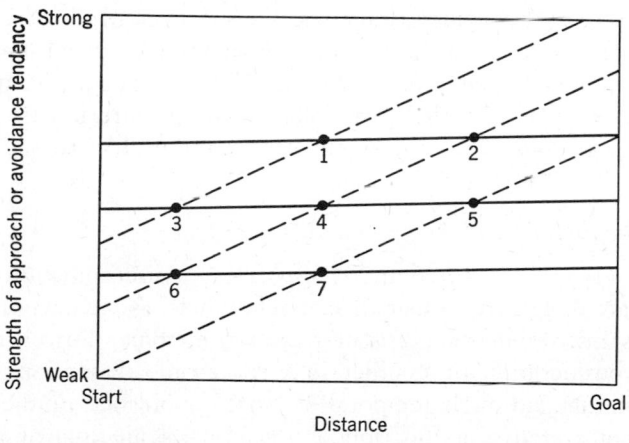

Figure 9–4. Schematic diagram representing three approach gradients (solid lines) and three avoidance gradients (broken lines) of differing overall strengths. Loci of conflict (numbered dots) are at points of intersection of any two opposing tendencies. Note the steeper slope of avoidance than approach gradients and the shifts in the locus of conflict with change in strength of either approach or avoidance tendencies. The set of dots in the center of the diagram (1, 4, and 7, forming a vertical line) suggests that when parallel increases (or decreases) in strength of opposing tendencies are made, the locus of conflict may remain at approximately the same distance from the goal. However, the functions shown are schematic only, and no implications of actual quantitative relations between any of the sets of variables are being made. Based on diagrams by Miller (1951c) and Brown (1957).

to incorporate temporal "distance" as well as spatial distances, and to include the continuum of qualitative similarity of new cues to those in earlier learning situations. With these extensions, Miller and his students (see Miller, 1951c) have shown that approach and avoidance tendencies are differentially generalized (the avoidance habits, having steeper gradients, are weakened more by generalization, thus shifting the conflict nearer the goal). The analogue to displacement phenomena is described by Miller (1948b), and confirming evidence is reported by Whiting and Sears (1949) in projective doll-play of children.

Dollard and Miller (1950) and Miller (1951c) suggest how the use of drugs and of psychotherapeutic procedures which either increase approach tendencies or decrease aversions can be manipulated in terms of the theory of conflict. They feel that the logic of the theory can explain, in terms of "movement" toward or away from goals that are both desired and feared, certain paradoxical effects of treatment. So, for example, the effects of an increase in positive motivation (where therapy is directed at positive factors only) will actually increase fear. This is derived from the assumed differences in steepness of gradients for approach and avoidance responses. Thus if we study Figure 9–4, we may see that raising the height of an approach tendency, without simultaneously modifying the corresponding avoidance tendency, may lead to a closer approach to the goal, followed by a more intense aversive reaction (e.g., intersections 3 would then shift to 1, 6 to 4 or 2, and 7 to 5).

Spatial, Temporal, and Discrimination Conflict

Brown (1957) has noted that temporal and discrimination-induced conflicts are in essence similar to spatial conflicts, as we have indicated. He offers an extended analysis of temporal conflicts, however, which permits consideration of conflict in a space-time dimension. (Brown points out that although temporal approach-avoidance gradients have been demonstrated as a function of the nearness in time of an event that is both desired and feared [Rigby, 1954], there has been no evidence supporting the greater steepness of temporal avoidance as compared with approach gradients.)

The intensity of a conflict that is remote in time would be expected to be less and to increase as the time of the event approaches. This is consistent with the analysis of spatial conflict, in which weak tendencies would come into conflict at a point closer to the goal than would strong tendencies. (Both assumptions are based on the increase in cues with nearness.) However, temporal conflicts (or spatiotemporal conflicts) might differ from simple spatial conflicts in several significant ways. As was observed in relation to the analysis of frustration behavior, conflict-generated cues might be expected to arise in anticipation of the conflict situation itself, and previously learned responses associated with conflict (as opposed to the tendencies involved in the conflict) might in turn differentially influence behavior in a spatiotemporal field. Brown speaks of the irreversibility of time (1957, p. 151), using as his example a soldier in combat awaiting a "zero-hour" to engage in an attack. The inevitability of the impending event suggests to Brown that there would be an increase in conflict with the passage of time. We have no argument with the logic of this analysis. However, before it is extended to include approach-avoidance situations, it would be well to examine the possibility that the subjective passage of time in anticipation of desired as opposed to feared or undesired events may not be equal (see Fraisse, 1963; Appley, 1964). If the two time scales are indeed different, the passage of clock time would not affect approach and avoidance tendencies equally, and conflict in temporal situations might not be as readily predictable in terms analogous to physical movement. By the same token, no spatial conflict is free from a time dimension. The differential steepness of approach and avoidance gradients in spatial conflict, for which experimental confirmation has been found, may be explained in a similar manner.

Clearly, this is put forward as a purely speculative notion for which no evidential support can be offered at this time. It is proposed in the hope that further research on temporal and spatiotemporal conflicts, particularly with human subjects, will include in their designs some means of measuring what we have called subjective time factors independently of the approach and avoidance responses themselves.

Mowrer (1960, pp. 424 ff.), in an analysis of conflict behavior in terms of "hope" and "fear," makes an interesting observation with respect to the actual behavior to be expected during conflict. Pointing out that approach and avoidance behaviors may be associated with *same* stimuli, he suggests that an algebraic summation should eventually occur, and that initial oscillatory behavior would be abandoned in the presence of such stimuli and the subject would *come to rest*. Subsequent changes (as in level of hunger or of fear, if these are the motivational variables involved) will cause oscillation to "break out" again. Thus Mowrer in effect considers only the oscillatory (vacillatory) behaviors to be conflict, and this to occur only at points of *approximate* equality of opposing tendencies (or underlying motive states). However, heightened muscular tension in states of inaction resulting from equal and opposite tendencies suggests that the balance is highly charged rather than neutral. This raises the question as to whether this motivational state is merely the sum of the two opposing tendencies or, as was suggested in the case of frustration, has a conflict-instigated drive increment added. Let us turn to this final point now.

Conflict as Drive

As we have already proposed that conflict is a special case of frustration, it would follow that our earlier conclusions with respect to frustration-instigated drive would be appropriate here as well. There is nothing new to be added at this point that has not already been said. However, we can observe that since in conflict the two action tendencies are in opposition, any drive-increment should be expected to increase both tendencies equally. Thus little or no "movement" could be expected, and the drive increase may be expected to increase somatic involvement, anxiety, and such action tendencies as may be associated with these conditions independently of the conflict which gave rise to the increased emotionality.

On the other hand, if Miller's hypothesis with respect to differential steepness of approach and avoidance gradients is correct, a somewhat different prediction might be made for approach-avoidance conflicts. The conflict-instigated drive increment should increase both tendencies to approach and to avoid. In light of the different gradients, however, the increase will upset the balance, leading to avoidance behavior, in turn increasing the relative strength of the approach behavior tendency, leading to approach behavior, etc. In other words, an increased vascillation would be predicted as the two tendencies shift from balanced to unbalanced state as a function of repeated mutual frustration and the resultant drive increment. Brown (1957, p. 142) has described this situation most aptly as "a kind of *pernicious homeostasis.*"

The above suggests that investigation of differential *components* of conflict behavior may well be worth the trouble. At the same time, the further specification of the nature of the gradients of approach and avoidance tendencies (i.e., specification of the functions they obey) will add considerably to our understanding of conflict and conflict resolution. At the moment, it appears that in *all* of the types of conflict, whether a conflict-instigated drive is posited or not, conflict resolution could not be expected without the intervention of factors outside the situation to break the self-maintaining cycle.

Summary

Conflict refers to the special case of frustration in which the interference with one response or action-tendency comes from an equal and opposite (incompatible) response tendency. Conflict may arise between motives, goals, or responses but is meaningfully conceived only in terms of incompatible action tendencies. Incompatibilities, however, can occur at not only motor, but neural, chemical, perceptual, or symbolic levels as well.

There are four main types of response conflicts: approach-approach, avoidance-avoidance, approach avoidance, and double (or multiple) approach-avoidance. Avoidance-avoidance conflicts can only occur in fields where barriers prevent escape, whereas no barriers are needed in any conflicts involving approach tendencies, as the individual is kept in the field by his own desires.

Miller's conflict theory proposes that gradients of approach and avoidance tendencies exist, with both tendencies growing stronger with nearness to the goal region. Avoidance gradients are steeper than approach gradients, and the height of both gradients varies with strength of their respective underlying drives. Evidence supporting Miller's analysis is described, and a schematic representation of the effects on conflict of differing approach and avoidance gradients is presented. The possible wide applicability of the Miller model is discussed as are certain needs for clarification and extension of evidence.

Similarities between spatial, temporal, and discrimination-induced conflicts are discussed as are certain possible differences. The possibility of conflict-induced drive and its consequences are also discussed.

STRESS

The term *stress* has come into wide use in behavior study only within the past two decades. But in this relatively short time it has all but preempted a field previously shared by a number of other concepts, including those which have been treated thus far in this chapter. Originating in the physical sciences, the term has the meaning of a force which, acting on a body, produces strain or deformation. Although sometimes used in this way in physiology and psychology, it seems gradually to have reversed this meaning, so that stress has come to represent the bodily condition under strain. The reason why this reversal is desirable will become evident when we discuss the concept of systemic stress. Both in the physical sciences and in biological and behavioral study, the concept of stress carries with it the connotation of an extreme condition, involving tension, perhaps damage, and some form of resistance to the straining force.

There are actually two stress concepts which are relevant to our considerations here, one primarily in physiology and psychobiology (systemic stress) and one in psychology (psychological stress). The two are closely related and since the limiting adjectives are not always used, they are often intermixed. In the hope that a discussion of each will help clarify the matter, we shall treat the two separately, although in describing each we shall necessarily involve the other.

Systemic Stress

The current popularity of the stress concept in psychobiology stems largely from the work of Hans Selye, the Canadian endocrinologist-physiologist. Since the mid-1930's, Selye has given the concept wide currency through an extensive series of papers and books (cf. Selye, 1936, 1950, 1951–1956, 1956a). He describes his work as an extension of the Bernard-Cannon concepts of adaptation and homeostasis (see Chapter 7) and sees stress as the state of the organism following failure of the normal homeostatic regulatory mechanisms of adaptation. Stress is manifested through the symptoms of a *General Adaptation Syndrome* (*GAS*) (see p. 443), a name chosen deliberately to emphasize the link. Neither stress nor the *GAS* is the same as adaptation, however, as we shall see.

Stress as Nonspecifically Induced Change. A main key to the understanding of Selye's concept of (systemic) stress is the distinction he makes between the *specific* effects induced by a stressor agent and the effects induced by such stimulation which are *not* specific to it. Thus he observes that whereas one stimulus (e.g., cold) may produce a vasoconstriction and a second stimulus (e.g., heat) a vasodilation, both (or either), if applied intensely or long enough, produce(s) *effects in common* and therefore not specific to either stimulus. These common changes, taken together, constitute the stereotypical response pattern of systemic stress. Selye "operationally" defines stress as "*a state manifested by a syndrome which consists of all the nonspecifically induced changes in a biologic system.*" Thus it has, he writes, "its own characteristic form of expression . . . but no particular, specific cause" (1959, p. 403). (It is for this reason that we believe the term stress is more appropriately used to describe a state of the organism rather than its varied instigating conditions.)

Stressor Agents. A large variety of stimulus events (both external and internal) have been shown to be capable of giving rise to stress. Such stimuli, or *stressor agents,* include heat, cold, infections, intoxicants, hemorrhage, restraint, muscular exercise, drugs, exogenous hormones, injury, shock, surgical trauma, and X-irradiation.[11]

Actually, *any* stimulus can serve as a stressor, depending on the con-

---

[11] Ganong and Forsham (1960), reviewing only a part of one year's work on the subject, identified some 19 stressor agents including, in addition to the above, the use of intense or novel stimuli and what they called "psychic" stressors.

text of its application. Significant is the fact that not only direct (surgical, pharmacological, or physical) intervention but indirect (neurogenic or psychogenic) stimulation can induce a (systemic) stress syndrome. Mason (1959), for example, has shown evidence for stress in monkeys induced by such subtle factors as the presence or absence of persons in a room, the change from one room to another, or the application of previously shock-associated stimuli. Christian (1959) has reported both laboratory and field studies in several species in which stress was produced by what he calls "sociopsychological" stimulation of size of animal colony (as distinct from mere physical crowding or space restriction).

Similar psychogenic factors have been shown to be effective stressors in human subjects as well. Basowitz et al. (1955) using paratroopers, Cook and Wherry (1950) studying submariners, Mason (1959) with pilots, and Davis et al. (1952) with combat infantrymen, among others, have demonstrated that life-threat and social-status threat situations could induce symptoms of systemic stress. The degree of stress in any instance depends on the type and intensity of the threat and on certain pre-stress sensitizing factors (see p. 448).

We have cited these examples particularly to emphasize again that not only systemic insults, such as injury or drugs, but such neurogenic and psychogenic stimulation as anticipation of pain, uncertainty, excess or deficiency of neural input, anxiety-provoking situations, or situations made noxious only as a result of prior conditioning can also serve as systemic stressor agents.

The specific responses to specific stressor agents (e.g., vasodilation to heat, antibody formation to infection) appear to be local or focal adaptations appropriate to the particular form of the stressor. When these adaptations are ineffective (as where the stressor is intense or its application prolonged) or when the stressor is nonspecific (as in neurogenic or psychogenic stimulation, or in low-grade infection), the *GAS* is invoked. The general effect of the stress syndrome appears to be the modification of bodily processes in such a way as to make available the energy resources normally kept in reserve or utilized for other functions, such as digestion or anabolism. (This is, of course, an oversimplification of the matter.)

The General Adaptation Syndrome (GAS). The syndrome by which the stress state is made manifest is called the *General Adaptation Syndrome (GAS).* Its characteristic pattern includes three stages: (1) an *alarm reaction,* including an initial *shock phase* of lowered resistance and a *countershock phase,* in which defensive mechanisms begin to operate; (2) a *stage of resistance,* in which adaptation is optimal; and

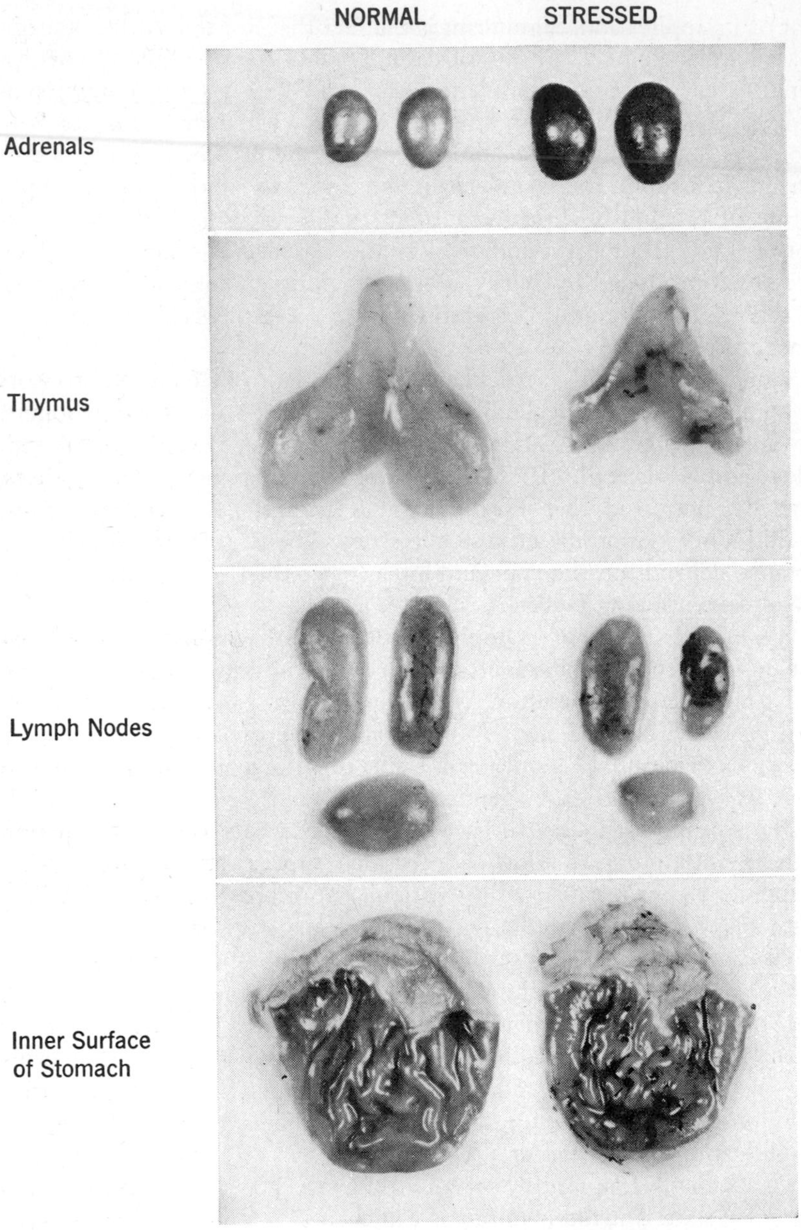

NORMAL   STRESSED

Adrenals

Thymus

Lymph Nodes

Inner Surface
of Stomach

Figure 9-5. Characteristic symptoms of stress syndrome. Note enlarged and discolored adrenals, involuted thymus and lymph nodes, and ulcerated stomach wall. Reproduced with permission from Selye (1952).

(3) a *stage of exhaustion,* marked by the collapse of adaptive responses.

The alarm reaction shows early (in its shock phase) an autonomic excitability, adrenaline discharge, and such symptoms as an increased heart rate, decreased body temperature and muscle tone, anemia, acidosis, transitory blood-sugar increase followed by a decrease, transitory blood leukocyte decrease followed by an increase, and gastrointestinal ulcerations. If noxious stimulation continues but is not too severe, countershock appears. This second phase of the alarm reaction is marked by adrenocortical enlargement and hyperactivity, and rapid thymus and other lymphatic involution.[12] Figure 9–5 illustrates four of the classical signs of the stress syndrome.

In the stage of resistance the symptoms of the alarm reaction seem to disappear. It is possible, however, that they are simply masked by adaptive systemic responding (as of the pituitary-adrenocortical system), for if noxious stimulation persists, this stage gives way to the final stage of exhaustion, in which the symptoms present in the alarm reaction reappear.

The *GAS* may be short-circuited by an intense or overwhelming stressor, such that no countershock or resistance develops, the organism going from the shock phase (in which resistance is far below normal) into exhaustion and death; or it may be foreshortened or prolonged, depending on the intensity and/or duration of the stressor and the state of the organism at the time of exposure.

Figure 9–6 illustrates some of the known (and hypothesized) processes of the stress syndrome and some of the symptoms of the *GAS.* Omitted from the diagram are both a number of details of the systems shown and additional systems which are probably involved. Likewise omitted are the many feedback loops that are known to exist between and among levels.[13]

---

[12] The listing of some of the symptoms of these two phases of the alarm reaction is intended to show what is meant by the stereotypic syndrome of stress (see Selye, 1950 or 1952, for more detailed symptom description). Under ordinary circumstances the appearance of these symptoms can be taken as a reliable measure of the presence of stress. Their absence, however, does not mean that stress is not present (cf. Selye, 1959).

[13] As an example, the hypothalamus is shown without separate identification of its neural, secretory or neurosecretory centers from which stimuli to the pituitary lobes emanate. It is now fairly well established that vasopressin and probably oxytocin, the posterior pituitary hormones, are actually neurosecretory materials produced in the hypothalamus and only stored in the pituitary. Vasopressin (the antidiuretic hormone) is known to act through the kidney, as well as contributing directly to general resistance. In addition, some claim has been made for vasopressin (or a factor like it) as a stimulant to the release of adrenocorticotrophic hormone (ACTH), although it could not be the only means of ACTH activation (see Ham, 1957; Bäjusz, 1960).

The diagram shows that several different mechanisms lead to what we have called "general resistance." (By this term we refer to all factors acting—via the biologic system generally—to neutralize or reduce the instigation(s) to stress.) The general resistance factors, in turn, act back upon the stressor, completing the main feedback loop. The fact that multiple pathways exist suggests that interruption of any one path would not be critical to the development of resistance. So, for example, although the diagram and the list of symptoms in the alarm

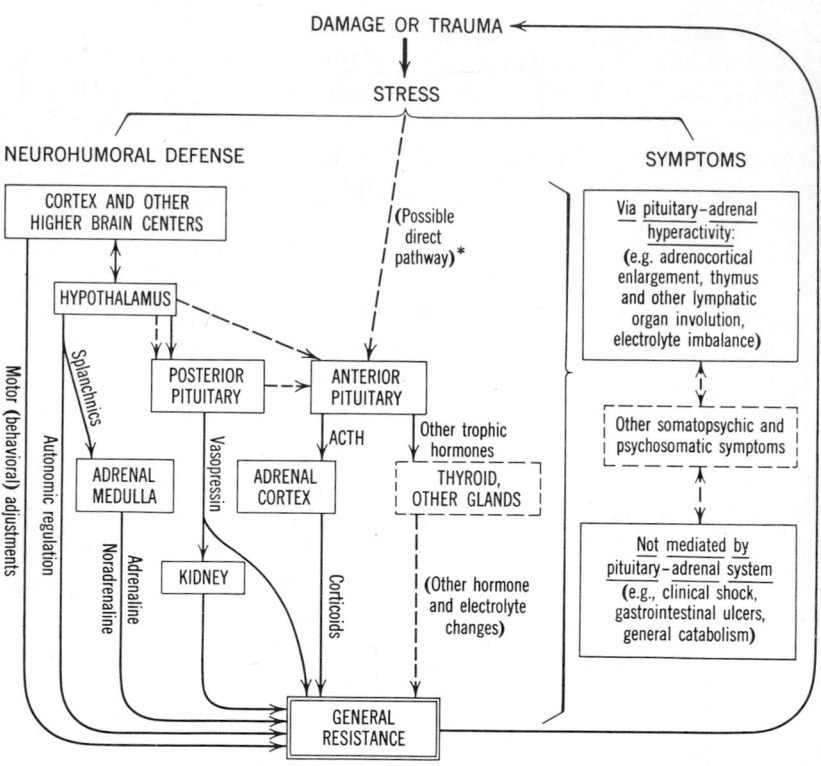

Figure 9–6. Partial schema of stress syndrome. (Solid lines represent known relations, broken lines uncertain relations.)

* Fortier (1951) and G. W. Harris (1955) have postulated possible direct humoral pathways to the anterior pituitary for certain systemic (as opposed to neural) stressors, in light of the observed release of ACTH from the anterior pituitary in the absence of connection with the hypothalamus. However, Ganong and Forsham (1960) challenge this idea on the basis that no pituitary activity has been observed when lesions are placed in the median eminence. Since to our knowledge the matter remains unsettled we have shown this possible direct pathway as tentative.

reaction tend to emphasize the role of the pituitary-adrenal system in the stress syndrome, neither adrenalectomy nor hypophysectomy eliminates the *GAS*. Such surgical interventions do, however, shorten the resistance stage (see Selye, 1959), suggesting a cumulative effect of the several parallel mechanisms.

Systemic Stress, Adaptation, and the "Diseases of Adaptation." Systemic stress results, we have said, from the failure of normal homeostatic adaptive responses to reduce or eliminate the sources of distress. The symptoms of stress (i.e., the *GAS*) are both an indication of maladaptation (e.g., in the lowered resistance of the shock phase of the alarm reaction) and of further adaptation (beginning in countershock and continuing through the stage of resistance). To limit or prevent stress is thus to limit or prevent the possibility of further adaptation, since the appearance of the alarm reaction, so far as we know, is a necessary precondition to the development of resistance. In other words, maladaptation (lowered resistance, disorganization) must precede adaptation (increased resistance, reorganization). The appearance of the shock phase of the alarm reaction is, however, no guarantee of further adaptation or recovery. As was earlier noted, a severe stressor (or a mild stressor acting on an already stressed organism) may lead to rapid exhaustion and death.

It is more than likely that the stage of exhaustion of the *GAS* is at least in part a function of the extraordinary physiological reactivity of the organism in the stage of resistance. In other words, the adaptive responses themselves may become stressors. Selye and his associates (see Selye, 1951–1956) have produced "experimental diseases" through exogenous administration of "adaptive" adrenal hormones. Damage to heart, kidney, liver, blood vessels, bones, and skin has been produced by normally nonpathogenic factors intensified through stress exposure.[14] The concept of psychosomatic medicine is in fact predicated on the hypothesis of self-damage through attempts at adaptation (cf. Wolff, 1953).

Timing, Adaptation, and Systemic Stress. There are a number of ways in which temporal factors enter into the determination of the stressfulness of events. First, there appear to be "critical periods" for the incubation of stress effects. The determinants of these are unknown, but it has been shown that early exposure to stressors can prevent the later effectiveness of stress exposure—a sort of "immunization" process

---

[14] This series of experiments by Selye and his associates has been criticized (cf. Ingle & Baker, 1953) because of the large doses of exogenous hormones employed. However, the reports of side-effects of ACTH and cortisone treatments (in presumably clinical doses) tend generally to support the point at issue.

(cf. Selye, 1961). By the same token, exposure to stress in combination with certain exogenous hormone treatments (see p. 447) may induce a more rapid stress reaction (cf. Selye, 1958, 1961). Selye refers to these processes as sensitizing or "conditioning" effects and considers that they play a significant role in determining stress thresholds. In other words, what we may call *latent stress factors* may be introduced by stress pre-exposure (or hormone sensitizing) during certain critical periods or in subliminal amounts. The effects of such latent influences are not apparent at the time of initial exposure, but appear during subsequent stress.

One conclusion from the work in this area is that slow adaptation, through systematically increased exposure to stimulation, may be able to raise stress thresholds, such that stimulus intensities earlier intolerable may be experienced without inducing full-blown stress responses. Conversely, hormonal sensitization tends to lower stress thresholds. Whether the thresholds are raised or lowered by these pre-treatments, however, is a function of the interaction of time and amount. Research on these parameters is as yet inconclusive, however.

Neuroendocrine and Neurovisceral Conditioning. It is known that conditioning (in the Pavlovian sense rather than in the sensitizing sense just discussed) is possible not only of motor and of exocrine reactions but of endocrine and visceral responses as well. Bykov (1957) reports a number of instances of interoceptive conditioning. For example, conditioned diuresis was established to a particular room, to a distinct stimulus (a horn), to injection of water into the stomach; inhibition of this response was likewise able to be controlled as a result of systematic pairing of stimuli. Heart and vascular conditioning, splenic conditioning, respiratory conditioning, and conditioning of HCl secretion have also been demonstrated in response not only to stimulation via the exteroceptive sensory pathways, but to physiologically neutral solutions after pairing with such hormones as thyroxin. Further, it has been shown that both chemical and neural stimulation of internal organs can serve as conditioned stimuli to overt responses which are induced through separate means.

In sum, the processes which compose the stress syndrome have been shown to be separately modifiable by experimental conditioning. It is reasonable to expect that they would be equally affected by the "chance conditionings" of everyday life, and that systemic stress processes, rather than being an isolated biologic system, would be directly involved in psychological adaptive sequences. Two recent studies illustrate this. Cook et al. (1960) showed that adrenaline, noradrenaline, and acetylcholine could serve as conditioned stimuli to a shock avoidance response (whereas control saline injections were ineffective). Gutmann and Jakoubek (1960) demonstrated a significant blood-sugar level rise in rats during successive waiting periods in anticipation of electric shock. Since we know from other studies (e.g., Ax, 1953; Funkenstein et al., 1957) that anger-producing situations lead to noradrenaline-like responses, whereas anxiety is associated with adrenaline-like reactions, the link between systemic and psychological stress appears to be a very real one.

Summary. Systemic stress is defined by Selye as a state manifested by all the nonspecifically induced changes in a biologic system. The stress response, or *General Adaptation Syndrome*, has a stereotyped order and form, involving neural, hormonal, and metabolic mechanisms in complex interrelation with each other. The determination of why, when, and the extent to which given agents may become stressors appears to be a function of three kinds of factors: (1) the innate toxicity of the agent—that is, its capacity to destroy tissue or function; (2) the unique "readiness" of the organism at the time of exposure to a given stimulus—as a function of the sensitizing effects of age, tissue state, previous exposure history, metabolic condition, etc.; and (3) the personal experiential background of the individual—rat or human —in terms of prior neural, humoral, metabolic, or psychosomatic conditioning. With this information as a background, we may now turn to a consideration of psychological stress.

Psychological Stress

Despite the popularity of the concept of stress in psychology and the vast quantity of research on the subject, there is surprisingly little uniformity in the conditions used either to induce or to measure it (cf. Lazarus, Deese, & Osler, 1952; J. G. Miller, 1953). In fact the term itself has been used sometimes to designate arousal conditions, sometimes for state variables, and sometimes to identify responses (cf. Pronko & Leith, 1956; Appley, 1961*a*). It is as though, when the word stress came into vogue, each investigator, who had been working with a concept he felt was closely related, substituted the word stress for it and continued in his same line of investigation. Thus stress has been used as a synonym for anxiety, conflict, ego-involvement, frustration, threat, and emotionality, generally, depending on a given writer's particular predilections. The need to spell out the relationships between and among these kindred concepts seems to us to be paramount. It is a task to which we feel obliged to contribute.

Let us first note that stress, when used in primarily psychological contexts, is not necessarily equivalent to systemic stress. Psychological stress is generally a *broader* term, including systemic stress but also the conditions preceding systemic involvement, such as those described for frustration and conflict. Like these others, therefore, it refers to a *state of the organism* resulting from some *interaction* with the environment. Additional identifying characteristics of stress will become apparent as we examine and compare some of the definitions which have been offered by psychologists.

Definitions of Stress. Lazarus, Deese, and Osler (1952), in an early review of the then burgeoning research on the effects of stress on performance, observed that "stress . . . is really a secondary concept, built upon the relationship between a primary concept, motivation, and the situation in which motivated behavior appears." More specifically, they conclude that "stress occurs when a particular situation threatens the attainment of some goal" (p. 295). This description resembles, of course, what we have earlier said about frustration, and does not distinguish the two conditions.

J. G. Miller (1953), by contrast, treats stress as a stimulus variable. He defines it as "any vigorous, extreme, or unusual stimulation which, being a threat, causes some significant change in behavior . . ." (p. A–4). On the other hand, if we were to change this to consider stress as the state of the organism resulting from such stimulation, the definition does denote the kind of stimulation that leads to stress, the requirement that a threat be involved, and that a significant change in behavior results. Pascal (1951) more clearly places the determinants within the individual when he defines stress "in terms of a perceived environmental situation which threatens the gratification of needs . . ." (p. 177). Here Pascal makes explicit the role of *perception* in determining stressfulness. Although it was implied by the notion of threat in the previous two definitions, we would consider the perception of threat as an important defining characteristic.

Basowitz et al. (1955), in their detailed report of a study of anxiety and stress in paratroop trainees, note that they began their investigation with a situational definition of stress in terms of "stimuli *more likely* to produce disturbances." They concluded, however, that "in future research . . . we should not consider stress as *imposed* upon the organism, but as its *response* to internal or external processes which reach those threshold levels that strain its physiological and psychological integrative capacities close to or beyond their limits" (pp. 288–289). And Schaffer (1954), in what he terms a neurophysiological hypothesis, suggests that stress "is brought about when a highly motivated organism is unable to find an adjustive response to the problem confronting it. This may occur," he writes, "under conditions variously described as trauma, frustration and conflict" (p. 332).

If we combine the critical features of stress from these various definitions with the notions with which we started, the following emerge:
(1) stress is a state of the organism, (2) it involves an interaction between the individual and the environment, (3) it is more extreme than
an ordinarily motivated state and may be the same as a state of severe
frustration or conflict, (4) a threat must be present, (5) the threat
must somehow be perceived, (6) the integrity of the organism is somehow involved, and (7) a normal adjustive (coping) response cannot be
found. As Schaffer has implied, not all of these features distinguish
stress from such related conditions as frustration and conflict. We
believe that such a distinction is desirable and possible, not merely to
avoid semantic confusion, but because the conditions represent at
least quantitatively different levels of reactivity. The next section represents a proposed distinction in terms of a concept of successive thresh-
olds.

Threat, Frustration, and Stress. In a previous definition, one of us
(Appley, 1962*a*) proposed that stress is "the state of an organism in any
situation where his general well-being is threatened, *and* where no
readily available response exists for the reduction of the threat" (p. 880).
By well-being he referred to a state contingent upon the regular (or
periodic) satisfaction of its motives. However, a condition of insufficiency alone would not produce psychological stress. As we noted in
discussing frustration (see p. 417), a simple condition of insufficiency
might lead to innate or acquired (habitual) coping behavior. The failure of such already available response modes would permit an increase
in arousal to the point where new, exploratory coping (either overt
or covert) takes place. We may call this level an *instigation threshold*.
Such a threshold defines the change from innate or habitual to new [15]
coping behavior or, conversely, it is defined by the exhaustion (or
anticipated exhaustion) of the repertory of *already existing* effective
coping responses.

Subsequently, should the goal-behaviors be interfered with, or such
interference anticipated, and the source of instigation persist, a second
threshold—the *frustration threshold*—will be reached. This is the point
at which the situation is perceived as likely to be beyond the capacities
of the organism's readily available coping potential. This is the point

---

[15] Newness here refers to the fact that these responses are not the usual
responses used. Included may be earlier, discarded habitual responses, as well as
responses acquired only at the higher level of arousal and somehow introduced
here as a result of this increased arousal level. However, the basic implication of a
requirement of change of response mode remains.

at which we may begin to speak of *threat perception*. The crossing of this threshold should give rise to anxiety and, as a result of increased (e.g., frustration-instigated?) motivation, to an intensification of (perhaps repetitive) coping behavior. Anxiety-related responses may now enter the picture. These in turn may lead to further intensification of response, introducing competing responses, or to escape responses, or all three, depending on the nature of the situation and of the responses innately or previously attached to anxiety. In short, it is at this threshold that a shift in pattern of response occurs, from exclusively task-oriented, problem-solving behavior to the inclusion of ego-oriented, self- or integrity-sustaining behavior. (See earlier discussion of ego-involvement, p. 418, and Chapter 14.)

It is, perhaps, only *if and when* both types of behaviors (task- and ego-oriented) have persisted for a while without any effective change in the situation that a third, or *stress threshold*, is reached. At this point we may observe the dropping out of all task-oriented behaviors, and the exclusive preoccupation of the organism with ego protection. This more extreme threshold may be identified with the *perception of danger* and a resultant further intensification of ego-defensive responses (desperation? panic?).

Finally, the exhaustion or anticipated exhaustion of ego-defensive behaviors may lead to a fourth, or *exhaustion threshold*, at which point we may speak of the *perception* [16] *of helplessness or hopelessness*.[17] Here the cumulative fatigue and inhibition, increased most rapidly during the previous period of exaggerated response, overtakes energized responding, and a drop in activity occurs.

Comment. If this analysis is at all plausible, several implications follow. First, the concept of stress in the proposed "model" fits all seven of the criteria which were set out in the discussion of definitions of stress. In addition, the "model" offers a framework for ordering a set of related concepts. Whereas frustration-associated behaviors are more highly energized than are instigation-associated behaviors, stress-associated behaviors are even more so. The cumulative fatigue and inhibition would in turn provide for a less energized final period associated with exhaustion. As one moves through time along an arousal continuum, the successive intrusion of more and more secondary (ego-protective)

---

[16] By perception as used here and elsewhere in this section we do not mean to imply the *conscious* awareness of a situation as requiring a particular type of response, etc. Unconscious "awareness," as indicated by autonomic responses, for example, or as reported in psychopathology, is quite sufficient to our meaning of perception (see Appley, 1962*b*).

[17] See Mowrer (1960) for an interesting discussion of the concept of hope as used in a related manner.

goal behavior should lead to an increase and then a decrease in the efficiency of behavior as measured relevant to the initial goal. Thus it should not be too difficult to accommodate the present proposal with the inverted U-shaped curve reported for autonomic activity (see Chapter 7).

By way of further comment, we are aware that we have not yet offered a definition of psychological stress in terms of our present proposal. We would now modify our earlier definition to state that stress is *the state of an organism where he perceives that his well-being (or integrity) is endangered and that he must devote all of his energies to its protection.*

One further comment relates to the possibility that the use of a threshold concept may suggest that there are sharp lines of demarcation between stages. We rather expect that the transition points of which we speak are *zones*, the width of which would be determined by the rate of change of probabilities of reversing one's course as one progressed through the zone. In other words, threat, danger, or hopelessness should be perceived by the individual in degrees of increasing likelihood with time in a situation (and inversely with the effectiveness of his coping behaviors) rather than as all-or-none perceptions.

Frustration Tolerance and Stress Tolerance. Individuals may be expected, on the basis of both innate and acquired factors (e.g., intelligence, metabolic rate, experience) to have developed response repertories of different extents. Since the richness of these repertories is intimately associated with the attainment of successive thresholds, it should be clear that the speed with which frustration or stress is reached would vary from person to person. Individual frustration and stress tolerances may differ also as a function of the intensity of the arousal conditions, the appropriateness of the available responses to the conditions of arousal, and the perceived consequences of failure to remove impinging arousal stimuli. The past history of success and failure of coping behavior (producing a factor sometimes called self-confidence) would be a determinant of this last condition. We shall return to the notion of stress tolerance a little later.

With this general sketch of step-ordered thresholds, let us give more detailed consideration to some of the conditions which have been found to give rise to stress and the patterns of stress response. It would not be inconsistent with our more restricted use of the term stress as defining a stage of an arousal hierarchy to recognize that the term is also used to describe the earlier stages in the entire sequence as well. In other words, conditions which lead to the arousal of the sequence would, if unchecked, produce stress. We may therefore, with due regard to caution, do well to accept the use of the term in this broader way. Doing so will permit us to examine the literature of stress without having to walk a semantic tightrope. At the same time, we must not lose sight of the gain we believe we have made from our analysis.

Conditions Giving Rise to Psychological Stress.[18] We may perhaps start with two general observations. First, that *any* stimulus (no matter how inane) may at some time serve as a psychological stressor, given the appropriate circumstances (e.g., the dripping water from a leaky faucet in the middle of the night). And second, that with the possible exception of extreme and sudden life-threatening situations, *no* stimulus is a stressor to all individuals exposed to it.

Holtzman and Bitterman (1952) have classified the great variety of methods which have been used to induce stress experimentally into seven main types of approach: (1) Disruptions of physiological homeo-stasis: this includes exposures to severe temperatures, drugs, starvation, sleep deprivation, etc. (2) Unpleasant or physically painful stimuli: included here are exposure to electric shock, air blast, water sprays, loud sounds, and other noxious stimuli. (3) Distractions, razzing, and time pressures: subjects are given tasks to perform and then harassed, criticized, forced to speed their performance, etc. (4) Real, contrived, or anticipated failure: either an impossible task is set or false standards are introduced, in either case assuring poor performance or task failure. (5) Social conflict and related procedures: the subject may be put in a leadership role in a group where cooperation is needed, and the group or a confederate in it so instructed to make cooperation impossible (see OSS Assessment Staff, 1948). (6) Conflicting per-ceptual cues: such tasks as mirror drawing, or naming of cards with a color name printed in ink of a different color. (7) Realistic situations threatening the individual's safety: fire rescue or parachute jumping, simulated battle situations using live ammunition, etc.

This list can be reanalyzed, added to, or modified. Groups 1 and 2, for example, involve manipulation of "natural" (physical or physiologi-cal) events, as do perhaps 6 and 7. On the other hand, groups 3, 4, and 5 are more clearly predicated on the assumption that the subject wants to "play the game"—that is, some presumption or manipulation of ego-involvement is necessary if these procedures are to be effective stress-inducers (see Chapter 14).

Lazarus, Deese, and Osler (1952) used only two broad categories to

---

[18] For more detailed reviews than can be given here, see Darrow and Henry (1949); Haggard (1949); Lazarus, Deese, and Osler (1952); Holtzman and Bitter-man (1952); Appley (1957); Janis (1958); and Korchin (1962); see also Selye (1956a).

classify stress-inducers: failure stress and task-induced stress. The former grouping included, as the name implies, methods intended to lead to failure experience, overlapping with categories 3, 4, and 5 of Holtzman and Bitterman, but also including what we would call frustration (again, it is so difficult in practice to see where one procedure leaves off and another begins). Task-induced stress involved situations (e.g., complex instructions, heavy load requirement, short time limits) which were presumably more manipulable by modifying tasks directly and less dependent on the manipulation of subjects' internal states via instructions. However, there is little question that the "personal equation" of interpretation would enter into both types of situations as a determiner of stressfulness.

All of the tasks which are used as psychological stress-inducers are effective only when they somehow threaten the life or the integrity of the individual exposed to them. In our earlier discussion of psychological homeostasis (see Chapter 7), and again in this chapter, we have spoken of the maintenance of ego- or self-integrity as basic to continued effective functioning. Thus when the organism perceives a (real or imagined) threat to the organization of the self, there should be a shift up the stress-arousal scale, with a changeover from what Rosenzweig (1944) called goal-persistent to ego-defensive behavior (see related discussion in Chapter 14).

The study of personality development in children reveals the acquisition of patterns of expectancy in relation to the self and the environment. As a result of experience, the world divides itself, so to speak, into the familiar and the unfamiliar, the predictable and the unpredictable, the certain and the uncertain. What we have been referring to as the integrity of the self or the ego is intimately associated with this "ordering" of the world and the self-identity which emerges from it.

If familiar stimuli are removed (or the individual is removed from the familiar environment) his ability to rely on habitual behaviors is disturbed (i.e., his repertory of effective coping responses is reduced), and he moves "up the stress ladder" to the protection of his orientation or stability (or, if extreme, his integrity) which the strangeness (unpredictability) of the environment will be perceived as threatening. (See our definition of stress, p. 453.)

Psychological stressors may then be classified in terms of the ways in which they contribute to (or detract from) orientation. Two main categories are seen: those involving either a deficiency or excess of stimulation and those involving ambiguity or conflict of stimuli. In either case the net effect will be to decrease certainty of orientation and hence to threaten well-being. Sensory deprivation studies (cf. Solomon et al., 1961) represent an extreme form of stimulus deficiency. However, psychological stressors need involve only the removal of the *familiar* rather than all stimuli.[19] Hence the child separated from its parents or the adult in a strange city or the soldier who loses his buddy or the rat in a new cage may be threatened in the midst of stimulation, as it were.

Under *deficit* situations can be included such categories as physical isolation (as in arctic weather stations, sentry duty, inactive observation posts, etc.), monotonous and repetitive tasks (as in many routine maintenance jobs, some vigilance tasks, etc.), and required inactivity or meaningless activity (as in "polishing" duties in fire stations or in military camps, "red tape," etc.). Any of these conditions of (relative) stimulus deficit will, when coupled with an inability to escape (e.g., because of military orders, impenetrable barriers), become stressors.

Excess of stimulation, either because of suddenness, amount, or continuity, or its unexpected (unpredictable) nature, may likewise precipitate a stress reaction. Janis (1951) studied the effects of heavy bombing of Britain during the Second World War on the civilian population. He found that stress reactions were largely the result of their "psychological unpreparedness" for the intense conditions of exposure they underwent. Rapid-fire requirements for the performance of detailed duties (overstimulation or information overload) may be stressful (see J. G. Miller, 1961). And as with deficit conditions, it is the *relative* overload that is critical.

Ambiguity and *conflict* of stimuli are stressors because the individual, although capable of responding, cannot know (in the first case) what response is called for, or (in the second case) is required to perform incompatible responses. Both conditions give rise to uncertainty, an artificial restriction of the response repertory, and, if unabated, to stress.

The sources of ambiguity or conflict may lie between one's own perceptions and those of others (where they disagree), or between contradictory information sources of equal credibility (these may both be social or nonsocial sources or a combination of the two). Ambiguity may result from a lack of information (e.g., a new gadget or a plastic model arrives but the manufacturer's instructions are missing) or lack of cues in the presence of information (e.g., one has a fine road map

---

[19] In the process of adjustment we develop ranges of tolerance for certain kinds and amounts of physical environments, foods, clothing, friends, pipes, manners of speech, etc. Depending on our tolerance level or our knowledge that we may escape at will, being placed in an environment devoid of these "props" can be severely disturbing.

but there are no road signs).

Finally, we may mention once again the procedures used to induce psychological stress which depend on the prior arousal of ego-involvement in the subject. These often involve contrived failure situations or threats to status.[20] It is important to keep in mind that such threats can operate as thwarting agents only if a prior motive state is assumed or established. Thus Mahl (1949), for example, measured gastric motility in ten students undergoing course examinations. He predicted and found an increase in motility in this "stress" situation. However, two of his subjects showed a decrease, instead. On closer investigation of these two cases he found that for different reasons the examinations were unimportant to them. Thus it is apparent that the two subjects who failed to show evidence of stress were not "involved," and in this sense immune to the normally stress-inducing capacity of the examination situation.

Perception and the Induction of Psychological Stress. Different individuals respond to stressors in different ways. Some enter into a stress state when exposed to a particular stimulus whereas others, as in Mahl's experiment, seem "immune" to the stress-inducing qualities of the same stimulus situation. Further, the same individual may enter into a stress state in response to one presumed stressor agent and not to another, or at one time and not another. We have already offered several partial answers to these paradoxes, but an important clue to the determination of these differences is the role of perception. In order to explain how a process can be threatening we must obviously resort to a perceptual (interpretive) determination of its "psychological significance." Stress, as many a disappointed investigator knows, "is in the eye of the perceiver!" Grinker et al. (1957) found that intentionally stress-inducing interview procedures were ineffective for that purpose in many of their hospital patients. On investigation they determined that the patients involved interpreted (perceived) the essentially hostile interviewing techniques in the framework of the therapeutic hospital setting. As such they accepted them as being necessary or "good for them," and thus nonthreatening.

Berkun et al. (1962), in attempts to study stress in soldier populations, reported similar effects of an overall frame of reference canceling out the effects of stress-inducing procedures. They placed men in simulated combat situations, involving some actual danger (of being shot accidentally, falling from a precarious perch, etc.). However, their subjects refused to accept as likely the possibility that the United States Army, or the investigators themselves, would expose them to real

---

[20] See Chapter 14 for further discussion of this type of experiment.

danger of injury or death outside of a war emergency.

In these examples we see the failure of threat or danger perception to develop even in situations in which it might reasonably be expected to occur. The subjects responded to the *larger contexts* in which these experiments were embedded. By the same token, it is not uncommon for subjects who have been invited into a psychology laboratory in order to perform some perfectly innocuous task to perceive (interpret) the procedures as insidious on the basis of their general expectation of what *should* happen in a psychology laboratory (or perhaps on the basis of their wish that something more "interesting" would happen).

It is clear that we mean by perception an interpretive-evaluative process from which the significance of events to the intrapersonal value system is inferred. Factors of set, attitude, predisposition, expectancy, and the like, must operate through some such mechanism, and what we have called the perception of threat or of danger must be a function of such an interpretive-evaluative "meaning-assigning" process. As one final example of the mediation of perception, we may note that social embarrassment or shame-induction is one commonly used method of inducing stress. However, such procedures are *in*effective in persons who are not aware of the social *faux pas* they are presumably committing or of the standards their behaviors are supposed to be violating. Thus, even despite the possible existence of a wish to please, a desire for social status, or a fear of social disapproval, no threat from the interaction of their responses and the environment is perceived, and no stress results.

Motivation, Vulnerability, and Stress. Any good bridge player will know what vulnerability means. In our context we are using it to suggest that a person will be vulnerable (i.e., stress-prone) in any situation in which a motive of some importance to his integrity is threatened. Threats to life cover a wide range of situations and most people are "vulnerable" with regard to these. Of greater interest to us here are the types of threats—to status, orientation, comfort, values or standards—which, though generic in nature, are defined highly selectively in individual cases. Thus one individual has an "investment" or identification with a place, person, idea, etc., and any challenge to these is threatening. (Minority group sensitivity to "jokes" about national origin, for instance, would be an example of a selective area of vulnerability.) We cannot go further into the dynamics of this interesting problem here. What is suggested is that psychological stress-inducing procedures fail to be universally effective because individuals are not equally vulnerable to all types of stressor agents. Insight may be gained into the variations of reactions of different individuals in so-called threat- and stress-inducing situations by taking account of the relative potencies of the motives being threatened in those situations (a profile of vulnerabilities), and the adequacy of the coping response repertories available. Stress induction is a complex function of the arousing stimuli, the relative vulnerabilities of the subject, and residual stress-reducing coping potential at any moment (see Appley, 1962*b*).

"Ego-Strength" and Frustration and Stress Thresholds. It is sometimes suggested that a factor of "ego-strength" may be measured as an index of overall ability to withstand threat. (What are popularly called optimism, hope, will power, etc., carry similar connotations; cf. Barron, 1953.) This may be defined as the subjective expectancy of response potential in excess of the minimum needed to meet the anticipated demands of a given situation. Although such a generalization is meaningful in distinguishing extremes, it may be misleading as an indicator of a general frustration- or stress-tolerance, for the reasons discussed under vulnerability and elsewhere in this section. There is rather a greater or lesser insulation from the effects of certain *kinds* of stressors as compared with others. The basic idea of tolerance thresholds is conceptually valid, but it seems more likely that a *series* of thresholds exists, related to the heights of the points on the vulnerability profile suggested earlier.

In sum, it appears to us that a stimulus must not only be of a given intensity to arouse anxiety, and a given higher intensity to lead to stress, but it must also be *of a given kind* for a particular person, related to his unique vulnerability profile.

The Nature of the Stress Response. We have spent considerable time, now, discussing stress without having identified the stress response itself. Actually, at least four response components are identified with the stress syndrome: systemic stress, emotionality, subjective feelings of distress, and defensive behavior. As might be expected from the foregoing discussion, correlational studies have been notoriously unsuccessful in relating the components to each other, or even reliably to more than a few specific stress-inducing procedures. Further, in describing any of these patterns of stress response we find it impossible to isolate those associated with stress *per se* from those often attributed to conditions of frustration, anxiety, conflict, distress, etc. Since it has been our thesis that these conditions form a related continuum anyway, this need not overly concern us.

1. *Systemic stress.* We can add little to what has already been said about systemic stress, except to indicate once again that there is good evidence of an intimate relation between the psychological and physiological components of stress (cf. Haggard, 1949; Darrow & Henry,

1949; Basowitz et al., 1955; Mason, 1958, 1959). The major overlapping "system in common" between the two is, of course, the autonomic nervous system, and it is to autonomic signs that most investigators turn for "hard" evidence of stress.[21] These are discussed next.

2. *Emotionality*.[22] Physiological symptoms of emotionality may include cardiovascular changes, sweating, pupillary dilation, breathing rate changes and breathing difficulty, general or specific gastrointestinal disturbances, headaches, anorexia, tension, tremors, palpitations, insomnia, etc. Distinctions need to be drawn between acute and chronic states and between situationally aroused and characteristic emotional responses, since some of the more severe symptoms would obviously not arise in short-term stress situations. Measures of GSR, heart rate, blood pressure and volume, electromyographic changes, etc., are frequently taken as indices of emotionality, anxiety, stress (and also fatigue). Systematic psychophysiological studies (cf. Wenger, 1948; Lacey, 1950; Malmo, 1959) have shown that autonomic responses are highly individually patterned, yet at the same time only casually related to subjective experience of emotionality. Thus an individual may consistently respond with an elevated breathing rate, another with a lowered heart rate, each responding in his own patterned manner repeatedly. Averaging responses across subjects has, as a result, obscured any relationships that may exist.

3. *Subjective feelings of distress*. A third category of stress response is the subjective awareness of bodily change. "I feel tense," "I'm anxious," "My head is going round and round," etc., express the subject's phenomenal feeling of stress or its antecedents. Korchin (1962) pleads for the study of these phenomenological data in their own right, and we would agree that this is desirable, despite the lack of correlation between such subjective expressions and physiological indices (see Mandler, 1958). For one reason, the verbal reports of felt distress reflect both stereotyped expression forms [23] and anticipations on the part of subjects of what kind of response they are expected to

---

[21] Until considerably more research has been completed in the area of autonomic response patterning it would be hazardous to attempt to say exactly how the patterns of systemic and psychological stress are interlocked. We suspect that they closely parallel each other, however.

[22] See, also, discussions of anxiety in Chapters 12, 14, and elsewhere in the book.

[23] We do not know if any studies have been done on the matter, but it seems likely that associative tendencies would be high among verbal labels of symptoms in any syndrome, as well known as the anxiety-stress syndrome. Hence, as a function of verbal fluency rather than discriminative responding, reports of subjective experience of such symptoms are likely to contaminate correlational studies with physiological indices.

give, what responses would please the experimenter, etc. Second, recent evidence (Berkun et al., 1962) suggests that care in measuring subjective distress may produce correlation with physiologic indices. And third, since we have given such emphasis to interpretive-perceptual responses in stress determination we believe that further study of felt stress, which should be closely related to the interpretive-evaluative perception mechanism, may further our understanding of it.

4. *Defensive behavior.* The ego-defense mechanisms are of course well known and need no elaboration here.[24] In our discussion of frustration we showed how alternative defensive adaptations could be engaged as a means of reducing or eliminating frustration, and in light of the hierarchical ordering we have here suggested for frustration and stress, it would seem that a shift in the forms of ego-defense would occur as one moved from frustration to stress to exhaustion. Thus, for example, only certain forms of ego-defense would be of use at or near the hopelessness threshold. These would include withdrawal, amnesic repression, and perhaps exaggerated forms of dissociative responses. In the extreme, the psychotic breakdown may be an ultimate defense against physical collapse, emotional exhaustion, and death, which continued stress would bring.

The Pattern of Psychological Stress Response.[25] Early in the development of the stress pattern there appears to be an intensification in all dimensions of behavior. Slight improvements can be recorded in the beginning, but as arousal continues deteriorative effects are noticeable in all aspects of performance, of judgment, and of relations with others and with oneself. Tendencies toward rigidity of response, inflexibility, inability to profit from experience and to use new information, inability to shift when shift is necessary or to persevere when required, suspiciousness, increase in hostility, irritability, increase in errors and decrease in speed of performance all appear. The degree of deterioration is generally correlated with the intensity of instigation.

By and large there is an increased interference with the ability to operate in the "real world," because of the intrusion of feelings (conscious or otherwise) of anxiety, uncertainty, dread, and finally helplessness or hopelessness. We suggested that the alternative end states could be psychosis, as a last final escape, or exhaustion and death. If we plot the progressive changes over time we see first an improvement

[24] Cf. Chapters 12 and 15 for further discussion of defense mechanisms; also the section on psychological homeostasis in Chapter 7.

[25] For more detailed descriptions of stress effects see Grinker and Spiegel (1945), Janis (1958), Lazarus and Baker (1956), Whitehorn et al. (1953), as well as references listed earlier in this section.

(as in performance) and then a decline. A systematic analysis in terms of our successive threshold notion might show patterns of responses coming into play and then being replaced by others, with an increase in ego-defensive behaviors at the expense of behaviors directed toward prior goal attainment at critical points (threshold points?) in the sequence. Because of unique intra-individual response patterning, simultaneous study of a series of physiological, phenomenological, and behavioral responses would have to be tried.

One interesting fact which has emerged from multiple-response studies is what may be called *response dissociation*. Thus Atkinson (1954) in a study of soldiers in an atomic bombing field exercise and Basowitz et al. (1955) in their study of paratroop trainees were able to draw distinctions between two types of threat reactions, one deriving from a basic insecurity about physical harm and a second from a fear of being shamed. The latter, affecting individual performance in group situations, appeared to be a serious problem for those who became anxious (e.g., about an impending parachute jump) *but remained in the group*. The effect of harm-anxiety, on the other hand, was to lead the man to withdraw, refuse to make further jumps, and so on. Basowitz et al. suggested that harm-anxiety may be of a more intense nature than shame-anxiety, related to earlier life trauma [and we might now add perhaps to the acquisition of different coping patterns], and might be related to the more severe hippuric-acid index of physiological disturbance under stress.

Temporal Factors and Psychological Stress. There seems little doubt that early stress exposure has an effect on later stress reactions, as was earlier suggested may be the case for systemic stress. Studies of infantile experience (see pp. 642, 685 ff.) suggest that the nature and timing of these early experiences may produce what we called latent stress effects which may be either positive or negative in their later summation with ongoing stress. We would suspect that the mediator in either case would be some form of emotional fractional anticipatory response redintegration (see discussion of Brown and Farber and Amsel hypotheses, p. 420), possibly in the nature of a conditioned neurovisceral or neurohumoral response (see p. 448).

A second type of temporal factor in stress is the delayed reaction observed in connection with acute episodes (see Basowitz et al., 1955; Grinker & Spiegel, 1945), but also over periods of at least several weeks. Surprisingly calm behavior during a crisis or a period of emergency may then be followed by overwhelming anxiety during a period free of threat "minutes and miles later" (Korchin, 1962, p. 19). Davis et al.

(1952) reported such delayed reactions in combat troops in the rear lines after battle, for example. Korchin (1962, p. 20) suggests that "this might represent a release phenomenon from the control of feelings and associated stress behaviors which had been necessary for adaptive behavior . . ." while the experience was in progress. He cites the findings of Basowitz et al. (1955)—that the group *least* disturbed during training had the highest post-graduation (three-week-later) rise in anxiety—in support of his interpretation of the after-discharge as a release phenomenon. We have no alternate explanation to offer, but find it of interest that such after-discharge (in the case of acute situations, at least) takes the form of a full-blown emotional reaction, rather than a gradual return to pre-stress level of arousal. Whether this is always the case we do not know, but reports of such delayed discharges are common enough in everyday experience.

Summary. Psychological stress is defined as the state of an organism in any situation where he perceives that his well-being is endangered, and he must devote all of his energies to its protection. It is proposed that stress is one stage of an arousal continuum, defined by successive instigation, frustration and stress thresholds, and followed by an exhaustion threshold marking a decline in arousal. The course of stress development is seen to be consistent with the inverted U-shaped function described for autonomic activity. Stress tolerance is described in terms of available response repertories and is thus seen to be primarily a function of learning.

Stress-instigating conditions are those which disturb physiological homeostasis or threaten the integrity of the self. They may take the form of deficit or excess of familiar (in contrast to all) stimulation, or stimulus ambiguity or conflict. The instigation of uncertainty is seen as a threat to acquired adaptation and hence to ego-integrity, giving rise to ego-protective responses which in turn successively interfere more and more with behaviors directed toward previous goals.

Perceptual interpretive-evaluative screening plays a primary role in determining the stressfulness of events. Individuals are differentially vulnerable to threat, suggesting a series of stress perception thresholds for different kinds of stressors. Stress responses involve emotionality, subjective feelings of distress and defensive behaviors as well as systemic symptoms. The pattern of stress responses is one of a temporary increase in organization and quality followed by a deterioration in performance and a gradual shift from prior goal-oriented to ego-defensive behaviors of increasing inappropriateness to the previous goal(s), and perhaps to the environment, culminating in complete withdrawal as a response to the perceived hopelessness of effective responding.

Response dissociation in stress is noted as is a temporal dissociation of stressful exposure and delayed stress response under certain circumstances.

GENERAL SUMMARY

This chapter has been concerned with an analysis of the concepts of frustration, conflict, and stress. All three are emotional states predicated on a prior motivated arousal and some form of interference with goal attainment. Frustration is the state of the organism resulting from the thwarting of goal behavior and is thought to have both drive and cue properties. It may, through a fractional anticipatory mechanism, be conditionable. Frustration may give rise to a variety of response patterns including aggression, regression, repression, and response fixation, which subserve the frustration-instigated motivation rather than the underlying (initiating) drive.

Conflict is a special case of frustration, where the source of thwarting is an incompatible response, motive, or goal. Conflict situations may arise between two equally attractive and mutually exclusive approach behaviors, two equally aversive alternatives in a situation where no escape is possible, between contradictory approach and avoidance tendencies in relation to the same goal or goal region, or in any combination of more than one approach and/or avoidance tendency where the resultant of forces is equal.

Miller's theoretical analysis of conflict behavior in terms of stimulus-response concepts is described and certain of its applications and implications discussed.

Both frustration and conflict are psychological conditions which threaten to disrupt the psychobiological homeostasis of the organism, and their development leads to a shift from task-oriented to ego-protective behaviors. A hierarchical relation is suggested among motivation-instigated, frustration-instigated, and stress-instigated behavior, with successive stages being defined by perceptual thresholds. A final stage of exhaustion (hopelessness) is also posited. Both systemic and psychological stress may be said to come into play with the appearance of stressor agents which initially give rise to moderate threat-related but not to stress behavior. Only after a degree or intensity of exposure which brings the well-being of the individual into question do the more extreme stress responses occur.

Of central importance to the concept of an instigation-frustration-stress-exhaustion continuum are the ideas of interpretive-evaluative perceptual thresholds through which ego-threats are recognized and ego-defensive behaviors come successively to replace earlier goal-related responses.

Systemic stress, manifested by the nonspecific reactions to stressor agents, occurs in relation to psychogenic and neurogenic as well as physical and metabolic stimulation. It consists of a multiple-pathway neurohumoral defense reaction which is specific in form but nonspecific in source or effect. Systemic stress response components are subject to modification through conditioning, and may in turn sensitize a later stress reaction, either increasing or decreasing its intensity.

Components of systemic and of psychological stress occur together, the two sharing in common at least the autonomic nervous system. Both systemic and psychological stress show unique intra-individual symptom (response) patterning, and it is possible that consistent (characteristic) response styles (combining psychological and somatic elements) may exist.

The concepts of frustration, conflict, and stress, along with ego-integrity-defense and other related concepts, describe aspects of an extended Bernard-Cannon adaptation theory. They are extreme conditions of homeostatic disturbance (if that concept may reasonably be extended to include acquired states) which induce successively more extended coping responses and involve successively larger segments of the organism's response system. Adaptation will result or the organism will succumb—as much a result of its own extremes of response as from any initiating condition.

Chapter 10

Motivation in Learning Theory:
Drive and Incentive

MOTIVATION AND LEARNING

In Chapter 2 it was pointed out that one very important avenue along which the concept of motivation rode to eminence during the present century is the study of learning. Beginning with Thorndike's studies, which led him to propose the law of effect, there has been a close and continuous relationship between motivation and learning, and it is sometimes very difficult to untangle one from the other. Motivation seems important as a factor in the instigation of behavior, essential for an organism to learn. Motivational states also may determine the effectiveness of "rewards" for what the organism does, again an apparently influential factor for learning. Motivation may have something to do with what learned acts will be exhibited in a given situation, that is, what features of the organism's acquired repertory will be displayed or performed. Motivation thus may contribute to the instigation, the reward and the display of behavior, and in all of these aspects it is intimately related to the learning process.

On the other hand, learning may have the greatest significance to motivation. We indicated, in Chapter 2, that when instinctual urges and unlearned behavior patterns came to have reduced credibility and emphasis, in the period 1910–1930, it was necessary to devise alternative explanations. It was an easy decision to assert that motives are learned and that many apparently innate behavior patterns are also in fact learned. The theoretical development and experimental investigation of these assertions have, of course, provided many problems for study, and much motivation literature has been concerned with them. If motives are learned, then learning contributes to motivation (see Chapter 11).

466

Learning and Behavior Theory

The psychological study of learning has resulted in the development of learning theory, the problem of which is the nature of learning, not of motivation. Because of the close relation between motivation and learning, however, learning theory has had to take account of motivation. In the process, learning theory has often been broadened, so that the term *behavior theory* becomes more appropriate than learning theory. By behavior theory we mean a theoretical development whose concepts permit application to phenomena other than those of the specific acquisition of responses. The most specifically and best developed behavior theories are probably those which grew out of a learning theory. Hence, learning theories will be our major present concern.

We shall deal here primarily with the *motivational* aspects of these theories, since their various concerns with problems of learning as such are tangential to the major interests of this book. Adequate summaries of the major theories may be found in Hilgard's books (1948, 1956), in the review by Estes et al. (1954), in papers by Spence (1951a, b), and Koch (1959).

In the title of this chapter we have given emphasis to *drive* and *incentive*. The theories we shall review here have stressed these concepts (positively or negatively), together with the notion of reinforcement. Certain learning theories, whose stress does not include these concepts, are excluded, among them the Gestalt or field theory of learning. Lewin's views are treated elsewhere in this book, as are those of the psychoanalysts.

We have confined ourselves, then, to a certain group of theories. They arose and were extensively developed in the period since about 1930. Theories of an earlier day tended to be highly general and speculative, perhaps more concerned with the definition of the subject matter of psychology (cf. Keller, 1937) than with the detailed derivation of phenomena. But in the early 1930's, Tolman (1932) described his theory of learning, together with its implications for situations other than those involving learning. He was followed by Guthrie (1935), Hull (1936, 1937), and Skinner (1938). More recently, the Hullian position has been modified in important aspects, notably by Mowrer (1947, 1956, 1960), Spence (1956, 1960), and others; and Tolman's position by MacCorquodale and Meehl (1953, 1954). We shall organize our presentation, however, around the four major viewpoints already indicated: those of Hull, Tolman, Guthrie, and Skinner, appropriately indicating the modifications that later writers have made in the respective systems.

HULLIAN THEORY

An influential formulation of a learning-behavior theory is associated with the name of Clark L. Hull. Starting in 1929, there was a series of papers and books by Hull that was initially concerned with trial-and-error learning and conditioning and that eventuated into a system, which Hull, as reflected in the title of his last book, *A Behavior System*, thought constituted an elementary general theory of behavior. Hull worked at Yale University during the development of his viewpoint. One of his early associates, K. W. Spence, has in his own right made significant modifications and contributions to the system. Spence, for about 25 years, worked at the University of Iowa, so that we may, from time to time, refer to this position as the Yale-Iowa, or Hull-Spence, formulation. Because of certain conceptions, it is often also referred to as S-R reinforcement theory, and sometimes as drive-reduction theory, although this last designation is inappropriate for Spence.

Other names associated with this general orientation include N. E. Miller and O. H. Mowrer. Mowrer is included, although his thought has deviated in recent years in important respects from the original formulation. There is, however, a significant historical relationship between his views and those of the Hullians. In this section, we shall be concerned with Hull's contribution to motivation theory, together with the additions and modifications made by the individuals already listed.[1]

Hull's Use of the Survival Model

Hull's formulation is rooted in the problem of organismic survival in an environment that is not especially nurturant. Survival is conceived

[1] Among the other names prominently associated with the Hull-Spence formulation are Judson Brown, John Dollard, I. E. Farber, Charles Osgood, Robert Sears, John Seward, and John Whiting. Dollard has provided sociological and psychoanalytic support to Miller's formulations and is implicitly considered in the discussion of Miller. Osgood and Seward have developed notions very similar to those of Spence and Mowrer with regard to the fractional goal response. Separate discussion of their contributions will therefore be omitted here. Sears' work is discussed in relation to acquired drive especially in connection with the effects of childhood experiences on the learning of motivation (Chapter 14). Whiting's notion—that acquired motives involve a frustration component—is outlined in Chapter 14. Brown and Farber are considered in Chapter 9 and in the discussion of acquired motivation (Chapter 14).

primarily in terms of those substances that must be taken in (e.g., air, water, and food) or eliminated in order for the *individual* to survive, and of those interactions (e.g., courtship, mating, and maternal behavior) necessary to *species* survival. As the following quotations suggest, behavior arises and is modified primarily in reference to the organism's needs. Conditions of need, Hull says, "activate more or less characteristic receptor organs . . ." (Hull, 1943, p. 18). "Animals may be regarded as aggregations of needs. The function of the effector apparatus is to mediate the satiation of these needs. . . . Drives become active in situations which, if more intense or prolonged, *would* become injurious" (1943, p. 65). "Usually organisms must act to reduce needs" (1951, p. 5). Elsewhere, this emphasis on adaptation becomes even clearer. In speaking of what effects of a response may reinforce it and cause it to be learned, Hull argued that a process of motivation reduction was essential. However, he realized that other conditions, like increase of stimulation or onset of a need, might be rewarding or reinforcing and that there may be more than one mechanism of reinforcement. But onset of a need, he said, ". . . would not have much adaptive value" (1943, p. 83) as a reinforcer.

So we see that Hull's thought stemmed directly from considerations of biological survival; it is obviously close to certain aspects of evolutionary theory and is continuous with the heavy emphasis placed on adaptation by the functionalist tradition in American psychology (see Chapter 2). Logan (1959, p. 304) has observed that, for Hull, if some characteristic had survival value Hull's confidence in the significance of the characteristic was increased. Nevertheless, Hull was a behavioristic or objective psychologist; no consideration of consciousness or purpose as cause was allowed to enter his argument.

If survival is conceived in essentially biological terms, then certain motivational states are apt to be accorded especial significance. These are the states, such as hunger, thirst, sex, and pain avoidance, most closely related to survival. And with Hull's stress on survival it is no wonder that he regarded these states as fundamental. Indeed, we could describe Hull's system as chiefly concerned with motivation, because, while he often seemed to and did focus on problems of learning, learning was, in the last analysis, only an instrumentality that permitted an organism to extend the range and variety of its efforts to satisfy its needs—and perhaps to anticipate their occurrence. As Hull's system developed, it became less and less concerned with the theory of learning and more and more concerned with other factors, including motivational ones, that influence behavior. In part this was a change forced by research findings, but it was not foreign to Hull's thinking.

Hull's system can be considered in terms of three main problems, dictated largely by his commitment to the survival model. First are the drives and the mechanisms of the drives he postulated. Second is the specification of the ways these drives affect behavior. And third, are the additional factors which control behavior, some of which, like drive stimuli, have a motivational basis but are not, in their functions, drives or motives.

Drives and Drive Mechanisms

Bodily need was, for Hull, the ultimate basis of motivation, and it arose from deficiencies of substances necessary to survival, or from an excess of substances inimical to individual or species survival. However, needs as such were not incorporated directly into the system. Rather, the systematic construct employed was *drive;* in his own words, "Since a need, either actual or potential, usually precedes and accompanies the action of an organism, the need is often said to motivate or drive the associated activity. Because of this motivational characteristic of needs they are regarded as producing primary animal *drives*" (Hull, 1943, p. 57). Presumably, drive was introduced because some needs, like that for oxygen, are not associated with the instigation of behavior [2] and because duration of deprivation, while associated with increasing need, is not always paralleled by increases in behavior, throughout the range of durations (see Chapter 5, pp. 239–240). Hence, drive is postulated as an intervening variable or construct; it could be assessed both by duration of deprivation (though as seen above this is an imperfect index) and by the intensity, vigor, or energy expendi-

---

[2] McClelland et al. (1953, p. 15) have criticized the survival model on the ground that some needs do not instigate behavior which might correct them, that is, some needs do not lead to drives. This criticism is clearly irrelevant. On the survival model one would expect either that the supply of needed substances (like oxygen) is ordinarily abundant and hence that the need is automatically satisfied or, alternatively, that organisms that do not respond to certain needs as drives would die out if the supply of necessary substances should suddenly change or if the absence of such a need-drive relationship were due to a mutation. The survival model is, of course, really a selective survival model which can call only on mutation and the particular environmental circumstances of an era to account for survival, modification, or dying out of a species. A different sort of argument against this model is that there are other motivations than those which are internal and homeostatic. Among them are exploration, curiosity, stimulation, and manipulation motives (see Chapter 6). These are often regarded as primary drives but are dependent on external stimuli. A further argument against Hull's conception is that stimulation or tension increments may be reinforcing (see section on reinforcement in next chapter).

ture in behavior. In the case of hunger, Hull (1951, 1952) somewhat modified this conception, adding to the drive proper, an "inanition component." This component is presumably responsible for the decreased behavior at extended intervals of food deprivation (see Chapter 5). However, behavioral intensity still does not follow duration of deprivation in a simple linear form, so that some conception of drive is presumably necessary beyond the notion of need. It would seem to us, from these considerations, that for Hull the behavior strength is the more important of the two variables from which drive strength may be inferred (duration of deprivation and behavior intensity), since it is from the behavioral indicators that the necessity for modification of the role of need as such seems partly to arise.

Primary Drives. The major primary drives, those associated with need states and part of the organism's innate equipment, that Hull listed are as follows (Hull, 1943, pp. 59–60): hunger, thirst, air, temperature regulation, defecation, urination, rest (after exertion), sleep (after wakefulness), activity (after inactivity), sexual intercourse, nest building, care of the young, and avoidance of or relief from pain (tissue injury).

Hull suggested that the onset of activities characteristic of the hunger, thirst, and sex drives is associated, respectively, with the following conditions: rhythmic and protracted contractions of the stomach, caused by the lack of nutritional elements in the blood; dryness in the mouth and throat, arising from a lack of water in the blood; and hormones in the bloodstream. Hull seemed to think these conditions caused restless behavior or activity and cited evidence (see Chapters 4 and 5 for review and evaluation) to indicate that increases in activity are associated with these local conditions. "The functional interpretation of this restless behavior is that an organism which moves about more or less continuously will in general traverse a wide area and consequently will be more likely to encounter food than if it remains quietly in one place" (Hull, 1943, pp. 62–63). A similar logic would presumably underlie the adaptive value of restless activity in the presence of other drives than hunger.

The local conditions of hunger contractions, or a dry mouth and throat,[3] seem to illustrate the way in which Hull thought needs are actualized into drives; the drives are essentially *stimuli:*

---

[3] It was seen in Chapter 5 that hunger contractions and a dry throat are no longer conceived as an adequate basis for phenomena of hunger and thirst. Animals without stomachs or with denervated stomachs, for example, continue to show hunger phenomena. The interpretation of these facts, however, is not entirely clear (see Chapter 5).

[Most primary needs] appear to generate and throw into the bloodstream more or less characteristic chemical substances, or else to withdraw a characteristic substance. These substances (or their absence) have a selective physiological effect on more or less restricted and characteristic parts of the body (e.g., the so-called "hunger" contractions of the body) which serves to activate resident receptors. This receptor activation constitutes the drive stimulus, S_D. In the case of tissue injury this sequence seems to be reversed; here the energy producing the injury is the drive stimulus, and its action causes the release into the blood of adrenal secretion which appears to be the physiological motivating substance (Hull, 1943, p. 240).

Needs then affect effector organs by way of receptors which can be stimulated, and differentially so, by energies set into action by the need states. When conditions in the body "deviate appreciably" from those optimal [4] to individual or species survival, "a state of need is said to exist, and a more or less persistent stimulation (S_D) arises. *This drive state (S_D) evokes . . ."* responses (Hull, 1951, p. 15, italics added).

Primary Reinforcement. Drives, then, are conceived as *stimuli,* and these stimuli act on particular kinds of receptors, elsewhere referred to as "drive receptors" (see later discussion). The function of these drive stimuli, as motivational variables, is to activate responses—either fairly specific innate connections (reflexes, innate or instinctive patterns of behavior) or general restlessness and activity, or both. Sometimes these innate acts and general restlessness do not accomplish a rectification of the organism's need conditions, and the animal dies. "If, however, any of the evoked movements chances to reduce the receptor discharge characteristic of a need (S_D), the stimuli and the stimulus traces operating . . . at the time acquire an increment of connection of such a nature that on subsequent occasions if any of these stimuli recurs in conjunction with the drive the reaction will tend to be evoked." This is the law of primary reinforcement (Hull, 1951, p. 15; cf., also, Hull, 1952, pp. 5–6). The close dependence, in Hull's thought, of learning on motivating conditions is evident in primary reinforcement.

We have now identified two fundamental features of Hull's system: the nature of primary motivation and the matter of primary reinforce-

---

[4] Hull did not specify what is meant by the word "optimal" here. Presumably he conceived an optimum physiological state (homeostasis) in terms analogous to those of body temperature. In this case the temperature usually remains within a rather narrow range, and symptoms of discomfort or distress are likely to appear when temperature deviates from this range. The food-taking, water-drinking, and other similar activities of animals show a considerable regularity (see Chapters 5 and 7) under ordinary conditions. This regularity may perhaps, in particular instances, be used to define an optimal condition, although factors of health, weight loss or gain, and so on, would have to be considered.

ment. We have presented their development in some detail, in order to indicate the important role of the conception of biological adaptation and survival in Hull's thinking. It seems quite clear that behavior essentially serves needs, as represented by drives, and that learning is a process whose biological function is to extend the range of the organism's adaptability beyond that provided by his innate or instinctive equipment. Although this sounds as purposive as McDougall's account, it must be emphasized, again, that there was no teleology or purpose in Hull's system.

These two conceptions, primary drive and primary reinforcement, were not considered by Hull or by his associates as providing a sufficient basis either for all motivation or for all reinforcement. Human beings, and even lower animals, are motivated and reinforced by conditions other than primary motivation and primary reinforcement. In 1943, in the *Principles*, Hull emphasized the role of secondary or learned reinforcement but did not stress a secondary or learned process of motivation. Later, however, he did so (Hull, 1951, 1952), and we will now deal with the resulting concepts.

Secondary or Learned Drive. Hull spoke of the conditions, like deprivation (C_D), which lead to the appearance of a drive state, and he stated that "*situations* associated with drives themselves become C_D's" (Hull, 1951, p. 21). This is the fundamental statement concerning secondary motivation or drive, and it was elaborated in the case of the secondary drive of fear: Let us suppose an instance of tissue injury, as might arise from being burned. There will be responses which escape (by withdrawal) the injurious stimulus. These responses will become associated with the stimuli of the situation because of the reinforcement due to the cessation of pain. An example would be hand withdrawal from a hot surface, which avoids further burning. Because of this learning, the stimuli of the situation can arouse the withdrawal responses, ahead of injury, on future occasions. These stimuli, then, are viewed as the conditions of drive arousal in the case of an acquired drive of fear. The responses they arouse also cause proprioceptive stimulation (many of the responses aroused by the situational stimuli would be internal ones—"fear"), and this proprioceptive stimulation comprises the drive stimulus, or stimuli, of the learned fear drive. These stimuli, being intense, are able to motivate behavior (Hull, 1951, p. 21).

Being burned is accompanied by the sight of, say, a stove (an antedating stimulus); thus the sight of a stove in the future might give rise to a tendency to withdraw the hand. The complex of stimuli produced by hand withdrawal, together with those from the stove and other environmental cues, can arouse fear reactions. Since fear is regarded as a secondary drive, we see something of the mechanism Hull thought underlaid secondary motivation. Secondary motivation could also presumably develop on the basis of the sex, hunger, and thirst drives. Hull points out, in the case of hunger, E. E. Anderson's concept (1941a, b) of the externalization of drive (see Chapter 11) and states: "Thus the hunger motivation became conditioned to the general external characteristics of the maze which became the C_D of the hunger drive, i.e., of a secondary motivation . . ." (Hull, 1951, p. 24).[5]

In the acquired or secondary drive of fear it seems that the previously neutral stimuli (e.g., the stove) become C_D's because they come to elicit responses similar to those aroused by the original tissue injury; in turn, these responses yield stimuli which are the secondary drive stimuli, so that the S_D's of this secondary drive are aroused by the C_D's *through the mediation of the responses* the C_D's elicit. Hull's formal statement of this does not explicitly mention response mediation (Hull, 1951, p. 25; 1952, p. 6) and hence has been criticized (cf. Hilgard, 1956, p. 129) as perhaps permitting stimuli (C_D's) to become directly associated with stimuli (S_D's), a kind of association not consonant with a general stimulus-response formulation. We think, however, that Hull meant that the occurrence of the S_D's was dependent on the response aroused by the C_D's; that is, the S_D's are response-mediated stimuli as just indicated. In theory, at least, this would obviate the criticism, a point which Hilgard also suggests. However, the evidence, as reviewed in Chapter 11, gives little support to this mechanism for the development of secondary motivation in the case of acquired drives based on hunger or thirst.

Secondary Reinforcement. Secondary reinforcement is the second learned factor which occupies a central role in the Hullian theory of motivation. It has received experimental confirmation many times. Operationally, the principle of secondary reinforcement states the fact that neutral stimuli, present during primary reinforcement, acquire themselves the property of being reinforcing stimuli. Thus they may maintain behavior, when primary reinforcement no longer occurs, or they may serve as "rewards" for learning acts which are never followed by primary reinforcement. Typical examples are provided by the per-

[5] Wolfe (1936) and Cowles (1937) showed that poker chips or discs could become valued objects (tokens) for chimpanzees if they were associated with food. With such chips as rewards, the animals would learn, and they would work to get them, indicating that the tokens also were incentives. These findings occurred only when the animals were hungry. Because the chips had little or no reward or incentive value when the chimpanzees were not hungry, these tokens are not taken to arouse an acquired drive.

sistence of a bar-pressing response, whose only effect is the click of the (now empty) food magazine, or by the learning of a turn in a simple T-maze, when the empty goal box on the side to which the turn leads is one in which the animal has previously experienced feeding. Secondary reinforcement not only serves to maintain behavior and develop new learning, but it has a central role in Hullian conceptions of behavior chains, which endure over considerable periods of time or distance. We shall see its importance later in the discussion of problems to which Hull applied his theory. Our present concern is with the mechanism of secondary reinforcement.

As we have seen, primary reinforcement is associated with a reduction in stimulation, that is, of S_D. In secondary reinforcement, a stimulus is presented, and superficially at least this fact seems to contradict the principle of primary reinforcement. In the *Principles* (1943, p. 97) Hull pointed out this fact but did not directly comment on it. His theory of secondary reinforcement, at that time, held that a stimulus could have secondary reinforcing value only so long as it continues to elicit the response that was associated with it when it developed secondary reinforcing properties (Hull, 1943, p. 92). Earlier, Hull had spoken of the possibility that *fractions* of the reaction conditioned to the secondary reinforcement could persist, even when the total reaction did not appear, and he mentioned such processes as salivation and other internal responses as examples (p. 91). A further discussion suggested that at least the first secondary reinforcing stimulus acquired its power because it can elicit, after conditioning, some part of the "need-reduction process" which the goal situation itself evokes (Hull, 1943, p. 100). This fractional component is usually referred to as g, or as r_g, and is often called a fractional goal reaction, or, in some circumstances, a fractional anticipatory goal reaction. In this formulation, then, Hull presumably accounted for the reinforcing effect of a secondary reinforcing stimulus.[6] The intensity of the occurrence of the r_g would determine how much reinforcing power a secondary reinforcer has.

The *Principles* presented secondary reinforcement as a primary mechanism in the law (as then stated) of habit formation. Later, Hull

[6] Hull recognized (1943, pp. 98–99) that even food might not be a primary reinforcer but instead be in fact a secondary reinforcing agent. Later research (see Chapter 5) has supported this suggestion. In the case of both food and water, reinforcing effects occur too rapidly for real need reduction to have taken place (cf. Osgood, 1953, p. 433). This may be the reason that Hull (1951, p. 20; 1952, p. 506) added a reduction in s_g to the mechanism of primary reinforcement (reduction in S_D).

thought that secondary reinforcement itself might be deduced as a secondary principle and therefore need not have the status of a primary law. His example, however, was changed, and he now spoke of the cessation of shock as a rat escapes from the shock compartment of an apparatus to a nonshock compartment, rather than of food reward. Not only does shock cease but so also do the stimuli which arise from the running itself, when the animal reaches the nonshock compartment. These cessations constitute primary reinforcement, and, in addition, a reduction of fear. Reduction in fear can be attached to the stimuli of the situation and to continuing traces of yet earlier stimuli. "As a result, on later repetitions of the objective conditions in question this relaxation generalizes forward on those traces, and gives rise to conditioned inhibitions . . . or . . . *anticipatory relaxations . . .* But relaxation of the muscular contractions reduces proprioceptive stimulus intensity and so reduces the drive stimulus wherever it occurs" (Hull, 1951, p. 27). This constitutes reinforcement. "It follows that any stimulus consistently associated with a reinforcement situation will through that association acquire the power of evoking the conditioned inhibition, i.e., a reduction in stimulus intensity, and so of itself producing the resulting reinforcement. Since this indirect power of reinforcement is acquired through learning, it is called *secondary reinforcement*" (pp. 27–28). Hull lists, in the next paragraph, most of the demonstrations of secondary reinforcement on which he had based his formulation of the mechanism of that process in the *Principles*. It is not clear to us, however, whether the cessation of activity, stressed in the later formulation, is in any major sense the same as or different from the earlier formulation which stressed g or r_g. The latter was discussed in conjunction with secondary reinforcement based on food, the former on relief from shock.[7]

A Negative Drive: Reactive Inhibition (I_R). Hull also spoke of a special negative motivation or drive—reactive inhibition. His first statement of this notion was as follows (1943, p. 278): "Whenever any reaction is evoked in an organism there is left a condition or state which acts as a primary negative motivation in that it has an innate capacity to produce a cessation of the activity which produced the state." This

[7] In his last publication (1952, pp. 14, 124–125) Hull added a corollary to his system, which dealt with secondary reinforcement by means of the "fractional antedating goal reaction." This appears to us to be comparable to the formulation used in his first book (1943, p. 100), and it is not entirely clear why Hull restored it specifically in *A Behavior System*, after discarding it in *The Essentials of Behavior* (Hull, 1952, 1951, respectively).

inhibitory condition varies with the effortfulness of the act in question but dissipates with time. But when present it is "a negative drive," much like pain or tissue injury. Recovery from this state (i.e., a reduction in the negative drive) is reinforcing, resulting in the conditioning of "cessation of activity" to stimuli or to stimulus traces present at the time the activity stops and therefore at the time drive reduction takes place (Hull, 1943, pp. 281–282). This learned cessation of activity is called conditioned inhibition (sI_R), a habit. As the reactive inhibition involves only the effector in motion, it is not a *general* negative drive state, and it presumably has relatively few of the general, functional properties of drives which are stressed in regard to the relationship of motivation to performance.[8] It seems to have been postulated mainly to account for certain phenomena associated with the extinction of conditioned responses, and Hull's later treatments of this problem did not develop it any further (1951, 1952).

Summary. We have now reviewed the drives and the conception of drives suggested by Hull, chiefly hunger, thirst, sex, pain avoidance, and reactive inhibition. We have outlined the conceptions of primary and secondary reinforcement and of acquired drive. Hull conceived drive as a stimulus (S_D) arising from a state of tissue need and having the general function of arousing or activating behavior. Except for innate behaviors which might be activated by specific S_D's, the behavior arising from the appearance of drive was conceived to be that of general restlessness, or activity, that is, drive as such mobilized the organism into general action but did not, without learning, lead to specific behaviors appropriate to particular motivations and goals (with the exception of innate connections, as noted). The intensity of the drive stimulus, Hull thought, was related in general to "the concentration of the drive substance in the blood" (1943, p. 240) and, as we have seen, the energy expended in behavior is an increasing function (within limits) of deprivation (see Chapters 5 and 11). Since the amount of blood-drive substance presumably would also increase with deprivation, we should expect that behavioral intensity or amount of activity would increase with drive (S_D) intensity, within the limits set by such a factor as inanition. Hull stated this, as follows, ". . . the vigor of an animal's struggle for food or water increases, other things equal, with the number of hours of food or water privation up to the point of beginning weakness from inanition" (Hull, 1951, p. 33); ". . . the various needs evoke actions which increase in intensity and variety as the need becomes more acute" (Hull, 1943, p. 65). The varia-

[8] Cf. Hilgard (1956, p. 138, fn. 42, p. 139).

MOTIVATION: THEORY AND RESEARCH

tions in intensity of the drive stimulus (S_D) presumably affect behavior as an example of the general principle called stimulus intensity dynamism.

Influence of Drives on Behavior

The initial formulations of Hull's theory provided an account mainly of learning and implied a dominant role for habit strength in determining behavior. As has been said, motivation played an important role, however, because reinforcement was conceived as drive reduction. But certain observations made by Tolman and his students questioned the role of reinforcement. Further, Tolman's group found that incentives, such as food, introduced in a goal box for hungry rats, had an immediate and dramatic effect in improving performance. Learning, which had not been very evident on prior, unrewarded, trials, "suddenly" became manifest. Furthermore, there was evidence that changes in reward had an effect on behavior that was immediate, a phenomenon difficult to explain on the basis of gradual changes in habit strength. As a result of findings such as these, Hull came to distinguish sharply between the *learning* of a habit and the *performance* or *use* of a habit —in short, between learning and performance. This is a distinction Tolman had earlier emphasized, and it is an instance of the influence of Tolman's thought on Hull's thinking.

In conjunction with this distinction, Hull developed further conceptions of the influence of drives on behavior, conceptions to which we now turn. He also changed the roles he had previously assigned to certain other factors, shifting them from variables influencing learning to variables influencing performance. We treat them in this section, also.

Relevant Drive. In addition to his emphasis on the point that drives act like stimuli, Hull also suggested the notion of a general drive state to which almost any drive may contribute and which therefore is not specific. The general formulation of this as presented in *Principles* was as follows:

. . . when blood which contains certain chemical substances thrown into it as the result of states of need, or which lacks certain substances as the result of other states of need, bathes the neural structures which constitute the anatomical bases of habit (sH_R), the conductivity of these structures is augmented through lowered resistance either in the central nervous tissue or at the effector end of the connection, or both. The latter type of action is equivalent, of course, to a lowering of the reaction threshold and would presumably facilitate reaction to neural impulses reaching the effector from any source whatever (Hull, 1943, pp. 240–241).

Hull pointed out, however, that this sensitization of a habit structure is not sufficient to evoke the reaction. "Sensitization merely gives the relevant neural tissue, upon the occurrence of an adequate set of receptor discharges, an augmented facility in routing these impulses to the reactions previously conditioned to them or connected" natively (Hull, 1943, p. 241). He further commented that this formulation suggests "the undifferentiated nature of drive in general, contained in Freud's concept of the 'libido' " (Hull, 1943, p. 241); Hull, however, did not suggest the primacy of any one drive, such as sex.

This general, nondifferentiated drive state ("generalized D") was conceived as a result of the contribution of any or all drives acting in the organism at a given time. No exceptions were made by Hull in his first formulation, although we obviously wonder whether such primary drives as the one for sleep (after wakefulness) or for rest (after exertion) or reactive inhibition (after response) contribute to it. Hull (1951, p. 40; 1952, p. 7) later restricted the earlier formulation by saying that "at least some drive conditions" can activate habits set up under other drives.

Behavior is thus seen to be a performance, determined by several factors, among them D, in addition to the associative one, habit (or sH_R).[9] D was conceived as multiplying habit to produce an excitatory potential (sE_R), which, more directly than either habit or drive, underlies the organism's performance. By letting sH_R stand for habit, sE_R for the excitatory potential, and D for drive, Hull's formulation may be written as

$$sE_R = sH_R \times D$$

If sE_R is taken as indicating that behavior will occur, then, when sE_R is zero, there will be no behavior. Thus, when D is zero, sE_R will be zero, and there will be no behavior mediated by the particular habit in question (or presumably any behavior at all). Similarly, if sH_R is zero, then, no matter what the value of D is, none of the behavior that particular habit mediates will be manifested. There will, no doubt, be other habits or innate (unlearned) connections (sU_R's), which the drive would act upon, so the organism would behave if D has a value greater than zero; but the particular behavior mediated by the habit shown in the equation could not appear. It is, in this formulation, the habit structure (or the innate connection) which confers on behavior its particular characteristics. As such, D can only energize these structures.

[9] Cf. Brown (1953), Farber (1954, 1955).

An example may help to clarify this discussion. If an animal is sated for food, water, sex, and so on, he is unmotivated. Presumably he would, then, be inactive, even though he is full of acquired habits, like bar-pressing or maze-running, and innate activities like grooming. If he has a bar-pressing habit, and is at the same time hungry, the bar-pressing will be activated by the drive (together with the stimuli afforded by the Skinner box). If he has no bar-pressing habit but is hungry and is in the Skinner box, he will behave; other response tendencies than bar-pressing will be displayed (grooming, exploring, sniffing, etc.).

If a habit has been learned under some drive condition to a level of great strength, the considerations just indicated would lead to the prediction that the strength of subsequent behavior it would mediate would depend on the drive strength at that subsequent time. In the *Principles*, Hull (1943) thought that the behavioral strength mediated by a constant habit strength would be a negatively accelerated, increasing function of the strength of the drive, because he conceived drive strength as changing with deprivation this way. Later, on the basis of research (see next chapter) that resulted in a more complex function, Hull (1951, pp. 38–39) accepted, for hunger, a functional statement of the strength of drive that represents this complexity: "The functional relationship of drive (D) to one drive condition (food privation) is: from $h = 0$ to about 3 hours, drive rises in a linear manner until the function abruptly shifts to a near horizontal, then to a concave-upward course, gradually changing to a convex-upward course reaching a maximum . . . at about $h = 59$, after which it gradually falls . . ." (pp. 38–39).[10] This function, of course, describes for a habit of constant strength the course of sE_R as the drive varies.

Irrelevant Drive. Another concept that needs mention here is the notion of alien or irrelevant drive. The general treatment we have summarized suggests that *any* drive, whether it was active or not at the time a habit was learned, would sensitize the habit structure in question. Alien or irrelevant drive may be defined as one which was not active at the time the habit it is now energizing was learned. Where both the alien and the relevant drive were active at the time of per-

[10] In this function Hull seems to include the inanition factor in drive. Strictly speaking, the drive itself "is an increasing monotonic sigmoid function of h . . ." (Hull, 1951, p. 38); the drive stimulus "is a monotonic increasing function of this state" (Hull, 1951, p. 39). Presumably, "this state" refers to the drive proper, set up by the C_D, although Hull may have meant to include the inanition factor which is also produced by the C_D. It would be hard, however, to understand how S_D could be a monotonic increasing function of the state arising from drive *and* inanition.

formance of a habit, their respective values would be summed, to produce the effective drive (Hull, 1943, p. 245; 1951, p. 40). This aspect of Hull's motivation theory has received a good deal of experimental attention, and this research is summarized in the next chapter.

Other Motivational Variables. In a former version of his theory, Hull (1943) suggested that in addition to the number of reinforcements (primary or secondary or both) a response received under given stimulating conditions, there were other variables which would affect the strength of the resulting habits. In later versions, however (Hull, 1951, 1952), habit strength as such was expressed as a function of number of reinforcements alone, but several factors were described as exerting an influence on the excitatory or reaction potential. These variables are the amount of the incentive (K) and the intensity of the stimulus which evokes the response (stimulus intensity dynamism or V).[11] The full constitution of reaction potential then is compounded of the multiplication of four factors: habit, incentive, drive, and stimulus intensity (Hull, 1952, p. 7). It should be observed here that we have not given the full account of the reaction potential effective for reaction evocation. The value reflecting the multiplication of D, H, V, and K would be attenuated by any reactive inhibition and conditioned inhibition present, and perhaps by its variability arising from the oscillation factor; the value would have to be larger than the "reaction threshold" for the response to appear.[12]

Some of what we have just discussed may be clarified if we stress again that reaction or excitatory potential is a function of both associative and nonassociative factors. The associative factor is habit; the nonassociative factors include drive, incentive, and stimulus intensity dynamism. While K is obviously related to motivation, since it is defined as the amount of incentive, and V may be a motivational term (Logan, 1959), the main influence of these factors has already been indicated; they simply multiply habit strength to produce sE_R. Drive, on the

[11] Delay of reinforcement (J) was thought at one time to influence sH_R (Hull, 1943) and later to influence sE_R (Hull, 1951). In the last formulation (Hull, 1952, pp. 126–133), J was derived from the principles of stimulus generalization and of the fractional anticipatory goal reaction. In essence, the derivation involves the assumption that with delay the stimulus situation at reinforcement is different from what it is at the time of response. Hence, the effective habit strength (s$\overline{H}_R$) at the time of response is decreased by the extent of this difference in terms of the generalization gradient. This effective habit strength, or s$\overline{H}_R$ value, of course, affects sE_R in terms of which Hull states the resulting corollary.

[12] In the compass of this book, we cannot enter into all of the details of Hull's system but must stress only the major motivational notions. Many concepts thus are only mentioned here.

other hand, has a more complex function in the system, as Hilgard (1956, p. 175) has observed: It is the basis for both primary and secondary reinforcement,[13] and it activates the habit strength into sEr. Both of these functions we have already discussed. In addition, drive provides distinctive stimuli, which enter into habit formation. Finally, the goal reaction itself provides an important basis for the organization of behavior. To these two matters we now turn, in order to complete our review of the major motivational facets of Hull's system.

Additional Factors Governing Behavior

Drive Stimuli. Motivation is often regarded as providing direction to or as a steering apparatus for behavior; that is, behavior *appropriate* to the motivation occurs. In Hull's system, this steering function is attributed to the distinctive *drive stimulus*, which accompanies the drive state and enters into the habit structure as an *associative factor* (cf. Brown, 1953; Farber, 1954, 1955). The following equation should clarify this point and relate it to the energizing function of drive:

$$sE_R = (^{S_E}_{S_D} H_R) \ (D_r + D_i),$$

where s_E and s_D are environmental and drive stimuli, respectively, and D_r and D_i are relevant and irrelevant (alien) drive, respectively. The drive stimulus, then, enters into the habit as does any other stimulus; that is, its directional or steering function relative to response is mediated by habit or association, not by motivation, although the origin of the S_D is, of course, a motivational one. This distinction means that drive, as such, is a general, nonspecific factor—one which energizes behavior tendencies more or less indiscriminately. But if the drive possesses a distinctive, discriminated stimulus, and if this stimulus has been associated with some response, then when the drive is active its associated response may occur, so long as other habitual (or innate)

---

[13] Although drive, as a motivational variable, is essential as a condition of reinforcement, strength of drive, at learning, was not considered by Hull as a factor determinative of amount of sH_R generated by a reinforcement. Amount of need or drive reduction, which in the *Principles* (Hull, 1943) was postulated to account for the effect of amount of incentive on sH_R, was dropped as a factor influencing sH_R when K was shifted to the status of a multiplier of sH_R in producing sE_R. Presumably, some minimal amount of drive (or S_D) reduction is required for reinforcement, but this point was never explicitly acknowledged or discussed. In this connection, it is stated that, in secondary reinforcement, the degree of such reinforcement is proportional to the intensity of the occurrence of a "fractional component of the need reduction process . . ." (Hull, 1943, p. 100). This apparent contradiction has never been resolved.

behavioral tendencies of greater strength are not present.[14] One possible source of such tendencies, in the presence of a strong irrelevant drive, would be its drive stimuli (S_{D_i}).

A further point here is that the drive stimulus, like other stimuli, is regarded as varying on both qualitative and intensitive dimensions. There are qualitative differences between hunger and thirst or between hunger and sex, for example, and quantitative differences among different intensities of hunger, of thirst, or of sex. Hull believed that if a reaction were learned under a drive of a given strength and then was elicited under the same drive at a different strength, the S_D at the time of elicitation would be different from what it was at learning. This difference would mean that there would be a less strong connection between the changed S_D and the reaction than there was between the original S_D and the reaction, according to the principle of the generalization gradient. Similarly, some generalization might be conceived as occurring between qualitatively different drives, like hunger and thirst, and this might mediate transfer of reaction from one drive to another.[15] Evidence was presented in Chapter 5 which supports the notions of drive discrimination and drive-intensity discrimination; there is also evidence for generalization along the drive intensity continuum. Drive stimuli function importantly, as associative factors, to steer behavior and to mediate transfer.

Goal Reactions. The goal reaction was mentioned as another of Hull's motivational concepts. Goal reactions are often regarded as simple, unitary processes like, for example, eating. Actually, of course, eating is a complicated group of events and reactions, involving the sight and smell of food, getting the food from receptacle to mouth, salivating, chewing, swallowing, social factors, etc. Hull was much impressed (1929) with the *anticipatory* character of the conditioned response, that is, that reactions conditioned to stimuli could, in many instances,

[14] It may be that certain drives, like those for sleep (after wakefulness) and rest (after reaction), have quite distinctive stimuli to which there is either a strong innate or a strong learned response. If so, such responses might, in the presence of the appropriate drive, be so strong as to dominate any other response tendency and hence give the appearance of not activating, as general drives, other response tendencies. This would be an alternative to a conception like that of a "negative drive" (reactive inhibition).

[15] Such a transfer might constitute an alternative theory to the one involving the notion of a "general unspecific drive state" in the explanation of the sensitization of habit structures by irrelevant or alien drives. See the discussion of Miller, in a later section of this chapter. There is also evidence that deprivation causing one drive may confound satiation of another (Verplanck & Hayes, 1953). This fact complicates the interpretation of generalized drive and of drive generalization (see Chapters 5 and 11).

precede in time the point of their original, unconditioned occurrence. Certain aspects of eating, of course, can only occur when food is present. Others, like salivation and licking the lips, do not require the presence of food for their activation; that is, they are *detachable, fractional* portions of the complex act of eating. Hull developed the conception that such detachable, fractional components of a response could, through learning, appear in a situation before the organism entered the actual eating situation; thus the term, fractional anticipatory or antedating goal reaction, is symbolized as r_g (the goal reaction itself being symbolized as R_G). Now any response has certain stimulational consequences—kinesthetic effects, for example. Thus, R_G and r_g will have such effects as S_G and s_g. And in s_g Hull found a construct which he used extensively. We have seen its role in secondary reinforcement, in which Hull suggested that secondary reinforcement depends on the occurrence of $r_g \rightarrow s_g$. Hull also used it in deriving phenomena involving the direction of behavior and even offered an explanation for apparent "purpose" in behavior, as well as other phenomena. We shall give examples illustrating its use through secondary reinforcement and in directional aspects of behavior.

An example of the use of secondary reinforcement is provided by the goal gradient, or the general phenomenon that a reward "which occurs sometime after a stimulus response event . . . is apparently able to work back and strengthen it" (Spence, 1947, p. 1). Hull (1932) first accepted this as a fact and suggested that the strength of conditioning depended on the remoteness in space or time of reward. Thus a given reinforcement would strengthen less a connection remote from it in time than it would one close in time. On the basis of this assumption, Hull (1932) offered an explanation of why it is, in a maze, that blind alleys are eliminated in favor of the true path, even though both are followed by reward. The answer, Hull suggested, is that reward follows sooner when the true path is taken than it does when the animal enters a blind alley. Over a number of trials this advantage will gradually build up in favor of the correct path, and blind-alley entrances will drop out. The goal gradient was shown empirically in a straight runway (Hull, 1934c). A number of deductions were made on this empirical finding, and on these assumptions, that are generally consistent with the findings from experiments on animal maze learning; the more rapid elimination of blinds near the goal than those distant from the goal is an example. These reasonable deductions concerning complex maze behavior gave Hull's use of the goal gradient the status of an important theoretical achievement.

However, Hull went on (1943) to show that the goal gradient may be derived from more fundamental principles. While early experiments on the delay of reward showed effectiveness for long delays (pp. 136–138), Perin (1943a, b) found that under well-controlled conditions the gradient of reinforcement was short, perhaps 20 to 30 seconds. Hull derived the longer gradient on the basis of secondary reinforcement, the possibilities for which were abundant in the earlier experiments. Hull then had two principles: the gradient of (primary) reinforcement and the goal gradient. The former was believed to be an effect of primary reinforcement whose effects persisted a short time; the latter was derived from this primary gradient through secondary reinforcement (Hull, 1943, pp. 142–146). Hull later modified this position in accordance with some suggestions from Spence (1947) to which we shall now turn (cf. Hull, 1952, p. 127).

Spence (1947) had available to him work which suggested that there may be no primary gradient of reinforcement at all (cf. Riesen, 1940; Perkins, 1947; Grice, 1948); thus he proposed that "all learning involving delay of the primary reward results from the action of *immediate* secondary reinforcement which develops in the situation" (p. 7).

Let us illustrate Spence's formulation by an example. Suppose an animal is rewarded for pressing the lever in a Skinner box but only after a delay of 60 seconds following the lever press. Learning occurs under these conditions, but is slower than it is when reward is immediate. Why? Spence argues that the stimulus situation at the time of the lever press is different from that which prevails at the time the reward occurs. These stimuli involve the external environment, as well as stimuli arising from the animal's movements, its viscera, etc. The two stimulus patterns are different, but they also have common or similar elements. The occurrence of the secondary reinforcing event (r_g) at the time of the bar press is seen to depend on the extent to which components of R_G will *generalize* from the stimulus situation at the time of reward to the stimulus situation at the time of the lever press. With variation in delay of reward, the amount of r_g will vary (inversely), and its potency as a secondary reinforcer is said to be a function of its amount or intensity. Hence gradients of reinforcement are derived through the mechanism of secondary reinforcement, itself dependent on r_g. A somewhat similar analysis can be made for the case in which our animal makes a series of reactions, as in a maze, on the way to the goal, but we will not deal with this situation here. Both instances are analyzed by Hull (1952, pp. 126–133).[16]

---

[16] Spence (1956) later interpreted these delayed reward cases on a different basis (see section on Spence) and also suggested that the chaining and the non-chaining situations involve separate mechanisms.

Perhaps implicit in the foregoing discussion is a suggestion of the way in which Hull used $r_g \rightarrow s_g$ as an integrator of behavior in a variety of situations. A further example may clarify the point. If a variety of stimulus situations has been associated with the consummatory response of eating (R_G), and we designate several of these stimulus situations as S_a, S_b, S_c, S_d, then in accordance with our previous discussion, it is also true that each stimulus situation can elicit the fractional goal reaction r_g, so that we may write:

$$S_a \rightarrow r_g, \ S_b \rightarrow r_g, \ S_c \rightarrow r_g, \ S_d \rightarrow r_g$$

We may further take one of these stimuli (S_a), for example, a light, and, in a simple locomotor situation, associate it with a turn to the right rather than to the left. For this stimulus, then, we would have the following situation:

$$S_a \rightarrow r_g \rightarrow s_g \nearrow^{R_{rt}}$$

But note that $r_g \rightarrow s_g$, now associated with a right turn, is also elicited by S_b, S_c, and S_d. We should have to predict, on this basis, a transfer of the right turn to these other stimuli, perhaps other lights or shapes or sounds, as follows:

$$\begin{array}{c} S_b \searrow \\ S_c \rightarrow r_g \rightarrow s_g \rightarrow R_{rt} \\ S_d \nearrow \end{array}$$

This example [17] indicates another major use of the $r_g \rightarrow s_g$ mechanism in Hull's system (cf. Hull, 1930, 1931, 1932, 1934a, b). Through it, Hull achieved a mechanism for transfer and integration of behavior which has some motivational relevance, in that r_g is always derived from some goal reaction. The appeal of Hull's system in its early phase (the decade of the 1930's) rested, for many psychologists, in his ability to use this and other mechanisms in the derivation of a variety of phenomena. The later system (cf. Hull, 1951, 1952) primarily reflected a detailed quantitative working out of the postulates of the system, and

[17] This example illustrates acquired or mediated generalization, which, of course, could occur on any common response. Hull, in many instances, emphasized the goal reaction, and we stress it here, since it is a factor in many circumstances involving motivation, and he used it in deducing phenomena called purpose, expectancy, foresight, and the like.

there was little effort devoted to further development along the lines just indicated.

Overall Summary of Hull's Position

Hull's system rests on the evolutionary problem of organismic survival. The chief concern seems initially to be with the organism's tissue needs, many of which give rise to *drives,* like hunger, thirst, sex, pain avoidance, and reactive inhibition. These primary, biological drives are conceived to act like stimuli, and when the drive stimulus is reduced by ingestion of food or water, interaction with a mate, avoidance or escape from noxious stimuli, or by rest, we have the condition of primary reinforcement, which strengthens the association between the stimulus situation and the responses which have preceded the reduction of the drive stimulus. These primary motivational mechanisms are supplemented by a conception of acquired or secondary drives (like fear) and by the notion of secondary reinforcement. While a primary drive condition is necessary to activity, reinforcement, and the acquisition of learned drives and secondary reinforcers, there are other functions assigned to the drive concept. One of these is to energize habits and unlearned response tendencies, so that they may be performed. Another is to provide distinctive internal (drive) stimuli, which may enter into habits and act as a directive factor in controlling behavior. A third is to provide for the goal reaction and the fractional goal reaction, which have important applications in secondary reinforcement and in the integration and mediation of the transfer of behavior. The goal gradient, transfer of responses among dissimilar stimuli, and the explanation of apparently purposive behaviors are among the phenomena to which an application of the fractional goal response has been made.

SPENCE'S DEVELOPMENT OF HULLIAN THEORY

We have already observed that Kenneth W. Spence contributed to Hullian theory during Hull's lifetime, and he has continued to do so in the years since Hull's death. Despite the close correspondence, in many respects, of Hull's and Spence's views, there have been differences, and certain of these differences relate to motivational conceptions within Hullian theory. As Spence (1956, 1960) has continued to work on his theoretical notions, motivational problems have been a chief concern.

The major differences between Hull and Spence may be summarized briefly. First, Spence has never advocated a tension-reduction theory of reinforcement, and he (1956) has espoused, at least tentatively, a two-process conception of learning for some learning situations. Hull, initially, treated incentives and their characteristics as factors affecting habit strength; later he shifted most of their influence to performance. Spence was always impressed by the role of incentives in performance, and a good deal of his later theorizing has dealt with incentive motivation. A second difference from Hull is in his idea of the manner in which incentives and drive combine. Spence has emphasized *emotion* or *emotionality* as a variable which contributes to general drive level. Except in the case of fear as an acquired drive, Hull did not. Finally, Spence has offered a theory of inhibition (Spence, 1960, Chapter 6) which stresses frustration as a source of response interference. He has not followed Hull's use of reactive inhibition. Our discussion of Spence's views is organized around these major points.

Motivation and Reinforcement

Spence does not deal, as did Hull, with the general problem of the survival of organisms but begins his treatment (Spence, 1956) by indicating that among the features of selective learning is the fact that the organism is *motivated*, and that this motivation may involve some "primary appetitional or primary aversive need, produced by manipulation of the organism's environment in the immediate past or present" (p. 29). Further, "The combination of the motivating state and the environmental situation impels the subject to respond and to continue responding to various aspects of the situation until a reinforcer is obtained or until removed from the situation" (p. 29). Reinforcers, it must be emphasized, are not necessarily construed as involving drive or drive-stimulus reduction; they are environmental events which increase "the probability of occurrence of responses they accompany" (p. 32), but this is an empirical statement, and speculations concerning the mechanism of reinforcement are not provided. Both primary and secondary appetitional and aversive processes can act as reinforcers. The appetitional ones involve consummatory acts (like eating) and the aversive ones a reduction or cessation "of an existing noxious stimulation (e.g., electric shock)" (Spence, 1956, p. 34).

Spence, like many authors, distinguishes two kinds of conditioning for analysis—classical and instrumental. An important point in this connection is that a classical conditioned response is also always formed whenever an instrumental response is learned; that is, for example, fractional eating or fear components are associated with the "preceding stimulus events that have the appropriate temporal relation" (Spence, 1956, p. 49). These fractional consummatory or fear responses are, of course, the familiar r_g's encountered in the section on Hull. Wherever *classical* conditioning occurs, Spence tentatively suggests that its development depends on reinforcement—that is, on the occurrence of the unconditioned stimulus (or on secondary reinforcement). However, Spence (1956, p. 151) does not believe that *instrumental* acts depend, for their acquisition, on reinforcement. They apparently are learned through stimulus-response contiguity, but the strength of the responses these instrumental habits mediate depends on the strength of the r_g's which occur in the same context. Hence, Spence has suggested a two-factor account for learning, with reinforcement (empirical law of effect) necessary for classical conditioning, and contiguity for instrumental conditioning. This formulation, quite tentatively proposed, is radically different from the one proposed by Hull, which regarded all learning as based on contiguity *with* reinforcement and which regarded reinforcement as reduction in S_D.

Most of the rest of Spence's theory is concerned with motivation; that is, most of the variables manipulated empirically and discussed theoretically are ones which can readily be classified as motivational. We can best understand these phases of his viewpoint by considering at length and with examples his treatments of incentive motivation, based on the $r_g \rightarrow s_g$ mechanism, and of emotionality as generalized drive.

Incentive Motivation [18]

We have already seen that incentive characteristics were used by Hull first as a factor governing the formation of habit strength, and later, as a consequence of the experiments of Crespi (1942) and of Zeaman (1949), as a factor governing excitatory or reaction potential. Spence (1956, p. 134) always regarded the matter of the effect of incentives on behavior as a motivational question, partly because of various findings reported in the literature and also because of the significance he saw in the fractional anticipatory goal response as a motivational as well as an associative factor. The motivational properties of this response would "vary with the magnitude or vigor with which it occurs" (Spence, 1956, p. 135); that is, presumably a large incentive would evoke a larger or more vigorous fractional goal response than would a small incentive.

It is not clear as to the mechanism by which incentives operate in this motivational fashion. Two possible conceptions are stressed by

[18] There is much in Spence's treatment of incentives that is similar to conceptions of incentives proposed by Seward (1950, 1951, 1952, 1953, 1956a), Logan (1960), and Amsel (1958, 1962). For Amsel's views, see Chapter 9.

Spence (1956, p. 135): ". . . the occurrence of these fractional goal responses results in a certain amount of conflict and hence in heightened tension or excitement. This heightened tension . . . might contribute to an increase in the existing state of general drive level, D. . . . Another possibility is that variation in the intensity of s_g provides an internal stimulus dynamism akin to Hull's notion of stimulus dynamism (V) resulting from different intensities of external stimulation." However, Spence suggests that this issue of the mechanism need not be resolved. Instead, incentive (K) can be used quantitatively to represent "the motivational property of the conditioned $r_g \rightarrow s_g$ mechanism . . . which is defined in terms of the experimental variables that determine the vigor of the latter" (i.e., $r_g \rightarrow s_g$) (Spence, 1956, p. 135). In other words the factors which affect the vigor of, say, the eating response, will empirically determine the size of K.

As r_g is a classical conditioned response, its strength is determined by such factors as the number of conditioning trials, the similarity between cues present at elicitation and those present at reinforcement, and by the properties of the goal object which occasion variation in the intensity or vigor of consummatory responses; as to the last problem, various experiments suggest that it may be time spent in the goal box, rather than amount eaten or size of the reward, that determines vigor of the consummatory reaction (see Chapter 11). However, it is also pointed out that variations in the concentration of sucrose in a reinforcing solution lead to variations in response rate.

[This variation in concentration] would be expected to elicit consummatory responses of different vigor. Classical conditioning of these different r_g's to cues in the apparatus would provide different values of K and hence different reaction-potential (i.e., E) values for the instrumental response under the different reinforcement conditions. Shifts in concentration of the reinforcer would produce changes in the vigor of the consummatory responses and through transfer changes in the vigor of conditioned fractional anticipatory goal response and thus the value of K [19] (Spence, 1956, p. 144).

As a factor determining response strength, K is assumed to interact with habit strength multiplicatively.

In a chain of responses, as might be found between the starting box and the goal box of a maze, Spence suggests that the value of K at different points of the maze would vary. This variation would be a function of the similarity between the stimulus situation at any point in the maze and the stimulus situation at the goal box where the con-

---

[19] Vigor of r_g is apparently indexed by rate of consumption, which varies with concentration of saccharin in solution (Spence, 1956, pp. 146–147; Sheffield, Roby, & Campbell, 1954).

summatory response is made. According to Spence, this similarity would ordinarily vary inversely with distance (or time) from the goal object, so that K would have a smaller value as it is elicited by cues distant in time or space from the consummatory reaction. This would generate a goal gradient, conceived in terms of variations in K, rather than in terms of variation in habit strength predicated on different amounts of secondary reinforcement (cf. Spence, 1947). In the other case of delay of reinforcement—that is, the one in which the subject remains in the same location following a response and before the goal object becomes available—Spence suggests that it is more complex than the serial response example, described earlier. Competing responses, which may interfere with the fractional antedating goal reaction, may occur in this second situation, especially when the goal object is long delayed; the incentive value of the antedating goal reaction would then be lessened.

It is quite clear that Spence's treatment of the K factor, as one influencing response strength but not habit strength, represents a major change from the *early* position taken by Hull. Also, the suggestion that in instrumental reward learning it is performance rather than habit strength which is influenced by the properties of the goal object removes this kind of learning from the reinforcement category. Spence clearly does not generalize this analysis very far; escape from a noxious stimulus, he suggests, will perhaps involve a very different theory (1956, p. 164).

Emotionality as Generalized Drive

Two kinds of primary or unlearned motivational states are postulated by Spence: the appetitional needs, like hunger and thirst; and the aversive or emotional drive states, like the pain from a noxious stimulus (e.g., electric shock). The appetitional needs are accompanied by distinctive stimuli or S_D's, which can acquire habit strength in the same fashion as external stimuli do. These various needs and drive states also "are assumed to contribute singly and in combination to the organism's general drive level (D)" (Spence, 1956, p. 166).

Spence follows Hull in indicating that in instrumental reward conditioning habit strength is not influenced by the strength of drive operative during acquisition. However, when such an acquired response is performed after learning, the strength of drive influences the strength of the response. The relationship suggested is as follows: ". . . response strength in instrumental reward conditioning situations has clearly been shown to be an increasing function, up to a point, of the deprivation time for the various need conditions. In the case of food and water deprivation, there appears to be a maximum period beyond which response strength actually decreases" (Spence, 1956, p. 169). However, Spence presents evidence that interfering responses may arise at the *shorter* deprivation intervals. When these responses are eliminated (Cotton, 1953), the relationship between response strength and deprivation interval is different. There is then little difference in response strength for different deprivation intervals. This (and other factors) permits at present no definitive conclusion concerning the relationship in question.

The strength of an aversive or emotional drive is treated somewhat differently. In the first place the conditions for variation in intensity of such drives lie in the intensity of the external, noxious stimulus. This is illustrated by the variation in performance of a conditioned eyelid reaction with the intensity of an air puff to the eye. There is some possibility here that, unlike the case of the appetitional drives, habit strength itself is influenced by the UCS intensity at acquisition (cf. Spence, 1956, pp. 174–176) and that an interpretation in terms of drive reduction is also possible. While Spence makes no final resolution of this point, he does state that ". . . whereas . . . reinforcement theory does not receive much support from studies involving appetitional needs, it . . . derive[s] considerable support from investigations employing aversive forms of motivation. This is possibly not unrelated to the fact that the experimenter has better control of the drive reduction in this type of situation" (Spence, 1956, p. 179).

In considering aversive stimulation, Spence's theory is that the drive mechanism "is an internal, emotional state or response of the organism (r_e), . . . aroused in different degrees with different intensities of such aversive stimuli as shock" (p. 180). Subjects will vary either because of constitutional or experiential factors in the degree to which they possess r_e, and this should mean that in various situations they should behave differently as a function of this r_e or D variation.[20]

Spence, like Hull, offers the proposition that all drives active in the organism will summate to produce a general drive level and that, at least under some conditions, this general D will activate the various habits that the organism has acquired. Spence is careful to indicate that the presence of competing reaction tendencies (for example, habits attached to the S_D's of irrelevant drives) may obscure relationships that might otherwise be expected and observed in the presence of generalized D. A careful analysis of the situation is necessary to determine whether this might occur.

[20] Much experimental work deriving from this formulation has been carried out recently in Spence's laboratory (cf. Chapter 14, and Spence, 1956, 1958).

Evidence from his laboratory convinces Spence that incentive and drive values are additive rather than multiplicative, as Hull assumed, but that their sum does multiply H in order to produce E, or excitatory potential. This is expressed symbolically as follows (Spence, 1956, p. 197):

$$R = f(\bar{E}) = H \times (D + K) - I_t$$

where I_t is an inhibitory factor.

Inhibition

Spence did not accept Hull's theory of inhibition and, as early as 1936, had suggested that nonreinforcement might act through frustration (Spence, 1960, pp. 96–97). Frustration, of course, can only occur after the development of an anticipation or an expectation of reward—that is, an $r_g \rightarrow s_g$ mechanism—and therefore would not appear in the early trials of the acquisition of an instrumental response, prior to the conditioning of r_g. As we have already seen, the occurrence of $r_g \rightarrow s_g$ has motivational properties.

With nonreward, however, this anticipation is frustrated, resulting in an emotional response (one of anger) (Spence, 1960, p. 98). This frustration response, with its stimulus consequences $(r_f \rightarrow s_f)$, can, through generalization, be aroused in advance of entrance into the (empty) goal box. The critical point is that other responses, competitive with the instrumental responses, can be elicited by the s_f. They are responses, either unlearned or learned in relation to the frustration stimulus, and to the extent that they successfully compete or interfere with the occurrence of the instrumental response, the instrumental response cannot occur. This is an interference theory of extinction (or inhibition) and depends on no specific additional motivational process, such as reactive inhibition.

Elsewhere, we shall see how Spence's analysis of motivation has yielded a number of experimental attacks on problems ranging from animal investigations to complex learning in human subjects. However, it should be made very clear that Spence does not pretend to have developed a formulation widely applicable to situations and species. Rather, his position favors the detailed working over of a limited number of problems in circumstances permitting precise control and manipulation of important variables. Whatever one may think of this approach (cf. Estes, 1957; Bruner, 1957, for varying opinions), Spence's contribution as such can only be evaluated in the light of the problem as he set it for himself. Some of the concepts we have reviewed are so closely tied to a limited experimental situation (e.g., the delay of reinforcement situation in the nonserial response case in the rat) that it is very difficult to extrapolate them to other situations, like problem-solving, or to other species, like monkeys and man. This is not perceived by Spence as his problem for the reasons already indicated. We shall, however, see in other writers of this same general persuasion, a much wider (and therefore necessarily looser) application of similar concepts.

Summary

Spence is primarily orientated to the general problem of selective learning, but he deals mainly with the two types of conditioning—classical and instrumental. The former depends on reinforcement as an empirical operation, and is highly important because fractional goal responses are formed through it. Such classical conditioning of goal response always occurs during instrumental learning. Instrumental learning develops by means of the principle of contiguity, but the *performance* of instrumental responses is governed by the incentive factor (K), which is acquired through the classical conditioning. As did Hull, Spence suggests that generalized drive will interact with habit strength to energize habit tendencies; he also stresses the role of incentives in this function and suggests that drive and incentive values summate and that their sum when multiplied by habit strength will (other things equal) yield the excitatory potential of a particular response. Spence has emphasized emotionality as a contributor to general drive level, and he has espoused a theory of inhibition based on competing reactions aroused by frustration of the $r_g - s_g$ mechanism, rather than on an independent motivational inhibitory variable.

N. E. MILLER'S FORMULATIONS

Equally closely associated with the Hullian viewpoint is Neal E. Miller, who has, perhaps, become most widely known for his applications of Hullian theory to a wide range of phenomena, while continuing to carry out an experimental program related to central issues of reinforcement theory. Miller has held to a tension-reduction theory of reinforcement and has also maintained a particular conception of the nature and functions of drive. All of the Hullian principles outlined in the earlier section of this chapter do not find full expression in Miller's work, but Hull, himself, in his last book (1952), seemed in some respects to have moved closer to Miller's position (cf. Hilgard, 1956, p. 123; Koch, 1954, p. 105 fn.). Miller (1959) has presented an extensive summary of his position, and somewhat informal treatments (Miller & Dollard, 1941; Dollard & Miller, 1950) in the context of application are available. Several differences, at least in emphasis, between Miller and Hull and between Miller and Spence, appear. Miller is an ingenious experimentalist, and many of his experiments have represented clever tests of those theoretical issues he apparently regards as having the greatest significance. A great deal of his later experimentation has concerned physiological mechanisms in motivation (see Chapter 5) and in reinforcement (see section on intracranial reinforcement in Chapter 11).

We shall here concern ourselves with Miller's description of the definition and function of drive, reinforcement, secondary reinforcement, and acquired drive, and his use of the drive generalization principle. Certain applications of S–R reinforcement principles by Miller are treated elsewhere, like the theory of conflict (Chapter 9) and the phenomena of learned drives and rewards (Chapter 11).

The function of motivation in Miller's position is very clear. "Without drives, either primary or acquired, the organism does not behave and hence does not learn" (Miller & Dollard, 1941, p. 21). Organisms can, of course, behave without learning, because there are usually innate or instinctive modes of adjustment which occur under drive states. Thus each primary drive will produce responses in "an innately determined preferential order" (p. 69), and this suggests that there is "distinctiveness or cue value" in connection with the drives (p. 69). Most of Miller's concern, however, is with learning or learned responses. It is important to note the emphasis placed on the cue value of the primary drive; Miller's concern with cues and their distinctiveness is much greater than is the case with other theorists of his camp.

Drive as Strong Stimulation

"A drive is a strong stimulus which impels action. Any stimulus can become a drive if it is made strong enough. The stronger the stimulus, the more drive function it possesses" (Miller & Dollard, 1941, p. 18). These three sentences summarize the definition and conception of drive which Miller follows. Strong stimuli may be internal, in which case they often are associated with deprivation conditions, like hunger or thirst, or they may be external, like pain-arousing stimuli.[21] These examples are illustrative of unlearned or primary drives. Acquired drives are similarly conceived as strong stimuli, but, as we shall see, these stimuli arise from responses made by the subject himself.

Miller takes the position that reduction in drive—that is, reduction

[21] Central processes, if they have *functional* properties of stimuli (or of responses), such as those of the nervous system, can also presumably operate as drives (Miller, 1959, pp. 242–243).

in the intensity of strong stimuli—is a necessary condition for learning. He is, therefore, a drive-reduction or a tension-reduction theorist (cf. Miller, 1951*b;* 1959, p. 256). This extends our prior description of his conception of motivation to add that he considers a stimulus to be a drive if its reduction is rewarding or reinforcing.

It is obviously difficult to offer criteria by which one will know when a stimulus is strong enough to be a drive and when it is not. Miller has never attempted to indicate such criteria, although he has suggested that the intensity of a stimulus may be relative to other stimulation in the situation (Miller & Dollard, 1941, p. 65; Miller, 1951*a*, p. 464). Fundamentally, the definition of a drive reduces to the impelling function of a stimulus and to the rewarding function of its reduction. "The ultimate test of drive and reward is their ability to produce the learning and performance of new responses" (Miller, 1951*a*, p. 436). The circularity in such a conception may be avoided if a drive condition, discovered through the production and learning of one response, is successfully used to produce and cause the learning of other responses (cf. Meehl, 1950). Such demonstrations have been made (cf. Miller, 1951*a*).

Reinforcement

Reinforcement, in the primary sense, is conceived as stimulus intensity reduction; thus food reduces hunger stimulation, and cessation of shock reduces pain. As these stimulus reductions take place, presumably the individual relaxes, both because of a decrease in tension and because fatigue from responding is, to Miller as to Hull, a drive, relief from which is afforded by rest, relaxation, or not responding. Stimuli associated with these relaxation responses occur contiguously with the reduction in drive intensity and with the reduction in fatigue; they will, on the reinforcement principle, acquire the ability to elicit these relaxation responses, and, once this is so, such stimuli function as rewards. They are learned rewards or secondary reinforcers. "For example, once the phrase, 'this is good,' has acquired the capacity to elicit relaxing, rewarding responses, these responses should be transferred to any new situation the subject learns to label as 'good' " (Miller, 1951*a*, p. 465).[22] An important aspect of the account given by

---

[22] At one time Miller and Dollard (1941, p. 65) suggested that acquired rewards could be effective "only in the presence of response-produced drives" and presumably could not be effective with only primary drives. However, Dollard and Miller (1950, p. 80) say: "Learned reinforcements are more effective in the presence of a drive, and even the presence of an irrelevant drive (i.e., hunger for a

Dollard and Miller (1950) of the functioning of motivational factors in human beings depends on the learned capacities of thoughts, words, and sentences to induce relief or relaxation and hence to function as rewards (see Chapter 11).

Acquired Drives

Perhaps more than any other investigator, Miller has been interested in and responsible for the study of acquired drives (cf. Miller, 1948*a*, 1951*a*). The empirical research on this point will be brought together in Chapter 11. The conception of acquired drives was sketched in the section which presented Hull's position. Briefly, it holds that responses, like the emotional ones in response to shock, are both productive of strong stimuli and learnable to other stimuli present in the situation. After they have been learned to the stimuli (external or internal), the stimuli may elicit them; the occurrence of these responses, however, produces strong stimulus consequences. Because strong stimuli are drives, this means that via the emotional responses the previously neutral stimuli have evoked a drive.

Suppose one has learned to be angry when he is called a derogatory name. Also he will react with anger to the anticipation of an insult or to the report that he has been called a name behind his back. The responses that ensue will be motivated by the anger, though just what they will be will also depend on what past experience in comparable or subjectively related situations has developed.

Drive Generalization: An Alternative to Generalized D

One of the most interesting developments in S-R reinforcement theory is the conception of generalized drive and the distinction it permits between habit and performance. Miller does not seem to use this particular notion, however. In relating experiments, for example, in which a habit learned under one drive was utilized under another drive, he has spoken of the drive stimulus *generalization* which mediates the transfer of the habit from one drive to another (Miller, 1948*b*, p. 161 fn., pp. 162–165; Dollard & Miller, 1950, pp. 174–175). He explicitly acknowledges that this transfer could be derived from Hull's conception of the role of alien drive but apparently prefers to use the drive-stimulus generalization mechanism.

learned reinforcement based on giving water to a thirsty animal) can increase their effectiveness somewhat. As with . . . other responses, it is difficult to be certain whether or not their effectiveness is reduced all the way to zero in the absence of any drive."

Summary

Miller's major motivational concepts are strong stimuli as drives, drive reduction as reinforcement, acquired drives, and drive generalization. His emphasis is placed on the stimulus aspect of motivation. This is paralleled by his emphasis in other contexts on the important roles of generalization and discrimination, both primary and mediated, in phenomena of human motivation and in intellectual functioning. Much more than Hull and somewhat more than Spence, he has stressed such aversive drives as pain. This may account for two features of his theoretical work: the heavy stress on the stimulus, perhaps deriving from experimental work in which the strong shock acts as a drive; and the use of a large number of emotion-denoting words (like fear, anger, disgust) in treating motivation. Such words may more often denote relatively transient *response processes* rather than enduring physiological states. If this is so, the Miller conception of response processes as yielding motivation ultimately should differ substantially from one that, like Hull's, emphasizes physiological states associated with operations of deprivation. Emotional responses as used by Miller may well have something in common with the affective and emotional bases of motivation outlined in Chapter 8, and it is our impression that stress on incentive motivation (Chapter 11) represents a shift in Miller's direction.

O. H. MOWRER'S FORMULATION

In the 1930's, O. H. Mowrer became a part of the Yale group and almost at once was identified with the study of fear and the application of the principles of learning to problems of neurosis and psychotherapy. He has also made significant experimental contributions to the study of learning and motivation and has been especially ingenious in developing experimental analogues of various human phenomena for use with lower animals. Throughout his work, Mowrer has made contributions to the theory of learning. He began as a monistic drive-reduction-reinforcement theorist in the Hullian tradition, later switched to a two-factor position, and has further revised his position in subsequent years.

Because of the limited scope of our present interest, we must forego here discussion of Mowrer's treatments of neurosis, personality, psychotherapy, language, and the analogues to human phenomena. Since fear is considered an acquired drive, we shall discuss Mowrer's contributions on this score. Too, we shall examine his revisions of reinforcement theory, not because of their relevance to the problem of learning but because so much of their content is centrally concerned with motivational concepts.

Anxiety or Fear

Mowrer's first major contribution to the study of anxiety (or fear as it is more commonly referred to by experimenters) stressed the importance of fear as a premonitory or warning cue of impending pain or danger to the organism (Mowrer, 1939, 1950a, Chap. 1) [23] and the proposition that fear is a learned reaction which many originally neutral stimuli can, through learning, come to elicit. Mowrer thought it probable that fear is not an innate reaction and that pain is. Fear would arise because of the anticipation of pain, or as Mowrer put it, *"anxiety (fear) is the conditioned form of the pain reaction,* which has the highly useful function of motivating and reinforcing behavior that tends to avoid or prevent the recurrence of the pain-producing (unconditioned) stimulus" (1950a, p. 17). Later, Mowrer (1950a, p. 17 fn.; 1956, p. 115) accepted the possibility that a noxious, intense stimulus may innately arouse fear as well as pain, but the fear component can be detached and be associated to other stimuli, which, in eliciting the fear, do not elicit the pain. In any case fear remains an acquired drive, capable of motivating responses and, when the fear is reduced, of rewarding them.

A number of experiments were carried out by Mowrer (cf. Mowrer, 1950a, Chaps. 3, 4, and 5) in the context of avoidance learning, which demonstrated the utility of regarding fear as an acquired drive. Even more generally, Mowrer has suggested that such

. . . key concepts as "attitudes" (sociology), "need for security" (social work), "tension" (psychiatry), and "anxiety" (psychoanalysis) all involve the assumption that human beings are capable of being motivated, not only by organic needs (discomforts) that are immediately present and felt, but also by the mere *anticipation of such needs* . . . Human beings have a strong impulsion to put as much "distance" between themselves and the brink of real privation as possible; and it is this "need for security"—not actual, immediate want—that keeps most men at their jobs and largely shapes their political, economic, and social ideologies (p. 29).

It is quite clear that Mowrer has seen anxiety, fear, or a more general concept, expectancy, as a highly general basis for motivation and that he would integrate the special concepts of the several disciplines identified in parentheses above in terms of this one general notion. In an-

[23] Since several of Mowrer's papers have been reprinted in his book (Mowrer, 1950a), further citations to the anxiety and other papers will be made to the book.

other connection, he (1950*a*, pp. 347–351) has stressed, in interpreting the results of a rat study, that hunger and thirst are probably accompanied by a *fear* of further hunger and thirst. In large measure, Mowrer would seem to suggest that *fear*, either of the pain arising from punishment or from persistence of other strong drives, is one of the most, if not the most, powerful learned motives in the human organism (cf. Mowrer, 1952, pp. 423–424). Mowrer's emphasis on fear or anxiety first arose perhaps when he saw that Freud's second theory of anxiety (see Chapter 12), which emphasized the warning function of anxiety, was capable of integration with Pavlov's notion of the signaling function of the conditioned stimulus (cf. Mowrer, 1950*a*, Chap. 1) and because of his interest in neurosis and psychotherapy (see Mowrer & Kluckhohn, 1944).

View of the Learning Process

Most of the thinking summarized so far represents Mowrer's thought when he still espoused a monistic conception of learning based on drive reduction. In 1947 he revised his conception of the learning process and began to advocate a two-factor theory of learning (Mowrer, 1947; 1950*a*, Chap. 9; 1951). This arose because he was puzzled by the problem of the acquisition of fear. It seems much more reasonable to assume that fears develop because pain or discomfort *begins* rather than because it ends. In a situation in which an animal is shocked, for example, it would appear to be the *onset* of the shock of which the conditioned stimulus (or sign) becomes premonitory rather than the *offset* or termination of the shock. Cessation of shock would presumably be required in a drive-reduction interpretation of such sign learning. Mowrer's doubts that drive reduction was involved in such learning led him and Suter (Mowrer, 1950*a*, pp. 278–293) to compare avoidance learning under two conditions. In one, the conditioned stimulus started

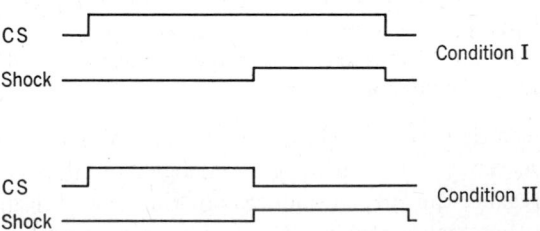

Figure 10-1. Diagram of relation of onset and offset of CS and shock (UCS) in the experiment by Mowrer and Suter (Mowrer, 1950*a*, pp. 278–293). A rise in the line for either stimulus indicates its onset; a fall in the line its offset.

before the shock and terminated with the shock; this condition presumably meets the requirement of drive (shock) reduction in conjunction with the signaling or conditioned stimulus, and drive-reduction theory would predict effective learning under these circumstances. In the other, the signal began before the shock but terminated with shock onset; under these circumstances drive reduction theory would presumably predict no learning or less than that under the first condition (Fig. 10–1). The results showed no difference between the conditions,[24] leading Mowrer to conclude that drive onset is a factor in learning. On this basis and other evidence, Mowrer concluded that a two-process or two-factor conception of learning is necessary: conditioning, which is "restricted to the process whereby emotions, meanings, attitudes, appetites, and cognitions are acquired . . . [and] 'solution learning' applying to all cases of overt instrumental habit formation" (Mowrer, 1951, p. 352). Conditioning is based on contiguity, and reinforcement is not essential to it; it involves primarily the autonomic nervous system. Solution learning, on the other hand, involves reinforcement and depends "upon the central nervous system and [seems] to involve responses which are mediated by the skeletal muscles . . ." (Mowrer, 1951, p. 352).[25]

More recently, Mowrer (1956, 1960) has modified his position still further. His new position can best be summarized in his own words:

. . . it is suggested that all learning is in the nature of sign learning, significance learning, meaning learning. When a stimulus (external or internal) is repeatedly paired, or correlated, with a bad experience, i.e., with drive increment, a meaning (fear) is learned which tends to prevent recurrence of that experience. On the other hand, when a stimulus (external or internal) is repeatedly paired with a *good* experience, i.e., with drive decrement, a meaning (fear decrement or hope) is learned which tends to insure recurrence of that experience. Thus habit formation and fear conditioning (incremental type), which were the two factors in the original version of two-factor learning theory, give way to incremental fear conditioning or secondary motivation and decremental fear conditioning or secondary reinforcement. These phenomena correspond, respectively, to the negative and positive valences, vectors, or expectancies of field theory and, at least loosely, to the two kinds of information—"on" and "off," "yes" and "no"—involved in servo (feedback) mechanisms (Mowrer, 1956, p. 121).

---

[24] This experiment and its interpretation have been critically discussed by Miller (1951b), Kendler (1951), and Sheffield (1951), and results by Sullivan (1950) do not support its interpretation.

[25] This conception is the diametric opposite of the one later advanced by Spence (see pp. 488–489).

Mowrer (1956, p. 123) stresses that instrumental responses are *guided* rather than strengthened by "hope" (secondary reinforcement) and by "fear" (secondary motivation). This formulation has been put more finely as follows:

Learning, I propose, is not a matter of strengthening or weakening connections between drives and overt behavior, but of the acquisition of "positive" (rewarding) and "negative" (punishing) feedback from stimuli that have accompanied past action or experience. If, in the past, a given act has been predominantly rewarding, then incidental stimuli, both external and internal, which have been associated with the act-reward sequence will take on . . . the capacity to produce secondary reward and thus to guide or direct the organism into the *same* or similar action in the future. If, on the other hand, a given act has been predominantly punishing, the incidental stimuli which have been associated with the act-punishment sequence will take on the capacity to produce a secondary drive increment ("fear") and will tend to guide the organism into *different* behavior (Mowrer, 1954, pp. 84-85).

Further, "Meanings, not means, attitudes, not actions—these are the most immediate outcomes of learning . . ." (p. 85).[26]

Summary

Considered here are Mowrer's contributions to the theoretical understanding and empirical study of fear (anxiety) as an acquired drive and his changing views on the problem of reinforcement. Starting from a monistic drive reduction viewpoint, he has espoused, first, a two-factor theory and, finally, a conception in which all learning is sign learning through contiguity. The meanings indicated by the signs are fear (corresponding to a drive-increment) or hope (fear-decrement or, generally, drive-decrement). The factors of fear and hope *guide* rather than strengthen instrumental activity, and stimuli (internal or external) provide the information on which fear and hope are based.

We believe that Mowrer's position has essentially reached emphasis on the incentive function of stimuli—that is, stimuli, external or internal, guide instrumental behavior in terms of their premonitory rewarding or punishing information. The stimuli acquire this information through association by contiguity. As Mowrer has indicated, this places him in a position close to conceptions of cognitive or field theory. Among the writers treated in this book, Mowrer's present views are

[26] This formulation represents, to Mowrer, a radical break with the Hullian viewpoint and a shift toward a Tolmanian view. Mowrer's book (1960) presents a more extensive review of the relevant literature and of the nature of his later formulation.

close to those of McClelland, Young, and Peak, as presented in Chapter 8, and to those of Spence (in certain respects) and Tolman, as outlined in this chapter.

GENERAL SUMMARY: HULL, SPENCE, MILLER, MOWRER

The Yale-Iowa point of view, presented through the ideas of Hull, Spence, Miller, and Mowrer, has stressed the role of motivation in activating both unlearned and learned behavior of organisms and in providing some of the conditions for the reinforcement of learning.

Hull conceived primary drives as stimuli, the reduction or elimination of which is reinforcing so far as the acquisition of responses is concerned. Drive also was of importance in the performance of habits, although, save for the minimum of drive necessary to permit reinforcement, drive strength was not important to learning. He presented a list of primary drives and provided for learned motivation through the concepts of secondary drive and secondary reinforcement. A negative fatigue-like drive was also postulated. Drive stimuli, which enabled the organism to act differentially with respect to different drives or to different intensities of the same drive, were conceived by Hull as important associative factors, that is, as stimulus elements which, together with external and other internal stimuli, entered into habits. Another important concept is associated with the goal response—namely, the fractional goal response. This fractional goal response could become anticipatory to contact with the goal itself and was the mediating basis for derivations of phenomena that involve such terms as purpose, direction, intent, and foresight. Hull's formulation was rooted in the conception of survival in an environment, one which thus stressed the important role of bodily need satisfaction. However, the essence of his view was an objective, essentially nonteleological, and mechanistic account of survival and adaptational processes.

Spence, in his development and modification of Hull's theory, has been less concerned with the general problems of adaptation and survival than with the analysis of certain learning problems. He has taken a view toward reinforcement that it is an empirical fact for some kinds of learning but has not been concerned with drive-stimulus reduction. He suggests that some kinds of learning do not involve reinforcement and that motivational control in such cases resides in characteristics of incentives (mediated by the fractional goal response). Incentives influence, not the learning but the performance of responses, and incentives interact with drive and habit strength to control the strength of responses. Drive for Spence, as for Hull, is a factor which may influence any habit, even those learned under other drives. Spence has stressed, in his empirical work, emotional drives like anxiety as set up by varying intensities of a noxious, unconditioned stimulus. His theory of inhibition emphasizes competing responses, arising from frustration of the fractional anticipatory goal response.

Miller defines drive as strong stimulation and has worked substantially with strong external stimuli (like shock) in establishing acquired drives. His work on acquired drives, conflict, and transfer of responses across drives has shown some of the breadth that Hull's concepts can achieve. Miller remains a drive-reduction theorist and, through his work on acquired drive, he has placed much stress on the role of response processes in setting up the strong stimuli that act as drives. Extensive studies of nervous-system processes in motivation and reinforcement have been prominent.

Mowrer shifted from a monistic drive-reduction position to a two-factor learning theory, in which the role of reinforcement is the opposite of that supposed by Spence in his own two-factor theory. Mowrer was led to this conception by his work on fear. He seems to regard fear as a highly generalized motivational state, being involved with the primary, internal drives as well as with noxious, external stimuli. Later, he has apparently abandoned a reinforcement position altogether in favor of one in which incentives become associated with hope (of reducing drive) or fear (of increasing drive). By these hopes and fears incentives then control behavior.

The Hullian point of view may in essence be described as a rigorous, objective, quantitative, and biologically flavored account of adaptational processes. It has preferred to deal with relatively simple situations and organisms, in the belief that the basic principles discovered will have wide applicability to other species and situations. It has stressed the testability of its deductions and has led to the execution of a great deal of experimental work (as well as controversy).

It is evident that major changes are appearing in the heritage which Hull developed. No longer is the monistic position on reinforcement agreed to universally, and external incentives and emotional drives seem bound to replace, to a substantial degree, the heavy emphasis on the internal, homeostatic drives, especially as neurophysiological research goes on to uncover the neurohumoral factors which probably underlie these drives. It is too early to guess the ultimate evaluation of history concerning the value and significance of the Yale-Iowa viewpoint. As one proceeds through the chapters of this book, however, it is apparent how many research topics have been initiated, influenced, or at least "flavored" by the Hull-Spence tradition.

EDWARD C. TOLMAN

A viewpoint as influential as Hull's and often in basic conflict with some of Hull's ideas was systematically formulated in 1932 by Tolman (1932). Subsequently developed in certain respects (Tolman 1938, 1949*a*, *b*, 1951, 1952, 1959), the system has remained much the same, although terminological changes have been frequent (Hilgard, 1956, MacCorquodale & Meehl, 1954). Tolman has had many supporters and adherents, and it is evident that S–R theory, in virtue of Tolman's work, has itself been modified. S–R theory, under the impact of criticisms and experimental results from the Tolman side, has had to develop accounts of concepts similar to expectancy.

Tolman has always identified himself as a behaviorist, but his behaviorism has had more in common with McDougall's purposivism, Gestalt psychology, Kurt Lewin's system, and, latterly, with psychoanalysis than have many behaviorisms. It is probably true that Tolman, ever since the 1920's, has stressed, almost more than any other theorist, the importance of motivational variables in reference to behavior. MacCorquodale and Meehl (1954, p. 178) point this out in indicating "the importance of Tolman's work in reducing the plausibility of the variant of the pure frequency-recency connectionism which was held by many prior to around 1930" (1954, p. 178). Stress on the *goals* involved in situations for a subject was a mark of Tolman's thinking from the start; among the properties of molar behavior he said (Tolman, 1932, p. 14) is its purposiveness, i.e., its *persistence* and *teachableness*. Molar behavior has ". . . the character of getting to or getting from a specific goal-object or goal-situation" (p. 10).

Differences from S–R Viewpoints

Before going on to describe the details of Tolman's treatment of motivation, we may observe in passing the outstanding differences between Tolman's position and those who follow the S–R viewpoint (particularly, Hull, Skinner, and Guthrie) in learning-behavior theory. These pertain to what is learned, on the one hand, and to the role of motivation and especially of reward on the other.

Although Tolman (1949*a*) admitted that there are several kinds of learning, some of which follow S–R principles, he held consistently to the notion that one kind of learning is the acquisition of expectancies or expectations (sign-gestalts, sign-significates). What this means is that organisms do not always learn specific responses, like, for example, a left or a right turn in a maze, but rather the *significance* or the *meaning* of the cues at a juncture in the maze, an expectation, in other words, of what lies beyond those cues. Put in other terms we could say for Tolman that organisms may learn "what leads to what," or associations between stimuli or signs. One evidence for this is that the responses used by an animal in getting from one place to another will often vary, rather than being fixed and invariable, when the situation, as in many of the experiments by Tolman and his students, permits such variation to appear. Such experiments, Tolman (1948) has said, show that what is learned has the nature of a *map*, rather than fixed responses or invariant *routes*. We need not pursue this subject further here, because this issue pertains mainly to the nature of learning. We may observe, however, that Tolman's emphasis on goals suggests that what organisms often learn in situations is the location where particular goals are to be found. This is a *cognitive* outcome.

The S–R formula means an association between a stimulus and a response. In denying that all associations involve responses, Tolman differs from the adherents of the S–R viewpoint. Some of the S–R theorists, but not all, believe that reinforcement is essential to learning. We have encountered this notion in Hull and Miller, who espoused a particular theory of reinforcement (drive reduction). At least in some situations Tolman has argued that reinforcement is not essential to learning. The best illustration is provided by the experiments on latent learning. In general, these experiments have been interpreted to show that hungry rats will learn something about a maze during explorations on which no reinforcements are given. That they learned something during the unrewarded exploration is shown when reward is later introduced. Performance then improves suddenly, leading to the inference that what was latently learned during the unrewarded trials is being manifested.[27] These findings led Tolman to suggest that incentive and reward affect the performance of what has been learned but not the learning process itself. (It was partly due to Tolman that Hull accepted the distinction between learning and performance.)

Emphasis on Goals and Incentives

To the student who surveys *Purposive Behavior in Animals and Men* (Tolman, 1932), it becomes obvious that much of the early experimental work by Tolman and his students investigated behavior as a

---

[27] We cannot here enter into the voluminous, controversial, and often conflicting literature of latent learning. The issue bears primarily on the subject of learning rather than motivation. For classification of experiments and review of evidence see Hilgard (1948, 1956), MacCorquodale and Meehl (1954), Thistlethwaite (1951), and Kimble (1961).

function of goals or rewards. Motivated animals were used, and it was recognized that behavior varies as a function of motivational conditions. More than that of most investigators, however, Tolman's program provided for the study of rewards. We will review this work in the next chapter. Here we may be content with a list of some of the variables studied: amount of reward, delay of reward, quality of reward, change of reward, and expectation of a particular kind of reward.

Tolman's Early Formulation of Motivation

The role of physiological motivational states in rat behavior was always recognized by Tolman. The rat's ultimate purpose, he said (1932, p. 28), is to get *"to a final physiological quiescence or from a final physiological disturbance or both."* In a state of drive the animal is in a state of demand for substances and situations which will provide physiological quiescences. It is clear, then, that Tolman, like Hull, felt drive (or need) to be a basic behavioral determinant, but Tolman, as in many respects did Lewin, emphasized not the restlessness that drive states may arouse but the *demands for goal objects* with which they are associated.[28] The ultimate or fundamental drives provide "the primordial bases for all behavior" (p. 271). The basic human appetites (drives) which Tolman listed in 1932 were food, sex, excretion, specific contact, rest, and sensorimotor hungers; and the human aversions were fright and pugnacity. He also spoke of second-order drives, like curiosity, gregariousness, self-assertion, self-abasement, and imitativeness (p. 291), which are "evoked primarily by external situations" (p. 294). He thought the second-order drives to be independent of the primary ones, though they could be attached to them. Personality mechanisms, like phobias, were also spoken of in 1932 in a motivational context. The primary and second-order drives were conceived as largely innate, whereas the personality mechanisms were acquired.

Tolman concluded his formulation of behavior processes in 1932 by indicating that there are four ultimate and independent causes of behavior, "stimuli, heredity, past training, and momentary initiating physiological states . . ." (p. 412). The role of motivation appears strongly in the following quote: "The organism responds to the given stimuli only, by virtue of an initiatory physiological state which, given his innate or acquired means-end-readinesses, gives rise to demands . . . one or more of which leads him to respond to the given S as presenting an appropriate means-object. These depending demands control

---

[28] The emphasis on incentive motivation by Spence, Mowrer, Amsel (see Chapter 11), and others is perhaps a restatement of this point.

the whole line of the S–R process" (Tolman, 1932, p. 407). As Hilgard summarized this point: "When drives are aroused, a state of tension ensues, leading to demands for goal-objects" (Hilgard, 1956, p. 201). Motivation also enters into learning of responses. Animals must be motivated to learn, and the presence of a goal object *confirms* an expectancy that the goal object would be located in a given place. While this notion of the confirmation of an expectancy sounds like a principle of reinforcement, Tolman (1952, p. 396) did not so regard it.

Tolman's Later Formulation

In many respects Tolman's later writings mainly contribute refinements and elaborations of the point of view outlined in 1932, especially in relation to motivational and personality variables (Tolman, 1942, 1943, 1945, 1949b). The fullest development and the most systematic presentation were made in 1951 (Tolman, 1951).[29] We will summarize this formulation now.

Behavior is a function of three independent or initiating variables: the stimulus situation, states of drive arousal and/or satiation, and individual difference variables. We shall be concerned with the second of these—drives—and the further concepts which are derivative from it. Tolman switches the usage of the words drive and need, as compared to his own earlier usage and that of Hull. Drive may be identified by means of consummatory behaviors, but "the real definition of drives . . . lies . . . in precise statements concerning the states of the underlying organs and tissues themselves" (Tolman, 1951, p. 280). The need which results from the initiating drive is "a readiness to get to and to manipulate in consummatory fashion (or to get from) certain other types of object" (p. 288). Even when drive is weak, needs may be aroused by stimuli; as when hunger is aroused by food, and needs may interact. Thus hunger can be aroused by drives other than that for food, as in compulsive eating. Tolman suggests a number of specific needs and also a "libido need," a sort of generalized need which varies among people and in the same person at different times as a sort of energy; it "has no specific goals of its own, but through contact with all the other needs . . . it adds magnitudes . . ." to them (Tolman, 1951, p. 289). The strength of any one need, like hunger, then, would be a joint function of hunger need as such, libido need, and the stimulus (food) situation. This libido need may have some similarity to Hull's generalized drive.

The list of primary needs Tolman gives in 1951 is much like the

[29] Another statement was later made by Tolman (1959). It does not seem to us to have the generality of the one in 1951, however.

earlier ones and includes hunger, thirst, sex, pain avoidance, aggression against outside obstacles, and a general exploratory, curiosity, or placing need. Secondary or "socio-relational" needs, which are largely innate (Tolman, 1951, p. 321 fn.), include affiliation, dominance, dependence, and submission. A set of tertiary or learned needs is also postulated, which consists "in wants to get to and from, to manipulate (as ways of getting to and from) certain relatively universal types of culturally provided goals . . ." (p. 321), like wealth and business success. These tertiary needs are assumed to be "subgoals connected by beliefs to more basic goals" (p. 321), though practically speaking they have a good deal of functional independence.

Needs may be measured operationally by the readiness of the individual to exhibit consummatory responses and by the vigor of behavior with reference to a standard goal object in an approach-avoidance type of situation.

Relations of Motivation to Other Concepts. Several other concepts are involved in Tolman's action model. We will deal with two of them. One is the belief-value matrix, which may be culturally shared or unique to an individual. It consists of beliefs that doing things or getting to objects, situations, or goals will gain satisfactions; these objects, situations, or goals represent categories. Thus one may believe that classes of objects or situations have the capacity to satisfy a need—in the case of hunger the class could be composed of restaurants, for example. As we understand it, the objects (types of restaurants) within the category will have varying *values* as to the expectation of the actor that the types of food they serve and their costs will, considering the state of his hunger and his pocketbook, satisfy his need. These belief-value matrices are acquired through experience and obviously function as an instrumentality in the service of needs.

The other concept is the behavior space. This consists of the environment and its objects as the actor perceives them: The objects have positive and negative valences, corresponding to particularizations of values from the controlling and activating belief-value matrix. Part of this behavior space includes the "behaving self," which includes need-pushes, corresponding to need deprivations. The behavior-space corresponds, more or less, to Lewin's concept of the "life space" or psychological environment (see Chapter 7). Such a concept emphasizes that the behaving person responds to his environment not as it would be assessed by a physicist's objective recording instruments but rather as he perceives the environment at any given time.

The need system and the belief-value matrix seem, in their interaction, to produce the behavior space and essentially to constitute what

Tolman would mean by personality. He states that personality "is a study of belief-value matrices—their integration or lack of integration —plus a study of need systems, the list of needs, the ways in which the individual needs do or do not enhance or depress one another, and their attachments to specific matrices" (Tolman, 1951, p. 353).

Summary

We have stressed the significance that Tolman has placed on motivational variables, which have often been translated mainly into demands and appetites for goal objects and into expectations as to what stimuli will lead to goal objects for which present drive or need produces a demand. Demands and expectations illustrate the *cognitive* aspect of his view. Tolman postulates a number of primary needs, like hunger (and a sort of general need, a libido), and second-order needs, like gregariousness. Even higher-order personality variables, which are learned, have a motivational status, such as the belief-value matrix which has an important role in determining the nature of the behavior space. Tolman has not formulated a motivational theory at a level of detail comparable to that espoused by Hull, but early he made the important point that motivational factors, while important to learning, may separately influence performance. Denying that reinforcement is basic to all learning, Tolman nevertheless seems to view behavior as arising essentially in the service of the organism's needs.

MacCorquodale and Meehl's Formalization of Expectancy Theory

MacCorquodale and Meehl (1953, 1954), while not especially advocating Tolman's expectancy viewpoint, nevertheless attempted to correct the looseness which has characterized many of Tolman's formulations. In doing so, they have recognized the role of motivational factors in an expectancy viewpoint. We may summarize this aspect of their treatment briefly as follows.

To begin with, an expectancy, as MacCorquodale and Meehl view it, involves three terms: S_1 is a stimulus whose perception gives rise to the probability that, if a response (R_1) is made, another stimulus, S_2, will appear. The notation for an expectancy is, therefore, ($S_1R_1S_2$). The probability that this response (R_1) will occur (a formulation similar to Hull's reaction potential) is said to be "a multiplicative function of the strength of the expectancy ($S_1R_1S_2$) and the valences . . . of the expectandum (S_2)" (MacCorquodale & Meehl, 1954, p. 246). Motivational factors enter into the valence of S_2; this is a function of its cathexis. The cathexis (or incentive value) arises from the number of times it has been associated with a consummatory response and also from the strength of the need (Hull's drive) for the cathected situation. Need strength (e.g., hunger) is related to duration of deprivation of the cathected situation (e.g., food).

It is quite clear that this view of the action potentiality of a response is quite similar to the formulation of Hull and of Spence (Hilgard, 1956, p. 450), in which a combination of drive and incentive (corresponding to need and to cathexis) multiplies habit strength (corresponding to expectancy). Other postulates in the MacCorquodale and Meehl formalization contain an equivalent of the term secondary reinforcement (Hilgard, 1956, p. 449).

MacCorquodale and Meehl have dealt with only the simpler aspects of Tolman's concepts (e.g., belief-value matrices are not considered). They have, however, preserved the important role which goal objects (the valenced expectandum) have always had in Tolman's system. It is of some interest that the incentive properties of objects have figured very importantly in the recent developments we have described for Spence and for Mowrer. A similar thread can be found in the affective theories of Young and McClelland (see Chapter 8), and it may be that a unification of motivation theory may ultimately develop around the incentive factor. If this happens, it will perhaps indicate that Tolman's emphasis, despite its informality and unrealized programmicity, was on the correct path, all along.

EDWIN R. GUTHRIE

We can be brief in our discussion of Guthrie, because his viewpoint in relation to behavior pertains largely to the nature of learning. His treatment is usually informal, and he never attempted the grand systematization of a behavior theory such as we saw in Hull and in Tolman. Yet his viewpoint has been influential and, in the case of motivation, has in many respects denied or attenuated the overweening significance that other theorists have accorded to it.

Guthrie's Explanation of Learning

To Guthrie learning occurs on the basis of a single contiguous occurrence of a stimulus and a response. Although this statement seems to belie ordinary experience, which suggests that repeated practice trials are necessary to learning, Guthrie would say that in each practice trial, new or different stimuli are being associated with the response. The argument is that to meet some criterion of learning, the learner may have to go through a number of trials, because the criterion may be that the response occur in a high proportion of the stimulus presentations. Guthrie's point is that no two stimulus presentations are identical, so that to condition a response to a substantial part of the varying stimuli within the loosely constant situation may require many trials (to meet the criterion). But learning occurs between each stimulus variant and the response completely on a single trial (Guthrie, 1935, 1942, 1952; Mueller & Schoenfeld, 1954; Hilgard, 1948, 1956). This position has received much further development in the hands of theorists such as Estes (1959).

Role of Reward and Punishment in Learning. Guthrie takes also an unusual position with respect to the role of reward (Guthrie, 1940). Strictly speaking, reward does not influence learning. Associations are formed between stimuli and responses, irrespective of rewards or other effects of the responses. Why is reward so much emphasized by students of learning? Guthrie's reply is that ordinarily the achievement of the reward removes the animal from the situation. This protects the S–R relationships formed there, since new and conflicting responses cannot be made in conjunction with the stimuli of the situation if the animal is no longer there. Similarly, punishment is important because of what it makes the organism do. Hilgard (1956, pp. 76–77) points out four things that, in Guthrie's terms, punishment may do: (1) Mild punishment may excite only and therefore enhance ongoing behavior. (2) But conflicting or incompatible responses may result from punishment, thus breaking up behavior patterns. (3) Punishment may also drive the organism to seek relief through escape; the acts of escape remove the animal from the situation, so, like rewarded acts, they will be retained. (4) Stimuli associated with punishment may come to evoke ahead of the punishment the responses which terminated it, thus producing avoidance.

Motivation in Guthrie's System

Motives seem to arise primarily through learning. "The problem of motive arises when it is necessary to explain how behavior becomes directed at certain ends, and this is a matter of learning . . ." (Guthrie, 1938, p. 92). The way in which motives affect behavior and learning is seen in that ". . . problems are persistent stimulus situations of such a nature that they keep the animal or the person disturbed and excited until some act is hit upon which removes the 'maintaining stimuli' and allows the excitement to subside.

"Such persistent and disturbing stimuli are sometimes called 'drive,'" like hunger spasms (p. 96).[30]

Drives or motives then are conceived as stimuli, as are many emotions (p. 103), and they are important mainly because they activate the

---

[30] This is reminiscent of Miller's statement that drives are strong stimuli. Early in his career, Miller was a student of Guthrie's.

individual; they make him respond until the maintaining stimuli are eliminated. It is important to note that "The drive remains faithful to the act that removed it because that was its last association" (p. 98). The recurrence of the drive stimuli will tend to re-evoke the previously successful act.

Guthrie admits that, in the maze, "Hunger is required to set the goal" (1952, p. 37). But he regards the goal differently than perhaps does Tolman. "Goal objects toward which behavior is getting . . . differ from simple stimuli in that the behavior toward them is 'driven' by stimuli which are usually internal. The animal may as justly be described as fleeing from the acute spasms of hunger as seeking its goal, food" (Guthrie, 1952, pp. 138–139). It is important to note that internal stimuli, arising from a state like hunger, are persistent over time (until food is eaten). This means that on subsequent occasions the final act in a sequence can advance temporally and appear on other occasions earlier than it did on the first one. This provides for anticipation and for short-circuiting of behavior, much in the fashion of the r_g in the Hull-Spence system.

Perhaps one other motivational implication may be mentioned, in addition to its activating, persisting, and time-binding roles. This is suggested when Guthrie observes that goal responses, when present, may increase the animal's energy. "The goal response with which the sight of the food is met by a hungry animal serves to energize eating. In the absence of food it can energize action," and, when food is not found in the goal box, the animal "is compelled to channel its excitement into activities other than eating" (Guthrie, 1952, p. 230). Goal responses would thus seem to have a general energizing role, as does their frustration.

Guthrie regards lists and classifications of drives as relatively unimportant. The important thing is what such stimuli make the organism do. He does, however, suggest that stimuli associated with a consummatory response, for example, eating, "can to some extent substitute for physiological hunger . . . This secondary drive dependent on association is called appetite by some writers and distinguished from real hunger" (Guthrie, 1938, p. 101). Furthermore, "interference with any action system under way may produce excitement" (p. 101).

Summary

Guthrie uses a minimum of motivational concepts, regarding drives or motives largely as persistent, strong stimuli which keep the organism active until some response it makes serves to eliminate the goading stimulus. Because of their persistence, motives maintain as well as arouse behavior, and they provide a basis for anticipation of events through response short-circuiting. Reward, as such, plays no part in Guthrie's treatment of learning.

B. F. SKINNER

For many years, Skinner has been working systematically from a highly objective, relatively atheoretical point of view on a program, the major fruits of which have been *Schedules of Reinforcement* (Ferster & Skinner, 1957) and *Verbal Behavior* (Skinner, 1957). While Skinner has always been chary of much theoretical involvement (cf. Skinner, 1950, 1959), in these last two books theoretical discussions are even more limited than they are in earlier writings, and concepts of drive and motivation are hardly mentioned (except insofar as the reinforcement operation involves the presence of a drive). We shall, therefore, be mainly concerned with the earlier treatments of Skinner's position (Skinner, 1938, 1953; Keller & Schoenfeld, 1950; cf. Verplanck, 1954; Hilgard, 1948, 1956).

Skinner made an early distinction between classical or respondent conditioning and instrumental or operant conditioning. In the latter, with which his work has been chiefly concerned, a response is, in the first instance, emitted by the organism. It is made to occur at a high rate and, frequently, in the presence only of certain external stimuli; these aspects of control are achieved through the operation of reinforcement. Skinner seems to accept an empirical law of effect for operant conditioning but he offers no speculations concerning its mechanism.

To Skinner a reinforcer is a stimulus which reinforces, that is, strengthens, a response. There are positive and negative reinforcers; if presentation of a stimulus (like food) achieves an increase in response rate we have a positive reinforcer. When the rate similarly changes on removal of a stimulus (like shock), we have a negative reinforcer (Skinner, 1953). Punishment is a separate case. The removal of a positive or the addition of a negative reinforcer constitutes punishment, and punishment effects only a suppression of responses, probably because it induces an emotional state, rather than eliminating responses, as does extinction (Estes, 1944). Skinner thinks punishment should not be used at all, since "The aversive stimuli which are needed generate emotions, including predispositions to escape or retaliate, and disabling anxieties" (Skinner, 1953, p. 183). This has been a major point in his advocacy of teaching machines (or programmed instruction) and in his design of a psychological Utopia (*Walden II*). Punishment is not a procedure to be followed in these situations.

Secondary Reinforcers and Generalized Reinforcers. Conditioned or secondary reinforcers in Skinner's system develop their reinforcing power "through being present when an original reinforcement is given" (Keller & Schoenfeld, 1950, p. 234); however, for this to happen, the stimulus in question must already be a discriminative stimulus for some response (p. 236).

Generalized reinforcers are secondary or conditioned reinforcers which have been "paired with more than one primary reinforcer" (Skinner, 1953, p. 77). Although secondary reinforcers usually work only when there is some state of deprivation present,

. . . one kind of generalized reinforcer is created because many primary reinforcers are received only after the physical environment has been effectively manipulated. . . .

We are automatically reinforced, apart from any particular deprivation, when we successfully control the physical world. This may explain our tendency to engage in skilled crafts, in artistic creation, and in such sports as bowling, billiards, and tennis (p. 77).

Environmental stimulation also seems to be reinforcing, even when such stimulation has not been associated with primary reinforcement. Skinner's example here is the reaction of a baby to the sound of its rattle. Perhaps reinforcement by environmental change has arisen in the course of evolution because of the favored position an organism would have "which is reinforced by its success in manipulating nature . . ." (p. 78).

Generalized reinforcers are an important concept to the study of human behavior, which seems so often controlled by rewards, like money, which have no simple relationship to primary rewards.

Drive

Skinner insists that drive is a concept that is introduced only "because much of the behavior of an organism shows an apparent variability" (Skinner, 1938, p. 341). For example, sometimes an animal will eat and sometimes not, even though the immediate circumstances are the same. The difference may lie in the difference between fasting and just having eaten. Fasting and feeding, or, more generally, the operations of deprivation and satiation, are the real defining operations so far as drive is concerned. As Skinner summarized his notion of drive:

In measuring the strength of a drive we are in reality only measuring strength of behavior. A complete account of the latter is to be obtained from an examination of the operations that are found to affect it. The "drive" is a hypothetical state interpolated between operation and behavior and is not actually required in a descriptive system. The concept is useful, however, as a device for expressing the complex relation that obtains between various similarly effective operations and a group of co-varying forms of behavior. The properties assigned to the state are derived from the observation of these relations (Skinner, 1938, p. 368).

Skinner refuses to think of drive as a stimulus, because stimuli have not been demonstrated for many drive states and, in the case of hunger, for example, the stomach contractions do not parallel the other evidences of the drive very closely (Skinner, 1938, p. 376).

As to the number of drives, Skinner states two points in answer to the implicit question. One is the further question, "In how many ways can an organism be deprived?" (1953, p. 148). He suggests that we also must ask:

How many kinds of behavior vary in strength independently of each other? On this basis we can distinguish between eating, drinking, sexual behavior, and so on, as well as between subdivisions of each of these fields. If the probabilities of eating two kinds of food always vary together we assume a common hunger; but if at certain times an organism eats salt more readily than sugar and at other times sugar more readily than salt, we find it necessary to speak of separate salt- and sugar-hungers (p. 149).

Reinforcement alone is not evidence for a drive. Thus, even though money, attention, affection, and so on, may be strong reinforcers, to postulate drives for each such reinforcer requires us "to show that it is possible to deprive or satiate an organism with given amounts of attention, approval, and so on, but we should also have to make sure that no satiation or deprivation is taking place in any of the primary areas associated with the generalized reinforcer" (p. 151). Addictions, on the other hand, qualify as acquired drives, because deprivation and satiation operations affect them, and, in general, reinforcers depend on the existence of some kind of deprivation state.

This discussion of drive identifies it virtually exclusively with operations of deprivation and satiation. It is not conceived as a stimulus, as a physiological or psychic state, as a response, or as pleasure-directed (Keller & Schoenfeld, 1950).

The drives usually mentioned in Skinnerian writings are hunger, thirst, sex, activity, pain avoidance, exercise, and sleep (Keller & Schoenfeld, 1950; Skinner, 1953).

Emotion

As in the case of drive, Skinner has not wished to accept a definition of emotion that defines it except in terms of its effects on behavior strength. In 1938, Skinner (p. 409) regarded emotion as very similar to drive, being a reference to a change in strength of behavior as a result of some operation. Keller and Schoenfeld (1950) also find it difficult to separate drive and emotion, though they mention, in the context of emotion, the operations of removing positive reinforcement and giving negative reinforcement and the intensity of stimuli. Skinner (1953) also suggests that drive and emotion are close, suggesting that "Any extreme deprivation probably acts as an emotional operation" (p. 165). On the whole, however, the conception of emotion in Skinner's formulation is unclear. It affects the state of response strength, but, as Verplanck says:

The operations, in the case of emotion, remain only vaguely specified. One seems to be the withholding of reinforcing stimuli (extinction), and the other the presentation of emotional stimuli, which are not independently defined. Unfortunately, . . . emotion appears frequently in the role of a *deus ex machina*, in that it is used to account for changes in strength which are observed when the conceptual system, taken with the experimental procedures, would otherwise lead to the expectation . . . that no change in strength would occur (Verplanck, 1954, p. 294).

Comment

The foregoing account is, we think, fair to Skinner's formulations of his viewpoint (cf. Skinner, 1959), but it in no way indicates his great influence. This influence has arisen from certain technical achievements in the control of behavior especially by means of intermittent reinforcement. By suitable manipulation of schedules of reinforcement very stable and persistent behavior can be obtained. Furthermore, by the judicious administration of reinforcements as an organism approximates some desired behavioral act ("shaping"), Skinner and his followers have been able to train animals to perform highly complex acts and to differentiate subtle differences of external stimulation.

As mentioned in passing above, the development of programmed instruction is one outcome of these achievements, and the Skinnerian methods have been successfully extended to many situations of behavioral study and control. Skinner himself in his novel *Walden II* has proposed a design for a Utopian society, based on the principles of positive reinforcement, response-shaping, generalized reinforcers, and schedules of reinforcement. Punishment as a means of social control would be shunned.

It is not possible in this book to consider these techniques of behavioral development and control in relation to motivational theory. It is worth noting, however, that much of the successful animal work has been conducted while the animal was under a considerable drive strength (e.g., 80 per cent of body weight).

Summary

Skinner's conception of drive and emotion is that they are behavioral changes induced by certain kinds of operations (deprivation, satiation, and the presentation of emotional stimuli). Beyond this, he does not go, in a theoretical analysis. Reinforcement, dependent on the existence of some deprivation, is the most significant feature of his system, and he has shown that behavior may be shaped and brought under control by various schedules of reinforcement (not reviewed here). Secondary and generalized reinforcers are important features of the system, in extending the notion of reinforcement beyond that of the primary rewards. Punishment acts only to suppress responses and has unfortunate consequences, so that Skinner feels it should be avoided.

GENERAL SUMMARY

Our review of learning-behavior theory has suggested that for most of the theorists considered motivational concepts have a centrally important role. To a large extent, these theories view biological motivation as the primary source or cause of the occurrence of behavior and of its strength, and as centrally involved in the development of those processes (habits, expectancies, incentives) which guide it to specific places and goals, or, in other words, make it seem to be purposive and directed. Behavior thus seems to serve the needs of the organism in the interest of organismic survival.

No theorist, in this group, has thought that unlearned motivational factors are sufficient, and much attention has been directed to learned motives and rewards and, more recently, to incentives as factors that come to activate and guide behavior through learning. These learned agencies develop their functions, however, in the first instance, through a relationship to primary or biological motivating factors and continue, in some measure, to be dependent for their existence on their biological background.

There are many differences among these theorists, concerning many issues. On such issues as the following we find disagreements: the number of innate drives postulated, the importance of reinforcement and the nature of its mechanism, the conceptual status of drive, the problem of generalized drive, drive as energizer of behavior or as instigator of demands for objects, and the role of incentives. Yet, despite these differences, these theorists as a group represent an objective, biologically oriented, experimental viewpoint, which, by and large, is consistent with the notion that work on difficult problems like motivation should begin with the simpler organisms and processes, leaving until later the application and verification of concepts in more complex organisms like man.

It may be noted here that many of these presumptions have been challenged, especially during the present decade. This challenge has ranged from attack on the derivation of the "higher" motives from the primary or homeostatic drives to serious suggestions that there are nonhomeostatic motives just as primary as are hunger, thirst, sex, and pain avoidance. Similarly, the notion that drives are like unpleasant stimuli, to be reduced or escaped or avoided, has been questioned. Recent advances in our understanding of the neurophysiology of primary drives and of reward processes have appeared to support some of these criticisms. In the next chapter and in Chapters 5 and 6, we review and attempt to evaluate some of the arguments and the evidence concerning these issues.

Chapter 11

Learning, Performance, Reinforcement, and Acquired Motivation

The theoretical viewpoints outlined in the last chapter, and the controversies which they have engendered, have stimulated a great deal of research. In this chapter, we bring together the empirical work relevant to a number of the issues and problems which have arisen because of theoretical and systematic questions.

The first problem to be discussed is the role that drive may or may not have in the acquisition of responses. Several theorists postulate no relationship between drive level and learning. Rather they consider drive as a factor governing *performance* of habits rather than *learning* of habits. This distinction between learning and performance and the effects of drive on performance constitute the second problem of the chapter.

A controversial central issue concerns the nature of reinforcement. The chief question here involves the notion of tension reduction. Later in this chapter the evidence, pro and con, on tension reduction in reinforcement is summarized.

No learning theorist believes that unlearned biological drives are sufficient to account for all motivational phenomena. Therefore, learned motivational mechanisms, incentives, and acquired drives have been postulated. The empirical status of these notions is reviewed in the final sections of the chapter. Additional relevant material will also be found in Chapter 14.

DRIVE, LEARNING, AND PERFORMANCE

Drive and Learning

There are three major ways in which the relationship of drive strength at the time of learning to the acquisition of responses has been investigated. In the first one, response measures *during learning* are compared for groups of subjects learning the task under different drive levels. The other two methods look to measures taken *after learning* for evidence that drive strength during learning made a difference. In the first of these other methods, subjects are trained under different drive strengths; then the strength of what was learned is studied under extinction (or some other "retention" procedure) during which all subjects perform under the *same* drive strength. The second of these methods uses a more complex procedure, known as a factorial design. In this design, a number of groups are again trained under several drive strengths. But during the test phase (e.g., extinction), each drive strength group is subdivided so that there is one subgroup which is tested (or extinguished) under each of the several drives used over all the groups during training. We will discuss these three kinds of studies in turn.

Comparison of Response Measures during Learning under Varying Drive Strengths. During acquisition the two chief measures of response learning employed are speed or rate measures and measures of errors or of correct responses. In certain responses, amplitude is also used. While the testimony of the literature is not unequivocal, much of the evidence points to an influence of drive on speed or rate of response measures but not on errors or correct responses.

Deese and Carpenter (1951) ran animals in a straight runway under either a very low-drive strength (1 hour food-deprivation) or under a high-drive strength (23 hours). The low-drive group showed little change in latencies of leaving the starting box over 24 trials, while the high-drive group reduced its latencies progressively to an asymptote at about the thirteenth or fourteenth trial. Hillman, Hunter, and Kimble (1953) used a multiple-unit, elevated T-maze and ran their rats under either a 2- or 22-hour thirst drive. During the 10 acquisition trials, the 22-hour group ran considerably faster than the 2-hour group, though there was no difference in the number of errors made. In the straight runway, similar findings for measures of speed have been reported by Lewis and Cotton (1957), by Barry (1958), and, for speed of making a bar-touching response, by Ramond (1954*a*, *b*). Measures of errors have not differentiated drive groups during learning in the experiments of Teel (1952) or Armus (1958) with rats or in experiments with monkeys reported by Meyer (1951), Miles (1959), and by Warren and Hall (1956).

These experimental results, for errors (or correct responses), conflict with other results. Variation in drive strength in all but two of these conflicting experiments, however, was provided by electric shock. Thus, Yerkes and Dodson (1908), Cole (1911), Dodson (1915), and

Hammes (1956) all employed shock variations and found that errors tended to be related to shock intensity, though with curvilinearity rather than a linear inverse relation perhaps being the rule. Mice, chicks, and rats were employed in one or another of these experiments. The animals were also often hungry, but this drive typically was not varied. However, Dodson (1917) did find that with variations in hunger from 24 to 48 hours, his rats learned best at 41 rather than at 24, 31, or 48 hours deprivation. Broadhurst (1957), using air-deprivation of from zero to 8 seconds, found, for his easiest discrimination task, that the number of correct responses during learning was a negatively accelerated, increasing function of time of air-deprivation (see Chapter 4 for further details of his procedure) up to 4 seconds. The differences, however, were small (Broadhurst, 1957, p. 348, Table 2). For the two difficult discrimination tasks, Broadhurst's data show that learning scores are superior for 2-second air-deprivation. Thus, if drive level is related to correct responses or to errors during acquisition, the data show the relation to be nonlinear.

These data of Broadhurst's indicate a relationship between task *dif-*

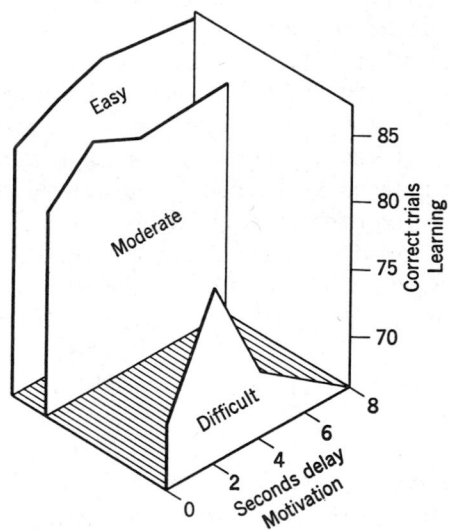

Figure 11-1. An illustration of the Yerkes-Dodson law. Motivation is varied by deprivation of air, and there are three levels of difficulty of discrimination tasks. The data show that the most effective performance on the easiest task was for the higher levels of motivation (4 and 8 seconds delay), whereas for the most difficult task, optimal performance occurred at a lower level of motivation (two seconds delay). Reproduced by permission from Broadhurst (1957, Fig. 2).

ficulty and the level of motivation which is optimal for best performance (i.e., fewest errors). Thus, a lesser motive strength (2 seconds) produces the best learning scores for the two most difficult discrimination tasks, whereas a stronger motive (4 seconds) does so for the easiest task (Fig. 11–1). This relationship is known as the Yerkes-Dodson law (Yerkes & Dodson, 1908), as it was first formulated by these investigators. Confirmation of it has been reported by Cole (1911), Dodson (1915), and Hammes (1956; see, also, Broadhurst, 1959). Again, except for Broadhurst's experiment, the varied drive was electric shock.[1] We are not aware of any experiments in which the Yerkes-Dodson law has clearly been verified when appetitive drives alone have been used.[2] Whether air-deprivation qualifies as an appetitive drive is uncertain.

Brush (1957) studied the effect of shock intensity on the acquisition of an instrumental avoidance task by dogs. He found no effect of shock intensity on latency of the avoidance responses, but he did find that the proportion of dogs acquiring the avoidance response increased with increments in shock intensity up to but not including the most intense shock (5.59 ma) he used. These results, like those of the other shock experiments just discussed, may indicate that aversive motivation (i.e., electric shock and perhaps air deprivation) affects speed, rate or latency measures and correct responses or errors differently from the ways in which appetitive motivation (e.g., hunger) affects them.[3] Speed of running curves for acquisition of an instrumental escape response from varying intensities of shock converged with trials (Campbell & Kraeling, 1953), rather than remaining parallel or diverging. Other results, however, have also been reported (Amsel, 1950*a*; Spence, 1956, p. 85, Fig. 20).

Drive strength, in instrumental responses, has been studied in one other way during acquisition. Elliott (1929*a*) found for rats in a multiple-unit T-maze that changing the drive employed from thirst to

[1] Most of the experiments which support the Yerkes-Dodson law, as well as those which find a relation between drive strength and errors, have employed discrimination tasks. Typically, shock (of varying intensity) has been given for incorrect responses; food reward has been given, usually, for correct responses, and hunger has *not* been varied. It has long been known that shock, given for wrong or even for correct responses, facilitates learning (cf., e.g., Tolman, Hall, and Bretnall, 1932; Muenzinger, 1934*a, b*). However, severe shock may instigate responses incompatible with learning, and it is likely that if this occurs it would result in greatest interference in the tasks of greatest difficulty. In sum, the meaning of these various experiments in which shock was used is not clear.

[2] Dodson's (1917) experiment, which used hunger, did not vary task difficulty.

[3] See pp. 528–529 for a similar possible conclusion in relation to factorial experiments.

hunger on the tenth day of the 20-day training period temporarily increased errors made and time taken to run the maze. Kendler (1945a) ran one group of animals under a hunger drive and another under both hunger and thirst in a simple T-maze. He found the combined-drive group to make more errors than the single-drive group. Braun, Wedekind, and Smudski (1957) used the following drive combinations in rats which were to learn a water maze: (a) 22-hour hunger, 35° C water temperature; (b) 0-hour hunger, 35° C; (c) 22-hour hunger, 15° C; (d) 0-hour hunger, 15° C. Swimming times from fastest to slowest were, for these groups, in this order: c, d, a, b. The combination of hunger and low temperature thus produced fastest swimming, but the relation of these drive combinations to errors was not very clear. Combining drives, then, or changing them during acquisition (Elliott), may have an effect on speed; its effect on errors, if any, seems to be to increase them.

The experiments we have summarized so far have concerned instrumental responses, that is, instrumental conditioning. Relevant data also are available from studies of classical conditioning. In classical conditioning, drive strength can be varied for appetitive drives by the usual deprivation operations, but for aversive motivation (such as a shock or a puff of air to the eye) it is the intensity of the unconditioned stimulus (e.g., the air puff or the shock) which provides the variation in motivation. The bulk of the relevant data have been obtained for classical aversive conditioning.

Passey (1948) and Prokasy, Grant, and Myers (1958) found that number of conditioned eyelid responses varied with the intensity of the air puff (UCS), there being more conditioning with the stronger than with the weaker intensities. Spence (1956) has reported confirmatory results (p. 67, Fig. 10) for percentage of conditioned responses, as well as for the amplitude of the conditioned eyelid responses (p. 111, Fig. 30). In addition, the drive strength of anxiety as measured by a questionnaire (see Chapter 14) is also related to measures of eye-*blink* conditioning. This is to say that high-anxious subjects yield more conditioned responses than do less anxious subjects.[4]

Measures of learning taken during the acquisition trials do, then, show some relations to drive strength. A general summary of the findings, which ignores a few conflicting data, is as follows: For instrumental responses, rate or speed measures vary positively with strength of appetitive drives but measures of correct responses or of errors do not. When aversive stimulation is involved, the evidence on rate, latency,

---

[4] For more details concerning these experiments and for references, see Chapter 14.

or speed measures for instrumental escape or avoidance is conflicting, but errors and correct responses do show some relation to intensity of the aversive drive. This is to say that errors tend to decline and correct responses to rise as aversive motivation increases, up to some magnitude of aversive stimulation intensity, and then to reverse themselves. There is some possibility that this point of reversal is related to task difficulty (Yerkes-Dodson law). For classical conditioning, conditioned responses appear to be more frequent and to have larger amplitudes as intensity of an aversive motive (UCS, e.g., air-puff to cornea) increases. Such findings also occur when drive strength is varied by comparing subjects scoring high or scoring low on an anxiety questionnaire.

Response Strength during Extinction as a Function of Drive Level during Acquisition. 1. *Constant drive strength during extinction.* There is a problem in the interpretation of the differences in response measures obtained under different drive strengths during acquisition (the preceding section). This is that it is difficult to know whether the responses vary with habit strength due to different drives or vary because the different drive levels affect not habit strength but performance. It will be recalled from the discussion of drive theory that several writers have suggested that drive level does not affect habit strength, but rather determines performance by multiplying habit strength. This multiplicative function would begin as soon as any habit strength at all develops. Curves for response measures under different drives should separate during acquisition, therefore, from an early point in the course of acquisition, even though habit strengths, under the different drive strengths, are the same. Since the problem of interest is whether habit strength varies with drive strength during learning, it is necessary to design experiments in which the roles of habit strength and other performance variables can be separated. The chief technique employed is to look for differences in habit strength during extinction. The argument here is that resistance to extinction or some other measure of "retention" is a measure of habit strength.

The first experiments on this problem used the procedure of training animals under different drive strengths and then testing all the animals for resistance to extinction or by other procedures under the identical drive strength. Thus, Finan (1940) gave his animals 30 reinforcements in a bar-pressing situation under either 1, 12, 24, or 48 hours of food deprivation and then, later, extinguished them under 24-hour deprivation. He found the greatest resistance to extinction in the animals conditioned under 12-hour deprivation. Strassburger (1950) and Carper (1953), using similar procedures, however, failed to find extinction differences as a function of drive strength during acquisition.

One problem with this kind of experiment is that, for some groups of animals, drive strength must be changed between the acquisition trials and the later test situation. We have already reviewed evidence that drive intensities can be discriminated (Chapter 5), so that such changes in drive, involving, as they probably do, changes in the drive stimulus between acquisition and extinction, do not provide pure tests (during extinction) of the effect of drive strength during acquisition. It is also possible that changing from a low to a strong drive is not quite the same thing as changing from a strong to a low drive. While this last problem can perhaps never be ruled out, an improved method for studying the general problem is afforded by factorial experiments.

2. *Factorial studies.* Factorial studies provide training of groups of animals under different drive strengths. In the test situation (e.g., extinction), however, subgroups of animals trained under each drive strength are tested under all of the drive strengths used during acquisition. In Table 11–1, this design is illustrated.

Table 11–1. Factorial design for studying the effects of drive on habit strength

Drive during test (e.g., extinction) >	0	6	12	24	
Drive during acquisition (hours of deprivation)					Mean values for habit strength
0					$\overline{X}$
6					$\overline{X}$
12					$\overline{X}$
24					$\overline{X}$
Mean value for extinction >	$\overline{X}$	$\overline{X}$	$\overline{X}$	$\overline{X}$	

Since, of the animals trained under any drive level (e.g., 6-hour hunger), some animals are extinguished under each of the drive levels used (0, 6, 12, 24), the mean value for each row (the marginal column at the right) shows the influence of drive during learning on extinction. The marginal values across the bottom of the table show the column means, which represent extinction at different drive levels with all drives during acquisition represented. It is customary to regard the row means as indicating habit strength and the column means as indicating the effect of drive on performance, with habit strength equalized.

So far as drive strength during acquisition is concerned, several experiments have found no influence on later performance as revealed in a factorial design. The experiments by Kendler (1945*b*), Teel (1952), and Hillman, Hunter, and Kimble (1953) for simple and multiple-unit T-mazes agree in this respect. On the other hand, several experiments do find an effect. These experiments usually involved complex mazes (Kimble, 1961, p. 413), and in the one study with a complex maze, in which no effect of drive strength was found on amount learned (Hillman, Hunter, and Kimble, 1953), the animals used were blind. Lewis and Cotton (1957) and Campbell and Kraeling (1954) found some effect of drive during acquisition on early extinction trials in a straight runway, when the measure was one of rate of response.

There are several difficulties, even with factorial experiments, in separating out the role of drive in influencing habit strength from other complicating roles which the drive levels may have. For instance, as previously noted, it is not at all clear that shifting the drive strengths from high to low is the same as shifting them from low to high. Neither Deese and Carpenter (1951) nor Davis (1957) found any marked effect on performance of shifting drive strength from high to low but did find marked effects for the reverse shift. Since drive shifts are involved in factorial designs and if the direction of shifts has different effects, this is an uncontrolled and perhaps uncontrollable complication.

Further, drive level could affect behavior not through an influence on a given habit strength but rather through influence on *what kind of habit is learned*. What is meant may be illustrated by experiments by Cotton (1953) and by Campbell and Kraeling (1954). After training his rats over 44 days to run a runway under each of several drive levels, Cotton then obtained additional runs such that, for each drive level (0-, 6-, 16-, and 22-hour food deprivation), he had 49 runs on which there were no competing responses to running. Competing responses were face-washing, scratching and biting, exploring the sides of the runway, etc. Running time for all trials showed a relation between speed and deprivation time, the relation being monotonic, that is, fastest running occurred for the longest deprivation, slowest for the shortest deprivation. However, there was *no relation* between deprivation time and running speed when only the trials on which there were no competing responses were considered.[5] Campbell and

---

[5] King (1959) found less difference in runs with competing and without competing responses than Cotton did, and his data seem to show that drive directly

Kraeling (1954) also observed that their animals behaved differently under different drive levels. Their high-drive animals, in the starting box, were orientated toward the door and wasted no time in running as soon as the door was opened. These behaviors were not seen in low-drive animals, which were lackadaisical about making the running response.

These findings suggest the following. Animals under low-drive strength are perhaps more receptive to stimuli—internal and external, other than the relevant drive stimuli—than are animals under high drive. This could mean that, since they make different responses in the situation, they learn different responses from those animals that learn under high-drive. To the extent that these different responses are compatible or incompatible with the responses required in a given situation, the animals would or would not make good learning scores. As Kimble observes (1961, p. 413), the fact that complex situations are more likely to show relations between drive strength and habit strength than are simple situations fits with this interpretation. That is, complex situations offer more stimuli and response alternatives than do simple ones, so that the animal, more "distractable" under low than under high drive, might learn many responses in complex situations incompatible with reaching the goal quickly and efficiently. Blinded animals, presumably less distractable than seeing animals, are equally efficient in learning a maze under several drive levels (Hillman, Hunter, & Kimble, 1953). This is only a shred of evidence, but it fits the general interpretation. The evidence reported by Bruner, Matter, and Papanek (1955) also fits this general interpretation. They found that animals under 12-hour food deprivation were apparently better able to perceive and, therefore, later to utilize a cue than were animals under a 36-hour period of food deprivation.[6]

The factorial experiments we have reviewed have not yielded a clear picture of the relation of drive strength to learning. Future experiments will be necessary to settle the issue, and they will somehow have to take account of the problem of changing drives as well as what is learned under different drive strengths. The experiments so far cited have used appetitive drives. Spence (1953) used a factorial design in

---

affects running speed. King used different animals at each drive strength, whereas Cotton used the same animals.

[6] Easterbrook (1959) has brought together literature suggestive that degree of emotional (or drive) arousal is inversely related to cue utilization; how this narrowing of the range of cues is related to task performance will depend, as he points out, on the relationship between the cues required in the task and those on which emotion brings the organism to focus.

eyelid conditioning, in which intensity of the air-puff (UCS) was suitably varied during training sessions on two successive days. The results suggest that UCS intensity on day 1 had an effect on the strength of conditioning as manifested on day 2. However, as Spence (1953; 1956, pp. 176–178) points out, an interpretation in terms of habit strength is not the only possible one; further experimentation, however, suggested to Spence that differential drive reduction in the case of UCS's of varying (aversive) strength may mediate variations in habit strength.

Performance of a Habit under the Acquisition (Relevant) Drive and under Irrelevant Drive

We turn now to the second problem in the relation of drive to learning and performance. This is the role of drive in the utilization of a habit once it is learned. Earlier we mentioned Hull's argument that habits are energized by drives. Two sources of such energization were suggested: one is the drive that was active at the time of learning. This is usually called the "relevant drive," even though its strength may differ from what it was during acquisition. The other source suggested was any other drive or drives active at the time of habit utilization, even though they were not active at the time of acquisition. Such drives, in this context, are sometimes referred to as "alien" drives or "irrelevant" drives. We consider the relevant drive question first.

Performance of a Habit under Relevant Drive. The basic design in this case is to train subjects under one drive strength and then to test them after acquisition under several strengths (sometimes including zero) of the same drive. Thus, one might train animals under 24-hour hunger and extinguish them after 0, 6, 12, 18, and 24 hours of hunger. Some learned response (usually, but not necessarily, an instrumental response) is involved.[7] There are two problems with this design. One is that the different drive strengths at extinction involve drive stimuli which are different in intensity from the drive stimulus present during acquisition. We have already touched on this problem, and a solution to it is possible by means of a factorial design as outlined in Table 11–1.

The other problem is more difficult. In order to have a picture of the influence of the acquisition drive, alone, on the performance of a habit, all other (irrelevant) drives should either be absent at the test or be equated under all strengths of the acquisition drive at test. It is difficult to be sure that either of these conditions is ever met.

---

[7] In some instances, this design has simply used a consummatory response, such as eating, under various drive strengths. See Chapter 5 for relevant findings.

Some of the earlier experiments are worth citing even though the problem of changing drives, and thus drive stimuli, is present. The combined data of Williams (1938) and Perin (1942) showed that resistance to extinction was greater if the drive strength at extinction was at 22-hour hunger rather than at 3-hour hunger, even though the number of reinforcements and drive strength during acquisition were constant. Perin (1942) also compared extinction, under drives of 1-, 3-, 16-, or 23-hour food deprivation, of a habit reinforced 16 times under 23-hour deprivation. Again, number of responses in extinction increased with drive strength during extinction. The extrapolation of the curve for these results to extinction at zero-hours' (relevant) drive suggested that responses would still occur at zero relevant drive, and such responses would presumably be due to irrelevant drive (see next section).

A number of experiments have examined the function relating instrumental behavior to drive strength at extinction. Koch and Daniel (1945) trained their animals on bar-pressing under 23-hour hunger and then, after carefully satiating them for food, tested them for extinction. Surprisingly (in terms of the extrapolation of Perin's data), very few responses were obtained and those that occurred appeared to be accidental.[8] Saltzman and Koch (1948) essentially repeated this experiment but, at extinction, used drive strengths of ½-hour, 1-hour, and 2-hour food deprivation. They found a few responses, as Koch and Daniel had at zero drive, for the 30-minute food deprivation group, and substantially more responses at 1-hour and 2-hour drive. The implication of this finding is that as drive strength increases from 0 to 2 or 3 hours, there is a rather steep rise in the behavior energized by the drive, followed, at further increments in drive, by additional but more gradual increases in strength in the behavior energized by the drive. Similar functions have been obtained in similar experiments by Horenstein (1951) and by Kimble (1951). Horenstein (1951) trained her animals under 23½ hours' hunger drive on a panel-pushing response and extinguished them under 0, 2, 12, or 23½ hours of food deprivation. Number of responses during extinction increased rapidly from 0 (hardly any responses) to 2 hours and then more slowly as drive strength continued to rise. A rather similar curve was found for latencies of additional animals run under 0, 1, 2, 6, and 23½ hour food deprivation following training under 23½ hours' drive. In this case, responses were reinforced, rather than extinguished. Speed of response (reciprocal of latency) rose sharply from 0- to 2-hour drive and gradually thereafter. Essentially similar findings were reported by

---

[8] We discuss the implications of these results more fully under irrelevant drive.

Kimble (1951), who used intervals since satiation of 10, 30, 50, and 60 minutes, 2, 8, 15, and 24 hours (training was under 24 hours). Kimble found little increase in behavior (as measured by latency) up to 1-hour drive but a rapid increase to 2 hours, and further, though not so rapid, increases thereafter. These several, highly similar experiments, then, have found results in close agreement with one another. Yamaguchi (1951) also studied this problem. He trained his animals under food deprivations of 3, 12, 24, 48, and 72 hours and extinguished each group of animals under the same drive strength. His results show increasing resistance to extinction up to 48 hours and, depending on whether the mean or median is used, uncertain results for 72 hours. Figure 11–2 shows a combined plot of the Koch-Daniel, Saltzman-Koch, and Yamaguchi results, taken from Yamaguchi's paper (1951). Horenstein's results are shown in Figure 11–3.

There are some discrepant results in the literature. Using a black-white discrimination situation and 23 hours' food deprivation during learning, Cautela (1956) extinguished his animals under 0, 6, 12, 23, 47, or 71 hours' drive. Resistance to extinction increased with drive up to 23 hours but went down for the longer deprivation intervals. Zeaman and House (1950) employed illumination as a drive condition and trained rats to escape from the illuminated (300-watt bulb) side of a two-compartment apparatus into the dark side by pushing open a door. Then they were tested in the apparatus for door-opening with both compartments dark, that is, no drive. The animals continued to respond, and their latencies were substantially shorter than those of a control group which had had no experience of light in the apparatus. Evidently, then, despite absence of the acquisition drive (a situation

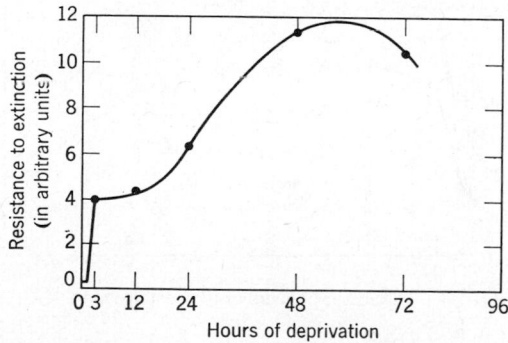

Figure 11–2. Resistance to extinction and hours of food deprivation. Reproduced by permission from Hall (1961, Fig. 9-5), who adapted it from Yamaguchi (1951).

comparable to that of Koch & Daniel [1945]) the habit continued to be expressed. Teel and Webb (1951) trained their rats under several drive levels in a simple T-maze and, after each day's training trials, satiated the animals for food and ran two additional trials in the maze. Over the thirteen days of satiated trials, their animals did perform and showed an increasing proportion of choices of the correct side of the maze. There are many differences between this experiment, the one by Zeaman and House, and those by Koch, Daniel, Saltzman, Horenstein, Kimble, Yamaguchi, and Cautela, but the conflicting results, despite the differences in experiments, perhaps should make us cautious about generalizations. In addition, the problem of changing drive strengths, and thus drive stimuli, between acquisition and extinction is present in these studies.

We have previously mentioned a number of experiments in which variations of drive strength *during acquisition* have been related to the degree of habit strength formed. Several of these studies can be mentioned again, as they also studied (factorially) drive strength during extinction. Such experiments presumably avoid the problem of changing drive strength. In terms of Table 11–1 our earlier interest was in variation of the marginal totals for *rows:* our present interest is in marginal totals for *columns.*

Teel (1952) used a T-maze and extinguished the running response

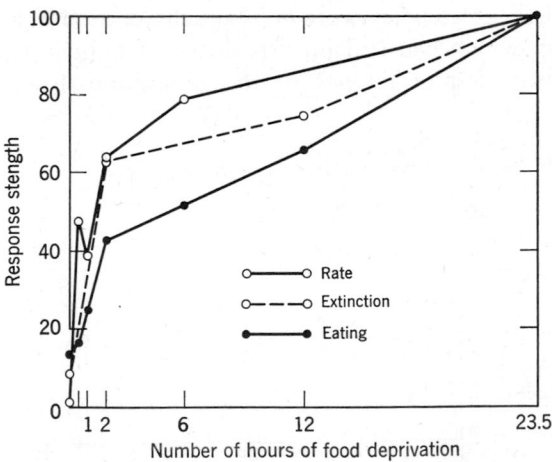

Figure 11–3. A plot of response strength (per cent of maximum score) as a function of hours of deprivation for three measures obtained in separate experiments. Reproduced by permission from Horenstein (1951, Fig. 5).

under 1, 7, 15, and 22 hours of hunger; each extinction drive group contained rats which had been trained at each of these four drive levels. Teel found no significant effect of drive level at extinction on extinction. Prokasy, Grant, and Myers (1958) found no effect of UCS intensity during the extinction of a conditioned eye-blink. Campbell and Kraeling (1954) extinguished a running response in rats and found no effect of extinction drive level (training drive was equalized) on either speed of the first six extinction trials or on number of trials to the extinction criterion.

Other factorial designs, however, have reported effects. Lewis and Cotton (1957) extinguished a running response under three drive levels. Running speed was slowest for one hour of deprivation, although no differences were obtained between the running speeds of the 6- and 22-hour deprivation groups. Barry (1958) found similar results. Deese and Carpenter's (1951) experiment included a reversal of drive conditions in their two groups of animals following the development of relatively stable rates of running the runway. They found that running speed increased sharply in animals switched from a 1-hour to a 23-hour hunger drive, but the animals switched from high to low drive did not change much. Davis (1957) found the same results for drive reversals when he measured latency of a panel-pushing response or activity in a type of stabilimeter. Hillman, Hunter, and Kimble (1953) switched drive strengths after the tenth trial of maze (multiple-T) learning. Running time decreased for animals switched from a 2- to a 22-hour drive (thirst) and increased for animals given the reverse shift. There was no effect on errors. Spence (1953) has reported that UCS intensity during extinction influences the number of responses obtained on the second day of eyelid conditioning.

One other set of data may be mentioned in connection with the role of the relevant drive in energizing responses. We have pointed out in the previous section that response measures *during learning* often differ as a function of drive during acquisition. But we did not stress another feature often found in these curves: the curves *diverge;* that is, not only is the performance of the high drive group at a higher level than that of the low drive group, but the difference tends to appear early in learning and to increase as training trials continue. Since number of trials (and thus reinforcements) is the same, this may mean that the habit strength, equal in the two drive groups in being multiplied by the diverse drive strengths, is being differently energized by drive. Figure 11–4 shows curves illustrating this point.

In summary, performance of a habit under relevant drive, in view of the results of experiments conducted in the 1940's and early 1950's, seemed to be a complex function of relevant drive strength, at least in the case of hunger. While there were some discrepant results, the picture suggested was as follows: little use of the habit under drive strength from 0 to 1 hour or so; rapid increase in habit utilization as drive strength increased up to 2 or 3 hours; then a more gradual rise in performance up to some maximum drive strength, and a decline thereafter. This picture involved the drives of hunger or thirst and was complicated by uncontrolled drive-stimulus intensity changes and,

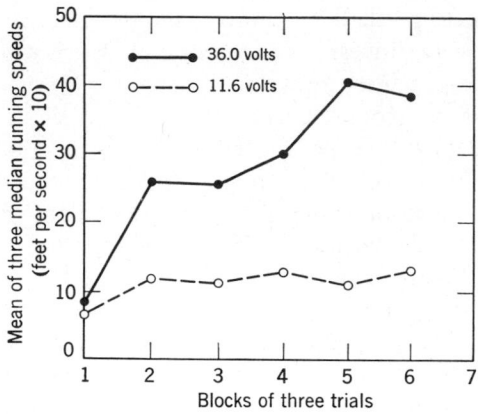

Figure 11–4. Divergence of two learning curves under different drive (shock) intensities. The response was running to escape the shock, and the measure plotted is speed. Reproduced by permission from Spence (1956, Fig. 20, p. 85).

perhaps, by uncontrolled irrelevant drive. Factorial designs have conflicted in their findings, some showing an influence of relevant drive level on performance after learning and some not. During acquisition it is found, not uncommonly, that learning curves of different drive groups diverge. This has been interpreted in the literature as showing that drive multiplies equal habit strengths.[9]

Performance of Habits under Irrelevant Drive. Hull proposed that habits could be energized by drives other than the acquisition drive. In the absence of the acquisition drive, the habit (if the appropriate

[9] It is possible, however, to interpret the divergence of these curves as arising from drive stimuli that are more vigorous or discriminable under strong than under weak drive strengths. Certain cases, however, such as anxiety or arousal induced by electric shock, are probably more readily analyzable as instances of energization than in terms of stimulus differences.

external stimuli were present) could be displayed so long as *some* drive was active. This proposition has led to a good deal of research (Webb, 1952). One set of studies arose in connection with satiation of the relevant drive; habits should still be displayed if other drives are active, and the extrapolation to zero relevant drive of Perin's data did, as we have seen, indicate that a substantial number of responses would be made. The findings of Teel and Webb (1951) and of Zeaman and House (1950) were consistent with these expectations (see, also, Earl, 1957), whereas those of Koch and Daniel (1945), Horenstein (1951), and Kimble (1951) were not. We have already reviewed these studies (in the last section). In none of them was irrelevant drive manipulated; relevant drive was "satiated" and performance was observed. In the studies with negative results, it is possible that, after satiation, there were no irrelevant drives active, or active in sufficient strength, to energize the habit. Or, it is possible that if an irrelevant drive were active it selectively elicited behavior incompatible with performance of the habit. Koch and Daniel (cf., also, Ellis, 1957) do observe that their satiated animals explored for a minute or two and then became quiescent. If we argue that this quiescence reflects a drive for rest, we could still say the animals were motivated but that the drive in question aroused responses incompatible with bar-pressing. Whether this interpretation solves any problem is open to question.[10]

Other experiments have manipulated irrelevant drive strengths, either in combination with relevant drives or concurrently with attempts to satiate the relevant drive. We speak briefly of the latter experiments first.

Webb (1949) trained his animals to obtain food under a 22-hour hunger drive by pushing open a door. Hunger was then satiated and the animals were next run to extinction, in the same situation, under 0, 3, 12, or 22 hours of thirst drive. Webb found, in general, that as thirst drive increased, there were more responses made during extinction and a longer time for extinction to occur. Brandauer (1953) obtained similar results. Miller (1948*b*) trained thirsty rats to run down a runway to water reward. He then satiated some of these animals for water but deprived them of food; the others were satiated for both food and water. On subsequent tests in the runway the hungry animals

---

[10] Hull (1951) did modify his assertion that irrelevant drives could energize habits by saying that "some" irrelevant drives could do so. He was not, however, specific. It certainly seems, intuitively, that a drive of rest, sleep, or reactive inhibition would not do so. Such drives might have an innately associated "response" of not responding or of sleeping, or such a response could, conceivably, be learned (see Chapter 4).

ran faster than the animals which were neither hungry nor thirsty.

These experiments seemed to demonstrate that a habit learned under one drive can be activated by another drive when the acquisition drive is satiated. However, as we pointed out in Chapter 5, there is an interaction between certain drives, especially hunger and thirst. Is it possible that these results might be due to the fact that water-satiated but hungry animals were really still thirsty, and conversely? Grice and Davis (1957) tested this possible interpretation. They trained hungry rats to make a panel-pushing response for food. Then the response was extinguished, in one group under hunger, in one under satiation for both food and water, in one under 22-hour thirst, and in one which was deprived of water and satiated for food. However, this last group was allowed to drink water to satiation just prior to extinction, and it gave more responses in extinction than did the thirsty group, perhaps because hunger, depressed when there is thirst so that the animal *appears* satiated for food, was "released" by the water taken just prior to extinction. The apparent transfer of bar-pressing from hunger to thirst might then be attributed to continuing hunger rather than to the energizing effect of irrelevant drive.[11]

There are other experiments to be considered, not involving satiation of the relevant drive. Wada (1922) found that knee jerks and strength of grip were increased when they occurred simultaneously with a stomach contraction; if the latter indicates hunger drive, this may illustrate the facilitation of other responses by an irrelevant drive. Kendler (1945a) found a thirst drive (added to hunger) to increase resistance to extinction of a food-rewarded habit in a Skinner box up to a strength of 12 hours but to reduce resistance at the higher level (22 hours) he used. Siegel (1946b) similarly found a decrement, though slight, in resistance to extinction when he added a 22-hour thirst drive to the relevant 22-hour hunger drive. Webb and Goodman (1958) trained rats to press one of two bars for food under 22 hours' food deprivation. After learning, the animals were satiated for food. First, a test for responsiveness under satiation was given (and there was little responsiveness). Then the box was flooded with water, and a significant increase in pressing of both bars occurred, but preponderantly of the previously rewarded bar. Jerome, Moody, Connor, and Fernandez (1957) had rats cross from one compartment to another under motivation to escape from light. The highest response rate was obtained when the animals were motivated not only by light-avoidance but also by a

---

[11] Grice and Davis found no differences in extinction between their thirsty group and the group satiated for both food and water, thus not confirming Webb's findings in this respect, either.

23-hour hunger drive. On the other hand, Sterling and Cooper (1957) found a decrement in responses to extinction when they added a 21-hour hunger drive to the relevant 21-hour thirst drive, as compared to extinction in a group run only under the thirst drive.

Although these various results are not very consistent, there is some agreement that the addition of one drive to another facilitates responses or increases resistance to extinction of habits. In the experiments just reviewed, the interaction of hunger and thirst is not a problem, since one of them was not used while the other one was presumably satiated.

The problem of energization of behavior by an irrelevant drive has also been studied in aversive motivation. Several experiments have involved the presentation of shock followed by tests of its aftereffects on other responses. Miller (1948*b*) trained rats under hunger drive to turn to one side of a T-maze for food. He then satiated their hunger. Part of the group was then given an electric shock on the elevated T-maze, but the other part of the group was placed there without shock. The shocked animals made fewer errors and ran faster to the side where previously they had found food than the nonshocked animals. This suggests that the T-maze habit was energized by the effects of shock (Miller's interpretation is a different one, as we will point out soon). Electric shocks administered to rats just prior to their being given an opportunity to eat or drink in a separate situation increase consummatory behavior (Siegel & Siegel, 1949; Siegel & Brantley, 1951; Amsel & Maltzman, 1950).[12] Nagaty (1951) studied extinction of a wheel-turning response developed as an avoidance reaction to shock. A buzzer was the signal to which the avoidance reaction was made. During extinction, one group received a shock just prior to the buzzer, another 20 seconds prior to the buzzer, and a third group received no shock. More responses were given in extinction by the two shocked groups than by the third, or nonshocked group. Amsel (1950*a*) added hunger to the anxiety presumably left over by shock experiences and found that running speed was enhanced by the addition of hunger to anxiety.

It may be concluded that the addition of postshock effects to other drives may act further to energize consummatory responses and other reactions. Reference to Chapter 14, where anxiety is discussed further, will add additional evidence to this point.

----

[12] Amsel (1950*b*) has shown that consummatory responses can also be decreased in the presence of anxiety, if, in the consummatory situation, the anxiety instigates responses incompatible with drinking. Negative results from the combination of shock effects with other drives (cf. Ellis, 1957; Franks, 1957; Moyer, 1957) may be due to such interfering responses.

We have now reviewed the major evidence concerning drive and performance. While none of the evidence on the problems and relationships we have considered can be said to be conclusive or entirely consistent, there does seem to be a basis for concluding that relevant and irrelevant drives do interact in some way with habit strengths to affect resultant performance.[13] Much of the research carried out has been conducted from the theoretical standpoint of Hull and Spence; that is, drive is considered as an energizer and as such it multiplies the existing habit strengths. In discussing Miller's viewpoint, we observed that he has not held to this formulation, preferring to use the concept of drive stimulus generalization as the mechanism by which a drive "energizes" a habit learned under an irrelevant drive or under a different strength of the relevant drive. Estes (1958) has developed this position in some detail,[14] applying his analysis chiefly to hunger and thirst. This analysis is reasonably convincing, but it seems less so when one thinks of energization of responses by shock, anxiety, or by light intensity when the original acquisition drive was, say, hunger or thirst. It is, of course, possible that both drive stimulus generalization and an arousal (see Chapter 8) or energization factor are or may be involved or that in some instances one mechanism is involved, and in other instances the other mechanism is involved.

[13] Another way to study this problem is to change the performance required and to do so under different drive strengths. Castaneda and Palermo (1955) stressed their elementary-school children subjects and gave one group a lot and another little training on a perceptual-motor task. Then relearning was undertaken, during which some of the relations in the task remained the same as before and others changed. The stress was associated with an increment in errors on the changed relations, as it should from Hull-Spence theory. Castaneda (1956) and Palermo (1957) have obtained similar findings (see, also, Birch, 1958; Shore, 1958). Buchwald and Yamaguchi (1955), working with rats, obtained different results. They trained their rats on a position habit on a T-maze under two drive levels. Then the position habit was reversed, half of each training drive group now being run on high and half on low drive. High-drive groups learned the reversal more quickly than low-drive groups. This result is the opposite of that predicted. Armus (1958), also using rats, found drive level to make no significant difference in a similar reversal situation. This failure to obtain a difference is also unexpected theoretically.

[14] Solomon and Coles (1954) failed to demonstrate, in rats, generalization of an imitative response, learned in a T-maze under hunger and food reward, to a shock-avoidance situation, in which imitation of a "leader" rat would have avoided shocks. Situational variables may have been different enough, however, to account for this failure.

REINFORCEMENT

It was evident, from our review of learning-behavior theories, that reinforcement is an important concept in several theoretical formulations. There is, of course, hardly any doubt that an empirical law of reinforcement is descriptive of many situations in which behavior is strengthened, and that the effectiveness of rewards or reinforcers bears some relationship to the drive or motive active at the time of learning. With such an empirical law of effect, we have, in this book, little concern, since this law is primarily a law of learning. On the other hand, the mechanism of reinforcement is a matter of concern to us insofar as the mechanism involves motivational factors. In conjunction with reinforcement, then, we shall discuss the problem of need or drive reduction as its mechanism, since this view of the way reinforcement works involves motivational assumptions. It is sometimes assumed that if an object or event acts as a reinforcer, a drive must therefore have been active.

There are a number of parameters of reinforcement over and above the simple fact of its occurrence. Such parameters include the quantity and the quality of the reward, delay of reward, changes in amount or quality of reward, derived or secondary reward, and partial or intermittent reward. Reward is also often found to have an effect that differs as it is removed in time or space from the act which is rewarded. This is to say that there are *gradients* of reinforcement. These various aspects of reinforcement have received a good deal of attention, as their behavioral effects are both interesting and important. A common interpretation of them is in terms of *incentive motivation;* that is, they are assumed to work because of the development of an incentive factor acquired through learning. After the discussion of the mechanism of reinforcement, we will take up the general problem of incentives and then indicate the applications of incentive theory to the various aspects and parameters of reinforcement.

Interpretations of Reinforcement

Kimble (1961) has outlined three interpretations of the critical factor in reinforcement: [15] (1) *tension reduction*, either by means of the reduction of needs, the reduction of drives, or the reduction of drive stimuli (this is the view of Hull and Miller); (2) *consummatory behavior*, whose occurrence could conceivably be reinforcing, without

[15] We will not concern ourselves here with the problem of whether reinforcement is essential for learning to take place. This problem is beyond the scope of a volume on motivation.

tension reduction (Sheffield has argued this in extending Guthrie's viewpoint); (3) the occurrence of *reinforcing stimuli* which have innate reward value but which do not afford tension reduction and whose reinforcement value is greater than is that of other stimuli involving equal amounts of consummatory behavior (the work of a number of writers leads to this alternative).

Need-Reduction. This is an extreme form of tension-reduction theories, and it assumes that reinforcement involves an actual change in depleted tissues, which is difficult to imagine in certain instances of reinforcement. When food is the reinforcer for a hungry animal, for example, the actual reduction of the tissue need would require time—the time for ingestion, digestion, and absorption. Reinforcement seems to occur too rapidly always to be dependent on this sequence of events, and, in addition, the phenomenon of secondary reinforcement is evidence against it. Secondary reinforcers do not seem to involve a reduction in the primary need state (Simon, Wickens, Brown, & Pennock, 1951; Miles & Wickens, 1953; Calvin, Bicknell, & Sperling, 1953b).[16]

On the other hand, it may be that a procedure which gets close to direct need reduction can be reinforcing. Coppock and Chambers (1954), with rats, and Chambers (1956a), with rabbits, successfully reinforced a response by means of intravenous administration of glucose. With rats, this response was one of head-turning. While these experiments would seem to indicate that more or less direct need reduction *can* reinforce behavior, it is conceivable that taste effects did accompany the intravenous feedings. Chambers (1956b) has also shown that rises in skin temperature in some areas of the body accompany the intravenous administration of glucose, and it is possible that such temperature changes could function as secondary reinforcement.

Miller and Kessen (1952) found that direct stomach feeding of milk was reinforcing, as rats learned a T-maze for this reward, although it was less reinforcing than the same amount of milk by mouth. Saline injections were used for incorrect responses, so bulk in the stomach was presumably not the critical variable (cf. Miller, 1957). Other side effects, however, as with the experiment by Coppock and Chambers, may have caused the superiority of the stomach milk over stomach saline. However, Miller (1957) has reported an advantage for stomach milk over stomach saccharin in reducing further food intake. This may

---

[16] An exception to this may be provided by Miller's experiments (see Chapter 5) in which milk by mouth had greater reinforcing power than milk by stomach and also reduced food intake more. It has not, however, been demonstrated that this additional reinforcing value of mouth milk is learned.

suggest the role of need reduction.

Reinforcement from Stimulation. Most of the other work on mechanisms of reinforcement has studied the effects of stimulation as reinforcers, and the fact that increased stimulation is reinforcing has been seen to contradict a tension-reduction viewpoint.[17] Where consummatory responses have been stressed, it is also believed that tension reduction is shown to be inessential to reinforcement. Certain of the experiments on exploratory behavior, reviewed in Chapter 6, have been offered as showing that tension or stimulus increases are reinforcing. Among other relevant studies are those by Montgomery (1954), who found that rats would learn a preference for that arm of a Y-maze which led to a complex (Dashiell) maze over the arm which led to an ordinary goal box, and by Montgomery and Segall (1955), who found that the complex maze would reinforce the learning of a white-black discrimination. Various other experiments reviewed in Chapter 6, especially those by Butler on reinforcement by visual stimulation in the case of monkeys, may be similarly interpreted. Kish (1955) and Barnes and Kish (1957) used an enclosure which contained a platform in each corner. One of them could be pressed down, whereas the other three were immobile. In both experiments it was found that, over time, the animals spent an increasing proportion of their own time on the movable rather than on the immobile platforms. Presumably, the sensory consequences of moving the platform were reinforcing. That sensory deprivation (Chapter 6) is an aversive state has suggested to some that tension reduction is an inadequate principle.

There is evidence that light-onset can reinforce a rat's behavior, despite the fact that the onset of a light results in increased stimulation.[18] The reinforcing illuminations have not been strong ones but, nevertheless, represent increases over the illumination present, prior to the response (e.g., a bar-press). Roberts, Marx, and Collier (1958) showed, among other things, that rats reared and fed in the dark responded to light-onset as a reinforcer. Thus, the reinforcing effects of light-onset cannot be attributed to secondary reinforcement, although, of course, light-onset can become a secondary reinforcer under appropriate conditions (Henderson, 1957; cf., also, Hurwitz &

---

[17] See Brown (1955) for a discussion of increased stimulation and tension reduction.

[18] Relevant experiments are by Kish (1955), Hurwitz (1956), Kling, Horowitz, and Delhagen (1956), Marx, Henderson, and Roberts (1955), Clayton (1958), Forgays and Levin (1958), Stewart and Hurwitz (1958). For studies of offset of light, see Munn (1950). Symmes and Leaton (1962) failed to find reinforcing properties for the onset of auditory stimuli in rats, though slight effects for mice have been reported by Barnes and Kish (1961).

Appel, 1959). Whether the animals were reared in the dark or in light, however, did make a difference in their response rate for the reinforcer of light-onset (see, also, Lockard, 1962). Those maintained in the light had higher rates. Hunt and Quay (1961) found that the experience of being vibrated in a cage is apparently an innate negative reinforcer, but that the negative reinforcement value could be reduced if the rats had lived in a vibrating cage over their life spans. Similar results were found in the case of flashing illumination by Meier et al. (1960). Maintenance level, then, can have an effect on the positive or negative reinforcers, but there are apparently inherent values as reinforcers (positive or negative) for some stimuli.

A similar argument can be made for tastes. We have already seen in Chapter 5 that there are preferences for dietary substances of which an animal has been deprived or for which his need has been increased by surgical procedures. In addition, there is evidence that food preferences may exist on the basis of the palatability of the foods, and P. T. Young (see Chapter 8) has argued that such preferences reflect not need or drive reduction but rather natively determined affective enjoyment. Certain experiments have been carried out with non-nutritive taste substances explicitly in order to test the drive reduction notion. Sheffield and Roby (1950) found that rats would learn a T-maze for the reward of saccharin, a non-nutritive substance, which tastes sweet to a human. Sheffield, Roby, and Campbell (1954) verified this finding and also showed that the saccharin solution was more effective in reinforcing learning than a nutritive but not so sweet solution of dextrose. There is substantial evidence in the literature that sweet tastes are reinforcing and that satiated animals will prefer and perform for them, whether they are nutritive or not (Guttman, 1953). A small drop of sugar solution, which can hardly reduce need or drive, is reinforcing for hungry animals (Smith & Duffy, 1957a). The primary interpretive problem so far as this work on taste is concerned is the extent to which the rewarding value of sweet tastes is learned.[19] There is some suggestive evidence that, under some conditions, the preference for saccharin may be partially extinguished (Smith & Capretta, 1956), but there is, as far as we can determine, no compelling evidence that all of the preference and reward value is learned. The significance of the findings concerning the reward values of tastes for the problem of tension re-

[19] Warren and Pfaffmann (1959) have been able to shift taste preferences in young guinea pigs toward a normally nonpreferred, bitter solution by permitting water intake only by means of the bitter solution in early life. This preference did not persist at a later test, which followed a period of time during which ordinary water was available.

duction depends on whether or not such rewards can be shown to acquire and to lose their reinforcing power through learning.

Intracranial Stimulation. Another development which has been said to challenge tension-reduction theory is the discovery of the rewarding effects sometimes associated with intracranial electrical stimulation (ICS). In 1954 Olds and Milner reported findings from studies begun earlier (Olds, 1955) which showed that electrical stimulation in some parts of the brain would reinforce bar-pressing of rats in a Skinner box. Electrodes had been implanted in the brains of these animals and a circuit was arranged such that when the bar was pressed a shock was administered to the brain (see Fig. 11–5). Initially, the rats were placed on the lever, thus depressing it, and if the animal did not respond, further such placements were made. The rats were in no way deprived and no rewards other than electrical stimulation were used. For some electrode placements, very high rates of responding for this "reward" were obtained; these placements were in the septal area of the brain. Other parts of the brain gave "neutral" values for the effect of stimulation on bar-pressing; that is, they neither facilitated it nor reduced it. Areas giving intermediate reinforcement values when stimulated were

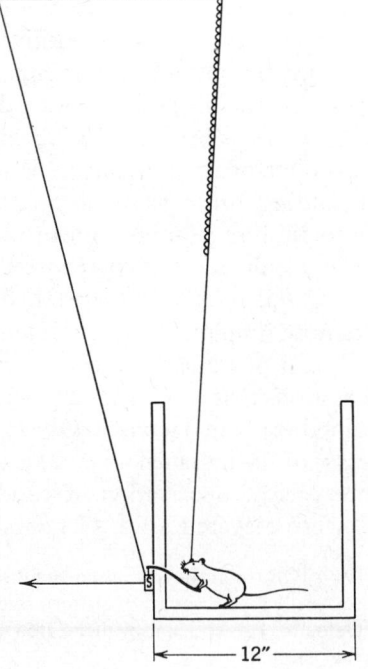

Figure 11–5. Diagrammatic sketch of bar-pressing device by which a rat administers electric shock to its own brain. Depression of the pedal closes a circuit and current enters the brain by means of implanted electrodes. Reproduced by permission from Olds (1958a, Fig. 1).

also found as were areas whose stimulation was apparently negatively reinforcing. Where a pronounced positive reinforcing effect was found, rather stable and high rates of responding were obtained. Rates as high as 7000 responses per hour have been reported (Olds, 1958a). When the current was turned off the rates of bar-pressing declined swiftly to near zero. Olds and Milner felt that they had discovered a primary reward procedure not dependent on drive reduction (Olds & Milner, 1954, p. 425).

Also in 1954, Delgado, Roberts, and Miller (1954) reported that electrical stimulation of certain areas in the cat's brain could arouse fear-like reactions. It was further found that stimulation in such areas could evoke a wheel-turning response previously learned to escape and avoid a shock to the grid floor of a compartment. The shock to the brain also was presented in one compartment of a two-compartment box; later, the cats learned to escape this compartment and enter a different one without any further shock in the first compartment. Furthermore, stimulation of the appropriate brain areas during feeding led to the development of an avoidance response to food. These experiments suggested that the centrally administered shock aroused a fear-like, emotional disturbance which could be conditioned, could be used as punishment, and could motivate learning (see, also, Delgado, Rosvold, & Looney, 1956; Cohen, Brown, & Brown, 1957).

While these two demonstrations of central mechanisms in positive reinforcement, fear, and avoidance are equally important, our present theoretical interest must be directed primarily to the positive reward case. This is because it is the positive case which has been usually taken as inconsistent with a tension-reduction account of reinforcement. We may summarize some of the more outstanding findings before considering their significance.[20] In addition to finding positive reinforcement from brain stimulation in rats, similar results have been reported for cats (Sidman et al., 1955; Roberts, 1958b), monkeys (Bursten & Delgado, 1958; Lilly, 1958), and the bottlenose dolphin (Lilly & Miller, 1962). Heath (1954) reported that stimulation of human subjects near or in the septal region elicits reports of sensations that seem pleasureable; similar findings for the human were obtained by Sem-Jacobsen (1958).

Brady et al. (1957) studied the effects of intracranial stimulation (ICS) in cats and rats under several intervals of deprivation of food and water. Lever-pressing rates for ICS were elevated after 48 hours'

---

[20] The papers of Olds (1955, 1956a, 1958a, b, 1959, 1962) may be consulted for details of the brain structures which do and do not yield reinforcing effects, positive or negative, on electrical stimulation. See, also, Delgado, Roberts, and Miller (1954), Zeigler (1957). We will not discuss them further here.

deprivation as compared to rates after 0 or 1 hour of deprivation, and 4- and 24-hour deprivation intervals produced intermediate rates. No reinforcement, other than electrical, was, of course, given. However, another experiment was run with one rat in which two bars were available, depression of one of which yielded brain stimulation (bar B) and of the other of which yielded water (bar A). Under continuous reinforcement on water (bar A), the animal satiated rapidly; his concurrent depressions of bar B, while rapid at first, dropped off markedly as satiation on water presumably developed. Such a drop-off did not occur, however, when bar A was reinforced on a variable interval schedule. In this case, it is unlikely that satiation developed. Olds (1958*b*) ran animals on a series of 1-hour bar-pressing sessions over 20 days. On alternate days the animals were hungry and not hungry. Later the animals were castrated and run during the presumed decline in androgen levels following castration and also after the injection of testosterone propionate, which raises the androgen level. Depending on electrode placement, either hunger or higher androgen level was associated with elevated bar-pressing rates. However, for electrode placements which showed an effect of androgen, there was either no effect or a reduced effect of hunger, and the reverse was also true.

These experiments suggest that ICS reinforcement rates can be affected by deprivation states, and the opposite effects of hunger and androgen suggest that there are separate reward systems for hunger and for sex. Margules and Olds (1962) implanted electrodes in lateral hypothalamic areas and, under food satiation, stimulated these areas. Twenty-eight of the 46 rats tested were found to eat at the onset of this stimulation and to continue to eat while the stimulation endured. Presumably, the eating "center" (see Chapter 5) was activated. The 46 animals were then tested for self-stimulation effects in a Skinner box, without food reinforcement. All of the animals tested for self-stimulation which had eaten in response to stimulation in the lateral hypothalamus also stimulated themselves in the Skinner box; only 4 of the 18 noneaters did so. Furthermore, hunger raised the level of self-stimulation among the animals which stimulated themselves, this effect being greater in the eaters than in the noneaters tested. Hence the eating center appears to be a strong self-stimulation center. Hoebel and Teitelbaum (1962) have confirmed and extended these findings. Self-stimulation by rats via an electrode implanted in the lateral hypothalamus was reduced or inhibited either by excessive eating or by ventromedial (satiety center) stimulation, but either ablation or anesthetization of the latter area exaggerated both feeding and self-stimulation of the lateral hypothalamus. As these authors observe, perhaps self-stimulation in the lateral hypothalamus yields effects similar to the gratification which eating affords.

There are other similarities between the rewarding effects of electrical stimulation of the brain and those from traditional reinforcers. Sidman et al. (1955) and Brodie et al. (1960) found that reinforcement schedules with ICS produced cumulative response curves similar to those given under food reinforcement schedules. Olds (1956a) found that a food-deprived and food-rewarded group performed somewhat better in a maze than a group rewarded only by electrical stimulation, although the stimulation group ran more rapidly in a runway. Olds (1958a) reported that animals would cross an electrified grid to receive brain stimulation on the other side and would withstand more grid shock in doing so than would food-motivated and rewarded animals. Bursten and Delgado (1958), working with monkeys, found that food rewards may be preferred to brain stimulation, and Kling and Matsumiya (1962) trained rats in a brightness discrimination task under either food or ICS reward and then to reverse the discrimination under the same motivating conditions. In the first discrimination task, there was no difference between the reinforcement groups, but the animals trained under ICS were slower to reverse the discrimination than animals initially trained with food reward. This suggests a degree of permanence for a habit learned under the reward of intracranial stimulation not always found by investigators. Rapid extinction of running in a straight alley for stimulation was reported by Seward, Uyeda, & Olds (1959), and Olds (1958a) reported retention of a maze overnight to be less for stimulation-rewarded than for food-rewarded animals. Rapid "extinction" of bar-pressing responses when the current is turned off has been reported many times (see Howarth & Deutsch, 1962). Stein (1958) has been able, however, to demonstrate secondary reinforcement for a tone associated with ICS.

As we mentioned earlier, high rates of response can occur under intracranial reinforcement, suggesting, since the reinforcement is continuous rather than intermittent, a virtual insatiability for this reinforcer. Olds (1958b) gave rats an hour a day of brain stimulation reward for bar-pressing for several weeks and then provided 48 hours' continuous stimulation reward for bar-pressing. Stable rates of bar-pressing during an hour run were observed for a month (and in some animals for as long as a year). The rates varied, probably as a function of electrode placement, from as few as 750 to as many as 5000 an hour. Subjects with hypothalamic implantations (Fig. 11–6) showed very high rates of bar-pressing during the 48-hour tests and no satiation (aside from physical exhaustion). Satiation effects did occur in subjects with telencephalic placements (parts of septal and amygdaloid regions). Insatiability, where Olds found it, would not be found for continuous reinforcement with food or water. Stein and Ray (1959) developed a technique by which rats could select their preferred intensity of intracranial electrical stimulation. They found that they could

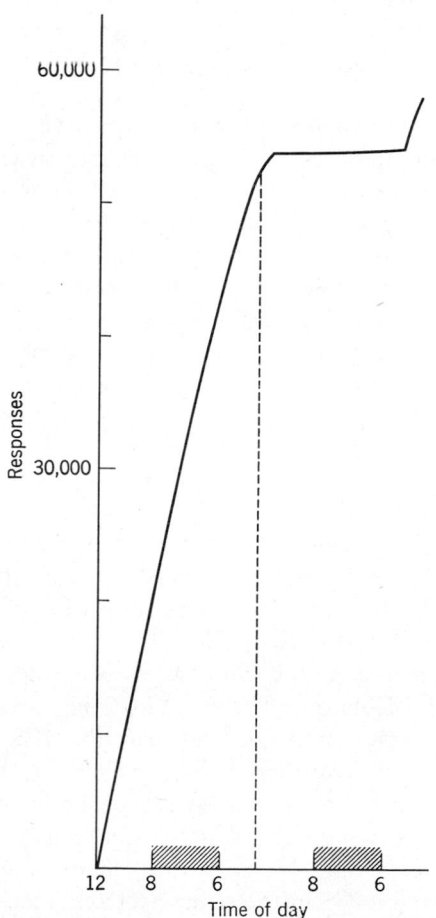

Figure 11–6. Cumulative response curve generated over a 48-hour period by a rat with an electrode implanted in the anterior medial hypothalamus. The ordinate shows cumulative response totals; the abscissa, time of day. The session began at noon, continued through the night (cross-hatching), all the next day, the next night (cross-hatching), to noon of the following day. The flat part of the response curve indicates a sleep period. The rate of self-stimulation was over 2000 times an hour in the waking periods. Reproduced by permission from Olds (1958a, Fig. 10).

and would do so and that the intensity selected "was always well above the reinforcing threshold; usually it was higher than most experimenters would care to assign . . . Exaggerated and even violent motor activity was often produced by the intensities selected . . ." (Stein & Ray, 1959, p. 571).[21]

Despite the rather consistent findings of positive reward from ICS, there are limitations that ought to be mentioned and findings that stimulation of a given area may have both positive and negative effects. These aspects of the problem involve the intensity of shock and its duration.

Olds (1958a, p. 317) reported bar-pressing curves for shocks ranging from 0 to 160 microamperes and administered to several different parts of the brain. All of the response curves rise, but most of them reach apparent asymptotic levels. For example, bar-press rates do not rise for shock intensities beyond about 10 or 20 microamps, in mid-forebrain areas, but rise up to 100 microamps in the posterior hypothalamus; the rate per hour at which these asymptotes occur varies a good deal—about 500 responses for the mid-forebrain to about 4000 for the posterior hypothalamus. Reynolds (1958), however, found that bar-press rates rose and then declined as current intensity increased, suggesting that the higher levels of shock were aversive.

Dual effects have been found by Roberts (1958a, b), Bower and Miller (1958), and Brown and Cohen (1959). In Roberts' first study it was found that cats would learn a T-maze if ICS in the posterior hypothalamus was turned off in the goal box, but they could not be trained to leave the starting box fast enough to avoid ICS altogether. This latter finding could be explained if the initial effect of the ICS is positively rewarding and if only as it continues does it develop aversive properties. Roberts (1958b) then, using a bar-pressing situation, found that cats would bar-press for the ICS, would learn to escape from the ICS, but would not learn to avoid it. Bower and Miller (1958) likewise found (in rats) areas of the brain in which onset of ICS is rewarding, but where, if it continues, it seems to become aversive since its offset is rewarding. These various findings of both rewarding and aversive effects of ICS in the same electrode placement complicate the picture of ICS effects considerably. Olds (1959, p. 384), however, has argued concerning these findings that "For the most part . . . [they] involve electrodes placed so that they stimulate a region between a dorsal negative-reinforcement system and a more ventral positive-reinforcement system in the hypothalamus and tegmentum." He would also explain Reynolds' results this way. Olds believes there

[21] See, also, Porter, Conrad, and Brady (1959).

are no conflicting or reversal effects if the implantations are made in areas distant from negatively reinforcing areas. With such pure placements, "all increases in electric current produce increases in response rate up to a certain asymptote characteristic of the region."

The experiment by Brown and Cohen (1959), however, seems to avoid this argument. They used cats with lateral hypothalamic electrode implantations. They used only those animals which, on stimulation, showed "rage" and locomotor reactions, and required each animal to learn an approach reaction in a runway for ICS and an avoidance reaction in a two-compartment shuttle box to a CS paired with the identical ICS. The animals learned both responses, indicating that the locus of ICS could hardly be designated as either a pleasure or as a punishment center.

ICS, Reinforcement, and Tension Reduction. Before, in our opinion, a full evaluation of the work with ICS can be given much more needs to be learned about it than we now know. However, we think it premature to judge that positive reinforcement by ICS (even if there were no puzzling aspect to it) necessarily invalidates a tension-reduction theory. While electrical stimulation may activate "reinforcement centers," there is no reason to assume that their normal activation is achieved this way. So far as food, water, and other reinforcers are concerned, the evidence (Chapter 5) now points to chemical or humoral factors in regulating neural eating, satiety, and drinking centers. While electrical stimulation may trigger off these centers, it may be that chemical deficits or excesses in the blood normally do so. This is to say that while electrical stimulation involves an increase in stimulation and no apparent tension or drive reduction, its effects may demonstrate another way in which reward centers can be triggered off, and it may not be a way in which it happens under natural conditions.

Consummatory Responses. Another approach to the problem of reinforcement, alternative to the one of tension reduction, is to emphasize that certain kinds of responses, for example, consummatory responses, in and of themselves, are reinforcing. This is the approach of Sheffield, and the reference experiment is one by Sheffield, Wulff, and Backer (1951). In this experiment, sexually inexperienced male rats were found to increase their speed of running in a runway, that is, they were reinforced, by being allowed access to receptive female rats. However, the copulation they were permitted was incomplete (they were not allowed to continue to ejaculation). Since they were inexperienced and presumably had never ejaculated, the experience of sexual stimulation could hardly have been secondarily reinforcing.

Hence, the acts involved in the pre-ejaculation response pattern were presumably reinforcing. Kagan (1955), in a sense, verified the results of the study by Sheffield, Wulff, and Backer, when he showed that rats would learn a T-maze for the reward of sexual interplay with a female whose vagina had been sutured closed. Findings suggesting a parallel interpretation were reported by Sheffield, Roby, and Campbell (1954). They found that the speed of making an instrumental response was highly correlated with the amount of saccharin consumed. This suggests that the intensity of a consummatory response is related to (presumably through its reinforcing characteristics) the strength of an acquired instrumental response.[22] Kagan and Berkun (1954) observed that rats would acquire a bar-pressing response when the only reinforcement was running in a wheel. The various experiments on manipulation (see Chapter 6), which demonstrate its rewarding value, are presumably pertinent here, also.

It is very difficult to distinguish between consummatory response as a reinforcer and the stimulation afforded by the objects involved or arising from the consummatory acts themselves as reinforcers. In either case, however, some kind of tension *increase* is seen as the reinforcing event, rather than a tension decrement.[23] Premack (1959) has suggested that differential rate of response is the critical reinforcing factor—that is, the activity with the higher rate of response (characteristic of most consummatory activities) can be a reinforcer. Unfortunately, most of the examples he cites can be given alternative interpretations, and we know of no critically supporting instances.

Summary

We have seen that tension reduction, as the mechanism underlying reinforcement, has come under attack. While direct need reduction has been found to be reinforcing, the evidence is scanty and capable of alternate interpretations. In any case, the demonstration that need reduction is reinforcing would not require that all reinforcement be either need or tension reducing.

The chief evidence contrary to tension reduction as the sole mechanism of reinforcement includes findings that light onset and the opportunity to explore and to be visually stimulated are reinforcing, that

[22] Alternative interpretations of this relationship, mediated through an incentive factor (K), can be made. See the section on incentives in this chapter.

[23] Campbell has conducted a number of studies which he has interpreted as showing that the intensity of consummatory *stimulation* is the critical event in reinforcement. We cannot follow his analyses here. See Campbell, 1955, 1956, 1957, 1958.

certain tastes may have intrinsic reward values, that electrical stimulation in certain areas of the brain is reinforcing, and that consummatory responses may reward behavior, even though need or tension reduction does not occur. In reviewing these findings, we have indicated, where appropriate, alternative interpretations and limitations. Nevertheless, the evidence to date is fairly substantial that reinforcers need not apparently reduce tension, at least as this process has often been conceived. It is at least clear that reinforcers have been discovered whose reinforcing effects would not be directly or readily predicted from a tension-reduction viewpoint.[24]

INCENTIVES [25]

The reinforcement function is not the only one which such objects as food may have. It is also possible to conceive them as arousing or motivating performance. In the latter, objects are considered as *incentives*, whereas in the former they are referred to as reinforcers or as rewards. The chief difference, in a functional sense, lies in what the object is supposed to do. As a reinforcer it strengthens a habit, but, as an incentive, it does not. Rather, it acts as an energizer of habits, in a manner similar to the way in which drive is said to energize habits.

Interest in incentives is not a new one (Gates, 1895), but the theoretical significance of incentive motivation began to be emphasized in the 1950's. In our opinion, it is a distinct possibility that the future development of ideas concerning motivation will mainly involve incentive motivation. This is partly because it is possible to interpret at least some drive phenomena in incentive terms (see Chapter 16). At any rate, in this section we summarize work on incentives in studies of animals, starting with a review of some of the early work with incentives and of the findings which brought incentive motivation its current prominence. Later, evidence in relation to subsequent theoretical developments will be brought together.

Reward Objects. Among the early findings relative to incentive was Simmons' (1924) demonstration that rewards vary in their effectiveness in producing learning in hungry rats. The most effective reward in this study was a combination of bread and milk plus return to the home cage, and it was followed, in order of effectiveness, by

[24] Later in the chapter, we briefly mention the problem faced in the acquisition of fear and whether it is shock onset or shock offset which is reinforcing. If shock onset does "reinforce" the acquisition of fear, this would be additional evidence contrary to tension reduction as the sole mechanism of reinforcement.

[25] In Chapter 15, there is another discussion of incentives, organized, however, around the study of incentives in the case of human subjects.

bread and milk alone, sunflower seeds, return to the home cage, and escape from the maze. Elliott (1928) trained rats on a multiple-unit T-maze, rewarding the experimental animals during the first nine days with a moist bran mash. On the tenth day, the reward was shifted to sunflower seeds (a less preferred food). A control group was trained, throughout, with sunflower seeds as the reward. During the first nine days, the experimental group's performance, as measured by both errors and time, was superior to that of the control group. However, with the change in reward, the performance of the experimental group deteriorated, becoming worse than that of the control group, that is, both errors and time increased. Tinklepaugh (1928, pp. 224–225) also observed disturbances in performance of monkeys when he substituted a less for a more preferred reward (a lettuce leaf replaced a piece of banana).

Reward objects, therefore, vary in their effectiveness, and the substitution of one for another affects performance (see, also, Elliott, 1929b). Young, in confirmatory experiments, found that rats would display differential running rates to sugar, wheat, and casein as incentives (Young, 1947) and that running speed increased when the incentive was changed from casein to a sugar (Young, 1948b).

Bruce (1930, 1932), using mazes, observed the deterioration in his rats' performance after reward was removed, and he pointed out that time and errors in a maze are affected not only by learning but also by reward (Bruce, 1930).[26] The obverse condition—the introduction of reward, following trials in a maze without reward—has also been studied. Blodgett (1929) and Tolman and Honzik (1930) found some, but not much, learning during unrewarded runs in mazes; when reward was introduced into the goal box on later trials, however, performance improved markedly. These experiments strongly suggest that the reward, after its introduction, energized habits formed during the unrewarded trials. (These are experiments in the area of latent learning, which has occasioned much controversy. We shall not concern ourselves further with this area and cite these experiments as perhaps indicating the motivating role of reward. See Thistlethwaite, 1951, Hilgard, 1956, and Kimble, 1961, for reviews of latent learning.)

Another way in which incentives have been shown to motivate behavior is by giving the animal a taste of the incentive before he makes his run. Bruce (1937), Morgan and Fields (1938), Anderson (1941d),

[26] We would now refer to these operations and results as involving "extinction." Bruce's study was an early one, however, in which removal of reward was carried out in instrumental responses.

and Maltzman (1952, p. 42) have made observations to this effect. These experimenters have given their rats small amounts of food or of water (the incentive being appropriate to the drive) just prior to the run in runway or maze and have found some facilitation of performance. Larger amounts of food or water given before the run, however, typically depress performance (presumably because of at least partial satiation of drive). It is as if the "taste" of food or water activates the animal to perform at a level superior to performance without it.

Amount of Reward

In addition to qualitative differences in incentives, permitting the subject to "pretaste" them, adding them or taking them away, etc., studies have also investigated the effect of systematic variations in the amount of incentives on learning and performance. This topic can also be referred to as amount of reinforcement, and it will be recalled that Hull, in 1943, made amount of reinforcement a variable controlling habit strength. Later he made it a variable affecting performance and having no influence on habit strength.

The early evidence (Grindley, 1929; Wolfe & Kaplon, 1941) had shown that measures taken during the acquisition of a response reflected variation in incentive magnitude (see, also, Logan, 1960, Figs. 12 and 13). Wolfe and Kaplon, for instance, found that the running speed of chicks in their tasks increased as the reward consisted of one-quarter of a piece of popcorn, a whole piece, or 4 one-quarter pieces. The experiments of Crespi (1942) and Zeaman (1949) put a new light on these findings. Both of these investigators ran their animals in runways in different groups, for varying amounts of reward. The runs were continued until performance seemed to be constant (asymptotic). Then the amounts of reward given were changed, and the effects of these alterations on running in subsequent trials were noted.

Zeaman (1949), for example, measured the latencies of the running responses of his rats for several amounts of food. The final level reached by the latencies at asymptote during the 19 acquisition trials was shortest for the animals rewarded with the largest amount of food (2.4 grams) and longest for the animals given the smallest reward (0.05 gram). Latencies for the other groups fell in between. One of the most interesting comparisons made by Zeaman, however, involved shifting, after the 19 acquisition trials, the 0.05-gram reward group to a reward of 2.4 grams and shifting the original 2.4-gram group to a reward of 0.05 gram. Latencies of both groups changed at once, the group now receiving a larger incentive shortening its latencies and the other group increasing its latencies (Fig. 11–7). This effect had also been noted by Wolfe and Kaplon (1941, p. 358) and Crespi (1942) and has been confirmed by Spence (1956, pp. 130–132) and, in a different design, by Metzger, Cotton, and Lewis (1957). Both Crespi and Zeaman reported, in addition, "contrast" effects. These refer to the fact that after change in amount of reward, the group whose reward was increased performed even faster than the group originally trained on this reward ("elation" effect), and the group which had its reward reduced performed even more slowly than the group originally trained

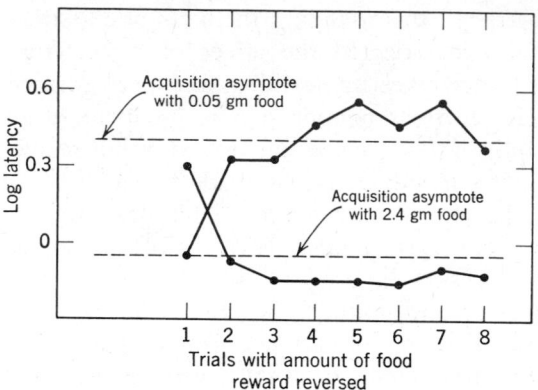

Figure 11–7. Effect of changing amount of reward for animals which have previously reached asymptote in latency of running a runway. Note that latency for the group whose reward was decreased (2.4 to .05 gram) shows longer latencies at once, and the group whose reward was increased from 0.05 to 2.4 grams reduces its latencies immediately. Reproduced by permission from Kimble (1961, Fig. 5.7), who adapted it from Zeaman (1954).

with the small reward ("depression" effect). The elation effect was not found by Spence or by Metzger et al., although O'Connor and Claridge (1958), working with imbeciles who performed a repetitive task, did find it. Depression effects were found by Spence but not by Metzger et al., or by O'Connor and Claridge. The contrast effect is, because of this conflicting evidence, uncertain, and Pereboom (1957) has been able to derive it, in any case, from a consideration of competing responses [27] (see, also, Pereboom & Crawford, 1958).

[27] Ehrenfreund and Badia (1962) found both contrast effects in animals under high drive (85 per cent body weight) but not under low drive (95 per cent body

Whatever may be the future status of the contrast effects, the influence of changes in amount of reward is to alter the rate or speed of performance rapidly. This is usually taken to mean that incentive magnitude has its effect on performance, not on habit (Pubols, 1960). It was observations such as these, as well as qualitative observations of behavior in conjunction with incentives, which led Spence (1956) to develop his theory of incentive motivation.

There are a number of other experiments in the literature in which the relationship between incentive magnitude and measures of performance has been studied. Seward (1951) and Pubols (1960) have reviewed this literature. Hutt (1954), using a bar-pressing situation, found that the rate of bar-pressing was affected both by the amount and the quality of the incentive, when these properties were varied factorially. Various concentrations of sugar solutions and of saccharin solutions also yield variations in response measures (Guttman, 1953, 1954; Young & Shuford, 1954, 1955). Shifts in concentrations of sweet substances effect shifts in response rates (Young & Shuford, 1954; Dufort & Kimble, 1956). Pubols (1960) concludes that these various findings indicate the effects of the variations of incentive to be on performance rather than on habit.[28]

Spence's theory, as outlined in an earlier section of the last chapter, suggests that the vigor of r_g is a critical variable in incentive motivation. There are several ways in which the amount of incentive factor could produce variations in vigor of r_g, aside from number of reinforced trials. A large reward might occasion stronger eating behavior than a small one, and a larger number of pellets might also do so to an extent greater than a small number or a single pellet. On the other hand, increases in size or number of pellets might have their effect

weight). They measured running speed in a straight runway. For further experiments on the effects of variable rewards see Logan (1960). Pubols (1960) has concluded that the bulk of evidence on the relation of drive to incentive functioning is conflicting.

[28] Time-independent measures, such as number of errors, trials, or correct responses are not clearly affected by incentive variations, so long as there is a magnitude greater than zero. There are other variations in effects depending on the methods used to vary incentives (Pubols, 1960, pp. 104–110). The studies we have reviewed have typically employed for each subject a single amount or concentration of the incentive. Another method is to use each subject at all levels of magnitude or concentration (the "differential" method—Lawson, 1957). Pubols (1960) is convinced that with the differential method, reward magnitude influences learning, at least until the animal has made successful discriminations among the magnitudes. Because this method is considerably more complex in its interpretation than the single (or absolute) amount method, we will not consider this work here.

through the greater time in the goal box which is required to eat them. If so, the r_g reactions could be better conditioned to the goal-box cues than with a small incentive. It is also possible that taste factors might differ in some way with size of incentive.

Mechanisms of Amount of Reward. A number of experiments have been directed to finding out what feature of incentive magnitude is critical to its motivational effects.

Spence (1956) reported studies whose results suggested that it is time in the goal box, rather than amount of food per se, which is critical to the effects of reward magnitude. D. E. Swisher (Spence, 1956, pp. 138–139) studied latency of bar-pressing. He used two groups of animals, one of which received a small food reward (0.05 gram), which they could consume in the apparatus in 30 seconds. The other group received a large reward (2.5 grams), which they were allowed to eat for 30 seconds in the Skinner box from which they were then removed to complete eating the pellet in a carrying case. Latencies for bar-presses over 40 trials did not differ, suggesting that size or weight of the reward was not important. R. S. Czeh (Spence, 1956, pp. 138–141) studied starting time in a runway. He trained three groups. One (I) received a large pellet and ate it in the goal box, as did the small-pellet group (III) which was given 30 seconds in which to do so. A second large-pellet group (II) ate for only 30 seconds in the goal box and was then removed to a feeding cage to eat the rest of the pellet. Groups II and III did not differ in starting times over the acquisition trials but Group I started faster than the other two groups. This suggests that time in the goal box (longer for Group I) rather than weight of the reward (different in Groups II and III, whose time in the goal box was the same) is critical to the reward-magnitude effect.

With water rewards for thirsty animals, Kling (1956) did not find time in the goal box (15 vs. 120 seconds) to be important in relation to speed of traversing a runway, but he did find that *drinking rate* was related to running speed. Fehrer (1956b) did not find any relation between time in the goal box or amount of drinking time allowed thirsty rats and the running time for a straightway or a U-shaped maze, but she did not assess consummatory rate.

In the studies cited by Spence, consummatory rate was not measured, but it is possible that it was the rate variable rather than the time in goal box per se which underlay the findings he reported. On the other hand, it is not impossible that different parameters of the consummatory response are involved in the effect of incentive magnitude for such different rewards as food and water.

Spence (1956) cited Guttman's (1953, 1954) studies as providing evidence favorable to the notion that vigor of r_g is related to the motivating value of an incentive. Guttman showed that rate of bar-pressing increased with concentration of the sucrose solution used as a reward and that, while rate of response increased with concentration of both sucrose and glucose (up to a limit), it was higher for sucrose (which is reported as tasting sweeter than glucose by the human). These experiments may be interpreted in the light of the findings of Sheffield and Roby (1950) and of Sheffield, Roby, and Campbell (1954) that rate of consummatory behavior increased with concentration of saccharin solutions and that this rate of intake was correlated with such performance variables as running speed. Rate of consummatory activity may, then, underlie the relations between sweet substances and performance variables, reported by Guttman. It is consistent with what we said in reference to a water incentive in connection with the experiments of Kling (p. 556). A perhaps comparable finding comes from the experiment of Sheffield, Wulff, and Backer (1951), who found a positive relation between running speed in a straightway and the amount of (incomplete) copulatory activity indulged in with the receptive female, which was the incentive.

Kraeling (1961) has reported an experiment which includes several aspects of consummatory responses. She used a straight alley which her rats traversed to a drinking tube at one end. In a factorial design, she varied concentration of a sucrose solution (2.5, 5.0, and 10.0 per cent) and durations of exposure to the solutions (5, 25, and 125 seconds). She measured running speed as a function, then, of concentration and exposure time and, also, actual caloric intake and number of tongue laps (a measure of consummatory response) during drinking. Running speed was chiefly related to concentration of sucrose, time of exposure not yielding a significant relation and there being no relation of speed to caloric intake. The functions relating running speed to concentration and to time of exposure were very similar to those relating concentration and exposure time to number of licks; both sets of functions were statistically significant relationships, and there were reasonably high correlations (.50 to .77) between running speed and number of licks. While these findings seem to support the interpretation that the effects of incentive magnitude are mediated by the vigor of the consummatory response, Kraeling cautions that another factor may be involved. This factor may be the intensity of the taste stimulation, that is, a kind of sensory consequence to some extent independent of rate of response. How the factor of amount of reward has its effects is not yet clear, but rate of response is still a definite possibility.

There are two other aspects of Spence's theory of incentive motivation which may be examined. One is the manner of combination of D and K, the other the generalization of r_g to other stimuli. We discuss each briefly.

Combination of Drive and Incentive

Evidence from studies in his laboratory (Spence, 1956, p. 197) and an experiment by Ramond (1954a) suggested to Spence that drive and incentive may combine by summation rather than by multiplication, as Hull had assumed. A number of experiments bear on this question, but the available evidence does not yield a clear-cut verdict on the matter.

Reynolds, Marx, and Henderson (1952) reported a rather complex interaction of drive level and incentive magnitude in a bar-pressing situation. Animals under high drive and high reward and under low drive and low reward extinguished more rapidly than high-drive low reward and low-drive high reward animals. Interactions were also reported by Seward, Shea, and Elkind (1958) for running speed and by Seward and Procter (1960) for latency of bar-pressing, but only when conditions of zero drive (hunger) and zero incentive (food) were employed. (It is questionable whether these zero conditions should be included; see, also, Seward, Shea, and Davenport, 1960.) Kintsch (1962) ran rats in a runway to a drinking tube under three drive levels and for three amounts of water reward, in a factorial design. The subjects were 23 hours thirsty at the start of a day's run but were brought to the appropriate drive level by prewatering. Kintsch found that latency of the running response was affected by both drive level and amount of water and that drive and incentive probably interacted in a multiplicative fashion.

In contrast, Reynolds and Pavlik (1958), using hunger and food incentive, found effects on latency of running for both these factors but no interaction. Similar results were found by Weiss (1960) in a runway and by Hulicka (1960a, b) for bar-pressing. Ehrenfreund and Badia (1962) reported a significant interaction between hunger and amount of food reward in relation to running speed measures, but they interpret the interaction to indicate not a multiplicative relation of D and K but rather a complex, additive one.

These experiments have varied in many details, such as the response measured, drives and drive strengths used, ways of establishing drive strengths, and in other ways as well. It is apparently too early for us to conclude that D and K do not combine multiplicatively, or, that they combine additively.

Generalization of r_g

The other aspect of Spence's theory involves the generalization of r_g to stimuli outside the goal box. The experiments we just reviewed, which showed that consummatory response rate was related to instrumental response speed, involved the measurement of consummatory responses in the goal box. It is an inference that variations in the vigor of this response occur also in the runway or maze and in the start box. Several experiments have been carried out to test, indirectly, the proposition that r_g generalizes as Spence's theory suggests that it does. The first studies were reported by Stein (1957). In one experiment he used a runway, and animals which were on 23-hour hunger. Each subject received 9 trials of running to the goal box, one group (control) receiving food reward there, and three experimental groups being rewarded by return to the home cage. Following this, 9 direct goal-box feedings were given the three experimental groups. Two of them were fed in the regular goal box (one group receiving 2 and the other 10 pellets there) and the third was fed in a *dissimilar* goal box. The argument is that direct goal box feedings would result in the conditioning of r_g to the goal-box cues. The regular goal box was similar to runway and start box, so, for the groups fed directly in the regular goal box, r_g should transfer to the start box and alley. This transfer should not be the case for the group fed directly in the dissimilar goal box, the dissimilarity between goal box and the start box and runway not providing a basis for generalization or transfer of r_g. In the groups in which r_g was to transfer, its vigor (based on 2 or 10 pellets) should vary. Stein measured running time in part of the runway and expected the 10-pellet, same goal-box group to run faster than the 2-pellet same goal-box group which, in turn, should have run faster than the dissimilar goal-box group (2 pellets). However, none of these expected differences was found and, in another experiment designed to correct difficulties with the first one, Stein likewise found no expected differences. Swift and Wike (1958) used a runway which their animals initially were permitted to explore, rather than running to the reward of immediate return to home cage. Two groups were then given direct feedings in the regular goal box (9 or 51 times), and two groups were fed directly in a dissimilar goal box (9 or 51 times). Runs were then made in the runway to the regular goal box. Number of feedings made no difference, but animals directly fed in the regular goal box ran slower on test trial 1, at equal speed on test trial 2, and faster on test trial 3 than the animals fed in the dissimilar goal box. The difference on trial 3 is in the direction expected on the basis of Spence's theory.

Gonzalez and Diamond (1960) also tested Spence's theory but found results opposite to what his theory would predict. In stage I of their experiment, one group was run in an alley into a goal box similar to the runway and another was run into a dissimilar goal box. These two groups can be symbolized as $RxBx$ and $RxBy$, respectively. Then each group was divided into halves and given feeding experiences in either Bx or By. Finally, in the third stage of the experiment the groups were run into the goal boxes in which they had been fed in stage II. Thus,

$$RxBx—Bx$$
$$RxBy—Bx$$
$$RxBy—By$$
$$RxBx—By$$

Running time declined significantly between stage I and stage III for groups $RxBy—By$ and $RxBx—By$. Running time for group $RxBx—Bx$ decreased, but not significantly, whereas running time for group $RxBy—Bx$ increased slightly. It is these latter two groups for which Spence's theory would predict reduced running time in stage III, as compared to stage I. The decreases in running time for the first two groups do not accord with the theory. A Tolmanian interpretation is given their findings by Gonzalez and Diamond.

We thus can find little present confirmatory evidence for the aspect of Spence's theory, which emphasizes the generalization of R_g to other, similar stimulus situations. Further work, however, is required before we can conclude that the theory is wrong.

Parameters of Reinforcement

In introducing the section on reinforcement and incentive, we noted certain parameters of reinforcement, discussion of which was postponed until the matter of incentive motivation was presented. We turn now to at least brief discussion of these aspects of reinforcement.

1. *Delay of reward and gradients of reinforcement.* It is widely known that the effectiveness of a reinforcer in determining response change is, under most conditions, greater when the reinforcer follows immediately on the response than when the reinforcer is delayed. Early interpretations of these findings and of running-speed gradients and error gradients in mazes and runways were made by Hull (see Chapter 10) in terms of different habit strengths developed under delays in reinforcement. Later evidence led to the substitution of secondary reinforcement for primary reinforcement in the case of delays or of response chains too long for primary reinforcement to function, and

Spence (1947) made a convincing argument that all, or almost all, delay effects could probably be accounted for in terms of secondary reinforcement. On this basis, delay of reinforcement would produce habit strengths through secondary reinforcement, and this problem would be of little concern in a book of motivation.

In 1952, however, Hull pointed out that there are two kinds of delay of reward situations. One is the response-chain case, in which the animal, in a runway or maze, makes a series of running responses or turns on his way to the goal. The length of this chain governs the delay of reinforcement for responses at given points in the chain. It is from analyses of situations like these that experiments yielding such phenomena as goal gradients, learning of shorter instead of longer pathways, etc., emerged. Hull's treatment of this case (as of the second case—see p. 485) remained in terms of habit strength.

Spence (1956, pp. 150–151) would now treat the response chain situation in terms of his theory of incentive motivation. (For further details of this treatment, see the theoretical section on Spence, pp. 490–491; and the discussion of experiments concerning Spence's theory, pp. 558–560.) We know of no further empirical work to bring to bear on Spence's reinterpretation of this delay of reinforcement situation.

The other delay situation is when the animal makes a response (e.g., a bar-press) and then must wait in the same situation for the reward to occur. Response learning is retarded in this case (the bar is commonly retracted during the delay). Spence (1956) gives essentially a *non*motivational interpretation of this case, suggesting that interfering responses engaged in during the delay compete with and prevent the rapid acquisition of the response being reinforced by the experimenter. We will not follow the evidence Spence cites for this conception, as it is nonmotivational in character.

2. Partial or intermittent reinforcement. This parameter of reinforcement (Jenkins & Stanley, 1950; D. J. Lewis, 1960; Kimble, 1961) refers to the procedure in which, during acquisition, not every response is reinforced. There are two kinds of intermittent or partial reinforcement situations. One is the discrete trials case, and, in it, only some of the trials are reinforced. The other is the free responding situation, in which there are no separate trials. In this case, reinforcement is not given for every response but after an experimenter-determined number of responses or period of time (referred to as "intermittent reinforcement" or a "schedule").

The outstanding findings from these procedures, in the discrete trials case, are that resistance to extinction is commonly greater after partial reinforcement than it is following reinforcement on every trial (con-

562 MOTIVATION: THEORY AND RESEARCH

tinuous reinforcement), and that, in the free-responding case, very large numbers of responses are made for a single reinforcement, and high rates of responding are maintained by only a few reinforcements. These phenomena, which are well established, raise theoretical problems of great magnitude and interest. The two cases may involve different principles, however, and most of the theoretical work has been devoted to the first case—partial reinforcement in the discrete trials situation.

Hypotheses concerning the discrete trials case have not, for the most part, involved motivational assumptions. However, one interpretation does suggest a motivational base for the partial reinforcement phenomenon, and we shall discuss it here. It has been proposed by Amsel (1958, 1962) and by Spence (1960), among others, and represents an application or extension of notions concerning r_g as a motivational factor.

The argument was developed by Amsel (1958) in the following way. In an instrumental learning situation, anticipatory reward responses (r_r or r_g) become conditioned or generalize to the stimuli antecedent to the goal box. On nonrewarded trials this r_r is frustrated, and, with enough trials, the frustration response is conditioned and occurs to the stimuli of the runway. The frustration response, of course, is accompanied by stimuli which arise from it ($r_F \rightarrow s_F$), and these stimuli, occurring in conjunction with the instrumental response, develop conditioned tendencies to elicit the instrumental response. These events would occur in nonrewarded trials, that is, a partial reinforcement situation. During extinction, of course, no rewards are given but in a group partially rewarded during acquisition, the s_F is connected to the running response and will continue to elicit it during nonrewarded trials. The response should occur longer during extinction than in the case of continuous reward, as here, during acquisition, no frustration occurred, and hence s_F is not associated with the instrumental running response.[29] Hence, the instrumental response would not be maintained during extinction after continuous reward by s_F.

It can be seen from the foregoing that Amsel's analysis predicts more resistance to extinction following partial rather than continuous reinforcement. The explanation makes use of the conditioning of a *stimulus*, arising from frustration of r_r or r_g, to the instrumental act, and this

[29] For other aspects of Amsel's theory, especially those dealing with the energizing function of the frustration response, see Chapter 9. Various other theorists have offered ideas similar to these; see Lewis (1960, pp. 21–22), Amsel (1958, p. 109; 1962, pp. 306–315), Spence (1960, p. 98). We shall not consider Amsel's discussions of discrimination learning in this book.

is then only indirectly and partially a motivational theory of the partial reinforcement case so far as extinction goes.

During acquisition, however, the frustration response ought to have a motivating effect on behavior. Spence (1960) points out that this effect should not appear early in training, because r_g is not yet conditioned to runway stimuli (see, also, Amsel, 1958). There should then, during acquisition, be a period of either no difference between a partial and a continuous reward group (or perhaps the latter should show initial superiority) followed by a period of superiority of the partial reward group, as r_g occurs and is frustrated on nonrewarded trials. Confirmatory data are presented by Goodrich (1959) in two experiments with a runway. For both starting speed and running speed there was little difference between 100 and 50 per cent reward groups for the first 15 or 20 trials, but thereafter, on both measures, the 50 per cent group started faster and ran more rapidly than the continuously rewarded group.

It is too early to tell whether this frustration approach to partial reinforcement can encompass the entire problem. Amsel (1958, 1962) has gathered together the relevant evidence.

The free-responding intermittent-reinforcement situation, characteristic method of the Skinnerians, is not encompassed by this interpretation. Spence (1956, p. 123) suggests a response-chaining formulation. That is to say, each bar-press or key-peck is but one response in a chain of responses which must occur before the reward is received. Spence says it is like the many steps an animal must take from the start box in order to get through a maze. This is evidently a nonmotivational interpretation of intermittent reinforcement.

3. *Secondary reinforcement and incentive.* Secondary reinforcement refers to the capacity of an original neutral stimulus to act in strengthening and maintaining habit strength after it has been associated a number of times with a primary reinforcer (see Myers, 1958; Kimble, 1961; Beck, 1961). We pointed out earlier that at least one theory of the mechanism of this kind of reinforcement involved the occurrence of r_g. Since r_g also is seen by some as the response whose frustration produces incentive motivation, it is evident that incentive motivation must be related to secondary reinforcement (Seward, 1950).

It is beyond the scope of this book to enter into a discussion of all of the work which has involved secondary reinforcement. However, we will discuss selected experiments which do suggest that secondary reinforcers may act as incentives do.

In the classic experiments of Wolfe (1936) and Cowles (1937), tokens were associated with food rewards in chimpanzees. When they were hungry, the chimps would not only learn for the token rewards but also would operate an apparatus which required lifting a weight to obtain them. They learned to operate this apparatus to obtain grapes (Wolfe, 1936) but went on to operate it when a token was the visible reward which would result from its operation. (The tokens were ultimately exchangeable for food.) Estes (1943) gave animals training consisting of the presentation of a tone followed by delivery of food in a Skinner box. Prior to this training, the animals had learned to bar-press for food. The association of the tone and food is "secondary reinforcement training," and Estes found that when he extinguished the bar-press the rate of bar-pressing was elevated if the tone was sounded. It is as if the tone "energized" the bar-pressing, as an incentive is supposed to do (see Estes, 1943; Walker, 1942).

Dinsmoor (1950) ran an experiment which enabled him to compare the incentive function with the secondary reinforcement function. He first gave 10 reinforcements in a Skinner box and then developed a discrimination such that for half the animals responses were reinforced when the light was on and for the other half responses were reinforced only in the dark. Then extinction was carried out, the animals being divided into three groups: one, a control, was extinguished under illumination opposite to that in which it had been reinforced; in another, the secondary reinforcement group, pressing the bar produced the illumination condition for 3 seconds associated earlier with reinforcement; in the third, the incentive group, extinction occurred under the illumination condition of acquisition but every bar-press reversed, for a 3-second period, the illumination. The return of the reinforcement illumination after 3 seconds could be construed as an incentive condition. Cumulative bar-pressing curves for groups 2 and 3 were virtually identical and considerably above the curve for the control group. This suggests equivalent effects for incentives and secondary reinforcers.

Gilbert and Sturdivant (1958) trained an experimental group by spraying their normal food with oil of anise for up to 13 days. Thus, the odor of this oil was associated with eating. In various control groups, this association was not established. Then the animals were tested in an activity box which had been sprayed with oil of anise. The activity displayed in this box by the experimental group was greater than that of the other groups, suggesting activation by the odor of oil of anise previously associated with eating (and r_g?). Marx and Murphy (1961) associated the sound of a buzzer with feeding in experimental groups and then trained their animals to run a runway to food in the food box. (Because of restraining apparatus, the buzzer did not become associated with running movements.) In the control animals, the buzzer sound occurred in the goal box but not in association with eating. Then extinction of the running response was carried out, and on certain trials of extinction the buzzer was sounded just after the animal was placed in the start box. Starting time was faster in extinction for the experimental animals on the buzzer trials than for trials without the buzzer. The difference was reversed for the controls. Again, a stimulus associated with feeding (secondary reinforcement training) is seen to energize behavior.

From the experiments we have just reviewed it appears that a secondary reinforcer can act as an incentive. On its face, it seems unlikely that a stimulus can perform both an incentive and a secondary reinforcing function, since one is an energizing, the other a "rewarding" role. A possible solution to this double-function paradox is provided in an experiment by Wyckoff, Sidowski, and Chambliss (1958), which raises questions concerning the status of the secondary reinforcement concept. These experimenters trained rats to approach a water dipper for water. As a rat touched the dipper a buzzer sounded. Later, bar-presses were rewarded by the buzzer in the experimental groups, but periods without bar-presses yielded the buzz in the control group. No significant differences in rate of bar-pressing were observed.

The critical feature of this experiment is that the bar was placed at the opposite side of the box from the dipper, whereas, usually, the bar is close in space to the point where reward is delivered. Also, in this experiment, the buzz was presented to the control animals, though not following a response (the secondary reinforcer is usually not presented to controls). An interpretation of these findings is that the buzzer, as a cue in the usual experiment on secondary reinforcement, keeps the animal near the bar and keeps the animal active so he bar-presses. In the ordinary secondary reinforcement situation, this would be true only for the experimental animals, giving them an advantage over controls.

It is by no means clear that all demonstrations of secondary reinforcement can be interpreted as artifactual so far as reinforcement is concerned, but it is a possibility. Such a reinterpretation, at the least, would resolve the paradox of the double function of reward and incentive presented by the experiments we reviewed earlier.[30]

[30] It will be recalled, from our discussion of Hull, that a stimulus-intensity dynamism was among the concepts proposed to account for performance. It is not entirely clear to us whether Hull intended to make this a motivational principle, but he did permit it to multiply habit strength in influencing performance. While there is evidence that stimulus intensity influences response strength

Summary

Reward objects vary in their effectiveness as reinforcers for learning or as instigators of performance, and changes in reward, including their introduction and their omission, often have marked effects on behavior. Small amounts of reward given before a performance may instigate vigorous or rapid performance, despite the reduction such prerewards must induce in the deprivation state.

That incentives probably affect performance, rather than habit strength, is indicated by the rapidity with which changes in behavior follow their sudden increase or diminution. It is still uncertain as to the mechanisms which mediate the effects of incentive magnitude, but rate of consummatory response seems, at present, to be a leading candidate.

It has been proposed by Spence that drive and incentive combine additively rather than multiplicatively as Hull assumed. Evidence on this issue is conflicting, as it is, also, on the question whether r_g can generalize, as Spence's theory would have it, from goal-box to runway cues, thereby energizing performance there.

Incentive motivational factors are related to such features of reinforcement, in addition to delay, as gradients of reinforcement, partial reinforcement, and secondary reinforcement. While the evidence is not abundant, it appears that the attempt to interpret these aspects of reinforcement in terms of incentive motivation is promising.

ACQUIRED MOTIVATION

In previous chapters, especially in Chapter 2, we pointed out that anthropological and sociological evidence from non-Western cultures and from social classes within cultures composed part of the challenge to instinct theory in the first decades of the twentieth century. As we have seen, the primacy of instinct theory [31] in motivational systems

(Hovland & Riesen, 1940) and that stimulus intensity influences performance but not learning (Kimble, 1961, pp. 342–345), it is possible that, rather than representing a dynamogenic factor in performance, principles of differential conditioning and generalization are sufficient to account for many of the relationships. Perkins (1953) and Logan (1954) have presented accounts based on these notions, and Champion's (1962) experiments seem to support their interpretations. We shall not pursue the matter further in this book.

[31] The discussion of ethology in Chapter 3 reveals the almost exclusively animal base of this revival of instinct theory. The few ventures of the ethologists into the human field are by analogy only and lack the sophistication these investigators have brought to the study of animal behavior. We have chosen, therefore, to deal with the present materials separately from the treatment of ethology.

was eliminated or much reduced by the attacks, both logical and evidential, that were launched upon it. Two questions, however, can be raised: What was the cultural and social evidence that was used? and What alternatives to instincts were advanced?

The present section is devoted to these questions. It begins by surveying briefly some of the material which shows that much behavior related to motivation varies widely in different cultures and different classes. This variation thus denies the universality of behavior patterns. Universality was an important basis for the inference that a behavior pattern is instinctive or unlearned, and the finding of variation made the inference of instinct less compelling than it otherwise would be.[32]

The widespread rejection of instinct left a systematic void. The behavior which instinct could "explain," however poorly, still remained to be explained. The simple, "sovereign principles" of social psychology (Allport, 1954), like suggestion, imitation, and sympathy, also no longer seemed adequate, whether they were given an instinctive base or not. Several alternatives, however, emerged, and it is the description and discussion of these alternatives to the instinct concept which is the second, and major, task of this section.

Both in classical psychoanalysis and in McDougall's system there were, as we point out in other chapters, provisions for the role of learning in motivation. But in classical psychoanalysis, the instincts (sex, aggression) in combination with anxiety were the major *drive-like* entities, and learning had its effects mainly in the complex defense mechanisms developed on this energetic basis. McDougall postulated more instincts than psychoanalysis did and also permitted combinations of them to be grouped in the complex structures he called the sentiments. But neither of these solutions is the same as those of drive theory or the kind of learned motive reviewed in this section.

Drive theory proposed the concepts of acquired drives and incentives as substitutes for instinct. Some drive theorists have suggested another alternative. This is that anxiety is the force underlying other, apparently learned motives. We have already spoken of incentives, and acquired drives will be treated here. Anxiety as the basic force is discussed in Chapter 14.

---

[32] The failure of Watson and Morgan (1917) to find more than a few adequate stimuli for the three innate emotional patterns they observed in infants and Watson and Rayner's (1920) successful demonstration that fear responses could be conditioned to neutral stimuli were also significant to the de-emphasizing of instinct. These findings have not always been substantiated by later workers. The historical importance of Watson's work and of his ultimate radical environmentalism (Watson, 1924) remains, however.

Cultural and Class Variations

Cultural Variations. Much cultural evidence is indicative of the variability which attends the customs, mores, standards of normality and morality, and the like of people around the earth. The vast majority of the earth's population does engage in such activities as, for example, eating, drinking, sleeping, and mating, and these behaviors as well as certain common institutions are found very widely if not universally (Kluckhohn, 1953). However, the *manner* in which common acts (e.g., eating, drinking) are performed or in which common institutions (e.g., the family) are organized may vary widely. Likewise there are some aspects of behavior which occur in some cultures that are virtually unknown in others; competitiveness and aggressiveness are illustrative. Even where activities are common over many societies and when the manner of their performance does not vary much (as in mating, for instance), the restraints and conditions under which such activities occur may be different. Acts which in one society may have little general significance may, in another, be embedded in a complex of religious or ritual significance.

Examples of these several kinds of variations can be found readily in many sources. Kroeber's *Anthropology Today* (1953) and Kluckhohn's review in the *Handbook of Social Psychology* (1954) are examples. Studies of national character also have relevance to the problem (e.g., Inkeles & Levinson, 1954). Some years ago, Klineberg (1940) examined systematically, in relation to cultural evidence, the status of each of the instincts which McDougall (1908) had postulated. As evidence contrary to the fully instinctual character of the behaviors McDougall had classified as instinctive, Klineberg could list data such as the following. So far as the parental instinct is concerned he noted that in some societies adoption of children into families other than that of the parents is a common practice. Infanticide, also, is a practice common in a number of societies. This evidence, Klineberg suggested, makes it suspect that there is a strong universal parental instinct. In relation to aggressiveness, he showed that warfare is not known to occur in a number of tribes, and where it does occur in other cases it can often be attributed to motives other than aggression, such as getting women, obtaining prestige and honor, securing property, replenishing the population of a tribe by means of prisoners, etc. Disputes may sometimes be settled in some societies by means other than direct fighting. Among Eskimos, singing of satirical songs was such an alternative. Klineberg concludes concerning aggressiveness that while it is widely distributed, its expression varies greatly. "Social factors determine the amount and to a large extent the very existence of aggressiveness" (Klineberg, 1940, p. 89).

While acquisitiveness is important in Western society, there are societies in which property is communal and others in which exchange of property, when it occurs, is always on even terms, never at a profit. The Zuñi, the Hopi, and the Arapesh are apparently noncompetitive peoples. This is illustrated for the Hopi by an incident quoted from Klineberg (1940, p. 106): "One teacher once tried the new method of lining them (the children) up against a blackboard with instructions to complete their sums as quickly as possible and turn to the front as soon as they had finished. She observed that as each child finished, he looked surreptitiously along the line to see how far the others had advanced, apparently unwilling to turn around until the others were also ready." Neither acquisitiveness nor competitiveness, then, can perhaps be regarded as instinctive.

Sexual behavior also shows many variations, as reflected across the world in widely different practices and attitudes concerning tabooing sexual play in young children, premarital sexual experience, homosexuality, marital fidelity, jealousy, and the like (Ford & Beach, 1951). Similarly, the kind of food that is eaten, the occasions of eating, and the manner of eating show great variations.

There are also differences in values that seem to be held in various societies. Among the Alorese (DuBois, 1944; Kardiner, 1945), shrewdness and chicanery have the status that competence and ability have in other societies, whereas honesty, strength, skill, and heroism are not highly valued or admired. The Alorese have little interest in beauty in graphic arts, though music is of some interest to them. Power and prestige, largely determined by wealth, are principal values. Such attitudes and values are in contrast to some of the apparent ones held in "Plainville," a small Midwestern town in the United States (West, 1945; Kardiner, 1945). Good character traits are reported, for Plainville, to be honesty, willingness to work, and performance of domestic duties. Esthetic interests are not strong in this Midwestern culture, but well-kept, neat, and freshly painted surroundings are valued. The Alorese have little interest in such matters. In Plainville, education, knowledge, and skill tend to be admired. Security and status are values to be achieved through success and perhaps wealth; power over others is not an evident value.

What has been said represents at least a sketch of some of the cultural facts of variation which, in some measure, are the kinds of findings that made the postulation of universal instincts a position difficult to defend. Variations are also found among social classes.

Class Variations. Many societies and nations, including the United States, involve a class system of greater or lesser formality and rigidity. Class lines are usually described in terms of educational and economic-occupational variables, but there are many other ways in which the people of a society or a country can be classified: for example, by age, sex, color, religion, place of residence, dialect grouping, or linguistic background. Some study has been given to the ways in which people, especially children, are affected by one or the other of these kinds of class membership. The argument, for our purposes, here, is that class membership may be a condition out of which variation in motivational characteristics develops. If true, such a result might point to experience, rather than to innate tendencies, as an important factor in motivation.

As is true of cultural studies, the literature on class membership is voluminous, and we can mention here only some illustrative examples. Hollingshead (1949) studied high school children in a Midwestern town. Among his conclusions was that the goals and values of middle-class children were very different from those of lower-class children. Academic success, social acceptability, material and cultural values involving relatively long periods of time were emphasized much more often in middle-class than in lower-class children. The school, Hollingshead argued, reflects the values of the middle class, and hence does not motivate the lower-class child as it does the middle-class child. McDonald, McGuire, and Havighurst (1949) asked children to keep diaries for a two-week period. The children were fifth, sixth, and seventh graders and came from four social classes. They found class differences in the extent of participation in organized recreational groups and in some of the leisure time activities reported by individuals. Leshan (1952) asked children of the lower and middle classes to tell stories, finding that the goals of the characters in the stories of the lower-class children were more immediate than those of the characters in the stories of the middle-class children.

Schneider and Lysgaard (1953) used a questionnaire and found that middle-class boys, more commonly than lower-class boys, tended to accept the notion of delay of impulse gratification. Negro boys respond to TAT pictures in terms suggesting that they tend to perceive the world as hostile and threatening in contrast to the perception of the world as essentially friendly by white boys of the same class (Mussen, 1953). Douvan (1956) compared achievement motivation responses in middle- and working-class high school students. She manipulated motivation by means of both monetary and symbolic deprivation and found the working-class students to be affected by the former and not the latter, whereas the middle-class children were affected by both. Rural boys had lower educational aspirations than urban boys, according to one survey (Haller & Sewell, 1957). Jewish parents inculcate in their sons values which lead to motivation for achievement to an extent greater than Italian-American parents (McClelland et al., 1958). Miller and Swanson (1958) compared children of entrepreneurial and of bureaucratic (large organizations) parents; self-control, self-denial, an active life, and independence were emphasized in the training of the children of the entrepreneurs, whereas dependency and passivity were more likely to be emphasized in the child training of bureaucratic parents.

This brief review of some of the evidence on the class variable indicates the kinds of differences frequently found when training practices and motivational matters are studied in representatives of different social classes. It should be pointed out also that sometimes such differences do not appear. We have highlighted the differences related to class, just as we have the differences related to culture, because it is out of such differences that alternatives to the instinct concept arose.[33]

FUNCTIONAL AUTONOMY

Before we turn to the acquired motivational concepts proposed by drive theory, we should also note another concept, that of the *functional autonomy of behavior*. This idea has been proposed as a solution to the problem of providing a noninstinctual base for those motivational processes that do not reflect basic, biological drives. Many years ago, as we mentioned in Chapter 2, Woodworth (1918) suggested that mechanisms can become drives. Evidently, Woodworth felt that in the process of acquiring a skill, or set of skills toward some end, the skill or skills themselves could develop a motivating power of their own, a power which would endure even though the end be no longer sought. "In short," he said, "the power of acquiring new mechanisms possessed by the human mind is at the same time a power of acquiring new drives; for every mechanism, when at that stage of its development when it has reached a degree of effectiveness without having yet become entirely automatic, is itself a drive and capable of motivating activities that lie beyond its immediate scope" (Woodworth, 1918, p. 104). Habits may become drives. Among the examples Woodworth gave were the "drives" learned during the development of skill in golf or chess or the mastery of a business. The persistence of such activities over long periods of time and their almost compulsive character probably suggested to him that they have drive value.

[33] For a more careful and thorough review of the literature of class differences, see Auld (1952).

Allport (1937) also spoke in this vein, and he invented the term "functional autonomy" to denote the behaviors which somehow have developed their own motive powers. He argues eloquently that while many activities, such as making money or climbing mountains, may originally have served some other motive, their persistence in many people despite the absence of the other motive necessitates their having developed drive value of their own; that is, they are functionally autonomous not only of their original motivational root but also of any other presently acting motive factors. Allport takes especial pains to deny that such persistent behaviors remain tied to infantile or biological sources, but admits that these sources may have been involved at the beginning.

Many psychologists (see, e.g., Bertocci, 1940; McClelland, 1942; Rethlingshafer, 1943) have not accepted this concept. Perhaps the major complaint is that functional autonomy does no more than *name* the phenomenon which it presumes to explain. Another objection is that there are other possible mechanisms which could account for the phenomenon.[34] Many such mechanisms are reviewed in this section and to them we now turn.

ACQUIRED DRIVE AND OTHER LEARNED MOTIVATIONAL NOTIONS POSTULATED BY DRIVE THEORY

As we have just seen, it has become commonplace to assert that most of the motivational characteristics of the adult human being are learned or acquired. However, mechanisms which mediate such acquired motivations have received theoretical analysis and empirical study only since about 1940 (cf. Mowrer, 1950a, Chaps. 1–5, inclusive). One of the first such notions was Anderson's (1941a, b, c, d) conception of the "externalization of drive" (see p. 581). Studies of the role of token incentives in controlling and reinforcing behavior were reported in 1936 by Wolfe and in 1937 by Cowles. Neal Miller discussed empirical studies of acquired drives in 1941, but full reports of his work were delayed for several years. Miller and Dollard (1941) showed how such behaviors as imitation and copying could be based on acquired motivational factors; later, they (Dollard & Miller, 1950) emphasized the role in human beings of verbal labeling responses in arousing motives and providing reinforcement.

Terminology. The terms *learned drive, acquired drive, secondary drive, psychogenic drive,* and *learnable drive* are all more or less equiv-

---

[34] Allport (1940) may be consulted for his reply to Bertocci and has further attended to the criticisms of functional autonomy more recently (Allport, 1961). Murphy's *canalization* concept is somewhat similar (Murphy, 1947, 1954).

alent and are often used interchangeably in the discussion of secondary motivation (Miller, 1951*a*). The chief criteria which have been employed to decide whether a given process is a learned drive as opposed to a habit are (1) its capacity to activate or energize other responses, (2) the rewarding or reinforcing value of its reduction or removal as indicated by the learning of new responses, and (3) the ability of the process, under some conditions, to suppress or inhibit other responses (Miller, 1951*a;* Brown, 1961). Conceptions of learned drive basically assert that responses which produce strong stimuli are the mechanisms of such drives. This has led Brown (1961) to speak of "learned sources of drive," rather than of learned drives.

In our earlier discussions, the term *drive* (or motive) usually refers to some process internal to the organism. Response produced stimuli would, of course, qualify under this criterion. The term incentive, on the other hand, is usually employed to denote some external object or stimulus situation which the organism approaches or avoids or which motivates another aspect of performance. While acquired drives and incentives are usually denoted by different operations, there are basic similarities between theoretical analyses of why it is that incentives work and analyses of learned drives as being dependent on response produced stimuli. We will point these out later. We will also suggest that most of the demonstrations of acquired drive are in fact demonstrations of motivational processes which are limited to relatively few situations. The motivation aroused by an incentive is also limited to the situations in which the incentive is present. This is a further similarity between acquired drives and incentives.

Acquired Motivation Based on Aversive Stimulation

Conditioned Fear. Miller (1941, 1948*a*) studied fear as an acquired drive. As evidences of the drive character of fear, he raised two questions: Once a fear response is learned, would it then instigate "random" behavior? and would its reduction reinforce the learning of new responses?

The apparatus Miller used consisted of two compartments, as displayed in Figure 11–8. One was white with a grid floor; the other was black with a solid floor. A door separated the two compartments. This door could be dropped (thus offering access to one compartment from the other) by the experimenter or by the rat under certain conditions. The animals were first tested in the apparatus with the dividing door open, so that their response tendencies could be observed. Then the animal was given 10 shock trials in the white compartment with the door between the compartments open. When the animal ran to the black compartment the door closed behind him, and he remained in the shock-free compartment for 30 seconds, after which he was removed to await the next trial.

After these shock trials, 5 *non*shock trials were given in which the experimenter opened the door as the animal approached it from the opposite end of the white compartment into which the animal had been placed. These trials were followed by 16 further nonshock trials, in which the door would drop only if the animal learned to rotate a little wheel above the door. Finally, another series of nonshock trials was run in which wheel turning would no longer drop the door but a

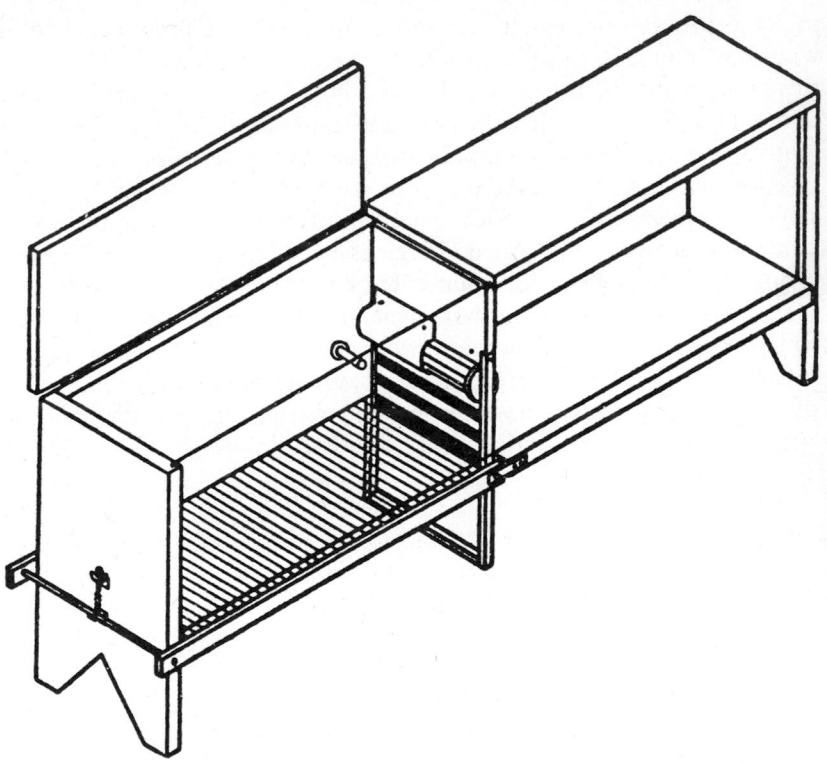

Figure 11–8. Apparatus used for the study of fear as an acquired drive. The left compartment is painted white, the right compartment black. Electric shock can be given through the grid floor of the white (left) compartment. The door between the compartments is painted with horizontal black and white stripes. It will drop out of the way, depending on conditions, when the experimenter presses a button or when the rat turns the wheel or presses the bar. Reproduced by permission from Miller (1951a, Fig. 1, p. 437).

bar-press response would. In this final phase the animal had to unlearn wheel-turning and learn bar-pressing.

Before shock the animals showed no apparent avoidance of or preference for either compartment. Running into the black compartment on being shocked was learned by all the animals, and they continued to do so on the 5 nonshock trials when the experimenter opened the door. Thirteen of the 25 animals learned to rotate the wheel to drop the door, and these 13 animals showed an improvement over the 16 trials in the speed with which they did so.[35] When the wheel became nonfunctional, 12 of these 13 animals eventually stopped rotating the wheel and shifted to bar-pressing, an act which they performed with increasing speed over 10 trials. Prior to learning the wheel-turning response, the animals displayed variable ("random") behavior, largely in the region of the door.

Miller interprets these findings as indicating that the cues of the white compartment became capable of eliciting responses originally produced by the shock. Since, in later trials, there was no shock, these responses—visceral and skeletal—constituted fear. Presumably, these responses produce strong stimuli, and these stimuli motivate or instigate the variable behavior out of which such skills as wheel-turning and bar-pressing emerged; escape into the black compartment would be fear-reducing and would hence reinforce the responses, themselves activated by fear, which preceded the escape.

In subsequent experiments, Miller and Lawrence (Miller, 1951a, p. 446; Fig. 6, p. 448) [36] varied the intensity of the shock given to different groups of rats in the initial training phase of an experiment similar to the one we have just described. During the nonshock trials involving bar-pressing, performance of the response was faster for animals which had received strong shocks than for animals which had received weak shocks. A very weak shock group showed no evidence of having acquired a fear-drive. Miller (1951a, Fig. 7, p. 449) also reports that a bar-pressing habit based on fear may persist for as many as 500 or 600 trials without shock; a number of variables influence this resistance to extinction, such as intensity of initial shock, and spacing of extinction trials (Miller, 1951a, p. 450).

[35] The 12 animals which did not learn the wheel-turning response developed, instead, a crouching response which was, of course, incompatible with wheel-turning. Later experiments, which eliminated the crouching response, were successful in getting all animals to learn the new response which dropped the door (Miller, 1948a, p. 93fn.).

[36] This experiment by N. E. Miller and D. H. Lawrence has never been fully published. The descriptions in Miller (1951a) as cited above are apparently adequate, however. See, also, Mathers (1957).

Several additional investigations have provided checks on factors in Miller's experiments and have extended the functions of fear that have been studied. May (1948) first trained his animals to cross a barrier between compartments to escape shock. Then he confined each animal in a pen (in the shuttle apparatus) where the experimental animals experienced the pairing of a buzzer with shock. Controls also were stimulated in the pen, some animals receiving shock alone, some the buzzer alone, and some unpaired presentations of the buzzer and shock.

The test trials consisted of placing the animal in one compartment of the shuttle apparatus, with the swinging door closed, and presenting the buzzer. The experimental animals, in far more instances than the various control animals, crossed the barrier at the sound of the buzzer. Analogously to Miller's findings, the buzzer presumably elicited fear in the experimental group. This fear response is probably so similar to the responses to direct shock (which in earlier training had been associated with escape) that it could mediate escape at the sound of the buzzer. In the control animals, the buzzer had not been paired with shock; thus it would not be expected to elicit a mediating fear response. The actual transfer of the hurdle-jumping response is probably dependent not only on the drive properties of fear but rather on the association between fear-like drive cues and the jumping response. However, the buzzer must have elicited the fear response in order for these cues to be available.

Brown and Jacobs (1949) suggested an alternative interpretation for the acquired drive results reported by Miller. Miller's rats had had five shock-free trials on which they could escape to the black compartment before they encountered the closed door for the opening of which the wheel-turning response was required. In other words, a running response, already learned, was blocked, and Brown and Jacobs suggested that a frustration-induced drive, rather than fear, might motivate wheel-turning and that its reduction might be reinforcing. They reported two experiments designed to evaluate this interpretation. In the fear-training part of one of these experiments a tone and light combination was the conditioned stimulus, and it was paired 22 times with shock in one compartment of an apparatus. No specific conditioned response was reinforced. Subsequently, the animals were placed in one compartment from which they could jump over a hurdle (after the door was opened by the experimenter) into the other, identical compartment. Fear, presumably aroused by the light-tone stimulus, would motivate the animal to behave, and the cessation of the tone and light, as soon as the jumping response occurred, would presumably result in fear reduction and thus reinforcement. Brown and Jacobs found that, compared to control animals (which were never shocked), the latency of hurdle-crossing in the experimental animals declined rapidly over 20 trials and remained significantly shorter for an additional 20 trials. This finding supports the notion that fear, learned as a response to the tone and light, was motivating and provided the conditions for the reinforcement of the hurdle-jumping response. Presumably there was no frustration-induced drive in Brown and Jacobs' experiment. Miller's interpretation is thus confirmed, in a different situation. Kalish (1954) performed a somewhat similar but more elaborate experiment. He confirmed the results reported by Brown and Jacobs and also showed that amount of fear was a function of number of fear-training trials and that it declined with extinction procedures (see, also, Gwinn, 1951).

Brown, Kalish, and Farber (1951) also investigated acquired fear, but their interest lay primarily in the energizing function of fear rather than in the role of its reduction as a reward. For fear-training, the experimental animals received 28 trials over four days in which a buzzer and light were paired with electric shock. Control animals also received both sets of stimuli but not in a paired arrangement. On three other trials, during each of these four days, the conditioned stimulus complex was presented without shock. Rather, the "popping" sound from a toy pistol was administered at the time the shock was due. If fear was being conditioned to the buzzer and light and if fear energizes other responses (like the startle response to the buzzer and light), then, in the experimental group, one would expect an increasing startle response to the sound of the cap pistol as conditioning proceeded and a decreasing effect as extinction was carried on. This, indeed, was what Brown, Kalish, and Farber (1951) found, supporting their interpretation that fear may energize other responses. Meryman (1952, 1953, cf. Brown, 1961, pp. 152–155) obtained confirmatory results in both rats and human subjects; in the latter the amplitude of GSR to a click was enhanced if the click occurred as a substitute for the shock following the presentation of the CS (another auditory stimulus).

Conditioned Emotional Response. Another technique for studying acquired fear-drives results in what is sometimes called a "conditioned emotional response." Estes and Skinner (1941) described the essential method. Rats were initially trained under hunger to press a bar for food, the schedule of reinforcement being at a four-minute fixed interval. After two weeks on this schedule, pairings of a tone and a shock (delivered through the floor of the apparatus) were made. Shocks seldom coincided with bar-presses. After twelve pairings of tone and shock, subsequent presentations of the tone alone were used. The tone now presumably elicited anxiety or a conditioned emotional response. The effects of the tone were a suppression of bar-pressing during the presentation of the tone. Estes and Skinner also showed that during extinction bar-pressing was depressed during the presentation of the tone and that the anxiety reaction itself is subject to extinction and spontaneous recovery. This last statement is an inference made by Estes and Skinner, based on the course of bar-pressing responses.

A number of investigators have used the conditioned emotional response to investigate other problems (cf. Hunt & Brady, 1951), but we shall not follow these lines of inquiry here. It is clear that conditioned fear may suppress certain responses, and this effect may be due to competing responses which the fear stimulus arouses and which interfere, in this case, with the bar-pressing response. Other evidence from similar experiments (Hunt & Brady, 1951) indicates that during suppression of bar-pressing, defecation occurs frequently; since defecation is often taken as an indication of emotional arousal this would suggest that this conditioned signal was emotionally arousing. Amsel (1950b) has also shown that conditioned fear can suppress such responses as drinking and that the suppression is accompanied by increased defecation. It may be that the anxiety has energized the response of defecation and that this and other emotional responses interfere with bar-depression and drinking. On the other hand, as Brown (1961) has argued, one could say simply that one of the consequences of an acquired drive may be the inhibition of some responses, without invoking competing responses.

Relationships to Avoidance Training and Punishment

Use of aversive stimulation is not limited to studies or demonstrations of acquired drives. Two other widely investigated phenomena involving such stimuli are escape and avoidance training and punishment.

Escape and Avoidance Training. In escape training, the organism receives the aversive stimulus (e.g., shock) but may escape from it by making some response. Frequently, some other external stimulus is used which coincides with or precedes shock onset; if the temporal precedence of the conditioned stimulus over the shock is long enough, the animal may learn to make a response which avoids the shock altogether. Escape training develops a response which removes shock but does not permit its avoidance. Avoidance training permits the organism to learn a response which entirely obviates the receipt of shock. Under suitable time arrangements of the neutral stimulus and the shock, the avoidance can emerge out of escape. Both of these procedures may be distinguished from classical conditioning employing aversive stimulation. In the latter, the shock is inevitable; that is, nothing the organism does can either avoid or escape the full duration of the aversive stimulus.

Solomon and Brush (1956) have described nine kinds of aversive training procedures, including the procedures we have already described. Avoidance (and escape) training differs chiefly from the acquired drive procedure in that interest focuses on the specific response which is instrumental to avoidance of or escape from a relatively specific stimulus situation. The learning of additional responses or the energization or suppression of another response is not of major concern in avoidance and escape training. The unconditioned aversive stimulus likewise continues to be presented, typically, in escape or avoidance training (except during test trials), and, even after successful avoidance is established, the animal may receive shock if he delays his response too long or otherwise fails to execute it effectively.

The boundaries among these kinds of experiments are not always well defined, and theoretical interpretations of avoidance training have often invoked fear or anxiety to account for the development of avoidance in the first place and to explain its persistence. Solomon and Wynne (1954) based their interpretation of avoidance on anxiety, but suggested a hypothesis to explain the fact that anxiety is not more manifest in animals with well-developed avoidance responses than it is. They argue that anxiety is "conserved" by the rapid occurrence of the avoidance response, as this prevents the anxiety from occurring; if anxiety does not occur it is not subject to extinction. Occasional dilatoriness on the part of the animal, however, would permit anxiety to occur and reinstate the waning avoidance response. Extinction of the response, therefore, could be very slow. Difficulties with this interpretation, however, especially in terms of available physiological evidence, have been pointed out by Solomon and Brush (1956, pp. 282–286). Physiological evidences of anxiety are not always obtained.[37] Other interpretations (Sheffield, 1948; Schoenfeld, 1950) have also been given.

Punishment. When aversive stimulation is presented because an organism makes a particular response or one of a class of responses, we speak of punishment. The goal of punishment is usually to eliminate or to make less frequent the occurrence of the response that is pun-

---

[37] Appley and Moeller (1962) have suggested that neuroendocrine differences may underlie escape and avoidance phenomena. Hypophysectomy apparently affects avoidance but not escape. Appley and Moeller propose a possible role for the pituitary in "anticipatory" (avoidant) responding in the absence of noxious stimulation.

ished. That this can be accomplished is not so much the problem as is the mechanism which permits this effect to occur, when it does. Thorndike (1927) had originally proposed that a reaction is weakened by punishment, but later he obtained evidence he thought was contrary to such a weakening effect (1932, 1935). This led Thorndike to propose that punishment strengthens or makes more likely behavior other than the punished-response without weakening this response itself.

Anxiety states were proposed by Estes (1944) to account for the effects of punishment, and he interpreted punishment as suppressing but not eliminating the punished response. Fear and avoidance interpretations of punishment have been suggested by a number of writers. Dinsmoor (1954, 1955) has offered an avoidance interpretation of punishment. In this he argues that punishment, like the avoidance situation, involves the development of secondary aversive stimuli which occur in the sequence of events which leads to the response to be punished. Behaviors which are incompatible with the occurrence of these secondary aversive stimuli, and thus prevent them, will be reinforced. This will in turn cause the suppression of the response which, if it occurred, would be punished.

Dinsmoor argues that in this account, as well as in his treatment of avoidance (cf., also, Schoenfeld, 1950), he has avoided concepts like anxiety and fear. While it is true that he has avoided the use of these terms, it seems to us that his statement is similar to the notion expressed by Brown (1961) that in speaking of acquired drive we should speak instead of learned sources of drive. In Brown's formulation these are often aversive stimuli arising from responses; certainly some of Dinsmoor's aversive stimuli would arise from responses. It may be that Brown's reformulation amounts to much the same thing as Dinsmoor's (and Schoenfeld's).

Acquired Motivation Based on Appetitional Primary Drive States

Interest naturally arises concerning the question of whether acquired drives can be based on stimulation arising from conditions other than aversive ones. Many writers object to the basing of all acquired motivation on original attempts to avoid pain. However, the relatively few experiments which have been designed to study the development of acquired drives based on hunger have not been consistently very successful.[38]

[38] If one conceives of hunger as a goading stimulus, of course, demonstrations of acquired drives would still essentially base them on aversive stimulation. With the possible exception of drug addictions, which could be said to be acquired drives,

Dashiell (1928) suggested that if external stimuli occur often enough in contiguity with drives, the external stimuli might acquire drive properties.[39] Anderson (1941*a*) used such a notion, calling it the "externalization of drive." He tested this idea in several ways. In one experiment, for example, Anderson (1941*c*) trained rats under hunger and food reward conditions for substantial numbers of trials in one maze and then transferred them to another maze task under conditions of satiation of hunger (and no reward). The animals showed learning in the second maze. Anderson believed that this evidence and evidence from other experiments supports the notion of drive externalization, but Siegel (1943) replicated the experiment without positive results.

Calvin, Bicknell, and Sperling (1953*a*) placed animals in distinctively striped and shaped boxes for 30 minutes each day for 24 days. One group received this experience under high drive, the other on a lower drive (22 hours and 1 hour food deprivation, respectively). After this training both groups were allowed to eat in the striped box after $11\frac{1}{2}$ hours of food deprivation. The original 1-hour group ate significantly less than the strong-drive group, suggesting that the distinctive box cues had become capable of arousing drive in the strong-drive group. Three attempts to verify these results, some of them attempting exact replications, have failed to do so, however (Siegel & MacDonnell, 1954; Scarborough & Goodson, 1957; Parkes, 1958).

Myers and Miller (1954) set up an experiment which in essence follows the logic of the fear-acquisition experiments by Miller that we have already described. A two-compartment box was used, and hungry rats learned to run from the white compartment to the black compartment through a door which opened when they touched it. This training was conducted under a 23-hour hunger drive, and different groups of animals received 0, 10, 30, or 70 training trials. Subsequently, all animals were satiated for food and put into the white compartment; in order to escape they now had to learn to press a bar which opened the door. All groups learned the response equally well, and Myers and Miller concluded that the learning was motivated by an exploratory drive, not by conditioned hunger (cf., also, Novin & Miller, 1962).

One property which distinguishes shock from hunger (and other primary appetitional drives) is its quickness of onset. It has been suggested that this property makes fear-learning possible on the basis of shock and the acquisition of drives on the basis of the more gradually developing appetitional needs difficult to demonstrate. Greenberg

we know of no evidence or experiment involving "drives" based on stimulation which would universally be regarded as nonaversive.

[39] A reading can be made of Woodworth (1918) to the same point.

(1954) injected rats with saline solution, in order to induce thirst quickly, and paired a blinking light with the thirst state. Measures of drinking taken later during stimulation from the light (without injection), however, gave no evidence for the acquisition of drive-eliciting properties by the light.

It must be concluded, on the basis of these experiments, that there is currently no evidence for the acquisition of drives on the basis of appetitional needs.

Situational Character of Acquired Drives

It is worth noting that in all cases of the demonstration of acquired fear drives the acquired drive appears, so far as available experimental evidence indicates, only in relatively specific environmental circumstances, for example, in a white compartment or at the presentation of a specific cue—a buzzer or a light-tone combination. In this respect, acquired drives, even though they may be mediated through stimuli arising from internal responses, are situation-bound. They do not seem to have the trans-situational character of primary drives, like hunger or thirst. It might be useful, then, to refer to the acquired drive of fear (the major one so far demonstrated) not only as involving a learned source of drive (cue to drive arousal) but also as a negative incentive condition as a source of drive. It is a negative incentive because it arouses escape or avoidance behavior.

Verbal Responses

It is interesting to note, in connection with situational specificity of acquired drives, that when Dollard and Miller (1950) and Brown (1953, 1961) refer to acquired drives in the human organism, they emphasize the role of self-administered verbal commands in arousing such motivational states. Such verbal processes can, of course, easily become independent of specific situations and thus show a greater parallel with primary drives in this respect than does fear in the case of lower animals. It is possible that verbal processes may be involved in instances of functional autonomy.

Estimate of These Acquired Motivational Notions

We have reviewed demonstrations that fear may be associated with cues and lead to variable and energized behavior and that reduction of fear (or, at least, removal of fear stimulation) appears to be reinforcing. Acquired motivations based on appetitive needs have not been demonstrated, although recent interpretations of incentive motivation may be a beginning solution to the problem of basing acquired motivations on appetitive situations. To date most of the experimental evidence concerning acquired drives has come from a few situations in the animal laboratory. While extrapolations to human behavior made by various writers are fairly plausible, especially when emphasis on verbal processes is made, there is still a long way to go before drive theory can be said to have successfully solved the problem of acquired motivation by means of its concepts. Another area of acquired motivation may be mentioned though it has received relatively little experimental or theoretical analysis. This is the area of addictions. It is possible that a wider attack on addictions with animal subjects would illuminate a number of problems of acquired motivation, especially those which seem to have the positive feature of approach, rather than the negative feature of avoidance.

Addictions

Powerfully motivated behavior is often reported in individuals who are "addicted" to certain drugs. Such addictions probably can be regarded as reflecting acquired motives or drives because there is no evidence that addictions develop without experience. Various hypotheses have been suggested as to the processes involved in addictions. Two of them involve aversive or unpleasant states, which the drug alleviates. One hypothesis stresses fear, anxiety, and inadequacy as representative of unpleasant feeling states which drugs may ameliorate. The amelioration of these feelings "explains" the addiction. Unpleasant withdrawal symptoms, caused by cessation of drug administration, constitute another aversive state which the drug may relieve. The second hypothesis emphasizes these states in explaining addictions. (It should be noted that physiological dependence on drugs and symptoms arising from their withdrawal occur only in respect to some drugs. Relief of anxiety, on the other hand, may perhaps be accomplished not only by drugs to which dependence may be formed but also by many others.) A third hypothesis as to the basis of addiction is that the euphoric or pleasant state which some drugs can apparently induce is the cause of the addiction. This basis could be independent of the others mentioned above, although in actual cases of drug addiction it is probable that more than one factor are involved.

Experiments have been carried out on animals which seem to support all three of these hypotheses. Masserman and Yum (1946) taught cats to perform a series of acts in order to obtain food. After the training was completed, electric shocks were given the cats at the goal so that they refused to work in the apparatus, presumably because of fear. Doses of alcohol, however, overcame this fear, and the mildly intoxicated cats would again work the apparatus to get food. The cats, after this sequence of training experiences, preferred a solution of milk and alcohol to plain milk, the latter having been the preferred liquid before their training. One might say at this point that the cats were addicted to alcohol or "alcoholic." When the fear of the apparatus was thoroughly extinguished, however, this preference for alcohol was lost. Conger (1951) trained hungry rats to approach one end of an alley to obtain food and then induced conflict by shocking them at that end of the alley. The animals would not, after this treatment, approach the food end of the alley, but after administration of alcohol they would once again do so. Presumably, the alcohol reduced the fear which kept the rats from approaching the food. Scarborough (1957) found that an alcohol group extinguished a bar-pressing response which turned off a shock more quickly than a control group, despite the fact that by the time extinction trials were given, the bodily effects of alcohol had dissipated. It is possible, however, that during the test trials (before extinction) the alcohol group animals learned that there was no shock on the grid-floor. Masserman (1946, p. 148) has reported further experiments indicating that drugs like nembutal, amytal, and morphine permit goal-directed behavior to reappear after it had been inhibited by punishment.

No physiological dependence was presumably established in these studies on alcohol, and they therefore relate to the first hypothesis, which stresses anxiety. A number of studies of morphine, however, with various species of animals have established a clear dependency (cf. H. D. Beach, 1957, pp. 104–105, for brief review). Spragg (1940) reported one of the best known studies. He used chimpanzees and gave them morphine injections twice daily in an injection room, somewhat removed from each animal's living quarters. After the injection, the animals remained in the injection room for a few minutes, presumably experiencing the effects of the drug there. Withdrawal symptoms began to appear prior to the time of injection about a month after the injections were started, suggesting the development of dependency on the drug. A few weeks later morphine-injection-seeking behavior was apparent. The animals would try to solicit injections, lead the experimenter to the injection room, and even though hungry would prefer the syringe to food if they had not had a shot for a while. Since these chimpanzees were normal ones it seems unlikely that fear, anxiety, or similar states were involved in the development of their morphine addiction. Their behavior of soliciting injections probably arose from the effects of withdrawal as suggested in the second hypothesis; how much they were directly affected by the euphoria which is reported by human addicts following morphine is unclear.

Beach (1957a) carried out several experiments with rats in which morphine addiction was developed. His experiments essentially involved determinations of goal-box preferences in a Y-maze after various training experiences. He ran his animals on a forced-choice trial, after a morphine injection, into their nonpreferred goal boxes, where they stayed for an hour. This training produced a preference shift to that goal box on later test trials. Dependence on the drug had been established before this training. This experiment indicated that relief from withdrawal symptoms could lead to learning a preference change, again confirming the second hypothesis. In another experiment, the morphine-dependent animals were run into the nonpreferred goal box twenty minutes after the injection. Presumably, relief from withdrawal symptoms had occurred prior to the run and the animals would experience only euphoria in the goal box. A change in preference did occur under these conditions, just as it had in the prior experiment. Tatum and Seevers (1929) found that dogs could learn cocaine-seeking behaviors; since cocaine is not supposed to develop dependency and withdrawal symptoms, this experiment also demonstrates the reward value of drug-induced euphoria. Thus hypothesis three presumably receives support.

One further experiment of Beach's was run after his rats had been taken off the drug and withdrawal symptoms had disappeared. He made a further test of preference for the two goal boxes. The animals which had presumably experienced both relief of withdrawal symptoms and euphoria in their originally nonpreferred goal boxes still retained their learned preferences for them. The animals which had experienced only the euphoria in these goal boxes, however, had lost their preference for them.

These experiments suggest that while anxiety, fear, or other aversive states may underlie addictions, such addictions may also arise from relief of withdrawal distress or from euphoria arising from the drug itself. Thus, to the extent that addictions illustrate acquired motives or drives, it is evident that several mechanisms may be involved. Further comparisons with other acquired drives must be limited because of inadequate knowledge both concerning other such drives and addictions themselves.

Comment Concerning Anxiety and Fear as Drives

It is especially true of fear, and it may be true of at least some anxieties, that the fear and anxiety reactions are based on anticipatory responses premonitory to the occurrence of a painful event. Electric shock or other noxious stimuli would be examples in point of such painful events. Two comments are in order.

One involves the cases of congenital insensitivity to painful stimuli, which we reviewed in Chapter 5. The two cases most fully studied and described were found to be essentially normal college girls, as far as motivational and personality assessments and their educational, social, and emotional histories were concerned. Yet, if in these girls anxiety or fear were a significant motivational force, it could presumably not have been predicated on the ultimate base of pain. We point this out while recognizing that anxiety, and even fear, may probably arise on many foundations other than the direct experience of pain. It is somewhat sobering, however, in the light of all the work we have reviewed and have still to consider which has stressed reactions to pain as the basis for fear or anxiety, to read about these apparently healthy but pain-free girls.

The other comment concerns characteristics in which acquired drives differ from biological drives and the problem of how fear is learned in the Miller experiments and in avoidance conditioning situations. Miller (1951a) points out that while reinforcement with food weakens biological drives, like hunger, and nonreinforcement strengthens such drives, the reverse would be the case for an acquired drive, like fear, which is governed by laws of habit formation. The strength of the latter would increase with reinforcements and decrease (extinguish) with nonreinforcements. These differences, together with the incentive-like character which acquired drives possess, clearly bring out the point that acquired drives are not equivalent to primary drives.

Another problem has been raised, specifically concerning the acquisition of the fear drives. The question involves the role of reinforcement. Many writers accept the notion that the instrumental avoidance response is reinforced by fear reduction in acquired drive and other avoidance learning experiments. But what reinforcing event underlies the acquisition of the fear itself? Miller (1951a, b) has maintained that the cessation of the pain reinforces the connection between the environmental stimuli and the emotional responses which are the bases of fear. But as has been pointed out (Solomon & Brush, 1956, p. 243) the fear response is also reduced (and hence reinforced) by a successful avoidance, once avoidance responding has been established. This point carries the implication that, in avoidance learning, fear will continue to grow over time, even without further shock, rather than extinguishing as it will ultimately do under most circumstances of nonreinforcement. It was out of such problems as this one that two-process conceptions of learning (such as those we have reviewed in Chapter

10) developed. In essence, they hold that fear is not learned on a basis of tension reduction but rather on the ground of contiguity between the environmental stimuli and the onset of the shock. This assumption has led to a variety of experiments, designed to test this and the other alternative. The hypothesis of conservation of anxiety (Solomon & Wynne, 1954) is a theoretical development also suggested in this context.

We shall not discuss this point further here, as the acquisition of a habit is a problem of learning and not of motivation. But it is noteworthy that, whatever the value of the concept of fear as an acquired drive may be to motivational theory, the nature of the process governing the acquisition of fear is still problematic.

SUMMARY

This chapter has reviewed the empirical findings related to a number of theoretical problems and issues arising in the context of motivational aspects of learning-behavior theories (see Chapter 10).

Drive strength, at the time of learning, seems to have an effect mainly on rate, latency, and speed measures, but its effects on correct responses or errors are not consistent. Measures which involve time are perhaps expressions of performance variables, rather than reflections of habit strength. There is some evidence that strength of aversive motivation may influence measures of habit strength, however. When the effects of drive strength during acquisition are studied later on, as during extinction, the bulk of the evidence shows that drive strength has little or no effect on the habit strength developed. A complication in this work, however, is that the habits learned under different drive strengths may be different ones.

Performance of a habit, once learned, has been studied under various strengths of the relevant drive and of irrelevant drives. Relevant drive, in the case of hunger, seems not to energize habits when drive strength is low but then to have an effect on performance which rises swiftly, at first, as drive strength increases, and then rises more slowly as drive continues to increase. There have been a number of problems in the design of experiments on this issue, however, and when improved designs have been used, the foregoing relationships are not at all clear.

Performance of habits seems to be affected, to some degree, by the presence of irrelevant drives, but the interpretation is complicated, especially in the case of hunger and thirst, by drive interactions. A stimulus generalization interpretation of the "energization function" of drives has been suggested by some authors.

Studies of reinforcement, reviewed here, have mainly been directed to the question of whether tension reduction is the critical factor in. reward. Direct need reduction has been found to be reinforcing, although side effects, which might serve as secondary reinforcement, have not been entirely ruled out. Stimulation, provided by the onset of illumination or by opportunity to explore or to manipulate the environment, has been successfully used as reinforcement. Intracranial electrical stimulation has powerful reinforcement effects, and this finding has been said to disprove tension reduction as the sole reinforcement mechanism. Problems with this conclusion were pointed out. Performance of consummatory responses, even in the absence of tension reduction, has reinforcement value. As ordinarily conceived, the tension reduction view of reinforcement confronts a number of problems if it is to be the sole mechanism of reinforcement.

Incentive motivation has received a good deal of attention in recent years. Its importance in controlling learning and performance has long been described, but the weight of the evidence now suggests that its effect is on performance rather than on learning. Theoretical interpretations of incentive motivation have stressed the role of fractional anticipatory goal responses, and a number of investigations have been concerned with aspects of this mechanism. Certain findings give it support; others do not.

Acquired drives have been postulated as alternatives to unlearned motives and to the hypothesized functional autonomy of motives. Cultural and class variations in behaviors related to motivation support the idea that much of human motivation is learned. While there is evidence that fear can be an acquired drive, this state appears to be less a drive than an emotional response elicited in specific situations. In the human, however, transfer from situation to situation may be mediated by verbal responses. Attempts to develop acquired drives in animals based on appetitive motivations have failed. Drug addictions probably qualify as acquired drives, but their investigation as motivational phenomena, at the present time, has not progressed very far.

Chapter 12

Psychoanalytic Motivation Theory[1]

Psychoanalysis has been described by one of its proponents as *the* basic theory of motivational psychology (Alexander, 1950, p. 32). But much of what has been written under the name of psychoanalysis has been either specific to mental disorders and/or their treatment, or much more general than a theory of motivation. The field has, without doubt, the most extensive literature of any part of psychology. Its ramifications invade most other fields of scholarship as well. As Rapaport has recently noted (Rapaport, 1959), specific applications of psychoanalytic theory and method have been made to normal as well as pathological behavior analysis, to anthropology and prehistory, literature, art, mythology, folklore, legend, language, religion, history, and society. Rapaport comments that not only has psychoanalysis ". . . asserted an all-inclusive applicability to the study of man," but it has also ". . . acted to make this claim good (p. 137)."

It would be practically impossible (and largely irrelevant) for us here to explore all of these claims. However, we are directly interested in those underlying assumptions, hypotheses, and findings of psychoanalysis that can be characterized as motivational in nature, and it is to this motivational core of theory that we shall direct our attention. The reader who wishes a more comprehensive view of the larger discipline would do well to refer to a more general source.[2]

FREUD AND THE BACKGROUND OF PSYCHOANALYSIS

Psychoanalysis began formally with the work of Sigmund Freud (1856–1939), and his name, at least, is known more widely throughout

[1] For an authoritative account written relatively recently, see Rapaport (1960). Toman (1960) has also written an introduction to psychoanalytic motivation theory.

[2] Useful recent reviews and surveys may be found in Blum, 1953; Hall, 1954; Hall & Lindzey, 1954, 1957; Harper, 1959; Pumpian-Mindlin, 1952a; Mullahy, 1948; Munroe, 1955; Rapaport, 1951a, b, 1959, 1960; Thompson, 1950; Thompson et al., 1955; and Toman, 1960.

the world than that of any other psychologist. Freud was a prolific as well as a lucid writer. His psychological works, covering a span of over fifty years, extend to some twenty-four volumes.[3]

For almost 80 of his 83 years, Freud lived in Vienna. The majority of his adult life was spent in private medical practice. An unwilling practitioner of medicine, Freud identified himself as a psychologist. He was more interested in the larger philosophy and science of life— its meaning and its means—than he was in the particular goals of treating particular patients with particular problems. From his own writings and from his biographers', it is apparent that he "backed into" the medical field and reluctantly took up a private medical practice as a means of consummating his long engagement to Martha Bernays in marriage. His interest remained with such deeper questions as the nature of life. It was perhaps this underlying interest that enabled him to make of his limited circumstances of clinical practice a laboratory for the investigation of the type of question we have noted. He found himself able to use his patients as subjects of study, and both derived from them and traced on their illnesses the theoretical conceptions he was later to call *psychoanalysis*.

We have said that psychoanalysis began with Freud. But, as Clara Thompson has put it (Thompson et al., 1955), it did not spring full grown from the brow of Freud. As a matter of fact, Freud lived at a time propitious for his discoveries. (The age-old argument of whether creative genius is a happenstance of the times or a function of the man need not concern us here.) Freud was, by his own admission, tremendously influenced by the revolutionary thinking taking place in the scientific world of his day. Through reading and through sometimes extensive personal contacts, he became familiar with the ideas of the then burgeoning new objective and experimental natural sciences. Needless to say, he was himself to become a major vehicle for the expansion of that scientific revolution to include psychology.

In his student days, Freud was much impressed by the then new Darwinian theories and their implications for human development. Darwin's *Origin of the Species* (1859), published when Freud was still a young child, had helped push open the flood gates of an objective biological science. Fechner's *Elemente der Psychophysik* (1860), published only a year after Darwin's and Wallace's dramatic reports on a theory of evolution, had made a strong case for the feasibility of a

[3] Freud, S., *The Standard Edition of the Complete Psychological Works of . . .*, Strachey, J. (ed. and transl.), 24 volumes, London: Hogarth, 1953 on. In addition, his neurological works fill several other volumes.

scientific study of man.[4] As a student, Freud found himself attracted to, and accepted the implications of, these new ideas. Through the physiologist Ernst Brücke, his early scientific mentor, Freud was directly exposed to the views of the Helmholtz school—that the laws of science were universally applicable and that physical and chemical explanations could be found for physiological events. Brücke was a member of the Helmholtz group, and his *Lectures on Physiology* (1874) formed a direct bridge for Freud from the naturalistic views of physics and chemistry to a conception of the living organism as a natural object, the orderly functioning of which could be understood in terms of energy transformations. Freud actually attempted to extend this hypothesis to cover psychological events, as had Herbart and Fechner, in somewhat different ways, earlier.

Helmholtz's ideas of energy conservation and exchange provided Freud with a model for his own theories of psychic energy and the dynamics of mental life. Freud later gave up the idea of a direct translatability of physical and chemical concepts to the psychological level (a view not unlike the philosophic position of reductionism today), but the influence of his early exposure to the antivitalism of the Helmholtz school was to remain with him. He made causality and determinism the cornerstones of his own work. Here we also find the foundation of Freud's conviction, so important to psychoanalysis: that a careful analysis of the mental processes, going *beyond* self-revealing conscious content—and thus studied naturalistically—could reveal the links on the particular causal chains of events in individual lives.

As part of the background of his development of psychoanalysis, we must note the fact that the first twenty or so years of his professional life were spent in a variety of positions, including work in neurology, neuroanatomy, and neuropathology as well as in clinical psychiatry. Rotating through a succession of hospital and university appointments, Freud had the opportunity to work and study with a number of distinguished (and some less-distinguished) scientists and physicians.

Through his contact with Meynert's clinic in Vienna, and particularly with Charcot at the famous Salpêtriere in Paris, and in his collaboration with Josef Breuer, Freud was drawn first to the problems of neuropathology in general and then to the particular problems of hysteria. This area, and the controversy over its etiology in organic or "psychic" disturbance, so interested Freud that he moved away from strictly neurological problems to the study of neuroses and their psy-

[4] C. Hall, in his *Primer of Freudian Psychology* (1954), dates the beginning of scientific psychology to Fechner's book.

chological origins. By 1895, when his collaborative *Studies on Hysteria* was published with Josef Breuer, Freud had already launched into the new dimension of psychoanalysis (although the first use of that term did not occur until the following year).

In describing the background from which Freud's theories arose, it is useful to recognize, as Rapaport (1959) has made so clear, that there were many converging influences whose traces can be seen not only in the content of Freud's work but in his nature as well. For example, Freud's exposure to the Helmholtz group's thinking and his extensive laboratory work in neurology and neuroanatomy are thought by Rapaport to have provided not only a broad background for Freud's aspirations to make his theorizing scientific but also some specific neurophysiological models (as we have noted above) for the theoretical systems Freud would later construct.

But Rapaport further points out that Freud's neurological work was actually more observational than experimental, and that this experience, in combination with his clinical work with Meynert, Bernheim, Charcot, and Breuer, inclined Freud toward reliance on careful observation and analysis rather than experimentation as a method of investigation.

Rapaport cites three additional sources of influence on Freud's professional development that are worth noting. First was his early exposure to Brentano and his "act psychology." Some of Brentano's concepts (intention, belief in reality) are considered by Rapaport to have influenced Freudian conceptions (e.g., the central role of instincts and the concepts of intention and of reality testing in Freud's ego psychology). Through Brentano, Freud was introduced to Kant and influenced away from the empirical views of "Anglo-Saxon" science. As Rapaport shows, Freud himself recognized the similarity of his views on unconscious determination to Kantian philosophy (Freud, S.; 1915*b*, p. 104).

Second and third sources of influence on Freud's thinking and writing were his interest in literature, and what Rapaport calls ". . . the Jewish tradition." These are seen to have played significant roles in his exposure to the subtleties of verbal communications and the nuances of language. These interests assisted him in expressing himself extremely well in writing (he was the recipient of the Goethe Prize for his writing) and at the same time permitted him to rely on the "intrinsic validity of his reasoning and descriptive writing" (Rapaport, 1959), in contrast to quantitative experimentation, as substantiating evidence for his theorizing.

Rapaport makes the final interesting suggestion that when viewed in terms of the broad *Zeitgeist*, Freud's idea of the relativity of man's behavior to his impulses followed upon Karl Marx's suggestion that man's view of the world was relative to his socio-economic status; and in turn was followed by Einstein's assertion that physical observation is relative to the observer's position. The three theories were, of course, independent observations of different types of events. The correspondence of the three ideas (if real as well as apparent) is indeed a worthwhile point to note in connection with the "spirit of the times."

We shall leave the further biographical development of Freud's life and the historic development of his thinking to others, as they have been so extensively explored.[5] It has been our intention only briefly to indicate the tradition and the setting in which Freud began. He was well trained and widely experienced in basic biological sciences and medicine. By the time he began his purely psychoanalytic work he had already earned a good reputation for his scientific papers on the nervous system, had published a number of well-received papers on neuroanatomic, neurophysiologic, and clinical subjects, and had written a book on aphasia in addition to the volume with Breuer on hysteria. He had also translated and partly edited several works of Charcot and Bernheim.

As Jones has shown (1953, vol. I), there is every evidence that Freud could have continued his strictly neurological work most successfully. His decision to reject the then currently accepted views on hysteria and to "fly in the face of authority" in persisting in the presentation of unpopular views was characteristic of Freud. To his credit, it must be noted that he was not only willing to propound and defend a position which was unpopular with his confreres and with the public at large, but he was a severe critic of his own work. Throughout his long professional career, Freud continually re-examined his own propositions and theories. When he recognized errors in his previous formulations, or when his continuing clinical practice and wide correspondence caused him to doubt an earlier position, he openly rejected his own views and revised his theories to reflect the new understandings he gained. And, unlike many other theorists, he continued to do this until his death at 83, despite a long and painful illness and despite the upheaval in his life as he was forced to flee his home in Vienna at the age of 81 to take refuge in London from the Nazi invasion of Austria.

As Jones has emphasized, in his exhaustive study of Freud and his works, this objectivity and continuous revision were sharply in con-

[5] Ernest Jones (1953–1957) presents a fascinating, detailed account of Freud's personal life and how he came to develop and carry forward his new ideas. Other, though less complete, accounts may be found in Bakan, 1958; Sachs, 1944; Wittels, 1924, 1931; and Rapaport, 1959.

trast to the often limited views of many of Freud's associates and followers who were (and are) more willing than Freud to make a cult of the psychoanalytic movement.

Let us turn now to the main topic of this chapter: the motivational theory in psychoanalysis. Although starting at the beginning—that is, with the founder of the movement, Sigmund Freud—we will at the same time start at the end, with Freud's posthumously published *Outline of Psychoanalysis* (1940), which, together with *The Problem of Anxiety* (1926) and *New Introductory Lectures on Psycho-analysis* (1933), bring together a fairly clear statement of the psychoanalytic position as Freud himself was able to finalize it. For our purposes, Freud's earlier views have only historic significance.[6]

THE QUESTION OF CONSCIOUSNESS

The psychology of Freud's time was predominantly a psychology of conscious content. In an attempt to parallel the discoveries of physics and chemistry, the "experimental psychologists" of the late nineteenth century were searching for the dimensions or elements of consciousness (see Boring, 1933). Their conviction that the proper field of study for their experimental philosophy was the content of the conscious mind prescribed introspection as their method and narrowed their focus to the correlates of physical stimulation in immediate experience.

Not all who wrote or worked in this new psychology were in agreement in this focusing on mental content, and some (e.g., Herbart, Lipps) had anticipated the importance of nonconscious processes.[7] But by far the main stream of psychological work was concentrated on an analysis of consciousness.

Freud did not reject consciousness as a primary source of data, but he saw such processes as having only ". . . an ephemeral quality . . . ," adhering to psychical processes only temporarily (1939). A psychology focused on consciousness would have many gaps in it, corresponding to the gaps in consciousness (1923, Chap. 1). For him, the unconscious was ". . . the true psychic reality. . . ."

[6] Robert Holt has pointed out (Personal Communication) that a contemporary statement of psychoanalysis based on Freud's own writing presents some difficulties, since Freud "had a tendency to leave earlier statements side by side with later ones that supplanted them." We have, despite this, tried to present the theory in as consistent a form as we could.

[7] Freud was neither the first nor the only theorist to dismiss consciousness in this way, as he himself notes in the *Interpretation of Dreams* (1900), though he did more to explore the nature of unconscious processes and to open the way for others to follow than had any of his predecessors. For a discussion of other theories see Miller (1942), Murphy (1932).

in its innermost nature it is as much unknown to us as the reality of the external world, and it is so incompletely presented by the data of consciousness as is the external world by the communications of our sense organs (1900, p. 542).

Consciousness plays the limited role of monitor, ". . . *a sense-organ for the perception of psychical qualities*" (1900, p. 544). All other aspects of mental life are unconscious (1940, Chap. 4). And it is on this that the investigator must concentrate.

THE NATURE OF THE UNCONSCIOUS

Freud was never embarrassed by not being able to "point at" the concepts with which he dealt. He was thus comfortably able to define the unconscious as ". . . any mental process the existence of which we are obliged to assume—because, for instance, we infer it in some way from its effects—but of which we are not directly aware" (1933, pp. 99–100).

This difficulty in specification was similar to the problems physicists have with terms like force, mass, attraction, etc., but in no way was it a handicap to the scientific usefulness of the concept involved.

Freud early conceived of the mental apparatus as topographically structured (1900). Nonconscious processes were of two kinds: *preconscious* and *unconscious*. The former included those processes which are able to become conscious—to slip in and out of consciousness, as it were—to be reproduced or remembered. The vast remainder of the mental processes are in the unconscious group. These ". . . have no such easy access to consciousness . . ." and can be brought to light only by the most devious routes and through the most penetrating analyses. It was to this large reservoir of experience that Freud reserved the name *unconscious proper*, and it was the one about which he was most curious.

How did material become unconscious? Why did it remain so? Under what conditions was it ever released? When, why, and in what form did it reappear? And, most important, how did its appearance, disappearance, and reappearance affect behavior? These were the questions which Freud sought to answer.

Now we must remember that Freud was an affirmed determinist. Behavior was caused. Since he had concluded that consciousness was too fragmentary to be a reliable causal basis for behavior, he felt sure that careful study of the operations of unconscious processes (and of the interrelations of the different levels of consciousness) would yield an underlying correlate system for behavior which would demonstrate scientific lawfulness.

Systematically analyzing unconscious causal chains, Freud was able to demonstrate dramatically that apparent errors in everyday speech and action—slips of the tongue, *faux pas*, accidents, etc.—were not such innocent happenstances as commonly thought, but were acts consistent with the motive structure of the personality involved.[8] Also, the contents of dreams and fantasies, whether these dreams or fantasies occurred in sleep or in waking states, were to be found meaningful when their latent aspects were analyzed in the context of unconscious motivation (see *Interpretation of Dreams* [1900]).[9]

In his continuing clinical observations on his patients, and with great care on himself as well (and to a minor extent even on his friends and relations), Freud confirmed his conviction that all behavior, no matter how slight or apparently insignificant, was at least in part unconsciously motivated. Such motivational bases might not be apparent in the behavior itself or in consciousness (this latter, itself understandable), but when the underlying unconscious chain of events that led to the behavior could be traced, causal relations became clear. What interested Freud greatly, and led to his later more developed conceptions of the workings of mind, was the fact that these relations, once presented to consciousness, were not recognized by his patients, and would often be strongly denied. This striking kind of finding, repeatedly observed, fit in with Freud's concern with an energy concept.[10] He was evolving a schema in terms of forces of relative strength which partly or wholly permitted material (and/or prevented it from) reaching a conscious state. This was a more fluid conception than the earlier topological divisions of levels of consciousness, and it included an energy concept.

[8] Many fascinating instances are traced by Freud in *The Psychopathology of Everyday Life* (1901).

[9] It may be useful here to call attention to Peters' criticisms (Peters, 1958) that Freud, by showing evidence for motivational determinism in *some* instances of errors and fantasies, was not entitled to draw the broad conclusion that *all* such cases are so determined.

[10] Robert Holt writes (personal communication to the authors): "The concept of energy was a pre-occupation of Freud's from the very beginning of his scientific work, considerably ante-dating any psychoanalytic model. When Freud was a student, energy was so much the rage, as stylish a concept as information is today, or perhaps even more so. The brilliant discoveries that the apparently different forms of physical energy (heat, light, mechanical, etc.) were interchangeable and interconvertible, was a profoundly exciting one, and it seemed to suggest that the work done by biological organisms, in all of the many different ways they used energy, could be looked on as a further instance of these transformations."

PSYCHIC ENERGY

Freud considered an energy concept essential, but never clearly or fully described the nature or the source of his early postulated "psychic energy." Examined historically, Freud's neurological training apparently led him to posit a kind of mechanical vibratory energy within the nervous system, deriving from the impingement of external, physical energy. This was consistent with neurological knowledge of the time. Later, when he went to a more purely psychological model, he seemed to treat psychic energy (and the later derived terms "libido" and "cathexis") as inferential abstractions without specific physical referents.

Hall (1954) has interpreted psychic energy to be one of the many transformations of metabolic energy. Organisms take in foodstuffs, metabolize and use them in a continual energy exchange with their environment. Some of the energy thus derived is used to drive the motor, some to heat the apparatus, and so forth. Energy could be transformed into electrical, thermal, chemical, and mechanical forms, a fact readily inferred from the different types of physical, chemical, and physiological measurements possible. Similarly, mechanical work is performed by the organism and can be measured in ergs, muscle fatigue, etc. Why, then, could one not conceive of a type of psychic energy to account for the kinds of *psychological* work performed inside the organism's nervous system—that is, thinking, perceiving, learning, remembering, and so on?

Freud himself was never so explicit. In his writings, he sometimes expressed psychic energy as the equivalent of excitation or stimulation, and other times he used a hydraulic model, in terms of storage and flow, not unlike the more specific model devised by Lorenz (see p. 70). Bellak et al. (1959) and Amacher (1962) show how Freud's thinking was influenced by the neurological concepts of his day and that he was fully aware of the changes taking place in physical theories of energy. As he shifted emphasis to a new conception of the mental apparatus, he simply never returned to a further elucidation or revision of the energy terms of his theory. It seems clear, however, that he never meant to imply anything vitalistic, mystical, or supernatural about his concept of psychic energy.[11] He presumed it likely that the method(s) of transformation of bodily to psychic energy, as well as

[11] Hall (1954) claims that Freud *explicitly* denied such qualities, and the late David Rapaport was also of this opinion (R. R. Holt, personal communication). We have been unable to document this claim directly, although it would be entirely consistent with his outlook to have written in this vein.

the reverse, could some day be known.[12] At any rate, he considered it quite consistent with the thinking of objective science to posit such a specific mental or psychic energy.

Further specification of quantitative and qualitative distinctions in psychic energy, and the circumstances of its production, distribution, and use, are intimately connected with the theory of instincts, so it is to this we will now turn.

THE PSYCHOANALYTIC THEORY OF INSTINCTS

The true purpose of the individual organism's life, Freud wrote in his final *Outline of Psychoanalysis,* is the satisfaction of its innate needs. These needs give rise to tensions, the forces behind which (the *instincts*) [13] ". . . represent the somatic demands on mental life" (Freud, 1938, p. 19). They are the ultimate cause of all activity.

In his *Instincts and Their Vicissitudes,* Freud (1915a) assigned four distinguishing characteristics to the instincts: their source, impetus, aim, and object. It may be instructive to look briefly at each of these.

1. *Source.* Internal bodily stimulation, whether produced as a result of chemical, mechanical, or other change, is "represented in mental life by an instinct" (Freud, 1915a, p. 64). These instinctual sources of stimulation are distinguished from the effects of external

---

[12] Freud, in essence posited a hypothetical state, disavowed any need for identifying its locus or mode of operation, and at the same time expressed his conviction that a means of translating this new type of energy into units of other types would some day be found. This theoretic problem, of some concern to philosophers of science, need not delay us here. Advanced students may wish to pursue further the question raised. For example, see MacCorquodale and Meehl (1948) on the distinction between hypothetical constructs and intervening variables.

[13] As many others have also pointed out, Freud actually used the German word *Trieb* (moving force), which was somewhat loosely translated as instinct. He did use the German *Instinkt* when speaking of *animal* (infrahuman) behavior, thus making the mistranslation even more obvious. Had the cognate term *drive* been used, much confusion would have been avoided and a more accurate picture of his intentions might have prevailed. As the word *drive* is not listed in Baldwin's dictionary (1911) and was apparently first introduced into psychological terminology by Woodworth in 1918, the word was probably not available as a translation of *Trieb* at the time Freud's writings were first translated into English. Hartmann, Kris, and Loewenstein (1949) compromise the matter by using the phrase "instinctual drives," whereas Colby (1955) and Rapaport (1959) speak directly of drives. In any case, what Freud described as *Trieb* appears in many ways to have closer affinity to the concept used by American learning theorists (see Chapter 10) than it does to that employed by the European ethologists (see Chapter 3). Fletcher (1957) offers an interesting and detailed comparison of the psychoanalytic and ethological concepts of instincts and their similarities with earlier instinct doctrines. Colby (1955) more briefly contrasts biological and psychoanalytic uses of the term.

stimuli on several grounds. First, they arise from the body itself (though they may be induced by some environmental manipulation, as in the withdrawal of a source of sustenance). Second, the instincts represent fairly constant (or as Fletcher has indicated, constantly recurring) stimulation as contrasted with the relatively momentary nature of external stimulation. And third, the organism may often escape external stimulation by removing itself from its presence. This is not possible with the stimulation from within.

2. *Impetus.* The impetus of an instinct is ". . . the amount of force or the measure of the demand upon energy which it represents" (Freud, 1915a, p. 65). This force or pressure is a function of the intensity of the need from which it arose, though Freud himself had little more to say regarding the impetus of the instincts, insofar as we can determine. His inclusion of impetus as an essential characteristic of the instincts shows us again his recognition of the necessity to think in energy terms, and perhaps his hope that eventual quantification of psychic energy could be achieved.

3. *Aim.* Although there are many avenues along which instinctual energy can be discharged, the aim of the instincts is basically to abolish the condition(s) of somatic stimulation from which they arose. Such "somatic modification . . . is experienced as satisfaction" (Freud, 1933, p. 133). In addition, since abolition of stimulation may not always be accomplished directly, instincts may have different intermediate aims. For example, in hunger, the final aim might be the abolition of stomach pangs, whereas intermediate aims would have to do with obtaining and consuming food. Fletcher draws our attention to the identity of this idea with the ethological concept of appetitive behavior (see p. 65 and Fletcher, 1957).

4. *Object.* Any person or thing in the environment or in the individual's own body that serves to satisfy the aim of an instinct may become its object. Although Freud considered the instincts themselves to be inherited, he did not believe that there was an innate connection between instincts and the object(s) through which satisfaction could be obtained. As a matter of fact, the object in or through which instinctual satisfaction is found may change ". . . any number of times in the course of the vicissitudes the instinct undergoes during life" (Freud, 1915a, p. 65), and this capacity for displacement is an integral part of the nature of instincts.[14]

---

[14] Freud paid considerable attention to this substitutability of one object for another as a means of instinctual gratification. It is the basis of his substitution and sublimation dynamisms.

The Nature of Instincts

The instincts are both *conservative* and *regressive*. They represent a kind of inertial force in organic life, an "organic elasticity," which conserves the organism by resisting change. One clinical manifestation of this regressive tendency of the instincts is the *repetition-compulsion*,[15] in which traumatic episodes are "relived" in the play experiences of children, in dreams and fantasies, and in therapy. Again, individuals tend to repeat over and over in their lives the patterns of interpersonal relation which have lost them friendships in the past, seeming never able to modify their behavior in each succeeding cycle. Freud saw the repetition-compulsion as a principle so important as to override the principle of pleasure, which ordinarily determined the primary processes of instinctual gratification (see later discussion). He used the concept of the repetition-compulsion also as a description of the ritual nature of tension-reduction procedures, showing how, again and again, each time the *status quo* is upset, the organism repeats the cycle of stimulus abolition. This automaticity is clear from the following quotation: ". . . the state, whatever it may be, which a living thing has reached, gives rise to a tendency to re-establish that state as soon as it has been abandoned" (Freud, 1940, p. 20). We should take note here of the fact, before moving on, that Freud saw this tendency to re-institute earlier forms as characteristic not only of individual lives but of the history of living matter. When he speaks of the re-establishment of earlier states he refers to both ontogenic and phylogenic conditions, and the earlier state may, at the extreme, be the inorganic state of the prehistory of the species (death being considered akin to this).

Freud based his descriptions of the nature of instincts on two grounds: his observations, and what he considered to be a "necessary postulate" regarding the functioning of the nervous system. This ran as follows: "The nervous system is an apparatus having the function of abolishing stimuli which reach it, or of reducing excitation to the lowest possible level, an apparatus which would even, if this were feasible, maintain itself in an altogether unstimulated condition . . ." (Freud, 1915a, p. 63). Now it is quite clear that this view of the nervous system, which was not without basis in the neurological thinking of Freud's middle years, is definitely not in keeping with our current

---

[15] Freud (1933, pp. 145–146) considered the repetition-compulsion to be an expression of the conservative nature of the instincts as well (an "instinct of recovery"), in much the same way as homeostatic mechanisms are seen to operate (see Jones, 1957, III, pp. 268–269) to conserve or restore what is (see Chapter 7). In this sense, conservative and regressive are two aspects of the same process.

understanding of nervous function. We recognize that the nervous system is continually active, and probably requires a certain amount of continuing stimulation in order to remain healthy.[16] Fletcher (1957) also criticizes this "postulate" in some detail and adds the further comment that the evidence for approach as well as avoidant behavior in the instinctual actions of lower species would be inconsistent with this view. Certain forms of tropistic behavior (see p. 41), for example, would require an extremely broad redefinition of what is meant by stimulus reduction in order to be included.

Freud introduced this "biological" postulate in an attempt to show how instinctual stimulation differs from external stimulation in the demands it places on the organism (e.g., relative persistence and inescapability), and even if we disregard the erroneousness of Freud's conception of nervous function, the distinction remains a valid one (see his definition of source, p. 598).

With regard to observation, we have already mentioned the clinical appearance of the repetition-compulsion, and can further suggest that insofar as general behavioral observation is concerned, the "tension-reduction" model,[17] of which Freud's neural postulate is an extreme example (in that it makes tension-reduction an innate function of the nervous system), would appear to be descriptive of large categories of behavior sequences.

As has been implied here, then, the validity of the description of the instincts as conservative and regressive need not rest on the assumption from which it is drawn. But to demonstrate that behaviors *may* subserve instincts whose sole aim is tension-reduction does not mean that all behaviors result from such "negative" instinctual sources, nor that they serve this aim. Yet it was Freud's belief that the instincts *are* the ultimate cause of *all* activity. He did, it is true, acknowledge a role for external stimulation, and, as we shall see later, ascribed an autonomous role to the ego as well. But basically, he held that the wide variety

---

[16] There is a wealth of neurological, neurophysiological, and neuropsychological evidence to support this point. Research on the electrical activity of the brain (Brazier, 1959), on the reticular system (Jasper et al., 1958; Magoun, 1958; Lindsley, 1957), and the recently reported series of studies on sensory deprivation (Solomon et al., 1961) clearly contradict Freud's postulate of an inactive nervous system.

[17] The "tension-reduction" model is perhaps the most widely met motivational hypothesis in biology and psychology today. It is the core assumption in the ethological position, provides the essence of most homeostatic models, is the key to the psychoanalytic theory of motivation, and was seen again (Chapter 10) as the fundamental motivational principle of one of the leading "schools" of American learning theory.

and complexity of creative human enterprises were motivated by instincts, the aim of which is the abolition of stimulation. This was, and is, a rather extreme and one-sided stand.[18]

Freud recognized the apparent paradox between his position and the "fact" that behaviors sometimes do not seem to be tension reducing (e.g., as in some instances of repetition-compulsion), but felt that it presented no insurmountable difficulty. The key to the solution lies in the fact that although the aims of the instincts are tension-reduction, the means for satisfying these aims are not immediately and directly available to the organism. Freud goes so far as to suggest that the whole fabric of civilization is a result of this inability of individuals to obtain direct and immediate gratification. Instinctual energy thereby becomes displaced onto persons, objects, and activities other than those directly subserving tension-reduction, and rather elaborate behavioral and social structures may result. The dynamics of such energic displacement both lead to and result from an elaborate personality organization, the workings of which constitute the processes of behavior. To gain some insight into these processes, we shall have to examine, at least briefly, some of the structural postulates that Freud employed in describing personality organization. But first we will look at the instincts themselves.

The Basic Instincts. Instincts derive from bodily needs. Since there are many body areas capable of producing stimulation, each is a potential source of instinctual energy, and thus a large number and variety of separate instincts can be distinguished. Freud recognized this possibility, and believed that eventually physiology would be able to sort out and classify these needs and their attendant instincts. Functionally, however, these component instincts appeared to reduce to two fundamental groups—the life and the death instincts.

The life instincts include those forces which subserve (1) reproduction and (2) life maintenance. The sexual instincts make up the first group, while such drives as hunger and thirst compose the second. Because of the importance attributed to them in the mental life of individuals, the sexual instincts were from the beginning explored quite extensively by the psychoanalysts, and an elaborate theory of psychosexual development was arrived at.

By sexual instincts, Freud meant those instincts based on stimulation from the different erogenous zones of the body.[19] These instincts de-

[18] Rapaport has offered a more moderate view on this point, which will be discussed later in this chapter.

[19] Distributed widely, these zones include foci in the regions of the body orifices—the mouth, the anus, and the genital sexual apparatus. Sexual, for Freud,

velop independently and successively, and only in puberty do they become coordinate in serving an overall reproductive function. Failure to progress through the stages successfully, due to traumatic or inadequate conditions of rearing, was held responsible for the various displacements of sexual energy (libido) onto inappropriate objects, persons, or activities. Thus certain perversions, for example, could be understood as inappropriate investments of sexual libido resulting from a fixation at one stage or some other breakdown in normal psychosexual development. By the same token, the enforced displacement of some of the libido of the sexual instincts, in the normal frustrations of development, was seen to provide the excess of energy usable for social and cultural activities. We shall come back to this point.

The facts of infantile sexuality, and its apparent importance in early development in shaping the personality organization, first led Freud to consider the sexual instincts as a separate basic group, and it was in this early stage of his theory that he thought to differentiate the types of energy, labeling the sexual energy *libido*, so as to differentiate it from that of the "ego instincts" (i.e., those of self-preservation). However, he also felt that the life-maintenance instincts play an important role as well, and, rather than being in opposition to each other, the two appear to function side-by-side as aspects of an overall life instinct, *Eros*. As his thinking developed, libido came to represent the energy of the life instinct generally, as contrasted to the energy of the death instinct.

The death instincts (alternately called the destructive instincts) were never so clearly defined as were the life instincts, although they are considered to be equally innate and as important as the latter in Freud's final presentation of his theory.

Three factors seem to have led to the concept of a death instinct: (1) dissatisfaction with the earlier explanation of aggression as a manifestation of the sexual instincts (the widespread occurrence of cruelty and destruction of the First World War profoundly impressed Freud); (2) the conviction that the repetition-compulsion principle was more

encompassed much more than just the adult genital sexual impulsion for which the term is commonly used. Infantile sexuality refers to the pleasure obtained from stimulating the mouth (through sucking, biting, etc.), the anus (through sphincter manipulation), and the genital areas (through rubbing or touching). Freud did not seek to equate infantile and adult sexuality, but chose the same term by way of emphasizing the relatedness of the two and the fact that pregenital "partial drives" or constitutional defects or unusual sensitivity of some zone may become incorporated as part of adult sexual activity (see Freud, 1905). Much public misunderstanding was engendered by early critics who could not or would not recognize the important distinctions that were being made.

fundamental and all-pervasive than the more limited sexual and self-preservative instincts could explain; and, most important, (3) the need to find a force to counteract the then monistic life instincts. Freud was, as we have indicated, a "psychic dualist." On the basis of his clinical observations, he was convinced that the personality was the battleground for the sometimes fierce struggle of opposing forces, and this intrapsychic conflict was so fundamental to the nature of organisms as to necessarily be rooted in the instincts.

But the broadest basis of all for the death instinct was seen by Freud to lie in the universal philosophic and scientific principle of entropy. Quoting Schopenhauer, Freud dramatically stated that "the goal of all life is death." But at the same time, he points out that this principle stands side by side with an opposing life instinct (Freud, 1933, p. 146). The life instincts, though eventually succumbing to death, in a way are permitted to "choose the time and place" in accordance with the needs they represent. They may postpone death, but obviously only up to a point.

Freud derived his death instinct in part from Fechner's stability principle. But, as Fletcher (1957) points out, Fechner's principle actually fits the conception of a dynamic homeostasis (see p. 317) better than it does the notion of death or disintegration. However, as Flügel (1949) has shown, Fechner described four different types of stability, one of which, "absolute stability," might be seen as the equivalent of death (see also Ashby's definitions of stability, p. 345). Freud and others have sought support for the concept of a universal principle of death in physics and in biology. But Jones (1957, Vol. III, pp. 276–277) cites Kapp (1931) and Penrose (1931) in physics and Brun (1953) in biology to show that such parallels are unfounded.[20]

Whether its universality could be established or not, the concept of a death instinct [21] was given a significant role by Freud in his motiva-

[20] As the reader will have surmised, there is a very close parallel between these arguments regarding the death instinct and the discussion with regard to open and closed systems, entropy, and homeostasis in the section on cybernetics in Chapter 7. An excellent discussion of this question is offered by Flügel (1949), some of whose points we shall summarize later.

[21] Alternatively using the terms "death instinct" and "destructive instinct," as well as "death wish," Freud never adopted a name for it, as he had used Eros to describe first the sexual instincts and then the life instincts. Nor did he find a name for the energy of the death instinct, as libido was used to describe its opposite. Jones (1957, Vol. III, p. 273) tells us that Freud did use Thanatos in this way in conversation, though never in writing. Stekel (1909) and later Federn (1952) have written of Thanatos as a death wish or instinct, and Flügel (1955)

tional system. Unlike the life instincts, the death instincts perform their work silently, and because of this, it is said, it has not been possible to identify their source very clearly. However, a vague attribution to the catabolic processes has been suggested (Freud, 1923, p. 56; Jones, 1957, Vol. III, p. 275).

Only in the case of aggression, which Freud attributed to the death instinct, are the manifestations visible. Normally operating internally, and having the goal of death (the individual is said to harbor an unconscious wish to die), the forces of Thanatos are fused with (and/or counterbalanced by) the forces of Eros. Aggression may be (and usually is assumed to be) diverted outward and manifests itself in sadism, destruction, and murder; later it may be turned inward again, as self-aggression sometimes breaks through as in masochism, self-mutilation, self-derogation, or defamation. As we earlier noted, the intensity of the hatred, violence, and destruction of the First World War helped convince Freud of the deep-rooted instinctual origin of aggression and of the need to account for it directly in his motivation theory.

Interaction of the life and death instincts. Freud's final description of the aims of the two basic instincts shows clearly how diametrically opposed they are: ". . . the aim of the first of these basic instincts is to establish ever greater unities and to preserve them thus—in short, to bind together; the aim of the second, on the contrary, is to undo connections and so to destroy things" (Freud, 1940, p. 20). How then could he account for ". . . the whole variegation of the phenomena of life"? The answer is a very simple one: the two instincts interact— "with and against each other"—thereby producing all possible combinations of effects. And indeed, many examples of behavior can be given in which elements of these polar forces can be detected. Freud offers the example of eating, which subserves the life instinct of maintenance, and yet includes the death-instinct-derived destructive acts of tearing, biting, chewing, etc. The commonly recognized painful elements of sexual excitement and intercourse further demonstrate such interaction, as do the more extreme behaviors of masochism and sadism. Finally of interest is the appearance of sudden shifts in balance between the two, as when love suddenly turns to hate (or the reverse). Our daily tabloids constantly remind us of these "love tragedies."

But to go any farther in our discussion of psychoanalytic motivation theory, we must give some attention to the structural concepts of the mind, for it is through these that the instincts are said to function.

finds this term appearing in the psychoanalytic literature since the early 1930's. Other analysts have used "mortido" or "destrudo" as a name for this death wish.

THE MENTAL APPARATUS

The tripartite division of the mind into conscious, preconscious, and unconscious portions was and is an extremely useful one clinically. However, as Freud went along, he found that these divisions did not correspond with what he was conceiving as the functional units of mental life. The unconscious (Ucs.) is not identical with the instincts or with the primary process. He found it necessary to treat separately of two aspects of what ·is not conscious, and to deal with an aspect of consciousness and unconsciousness simultaneously as a single entity. Ultimately, the terms unconscious, preconscious, and conscious became merely descriptive.

To deal with the phenomena more adequately, Freud evolved a second tripartite division, this one even less operational. Its three components, called the *id, ego,* and *superego,* more closely corresponded to the functioning units of the mental apparatus, as he saw them. These, then, became the structural units of the mind—or, as modern psychoanalysts prefer, a structural model of the personality. The dynamics of behavior could now be examined as a function of the interaction of these parts.

The Id. The oldest, most primitive of the mental provinces is called the *id.*[22] "It is the obscure inaccessible part of our personality . . . [and can be imagined only as] . . . a chaos, a cauldron of seething excitement . . ." (Freud, 1933, pp. 103–104). "It contains everything that is inherited, that is present at birth, that is fixed in the constitution —above all . . . the instincts . . ." (Freud, 1940, p. 14).

The id is the reservoir of instinctual energy. Freud therefore presumed it to be in direct contact with somatic processes from which these instinctual needs derived, but he would not speculate as to where or how this occurred. Basically, he saw the id as unorganized, illogical, timeless, knowing "no values, no good or evil, no morality" (Freud, 1933, p. 105).

The id is regulated by the two principles by which the instincts operate, namely, the *Nirvana principle* [23] and the *pleasure principle.*

---

[22] Freud used the German words *Es* (It) and *Ich* (I) to represent the impersonal and personal parts of the mind, respectively. As Jones (1957, Vol. III, p. 280) and Healy, Bronner, and Bowers (1930, p. 37) have noted, the translation of these terms into their Latin equivalents, *Id* and *Ego,* makes them less confusing when used in English contexts than would the English words *It* and *I* be, which is certainly the case.

[23] Freud credits Barbara Low with suggesting this name, which he first applied to the pleasure principle (Freud, 1920, p. 76). But after he evolved the life-death instinct polarity, he came to see a difference in the operating principles of the two

The first of these principles, Nirvana, states that the organism seeks to maintain "at as low a level as possible the quantities of excitation flowing in to it." This will be recognized as the primary aim of the death instinct, and as Fletcher (1957) reminds us, is based on the same "necessary postulate" of nervous function, thus subject to the same criticisms (see p. 600). The regulation of the energies of the id is shared by the Nirvana and pleasure principles. The latter, related to the life instincts, is also concerned with tension reduction, but not in the absolute and quantitative way described earlier. The pleasure principle has as its goal the increase of *affective* pleasure and the decrease in *affective* unpleasure or pain.[24] But Freud recognized that there are such things as "pleasurable tension and 'painful' lowering of tension." He therefore referred the operation of the pleasure principle to an ill-defined "qualitative" aspect of tension reduction. "It is probable . . . that what is felt as pleasure or unpleasure is not the *absolute* degree of the tensions but something in the rhythm of their changes" (Freud, 1940, p. 16). This was, unfortunately, as far as he carried the distinction. We think it is important to note his recognition of such a difference, however, despite the fact that many psychoanalysts today tend to disregard this point and to treat the pleasure principle as though it were a single tension-reduction hypothesis. It would seem worth noting that this distinction has some resemblance to the kind of distinction McClelland and Peak have more recently introduced (see p. 374 and p. 386), and to the adaptation-level hypothesis of Helson (see p. 336) on which McClelland draws. Once again, our attention is drawn to the two kinds of stability implied by these two principles, and we shall come back to this important matter once more (see p. 615 below).

The *primary process*, the means by which the id operates, consists in discharging instinctual energy [25] as soon as possible, and in disregard of reality. Ordinarily, such energy will be discharged, in the derivative forms of *impulses* or *wishes*, through any directly available motor channel. Thus reflexive bladder-emptying, spitting, blinking, thrashing

and assigned Nirvana as the regulating principle of the death instinct, seeing the pleasure principle as evolving out of a struggle of the life and death instincts and, as a result of the victory of the former, serving to modify the Nirvana principle in regulating the id.

[24] Rapaport (1959) makes the specific point that in Freud's theory, pleasure and unpleasure are *not* affects but abstract concepts, only roughly coordinate with feeling states. We would agree that this interpretation fits Freud's meaning better, but there is no question that Freud intended the analogy at least to a change in affective tone as the guiding cue system of the pleasure principle.

[25] Freud uses the word *cathexis* to represent psychic energy occupying or investing a particular channel or process.

would be used as means of direct discharge. However, many wishes cannot be fulfilled so easily (as, for example, hunger, where ingestible food must be present in the mouth). In these cases, the primary process produces, from the memory system of the organism, a mental image of the desired object and, by cathecting it as if it were real, fulfills the wish. Now it will be recalled that the id is irrational and illogical. It is unable to distinguish between image and reality. Some of what one observes in the play of children, in the dreams and fantasies of normal adults, and in the hallucination of psychotics can be considered instances of this process.[26]

It is obvious that a hungry person cannot live on images alone (!), and that bread exists only in reality. Thus the primary process must fall short of its objective of wish fulfillment; it can reduce tension only temporarily. By virtue of this impasse (and with successive occurrences of it) a portion of the id becomes differentiated into a new structure capable of perceiving reality, and able to mediate between the id and the external world. This new structure is the *ego*.[27]

The Ego. Like the id, the ego "pursues pleasure and seeks to avoid unpleasure" (Freud, 1940, p. 16), but its pursuit takes account of the requirements of external reality, and is thus said to be governed by the *reality principle*. As the ego develops, so does the reality principle come to replace the pleasure principle for that part of the id differentiated as ego, "forced upon the ego" as it were in the interest of self-preservation. The organism is now governed by the pursuit of realistic gratification: it discharges instinctual energy by realistic interaction with the environment. Freud writes: "Actually, the substitution of the reality-principle for the pleasure-principle denotes no dethronement of the pleasure-principle, but only a safeguarding of it. A momentary pleasure, uncertain in its results, is given up, but only in order to gain in a new way an assured pleasure coming later" (Freud, 1911, p. 18). The ego develops out of ". . . what was originally a cortical layer [of the id], provided with organs for receiving stimuli and with apparatus for protection against excessive stimulation" (Freud, 1940, p. 15). It thus mediates between the id and the external world. The ego thereby controls the motor apparatus, and any overt expression of a wish must

[26] The distinction between the primary process and the more rational secondary process was first made in Freud's *Project* (1895), in some detail in relation to the analysis of dreams (Freud, 1900), and later extended to describe id function. Jones (1953, Vol. I) considers this distinction to be one of Freud's truly great discoveries.

[27] A recent reformulation of this proposition by Hartmann, Kris, and Loewenstein (1946) is discussed later in this chapter (see p. 636).

channel through it. Thus the ego withholds the discharge of cathexis until, by reality testing, it can determine that an appropriate object is actually present in the environment.

The ego performs its task by (1) observing accurately what exists in the external world (perceiving), (2) recording these experiences carefully (remembering), and (3) modifying the external world in such a way as to satisfy the instinctual wishes (acting). Failing this last, the ego must hold off the discharge of energy until such modification can be brought about or an appropriate substitute found.

The *secondary process*, the ego's principal mode of operation, involves continuous reality testing by comparison of the memory images of previous satisfiers with those present in the environment. Realistic thinking allows trial exploration of the environment without danger to the organism. In Freud's words, the ego "interpolates between desire and action the procrastinating factor of thought." In order to accomplish its functions, the ego is highly organized, in contact both with the conscious perceptions of reality and with the libidinal desires of the id, and performs its "executive" function by virtue of its primarily autonomous apparatuses of perceiving, remembering, thinking, and acting. By way of summary, let us quote Freud's last description of ego activity:

Its psychological function consists in raising the processes in the id to a higher dynamic level . . . ; its constructive function consists in interposing between the demand made by an instinct and the action that satisfies it, an intellective activity which, after considering the present state of things and weighing up earlier experiences, endeavors by means of experimental actions to calculate the consequences of the proposed line of conduct. In this way the ego comes to a decision whether the attempt to obtain satisfaction is to be carried out or postponed or whether it may not be necessary for the demand of the instinct to be altogether suppressed as being dangerous . . . (Freud, 1940, p. 110).

Finally, we turn to the question of energy in the ego. Freud, in his earlier writings (before 1923), saw the ego as having its own energy supplies (the ego instincts). He then changed his view to suggest that *all* energy comes via the id. The ego, by virtue of its position as a mediary between the id and reality (where energy is discharged), is able to "capture" libido from the id and thus become the storehouse of all libidinal reserves. This is accomplished by what Freud calls the "trick" of the ego in identifying itself with desired objects (i.e., by offering itself to the id as a love object) and so obtaining the libidinal cathexes which these objects themselves would ordinarily receive. Likewise, when cathexes are withdrawn from objects in the real world, the energy resides in the ego.

That the ego must use considerable energy for its psychological functions is apparent. In addition, as we shall see shortly, energy is needed for the production of anxiety, an activity exclusively attributed to the ego. However, there is some disagreement as to where this energy derives. Holt (in personal communication) has drawn our attention to the fact that Freud, despite his stand on id-derived energy, continued to imply, occasionally, a nondrive source of neutral (hyper-cathectic) energy freely available to the ego for its everyday work. Hartmann (1958) has recently revived this earlier view that the ego "apparatuses of primary autonomy" have their own sources of energy, a position concurred in by such other major current psychoanalytic theorists as Rapaport, Gill, and Holt. Holt (personal communication), for example, argues that R. W. White's collection of evidence about effectance and competence should strongly suggest the need to assume a second source of energy (see p. 615).

The Superego. The third aspect of the personality, and the last to become differentiated in the child's growth,[28] is the *superego.* Just as the ego develops from the id, the superego forms a part of the ego and yet remains functionally separable. Through the ego's contact with the outside world during the child's long period of dependency on its parents, certain consistent patterns of influence are experienced and internalized via identification. These patterns reflect the values—that is, the ethics, morals, ideals, and taboos—of the culture as they are interpreted by and through the parents or their surrogates. These values are represented to the child in terms of the rewarding and punishing responses of the parents (or their surrogates) to the actions of the child.

Adapting to reality—particularly the reality of frustration, the actual loss of a parent, or the loss of an early relationship to a parent—the child identifies himself with his parent (thus assuring a greater frequency of reward and a lesser frequency of punishment). He incorporates, or *introjects,* values insofar as they are components of his conception of the parent.[29] The ego, or rather the superego (which is what this introjected portion of the ego is called), thus acquires an internal means of judging good from bad, and awarding itself either

---

[28] Quite a few modern theorists agree with Melanie Klein that the superego develops *very* early, about as soon as the ego.

[29] Freud notes that in the case of the loss of a love object, ". . . one often compensates . . . by identifying . . . ; one sets it up again inside one's ego, . . . object-choice regresses . . . to identification" (Freud, 1933, p. 91).

self-esteem, shame, or guilt, as previously it was possible to distinguish pleasant from unpleasant (the function of the id), and real from unreal (the function of the ego).

The superego contains two subsystems: the *ego ideal*, a sort of idealized abstraction (sometimes unreal) of the values for which rewards have been obtained; and the *conscience*, representing unresolved tensions and punished or forbidden areas of activity.[30] Behaviors, but more important still, thoughts preceding behaviors (now available to the superego as part of the personality), are assessed with regard to their approximation to these abstracted good-bad concepts in the superego. Ideas or actions which approach the model of the ego ideal give rise to an increase in self-respect, or pride, much as though ". . . it had made some precious acquisition"; whereas thoughts or acts that receive the censure of the conscience give rise to feelings of guilt, shame, and dread, the latter corresponding ". . . precisely to a child's dread of losing his parents' love" (Freud, 1940, p. 122).

Psychoanalysts point out that although it is derived from the parental model, the conscience is often considerably more severe (and the ego ideal more ideal) than the real model set by the parents. This would appear to occur because it is the perceived and fantasied parent—actually the model of the parents' superego—which is incorporated, rather than the real one. (Thus the phrase "do as I say, not as I do" might not be inaccurate!)

It is characteristic of the superego to "strive for perfection," as contrasted with the ego's striving for reality. The superego contains not only the model of the perceived parental personality, but also the ethnic, national, and family traditions, the demands of the immediate social milieu, and the later influences of others, such as teachers, admired public figures, and even abstract social ideals [31] (Freud, 1940, p. 17). But each of the later influences is in turn reacted to or incorporated as a function of the earliest superego structure evolved in the relations with the parents.

Insofar as the objectives of the superego are "perfection" rather than "reality," it would be inevitable that a source of conflict between the

---

[30] After making these formal distinctions, Freud did not always follow them very consistently.

[31] Schafer has recently re-examined Freud's development of the superego concept, and concludes that Freud intended there to be a "loving and beloved aspect of the super-ego" (Schafer, 1960, p. 186), as well as a self-punitive one. Thus as object hate is transformed into self-hate, so ". . . in the benign aspect of the super-ego . . . object love is turned around . . . into self-love or narcissism felt as pride and security in relation to society and destiny as well as one's own conscience and ideals" (p. 187).

ego and the superego would exist. And insofar as the superego, representing the moralistic side of the personality, would oppose those instinctual aims of the id that society requires to be inhibited (i.e., sexual expression), a conflict with the id might also be expected. Indeed, in its functioning, the superego is said to side at times with the ego against the id, and at times with the id against the ego, depending on the coincidence of goals of the moment.

RELATION OF QUALITATIVE AND STRUCTURAL ASPECTS OF MIND

A word seems in order regarding the relationships between the two tripartite divisions of mind. On the one hand, Freud had made a good case for a division into the systems of conscious, preconscious, and unconscious, and then later on, he presented arguments for reconceptualization in terms of id, ego, and superego. How are these related?

In the first place, we must recall that these are both structural abstractions, bearing no direct relation to neurological or physiological reference points in the brain or elsewhere. The topographical systems (Ucs. and Pcs.-Cs.) constituted a preliminary model which was useful in describing *levels of availability* of materials in the mind. For various reasons (internal inconsistencies, etc.) Freud abandoned this model for the new structural one of id-ego-superego. Conscious, preconscious, and unconscious were retained as *qualities* of mental processes, rather than as structural systems.

Figure 12–1 presents two diagrams, which Freud proposed at different stages of his work, possibly representing the relation between the mental qualities and the structural system variables. The first was offered in 1923 (p. 29), while the second appeared in Freud's *New Introductory Lectures* in 1933 (p. 111).

We can see from these diagrams that no clear boundary lines are drawn between the qualities of consciousness, nor are there sharp lines of demarcation between the divisions id-ego-superego. These were left deliberately vague, and Freud warned his audience *not* to ". . . imagine sharp dividing lines such as are artificially drawn in . . . political geography." One ". . . cannot do justice to the characteristics of the mind by means of linear contours . . ." (1933, p. 110). He sought only to relay relative relations of parts—as for example that access of the id to the external world lies through the ego. And even upon presenting the second diagram, Freud offered the correction that the space devoted to the unconscious id ". . . ought to be incomparably greater than that given to the ego or to the preconscious" (1933, p. 110).

The reader may note a section marked "repressed" in both diagrams. The significance of this area will be discussed in the next section of this chapter, but we may here note that in the case of repressed materials in the unconscious there is a barrier to free movement from one system to another (in either model).

Examining the relationships, we see that the id is entirely unconscious, having no access to consciousness except through the ego. The ego, on the other hand, spans all three levels of consciousness, as does the superego. Thus we could expect direct "communication" between the ego and the superego, the ego and the id, or the id and the superego. The first of these alone could occur at the conscious or preconscious level. Since the id is the repository of the instincts, it is clear that at no time are the instincts present in consciousness, except via a transformation into ego or superego derivatives.

The fact that biological energies become psychic energies in the id, but yet can find expression only through the "executive" function of the ego, places emphasis on the nature of the early ego development and the adequacy with which the integration is effected among the three agencies of mind and reality. Neuroses and psychoses as well have their origin here. Since the ego develops in relation to the real external world, pathology may be defined in terms of a loss or distor-

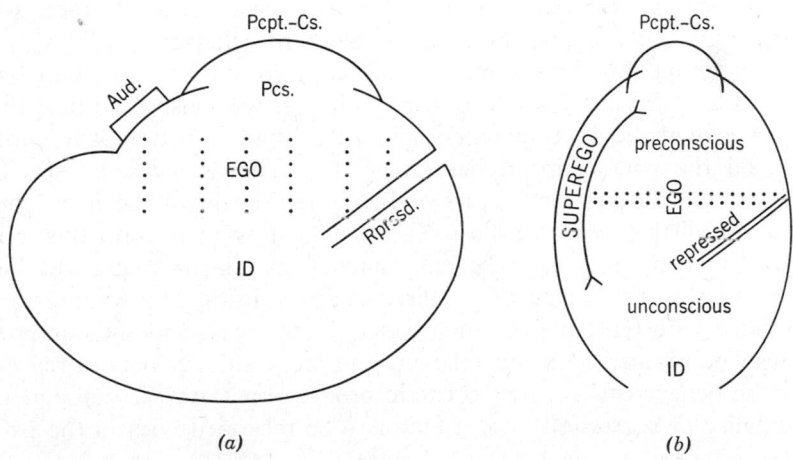

(a)   *(b)*

Figure 12–1. Two diagrammatic representations of mental apparatus. Figure 12–1*a* is modified by permission from Freud (1923, p. 29), and Figure 12–1*b* from Freud (1933, p. 111).

Pcpt. Cs. = perceptual-conscious system; Pcs = preconscious; Rprssd = repressed, Aud. = "auditory lobe."

tion of reality contact. In the case of the neuroses, reality is ignored rather than denied, whereas in the psychoses, the ego, in the service of the id, withdraws from a part of reality (Freud, 1924). Freud summarizes this for the psychoses by saying

This is in complete agreement with the clinical experience that the precipitating cause of the outbreak of a psychosis is either that reality has become intolerably painful or that the instincts have become extraordinarily intensified—both of which, in view of the rival claims made by the id and the external world upon the ego, must produce the same effect upon it (1940, p. 114).

Thus *ego strength* is, in the final analysis, the principal measure of mental health. But let us emphasize, once again, that the strength of the ego may be measured only in terms of the adequacy with which it can maintain an effective integration of the three aspects of personality in relation to external reality. And we come back, therefore, to the realization that although this excursion into parts of the personality is useful to an understanding of the functions of the living organism, in the final analysis, they do not exist as separate entities, but as a more-or-less integrated whole.

THE DYNAMICS OF BEHAVIOR

Having now briefly examined the nature of the instincts and the hypothetical systems of the personality in which they operate, we next turn to a consideration of the dynamics of behavior.

Throughout this discussion, we must keep in mind the dictum that "the child is the father of the man." That is, we must recognize the importance of the developmental point of view to any attempt to comprehend the personality dynamics of the adult. Freud laid especial emphasis on the first few years of life as setting down the basic patterns for all that was to follow.[32] Actually, he went beyond this. His views of evolution were what are called Lamarckian—that is, he believed in the inheritance of acquired characteristics. His writings are sprinkled with references to such concepts as a racial unconscious, and, as may be recalled from his characterization of the instincts as regressive, he believed that a phylogenetic progression (and the consequent possibility of regression) was a factor to be reckoned with in the psy-

[32] Hall and Lindzey (1957) point out, however, that despite this emphasis, Freud rarely studied children directly, drawing upon the adult recollections of his patients as the primary data source for his understanding of early development. Of course other psychoanalysts (e.g., Anna Freud [1945], Erikson [1950], Melanie Klein [1932]) have made rather extensive studies of children within the framework of psychoanalytic theory.

chic life of the individual (e.g., see earlier discussion of death instinct).

The libidinal wishes—arising in the soma—are first expressed directly via the primary processes of the id in accordance with the Nirvana and pleasure principles. Change occurs as a consequence (although perhaps not exclusively so) of the failure of primitive behavior to fulfill adequately the purposes of tension-reduction.[33] This change, described as a modification of the id into ego ("the taming of the passions"), is the first imposition of organization on the otherwise loosely ordered, illogical, raw structure of mind. This is accomplished by interposing a series of psychological structures between the impulses of the id and the real world in which the energy of these impulses must find release. One must recognize the importance of necessity here. This structuring comes about only because survival would be impossible without it. (There is no intended implication of teleology here. It is not the "purpose" of the personality to survive, in the sense that it "chooses" to do so. It is rather meant that organisms that do survive do so as a result of the development of intermediary ego structures and functions.) The interpolated functions—the carrying out of psychological work of the organism—consist in such processes as perceiving, remembering, judging, discriminating, abstracting, generalizing, thinking, and reasoning, as well as feeling and acting. Through them, the organism may act *selectively* in the environment, may use prior experiences of successful and unsuccessful energy release (that is, those behaviors which produced pleasure as opposed to those which did not or which caused pain) in determining whether and how to act or to withhold action, and so on.

Since the effectiveness of action in the outside world depends not only on physical reality but on the more arbitrary social "reality" of the culture in which the individual lives, a special aspect of the ego must deal with this, and the superego is conceived for this purpose (see later discussion, in Erikson's work, of ego identity).

We have tried to stress the fact that "higher level" functioning comes about only as a result of the failure of simpler levels of function to

[33] R. W. White (1959, 1960) and Rapaport (1960) have each attacked this view that change results from failure to reduce drives. White claims that this libido theory is inadequate to account for exploratory, manipulative, and play activities in the absence of known primary drives. He offers instead a *competence* model, in which such activities are motivated by *effectance*, namely, the production of environmental change, and lead to the development of a sense of competence. Rapaport (1960), on the other hand, denies that psychoanalytic theory *is* a simple tension-reduction theory, pointing to repeated emphasis (in treatments of conflict, defenses, and anxiety) on tension-maintaining and tension enhancing behaviors. (See discussion of new ego theories later in this chapter.)

achieve tension release.[34] Thus frustration or conflict (either real or imagined) is at the core of all personality growth. But how do the changes take place?

Identification, Displacement, and Sublimation

Contributing significantly to the maturation of behavior are three processes or mechanisms which we have already met in our earlier discussions: *identification, displacement,* and *sublimation.* The last of these, akin to the more generalized notion of neutralization (see Rapaport, 1960), is possibly the most important.

We have used *identification* to refer to the process by which the child seeks to model its own behavior after that of the parent or another person—and thus makes more likely the gratification of its needs (since the model chosen would ordinarily appear much more successful than the child in obtaining satisfactions). The models are usually the parents, first, but children tend to incorporate features of other personalities, and of impersonal objects and ideas as well, as their experience widens. In the final analysis, we could speak of the incorporated model as a montage of impressions from many sources. It may be noted that one important dimension of individual differences is the harmoniousness of integration of these impressions (see Erikson, 1950, 1953).

The concept of *displacement* is used in several different ways by Freud. Displacement generally refers to the attachment of energy (cathexis) to objects other than those originally chosen as means of tension release. This comes about either because of the unavailability of the original object in the real world, or because of the opposition to instinctual wishes or fears by anticathexes within the personality. Displacements may replace displacements so long as energy discharge does not take place (and provided sufficient energy remains). When used in connection with the primary process, displacement refers to an unrealistic, self-defeating, fluid transfer of psychic energy from one representation to another. In this case, each successive displacement may be less appropriate than the prior choice, and a less complete energy discharge takes place. On the other hand, in the secondary process, displacements may lead to choices that are *more* appropriate, as a function of the operation of the reality principle, energy being directed toward objects that can be attained, and away from those that can't. Thus, for example, if a wife is a displacement for a mother, it is obvious that realistic and virtually complete discharge of genital sexual

---

[34] The reference here is not to tension as a *felt* state, but an abstract concept referring to accumulation of cathectic energy.

tensions can occur via the displacement, but *not* without it! [35] Changes of this sort are clearly adaptive.

Freud used the term *sublimation* to describe the deflection (i.e., displacement or channeling) [36] of instinctual energy from its original (libidinal) aim to some socially desirable activity or object, as, for example, the creative products of the arts and sciences. This process has sometimes also been called *substitute-formation* or *externalization*. Such substitutions, or displacements, lead to the inclusion of a large number of activities and objects—some only remotely associated with primary tension-release—in the ego structure. This essentially adaptive ego structure formation becomes the basis for many of our varied and complex interests and social actions. In essence, whenever the direct expression of instinctual energies is threatening to the organism (see next section), they are aim-inhibited (i.e., desexualized). And since only a portion of the energy thus inhibited can be utilized in relation to substitute objects or actions, a residue of neutralized, undischarged energy may be available to the ego. The ego, thus supplied with neutral energy, does not passively react to stimulation, but actively *scans* the environment, storing up information useful to future tension-release.[37] Even more important, the ego can use this neutral energy as an auxiliary source to sustain other motivated behaviors, including the anticathexes required to defend against direct libidinal discharge. (The new ego psychology of Hartmann, Erikson, Rapaport, and others [see p. 635] has greatly elaborated this important, though never completed, area of Freud's work.)

Freud further implied that excess residual energy in the ego could partly be discharged as "nervousness," restlessness, or anxiety, although this was at most an incidental by-product of its accumulation in the ego.

Finally, a word about the directions of displacements. As one may infer from the reasons they occur, displacements follow lines of similarity of available objects or behaviors to those originally cathected.[38] Both the direction and the distance of displacement would be deter-

---

[35] We are indebted to R. R. Holt for this illustration.

[36] This concept of displacement is similar to Murphy's (1947) notion of canalization (see p. 637).

[37] There is a striking similarity between this suggestion and the function assigned to a similar mechanism in the cybernetic system (see p. 356).

[38] It is useful to note that mediated as well as actual similarity is meant here. Thus, on a verbal scale, *boy* and *toy* may be closer than *boy* and *doy* by virtue of meaningful association as well as sound. By the same token, *boy* and *man* might be closer than either of the above pairs. Displacement may occur along scales of similar sound, appearance, meaning, feeling, or, as in octaves in music, direct sensory or other bases.

mined as the resultants of social approbations and disapprobations, as
these have previously been incorporated in the superego.

Anxiety, Repression, and Defense

Anxiety. Freud defines anxiety as a uniquely unpleasant feeling state,
accompanied by certain specific efferent or discharge phenomena, and
the perception thereof (Freud, 1926, p. 70). The prototypic experience
of anxiety, for man at least, is the trauma of birth. The sudden and
intense stimulation which normally accompanies the change from a
protective intra-uterine environment to the uncertain and demanding
realities of life constitutes the first real danger situation which the
organism must face. The apparently automatic physiological responses
of anxiety, which are evoked at this time, would appear to serve a
useful purpose in facilitating the necessary adjustments of breathing
and heart function which permit the new organism to survive. Anxiety,
thus, is an adaptive response to this first danger, and its mobilizing
effects may be said to be generally useful in situations where excessive
stimulation requires extraordinary response.

Possibly on the basis of this early experience, the organism responds
with (or *redintegrates*) anxiety in later situations of excessive or unusual stimulation, that is, in situations of danger. In terms of Freud's
structural system, anxiety is said to be the response of the ego to stimulation it is unable to control. We have here tried to suggest that such
excessive response may be quite appropriate to the demands of the
situation for increased capacity, as for flight from a threatening environment. However, the anxiety is itself an unpleasant state, and one
which the organism would ordinarily seek to minimize or avoid entirely. As a result of learning (e.g., see Mowrer's hypothesis, p. 499), the
individual responds with anxiety to the *expectation* of danger—"feels
anxious *lest* something occur," as Freud put it (1926, p. 112). This
apprehensive signal then permits the ego to act in advance and thereby
protect itself from a further development of noxious (painful) stimulation.

The dangers of which we have so far spoken are *real* dangers, threatening the organism from the outside, and the anxiety developed in
these instances is said to be *real* anxiety. But there are two other ways
in which the ego can be overwhelmed: by excessive stimulation from
the instincts (the id), and by excessive pressure from the superego.
These, respectively, arouse what are called *neurotic anxiety* and *moral
anxiety* (or *guilt*). In all three types of anxiety, the affective experience
is in the ego, and what is feared has its eventual referents in reality.
In the case of neurotic anxiety, however, what is feared is that exces-

sive libidinal energies will be discharged onto the outside world and will result in punishment (loss of bodily integrity, or castration) or withdrawal of love (which the child sees as punishing). In the case of moral anxiety, the child has already introjected into its superego the moral code of its culture, and thus punishment is in the form of reprobation by conscience, experienced as feelings of guilt.

To sum up what has been said so far, a real danger (excessive or painful stimulation) may overwhelm the organism and perhaps destroy it. As a result of its past experiences, the perception of impending danger—from *any* source, inner as well as outer—gives rise to a release of anxiety in the ego, which serves as a *signal* of impending catastrophe, and permits the ego to engage in anticipatory defensive action. What is to be avoided is that condition of intense stimulation which occurred in earlier traumata [39] and the sense of helplessness that accompanied it (i.e., the reinstitution of the infantile state). Freud neatly summarizes these points as follows:

The danger situation is the recognized, remembered and anticipated situation of helplessness. Anxiety is the original reaction to helplessness in the traumatic situation, which is later reproduced as a call for help in the danger situation. The Ego, which has experienced the trauma passively, now actively repeats an attenuated reproduction of it with the idea of taking into its own hands the directing of its course (1926, pp. 114–115).

Beginning with the birth trauma, a successive series of situations in the development of the individual (due to his continuing condition of dependency) provides a basis for both the reinstitution of the feeling of helplessness and for the attendant experience of anxiety. The repeated (normally occurring) instances of separation from the mother (which are not understood by the infant as temporary, but represent permanent object-loss, loss of love, and of the source of nurturance), castration threat in pre-adolescence, and threat of social ostracism and loss of love (with attendant threat of loss of means of instinctual gratification) in adolescence and adulthood all serve to redintegrate the earlier trauma (Freud, 1926, 1933).

Finally, let us examine the relations among the three types of anxiety once again. Real or objective anxiety is the first type to occur, and, as we see it, is an inevitable part of mammalian life. This is described as an "intelligible reaction to danger." It consists in the alerting

[39] Freud writes: ". . . what is feared, the object of the anxiety, is always the emergence of a traumatic factor, which cannot be dealt with in accordance with the norms of the pleasure-principle" (1933, p. 129). And, in another context: ". . . a *traumatic* situation . . . [is] . . . our experience in a situation of helplessness . . ." (1926, p. 114).

of the organism, followed by coping behavior in an attempt to avoid or reduce the danger. In instances of sudden or intense stimulation, it is possible that the signal aspect will fail, resulting in paralyzing and unadaptive fear.

Neurotic anxiety may appear as "free-floating, general apprehensiveness" or dread, as in the case of the anxiety-neuroses; as an unwarrantedly intense fear associated with an object, idea, or class of objects in reality, as in the phobic reactions (e.g., fear of high places, enclosed spaces, etc.); or as a specific hysterical symptom or a panic reaction for which no apparent cause can be determined. Neurotic anxiety has been identified as a fear of excessive instinctual demands, although as in the examples just mentioned the fear appears often to be displaced on some aspect of the environment. Finally, in moral anxiety, the fear of punishment (a real danger) is internalized, appearing as guilt or shame, and again can be traced to a fear of loss of love, this time mediated by the introjected representation of the parent figure.

It can be seen that in all three types of anxiety, the referent is an anticipated *real* threat from the environment. In neurotic anxiety the attempt to gratify the instinctual needs could bring about a real danger; and in moral anxiety, the dread of punishment similarly lies behind the guilt or shame. Thus the distinctions which have been made with such care would hardly seem worth the effort. Because of the unconscious nature of the internal demands, however, a useful purpose is served by distinguishing between fear of the known (objective) danger and of the unknown (instinctual, moral) danger. In these instances, and particularly in the case of neurotic anxiety, the fact that the object is unknown (unrecognized) rules out the possibility of taking effective action in the environment. As a consequence, the ego turns to more circumspect means of protecting itself—to repression and the other "mechanisms of defense."

Repression and Defense. It is clear that that against which the ego must defend itself is the outbreak of uncontrollable anxiety. If its integrity is threatened from the outside, the ego can either flee or attempt effective motor action to remove the danger. If it is threatened from the inside, however, the defenses of the ego must take another course. Here the primary weapon is exclusion from consciousness. We will remember that the ego controls both access to consciousness and access to action. When an instinctual impulse that would endanger the organism becomes strong, the ego attempts to isolate the instinctual energy by forming an anticathexis around it. That is, the ego "blocks" the energy of the instinct with an equal amount of energy so that it cannot force its way into consciousness. This mechanism is known as *repression*. A dangerous thought or idea is forced out of consciousness as a result of giving rise to the "alarm" signal of anxiety.

But repression is not always successful. The ego may be too weak to provide sufficient energy for successful repression, or the libidinal energy may be reinforced (as in puberty) by additional resources from newly matured body function. In these instances, the repressed impulse is said to break through to consciousness and thus give rise to anxiety. Frequently, the result of repression is to force a displacement, a sublimation, or a symbolic expression of the repressed wishes. In this way they may find expression in consciousness without arousing the anxiety of the ego. Thus an infantile erotic urge can be transformed into an esthetic interest, hostility to the father can be displaced onto the "authorities," and so on. Still another way in which the energy of the repressed can express itself is through the formation of symptoms, or some other substitute formation. Evidence that the repressed material is not simply abolished in the process of repression is the common observation that it "breaks through," albeit usually in distorted form, in such periods when the ego is not on its guard—as in dreams, errors, and accidents.

Psychoanalysts have described a score of other mechanisms through which the ego may act in its attempts to preserve itself from being overwhelmed.[40] Although they differ considerably one from another, there is no sharp line of demarcation between any two similar mechanisms. Fundamentally, they all do two things: (1) they operate unconsciously—else their very purpose would be lost, and (2) they characteristically deny, distort, or falsify the ego's perceptions of events either internal, external, or both.

Among the more important of the mechanisms, in addition to repression, are the following:

1. *Regression*, whereby the ego retreats to an ontogenetically earlier pattern of coping behavior, usually one which had been unusually successful at an earlier stage of development or, on the contrary, one which had provided inadequate satisfaction and thus prevented its integration with more mature levels of behavior. (Such an earlier behavior mode and/or stage of development is said to have been *fixated*.) Examples of regression would include the wife who resolves an argument with her husband by "going home to mother," or the

[40] Fascinating as they are, intrinsically, it is beyond the scope of our purposes here to give more than cursory descriptions of a few of the mechanisms of defense. Excellent discussions of these mechanisms may be found in Anna Freud's *The Ego and the Mechanisms of Defense* (1936) and in Otto Fenichel's *The Psychoanalytic Theory of Neurosis* (1945).

college athlete who breaks into tears after making an error in an important play. Fixations, which come to light as a result of regression, provide useful clues to the areas of personality development where unusual difficulties were encountered by the individual in earlier life (i.e., when either successes or failures prevented normal progressions).

2. *Projection* is the mechanism whereby an unacceptable feeling toward an object or person is rejected from consciousness and attributed to that person or object rather than to the self. Thus "projected" into the outside, the emotion can be handled as a real danger and dealt with more effectively. "I hate you!" is dangerous, but if "You hate me!" I can be excused for treating you badly. By assigning features of the self to others, the individual may escape feelings of shame or guilt which would otherwise result if the ego were forced to recognize these undesirable (painful) feelings as its own. A mechanism which is in some ways the counterpart of projection, namely, *introjection* (see p. 610), is a process by which a person incorporates features of other people or objects into the self, thus enhancing the value of the ego. When used as a mechanism of defense, introjection, as with projection, creates a delusion of identity, as when adolescents copy the mode of dress or hair style or other mannerism of a favorite film idol, thus symbolically "acquiring" the talents or other desirable attributes of the other and thereby reducing feelings of inadequacy and failure. All too often, this symbolic and magical nature of introjection results in the taking-on of an undesirable quality, almost as a substitute for the desirable one, which may not be reproducible in one's self (e.g., as the imitation of a talent or strength beyond the capacity of the imitator at the time).

3. *Reaction formation*, as a defense mechanism, follows the adage "if you can't beat 'em, join 'em!" Here, the anxiety-producing affect is directly reversed in consciousness, hostile feelings being replaced by feelings of undue concern for the other person, for example. Reaction formations may be distinguished from genuine emotions by their inappropriate intensity and persistence. "Thee protesteth too much" exemplifies the suspicion which is attached to such strong shows of affect.

The above will perhaps serve to illustrate some of the diverse forms which defense may take. Repression and the more exaggerated use of any of these defenses, resulting in symptom formation, already mentioned, are two other main avenues along which defense may be directed. A. Freud (1936), Fenichel (1945), and others, have stressed the developmental aspects of pathological defenses. A basic tenet of psychoanalytic theory and therapy is the assumption that neuroses have their beginnings in the earliest attempts to cope with the environment. The mechanisms of defense against anxiety that appear early and are successful may be expected to set the pattern for later reactions to danger. In this way the personality develops: from crisis to crisis, as it were, along the paths of successful solution.

Two further items must be mentioned before we conclude this section. First, to point out the circular problem that develops with the ego defenses. Anxiety arises when the organism anticipates a danger. The anxiety is used as a signal for defense, and thus the danger is avoided. But the success of the defense precludes the possibility of determining if the alarm was real or not. Cues in the environment then may incorrectly set off the cycle, and the ego has no way of discovering the error. This would appear to be the case in neurosis, and partly accounts for the fact of resistance in therapy and the often-observed and related phenomenon that patients in psychotherapy appear to get worse before they get better.[41] In fact, psychotherapists are convinced that one of the greatest hurdles in therapy is the overcoming of the initial resistance, which will permit the patient to test reality sufficiently to discover the fact that the ego has been issuing a "false alarm."

In the second place, we want to emphasize that in all that has been said, no sharp distinction is to be drawn between the normal and the abnormal (Freud, 1940). Freud made a useful distinction between successful and unsuccessful defense, and taught that sublimation (the substitution of socially desirable modes of tension release for less adaptive means of impulse gratification) is the "normal" way of adjusting. However, as he made clear early in his work,[42] any of the mechanisms of defense may make their appearance—perhaps all do—in any individual. Quantitative criteria (e.g., how much energy is immobilized in anticathexes, how much distortion of reality exists) rather than qualitative distinctions (e.g., presence or absence of this or that mechanism) need ultimately to be drawn.[43]

[41] This phenomenon is also often attributed to the "transference neurosis" in psychoanalysis.

[42] In his lectures at Clark University in 1909, Freud cautioned his audience that ". . . neuroses have no peculiar psychic content of their own which is not also to be found in healthy states . . . neurotics fall ill of the same complexes with which we sound people struggle. It depends on quantitative relationships, on the relations of the forces wrestling with each other, whether the struggle leads to health, to a neurosis, or to compensatory over-functioning . . ." (1910, p. 215).

[43] Holt (1960) offers an excellent recent discussion of these points on the basis of the post-Freudian developments in Ego Psychology.

Comment. This now concludes our presentation of "basic" Freudian motivation theory, except as we shall put forward some of the post-Freudian contributions in the next few pages. The informed reader may notice that we have omitted discussion in any detail of many of the more popularly known features of psychoanalytic theory. Thus, for example, there has been no more than cursory mention of the important stages of psychosexual development, of the Oedipus complex, of symptoms, of neurosis, and of psychoanalytic therapy. These are of great interest and importance to psychology in general and to psychotherapy in particular. But our focus must remain, as we indicated in the introduction to this chapter, on the core of psychoanalysis and its underlying metapsychology (see Rapaport & Gill, 1959), as these bear on motivation; and we hope that our presentation has properly reflected the essence of this central aspect of the psychoanalytic viewpoint.

OTHER MAJOR VARIANTS ON PSYCHOANALYTIC THEORY

Both during Freud's lifetime and since his death in 1939, a number of other psychoanalysts have offered ideas of their own—some extending and some contradicting the basic theoretical tenets set forth by Freud. The sheer volume of the psychoanalytic literature precludes any faithful attempt to note all of the variants. We shall instead select what appear to us to be the more significant variations, modifications, and extensions. From a brief discussion of each of these, it should be possible to see the direction(s) in which psychoanalytic theory has begun to move.

Jung and Adler

Although quite different both as individuals and in the contributions they have made, Carl Jung (1875–1961) and Alfred Adler (1870–1937) are usually thought of together by virtue of the fact that they were the first (along with Wilhelm Stekel) of the persons identified with Freud's intimate circle to break with "orthodox" (i.e., Freudian) psychoanalysis and attempt to form new schools, and they both did so around the same time (circa 1912). Both disagreed with Freud's then heavy emphasis on the sexual basis of cathectic energy. Each had a different concept of the nature of primary motivation and early conflict, in both cases emphasizing more than Freud the role of sociocultural factors and of parent-child relations in the etiology of neurosis.

Jung's Views. In rejecting Freud's early libido theory, Jung rather conceived of sexual energy as only *one* form of an undifferentiated psychic energy, the *primal libido,* or general life force. (Actually,

Freud came to subsume sex under a wider life energy, Eros, as well [see p. 602].) Although he did not explicitly posit a death wish, Jung's conception of energy utilization had much in common with Freud's. He accepted the first and second principles of thermodynamics as models for his energy system. Thus energy may be shifted or redistributed (i.e., displaced) but not lost from the system, and the ultimate aim of life is a balanced state of tension (self-actualization) in which opposite systems in the personality, or values, are evenly energized. Any imbalance leads to tension until the energy can be redistributed. Energy is used for the satisfaction of inborn (instinctual) needs first, but as development produces greater efficiency, excess energy becomes available to higher functions—social and cultural activities. Although the terminology is different, the net effect is the same as would be predicted by Freud's theory of energetics.

Jung saw the organism as developing its own unique individuality, striving ever toward the realization of *self*. The forces of society cause the inhibition not only of sexual (i.e., socially "bad" impulses, as Freud had seen them), but healthy impulses as well. Man is made up of opposing tendencies: of maleness and femaleness, of introversion and extraversion. Self-realization (see Chapter 13) is the attainment of a balance of these forces. Neurosis is a result of an imbalance of these tendencies, as a consequence of uneven emphases in development.

Jung emphasized the role of the mother, not as sex object but as source of nurturance, in determining direction of growth. A second important influence is the pattern of relation between the parents. Not the overt or formal relations, but the concealed discords and tensions of the home, which are absorbed by the child from the emotional atmosphere around him. Jung thus turned the focus of the problems of adjustment from the child as a bundle of sexual energy requiring harnessing to the child-parent interaction, in which unfolding patterns of character are developed or repressed as a result of the sometimes neurotic handling by the parents. This shift in emphasis can be seen as tending along the same direction Freud later followed as he moved from a primarily sexual libido theory to the greater emphasis on ego development. The emphases were admittedly different, however, since Jung was inclined to stress the dignity and meaning of self-actualization and the full life, whereas Freud saw this always in terms of impulse and defense.

On the other hand, Jung did not disagree with Freud's biological emphasis. *Both* biological and social features have importance in his theoretical system. Perhaps the best known feature of Jung's thinking is the concept of the *collective unconscious*. This has similarity to

Freud's racial unconscious, but is more extreme and more elaborate. Like Freud, Jung assumed the inheritance of acquired characteristics, an assumption quite generally rejected in biological science today. The collective unconscious contains the experience of all mankind, the "wisdom of the ages," accumulated over the centuries and somehow transmitted from generation to generation. It is an underlying substratum of the personal unconscious, which later contains the experience of the individual life. Jung explained the allegedly universal appearance of certain symbols, regardless of differences in culture, by the presence and functioning of the collective unconscious. (An alternative and perhaps less extreme explanation might be found in the universality of certain essential human biological structures and functions, from which common symbolic abstractions—the universality of which has not been adequately demonstrated to begin with—might independently arise in different cultures.)

Even before his association with Freud, Jung had shown an interest in the mystical and occult. His writings clearly show this influence. When Jung and Freud broke with each other, Freud bitterly denounced Jung's departures from psychoanalytic theory as ". . . unintelligible, obscure, and confused . . ." (1914, p. 350). This vein of criticism has been characteristic of Freud and the traditional psychoanalysts ever since (see Jones, 1955, Vol. II). As Clara Thompson (1950) has pointed out, the mysticism attached to Jung's hypothesized collective unconscious, for example, is even more evident in his later writings (Jung, 1933, 1938, 1939). Jung has peopled this unconscious with *archetypes*, or universal (unconsciously given) idealized images, which play an active role in behavior determination. Thus each man has his female archetype, the *anima*, and each woman her masculine archetype, the *animus*, which contribute to their own bisexuality and their behavior toward the opposite sex. Experience with the mother and with other women is shaped in part by the anima archetype and in part by the nature of the experience itself. Jung has elaborated the concept of archetype to the point where each aspect of the person has its counterpart in the collective unconscious and is influenced by this inherited idealized image.

In addition to the causal, antecedent (i.e., biological, ancestral) determiners of development, Jung stresses purposive or teleological factors. The aims and goals of man, his forward-looking aspirations, his destiny (in sharp contrast with Freud's views) are considered to be equally as important as the causal determiners. Whereas Freud appeared to view man as being essentially "pushed" by his instincts, Jung sought to emphasize the meaning and essential dignity of life and the striving for self-actualization.

Out of the intrinsic conflicts of the different aspects of his personality (out of oppositions of systems, complexes, archetypes, functions, values, etc.) man evolves a transcendent personality, the *self*. This is different from the ego (which is entirely the conscious self for Jung), and is an all-inclusive, integrative, balanced, actualized concept—one rarely achieved completely, but representing the ideal of development —the whole person (cf. Freud's concept of ego-ideal).

As did Freud, Jung draws primarily on clinical evidence to support his theoretical postulates, and secondarily and extensively (but selectively) on the analysis of myths, dreams, and symbols, not only of Western man but of other cultures, too (Jung & Kerenyi, 1949, Jung, 1956; Progoff, 1953). That these dramatically support many of his interpretations will not be surprising. They do not, unfortunately, provide a means of critical scientific validation, however, and the very nature of the concepts described makes it even more difficult than in the case of Freud's concepts to conceive of adequate evaluative procedures in the laboratory. Jung did contribute to the development of an interesting investigative method, which has been widely used by others as a laboratory tool, although Jung himself did not use it after the first few years, and never in any really systematic way. This was the *word-association procedure*, and the assessment of affect in connection with the produced associations. However, these techniques do not lend themselves to tests of Jung's archetypes or their hypothesized ancestral origins. How these can be assessed remains in question.

Adler's Views. Adler, like Jung, did not accept Freud's early insistence that sexual libido was the primary basis of human motivation. He saw the smallness, weakness, and helplessness of the infant as giving rise to a generalized attitude of inferiority (at first associated with a particular organ, the penis, though he later abandoned this view). Such a feeling would be universal, for all children have this completely dependent relation to their environments. Paralleling the frequently observed organic compensations for weak, injured, or absent body parts (Adler, 1917), Adler posited a psychic compensatory mechanism—a *striving for superiority*. This was for him the sole means of channeling energy to behavior. Not separate drives, but an all-consuming drive toward more complete development pushes the ego to greater and greater accomplishment. Sex, rather than being an all-important primary drive, is subsumed as one means to power and superiority. Perfection, rather than pleasure, is the ruling principle of life.

This emphasis on orientation toward the future (see Chapter 13), like that of Jung, emphasizes the conception of human dignity and worth, in contrast to what Adler considered Freud's more "degrading" view. But Adler went considerably further in this direction. He attributed to what he called the *creative self* the capacity to take hold and shape the personality along its own particular *style of life*. As Hall and Lindzey recently observed (1957), this coincides with the poetic and popular view of man as captain of his fate.[44]

Finally, we may note Adler's agreement with Freud and Jung that motivation is of innate origin. But in lieu of Freud's biological instinctual drives, and of Jung's unconscious images, Adler proposed an inborn *social interest* as the primary driving force. This social interest must be carefully nurtured if it is to develop properly. Thus Adler gave great emphasis to differences in the social environment as determiners of personality development,[45] an emphasis which has now been incorporated in the mainstream of psychoanalytic thinking. Adler was a prime mover in the establishment of child guidance clinics, and gave impetus to studies of the role of the child in the family constellation, of educational practices, and of the effects of early child-rearing practices on later style of life. While applauding these new insights, Thompson (1950) says that Adler's emphasis on the future striving of the organism may have led to an unbalanced neglect of causal factors in his overall theoretical position.

Other Variants on the Freudian Theme

Since the 1920's, a quite impressive number of variants on the Freudian psychoanalytic theme have appeared. Among the better known advocates of these variations were four men who, like Jung and Adler, were personally associated with Freud. Though none achieved the eminence of these two early deviants, each contributed some unique addition, modification, or re-emphasis, to psychoanalytic theory. Space permits us to mention them only briefly in passing.

Otto Rank (1929, 1945) has already been mentioned as emphasizing the importance of the *birth trauma*, and thus focusing on the role of

[44] There is no question of the appeal of such a view—but its popularity at the polls, as it were, cannot replace the more sober question of its scientific validity, a matter much more difficult to decide. As Freud pointed out, there is a real danger, even in science, that people may be more swayed by the degree to which a theory flatters or disturbs their self-concepts than by the objective evidence.

[45] Clara Thompson (1950) considers Adler's work to have been pioneering in having called attention to the total personality in its struggle for adaptation, and in the resultant focus on cultural factors.

the mother. His *"will therapy"* elaborated the conflict of the positive, creative will and the urge to return to the womb, the state of complete surrender and dependency before birth. Like so many others, Rank placed emphasis on the importance of social interaction in the etiology of conflict and neurosis.

Wilhelm Stekel (1949, 1950) contributed largely to the exploration of new and shorter therapeutic procedures; he also saw the role of current conflicts in the patient's adult life as important in neurosis. He recognized the role of the therapist's personality in his interaction with the patient, a fact which Sullivan and others have greatly extended.

Sandor Ferenczi (1952), like Stekel, experimented with variations in the technique of psychotherapy by manipulating the role of the therapist. He considered the therapy relation as a situation in which to "work through" earlier unsuccessful interpersonal attitudes, a view much more elaborated in the techniques of Moreno (1946) and Alexander (1956).

Wilhelm Reich (1933) rejected Freud's death-instinct concept, finding the earlier idea of a sexual libido entirely adequate. Harper (1959) describes Reich in this regard as "out-Freuding Freud!" Reich recognized the way in which various types of defenses take on muscular, postural, vocal, and other somatic forms, and the role of bodily tensions, as cues to emotional states, a view we have already seen greatly emphasized and widely explored elsewhere (see discussion of Freeman, Chapter 7). He also broadened the originally narrow list of defenses and was instrumental in developing the modern view of the multiple *layering* of defenses (e.g., see Hartmann, 1958). Reich also introduced the important concept of character defense (and character armor), and, in his analysis of character structure, he anticipated Kardiner's concept of a "basic personality structure" (Kardiner, 1939) as a product of the cultural forces of a given society. Reich went on to develop a rather unique form of "orgone therapy" and to emphasize orgastic potency as a criterion of mental health. His orgone theory has had little support among psychoanalysts or, as Thompson (1950) maintains, from the evidence (e.g., the potency of schizophrenics), although since it is extremely difficult to quantify or judge the nature of orgastic experience, the hypothesis about potency and mental health is not easy to test.

The Emphasis on Culture

A number of Freud's critics have claimed that he ignored the influence of social and cultural factors in the formation of personality and the etiology of neurosis in favor of a strictly biological view. This

is not entirely correct. Freud did emphasize the somatic origin of instinctual drives and the primary importance of constitutional factors.
Even the ego was seen as developing in the service of the drives. But
in describing the development of the ego, and particularly of the
superego concept to which he paid increasing attention, Freud acknowledged the significance of the shaping role that culture plays in
determining (and/or in modifying) personality structure. Thus, if one
recognizes the constitutional base from which he started, it is then
possible to accept Hartmann's opinion that "Freud's view united the
biological and sociological points of view" (Hartmann, 1958, p. 32).

Many of Freud's followers did, however, give greater emphasis to
social and developmental factors in shaping and even directing the
lives of their patients. Three theorists in particular, from among many
others who could be mentioned, have come to represent the "cultural
school" of psychoanalysis. These are Karen Horney, Erich Fromm,
and Harry Stack Sullivan.[46] Their separate and common emphases on
interpersonal factors in the etiology of neurosis have, they say, taken
them far "beyond Freud." As these positions are clearly relevant not
only to neurosis but to the motivational assumptions of psychoanalysis,
they are worth our attention here.

Horney's Views. Karen Horney (1885–1952), trained as a Freudian
psychoanalyst in Berlin, considered her work as extending and modifying Freud, not as "non-Freudian." She accepted Freud's basic ideas of
psychic determinism and the importance of unconscious motivation,
but rejected both the primary role of instincts and the structural system of the personality Freud had elaborated. In the place of Freud's
life and death drives, Horney conceived of the helpless infant as seeking *security* in a potentially hostile and dangerous world. Feelings of
insecurity may give rise to a basic anxiety as a result of many possible
combinations of parent attitudes or behavior, lack of warmth or guidance, dominance, disparagement, overprotection, etc. When this happens, the person (Freud's ego?) develops various *strategies* in an attempt to cope with these untenable feelings. These strategies may take
many forms—Horney calls them *neurotic needs* because they are so
often irrational—and may become institutionalized (i.e., functionally
autonomous, in Allport's sense) as modes of defense against anxiety.
Some of these needs are for affection and approval, for prestige, for
independence, for power, etc. All of them reduce to tendencies to move

[46] Abram Kardiner (1939, 1945) and Camilla Anderson (1957) are at least two
others who have been described as belonging to this "social psychological" or
"dynamic culturalist" point of view. (See Hall & Lindzey, 1957; Harper, 1959;
Thompson, 1950 for further discussion of this school.)

(1) toward, (2) away from, or (3) against people. An imbalance of these three "orientations" leads into neurosis and the further protective defenses of the neurotic (i.e., the Freudian defense mechanisms). The *psychological vicious circles,* made up of defenses against difficulties produced by defenses (cf. Reich's layering of character defenses), of the anxiety-producing conflicts of neurotic goals make neuroses resistant to the modifying influences of reality.

Horney conceived of a tripartite division of the personality with some resemblance to Freud's ego-id-superego scheme, which she rejected. She spoke of the *idealized self-image* (a kind of abstracted, perfect self-percept) and the *actual self* (the person as he actually is) as being in conflict. The *real self* (that which the actual self could potentially become, though far from the unreal idealized self) can emerge only when the self-restrictive influence of the neurotic idealized image is counterbalanced (though not overwhelmed).

Horney was outspoken in her centering of the causes of neurosis in the cultural pressures of early childhood and attempted in her writings (1937, 1939, 1945, 1950) to show how each of the developmental conflicts Freud ascribed to instinctual sources could be explained in terms of social forces, rather than the innate biological nature of man. Specifically, for example, Horney reinterpreted the repetition-compulsion, which Freud had seen as a result of biological necessity, in terms of the dynamic requirements of the adult personality in relation to contemporaneous pressures. She supports this and other reinterpretations by reference to case materials drawn from her own patients. Like several of the others already discussed and those yet to be discussed, Horney could not agree that the detailed exploration of the events of early childhood by adult patients was as important as contemporaneous analysis, and she was suspicious that patients' curiosity about these early years tended to contaminate the therapeutic process. She felt that Freud may have arrived at the concept of repetition-compulsion, as he had the theories of fixation, regression, and transference, out of an erroneous bias produced by his biological (genetic) point of view.

Fromm's Views. Erich Fromm (1900–　), unlike the others so far discussed in this chapter, was trained in sociology and psychology before taking his psychoanalytic training and becoming a therapist. His theories may be described as social philosophy rather than strictly psychological theories, though they make several assumptions which are of interest to us here. Fromm emphasizes the fundamental loneliness of man, a condition distinctly human, and stemming from man's success in freeing himself from immediate dependence on nature. In the process of physical and social evolution, though, this freedom has led to loneliness, and in turn to a need to escape from freedom. The central problem of human motivation is not the satisfaction of instinctual drives, but rather the solution of the problems society has created —the avoidance of the pressures that force man to seek escape, from his individuality and from his freedom, into conformity, dependence, and slavery. Fromm considers *self integrity* to be the elusive but primary target of man. To discover his "true self," to use the society he has created instead of being used by it, to relate himself to his fellow man on a basis of love and brotherhood, ". . . to transcend nature by creating rather than by destroying" (1955, p. 362), these are man's true goals. The nature of man's condition has created distinctly human needs—for identity, rootedness, transcendence, relatedness, and orientation—which may be met in many ways. Unfortunately, societies generally create undesirable means for meeting man's needs. And they create political and social institutions that produce conflicts within him by satisfying certain of his needs at the expense of others (e.g., as permitting identification with a national or industrial symbol—the fatherland, flag, company—but frustrating his needs for individual identity and integrity). Similar to Adler, Fromm's theories are highly palatable, and his analyses plausible. Such descriptive analyses of cultures, however, though extremely well drawn, defy the kind of precision required of scientific proof.

Thompson, who was herself a member of this group, suggests, in relation to Fromm's and other of the cultural-determinists' theories, that although they may appear as pessimistic as Freud [47] in describing the conflict and resultant destructiveness everywhere in view, they ascribe this to social rather than innate biological pressures. This at least offers the theoretical hope that new constructive forces may be introduced, and man's human condition made more human.

Sullivan's Views. Harry Stack Sullivan (1892–1949), because of his many substitutions of his own terms for Freud's, gives the impression of departing most extremely from psychoanalytic theory. Sullivan defines the unit of study as the *interpersonal relation*, rather than the individual. Granting a biological substrate, he sees the personality as emerging out of interactions with other human beings and as a product of the social forces that act upon the individual from day to day, beginning with birth. Thus, although acknowledging the role of heredity in determining individual differences in capacity and the maturation of physical functions as necessary before certain phases of development

[47] Holt reminds us (personal communication) that Freud's pessimism was personal, and *not* a necessary consequence of his theory.

can occur, he nevertheless rejects Freud's idea of an unfolding (instinct-based) development and substitutes for it an emphasis on social interaction (i.e., stages set off by the acquisition of language and other interpersonal criteria).

Sullivan's theory is one of tension reduction, in this respect very much like Freud's, based on the accumulation and discharge of energy. For the instincts, Sullivan substitutes two (interrelated) human need realms: *satisfaction* (of needs arising as a result of biological processes) and *security* (pertaining "to the social order rather than to the peculiar properties of our somatic organization" [1947, p. 6]). Sullivan posits an innate power motive which is frustrated by the infant's helplessness. This sense of powerlessness—or insecurity—is allayed by social conditioning—an "accultural evolution"—as the infant learns to control the environment through social interaction. Loss of means or of agencies of satisfaction would restore insecurity. Thus security needs are the direct (and uniquely individual) outgrowth of conditioning experiences in relation to other people. Interference with need gratification (which occurs more predictably in the case of security) leads to anxiety (or, in the extreme, terror). Anxiety is early transmitted to the infant by the "mothering one" in such subtle ways as by manner of handling and breast feeding. Sullivan describes this process of communication as *empathy*, and points to its nonverbal, nonovert character, though he is unable to suggest a mechanism for such "emotional contagion and communion." Succeeding experiences of frustration, discomfort, separation, etc. lead to further increase of anxiety and concurrent protective personality *dynamisms*. Dynamisms are similar to what others have called defenses, personality traits, habits, or characteristic modes of expression (covert as feelings, emotions, or attitudes, or overt as actions). The dynamisms are built up out of experiences with rewards and punishments, and correspond to the "correct" and "incorrect" behaviors as socially defined.

Most important of the dynamisms is the set of attitudes built about the self. These attitudes, particularly, develop out of the person's experiences of anxiety and, like Freud's two-sided superego, provide models of "good-me" and "bad-me" to guide behavior. Like the superego, too, the self-system develops from the idealized (and in ways irrational) aspects of society, and thus sets standards of behavior which may be quite arbitrary. (There are, of course, common threats which elicit real anxiety in *any* society [e.g., the threat of castration]. But there are types of social *faux pas* that would embarrass an American as contrasted with a Hindu or Chinese, for example, to illustrate the cultural arbitrariness of many of the situations that elicit anxiety in a given society.) Preserving the self from anxiety may lead to an isolation of the self-system from change or growth with experience, a process remarked upon by many of the psychoanalytic theorists, beginning with Freud (e.g., Horney's vicious circles).

The self is a developmental product of early experiences with rewards and punishments, not an inborn potential, as Fromm or Adler had seen it. It is made up of the "reflected appraisals" of others, and in turn (like Freud's ego) monitors what will be attended to and what will be neglected or distorted. However, the self-dynamism can be changed, in later life, provided sufficient new experience with *significant* adults supports such change (e.g., as in therapy, but otherwise as well).

Sullivan describes three developmental levels of cognitive experience or symbolic activity. First, preconceptual or *prototaxic* experience, which is the direct and simple sensory contact ("instantaneous records of total situations" [Mullahy, 1945, p. 125]). This is the earliest type of experience, the momentary camera-eye experiences on which memory is based. Second, *parataxic* and autistic processes, in which experiences can be differentiated into their component parts, although they as yet appear as concomitant rather than logically or causally linked events (cf. Freud's primary process). And finally, *syntactic* thinking, based on consensually validated evidential experience (e.g., logical or scientific thinking, in terms of agreed-upon language and metric symbols; cf. Freud's secondary process). Not all people develop to this third cognitive level, parataxic thinking being far more common. *Parataxic distortion* is the process wherein the idealized or fantasied personifications of parents, heroes, villains, others, or self are interacted with as though they were real (cf. Freud's concept of transference). Ideas of parental omniscience, the omnipotence of real or fantasied heroes (legendary or personally contrived), and distorted generalizations of the self and self-other relations are substituted for realistic appraisals and self-modifying or self-enhancing activities. These distortions are retained, as we have earlier noted, because of the irrational conviction that they are anxiety reducers. They may be removed only through progression to syntactic levels of cognition (i.e., through reality testing), a process most difficult to achieve.

Finally, we may note Sullivan's awareness of relativity in his conception of stereotypes as shared parataxic distortions, ostensibly built upon consensual validation, but in fact a function of the common anxiety and common distorted self perception of the group members.

Comment. The reader may have perceived, in all of the post-Freudian theories we have so briefly sketched above, a common emphasis on the role of social determiners, whether based on an innate core or not, in shaping the *basic* motivational forces that contribute to the adult personality. These social factors direct the energies of the organism toward the satisfaction of goals within the framework of societal structures. None of the theorists has denied the facts of biology, though there is considerable variation in what they ascribe to inborn and what they ascribe to acquired characteristics.

With regard to the changes they have sought to introduce into psychoanalytic theory, these may be crudely summarized as primarily a rejection of the notion of strict biological determinism in favor of a more clearly sociological approach. They have each attempted, in the main, to draw upon their own interpretations of the many-faceted fabric of civilized society for concepts to explain human motivation, in contrast to what appeared to them to be Freud's effort to build a personality structure and a motivational system from the inside out, in terms of displaced biogenic energy.

In general, though, despite linguistic differences and emphasis, there is no striking departure from the structure of Freud's motivational theory. The role of anxiety remains central, development leads to structural modification in response to reality considerations, and tension-reduction or anxiety control is the most significant motivational construct in psychological development (or failure of same). The downgrading of the role of the instincts is perhaps the major departure in these views.

THE NEW EGO PSYCHOLOGY

We return now to the "mainstream" of psychoanalytic thought to examine the direction it has followed since the death of Freud. In his later writings, Freud had begun to give more attention to the role of the ego, and it is in this area that current psychoanalytic theory has most rapidly developed.

Virtually no one today accepts Freud's idea of a "death instinct," although the aggression (see Chapter 14) which he had posited as emanating from this source is considered by many psychoanalysts to be innate (Bellak, 1956; Hartmann, Kris, & Loewenstein, 1949). The life instincts are presumed to have their origins in specific somatic areas. It may then be suggested that those who seek a bodily source for aggression (general excitement) examine its possible relation to such nonspecific organic centers as the hypothalamic-pituitary-adrenal system and the reticular formation.

In any case, there seems to be a trend away from what is called premature neurologizing and physiologizing of psychoanalytic concepts (see Bellak et al., 1959) in favor of a working out of primarily psychological structures to account for the ways in which social and cultural variables combine with developmental factors to influence the shaping of personality.

Freud himself had never abandoned the id as the most important of the structures of the personality, but he had begun to elaborate a more independent role for the ego as the executive controller of instinctual energy and the preserver, through judicious use of anxiety and defense, of the integrity of the individual. Hartmann (1939, 1950, 1958) and Hartmann, Kris, and Loewenstein (1946, 1949) have emphasized the independence of the ego not only in function but in origin as well.

The concept they propose is that the infant is at the beginning in an undifferentiated stage, containing both the instinctual drives in an elementary (undeveloped) form and rudiments of the ego—the apparatuses of *primary autonomy*. In the process of development, these elements are pulled together and differentiated from the id to form the ego. These primary, inborn ego structures are the basic capacities —to perceive, learn, remember, think, and act—which different individuals have in varying degrees. They provide a means of pre-adaptation [48] to the "average expectable environment" (Holt, 1960, p. 255) and, together with the acquired apparatuses of *secondary autonomy* (e.g., habits, defenses), make up the ego structure, man's "organ of adaptation" (Hartmann, 1939). The autonomous ego draws its energy from sources in its own apparatus and/or from a reservoir of *neutralized* sexual and aggressive libido, using it for aims independent of these sources, however.

Rapaport (1951b, 1958) has extended this notion of autonomy to include autonomy from the environment, too. In this he contrasts normal behavior to that of the stimulus-bound behavior of brain-damaged individuals. The highly developed ego structure permits *selective* responding to environmental stimulation.

The ego apparatuses develop in accordance with their own nature and along lines permitted by the particular social organization of the environment, which combination of determinants mutually limit the mode and adequacy of adaptation. Hartmann uses the term *social compliance*, paralleling Freud's somatic compliance concept, to describe this channeling of energy along socially conditioned avenues. (Mur-

---

[48] There is of course an implicit circularity in this argument. Since man can be shown to adapt to a variety of social environments, we may infer such a pre-adaptation and can then demonstrate the presence of a pre-adaptability on the evidence of such adaptation.

phy's earlier term, *canalization*, expressed much the same idea [1947].)

Rapaport (1959, 1960) offers two very cogent analyses and reviews of these contributions. He suggests a *threshold* concept—for both sensory stimuli and drives—as a mechanism of the ego. He accepts this idea of drives triggering action in an autonomous ego, but considers the ego capable of functioning even when not directly gratifying specific drives. He raises the very significant question, however, of the source of energy for the nontension-reducing functions of the ego.[49] Neutralized libidinal and/or aggressive energy is one answer that has been given to this question, but considerable interest remains in the processes by which such energy can be detached from its drive source in the first place and the conditions which lead to its release in the second. As can be recognized, this problem is not unique to analytic theory, being one which runs through all of the theories of motivation of the tension-reduction variety.

Thus, within orthodox psychoanalysis as well as in the various deviant groups to which psychoanalysis has given rise, the new direction is an attempt to develop a comprehensive understanding of social factors not as by-products of an unfolding developmental process but as codeterminants of that development itself.

Erik H. Erikson (1950, 1956, 1959) must certainly be mentioned as one of the more important contributors to ego psychology. His *Childhood and Society* (1950) greatly extends Freud's biological developmental theories in an *epigenetic* concept, in which eight built-in stages of ego development span the complete life cycle. Erikson, drawing extensively on anthropological field data, sees a developmental progression through a series of crises or fateful encounters: trust vs. basic mistrust, autonomy vs. shame and doubt, initiative vs. guilt, industry vs. inferiority, identity vs. role diffusion, intimacy vs. isolation, generativity vs. stagnation, and ego integrity vs. despair.

Development occurs in a family or social context and involves a mutual shaping, in which ". . . society (mediated by the caretaker persons) meets each developmental phase with institutions specific to it, and for each [behavior] mode provides social modalities which enable the individual's behavioral patterns to find socially useful and adaptive opportunities" (Holt, 1960, p. 260).

---

[49] This may be recognized as similar to the phenomenon Allport (1937) labeled "functional autonomy." As Holt (1960, p. 256) notes, however, Hartmann's concept refers to *relative* not absolute autonomy, since ego structures may be weakened or overwhelmed (as in psychopathology) and do not retain their autonomy under such circumstances.

His central concept of *identity* may be grasped from the following brief quotes:

The growing child must, at every step, derive a vitalizing sense of reality from the awareness that his individual way of mastering experience (his Ego synthesis) is a successful variant of a group identity and is in accord with its space-time and life plan. . . . Ego identity gains real strength only from . . . recognition of real accomplishment—i.e., of achievement that has meaning in its culture (Erikson, 1950, p. 208).

Identity is thus both a social *and* individual concept, a view parallel to that expressed by Hartmann, Rapaport, and others. The attainment of identity is a characteristic of the developing ego, and not the super-ego. In this distinction we can see the shift in emphasis from the earlier traditional psychoanalytic view most clearly.

Two important developments have resulted from this "new look" in psychoanalysis. First, there has been an increased interest on the part of psychoanalytically trained investigators in the direct study of developmental processes in childhood (as contrasted to the inferences drawn from remembered incidents of childhood produced by adult patients). Some of this work has been reported in the annual volumes of *The Psychoanalytic Study of the Child* (Anna Freud et al., 1945 on), and will be further discussed. The second development has been a growing rapprochement between psychoanalysis and psychology proper, a movement which is bound to enrich and broaden the scope of both disciplines. It should specifically provide the nonpsychoanalytically trained psychologist with a better understanding of the wealth of clinical material which led to the formulation of analytic concepts (as well as a more precise understanding of what the psychoanalyst means by his terms), while at the same time making available to the analyst the quite extensive data from normal developmental studies and the highly developed methodologies of experimental psychology as a means of testing psychoanalytic hypotheses.

CURRENT STATUS OF PSYCHOANALYTIC MOTIVATION THEORY

In an extensive and highly provocative series of papers, Rapaport and others have been trying to draw together the general outlines of current psychoanalytic theory, fully recognizing the difficulty of their tasks (see Rapaport, 1951*b*, 1958, 1959, 1960; Gill, 1959; Rapaport & Gill, 1959; Pumpian-Mindlin, 1952; Knight & Friedman, 1954). They have tried to indicate the variables with which psychoanalysis is concerned, the concepts and principles that seem to have some likelihood of endurance, and the areas in which gaps in the theory seem most evident. Here we can only highlight some of the main points of these discussions as they may be relevant to the psychoanalytic theory of motivation.

1. *Energy concept.* Most psychoanalysts assume a biological substratum, deriving energy from metabolic sources.[50] Energy is transformed through unknown mechanisms into forms usable for psychological work. A distinction is made between cathectic (psychic) energy (whether called this or not) and muscular energy.

2. *Source of motivation.* There is no general agreement on specific instincts or drives, although the tendency is growing to use the latter term (which is cognate with Freud's term *Trieb*) and to avoid the implication of specific energies earmarked for specific need gratifications. There is fairly good agreement that life drives (hunger, thirst, sex, etc.) make up one main group of motive forces, and that aggression (though not a death instinct) is a motive force to be dealt with.[51] Whether aggression derives from bodily sources (e.g., endocrine or neuroendocrine function) or is simply coordinate with such organic and physiological events remains an open question. The traditional Freudian view implied an innate need to hurt and destroy. The new Ego Psychology perhaps will allow the option of assessing anger and its concomitants as a result of the inevitable frustrations and conflicts of early development. In either case, the matter will be as difficult to resolve for this theory as it is for the ethologists (see Chapter 3). It is part of the age-old—perhaps meaningless—argument of nature vs. nurture.

3. *Unconscious motivation.* Undoubtedly Freud's most significant and lasting contribution has been his elucidation of unconscious processes. The idea of unconscious forces at work in the mental life has received almost universal acceptance and has the widest implications. It has permanently changed the course of psychological science, and its ramifications have had a broad impact on man's thinking in the humanities, the arts, and throughout the social sciences. The distinction between irrational primary processes (as described in dreams and fantasies, for example) and the rational secondary processes of organized personality, and the demonstration of motivational significance in both types of processes, will remain a contribution of great value whether identified with the particular structural units of the id-ego-superego or some other schematic conception of the personality.

4. *Interaction of drives and structures.* Many classifications and

---

[50] Goethe, whose work so inspired Freud, summed this point up very succinctly in the phrase "Mann ist was Mann isst!" (Man is what he eats!).

[51] Anxiety, an important third category here, will be dealt with later (see p. 641).

reclassifications have been attempted of the instincts or drives on the one hand and of the structure of personality on the other. No agreed-upon groupings have resulted, although there appears to be universal agreement on the need for both classes of variables. More important is the consensus that development results from the integral interaction of biogenic factors *and* environmental influences (i.e., learning). Rapaport (1959, p. 152) has summarized it this way:

Human behavior is neither merely learned (imprinted by repeated experience), nor preformed and merely unfolded in the course of a "maturation" process. . . . [It] develops according to the "ground plan" (Erikson) of an epigenetic process (of which libido development and ego development are specific aspects) through a sequence of developmental crises, whose solution depends as much on the solutions of previous crises [i.e., kinds of solutions not successes or failures] as on the environmental (social) provisions which meet it (Freud, Hartmann, Erikson, Kardiner, Sullivan).

5. *The tension-reduction hypothesis.* Underlying the psychoanalytic theory generally is the hypothesis that motivation results from the arousal of tension(s) and the organization of behavior around tension reduction. This principle has been given various names—the pleasure principle, constancy, wish fulfillment, stability, least effort, entropy, and, in aspects, the death instinct. Each name and description differs somewhat in meaning, but the common core of all is movement from state(s) of greater to state(s) of lesser upset, activation, or tension.

6. *Relative autonomy of structures.* Both primary and secondary apparatuses of ego autonomy—those mediating abilities and capacities (e.g., perception, memory, reflexes) and those involving defenses, modes, and controls, respectively—evolve considerable independence from both instinctual and environmental influence. In our present state of knowledge of neuropsychology and neurophysiology we are unable to identify the bases on which such relatively permanent structures are formed or why they retain their particular forms and relations. On a behavioral basis, however, it is possible to recognize apparently autonomous functional organizations (e.g., attitudes, habits, percepts, consistent thought patterns, responses). These systems are only *relatively* autonomous, however, and subject to influence from drives and conflicts under unusual conditions (e.g., trauma, decompensation). So, for example, perception and memory may, under conditions of strong motivation, be subject to encroachment by wishful distortions. Even such apparatuses of primary autonomy as vision proper may be drawn into conflict and temporarily put out of operation completely, as in hysterical blindness. It is on the assumption of relative autonomy (or

its converse, relative modifiability) that psychotherapy, and even education, becomes at all feasible.

7. *Anxiety and defense.* Second in importance only to the emphasis on unconscious motivation as a contribution of the psychoanalytic writers to an understanding of motivational processes has been the description of the role of anxiety in the economy of the personality (Freud, 1926), and the elaboration and description of the mechanisms of defense (A. Freud, 1936; W. Reich, 1945; Fenichel, 1945). The significance of the central role of anxiety is seen in several ways. First, it provides an additional link between the biological energy substrate and social behavior. Cues, in themselves innocuous, may become motivators through their invocation of anxiety. Second, by positing anxiety as an arousable state, one can subsume apparently tension-increasing behaviors under the tension-reduction hypothesis. Third, the assumption of a central "self-punishing" agent makes more plausible the otherwise-confusing facts of the tenacity of neurotic symptoms and the related phenomenon observed in learning studies, the resistance of avoidance responses to extinction (cf. Mowrer, 1950a). This persistent behavior is observed in the absence of any apparent state of deprivation or present environmental threat (Chapter 11). The persistence of the sometimes highly contrived behavior patterns described as defense mechanisms is also made more plausible when an internal state of discomfort (anxiety) is posited. A fourth aspect of anxiety must also be mentioned, namely, the link which it provides between a present situation and the individual's past. By positing such a self-arousal state in the ego (or the memory system), the intensity of arousal may be correlated not with the evoking stimulus but with the significance of the aroused memory in the life history of the individual. This is certainly one of the core concepts in psychoanalytic motivation theory.

The defense mechanisms themselves—displacement, repression, substitution, symbolization, isolation, projection, reaction formation, etc. —are very useful and accurate clinical descriptions of behavior. As Rapaport (1959) has noted, their closeness to an observational base, unlike some of the more abstract concepts of psychoanalysis, makes their survival as concepts quite likely. That they are mechanisms of *defense* relates to the prior hypothesized role of anxiety in the motivational system, and this seems well enough established.

Although there are always subtle distinctions in definitions, the fact that anxiety [52]—or emotional arousal—is given an important place in

[52] We have here restricted our treatment of emotion to a discussion of anxiety, which is by far the most significant and best treated of the emotions in the

most motivational theories, and in behavior theories generally, and the further fact that considerable progress is being made currently in the psychophysiology of emotion, augurs well for the closer rapprochement of psychoanalytic and other theories of motivation.

8. *Conflict.* Psychoanalytic motivation theory is above all else a theory of intrapsychic conflict. Neuroses, and even psychoses, are seen as derivative developments of otherwise irreducible intrapersonal tensions resulting from mutual inhibition of opposing dynamic forces. The conflict has been variously assigned to opposing instincts or drives, id vs. ego, ego vs. superego, id vs. superego, actual vs. idealized self, drive-energy vs. structure, opposing modes of gratification, impulses or wishes vs. countercathexes, and many other hypothesized structural and/or functional units within the personality. In all cases, it reduces to a clashing of forces, the mutual reduction or satisfaction of which is somehow precluded. Freud tried to epitomize this essential nature of man in his concepts of the life and death instincts, but the concept of conflict reappears as between the individual and society, and then the intrapsychic representatives of biological and social forces. The personality itself is conceived as a product of necessity, born in conflict and guaranteed survival, in a sense, out of the natural contradictions of societal structuring of the environments of developing human organisms.

9. *Early experience.* Not only psychologists, but all of literate mankind has come to recognize the importance of early experience to later development, particularly as a result of Freud's writing. Prior to Freud's time, preverbal and early childhood experiences had tended to be discounted as being able to be replaced by adult reason. Freud argued that the effects of such experiences, though perhaps never verbalized or verbalizable, provide an important foundation (perhaps even the mortar) for the personality structure. Freud's specific hypotheses about the precise stages of psychosexual development (especially as these were tied to the underlying early assumption of an all-pervading sexual libido) may well be replaced. Indeed, they had begun to be modified by Freud himself in his later writing, and have been extensively developed and changed by Erikson. But the role of early experiences as sources of anxiety and as models for later behavior development and persistence has probably now been established.

Considerable clinical evidence from adult psychoanalysis is being accumulated in support of this contention, as well as a growing number of developmental studies (cf. Spitz, 1950; Bowlby, 1951; Ribble,

psychoanalytic literature. For a more extensive treatment of the psychoanalytic theory of affects, see Rapaport (1953).

1944; Whiting & Child, 1953) and of experimental animal studies (cf. Thompson, 1955; Thompson & Schaefer, 1961).

10. *Main limitations.* We have tried to show the changes that have been introduced in psychoanalytic theory, and it must be clear, even from this brief presentation, that attempts are being made to make the system adequate to account for all of the types of behavioral phenomena. In its present state, an unfortunate confusion exists in the plethora of overlapping concepts and nonoperational terms. Despite the confusion of language, however, one has the impression of an increasing realism in psychoanalytic thinking. Having demonstrated the "intrinsic validity" of many of the basic ideas of unconscious motivation, some (though not all) of the theoretically oriented psychoanalysts have now turned to developmental and experimental studies as further means of clarifying as well as testing their ideas.

In addition to the confusions of language, then, we may add that the main limitations of psychoanalytic theory are the lack of an adequate theory of structure acquisition or change (i.e., a learning theory) and the insufficient recognition, so far, of the importance of seeking evidence outside the clinical setting. All three limitations, although quite difficult to surmount, are at least now being approached.

11. *Addendum.* The search for better models goes on. We pointed to the efforts of Rapaport, Gill, and others to restate psychoanalytic theory more comprehensively. Hartmann, Kris, Loewenstein, Rapaport, Holt, and others have most provocatively extended the treatment of the ego apparatuses in an attempt to deal with phenomena of adaptation as ego functions and to point up the relative autonomy of ego functions. Erikson has recast Freudian developmental theory, extending its range through the entirety of the life cycle and showing how ego development is continually modified by the nuclear conflicts of successive social realities and individual needs and capacities. Erikson substitutes the struggles for identity and integrity for the countering of libidinal urges as the main organizing forces of the maturing ego.

A word should be added about another recent attempt to update Freud's metapsychological model. This was Kenneth Colby's *cyclic-circular model*, which appeared in his monograph, *Energy and Structure in Psychoanalysis* (1955). This was an extremely complex and elaborate model, which Colby has since abandoned as too abstract in favor of exploring models in the form of computer programs (Colby, personal communication). However, his purposes in presenting his model are worth mentioning. He wanted to remind his analytic colleagues that Freud himself was a model builder and expected his id-ego-superego structural model to be superceded on the basis of new informa-

tion, just as he himself had practically abandoned his earlier Systems
Cs.-Pcs.-Ucs. Colby objected to the attempts of the new ego psychology movement to enlarge and assign new functions to the ego concept,
since this made it no longer possible effectively to characterize this
overburdened part of Freud's structural system. However, he did agree
that the assigned functions corresponded to observations and had to be
accounted for. His cyclic-circular structural model was such an attempt.
It was cast in terms of a "three-dimensional manifold," attempting to
account for structure and function (energy) simultaneously. Using
modern notions of open-systems and continuous neural activity, Colby
tried to provide a neurophysiological basis for his speculative model.
Although his model was an intriguing tour de force, Colby anticipated
that further knowledge would force the abandonment of a visually
representable model (even in three-dimensions) for some form of
mathematical expression instead. And this is exactly where he is now
spending his efforts.

TYPES OF SUPPORTING EVIDENCE

In discussing evidence for psychoanalytic theories it is necessary to
distinguish between the empirical *sources* from which the theoretical
structure was derived and the independent means of *validating* these
hypotheses. As is generally well known in science, the test of a hypothesis can be made only after a sufficiently clear set of variables has been
identified and objective conditions of observation have been provided
for the affirmation that the variables do indeed relate to each other
in the manner prescribed. We see at once the difficulties which meet
us in applying this approach to psychoanalysis. The complex raw data
are not usually directly available to observation, and when made so
in some artificial way, appear to lose their dynamic quality. This type
of problem is not unknown to other life-sciences investigators who
seek to understand vital biological processes in the living organism,
only to find that the means available for precise assessment permit *in
vitro* study only. One then does what he can do outside of the living
individual and cautiously infers what might have been the case had
direct investigation been possible.

The primary type of evidence for psychoanalytic theory is the reconstructed life history produced by patients during analysis and their
behavior in the analytic situation. Supporting data have also been derived from clinical and naturalistic observation of infants and children,
and from experimental studies of the effects of environmental change
on behavior, including the exploration of unconscious motivation
through the use of projective techniques, hypnosis, and drugs. We

shall discuss each of these briefly, beginning with the analytic case studies.

The Psychoanalytic Case Study

In Freud's time, and to a large extent still, the most usual source of data for both psychoanalytic theorizing and verification of psycho-analytic hypotheses is the series of oral reports of patients undergoing therapy. As we know from our review of these hypotheses in this chapter, however, they deal largely with developmental factors and interactions of hypothetical aspects of the personality with the environment and with each other which occurred long before the patient presents himself for analysis. Thus the raw data of study are not directly available to the analyst but must be inferred from what is expressed (in words and acts) *about* these earlier periods. Further, since the hypothesized personality processes produce a certain amount of self-distortion and deception, it may be assumed that patients' reports will not directly reflect the operation of the underlying processes but will be reconstructed in such a manner as to obscure their nature. The analyst, then, must *interpret* what is expressed to him. By so doing, he may influence the course of subsequent productions. Indeed, this is what he *seeks* to do in his role as therapist. If, then, the research-minded analyst seeks to "test" analytic hypotheses against the "reality" of his observations, he finds himself embarrassed by the degree to which the very hypotheses he wishes to test have shaped the material on which his test is to be conducted.[53]

Freud was early accused of "tracing" the pattern of illness he wished to find on his patients, and to some extent this type of problem is insurmountable! Glover (1956) argues that greater precision of language and of diagnostic categories and a more conscientious and less selective sharing of therapeutic experiences among analysts might, in ten or twenty years, produce the kind of data that could serve as ground for testing some of the crucial analytic hypotheses. The attempts by Dollard et al. (1953) and by the Rogers group (e.g., Rogers & Dymond, 1954) to record and analyze verbatim therapeutic protocols, and thus provide a beginning basis for interpatient comparisons and inter-therapist analysis, are an example of steps in this direction. Bellak (1956) has also made approaches to this type of objectivity. But these attempts have been directed largely to studies of the therapeutic process rather than the validation of underlying hypotheses.

The Menninger Project. A psychoanalytic research group at the

---

[53] The word *contamination* is usually used for a similar situation which arises in an experimental study.

Menninger Clinic has been doing a systematic "naturalistic study of clinical data" (Wallerstein, 1961, p. 12) in an attempt to evaluate psychotherapeutic processes and outcomes and as a means of testing and of more clearly articulating the psychoanalytic theory of therapy.

To control for contamination they worked out "*in advance* the specific predictions, the [theoretical] assumptions on which they are based, the contingencies to which they relate . . . , and the evidence that will be necessary to confirm or refute them" (Wallerstein, 1961, p. 13; see also Wallerstein & Robbins, 1956). They further independently matched patient profiles and took care to isolate evaluative procedures from persons who might influence therapeutic outcome or post-treatment evaluations. The late Helen Sargent (1961), a member of the research team of this project, argued for the *relative* meaning of objectivity in science, pointing to interesting parallels between inference processes in clinical psychology and nuclear physics (as, for example, the unavailability to direct observation of such postulates as ego in psychology and neutrino in physics). She expressed the view of this psychoanalytic research group that *reality* (observer agreement), *relevance* to (or agreement with) known facts, *import* (for hypotheses suggested by observations), and *utility* (hypothesis confirmation) might be more important than traditional concepts of reliability and validity in assessing intrapsychic change. (We may note here, parenthetically, that there is no necessary contradiction between the sets of criteria Dr. Sargent accepts and rejects. She herself points to precedents in psychophysics, for example, for relativistic interpretations of so-called objective events. At any rate, the "heretical" proposals—or rationalizations—which are introduced to underscore the *scientific* nature of this major project appear unnecessary, when one contrasts the systematic approach of this group with the typical anecdotal and highly selective reporting of cases usually appearing in the psychoanalytic literature.)

The Menninger project has not, at this writing, reported any of its analyses. We indeed hope that the results of this program will allow inferences about the validity (and/or utility) of underlying psychoanalytic hypotheses as well as therapeutic processes based on psychoanalytic theory.

The Bethesda Project. A second programmatic approach to the analysis of analytic psychotherapy, with possible inferences for psychoanalytic theory validation, is in progress at the National Institute of Mental Health in Bethesda. Shakow (1960) and Cohen and Cohen (1961) have presented preliminary reports of the work of this group, which consists essentially of the accumulation and analysis of sound motion-picture records of psychoanalytic interviews. Shakow and his associates (see Sternberg et al., 1958) agree with Glover and with the Menninger group as to the unreliability of the therapist as either objective experimenter or recorder. Film-recorded sessions preserve the raw data intact and allow analysis and reanalysis along any dimensions investigators may select. To the extent that this type of information has relevance for validation studies of underlying analytic conceptions, we now have truly comprehensive records for the first time. The challenge of meaningful hypothesis-testing from this mass of data still remains. To date, the Bethesda group has made little systematic progress in their analyses.

Comment. As for the general run of psychoanalytic case reports, Glover's (1956) depreciation of their value as a source of validating data is well taken. Each analyst, himself trained by an analyst, has (or acquires) an emotional investment in the particular point of view to which he has been indoctrinated, etc. Further, the goals of objective investigation of hypotheses, on the one hand, and of psychotherapy, on the other, are often in conflict. Since most psychoanalysts are therapists by training, interest, and source of income, Glover doubts if they will ever voluntarily provide a useful objective source of data for their own or for independent, unbiased evaluation of psychoanalytic hypotheses. The Menninger and Bethesda projects may prove to be worthwhile exceptions to Glover's fears.

Internal Consistency. In fairness, it should be pointed out that Freud, and many of his associates and followers, did not ignore the problem of validity but relied on the *method of internal consistency*, as it has been called, to verify their hypotheses. Rather than cross-case validation, or statistical study, they reasoned that "if-then" relations within cases provide a means of validation. Thus, taking symptom formation as an example, if a patient presents a particular hysterical symptom and, in the course of therapy, a relation is "discovered" between the symptom and some early traumatic episode, a hypothesis of relationship may be said to exist. If, on working through this early period, the symptom can be understood as a defense against anxiety and can be done away with on the reduction of the anxiety, then, *ipso facto,* the theory of symptom development as anxiety defense has been "proved." Those trained in the rigorous logic of the scientific method will immediately object to the "looseness" of this line of thinking, but considering the highly complex nature of the variables involved, it is easy to see why this type of reasoning would be considered sufficient proof for the existence of the underlying chain of events. At any rate, considerable evidence of this sort has been amassed in the psychoanalytic literature, and it is pointed to whenever attacks are made on psychoanalytic theory as being unsubstantiated speculation. To Freud's credit, we should remember that he applied his criterion, however inadequate it may appear to his critics, with unfailing rigor. The sharp revision of the anxiety theory (1926) and the gradual changes from a libido to an ego theory, which we have traced in this chapter, were the results of internal inconsistencies, which showed the need for modification of the theoretical framework. This method, then, can produce change in a theory on the basis of contradictions, as well as support a theory on the basis of internal confirmation.

We must here make the obvious point, however, that although this type of thinking has some merit and may suffice as a rationalization for therapy, it cannot substitute for eventual precise and independent verification as scientific theory. This is particularly true when it is being evaluated as a theory of motivation for general psychology.

Three further points need to be stressed as well. First, we have said that such internal proof may be acceptable as a rationalization for therapy, but in fact this would be permissible only if therapy as such could independently be determined to be successful. The evidence for the success of psychoanalytic therapy is itself far from satisfactory and therefore provides very little by way of confirmation of the vaguely validated underlying postulate system. Second, the fact that alternate, and sometimes quite opposite, theoretical assumptions may be used to explain the same symptom-acquisition or symptom-remission places more of a burden on the direct validation of theory (as contrasted with inferred validation as a result of therapeutic success). Finally, of course, inferred validation is not to be dismissed if, at least, it can be itself indirectly corroborated by investigations using more than one method. It is to recent attempts to obtain such independent verification that we now turn.

Clinical Observations of Infants and Children

Since many of the analytic hypotheses concern early development, a reasonable source of supporting data for analytic theories might be expected to be found in direct observations of young children.[54] In fact, a considerable amount of such clinical material abounds in the literature, particularly in the annual volumes of *The Psychoanalytic Study of the Child* (A. Freud, et al., 1945 on). Unfortunately, such reports of observations lack the rigor of experimental studies, on the one hand, and the

[54] A more extensive treatment of some of these studies will be found in Chapter 13.

intensity of analytic case materials, on the other. Further, they inevitably suffer from problems of adequacy of representative sampling.

In 1949, Orlansky reviewed a series of such studies, with a view to assessing the state of knowledge of relations of infant-care conditions to personality formation. He included studies of nursing experiences (breast vs. bottle feeding, length of breast feeding, self-demand vs. scheduled feeding, weaning, and thumb-sucking), "mothering," sphincter training, restraint of motion, and infant "frustration" and "aggression." After a careful examination of the research literature then available, Orlansky concluded that ". . . personality is not the resultant of instinctual infantile libidinal drives mechanically channeled by parental disciplines . . ." (1949, p. 39), but a result of unique person-environment interactions. He felt that "orthodox Freudian theory" was less adequate than such neo-Freudian sociocultural theories as Horney's (1939) or Fromm's (1941) in dealing with the facts (particularly the cross-cultural evidence) of child-rearing practices as contributors to personality structure.

Lowrey (1940), Goldfarb (1944), Bowlby (1951), Freud and Burlingham (1944), Ribble (1943, 1944), and Spitz (1945, 1946a, b, 1950) have all presented observational data to support the desirability of close, warm "mothering" for young children. Their investigations included semi-structured stimulus situations in which both specific responses and gross physical and motor developmental changes were studied, over a period of time, in relation to the type of mother-child setting provided in early life. Spitz, for example, reports a series of comparisons of infants reared in a foundling home, a nursery, and private homes. Taking successive behavior samples, noting changes in developmental level (as compared with Hetzer-Wolf baby test premeasurements), and observing changes in responses to standard stimulus settings, Spitz showed how "hospitalism" and "anaclitic depression" resulted from a lack of close mother-child relation or from separation of mother and child, respectively. He concluded that an early "affective interchange" is essential for healthy emotional, physical, and behavioral development. In further experimental clinical studies, Spitz has attempted to determine the developmental stages at which certain social behaviors emerge (e.g., smiling, anxiety) and the relation of the type of environment to this emergence pattern.

Pumpian-Mindlin (1952b) considers Spitz's studies as significant steps in progress in the experimental-observational testing of analytic hypotheses. Pinneau (1950, 1955a, b), on the other hand, has severely criticized the work of Spitz and of Ribble and L. Fischer (1952), as well, on the basis that their study designs and procedures and their sampling were hardly adequate to support the wide conclusions drawn. In an exchange between Pinneau and Spitz (1955), a number of the difficulties of this type of research became apparent.[55] For example, the matching of subject samples in natural environments, the control of "irrelevant" variables, the background factors which produce the samples (e.g., foundling-home children are possibly different to begin with from children either born in a prison nursery to unmarried mothers or reared in private homes by their own parents), etc., make it difficult to know whether the differences observed are due to the variables studied or not.

Pinneau makes it clear that he is not challenging the actual validity of the conclusions drawn by Spitz and the others, but rather the right of these authors to draw such sweeping conclusions from the poorly controlled (and therefore inconclusive) evidence they were able to amass. And, admittedly, despite the best intentions of the most honest investigators, obtaining objective and critical information on early behavior in human infants is an extremely difficult job. We cannot but hope to encourage more studies of the observational-experimental sort. But we must recognize that studies in natural settings, especially with humans, will always have to be interpreted cautiously because of the poor controls which usually characterize such situations.

The difficulties associated with this particular area of investigation are succinctly summarized by Garner (1954) in a review of a collection of papers and reports of observations by Klein et al. (1952). She writes: ". . . there are no conventional, generally accepted psychological methods for interpreting the emotional significance of infant behavior. Consequently, there are many theories, little data, and deep frustrations" (p. 191).

The more generous financial support of research in this past decade has provided the opportunity for more ambitious as well as more systematic observational programs. We are now getting an increased number of reports of large-scale observational studies of children as well as studies of parent-child interactions and of parents' attitudes via interviews and questionnaires (cf. Sears, Maccoby, & Levin, 1957; Escalona & Heider, 1959; Barker & Wright, 1955). Although these investigations do not always involve the use of precise experimental controls, they at least give careful descriptions of the *total* settings in which the data are gathered. If a sufficient number of such studies accumulates, consistency of finding across enough different uncontrolled situations may provide some type of supporting (or questioning) evidence for theoretical hypotheses.

[55] The ethical considerations here involved will be discussed in the next section on experimental studies.

Experimental Studies

Ideally, one would test, directly in the laboratory, the hypotheses stemming from psychoanalytic theory. However, on at least two grounds, such direct validation is impossible. First is the obvious difficulty in translating many conceptual abstractions (such as psychic energy, repression, or death instinct) into quantitative terms and in arriving at acceptable operations for the manipulation of such intrapsychic variables, or for the measurement of change in their state. Second, and really most important, is the fact that such tests would require severe manipulation of the environments of human beings, a possibility ruled out by the ethical code of psychological investigators. For example, to test the hypothesis that early-occurring traumatic experiences prevent "normal" ego-development and thus lead to an unstable or asocial personality structure, the experimenters would need to traumatize some children deliberately to observe if the effects were as predicted. Obviously, the ethical investigator, no matter how eager to determine the validity of this hypothesis, would be unable to induce a condition in his subjects, the effects of which might be permanently damaging.

Studies of Early Environment. Because of these limitations, most of the "objective studies" of psychoanalytic hypotheses have been of the observational or "counting" type. Standardized observation, interviews, ratings, and questionnaires have been used, but these have done little more than tally the frequency of occurrence of an event or a condition, usually naturally observed or recalled, as a function of presumed antecedents.

Sears (1943, 1944) has reviewed a large number of observational studies of non-nutritive sucking in infants reared "normally." These naturalistic studies (e.g., Pratt, Nelson, & Sun, 1930; Levy, 1928; Jensen, 1932; Halverson, 1938; and MacFarlane, 1939) led to the conclusion that there is an innate sucking need. This was further supported by such classic experiments as Levy's (1934) with puppies, in which litter-mates were given breast, small-hole nipple and large-hole nipple feedings, with the greatest amount of non-nutritive sucking being found in those puppies receiving the least amount of nutritive sucking (i.e., the puppies using nipples with large holes). These studies,[56] widely accepted as demonstrating the existence of the oral stage of psychosexual development, were also taken as at least indirect evidence for the instinctual nature of libido.

More recently, however, Davis et al. (1948), in an excellent demonstration of the value of experimental manipulation of the environment

[56] See, also, discussions of studies in Chapters 4 and 13.

to the establishment of scientific information, studied sucking behavior in infants who were *cup*-fed from birth. In the absence of initial sucking experience, *no* evidence of a sucking need was found. In other words, the presumedly innate sucking need is apparently a function of the "natural" rearing practices to which infants are exposed. We would agree with Hilgard (1952) that studies such as this are quite necessary to the ultimate separation of fact from fancy. Actually, data from questionnaire studies (e.g., Hamilton, 1929; Hattendorf, 1932; and Landis et al., 1940) and from observations in other cultures (e.g., Mead's study of the Arapesh, 1935; Malinowski's study of the Trobriand Islanders, 1927) have given only partial support to some of Freud's generalizations about cross-sex identification, the Oedipus complex, the desexualized latency period, etc.

Observational studies, and even experimental studies in naturalistic settings, thus require extremely broad sampling, as a minimum, before they can be offered as evidence. Even then, as we have earlier pointed out, it is difficult to separate out the possible influences of simultaneously operating variables. Experimental studies require careful replication and testing along the whole range of any variable as well (as may be evident in comparing the studies and findings of Levy and Davis et al., for example).

Animal Experimentation. A number of investigators have developed experimental analogues of psychoanalytic concepts and sought to test them with animal subjects.[57] J. McV. Hunt (1941), for example, used food deprivation in infant rats to study the effects of frustration on later food-related behavior. He found that rats having such experience would later hoard significantly more food than did rats spared this early traumatic experience. Hunt's findings have since been confirmed by other investigators (see Morgan, 1947). Similar effects of early experience on later behavior, especially under stressful conditions, have been reported for a number of years, as on aggression (Scott, 1958) and regression (Mowrer, 1940).

Miller (1948*b*), in a most ingenious experiment, suggested that the psychoanalytic concept of *displacement* might be understood in terms of the learning theory concept of *generalization*. He proceeded to demonstrate how rats, taught to avoid a shock by striking each other, would "displace" this learned aggressive response onto a doll present in the experimental chamber in the absence of the second rat or, secondarily, onto the walls of the chamber in the absence of rat and doll.[58] Dollard and Miller (1950) have made extensive use of such analogies in their

[57] See, also, discussions of studies in Chapters 4 and 13.
[58] But see discussion of this study in relation to aggression in Chapter 14.

learning theory interpretation of personality. In fact, their analysis draws heavily on psychoanalytic concepts, in turn providing these concepts with a measure of experimental support.

Hilgard (1952, 1956) has pointed up the inherent weaknesses of both experimental analogues utilizing animals and inferences based on manipulations of early environments. In the first instance, there is the questionable assumption, especially when one is dealing with presumed intrapsychic events, that the variables being manipulated in animal studies are the same as, or even analogous to, those in humans. Rapaport (1959) has expressed similar, and even stronger, reservations. And in the second, Hilgard disputes the possibility of separating out the influences of the earlier experience(s), in such studies as Hunt's, from those concurrent with the later effect(s) being tested. This criticism is actually made with respect to child-rearing conditions, which are even less controllable, or even assessable, than those under which laboratory animals are reared.

The Use of Projective Techniques. Truly experimental studies with human subjects have been few, for the many reasons already noted. The closest examples to be found are those studies using projective techniques. They have usually been especially designed to elicit responses predictably associated with particular developmental stages or experimentally induced conditions. Friedman (1952), for example, used a story-completion task to show that during the latency period (ages 7 to 12) children more often gave castration-type endings to stories than did either younger or older children. These results were interpreted as consistent with the psychoanalytic prediction of less castration anxiety during latency.

Along similar lines, Blum (1949) developed the Blacky Test as a means of validating psychoanalytic hypotheses regarding psychosexual development. The test consists of a series of 12 cartoons depicting Blacky, a male or female dog (depending on the sex of the test subject) in relation to "Papa," "Mama," and a sibling dog. The cartoons and instructions were cleverly designed to elicit responses that could be categorized as "oral eroticism," "oral sadism," "castration anxiety" (males), "penis envy" (females), etc. In Blum's original study, using normal college men and women, 14 of 15 analytic hypotheses were confirmed. However, as the author himself makes clear in discussing his findings, one could always quibble with the construct validity of the various parts of such an instrument. Later studies using the Blacky Pictures (Blum & Hunt, 1952; Blum & Miller, 1952) continued the cautious hopefulness that the instrument would prove useful in providing independent validation for psychoanalytic concepts.

Friedman's fable completions and Blum's Blacky Pictures are only two of a host of other possible devices that have been and can be used to elicit thought content. Other forms of sentence completion, picture interpretation, self-ratings, and word-association techniques (this last a traditional psychoanalytic tool [see Kubie,1952]) are also of value in providing a means of escaping the censor in attempting to assess unconscious content and through such assessment verifying theoretical claims about its nature.

Studies of Memory, Thinking and Perception. From experimental psychology and from social psychology have come large numbers of studies of selective remembering and forgetting (see Zeller, 1950a; Hilgard, 1956) and of perceptual defense (see Hall, 1961). These generally lend support to the psychoanalytic concept of repression and point the way to an understanding of its mode of operation. Generally, pleasant memories tend to be retained longer than unpleasant ones, memories associated with taboo areas tend to be recalled less well, and some form of denial mechanism—a defensive "nonseeing" or at least nonreporting of anxiety-related percepts—appears to be clearly demonstrable.

Studies of the organization and pathology of thought (see Rapaport, 1951a) help to illuminate the relationships between consciousness and the unconscious and the distortion processes of repression and secondary elaboration in pathological cases.

Hypnosis, Drugs, and the Experimental Implantation of Mental Content. Finally, we may point to the recently expanding areas having to do with contrived or experimentally induced conditions. Through the use of hypnosis or hypnagogic drugs, investigators have been able to approach more closely the "more highly charged storm centers" of the mental apparatus (see Pumpian-Mindlin [1952a] for a discussion of some of this work). Dreams can be "seeded" with specific content, the modification of which can then be traced. Experimentally induced conflicts, like miniature neuroses, can be studied at close quarters, and the use of psychogenic drugs has even permitted exploration of more serious disorders.

Summary

There are, then, a number of possible ways, in addition to the analytic case approach, by which psychoanalytic hypotheses can be evaluated. That these methods are indirect and require a degree of language translation and concept definition is readily acknowledged by their proponents. The laboratory analogues have been generally supportive of psychoanalytic hypotheses, but, as Hilgard (1952) has warned, they have thus far dealt with only the ". . . most superficial aspects of psychoanalytic theory, while many of the deeper problems are scarcely touched" (p. 43). The newer methods noted above and the renewed interest of many within the psychoanalytic camp (see e.g., Rapaport, 1959, 1960; Rapaport & Gill, 1959; Toman, 1960) in pressing forward toward more systematic (and thus testable) statements of the analytic position, give hope of a real rapprochement between psychoanalysis and the main body of scientific psychology.

A FINAL WORD

It is probably unnecessary to recapitulate here the many specific criticisms which have been made of this or that aspect of Freudian theory. They have come both from within the camp of the psychoanalysts and from many other sources as well. Outside the scientific area a highly emotional debate raged for a long while as to the "desirability" of the sweeping claims made by or attributed to psychoanalysis—a debate stimulated by the perceived threat to vested interests in theological and politico-philosophic positions. Interestingly enough, this debate has largely subsided, with a wider acceptance of and accommodation to psychoanalysis in the literary world, for example, than it has ever received in the scientific community.

Within science, the criticisms have focused on the untestability of the many poorly defined analytic concepts and the limited evidence on which the system rests. Unfortunately for its acceptance as scientific theory, many of its practitioners and supporters, themselves largely untrained in the rigors of scientific evidence accumulation, defend their positions either by rejecting the very notion of and need for independent testing or by presenting voluminous subjective case records as "proof" of their point of view.

It is encouraging that, in the past two decades particularly, a new vitalization of psychoanalytic theory *and* research has been taking place. As has been noted, the contributions to the "new psychoanalysis" of Hartmann, Kris, Erikson, the late David Rapaport, Toman, Colby, the research groups at Menninger, New York University, the National Institute of Mental Health, and the various psychiatric institutes make us aware that Freudian psychoanalysis is far from passing into the history of psychology with the death of its founder. It has apparently rededicated itself, and is at last making its bid for serious consideration as scientific theory.

Chapter 13

Self-Actualization and Related Concepts

In the other chapters of this book, the models described are essentially concerned with this fundamental problem: to explain some part of or all the conduct of organisms by means of motivational processes. By and large, conduct has been accepted as it occurs, and assumptions concerning motivational factors have been made as necessary, in the view of the theorist, to account for this conduct. Although the widely varying assumptions and the lack of critical and decisive evidence relative to them (which we have seen and will see again) are clear indications that the field of motivation is a poorly developed one, these attempts may at least be said to fall within the ordinary operations of a scientific approach: phenomena are observed and described, efforts are made to define and demonstrate factors which antedate, explain, control, or underlie them, and these factors are integrated loosely or firmly into a theoretical formulation. Such formulations are usually as parsimonious as possible, testable at some level, and usually neutral in a valuational sense, that is, they do not judge conduct. As theories, they are assessed in terms of how well they account for the evidence and what their testability is, but not in terms of criteria other than these or similar ones.

In recent years, two movements have shown an accelerating development which, in certain respects, deviates from these ordinary operations of a scientific approach. One of them, stemming generally from humanistic studies and philosophy, is *existentialism;* the other, stemming largely from psychology and psychiatry but also from sociology, we here refer to by the phrase "the emphasis on *self-actualization.*" To us, the two movements appear to have many similarities, but there also seem to be some differences. Because we find it of greater relevance to the field of motivation, we shall confine ourselves largely to the emphasis on self-actualization, prefacing our discussion of this topic with a brief consideration of existentialism.

656

EXISTENTIALISM

Although such thinkers as Socrates, St. Augustine, Duns Scotus, and Blaise Pascal are often mentioned as precursors of modern existentialism, it is safe to say that in the West, existentialism has fully emerged only recently, starting with the work of Sören Kierkegaard (1813–1855) and Friedrich Nietzsche (1844–1900). It is represented in the contemporary period by Karl Jaspers, Martin Heidegger, and Jean Paul Sartre, among others.

There are a number of points characteristically discussed in the existentialist viewpoint. One is the collapse of religion, which characterized the nineteenth and twentieth centuries. Nietzsche, for example, said that God is dead. It is true that many people still go to church and profess belief, but to the existentialists this kind of religion is apparently much less fully involving and meaningful to its communicants than were earlier Christianity and other faiths. In reading existentialist literature, one feels that the loss of faith is a highly significant factor in leading to the development of existentialist thinking. With this loss of faith, of course, must come also a sense of the brevity of human life; immortality in an after-life is a belief that disappears with loss of faith. In addition, however, the existentialists emphasize the transitoriness of human thought, institutions, and achievements in general. Barrett (1958) expresses this as the realization of human finitude; it seems to be a part, at least, of what is referred to as "the encounter with nothingness." That is, the values, goals, and beliefs of societies which transcend the individual's life are, to that individual, meaningless beyond his individual life.

A second aspect of existentialist thought is to deny the supremacy of reason, or rationality. This denial takes several forms. One is to stress that there are strong, irrational impulsions in human nature, a point emphasized by Schopenhauer, who influenced Nietzsche and, in his later years, Kierkegaard. These forces are not to be denied. Rather, one must recognize and come to terms with them. Another form is the emphasis on the individual, direct experiencing of life, rather than dependency on mediate experience such as is provided by books, newspapers, magazines, and, in the modern day, radios and television. There is something of the Romantic concern with direct experience of nature in many of the existentialists. What is abstract, classified, or general tends to be rejected as against the concrete, specific, or unique in experience. A third form is the emphasis on the subjective *experience* of truth as a sufficient *criterion* of truth. External or intersubjective testability of propositions is not seen by the existentialists as a critical feature that must be possessed by what is true.

A third point which existentialists make is that scientific and technical achievements have not solved the problem of man's existence but rather have placed difficulties in the way of man's solution of this problem himself. One difficulty arose, it is argued, from the success of Science. This success led to a belief, more prevalent in the nineteenth than in the twentieth century, that there is a perfect order in nature which reason, in the guise of Science, would discover. From Science, this belief holds, there would derive an ascending curve of progress under the envelope of which human problems would disappear. Such a rational view, the existentialists argue, ignores the irrational forces in man and the vast uncertainties in basic issues of Science itself (as examples, Heisenberg's principle and Gödel's proof). Such a view of human destiny, that is of human beings living in a rationally ordered society, implies that human beings can be manipulated as things are. Such manipulation the existentialists would not accept, even if they thought it fully possible. The manipulation and control of natural objects, in the interests of scientific and technical "progress," they feel, are bad enough.

A fourth point is that in the highly technological, mass production society, which has emerged in the last century or so, and especially in recent decades with their emphasis on mass communication, propaganda, and conformity, the individual being is lost. Karl Jaspers, as Barrett (1958, p. 28) summarizes it, "sees the historical meaning of existential philosophy as a struggle to awaken in the individual the possibilities of an authentic and genuine life, in the face of the great modern drift toward a standardized mass society." Barrett further suggests that since the First World War Western society is "in a state of dissolution"; he indicates what this means for the individual as follows:

The individual is thrust out of the sheltered nest that society has provided. He can no longer hide his nakedness by the old disguises. He learns how much of what he has taken for granted was by its own nature neither eternal nor necessary but thoroughly temporal and contingent. He learns that the solitude of the self is an irreducible dimension of human life no matter how completely that self had seemed to be contained in its social milieu. In the end, he sees each man as solitary and unsheltered before his own death. Admittedly, these are painful truths, but the most basic things are always learned with pain, since our inertia and complacent love of comfort prevent us from learning them until they are forced upon us. It appears that man is willing to learn about himself only after some disaster . . . (1958, p. 30).

May et al. make a similar point this way:

When a culture is caught in the profound convulsions of a transitional period, the individuals in the society understandably suffer spiritual and emotional upheaval, and finding that the accepted mores and ways of thought no longer yield security, they tend either to sink into dogmatism and conformism, giving up awareness, or are forced to strive for a heightened self-consciousness, by which to become aware of their existence with a new conviction and on new bases (1958, p. 17).

In the following quotation, Ellenberger presents a clear summary of this aspect of existentialism:

Some of the main features of the structure of human existence had already been outlined by Kierkegaard. Man is not a ready-made being; man will become what he makes of himself and nothing more. Man constructs himself through his choices, because he has the freedom to make vital choices, above all the freedom to choose between an *inauthentic* and an *authentic* modality of existence. Inauthentic existence is the modality of the man who lives under the tyranny of the *plebs* (the crowd, i.e., the anonymous collectivity). Authentic existence is the modality in which a man assumes the responsibility for his own existence. In order to pass from inauthentic to authentic existence, a man has to suffer the ordeal of despair and "existential anxiety," i.e., the anxiety of man facing the limits of his existence with its fullest implications: death, nothingness. This is what Kierkegaard calls the "sickness unto death" (in May et al., 1958, p. 188).

The foregoing paragraphs represent an abbreviated review of some of the major aspects of existentialist thought. Even more difficult to reduce to brief compass are their positive assertions as to what a man can do or can try to do. A great deal is made of the difference between existence and essence; the essence of a thing cannot be discovered (if there is an essence at all), the argument goes, unless its existence is first realized and accepted. Barrett (1958, p. 84) illustrates this point by indicating that Plato and Aristotle would ask, "What is Man?", whereas St. Augustine would ask, "Who am I?" Barrett goes on to say,

. . . this shift is decisive. The first question presupposed a world of objects, a fixed natural and zoological order, in which man was included; and when man's precise place in that order had been found, the specifically differentiating characteristic of reason was added. Augustine's question, on the other hand, stems from an altogether different, more obscure and vital center within the questioner himself: from an acutely personal sense of dereliction and loss, rather than from the detachment with which reason surveys the world of objects in order to locate its bearer, man, zoologically within it. Augustine's question, therefore, implies that man cannot be defined by being located in that natural order, for man, as the being who asks himself, Who am I?, has already broken through the barriers of the animal world (p. 84).

To answer Augustine's question lies in the realm of existence, whereas Plato's and Aristotle's question is answerable in terms of essences or properties of things.

What the existentialists then seem to ask, first, is that Man realize what he is, that is, a being who will someday die, who has strong irrational forces within him, and who cannot realistically be comforted by religious, political, scientific, or other illusions. To reach, appreciate, and live with these realizations is a task that is difficult and fraught with anxiety or dread. But only if such realizations are achieved can man achieve a natural, holistic, and individual life. The existentialists, however, do not provide specific guidelines for a way of life or indicate what the future of an existentialist man or society would be like. Perhaps it would be nonexistential for them to do so. Mystic, religious states may represent one solution.

May et al. (1958), on the other hand, emphasize that the realization of one's potentials can occur once being as existence is accepted and understood. In this point, they seem close to the viewpoint that we have called the emphasis on self-actualization. Since the adherents of this viewpoint have many more things to say that are directly relevant to the problem of motivation than have the existential philosophers, we shall leave the latter at this point. The similarities in their thought and the thought of those who emphasize self-actualization will, we think, be evident as we proceed.

THE EMPHASIS ON SELF-ACTUALIZATION

We made the point, a moment ago, that existentialism appears to depart from the ordinary scientific canon under which efforts are made to describe, explain or control, and to theorize about phenomena. The existentialist approach seems to involve an acceptance of phenomena as they are and, within the framework provided by these phenomena, to urge men to find their ways of life in terms of what is true and important to them and their self-realization. Existentialism is thus suggestive of a way of life, similar to that developed in such Oriental systems as Zen Buddhism, based on a close analysis of the conditions and meaning of existence.

Although many, if not most, of the writers who emphasize self-actualization retain a scientific orientation,[1] they, like the existentialists,

[1] For a statement integrating his scientific and therapeutic commitments, see Rogers (1955a). More generally, see Royce (1959).

seem to be primarily concerned with stating the conditions and pre-requisites for living a satisfactory human life. While these prerequisites and conditions may be discovered through scientific analysis (rather than through philosophical consideration), it is important to note here that this is a *different goal* for science from the ones stressed elsewhere in this book. The whole of human life, rather than specific aspects of it, is the problem to which the emphasis on self-actualization is dedicated.

There are three essential points around which a discussion of the emphasis on self-actualization may be organized. One is the conception of human nature; that is, what are the essential properties of being human and what would be the characteristics of human life were these properties to be fully realized? To some extent, at least, these are motivational questions. A second point is the factors which *prevent* the realization of their human potentials by most people; this, too, involves motivational questions. The third point, which overlaps with the first, concerns the nature of motivation in the self-actualized person. We shall discuss these three points in a moment.

First we briefly sketch some aspects of the development of the emphasis on self-actualization and indicate the major theorists we have placed in this category.

Development of the Emphasis on Self-Actualization

We can describe this emphasis as stressing the *uniqueness* of the individual, as emphasizing a *holistic* or *organismic* and *phenomenological* approach to human experience and conduct, and as insisting that the individual must discover his *real self* and make the best of it in order to be healthy, no matter how difficult this task is.

While the uniqueness of man among the creatures of earth has been held for centuries, it was particularly stressed in the German movement known as Geisteswissenschaft or Kulturwissenschaft in the years immediately preceding and following the turn of the twentieth century. Stressed here was the idea that methods for the study of human personality and culture should not be the reductive, analytic, nomothetic methods of natural science (Naturwissenschaft), but that methods used should reflect the unique, individual integration which is achieved by each person. Personal autobiography, other personal documents, and similar sources of information were considered more appropriate to the study of personality and cultural history and movements than such techniques as test scores, laboratory procedures, and the like.

A chief interpreter and advocate of this viewpoint in the United States is Gordon Allport (1937, 1942, 1960, 1961), who has insisted that methods must be used to study the unique, undivided personality [2] and that the motivations of normal adults are (1) functionally autonomous, rather than dependent on bodily needs or infantile deprivations, (2) frequently known in awareness, rather than unconscious, and (3) highly individual, rather than shared with other men. He has also argued that ego and self-concepts must find a place in contemporary psychology (Allport, 1943). Allport has kept alive a point of view in American psychology which, until recently, found little general support. Much in the emphasis on self-actualization is consistent with his position.

The organismic-holistic emphasis has also been stressed in medicine and neurology and by Gestalt psychology (Hall & Lindzey, 1957, pp. 296–297). The chief point in the organismic argument is that organisms function as wholes, as integrated units, rather than as part-systems. The study of a particular response system or intellectual process would, it is argued, be most profitably pursued if the entire organism is considered, as compared with the artificial and limited situation which arises when the effort is made to isolate a system and to study it by itself. Kurt Goldstein (1939, 1942) has made much of this point in his studies of brain-injured persons.

Gestalt psychology has emphasized holism in the study especially of perception and problem-solving, in which, it is argued, one can best understand the nature of the processes involved by viewing them as belonging in an integrated and interrelated *field* of events and processes. In perception, for example, a stimulus may be seen quite differently as it appears in one configuration or in another. The classical Gestalt psychologists did not directly stress problems of personality and motivation, but their field-orientation has been influential in these areas.

Phenomenology [3] refers usually to a way of looking at experience. It was developed by Edmund Husserl (1859–1938), a student both of Brentano and Carl Stumpf. Husserl insisted that one must take experience as it comes, in order to know it, without analysis, without interpretation, and the like. To know the world, for example, one must observe what is there in experience, uninfluenced by theories of reality, sets to observe this or that, or in this or that way. Openness to direct experience and the description of that experience in essentially unsophisticated ways are seen as basic to the understanding of the world (and, in its existentialist form, the inner world). The Gestalt psychologists have tended to be phenomenologists, as have the organismic theorists. Allport's emphasis on the importance of consciously experi-

[2] Cf. Meehl (1954).
[3] For brief historical accounts, see Boring (1950), MacLeod (1947).

enced motivations is similarly an expression of a phenomenological viewpoint. Much of what is said by those who emphasize self-actualization (and existentialism) can be summarized as the desirability of and the necessity for people to experience the world and themselves as they are, rather than as some theory, belief, or convention would make them appear.

The essential meaning of the concept, self-actualization, is found in the discovery of the real self and its expression and development. We have already seen, in the discussion of existentialism, some of the precursors of this concept. Another influence, in our view, was provided by some of the early dissidents from Freud's thinking, notably Adler, Jung, and Rank. As we noted in Chapter 12, all of them disagreed with Freud's emphasis on infantile sexuality as the primary basis of conduct, each offering a substitute emphasis of some relevance to the present discussion of self-actualization. We shall now deal with each, briefly.[4]

Adler, it will be recalled, early emphasized that organ inferiority was a source of compensatory striving and that aggressive and power motives were important constituents of the motivational life of man. Later on, his ideas shifted to a major extent, so that he came to emphasize social interest and striving for perfection (which is like self-actualization, cf. White, 1957, p. 2; Hall & Lindzey, 1957, p. 120) as motives. Inferiority feelings, not limited to those arising from organ deficiencies, continued to figure prominently in his system, because the young child is inferior, physically and otherwise, to many if not all of the people of his environment. However, a loving and trustworthy social environment, especially that provided by the mother, could channel the striving arising from inferiority feelings into a constructive working toward perfection, a channel oriented to the interests and welfare of others as well as of the self, rather than a compensation through striving for superiority or dominance over others. We would interpret these ideas to mean that if a sufficient feeling of personal worth can be achieved early in life, then the individual's natural *social interest* will be able to express itself satisfactorily in his relations with others.

Adler's emphasis on social interest (*Gemeinschaftsgefühl*) and on the feeling of personal worth or value was accompanied by a belief in the uniqueness of the self. He admitted the role of conscious processes in personality and emphasized the point that goals or expectations relative to the future are quite important to the motivation of men. While

---

[4] For secondary accounts of these writers and for references, see Mullahy (1948), Blum (1953), Munroe (1955), Hall and Lindzey (1957). Ansbacher and Ansbacher (1956) have recently provided an extensive selection from Adler's writings. See, also, Progoff (1956).

these features do not exhaust the many facets of his system, they do, with what has already been said, indicate the major notions that have similarity to those in the emphasis on self-actualization.

C. G. Jung (1875–1961) was the next major deviator from Freud (see Chapter 12). Jung's system is quite complex, and many of his concepts have little directly to do with motivation or with the emphasis on self-actualization. Like Adler, however, Jung stresses the future in his account of conduct, that is, the goals or aims of the individual. Jung called this aim "self-actualization," and, as Hall and Lindzey (1957, p. 96) say, this "means the fullest, most complete differentiation and harmonious blending of all aspects of man's total personality." They indicate that Jung was the first to use this phrase, and Mullahy (1948, p. 160) has brought out Jung's emphasis on the potential for individuality of people rather than conformity.

A third major deviationist from Freud, who may be seen as stressing self-actualization, was Otto Rank (1885–1939). Rank felt that only through the expression of individuality could we be creative, and he referred to the person who achieves this expression as the "artist." Standing in the way of this achievement is the anxiety which separation from the mass or herd brings; to reach individuality one must necessarily experience this anxiety but not be permanently set back by it. The trauma of birth provides the first experience of separation and anxiety, and further development and individuation of the person involves more separation and anxiety like that of birth. Most people—the "average man"—according to Rank, do not attempt to achieve individuality. They conform to external demands, first of the mother and father, later of society. But the artist faces and resolves the conflict between this symbiotic union (which is a sort of "death") and his individuality (a sort of "life-force"). The neurotic individual lies between these two poles; he cannot accept the symbiotic union but is yet not free to express individuality without guilt and anxiety (Munroe, 1955). In Rankian terms he is probably psychologically closer to self-actualization than is the average man, because his neurosis at least expresses a movement toward individuality. For Rank, one could say, the suffering of the neurotic is valuable because it shows him to be on the way to an expression of individuality, which those who remain "average" cannot achieve.

We have seen already the influence of the organismic view of personality, with its stress on holism and uniqueness, and of phenomenology and Gestalt psychology on the development of the emphasis on self-actualization. Adler, Jung, and Rank represent a third anticipatory influence, one which is receiving contemporary recognition. There is another, somewhat indirect influence which we think turned the thoughts of theorists away from certain Freudian conceptions and led some of them, ultimately, to the emphasis on self-actualization. This is cultural anthropology and sociology.

Prior to the 1920's and 1930's the tendency of psychoanalytic, psychiatric, and psychological theorists of motivation and personality was to emphasize man's biological characteristics and to ignore, in large measure, the fact that he functions in a social environment. A biological determinism often assumes that human nature is much the same everywhere. However, sociology and cultural anthropology discovered that man is not the same wherever he exists. While he must, wherever he is, eat, sleep, drink, procreate, etc., the *ways* in which he does these things and the rules governing these performances may vary widely as a function of the social class or caste to which a man belongs, the geographical area within a country in which he lives, and the culture of which his nation or his group is a participant. In addition, man's values, goals, morals, beliefs, and even his definitions of normality and abnormality can be seen to be influenced, not biologically but socially or culturally. Such a relativism certainly does not accord well with the prior role assigned to a more or less fixed biological constitution.

These ideas from sociology and anthropology have had a widespread effect on the behavioral sciences. Their significance to our present concern arises from the fact that many of the presuppositions of classical psychoanalytic theory were thereby challenged (Thompson, 1950) and led, at least in part, to the theories of Erich Fromm and Karen Horney, who in many respects stand at the forefront of those who emphasize self-actualization.[5]

We summarize this section concerning the development of the emphasis on self-actualization by simply listing the influences we have mentioned: the organismic view of the person, with its emphasis on wholeness and uniqueness; phenomenology; Gestalt psychology; Adler, Jung, and Rank, who, in their deviations from Freud, brought out the importance of individuality and man's orientation to future goals; cultural anthropology and sociology, which directed attention away from biological characteristics and toward the socio-cultural environment. Table 13–1 contains the recent and contemporary theorists we would place together as emphasizing self-actualization or some closely kindred concept. We cannot here discuss each of them in detail and

---

[5] Among those notably influenced by the socio-cultural findings was Harry Stack Sullivan. Although he did postulate a tendency to mental health (Sullivan, 1947, p. 49), we find the structure of his theory, though not its content, similar to that of classical psychoanalysis.

will content ourselves in the next sections with presenting the chief
outlines of this position through a fairly detailed description of the
relevant views of three "specimen" theorists.

Table 13–1. List of recent theorists classified as emphasizing self-actualization and the term each uses.*

> Kurt Goldstein (1939): Self-actualization
> Erich Fromm (1941): The productive orientation
> Prescott Lecky (1945): The unified personality; self-consist-
>   ency
> Donald Snygg and Arthur Combs (1949): The preservation
>   and enhancement of the phenomenal self
> Karen Horney (1950): The real self and its realization
> David Riesman (1950): The autonomous person
> Carl Rogers (1951): Actualization, maintenance, and enhance-
>   ment of the experiencing organism
>   Fully functioning person (1955*b*)
> Rollo May (1953): Existential being
> Abraham Maslow (1954): Self-actualization
> Gordon W. Allport (1955): Creative becoming

---

* A number of theological writers, like Martin Buber and Paul Tillich, could
be included. We here confine our consideration to psychoanalysts, psychologists,
psychiatrists, and sociologists.

Nature of the Emphasis on Self-Actualization

Conception of Human Nature. From the discussion in the last chapter, the inference can be drawn that Freud's theory is based on the implicit assumption that the irrational and evil character of human nature is basic. Whether true or not, it is clear that Freud personally
had no great belief in human goodness and was not very optimistic
as to the course of human destiny. Most of the other viewpoints
treated in this book would probably take a neutral view in relation
to the valuation of human nature. Many of those who emphasize self-
actualization take quite another view. Perhaps the most clear-cut statement has been made by Rogers (1955*b*, pp. 14–15), ". . . the basic
nature of the human being, when functioning fully, is constructive
and trustworthy." When freed of defensiveness and open to experience, "his reactions may be trusted to be positive, forward-moving,
constructive." He will socialize himself, because of his needs to affiliate and communicate with others. "I have little sympathy with the
rather prevalent concept that man is basically irrational, and that his
impulses, if not controlled, would lead to destruction of others and

self. Man's behavior is exquisitely rational, moving with subtle and ordered complexity toward the goals his organism is endeavoring to achieve." [6] Adelson (1956, p. 68), commenting on Allport's (1955) somewhat similar views, has this to say, ". . . [there] is a commitment to a particular moral philosophy. Parrington called it 'the doctrine of human excellence.' Man is born without sin, aspiring to goodness, and capable of perfection; human evil is exogenous, the betrayal of man's nature by cruel circumstance." Harsh (1957), commenting on a book to which a number of self-theorists contributed (Moustakas, 1956), says, "A crowning premise concerns the inherent goodness of man. The consensus is that, if freed from the fetters of society, man could reach new heights of happiness and achievement. Fromm and Horney illustrate the false goals set by societies, but there is no comment on past failure of naturalistic Utopias." Clearly, the spirit of Jean Jacques Rousseau rides again (cf. Chapter 2).

Characteristics of the Self-Actualizing Person. We shall discuss in some detail later the reasons offered by these theorists for the fact that most of us possess unfortunate characteristics and also inquire into certain motivational assumptions which underlie the point of view toward human nature just indicated. First, we need to examine more intensively the characteristics these writers spell out for human nature. These characteristics generally are those that the self-actualized or the fully functioning person would have; that is, he would show what is the best and also the possible that human nature offers in such areas as perception, cognition, creativity, self-realization, and interpersonal relationships. Specifically, we indicate here the description that Fromm, Maslow, and Rogers give, respectively, for the productive orientation, the self-actualizing person, and the fully functioning person.

Fromm (1941, 1947, 1955) describes several "orientations" man's conduct may take. All of these are shaped to a major degree by the kind of society in which he lives, because the human being, unlike the lower animal, does not possess fixed, immutable behavior patterns. Man can therefore adjust himself to a wide variety of social circumstances, but most of these adjustments, Fromm argues, are antithetical to the full realization of his human nature. The orientations of this type are called "nonproductive" and include the exploitative and the

[6] Quoted by permission. May et al. (1958, p. 82), while generally indicating approval of Rogers' viewpoint, observe, ". . . Rogers' viewpoint is more optimistic, whereas the existentialist approach is oriented more to the tragic crises of life . . ." Elsewhere (p. 22) they mention the importance of admitting "irrational urges or poetic visions" to awareness. Rogers, in his emphasis on rationality, would appear to subscribe to what Barrett (1958) takes as a major fault in the Western enlightenment, which Existentialism has pointed out.

hoarding orientations dominant in the nineteenth century and the receptive and marketing orientations dominant in the twentieth. Only the productive orientation permits the satisfactory realization of human potentials.

What is the character of the productive orientation? We can best answer this question by indicating some of the ways in which this orientation is expressed (Fromm, 1955). One way is through relatedness to other people, the productive expression of which is Love. To Fromm, *"Love is union with somebody, or something, outside oneself, under the condition of retaining the separateness and integrity of one's own self.* It is an experience of sharing, of communion, which permits the full unfolding of one's own inner activity" (1955, p. 31). This kind of love, "the mystical experience of union" (p. 32), includes erotic love, maternal love, the feeling of human solidarity, and also self-love (Fromm, 1939); it is a cardinal point that one cannot love others unless he loves and respects himself. In addition to love, the productive orientation is expressed in other ways, in ". . . *thought* . . . in the proper grasp of the world by reason. In the realm of *action* . . . in productive work, the prototype of which is art and craftsmanship. In the realm of *feeling* . . . in love . . ." (Fromm, 1955, p. 32). Such love includes the attitudes of care, responsibility, respect, and knowledge with regard to the other.

In the productive orientation the individual is creative rather than destructive, and he realizes and accepts himself as an individual, rather than conforming to convention and losing himself in the herd. He is aware of himself, and he thinks, acts, and feels in reference to his own needs as well as with reference to those of others. Fromm has considered what kind of society would best fit with a productive orientation. He calls it "humanistic communitarian socialism" and describes it thus:

A society in which man relates to man lovingly, in which he is rooted in bonds of brotherliness and solidarity, rather than in the ties of blood and soil; a society which gives him the possibility of transcending nature by creating rather than destroying, in which everyone gains a sense of self by experiencing himself as the subject of his powers rather than by conformity, in which a system of orientation and devotion exists without man's needing to distort reality and to worship idols (Fromm, 1955, p. 362).

Maslow (1954) presents a list of 15 characteristics of the self-actualized person, and he devotes especial attention to a few of them. All these characteristics represent empirical findings from Maslow's (1954) study of self-actualizing people. Unfortunately, he tells us little about the nature of this sample or the methods used in studying these people. Furthermore, several of the characteristics overlap with one another.

The 15 characteristics are as follows (Maslow, 1954, Chap. 12), and the similarity of the characteristics to those listed by Fromm is evident.

1. *More efficient perception of reality and more comfortable relations with it.* This means that self-actualized people readily detect falseness and spuriousness in other people and judge people accurately. They also distinguish "far more easily than most the fresh, concrete, and idiographic from the generic, abstract, and rubricized" (Maslow, 1954, p. 205). Therefore they live closer to reality and to nature than most people do. They also tolerate uncertainty and ambiguity more easily than do others.

2. *Acceptance of self and of others.* These people have relatively little guilt, shame, or anxiety; that is, they accept themselves and their various characteristics and are not defensive.

3. *Spontaneity.* They are especially spontaneous in their thoughts and other covert tendencies and are so, also, in their behavior. But unconventionality is not a mark of their behavior, for their unconventionality is not put on to impress others and may even be suppressed in order not to distress others.

4. *Problem centering.* They are not ego-centered but rather oriented to problems outside themselves, important problems to which they are devoted in the sense of a mission in life.

5. *Detachment; the need for privacy.* They do not mind solitude and even seek it; their objectivity is an expression of their detachment.

6. *Autonomy: independence of culture and environment.* They have relative independence of their environments, as prior characteristics would suggest.

7. *Continued freshness of appreciation.* ". . . they derive ecstasy, inspiration, and strength from the basic experiences of life" (Maslow, 1954, p. 215), even on occasion from things they have seen, heard, or done many times.

8. *Mystic experience or the oceanic feeling.* These are experiences which may arise in a variety of settings; they are "feelings of limitless horizons opening up to the vision, the feeling of being simultaneously more powerful and also more helpless than one ever was before, the feeling of great ecstasy and wonder and awe, the loss of placing in time and space, with, finally, the conviction that something extremely important and valuable had happened . . ." (Maslow, 1954, p. 216).

9. *Gemeinschaftsgefühl or social interest* (Adler's term). This is a "feeling of identification, sympathy and affection" for mankind (Maslow, 1954, p. 217), even though the self-actualizing person is troubled by the many shortcomings of the species.

10. *Interpersonal relations.* These are very deep and profound and are present usually with only a few rather than with many individuals. Such hostility as is shown is reactive in a situation, rather than chronic.

11. *Democratic character structure.* They respect people and can learn from and relate to them, irrespective of birth, race, blood, family, etc.

12. *Discrimination between means and ends.* The self-actualized discriminate ends or what they are striving for from the means for accomplishing the ends to an extent that most people do not. On the other hand, they can often enjoy the means or instrumental behavior leading to an end, which more impatient persons would dislike.

13. *Sense of humor.* These people tend to be philosophical and nonhostile in their humor.

14. *Creativeness.* Each one has "a special kind of creativeness or originality or inventiveness that has certain peculiar characteristics" (Maslow, 1954, p. 223). (Further attention is given this matter later.)

15. *Resistance to enculturation.* They get along in the culture but are detached from it; that is, they are essentially autonomous of it although not especially unconventional in a behavioral way, as was said before.

Before turning to somewhat fuller discussions of Love, the peak experience, and creativity in self-actualizing people, we should perhaps mention that Maslow (1954) says these people are not perfect. They have many ordinary human failings, and, on occasion, they can be ruthless, alienative of others, detached, and so on.

Love. Maslow (1954, Chap. 13, 1955) describes healthy love as "in part an absence of defenses, that is to say, an increase in spontaneity and in honesty" (p. 239). "In such a relationship it is not necessary to be guarded, to conceal, to try to impress, to feel tense, to watch one's words or actions, to suppress or repress" (pp. 239–240). Self-actualized people "have the power to love and the ability to *be* loved" in this way (Maslow, 1954, p. 241). Their sexual experience may reach the "most intense and ecstatic perfection . . ." (p. 242), often approaching the level of mystic experiences (see p. 669). Maslow cites with agreement Fromm's statement that care, respect, responsibility, and knowledge are integral to the love relation in the self-actualized, but he adds "fun, merriment, elation, feeling of well-being, gaiety" (p. 251) to this rather sober list. The self-actualized person does not *need* love, since at one level his love-need has been satisfied; hence his reaction to the "other" is not as a means to some end but rather is an end in itself, so that enjoyment, admiration, delight, contemplation, and appreciation, rather than use, are its characteristics, while at the same time the individuality of the lovers is preserved. Maslow (1955) has called this kind of love B-love (i.e., love for the other person's Being) as opposed to D-love (i.e., deficiency love, or selfish or neurotic love).

Creativity. As may be readily surmised from what has been said already, creativity is more prominent in self-actualized people than in others. In two papers, Maslow (1958*a, b*) has elaborated the nature of creativity as he sees it, in science and in self-actualizing people. Concerning scientific creativity, Maslow (1958*b*) emphasizes the importance of what a Freudian theorist would call "primary process" in creative work (see Chapter 12). This is "the primary creativeness which comes out of the unconscious . . . the source of new discovery —of real novelty—of ideas which depart from what exists at this point" (p. 2), and he considers at length the factors which block the expression of this kind of creativity. He admits another kind of creativity termed "secondary creativity" which occurs in rigid, constricted people, for example, some of the prominent scientists studied by Anne Roe (1953). He refers to the product of secondary creativity as "secondary science." [7]

More pertinent to our discussion is the nature of creativity in self-actualizing people (Maslow, 1958*b*). Maslow differentiates this kind of creativity from productive creativity as reflected in poetry, art, music, invention, science, etc. Self-actualizing creativity is potential in *anyone* and requires no special talents or abilities. It appears in every-day life as an expression of a personality which is perceptive, spontaneous, expressive, "child-like," and which shows no fear of the unknown; in short, creativity of this kind is described essentially in terms of the characteristics of self-actualizing people, and emphasis is again placed on the ability to deal with and to use primary process.

The Peak Experience. In three papers, Maslow (1957, 1958*a*, 1959*b*) has discussed two types of cognition, those which he refers to as cognition of being (or B-cognition) and as cognition organized by deficiency needs (or D-cognition). B-cognition appears in "moments

---

[7] Later on, in the same paper, Maslow seems to speak positively of secondary process, in contrast to the pejorative tone implied in "secondary science." A great deal of "secondary process" is needed to evaluate, order, and carry out the "ideas" of primary process. The healthy person, he says, fuses primary and secondary processes, that is, they indulge in "regression in the service of the Ego."

of highest happiness and fulfillment" (Maslow, 1959a, p. 45), referred
to as *peak-experiences*. These experiences occur in a variety of circumstances, such as "in the B-love experience, the parental experience,
the mystic or oceanic, or nature experience, the aesthetic perception,
the creative moment, the therapeutic or intellectual insight, the orgas-
mic experience, certain forms of athletic fulfillment" (Maslow, 1959a,
pp. 44–45). We should note, here, that such experiences are not restricted to self-actualizing persons but can come to anyone at any
time; perhaps they are more frequent, intense, and perfect, however,
in the self-actualizing than in the average person. There are several
features that cognition of being in the peak experience possesses. Very
briefly, they are as follows: experience is a whole or a complete unit,
"as if it were all there was in the universe . . ." (p. 45); the percept
receives the individual's complete attention, concretely and not as a
member of a class; the nature of the percept is more directly seen,
aside from human needs and uses; the perception is richer in B-cognition than in D-cognition with repetition; perception can be object-
centered and the self can be forgotten in the contemplation of the object; the experience is an end in itself; there is disorientation in time
and space; the experience is always a good one, perfect and complete;
the experience has the character of perception of the absolute; it tends
to be a passive and receptive kind of cognition; there is the emotional
reaction of wonder and awe; the experience of unity can include the
whole world, or just a small part of it, like the loved one; it is a concrete perceiving "as a perception of all aspects and attributes of the
object simultaneously or in quick succession" (Maslow, 1959a, p. 56);
conflicts and inconsistencies are often resolved; the world and persons
are accepted, completely, lovingly, and uncondemningly; perception
tends to the idiographic; there is a loss of defensiveness, control,
anxiety, and the like.

   This list, which seems to contain several internally overlapping
features, as well as features which overlap with the 15 characteristics
of self-actualizing persons and the properties of creativity and B-Love
previously given, contains items which figure prominently in mystical
and theological discussions. Maslow recognizes and is not troubled by
this correspondence. The list also contains items which in some form are
found in the experience of psychotics; this does not concern Maslow,
as the experiences he describes are transient matters which the individual understands for what they are. There are other problems, such
as the validation of some of the experiences in B-cognition, the question of action rather than contemplation, fatalism, indiscriminate acceptance of others, over-estheticism, which Maslow (1959a, b) recog-

nizes. Maslow's evidence convinces him that these problems have had no practical reality in the case of his subjects.

Carl Rogers (1955*b*) addressed himself to the description of what a person would be like following an optimal experience of psychotherapy. He finds three major characteristics. First is *openness to experience,* the opposite of defensiveness; all experience would be "received," without distortion, whether it originated in the external world or inside the person. "Availability of experience to awareness" is a phrase expressing something of the same meaning. Second, the individual would *live in an existential manner;* that is, he would become "a participant in and an observer of the ongoing process of organismic experience, rather than being in control of it" (p. 7). He would not display rigidity, tight organization, or impose on experience some structure. Third, such a person would *trust his feeling of what is right* in situations and find, in fact, that such feelings served as a good and trustworthy guide to behavior. These characteristics are pulled together in the following summary of what a fully functioning person is like:

He is able to live fully in and with each and all of his feelings and reactions. He is making use of all his organic equipment to sense, as accurately as possible, the existential situation within and without. He is using all of the data his nervous system can thus supply, using it in awareness, but recognizing that his total organism may be, and often is, wiser than his awareness. He is able to permit his total organism to function in all its complexity in selecting, from the multitude of possibilities, that behavior which in this moment of time will be most generally and genuinely satisfying. He is able to trust his organism in this functioning, not because it is infallible, but he can be fully open to the consequences of each of his actions and correct them if they prove to be less than satisfying.

He is able to experience all of his feelings, and is afraid of none of his feelings; he is his own sifter of evidence, but is open to evidence from all sources; he is completely engaged in the process of being and becoming himself; and thus discovers that he is soundly and realistically social; he lives completely in this moment, but learns that this is the soundest living for all time. He is a fully functioning organism, and because of the awareness of himself which flows freely in and through his experience, he is a fully functioning person (Rogers, 1955*b*, p. 10).

The many characteristics of the descriptions given by Fromm, Maslow, and Rogers show much overlap and agreement. It is difficult to epitomize these descriptions but perhaps the following features are the most significant: It is possible for the human being, on his nature, to be open to experience, that is, not defensive; to love others and the self without admixtures of aggression or of manipulative needs; to act ethically, morally, and for the social good; to be expressive of his potentials in an autonomous, self-realizing way; to be spontaneous and creative; to be curious and exploratory.

Factors Which Limit or Prevent This Kind of Development. An important thing to recognize is that the characteristics we have just summarized are seen, in one way or another, as being potential in everyone; that is, they are basic characteristics of human nature. Why, then, are they expressed only in the few, rather than in the many? Two chief and interrelated sets of factors are offered by the writers we have examined as standing in the way of self-actualization. One may be referred to as prevention by society; the other as prevention due to dominance by "lower needs." We shall discuss these factors as they are described respectively by Fromm and by Maslow. Rogers has been less explicit than these two writers in his discussion of the matter.

Fromm's fundamental point is that with the emergence of the human being there is a *break* in the evolutionary scale of animals. This break is characterized by the points that in the human "action ceases to be essentially determined by instinct; nature loses its coercive character; . . . action is no longer fixed by hereditarily given mechanisms." Furthermore, "When the animal transcends nature, when it transcends the purely passive role of the creature, when it becomes, biologically speaking, the most helpless animal, *man is born.*" When this happened ". . . a new species arose, transcending nature—*life became aware of itself*" (Fromm, 1955, p. 23).

Awareness and reason, Fromm argues, are man's curses as well as his blessings. They are his curses, because they enable him to rise above nature but at the same time realize "his powerlessness and the limitations of his existence," for example, death (Fromm, 1955, p. 24). Man lacks instincts and strength, and at birth he is helpless—all these lacks prepare him for life in nature less well than animals. Thus ". . . he has fallen out of nature, as it were, and is still in it . . ." (Fromm, 1955, p. 25). Man must *discover* or *make* his way in nature, rather than having his way prepared for him through unreasoning instinct; the life of the lower animal is psychologically easier than man's—his instincts give him his ways of conduct, and his presumed lack of awareness and of reason prevents his seeing or having the problems which are fundamental in the human. Man must discover the significance of his existence, what he lives for over and above the satisfaction of the physiological needs. His human needs remain to be expressed, even though the physiological ones are satisfied; cultures provide the patterns whereby these human needs are expressed and whereby the question as to the meaning of existence is answered, but some cultures provide better satisfactions and answers than others. Only when the most satisfactory solutions to these needs and this problem are possible, can the productive orientation become characteristic of a society (as it would, presumably, in Fromm's "sane society"). The needs Fromm mentions (1955, pp. 27–66) are five in number: (1) to be related to others through productive love; (2) to be transcendent, that is, to create rather than to destroy; (3) to have roots, that is, to feel that he belongs to or is a part of the world or the brotherhood of man; (4) to have a sense of personal or individual identity, to be unique; (5) to have a frame of reference in terms of which to perceive and understand the world.

Every human being starts life in a helpless state, so that he must be cared for, protected, and given security by others. While this situation is a necessary one in early childhood, it becomes decreasingly so as the child gets older; the extent of its potential decline, however, is contingent upon the state of development of society and its technology. Fromm has argued (1941) that only in recent times has man's control over nature in the service of his needs reached the point at which he can stand alone, in independence or autonomy of family and other kinds of dependent relationships. In a word, Fromm believes man can now be free. That he has not become free and productive arises because he is afraid to break the ties that give security and to become an individual. Our society, further, blocks the road to freedom and individuality by the false goals and the conformity on which it insists. To withstand the anxiety and the loss of security, which becoming an individual causes, is extremely difficult—it is like the re-experiencing of birth, and to Fromm, as to Rank, this step is seen as a rebirth.

It appears to us that Fromm holds modern society responsible for man's failure to progress beyond the nonproductive orientations; that is, society and its members reject, punish, ridicule, and threaten the individual who seeks to become himself, rather than aiding and abetting him. Were insecurity and anxiety not enforced from without, as we understand Fromm, the task of becoming productive, while perhaps never easy, would be more likely to be accomplished by more people than at present; this is a main emphasis in his design of the sane society, that is, humanitarian communitarian socialism.

Maslow also would condemn many features of contemporary society and culture. However, his discussion of the emergence of self-actualization is differently cast. It assumes a hierarchy of basic needs, with self-actualization at the top, and it further assumes that for higher needs to function there must have been a prior satisfaction of the lower needs. It is a more explicitly motivational theory than is Fromm's. We turn now to a discussion of this view, remarking in passing that there is no necessary inconsistency or disagreement between Fromm and Maslow; each has developed the factor that seemed strongest to him and could accept the other's ideas as complementary to his own.

Before listing the needs in the Maslow hierarchy, we point out several features to keep in mind. One is that these needs are believed to be universal; Maslow refers to them as "instinctoid" by which he means that many of them, especially the higher ones, are not strong enough to be apparent unless conditions favor their manifestation. Under favorable conditions, however, they *will* appear. Another point is that a lower need may be sufficiently satiated at some time so that it will no longer appear with major or dominant impetus in the individual's behavior except under very unusual conditions. Satiation of a lower need is seen as a condition on which the appearance of a higher one depends.[8]

At the base of the hierarchy (Maslow, 1954, Chap. 5) are the *physiological needs*, like hunger, thirst, etc. Maslow emphasizes that if one examines such needs in great detail there are very many of them, as is seen in the case of hunger when the variety of specific hungers (see Chapter 5) is considered. These needs are the most prepotent ones and, if unsatisfied, can dominate the individual, as in the case of the starving man or the man dying from thirst. However, in our society such needs are seldom dominant, at least in the greatest segment of the population. That is to say, they are chronically gratified; few people fear starvation, for example. But during times of disaster, as in the Great Depression of the 1930's, chronic gratification is not the case, and starvation, or the fear of it, can make hunger dominate conduct.

Next in line are the *safety needs*, which also may dominate behavior. Normally in our culture, these are seen mainly in children and are said to underlie both the infant's reactions to strangers, sudden noises, the threat of being dropped, etc., and the older child's desire for routine. Various security measures which adults take, such as tenured positions, savings, and all sorts of insurance are seen as means of providing safety from the kinds of things which would upset security. Normally, adults are not dominated by the safety needs in a well-ordered or regulated society, and they are seen in action mainly "in emergencies, e.g., war, disease, natural catastrophes, crime waves . . ." and similar

---

[8] Some needs, for example, hunger, can never be satiated permanently. However, they can be satisfied often enough, so that fear of their frustration is not significant.

conditions (Maslow, 1954, p. 88). They are, however, often seen in neurosis.

The *belongingness* and *love needs* arise when the physiological and safety needs are relatively quiescent:

Now the person will feel keenly, as never before, the absence of friends, or a sweetheart, or a wife, or children. He will hunger for affectionate relations with people in general, namely, for a place in his group, and he will strive with great intensity to achieve this goal. He will want to attain such a place more than anything else in the world and may even forget that once, when he was hungry, he sneered at love as unreal or unnecessary or unimportant (Maslow, 1954, p. 89).

These needs, Maslow says, are often frustrated in our society and are a common basis for maladjustment and psychopathology. It should be noted that this is not B-Love, which we mentioned earlier, but rather D-Love. B-Love can only emerge when D-Love and other basic needs have received some measure of gratification.

The *esteem needs* are the next to appear in the hierarchy. These represent ". . . a need or desire for a stable, firmly based, usually high evaluation of themselves, for self-respect, or self-esteem, and for the esteem of others" (Maslow, 1954, p. 90). There are really two subsets of needs in this category. One is "the desire for strength, for achievement, for adequacy, for mastery and competence, for confidence in the face of the world, and for independence and freedom. Second . . . the desire for reputation or prestige (defining it as respect or esteem from other people), status, dominance, recognition, attention, importance, or appreciation" (Maslow, 1954, p. 90). It is emphasized that the regard of others must be a deserved one. The gratification of these needs brings "feelings of self-confidence, worth, strength, capability, and adequacy . . ." (Maslow, 1954, p. 91).

These are the needs that fall in the hierarchy beneath *self-actualization*, the highest need of the hierarchy (*cognitive* and *aesthetic needs* are also mentioned but not stressed). We have already discussed the characteristics of self-actualizing people and will further discuss the motivational character and implications of this ultimate need in the next section. Certain other points should be made about the needs already described.

The hierarchy as we have described it is not absolutely fixed, although to discuss variations from the pattern indicated would require a more detailed presentation than space permits. Also, it is not necessary, or, in some cases, even possible that a lower need be permanently and finally gratified. It is better to say that the need is *largely* gratified or that there is a history of extensive gratification of the need; under these conditions, higher needs may appear. It must also be pointed out that gratification is only satisfactorily achieved for a need when "intrinsically appropriate satisfiers" are involved. "For the love-hungry, there is only one genuine, long-run satisfier, i.e., honest and satisfying affection. For the sex-starved, food-starved, or water-starved person, only sex, food, or water will ultimately serve" (Maslow, 1954, p. 110). Thus satisfiers are not developed through contiguous association, as in secondary reinforcement or learned incentives (see Chapter 11).

Maslow argues that the failure to satisfy the basic needs leads to deficiency conditions, analogous to a vitamin deficiency. He argues that gratification of these needs is essential to psychological health. These needs are basic because (1) the absence of their satisfiers prevents psychological health, (2) the presence of the satisfiers prevents illness, (3) restoration of the satisfiers overcomes the illness, (4) the satisfier is chosen by the deprived person over other satisfactions, and (5) in healthy people such needs are absent (Maslow, 1955).

The assumption that the basic needs are "instinctoid" is essential to Maslow's position. It is also essential to all positions within the emphasis on self-actualization, because of the rejection of the value of much that society gives the individual, the rejection of the hypothesis of cultural relativity, and because of the universality postulated for human nature. Maslow at least recognizes this assumption openly [9] and after listing a dozen mistakes of past instinct theory (Maslow, 1954, pp. 126–136), he goes on to advance arguments to support the instinctoid nature of the basic needs. He argues that associative learning cannot account for these needs, nor could the older instinct theory. He points out that although instincts may drop out as we move up the phyletic scale, there is no good reason that others, albeit "weaker"

---

[9] Maslow (1959c, p. 14) comments that most of the writers in the self-actualization group, while insisting that man's nature or real self is good, trustworthy, and ethical, have "very definitely ducked the crucial statement about this inner core, i.e., that it *must* in some degree be inherited or else everything else they say is so much hash." And again, "We can't affirm *both* that culture does everything and anything, and that man has an inherent nature. The one is incompatible with the other." From a theory of acquired motivation one could probably derive the kinds of motives postulated for the self-actualizing person, given certain socio-cultural conditions. But this would not satisfy those who emphasize self-actualization; it is their belief that these motives are basic in human nature and that their frustration not only damages psychological health but leaves the person dissatisfied and driven to find "adjustment" in unsatisfactory and dangerous compromises.

ones, might not be added. He thinks cultural evidence shows the universality of the needs but admits its lack of definitiveness. The five arguments just listed for the basic character of these needs also argue for their instinctoid nature. He argues, finally, that cultural anthropologists no longer adhere fully to the doctrine of cultural relativity (Maslow, 1954, pp. 143–144).

We shall attempt some evaluation of these arguments in the final section of this chapter. It is interesting to note, however, that Maslow went to some length to marshal data from studies of animals, children, and other cultures to demonstrate that destructiveness is not instinctoid (Maslow, 1954, Chap. 10). Later (Maslow, 1959c, pp. 14–15) he admits uncertainty on this point. But it is quite clear that his position, like those of the other theorists who emphasize the individual as against society, must find that destructiveness and aggression are reactive or are learned if chronic; otherwise they could never justify the view that the individual's true self is such that social controls of it are unnecessary and even harmful.

Motivation in the Self-Actualizing Person. We shall briefly mention here what Rogers and Maslow say on this topic. Fromm's views are implicit in what has been said of him already.

Rogers (1955b) comments that the behavior of the fully functioning person would be dependable and, after the fact, understandable or "postdictable," but that it would not be predictable. The reason for unpredictability lies in the view that this kind of person would respond fully to the uniqueness of the particular constellation of external and internal stimuli operative at any moment. The maladjusted person's behavior, on the other hand, should be specifically predictable, because it is repetitive, rigid, and arises from rather undifferentiated perceptions of stimuli. The principle involved here is that "some loss of predictability should be evident in every increase in openness to experience and existential living" (Rogers, 1955b, p. 16).

A comparable judgment would follow from Maslow's discussion of self-actualizing people. The motives common to men are the lower needs in the hierarchy, the deficit needs, that is, those below the level of self-actualization. Where knowledge as to the existence of these needs is present, behavior should be predictable, and perhaps predictive accuracy would increase as one goes down the hierarchy. But in the self-actualizing person these needs are essentially gratified, and the directions of his behavior are governed by his need for self-actualization, that is, the tendency for one "to become actualized in what he is potentially. This tendency might be phrased as the desire to become more and more what one is, to become everything that one is capable of becoming" (Maslow, 1954, p. 92). One might be able to predict what such people would do, in general, from a knowledge of their capacities or potential capacities, but a prediction based on motivational variables per se would, on this analysis, not be possible.

One can almost question whether self-actualizing persons are motivated at all, at least in the usual sense of the word. Maslow has stressed that some of their behaviors arise out of sheer enjoyment of using their capacities and that they need not behave in accord with a functionalist model of behavior; that is, that some purpose or goal ulterior to the behavior itself must motivate the behavior. Elsewhere he has put the point like this:

. . . we must construct a profoundly different psychology of motivation for self-actualizing people, e.g., expression motivation or growth motivation, rather than deficiency motivation. Perhaps it will be useful to make a distinction between living and *preparing* to live. Perhaps the concept of motivation should apply *only* to non-self-actualizers. Our subjects no longer strive in the ordinary sense, but rather develop. They attempt to grow to perfection and to develop more and more fully in their own style. The motivation of ordinary men is a striving for the basic need gratifications that they lack. But self-actualizing people in fact lack none of these gratifications; and yet they have impulses. They work, they try, and they are ambitious, even though in an unusual sense. For them motivation is just character growth, character expression, maturation, and development; in a word self-actualization (1954, p. 211).

We may conclude the discussion of this section by summarizing Maslow's comparison (1955) of growth-motivation and deficiency-motivation. In the growth-motivated self-actualizing person, impulses are desired and welcomed rather than rejected and feared; gratification of impulse increases rather than decreases motivation; that is, growth is rewarding and the desire for it is increased by gratification. Gratification of growth motives produces health, whereas satisfaction of deficit needs only prevents illness, and gratification of growth motives causes the pleasure of production and creation. In a sense, however, these motives are never gratified, as a deficit need is, because growth is continuing. Growth motives, as we have suggested, are idiosyncratic and are less dependent on other people than are deficit needs for their gratification; growth-motivated people are, therefore, less dependent on other people than are deficit-motivated people and can perceive people disinterestedly, just as they can perceive the world objectively. Their perceptions are not distorted by their deficit needs; egocentricity and self-consciousness are less apparent. They are able to solve their problems by themselves, ordinarily, rather than having to seek help from others.

These contrasts between growth-motivation and deficiency-motivation would, we think, characterize also the views of Rogers, Allport, and Fromm, as well as of Maslow.

EVIDENCE

We now attempt an evaluation of the points of view just reviewed, in terms of such evidence we can find, that has some pertinence to the issues involved. This is not an easy task. Much of the support mentioned by the theorists concerned is not available as published evidence, and some of the support is, rather than evidence, more in the form of argument. Other evidence cited is, when all of the relevant papers are examined, not at all clear-cut. Because of such problems, we shall, ourselves, indulge in a bit of argument, recognizing, however, that evidence is usually preferable to dialectic. Three major issues seem to pervade the problem of evaluation, and we deal with them in succession: the nature of human nature in healthy persons; the problem of an hierarchy of needs; the problem of basic need gratification.

The Nature of Human Nature in Healthy Persons

As has already been evident, the view of basic human nature advanced by Allport, Fromm, Maslow, Rogers, and others who emphasize self-actualization is highly favorable; that is, they seem to assert its potential for goodness and are optimistic as to the possibility of the realization of this potential, given suitable conditions. Some evidence is advanced to support this view. Before turning to it, however, we may observe that this kind of general view was prominent in the eighteenth and early nineteenth centuries; one of Freud's achievements, it is commonly said, was the discovery of the impulsive, irrational, amoral nature of man. Freud found so much evidence for destructiveness, sadism, masochism, hostility, and the like, that he postulated a death-aggressive instinct. The views of those who emphasize self-actualization are, then, far removed from his. Disagreement with Freud, of course, does not prove the theorists of self-actualization wrong. Many writers have rejected Freud's death instinct, attributing aggression and similar phenomena to frustration or other external sources. No doubt those who emphasize self-actualization would accept this solution. But they will not go one step further, to the attribution of most of the basic major human traits to social influences. This step founders on the rock of cultural relativity, acceptance of which means that the culture or society sets the norm of human nature and its health. Those who stress self-actualization do not typically accept cultural relativity. Instead, they postulate innate good—as the basic human nature (Maslow's instinctoid basic needs) whose expression is consistent with psychological health and is not inimical to human society.

In several places, Maslow (1954, 1959c) has indicated lines of evidence which he believes support his view of human nature. One kind of evidence is provided by experiments indicating that the body is capable of considerable self-regulation in the interests of homeostasis; another indicates that dietary self-selection, in both children and animals, provides within limits a satisfactory variety and quantity of food. (These topics are treated, respectively, in Chapters 7 and 5, and we will not go into this evidence here.) This evidence, to Maslow, indicates that organisms, left alone, make wise choices. The point, we think, is that such data are taken to verify the belief that organisms can know their needs and can act appropriately with reference to them. Maslow argues, then, that we can take the testimony of healthy people concerning what their needs are, the testimony of neurotic people concerning what their needs are, and so on. This is a rather large jump from the kinds of data involved in experiments on homeostasis and dietary self-selection, as reference to Chapters 5 and 7 will indicate.

Another evidence for his view of human nature, suggested by Maslow, is that children are natural, spontaneous, undefensive, curious, and, in their way, creative to an extent greater than the typical adult or older child in our culture. This is a point with which it is difficult to disagree, although we can find few satisfactory data that would directly validate it in other than an impressionistic way. Again, of course, it is difficult to say why such characteristics are taken as supporting a universal view of human nature without also mentioning that children are often irritable, impulsive, short-sighted, aggressive, egocentric, and bound by physiological needs. Many psychologists accept the notion that the thinking, conception of reality, and similar processes in children are at developmental levels different from and, in a sense, inferior to those of the adult. It is difficult either to accept or fully evaluate this argument from Maslow.

The potential for creativity, that is, creativity which makes use of the primary process in the unconscious, is also stressed by Maslow as indicating a valuable aspect of unfettered human nature. Perhaps not everyone would evaluate this phenomenon as would Maslow. It obviously and admittedly requires the operation of secondary process to sift out the good from the not-so-good products of primary process and to work what is good into a form suitable for evaluation, trial, and verification. And there is considerable question as to the status of "primary process" itself. Does it represent material from the unconscious? Does it actually represent "raw" human nature? Isn't it largely determined by low-level needs?

Evidence from psychotherapy is advanced by both Maslow and Rogers as indicating the potential for growth of the human being, the pressure to achieve mental health that people have, and their response to being accepted by the therapist. Rogers cites many excerpts from therapeutic sessions to support these statements, and Maslow generalizes that these points are verified by other therapists.

In this book, we cannot enter into a full survey of the literature on the outcomes of psychotherapy. However, we shall briefly summarize our impressions of this literature. It is true that some therapists and some patients have written glowingly of the results of therapy. On the other hand, Freud himself did not claim great achievements for his therapy in many of his patients. Other therapists report failures and instances of little progress. A group of psychologists (Boring et al., 1940), who reported on their experience as analysands, were not uniformly enthusiastic. The research literature on therapeutic outcomes is not encouraging. One problem, of course, and a difficult one, is to decide how outcomes are to be measured and what outcomes are to be examined.[10] Beyond this problem, there is evidence that many patients leave treatment before very many sessions and before (probably) they have been helped. The majority of patients who start and remain in psychotherapy are from the upper socio-economic-educational groups. Some psychologists (e.g., Eysenck, 1952) believe that psychotherapy has no proved value whatsoever, on the basis of the kinds of evidence they have collected. Others, using ratings and tests of various kinds (e.g., Rogers & Dymond, 1954), have found substantial evidence of change. Our general conclusion would be that the present public evidence on the changes and outcomes resulting from psychotherapy is hardly supportive of the kinds of assertions made by Maslow and by Rogers if they are made as universal generalizations. We do not think that present, reported therapeutic outcomes, whatever the kind of therapy, support a particularly positive view of human nature.

Maslow's major support for his view of human nature comes from his study of self-actualizing people. As we have said before, little has been published concerning the characteristics of this sample of people, that is, how they were selected or how they were studied. They are supposed to be psychiatrically healthy, and they have presumably

---

[10] Jahoda's book (1958) is instructive as to the definition of positive mental health. See also relevant discussion in Chapter 12.

been studied intensively. But we know little more which would help us evaluate the claims that their self-actualizing characteristics are potential in all of us. For example, some questions we would raise are these: Are they very bright, especially talented, highly educated, favorably employed? What are their ages, their sex distribution, their marriage statuses, the number of their children, their areas of residence, their economic level? Basic questions such as these cannot be answered from the available information. (We don't even know how many self-actualized subjects there are.) And it is just possible that some factor of intelligence, talent, employment, etc., may make them completely unrepresentative of the rest of us and, therefore, an unsuitable sample from which to generalize about the species.[11]

The Problem of a Hierarchy of Needs

Maslow's formulation that needs or drives are arranged in a sort of dominance hierarchy does, we think, receive at least partial support from various kinds of evidence. That the support is partial is because the evidence concerns only the needs at the two lower levels of his hierarchy, the physiological and anxiety (security) needs.

There are many reports in the literature of the dominating effects of severe hunger, cold, heat, thirst, and fear. A representative account for hunger is provided by Keys et al. (1950) from the semi-starvation experiments carried out with conscientious objectors at Minnesota. Their subjects, after a time, thought of little else but food, and many of their normal activities and interests (presumably arising from "higher" motives) succumbed to the constant hunger. Wolf (1958) has reprinted a number of accounts in which severe and prolonged thirst is seen to have similar effects. Farber, Harlow, and West (1957) concluded that the effects of brainwashing techniques owe much to a state of the prisoner which they label "debility, dependency, and dread." Reports from concentration camps and areas in the world where severe catastrophe or other stress has occurred (see Chapter 9) are often indicative that normal interests and values and acceptable social behavior cannot withstand for very long against the demands of the physiological needs and severe insecurity. Also, often implicated in such cases, is the collapse of ordinary social standards and controls so that directing frames of reference are lost (Sherif & Cantril, 1947, Chap. 12; see also, Kilby, 1948).

Goldstein (1942) has emphasized the importance to brain-injured

---

[11] Maslow (1954) has identified some public figures as being self-actualized, and they are certainly not representative of the population at large in many of their characteristics and circumstances of life.

patients of avoiding "catastrophic" situations, that is, situations with which, because of the injury, they are no longer able to cope. Such catastrophe-avoiding behavior stands in the way of the expression of other and higher interests and motives. Less dramatic but definite effects have been reported that hunger and thirst reduce exploratory behavior in rats, and interference from hunger in the performance of tasks has been reported for monkeys by Harlow (1953*b*, p. 32) and for chimpanzees by Birch (1945). Additional material pertinent to these points was mentioned in Chapter 5, in the discussion of factors involved in drive-related behavior.

It seems well authenticated that certain kinds of drive states, that is, the physiological needs involved in individual survival and those involving pain and threat like anxiety and insecurity, can under certain severe conditions come to dominate the organism's behavior, as they do not dominate it at other times. To this extent, then, Maslow's notion of the hierarchy of needs receives support. However, we hasten to add that nothing we have said so far validates the hierarchical hypothesis in relation to the needs lying above the safety needs, such as belongingness and love. These needs have seldom been studied. What relevant material there is is brought out in the immediately following section.

The Problem of Basic Need Gratification

As we have seen already, the condition for the emergence of higher needs is the gratification of the lower needs. As we understand this point, it really has two related aspects. In the first place, certain needs cannot be gratified out of existence, because normal bodily processes regularly re-create them. Hunger and thirst are examples. What need gratification would mean in such cases, we assume, is that moderate degrees of hunger or thirst, for example, would not be terribly upsetting to the organism. If there were a history of regular need gratification, then the recurrence of a need state would not fore-ordain, so far as the individual's experience is concerned, that gratification will not be forthcoming or that the need state will get worse. A history of need gratification, then, would mean that the response to a need would not be so compelling or urgent or anxiety-laden as it would be if in the past the individual had repeatedly experienced strong, debilitating needs. He should be able to withstand deprivation more readily against a background of need gratification than against a history of frequent frustration. Both J. McV. Hunt (1941) and Mowrer (1950*c*) have presented arguments in a somewhat similar vein. We reviewed relevant evidence in Chapter 4.

In the case of other basic needs, however, Maslow seems to say that gratification can more or less eliminate them from further status in the organism's repertory. Perhaps the needs for security, love (D-Love) and belongingness, and esteem fit here. Once sufficiently gratified they not only no longer dominate but also they do not appear again in the organism's behavior. What kind of evidence is pertinent to this point?

There are three general kinds of evidence usually cited. One concerns sucking behavior. Certain experiments suggest that frustration of sucking activity causes a great deal of non-nutritive sucking, implicating a frustrated need. Non-nutritive sucking, however, in these experiments did not appear in any magnitude when adequate sucking occurred during regular feeding.[12] We may indicate that the evidence presently supports the existence of a sucking need in dogs, though not in humans, and of a need for contact with a soft object in monkeys. The evidence in favor of Maslow's point from these experiments is, at best, limited.

A second kind of evidence is the effects of inadequate mothering on human behavior, both in the period of infancy and at later ages. The third type of evidence concerns the effects of restoration of adequate mothering to deprived children or the satisfaction of love needs in psychotherapy. There is little satisfactory information on these points. We mention some of it in connection with the second kind of evidence.

Few people would question that parental care is a potential source from which many of the characteristics and traits of children arise. Similarly, there is widespread belief that patterns of neurosis, psychosis, delinquency, and other disturbed behavior derive from the child-parent interaction. Such relations as these usually represent the effects of long-continued, disturbed parent-child relations, as indicated in Levy's work (Levy, 1937a, b, 1943, 1951) and that of Bettelheim (1950, 1955). Bowlby (1951) and Brody (1956) have brought together much of the relevant literature (see, also, Stagner, 1948). In such long-continued relations a complex of factors is, of course, involved, and specific drive conditions are not clearly responsible.

More specific studies of the reactions by infants to aspects of mothering are available. Escalona (1945) indicated that a high proportion of the four-week-old infants who refused the breast had mothers who were excitable and "high-strung." Fries (1946) found startle reactions in infants cared for by a certain kind of nurse, and Escalona further found that food likes and dislikes of infants paralleled the preferences of the adults who gave them their feedings. The most widely cited

[12] See, also, the discussion of this evidence in Chapters 4 and 12.

studies of the general problem of maternal deprivation in infancy, however, are those of Ribble and of Spitz (see, also, Chapter 12).

Ribble (1939, 1941, 1943, 1944) has argued from observations of several hundred infants that the physical and psychological status of the newborn and young infant is a precarious one, and that extensive mothering activities are necessary if the infant is to survive physically and develop psychologically. Mothering involves close bodily contact between mother (or surrogate) and child, as occurs in breast feeding, rocking, cuddling, etc. Ribble reports marked physical and emotional effects of the absence of adequate mothering, such as a negativistic excitement or a regressive quiescence. These reactions are said to arise because of the failure of the child to receive the mothering contact. Cases are cited in which dramatic recovery occurs, following the institution of mothering activity by a substitute. Ribble's account has suffered for several reasons. She buttressed her report by a great deal of dubious physiological theorizing (Pinneau, 1950; Stone, 1954) and wrote in a rather emotional tone (Orlansky, 1949). Further, she did not describe her sample of cases very well, the exact conditions under which they lived and were studied, or just how they were studied.

Spitz has emphasized the importance of the mother-child relationship by studying the effects on the child of being separated for several weeks from the mother. In one study (Spitz, 1946a) he described such depressive symptoms in infants separated from the mother as a drop in developmental quotient (as measured by an infant test), a sad, apprehensive appearance, expressionless eyes, a sort of dazed, withdrawn, emotionless facial expression, inactivity, and autoerotic behavior. A more severe form of this kind of depression was also observed and was called "hospitalism" (Spitz, 1945, 1946b, 1951). High infant mortality rates were also reported. Spitz' studies were carried out in two institutions (and included babies living at home as controls), and Spitz interprets his findings as showing that maternal separation from the infant is the responsible factor in the unfavorable conditions described above. Maternal separation means that the care of the child was taken over by institution personnel. Although these nurses were described favorably in terms of their attitudes toward children, each of them had the care of about eight babies. Each baby, therefore, could receive little attention and was left alone much of the time. It is important to note that the limited human or mothering contact is stressed; the care was neither abusive nor physically neglectful.

Like Ribble's studies, those by Spitz are difficult to interpret (Pinneau, 1955a, b; cf. Stone, 1954). Pinneau (1955a) shows, for example, that much of the change in developmental quotient reported in one study occurs *before* the children were separated from their mothers, according to statements by Spitz. In his reply to Pinneau, Spitz (1955) did not mention this point, which is perhaps the most important one of all those that Pinneau made. While we believe that both Ribble and Spitz, as well as other workers, are reporting observed facts, difficulty arises in attempting to determine how widely they can be generalized and just what factors in the situations studied led to the results obtained. Unfortunately, the reports available do not answer all one's questions. We shall cite other reports, which, on face value, seem to give contrary evidence.

Anthropological comparisons of the child-rearing practices in various societies have sometimes been seen to reveal relationships between childhood experiences and adult personality characteristics. Orlansky (1949; cf., also, Stevenson, 1957), however, reviewed the relevant evidence and found little consistent support for this view. Some recent evidence, more directly germane to the Ribble-Spitz studies, has been obtained in the Kibbutzim of Israel. The Kibbutz (Spiro, 1958) is an Israeli collective settlement, in which children do not live with their parents but live instead in a house with like-aged children and are cared for by nurses. Contact with the true mother is intermittent, although continued throughout childhood and adolescence, and the primary adult involved is a nurse who is responsible for several children at the same time. A number of investigations have been made of children reared in Kibbutzim. At least some of the features of institutional maternal deprivation emphasized by Ribble and Spitz are found in the Kibbutzim. Yet Caplan (1954) reported no apparent disturbances of any severity in adults reared in this situation. Faigin (1958) and Rabin (1957, 1959) also find little difference between children reared in Kibbutzim and in homes. Rabin (1957) suggests greater maturity of the children in Kibbutzim than in his controls, as reflected in Rorschach findings.

There are a number of other reports in the literature whose results seem to conflict with those reported by Spitz and by Ribble. A number of years ago, Wayne Dennis (1938, 1941) reared two infants under conditions of minimal social stimulation for several months, starting at an early age. The children developed normally, except in certain motor performances in which retardation seemed likely to be due to lack of specific practice. Lewis (1954) reported on 500 children who entered a children's center in England. Although there were disturbances in the children, they seemed more related to features of the mother's personality than to maternal separation. Dennis and Najarian (1957) reported on babies reared from an early age in a

Lebanese orphanage, in which each staff member cared for 10 children. They indicate that adult-child contacts were quite limited, and the infants spent much time alone. Some developmental retardation was noted, but it seemed to arise from a lack of learning opportunity rather than from maternal deprivation in an emotional sense; the children maintained emotional responsiveness, and, "There is nothing to suggest that emotional shock, or lack of mothering, or other emotion-arousing conditions, were responsible for behavioral retardation" (Dennis & Najarian, 1957, p. 12).

Rheingold (1956) compared control infants in an institution with other infants for whom she consistently served as "mother" for several hours a day over eight weeks. The control cases were cared for by a variety of aides and nurses and were alone a good deal more of the time than were the experimental subjects. While the latter subjects did develop considerably more social responsiveness to the experimenter than did the controls, there were no significant differences between them on various developmental tests involving bodily skills and infant "intelligence." Bowlby, Ainsworth, Boston, and Rosenbluth (1956) found a group of children who had spent from several months to two years isolated from their families because of hospitalization for tuberculosis. The children were thus not separated from their families because of rejection or parallel emotional reasons. As compared with matched controls, the tuberculous children were equal in IQ but there were more emotional and personality disturbances. However, the degree of these disturbances was less than expected, leading Bowlby et al. (1956) to believe the dangers of separation to have been overstated in earlier reports.

We are thus left with a considerably different view of the results of maternal separation than we obtained from the Spitz and Ribble studies.[13] It is no longer as clear as these studies implied that affective frustration arising from maternal separation persists until appropriate gratifiers occur, or, put another way, that development must necessarily be impeded by a lack of maternal affection. Baldwin (1956, p. 265) summarized the situation as follows (this was prior to the appearance of some of the studies we have mentioned): "We have, therefore, an interesting and reasonably well-confirmed relationship to work with, but in the 15 years of work on this topic, we are still quite uncertain about what is in institutionalization that has the effects, and we are not even sure just what the effects are except that they are bad." He goes on to say, "If we knew how often an environment challenged, gratified or frustrated a child; if we knew how often it

[13] See, also, our discussion of these studies in Chapter 12.

reinforced his approaches to people; if we knew how much it stimulated or failed to stimulate a positive action from the child, we would be in a better position than we are to understand its effects." We believe, with Baldwin, that a detailed analysis of the child-environmental interactions, such as has been suggested in D. M. Levy's (1958) recent work, and of the effects of reinforcement for specific acts (cf. Brackbill, 1958; Rheingold, Gewirtz, & Ross, 1959) will provide a much clearer picture of the importance of need gratification in the early stages of child development. Since this is the major area of empirical support for many of Maslow's contentions about the hierarchy of needs and the role of basic need gratification, we must conclude that his point of view receives little clear or consistent support. It is also true that giving love does not seem sufficient to cure psychosis, neurosis, or delinquency. Fromm-Reichmann (1954, 1955) has pointed this out strongly in discussing the treatment of schizophrenia.

SUMMARY AND CONCLUSION

The viewpoints reviewed in this chapter, existentialism and the emphasis on self-actualization, are concerned, in the first instance, with stating what a satisfactory human life can be. The existentialists point out the fact of human finitude—a circumstance which must be accepted in order for one to achieve real or genuine existence as a unique individual. Conformity and the illusions afforded by religion, politics, and science must be given up in order for a man to live existentially, but to give up such crutches occasions anxiety and dread. Except for the anxiety brought on by discarding the false security afforded by conformity and the other illusions, the existentialists do not speak much in motivational terms. However, their ideas have much in common with the emphasis on self-actualization, in which motivational concepts seem to enter.

It is a cardinal thesis of those who emphasize self-actualization that human nature, in general, has an inherent capacity to realize itself. Such a realization would have much in common with the existentialists' conception of the conditions for a satisfactory life. Human nature, to the theorists of self-actualization, is constructive, trustworthy, rational, unique, and individual. It requires a proper set of circumstances in order for it to emerge, but these circumstances are not readily provided by contemporary society. This is to say, as we said for the existentialists, that society tends to force conformity and illusion upon the individual. It requires courage in order to achieve self-actualization, as reaching such an achievement involves much anxiety and insecurity. Some theorists emphasize less the general obstacles which society places in the way of self-actualization and emphasize more the notion that ungratified, deficit needs stand in the way of the dominance of the self-actualization or growth needs. Such an argument conceives that needs exist in a hierarchy, such that some measure of gratification for the lower, deficit needs is a prerequisite for the emergence of the higher, growth-related needs. Social and economic conditions, however, may impede the gratification of lower-order, deficit needs.

The motivation of the self-actualizing person is said to be different from that of the person who has not reached self-realization. The behavior of the latter is predictable, on motivational grounds, whereas the behavior of the former is not. This assertion of unpredictability arises from the idea that motivation in the self-actualized is unique and devoted to the realization of his individual potentials. The behavior of the self-actualized person may be understandable, after the fact; that is, it is postdictable, but it is not predictable. It is sometimes said, in this connection, that a different sort of motivation will be required for the self-actualized person from what is appropriate to the non-self-actualized.

These various ideas about self-actualization constitute a break with much psychological theorizing about motivation and, together with the notions of the existentialists, comprise almost a program of what human life should be. However, the evidential basis for these ideas and this program is, we think, a limited one. Whether human nature, unspoiled by society, is as satisfactory as these viewpoints lead us to believe is certainly questionable. And it will be difficult either to confirm or to infirm this proposition, on empirical grounds. While there is some evidence that intense physiological and safety needs can dominate behavior, evidence for the hierarchical relationship of other needs is wanting. Furthermore, evidence on another point—that frustration of basic needs is crippling and, also, that gratification of such needs is health-giving—is at best equivocal.

In relation to the functions of the motivation construct, summarized in Chapter 1, the existentialists can hardly be appraised, as they develop only indirectly their motivational notions. For Maslow, the self-actualization theorist who is most explicit about motivation, some comment is in order. While low-level needs, in high strengths, dominate and perhaps energize behavior, the emphasis here seems to be on the directional function of motivation. Thus specific and intrinsic gratifiers are required to satisfy lower needs, and behavior would be seen as directed to the satisfaction of these needs. The needs of the self-actualized person, arising from the necessities of his own growth, would, also, mainly impart direction to his behavior.

The emphasis on self-actualization (and its philosophical relative, existentialism) suffers, in our opinion, from the vagueness of its concepts, the looseness of its language, and the inadequacy of the evidence related to its major contentions. It is difficult to see how it can foster meaningful investigations in view of its vague language. The first prerequisite for further development and evaluation of this viewpoint, it seems to us, is the formulation of the important ideas in language that is relatively precise. It then may be possible to carry out investigations related to the basic premises.

Chapter 14

Some Aspects of Human Motivation

A number of "motives" are often mentioned when human behavior is discussed. Included are achievement, affiliation, power, aggression, dependency, fear, and anxiety. While these states are usually conceived to be learned motives, they have been studied, typically, in cross section, rather than developmentally or historically. Hence, their systematic status is not as clear as is the case with acquired motivational variables discussed in Chapter 11. Not all writers would accord them acquired drive or motive value. Yet, a substantial literature has grown up concerning these states.

The present chapter is devoted to the discussion of these concepts. It begins by considering the view that the master motive is anxiety and that anxiety underlies other apparent motives. It continues with discussions of anxiety as measured by questionnaires and of a number of motives studied mainly by means of a projective test, the thematic apperception test, including achievement, affiliation, and certain others. Finally, it reviews the status of dependency and aggression and considers the role of experience in the development of motivational systems such as those just mentioned.

ANXIETY AS THE FORCE UNDERLYING OTHER APPARENT MOTIVES

As was said a moment ago, not all writers agree that achievement, power, etc., represent independent motives. Rather, they are seen as deriving from a more basic condition, anxiety. In Chapter 10, it was pointed out that Mowrer (1950*a*, pp. 29, 347–351) offered as an explanation for many so-called human needs the possibility that an *anticipation* of privation underlies them all. A similar argument has been suggested by Brown (1953, 1961). We will now consider Brown's argument and certain experiments which are pertinent to it.

As an example, Brown uses the desire for money. He rejects the notion that there is a drive or motive for money, or an economic motive (as well as many other so-called motives) and explains the value of money in the following, hypothetical way. He suggests that very young children, in the course of the many painful experiences they have with accidents, falls, illnesses, and the like, come to associate the worried, anxious speech and appearance of their parents with these experiences; hence these features of their parents' behavior become capable of arousing anxiety in the children. If then the parents speak and act in a similar fashion concerning money problems, it is possible that the child's anxiety reactions will also transfer to the topic of money, or more specifically, the absence of money. Getting money, of course, would reduce this anxiety, and the behaviors which accomplished this obtaining of money would therefore be strongly reinforced. With sufficient experience of this kind the child could emerge as apparently highly motivated to obtain money or economic success. However, the underlying motive, in this analysis, would be anxiety (perhaps in combination with other drives). Brown sees no reason to postulate a motive for money or for such other goals as praise, prestige, affection, eminence, and so on. Such goals as money could well derive from anxiety (or some other basic drive).

Brown's analysis was speculative and hypothetical. Two sets of experiments, one concerned with social deprivation and the other with social affiliation, however, will now be reviewed with respect to this interpretation.

Social Deprivation in Young Children

Gewirtz and Baer (1958a, b; cf., also, Gewirtz, Baer, & Roth, 1958) attempted to set up social deprivation, social satiation, and a nondeprivation condition in children prior to having the children play a game, during which some of their responses were reinforced (given approval) by the experimenter. The game involved placing a marble in one of two holes, and the experimenter said "Good" or "Fine" or some equivalent expression when the child placed the marble in the correct hole. These reinforcements were given on a fixed-ratio basis. The nondeprived children started to play the game at once on reaching the experimental room. The deprived children were required to wait alone for 20 minutes before starting the game or being told what they were to do, whereas with the satiated children the experimenter maintained a friendly, interested conversation for the 20 minutes before the game was started.

The approving responses of the experimenter increased the correctness of the performance of the task in all three groups, but the effect was greatest for the deprivation, next for the nondeprivation, and least for the satiation groups. Also, questions, comments, and attention-seeking behaviors were more frequent and more intense in the deprivation group than in the nondeprivation group. These results led Gewirtz and Baer (1958*b*) to conclude that the deprivation of social reinforcers had set up a drive for social reinforcers, whereas the satiation condition reduced it. Presumably, they mean an independent, basic drive.

In a series of papers, Walters and his associates have objected to this conclusion on the ground that anxiety was aroused by the deprivation procedure and is responsible for the social behavior and the effectiveness of the social reinforcer. With college students, Walters and Karal (1960) found social deprivation and satiation to have no effect on rates of verbal response in an interview situation and to have inconsistent effects on responsiveness to social reinforcers. Walters and Ray (1960) experimented with first- and second-grade boys, using the same game as that employed by Gewirtz and Baer. Their experiment employed four conditions: in one the child was isolated for 20 minutes under conditions designed to arouse some anxiety, and in another the isolation was not accompanied by anxiety; there were two satiation conditions, in one of which there was induced anxiety but not in the other. The results showed that improvement of performance was true of both anxiety groups; improvement was somewhat greater for the isolated anxious than for the satiated anxious group. Neither nonanxious group showed any change in performance. Walters, Marshall, and Shooter (1960) used adolescent boys in an autokinetic judgment situation under conditions of anxiety and isolation. Anxious subjects were found to be more suggestible and to be more easily conditioned to give a class of judgments than nonanxious subjects, but isolated and nonisolated boys did not differ in these measures.

These experiments, together with others he has performed, have led Walters to reject the hypothesis of a social drive and to attribute any effects of isolation to anxiety. While his experimental results seem to support this interpretation, especially since isolation per se seems to have had no reliable effects, it must be remembered that there is no direct evidence that the isolated children in the Gewirtz-Baer experiments were anxious. It is also possible that some state other than anxiety was involved in Walters' experiments.

Social Affiliation

Schachter (1959) has reported a number of experiments, the purpose of which was to study the relationship of affiliative behavior to anxiety. Typically, his subjects were female college students who received point credits on their final examination in an introductory psychology course for participating in an experiment. Most of the experiments followed this procedure: A small group of girls who were strangers to one another reported for the experiment and were greeted by a man in a white coat with a stethoscope in his pocket; he introduced himself as a physician in the Department of Neurology and Psychiatry. In the room was an array of electrical equipment. The man (who called himself Dr. Gregor Zilstein) gave a talk about the importance of research on the effects of electric shock and then told the girls about the experiment in which they were to participate. In one group (high anxiety) the girls were told that they would receive severe, painful, but not harmful shocks, whereas another group (low anxiety) was told they would receive mild shocks, shocks that rather than being painful would feel like a "tickle" and would be harmless. All the girls were told that physiological responses would be recorded during the shock experiences.

Before proceeding, the girls first filled out one or both of two questionnaires, which measured their degree of anxiety for the shock experiment. Then the girls were told there would be a delay before the experiment began and that they could wait either alone in a comfortable room which had books and magazines or together in a classroom with other girls. The girls were given a questionnaire on which their preference for waiting alone or together and a scale on which the intensity of their desire to wait alone or together were measured. Finally, the subject was given a choice between remaining for the experiment and leaving. If she chose to leave, of course, credit was not to be given her for participation in the experiment. This ended the experiment, and Zilstein then explained its character and purpose.

The first experiment showed significantly different measured degrees of anxiety for the high and low anxiety groups, and almost a third of the girls in the high anxiety group refused to continue whereas none in the other group refused. The manipulation of anxiety therefore seemed effective. And 20 of the 32 girls in the high anxiety group chose to wait with others as compared to 10 of 30 girls in the low anxiety group. This difference was significant as was the difference between the intensity of the desire of the girls in the two groups to be with others. This experiment then suggests that anxiety leads to affiliative behavior in college women.

In a second experiment, the subjects (different girls) were run individually, all under the high anxiety condition. Here they were given, in one group, a choice between waiting alone or waiting with other girls taking part in the same experiment. A second group's choice was between waiting alone or with other girls who were waiting to talk to a professor or advisor. Six of the 10 girls who were told they could wait with other subjects chose to do so, but none of the 10 girls in the second group chose to wait with the advisees. This difference, as well as the intensity of their feeling about waiting with others, was significant. As Schachter observes, this suggests that misery loves miserable company, not just any company.

A further experiment used groups of college girls again, and the high-and-low-anxiety manipulations. There were two other conditions at the time of choice; in one the choice of waiting with others also carried a prohibition of talking to them about anything, and in the other permission to talk about anything except the experiment. Thus there were four groups: high-anxiety-silence, low-anxiety-silence, high-anxiety-irrelevant-talk, low-anxiety-irrelevant-talk. Comparison between the induced levels of anxiety did not yield differences, and the subjects had to be reassigned on the basis of their expressed anxiety. If they refused to continue in the experiment or if they checked the two points on the anxiety scale indicating the highest degree of anxiety, they were classified as truly anxious. All other subjects were classified as true low anxiety. This resulted in reducing the number of subjects in the high anxiety groups, although reclassification worked both ways: that is, some subjects subjected to the high anxiety conditions were reclassified as true low anxiety whereas some subjects under low anxiety conditions were reclassified as truly anxious. On the basis of these reclassifications the truly anxious subjects tended, to an extent greater than the true low anxiety cases, to prefer to be with others under either silence or irrelevant talk conditions. Anxiety, again, as defined, was found to be related to affiliation.

These results, however, suggested to Schachter that a subject variable, in addition to or in interaction with experimentally manipulated anxiety, was controlling the choices of waiting with others or alone.

Schachter reasoned that individuals who are the first born in a family have probably had anxiety and pain relieved by people to an extent greater than later-born people. Presumably, the mother is more worried and sensitive to the expressions of anxiety of a first-born than she is to those of a later-born. With a second child her behavior is perhaps more casual and, of course, she is likely to be busier than she was when she had but one child. Hence, the first-born should receive more attention from others, especially from the mother, than the later-born, when he is anxious. And the later-born, also, may experience pain and anxiety from others—especially older siblings—and thus may be more chary of affiliative behavior under anxiety than the first-born. On these bases it follows that first-born children should affiliate more under

MOTIVATION: THEORY AND RESEARCH

anxiety than later-born; and it is possible that such differences may carry over into later years.

The data from the earlier experiments were then re-examined with respect to ordinal position of the subject's birth. The data are quite consistent when analyzed in several ways and when the experiments are treated separately or pooled. For example, under high anxiety, 32 of 48 first-born subjects chose to wait with others, whereas only 21 of 60 later-born subjects did so. This represents a $\frac{2}{3}$ vs. $\frac{1}{3}$ split and is significant. Under low anxiety, however, the choices of first-born subjects do not differ significantly from those of later-born subjects: 14 of 45 and 23 of 56 chose to wait with others, respectively. The anxiety scales show the first-born to be more anxious under high anxiety and that more of them refuse to continue the experiment than is the case with the later-born; these measures, under low anxiety conditions, do not differentiate the first- and the later-born. And the differences in affiliative behavior remain when only truly anxious subjects, whether first- or later-born, are used. Thirty-two of 40 truly anxious first-born subjects chose to wait with others as against 11 of 36 later-born truly anxious subjects. It is apparently clear, then, that anxiety tends to lead first-born subjects to show affiliative behavior.[1] It tends not to do so in later-born subjects; there is evidence, also, that the tendency to choose to wait with others declines rapidly as the exact ordinal position of a subject in his family increases.

While anxiety seems to be related to the affiliative tendency in interaction with characteristics of people, the results of an experiment with hunger showed no relationship to ordinal position of birth. In this experiment, Schachter gave his subjects an opportunity to take one of four tests after an adaptation period, spent either alone or with another person. Male college subjects were used. Those who had gone without food for 20 hours chose predominantly to spend the adaptation period with another subject and gave social reasons for their choice. Subjects who had experienced six hours' hunger or who had just eaten preferred in the majority to be alone during the adaptation period. These findings, based on males, together with those of the earlier experiments, based on females, indicate that either or both hunger and anxiety may underlie affiliative behavior. While it may be that hunger states are also

---

[1] Schachter has summarized data from the literature which, he suggests, give further evidence that first-born tend to affiliate under stress conditions while later-born do not. Fewer first-born are chronic alcoholics, more enter into and stay longer in psychotherapy, and fewer become fighter-pilot aces than later-borns. First-born nursery school children are more dependent and first-born college males are more conforming than later-born cases (Schachter, 1959, pp. 62–89).

capable of arousing anxiety, the operations in the hunger experiment were not anxiety arousing.

The relationships between anxiety and hunger on the one hand and affiliation on the other that Schachter has found can be given a number of interpretations. What value does affiliation have for the anxious or the hungry subject? One further experiment, directed to this question in the case of anxiety, may be summarized. Whether a similar analysis is appropriate to hunger (and other states) is a question for further re-search.

The experiment in question was conducted by Wrightsman (1959) and has been summarized by Schachter (1959). Each subject reported to a "nurse," who escorted him to a room, in which there was medical equipment and where he heard a tape-recorded message. This message indicated that he was about to receive a hypodermic injection which would either raise or lower his blood glucose level to near-danger points. Following this message, the subject (male or female) rated his state of anxiety. Next, the subject either waited alone for five minutes, waited with three other subjects in silence for five minutes, or waited with three other subjects for five minutes with freedom to talk about anything including the experiment. At the end of the five minutes, the subject took two measures of anxiety and indicated whether he wished to continue in the experiment. This ended the experiment.

The conditions of waiting alone, silent togetherness, or talkative togetherness showed no difference for the later-born subjects in the reduction in anxiety occurring between the initial measurement and the later one. There was less reduction for first-born subjects for the alone condition than for either of the together conditions. There was some evidence for the first-born cases that talking was less effective than simply being together with others in silence. Discussion may be anxiety arousing as well as anxiety reducing, and it is true that in the 17 silent-together groups anxiety levels either did not change at all or decreased, whereas in the together-talk condition some groups actually showed an increase in anxiety.

The range of anxiety in the groups was not as great in the together groups at the second assessment as it was initially when the subjects were alone; this increase in homogeneity from first to second testing is significantly smaller for the subjects who remained alone throughout. Schachter believes that a social comparison process was responsible for the homogenization of anxiety level that occurred in the talk group; various analyses lead him to reject the homogenization of the together-silent group as a statistical artifact. In summary of these points, Schachter (1959, pp. 121–122) states:

It has been hypothesized that the emotions, like the opinions and abilities, are evaluated by social comparison processes . . . (T)his hypothesis demands the demonstration that when discrepancies of emotional state exist among the members of a group, social influence and rejection processes are active. The decrease in discrepancy of anxiety states after a period of interaction in the "Together Talk" condition is evidence that social influence processes are operative. The failure to reduce discrepancy in wide-range groups is an indication of rejection.

This leads Schachter to the conclusion that both anxiety reduction and self-evaluation are involved in the affiliative behavior he has studied. Hunger can also lead to affiliation. Schachter's work, in some respects, is a confirmation of Brown's suggestion that apparent motive states may have more basic factors underlying them.

A number of experiments have been reported which have verified some of Schachter's findings. Included is one by Sarnoff and Zimbardo (1961), who, however, have raised some questions about the meaning of Schachter's results. In its essentials, the argument is that in Schachter's experiments it was fear, not anxiety, that was engaged, since his experiments involved the threat of direct physical pain. Anxiety, on the other hand, Sarnoff and Zimbardo argue, is most likely to arise from arousal of repressed motives, and the consequence of such anxiety arousal may be avoidance of others. This avoidance could occur because the individual needs to gain self control, or because he hesitates to reveal the fact that apparently innocuous stimuli make him anxious. Anxiety, then, should not lead to social affiliation; fear on the other hand should do so.

An elaborate experiment was carried out by Sarnoff and Zimbardo to test their expectations. Under strong fear (of electric shock) they found more of a desire to affiliate with others than under low fear. Also, first-born and only children showed more of a wish to affiliate under fear than did later-born subjects (the subjects in this experiment were males). Anxiety was manipulated by arranging things such that the subject expected he would have to engage in oral activities. Subjects in the induced high anxiety condition expected to be required to suck on such things as their thumbs, a baby bottle, nipples, pacifiers, and the like. Low anxiety subjects, however, expected to put into their mouths objects that involved blowing, like whistles, balloons, and pipes. High anxiety subjects under these conditions showed much less of a desire to affiliate with others during a waiting period than low anxious and fearful subjects. These results are taken by the experimenters as supporting their expectations.

Whether Sarnoff and Zimbardo were successful in creating "anxiety" in their subjects or whether some other state like "embarrassment" or "shame" was created is impossible at this point to say. However, the results are clear in indicating that there are limits to the kinds of aversive states which will lead to affiliative behavior. What is suggested is that if affiliative behavior can be anticipated by the individual (on the basis of past experience) as offering relief from an unpleasant state, the unpleasant state may motivate social affiliation. On the other hand, solitude may, in the case of some unpleasant states, be more relief-giving than affiliation, or, if not relief-giving, it may not engender more un pleasantness than would affiliation. Under such conditions the individual would not affiliate.

Fear, anxiety, and perhaps other aversive conditions can probably underlie many other apparent motives, like affiliation or the desire for money. Whether all such apparent motives can be reduced to this mechanism is, of course, impossible to judge at the present time. And it should be observed that a given kind of behavior (or apparent motive) would only arise on the basis of an aversive condition if that behavior, in the individual's past, had been found to have the value of reducing the aversive condition. Individual differences, one would expect, would be marked in such instances. And a further troublesome problem for any interpretation based on anxiety as derived from pain is the apparent normality of personality and motivation of cases of congenital insensitivity to pain (see Chapter 5). If these individuals have anxiety as we have said already, it must have been developed on some basis other than anticipation of pain.

ANXIETY MEASURED BY QUESTIONNAIRES

Two major approaches to the study of anxiety by means of questionnaire measures have characterized much research on anxiety since about 1951. One is to consider anxiety as a drive state, which, in sum with other drive states, multiplies habit strengths. The other is to consider anxiety as a source of stimuli for responses, which may or may not be compatible with the behavior required in a particular situation. Representative of the first approach is work with Taylor's *Manifest Anxiety Scale (MAS)*. The second approach is typified by the use of Mandler and Sarason's *Test Anxiety Questionnaire* with both adults and children. We consider these approaches in turn.

The Taylor Manifest Anxiety Scale

This scale (Taylor, 1951, 1953) was constructed by giving approximately 200 items from the *Minnesota Multiphasic Personality Inventory* to five clinical psychologists who were asked to select those items

which indicated manifest anxiety (as defined in accordance with a
description by Cameron [1947] of chronic anxiety reactions). The 65
items on which 4 of the 5 judges agreed were combined with 135
buffer items into the first version of the *Manifest Anxiety Scale,* which
the subject was given under the title *Biographical Inventory.* In subsequent revisions, 15 of the anxiety items were eliminated because of
their failure to correlate highly with the total anxiety score, and the
buffer items were modified. The test was given to almost 2000 students in introductory psychology courses over the three academic years
1948–1951 at the State University of Iowa, and scores ranging from
1 (low anxiety) to 46 (high anxiety) were obtained. The median score
for this group was about 13 (mean, 14.56) and the distribution shows
a bunching of cases at the low score end of the distribution, with a
long tail toward the upper end of the distribution; that is, the distribution is skewed to the right, in the direction of high anxiety scores.
Mean scores for men and women were not significantly different, and
a large group of airmen in basic training and a group of night-school
students at Northwestern University showed essentially the same distribution. Test-retest reliability of the scale is satisfactory (.81 to .89),
with the intervals between administrations ranging from three weeks
to seventeen months. The absolute level of mean scores in the original
scale, for such repeated testings, remained constant. There is evidence,
however, that the type of filler item used affects the scores obtained
in the anxiety items (Taylor, 1953, p. 287),[2] and there was a decline
in mean scale scores over a four week retest interval for a revision of
the scale; nevertheless the test-retest correlation for these two sets of
scores was .88. Some evidence that the test has validity was reported
by Taylor (1953, p. 290), who found that neurotic and psychotic subjects yielded a distribution on the scale skewed to the low end of the
distribution; their median score of 34 fell between the 98th and the
99th percentiles of the normal college population. Other evidence concerning the validity of the scale will be presented in a later section.
Table 14–1 lists some representative items and the responses indicative
of anxiety.

Theoretical Rationale for the Manifest Anxiety Scale. Taylor (1956)
and Spence (1958) have specified in some detail the rationale for the
development and use of the anxiety scale. Briefly, this rationale lies in

---

[2] Further revisions of the scale have been made, but we will not follow them
in detail (Taylor, 1953, p. 288). There are also available a short form of the scale
(Bendig, 1956), forced-choice forms (Heineman, 1953; Christie & Budnitzky,
1957), children's forms (Castaneda, McCandless, & Palermo, 1956; Sarason, Davidson, Lightfall, & Waite, 1958), and a short form for children (N. Levy, 1958).

the multiplicative relationship of drive to habit (Hull, 1943) and the attempt to study this relationship in human subjects. That is, if the Hullian assertion that available drives multiply available habits is valid, then variations in a human drive like anxiety in conjunction with variations in habit factors ought to lead to implications that could be tested by systematic experimentation. The argument here is essentially the one we reviewed in Chapter 11 (pp. 529–538). Persons with a high drive state should do better in performance than those with weak drives, when the two groups have habits appropriate to the performance situation; the opposite prediction would follow, however, if both groups have strong habits which are inappropriate to or are wrong in the situation. This is because the multiplication of the strong habit by the strong drive in the strong drive group will make such a habit very persistent; it will be less so and therefore more easily overcome in the low drive group.

Table 14–1. Representative items from the Taylor *Manifest Anxiety Scale* and the answer indicative of anxiety (from Taylor, 1953, pp. 286, 288)

I have very few headaches. (False)
I cannot keep my mind on one thing. (True)
I practically never blush. (False)
I have nightmares every few nights. (True)
I sweat very easily even on cool days. (True)
I am easily embarrassed. (True)
I am happy most of the time. (False)
I do not have as many fears as my friends. (False)
I certainly feel useless at times. (True)
I am very confident of myself. (False)

How does the *Manifest Anxiety Scale* relate to this argument? As Taylor (1956, p. 306) put it, the assumption is that "scores on the scale are in some manner related to emotional responsiveness, which, in turn, contributes to drive level." Thus, individuals with high anxiety scale scores may be chronically responsive in an emotional manner, or, alternatively, they may be readily susceptible to arousing stimulation and react with anxiety in relation to situations that have some emotional implication. On either of these interpretations they would have higher emotional arousal than would people with low anxiety scale scores in general, or at least in many situations. Which of these interpretations is valid was to be determined by experimental evidence. Spence (1958) has presented the same rationale for the use of the *Manifest Anxiety*

Scale, referring to the emotional responsiveness as an intervening variable, designated r_e.

Experiments Directly Pertinent to This Theoretical Rationale.

1. *Conditioning.* The first experiments were carried out by Taylor (1951) with the classical eyelid conditioning situation. Taylor used subjects who scored either in the upper 12 per cent or in the bottom 9 per cent of the MAS distribution. These two groups were quickly differentiated during the conditioning procedure, the high MAS group showing much more rapid conditioning than the low anxious group. A number of other eyelid-conditioning experiments have yielded very similar results, in most cases significant statistically (Hilgard, Jones, & Kaplan, 1951; Taylor, 1956; Spence, 1956, 1958; Spence & Ross, 1957). In the classical conditioning situation, what is involved is the association of a conditioned stimulus with a response whose occurrence is practically guaranteed by the presentation of the unconditioned stimulus. In eyelid conditioning, for example, the eyeblink response is elicited by a puff of air to the cornea of the eye. This means that there are few, if any, responses competitive to the CR that develops when the CS is paired with the UCS. If drive multiplies the developing habit strength, then high drive subjects should, as they are, be superior to low drive subjects in this task. Spence (1958) has also shown that intensity of the air puff to the eye (see Fig. 14–1) as well as a threat of shock have more effect on conditioning in high anxious than in low anxious subjects. Presumably, the puff intensity and the threat are factors which add to the subject's drive level.

Bindra, Paterson, and Strzelecki (1955) failed to find a difference between high and low anxious *Ss* when they conditioned a salivary response, and Bitterman and Holtzman (1952), conditioning the GSR, obtained a difference in the expected direction which was not significant. The latter experiment used subjects not as widely separated on the MAS as the subjects have been in the typical eyelid conditioning studies. The correlation between MAS and eyelid conditioning scores is only about .25 (Taylor, 1956, p. 307), so that conditioning differences are likely to be obtained only with extreme groups. The study by Bindra et al., of course, did not involve conditioning on the basis of a noxious stimulus. This could suggest that the differences in anxiety are mainly operative in relation to situational factors; that is, MAS anxiety is an acute, situational, rather than a chronic, condition.

High MAS scoring subjects tend to extinguish CR's more slowly than low anxious subjects, but the differences are small. In differential conditioning, in which one CS is reinforced and another like, but different, stimulus is presented but not reinforced, some of the predictions as to differences between high and low MAS subjects have been confirmed, but the evidence concerning others is questionable. Greater response strength has been shown by anxious subjects rather than by low anxious subjects to the positive CS, as it should, but differences on the negative CS have not been significant and differences between the responses to the positive and the negative stimuli, while usually in the predicted direction, have failed to be significant, statistically (Spence & Farber, 1953, 1954; Spence & Beecroft, 1954; see, however, Runquist, Spence, & Stubbs, 1958).

Evidence concerning generalization of conditioning has been reported by Rosenbaum (1953), who found more generalization in high than low anxious subjects when the groups were given intermittent, strong shocks. Wenar (1954) trained high and low anxious subjects to respond by pressing a key to signals (including shock), then tested for reaction time to these stimuli in a series in which the interstimulus intervals were different from what they were during training. This is a sort of temporal generalization, and Wenar found shorter times to the stimuli for reactions of the high than for those of low anxious subjects. Kamin and Clark (1957) found the reverse, however, when they tested simple reaction time or reaction time motivated by shock avoidance. However, they were not concerned in this study with generaliza-

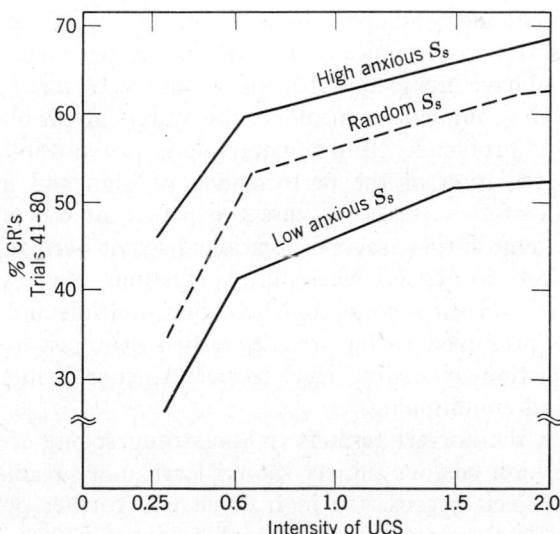

Figure 14-1. Per cent CR's as a function of type of subject and intensity of air puff (UCS) in lb/in.^{2} Reproduced by permission from Spence (1958, Fig. 3).

tion effects. S. A. Mednick (1957) reported some evidence that high MAS subjects generalize more than low MAS subjects when the stimuli are an array of lights, and M. T. Mednick (1957) found more generalization mediated by interword associative connections in high than in low anxious subjects.

Direct measurements of emotional responsiveness have been obtained and compared to conditioning rate. Runquist and Ross (1959) used pulse-rate changes or skin conductance to measure subjects' emotional responsiveness, and Runquist and Spence (1959) used muscle action potentials to assess the same variable. The more emotional subjects in these experiments showed more rapid eyeblink conditioning than the emotionally less responsive subjects. We consider a little later the relation between such measures of emotional responsiveness and MAS scores.

In general, the findings of the experiments involving classical conditioning have favored the propositions advocated by drive theory and thus suggest that MAS does measure a drive. Methodological differences may explain occasional failures to verify the other findings (cf. Hilgard, Jones, & Kaplan, 1951; Caldwell & Cromwell, 1959; Prokasy & Truax, 1959). Confirmatory data, however, not based on the use of MAS, for the relation between anxiety and conditioning are reported by Welch and Kubis (1947a, b) for the GSR.

2. *Complex processes.* In addition to classical conditioning, the Iowa investigators extended the application of the theory of generalized D and their research to complex processes. In the pertinent studies the tasks employed have included verbal and stylus mazes, serial and paired-associate learning, immediate memory, the water-jar problem, and rational learning problems. Unfortunately, it is not possible to give a satisfactory prediction of the performance of high and low anxious subjects in all of these tasks, because the nature of the processes involved in learning in these several situations has not been fully worked out. We indicate in general what the expectations were. These situations differ from classical conditioning in that multiple and competing responses are presumed to be present, rather than just a single one. Hence the relation of anxiety level to performance is more complex than in classical conditioning.

If, however, the correct response is the strongest one of the several available, the high anxious subject should learn more readily than the nonanxious subject, because the high drive will further potentiate, in him, the already dominant (and correct) response. When the reverse situation holds, and the strongest response available is incorrect, then the high anxious subject should be handicapped because, again, the dominant but incorrect response will be potentiated more in him by the higher drive level than in the nonanxious subject. Eventually, of course, this situation could reverse itself if, in the anxious subject, the correct response does somehow become dominant through learning (Hill, 1957).[3]

The clearest test of this kind of theorizing is provided by a paired-associate learning task. In such a task, the subject must learn to give a particular response to a specific stimulus. Complications arising from serial order are avoided by presenting the stimuli in different sequences from trial to trial. Taylor and Chapman (1955) used paired nonsense syllables in which intralist similarity was at a minimum; the anxious group outdid the nonanxious group on this task, making fewer errors and requiring fewer trials to reach criterion. Spence, Farber, and McFann (1956) used pairs of words. There was minimal similarity between words, thus minimizing competition, and the response words in the pairs had an initially high probability of occurrence to the relevant stimulus words, pre-experimentally. Anxious subjects learned this list faster than nonanxious subjects. Several other experiments have yielded findings more or less consistent with these and have added that paired associates involving competition (difficult) are more readily learned by the nonanxious than by the anxious subjects (Ramond, 1953; Spence, Taylor, & Ketchel, 1956; see Spence, 1956, 1958). Chiles (1958) used a list in which half of the pairs were difficult and the rest easy. Drive was manipulated by using shock or by not using it. The shock group (high drive group) did better than the nonshock (low drive) group throughout on the easy items and, after initial inferiority, also did better on the hard items. These results closely approximate the theoretical expectation. With the growth of habit strength on the difficult items, the high drive subjects would, later in learning, do better on these than the low drive group because of the multiplication of habit by the higher drive.

Some additional supporting evidence has been obtained in situations where difficulty has been defined in terms of competition arising from items in a serial list, which are similar, as compared to easier lists, in which such intralist similarity has been minimized. Mazes and serial

---

[3] Other Hullian principles, such as the reaction threshold and the oscillation of reaction potential, make the theoretical situation very complex (Taylor, 1956, pp. 304–306; Hill, 1957, pp. 491–492), and there is also the problem whether it is the relative or absolute differences in reaction potential which are critical to the outcome of response competition. Knowledge of the subjects and tasks used in the pertinent studies is inadequate to bring these principles to bear on prediction in any satisfactory way.

verbal lists have been employed. Because theoretical expectation is not entirely clear and worked out and because, despite several positive findings, there are also negative findings in the literature, we will not discuss these investigations here (for reviews, cf. Taylor, 1956, pp. 308–310; Jensen, 1958, pp. 313–317; I. G. Sarason, 1960, p. 406; Martin, 1961, pp. 246–247; Hall, 1961, pp. 180–186; Brown, 1961, pp. 259–263). Conflicting results have also been found in differences between high and low anxious subjects in studies of transposition (Stevenson & Iscoe, 1956; Bendig & Vaughan, 1957) and rigidity in a problem-solving task (Maltzman, Fox, & Morrisett, 1953; Cowen et al., 1957; see, also, Grant & Patel, 1957).

From what we have said, it is clear that the *Manifest Anxiety Scale* and the theory in which it was embedded generated a great deal of research in a decade's time. Some situations have yielded results consistent with theoretical expectation. In other situations the results have been conflicting. But what of the scale itself? To what extent can it be regarded as a valid measure of anxiety?

Correlates of the Manifest Anxiety Scale. The rationale we sketched, a few pages back, for the use of the *Manifest Anxiety Scale* accepted the scale as a measure of anxiety-drive. Further, anxiety, as measured, was treated theoretically as a measure of at least a part of effective generalized drive. The fact that a number of experiments yielded results consonant with expectations from general drive theory lends some support to the interpretation of the scale as measuring drive. However, as we have seen, there are conflicting results, and, also, there has been objection to the construct validation procedure (Jessor & Hammond, 1957; Kausler & Trapp, 1959; Hill, 1957). The objections have been that item-selection for the *Manifest Anxiety Scale* was not dictated by theoretical requirements but rather by clinical agreement that a statement was related to a clinical definition of anxiety and, furthermore, that factors other than the relation of the MAS scores to anxiety may account for those results that have accorded with theoretical expectation.

What correlates does the manifest anxiety have?

Physiological measures. Since anxiety has been considered to be a sort of emotional reactivity (e.g., Spence's concept of reactivity), it has been logical to determine whether the anxiety scale scores are related in any way to physiological measures of reactivity. Several such comparisons have been made with negative results (I. G. Sarason, 1960, p. 408), but Runquist and Ross (1959) did find a low but significant correlation of $+.22$ between a combination of GSR changes and heart rate and MAS scores. The investigations of this problem made so far can be criticized because only one or two measures of physiological reactivity have been used. The available data, to date, do not give much credence to the notion that MAS measures physiological reactivity.[4]

Other characteristics. Many other studies have compared MAS scores with ratings of anxiety and with scores on tests of intelligence, neurotic tendency, and other personality traits. Scores made by persons in various diagnostic categories also have been compared, and the MAS has been studied in several factor analyses.

Anxiety scale scores have been found to be negatively correlated with intelligence, though perhaps twice as many studies have found no correlations (I. G. Sarason, 1960, pp. 407–408).

Ratings of anxiety by clinicians have been sometimes found to be highly correlated with MAS scores and sometimes not, although almost all correlations reported are positive, and their median value is about .40 (Taylor, 1956, pp. 316–318). Psychiatric patient groups have usually scored higher on MAS than nonpatient groups, although differentiations between diagnostic groupings have not always been successful with the MAS (Taylor, 1953, 1956; Taylor & Spence, 1954).

Perhaps the highest correlations reported between MAS scores and other measures have been those with neurotic tendency and with psychasthenia. Deese, Lazarus, and Keenan (1953) found a correlation of .81 between the MMPI psychasthenia scale and MAS scores, an *r* which was reduced to .40 when overlapping items were eliminated. Brackbill and Little (1954), Eriksen (1954), Eriksen and Davids (1955) found high correlations between these scores, the values reaching .92 when the two scales included the overlapping items. Franks (1956) obtained a correlation, also of .92, between MAS scores and scores on the *Maudsley Medical Questionnaire,* a measure of neuroticism, and Bendig (1957) also found a high correlation between MAS scores and neuroticism. Davids (1955) found high correlations (.76 to .83) between MAS scores and scores on the *Psychosomatic Inventory* (McFarland & Seitz, 1938). Self ratings of anxiety were correlated with the MAS scores between .60 and .74 and between .74 and .84 with the *Psychosomatic Inventory.*

The foregoing correlations are illustrative only of the kind of traits with which the MAS scores have been found to be related. It is not at all clear that such correlations invalidate the Taylor Scale as a measure of anxiety, because anxiety is thought to be a significant factor in neurosis. However, neurosis involves characteristics other than anxiety pure and simple, and the implication is that the Taylor Scale is tapping

[4] Among the studies reporting negative findings are those by Berry and Martin (1957), Raphelson (1957), and Silverman (1957).

a number of characteristics and that its scores probably are not simple or pure measures of anxiety. Factor analyses in which Taylor Scale scores have been used have, in fact, indicated that the MAS is a complex instrument, requiring several factors to account for the correlations it shows with other procedures (Martin, 1958, 1959; Holtzman & Bitterman, 1956; O'Connor, Lorr, & Stafford, 1956; Bendig, 1958*a*).

Summary. We have seen that Taylor's *Manifest Anxiety Scale* was conceived as a measure of anxiety drive and that, in accordance with the theory of generalized drive, high anxious and low anxious subjects were expected to differ in theoretically predictable ways in various learning tasks. While theoretical expectation received considerable confirmation in studies involving classical, defensive eyeblink conditioning, the results for more complex learning situations have not been very consistent, even though a number of them are in accord with expectation. A major problem with this area of study has concerned the adequacy of the MAS as an indicator of anxiety, and a great deal of attention has been paid to its relations to rated anxiety, diagnostic groupings, physiological indices of emotional reactivity, and to other traits and characteristics. The resulting enormous literature has indicated that anxiety scale scores are, or may be, related to many other variables. However, little relationship has been found between MAS scores and physiological reactivity, and it is clear that there is some relation between MAS and neuroticism, especially psychasthenia. The development of the MAS has led to a great deal of research, but the meaning of much of it is quite unclear. The basic problem has been whether it measures the drive presumed to be involved or whether it measures nonmotivational variables which affect performance in the same or similar way that the drive was expected to, theoretically.

Test Anxiety

A conception of the role of anxiety alternative to the Taylor-Spence notion that anxiety has its major effects as a part of general drive level has been offered by Mandler and Sarason (1952). They stress the point that the existence or the instigation of anxiety leads to responses on the part of the subject which are of two types and which have been acquired in his prior experience as a means of reducing anxiety. One type of response is related to task completion, and if responses of this kind occur, the subject would go on to complete the task effectively. The other type, however, consists of responses not connected with or relevant to the task, such as "feelings of inadequacy, helplessness, heightened somatic reaction, anticipations of punishment or loss of status and esteem, and implicit attempts at leaving the test situation. It may be said that these responses are self rather than task centered" (Mandler & Sarason, 1952, p. 166). Responses of this type would tend to interfere with task completion. Mandler and Sarason's conception considers anxiety as a drive in the sense of a strong stimulus but emphasizes the responses which are associated with the drive stimulus and which it arouses rather than the energizing consequences of the drive.[5]

Mandler and Sarason (1952; Sarason & Mandler, 1952) have developed and described a test anxiety questionnaire which is designed to measure anxiety reactions which occur in test situations. The questions concern a student's subjective reactions before and during a test situation, such as individual and group intelligence tests and course examinations. Reactions surveyed by the questions include such items as uneasiness, acceleration of heartbeat, sweating, emotional interference and worry both before and during a testing situation. A satisfactory distribution of scores from the 37 anxiety items finally used was obtained, and the reliability of the scale (corrected split-half) was represented by a coefficient of .91.

Mandler and Sarason validated their scale by taking high-scoring and low-scoring groups of subjects from the extremes of the distribution of scores on the scale and testing them as follows. First, the subject was told he was to be given a number of intelligence tests and, after sample tests, he was given six trials each on a Kohs block-design and a digit-symbol test, the tests being presented alternately.

Following this part of the experiment, the subject was either told nothing before going on, or was told that he had done very well (success) or very poorly (failure) in the first part. Suitable dramatics were employed to give reality to the success and failure. Then the next part of the experiment was run; this consisted of six trials each on another block design and another digit-symbol test, presented alternately. The experimenter did not know at any time to which anxiety group the subject belonged, but he rated each subject on a five-point scale for the amount of overt anxiety shown. A point correlation (phi) between his ratings and the test scores was significant (.59).

In the first part of the experiment, the high anxiety group took longer and showed more variability than the low anxiety group on the first five of the trials on the block-design test, but there was no difference on the sixth trial. This (and parallel data from the neutral groups) is taken to mean that, in a task like the block-design test, in which completion occurs on each trial, the originally interfering anxiety responses become compatible with good performance, so that by trial six the two

[5] A parallel interpretation of frustration has been made by Child and Waterhouse (1952, 1953). See Chapter 9 for a treatment of their views.

anxiety groups do not differ. Poorer performance and an increase in variability over trials in Part One of the experiment were also found on the digit-symbol task for the high anxiety group; on this test no subject completed the task so that the anxiety-induced responses could not become associated with task completion. Presumably this is why variability increased with trials in the high anxiety group, which it did not do with the block-design test.

After the failure, success, or neutral instructions, the neutral high anxiety group performed somewhat better on the second block-design test than the other two high anxiety groups, but the failure and success groups did not differ from each other. The low anxiety group after failure performed significantly better than the low anxiety neutral group, and the low anxiety success group was intermediate to these two groups. The low anxiety failure group performed significantly better than the high anxiety failure group.

The general interpretation of these results is that high anxiety subjects respond to evaluation with *responses* that, at least initially, interfere with performance; the low anxiety groups seem to be energized rather than made to emit interfering responses by evaluation. It is not clear whether the low anxiety groups can be said to be made anxious by evaluation; in them, perhaps, achievement was aroused. The high anxious groups, whether aroused to achieve or not, respond to the arousal operation with task-interfering responses.

Sarason, Mandler, and Craighill (1952) made further observations in subjects classified by their scale as high or low anxiety. In one experiment, a subject was given a digit-symbol test and told that he was or was not expected to finish it in the time allowed. The performance, over several trials, of low anxious subjects was better for the expected-to-finish than for the not-expected-to-finish instructions, indicating a motivational effect; for high anxious subjects the direction of the difference was reversed on some of the trials, suggesting interference from the stress of expectation to finish. High and low anxious subjects performed a stylus maze under either ego-involving or task-orientation instructions. Low anxious subjects did better under ego-involving than under task-orientation conditions, but the reverse occurred for the high anxious subjects. Again, the high anxious subjects are adversely affected by challenging, evaluative instructions, whereas the low anxious subjects benefit.

There is a good deal of evidence in the literature that under stressful conditions, such as those involving reported success and failure, situations implying an evaluation of intelligence or other abilities, or, generally, ego-involvement, subjects who make high scores on anxiety scales are adversely affected, whereas subjects who make low scores are either not affected at all or are motivated to improve their work. The tasks employed in such studies [6] are usually complex ones, but the interpretation of the impaired performance of high anxious subjects under stress has not emphasized competition from intratask factors so much as competition from the responses which high anxious subjects make to their own anxiety when it is aroused in the stressful circumstances.[7]

This interpretation, as Taylor (1956) points out, implies that anxiety as a drive would always improve performance were it not for the interfering responses aroused by the anxiety (drive stimulus). Drive theory, too (Spence, 1958), recognized responses to the drive stimulus and drive theory could accept their interference as a factor detrimental to the performance of high anxious subjects. The effect of drive on the habit strengths of the correct and incorrect responses aroused by the stimuli of the task, as outlined in the discussion of the rationale for the use of the *Manifest Anxiety Scale*, would, however, have to be considered in any predictions about the relative performances of high and low anxious subjects in any particular task.

Evaluation of Anxiety as a Drive

The meanings and theoretical conceptions of anxiety are various (May, 1950), and it is by no means easy to settle on criteria of anxiety on which there would be widespread agreement (Krause, 1961). Although it is not totally adequate as a conception, the report of "feeling afraid" was seen by Krause (1961) as having the widest acceptance in the literature as an indicator of anxiety. While there is thus a concordance between what is taken in the literature and what has been used in Schachter's rating scales, the *Manifest Anxiety Scale*, and the

[6] The literature has been brought together by Taylor (1956, pp. 310-316), Martin (1961, pp. 246-249), and I. G. Sarason (1960, pp. 404-406). See, also, Lazarus, Deese, and Osler (1952) and Chapter 9.

[7] A monograph by S. B. Sarason, Davidson, Lighthall, Waite, & Ruebush (1960) has reported a great many investigations of children differentiated by means of a test anxiety scale and, also, a general anxiety scale. Much attention is also devoted in the monograph to prior work on fear and anxiety in children and certain theoretical formulations and methodological problems. Test-anxious children show inferiority in situations containing cues suggesting evaluation by authority figures but are less inferior or not inferior to nonanxious children in situations in which such cues are absent, that is, which are not test-like, or in situations in which performance is not impaired either by dependency or by cautiousness.

Test Anxiety Questionnaire as indicating anxiety, we may point out that Krause suggests self-reports to be a sufficient but not a necessary indicator of anxiety. Other supporting indicators, such as flight or paralysis, the presence of suitable stressors for the anxiety and flight reactions, and a concomitant physiological activation are all conjointly required for us to be certain that a state of anxiety exists.

It is worth noting that where more than one self-report scale of anxiety has been used, the intercorrelations, while often positive, are not high. The same point can be made concerning the relation between ratings of anxiety by judges and physiological measures and self-report scores. Factor analyses of the self-report scales have shown them to be complex, with loadings on many factors some of which may have little to do with anxiety. On the other hand, high correlations are sometimes found between scores on the self-report anxiety scales and measures not presumed to stand directly for anxiety, such as neuroticism. It seems clear that there is considerable uncertainty concerning what anxiety scales and ratings are currently measuring. It would seem that much more work concerning what the procedures for measuring anxiety mean must be carried out before such procedures can be satisfactorily employed to gauge either the role of anxiety as a drive in behavior or the adequacy of theories which have offered varying interpretations of how anxiety relates to behavior.

An interesting and potentially valuable way of studying anxiety measures has been used by Mandler and his associates. It is probably too early to reach definitive conclusions from this work, but the procedures have interest. Briefly, the notion is to obtain ratings from the subject and from an interviewer of the extent of the subject's autonomic responses to stress situations and of his awareness of them. Actual recordings of physiological reactions are made under stress. It is therefore possible to compare a subject's estimate and awareness of his physiological reactions to stress with the ones he actually makes. Comparisons with anxiety scale scores are also possible. For example, Mandler et al. (1961) have evidence suggestive that the *Manifest Anxiety Scale* is perhaps a measure of activation or arousal but not of emotionality, which is another aspect of anxiety. What this may mean to performances of high and low scoring subjects on MAS on other tasks remains to be worked out, but clearly it will be of great value to have more knowledge of what anxiety scale scores mean than has been available in the past (see, also, Mandler, Mandler, & Uviller, 1958; Mandler & Kremen, 1958).

AROUSAL, MEASUREMENT, AND CORRELATES
OF OTHER MOTIVE STATES

The literature of the behavioral sciences is replete with motivational terms and references. Many such terms and references are little more than figures of speech. Others, however, denote concepts which have led to attempts to arouse, measure or determine correlates of the states to which the concepts refer. Many procedures have been used, both for arousing motivation and for assessing its existence and its intensity. The correlates studied have been diverse. Some of the concepts, procedures for measurement, and for arousal, and the correlates studied, have been examined systematically with reference to each other. The study of others has not been so systematic. In this section we sample this diversity of materials: the arousal of motives; the measurement of various characteristics, after arousal of motives, or cross-sectionally, often thought to be motivationally relevant; the study of correlates of the motives, aroused or simply measured. We begin with concepts and procedures which are designedly motivational and whose study has been relatively systematic, going on to some of the concepts and procedures whose motivational status is less clear. On this course, we digress from time to time to raise questions and issues.

THE AROUSAL AND MEASUREMENT OF "NEEDS" BY
MC CLELLAND, ATKINSON, AND THEIR ASSOCIATES:
ACHIEVEMENT, AFFILIATION, POWER, FEAR, SEX,
AGGRESSION, FEAR OF FAILURE

Achievement

Rationale and Experimental Arousal. In 1947, David C. McClelland and his co-workers began a series of studies designed to establish (1) a satisfactory procedure for measuring a human motive (presumably a learned motive) and, if this first venture was successful, (2) to study the correlates in behavior of the motive and, (3) to study the factors involved in its differential development in people. We shall discuss the first two facets of this work here, reserving to the final section of this chapter the third of these problems.

Two basic propositions underlay this work. One comes from psychoanalysis and from projective measurement generally; it holds that motivation may have effects on fantasy (cf. Murray, 1938). The other notion comes from work on animal motivation and is the point that motives can be aroused by suitable conditions and that degree of arousal can be varied by altering the conditions of arousal (McClelland et al.,

1953, p. 3). Actually, attempts were also made to study the effect of motive arousal on perception as well as on fantasy (thematic apperception). While the hunger drive was found to influence both these kinds of behavior (R. N. Sanford, 1936; McClelland & Atkinson, 1948; Atkinson & McClelland, 1948), the results for arousal of a need for achievement were better for fantasy than for certain perceptual measures (McClelland, Atkinson, & Clark, 1949a; McClelland et al., 1949b). It is therefore with thematic apperception that we are chiefly concerned.

The first experiments were carried out, not with a learned motive, but rather with hunger. The reason for this was that Atkinson and McClelland (1948) desired first to establish that fantasy would reflect a state, hunger, which everyone agrees is in fact motivational. They used U.S. Navy personnel, who were asked to write stories organized around standard questions [8] in response to six pictures. The pictures used were thought to be related to such aspects of hunger-satiation as deprivation, food, place of eating, and the like, and the subject thought he was taking a test of creative imagination. A procedure for scoring the stories in terms of imagery, themes, needs, activities, goals, and other variables that the stories expressed was devised. Since the subjects wrote their stories under 1, 4, or 16 hours of food deprivation, characteristics of the stories which differed as a function of food deprivation were sought. For example, the frequency with which food deprivation was the central focus of the story increased with food deprivations of 4 to 16 hours, whereas food imagery—that is, any reference to food or eating—did not change with food deprivation. A scoring system was developed on the following bases: items that showed an increase between short and long deprivation were given each a +1 or +2 (depending on the size of the shift); characteristics that showed a decrease in the stories from little to greater hunger were given negative values (e.g., goal activity, i.e., eating). Characteristics that did not change were not scored. Mean need-food scores based on this system did differentiate the 1- and 4-hour groups from the 16-hour group. Such differentiation is not surprising, since the total need-food scores were based on scoring elements that had already differentiated these groups. However, the general point—that thematic apperception or fantasy, if suitably scored, can differentiate need or motive states— was considered confirmed.

[8] "(1) What is happening? Who are the persons? (2) What has led up to this situation? That is, what has happened in the past? (3) What is being thought? What is wanted? By whom? (4) What will happen? What will be done?" (Atkinson, 1958a, p. 48). The paper by Atkinson and McClelland (1948) is abridged as Chapter 2 in Atkinson's (1958a) book.

The next experiment followed a design similar to, if more complex than, that of the one with hunger. In this second experiment (Mc-Clelland et al., 1949*b*, 1953; Atkinson, 1958*a*, Chap. 3) several conditions were established to create different degrees of the need for achievement (nAch), subjects wrote stories around the four questions in response to pictures designed to be related to achievement, and a scoring system based on shifts of story characteristics between arousal conditions was developed to measure nAch.

The subjects were male college students, and the experiments were conducted by graduate students during class periods; the instructor introduced them. In most of the six conditions of the experiments there were two phases. One involved the taking of a series of seven tests: anagrams, two scrambled word tests, and four paper-and-pencil motor tasks. These tests were followed by the test of "creative imagination," consisting of pictures selected to be related to achievement situations.

The achievement orientation was established around the series of seven tests. All groups wrote stories under essentially the same conditions. The six conditions of achievement arousal were as follows:

Relaxed. The instructor introduced the graduate students who, he said, were trying out some tests. The test administrator spoke in a vein to indicate that it was the tests, not the students, that were being tested; the tests were said to be new, still being developed, and data were being collected to improve them.

Failure. A very different attitude attended this procedure. The instructor introduced the experimenters, who passed out the test materials with no explanation. The first test was administered at once, with emphasis on paying attention closely as it was timed. After it was finished, the subjects scored their papers and obtained their scores. They then completed a short questionnaire, which asked, among other things, for class standing, IQ, and an estimate of their general intelligence. Then one of the experimenters spoke about the test just completed and those to come. He emphasized that the series of tests measured general intelligence, a person's ability as a leader, that they were used during the Second World War to select people for high administrative positions in the Federal government. Different schools, he emphasized, were being surveyed to discover which educational institutions had students with administrative abilities as shown by high scores on the tests. The subjects were told of a rival institution which excelled in the number of such students.

After this presentation, which was, of course, false, the experimenter quoted norms on the first test which were so high that almost every one failed, that is, placed in the bottom quarter of the announced norms. The remaining six tests were then given, after the first test was said to be the best single one in the battery. On completion of the next six tests, the students scored their work so as to obtain a total score for all of them and again were given false, high norms. This procedure was then followed by the test of creative imagination.

These instructions, which are called ego-involving, seemed to be believed, since the students worked quietly and hard and expressed dismay when the norms were announced. In contrast, the students under the relaxed condition seemed to enjoy the test, as they would enjoy some parlor games.

Neutral. This group was oriented to the *tasks* but was asked to take them seriously and to do their best, so that satisfactory norms could be developed. (Apparently, no norms were announced.)

Success-failure. The norms announced after the first test for this group provided success, as they were so low that almost everyone's score was a good one. After the next six tests, however, the norms quoted were very high, producing failure. This group was used to accomplish very high nAch arousal, and the neutral group was designed to be aroused to a level intermediate to those of the relaxed and the failure groups.

Achievement-oriented.[9] In this condition, the instructions for the paper-and-pencil tests were those used for the failure condition but no norms were announced.

Success. The instructions again were those for the failure conditions, but the norms announced both after the first test and after the next six were so low that most of the subjects believed they did well on the tests.

While the test of creative imagination obviously differed in form from the other seven tests and while the instructions for it clearly indicated that there were no right or wrong answers, there was no break between it and the other tests suggestive that it was not a part of the total battery, under any of the instructional conditions. However, dif-

---

[9] This condition is reported by McClelland et al. (1953, pp. 102–104) and is presented as the extreme of a continuum represented by the relaxed, neutral, and achievement-oriented conditions. In the earlier report (McClelland et al., 1949*b*, p. 244) a similar condition, there referred to as "ego-involved," was used, but data were not reported because the stories obtained were so tense, inhibited, and cautious that meaningful analysis was not possible. Data for the success condition were not reported in this paper either. In the neutral condition (McClelland et al., 1953, p. 102), a 12-minute anagrams test was used *after* TAT administration; the 12-minute anagrams test was used in the achievement-oriented condition *before* the TAT (McClelland et al., 1953, p. 103). Both of these groups then seem to have been tested differently from the others.

ferent experimenters administered the two phases of the experiment.

Scoring System. The stories written under the various achievement conditions were analyzed along the general lines involved in scoring the stories written under hunger. We present, first, the general model involved which underlies the scores, then the scoring categories themselves and their manner of combination,[10] and, finally, evidence concerning the validity of the scores relative to the experimental manipulations.

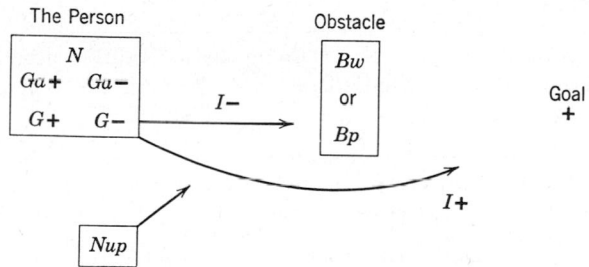

Figure 14–2. Behavioral sequence showing position of scoring categories. Reproduced by permission from McClelland et al. (1953, p. 109).

Figure 14–2 shows the model adopted by this group of workers (McClelland et al., 1953, pp. 108–109). The model conceives a behavioral sequence as getting under way when the person experiences a motive or need (N), and he may anticipate goal attainment ($Ga+$) or failure ($Ga-$). He will engage in activities which are instrumental to goal attainment; it may be successful ($I+$) or unsuccessful ($I-$). Obstacles outside in the world (Bw) or personal, that is, internal (Bp), may block his goal-directed behavior. Positive affect ($G+$) may be experienced on goal attainment or negative affect ($G-$) on failure and frustration. Someone else may help or sympathize with him (Nup), that is, he may receive nurturance from another.[11]

[10] There have been at least three systems for scoring nAch. The first two (McClelland et al., 1949*b*; Atkinson, 1950) were superseded by system *C* (McClelland et al., 1953, Chap. IV, reprinted with abridgement as Chap. XII in Atkinson, 1958*a*). We shall deal only with system *C* here. McClelland et al. (1953, Table 5.2, p. 149) report intercorrelations of scores based on system *C* of .90 and .87 with the earlier systems.

[11] The *p* in *Nup* refers to "press," a term used by Murray (1938) to indicate the effects of the environment on an individual. The abbreviation nAch for need achievement was also used by Murray. The Thematic Apperception Test

In setting up a scoring system for nAch, the selection of items was accomplished by determining which items differed in the stories written by males under the relaxed, neutral, and achievement-oriented conditions and, for certain items, under the relaxed, success, failure, and success-failure conditions. Certain types of imagery did not shift with the changes in the conditions under which the stories were written, one being hostile press, another being the adoption of substitute goals or actions when obstacles to achievement arise. The items which did change and which are utilized in making up an individual's nAch score are listed in Table 14–2 and are briefly described now.

Table 14–2. Scoring system for obtaining an individual's nAch. (Reproduced by permission from McClelland et al., 1953, p. 148, Table 5.1.)

Category *	Score
Unrelated imagery	−1
Doubtful imagery	0
Achievement imagery	+1
Need (*N*)	+1
Instrumental activity	+1
Positive anticipatory goal state	+1
Negative anticipatory goal state	+1
Personal obstacle	+1
Environmental obstacle	+1
Positive affective state	+1
Negative affective state	+1
Nurturant press	+1
Achievement thema	+1

---

* The statistical and logical bases for the inclusion of all of these categories are not of the highest order. There is question about the independence of some of the categories. Some of the categories reached significance only when the conditions involving success or failure were included; it is not clear that these conditions are linearly related to the relaxed, neutral, and achievement-oriented conditions. Not all of the items scored "+" change consistently in the direction of greater arousal even among the relaxed, neutral, and achievement-oriented conditions (cf. McClelland et al., 1953, Figs. 5.1 and 5.2, pp. 140–145).

Achievement imagery. The overall definition of nAch is that the subject show concern over competition with a standard of excellence; such concern may not be stated explicitly, but there must be enough

(TAT) was introduced by Morgan and Murray (1935), but its use by the McClelland group differs in important respects from its clinical use as well as its original use.

evidence to justify the inference that there is such a competition. Achievement imagery is scored when competitive activity is mentioned, so long as it is not purely aggressive, or when the story expresses for a character affective reactions, such as pride or disappointment, over the outcome so far as goal attainment is concerned. Self-imposed requirements for good performance and descriptions of instrumental acts such as that they are being carefully or seriously undertaken also qualify for the scoring of achievement imagery. The inference of achievement imagery can be made for stories which suggest unique accomplishments, such as an artistic creation or an invention, or which suggest long-term goals of an achievement sort. Only if a story is scored for achievement imagery are the remaining categories for scoring nAch applied to it. Thus, stories with imagery which is unrelated to or doubtfully related to achievement would receive no further scores.

Statement of need for achievement. This is scored when a character in a story explicitly states the desire to achieve something, such as expressing a desire to be a doctor or to succeed in some activity.

Instrumental activity. This is an indication in the story that something is being done, overtly or covertly, to attain an achievement goal.

Anticipatory goal states. Goal attainment or frustration or failure to reach the goal is indicated by a character in the story.

Obstacles. A personal obstacle (such as failure of nerve) or an external obstacle (such as being drafted) could cause difficulties in the way of goal attainment by a character in the story.

Affective states are scored when the story describes emotional reactions to goal attainment or to frustration.

Nurturant press is scored when the story describes assistance received by a character from someone else in reference to achievement. Helpful advice or encouragement by a teacher, parent, or other significant figure would qualify.

Achievement thema. If the central plot of the story concerns achievement, then it would be scored for Achievement thema.

Achievement score. Each story written by a subject is scored by means of those categories which are appropriate to it and the scores for that story are summed algebraically; then the scores for all the stories written by a subject are summed to obtain his total score. For the scores of 30 subjects listed by McClelland et al. (1953, Appendix II), the total nAch scores ranged from -3 to $+21$. The highest score for any of the 120 stories written by these 30 cases was $+7$. A score of $+9$ for one story has, however, been reported (p. 186).

Group differences. Mean nAch scores were reported by McClelland et al. (1949*b*, p. 249, Table V), as —1.00 for the relaxed, 3.13 for the neutral, 5.82 for the failure, and 6.00 for the success-failure conditions. This progression of means is what one would expect if the different groups do in fact represent differential degrees of arousal of nAch. In a later report, using a different scoring system, McClelland et al. (1953, p. 184, Table 6.9) give mean nAch scores of 1.95 for the relaxed, 7.33 for the neutral, 8.77 for the achievement-oriented group, 7.92 for the success, 10.10 for the failure, and 10.36 for the success-failure groups.[12] Lowell obtained a mean nAch score under neutral instructions of 5.05 and under achievement-oriented conditions of 9.05 (McClelland et al., 1953, Table 6.1). For both male high-school students and for male Navajo ninth-graders, higher nAch scores are obtained under achievement-oriented than under neutral conditions (McClelland et al., 1953, Tables 6.2, 6.3, p. 167, p. 170). Field (1951) obtained mean scores of —1.46 for males under relaxed conditions and of 3.46 under failure conditions. Clearly, the relaxed and neutral conditions show lower nAch scores, at least in males, than the various conditions which explicitly involve achievement, failure, success, success-failure, and achievement-orientation. We should note that Field's findings were obtained entirely independently of the McClelland group. Noteworthy in these findings is that the arousal procedures and the scoring system, first developed chiefly with male college men in Connecticut, seem to hold for male high-school students in Connecticut, male Navajo ninth-graders, and male college students, in both day and evening sessions at the University of Maryland.

Reliability of scores. Two kinds of reliability must be considered in dealing with projective measurement. The first arises from the fact that the protocols obtained from the subjects must be scored in terms of the scoring system by judges or scorers. Good interjudge scoring agreement has been reported, even when one judge had relatively little experience with the scoring system. Experienced judges agreed on 91 per cent of the scorings of various categories, and the scores provided by the two judges were intercorrelated at .95. Rescoring by the same judge six months later yielded comparable values. Scores provided by inexperienced judges correlated well with those assigned by experienced judges (McClelland et al., 1953, pp. 185–187). Scoring manuals and

[12] In the book (McClelland et al., 1953), the shifts of score categories among the relaxed, neutral, and achievement-oriented categories seem to be the basis of selection of categories for nAch score. In the earlier paper (McClelland et al., 1949*b*) the scores were based on shifts between the relaxed and the failure conditions (pp. 248–249).

examples are provided by McClelland et al. (1953) and by Atkinson (1958*a*).[13]

The second kind of reliability refers to the consistency of nAch scores obtained from the same subject at different points in time. One estimate of reliability reported was determined from two sets of three pictures each, administered at the same time. The *r* was .64 (corrected it was .78) (McClelland et al., 1953, pp. 190–191). However, *r* between scores obtained from two sets of pictures given a week apart was only an insignificant .22 (p. 192). Nevertheless, the two forms agreed in 72.5 per cent of cases in placing subjects above or below the medians in the score distributions. Krumboltz and Farquhar (1957) have reported a test-retest reliability coefficient over a nine-week period of only .26. Although these values question the stability of nAch scores in the individual, indirect evidence of reliability does come from findings that nAch scores are related to other behaviors. This suggests though it does not prove that nAch is a fairly stable characteristic. It may be that the test-retest method is not appropriate to this kind of instrument. However, Haber and Alpert (1958) have reported a test-retest reliability of .54 (corrected to .70) over a three-week interval.[14]

Sex differences. High school girls did not show higher nAch scores under achievement-oriented conditions than under neutral conditions [15] (McClelland et al., 1953, p. 172), and similar findings were obtained with college women (p. 175). In both cases the scores under both conditions were relatively high. Field (1951) also found no difference in nAch scores for college women under relaxed and failure ego-involvement conditions, although he obtained the usual difference between the two conditions for men. He also found higher nAch scores under relaxed conditions for women than for men.

Are there procedures which will alter nAch scores for women? Field studied another set of arousal conditions and obtained stories to them, applying the nAch scoring system to the stories. These arousal conditions were termed social acceptability. In the failure and success operations of this condition, subjects were told, after a talk stressing the importance of social acceptability, that a committee had made, for the group of which the subjects were members, a judgment of the acceptability of each member under the condition that the group was to be reduced in half. Each subject received a confidential rating, "A" if he

[13] Satisfactory agreement among scorers has also been reported by Sadacca, Ricciuti, and Swanson (1956).

[14] See also Reitman and Atkinson (1958).

[15] They did show higher nAch scores to pictures containing males than to pictures containing females. The same difference was found for high school males.

had been accepted (success), "R" if he was to be rejected (failure). The TAT stories were written following these rather drastic maneuvers.[16] Both male and female college students were subjects in success and failure conditions as well as in a separate relaxed condition.

The nAch scores of the males were not affected by these conditions of social acceptability, but both the success and failure conditions of social acceptability raised the nAch scores of women. We have already seen that the converse findings were obtained by Field under achievement-arousing conditions. The McClelland group (1953, p. 181) says that emphasis on social acceptability will nearly always arouse nAch in women.

Alternative measures of nAch. One method which produced results not at all comparable to those from the projective method of assessing nAch was called (de Charms et al., 1955) value achievement or vAch. This measure was composed of nine questionnaire items (e.g., "I set difficult goals for myself, which I attempt to reach"), to each of which the subject checked the extent of his agreement; the sum of his responses was his vAch score. This score showed a low, positive and significant relation with nAch scores ($rho = .23$). However, McClelland and his associates regard it more as a measure of a conscious desire for achievement rather than as a measure of the motivation to achieve. The relations between vAch and other behaviors showed that vAch is associated with conformity, deference to expert opinion, and valuation of people in terms of their success and failure. NAch showed none of these relationships, and it related to various other behaviors to which vAch did not. Measurement of nAch, therefore, by direct questions concerning evaluations of achievement, is not appropriate.

A measure of motivation called the *Iowa Picture Interpretations Test* (IPIT) has been described by Farber (1955) as well as others. In this test a series of TAT pictures is presented one at a time and with each one there are four alternative interpretations, one of which the subject is to select. One alternative reflects achievement and the others blandness, insecurity, and hostility. The subject ranks these four statements for each picture, and the measure of his motives is the sum of his ranks for each kind of statement across pictures. While correlations between achievement scores on this test and TAT nAch are low and insignificant (Hurley, 1955), other data (cf. Brown, 1961, p. 252) suggest that IPIT is related to other behaviors much as are nAch scores from TAT's. Bendig (1958b) found little or no relation between TAT nAch and achievement scores from the *Edwards Personal Preference Schedule.*

[16] Field's (1951) dissertation has never been published. However, a rather full account of it is presented in McClelland et al. (1953, pp. 177–181).

French (1956*b;* see selection 16 in Atkinson, 1958*a*) developed a measure of both achievement and affiliation motivation by modifying a procedure developed by Sherriffs (1948). The subject is presented with a set of items each of which describes behavior that is characteristic of a man. The subject is to write a statement as to why the man behaves as he does, and these statements are scored in terms of achievement for items related to achievement imagery and for affiliation for the appropriate items. Trained scorers reach high levels of agreement in scoring the statements. Relations to other behaviors of the scores from French's procedure suggest validity for both the achievement and affiliation measures. We review these findings in a later section.

There are, then, alternative methods to the TAT, some of which may get at the same things as the nAch score of the McClelland system. However, most of the available research utilizes the McClelland scoring system. Analyses of this scoring system have also been made which carry it somewhat beyond what we have said so far. We shall consider both these analyses and the research relating nAch TAT scores to other behavior in a later section. First, we describe very briefly the techniques used for developing TAT measures of several other motives.

Affiliation

The development of scoring systems for various other needs has followed the logic we have already outlined for hunger and achievement. That is, stories written under a relaxed or neutral condition and under a condition designed to arouse the motive to be measured are compared, and characteristics which differentiate the stories written under the two conditions are the bases of the scoring system for that need. The pictures used and the scoring items which result differ from those used for nAch. Most of these other need scores have not been as fully replicated or related to other behaviors as has the nAch score, and the scoring systems therefore must be regarded as not so well established as the one for nAch. (The scoring for the affiliation and power motives is described in Atkinson [1958*a*].) Where relations with other behaviors have been studied for these needs, this work will be found in a later section of this chapter. In the present section we deal with the operations used to arouse the need for the purpose of finding story items which might measure it.

Shipley and Veroff (1952) selected two equivalent college fraternity groups and subjected them to the following operations in order to arouse nAffiliation in one group (*A*) but not in the other (*B*). The groups were tested in a room in their fraternity houses. Group *A* was given a sociometric procedure to arouse nAffiliation, followed by the

TAT pictures. In the sociometric test, each subject stood up in turn as his fraternity brothers rated him on 15 adjectives such as aggressive, antisocial, conceited, friendly, intolerant, modest, sympathetic, timid. At the end of the procedure each subject wrote down the names of the three brothers he would choose as close personal friends. A second experimenter gave the TAT. The control group (*B*) wrote TAT stories (in a group) after checking a food preference list. Presumably, being rated, rating others, and choosing people as friends made the group members sensitive to affiliative relations or, in the language of the investigators, aroused the affiliation motive in group *A*.

A second method for arousing nAffiliation was used in another study by Shipley and Veroff. In this experiment TAT stories were obtained from freshmen who had been accepted into fraternities and from freshmen who had been rejected by fraternities they had wished to join and who were disappointed over the rejection. The TAT was given a month after the rushing season had ended.

Based on the two sets of data, a scoring system for nAffiliation yielded a higher mean score for the aroused group in the first study and for the rejected freshmen than for their respective control groups.

Atkinson, Heyns, and Veroff (1954) developed another measure of nAffiliation, one emphasizing "separation imagery" less than the one developed by Shipley and Veroff. Atkinson et al. used different pictures and used the sociometric rating procedure that Shipley and Veroff had used as the arousal procedure. However, their control or comparison group was tested in a college classroom under task orientation conditions. A scoring system derived from the two sets of stories differentiated the two groups at a satisfactory significance level. We thus have two systems for scoring nAffiliation, but we know of no evidence of their comparative values. We should note that in both of these reports the scoring systems were developed from and applied to the same subjects. Cross-validation of the scoring systems was not reported in either study.

Power

Veroff (1957) obtained TAT stories from two groups in order to set up a scoring system for a power motive. The aroused group was a set of candidates for positions as student leaders in a Midwestern university. These individuals had declared their candidacy and campaigned for a month, and they were tested as they waited in a group to see how the two days of balloting had turned out. The comparison group was composed of students in an undergraduate class in psychology, tested in the classroom under task-orientation conditions. The scores of the two groups on the scoring system (developed from their own stories) were significantly different. There is some possibility, however, that this nPower measure is related also to a "recognition motivation"; some relation to nAch is reported, but this finding is discounted because nAch scores do not relate as nPower does to such variables as the Social Value Dimension of the *Allport-Vernon Study of Values,* as interest in the job, satisfaction of being a leader, and the like. The correlation between nAch and nPower, while significant, is low ($r = .27$).

Fear

Walker and Atkinson (1958) developed a measure of fear in TAT stories, following the lead of Murray (1933), who observed in young children that faces in pictures were seen as more malicious or threatening after fear-provoking stimulation than without it. Escape from threat was the kind of theme they looked for in the stories to the two pictures which they used, and they refer to the scores as fear-related. The test was administered to Army personnel in the field. One condition (A) was testing under the relatively relaxed, routine conditions of Army life. A second condition (B) was testing 10 hours before an atomic explosion was to be detonated near the camp where the men, who were to participate in the maneuvers related to this explosion, were stationed. The third condition (C) was testing the men while they were located in trenches 4000 yards from the detonation, immediately after the explosion. Condition four (D) involved testing 10 hours after the explosion, and condition five (E), two weeks afterward in a remote, regular Army post. All groups were tested two times, and various other control groups were tested twice, also, in order to determine the effects of repeated testing alone.

The stories were scored for fear-related motivation, defined by expressed sequences of behavior showing attempts to cope with the threat of physical injury. The scoring system was an a priori one, applied to the stories written under the various conditions. Conditions B, C, and D yielded stories generating higher fear-related motivation scores than were obtained for the pertinent control groups, with the greatest difference being for conditions C and D.

Sex

Clark (1952, 1955) studied TAT stories written by college men after they had viewed a series of slides of attractive nude females (arousal conditions) or after having seen a series of neutral slides such as landscapes (control condition). The slides of females were life-size and were to be rated for attractiveness; the neutral slides were rated for aesthetic value. This experiment was run in a classroom situation. A parallel experiment was run in which the nude female slides were presented and the stories obtained at a fraternity beer party. The parallel control condition, also a beer party, involved no slides but just the writing of stories under the influence of alcohol as a test of "creative imagination."

Manifest sexual material in the stories of the aroused group in the classroom situation was less frequent than in its control group. Under alcohol, however, the aroused group expressed more manifest sexual imagery than its control group. Both groups under alcohol expressed more sexual imagery in their stories than both the classroom groups.

Clark (1952, 1955) analyzed the stories of the nonalcoholic (classroom) aroused condition for the expression of sexual symbolism. He found much more sexual *symbolism* in these stories than in the stories of the control group. Presumably anxiety, for the aroused subjects run in the classroom, inhibited their *manifest* sexual expression (cf. Mussen & Scodel, 1955), so they resorted to symbolism. The groups run under alcohol showed little sexual symbolism; these were the groups, of course, which showed a good deal of manifest sexuality. Other findings, together with those we have just mentioned concerning symbolism, indicate that manifest expressions of need states in TAT stories may not fully represent or be linearly related to the motive state if anxiety is associated with it.

Aggression

Feshbach (1955) studied the role of fantasy as expressed in TAT stories in reducing the strength of aggression; in doing so he identified characteristics of stories which reflect aggression. Feshbach used three groups. In one, the Insult-Fantasy group, aggression was aroused by an insulting experimenter, and this group was asked to write stories to four TAT pictures before reflecting, terminally, their aggression by means of a sentence completion test and a questionnaire dealing with the experiment, the experimenter, and psychological research. The same terminal measures were used for the Insult-Control group, which was insulted but was given nonfantasy tests to do (such as paper and pencil aptitude tests), rather than the TAT. A third group was not insulted at all but was given the TAT pictures to which to write stories and the terminal measures. On the attitude questionnaire, both insult groups showed more aggressive responses than the noninsult group, and the Insult-Control group was typically more aggressive than the Insult-Fantasy group. Somewhat similar results were found for aggression expressed on the sentence completion test.

The TAT stories were rated for aggression on a five-point scale. The stories of the Insult-Fantasy group were somewhat more aggressive than those of the non-Insult-Fantasy group. A correlation between aggression scores in the stories of the Insult-Fantasy group and amount of aggression in the attitudes (questionnaire) toward the experimenter was significant ($r = -.25$). Both of these findings suggest, though not strongly, that aggression was reduced by fantasy in the Insult-Fantasy group, and that this may account for their reduced aggression as compared to the Insult-Control group on the final questionnaire and sentence-completion test.

No general method for scoring aggression on the basis of TAT stories arises from this experiment, but the results give some hope that such a measure could be developed.

Fear of Failure and Hope of Success

Certain curvilinear relations between nAch scores and other behaviors (see p. 732) seem to arise because subjects in the mid-third of the nAch score range show performance decrements apparently associated with fear of failure. The presence in the TAT stories of these subjects of a number of negatively toned responses ($I-$, $Ga-$, Bp, Bw, $G-$) led Moulton (1958) to re-examine the data from an earlier study by Atkinson (1953) in an effort to develop a measure of fear of failure. Atkinson had studied recall of uncompleted tasks, and Moulton took inability to recall uncompleted tasks as an indication of fear of failure. A system for scoring manifestations of failure in the stories was developed from these data, and all the stories of Atkinson's study were re-analyzed with it. The Fear-of-Failure score was found to be negatively related to the recall of uncompleted tasks. These scores were subtracted from a Hope-of-Success score, based on positively valued achievement-related items from the nAch scoring system. This was called a Net Hope-of-Success score, and it and the uncorrected Hope-of-Success score correlate well and positively with recall of uncompleted tasks under achievement orientation but not under relaxed conditions or at all significantly with memory for completed tasks. Various other findings indicate that the Hope-of-Success (or Net Hope-of-Success) scores are measures of a positive motive for achievement, whereas fear of failure is not. The corrected scores show more linear relations with other variables than the original nAch score. A study by Clark, Teevan, and Riccuiti (1956) also showed that the mid-score subjects on nAch have more negative subscores and fewer positive subscores than subjects whose nAch scores are at the extremes.

The differentiation of fear of failure from hope of success indicates that the original nAch scoring procedures were conglomerates. This conclusion seems also pertinent to the *Manifest Anxiety Scale* and similar procedures. Motivation measurement, in the human, has not reached a high level of development when the measurement instruments are as conglomerate as these seem to be.

So far as the needs studied by McClelland and associates are concerned, there is also the question whether they are independent. Little attention has been paid to this issue, but Applezweig, Moeller, and Burdick (1956) reported a significant negative correlation ($-.45$) between nAffiliation and nAch scores taken from the same stories. The independence of these motives is an important issue and should receive further study.

Relations to Behavior

Investigation of the relationships of need scores (chiefly, nAch) to other behavior can be divided into two broad classes. The first, earlier, and simpler class consists of direct comparisons of performances on other measures for subjects whose scores on nAch vary. We will review this group of investigations first. The second class is more complex, in the sense that situational cues, probabilities of outcome, and other variables are involved, as well as nAch. The role of picture cues in the extent of achievement imagery found in the TAT stories will also be considered here. Studies of the origins of nAch will be treated in the final section of this chapter.

Direct Comparisons of Need Scores and Other Measures

In most of the comparisons of nAch and other behaviors, the score for nAch was obtained from the subjects under the neutral condition. This condition presumably permits the stories to be influenced by the individual's usual nAch to an extent greater than would be the case where the situational pressures for achievement are pronounced, as they are in the achievement-oriented failure and success conditions. These arousal conditions were used mainly to develop a valid scoring system and to study story characteristics [17] under various arousal levels. It is the natural condition, however, in which the individual difference, which nAch represents, is measured.

Lowell (1952) compared the performances of high and low scoring subjects on nAch on a scrambled-words test and an arithmetic test. The scrambled-words test consisted of a 10-page booklet, each page of

---

[17] Extensive analyses of the effect on story characteristics of the various arousal conditions are reported by McClelland et al. (1953, Chap. V). We will not review all of this material here.

which contained 24 scrambled words, that is, familiar words with their letters disarranged. The subjects worked 2 minutes on a page and were to make a word out of each set of disarranged letters. The additions test, given at a different session, consisted of 10 pages of addition problems. On the scrambled-words test, the high achievement group started at about the same performance level as the low achievement group but quickly improved their performances so that in the last of the 10 two-minute periods they were unscrambling about half again as many words as they had in the first 2-minute interval. The low achievement group, however, showed relatively little change over the 10 intervals. Evidently, the high achievers *learned* to perform this task more quickly and efficiently over the time they worked on it, whereas the low achievers did not. Neither group showed a performance gain over the period taken by the arithmetic test, which, of course, called for operations which had been well learned by all the subjects in school long before the experiment. However, the high-need achievers worked approximately 20 per cent more problems in each time interval than the low-need achievers. These findings suggest effects on learning and performance of nAch which are consistent with the view that it functions as a motive, variations in which relate to other behaviors.

One problem with this interpretation of these results is that the verbal scores of the scholastic aptitude test (ACE) of the high-need achievers are higher than those of the low-need achievers. However, the correlation between scrambled-word output and nAch is only reduced from .48 to .44 when the effects of the intelligence test scores are taken out by partial correlation. There is also evidence that on an anagrams test the performance of high-need achievers is better maintained through time than is that of low-need achievers; the performance of the latter tends to fall off during the middle minutes of this task to an extent greater than does the performance of the high-need achievers (McClelland et al., 1953, pp. 227–229). French and Thomas (1958) found high need achievers to persist longer in trying a problem-solving task than low-need achievers.

A number of behavioral characteristics have been related to nAch scores, but the size and character of the relations have not always been consistent. College grades have sometimes been found to be correlated with nAch, sometimes not (McClelland et al., 1953, pp. 237–242).[18] Certain linguistic measures were compared for high- and low-need

[18] Positive relations between nAch scores and high school grades have been reported by Ricciuti (1954) and Ricciuti and Sadacca (1955), whereas minimal or no relations between nAch and college grades were found by Ricciuti (1954) and by Applezweig (see Applezweig et al., 1956).

achievers for an essay they had written. High-need achievers tended to use more abstract nouns and anticipatory tenses than did low-need achievers; the latter employed more negations and dependent clauses than the former. Variations in essay length did not differentiate level of nAch at a significant level, but both groups wrote longer essays than did subjects with intermediate nAch scores; this intermediate group, however, produced more Rorschach responses than the other groups (McClelland et al., 1953, Chap. VIII). A number of other comparisons have produced relatively small differences; included are analyses of sentence-completion data, certain Rorschach score category differences, and other test scores. Such differences as have been obtained have not been tested in replications of the original studies (McClelland et al., 1953, Chap. VIII).

McClelland and Liberman (1949) determined perceptual recognition thresholds for subjects whose nAch scores varied, using 10 neutral words, 10 security-related words (e.g., nurture, threat), and 10 achievement-related words (e.g., success, failure). Subjects whose nAch scores were above the mean nAch score recognized the positive achievement words more quickly than the remaining subjects, but this finding held for only one scoring system. McClelland and Liberman then combined the nAch scores with a score indicating how well a subject had maintained his performance on the midsection of the anagrams task, and compared the recognition times of low, middle, and high nAchievers on positive security and achievement words. They found that the high-need achievers recognized the positive achievement words more quickly than the middle and low groups, but also that the middle group on nAch was significantly *slower* in recognizing the negative achievement or failure words than the high and low groups. This suggests that the intermediate score range on nAch may reflect a motive for achievement which is basically a fear of failure rather than a positive striving to achieve; the latter perhaps characterizes the high scores.

We will encounter this difference again as we consider nAch further, and it was undoubtedly involved in some of the findings we have already reviewed. (Re-analyses of their data have not been reported by Lowell or other investigators.) Moulton et al. (1958) measured nAch scores of samples of high-school and of college students under neutral conditions on one day and then tested recognition thresholds to success, failure, and neutral words on a second day. For half the subjects, the recognition thresholds were obtained under neutral conditions, but for the other half the recognition tests were carried out after an achievement-arousing procedure involving testing. Under neutral conditions there were no significant differences in recognition thresholds between high and low need achievers, but under motive-arousal conditions the high nAch groups had significantly lower thresholds for both success and failure words than the low achievement groups. These differences arose primarily from the slower recognition times (as compared to neutral words) for both success and failure words manifested by the low achievement group.[19]

NAch score was related to level of aspiration in an investigation by Atkinson (cf. McClelland et al., 1953, pp. 244–248). Students were asked to report to their classroom prior to the hour at which they were to take a final examination in a psychology course. Early attendance was voluntary and about half the class came. A TAT was given them to provide nAch scores, and they were also asked to indicate what grade they expected to make on the final examination which was to follow. Certain other data were also obtained. The obvious correlation between nAch score and expected examination grade (level of aspiration), while positive, was low and insignificant; however, a further analysis revealed a relationship. A comparison was made of the location of each student in the midterm class distribution and in the overall college grade-point-average distributions. For some of the students the location of the midterm standing and their overall grade-point standing was congruent; that is, their midterm standing in the course was about what their overall standing was, relative to other students. For this group the correlation between nAch and expected grade was low (negative) and insignificant. For the rest of the students, class standing was incongruent with overall standing; that is, in the class, they were doing either better or worse than usual. For these students the correlation was +.45, significant in itself and significantly greater than the one for the students whose standings were congruent. These findings suggest that when reality determines level of aspiration there is little relation between nAch and level

---

[19] Atkinson and Walker (1956) measured nAffiliation in 93 college students and then conducted a perceptual test for one group under neutral conditions and for another group under conditions presumably of arousal of this need (sociometric rating procedure). The perceptual task consisted of the presentation, at well below threshold illumination and exposure intervals, of slides, each of which contained four figures; one figure was a face (or several faces), the others were neutral, such as house furnishings. The subjects were asked to designate in which quadrant of the slide "the picture *stood out the most* or was *most clear* to them." The subjects who scored high in nAffiliation reported significantly more often than the others that the quadrant which actually had a face in it was the one in which the picture was most salient. However, there was no significant effect of the arousal as compared to the nonarousal condition.

of aspiration; when the facts of reality conflict, however, level of aspiration does relate to nAch score.[20]

Summary. There is some evidence, from one study, that learning and performance of verbal and numerical skills are related to nAch scores. Evidence concerning other verbal performances, such as essays, and school grades is not at all clear but does not suggest any strong relationships. Perceptual word recognition scores show differences among nAch levels, but these differences seem mainly to arise because middle (and sometimes low) nAch scores are associated with delayed recognition of certain words, for example, failure words. Although one might expect nAch scores to be related to level of aspiration, it has not been easy to demonstrate a relation between them; some evidence, however, does suggest a relation.

The foregoing evidence shows that nAch scores are related to other behaviors, but not strongly. It is difficult to compare studies, because the methods of separating high from low levels of nAch have varied, and studies in this area have seldom been replicated. It is not always clear that there should be a relation between nAch and some of the dependent variables studied. More sophistication is found in the studies involving complex relations between nAch and behavior.

Complex Relations of nAch and Other Behaviors

The studies to which we now make reference are more complex than most of those so far mentioned in that possible interactions of nAch score with other factors have been taken into account. In the case of a motive, like nAch, there are perhaps four possible sets of variables that will influence either the nAch score itself or its relations to behavior or both. Three of these sets of factors are manipulable experimentally, and one is not. The manipulable ones are the number of achievement-related cues that the pictures contain, the instructional-situational cues for achievement (e.g., neutral vs. achievement-oriented), and various aspects of the behavior or task itself, including the scoring system, or the circumstances under which it is carried out. The nonmanipulable variable, of course, is the set of internal determinants of nAch, which the subject carries with him. While few of the studies have involved all of these factors, any adequate synthesis of results must take account of them. We turn now to the relevant investigations.

Variations in Pictures and in Situational Cues. McClelland et al. (1953, pp. 199–201) selected five pictures which had many characteristics in common but three of which (*B, C, D*) seemed, *a priori*, to contain

---

[20] Ricciuti and Schultz (1958) have found a low degree of relation between nAch scores and level of aspiration in performance situations.

many more achievement related cues (work situations were depicted) than the other two (A, E). The mean nAch score for B, C, and D together was 2.28; for A and E it was 0.50, a significant difference. The difference between high- and low-need achievers (nAch level based on scores for seven other pictures) for pictures with few achievement cues (A, E) was 2.26 and for the high-cue pictures was 2.35 (McClelland et al., 1953, pp. 202–203). This suggests that there is not an interaction between nAch and picture cues, since the difference between high and low achievers was constant across pictures varying in picture cues.

In further studies, one high-cue and one low-cue picture were used and different subjects responded to both under relaxed or achievement conditions. NAch scores to both pictures were greater under achievement conditions than under relaxed conditions (McClelland et al., 1953, 203–204); as the data were presented, one cannot tell whether there was a significant interaction between arousal condition and picture cues, though it is possible that there was. In general, from these studies, we can conclude the following: under most conditions, high-need achievers will obtain higher scores than low-need achievers, but the difference will be maximal for pictures with minimal cues in a situation of maximal arousal (McClelland et al., 1953, pp. 206–207). Instructional cues and picture cues also exert, at the levels studied, a significant effect on nAch score, so the joint operation of these three variables seems to be clear.

Demonstrations of the significance of the variable of picture cues suggest that "norms" for pictures might be established. Jacobs (1958) obtained judgments from subjects as to which ones of a list of concerns (or "motives") might be dominant in the minds of the characters in a series of pictures he showed them. The 14 concerns covered a range of problems, and there were 12 pictures. The pictures were found to have quite different cue values. By looking at Jacobs' data (1958, Table I, p. 623) one can select pictures whose cue value, as judged, would be greatest for achievement, affiliation, power or influence, etc. For example, the two pictures rated highest for achievement show, in the one, a man trying to shoot a basket in a basketball game and, in the other, two men working on a machine. For affiliation, the highest ranked pictures are one of a conference and one of a club scene; the same two received the highest rankings for power or influence.

Birney (1958a) used a version of Jacobs' rating and ranking procedures in order to select pictures varying in nAch cue value for his study. He found that ratings of achievement cue value were correlated positively and significantly with the percentage of another group of subjects who showed achievement imagery in stories they wrote to these pictures. The affective tone of the stories was also predicted by ratings of affective tone of the pictures, but specific imaginative content (N, I, etc.) was not well predicted from picture ratings. Birney (1958b) found that nAch and task performance were positively related when a student was the experimenter but not when a faculty member was the experimenter. Comparison of two student experimenters yielded no difference, according to Haber and Alpert (1958). They used information from the Jacobs and Birney studies in order to select two sets of high and low cue-value pictures. To be considered a high-cue picture, 75 per cent of the subjects writing stories for it had to use achievement imagery in their stories; in addition, raters had to agree that the picture was high in suggested concern with achievement; and the picture could not have (by ratings) concerns other than the concern with achievement. Correspondingly, a picture was considered to have low nAch cue value only if it produced achievement imagery in 25 to 50 per cent of the subjects and if it was rated as having very few achievement cues.[21] In passing, it can be noted that rankings of pictures for achievement correlate well (.71) with proportion of subjects yielding achievement imagery to them when different subjects are used, but the correlation is low (and positive) when it is between the rank the same subject gives a picture and the achievement imagery his story for it contains; when this latter correlation is done by picture rather than across subjects, it too is low but positive.

Using two sets of three high-value pictures and three low each, Haber and Alpert ran two groups of subjects at two different times each. One group (I) was run both times three weeks apart under relaxed conditions; the other (II) was run first under relaxed conditions and then under achievement orientation. The relaxed and achievement situations were very carefully defined in terms of instructions given and behavior of the experimenters. The mean scores for the groups are shown in Table 14–3.

Table 14–3. NAch scores for different pictures and different orientations and sessions in the Haber-Alpert (1958) experiment. Each group run in two sessions.

Condition	Session	High achievement picture cues	Low picture cues
Relaxed	Session I, Grp I	6.00	3.27
Relaxed	Session I, Grp II	7.89	2.22
Relaxed	Session II, Grp I	6.38	2.00
Achievement Oriented	Session II, Grp II	8.37	4.42

[21] It is not clear from the Haber and Alpert report how the third criterion, concerns with achievement, was applied to the low-cue pictures.

It can be seen in the data for both sessions that picture cues make a considerable difference in nAch scores, for both groups. There is also an increase in nAch scores for both kinds of pictures under arousal conditions (Session II) for the group (II) which underwent arousal, but it is slight for the high-value pictures. The change under arousal for the low-value pictures is greater, and also it can be noted that the score for Group I goes down in Session II (relaxed) rather than increasing. We see again, then, that picture cues and arousal situation both determine nAch score, and in fact probably interact significantly (pictures by situations interaction is significant for Group II, at $p < .05$).

Tasks and Performance Situations. Atkinson (1953) studied recall for tasks, the performance of which had been completed or had not been completed. His study is an investigation of the Zeigarnik effect (Zeigarnik, 1927) that, typically, the recall for incomplete tasks is better than it is for completed tasks. Twenty similar paper-and-pencil tasks were used by Atkinson with a time limit so that the shorter tasks were completed and the longer ones were not. Three groups worked the tasks and took the TAT nAch test immediately thereafter; one group was task-oriented, one relaxed, and one ego-involved. The results showed that high-need achievers tended to recall more incomplete than complete tasks under ego-involved conditions but showed small differences (in the same direction) under task and relaxed orientations. The low-need achievers, however, manifested an opposite pattern. They recalled more incomplete than complete tasks under the relaxed orientation, showed a small difference in the same direction under task orientation, but recalled slightly more completed than uncompleted tasks under the ego-involved condition. It would appear from these results that the low-need achievers were made uneasy (or fearful of failure) by the ego-involved condition which implied a test of their ability and that perhaps they resolved their uneasiness by recalling the tasks they had successfully finished. The high-need achievers, on the other hand, apparently are motivated differently by ego-involvement and remember the tasks they had failed to complete to an extent much greater than their memory for completed tasks.[22] The circumstances of task performance thus interact with nAch level to control, in this case, a memory performance.

French (1955) used a digit-letter substitution test which could not be completed within the allotted time. French selected 15 high and 15 low

---

[22] A number of findings related to these results as well as to other issues concerning motivation measurement in fantasy, and a general discussion of methodological problems, issues, and findings, are available in a paper by Reitman and Atkinson (1958).

need achievers (from Air Force officer trainees), on the basis of her nAch procedure for each of three groups and, 5 months later, had them take the digit-letter test with no special instructions. Immediately thereafter, however, one group was given instructions for the relaxed orientation, one ego-involving instructions, and one instructions that the five men making the best scores would be allowed to leave early and have some free time. (Free time in the tight schedule of officer candidates in the Air Force is highly valued.) Then an alternative form of French's test for nAch was given, followed by administration of a second code test. The initial nAch scores, obtained 5 months earlier, were correlated positively and significantly with the nAch scores under arousal conditions and, in the ego-involvement condition, they were correlated with performance scores though not in the other two (relaxed and leave-early) conditions. Change of performance score from the unmotivated to the motivated condition at the second testing showed the motivation of the high nAchievers to be engaged by both the ego-involving and the leave-early conditions but not that of the low-need achievers. Under the relaxed orientation, there was a significant correlation between nAffiliation scores and performance; apparently the friendly experimenter under these conditions engaged the affiliation motive but not, of course, the achievement motive.

It is clear from French's results that the conditions present at the time the performance and motivation are measured are significant to the results obtained. French (1956a) showed that the selection of work partners with whom one performs a task is related to motivation. Given choices, high nAchievers who are low in nAffiliation will select partners who are competent, rather than friends; subjects high in nAffiliation but not in nAchievement tend to select friends rather than competent work partners. Atkinson and Reitman (1956) used subjects on whom both nAch and nAffil scores were available and assigned some of them to work alone under achievement-orientation conditions. The rest worked in a group situation rather than alone but also under an achievement orientation with a monetary prize; it was believed that the group situation aroused affiliation motives as well as nAch and financial motivation, so that it was a multi-incentive condition. Some evidence was obtained that the overall performance in the multi-incentive condition showed a higher output than in the alone condition. However, the high-need achievers did better in the alone condition than the low-need achievers, whereas they did not differ in the multi-incentive condition. High scorers on nAffiliation attempted more problems than low scorers in the multi-incentive condition, whereas they did not differ in the alone condition. This is presumably due to arousal of nAffiliation in the multi-incentive situation, unless one wishes to argue that nAch was engaged in the nAffiliation subjects in the group situation.

French (1958) constituted several groups of four subjects each so that each group was homogeneous in the motive patterns of its members; the members in each group were either high in nAch and low in nAffil or the reverse. Each group worked on a "verbal assembly" problem which required them to put phrases or short sentences together to make a story. Each subject had 5 such phrases, and the group was to use all of its 20 phrases and to arrange them solely by oral communication. The group performance was scored. Two additional conditions were involved. In the first one, some of the groups worked under the instruction to agree on a single, final solution (group orientation); others did not have to reach agreement (individual orientation). The other condition involved a type of feedback. Each group was interrupted and the experimenter commented on its performance. One type of feedback emphasized efficiency in performing the task (achievement feedback); the other how well the group members were getting along together (feeling feedback). The high-need-achiever groups performed much better than the affiliation-need groups under both group and individual orientations so long as the feedback concerned task efficiency. The affiliation group performed better under the group orientation than it did under the individual orientation with both types of feedback and did better for feeling feedback than for task feedback. Under feeling feedback and group orientation, the affiliation groups performed better than the achievement groups, the only instance of clearly better performance for the affiliation groups than for the achievement groups.

These results, together with those of Atkinson and Reitman, and the other results we have cited from French and from Atkinson strongly suggest a complex interaction of motive, arousal conditions, task characteristics, and situation of performance as determinative of performance rather than any simple relation between need and performance. Hardy (1957) found conformity to social pressure to be jointly determined by nAffiliation and conditions of social support from the group. Samelson (1958) found somewhat similar results. Krebs (1958) found nAchievers to maintain independence in situations of conformity. Situational factors in the role of nAch have been stressed further by Applezweig, Moeller, and Burdick (1956) and by Atkinson and Raphelson (1956).

Atkinson (1958b) studied the interrelations of nAch, the value of an incentive, and the probability of obtaining it. High and low nAchievers were used as subjects and the incentive for performance was either $1.25 or $2.50. However, each subject was told how likely it was that he would obtain the incentive. That is, it was said that the incentive would be given to one of 20, one of 3, one of 2, or three of 4 students in his group. High nAchievers worked harder at the intermediate probabilities of obtaining the incentive ($\frac{1}{3}$ and $\frac{1}{2}$) than at the extreme probabilities ($\frac{1}{20}$ or $\frac{3}{4}$). There was no real difference between high and low nAchievers at probabilities of achieving incentives at odds of $\frac{1}{20}$ or $\frac{3}{4}$, but the high nAchievers worked harder at probabilities of $\frac{1}{2}$ and $\frac{1}{3}$, especially the latter. High nAchievers seem to want to test themselves against a standard but not in relation to extreme odds. Few differences were found for the larger amount of money; presumably this sum was sufficient to motivate all the students to perform at almost any probability of pay-off.[23]

Atkinson (1957) has interpreted some of the interactions shown in the case of nAch in the following way. While nAch is a stable disposition, it must be *engaged* by situational cues. He suggests that the degree of arousal is some function of motive strength and expectancy of goal attainment in the situation; incentive value is also involved. If nAch is not engaged, high nAchievers will not perform differently than low nAchievers. However, as measured, nAch is complex, probably comprised of both a motive to succeed and one to avoid failure. Which one is dominant in an individual will, of course, determine just how the interaction of motive, situation, expectancy and incentive value will turn out. Naturally, the success or failure in a situation will alter the relations among these variables. (Further details of this formulation will be considered in the next chapter, since it is similar to treatments of level of aspiration. See pp. 773–775.)

Comment. This completes our review of the work of McClelland and associates. They have carried out a great deal of work, but its final evaluation is difficult. Many of the findings require replication before they can be considered established, and the independence of the various needs should be shown. Also, many of the needs, as measured, represent complex conglomerates rather than pure motives. Furthermore, as we bring out in Chapter 15 in the discussion of methods of arousing and measuring motivation, there has been question whether nAch and the other motives as conceived, measured, and manipulated really are

---

[23] Parallel findings have been reported by McClelland (1958a) for children, and he has found high nAchievers to have preferences for financially risky occupations. Various studies have compared nAch with personality measures (cf. Atkinson, 1958a, Chaps. 26, 27, 28; Minor & Neel, 1958; Wertheim & Mednick, 1958; Lazarus et al., 1957), anxiety, and other scales (Raphelson, 1957; Raphelson & Moulton, 1958; Bendig, 1958b; Kausler & Trapp, 1958). We will not summarize these relationships here.

motivational rather than being habits or modes of responding to situational cues.

Nevertheless, it must be said that the work of McClelland and his associates represents one of the few systematic and coordinated empirical approaches to the study of human motivation that has yet been made. Accepting, from animal work, the notion that motives can be aroused, they attempted to measure this arousal by means of a clinical technique, that of fantasy. Furthermore, they went on to try to find relations between the measurements of motives to behavior in other situations.

Aside from problems such as the crudity of their measures, possible correlations of nAch scores with intellectual variables, questionable expectations as to how performance would relate to motives, failure to replicate many of the findings, and the like, this work is also faced with a serious conceptual dilemma. This is that it is unclear whether nAch (and the other motives) represents a habitual mode of responding to certain cues or whether it represents something else, an energizing factor not reducible in its operation to habit. The whole field of motivation, at present, is embarrassed by this dilemma.

THE STUDY OF OTHER MOTIVES: DEPENDENCY AND AGGRESSION

Fear, anxiety, achievement, affiliation, power, and sex, which we have discussed already, do not begin to exhaust the lexicon of presumably learned motive states. In the literature, however, relatively little systematic study has been afforded motives, aside from those just listed. Two exceptions, however, are dependency and aggression, which we discuss now.

Dependency

Dependency, shown in behavior that elicits aid, assistance, comfort, etc., from others, is a term commonly employed in clinical discussions of the motivations of both children and adult patients, especially in reports based on projective test materials. So far as we are aware, however, it has received relatively little direct study of a systematic kind with adults. Sears et al. (1953), on the basis of studies in children, have suggested that it is an acquired drive, one that is or may be developed very early in a child's life.

An important distinction, made in conjunction with dependency by Sears and his associates, is the demarcation of instrumental acts from the drive properties of dependency. The instrumental acts are said to develop first; dependency arises because adults, especially the mother, perform such various nurturant acts toward the child as feeding, warming, drying, snuggling. The child learns to secure the help of his mother when pain, hunger or other factors distress him. Presumably, the actions the child learns include acts that will attract the mother's attention, and, if she has nurturant tendencies, she will respond to and reinforce his attention-getting or dependent behavior.

If this were the whole story, we could dismiss dependent behavior as an instrumental act motivated by other needs, for example, hunger, thirst, pain, or anxiety. However, Sears et al. (1953) suggest that an acquired drive may also develop. The argument, first proposed by J. W. M. Whiting,[24] is that those actions sometimes followed by reward and sometimes by punishment will develop into a secondary motivational system. Reinforcement leads to expectancy of reward, and nonreinforcement leads to an expectation of failure to obtain the reward. These two expectancies, being incompatible, will conflict; conflict-induced drive is seen as the energy source of such a motivational factor as a dependency motive, according to this analysis. Sears et al. (1953) point out that it is almost impossible to prevent at least some frustration in infants so that the expectancy of nonreward can readily develop during the period of infancy. The dependency drive presumably has as its goal the elicitation of nurturant maternal acts. Instigators of this acquired drive would be the parent and similar people, various drive states in the child, and other discomforts and frustrations; and later on, symbolic factors might arouse it.

Unfortunately, the investigations of dependency have seldom involved efforts to arouse or to measure the drive aspect just described. Typically, investigators have measured behavior or projective test performance in children in order to assess dependency status and then have looked to aspects of parent care for relations between parent care and dependency. An exception to this rule is provided by Hartup (1958), who compared the performance of two groups of nursery-school children on two tasks. The first group performed the tasks after 10 minutes of nurturance by the experimenter; the second group received 5 minutes of nurturance after which the adult withdrew. Five minutes later the subjects of this second group performed the tasks. The girls of the second group performed better than the girls of the first group, perhaps reflecting the energizing of behavior by a drive

---

[24] So far as we know, Whiting's hypothesis was developed in a paper in 1949 that has not been published and which we have not seen. It is described in Sears et al. (1953, pp. 180–181) and in Miller (1951a, pp. 466–467). It has some resemblance to frustration-induced drive and to the theory of incentives (cf., pp. 420–422). See, also, Whiting and Child (1953).

induced by the adult's withdrawal. Among boys, however, only those high on measured dependency performed better following the withdrawal of the adult. Beller (1959) also reported more dependent behavior in children when adult availability was limited than when it was not, and he found a relation between dependent behavior and the amount of the child's initial dependency. On the ground that adult unavailability might lead to conflict between expectancies of reward and nonreward, these studies perhaps involved a dependency drive.[25] However, it is also possible to say that adult unavailability was a cue for performance on the basis of past reinforcement in similar circumstances.

Sears et al. (1953) studied dependency behavior in nursery-school children and related it to various aspects of their home environments. The children's behavior was rated by their teachers on such characteristics as seeking help, praise and approval, physical contact, attention, or nearness in relation to the teacher or other children. Behavior observations were also made, independently of these ratings, on dependent behaviors such as securing attention, reassurance, being near the teacher, and the like. Various aspects of home experience, child training, and maternal attitudes were obtained through an interview with the child's mother.

One problem with this investigation is that the various ratings and observations are not highly intercorrelated; also, there are substantial correlations between some of the dependency measures and the activity of the child as rated by the teacher. Any conclusions must also be constrained by the sex differences present in these measures and by their interrelations with one another and with the mothers' interview material.

Within the limits of problems such as these, Sears and his co-workers conclude that infant feeding frustration, especially severe weaning, is related to nursery-school dependency behavior, a relation closer for girls than for boys, and closer for dependency to the teacher than to other children. Toilet training factors were unrelated to dependency behavior. Various other relations also were found, at least for some subgroups, between dependency and current frustrations at home as well

[25] The experiments of Gewirtz, reviewed earlier in this chapter, are also pertinent here, since Gewirtz used social isolation to induce a motive for social interaction. However, as we described it earlier, this "drive" could be interpreted alternatively as anxiety. The work of Spitz and others, reported in Chapters 12 and 13, involving maternal separation, could be interpreted as involving dependency. Dependent behavior was not the consequence of maternal separation, however, which studies such as Spitz' have emphasized.

as the punitiveness of the mother. None of these relations was very strong, but it appeared to these investigators that feeding frustration in these children was central to the establishment of the dependency drive.[26] Whether an interpretation based on reinforcement of the behaviors which define dependency is equally cogent is not considered by the Sears group.

One study of college men brings out the significance of conflict over dependency desires in relation to the frequency of TAT dependency themes. Fitzgerald (1958) secured sociometric ratings and interview measures of dependency and dependency-related behavior, and scored TAT stories and sentence completions for dependency themes. He found no correlation between TAT dependency score and interview and sociometric measures of dependency, but he did find significant, though low, positive correlations between the dependency score for incomplete sentences and dependency in interview and on sociometric variables. He also compared number of dependency themes in TAT and sentence completion for subjects rated as having much conflict over dependency; dependency responses on the TAT were much more frequent for the "conflicted" subjects than for those free of important dependency conflicts. Data for the sentence completion test showed differences in the same direction but were not significant.

Our sampling of the literature has shown little direct investigation of dependency behavior as a phenomenon, let alone as an acquired drive. Present evidence is consistent with an interpretation alternative to a drive status for dependency; this is that dependent behavior serves other states (like anxiety) and that its apparent strength in some children and adults arises from its reinforcement in the context of a variety of other motives.

Aggression

Behavior which may be characterized as aggressive, hostile, war-like, or destructive has received more attention from theorists than has dependency. Most of the early theorists included an instinct for this kind of behavior in their lists of instincts, and the prevalence of aggressive, hostile actions—ranging from war to sibling rivalry—has maintained the status in most motivational systems of some concept or entity which refers to aggression. The major theoretical motivational interpretations of aggression may be classified as follows: (1) as being of instinctive origin, (2) as being reactive to frustration, (3) as an acquired drive. We must also add a fourth interpretation which is not

[26] Other evidence on these relations has been reported by Heathers (1955a, b), Stendler (1952, 1954), Whiting and Child (1953), and Antonovsky (1958).

a motivational one: As has been suggested for dependency, aggressive behavior, in individuals who manifest it, is learned because it is reinforced. We summarize these conceptions in turn.

1. *Aggression as instinctive.* The most prominent theory of aggression as an instinct is, of course, Freud's (see Chapter 12). His last theory, it will be recalled, suggested a death instinct, which incorporated destructive, hostile, and aggressive impulses. Freud was led to this formulation partly because his tendency to think in polarities required an opponent to the life instincts. But he was also impressed by the amount of destructive, aggressive behavior he observed in his patients and in the world about him. Some psychoanalysts accept the death instinct (cf. Buss, 1961, pp. 187–188), but others accept it only partially, limiting their conceptions to an instinct for aggression alone. This instinct is directed primarily toward others, at least originally, whereas the death instinct includes a primal masochism (Buss, 1961, p. 190). An instinct for aggression toward others is a postulate less sweeping in character than the death instinct.

2. *Aggression as reactive.* Many psychoanalysts reject both the death instinct and an instinct for aggression and derive aggressive behavior in other ways. Saul (1956) stressed the origin of aggression as arising in unfortunate childhood experiences, and Horney (1945) suggested that aggressive behavior was one way in which a person can cope with basic anxiety (see Chapter 12). In both of these interpretations, aggression is a reaction to something else.

Perhaps the most widely known theory of aggression as a reactive process is the frustration-aggression hypothesis. Originating with Freud before he shifted to the conception of a death instinct, it was taken up, developed, and investigated by the Yale group in the 1930's. The first formulation (Dollard et al., 1939, p. 1) stated that aggression always occurs because of frustration and that frustration always leads to aggression. Miller (1941), however, soon reduced the scope of this generalization by indicating that aggression is only one of a number of possible responses to frustration. He still held to the notion, on the other hand, that aggression always presupposes frustration. The frustration-aggression hypothesis has led to research and it has been widely influential. Its adequacy, however, is limited, as we shall see.

3. *Aggression as acquired drive.* There appear to be somewhat different conceptions of aggression as an acquired drive. One of them stresses the role of anger, the other the role of conflicting expectations concerning the reinforcement of aggressive behavior.

Miller and Dollard (1941, pp. 61–64; see, also, Dollard & Miller, 1950, pp. 82–84) suggested that anger is a learnable drive; that is, they postulate such reactions as threshing about, striking, clawing, and internal visceral responses as occurring innately to situations which produce "anger." If these responses, or some of them, can be attached to previously neutral cues, then the cues will initiate the anger response. Since aggressive behavior is at least one of the consequences of anger, aggressive behavior would be a possible consequence of the presentation of the cues which now elicit anger.[27] A reduction in anger would be reinforcing.

Buss (1961),[28] in an extensive review of the field of aggression, has indicated that in his view the only aspect of aggressive behavior which may be considered at all in drive terms is the emotional response of anger. Unless aggression is "angry aggression," Buss would see no reason for a drive interpretation of aggression, and, in any case, he himself sees little virtue in referring to anger as a drive. We return to this viewpoint in a moment.

The other interpretation of aggression as an acquired drive is offered by Sears et al. (1953) and is similar to their conception of the acquired drive of dependency (see p. 741). The goal response of aggression, they point out, is injuring another, and the child discovers that he can obtain compliance with his wishes by hurting someone else. Aggression so far would be only an instrumental response motivated by various needs and rewarded by getting one's way, but again the drive is said to arise from a conflict between the expectations that the behavior will be successful and that it will not be successful. Presumably, in experience, aggressive behavior is both rewarded and punished, and hence the conflict and the induced drive. It will occur, however, only when *instigated* by people, at least until symbolic factors permit its internal instigation.

4. *Nonmotivational interpretation of aggression.* Buss (1961), indicating that aggressiveness is or may be an enduring and pervasive personality characteristic, emphasizes the role of habit: "Aggression is the habit of attacking" (Buss, 1961, p. 198). Four factors determine the strength of aggressiveness in an individual. One of these is the frequency and intensity with which attack, frustration, and annoyers (the antecedents of aggression) have been experienced. "The individual

---

[27] Miller and Dollard (1941, pp. 63–64, fn.) indicate that aggression will occur if it is the response most strongly learned to the anger. It appears that this formulation is a theory of how frustration may lead to aggression; anger, established by frustration, will, under appropriate circumstances, mediate between the frustration and the aggression.

[28] See also, for reviews of the literature, Berkowitz (1958, 1962) and McNeil (1959).

who has been the recipient of many anger stimuli is more likely to be chronically aggressive than the one who has been the recipient of few anger stimuli" (Buss, 1961, p. 198). Second is the extent to which reinforcement has followed aggressive or attacking behavior; reinforcement here may come from reduction of anger, from eliminating noxious external stimuli, or from the attainment of various rewards. Such rewards need not be directly related to the expression of anger, as would be hurting another; as we understand it, food, success, prestige, dominance, achievement could reward aggressive behavior. Punishment, on the other hand, would weaken aggressive behavior through conflict-aroused inhibition, if not through reduced habit strength. Nonreward of aggression (i.e., extinction) would reduce habit strength. A third factor in determining the strength of aggressiveness is "social facilitation." Buss suggests that the peers and older members of the individual's group or family may provide models of aggressive behavior. In a highly aggressive group or family, the individual will probably be rewarded for initiating aggressive behavior; he will also often be attacked so that he will be frequently angry. The final factor related to aggressiveness is temperament—that is, the extent to which the individual is impulsive, to which he is active, to which he reacts intensely to situations, and to which he is independent. These temperament variables, Buss believes, appear early in life, but it is not clear as to what extent they are constitutional or specific only to aggression.

Empirical Study of Aggression

Is It Instinctive? It is probable that many behavioral scientists, especially in the United States, would deny that there is an instinct for aggressiveness (but see Chapter 3, on ethology). At one time, Maslow (1936), who had made extensive studies of dominance relations among primates, suggested that there is a "dominance drive." In a later discussion of aggressiveness in animals and primitive societies (Maslow, 1954, Chap. 10), however, he could find little or no ground on which to assert that there is an instinct for aggressiveness or destructiveness.

Dominance relations and fighting are widely observed phenomena in birds, mammals, and in some reptiles, but students of these matters tend to look to a variety of variables for their explanation. Competition for food and sexual privileges and territoriality are some of the factors of which fighting and dominance seem to be functions, and relations between these behaviors and factors, such as age, sex, deprivation states, hormonal levels, and neural structures, have been reported. A sampling of reviews of animal behavior in a number of species reveals much evidence of fighting and dominance but no reference to an "instinct" for aggression. Temperamental variables, which may have a genetic component, are probably related to aggressiveness, but they do not, of course, comprise an instinct for aggression.[29] Scott (1958) made a careful survey of the literature of animal aggression and included some cultural materials for human societies. He could find no convincing evidence for the existence of an instinct or a drive of aggression, apart from learning. He points out that some animals, such as clams, do not fight at all, and that individual differences, associated with sex, genetic history, ecological factors, and many other variables, govern the amount of fighting displayed in the members of other species.

Kardiner (1945) observed that a war-like group of American Indians (the Comanches) were aggressive not because of childhood frustrations but because raiding and confiscation of property were profitable. Marler (1957) found that fighting in chaffinches could be reinforced if it led to food-getting. There is also evidence from experimental work with rats and human subjects that aggressiveness may be increased by means of reinforcement (cf. Miller, 1948b, but see Ulrich & Azrin, 1962).

Antecedents and Arousal of Aggression. Aggression is sometimes aroused experimentally by frustrating, insulting, or failing a subject in a laboratory situation or task. On the other hand, aggression may not be actually aroused at the time of an investigation. Rather it may be measured in the "resting state," and the variations among subjects in the amount of aggression they display may be correlated with various kinds of antecedents. While direct arousal perhaps more clearly involves motivation than do resting state measures, we will include some examples of correlated antecedents to aggression.

1. *Frustration.* On the frustration-aggression hypothesis one would naturally expect frustration to be the method of choice for setting up aggression. We think of a behavioral event as involving (1) the instrumental acts involved, (2) the presentation of the reward or reinforcer, and (3) the consummatory response to the reinforcer. The sequence can be interrupted at any one of these three points, and it is necessary, in defining frustration, to indicate to the interruption of which one it refers. The instrumental response can be disturbed by barriers, by preventing or blocking it, by interrupting it, or by causing it to fail; distraction during its performance and pitting competing responses against it (thus generating conflict) are other ways in which the instrumental behavior may be impeded or made ineffective (Buss, 1961, pp.

[29] Pertinent reviews are by Bindra (1959), Crawford (1939), Collias (1951), Munn (1950), Nissen (1951), Smith and Ross (1952), Scott (1958), and Fuller and Thomson (1960).

18–19). Omission of reward can be frustrating; Amsel (1958), as well as others, has spoken of this as "frustrative nonreward" (see Chapters 9 and 11). Or the reward can be presented but the consummatory response prevented. Perhaps if after task completion the subject is told that he has failed or that his performance is poor or unsatisfactory, he will be frustrated, because these outcomes conflict with expectation of success or approval.[30]

Instrumental behavior was interrupted by Miller and Bugelski (cf. Dollard et al., 1939, p. 47), who asked pairs of subjects to perform a task in a cooperation and competition situation. However, a bogus partner participated in the pairs, and he frustrated the other partner by doing his part incompetently and by disrupting the work generally. The frustrated partners made many self-critical remarks and reduced their estimates of themselves on a personality scale, both kinds of results suggesting that the subject was turning his aggression inwardly. The Office of Strategic Services (1948) used a similar procedure in their assessment methods. "Helpers" were assigned who actually frustrated the supervisory efforts of the person being assessed by bungling their work and pestering him. Frustration was presumably produced and occasionally led to physical violence (aggression) on the part of the supervisor.

Lindzey and Riecken (1951) arranged their experiment so that the "real" subject would do more poorly than the other subjects, who were stooges. The task was card-sorting, and each member of the group was to receive a monetary prize if the performance of each subject, real or stooge, was up to certain standards. Since the procedure was arranged so that the real subject did not do so well as the others, he was frustrated and sometimes his performance "prevented" anyone from receiving the prize. Anger was aroused in the real subjects who mainly expressed aggression, however, toward themselves. Since the source of the frustration was apparently the real subject, aggression could only be expressed inwardly, in contrast to the OSS situation.

Consummatory responses were blocked by Sears, Hovland & Miller (1940), who hired male subjects in order, ostensibly, to study fatigue. The subjects were kept awake all night, and smoking was prohibited (all were habitual smokers). Restraints on activity, conversation, and other diversions were imposed for periods of time, and

---

[30] Some of these operations, such as omission of reward, are typical of extinction and of intermittent and secondary reinforcement. Presentation of reward without consummatory response was accomplished by Grindley (1929) by putting a glass barrier in front of the reward. He found this operation to have secondary reinforcing properties, at least for a period of time.

a meal they had expected was not forthcoming. Aggression was manifested toward the experimenters, and drawings made by one subject
showed violent and hostile themes. In all of these experiments, aggression was probably not expressed as intensely as it might have been had
the social situation not involved some constraints, and whether aggression is shown outwardly or toward the self is a function of both the
social situation and the perception of the source of the frustration.

Another variable which might be important to the frustration is the
strength of the instigation to the responses which are blocked. Sears
and Sears (1940) studied the reactions of a five-month-old baby to
interruptions of bottle feeding; the interruptions were imposed, on
different occasions, after varying amounts of feeding had already been
accomplished. Latency of crying was the measure observed, and the
earlier in the feeding the bottle was removed the sooner the crying
occurred. According to Sears and Sears, frustration was greater when
the interruption occurred early than when it occurred late. (One could
argue of course that hunger also was greater for early interruptions.)
Haner and Brown (1955) required children to fill a number of holes
in a board with marbles, requiring all the holes to be filled for a reward.
The child pushed a plunger at the sound of a buzzer, which signaled
the end of a trial, and the force of this response was measured. The
subjects were failed after varying numbers of holes were filled; the
closer the subject was to the goal of filling all the holes when failure
occurred, the stronger was his push on the plunger. Presumably, nearness to the goal increases the instigation to the task, and the strength
of frustration is greater as strength of instigation increases.[31]

Doob and Sears (1939) and Allison and Hunt (1959) used questionnaires to study this problem. College students reported on the likelihood of their responding to various instances of frustration with aggression or anger. The probability of such responses increased with the
judged strength of the frustrated response tendencies.

A number of other studies related to the frustration-aggression hypothesis will not be considered here because they confound frustration
with other variables or because of failures of replication.[32] In general,
the status of the frustration-aggression hypothesis is not high, at the

[31] It can be questioned whether crying and plunger-pushing are aggressive
responses. However, if frustration increases response strength it is manifesting
the energizing function of drive, whether the response is an aggressive one or not.
The findings of the Haner-Brown experiment were not confirmed by McDonough
(1958) with children or Roehl (1959) with adults.

[32] Failures of replication include the widely cited report of a negative correlation between the price of cotton and incidence of lynchings in the South (cf.
Hovland & Sears, 1940; Mintz, 1946).

present time. Frustration does *not* always lead to aggression, especially when the frustration is not perceived as threatening, emotion-arousing, or arbitrary (Maslow, 1941; Sargent, 1948; Zander, 1944; Pastore, 1950, 1952; Appley, 1962*a*). Alternative responses aside from aggression have been admitted as possibilities arising from frustration by Miller (1941), and various alternative responses have in fact been observed (cf. Hall, 1961, p. 237). Other aspects of this hypothesis will be summarized after the discussion of further antecedents of aggression. However, it is clear that whether aggression will occur as a response to frustration is partly determined by the instrumental value it has in the situation in which frustration is experienced (Buss, 1961, pp. 24–25), by individual differences (Block & Martin, 1955), and by the extent to which reinforcement has followed aggressive responses (Davitz, 1952; Otis & McCandless, 1955).

2. *Noxious stimuli.* Buss (1961) identifies noxious stimuli (annoyances, attack by someone else) as potential instigators to aggression and apparently regards them as not necessarily frustrating.[33] Little has been done so far as annoyances (like someone's rasping tone of voice) are concerned (cf. Cason, 1930), but insult and attack by the experimenter have been used, and Buss (1961) cites an unpublished study by Gillespie (1961) in which verbal insult or attack was found to arouse more aggression than frustration of task performance.

We have already described the experiment by Feshbach (1955) in which a group was insulted by the experimenter, and evidence of aggression was found in the TAT and in other measures which were used. McClelland and Apicella (1945) employed as an experimenter a college student who knew all the subjects to at least some extent. He failed the subjects on a task and then insulted them for their poor performances, by derogating and cursing them. A substantial proportion of the subjects' reactions to this treatment evidenced anger and aggression. Various other experimenters have combined insults with frustration (failure) and have obtained aggressive responses (Cox, 1952; Funkenstein, King, & Drolette, 1957; Weiss & Fine, 1956; Zuckerman, 1955). Aggression has also been obtained when insults emanate from participants who are associates of the investigator, either as "experimenters" or as "subjects" (Ax, 1953; Thibaut & Coules, 1952; Margolin, 1954).

In these experiments, then, aggression has been situationally aroused by means of insult, which presumably gave rise to anger which led to aggression (or to which the subjects responded aggressively from

[33] Dollard et al. (1939) suggested overreaction to minor annoyances as an indicator of frustration.

habit). These experiments, together with those on frustration, do not tell us a great deal about aggression. We know that it can be aroused and measured in the laboratory and what some of its antecedents are. Other work has studied antecedents of aggressiveness as a characteristic of individuals independent of specific arousal. To these studies we now give brief attention.

3. *Correlated antecedents of aggression.* Sears et al. (1953) studied aggression in nursery-school children, measuring it, as they had measured dependency, by means of teachers' ratings and behavior observations, and inferring antecedents of aggression by means of interviews with mothers. As with the dependency measures, the various indices of aggression showed intercorrelations considerably less than perfect, and activity showed some relations to aggressiveness. There was little evidence that scores on aggression were related to measures of infant and current frustration or with other aspects of early childhood experience in the home, as reported by the mothers. However, there was a relation between aggression, among boys, and the extent of the mothers' *reported punitiveness* for aggressive behavior.[34] Walder (1961), with older children, has reported a high relation between intensity of the punishment by fathers for aggression and aggressiveness in their sons; a similar relation, though not so consistent, was found for girls. (Whether this reflects a causal relation cannot be decided.) Social and economic variables are also related to children's aggressiveness; that is, aggression in children was inversely related to socio-economic status of the home, length of residence in the United States, residence in a rural area, and degree of parents' participation in the community (Walder, 1961). Bandura and Walters (1959) found, in adolescent, aggressive, antisocial boys, that aggressiveness was related to the mothers' permissiveness in allowing the boys to express aggression toward them and to the degree of punitiveness in response to aggression from other adults on the part of the parents of the boys.

There is a good deal of evidence, although in detail it often shows inconsistency, that aggressiveness in children is related to a variety of factors associated with their homes and other social settings. Sociological variables are probably indicative of other, more direct, factors. Thus, parental reactions to aggression, parental expression of aggression, peer relations, and acceptability of outlets for aggression are probably the factors which are specifically influential in shaping the relations between social class, for example, and aggressiveness in children. Undoubtedly, there are many things which will make a child angry;

[34] See, also, Sears, Maccoby, and Levin (1957).

whether he will become aggressive, chronically or temporarily, however, depends on many other factors.

The Problem of the Measurement of Aggression. The most obvious technique for assessing aggression is to measure its actual occurrence in overt physical or verbal form in some situation or over time. This has been done (e.g., Sears et al., 1953). However, two questions have led to stress on indirect techniques for measuring aggression (aside from the impracticality of direct observations). One concerns the adequacy of overt aggression as a measure of the amount of aggression induced by some operation. Factors in the situation or in the person may prevent full overt expression. The other question relates to individual differences. People obviously differ in aggressiveness (whether conceived as a motive or as a habitual mode of expression) as a more or less permanent characteristic. How may this characteristic be assessed?

A variety of techniques has been used to measure aggression. Questionnaires and inventories (both situationally specific and general), ratings, and projective tests are the chief classes of instruments which have been used. We shall speak briefly here of inventories and projective procedures.[35]

Three chief ways have been used to determine whether aggression is measured by a technique. One is to compare groups believed or known to differ in aggressiveness (by an independent criterion) on some procedure. Another is to scale materials so that they reflect aggression differentially; more aggressive people should be differentiated from less aggressive people on the basis of their responses to such material. The third is to compare responses to some technique in subjects in whom anger or aggression has been aroused and in subjects in whom it has not been aroused. This last procedure is the one most directly relevant to motivation. In the other two, it is not at all clear that the *motive* or *drive* of aggression is being measured. The chief instruments used in the study of aggression are the Rorschach, the Thematic Apperception Test (TAT), modifications of the TAT, inventories, and, with children, doll play.

The Rorschach Test. Buss (1961) has summarized evidence that scores for the content of Rorschach responses (cf. Elizur, 1949; Mur-

---

[35] Buss (1961, pp. 46–51) has characterized these methods, as we have done, as indirect. He proposes, as a direct measure, an "aggression machine." In this device the subject's aggression is measured by the intensity of an electric shock he gives to another "subject" who is an accomplice and is said to be learning a task. No shock is actually delivered to the accomplice. The subject has been given the "feel" of the shocks he thinks he is delivering to the accomplice, however, ahead of time. Even this technique is probably limited by inhibitory aspects of social situations.

stein, 1956) will distinguish normal subjects on the basis of variations of aggressiveness, as assessed sociometrically. However, self-report is closely related to these differentiations, so that this evidence is not indicative that the Rorschach is tapping "deep" or "unconscious" aggression. Discriminations on the basis of Rorschach content have been made successfully in prisoners, psychiatric patients, and patients in psychotherapy; in each kind of sample some external measure of aggressiveness was compared with the Rorschachs—for example, prisoners who had committed assaultive crimes vs. prisoners who had committed nonassaultive crimes, violent psychiatric patients vs. nonviolent patients, patients rated aggressive by their therapists vs. those not so rated. Typically, the Rorschach content scores of overtly aggressive prisoners, patients, or patients in therapy show more aggressiveness than those of the comparison group. Buss (1961, p. 137) concludes from this: "Thus hostile responses on the Rorschach are best regarded in terms of response sampling of a larger population of hostile responses, rather than in terms of drainage of a reservoir of hostility." Induction of aggression by frustration (Gluck, 1955a) was not reflected in Rorschach content; overt examiner aggressiveness reduced and covert examiner aggressiveness increased hostile Rorschach content (Sanders & Cleveland, 1953). Formal Rorschach scores yield, at best, small relations with measured or induced aggressiveness (Buss, 1961, pp. 135–137).

Thematic Apperception. When the TAT is used with clinical or deviant samples or when aggression scores on it are compared with patients' known aggressiveness, the results, as Buss (1961, pp. 140–141) summarizes them, are as follows: "First, the TAT is a good measure of anti-social aggression but not of milder and more social forms of aggression. Second, using case histories as a source of criterion measures of aggressive behavior yields positive results, while ratings of hospital behavior yields negative results (except for outbursts of rage which approach antisocial aggression)." Various comparisons in college students and normal adolescent boys yield inconsistent or negative results. Among institutionalized and disturbed adolescent boys, some relations between aggressiveness and TAT scores were found.

Several investigators have studied the effect on TAT aggression scores of manipulations designed to anger the subject. Thus, Bellak (1944) counted the number of aggressive words in the TAT stories during criticism by the examiner. He found more aggression in the stories during the period of criticism than in the stories produced without criticism. Lindzey and Kalnins (1958) also found evidence of aggression in the TAT stories of college men who were frustrated by failure in an experimental situation. We have mentioned before the study by Feshbach (1955) in which TAT aggression was greater in a group of college students who had been insulted than in a control group. With other kinds of subjects, however, operations of these kinds have not always been successful (Matarazzo, 1954; Gluck, 1955*b*).

A number of investigators have employed modifications of the TAT. The chief modification has been to select pictures which are related to aggression, while retaining enough ambiguity so that they do not "require" an aggressive response. Themes of fighting might, for example, be readily perceptible in the pictures, along with other possibilities. Such pictures have been successful in eliciting stories which vary in aggressiveness as do other measures of aggression applied to the same subjects (Kagan, 1956; Lesser, 1957, 1958*a*). It is an important finding from these studies that some, but not too much, structure toward aggression be provided in a TAT picture if it is to assess aggression (see also the section on the TAT pictures used in studies of nAch, p. 734). The standard TAT has very few pictures that lead to many aggressive responses (Auld, Eron, & Laffal, 1955).

Even with a modified set of pictures, however, other variables may affect the measurement. Thus, Lesser (1957) found an overall correlation of only .07 for his group of schoolboys between TAT aggression scores and teachers' ratings of behavioral aggression. He was able, however, to divide his subjects into a group whose mothers encouraged aggression and another group whose mothers discouraged aggression. For the former group the correlation between TAT aggression scores and behavioral aggression was .43; for the latter group it was —.41. Both values were significant.

In conclusion to the brief discussion of projective measurement of aggression, it is clear that content scores based on the standard instruments can be found to be directly related to overt and assaultive aggressive trends but probably not to other kinds of aggression. Relative unambiguity of TAT pictures seems to be a desirable feature so far as getting valid evidence of aggression is concerned (cf. Kagan, 1959), and such variables as maternal approval or disapproval of aggression in schoolboys (Lesser, 1957) and amount of anxiety over aggression (Mussen and Naylor, 1954) also appear to affect the adequacy of the measures. Arousal of anger may lead to aggressive themes in TAT stories.

On the basis of these results, it can be concluded that aggression *can* be measured by projective procedures, the relation tending to be direct; that is, the more overt aggression there is, the more projective aggression there is likely to be. Further, it may require special stimulus materials, special scoring, and knowledge of other variables in order to obtain valid measurements. The standard projective tests are not a "Royal Road" to the uncovering of hidden aggressive tendencies.

Other measures. Inventories consist of sets of questions to which the examinee is to select an answer from alternatives which are provided him. Three illustrative questions (Buss, 1961, p. 171) follow: "Once in a while I cannot control my urge to harm others." "If somebody hits me first, I let him have it." "I never get mad enough to throw things." Such inventories have been constructed to measure aggression, but, while some positive findings have emerged, they have not been exploited much as yet. It is Buss' opinion (1961, Chap. 9) that they have considerable potential in this respect. Buss believes that the projective measures mainly get at aggressiveness of which the subject is aware and sees no reason that such aggressiveness cannot be measured by inventories. Inventories are commonly applied as measures of enduring, characteristic trends, although in one study (Walters & Zaks, 1959) situational frustration was found to raise aggression scores on an inventory.

With young children, a major method for the study of aggression has been doll play (Levin & Wardwell, 1962). Although the specific details of equipment and procedure vary, in general the child is provided a roofless doll's house and a number of miniature dolls representing adults and children of several ages. The child is told that he can make the dolls do whatever he wants them to, and he is encouraged to play with them freely and imaginatively. Most children will display some aggressive acts in the course of using these materials, although, of course, many other themes may also be manifested.

Yarrow (1948) found that failure on an impossible task increased the amount of doll play aggression shown by nursery-school children (see, also, Bach, 1945). Isch (1952) observed the mother-child interaction and then studied the doll play of the children. She found the doll play to display aggression in relation to aggression or rejection by the mother toward the child. These experiments presumably deal with "angry" aggression. Most of the other studies of doll play have related aggressiveness to such variables as frustration and punishment (for aggression) at home, the aggressiveness of the child at home or in school, characteristics of the children studied (such as age and sex), and changes in aggressiveness over more than one doll-play session. These studies have been reviewed by Buss (1961) and by Levin and Wardwell (1962). In the second session the child displays more aggression in doll play than in the first session; presumably this occurs because the child learns that he can express aggression in doll play without punishment (or, perhaps, he is reinforced for expressing aggression). Introducing a stranger into the second session rules out this increase, but it takes place when the mother attends the second session, a result that was unexpected (Levin & Turgeon, 1957). Some evidence has been reported that children who are severely punished at home for aggression manifest large amounts of doll-play aggression (Hollenberg & Sperry, 1951). However, Levin and Sears (1956), using a wider population sample, found it necessary to complement the variable of severity of punishment with such factors as sex of the child, the parent administering the punishment, and the child's identification with the parent. For example, boys who are highly identified with their fathers and who are ordinarily punished by their fathers show much doll-play aggression. In girls, the relationships are much less clear.

Other Aspects of Aggression

Aggression is subject to a number of influences, at least theoretically. Punishment and reinforcement and opportunities for displacement and catharsis are among the more important of these factors.

Punishment and Reinforcement. Aggressive behavior is often met with punishment. Hollenberg and Sperry (1951), in one of their experiments, used preschool children as subjects, each one of whom served in four doll-play sessions. Verbal punishment for doll-play aggression was administered to one group during the second session. This group showed no increase in aggression between the first and second sessions and showed a decline at the third session; however, when permissiveness was reinstated in the third session, aggressiveness went up again at the fourth session. Meanwhile, the control group had shown an increase in aggression from session to session, a finding commonly seen in repeated doll play under permissive conditions.

Other investigations of punishment have not used *actual* punishment but have either inquired by questionnaire as to the amount of aggression an adult subject thinks he would display in view of the punishment various acts might generate, or the subject has been allowed to express aggression verbally toward persons of varying status and authority. It is likely that he would expect punishing effects from expression of aggression toward persons of status and authority. After frustration, subjects will express more aggression toward a student (Worchel, 1957) or to an Army private (Reiser et al., 1955) than to a faculty member or an Army captain. Questionnaire studies find that subjects think they will or will not express aggression as a function of the amount of punishment they expect (Doob & Sears, 1939) or as a function of the person to whom the aggression is expressed

(Cohen, 1955; Graham et al., 1951). Thus college women believe they would aggress more toward peers than toward professors. Buss (1961, pp. 56–59) has pointed out that the effects of punishment on aggression are complex and that the effects of punishment will often be only temporary unless alternative instrumental acts are available. We should note that in these investigations punishment was described as a direct consequence of aggression; in other studies, such as the one just described, in which severely punished children have expressed much aggression in doll play, the aggression occurs in a permissive situation, not in the ones in which the punishment took place.

As we have noted already, doll-play aggression tends to increase with repeated sessions, even with the child's mother present. One possible explanation for this increase is that the child interprets the permissive environment as rewarding of his aggressive behavior. Or perhaps he does not expect punishment in this social situation. Another is that, with an adult present (the mother or a familiar teacher or experimenter), he does not control his aggression, assuming that the adult will exercise control if he goes too far. Siegel and Kohn (1959) found a decline in aggressive play in two children left alone together, whereas aggression increased with an adult present. This may support the responsibility hypothesis, but one could argue that, alone together, neither child would be aggressive toward the other with no adult present to stop counteraggression. It could also be said that aggression may serve to gain adult attention and without an adult cannot be used to this end. Other findings of increasing aggression either between or within sessions of doll play have been reported by P. S. Sears (1951), Pintler (1945), Phillips (1945), and Hartup and Himeno (1959). (See, also, Levin & Wardwell, 1962, p. 42.) Some investigations cited in the next section also support the notion that aggressive behavior may be strengthened by reinforcement (cf. Davitz, 1952). But, first, we should mention that punishment, or fear or anxiety over aggression, probably rising from anticipation of punishment or loss of affection, is basic to the conflict analysis that has often been applied to various aspects of aggressive behavior and its inhibition (see Chapter 9; Lesser, 1958b; Miller, 1944; Sears et al., 1953, pp. 215–220).

Displacement and Catharsis. It has often been said, following psychoanalytic theory, that the energy of aggression is displaceable; that is, it can be directed toward an object other than the one to which it would be most appropriate. Thus aggression toward a frustrating agent such as an authority figure, inhibited because of the feared consequences of aggression toward such a figure, may find its mark in some innocent person, animal, or thing, toward whom or which aggression may be safely expressed. It is evident that such a concept implies that aggression must be "drained off."

Buss (1961) suggests that there are two kinds of displacement. In one, anger lowers the threshold for the occurrence of aggression on mild provocation. This is perhaps similar to the drainage hypothesis. The other kind of displacement arises when aggressive responses are *transferred*, without anger, from one stimulus to another on the basis of similarity between the stimuli. Miller's (1948*b*) experiment illustrates the latter kind. He trained two rats to strike at each other in order to terminate electric shock. Later, in the absence of one rat the striking response, in perhaps half the animals, generalized to a celluloid doll also present in the compartment. This shows the transfer of an instrumental aggressive response (without anger but under fear) from one stimulus to another similar one. However, we do not think it is especially relevant to the catharsis type of displacement hypothesis as we have just stated it. Stimulus generalization predicts transfer of aggression to objects similar to the original object of aggression (within the limits set by conflict over fear of counter-aggression and by availability of other objects). Displacement of angry aggression, however, could occur to any initiating stimulus, response to which was facilitated by the lowering of the threshold for aggressive responses, due to anger.[36] While this would seem to be Buss' prediction, it is possible that it is too simple. The displaced aggressive reaction could still be more likely to some people, who resemble the frustrating agent in some way, than to others, and it could also be inhibited toward some people (despite provocation) due to fear of consequences but not inhibited to others. Unfortunately, clear-cut evidence on these possibilities is not available, but anecdotal evidence can, no doubt, be found to fit any one of them.

Catharsis, in this context, refers to the reduction of instigation to aggression by means of expression of aggression; it also implies a drainage hypothesis. A number of studies (Buss, 1961, pp. 80–84) have investigated the effect of catharsis in the absence of anger. In such studies a measure of aggressiveness is usually applied both before and after an opportunity for catharsis has been given. Cathartic opportunities have included active aggression in doll play, movies involving fighting and aggression (the spectator being passive), and aggressive role-playing. In general, the findings of such studies show no decrement in aggression and sometimes indicate that aggression has increased in the post-test.

[36] A major application of the displacement notion is the scapegoat hypothesis (Dollard et al., 1939; Miller & Bugelski, 1948) as an explanation of prejudice. A careful review of the literature reveals little consistent evidence in favor of the scapegoat hypothesis, however (Buss, 1961, pp. 245–258).

Possible here is an interpretation that the expression of aggression has been reinforced, and it is unlikely that angry aggression has been involved in these situations.

Catharsis has also been studied for angry aggression. Feshbach (1955) found a reduction in aggression in an insulted group after aggression had been expressed in TAT stories. In a later study, Feshbach (1961) arranged to insult some of his college subjects and not to insult others. Some members of each group saw a prize-fight film and the others a nonaggressive film. The insulted group which saw the fight film manifested less aggression later than the insulted group which saw the nonaggressive film. There was some evidence that there was more later aggression in the noninsulted aggressive film group than in its control. Some additional experiments on this problem give only partial support to these findings, but various differences in procedure might account for the failure to obtain better agreement. Buss (1961) thinks the evidence supports the notion that, in the presence of anger, catharsis, whether achieved actively or passively (as through a film), can reduce the instigation to later aggression.

Hokanson and Shetler (1961) measured systolic blood pressure prior to frustrating their subjects, after frustration, and following an opportunity to express aggression physically toward either a high or low status experimenter by administering electric shock to him. The shocks were given ostensibly to signal incorrect responses in a guessing task. The frustration manipulation increased systolic blood pressure, as compared to a control condition, and expression of aggression toward the low-status experimenter reduced systolic blood pressure. This measure remained high in the absence of an opportunity to express aggression. Systolic blood pressure declined with respect to the high-status experimenter, however, in time, irrespective of the opportunity to express aggression.

These results suggest support for a cathartic effect of aggression, under some conditions. How the aggression toward the high-status experimenter was resolved, however, is problematic. Overt aggression was not necessary to its resolution, as it is not, in any evident way, when one watches a fight movie.

This review of aspects of aggression shows aggressive behavior to be complexly determined. When it is punished, aggressive behavior tends to decline in frequency, and subjects report that their expression of aggressive behavior is probably related to the amount of punishment they think it would engender. Their hesitation to express it to certain status figures is probably related to anticipated consequences. On the other hand, aggression tends to increase when it is reinforced.

Whether aggression is displaceable to related objects or, alternatively, whether angry aggression is simply released by *any* annoying stimulus is not clear on the basis of present evidence. While the transfer of an instrumental aggressive response from one stimulus to another does not necessarily indicate the discharge of angry aggression, we still think such a discharge is hypothetically tenable. There is some evidence that angry aggression is capable of being discharged either in fantasy or by witnessing aggression. The question whether it is displaced to less risky objects than the original object of the aggression needs further study.

Summary of Dependency and Aggression

Dependency and aggression are widely regarded as strong motives. Instinctive status has been accorded to them, especially to aggression, but the bulk of the literature surveyed here regards them as acquired drives or learned motives. It is clear that either dependent or aggressive behavior may represent response tendencies instrumental to obtaining reinforcement related to motive states other than dependency or aggression. In short, both dependency and aggression may represent habitual ways of responding in certain situations; where this is true, it is unnecessary to posit independent motivational status for dependency and aggression.

Dependency has been studied mainly in young children, and certain factors in the home, such as infantile feeding-frustration, show some correlation with the incidence of dependent behavior. Dependency has seldom been investigated as a factor in the energization of other responses. Our review has yielded little systematic information pointing to drive status as opposed to instrumental status for it.

In treating aggression, we have reviewed a number of hypotheses as to its character and a number of factors governing its occurrence. Aggression has been seen as a *reaction* to certain stimuli, as a learned drive, and as a trait or habit arising through reinforcement. In the studies summarized, noxious stimuli have been the most effective instigators of aggression, whereas frustration (to which aggression would be a reaction) has not been very effective. This latter finding in part is due to situational aspects of frustration, which often permit subjects not to see an event as frustrating, though, objectively, it is. Much of the work on aggression has found correlates of aggressive behavior in the home-environment and in current experiences there. One problem which looms large in the study of aggression, as it does in dependency and other learned motives, is the one of measurement. Part of this problem arises from the fact that aggression can be behavior arising from anger or it can be a trait, present without anger.

When trait aggression is separated from angry aggression, there is some evidence that the two respond differently to various experimental manipulations. Thus, angry aggression, closest to what is meant by a drive or a motive of aggression, is usually short-lived and responsive to catharsis. Trait aggression is conceived to be enduring, and catharsis does not affect it.

As a habit or trait, aggression can arise in several ways. Aggressive behavior can be reinforced because it secures rewards related to many organismic needs and desires—food, sex, money, status, dominance, and so on. In this case, the aggressive behavior has little to do with a motive or drive of aggression. On the other hand, aggression, even when motivated by anger, can be rewarded—it may make another back down, obtain approval for standing up for one's rights, obtain relief for the state of anger. When such rewards follow an anger-aggression sequence, the sequence may be strengthened so that the individual becomes quick to anger and quick to aggressive action.

THE ROLE OF EXPERIENCE

The notions of acquired motivation and, to a certain extent, of social motivation (see Chapter 15) lead us to look to prior experience for the antecedents to and the development of contemporary motivational factors. This is an area to which we have been sensitive throughout this book. At this point, we summarize the various references to the role of early experience made in the preceding pages.

The story began in the second chapter, with our references to the rejection of the instinct concept and to early experiments on the conditioning of emotional responses. Our discussions of native behavior patterns in Chapters 3 and 4 made reference to the role of experience in a variety of contexts, from species-specific behavior to sex and hoarding. Heavily emphasized in relation to hunger, thirst, and pain avoidance (Chapter 5) was the role of past experience in controlling characteristics of consummatory responses and (Chapter 6) general activity.

Certain theories have highlighted notions of acquired motivation, as the discussions of hedonic and emotional factors and of drive theory show. Reactions to frustration, conflict, and stress were seen to be modified by infantile and later experiences, at least in several instances. When we came to psychoanalysis and self-actualization, there were many references to characteristics of parent-child interaction, mothering, separation, etc., as variables significant to the child's motivational development and status. In Chapter 11, we reviewed a number of studies of class and cultural differences in motivational variables, and in this chapter we pointed to child-parent interactions, again, in discussing aggression and dependency. Anxiety, too, can be derivative from earlier experiences.

In most of the human work reviewed in prior parts of this book, the time spans covered have been relatively brief, as in certain studies of effects of maternal separation on infant behavior. Where time spans are longer, the character of the early experience or of the subsequent effects has not been very specific. In this section, we therefore add one final example: the relations McClelland believes exist between nAch in later life and certain experiences during development. We conclude the section by reviewing the analysis made by Gewirtz (1961), which is one of the most detailed specifications we have encountered so far as the development of motivation is concerned.

The Origins of Need Achievement

It will be recalled that, in the McClelland formulation of the nature of motivation, all motives are learned (pp. 374–386). In the case of achievement motivation, which is the motive most thoroughly studied by the McClelland group, the motivation involves performance in the context of standards of excellence and is a desire to have the performance stand well in evaluation against such standards. Hence, it would be argued that the history of someone who has high nAch must be one of competition with performance standards or one in which the individual was expected by himself to do things well.

On this hypothesis several investigations were carried out. Thirty men on whom nAch scores were available rated their parents on several behavioral variables, and a psychiatrist also rated the parents on these variables after an interview with the subjects. A combination of these ratings into an overall rating of *severity* of upbringing, and both the sons' and the psychiatrist's ratings of severity, correlated significantly ($r = .40$) with achievement scores. Further data were obtained from the subjects concerning personality traits of their parents. Here negative correlations were found between achievement scores and the parental trait of being friendly and helpful and the characteristics of being successful, clever, and self-confident. McClelland et al. (1953, p. 281) summarize these various findings as follows: "College males who give evidence of being very 'close' to their parents in their admiration of them and perception of them as particularly loving and helpful do not for the most part score high on *n* Achievement. On the contrary, it is the students who see their parents as 'distant'—unfriendly, severe, unsuccessful—who have high *n* Achievement scores." These findings, however, were reversed for male high-school students.

Better investigations of the origins of nAch involve measures of parent behavior independent of the individuals whose nAch is being assessed. The family or parent variable looked for is *independence training*, that is, pressure on the child to master various skills and tasks early so that he can do them by himself, independently of his parents. In one study (McClelland & Friedman, 1952; McClelland et al., 1953, pp. 289–297), folk tales of several North American Indian tribes were collected and scored for nAch. Independently, the stress on independence training of these cultures was rated. Significant relations, in the anticipated directions, were found between nAch and the existence of initial indulgence of the child in the culture (negative), and the age at which independence training started and severity of the training.[37]

Somewhat indirect evidence of a similar kind of relationship was obtained by McClelland et al. (1955). They administered questionnaires concerning independence training and educational level to groups of parents who were classified as Protestant, Jewish, Irish-Catholic, and Italian-Catholic. The reason for using these religious groupings is that, according to Max Weber (1930), capitalism was fostered in Protestant countries more than in Catholic countries because Protestantism emphasized the moral value of success in worldly affairs, whereas this was not so true in Catholicism. McClelland reasoned that if Weber is right, independence training should be stressed more by Protestants than by Catholics, since presumably Protestants have higher nAch scores than Catholics. The Jewish group was expected to be like the Protestants.

The data show that Protestants and Jews expect children to have mastered certain items indicative of independence training at earlier ages than do Catholics, and this source of variation is significant. Educational level and sex of parent also were significantly related to age of expected independence training—the more highly educated parents and mothers at any educational level expecting earlier development of independence than the less educated parents and the fathers.

A last study in this tradition was reported by Winterbottom (1958). She interviewed mothers of 29 eight-year-old boys concerning various aspects of independence training and also measured nAch of the boys by means of a procedure suitable for their age. She found evidence of a strong relationship between nAch, on the one hand, and independence training, on the other. While the mothers of the high and low nAch boys did not differ in the *number* of demands for independence they made, the mothers of the high nAch boys made them *earlier* than

[37] Child, Storm, and Veroff (1958) have conducted a parallel study which offers little support to these findings. Certain methodological problems in their own study, however, have led them to refrain from offering their results as a disconfirmation of Friedman's investigation.

the mothers of the other boys. Some of the items which differentiated the two groups in terms of age at which they were demanded were: to stand up for one's rights, to know one's way around the city, to go out to play, to try hard things for oneself. Nondifferential items include eating alone without help, earning spending money, doing tasks around the house. The mothers of the boys scoring high on nAch also evaluated the children's accomplishments higher and were more rewarding than the other mothers.[38]

These studies point to the kind of investigation which examines the relation between a relatively specific motive and fairly specific kinds of early experiences hypothesized to be related to the motive in question. Obviously, much more work is required to confirm the relation between independence training and nAch, as well as to find relations between early experiences and other motives.

Gewirtz' Analyses

Gewirtz (1961) has made a close analysis of the conditions under which social motivation and attachment may develop in the human infant or child. Unlike earlier analyses, he focuses not on needs or drives but rather on the evoking and reinforcing functions of environmental stimuli and the development of generalized reinforcers.

Gewirtz departs in certain respects from other analyses of social motivation and attachment based on learning theory, although his is a learning viewpoint. He stresses the following points:

1. The biologically satisfied infant is yet highly responsive to stimuli; his activation is *not* considered to be dependent on hunger, thirst, or aversive states.

2. An environment which provides many stimuli will evoke many behaviors, including emotional-startle responses. Habituation of these latter responses can occur if they are elicited often enough.

3. There are many varieties of reinforcing stimuli; reinforcers are not limited to need-reducing stimuli. The determination of what stimuli will be reinforcers is presently an empirical question.

4. Many of the reinforcing stimuli the child receives are provided by or occur in the context of the care-taking person (e.g., the mother). As a consequence, the caretaker can become a powerful generalized reinforcer, so long as certain conditions are met. Such conditions include the discriminability of the caretaker from others, and the application

---

[38] Chance (1961), studying school achievement in first-graders, found the early independence training group to achieve less well than the late independence training group.

of reinforcers in suitable contiguity to social behaviors. Attachment may be said to have developed to the caretaker when that one uniquely appearing person appears to be the *preferred* source, so far as the child is concerned, of various reinforcing stimuli.

There are many other aspects of Gewirtz' analysis, the discussion of which cannot be entered into here. Suffice it to say that Gewirtz looks on the model of operant conditioning as the critical and useful one in the development of social motivation and attachment and that these latter terms refer to social objects who by virtue of their administration of reinforcers (or through generalization) have become generalized reinforcers. It is evident, then, that the maintenance of social behavior, for Gewirtz, lies in the environment. In this sense, it is an incentive-like theory of social motivation and attachment so far as it has been taken.

Gewirtz has pointed out that the reactions of children to maternal separation and deprivation of mothering (see pp. 685–690) would be interpreted differently from his analysis than from a need orientation. It is the presence or absence of discriminative or reinforcing stimuli and the occurrence of reinforcers contingent on certain behaviors that would be invoked. Thus, apathy in a child might reflect the point that few stimuli in the environment evoke or maintain behavior. Marked emotional reactions after separation might arise from failure of the new caretaker to administer reinforcements effectively or might occur because of the occurrence of stimuli to which habituation had not occurred.

This analysis offers a quite different interpretation of certain phenomena from others we have considered. It is too early to tell how fruitful it will be, but it offers considerable promise.

SUMMARY

In the present chapter several widely postulated human motives were treated in terms of their systematic status and empirical study. The following general comments may be made by way of summary.

It has been suggested that many motives are not really independent motives at all but, instead, identify behavior aroused by fear and anxiety and are reinforced by reductions in fear and anxiety. Experimental work on social behavior in children and affiliative behavior in adults has yielded evidence consistent with this interpretation. Other interpretations, however, are possible, and it is not clear how widely the anxiety interpretation can be generalized. There is evidence, for example, that anxiety does not always lead to affiliative behavior.

Various other learned motives have been studied. Anxiety has been measured by means of a questionnaire and has been conceived as an emotional response which acts as a general source of drive. Extensive experimental work has resulted in some support for this interpretation in simple learning situations. In complex situations of learning and performance, the evidence has not been consistent. Furthermore, anxiety as measured has not shown the relations to physiological arousal that it might be expected to have.

Achievement, affiliation, power, and several other motives have been studied by means of arousal operations and assessment by fantasy. Measures of several such motives are now available. Achievement has received extensive study in relation to other performances. It appears now that achievement as measured relates to other behaviors, at least to some extent, but that the relationship is a complex one, involving not only the achievement motive but also characteristics of the situations and performances in which it is embedded. Motive status for achievement has been questioned.

Dependency and aggression have also been treated as learned motives. As with achievement, however, it is possible to see them not as motives but as learned modes of operation reinforced in relation to other drives, such as hunger and pain avoidance. Research on dependency has emphasized its correlates (in children) in the home environment, and there is little evidence for its drive or motive status. Aggression has received more attention. When it is accompanied by anger, it perhaps operates as a drive, and there is some evidence that expression of anger has a cathartic effect. Most of the work on aggression has not involved anger. The trait of aggression is related, again, to variables in the home, and it seems to be measurable by a variety of techniques, many of them essentially similar to self-report procedures.

Chapter 15

Social Motivation

The hypotheses and findings we reviewed in the last chapter were developed to a large extent in the context of drive theory. This is to say that learned motive states, such as fear and anxiety, aggression, and dependency, have been conceived as logically equivalent in status, character, and function to such drives as hunger and thirst. This equivalence has not been so explicit for achievement and the other motives studied by McClelland and his associates. Even here, however, the focus has been on internal, enduring characteristics of the individual as at least a major variable in his achieving, affiliative and power-related behavior.

In the case of human motivation, as in animal motivation, it is possible to lay stress on external and situational factors, rather than on internal, enduring states. There is a considerable tradition of investigation which has placed its emphasis on circumstances external to the individual. We have brought this work together in the present chapter on social motivation, since many, if not all, of the situational factors involved are implicitly, if not explicitly, social in nature.

Our first concern is with incentives, as applied to human beings (our chief references to incentives, heretofore, have involved animals, in Chapter 11). The classical studies dealt with knowledge of results, the level of aspiration, rivalry, competition, and related matters. Work with rivalry, competition, and the effects of audiences led more or less naturally into the modern concerns of group dynamics, such as conformity, goals of groups, and whether social situations create motivations which might not otherwise exist. These problems are treated in this chapter.

Techniques for the study of human motivation commonly involve interactions between an experimenter and the subject. Studies involving such interactions have been mentioned in the prior chapter, but further work on the interruption of tasks and on ego-involvement is brought together in the present one. So, also, are considerations of the problem of the motivation for social behavior, which have led to the formulation of a theory of cognitive dissonance.

The procedures for the arousal and measurement of motives in human beings, reviewed in this and the preceding chapter, themselves contain many uncertainties. We raise various methodological issues about these procedures in this chapter and offer some comments as to the relations to motivation of such concepts from personality theory as trait, attitude, value, and style.

THE VALUE OF INCENTIVES

The study of acquired motivation, as represented in the last chapter, had its inception, as we earlier observed, around 1940. Prior to 1940, however, there was a considerable interest in acquired motivation, revolving mainly around the topic of incentives (see Diserens & Vaughn, 1931; Dashiell, 1935). Incentives refer to objects, such as rewards, or to situations and conditions, such as knowledge of results, competition, and cooperation, which are used for purposes of arousing the motivation to perform. Perhaps the first study of motivation ever published (Gates, 1895) studied incentives in animals, a topic we treated in Chapter 11.

The initial investigations of incentives seem to have been directed to the solution of such relatively practical problems as the role of incentives in controlling school or industrial performance and the value of social factors in influencing behavior. It often had little theoretical or systematic implication. Research since the 1930's has not ignored these kinds of problems, but it has had considerably greater theoretical and methodological sophistication. There is, perhaps, little continuity between the early work on incentives and the later work on similar problems, but there is some merit in mentioning the earlier work in the context of the later.

As we have said, the early studies of motivation in human beings were concentrated on the following topics: knowledge of results, praise and reproof (or blame), encouragement and discouragement, the influence of audiences and partners, rivalry, cooperation, and competition. These divide themselves into two groups, the first three dealing directly with individual performance, the last four more clearly involving social variables. We will discuss the social variable group a little later.

The topics can be dealt with at two levels of specificity. One is to apply knowledge of results, praise, reproof, etc., to *specific responses* in a task; the other is to provide such incentives to *overall performance*. This second approach typifies the early work in this field.[1] We briefly cite illustrative experiments.

---

[1] A parallel area in the study of learning has been concerned with the effects of rewards and punishments on the acquisition of correct responses. Much of this work was instigated by the law of effect (cf. Postman, 1947).

Knowledge of Results

Knowledge of results is a factor commonly thought to have motivational aspects. However, it undoubtedly has nonmotivational values as well, since information is provided by the knowledge. The term refers to procedures by which the subject is informed of the quality or quantity of his performance. Johanson's (1922) experiment is illustrative. He measured the speed with which a subject pressed a telegraph key on signal. Under one condition, the subject received no information about the speed of his reactions; in another, he was told the speed of his reaction before the next trial. The latter group performed its reactions more quickly than the former group, on the average. Ammons (1956) has reviewed the literature of this problem and concludes that knowledge of results, typically, achieves better performance than no knowledge of results, and that at least some of this effect may be attributed to the interest, attention, and avoidance of boredom which knowledge of results can provide. It is clear, however, that information, as well as motivation, is yielded by knowledge of results, and it is not certain, in the generality, how much of the advantage is due to the motivation or to the information provided by the knowledge of results.

Knowledge of results, of course, provides a standard by which a subject can judge his performance against his past efforts or against some standard which has been provided for him by the experimenter. The procedures known as praise and reproof (or blame) and encouragement and discouragement typically have involved a general evaluation by the experimenter of the overall performance of a group or of individuals as good or bad or as satisfactory or unsatisfactory. There is, thus, some knowledge of results in these procedures, although it is rather unspecific, and the evaluation of his work cannot be or is not usually made by the subject himself. Hurlock's (1924, 1925) often-cited experiments represent the measures employed. Hurlock used three groups of grade-school children. At one session the children took one intelligence test and at a second session another form of the same test. Prior to this second test, one group was complimented on the very high scores they had made as well as on the neatness of their papers. Another group, however, was reproved for their prior performance; they were told their marks were low and their papers slovenly. A third group was retested without praise or reproof. Hurlock found that both the praise and reproof groups raised their scores at the second testing as compared to the control group and that there was little difference in the praised and reproved groups. In a later experiment, Hurlock's subjects took one brief arithmetic test a day for five days. One group, the control, took its tests by itself with no special procedures. The rest of the subjects worked in the same room; one group of these (the ignored group) received no praise or blame but heard these manipulations being used with the others. A second group was singled out by calling out the individual names. The children came before the class, where they were praised for the preceding day's performance. The third group was treated much as was the second group except that they were reproved for their prior day's work. The results showed, as had the prior experiment, that performance improved for both the praised and reproved groups after the first occasion of these procedures; thereafter, the performance of the reproved group fell off while that of the praised group continued to show further gains. The reproved group and the ignored group performed at higher levels throughout than did the controls. These experiments have been interpreted as showing that praise is better than reproof in inciting performance, because it is more enduringly effective than reproof. (Another interpretation is that the reproved children quit trying to do better, since their efforts are never rewarded.) Schmidt (1941), however, in a similar experiment, was unable to confirm this generalization, finding that the results obtained varied with the sex of the subjects as well as with which one of the two experimenters was carrying out the manipulations. Schmidt concludes that situational factors are very important in determining if the praise or reproof maneuver "takes."

This early work on incentives, very briefly represented here, does not seem to have led to entirely satisfactory general conclusion, perhaps because the effects of praise and reproof are more complex than these experiments would seem to suggest. We turn now to the level of aspiration and the related area of success and failure for further work related to incentives.[2]

Level of Aspiration

The studies of incentives we have reviewed so far are rather gross; that is, the performances of groups are compared after different treatments. Little can be discovered in this way about how the individual sets his goal and reacts to his own performance or to evaluations of that performance by others. A technique which has had much use in the study of the factors involved in and the processes of goal setting, the level of aspiration, was developed by Kurt Lewin (1935, pp. 250–

[2] There is a large literature on incentives in industry (cf. Viteles, 1953) and much work also exists on the relation of job attitudes to measures of job performance (cf. Brayfield & Crockett, 1955; Herzberg et al., 1957, 1959). We will not review these materials here.

254) and his students. In this procedure the subject is asked to state what his performance will be on some task on the next trial of the task. A simple illustration will indicate the procedure. Suppose a subject is asked to carry out a series of trials in throwing darts at a target. He may be asked to say, before any trials, how well he expects to perform in terms of markings on the target on the first trial. After completing the trial and seeing how well he performed, the subject is asked to state how well he expects to do on the next trial. Again he throws, sees the result, and indicates how he will do on the third trial, and so on. It is possible, perhaps, to alter his feelings of success and failure by ascribing certain levels of performance to groups with which he can compare himself, for example, athletes or nursery-school children. In certain tasks in which the subject cannot actually see how well or poorly his effort turns out, the experimenter can report on the performance, indicating success or failure (regardless of actual outcome) according to experimental requirements.

These procedures are not without difficulties. A serious problem is that the subject's prediction will vary as he is asked to state it in different ways. Diggory (1949), among others, found that the discrepancy between the subject's last performance and his aspiration level was about twice as great when he was asked to state what he "hoped" to do on the next trial as it was when he was asked what he "expected" to score on the next trial. It is clear that many subjects hope to do better than they expect, realistically, to do. The variability of actual performance on the task is important, too (Sutcliffe, 1955). Where there is little variability, the subject's goal can be realistically governed by knowledge of his probable performance; this is not the case when his performance varies widely from trial to trial. Ricciuti (1951) has stressed the many procedural variations characteristic of this area of experimentation, and Spitzer (1958) points out various problems in the methods used to run and score level of aspiration experiments.

A quite widely accepted generalization from experiments on level of aspiration is that successful performance leads to an increased level of aspiration and that unsuccessful performance (failure) leads to a reduced level of aspiration (Lewin et al., 1944; Child & Whiting, 1949). Knowledge (whether true or false) of what other groups have achieved or of what members of one's own group have achieved will also affect goal-setting (Lewin et al., 1944). Individual differences, sometimes related to past history of success and failure in other activities such as school, may be important determiners (Lewin et al., 1944; P. S. Sears, 1940, 1941; Escalona, 1948; Sumner & Johnson, 1949). Age differences may also be important (Sears & Levin, 1957). Regularity of success was associated with quicker development of expectation of failure when success stopped than it was for mixed success and failure within a series of mazes (Gilinsky & Stewart, 1949).[3] Yacorzynski (1942) measured the effort used on a task and the aspiration level. He found that as predictions of success decreased, effort tended to increase.

The literature in which the level of aspiration has been involved is extensive, and we do not attempt to encompass it all here (cf. Lewin et al., 1944; Spitzer, 1958). Rather, we turn now to theoretical analyses of the determinants of the level of aspiration and related processes. The complexity of the factors governing the setting of a goal is suggested by these analyses. We shall go beyond the level of aspiration situation as such, because a number of parallel situations have been analyzed in comparable ways (S. Siegel, 1957; Edwards, 1954; Feather, 1959).

One of the major findings is that the value of an incentive or the goal of performing a task at a given level appears to be modified by the subject's expectation of achieving it, that is, by his subjective estimate of the probability that he will attain it (for short, subjective probability). If one is throwing darts, he presumably wants or hopes always to hit the bull's-eye. If this is so, then the level of aspiration would always be to perform at the highest level the task permits. But subjects do not, typically, state their aspiration levels so highly or so consistently. Rather, their stated aspiration levels appear to be modulated by other factors, such as anticipated failure to achieve at a given aspiration level. The subject appears to strike a balance between the likelihood of success and the likelihood of failure in obtaining an incentive or achieving a given performance level.

Consider, for purposes of illustration, the dart-throwing situation. There is a target with a bull's-eye in the center and three concentric rings surrounding the center. Let us score a bull's-eye as 5, and scores of 4, 3, and 2 for a throw which hits within the respective consecutive rings, and a score of 1 for a throw which hits the target outside any of the rings. Most subjects would value most a score of 5 and least a score of 1. On the other hand, failure to achieve a 5 would not be particularly embarrassing, whereas failure even to hit the target would be. The value, then, of success at a score of 5 is much greater than that of any other score, but the negative value of failure at 5 is less than the negative value of failure at the other levels. On this basis the subject should always state his aspiration at 5. As he does not, it is a reasonable inference that the values of success and failure at any performance level are weighted (Lewin et al., 1944) by a subjective probability factor. The

---

[3] This outcome is similar to the findings for extinction following continuous and intermittent reinforcement (see Chapter 11).

value of a score of 5 is great but the subjective probability of achieving it is low. Similarly the negative value of failure at a score of one is high, but again (perhaps) the probability of failing at that level is low. Similar calculations applied to the other three levels of task performance would, in most cases, result in an announced aspiration level for an intermediate value of task performance, that is, scores 2, 3, or 4. This analysis follows the one presented by Lewin et al. (1944) (see, also, Cartwright & Festinger, 1943).

There are probably differences among situations in the ways in which various factors influence subjective probabilities, on the one hand, and incentive values on the other. In a performance situation such as dart-throwing, for example, telling adult subjects that school children easily make bull's-eyes may make the values of achieving at all other levels very low and the negative value of failure at all other levels very high. Such a situation could bring great pressure on the subject to aspire to a score of 5, despite low subjective probabilities for that score. On the other hand, the value of different amounts of monetary incentives may be more independent of the alleged performances of such reference groups, and, in this case, the subjective probability factor may enter more heavily. Evidently, then, the value of a given incentive may vary as a function of various group standards of which the subject is aware and as a function of personality factors which lead him to desire to achieve or perform well or poorly. His own history of achievement, both within the task and aside from it, may influence the subjective probability relevant to the aspiration level he will state or the incentive which will motivate him. Considerations such as these certainly imply that simple rules governing the use and effectiveness of incentives will not be forthcoming, and suggest, furthermore, that "cognitive" factors, that is, those which enter probability estimates, are involved, as well as affective (motivation) factors, in determining the effects of incentives on behavior.

A number of writers have developed notions very similar to those we have just described. They have been compared by Feather (1959). The writers are Rotter (1954), Tolman (1955), Edwards (1954, 1955), and Atkinson (1957). Their formulations vary in details from the one by Lewin et al. (1944) and from one another, but all of them emphasize the role of expectation or subjective probability. Rotter holds that the potential of occurrence for a given behavior is a function of both the expectancy that reinforcement will follow that behavior in a given situation and the value that the reinforcement has. Here reinforcement value and expectancy appear to be independent, whereas in Lewin's formulation they are inversely related. Tolman argues that performance of a behavior will depend (in the case of a rat in a food-reward situation) on the need for food, the value (or valence) of the anticipated food, and the expectancy that the food will be forthcoming as positive factors, and the work involved in making the response to get the food on the negative side. Atkinson uses six variables in dealing with the motivation for specific behaviors: the subjective probability (expectancy) of (1) success and (2) failure, (3) the positive incentive value of success, (4) the negative incentive value of failure, (5) the achievement motive, and (6) the motive to avoid failure. Edwards, working in the context of decision theory (Edwards, 1954, 1961; cf., also, S. Siegel, 1957), has argued that decisions must involve both utility (value of incentives) and subjective probability. He believes that choices are made by people to maximize subjectively expected utility; choice is considered to be a function of the factors of expectancy and utility, which are independent.[4]

In summary, there appear to be a number of variables which influence the effectiveness of incentives aside from incentive value itself; probability of success, probability of failure, and motive or need states must be considered. While the problem of incentives is an important one, it is likely that no simple motivational formulation—that is, one which ignores subjective probability, group standards, and past experience—can encompass all of the facets of this problem.[5]

SOCIAL FACTORS AND SOCIAL PROCESSES
Social Factors

Most of our considerations of motivation in this book deal with some state of the individual, thought to exist because of biological reasons or because an external situation (an incentive) can arouse it. The external situations treated so far have, for the most part, been nonsocial or, at least, not explicitly social. The behaviors associated with motivational states, also, have been discussed without particular concern with whether they were social or not.

In introducing the topic of incentives, we mentioned the influence on behavior of such factors as audiences, partners, rivalry, cooperation, and competition. They represent an attempt to explore directly the

---

[4] Irwin (1958) has argued that *preference* is a phenomenon uniquely definitive of motivation. While he has worked on decision processes, his experiments do not seem to us to involve clearly motivational variables.

[5] A further complication is brought out in studies of factors leading to job satisfaction (Herzberg et al., 1957, 1959). This is that there may be one set of factors which leads to positive job satisfaction and another set which, while not involved in positive satisfaction, may be sufficient to arouse job dissatisfaction.

influence of social factors on human performance and perhaps constitute initial studies in empirical and, especially, experimental social psychology. Cartwright and Zander (1960) refer to them as providing experimental techniques which, among other influences, fostered the development of group dynamics. We shall indicate briefly the character of this early work, leading from it into certain other aspects of social process.

The initial studies of social factors in relation to behavior were carried out in the context of a controversy over the concept of group mind (Cartwright & Zander, 1960, p. 18). This controversy concerned the issue of whether, in a group, there is or is not a factor or a process which transcends the particular individuals involved. An alternative to the group mind was to argue that the group's properties contain nothing not already present in the individual members of the group. While early work was carried out by A. Mayer in 1903 and by Meumann in 1904 (Sherif & Sherif, 1956, p. 126), the most influential investigations were done by F. H. Allport (1920, 1924). His research followed the lead of Moede (1920) and was an experimental comparison of behavior when the individual worked alone and when he worked in the company of others who were also carrying out the same tasks. An effort was made to minimize rivalry and competition among individuals in the latter situation, and there was no overt interaction among them. The effort was to create a situation of just being in the presence of others as opposed to being alone. Allport's subjects were engaged in such tasks as free chain associations, letter cancellation, reversible perspective, multiplication, reasoning tasks, and judgments of odors and weights. Allport found evidence of social facilitation in that at least some subjects on some tasks showed a quantitative increase in output under social conditions. He also found some disruptive effects, arising from distraction and excitement. Qualitatively, the reasoning products developed in the social situation were often not as good as those from the alone condition. Extremity of judgment was reduced in the social as compared with the individual situation. Allport interpreted his findings not as requiring a concept of group mind but invoked notions about the individual to explain his findings. A number of other experimenters continued Allport's work (e.g., Dashiell, 1930; cf. Dashiell, 1935), and conflicting results and individual differences suggest that factors in addition to the presence or absence of other people are involved.

Several early experiments were made on the effects of rivalry or competition (cf. Dashiell, 1935; Young, 1936; Sherif & Sherif, 1956). In general, the results indicate that putting children or college students in a competitive situation with others increases the quantity or speed but not necessarily the quality of their work. There are individual differences, too, some subjects responding well and others poorly to the competitive situation. Sims (1928), in addition, found that competition between two paired individuals was more productive of increased performance than was pitting two groups of subjects against each other; in the latter the individual's score became a part of the score of his group.[6]

A final type of social influence, investigated in early studies, was that of prestige suggestion—group and majority or expert opinion (cf. Dashiell, 1935; Sherif & Sherif, 1956). Various reactions, opinions, and judgments of subjects were shown, on the whole, to be susceptible of change in the direction of group, majority, or expert opinion.

Work of this sort has tended, since the 1930's, to merge into the general topics of group dynamics (or group processes and their effects), conformity, social pressure, and opinion change, and into the problem of ego-involvement. Some of the complications involved in the study of ego-involvement were brought out in the discussions of anxiety and achievement motivation; and we go into this problem again a little later.

Social Processes

There are many phenomena in the general domain of social psychology which have motivational features. Certain theories about motivation have arisen in the context of investigations of social processes. Group properties such as attractiveness, cohesiveness, communication patterns, leadership and other roles, and the effects of group standards undoubtedly are predicated in part upon motivational patterns of individuals, interact with them, and modulate their effects. Within the compass of a book such as this, it is impossible to treat the entire range of social phenomena from a motivational point of view or to review the various aspects of personality and its organization which are relevant (cf. Mann, 1959). Under the present topic, we have chosen two to discuss as illustrative: *conformity* and *needs created in social situations*. In the section following this one we look at motivational theories, such as *cognitive dissonance*, which, while not only socially relevant, have had their origins in the treatment of social behavior and behavior studied in social settings.

---

[6] Many experiments in this general area are summarized in tabular form by Murphy, Murphy, and Newcomb (1937, pp. 470–499). Cf., also, Kelley and Thibaut (1954) and Lorge et al. (1958).

Conformity

When one is a member of a group, there are a number of reasons that he will tend to change his way of acting, thinking, believing, or feeling in the direction of the norms of the group (Cartwright & Zander, 1960, pp. 165–188). The pressures of others are brought to bear on the individual, and frequency of interaction is a factor. As a group member, one must—if the group is to maintain itself, to achieve, and to provide at least some satisfaction for its members—forego some of his individuality. The fact of increased uniformity as a result of group membership is well established in many instances. The mechanisms of the development of uniformity are often unspecified or little understood.

A situation developed by Asch (1952, 1956) has received a good deal of attention in relation to group influences on judgment. (We consider Asch's situation here, recognizing that it had precursors in such experiments as those of Sherif [1935].) Asch constituted groups of subjects for the purpose of making perceptual judgments (e.g., to match the length of one line with one of three other lines). In some of the experiments, groups of as many as eight subjects were employed, all but one of them accomplices of the experimenter. The lone "real" subject, then, could be subjected to the influence of majorities of various sizes. Typically, the procedure was to ask each subject to announce his judgment publicly. The accomplices would make erroneous judgments, and the object of the experiment was to observe what the critical subject would do in the conflict between the evidence of his senses and the pressure to conform to what the rest of the group apparently saw. A number of subjects in this situation "yielded" to the majority and shifted their judgments from accurate ones to inaccurate-but-group-sanctioned ones. Others continued to give veridical judgments, being able, apparently, to maintain their "independence" despite the pressure of the majority. Many variations were made in this basic design by Asch and different outcomes were obtained. However, the major finding of concern to us here is the fact of individual differences. Can these differences be attributed to motivation?

Several experimenters have examined this question, and we describe three studies here. Moeller and Applezweig (1957) used a forced-choice questionnaire to select female college subjects with high motivation for either social- or self-approval. The inventory gives behavior samples together with four possible reasons for each behavior, which the subject orders according to likelihood as the reason for the behavior. Subjects were selected who were high in giving reasons related to social-approval but low in giving reasons related to self-approval; they were contrasted with subjects with the reverse pattern as well as with subjects who were high in both social- *and* self-approval patterns. An Asch-type of situation was then used with these subjects. It was found that the subjects high in social-approval yielded more often to the majority than the girls high on both needs. The latter worried about their nonconformity, whereas girls low in social-approval needs did not. One, then, can be aware of and be affected by group pressure (as in the high-high group) but not show conformity. Krebs (1958) studied male college students classified as to level of need achievement and scores on a self-report measure of independence training. A conformity situation involved memory for whether a given slide had been presented in one set or in another. The greatest conformity was found in subjects who were low in nAch and who also reported lateness of independence training. Samelson (1957, 1958), however, did not find any significant relations of conformity, in the situation he used, to nAchievement or nAffiliation, although there was a slight, negative relation between nAch and conformity. This finding is at least consistent with Krebs' report.

Much more experimentation will be required before we can understand the relations between individual motivation, perceptions of group pressures, the kinds of reactions group pressures arouse, and other aspects of group behavior. Furthermore, it may be that the social situation *creates* motives over and beyond those brought to the situation by the individual. To this problem, we now turn.

Do Social Situations Create Motives?

This question probably has a number of ways in which it can be answered, depending on definitions of terms and on the situations to which one refers. We shall discuss it in two contexts, the question of group goals, on the one hand, and the matter of motives or needs as a function of social situations, on the other. It could also be discussed in another way, that is, that the group situation creates no new motives but, instead, offers ways of achieving motive expression characteristic of the group setting. This alternative should be held in view during the ensuing discussion.

1. *Group goals.* We can argue that, if there is such a thing as a group goal, it is a composite of the goals of the individuals who constitute the group. Cartwright and Zander (1960, pp. 347–349) point out certain difficulties with this formulation. They prefer to speak of a goal as a property of a group, without worrying in much detail con-

cerning the origins and other aspects of such group goals. However, they do indicate that an important matter is the extent to which the group member accepts the group goal. This, they suggest (p. 357), is a function of the individual's motives, his judgment of the relative positive and negative weights for him of engaging in the activities necessary to achieve the group goal, and his subjective estimate of the probability that the group goal will be achieved. It is quite clear that the nature of group goals, their method of being set, the influences upon them, and their effects are all important. Also critical are such complex factors as the clarity of the group goal, the interdependence of the group members in achieving the goal, the cohesiveness of the group, and the degree of commitment and participation of the individuals so far as the group goal is concerned (Cartwright & Zander, 1960).

As an illustration, we may cite the experiment by Horwitz (1954), who was concerned with the question of whether group goals function the same as do individual goals. He set up a situation in which groups of girls each represented a sorority in a contest with groups from other sororities. The group's task was to instruct the experimenter as to moves to make in completing a series of jig-saw puzzles, and a certain degree of agreement had to be achieved for the experimenter to act. The subjects made choices independently as to what the next step was to be and did not know what each other member had decided. They continued to make choices until the stipulated level of agreement was reached, on any given trial. After a certain degree of progress had been achieved on each puzzle, the group voted on whether to continue working on it or to stop and go on to the next one. The votes for choices and for continuing or stopping were recorded, but, since the subjects did not know how the others had reacted, they did not actually determine either the placement of pieces or continuation or interruption of the task. The experimenter announced that a task was to be continued; that is, he said the group vote was to go on or not to go on with the task. The subjects recalled the names of the puzzles at the end of the series. As has been reported for individual subjects, the recall was better for the interrupted tasks than for the completed tasks. In addition, however, Horwitz found that an important factor in recall was the previous agreement of the individual with the group "decision." This information does suggest, then, that group goals and motives can be established and function in a manner similar to the way they work with individuals. It further indicates that there will be individual variations in the way and extent to which the group members will be affected by the group goal.

2. *Creation of motives by a social situation.* Horwitz (1956) has argued that at least some motives (his term is *needs*) are generated in social environments. He appears to conceive such motives as paralleling, for the social or psychological case, such physiological motives or drives as hunger and thirst. As a major illustration of this point of view, we consider Horwitz' discussion of aggression or hostility. This he views as a motive that arises from deficiencies relative to goal striving in the psychological environment.

The argument is predicated on the assumption that in a social situation individuals have a *weight* or *power* in decisions of a group that will affect the degree of need satisfaction they can obtain in the social context. To demonstrate that this power or weight is a critical factor in determining hostile or aggressive reactions under identical conditions of frustration, this experiment was carried out: Groups of students were given the task of learning how to make some objects under the guidance of a teacher. Prior to engaging in the task, the situation was so structured that, in one kind of group, control over how the instruction was to proceed was vested in the teacher but in other groups (to different degrees) it was vested in the group itself. In all groups, however, the teacher followed his own wishes so far as instructional procedures were concerned. Verbal aggression and unfavorable ratings of the personal characteristics of the teacher were largely absent in the group that had not been given any power over the procedures of instruction, but both increased with degree of pre-arranged power vested in the other groups. The point is that a social relation accounts for these differences, since the actual behavior of the teacher was the same in all instances. The expression of aggression here is associated with the loss of power, according to Horwitz, rather than with the frustration of desires to have the instructional procedures carried out in a certain way.[7] Horwitz reports a number of experiments which, he believes, show that the social situation is capable of creating motives. What the ultimate merits of this approach will be remains, however, to be established, since other interpretations may be possible. It is a plausible hypothesis that any change in rules might arouse aggression, aside from the factor of "power." Would a group given no authority over teaching procedures react with aggression if authority was turned over to them suddenly? It might, and if it did, this would, in Horwitz' terms, arise from an *increase* rather than from a decrease in power.

---

[7] The reader will recall similar discussions relative to the frustration-aggression hypothesis. "Threat" and "arbitrariness" were found necessary to aggression, not frustration alone (see Chapters 9 and 14).

Interruption, Ego-Involvement, Uncertainty, and Dissonance

There is a considerable tradition in the study of motivation that departs from the postulation of internal motive states or specific incentives. Horwitz, whose work we have just discussed, is partially representative, since he looks to the situation for the creation of motives rather than to the individual. Emphasis has also been placed on motivations induced by the tasks in which an individual is engaged, by success and failure as they are related to self (ego)-esteem, by uncertainty as to what to believe or think about events or oneself, and by the aftereffects of making a choice among alternatives. This section is devoted to reviewing this material.

The sophisticated reader will discern that the tradition under consideration has a familial relation to Gestalt psychology, more specifically to the extensions of Gestalt theory to problems of personality dynamics initiated by Kurt Lewin. Gestalt psychology is not usually treated in discussions of motivation, because it spoke very little of motive, drives, incentives, etc. Yet its conception of stresses and strains within an organism-environment field to the resolution of which behavior is devoted is a dynamic one (Heider, 1960). Certainly it influenced Lewin and, through him, many other investigators. Not all of what we consider in this connection is actually social motivation; but we consider it in this chapter, because it has been the social psychologists, to a large extent, who have been responsible for the development of concepts in this framework.

Interruption of Activity. In Chapter 7 we provided a brief account of the major features of Lewin's theoretical system. One of the central experimental problems of the early work carried out by Lewin and his students was the investigation of the persistence of an activity in an individual's behavior. It was postulated that acceptance of a task created a motivation (intention, quasi-need) to carry it through to completion. That this is true was demonstrated in several ways. One was by determining the extent to which activities, once interrupted, would be resumed if opportunity to do so was given; another procedure was to see if recall for incomplete activities would differ from that for completed activities. Still another procedure was to study whether substitute activities would affect the resumption of another activity interrupted before the substitute tasks were performed. Finally, study was made of whether the tension accompanying a task could be discharged by having the subject perform it over and over.

The first investigation was Zeigarnik's (1927) study of memory for completed and uncompleted tasks. She had her subjects carry out a series of tasks, half of which were carried to completion; in the other half performance was interrupted before task completion. In 26 of the 32 subjects (Zeigarnik, 1927, Table 1, p. 9), there was better retention for the names of the uncompleted tasks than for the completed tasks on a subsequent recall test. Presumably, the tension state corresponding to the task continued to a greater extent for the unfinished than for the completed task, thus causing better recall of the former. Later studies have verified these findings but have stressed that individual differences and the threat-value to the person of failure (uncompletion) are conditions under which these findings may not always hold. (We consider these points further in the next section.)

Ovsiankina (1928) interrupted the subject's task performance but a little later left him free in the situation where his unfinished work lay. She observed whether the subject would resume it. In a high proportion of instances, the subjects did in fact resume their interrupted work, though they had not been told to do so.

Karsten (1928) had her subjects repeat the same task again and again, although the subject was presumably free to stop when he had had enough. The subjects did show satiation but apparently tried to overcome it by various devices of variation in the task. They showed inattention and fatigue after a time. Karsten also demonstrated transfer of satiation from one task to a slightly different version of the tasks (co-satiation).

Lissner (1933) found that if other activities were provided following interruption they could, under some circumstances, satisfy the need to resume the interrupted activities. The successful substitute tasks, however, had to be similar both in character and in difficulty. Mahler (1933) found that the more real the substitute tasks were, as compared to talking or thinking, the greater the substitute value they had.

The experiments we have just summarized are representative of the early work, which suggests that a motive of some kind can be induced by the acceptance of a task and the initiation of work upon it. As in the case of recall for uncompleted tasks, later experiments have pointed to additional factors that may be involved. H. Nowlis (1941) found that praise or failure for the incomplete performances yielded reduced resumption of the tasks as compared to a neutral condition. Grosslight and Child (1947) found that subjects given repeated success over 10 trials gave up the task more quickly when reward was removed and engaged in more substitute activities than did subjects who had one or two failures intermixed with 8 or 9 successes in the first two trials.[8]

[8] This finding seems to parallel results for extinction following continuous or intermittent reinforcement.

Keister and Updegraff (1937) were able to increase the persistence and maturity of reactions by preschool children in performing a difficult task if they had previously trained the children on a series of tasks of progressively greater difficulty. Horwitz et al. (1953) found that group characteristics such as cohesiveness and agreement and feedback about performance were variables affecting rate of satiation for a task. Evidently, the processes involved in setting up motives by means of interrupting tasks or satiating motives by performing tasks are complex and numerous. Whether interruption sets up a motive irrespective of how the person "perceives" the situation is a problem deserving more study than it has had.

Ego-Involvement. The term "ego-involvement" is used to refer to circumstances in which attitudes relative to the person himself and his possessions, the people, groups, values, and institutions with which he is involved are engaged (Sherif & Cantril, 1947; Sherif & Sherif, 1956). A variety of experimental operations have been used in studies of ego-involvement (Iverson & Reuder, 1956), but they tend to focus on threats to the individual's identity, status, or importance; Iverson and Reuder suggest that in most of the experiments a situation is devised containing "the possibility of interference with or deprivation of the need to enhance or to maintain one's feeling of self-esteem" (p. 149). The chief operations employed have been as follows: (1) Involvement set up by instructions, that is, telling the subject he is taking an important intelligence or personality test,[9] or by providing that the subject "fail" in his performance on such a test or other task. (2) Providing material which will involve him in some way, as by using a story which disparages his sex, or by labeling the subject's products abnormal or as failures, or by using materials consonant or dissonant with his attitudes. (3) Classification of subjects as anxious or as having high or low self-esteem on the basis of ratings or questionnaires and then subjecting them to procedures of the first two types (Iverson & Reuder, 1956).

We have already seen the use of procedures such as these in our discussions of achievement, manifest anxiety, and test anxiety in the last chapter. Among the findings that are fairly stable in this area is the one that reactions to ego-involvement vary with intra-individual variables. People with high nAch and/or low anxiety tend to improve performance under such threats; the performance of high-anxious or low nAch subjects tends to be affected adversely. The bulk of the work on

[9] These procedures can work only in a culture which prizes intellectual capability and certain traits of personality. The procedures probably succeed best with persons from the middle-class in the United States, where they have been most widely used.

ego-involvement has been concerned with its effects on a variety of performances: on retention, perception, motor responses, problem-solving, preferences and judgment, set, and level of aspiration. The major findings in the area of retention may be briefly summarized (after Iverson & Reuder, 1956; Hall, 1961) as illustrative both of the problem of ego-involvement and of the difficulties in investigating it.

Retention and Ego-Involvement. Alper (1946) compared the learning and retention of nonsense syllables and digits when the learning task was presented as measuring intellectual ability (ego-involvement) and when it was not. There was no difference in learning scores, but the ego-involved subjects showed no loss in retention over 24 hours, whereas the control subjects did. Alper (1948a) found that ego-involvement was related to memory gains over a retention interval (reminiscence), gains not found in a task-oriented condition. Other, somewhat comparable studies have not verified Alper's results (Chansky, 1956; Russell, 1952). However, differences in procedures, tasks, and subjects may be responsible. Failure experiences (as opposed to ego-involvement alone) have had a detrimental effect on performance in a number of experiments. Representative are the experiments by Sears (1937), McClelland and Apicella (1947) and Zeller (1950b, 1951). Typically, adverse effects on retention of tasks learned first have been found after failure on a second task, and the adverse effects have persisted for as long as three days. In some experiments, later experiences of success have led to recovery of retention, as has hypnosis (Zeller, 1950b, 1951; Rosenthal, 1944). It is evident that these experiments have some relationship to the psychoanalytic mechanism of repression (Zeller, 1950a), as well as, perhaps, to the study of praise and reproof outlined in an earlier section.

In a number of experiments the problem of selective recall has been investigated. T. S. Kendler (1949) found better recall for puzzles on which her subjects had had "success" than for those on which they had "failed," despite their having worked longer on the latter puzzles. A number of experiments have found that recall is superior for material that agreed with a subject's attitudes, values, or beliefs, for material favorable to his sex or color, for material produced by the subject such as associations, and for story titles labeled normal rather than abnormal, etc. For example, Edwards (1941) presented to pro- and anti-New Deal subjects a speech composed half of pro- and half of anti-New Deal statements. Each kind of subject remembered better the statements consistent with his attitudes. However, in this, as in the many other experiments on this problem, it has been difficult to equate knowledge of and familiarity with the subject matter which is and is not consistent with the subject's attitude. In direct recall and selective recall, there are other studies that did not obtain such clear differences as those we have mentioned. This is a difficult area in which to work and to make comparisons among investigations. Differences in tasks, subjects, and the effectiveness of ego-involvement procedures are among the factors which may account for variability in findings.

One result which appears to have some generality is the fact that after failure there is often better memory for completed than for uncompleted tasks (Rosenzweig, 1943; Rosenzweig & Mason, 1934; cf. Glixman, 1948, 1949). This is especially true in subjects who are threatened by failure (Atkinson, 1953; Eriksen, 1954). Evidently the threat, in some people, motivates retention of what they have done well (completed). In others, however, it apparently acts as a challenge so that they recall what they have not finished.

We should point out that ego-involvement procedures are by no means simple or clear in a conceptual sense. One could interpret their effects as being that of arousal or activation or as instigating some more specific motive, such as anxiety or fear of failure or hope of success. On the other hand, one might interpret them as cueing off reactions to threatened failure; in some subjects such habits might be incompatible with and in others might be compatible with effective performance of the particular task involved. These possibilities are discussed later in this chapter.

In conclusion, we reiterate that the procedures of ego-involvement are probably heterogeneous. They depend for effectiveness on their plausibility; that is, they must be taken seriously by the subject. (Checks on the effectiveness of the manipulation should be made.) In addition, there are individual differences in response even to effective manipulations. Finally, tasks on which the effects of the procedures are to be studied may vary in what they require of the subject and in the relations that the responses they involve have to the effects of ego-involvement.

Uncertainty. In 1950, Festinger pointed out that it is often necessary, if a group is to achieve a goal, that there be uniformity in certain respects among the group members. This point was made in the context of factors leading to communication, and it was suggested that communication among group members might arise when discrepancies in matters of opinion, attitude, or belief were present. Such communication might foster opinion or attitude change in some members of the group, thus increasing uniformity. However, if communication decreased uniformity, the group might be fractionated. A number of factors were suggested of which the tendency to communicate in the presence of discrepant opinions, attitudes, and beliefs would be a function. Among them were the amount of the discrepancy, the importance or relevance of the disagreement to group functioning, the cohesiveness of the group, the status of the individual group member and his "influenceability," etc. Festinger (1950) pointed out that the importance of communication would be enhanced when there was no objective or physical standard against which to judge the validities of opinions, attitudes, or beliefs. If a clear physical criterion exists, as would be the case in the comparison of lengths of objects by means of a meter stick, communication would not be so necessary as it would be in the case of an attitude or belief about some social issue, where the facts are ambiguous or difficult to ascertain. Implicit is a desire on the part of the individual to have his judgments validated by external criteria.

Festinger later (1954*a*, *b*) spoke of a "drive for self-evaluation," or of a desire "to know that one's opinions are correct and to know precisely what one is and is not capable of doing" (1954*b*, p. 217). This motivation is perhaps an instance of a general motive to know the environment, and in many instances it would require social behavior for its resolution. Social behavior, under this motivation, would arise, as suggested, when no direct or simple test can be used to obtain the required information from the environment directly. When direct testing of the environment cannot be carried out, ". . . the person 'tests himself' against, or more specifically, compares himself with other persons" (Festinger, 1954*b*, p. 195). If others agree with one's opinion, then one may feel that it is correct. If they disagree, one may not be so sure. Of course, the significance of the social comparison depends on who the others are and what the importance of the issue is. Abilities, as well as opinions, attitudes, and belief, would be tested in a similar way, and we can generalize by saying that uncertainty about one's characteristics may lead to communication and affiliation, when data cannot be obtained from nonsocial sources.[10]

Experiments have been performed to determine whether this formulation is a sound one. We describe one as an illustration.

[10] Festinger, as the course of our discussion suggests, seems to shift from a formulation rooted in the problem of communication in the interest of group functioning to a formulation that postulates a need to know the environment, a motive which *individuals* have. As he discusses this motive, it appears as an autonomous one. One could, however, argue that such a "motive" is acquired through many experiences in which accurate reporting of the environment is reinforced and inaccurate reporting is punished (cf. Dollard & Miller, 1950). Such reporting could be an instrumental response, then, rather than a motive, and it may be anxiety-avoidance which is the motive underlying the desire to

Festinger, Gerard, and others (1952) had subjects indicate their opinion on some issue and then, later, state their confidence in their expressed opinions. Prior to this expression of confidence, a fictitious census of the opinions of the group on the issue was made known to each subject. For some, the group consensus agreed with them; for others it did not. For those who thought the group agreed with them, confidence in their opinions was high, whereas confidence was low for those who thought the group did not agree. Comparison with the (fictitious) group consensus, then, affected confidence of judgment. It is reasonable to expect, further, that vulnerability to opinion change might be high in those with little confidence.[10]

Conditions Related to Dissonance. A development in motivational theory, which began to reach major status in the 1950's, involves the notion that *discrepancy* is an important condition relevant to motivation. The discrepancy may lie in the relation of expectation to outcome, in the relation of one piece of knowledge to another, in one's evaluation of an object relative to another's evaluation of an object, between what one says and what one does, etc. We have already encountered the concept of discrepancy in views previously discussed, for example, those of McClelland, Hebb, and Peak. Especially in social psychology, however, the general notion of discrepancy as a condition for motivation seems to have had a wide appeal.

Much of the work on discrepancy (balance-theory, principle of congruence, etc.) has been concerned with problems of attitude and opinion change and interpersonal perception. Among the writers involved have been Heider (1946, 1958, 1960), Newcomb (1953a, b, 1959), Osgood (Osgood & Tannenbaum, 1955; Osgood, Suci, & Tannenbaum, 1957; Osgood, 1957, 1960), Abelson and Rosenberg (1958), Cartwright and Harary (1956), and Jordan (1953). We cannot treat the views of all these writers and their research within the confines of our present space. We will instead describe one discrepancy theory which has received considerable attention, namely, Festinger's theory of cognitive

know the environment so that accurate reports can be made. (People are often shamed for seeing things differently from the ways others see them.)

It is also important to consider that the situation may be perceived not as requiring agreement but rather as necessitating disagreement. One may not trust group judgments or he may see disagreement as advantageous. Under such circumstances the group would not exert pressure to uniformity. In the experiment by Festinger, Gerard et al. (1952), the results might have been different had a confidence rating been expressed prior to the making known of the group census. Perhaps commitment or "face-saving" would operate to maintain the "confidence" of the group members in their judgments, whatever the outcome of the group census.

dissonance (1957, 1958, 1961). We selected this formulation because it is explicitly motivational, it has high generality (and may encompass much of the other views just listed), and because a great deal of research has been generated by it in its brief career. Brehm and Cohen (1962) have brought the research together that has been concerned with dissonance and have evaluated and extended the theory and compared it to other models.

Festinger (1957) has postulated that cognitive dissonance is or gives rise to a tension state, which is motivational in character. "Just as hunger is motivating, cognitive dissonance is motivating. Cognitive dissonance will give rise to activity oriented to reducing or eliminating the dissonance. Successful reduction of dissonance is rewarding in the same sense that eating when one is hungry is rewarding" (Festinger, 1958, p. 70). But what is cognitive dissonance? To answer this question, we must first say that there are cognitive elements or pieces of information or bits of knowledge that may be related to oneself, to others, or to the nonsocial environment. Further, we must add that these elements exist or may exist in relation to one another. The chief relations of importance are consonance or dissonance. With elements that are consonant, there is no disparity, there is no inconsistency; no tension arises because having one element is compatible with having the other. Or, we could say, one element psychologically implies the other, or one leads to the other. If you are a good golfer and on a given day your golf score is a good one, these two elements are consonant; one implies the other.

But elements may be dissonant. Being a good golfer does not imply or lead to a round of golf in which you do not break 100. This is the obverse of what being a good golfer implies.[11] Dissonance arises when, in the presence of one element, the obverse of that element is also present or implied. And having such dissonant elements is to have motivational tension. In our example, one might find excuses for his poor round, take a lesson, or perhaps engage in additional practice; these would be behaviors activated by the dissonance and directed to resolving it. It is even possible that, with repeated poor performance, one would change his evaluation of his skill; or perhaps reformulate his opinion to assert that he is a good golfer who has a lot of bad days!

Some cognitions are irrelevant to one another, and neither dissonance nor consonance would arise concerning them. Thus a poor round of golf presumably has nothing to do with one's proficiency as a scientist. One's knowledges in this case are not relevant to one another and there-

[11] It is obvious that different frames of reference would lead to differing definitions of what a good golfer would be.

fore neither consonant nor dissonant.

The amount of dissonance generated is a function of other conditions. One is the importance of the elements. An individual may experience little dissonance in the presence of a poor golf score if being a good golfer has little importance to him. A second factor is the ratio of dissonant to consonant cognitions, with each element weighted as to its importance. A single poor round in a season of golf would not be very dissonant to the notion of being a good golfer; if half the rounds of a season were poor, the dissonance would be much greater. In addition, elements may differ in their resistance to change. Thus, cognition may be that one is a good athlete. Elements incompatible with this cognition might produce much greater dissonance than they would with being a good golfer alone. The more general cognition then might be more resistant to change than the more specific one about golf.

It is worth mentioning here that Festinger's analysis has many parallels in other formulations. Already mentioned is the point that, in the treatments of McClelland, Peak, and Hebb, *discrepancy* from a prevailing adaptation level figures as the important condition to motivation. *Discrepancy* is surely similar to *dissonance*. Furthermore, the example we have just given concerning one's cognition of being a good golfer or a good athlete implicates notions of self-concept or image and of self-consistency. These have parallels in Lecky's formulations (see Chapter 7) and in other theories of the self. It is obvious that the resolution of dissonance reduces tension or, put another way, restores equilibrium or balance, a homeostatic-like conception.

Festinger's analysis was applied primarily to post-decisional situations.[12] If one has already made a choice between two makes of automobile, he is post-decisional. However, the bad features of the car he has chosen and the good features of the one he has rejected still exist, and their existence creates dissonance: the bad features with the knowledge that one car was chosen, the good features with the fact that one was rejected. (There will, of course, be other features of the two cars consonant with their acceptance and rejection.) According to Festinger's analysis, one would then be motivated to reduce the dissonance by maximizing elements that would be consistent with the facts of the decision. One might read new car advertisements for the make he has selected and seek out someone who, he has heard, has had trouble with the model he rejected.[13] Brehm and Cohen (1962, Chap. 13) have pointed out, in their discussion of dissonance theory and conflict theory,

---

[12] But see Festinger (1961); also see Brehm and Cohen (1962, Chap. 13).

[13] There is much in this example that resembles the mechanism of *rationalization*. Festinger, however, does not employ this term.

that restriction to post-decisional events may not be a necessary feature of the dissonance formulation. However, much of the research stimulated by Festinger's theory has pertained to such post-decisional phenomena.

Brehm and Cohen (1962) have emphasized the role of *commitment* to a behavior, attitude, or opinion in generating dissonance and in mediating deductions from the general theory that are not obvious. If one *agrees*, that is, commits himself to listen to a disagreeable political exposition by someone he does not like, the prediction, on the basis of dissonance and commitment, is that liking for the expositor will increase. (Presumably, he does not change his political views.) Working out this derivation will permit the reader to test his understanding of dissonance theory and the role of commitment. It should be added that in committing himself to listen to the discrepant political views, the auditor presumably *chose* to do so. Brehm and Cohen (1962) emphasize that, in their view and in terms of a good deal of evidence, commitment to behavior which is discrepant is essential to dissonance arousal. Further the degree of freedom which the subject thinks he has in choosing to engage in the discrepant behavior determines the magnitude of the dissonance aroused. Commitment and choice appear to involve extensions of Festinger's theory and would interact with the other factors in dissonance arousal and its magnitude, which we have already mentioned.

Evidence. Brehm and Cohen (1962) review nearly fifty experiments and other papers concerning the theory of cognitive dissonance. We cannot encompass all of this material here, but we will indicate in summary form the major findings concerning the arousal of dissonance and the consequences of dissonance arousal. We will also summarize several experiments in more detail, so as to indicate, especially in relation to other motivational states, the kind of experiment dissonance theory tends to foster.

According to Brehm and Cohen's (1962, pp. 302–309) summary, the amount of dissonance arousal increases under the following conditions (each statement is supported by from one to seven experiments):

1. The more attractive the rejected alternative when the person chooses between attractive alternatives.
2. The more negative the characteristics of the chosen alternative when the person chooses between two courses of action.
3. The greater the number of rejected alternatives when the person chooses between attractive alternatives.
4. The less the cognitive overlap between attractive alternatives.

5. The more recent the decision to choose between attractive alternatives.
6. The more important the relative cognitions surrounding a decision.
7. The less the amount of positive inducement for commitment to discrepant behavior, that is, (*a*) the smaller the financial incentives or prizes for commitment . . . (*b*) the less the justification for commitment . . . (*c*) the more negative the characteristics of the inducing agent.
8. The greater the choice in commitment to discrepant behavior.
9. The less the coercion applied in order to induce discrepant commitment.
10. The less the person's ability or self-esteem would lead him to perform a discrepant act.
11. The more the person has to engage in the negative behavior (i.e., the more discrepant behavior to which he is committed).
12. The more negative information the person has about the discrepant situation to which he is committed.

The modes of dissonance reduction that have been measured are summarized by Brehm and Cohen as follows: changes in opinions in relation to a number of issues; changes in evaluations of people, groups, objects, foods, etc.; selective exposure to information; selective recall; perceptual distortion; and such behavioral changes as ordering things to eat, amount of water drunk, job productivity, modifications in performance so as to produce failure, and conforming to a group-norm.

Some Illustrative Experiments. We have chosen five experiments as illustrative. The first two were selected because the derivations from dissonance theory are not entirely obvious. The remaining three were chosen because they deal with drives.

1. *Dull motor tasks.* Festinger and Carlsmith (1959) signed up subjects for a two-hour experiment, and when each subject arrived he was asked to perform two dull, repetitive motor tasks; in one he packed spools into a frame, emptied it when it was full, and then repeated the process. In the other, he turned pegs a quarter turn, then another quarter turn, and so on. Each task took a half-hour. After this time had elapsed, the subject was told that he was serving in an experiment concerned with the effects of set on performance. He had been in a no-set condition, but the other condition involved establishing a set that the tasks were interesting, fun, and enjoyable. This latter set, he was told, was induced by an employee who posed as a subject who had just completed the experiment. Both experimental and control subjects were

treated alike to this point.

For the experimental subject, the procedure then went as follows. He was told that the employee who ordinarily induced the set that the tasks were interesting was not present that day. The next subject due was supposed to receive the set treatment, and the experimenter requested the subject who had just completed the motor tasks to act as a substitute. It was implied that he might be asked again to do so at a later time. Further, the subject was offered either $1.00 or $20.00 to perform this role, and, if he agreed, he was paid at once.

After agreement, the experimental subject was introduced to the next "subject" (actually an employee), was left alone with her, and proceeded to induce the set that the tasks to come were enjoyable and interesting (this interaction was tape-recorded). Following this, the experimental subject was thanked and told that the experiment was over. However, before he left, he was asked to see someone else who was making a survey of how students felt about participating in experiments. (The fact of this survey had been announced in class some time before.) In this interview (which the control subjects were also given) the major purpose was to get a rating of how interesting the motor tasks had been.

The control subjects had performed the tasks but had not participated in the rest of these events. Their ratings, therefore, provide a base against which to compare the ratings of the two sets of experimental subjects—those receiving $1.00 and those receiving $20.00 for presumably acting as a substitute experimenter. It was found that the control subjects rated the tasks on the negative side of a scale for enjoyability. The $20 subjects rated them only slightly more enjoyable than did the control. The $1 subjects, however, rated the tasks at almost +1.5 for enjoyability (maximum possible was +5.0), significantly higher than the ratings by the controls or the $20 subjects.

The dissonance theory interpretation of this finding is as follows. The experimental subjects all had a cognition that the motor tasks were dull and that they had told someone else the tasks were fun. Thus, there was dissonance in all. For the $20 subjects, however, the dissonance is not so great as for the $1 subjects, because the fact of a $20 payment presumably justifies their deception. One dollar, however, is not enough to justify the deception. So the $1 subjects had more dissonance and resolved it by evaluating the tasks as fairly interesting. (Evaluations of the actual statements made in inducing the set by the two sets of experimental subjects showed no reliable difference.)

2. *Sex discussion.* Aronson and Mills (1959) recruited college girls to participate in a discussion group on the psychology of sex. When

the subject arrived, she was told that the group was not a face-to-face group but rather that the discussion was carried on by means of ear-phones and microphones. This was to reduce the embarrassment that a face-to-face discussion would create. It was explained to the subjects that before admitting them to the group a screening procedure was used, in order to pick participants who would not be overly embar-rassed by the topics. The male experimenter then proceeded to ad-minister one of two kinds of "screening" procedures (no such screen-ing was given a control group). One procedure was designed to be very embarrassing; the subject read aloud (in the presence of the male experimenter) obscene words and two vivid descriptions of sexual activity. In the other procedure (mild) the subject read five words related to sex but which were not obscene. The subject was told that her reactions to these procedures would be observed and her accept-ance as a group member would depend on the clinical evaluation of her reactions. In fact, all subjects were told they were acceptable.

The subject was then permitted to listen to the "on-going discussion" of the group she was to join but, on reasonable pretexts, was enjoined from saying anything in this first session. The discussion was actually taped and was designed to be dull and uninteresting. After the "discus-sion" was over, each subject gave an evaluation of it. The major find-ing was that the ratings made by the severely embarrassed subjects (in the screening procedure) were significantly different from both the control ratings and the ratings of the subjects who had had a mild screening (the latter two groups did not differ). The direction of the difference was that the group with severe screening gave much more favorable reactions to the group and the discussion than was the case with the other two groups.

Again, the person after severe screening had a cognition of the em-barrassment of the screening procedure and of the dullness of the dis-cussion. Thus dissonance was created, and it was resolved by enhancing the valuation of the group and the discussion. The other two groups (control and mild screening) had the cognition of a dull discussion but had either no cognition of embarrassment or one of very mild embar-rassment. There was, thus, little or no dissonance in these groups.

3. *Hunger.* In an experiment by Brehm and Crocker (Brehm & Cohen, 1962, Chap. 8) subjects were asked to go without breakfast or lunch and to report to the laboratory in the afternoon. When the sub-ject arrived, his attention was called to sandwiches, milk, and cookies, which were in sight. He then rated his degree of hunger and took motor and intellectual tests for 15 minutes. After this, the dissonance manipulation (high or low) was introduced.

In this manipulation, the subject was told that he was one of the subjects from whom, if they were willing, an additional period of hunger and more testing in the evening would be asked. (The subjects had previously been asked to keep the evening free.) Food was promised at the end of the evening session. In the high dissonance condition, no tangible inducement was given the subject for extending his participation in the experiment. In the low dissonance condition, a $5.00 payment was offered for further participation. In each condition, the subject chose whether or not to continue, and most of them did so.

Immediately after this treatment, the subject re-rated his hunger and was asked to order the number of sandwiches, cookies, and cartons of milk he would desire after the evening session. In fact, this ended the experiment.

The high dissonance subjects rated themselves less hungry and ordered fewer of the food items for the later meal than did the low dissonance subjects. Presumably, the differences in dissonance forced differential evaluations of common deprivation intervals. Because of some methodological problems in this experiment, it was repeated using thirst as the drive.

4. *Thirst.* Brehm (Brehm & Cohen, 1962, Chap. 8) asked his subjects to drink no liquids from bedtime to the next afternoon, at which time they reported to the laboratory. On arrival, the subject rated his degree of thirst. After performing several tasks, the experimental subjects were induced to go without liquids for approximately another 24 hours. (Control subjects did not receive this treatment.) In the inducement, either $5 or $1 was offered to induce low and high dissonance, respectively. Two further tasks were performed and degree of thirst was again rated. The subject was then told that he could drink —the last time he could do so until the next afternoon. He was permitted to drink and the amount drunk was recorded. This ended the experiment.

The results for males, in whom there is evidence that the manipulations were successful (they were not for females), show that the high-dissonance condition ($1.00 payment) is associated with a decline in rated thirst from the first to second rating; this is not true of the low-dissonance condition. In addition, the high-dissonance subjects actually drank less water than the low-dissonance subjects, a finding consistent with the ratings of thirst though it did not reach statistical significance.

There are some problems of interpretation of the results of this experiment, as the controls also showed a decline in rated thirst. However, in the two experiments on thirst and hunger, the findings concerning rated hunger and thirst, amount of food ordered, and amount of water drunk do differentiate the high-dissonance from the low-dissonance subjects. In these measures, the high-dissonance subjects behave as if they were less hungry or thirsty than the low-dissonance subjects. Presumably, the drive state was undervalued in order to reduce the dissonance between the drive condition and the fact of further commitment to deprivation, in the presence of an inadequate incentive for doing so. As Brehm and Cohen (1962) point out, this suggests that drive states are subject to cognitive valuation arising from dissonance. Our discussion of hunger and thirst in Chapter 5, of course, has already indicated that consummatory behavior is subject to the influence of a number of variables, in addition to deprivation.

5. *Avoidance motivation.* In an experiment by Cohen and Zimbardo (Brehm & Cohen, 1962, Chap. 8) the subject's motivation to do well was aroused by suitable comments concerning the task he was to perform. Then he was asked to read aloud and to memorize a poem, after which he recited the poem from memory and discussed its psychological implications. His recitation and discussion were made under conditions of delayed auditory feedback (DAF); the DAF experience lasted about five minutes. DAF is a stress condition, and it is difficult to speak and think well or coherently during it.

The dissonance manipulation involved getting the subject to agree to return for a 50-minute DAF session; all subjects were to be paid $2.00 for this further participation. High dissonance was created by telling the subject that he would perform very poorly in the 50 minute session, low dissonance by telling him that he would do just about average. In addition to several questionnaires and rating scales, the subjects were given two further choices. One was that instead of a second session under DAF they could participate (for the $2.00) by scoring some GSR records the experimenters had. Before this, however, they were shown the dial setting for the DAF session they had just completed. It was set very high at this point, and it was explained to the subject that the difficulty of the DAF situation is a function of how high the setting is. Then they were asked to set the dial at the level at which they would like to begin the 50-minute session and were told that the dial would remain at this setting for half of the next session.

The major results of the experiment were as follows. Nine of the ten low-dissonance subjects decreased the dial setting for the 50-minute session, thus providing an easier task for themselves. Only two of the high-dissonance subjects reduced the dial setting, and the rest kept it at about the level they had presumably already experienced. The mean changes for the Highs is +.03, for the Lows −3.42, a significant difference. None of the high-dissonance subjects expressed a desire to change tasks, whereas four of the ten low-dissonance subjects preferred to change. When asked to recall advantages and disadvantages of research with DAF, as expressed in an exposition the subject read, the Highs tended to recall fewer disadvantages than the Lows and more advantages than the Lows. The high-dissonance subjects also tended to rate their success motivation lower than the Lows and to feel more coerced to continue in the experiment than the Lows.

In general, the dissonance interpretation of these various differences is that having committed themselves to more failure, the high-dissonance subjects reduce their avoidance of failure to a greater extent than the low-dissonance subjects. This is evidenced by their setting the dial at a level where failure is likely, by sticking to the DAF task, by reducing success aspiration, and by the feeling of coercion.

These last three experiments are interpreted by Brehm and Cohen as showing that dissonance can affect other motivations. They feel that cognitive factors may be quite important to motivation, especially in relation to consummatory behavior and in the effects of motivation on various psychological processes.

Comment. In its short life-span, dissonance theory has generated a good deal of research and has been plausibly applied to the results of experiments already reported in the literature. Nevertheless, there are a number of questions which can be raised concerning it and about the evidence taken to be supportive of the theory.

One problem is that, so far, the manipulation of dissonance has been achieved almost entirely through elaborate instructional procedures which deceive the subject as to what is being done. Critical is whether these procedures "take," that is, whether the subject believes in and is influenced by them. Measures of commitment and freedom of choice have been used, chiefly by means of rating scales. We review problems of arousal and measurement later in this chapter, and the comments made there apply to the dissonance experiments. The definition of cognitive elements, their measurement and the assessment of degrees of disparity among them are factors critical to the further development of the dissonance formulation.

We have already said that there seem to be parallels in dissonance formulations to other theories which emphasize discrepancy, self-consistency and homeostasis. We can add that conflict theory (Chapter 9) also offers parallels. Much more needs to be done than has been done so far to determine whether the dissonance formulation leads to deductions not possible on the basis of other viewpoints. It is also worth noting that ego-involvement as well as anxiety, achievement, level of aspiration, and other topics treated in this and the preceding chapter involve operations similar in many respects to those used in experiments on dissonance. Dissonance theory (and its research) needs more anchoring in the concepts and methods of prior work than it has had to date.

PROBLEMS OF AROUSAL AND MEASUREMENT

The classical operation for establishing a motivational or drive state is deprivation. There are problems of interpretation with the consequences of this procedure, as we have suggested in Chapter 5. Nevertheless, what one is to do when he wishes to utilize deprivation is clear. With rare exceptions, deprivation has not been employed in studies of human motivation, although human motive states are commonly conceived as deprivation states. There are typically two broad classes of methods by which human individuals are classified as to motivational status. One is by means of a psychometric procedure—an anxiety scale, a thematic apperception test, a questionnaire or inventory, a self-rating procedure, or ratings by others. The questions and scales used characteristically are selected to get at motivational factors by means of expert judgment or by the criterion that they discriminate groups which ought to differ in the motivational characteristic involved. Sometimes the items are selected because under arousal conditions responses to them have changed appropriately.

The second kind of method employs arousal conditions to establish the motivated state. Threats of shock, embarrassment, stress, failure, and all the procedures referred to as ego-involving figure here, as would the manipulations of the experimenter in creating dissonance. Sometimes a procedure is used to assess the effectiveness of the arousal manipulation; when such procedures are employed they are usually rating scales.

It is not uncommon that both kinds of procedures are combined: the effects of arousal are studied in people classified as to motivational status by some psychometric procedure, or a psychometric procedure is used to assess the effect of the arousal operations.

Whether psychometric classification or an arousal procedure be used, the motivational effects are typically evaluated through some performances—learning, perception, memory, group behavior, physiological measures, etc. Some expectation as to how the motivation state *ought* to affect such behaviors is usually entertained, although the rationale for such expectations is often cloudy.

There are three problems here, and we take them in the following order: arousal, measurement, and the relation of the task to the motive state aroused or measured.

Arousal

We have already said, in discussing ego-involvement, that the arousal manipulation can be problematic. Typically, it is verbal, and it depends for its success on the credulity of the subjects and the effectiveness of the operators who try to induce arousal. An unconvincing speech may well arouse the subjects not at all. Some subjects may be taken in, others not. Some experimenters use many props and prepare their arousal operations carefully. Others do not. It is no wonder that experiments in which the "same" arousal operation has been employed often do not yield the same findings.

The important theoretical question, however, is what do arousal operations arouse? A second question is, if they arouse anything do they arouse the same thing or the same thing in the same degree in all subjects?

The first question is intimately related to the conceptual status of motivation. For many, arousal induces an emotional state, which has motivational properties. But the operations of arousal may have many cue values which can elicit habits as well as, or perhaps instead of, an emotional state. Are these habits motivational ones? What is the character of the habits: instrumental acts, goal expectancies? The answer to these questions lies in part in theory, that is, what are the hallmarks of a motivational state? In part, the answer is empirical: Are there evidences of emotional states as a consequence of arousal? Are the evidences physiological? verbal? instrumental acts (verbal or nonverbal)? expectations? On the basis of what we now know we cannot answer these questions generally, but work such as that being carried on by Mandler (see p. 714) is important to getting answers. We have a bias in favor of the notion that if arousal generates a motivational state there ought to be correlative evidence from physiological indices. But it is possible that physiological responses may be short-circuited in the adult subject, even though they may have been present at an earlier age.

Another important avenue to the investigation of responses to arousal is their history. How were they learned? Under what circumstances? Under what reinforcements?

It is clear from the literature that a given arousal condition will elicit varying reactions from different people, even when all of them are taken in. We have seen differential reactions to achievement arousal in the notions of success motivation and fear of failure, in differential effects of threat in highly anxious as opposed to nonanxious subjects, in first born and only children and in the later born, etc. The careful experimenter must provide ways of identifying these kinds of individual differences in reactions to his inductions and not lump all his subjects into one group unless these differences are taken account of. Perhaps this kind of difference points, as strongly as anything, to the role of learning in the responses to arousal. Constitutional differences could be involved, however. Historical research seems again to be indicated to bring out the developmental factors and experiences important to the varying reactions to arousal.[14]

Measurement

There are two cases here. One is estimates made by the subject or by an external observer of motivational status in the absence of arousal. The other is estimates made, again by the subject or by external observers, of motivation induced by an arousal manipulation.

Absence of Arousal. Perhaps the majority of motivational measurements are made under these conditions. The subject responds to questions about his past reactions (e.g., somatic symptoms), takes a projective test, rates or answers questions about his goals, wishes, desires, expectations, preferences, interests, values, sentiments, attitudes, etc., is rated after an interview or other observational situation, or performs some task such as level of aspiration. While the situation may provide some sort of arousal, it is not specific, planned, or controlled. The items, rating scales, observations, or tasks used may be justified because of face validity (e.g., symptoms of physiological reactivity), differences between groups believed to differ in a motive (e.g., anxious persons vs. nonanxious persons), the fact that goals, preferences, or aspirations are called for, because theoretical considerations are vaguely relevant (as in the classification of water responses as implying oral motives in projective tests), or because the items involved have differentiated aroused groups from nonaroused groups in the past (e.g., the McClelland system for scoring nAch).

Under conditions of no arousal, the subject must respond in these situations in terms of the stimuli which they provide. Presumably, these stimuli elicit responses according to their relative strengths, but these strengths could represent habitual ways of responding rather than motivational factors (cf. Buss, 1961; Farber, 1954, 1955). It would appear that a number of factors (each in itself of different strength) may be involved in these responses (McClelland, 1958*b*), such as traits, neuroticism, situational expectations (Rotter, 1960), response biases, and many others. It seems unlikely that scores based on such procedures

---

[14] Relevant evidence may be found in such sources as Wenger (1948), Terry (1953), Ax (1953), Block (1957), Davis (1957), Lacey and Lacey (1958).

are pure measures of motivation if, indeed, they measure motivation at all.

One might argue that the fact that the subject chooses this rather than that (Irwin, 1958) or responds in one way rather than another indicates that motivation is being measured, at least indirectly. This would follow if one conceives motivation mainly as a regulator of directionality. (However, it is recognized that habits also direct.) Or, one could suggest, a past history of reinforcement has dictated the choice of which behavior will appear, and reinforcement depends on motivation. These ideas may, of course, be true. But two points are in order. One is that if reinforcement has strengthened a preference or a behavior so that it is now selected, this is tantamount to saying that habit is governing the selection. To call this motivation would be to regard certain habits as motivational. The other point is that while past reinforcement may have strengthened the current choice or the current behavior, it is not necessarily true that the motive involved in the past reinforcement is the same one that the choice or the behavior is now taken to indicate. We saw, for example, in the discussion of aggression, how aggressive behavior might be rewarded and thus strengthened because it secured other goals. Thus the subject could be behaving aggressively but not be motivated aggressively; aggression in such a case could be a habit of wide generality, learned originally on the basis of rewards for such motives as hunger, sex, achievement, affiliation, or what not.

Measures under conditions of non-arousal, then, have serious limitations as measures of motivation. We do not know whether what is measured is a motive, a habit, or some combination of both.

Presence of Arousal. But what of the case when an arousal operation has been conducted, and the subject answers questions, rates his feelings, tells stories, expresses an aspiration, or is rated or otherwise assessed by others? The questions, rating scales, and the like, will be relatively specific to the specific manipulations, whereas in nonarousal conditions they will refer to situations more generally.

Here, we also have cues. The cues arise in the situation and from the aroused state, if it occurs. Perhaps the situational cues alone can produce the behavior "indicative" of the motive. These cues can, as in the nonarousal case, elicit habitual ways of responding. So can cues arising from actual arousal. The same problems of interpretation arise here, as in the nonarousal condition.

There seems to be no way to be sure that what the subject says, does, or chooses is indicative purely or even loosely of a motivational state.

If there is physiological evidence of arousal, of course, most people would agree that motivation exists. This is despite the fact that physiological responses may be cued off as habits in the situation. But they can presumably energize other responses and their cessation may be rewarding, features not true of other kinds of habits, especially instrumental ones, cued off by the situation or by the physiological responses themselves.

There is, of course, another way out. This is to look at some task performance as it is affected by variations assessed either in arousal or nonarousal conditions. To this we turn next.

The Task. One can argue that a measurement on which people differ or a manipulation to which people have been subjected is valid for the establishment of a motivational state if measurements of performance on some *other* task reveal differences consistent with expectation on the hypothesis that such a state did exist. This is essentially the argument of construct validity (Cronbach & Meehl, 1955). Thus if it is expected that a motive will facilitate or energize some performance and if people who score high on a measure of the motive or whose motive has been aroused do in fact perform better than low-scoring people or people in whom no arousal has been attempted, then one may infer validity for the measurement or the arousal operation because the expected effects have been obtained.

This line of argument underlies much of the work on human motivation which we have surveyed. It is theoretically sound, but it runs into certain practical difficulties. One is the question whether the critical task can be influenced by other variables than the motive in question. If it can be, then there is no assurance that the measurement or arousal operation has been validated by the performance differences, unless all other relevant variables have been controlled. Unfortunately, knowledge of what variables are relevant is often lacking, so that they cannot readily be held constant. An illustration is provided by the work with the *Manifest Anxiety Scale* (see Chapter 14).

A second problem arises in connection with the expected consequences of the motive differences on task performance itself. So little is usually known about the properties of the task and the processes involved in it that it is often moot as to whether motive arousal will facilitate, inhibit, or have no effect on its performance. We have seen this problem in stark relief, also in connection with work on the *Manifest Anxiety Scale*.

Establishing construct validity, then, is not a simple or an easy task. The dependent performance must be understood in terms of all the variables which affect it and of the processes involved in it. And there

must be explicit bases for expectations that the motive state will interact with these processes at all and, if they do, in what direction. Most
of the research of the construct validation type in the area of human
motivation does not satisfy these requirements.[15]

In summary of the problems of measurement and arousal, we must
conclude that there are many difficulties in the interpretation of the
research that has been carried out. Some of the difficulty is methodological but some of it is conceptual. The latter difficulty goes to the root
of the theoretical status of motivation: Does it only energize and provide the conditions for reinforcement or may it also direct? If the last,
how may it be distinguished from habit?

RELATIONS OF MOTIVATION TO PERSONALITY CONCEPTS

Our discussion of various motives may have led the reader to wonder
about other terms frequent in the lexicon of the behavioral sciences.
Among them are the various terms such as trait, attitude, value, sentiment, temperament, interest, preference, and so on. Such terms include
several (e.g., trait, value, interest) which Littman (1958) refers to as
motivational terms, because they designate something that is "active"
rather than "passive." (Terms of passivity include such words as aptitude, ability, imitation, closure, according to Littman.) Why have we
not discussed them heretofore?

Before answering this question, a further comment is necessary. This
is that the terms like trait, etc., are *descriptive* terms for behaviors characteristic of the organism, whatever their theoretical status. But there
is another way in which a relation of personality to motivation can be
formulated. This is that the way in which a given motive is manifested
or dealt with in behavior is a function of the particular personality
constellation in which it is embedded. We discuss in this section these
two points: descriptive personality terms, on the one hand, and motives
in relation to personality constellations, on the other.

Descriptive Personality Terms

The most commonly used terms in the study of personality, and the
ones to which some systematic attention has been paid, are *trait, attitude, value*, and *preference*.

Trait, Interest, Value. The word *trait* generally refers to a consistent pattern of behavior which an individual shows over a fairly wide
spectrum of situations. Thus, if one is characterized as sociable, we are
saying that he has a trait and we mean that the person tends to like and

---

[15] See, for further discussion of these problems, Jessor and Hammond (1957),
Kausler and Trapp (1959), Hill (1957), Spence (1958).

seek out people, to be with them much of the time, and, perhaps, to be unsatisfied without them.

As we have used the term trait in the example just cited, there is perhaps little to suggest any particular theoretical interpretation of the trait concept. And the term trait is commonly used primarily as a descriptive term, of theoretical neutrality. However, G. W. Allport (1937) suggested that some traits are dynamic, having motivational significance. Any restlessness over the absence of people and any urge to find them might suggest a motivational quality to the trait of sociability. However, this usage has not been common and, to our knowledge, has not led to empirical testing. In any case, traits undoubtedly involve much that is habitual rather than motivational. In the case of persistence, a trait that has received a good deal of attention (Ryans, 1939; Feather, 1962), Feather (1961, 1962) has shown that an analysis in terms of the achievement motive (and other factors) has value. Whether in other traits various kinds of motives can be found remains for further investigation to reveal.

Another approach to the study of personality traits is through factor analysis of correlations among a variety of test scores, behavioral ratings, physiological indices, and so on. Motivational variables or motivational traits are sometimes listed among the outcomes of these procedures (cf. Eysenck, 1953; Cattell, 1957, 1959; and Guilford, 1959). As arousal operations have not typically been involved in these studies and as theoretical analysis has not progressed far, we will not treat the results of factor analysis further.

Interest and value are usually measured by having the subject make choices between descriptions of activities, goals or beliefs (Guilford, 1959; Dukes, 1955; Hill, 1960). That is, the subject is asked to state or to manifest preferences (Irwin, 1958). With none of these terms, however, has the role of habit been separated from the role of motivational factors, and the relative contribution of these variables has not been assessed. Measured interests, values and preferences have some predictive value in relation to other behaviors and therefore have some practical utility, as do trait measurements. Because of their uncertain conceptual status and because manipulations of arousal and satiation have not been devised relative to interest, value, and preference, we shall not go further into their analysis here. These terms all represent complex resultants of many factors and it is not at all clear that they are, in any sense, uniquely motivational.[16]

[16] The uncertain status of concepts like trait, interest, value, and preference arises in part because the items used in their measurement and the names applied to the measuring scales have been rather arbitrary. Also, these measurement

Attitude. This term is a central one to much of social psychology and typically refers to evaluations which people make of objects or representatives thereof. Thus, one may be favorable or unfavorable in his evaluation of a piece of legislation, a given skin color, and the like. Some theorists do not consider attitudes to be motivational in character, but others do. Among the latter, Katz and Stotland (1959) are representative. They suggest that attitudes have an *affective* component and regard this component as central to the attitude concept, as being the unique factor which distinguishes attitudes from other cognitions and which confers upon an attitude its attribution to objects of good or bad qualities. It appears to us that this formulation of attitude has much in common with McClelland's theory of motivation (pp. 374–386).

However, we again do not find in the literature of attitude studies investigations which have been designed to elucidate in any uniquely motivational way this affective component of attitudes. As with the various other terms we have just considered, it seems that attitudes and their expression are quite complex, influenced by many variables. Until further analysis can be made of the attitude concept and until empirical work can show the value of a motivational conception of attitude, it is largely an assertion of faith that it is useful to conceive attitudes as motivational variables.

Motives in Relation to Personality Constellations

It has already been pointed out that different levels of some motives, for example, nAch, may represent different motive states rather than different amounts of the same motive. We have also seen that relations of the task to the motive and to responses instigated by motivational stimuli are important factors in how a motive will affect behavior. A somewhat different emphasis stresses that a given motive will have effects which will be conditioned by personality factors which themselves, perhaps, are not directly motivational.

This point has been made by Klein (1954). He has used the concept of "cognitive control" to refer to a manner or style of performance which cuts across a number of situations. In one experiment, Klein selected subjects who were highly susceptible to interference and another set of subjects not interference prone. Interference was measured by requiring that color names be called out loud in a situation in which color names were printed in incongruent colors (e.g., the word "green" printed in red). Then these subjects were made thirsty by

procedures have usually been developed for practical purposes, and theoretical issues have not been important or of interest to those who have developed the measures.

means of a dry meal and were put through several tasks involving thirst relevant stimuli. It was found that the high interference and the low interference subjects differed markedly in the way they responded to these tasks, though presumably the thirst need was aroused equally in both groups. In one condition the subject was to reproduce the size of a standard disc by adjusting another disc; on the latter there was either a thirst relevant symbol or a symbol irrelevant to thirst. The high-interference group underestimated and the low-interference group overestimated the size of the standard disc in terms of their adjustments of the variable disc. Further, the errors made by the low-interference subjects were affected by thirst but were not affected in the high-interference subjects. In several other situations, the high and low interference subjects differed in the ways in which they responded under the thirst need, but it is not at all clear that thirst is essential here. The point of Klein's argument is that perhaps the effects of *any* motive are filtered through the constraints provided by cognitive controls.

Somewhat similar findings have been reported in relation to nAch by Lazarus and Baker (1956) and Lazarus et al. (1957). This is to say that controls or regulatory factors in the subject's personality will modulate or control the way he responds to a need and the way in which the need or motive is reflected in behavior. Such findings suggest that it is no simple matter to trace out motivational effects in the behavior of people and that individual differences in controls, maturity, and perhaps many other variables must be considered in predicting the effects on behavior of the arousal of a motive.

SUMMARY

This chapter, unlike the last one, is not much concerned with motivational concepts which are modeled on basic drives but rather deals for the most part with external and situational factors which have been thought to have motivational effects on human beings.

Among the first studies of human motivation were those which dealt with incentive conditions such as knowledge of results and praise and reproof. While some generalizations can be made from these studies, for example, knowledge of results is helpful to performance and praise is often more effective than reproof, further work indicates that simple rules governing the effects of incentives are inadequate. Level of aspiration and related techniques indicate that individual motives, the value of the incentive, and the subjective probability of obtaining the incentive must all be taken into account.

An early interest in the study of human motivation was the study of the effects on behavior of such factors as competition, rivalry, and audiences. Effects were obtained, but they were not easy to interpret or to generalize. These investigations contributed, however, to the study of conformity and to study of the question whether social situations can create motives. Some evidence has been found that conformity is related to individual motive patterns, and there are experiments whose findings suggest that goals can be created by a group situation and that the group goals will influence the behavior of individuals much as do personal goals.

Tasks, it is sometimes suggested, create their own motives, and experiments on the interruption of tasks, memory for completed and uncompleted tasks, resumption of interrupted tasks, and discharge of task tensions by means of substitute activities have provided evidence that, under some conditions, task-related motives do develop.

A good deal of research has been done indicating that threats to self-esteem (ego-involvement) can motivate people. Work on retention reviewed in this chapter (as well as work cited in the preceding chapter) indicates this fact but also brings out the point that there are individual differences in responses to such threats. After interruption of a task, some people are apparently threatened, as they remember interrupted tasks less well than completed tasks. The converse is also true for other people, however.

In order to explain the occurrence of communication among people, it has been suggested that uncertainty about features in the environment is one reason that people talk to each other. Uncertainties may be resolved through communication; and some experiments support this factor as a basis for communication. A more general theory of motivation has, however, emerged from work on uncertainty and communication. It is the theory of cognitive dissonance. This theory states that when cognitive elements are inharmonious, a tension will be created. This tension motivates behavior for its reduction, and experiments on a variety of topics offer some support for dissonance theory.

In dissonance theory, as with other aspects of social motivation, problems of arousal and measurement are important and knotty. Much of the work on social motivation (as well as on acquired motivation) rests on procedures for arousal and measurement whose relation to motivational variables is anything but clear-cut. The expression of motivation in the adult human being is modulated, in all probability, by personality mechanisms, so that direct evidence of motivational factors is seldom seen. While there have been much research and many provocative hypotheses concerning social motivation, there is yet a good deal of unclarity in the present conceptual status of this work.

Chapter 16

Toward a Unified Theory of Motivation

We come now to our final summing up. Although not exhaustive, we have tried to offer a fairly extensive treatment of all the major and and most of the minor theoretical positions that exist in the field of motivation. In each instance we sought to present a straightforward and sympathetic account of the assumptions, propositions, and supporting evidence for a particular theory or closely related group of theories. At the same time an attempt was made to indicate some of the limitations of each position, both as seen by others and as seemed apparent to us.

CURRENT STATUS OF THE FIELD

It is clear that a comprehensive, definitive psychology of motivation does not yet exist. Nor, for that matter, would it be reasonable to expect that one should. On the other hand, the vastness of the literature on motivational concepts and the large quantity of research on motivational phenomena have provided a foundation on which a psychology of motivation can conceivably be based.

In this final chapter we should like to point to some significant areas of agreement that we find to exist among the different theoretical positions and which are generally supported by the available evidence. We also identify some shortcomings and suggest some conceptual clarifications. The reader should keep in mind that our generalizations here, and certainly all of those made by the writers whose work we have reviewed in the preceding chapters, are limited by the as yet unknown generality of the observations on which they are based. The empirical data available are, at best, selective samples, largely of mammalian behavior and of only certain species and strains. Like an immense jig-saw puzzle or the fabled story of the blind men and the elephant, one may draw conclusions about the nature of the whole picture (or elephant) on the basis of the few pieces one has been able to put together (or the limited area to which one has been exposed). With the addition of more information, the previous generalization is suddenly found wanting, and new hypotheses—even sometimes directly contradicting the previously held ones—take on self-evidence. And the process may then repeat itself again and again. In the prescientific era beliefs could exist indefinitely in the absence of a criterion of evidence. By the rules of science, on the other hand, we are obliged to discard generalizations when they are contradicted by facts or modify them to incorporate the implications of the new facts.

Unfortunately, in the field of motivational psychology, we are rather in the position of the blind men. Each investigator explores an area of the subject most readily available to him or amenable to his tools or methods. His conclusions may derive from his methods and fit his facts. Where controversies appear to exist we generally find that investigators have (1) observed different species, strains, age groups, sexes, etc.; (2) used mutually exclusive observational methods; (3) observed different aspects of behavior; (4) employed different units or methods of measurement; (5) controlled different variables; (6) generalized from too few instances; or (7) inferred events to be occurring when they could not be observed directly. Where hypothetical constructs or intervening variables have been employed—and this has been a major device for motivation theorists—care has not always been taken to provide sufficient referents for others to clearly identify the variable intended. Loose defining and terms with surplus meaning, use of common terms in different contexts (e.g., instinct), and arguments by analogy have all added to the profusion of language and the impression of conflict of ideas in motivation theory.

We have throughout the book attempted to call the reader's attention to the above limitations wherever it seemed necessary, and will not restate these points here. Suffice it to say that we believe *some* of the differences between and among theoretical positions may be expected to disappear with the clarification of meaning and implications of terms used by each—a goal to which this book may, we hope, have made a contribution—and with the continued accumulation of empirical data, particularly studies applying methods of one approach to pet problem areas of others. The behaviorists' invasion of the ethologists' domain and the stimulating experimental and theoretical rebuttals by the ethologists are worthwhile demonstrations of this, as are the learning theorists' developments of animal analogues intended to demonstrate as well as to test psychoanalytic hypotheses.

Expecting regular changes to occur as work progresses in the field, we may nevertheless try, in the remaining few pages, to indicate some of the concepts that appear to underlie all the points of view presented. We feel that these may provide a common basis for a set of fundamental laws of motivation which should ultimately emerge. The reader is warned not to allow our choice of terms to becloud the basic point that the concepts discussed are seen as compatible with *all* current theories. Despite our sometimes apparent personal biases, in this section we are not choosing sides, as it were, but choosing ideas, so to speak, on which all sides might agree.

EQUILIBRATION

The need-reduction model, when applied to hunger and thirst phenomena, for example, suggests a growth of impelling force-to-action, consummatory eating or drinking behavior, and force-, tension-, or need-dissipation. If one examines the matter in any detail (as we have done in Chapters 5 and 11, as well as elsewhere in the book), it is apparent that the model is far too simple. It is by no means clear *how* the need impels action, or *why* the action ceases long before the need could actually be reduced physiologically, or if, without learning, the need impels action at all. Despite this, however, a quite regular pattern of phenomena is observed: deprivation (tension increase) → action → satisfaction (tension decrease). Even if we ignore the problem of need vs. drive as impulse to action, the arousal-action-reduction sequence appears to describe what happens in a large number of instances of so-called motivated behaviors.

Actually, the need-reduction pattern can be equally well described in terms of an equilibration model. Thus, it presumably starts whenever disequilibrium of a system occurs and is followed by equilibrating responses, which in turn cease when a balanced state is achieved. Need-reduction [1] may then be one illustration of an equilibration model, but such a model can also include acquired states for which no physiological needs can be reasonably postulated—such as affiliation or achievement or love or esteem, etc. The difficulty which the need-reduction model has in dealing with these and other acquired and seemingly functionally autonomous states may be obviated in an equilibration model. In fact, we think an equilibration model is sufficiently descriptive of motivated behavior sequences generally to assume the status of a fundamental principle. This is not to say that all behavior that is considered motivated can necessarily be explained by this principle, but rather that whenever a state of disequilibrium is induced in a healthy organism, as a result of either endogenous or exogenous fac-

---

[1] To the extent that the drive concept is used in the sense of or analogously to a need-reduction model, the limitation here noted would apply to drive as well.

tors, a program of equilibrating responses may be presumed to occur and continue until the disequilibrium is in some manner reduced or abolished.

In Chapter 7 we have spelled out in some detail a number of models of equilibration systems. It is not our purpose here to recommend that one or another of these be adopted as *the* system to explain motivation. Rather we are of the opinion that the equilibrium–re-establishment idea around which these theoretical systems are built is in fact fundamental to all motivation theories. Both ethological and psychoanalytic instinct theories (Chapters 3 and 12) involve tension build-up and release as a core concept. Some of the observational data and minor theories associated with bodily conditions, and other drive-like patterns (Chapters 4, 5 and 6), invoke similar notions in relation to endogenous, rhythmic physiological processes. And compatible ideas are found in the theories of arousal (Chapter 8), conflict and stress (Chapter 9), drive (Chapters 10 and 11), and acquired and social motivation (Chapters 14 and 15).

Only perhaps in some cases of acquired and social motivation, self-actualization (Chapter 13), and possibly the hypothesized "spontaneous" activity and exploration (Chapter 6), is the applicability of the equilibration model challenged. And yet a careful examination of these phenomena and the interpretations which they have been given shows two ways in which they are consistent with our hypothesis. First, the self-actualizing theories actually do *assume* the operation of biological homeostatic processes prior to, and underlying, the development of higher order "needs." Maslow, for one, suggests that D-type people— those we can reasonably suppose to be the vast majority of the populace —behave almost completely in accordance with an equilibration model. His self-actualizers, on the other hand, apparently grow "beyond" such processes. It would appear that such individuals (and they are rare) develop quite high tolerance or variability limits in regard to lower order disequilibrations, apparently based on successful experiences in satisfaction of these basic needs. However, even in these individuals there would appear to be limits to the amount of frustration which can be tolerated without readjustment processes being put into operation. Unfortunately, the writings of the self-actualizing theorists are not specific enough on this matter to be sure that this inference is correct. It is our impression that it is, however. Of course, it is possible that voluntary readjustive processes could be so controlled in these individuals, as a function of strong habit patterns or by strong acquired motive patterns (cf., for example, Young's findings on preferences in rats, Chapter 5) in conflict with homeostatic adjustive processes, as to induce death before readjustment (cf., also, Chapter 9). These possible exceptions would not appear to damage our case for the application of an equilibration model, however.

The second argument in favor of an equilibratory interpretation of self-actualizing behavior has itself little direct evidential support but can be supported inferentially by such data as those on adaptation level theory (Chapter 7) and social motivation (Chapter 15). This position holds that induced, acquired, or learned tensions (be they cortical, subcortical, neurohumoral, or whatever) may provide base lines or mean levels, deviation from which leads to adaptive responding. The classical story of the nineteenth-century French colonial officer wearing his white gloves and uniform tie, even when on isolated duty in the heat of the midday Sahara sun, might be an illustration of such an artificial norm, deviation from which is upsetting for the individual concerned.

The objections which a number of psychologists have raised to an equilibratory principle have been based on the argument that there is more to life than the activities appropriate to bed, board, and bath! We submit that this is a spurious argument. Only a few extremists seriously suggest that motivation arises exclusively from, or is governed entirely by, these bodily considerations.[2] Even those critics who reject the primacy and dominance of bodily needs do, nevertheless, *accept* equilibration as a motivational principle for a good segment of behavior. The arguments are really on the subissues of (1) whether the equilibration notion is as appropriate to exogenous as well as endogenous processes, and (2) whether sources of disequilibrium can arise from learned as well as unlearned sources. How, for example, can equilibration underlie incentive motivation or exploration? And how can equilibration explain instances of compulsive conformity to artificial (and biologically meaningless) norms? Self-denial of any sort would seem to be a contradiction of a simple homeostatic principle. And yet we know that these phenomena occur. Perhaps we can once again remind the reader that although such apparent exceptions to a universal equilibratory principle may require additional or supplementary explanation, they no more restrict or invalidate the principle of equilibration than does the fact that objects heavier-than-air rise from the ground destroys the principle of gravity.

The appealing attempts to picture man as essentially good rather than evil, as growing or becoming rather than as defensive or conserva-

---

[2] One could possibly have accused early Freudian thinking of holding such a view, but the recent developments in ego psychology (see Chapter 12) have surely reprieved the psychoanalysts from this charge.

tive, and as independent of his biological self are reminiscent of the theological arguments of an earlier day, particularly of those raised against evolutionary theory. In any case, they are of little heuristic value. We do not dispute the significant, essential differences between man and animal implied in these views when we commend an equilibratory hypothesis for consideration as universally applicable. Nor do we neglect the difficult technical problems which must be overcome in order to arrive at an understanding of the *modus operandi* of posited equilibratory mechanisms beyond those immediately sustaining the balances of the fluid matrix of the body. By the same token, demonstrations of the existence of exploratory behaviors in rats, of curiosity or manipulatory behaviors in mammals, and of "growth tendencies" in humans, all appearing to be functionally independent of directly present biological privation, are insufficient bases, in themselves, to reject such a principle, unless these studies in turn provide clues to a different origin and meaning of these behaviors.

Finally, while proposing the universality of an equilibratory principle, we would nevertheless consider it essential to pursue experimentally the two subissues just noted, namely, (1) the possible mechanisms by which this principle is made operative in relation to exogenous processes, and (2) the role of learning in establishing equilibratory norms and disequilibratory criteria and thresholds. It is likely that at least partial answers to these questions will be found in research areas which have recently attracted much interest for other reasons: (1) studies of sensory deprivation and sensory overloading, (2) effects of early (including prenatal) experiences on later behavior, (3) neurohumoral activation mechanisms, and (4) social influences on normative behaviors. Data from the first two of these areas are already suggesting the remarkable resilience of living systems under extreme and unusual circumstances, as well as the persistence of latent sensitizing factors which combine with later stimulus effects to either facilitate or disrupt ongoing behaviors. Information in the third field points to the capabilities of living systems to organize and reorganize themselves in many alternative ways. We have long been aware of the concept of normative behavior and its docility. Perhaps more definitive research in the fourth of these areas, in this next decade, will reveal more clearly the nature of the mechanisms of social influence and more particularly the ways in which organisms incorporate change and yet appear to retain their integrity. Starting from the assumption of a dynamic, equilibratory series of systems as a model for the behaving organism will, we think, provide a fruitful point of departure.

Some More Specific Questions

In sum, then, it is clear that we find the motivation concept to have value and that the framework provided by an equilibration model is one which we think has general utility for motivation. These points, however, are very general ones, and it is desirable to be more specific about issues, functions, and mechanisms in motivation. We therefore turn now to several more specific questions. First, we deal with the concept of drive and with the reasons that this concept and parallel hydraulic-like mechanisms no longer seem to be satisfactory. Second, we suggest possible mechanisms which may fulfill these functions; such mechanisms are functional substitutes for drive but do not have its difficulties and accord more adequately with the facts. We are not, therefore, merely replacing one word by another. Next, we ask, what functions must the motivation concept discharge? This will return us to one of the central problems of our first chapter. Finally, we sketch the applicability of the suggested mechanisms to major facts and theories as outlined in this book.

DRIVE

Much of the thinking about motivation in this century has been organized around the concept of drive. Although the term was introduced by Woodworth in 1918, its conception as an effect of deprivation perhaps owes its origin more to other sources than to Woodworth. Jennings and Craig stressed the restlessness which accompanied deprivation, and Cannon, of course, suggested that the restlessness arose from the stimuli set up by deprivation—stomach contractions in the case of hunger, and local dryness in the mouth and throat in the case of thirst. Moss, Warden, and Richter presented evidence that deprivation did instigate activity—crossing an obstruction to obtain an incentive, running in a wheel, or moving about a stabilimeter cage. That the deprived animal would be active made good evolutionary, functionalist sense: the active animal could survive, as by being active he would move about his environment, thus increasing his chances of encountering needed objects. It is thus clear that the fundamental operation of drive was *deprivation,* and it was conceived as resulting in deficits (as in hunger) or excesses (as in sex) which provided stimuli that goaded the organism into activity. We will speak of this conception as the drive-stimulus model.

There were other observations which seemed to fit well with the control of behavior by drive, or operationally, by deprivation. Consumption of food or water, for example, was observed to be related to deprivation, that is, deprived animals ate or drank more when given the opportunity than undeprived animals. It was found that animals, maintained in cages in which food and water were always present, would eat periodically, that is, there was a cyclicity to their episodes of eating. This cyclicity was attributed to drive, arising over the brief (two-hour) period of "self-imposed" deprivation. Cyclicity appeared, also, in the activity of female rats, correlated with stages in the oestrus cycle.

Drive was further observed to be necessary for learning; for example, an animal deprived of food or water would learn a maze, if suitably rewarded, to a greater extent than would an *un*deprived animal, which was offered a similar reward. Further, if the incentive object was appropriate to the drive (e.g., food to hunger) learning was accomplished more readily than it was when the incentive was not appropriate to the drive.

In *summary*, the deprivation operation was found to have important effects on behavior: it made animals restless and active, caused them to cross obstructions to obtain incentives, led them to learn, was associated with cyclic features of their behavior, and yielded augmented consummatory behavior.[3] The drive construct was introduced to describe the goading effect on animal behavior of stimuli arising from tissue deficits or from excesses of certain substances. The implication was that the behavior was an automatic response to the goading stimuli and that the behavior was a regulatory mechanism whose function was to eliminate the spurs to action provided by the drive state.

This conception of drive had its parallels elsewhere. Classical psychoanalysis also developed a model, the functional properties of which seem similar to those we have just outlined. The model, however, rather than being one which stressed goading stimuli, was a hydraulic one. Instinctual or drive energy was seen to accumulate, as would water flowing into a closed container, and if undischarged, the accumulation would ultimately burst the vessel. Behavior again was seen as regulative so far as this energy accumulation, or tension condition, is concerned. There is an implication of an inexorable accumulation of energy which stirs the organism into regulatory activity. This amounts to much the same thing logically and functionally as the drive-stimulus model.[4]

---

[3] Later evidence has led to a re-evaluation of these findings as supportive of a drive-stimulus model. See discussion on pp. 816–821.

[4] Freud did speak of tension arising from stimuli, especially in the newborn infant. He seemed here to stress external stimuli and, so far as we can judge,

Deprivation, in Freud's model, arises from the failure to discharge the accumulated tension rather than from the depletion of tissues. This emphasis comes perhaps from the fact that Freud devoted little or no attention to hunger or thirst.

A corollary to the drive stimulus model was that all motivation had its origin in the biological drives arising from deprivation of food, water, sexual behavior, or from pain, and that other acquired motivations were derived from these states. A corollary from the hydraulic model was that widely varied behaviors had their ultimate motivational origin in libido and aggressive drives or in anxiety, the varied behaviors being highly elaborated devices ("defenses") to accomplish the reduction of the energy accumulations or to prevent their further development.

As earlier noted, much of the protest against these models of motivation has taken the form of insistence that there are exogenous "motives," such as exploration, manipulation, and curiosity, and that tension increments may be rewarding as well as tension decrements. Many of the arguments for "growth motivation" and for drives which are independent of hunger, thirst, sex, aggression, and pain, have, we think, been misdirected. They have not questioned the existence of these drives but rather have insisted that there are *other* "drives" as well. Deprivation, the classical defining operation of drive, however, does not apply to most of these other proposed drives.

We think the problem is with the drive concept itself, whether conceived in stimulus or in hydraulic terms. We believe that it presents certain insurmountable difficulties which severely limit its usefulness. In the next section we identify these difficulties as a prelude to the introduction of alternative concepts or mechanisms which may be capable of handling the valid observations that led to the drive notion, as well as the objections which have been made to it.

Difficulties with Drive

The drive-stimulus model, as has been noted, was developed mainly on the basis of the deficit conditions of hunger and thirst. Its applicability to such conditions as underlie sexual, maternal, migratory, and other behaviors has never been clear. None of these behaviors is a response to a tissue *deficit*. Whether they reflect some kind of bodily excess is perhaps a moot point.

In the case of sexual behavior, for example, a state of hormonal readi-

did not emphasize internal stimuli associated with energy accumulation. The ethologists have also used a hydraulic model, and the stimuli they mention are chiefly external ones, the "sign" or "releasing" stimuli.

ness is presumably essential for its occurrence. (This, however, is not always the case, especially in sexually experienced primates and man.) But there is no evidence of which we are aware that this hormonal level is modified, that is, reduced, by sexual behavior. It is true that the male ejaculates, but the seminal fluid does not contain androgen. If the hormonal level is affected by ejaculation, the effect must be an indirect one. Females do not ejaculate, so that there can be no question of an immediate reduction of hormonal level as a direct result of female sexual behavior. Local genital stimulation, it might be argued, could serve as the goad to sexual behavior in both sexes. However, there is evidence (Chapter 4) that sexual behavior can be maintained in a variety of species in the absence of genital stimulation. Unfortunately, this evidence does not permit a clear conclusion as to whether sexual behavior would appear in *inexperienced* organisms without genital stimulation though with adequate hormonal levels.

There is the phenomenon of sexual exhaustion but the mechanism of the exhaustion is not at all clear. If hormonal levels in the blood do not change, the exhaustion may be due to transient changes in genital structures themselves or to changes in their responsiveness to stimuli. A new mate, substituted for the former one, may more quickly reactivate an animal to sexual behavior. This would hardly be the case if prior sexual activity had drained away the substances (hormonal or otherwise) necessary to arouse sexual behavior. (More work is required for understanding of the processes by which a new partner restores sexual behavior, as well as of the limits of this effect.)

While sexual behavior tends to be somewhat episodic, this characteristic may have little or nothing to do with blood hormone levels. We have seen that there is no evidence that sexual activity reduces hormones, and recovery from sexual exhaustion (in the male rat) is complete after 24 hours of rest—that is, no further intensification of sexual behavior seems to occur with deprivation beyond 24 hours. One might well wonder whether, in the intact male, blood androgen levels ever change, aside from aging and disease. If they do not, they could scarcely account for sexual behavior when it does occur.

What we have just said for sex could be applied to other "drives" as well. Perhaps the reader will wish to think of other drive states along the lines of this discussion. At any rate, it should be clear that the deficit-induced or the excess-induced drive-stimulus model of drive has little or no applicability to sex.

Does the hydraulic model fare better? We think not. The discussion of sexual motivation in conjunction with the drive-stimulus model applies as well to the hydraulic model. So far as aggression is concerned, no deprivation condition or physiological basis has ever been discovered, and there seems to be no reason to suppose that an accumulation of "aggressive energy" takes place over time (see discussions in Chapters 12 and 14).

The Case of Hunger. If there are a number of "drives" which do not fit well with either the drive-stimulus or the hydraulic model, what of hunger on which the drive-stimulus model seems to have been constructed? To this question we now turn.

There are several kinds of information which are not consistent with the notion of an automatic activation of certain behaviors by means of food deprivation.[5] One is that consummatory behavior is not, on initial occurrences of deprivation, adequate to overcome the deficit. Animals do not start to eat at once or to utilize fully the period available for eating until they have experienced deprivation a number of times. Adjustments to restricted feeding schedules may take as long as 15 days. While this slow adjustment can be interpreted as a reflection of gradually accumulating bodily deficits, it is also possible to make a learning interpretation of the findings and to say that animals *learn* to be hungry or thirsty. Further, Richter's demonstration of *cyclicity* in the eating behavior of rats with food freely available to them has been shown to be true only of the "average rat." When eating records of individual animals are examined, randomness, rather than cyclicity, appears. Such random eating would not be predicted by a drive-stimulus theory which would require responses to the periodic onset of drive after given intervals of self-imposed deprivation.

The evidence that small feedings prior to a maze run augment speed of running would not be expected on the basis of a simple drive interpretation. The feedings should reduce the drive and therefore the instigation to running. Preferences for certain tastes can be developed which actually prevent the animal from making up deficiencies of needed substances. The drive-stimulus model is not easily able to account for specific hungers, and, of course, food-related behavior is known to persist in the absence of stimulation from the stomach. Central theories of hunger seem well supported by neurophysiological findings. The mechanisms operative in prefeeding, preference, specific hungers, persistence of hunger in gastrectomized animals, and hypothalamic control of eating are not well understood, and local stimula-

---

[5] It is important to note that measurements of drive in the obstruction box always involve the presence of a relevant incentive with which the animal's past experience has made him familiar. Such measurements thus involve more than the operation of drive alone; they represent the interaction of incentive and deprivation states.

tion, in conjunction with past experience, may be more important than available experiments have indicated. Nevertheless, it is difficult to place much confidence in a drive-stimulus model in the face of all of these phenomena.

As indicated earlier, activity increments associated with deprivation have been interpreted as reflecting the automatic spur to restlessness provided by drive. Do these increments constitute validation of drive-stimulus conceptions?

In Chapter 6 we reviewed findings which permit an alternative interpretation of the relationship of activity to food deprivation. Several experiments have shown that under constant environmental conditions activity, as measured in a stabilimeter cage, does not increase with starvation. Further, it has been shown, for both the stabilimeter and the running wheel, that activity increments in relation to deprivation appear mainly when feeding occurs at regular intervals. The activity appears to reflect an *anticipation* of feeding-time rather than a response to deprivation per se. Obviously, such anticipations are learned. It is worth noting here that students of animal learning typically provide for several days of adaptation to a regular feeding schedule before they start the animals on the learning task. This procedure permits the animals to anticipate feeding at about the time they are to learn the task and thus to be maximally active during the period of the learning trials.

In addition to the interpretation that the relation of activity to deprivation is based on learned anticipations of the time of feeding [6] rather than reflecting automatic energization of activity by increasing drive, there is another possibility: activity may maintain bodily temperature, and it is this temperature regulation that is critical to the relation between activity and deprivation. Stevenson and Rixon (1957) [7] showed that increases in running (wheel) activity over several days of starvation were much greater when environmental temperatures were low than when they were high. In further experiments, they measured skin and colonic temperatures in rats over six days of starvation. Some of the animals were put into slings to restrict their muscular activity, whereas others were permitted to move about a cage (not a wheel) normally.

[6] Internal stimuli may be important to such anticipations. Bash (see Chapter 5) found that increments in activity prior to feeding disappeared after gastrectomy, although various other features of food-deprived behavior remained. See, also, White (1959) and Hunt (1960).

[7] We are indebted to Professor John F. Hall for calling our attention to the paper by Stevenson and Rixon. Several of the points made in the discussion of this paper arose in conversation with Professor Hall.

Skin and colonic temperatures declined over the six days of starvation in the animals restricted in the slings, but the freely moving, starved animals showed no such decline, their temperatures, insofar as they changed at all, rising. Rats confined to slings but fed there also showed no decline in body temperature.

This experiment seems clearly to demonstrate that activity may serve to maintain body temperature. We have seen (Chapter 4) that rats will be reinforced for and will maintain bar-pressing when it results in a warming of a cold environment. It is entirely possible that they can learn to be active in order to maintain body temperatures that otherwise would decline because of food-deprivation.

Certain other implications of the relation of activity to body temperature may be mentioned. In Chapter 6 the finding was reported that young rats show increments in stabilimeter activity under food deprivation even when the environment is a constant one. It is possible to interpret this finding (not obtained with rats over 100 days of age) as follows: The younger animals were probably less well covered by insulating layers of fat than were the older ones and, in any case, starvation might deplete fat in younger animals faster than in the adult ones. Perhaps, then, the younger animals showed activity as a heat-regulating device. It is also possible that because of their smaller size the young animals could move about the relatively small cages enough to maintain bodily heat, whereas the larger, older animals did not have enough room to use this procedure effectively. For them, perhaps, curling up inactively in a corner was a more effective means of heat conservation than activity would be a means of heat production.

On the basis of our present knowledge, it is not possible to be sure why in other experiments activity has not occurred during deprivation. Cage size and environmental temperatures are probably important factors, however. In sum, we can say that activity can be learned as a response to anticipation of feeding; it may also serve directly as a means of maintaining bodily temperature and can perhaps be learned in response to deprivation on this basis when circumstances permit. As an effect of deprivation, activity is not a simple matter and can hardly be seen as an automatic response to drive stimulation.

Another finding commonly cited to support the relation between activity and deprivation is the relation between running cycles and the oestrus rhythm. In the light of the prior discussion, it is worth noting that Brobeck, Wheatland, and Strominger (1947) found that a decline in body temperature preceded the increase in running occurring with oestrus. It is therefore possible that running in oestrus is a heat-regulating activity rather than an evidence of sexual agitation on the part of the female.

These findings with respect to the relation of activity to temperature regulation are consistent and clear, so far as they go, but further systematic study is needed of this relationship and of other possible relationships between other bodily conditions and activity. Until considerable additional data are in hand, it would be premature to go beyond the speculative statements so far offered.

In sum, we think the arguments and the evidence presented in this section are disabling to the concept of drive. Let us be clear: deprivation is still, in certain instances, a powerful means of activating behavior. The question is, "Why?" If drive, established by deprivation, is not adequate, how may the effects of deprivation, when they occur, be explained? Can an explanation for the effects of deprivation be developed which will apply to or parallel explanations for those motivated behaviors in which no operation of deprivation is clearly present?

SOME POSSIBLE ALTERNATIVES

In the discussion of activity as an effect of deprivation, we pointed to evidence that activity appears following food-deprivation only when the animal may *anticipate* the occurrence of feeding. What this suggests is that stimuli, regularly associated with feeding, can elicit anticipations. The stimuli may be internal or external, and the anticipation may be some sort of fractional goal response; while r_g is an example of what we mean by an anticipation or expectancy, we do not wish to identify all anticipations as r_g's. Further investigation will be required to uncover the character of anticipations; for example, whether they may be central as well as peripheral in origin. We think anticipation can account for the phenomena associated with prefeeding, preference, and persistence of hunger in gastrectomized animals, and many of the findings which led Beach (Chapter 4) to speak of sexual "appetite," rather than of sexual drive, seem to reflect an anticipatory process.

In all of these cases, as well as in the instance of activity, the central observation is that behavior displays an augmentation of vigor—an invigoration, so to speak—over the level of vigor that would be present in the same stimulus situation without anticipation. It is as if the anticipation arouses or excites the organism, alerts it, enhances its responsiveness to the available stimuli. Why anticipation should have these effects is not clear, but it might be due to momentary frustration of anticipations, to an increase in total level of organismic stimulation, or to many other factors. Our impression is that anticipation brings or may may bring about a state of arousal akin to the arousal of which activation theorists speak (Chapter 8). This has led us to refer to this mechanism as an *anticipation-arousal mechanism.* However, it is perhaps not necessary to imply an intervening arousal state, and a term which does not do so is *anticipation-invigoration mechanism (AIM)*.

This formulation has much in common with other suggestions contained in the literature. Something like the anticipation-invigoration mechanism has been suggested by Seward, Sheffield and Campbell, Amsel, Spence, and Brown and Farber; and it is analogous to mechanisms proposed by Mowrer, Young, and McClelland, among others. The emphasis on incentives, long characterizing Tolman's work in conjunction with expectation, is, of course, a predecessor.

We conceive the invigoration, coming from anticipation, to be dependent on the stimuli which have regularly antedated or accompanied consummatory behavior. As indicated already, these stimuli can be either internal or external. Such stimuli, of course, may also play a role in guiding or directing the behavior which ensues and which anticipation has aroused, to one degree or another. Where the stimuli in the situation (including any arising from the deprivation state) have been previously associated with specific instrumental responses, such as making a right turn in a T-maze, these responses will occur, their latency and speed (indices of vigor) being dependent on arousal.[8] When the stimuli present are *not* associated with particular responses or response sequences, one would expect restless, agitated, variable behavior to be the effect of arousal. What we are stressing is that stimuli, including any coming from internal features of the deprivation state, may have a double function: they come through learning to evoke anticipations (and thus arousal) and they serve (after learning) as cues for responses.[9]

The deprivation operation may turn out to be essential, at least in the case of hunger, to the process of establishing anticipations. Stimuli arising from deprivation may be integral to the occurrence of previously established anticipations. But invigoration occurs, not as an inevitable consequence of deprivation but as an effect of anticipations instigated by stimuli that have accompanied feeding. On the other hand, anticipations may develop or occur in the absence of depriva-

---

[8] Such stimulus-response associations could have been acquired under a deprivation state different from the one that is currently present.

[9] Neal Miller has proposed a drive and a cue function for stimuli. The drive function, however, is correlated with stimulus intensity. In our formulation the stimulus intensity is not critical to the evocation of anticipations.

tion: cues associated with a sweet taste or with sexual satisfaction may arouse an organism, even though it is sated for food and has not been subjected to prolonged sexual abstinence.

We do not propose that anticipation is a sufficient mechanism to account for all the phenomena to which the concept of motivation is relevant. In the first place, there is too little information for dogmatism on any point, and we have purposely avoided doing more here than suggesting that anticipation can serve as a fundamental process underlying motivation. In the second place, and more important, anticipation can only work *after* learning has occurred. What can we say of cases in which learning is unnecessary for motivated behavior to occur?

In answering this question, we have found Beach's (1956) account of sexual arousal (SAM, see Chapter 4) a plausible one, although the discussion which follows will indicate one or two of its problems. Beach argues, essentially, that stimulation is necessary to arouse sexual behavior in an organism that is hormonally "ready" for it. In other words, sexual behavior depends on two conditions: adequate hormonal levels *and* adequate external stimulation. (In the human, symbolic stimuli may replace direct stimulation.) Hormonal readiness alone, Beach has observed, is not a sufficient condition for sexual behavior to occur. It is doubtful, as a matter of fact, that a hormonally "ready" rat is sexually aroused at all in the absence of certain stimuli. When an oestrus female is present, however, the male shows interest, but he does not attempt copulation until some time has passed. This interval is occupied by interactions of the animals (see Chapter 4) which apparently increase the sexual arousal of the male to some level at which he will begin copulation. (Beach refers to this as the "copulatory threshold.") And without the hormonal factor (as in prepuberal castrates), the stimulation from the receptive female is not sufficient to engage the animal's sexual interest. The arousal depends on the stimuli from the female in the presence of an adequate hormonal state.

In experienced animals, anticipations set off by cues from the mate or from the situation can lead to arousal. But there is a strong implication in work on sexual, maternal, migratory, and other such phenomena that arousal can occur initially without experience. In accounting for this, Beach suggests, as did Lashley (1938a) in writing of a variety of instinctive behaviors, that the hormonal state sensitizes the animal selectively with respect to stimuli. Thus the hormonally ready male rat is more likely to respond to and be aroused by the receptive female than he would be if not hormonally ready or than he would be if the stimuli were nonsexual.

The basis for this selective sensitization is unknown but is presumably innate. It is, of course, possible that it does not exist at all. Investigations of sexual (and other "instinctive" behaviors) usually do not test the relative arousal value of instinct-related stimuli (like a receptive female) and of other unrelated stimuli. It is possible, but it is only a speculation, that a hormonally ready animal is generally more responsive to a wide variety of stimuli than one which is not ready and that the evidence of *selective* sensitization has appeared because investigators have usually employed only the stimuli in which they happened to be interested. We have already mentioned that under controlled, constant, environmental conditions the activity increments expected under food deprivation do not always occur. However, when stimuli are introduced, activity *does* increase, and the increment is larger in deprived animals than in satiated animals. This suggests that the deprivation sensitizes the animal to external stimuli (even though they may be unrelated to the provision of food) so that they have augmented arousal value; perhaps other states of readiness, like that for sexual behavior, have similar general effects.

Whatever the mechanism by which selective sensitization occurs, if in fact it does, the presence of the appropriate stimuli serves to excite or arouse the animal.[10] This may be an innate effect, probably modifiable by learning. In addition, the stimuli can guide or elicit the responses which comprise the instinctive act sequence. The occurrence of responses from this sequence may contribute further to arousal and to the subsequent unfolding of the later innate acts in the sequence. In any case, arousal is the key factor, so far as motivation is concerned, in behavioral events in which sensitization is critical. We may speak of a *sensitization-arousal* or *sensitization-invigoration mechanism* (*SIM*) which parallels the *anticipation-arousal* or *anticipation-invigoration mechanism*.

When the behavior energized either by *anticipation-arousal* or by *sensitization-arousal* occurs and leads to consummatory behavior, the aroused state must be affected in some way. The feedback from consummatory behavior, sometimes described as reinforcing, evidently permits a given arousal episode to be terminated. Whether this results from satiation, habituation, enjoyment, or some other process is as yet unclear.

---

[10] Selective sensitization of receptors was proposed by Richter (see Chapter 5) as a means of accounting for specific hungers. He suggested that sensory thresholds for needed substances were lowered. Tests of this proposition have not confirmed it. A learning interpretation of specific hungers has plausibility, but more work is required to establish its likelihood.

Is there any point to our emphasizing arousal [11] based on stimulus-induced anticipations and on responses to stimuli to which the animal is sensitized? That is, do these notions have advantages over drive? Aside from the point that we think these ideas agree better with the facts than the drive notion, there is another important implication. If behavior is determined significantly by internal drives, waxing and waning in terms of deprivation and satiation, there is little that can be done to modify the behavior, short of eliminating the drives (perhaps an impossible task in some cases) or encouraging their indirect expression in alternative ways (as by "sublimation"). However, to the extent that behavior is determined by learned anticipations, it is possible to conceive the modification of behavior by means of eliminating or altering the expectations; while no concrete suggestions for doing so can be made at this time, procedures for changing expectations should in principle be less difficult than those for eliminating drives or changing responses to them. And further, on an expectation conception of motivation, one would not be concerned with the possible accumulation of energy based on biological or "psychic" sources.

FUNCTIONS OF MOTIVATION

In Chapter 1 we listed the functions to which motivation has been assigned, and we pointed out there that there has been a highly general "conceptual commitment" to motivation, as expressed in the phrase "all behavior is motivated," or in the idea that without motivation there would be no behavior. As an expression of a conviction that behavior is *determined*, this commitment is one with which we should not care to argue. As a postulate that motivation has an overriding importance in the analysis of behavior, however, this assertion must give us pause.

Aside from this deterministic implication, however, two meanings seem to stem from the commitment to motivation. One has a purposive cast, in the sense that behavior is seen as *directed* to the satisfaction of the organism's needs. Such a view tends to ignore the possibility that behavior may arise from factors independent of motivation. More importantly, however, it asserts the directed character of behavior without specifying how the direction comes about. It is clear

---

[11] Hunt (1963) has also made arousal the central concept in motivation. An incongruity-congruity principle is responsible for the arousal in his view. Anticipation and sensitization might be analyzed in terms of this principle, but we prefer to leave them relatively specific, as the more specific a suggestion is the easier it is to test and thus to disprove.

that behavior often has a directional character, but it is also evident that this direction can come about as a result of many determinants, including (1) innate structures, (2) abilities, (3) control by external stimuli, and (4) mediation by habit, perhaps as well as by motivation. The factors that control behavior are multiple. If motivation does direct behavior, this can occur only through the stimuli which motivational states provide—the stimuli to which such states sensitize the organism, the incentive objects to which they orient it, or the activation of innate or habit structures. Such mechanisms involve much more than the mere assertion that motives direct behavior.

It is said that without motivation there would be no behavior, and this is the second meaning of the commitment to motivation. The unmotivated organism is an inactive one, quiescent, perhaps sleeping.[12] But it is clear to us that a *living* organism is never *totally* inactive; when it is, it is dead. The issue of activity vs. inactivity is a false one, although the problem of levels or degrees of activity is a real one. Activity is a property of living organisms, and its sheer existence does not constitute a motivational or, indeed, a psychological problem.[13]

We think it is evident from this discussion that motivation does not need to be invoked to account for the directional property of behavior or for the fact that behavior occurs. However, as indicated in the discussion of mechanisms, we do think that the motivation notion is needed to account for the invigoration of behavior. Whether or not this invigoration will energize many responses, a few, or only one, will depend on the stimulus situation. In the presence of a strong stimulus-response association, only one response will be evoked. In the absence of any prepotent tendencies a variety of responses may be energized.

RELATIONSHIPS OF MECHANISMS TO MOTIVATIONAL
FACTS AND THEORIES

The facts and theories of motivation have been reviewed in Chapters 3 through 15. In general, the facts that have been gathered relate closely to the theories under whose aegis they were collected or pertain especially to the particular area of inquiry in which they are embedded. Hence, the evaluation of the two mechanisms will proceed sequentially

[12] It is amusing to note that while the phenomenon of inactivity is taken by some theorists as indicating absence of motivation, they often also postulate drives for sleep or for rest.

[13] This point has been made by Bindra (1959), Cofer (1954), Hebb (1949), Hunt (1960), McClelland et al. (1953), Murphy (1947), and White (1959), among others. While Hebb (1955) seemed to retract his earlier position, it seems to us that the facts of arousal with which he was mainly concerned do not bear directly on this issue.

through the topics of this book and will treat simultaneously of fact and theory. The mechanisms will be examined in each context, and usually it will be true that for a given topic one is more relevant than the other one.

Ethology (Chapter 3)

The major ethological observations relate the occurrence of specific acts or behavior patterns to specific stimuli under conditions of hormonal "readiness." [14] In general, it appears that these findings can be accommodated by the *sensitization-invigoration mechanism*, since much of the ethologists' work suggests that the organism becomes sensitive, for example, seasonally, to certain stimuli. On the occurrence of the stimuli, the instinctive series of acts is aroused or released, and each element in the chain is released in turn by stimuli emanating from the prior response, or from a response of another organism in the case of social behavior (e.g., sexual and fighting behavior).

The ethologists, however, have used a hydraulic model, emphasizing the building up of energy, apparently due to hormonal changes, which at high levels can discharge without an adequate stimulus. This is vacuum activity. There are also displacement activities, but these seem to arise when a response, released in a situation, is blocked by incompatible responses released by other features of the situation.

Our previous discussion of the *sensitization-arousal mechanism* implied that there is an adequate stimulus to which the physiologically ready animal is sensitized and which raises the arousal level when it occurs. This is, of course, an oversimplification. There is probably a *band of stimuli* which can function this way. What we mean here is that stimuli varying over some range of intensity, color, size, patterns, etc., can arouse the sensitized animal. Perhaps band width is a function of degree of physiological readiness, so that the animal will be sensitive to less than adequate stimuli under high readiness and therefore be aroused by them.

As pointed out in Chapter 3, we do not know how often vacuum activities occur; thus it is not possible to estimate how severe a problem they pose for this mechanism. However, it is likely that there are some stimuli to which the sensitized animal responds, in so-called vacuum activity, even though the stimuli present are not obviously adequate

---

[14] Certain facts, such as the release of alarm reactions by specific stimulus patterns, are apparent exceptions to this statement but perhaps do not involve motivation (however, see Schneirla, 1959a). The fact of imprinting is not a motivational problem, either, although motivation variables may affect its occurrence.

ones. Vacuum activity thus may represent behavior occurring when the band width for stimuli is very wide.

Bodily Conditions: Maternal, Parental, Sexual, and Other Behaviors (Chapter 4)

In outlining the *sensitization-arousal mechanism*, we spoke of sexual behavior in the male rat which provided the model for the mechanism. (Beach, 1956, has suggested that this model is also applicable to the human male, with the addition of symbolic and fantasied stimuli.) It is probable that the female's sexual behavior also is aroused by stimuli from the male to which she is sensitized.

In sexual behavior, the actual pattern of acts which occurs, whether it is innate, acquired, or an admixture of both, is not a motivational problem, as it is mediated by innate or learned structures. The arousal of the sensitized animal under appropriate stimulation (including the act sequence on the part of the mate) presumably energizes the appropriate structures and controls the vigor of the responses they mediate.[15]

The same formulation can be applied to many other instances of behavior described in Chapter 4: maternal, nesting, retrieving, nursing, sucking and incubation behaviors, migration, homing and hoarding, respiration, and temperature regulation. The critical matter in all of these cases is, for motivation, the condition which activates or energizes the relevant response patterns, whether these are innate or acquired. In maternal behaviors—retrieving, incubation, feeding, and migration, for example—there is a hormonal state in the presence of which the animal reacts to and is presumably aroused by stimuli to which it is less likely to react if the hormonal state is not present. The *sensitization-invigoration mechanism* seems appropriate to these instances.

In other instances, a hormonal state does not seem to be initially involved. However, invigoration seems to occur under extremes of temperature and, under appropriate external conditions, leads to rectifying instrumental behavior, much of which may be learned; nesting behavior occurs under these conditions, although nest-building itself may, in many species, be unlearned. The arousal conditions which underlie hoarding and homing cannot now be specified; in hoarding, the evi-

---

[15] It is unfortunate that in the case of sexual arousal, as in the cases of other arousal conditions described in Chapter 4, little attention has been devoted to the question whether the arousal can energize responses other than those specific to the stimuli to which the animal has been sensitized. Can, for example, sexual or maternal arousal energize responses learned and reinforced under food deprivation?

dence conflicts as to whether a deprivation condition is involved and whether past experience is essential. Homing has been studied largely from the viewpoint of the cues which control it rather than from the aspect of its invigoration. It occurs, of course, when the bird is away from "home," and perhaps the alien environment is capable of arousing the bird and thereby energizing whatever mechanisms underlie the homing performance proper.

The mechanisms of sucking and contact-related behavior are too little understood at present to enable us to attempt an application of either mechanism to them. In the cases of reactive inhibition, fatigue, and sleep, it seems likely that the states themselves, either directly or through a sensitizing process, instigate responses appropriate to the rectification of the initiating conditions. It is also possible that *anticipation-arousal* can occur when the relief of these states is prevented.

Bodily Conditions: Hunger, Thirst, and Pain Avoidance (Chapter 5)

The description of hunger and thirst in Chapter 5 revealed that the control of eating and drinking resides in hypothalamic and other neural centers and that these centers are probably themselves regulated by the constitution of the blood, or by temperature, in the case of hunger, and by cellular dehydration, in the case of thirst. It is important to note that in experiments related to the functioning of these centers and to the factors which control them, incentive objects—food or water—are always present, and experienced animals are always used. At the level of actual behavior, then, the animal, sensitized by past experience to food or water stimuli through the activity of the neural centers, is in a state to be aroused by these stimuli and thus to have consummatory responses invigorated. Since naive animals have never been used in experiments in which neural centers have been stimulated, it is not possible to decide whether a *sensitization-arousal mechanism* or an *anticipation-arousal mechanism* (or both) should be invoked to deal with the consummatory behavior involved.

In many hunger experiments, however, it seems likely that the anticipation-arousal mechanism would apply. Experience seems to be essential for the deprived animal to start eating quickly and to continue eating in the time available. We would interpret these findings as requiring that the animal learn that the cues of the eating situation are associated with food. These cues (and the food itself) can then arouse anticipatory feeding responses, such as salivation, lip-licking, swallowing, and the like. If these responses have arousal effects, the eating responses would be invigorated. It is possible that the arousal effects would be greatest after the animal has been frustrated because of his being removed, on initial trials in the situation, before hunger was completely satisfied. Components of the eating response, conditioned to the invigoration arising from frustration, could then elicit this arousal on subsequent introduction to the situation, invigorating the eating responses.

In other experiments on hunger and thirst, in which incentives are present, it has always been possible for the animal, over trials, to learn anticipatory responses to the cues of the situation. Thus, in obstruction box experiments the animal repeatedly runs from starting box to incentive, and it seems likely that the cues of the starting box come to arouse anticipatory responses which can then invigorate the running response. Similarly, in other situations, such as running a runway, pressing a bar, or pushing a lever, a parallel analysis may be made. Young has described the state of readiness manifested by animals in the starting box of an apparatus after they have run down an alley to sweet tastes. It seems clear that this readiness represents a condition of invigoration, probably mediated by the anticipatory reactions learned as a result of prior runs to this reinforcement. Whether sweet tastes (for some species) have the capacity to arouse especially vigorous consummatory responses on the basis of learning or because of innate reactions is a problem to which an answer is of interest but not essential to the present argument. Studies of specific hunger have not been sufficiently analytic, in most instances, to permit a judgment of whether the anticipation-arousal mechanism can account for their findings.[16]

Pain avoidance, in studies of motivation, has been of importance mainly to the notion of acquired motivation. We deal with it in terms of the invigoration mechanisms in discussing drives.

Activity and Exploration (Chapter 6)

The discussion of activity in Chapter 6 could reach no satisfactory general conclusion as to the existence of an independent drive for restless and running activity. It is evident, however, that activity variations bear some relationship to hunger, and our description of the *anticipation-invigoration mechanism*, a few pages back, indicated how this mechanism could deal with such variations. The literature clearly suggests that activity is affected by variations in the health and physiologi-

[16] Choice of one substance over another may be due to learned preferences, although the preference may have been originally learned because one substance elicited more vigorous consummatory responses (and therefore more vigorous anticipatory responses) than the other. We do not agree with Irwin (1958) that choice or preference is a unique sign of motivation.

cal status of the animal, and it is perhaps possible that in the healthy, rested animal it is external stimuli (including temperature), as much as anything, which arouse him to be active. Running activity in the wheel does seem to carry its own stimuli for continued running.

Exploratory behavior in the several forms which we described in Chapter 6 has been interpreted by Berlyne as involving arousal. The novel stimulus, or the sudden, incongruous, intense, or changing one, he has argued, creates an emotional arousal state. We have also seen that stimulus deprivation may lead to arousal. In the case of novel stimuli, where fear does not occur, Berlyne indicates that the arousal state is reduced by exploration, manipulation, inspection, and so on. In sensory deprivation, arousal is reduced by the reintroduction of familiar sensory input (see, also, Lana, 1960, 1962). Both the novel stimulus and the reduction of stimuli represent deviations from a previously existing state. Such deviations may disrupt ongoing anticipations and add to the invigoration these anticipations may already have engendered. Perhaps more likely is the possibility that such deviations have been associated, in the individual's past, with circumstances in which he has received punishment, been frightened, or obtained rewards. The current deviation, then, could cue off anticipatory arousal, based on the relevant anticipations, which would invigorate those responses of greatest strength in the situation. Approach responses could often be called exploratory, of course.

Homeostatic Models (Chapter 7)

The proposed mechanisms are conceived in the framework of equilibrating processes; that is, arousal, however instigated, leads to behavior, the consequence of which is to restore, at least momentarily, balance to a disturbed system. Evidently, then, our conceptions are consistent with the main, general presuppositions of homeostatic models. Suggesting that arousal may underlie exploratory or other similar behaviors permits the incorporation into this framework of findings that have often been held to be inconsistent with homeostatic and tension-reduction models.

Hedonic and Activation Theories (Chapter 8)

In the conceptions of both P. T. Young and of McClelland the chief motivational factor is an affective state. McClelland refers to affective arousal and indicates that its existence could be assessed by physiological measures, which in other contexts are said to measure arousal. Young, as indicated a moment ago, points to proprioceptive tension in the animal waiting to run to a sweet-tasting object, and this tension would seem to qualify as arousal. In both cases, aspects of the situation, after experience, seem to cue off the affective arousal and the proprioceptive tension, and McClelland explicitly deals with affective arousal as arising from an anticipation of a change in an affective state. Thus, both of these formulations seem to accord well with the *anticipation-invigoration mechanism.*

Arousal and activation theories have chiefly emphasized the points that behavior is more efficient under certain general activation levels than it is under others and that tension increases may be rewarding if they raise general arousal to some optimal point. We have already commented on the latter point in our discussion of equilibration, and elsewhere. As to the former, it seems consistent with the notion that arousal can invigorate responses: too low an arousal level would not do so, and thus behavior would be inefficient; too high an arousal level, in the absence of prepotent response tendencies, might disorganize behavior through the competing responses it could engender.

Activation theory has paid relatively little attention to the conditions of arousal, except in a general way.[17] Stimulation is essential for arousal, but the implication has been that almost any stimulation will do. Our emphasis on the stimuli involved in sensitization-invigoration and anticipation-invigoration ties arousal to relatively specific circumstances and also provides for stimuli which can evoke specific habit or innate structures, which in turn give direction to the resulting behavior.

Frustration, Conflict, and Stress (Chapter 9)

A reading of Chapter 9 will reveal that the major motivational consequence of frustration, conflict, and stress is arousal. Blocking of sequences leading to goals—either because of competing responses or some other mechanism—underlies frustration and conflict, and overloading the organism seems to constitute stress. What is perhaps often involved here is the disruption of anticipations or perhaps the generation of arousal by too many stimuli to which the organism has been sensitized. In general, these conditions are probably characterized by high states of arousal, and in the absence of prepotent tendencies, these states will invigorate a wide variety of responses. Whether they are adaptive, of course, will depend upon their relationships to the requirements of the situation. Theories of frustration-induced drive (Amsel, Spence) and of conflict (Brown and Farber, Neal Miller) seem to fit well with the *anticipation-invigoration mechanism.* This is hardly

---

[17] Duffy's (1962) book appeared too late for us to take account of it in the preparation of this manuscript.

surprising, since Amsel's theory, at least, was one source of its formulation.

Systemic (particularly hormonal) involvement in psychological stress further suggests that a *sensitization-invigoration mechanism* may be significant in certain stress phenomena.

Drive Theory (Chapter 10)

Our rejection of the concept of drive is pertinent especially to the theories of Hull and Neal Miller, but we do not think it affects the general structure of their formulations. This is because many of the phenomena which led to the notion of drive can be handled as well by the mechanisms of *anticipation-invigoration* and *sensitization-invigoration*. In actual fact, much neo-Hullian theorizing, as seen in the work of Spence, Amsel, and Mowrer, for example, has been in the direction of incentive motivation, and the nature of incentive motivation theory has much in common with the *anticipation-invigoration mechanism*. As we point out momentarily, acquired drive seems to fit this mechanism as well, and this fact is relevant to Miller's ideas. We conceive the invigoration feature as functioning in part as generalized D was supposed to function, thus preserving one of the most interesting aspects of drive theory—the separate mechanisms governing learning and performance. (In a book on motivation, we need make no commitment to a theory of the nature of learning.)

Perhaps the major importance of drive, in the eyes of many students of learning, is that it makes animals active and responsive when they are placed in learning situations. While this is true, we may point out again that the operations of deprivation do not require interpretation in terms of drive. Typical in studies of animal learning is a phase of habituation to a feeding rhythm. It is quite likely, as we earlier noted, that this procedure provides that the animal anticipate feeding at the time set for learning. These anticipatory feeding responses invigorate instrumental behaviors.

Tolman, whose work was concerned with incentives and with expectations (anticipations), did not describe a mechanism comparable to arousal. However, we can see no difficulty in incorporating the many observations made by him and his students concerning incentives in the *anticipation-invigoration mechanism*. A similar point may be made for Guthrie, who actually wrote briefly of a similar mechanism. The major aspect of Skinner's work which would not be dealt with in the terms outlined above is that on reinforcement schedules. We do not yet know whether these schedules require a motivational interpretation, but it is possible that the *anticipation-arousal mechanism* may be capable of incorporating some of the phenomena of the schedules.

Learning, Performance, Incentive, Reinforcement, and
Acquired Drive (Chapter 11)

Our summary concerning the relationship of deprivation (drive) to acquisition of responses did not yield a clear conclusion. This was very possibly due to the fact that, in many cases, different habits are learned under short deprivation durations from those learned under long deprivations. And it was the distractibility of the animal under short deprivations that was seen as giving rise to the differences. Conversely, longer deprivation periods provide greater opportunity for cues to become associated strongly with anticipations. Thus, prepotent responses would be increasingly likely to be evoked by anticipations under long rather than short deprivations.

Our discussion of acquired drive brought out the fact, so far demonstrated only in avoidance situations,[18] that such drives consist of emotional responses to situational cues, the responses being anticipatory to the occurrence of shock. These responses constitute arousal and are seen to invigorate further behavior. Clearly this phenomenon is an illustration of the *anticipation-invigoration mechanism.*

We should note that in avoidance learning it has been found that while arousal may be essential to the *formation* of an avoidance response, it is not necessary to the *maintenance* of the response, suggesting that the arousal can be short-circuited. This is an important matter, as it means that measurable arousal will not always be present when responses which are well-learned are involved. However, in the history of such responses, a period in which the occurrence of arousal could be observed would be demonstrable.

The Psychoanalytic Model (Chapter 12)

Insofar as the psychoanalytic model employs a drive-like concept, our rejection of the notion of drive is critical to the presuppositions of the model. However, it is by no means clear just what the drive-like conception of psychoanalysis is or how important it is to the structure of the model. It is obvious that a significant aspect of the point of view involves arousal by objects and other stimuli (e.g., symbolic, internal stimuli). The arousal may occur in relation to desired objects and also in relation to fear- and anxiety-inducing or -arousing objects and stimuli. The frequent use, in psychoanalytic writings, of emotion-denoting words clearly implies that arousal is tied to situations and

---

[18] Wright (1963) has reported a new demonstration of acquired motivation based on hunger. He interprets his findings, not in terms of acquired drive, but as evidencing emotional frustration arising from conditioned anticipations.

stimuli. The analytic mechanisms are instrumental or adjustive devices for adaptation to arousal, so that in themselves they are not, strictly speaking, motivational concepts. We are unable to be certain of the applicability of the *sensitization-invigoration* and *anticipation-invigoration mechanisms* to psychoanalysis, but it is our impression that the critical arousal feature of the psychoanalytic model is, at least logically and theoretically, in accord with these mechanisms.

Turning to the new ego psychology, we believe that the concepts it has introduced are essentially structural ones, and no motivational mechanisms seem to have been proposed beyond those already postulated by classical psychoanalysis.

Self-Actualization (Chapter 13)

So far as the ultimate motive which this group postulates—that of self-actualization—it is very difficult to decide just what the motive consists of, let alone to decide whether our mechanisms have relationships to it. The emphasis is on individual growth, but the directions of growth are not spelled out as they differ from individual to individual. At a general level we could say that whatever the goals or satisfactions of growth may be, it seems likely that they give rise to anticipatory reactions before they are achieved. If so, this would provide the invigoration mechanism which would then energize the specific course of acts which are involved in the realization of growth.

Some Major Human Motives (Chapter 14)

The major motives we outlined in Chapter 14 were anxiety, achievement, dependency, and aggression. It is clear that arousal is the main function of anxiety, as a motive. Anxiety is, almost by definition, an aroused state. And, also almost by definition, the arousal occurs because of anticipation of future events. Thus anxiety, as did acquired drive in the case of fear, fits the *anticipation-invigoration mechanism* rather well. What the arousal will invigorate, of course, will depend on the responses available, and they may or may not be compatible with performance of the task in which the individual is engaged.

In achievement, too, current theorizing implies that certain cues, acting on a person with a strong need for achievement, will trigger anticipations of enjoyment (in McClelland's sense) or, more generally, satisfaction through the accomplishment of something. Presumably these anticipations are arousing and would invigorate responses suitable to reaching the goal. Arousal should also occur in people who "fear" failure, but the responses invigorated here would probably not be identical with those aroused by a "positive" achievement goal. Similar accounts could be given of affiliation, power, and the other needs in the McClelland list.

Long-term achievement or other enduring motives are more difficult to conceive in terms of anticipation-arousal. One possibility is that long-term achievement, for example, consists of a series or chain of short-term episodes, each one of which contains arousal due to anticipation of its specific goals. Another possibility, consistent with our earlier discussion of the *anticipation-invigoration mechanism*, is that arousal drops out with sufficient experience of the achievement motive sequences, and the practice of working to achieve becomes habitual. The argument for so-called functionally autonomous motives may be dealt with in this way. There are insufficient data available, however, to permit a decision on these points.

We saw in Chapter 14 that dependency and aggression are not very well understood and that there is some question about their independent motivational status. However, emotional arousal (as in anger) cued off by situations or noxious stimuli was seen as qualifying as motivational. In general, this account seems to fit reasonably well with our description of *anticipation-invigoration*, especially if the blocking of anticipations constitutes a motivational state of affairs.

Social Motivation (Chapter 15)

Many of the topics we discussed in Chapter 15 were more or less concerned with ego-involvement. Included were direct studies of ego-involvement as well as those of incentives, competition, interruption and resumption of tasks, substitute value, and the level of aspiration. These studies generally involve some procedure for arousing the subject; he is led to anticipate either failure, frustration, or embarrassment. It is clear that arousal is involved in most of these situations and that anticipation is often, if not always, involved. We think the *anticipation-invigoration mechanism* is germane to this kind of phenomenon.

The other chief topic of Chapter 15 concerned dissonance formulations. There is no question that arousal is postulated here, since dissonance or imbalance is an arousal state almost by definition. The anticipatory aspects of the formulation are not entirely clear, although in a good many experiments the subject is asked to commit himself to do something. It is conceivable that the anticipation of the consequences of what he is to do (which is usually contrary to an attitude, opinion, or preference he has) or of the consequences of failure produces the arousal. If this is so, as seems likely, then the dissonance formulation would fit nicely with the *anticipation-invigoration mechanism*.

GENERAL COMMENT

In advancing the notion of arousal, as expressed in the *sensitization-* and *anticipation-invigoration mechanisms,* we recognize that we have not been very specific. It would take many more pages than we have written and a great many more experiments than have been performed to present these concepts rigorously and to test their adequacy. The purposes we have served by this discussion, however, are as follows:

1. We wished to point out that the drive concept is without utility. As a matter of fact we think it is worse than this—it is a liability. Nevertheless, we recognized that to reject drive without the positing of plausible alternatives would not be constructive, and we have made arousal, we think, an attractive alternative. However, we also feel that arousal, without some anchoring, is a slippery notion, and we have therefore attempted to anchor it to internal and situational stimuli by means of sensitization and anticipation. There are good precedents for both of these anchors.

It should be clear that in rejecting drive we do not mean to imply that the enormous amount of research which has been conducted within that framework is also being rejected. On the contrary, we believe that the experimental work composing the research literature of drive is fundamentally sound, whereas its interpretation in terms of the drive conception has been unfortunately limiting. The proposals made in this chapter, then, are intended as an interpretive reconceptualization—a new and more fruitful way, we hope, of conceptualizing the facts of motivation—rather than a rejection of these facts.

2. Another reason for this discussion is that we think motivation has been expected to and been used to explain too much. In rejecting drive, we have also rejected the notion that all behavior is motivated, and we have emphasized that the *directional* component of behavior is determined by innate or habit factors brought into play by situational stimuli in combination with arousal, as well as by nonpsychological factors in the situations in which behavior occurs; hence the emphasis on *invigoration* as a motivational term in our formulations.

3. Motivation is too often postulated as a *deus ex machina* and, as has been the case in the past with instinct, has seemed to explain without doing so. In emphasizing invigoration, we have sought to set a condition that must be satisfied if we are going to say that motivation is operative. That is, there must be some evidence that an invigoration process has been evoked before we can say that behavior reflects motivation. Unfortunately, no single criterion measure will satisfy this requirement. Our choice of the term invigoration in lieu of arousal was

intentional and necessary, we believe, because the latter term commonly implies an emotional state, direct evidence of which is not always present when a motivational process is at work. In instances in which the arousal phase has been short-circuited, for example, we shall probably need to rely either on individual historical evidence or on a behavioral criterion (e.g., response vigor). The use of contemporaneous measures of autonomic functioning so commonly employed as evidence of arousal is also limited, since such indices are themselves subject to the influence of differential learning and of adaptation effects which may not identically affect the underlying invigoration process. By the same token, however, it should be clear that even in the use of behavioral evidence, such as increments in response vigor, care must be exercised to determine whether the greater vigor of a response represents an increase in motivation or is the result of the discriminative *learning* of a response of greater intensity. Perhaps our distinction between *sensitization-invigoration* and *anticipation-invigoration* will encourage the search for different kinds of criteria, either in selective neurophysiological measures or in behavior, related to the two sources of invigoration, rather than reliance on a single undifferentiated type of index (e.g., autonomic functioning) which, as has been noted, we really have no reason to expect to be present on all occasions of response invigoration.

4. Finally, not only in the matter of criteria but in other ways as well, we hope that the suggested mechanisms will point the way to more analytic experimentation in areas where, to date, only rather general information is available. Thus, for example, in studies of specific hungers and of cognitive dissonance, to mention but two areas, we need more detailed accounting of anticipations (or sensitizations) and of degrees of arousal. With such concept-related data in hand we shall be better able to assess the usefulness of these and other proposed mechanisms and to move forward more rapidly in the construction of the motivational aspects of a comprehensive behavior theory.

Bibliography-Author Index

(The pages on which citations occur are given in brackets)

Abelson, R. P., & Rosenberg, M. J. (1958) Symbolic psycho-logic: A model of attitudinal cognition. *Behavioral Sci.* 3, 1–13. [788]

Abramson, H. A. (Ed.) (1957) *Neuropharmacology*. Transac. Third Conf., New York: Josiah Macy, Jr. Found. [150]

Adams, O. S., & Chiles, W. D. (1960) *Human performance as a function of the work-rest cycle*. Wright Field, Ohio: USAF WADD Tech. Rep. 60–248, Contract No. AF 33(616)-6050. [164]

Adelson, J. (1956) On man's goodness. *Contemp. Psychol.* 1, 67–69. [667]

Adler, A. (1917) *Study of organ inferiority and its physical compensation*. New York: Nerv. and Ment. Dis. Publ. Co. [627]

Adlerstein, A., & Fehrer, E. (1955) The effect of food deprivation on exploratory behavior in a complex maze. *J. comp. physiol. Psychol.* 48, 250–253. [290]

Adolph, E. F. (1941) The internal environment and behavior: III. Water content. *Amer. J. Psychiat.* 97, 1365–1373. [248]

Adolph, E. F. (1943) *Physiological regulations*. Lancaster, Pa: The Jacques Cattell Press. [256]

Adolph, E. F. (1948) Water ingestion and excretion in rats under some chemical influences. *Amer. J. Physiol.* 155, 309–316. [247]

Adolph, E. F. (1950) Thirst and its inhibition in the stomach. *Amer. J. Physiol.* 161, 374–386. [252]

Adolph, E. F. (1957) Ontogeny of physiological regulations in the rat. *Quart. Rev. Biol.* 32, 89–137. [257]

Adolph, E. F., Barker, J. P., & Hoy, P. A. (1954) Multiple factors in thirst. *Amer. J. Physiol.* 178, 538–562. [257]

Adolph, E. F., et al. (1947) *Physiology of man in the desert*. New York: Interscience Publishers. [247]

Adriaanse, A., (1947) *Ammophila campestris* Latr. und *Ammophila adriaansei* Wilcke. Ein Beitrag zur vergleichenden Verhaltensforschung. *Behavior* 1, 1–35 (cited by Tinbergen, 1951). [8]

Adrian, E. D., Bremer, F., & Jasper, H. (Eds.) (1954) *Brain mechanism and consciousness*. Oxford: Blackwell Scientific Publications. [402]

Adrian, O. M. (1960) Discussion. In Wolstenholme, G.E.W. and O'Connor, Maeve (Eds.) *Ciba Foundation symposium on the nature of sleep*. Boston: Little, Brown and Co., p. 386. [168]

Aiken, E. G. (1957) *Response reversal and fatigue*. Fort Knox: U. S. Army Med. Res. Lab. Report No. 289. [139]

Airapetyantz, E. S., & Bykov, K. M. (1945) Physiological experiments and the psychology of the unconscious. *Philos. and phenomenol. Res.* 5, 577–583. [265]

Albino, R. C., & Long, M. (1951) The effect of infant food-deprivation upon adult hoarding in the white rat. *Brit. J. Psychol.* 42, 146–154. [124]

Aldrich, C. K. (1955) *Psychiatry for the family physician*. New York: Blakiston Div., McGraw-Hill. [323]

Alexander, F. (1950) *Psychosomatic medicine*. New York: W. W. Norton. [589]

Alexander, F. (1956) *Psychoanalysis and psychotherapy*. New York: W. W. Norton. [629]

Allan, H., & Wiles, P. (1932) The role of the pituitary gland and parturition. I. Hypophysectomy. *J. Physiol.* **75**, 23–28.   **[111]**

Allee, W. C., Emerson, A. E., Park, O., Park, T., & Schmidt, K. P. (1949) *Principles of animal ecology.* Philadelphia: W. B. Saunders.   **[307, 327]**

Allee, W. C., Nissen, H. W., & Nimkoff, M. F. (1953) A re-examination of the concept of instinct. *Psychol. Rev.* **60**, 287–297.   **[78]**

Allison, J., & Hunt, D. E. (1959) Social desirability and expression of aggression under varying conditions of frustration. *J. consult. Psychol.* **23**, 528–532. **[750]**

Allport, F. H. (1920) The influence of the group upon association and thought. *J. exp. Psychol.* **3**, 159–182.   **[776]**

Allport, F. H. (1924) *Social psychology.* Boston: Houghton-Mifflin.   **[43, 776]**

Allport, G. W. (1937) *Personality: A psychological interpretation.* New York: Holt.   **[314, 318, 322, 572, 637, 661, 804]**

Allport, G. W. (1940) Motivation in personality: Reply to Mr. Bertocci. *Psychol. Rev.* **47**, 533–554.   **[572]**

Allport, G. W. (1942) *The use of personal documents in psychological science.* New York: Soc. Sci. Res. Council, Bull. No. 49.   **[661]**

Allport, G. W. (1943) The ego in contemporary psychology. *Psychol. Bull.* **50**, 451–478.   **[662]**

Allport, G. W. (1953) The trend in motivation theory. *Amer. J. Orthopsychiat.* **23**, 107–119.   **[329]**

Allport, G. W. (1954) The historical background of modern social psychology. In Lindzey, G. (Ed.) *Handbook of social psychology.* Cambridge: Addison-Wesley Press, Vol. I, pp. 3–56.   **[44, 51, 567]**

Allport, G. W. (1955) *Becoming: Basic considerations for a psychology of personality.* New Haven: Yale University Press.   **[320, 666, 667]**

Allport, G. W. (1960) *Personality and social encounter.* Boston: Beacon Press. **[661]**

Allport, G. W. (1961) *Pattern and growth in personality.* New York: Holt, Rinehart & Winston.   **[572, 661]**

Almquist, J. O., & Hale, E. B. (1956) An approach to the measurement of sexual behavior and semen production of dairy bulls. *Proc. 3rd. Internat'l. Cong. Anim. Reproduc.*, London: Brown, Knight and Truscott, Ltd., pp. 50–59. **[193]**

Alper, Thelma G. (1946) Task-orientation vs. ego-orientation in learning and retention. *Amer. J. Psychol.* **59**, 236–248.   **[785]**

Alper, Thelma G. (1948a) Task-orientation and ego-orientation as factors in reminiscence. *J. exp. Psychol.* **38**, 224–238.   **[785]**

Alper, Thelma G. (1948b) Memory for completed and incompleted tasks as a function of personality: Correlation between experimental and personality data. *J. Pers.* **17**, 104–137.   **[363]**

Amacher, P. A. (1962) The influence of the neuroanatomy, neurophysiology and psychiatry of Freud's teachers on his Psychoanalytic theories. Unpubl. doctoral dissert., University of Washington.   **[597]**

Ames, A., Jr. (1946) *Some demonstrations concerned with the origin and nature of our sensations (what we experience).* Hanover, N.H.: The Hanover Institute (mimeo).   **[318]**

Ammons, R. B. (1956) Effects of knowledge of performance: A survey and tentative theoretical formulation. *J. gen. Psychol.* **54**, 279–299.   **[770]**

Amsel, A. (1949) Selective association and the anticipatory goal response mechanism as explanatory concepts in learning theory. *J. exp. Psychol.* **39**, 785–799. **[265]**

Amsel, A. (1950a) The combination of a primary appetitional need with primary and secondary emotionally derived needs. *J. exp. Psychol.* **40**, 1–14.   **[523, 537]**

Amsel, A. (1950b) The effect upon level of consummatory response of the addition of anxiety to a motivational complex. *J. exp. Psychol.* **40**, 709–715. [537, 578]

Amsel, A. (1951) A three-factor theory of inhibition: An addition to Hull's two-factor theory. *Amer. Psychologist* **6**, 487 (Abstr.). [420]

Amsel, A. (1958) The role of frustrative nonreward in noncontinuous reward situations. *Psychol. Bull.* **55**, 102–119. [420, 421, 489, 562, 563, 749]

Amsel, A. (1962) Frustrative nonreward in partial reinforcement and discrimination learning: Some recent history and a theoretical extension. *Psychol. Rev.* **69**, 306–328. [420, 489, 562, 563]

Amsel, A., & Maltzman, I. (1950) The effect upon generalized drive strength of emotionality as inferred from the level of consummatory response. *J. exp. Psychol.* **40**, 563–569. [537]

Amsel, A., & McDonnell, R. (1951) Discrimination of pain from conditioned pain in the rat. *J. comp. physiol. Psychol.* **44**, 457–461. [265]

Amsel, A., & Roussel, J. (1952) Motivational properties of frustration: I. Effect on a running response of the addition of frustration to the motivational complex. *J. exp. Psychol.* **43**, 363–368. [421]

Amsel, A., & Ward, J. S. (1954) Motivational properties of frustration: II. Frustration drive stimulus and frustration reduction in selective learning. *J. exp. Psychol.* **48**, 37–47. [421]

Amsel, A., & Work, M. S. (1961) The role of learned factors in "spontaneous" activity. *J. comp. physiol. Psychol.* **54**, 527–532. [277]

Anand, B. K. (1961) Nervous regulation of food intake. *Physiol. Rev.* **41**, 677–708. [222, 225]

Anand, B. K., & Brobeck, J. R. (1951) Hypothalamic control of food intake in rats and cats. *Yale J. biol. Med.* **24**, 123–140. [217]

Anand, B. K., Dua, S., & Schoenberg, K. (1955) Hypothalamic control of food intake in cats and monkeys. *J. Physiol.* **127**, 143–152. [219]

Anastasi, Ann & Foley, J. P., Jr. (1948) A proposed reorientation in the heredity-environment controversy. *Psychol. Rev.* **55**, 239–249. [43]

Anderson, Camilla (1957) *Beyond Freud.* New York: Harper. [630]

Anderson, E. E. (1937) Interrelationship of drives in the male albino rat: I. Intercorrelations of measures of drives. *J. comp. Psychol.* **24**, 73–118. [189, 255, 267, 271]

Anderson, E. E. (1938) The interrelationship of drives in the male albino rat: II. Intercorrelations between 47 measures of drive and learning. *Comp. Psychol. Monog.* **14**, Whole No. 72, pp. 1–119. [186, 187, 238, 255, 267]

Anderson, E. E. (1941a) The externalization of drive: I. Theoretical considerations. *Psychol. Rev.* **48**, 204–224. [474, 572, 581]

Anderson, E. E. (1941b) The externalization of drive: II. The effect of satiation and removal of reward at different stages of the learning process of the rat. *J. genet. Psychol.* **59**, 359–376. [474, 572]

Anderson, E. E. (1941c) The externalization of drive: III. Maze learning by non-rewarded and by satiated rats. *J. genet. Psychol.* **59**, 397–426. [572, 581]

Anderson, E. E. (1941d) The externalization of drive: IV. The effect of prefeeding on the maze performance of hungry rats. *J. comp. Psychol.* **31**, 349–352. [552, 572]

Andersson, B. (1953) The effect of injections of hypertonic NaCl-solutions into different parts of the hypothalamus of goats. *Acta physiol. Scand.* **28**, 188–201. [254]

Andersson, B., & Larsson, S. (1961a) Physiological and pharmacological aspects of the control of hunger and thirst. *Pharmacol. Rev.* **13**, 1–16. [222]

Andersson, B., & Larsson, S. (1961b) Influence of local temperature changes in the preoptic area and rostral hypothalamus on the regulation of food and water intake. *Acta physiol. Scand.* **52**, 75–89. [226]

Andersson, B., & McCann, S. M. (1955a) A further study of polydipsia evoked by hypothalamic stimulation in the goat. *Acta physiol. Scand.* 33, 333–346. [254]

Andersson, B., & McCann, S. M. (1955b) The effect of hypothalamic lesions on the water intake of the dog. *Acta physiol. Scand.* 35, 312–320. [254]

Andreas, B. G. (1958) Motor conflict behavior as a function of motivation and amount of training. *J. exp. Psychol.* 55, 173–178. [431]

Andrews, T. G. (1940) The effect of Benzedrine sulfate on syllogistic reasoning. *J. exp. Psychol.* 26, 423–431. [145]

Angyal, A. (1941) *Foundation for a science of personality.* New York: Commonwealth Fund. [347]

Anliker, J., & Mayer, J. (1957) The regulation of food intake. Some experiments relating behavioral, metabolic, and morphological aspects. *Amer. J. clin. Nutrit.* 5, 148–153. [224]

Ansbacher, H. L., & Ansbacher, Rowena R. (Eds.) (1956) *The Individual-Psychology of Alfred Adler.* New York: Basic Books. [663]

Antonovsky, H. F. (1958) A contribution to research in the area of the mother-child relationships. *Child Develpm.* 30, 37–51. [744]

Appley, M. H. (1957) Psychological stress. (Appendix II of *A study of operational safety requirements in the submarine polaris missile system.* Electric Boat Div., General Dynamics Corp.) Feb., 1957, (dittoed). [313, 454]

Appley, M. H. (1961a) *Motivation and psychological stress.* Paper presented to Psychology Colloquium, Southern Illinois University, Carbondale, Illinois, Sept. 1961. [449]

Appley, M. H. (1961b) Neuroendocrine aspects of stress. In Flaherty, B. E. (Ed.) *Psychophysiological aspects of space flight.* New York: Columbia University Press, pp. 139–157. [217, 313]

Appley, M. H. (1962a) Motivation, threat perception, and the induction of psychological stress. *Proc. Sixteenth Internat. Congr. Psychol., Bonn* 1960. Amsterdam: North Holland Publ. Co., pp. 880–881. [451, 751]

Appley, M. H. (1962b) *Psychological stress.* Paper presented to Psychology Colloquium, University of Toronto, November 1962. [452, 459]

Appley, M. H. (1964) *Temporal factors and isolation.* Paper presented to Naval Medical Research Institute Seminar, University of Delaware, Newark, June 1963. [439]

Appley, M. H., & Moeller, G. (1962) *Escape and avoidance learning and the pituitary-adrenal system.* Paper presented to Psychology Colloquium, University of Illinois, May 1962. [313, 579]

Applezweig, M. H. (1951) Response potential as a function of effort. *J. comp. physiol. Psychol.* 44, 225–235. [90, 155]

Applezweig, M. H., Moeller, G., & Burdick, H. (1956) Multimotive prediction of academic success. *Psychol. Reps.* 2, 489–496. [730, 731, 739]

Arden, F. (1934) Experimental observations upon thirst and on potassium overdosage. *Australian J. exper. biol. and med. Sci.* 12, 121–122. [251]

Armington, J. C., & Mitnick, L. L. (1959) Electroencephalogram and sleep deprivation. *J. appl. Physiol.* 14, 247–250. [174]

Armstrong, E. A. (1947) *Bird display and behavior.* London: Cambridge University Press. [60, 71]

Armstrong, E. A. (1950) The nature and function of displacement activities. In Society for Experimental Biology, Symposium No. 4: *Physiological mechanisms of animal behaviour.* New York: Academic Press, pp. 361–384. [60, 70, 71, 72, 73, 77, 92, 93]

Armus, H. L. (1958) Drive level and habit reversal. *Psychol. Reps.* 4, 31–34. [521, 538]

Arnold, Magda B. (1945) Physiological differentiation of emotional states. *Psychol.*

Rev. **52**, 35–48.   [314, 315, 392, 394]

Arnold, Magda B. (1960) *Emotion and personality:* Vol. I. *Psychological aspects.* Vol. II. *Neurological and physiological aspects.* New York: Columbia University Press.   [391]

Aronson, E., & Mills, J. (1959) The effects of severity of initiation on liking for a group. *J. abn. soc. Psychol.* **59**, 177–181.   [793]

Asch, S. E. (1952) *Social psychology.* Englewood Cliffs, N.J.: Prentice-Hall.   [55, 778]

Asch, S. E. (1956) Studies of independence and conformity: I. A minority of one against a unanimous majority. *Psychol. Monog.* **70**, Whole No. 416.   [778]

Aschoff, T. (1962) Timegivers of 24-hour physiological cycles. In Schaefer, K. E. (Ed.) *International symposium on submarine and space medicine:* Vol. I. *Man's dependence on the earthly atmosphere.* New York: Macmillan, pp. 373–380.   [163, 169]

Aserinsky, E., & Kleitman, N. (1955) A motility cycle in sleeping infants as manifested by ocular and gross bodily activity. *J. appl. Physiol.* **8**, 11–18.   [163]

Ashby, W. R. (1940) Adaptiveness and equilibrium. *J. ment. Sci.* **86**, 478–483 [344, 345]

Ashby, W. R. (1950) The stability of a randomly assembled nerve-network. *EEG and clin. Neurophysiol.* **2**, 471–482.   [355]

Ashby, W. R. (1952) *Design for a brain.* (rev. ed., 1960). New York: Wiley [342, 344, 345, 347, 348, 350, 351, 352]

Ashby, W. R. (1954) The applications of cybernetics to psychiatry. *J. ment. Sci* **100**, 114–124.   [348]

Ashby, W. R. (1956) *Design for an intelligence-amplifier.* In Shannon, C. E., & McCarthy, J. (Eds.) *Automata studies.* Princeton: Princeton University Press, pp. 215–234.   [342, 345]

Atkinson, J. W. (1950) Studies in projective measurement of achievement motivation. Unpubl. doctoral dissert., University of Michigan.   [719]

Atkinson, J. W. (1953) The achievement motive and recall of interrupted and completed tasks. *J. exp. Psychol.* **46**, 381–390.   [317, 729, 737, 786]

Atkinson, J. W. (1954) Theoretical basis of projective measures of fear. In *Symposium on motivation.* Washington, D.C., Research and Development Board, Dept. of Defense, 61–67.   [462]

Atkinson, J. W. (1957) Motivational determinants of risk-taking behavior. *Psychol. Rev.* **64**, 359–372.   [740, 774]

Atkinson, J. W. (Ed.) (1958a) *Motives in fantasy, action, and society.* New York: Van Nostrand.   [2, 8, 716, 717, 719, 723, 725, 740]

Atkinson, J. W. (1958b) Towards experimental analysis of human motivation in terms of motives, expectancies, and incentives. In Atkinson, J. W. (Ed.) *Motives in fantasy, action, and society.* New York: Van Nostrand, pp. 288–305.   [739]

Atkinson, J. W., Heyns, R. W., & Veroff, J. (1954) The effect of experimental arousal of the affiliation motive on thematic apperception. *J. abn. soc. Psychol.* **49**, 405–410.   [726]

Atkinson, J. W., & McClelland, D. C. (1948) The projective expression of needs: II. The effect of different intensities of the hunger drive on thematic apperception. *J. exp. Psychol.* **38**, 643–658.   [716]

Atkinson, J. W., & Raphelson, A. C. (1956) Individual differences in motivation and behavior in particular situations. *J. Pers.* **24**, 349–363.   [739]

Atkinson, J. W., & Reitman, W. R. (1956) Performance as a function of motive strength and expectancy of goal attainment. *J. abn. soc. Psychol.* **53**, 361–366. [739]

Atkinson, J. W., & Walker, E. L. (1956) The affiliation motive and perceptual sensitivity of faces. *J. abn. soc. Psychol.* **53**, 38–41.   [733]

Auld, F., Jr. (1952) Influence of social class on personality test responses. *Psychol. Bull.* 49, 318–332.   [571]

Auld, F., Jr., Eron, L. D., & Laffal, J. (1955) Application of Guttman's scaling method to the TAT. *Educ. Psychol. Meas.* 15, 422–435.   [755]

Ax, A. F. (1953) The physiological differentiation between fear and anger in humans. *Psychosom. Med.* 15, 433–442.   [332, 449, 751, 800]

Bach, G. R. (1945) Young children's play fantasies. *Psychol., Monog.* 59, Whole No. 272.   [756]

Bachrach, W. H. (1953) Action of insulin hypoglycemia on motion and secretory functions of the digestive tract. *Physiol. Rev.* 33, 566–592.   [212]

Baer, D. M., & Gray, P. H. (1960) Imprinting to a different species without overt following. *Percept. mot. Skills* 10, 171–174.   [90]

Bailey, C. J. (1955) The effectiveness of drives as cues. *J. comp. physiol. Psychol.* 48, 183–187.   [265]

Bailey, C. J., & Porter, L. W. (1955) Relevant cues in drive discrimination in cats. *J. comp. physiol. Psychol.* 48, 180–182.   [265]

Bailey, P., & Davis, E. W. (1942) The syndrome of obstinate progress in the cat. *Proc. Soc. exper. Biol.* 51, 307.   [354]

Bäjusz, E. (1960) Neuroendocrine relationships. In *Progress in neurology and psychiatry.* Vol. 15: New York: Grune and Stratton, pp. 233–251.   [445]

Bakan, D. (1958) *Sigmund Freud and the Jewish mystical tradition.* New York: Van Nostrand.   [593]

Baker, R. A. (1953) Aperiodic feeding behavior in the albino rat. *J. comp physiol. Psychol.* 46, 422–426.   [240]

Baker, R. A. (1955) The effects of repeated deprivation experience in feeding behavior. *J. comp. physiol. Psychol.* 48, 37–42.   [240, 241]

Baldwin, A. L. (1956) Child psychology. *Ann. rev. Psychol.* 7, 259–282.   [689–690]

Baldwin, J. M. (Ed.) (1911) *Dictionary of philosophy and psychology.* 3 vols. New York: Macmillan.   [43, 598]

Ball, J. (1934) Sex behavior of the rat after removel of the uterus and vagina. *J. comp. Psychol.* 18, 419–422.   [177]

Ball, J. (1937) A test for measuring sexual excitability in the female rat. *Comp. psychol. Monog.* 14, 1–37.   [189]

Ball, J. (1940) The effect of testosterone on the sex behavior of female rats. *J. comp. Psychol.* 29, 151–165.   [181]

Bandura, A., & Walters, R. H. (1959) *Adolescent aggression.* New York: Ronald Press.   [752]

Barber, T. X. (1959) Toward a theory of pain: Relief of chronic pain by prefrontal leucotomy, opiates, placebos, and hypnosis. *Psychol. Bull.* 56, 430–460.   [260, 261, 262, 263]

Bard, P. (1935) The effects of denervation of the genitalia on the oestral behavior of cats. *Amer. J. Physiol.* 113, 5–6.   [177]

Bare, J. K. (1949) The specific hunger for sodium chloride in normal and adrenalectomized white rats. *J. comp. physiol. Psychol.* 42, 242–253.   [231, 233]

Bare, J. K. (1959) Hunger, deprivation, and the day-night cycle. *J. comp. physiol. Psychol.* 52, 129–131.   [243]

Barker, J. P., Adolph, E. F., & Keller, A. D. (1953) Thirst tests in dogs and modifications of thirst with experimental lesions of the neurohypothesis. *Amer. J. Physiol.* 173, 233–245.   [249]

Barker, R. G., Dembo, Tamara, & Lewin, K. (1941) Frustration and regression: An experiment with young children. *Univ. Ia. Stud. Child Welf.* 18, No. 1, 1–314.   [363, 424, 425]

Barker, R. G., & Wright, H. F. (1955) *Midwest and its children.* Evanston: Row, Peterson.   [650]

Barmack, J. E. (1938) The effect of Benzedrine sulfate (benzyl methyl carbina-mine) upon the report of boredom and other factors. *J. Psychol.* **5**, 125–133. [145]

Barmack, J. E. (1940) The time of administration and some effects of 2 grs. of alkaloid caffeine. *J. exp. Psychol.* **27**, 690–698. [145]

Barnes, G. W., & Kish, G. B. (1957) Reinforcing properties of the termination of intense auditory stimulation. *J. comp. physiol. Psychol.* **50**, 40–43. [541]

Barnes, G. W., & Kish, G. B. (1961) Reinforcing properties of the onset of audi-tory stimulation. *J. exp. Psychol.* **62**, 164–170. [541]

Barnett, S. A. (1958) Experiments on "neophobia" in wild and laboratory rats. *Brit. J. Psychol.* **49**, 195–201. [291]

Barrett, W. (1958) *Irrational man; a study in existential psychology.* Garden City, N.Y.: Doubleday. [657, 658, 659–660, 667]

Barron, F. (1953) An ego-strength scale which predicts response to psycho-therapy. *J. consult. Psychol.* **17**, 327–333. [459]

Barry, H. (1958) Effects of strength of drive on learning and extinction. *J. exp. Psychol.* **55**, 473–481. [521, 533]

Bartlett, F. C. (1943) Fatigue following highly skilled work. *Proc. Roy. Soc., B.* **131**, 247–257. [138]

Bartlett, F. C. (1953) Psychological criteria of fatigue. In Floyd, W. F., & Welford, A. T. (Eds.) *Symposium on fatigue.* London: H. K. Lewis & Co., pp. 1–5. [138]

Bartley, S. H. (1951) Fatigue and efficiency. In Helson, H. (Ed.) *Theoretical foundations of psychology.* New York: Van Nostrand. [139]

Bartley, S. H. (1957) Fatigue and inadequacy. *Physiol. Rev.* **37**, 301–324. [135, 139]

Bartley, S. H., & Chute, Eloise (1947) *Fatigue and impairment in man.* New York: McGraw-Hill. [135, 136, 137, 139, 140, 316, 332]

Bartoshuk, A. K. (1955) Electromyographic gradients as indicants of motivation. *Canad. J. Psychol.* **9**, 215–230. [397]

Bash, K. W. (1939*a*) An investigation into a possible organic basis for the hunger drive. *J. comp. Psychol.* **28**, 109–135. [208]

Bash, K. W. (1939*b*) Contribution to a theory of the hunger drive. *J. comp. Psychol.* **28**, 137–160. [209, 210]

Basowitz, H., Persky, H., Korchin, S. J., & Grinker, R. R. (1955) *Anxiety and stress.* New York: McGraw-Hill. [443, 450, 460, 462, 463]

Bass, A. D. (Ed.) (1959) *Evolution of nervous control from primitive organisms to man.* Washington, D.C.: A.A.A.S. [150]

Bass, M. J., & Hull, C. L. (1934) The irradiation of a tactile conditioned reflex in man. *J. comp. Psychol.* **17**, 47–65. [153]

Bastock, M., Morris, D., & Moynihan, M. (1954) Some comments on conflict and thwarting in animals. *Behavior* **6**, 66–84. [93]

Bayer, E. (1929) Beiträge zur Zweikomponententheorie des Hungers. *Zeitschrift f. Psychol.* **112**, 1–54. [242, 243]

Beach, F. A. (1937) The neural basis of innate behavior: I. Effects of cortical lesions upon the maternal behavior pattern in the rat. *J. comp. Psychol.* **24**, 393–436. [110, 117]

Beach, F. A. (1938) The neural basis of innate behavior: II. Relative effects of partial decortication in adulthood and infancy upon the maternal behavior of the primiparous rat. *J. genet. Psychol.* **53**, 109–148. [117]

Beach, F. A. (1940) Effects of cortical lesions upon the copulatory behavior of male rats. *J. comp. Psychol.* **29**, 193–239. [184]

Beach, F. A. (1941*a*) Copulatory behavior of male rats raised in isolation and sub-jected to partial decortication prior to the acquisition of sexual experience. *J. comp. Psychol.* **31**, 457–470. [184]

Beach, F. A. (1941*b*) Female mating behavior shown by male rats after adminis-tration of testosterone propionate. *Endocrinology* **29**, 409–412. [181]

Beach, F. A. (1942*a*) Analysis of factors involved in the arousal, maintenance and manifestation of sexual excitement in male animals. *Psychosom. Med.* 4, 173–198.   [65]

Beach, F. A. (1942*b*) Analysis of the stimuli adequate to elicit mating behavior in the sexually inexperienced male rat. *J. comp. Psychol.* 33, 163–207.   [186, 194, 196]

Beach, F. A. (1942*c*) Effects of testosterone propionate upon the copulatory behavior of sexually inexperienced male rats. *J. comp. Psychol.* 33, 227–247. [196]

Beach, F. A. (1942*d*) Sexual behavior of prepuberal male and female rats treated with gonadal hormones. *J. comp. Psychol.* 34, 285–292.   [179]

Beach, F. A. (1942*e*) Male and female mating behavior in prepuberally castrated female rats treated with androgens. *Endocrinology*, 31, 673–678.   [181, 182]

Beach, F. A. (1942*f*) Copulatory behavior in prepuberally castrated male rats and its modification by estrogen administration. *Endocrinology* 31, 679–683. [179, 180]

Beach, F. A. (1943) Effects of injury to the cerebral cortex upon the display of masculine and feminine mating behavior by female rats. *J. comp. Psychol.* 36, 169–198.   [184]

Beach, F. A. (1944*a*) Effects of injury to the cerebral cortex upon sexually-receptive behavior in the female rat. *Psychosom. Med.* 6, 40–55.   [184]

Beach, F. A. (1944*b*) Relative effects of androgen upon the mating behavior of male rats subjected to forebrain injury or castration. *J. exp. Zool.* 97, 249–295. [184]

Beach, F. A. (1945) Hormonal induction of mating responses in a rat with congenital absence of gonadal tissue. *Anat. Rec.* 92, 289–292.   [177]

Beach, F. A. (1948) *Hormones and behavior.* New York: Hoeber.   [175, 176, 177, 181, 183, 191]

Beach, F. A. (1950) The snark was a boojum. *Amer. Psychologist* 5, 115–124. [122]

Beach, F. A. (1951) Instinctive behavior: Reproductive activities. In Stevens, S. S. (Ed.) *Handbook of experimental psychology.* New York: John Wiley, pp. 387–434.   [108, 110, 117, 175, 179, 180, 181, 182, 183, 184, 185, 191, 192, 196, 197]

Beach, F. A. (1955) The descent of instinct. *Psychol. Rev.* 62, 401–410.   [25, 44, 56, 100]

Beach, F. A. (1956) Characteristics of masculine sex drive. In Jones, M. R. (Ed.) *Nebraska symposium on motivation, 1956.* Lincoln: University of Nebraska Press, pp. 1–32.   [175, 187, 189, 194, 197, 198, 823, 828]

Beach, F. A. (1958) Normal sexual behavior in male rats isolated at fourteen days of age. *J. comp. physiol. Psychol.* 51, 37–38.   [196]

Beach, F. A., Carmichael, L., Lashley, K. S., Morgan, C. T., Stone, C. P., & Hunter, W. S. (1947) Symposium on heredity and environment. *Psychol. Rev.* 54, 297–352.   [43]

Beach, F. A., & Holz, A. M. (1946) Mating behavior in male rats castrated at various ages and injected with androgen. *J. exp. Zool.* 101, 91–142.   [177, 179]

Beach, F. A., & Holz-Tucker, A. M. (1949) Effects of different concentrations of androgen upon sexual behavior in castrated male rats. *J. comp. physiol. Psychol.* 42, 433–453.   [186]

Beach, F. A., & Jaynes, J. (1954) Effects of early experience upon the behavior of animals. *Psychol. Bull.* 51, 240–263.   [100]

Beach, F. A., & Jaynes, J. (1956) Studies of maternal retrieving in rats: III. Sensory cues involved in the lactating female's response to her young. *Behaviour* 10, 104–125.   [111]

Beach, F. A., & Jordan, L. (1956a) Effects of sexual reinforcement upon the performance of male rats in a straight runway. *J. comp. physiol. Psychol.* 49, 105–110. [187]

Beach, F. A., & Jordan, L. (1956b) Sexual exhaustion and recovery in the male rat. *Quart. J. exp. Psychol.* 8, 121–133. [187, 188, 189, 198, 199]

Beach, F. A., & Rasquin, P. (1942) Masculine copulatory behavior in intact and castrated female rats. *Endocrinology* 31, 393–409. [181]

Beach, H. D. (1957) Morphine addiction in rats. *Canad. J. Psychol.* 11, 104–112. [584, 585]

Beck, R. C. (1961) On secondary reinforcement and shock termination. *Psychol. Bull.* 58, 28–45. [563]

Beebe-Center, J. G. (1932) *The psychology of pleasantness and unpleasantness.* New York: Van Nostrand. [382, 383, 385]

Beebe-Center, J. G., Black, P., Hoffman, A. C., & Wade, M. (1948) Relative per diem consumption as a measure of preference in the rat. *J. comp. physiol. Psychol.* 41, 239–251. [233]

Beecher, H. K. (1957) The measurement of pain: Prototype for the quantitative study of subjective responses. *Pharmacol. Rev.* 9, 59–209. [261]

Bélanger, D. (1957) "Gradients" musculaires et processus mentaux supérieurs. *Canad. J. Psychol.* 11, 113–122. [397]

Bélanger, D., & Tétreau, B. (1961) L'influence d'une motivation inappropriée sur le comportement du rat en sa fréquence cardiaque. (Influence of irrelevant motivation on behavior and heart rate of the rat). *Canad. J. Psychol.* 15, 6–14. [397]

Bellak, L. (1944) The concept of projection. *Psychiatry* 7, 353–370. [754]

Bellak, L. (1956) Psychoanalytic theories of personality. In McCary, J. L. (Ed.) *Psychology of personality.* New York: Logos Press. [635, 645]

Bellak, L., Ostow, M., Pumpian-Mindlin, E., Stanton, A. H., & Szasz, T. S. (1959) Conceptual and methodological problems in psychoanalysis. *Annals N.Y. Acad. Sci.* 76, 971–1134. [597, 636]

Beller, E. K. (1959) Exploratory studies of dependency. *Trans. N.Y. Acad. Sci.* 21, 414–426. [743]

Bellows, R. T. (1939) Time factors in water drinking in dogs. *Amer. J. Physiol.* 125, 87–97. [248, 252, 253]

Bellows, R. T., & Van Wagenen, W. P. (1938) The relationship of polydipsia and polyuria in diabetes insipidus. *J. nerv. ment. Dis.* 88, 417–473. [255]

Bellows, R. T., & Van Wagenen, W. P. (1939) The effect of resection of the olfactory, gustatory, and trigeminal nerves on water drinking in dogs without and with diabetes insipidus. *Amer. J. Physiol.* 126, 13–19. [247]

Bendig, A. W. (1956) The development of a short form of the Manifest Anxiety Scale. *J. consult. Psychol.* 20, 384. [702]

Bendig, A. W. (1957) Extraversion, neuroticism, and manifest anxiety. *J. consult. Psychol.* 21, 398. [709]

Bendig, A. W. (1958a) Identification of item factor patterns within the Manifest Anxiety Scale. *J. consult. Psychol.* 22, 158. [710]

Bendig, A. W. (1958b) Manifest anxiety and projective and objective measures of need achievement. *J. consult Psychol.* 21, 354. [724, 740]

Bendig, A. W., & Vaughan, C. J. (1957) Manifest anxiety, discrimination, and transposition. *Amer. J. Psychol.* 70, 286–288. [708]

Benedict, Ruth (1946) *The chrysanthemum and the sword.* Boston: Houghton-Mifflin. [326]

Bentley, M. (1928) Is "emotion" more than a chapter heading? In Murchison, C. (Ed.) *Feelings and emotions—The Wittenberg symposium.* Worcester, Mass.: Clark University Press, 1928, pp. 17–23. [368]

Berg, I. A. (1944) Development of behavior: the micturition pattern in the dog. *J. exp. Psychol.* 34, 343–368. [134]

Berkowitz, L. (1958) The expression and reduction of hostility. *Psychol. Bull.* **55**, 257–283.   [746]

Berkowitz, L. (1962) *Aggression: A social psychological analysis.* New York: McGraw-Hill.   [424, 746]

Berkun, M. M., Bialek, H. M., Kearn, R. P., & Yagi, K. (1962) Experimental studies of psychological stress in man. *Psychol. Monogr.* **76**, 15, Whole No. 534. [457, 461]

Berkun, M. M., Kessen, M. L., & Miller, N. E. (1952) Hunger reducing effects of food by stomach fistula versus food by mouth measured by a consummatory response. *J. comp. physiol. Psychol.* **45**, 550–554.   [216]

Berlyne, D. E. (1950) Novelty and curiosity as determinants of exploratory behavior. *Brit. J. Psychol.* **41**, 68–80.   [290, 292]

Berlyne, D. E. (1951) Attention to change. *Brit. J. Psychol.* **42**, 269–278.   [286]

Berlyne, D. E. (1954) An experimental study of human curiosity. *Brit. J. Psychol.* **45**, 256–265.   [298]

Berlyne, D. E. (1955) The arousal and satiation of perceptual curiosity in the rat. *J. comp. physiol. Psychol.* **48**, 238–246.   [291]

Berlyne, D. E. (1957a) Attention to change, conditioned inhibition (sIr), and stimulus satiation. *Brit. J. Psychol.* **48**, 138–140.   [286]

Berlyne, D. E. (1957b) Conflict and information-theory variables as determinants of human perceptual curiosity. *J. exp. Psychol.* **53**, 399–404.   [297]

Berlyne, D. E. (1958a) The influence of complexity and novelty in visual figures on orienting responses. *J. exp. Psychol.* **55**, 289–296.   [287]

Berlyne, D. E. (1958b) The influence of the albedo and complexity of stimuli on visual fixation in the human infant. *Brit. J. Psychol.* **49**, 315–318.   [297]

Berlyne, D. E. (1958c) Supplementary report: Complexity and orienting responses with longer exposures. *J. exp. Psychol.* **56**, 183.   [288]

Berlyne, D. E. (1960) *Conflict, arousal, and curiosity.* New York: McGraw-Hill. [278, 286, 292, 294, 295, 297, 298, 300]

Berlyne, D. E., & Slater, J. (1957) Perceptual curiosity, exploratory behavior, and maze learning. *J. comp. physiol. Psychol.* **50**, 228–232.   [292, 294]

Bermant, G. (1961) Response latencies of female rats during sexual intercourse. *Science* **133**, 1771–1773.   [187, 189]

Bernard, C. (1859) *Leçons sur les propriétés physiologiques et les alterations pathologiques des liquides de l'organisme.* Vols. I and II. Paris: Balliere. [303, 307]

Bernard, L. L. (1924) *Instinct: A study in social psychology.* New York: Henry Holt. [37, 42, 56, 61]

Bernstein, A. (1955) Some relations between techniques of feeding and training during infancy and certain behavior in childhood. *Genet. psychol. Monogr.* **51**, 3–44.   [114]

Bernstein, L. M., & Grossman, M. I. (1956) An experimental test of the glucostatic theory of regulation of food intake. *J. clin. Investig.* **35**, 627–633. [225]

Berrien, F. K. (1962) Homeostasis of groups. *Trans. N.Y. Acad. Sci.*, Ser. II **24**, 528–535.   [365]

Berry, J. L. & Martin, B. (1957) GSR reactivity as a function of anxiety, instructions, and sex. *J. abn. soc. Psychol.* **54**, 9–12.   [709]

Bertalanffy, L. von (1950) The theory of open systems in physics and biology. *Science* **111**, 23–29.   [344]

Bertalanffy, L. von (1951) Theoretical models in biology and psychology. *J. Pers.* **20**, 24–38.   [344]

Bertocci, P. A. (1940) A critique of G. W. Allport's theory of motivation. *Psychol. Rev.* **47**, 501–532.   [572]

Bettelheim, B. (1955) *Truants from life: The rehabilitation of emotionally disturbed children.* Glencoe, Ill.: The Free Press.   [686]

Bettelheim, B. (1950) *Love is not enough*. Glencoe, Ill.: The Free Press. [686]

Bevan, W., & Grodsky, M. A. (1958) Hoarding in hamsters with systematically controlled pretest experience. *J. comp. physiol. Psychol.* 51, 342–345. [125]

Bexton, W. H., Heron, W., & Scott, T. H. (1954) Effects of decreased variation in the sensory environment. *Canad. J. Psychol.* 8, 70–76. [279, 281, 282, 408]

Billingslea, F. Y. (1940) The relationship between emotionality, activity, curiosity, persistence, and weight in the male rat. *J. comp. Psychol.* 29, 315–325. [273]

Bills, A. G. (1927) The influence of muscular tension on the efficiency of mental work. *Amer. J. Psychol.* 38, 227–251. [393]

Bills, A. G. (1931) Blocking: A new principle of mental fatigue. *Amer. J. Psychol.* 43, 230–245. [141]

Bills, A. G. (1937) Fatigue in mental work. *Physiol. Rev.* 3, 436–453. [141]

Bills, A. G. (1943) *The psychology of efficiency*. New York: Harper & Bros. [139, 141]

Bilz, R. (1941) Zur Psychophysik des Verlegenheitskratzens. *Zentralbl. Psychother. und ihre Grenzgeb* 13, 36–50 (cited by Tinbergen, 1951). [83]

Bindra, D. (1947) Water-hoarding in rats. *J. comp. physiol. Psychol.* 40, 149–156. [123, 124]

Bindra, D. (1948a) The nature of motivation for hoarding food. *J. comp. physiol. Psychol.* 41, 211–218. [124]

Bindra, D. (1948b) What makes rats hoard? *J. comp. physiol. Psychol.* 41, 397–402. [126]

Bindra, D. (1957) Comparative psychology. *Ann. rev. Psychol.* 8, 399–414. [103]

Bindra, D. (1959) *Motivation: A systematic reinterpretation*. New York: Ronald Press. [2, 12, 117, 118, 122, 123, 124, 234, 235, 748, 826]

Bindra, D. (1961) Components of general activity and the analysis of behavior *Psychol. Rev.* 68, 205–215. [270]

Bindra, D., Paterson, A. L., & Strzelecki, J. (1955) On the relation between anxiety and conditioning. *Canad. J. Psychol.* 9, 1–6. [704]

Bindra, D. & Spinner, N. (1958) Response to different degrees of novelty: The incidence of various activities. *J. exp. anal. Behav.* 1, 341–350. [291]

Bingham, H. C. (1928) Sex development in apes. *Comp. psychol. Monog.* 5, 1–165. [196]

Birch, D. (1958) Motivation shift in a complex learning task. *J. exp. Psychol.* 56, 507–515. [538]

Birch, H. G. (1945) The role of motivational factors in insightful problem solving. *J. comp. Psychol.* 38, 295–317. [685]

Birch, H. G. (1956) Sources of order in the maternal behavior of animals. *Amer. J. Orthopsychiat.* 26, 279–284. [96]

Birney, R. C. (1958a) Thematic content and the cue characteristics of pictures. In Atkinson, J. W. (Ed.) *Motives in fantasy, action and society*. New York: Van Nostrand, pp. 630–643. [735]

Birney, R. C. (1958b) The achievement motive and task performance. *J. abn. soc. Psychol.* 56, 133–135. [736]

Bitterman, M. E., & Holtzman, W. H. (1952) Conditioning and extinction of the galvanic skin response as a function of anxiety. *J. abn. soc. Psychol.* 47, 615–623. [704]

Bjerner, B. (1949) Alpha depression and lowered pulse rate during delayed actions in serial reaction tests; Study in sleep deprivation. *Acta physiol. Scand.*, Suppl. No. 65, 19, pp. 93. [171]

Blake, R. R. (1958) The other person in the situation. In Tagiuri, R., & Petrullo, L. (Eds.) *Person perception and interpersonal behavior*. Stanford: Stanford University Press, pp. 229–242. [339, 340]

Blake, R. R., Mouton, Jane S., & Hain, J. D. (1956) Social forces in petition-signing. *Southwestern Soc. Sci. Quart.* 36, 385–390. [340]

Blake, R. R., Rosenbaum, M. E., & Duryea, R. A. (1955) Gift-giving as a function of group standards. *Hum. Relat.* 8, 61–73.   [340]

Block, J. (1957) A study of affective responsiveness in a lie-detection situation. *J. abn. soc. Psychol.* 55, 11–15.   [800]

Block, J., & Martin, B. C. (1955) Predicting the behavior of children under frustration. *J. abn. soc. Psychol.* 51, 281–285.   [751]

Blodgett, H. C. (1929) The effect of the introduction of reward upon the maze performance of rats. *Univ. Calif. Publ. Psychol.* 4, 113–134.   [552]

Bloomberg, R., & Webb, W. B. (1949) Various degrees within a single drive as cues for spatial response learning in the white rat. *J. exp. Psychol.* 39, 628–636.   [265]

Blum, G. S. (1949) A study of the psychoanalytic theory of psychosexual development. *Genet. psychol. Monogr.* 39, 3–99.   [653]

Blum, G. S. (1953) *Psychoanalytic theories of personality.* New York: McGraw-Hill.   [589, 663]

Blum, G. S. & Hunt, W. F. (1952) The validity of the Blacky Pictures. *Psychol. Bull.* 49, 238–250.   [653]

Blum, G. S., & Miller, D. R. (1952) Exploring the psychoanalytic theory of the "oral character." *J. Pers.* 20, 287–304.   [653]

Bolles, R., & Petrinovich, L. (1954) A technique for obtaining rapid drive discrimination in the rat. *J. comp. physiol. Psychol.* 47, 378–380.   [265]

Bonney, W. C., & George, C. E. (1958) *Studies of Adaptation Level phenomena in personality.* Tech. Rep. No. 2, Proj. NR 171–054, Contr. Nonr. 02119(01) College Station: Texas A. & M. Research Foundation, August 1958.   [341, 365]

Bonvallet, M., Dell, P., & Hiebel, G. (1954) Tonus sympathétique et activité électrique corticale. *EEG clin. Neurophysiol.* 6, 119–144.   [403]

Boring, E. G. (1915) Processes referred to the alimentary and urinary tracts: a qualitative analysis. *Psychol. Rev.* 22, 306–331.   [134]

Boring, E. G. (1933) *The physical dimensions of consciousness.* New York: Appleton-Century.   [594]

Boring, E. G. (1942) *Sensation and perception in the history of experimental psychology.* New York: Appleton-Century-Crofts.   [205, 206, 244, 245, 246, 260]

Boring, E. G. (1950) *A history of experimental psychology* (2nd. ed.) New York: Appleton-Century-Crofts.   [29, 31, 32, 36, 38, 40, 41, 42, 46, 47, 48, 49, 390, 413, 662]

Boring, E. G., Landis, C., Brown, J. F., Sachs, H., & Willoughby, R. R. (1940) Symposium: Psychoanalysis as seen by analyzed psychologists. *J. abn. soc. Psychol.* 35, 3–55.   [683]

Bornemann, E. (1952) Developmental lines of research on fatigue. *Mensch u. Arbeit.* 4, 5–9.   [139, 140]

Bousfield, W. A. (1933) Certain quantitative aspects of the food-behavior of cats. *J. genet. Psychol.* 1933, 446–454.   [239]

Bousfield, W. A. (1934) Certain quantitative aspects of chickens' behavior toward food. *Amer. J. Psychol.* 46, 456–458.   [239]

Bousfield, W. A., & Elliott, M. H. (1934) The effect of fasting on the eating behavior of rats. *J. genet. Psychol.* 45, 227–237.   [241]

Bower, G. H., & Miller, N. E. (1958) Rewarding and punishing effects from stimulating the same place in the rat's brain. *J. comp. physiol. Psychol.* 51, 669–674.   [548]

Bowlby, J. (1951) *Maternal care and mental health.* Geneva: World Health Organization Monogr. No. 2.   [642, 649, 686]

Bowlby, J., Ainsworth, M., Boston, M., & Rosenbluth, D. (1956) The effects of mother-child separation: A follow-up study. *Brit. J. med. Psychol.* 29, 211–247.   [689]

Bowman, K. M., Miller, E. R., Dailey, M. E., Simon, A., & Mayer, B. F. (1950) Thyroid function in mental disease: A multiple test survey. *J. nerv. ment. Dis.* 112, 404–424. **[325]**

Brackbill, G., & Little, K. B. (1954) MMPI correlates of the Taylor scale of manifest anxiety. *J. consult. Psychol.* 18, 433–436. **[709]**

Brackbill, Y. (1958) Extinction of the smiling response in infants as a function of reinforcement schedule. *Child Develpm.* 29, 115–124. **[690]**

von Bracken, H. (1952) On the psychopathology of fatigue symptoms. *Mensch u. Arbeit.* 4, 56–68. **[140, 143]**

Bradley, P. B., & Key, B. J. (1958) The effect of drugs on the arousal responses produced by electrical stimulation of the reticular formation of the brain. *EEG clin. Neurophysiol.* 10, 97–110. **[145]**

Brady, J. V. (1958) Emotional behavior and the nervous system. *Trans. N.Y. Acad. Sci.* 18, 601–612. **[313]**

Brady, J. V., Boren, J. J., Conrad, D., & Sidman, M. (1957) The effect of food and water deprivation upon intracranial self-stimulation. *J. comp. physiol. Psychol.* 50, 134–137. **[544]**

Bramwell, J. M. (1921) *Hypnotism: Its history, practice, and theory* (3rd. ed.) London: Rider. **[49]**

Brandauer, C. M. (1953) A confirmation of Webb's data concerning the action of irrelevant drives. *J. exp. Psychol.* 45, 150–152. **[535]**

Braun, H. W., Wedekind, C. E., & Smudski, J. F. (1957) The effect of an irrelevant drive on maze learning in the rat. *J. exp. Psychol.* 54, 148–152. **[524]**

Brayfield, A. H., & Crockett, W. H. (1955) Employee attitudes and employee performance. *Psychol. Bull.* 52, 396–424. **[771]**

Brazier, Mary A. B. (1950) Neural nets and integration of behavior. In Richter, D. (Ed.) *Perspectives in neuropsychiatry.* London: H. K. Lewis. pp. 35–45. **[354, 355]**

Brazier, Mary, A. B. (1959) *The central nervous system and behavior.* Transact. First and Second Confs., New York: Josiah Macy, Jr. Found. (2 vols.) **[149, 150, 356, 601]**

Brazier, Mary, A. B. (1960) *The central nervous system and behavior.* Transact. Third Conf., New York: Josiah Macy, Jr. Found. **[149, 150]**

Brecher, G., & Waxler, S. H. (1949) Obesity in albino mice due to single injections of gold-thioglucose. *Proc. Soc. exp. Biol. Med.* 701, 498–501. **[224]**

Breed, F. S. (1911) The development of certain instincts and habits in chicks. *Behav. Monog.* 1, No. 1. **[258]**

Brehm, J. W., & Cohen, A. R. (1962) *Explorations in cognitive dissonance.* New York: Wiley. **[789, 790, 791, 794, 795, 796]**

Bremer, F. (1954) The neurophysiological problem of sleep. In Delafresnaye, J. F. (Ed.) *Brain mechanisms and consciousness.* Springfield: Charles Thomas, 137–158. **[166]**

Bremer, F. (1960) Neurophysiological mechanisms in cerebral arousal. In Wolstenholme, G. E. W., & O'Connor, Maeve (Eds.) *Ciba Foundation symposium on the nature of sleep.* Boston: Little, Brown and Co., pp. 30–49. **[166]**

Breuer, J., & Freud, S. (1895) *Studies in hysteria.* New York: Nerv. and Ment. Dis. Public., 1937. **[591]**

Brillouin, L. (1956) *Science and information theory.* New York: Academic Press. **[345]**

Britt, S. H., & Janus, S. Q. (1940) Criteria of frustration. *Psychol. Rev.* 47, 451–470. **[414, 419]**

Broadbent, D. E. (1953) Neglect of the surroundings in relation to fatigue decrements in output. In Floyd, W. F., & Welford, A. T. (Eds.) *Symposium on fatigue.* London: H. K. Lewis & Co., pp. 173–178. **[138, 139]**

Broadhurst, P. L. (1957) Emotionality and the Yerkes-Dodson law. *J. exp. Psychol.* 54, 345–352. **[134, 522]**

Broadhurst, P. L. (1958) Determinants of emotionality in the rat: III. Strain differences. *J. comp. physiol. Psychol.* **51,** 55–59.   **[410]**

Broadhurst, P. L. (1959) The interaction of task difficulty and motivation: The Yerkes-Dodson law revived. *Acta Psychol.* **16,** 321–338.   **[523]**

Brobeck, J. R. (1946) Mechanism of the development of obesity in animals with hypothalamic lesions. *Physiol. Rev.* **26,** 541–559.   **[219]**

Brobeck, J. R. (1955a) Regulation of energy exchange. In Fulton, J. F. (Ed.) *A textbook of physiology* (17th ed.) Philadelphia: Saunders, Chap. 56. **[132, 226]**

Brobeck, J. R. (1955b) Neural regulation of food intake. *Annals N.Y. Acad. Sci.* **63,** Art. 1, 44–55.   **[217, 221, 226, 227, 242]**

Brobeck, J. R. (1957) Neural control of hunger, appetite and satiety. *Yale J. biol. Med.* **29,** 565–574.   **[226, 227]**

Brobeck, J. R. (1960a) Food and temperature. *Recent progr. hormone Res.* **16,** 439–466.   **[222, 226]**

Brobeck, J. R. (1960b) Regulation of feeding and drinking. In Field, J. (Ed.) *Handbook of physiology, Sect. 2, Vol. 2.* Baltimore: Williams and Wilkins. **[222]**

Brobeck, J. R., Larsson, S., & Reyes, E. (1956) A study of the electrical activity of the hypothalamic feeding mechanism. *J. Physiol.* **132,** 358–364.   **[221]**

Brobeck, J. R., Tepperman, J., & Long, C. N. H. (1943) Experimental hypothalamic hyperphagia in the albino rat. *Yale J. biol. Med.* **15,** 831–853. **[217]**

Brobeck, J. R., Wheatland, M., & Strominger, J. L. (1947) Variations in regulation of energy exchange associated with estrus, diestrus, and pseudopregnancy in rats. *Endocrinology* **40,** 65–72.   **[820]**

Brodbeck, A. J. (1950) The effect of three feeding variables on the non-nutritive sucking of new-born infants. *Amer. Psychologist* **5,** 292–293.   **[114]**

Brodie, B. B., & Costa, E. (1962) Some current views on brain monoamines. *Psychopharm. Serv. Cent. Bull.* **2** (5), 1–25.   **[146]**

Brodie, D. A., Moreno, O. M., Malis, J. L., & Boren, J. J. (1960) Rewarding properties of intracranial stimulation. *Science* **131,** 929–930.   **[546]**

Brody, Sylvia (1956) *Patterns of mothering: Maternal influence during infancy.* New York: International Universities Press.   **[686]**

Brooks, C. McC. (1937) The role of the cerebral cortex and of various sense organs in the excitation and execution of mating activity in the rabbit. *Amer. J. Physiol.* **120,** 544–553.   **[177]**

Brouha, L. (1954) Fatigue—measuring and reducing it. *Advanced Mgmt.* **19,** 9–19. **[144]**

Browman, L. G. (1942) The effect of bilateral optic enucleation on the voluntary muscular activity of the albino rat. *J. exp. Zool.* **91,** 331–344. **[132]**

Browman, L. G. (1943) The effect of controlled temperature upon the spontaneous activity rhythms of the albino rat. *J. exp. Zool.* **94,** 477–489.   **[132]**

Brown, F. A., Jr. (1962) *Biological clocks.* Boston: D. C. Heath.   **[169]**

Brown, G. L., & Burns, B. D. (1949) Fatigue and neuromuscular block in mammalian skeletal muscle. *Proc. Roy. Soc. B.* **136,** 182–195.   **[137]**

Brown, G. W., & Cohen, B. D. (1959) Avoidance and approach learning motivated by stimulation of identical hypothalamic loci. *Amer. J. Physiol.* **197,** 153–157. **[548, 549]**

Brown, J. S. (1948) Gradients of approach and avoidance responses and their relation to level of motivation. *J. comp. physiol. Psychol.* **41,** 450–465. **[436]**

Brown, J. S. (1953) Problems presented by the concept of acquired drives. In Brown, J. S., et al. *Current theory and research in motivation: A symposium* Lincoln: University of Nebraska Press, pp. 1–21.   **[12, 13, 479, 482, 582, 693]**

Brown, J. S. (1955) Pleasure-seeking and the drive reduction hypothesis. *Psychol. Rev.* 62, 169–179. [541]

Brown, J. S. (1957) Principles of intrapersonal conflict. *Conflict Resolution, 1,* 135–154. [436, 437, 438–439, 440]

Brown, J. S. (1961) *The motivation of behavior.* New York: McGraw-Hill. [2, 8, 12, 13, 300, 415, 416, 419, 420, 421, 422, 573, 577, 578, 580, 582, 693, 708, 724]

Brown, J. S., & Farber, I. E. (1951) Emotions conceptualized as intervening variables —with suggestions toward a theory of frustration. *Psychol. Bull.* 48, 465–495. [370, 379, 419, 420]

Brown, J. S., Harlow, H. F., Postman, L. J., Nowlis, V., Newcomb, T. M., & Mowrer, O. H. (1953) *Current theory and research in motivation: A symposium.* Lincoln: University of Nebraska Press. [2]

Brown, J. S., & Jacobs, A. (1949) The role of fear in the motivation and acquisition of responses. *J. exp. Psychol.* 39, 747–759. [576]

Brown, J. S., Kalish, H. I., & Farber, I. E. (1951) Conditioned fear as revealed by magnitude of startle response to an auditory stimulus. *J. exp. Psychol.* 41, 317–328. [577]

Browne, R. C. (1953) Fatigue, fact or fiction? In Floyd, W. F., & Welford, A. T. (Eds.) *Symposium on fatigue.* London: H. K. Lewis & Co., pp. 137–142. [141, 143]

Brožek, J. (1962) Current status of psychology in the U.S.S.R. *Ann. rev. Psychol.* 13, 515–566. [149]

Bruce, R. H. (1930) The effect of removal of reward on the maze performance of rats. *Univ. Calif. Publ. Psychol.* 4, 203–214. [552]

Bruce, R. H. (1932) The effect of removal of reward on the maze performance of rats: II and III. *Univ. Calif. Publ. Psychol.* 6, 65–73, 75–82. [552]

Bruce, R. H. (1935) An experimental investigation of the thirst drive in rats with especial reference to the goal-gradient hypothesis. *Psychol. Bull.* 32, 677–678. [248]

Bruce, R. H. (1937) An experimental investigation of the thirst drive in rats with especial reference to the goal-gradient hypothesis. *J. genet. Psychol.* 17, 49–60. [552]

Bruce, R. H. (1941) An experimental analysis of the social factors affecting the performance of white rats: I. Performance in learning a simple field situation. *J. comp. Psychol.* 31, 363–377. [258]

Brücke, E. (1874) *Lectures on physiology.* Vienna: University of Vienna. [41, 591]

Brun, R. (1951) *General theory of neurosis.* New York: International Universities Press. [92]

Brun, R. (1953) Über Freud's Hypothese von Todestrieb. *Psyche.* 7, 81–111. [604]

Bruner, J. S. (1957) Mechanism riding high. *Contemp. Psychol.* 2, 155–157. [493]

Bruner, J. S. (1958) Social psychology and perception. In Maccoby, E., Newcomb, T. M., & Hartley, E. (Eds.) *Readings in social psychology,* (3rd. ed.). New York: Holt. [4]

Bruner, J. S., Matter, J., & Papanek, M. L. (1955) Breadth of learning as a function of drive level and mechanization. *Psychol. Rev.* 62, 1–10. [528]

Brunton, T. L. (1883) On the nature of inhibition, and the action of drugs upon it. *Nature* 27, 419–422. [147]

Brush, F. R. (1957) The effects of shock intensity on the acquisition and extinction of an avoidance response in dogs. *J. comp. physiol. Psychol.* 50, 547–552. [523]

Buchwald, A. M., & Yamaguchi, H. G. (1955) The effect of change in drive level on habit reversal. *J. exp. Psychol.* 50, 265–268. [538]

Bujas, Z. (1957) Testovi umora (Tests of fatigue) *Arh. Hig. rada* 8, 211–214. (Abstract cited: *Psychol. Abstr.* 1959, 33, No. 3036.) [144]

Burch, N. R., & Greiner, T. H. (1958) Drugs and human fatigue: GSR parameters. *J. Psychol.* 45, 3–10.   [144, 146]

Bursten, B., & Delgado, J. M. R. (1958) Positive reinforcement induced by intra-cerebral stimulation in the monkey. *J. comp. physiol. Psychol.* 51, 6–10. [544, 546]

Bury, J. B. (1932) *The idea of progress: an inquiry into its origin and growth.* (1st ed.) New York: Macmillan Dover reprint: 1955.   [34]

Bush, R. R., & Whiting, J. W. M. (1953) On the theory of psychoanalytic displacement. *J. abn. soc. Psychol.* 48, 261–272.   [423]

Buss, A. H. (1961) *The psychology of aggression.* New York: Wiley.   [745, 746, 747, 748, 751, 753, 754, 756, 758, 759, 760, 800]

Butler, R. A. (1953) Discrimination learning by rhesus monkeys to visual-exploration motivation. *J. comp. physiol. Psychol.* 46, 95–98.   [284]

Butler, R. A. (1957a) The effect of deprivation of visual incentives on visual exploration motivation in monkeys. *J. comp. physiol. Psychol.* 50, 177–179. [285]

Butler, R. A. (1957b) Discrimination learning by rhesus monkeys to auditory incentives. *J. comp. physiol. Psychol.* 50, 239–241.   [285]

Butler, R. A. (1958) The differential effect of visual and auditory incentives on the performance of monkeys. *Amer. J. Psychol.* 71, 591–593.   [285]

Butler, R. A., & Alexander, H. M. (1955) Daily patterns of visual exploratory behavior in the monkey. *J. comp. physiol. Psychol.* 48, 247–249.   [284]

Butler, R. A., & Harlow, H. F. (1954) Persistence of visual exploration in monkeys. *J. comp. physiol. Psychol.* 47, 258–263.   [284, 285]

Bykov, K. M. (1957) *The cerebral cortex and the internal organs.* (Gantt, W. H., ed. and transl.) New York: Chemical Publ. Co.   [431, 448]

Caldwell, D. F., & Cromwell, R. L. (1959) Replication report: The relationship of manifest anxiety and electric shock to eyelid conditioning. *J. exp. Psychol.* 57, 348–349.   [706]

Calvin, A. D., & Behan, R. A. (1954) The effect of hunger upon drinking patterns in the rat. *Brit. J. Psychol.* 45, 294–298.   [264]

Calvin, J. S., Bicknell, A., & Sperling, D. S. (1953a) Establishment of a conditioned drive based on the hunger drive. *J. comp. physiol. Psychol.* 46, 173–175. [581]

Calvin, J. S., Bicknell, E. A., & Sperling, D. S. (1953b) Effect of a secondary reinforcer on consummatory behavior. *J. comp. physiol. Psychol.* 46, 176–179.   [540]

Cameron, N. (1947) *The psychology of behavior disorders: A bio-social interpretation.* Boston: Houghton-Mifflin.   [702]

Campbell, B. A. (1955) The fractional reduction in noxious stimulation required to produce "just noticeable" learning. *J. comp. physiol. Psychol.* 48, 141–148. [550]

Campbell, B. A. (1956) The reinforcement difference limen (RDL) function for shock reduction. *J. exp. Psychol.* 52, 258–262.   [550]

Campbell, B. A. (1957) Auditory and aversion thresholds of rats for bands of noise. *Science* 125, 596–597.   [550]

Campbell, B. A. (1958) Absolute and relative sucrose preference thresholds for hungry and satiated rats. *J. comp. physiol. Psychol.* 51, 795–800.   [550]

Campbell, B. A., & Kraeling, Doris (1953) Response strength as a function of drive level and amount of drive reduction. *J. exp. Psychol.* 45, 97–101.   [523]

Campbell, B. A., & Kraeling, Doris (1954) Response strength as a function of drive level during training and extinction. *J. comp. physiol. Psychol.* 47, 101–103. [527–528, 534]

Campbell, B. A., & Sheffield, F. D. (1953) Relation of random activity to food deprivation. *J. comp. physiol. Psychol.* 46, 320–322.   [274, 275]

Campbell, B. A., Teghtsoonian, R., & Williams, R. A. (1961) Activity, weight loss, and survival time of food-deprived rats as a function of age. *J. comp. physiol. Psychol.* 54, 216–219. [275]

Cannon, W. B. (1918) The physiological basis of thirst. *Proc. Roy. Soc. London, B.* 90, 283–301. [245, 246]

Cannon, W. B. (1927) The James-Lange theory of emotions: a critical examination and an alternative theory. *Amer. J. Psychol.* 39, 106–124. [369, 391]

Cannon, W. B. (1929) *Bodily changes in pain, hunger, fear and rage.* (2nd ed.) New York: Appleton. [205, 207]

Cannon, W. B. (1932) *The wisdom of the body.* New York: W. W. Norton (2nd. ed., 1939). [207, 302–303, 304, 305, 307, 309, 310, 317]

Cannon, W. B. (1934) Hunger and thirst. In Murchison, C. (Ed.) *A handbook of general experimental psychology.* Worcester, Mass: Clark University Press, pp. 247–263. [205, 207]

Cannon, W. B. (1941) The body physiologic and the body politic. *Science* 93, 1–10. [303]

Cannon, W. B. (1945) *The ways of an investigator.* New York: W. W. Norton. [303]

Cannon, W. B., & Washburn, A. L. (1912) An explanation of hunger. *Amer. J. Physiol.* 29, 441–454. [206, 207, 209]

Caplan, G. (1954) Clinical observations on the emotional life of children in the communal settlements in Israel. In Senn, M. H. (Ed.) *Problems of infancy and childhood.* Trans. 7th Conf. N.Y.: Josiah Macy, Jr., Found. pp. 91–120. [688]

Carlson, A. J. (1916) *The control of hunger in health and disease.* Chicago: University of Chicago Press. [205, 206, 207, 208, 210, 212, 215, 217]

Carlson, A. J., & Johnson, V. (1953) *The machinery of the body.* (4th ed.) Chicago: University of Chicago Press. [133]

Carlton, P. L., & Marks, R. A. (1957) *Heat as a reinforcement for operant behavior.* Fort Knox: U.S. Army Med. Res. Lab. Report No. 299. [133]

Carmichael, L. (1926) The development of behavior in vertebrates experimentally removed from the influence of external stimulation. *Psychol. Rev.* 33, 51–58. [79]

Carmichael, L., & Dearborn, W. F. (1947) *Reading and visual fatigue.* Boston: Houghton-Mifflin. [144]

Carmichael, L., Kennedy, J. I., & Mead, L. L. (1949) Some recent approaches to the experimental study of human fatigue. *Proc. Nat. Acad. Sci. Wash.* 35, 691–696. [139]

Carpenter, C. R. (1942) Sexual behavior of free ranging rhesus monkeys (*macaca mulatta*). I. Specimens, procedures and behavioral characteristics of oestrus. *J. comp. Psychol.* 33, 113–142. [193]

Carpenter, J. A. (1956) Species differences in taste preferences. *J. comp. physiol. Psychol.* 49, 139–144. [233]

Carper, J. W. (1953) A comparison of the reinforcing value of a nutritive and a non-nutritive substance under conditions of specific and general hunger. *Amer. J. Psychol.* 66, 270–277. [319, 525]

Carr, R. M., & Williams, C. D. (1957) Exploratory behavior of three strains of rats. *J. comp. physiol. Psychol.* 50, 621–623. [294]

Carr, W. J. (1952) The effect of adrenalectomy upon the NaCl taste threshold in the rat. *J. comp. physiol. Psychol.* 45, 377–380. [234]

Carthy, J. D. (1956) *Animal navigation: How animals find their way about.* London: George Allen & Unwin. [127, 128, 129, 130]

Cartwright, D. (1959) Lewinian theory as a contemporary systematic framework. In Koch, S. (Ed.), *Psychology: A study of a science.* Vol. 2, New York: McGraw-Hill, pp. 7–91. [357, 358, 359, 362]

Cartwright, D., & Festinger, L. (1943) A quantitative theory of decision. *Psychol. Rev.* **50**, 595–621.   **[774]**

Cartwright, D., & Harary, F. (1956) Structural balance: a generalization of Heider's theory. *Psychol. Rev.* **63**, 277–293.   **[788]**

Cartwright, D., & Zander, A. (1960) *Group dynamics: Research and theory.* (2nd. ed.) Evanston, Ill.: Row, Peterson.   **[776, 778, 770, 780]**

Cason, H. (1930) Common annoyances: A psychological study of everyday aversions and annoyances. *Psychol. Monog.* **40**, Whole No. 182.   **[751]**

Castaneda, A. (1956) Effects of stress on complex learning and performance. *J. exp. Psychol.* **52**, 9–12.   **[538]**

Castaneda, A., McCandless, B. R., & Palermo, D. S. (1956) The children's form of the Manifest Anxiety Scale. *Child Develpm.* **27**, 317–326.   **[702]**

Castaneda, A., & Palermo, D. S. (1955) Psychomotor performance as a function of amount of training and stress. *J. exp. Psychol.* **50**, 175–179.   **[538]**

Cattell, R. B. (1957) *Personality and motivation: Structure and measurement.* New York: World Book.   **[804]**

Cattell, R. B. (1959) The dynamic calculus: concepts and crucial experiments. In Jones, M. R. (Ed.) *Nebraska symposium on motivation 1959.* Lincoln: University of Nebraska Press, pp. 84–134.   **[804]**

Cautela, J. R. (1956) Experimental extinction and drive during extinction in a discrimination habit. *J. exp. Psychol.* **51**, 299–302.   **[531]**

Chambers, R. M. (1956a) Effects of intravenous glucose injections on learning, general activity, and hunger drive. *J. comp. physiol. Psychol.* **49**, 558–564. **[540]**

Chambers, R. M. (1956b) Some physiological bases for reinforcing properties of reward injections. *J. comp. physiol. Psychol.* **49**, 565–568.   **[540]**

Champion, R. A. (1962) Stimulus intensity effects in response-evocation. *Psychol. Rev.* **69**, 428–449.   **[566]**

Chance, June E. (1961) Independence training and first graders' achievement. *J consult. Psychol.* **25**, 149–154.   **[765]**

Chansky, N. M. (1956) Threat as a factor in recall in a retroactive paradigm. *J. Psychol.* **41**, 3–10.   **[785]**

Chapman, R. M., & Levy, N. (1957) Hunger drive and reinforcing effect of novel stimuli. *J. comp. physiol. Psychol.* **50**, 233–238.   **[294]**

Chapman, W. P., & Jones, C. M. (1944) Variations in cutaneous and visceral pain sensitivity in normal subject. *J. clin. Investig.* **23**, 81–91.   **[261]**

Charlesworth, W. R., & Thompson, W. R. (1957) Effect of lack of visual stimulus variation on exploratory behavior in the adult white rat. *Psychol. Reports* **3**, 509–512.   **[290, 294]**

Child, C. M. (1924) *Physiological foundations of behavior.* New York: Holt. **[303, 304, 306, 307, 314]**

Child, I. L., Storm, T., & Veroff, J. (1958) Achievement themes in folk tales related to socialization practice. In Atkinson, J. W. (Ed.) *Motives in fantasy, action, and society.* New York: Van Nostrand, pp. 479–492.   **[764]**

Child, I. L., & Waterhouse, I. K. (1952) Frustration and the quality of performance: I. A critique of the Barker, Dembo and Lewin experiment. *Psychol. Rev.* **59**, 351–362.   **[425, 711]**

Child, I. L., & Waterhouse, I. K. (1953) Frustration and the quality of performance: II. A theoretical statement. *Psychol. Rev.* **60**, 127–139.   **[419, 425, 711]**

Child, I. L., & Whiting, J. W. M. (1949) Determinants of level of aspiration: Evidence from everyday life. *J. abn. soc. Psychol.* **44**, 303–314.   **[772]**

Chiles, W. D. (1958) Effects of shock-induced stress on verbal performance. *J. exp. Psychol.* **56**, 159–165.   **[707]**

Cho, J. B., & Davis, R. T. (1957) Preferences of monkeys for objects other than food. *Amer. J. Psychol.* **70**, 87–91.   **[296]**

Christensen, E. H., Krogh, A., & Lindherd, J. (1934) Investigations on heavy muscular work. *Quart. Bull. Hlth. Organ., League of Nations* **3**, 388–417. [136]

Christian, J. J. (1959) The roles of endocrine and behavioral factors in the growth of mammalian populations. In Gorbman, A. (Ed.) *Comparative endocrinology.* Columbia University Symposium, Cold Spring Harbor. New York: Wiley, pp. 71–97. [443]

Christie, R., & Budnitzky, S. (1957) A shortened forced-choice anxiety scale. *J. consult. Psychol.* **21**, 501. [702]

Christman, Ruth C. (1950) (Ed.) *Pituitary-adrenal function: A symposium.* Washington, D.C.: A.A.A.S. [308]

Cizek, L. J., Semple, R. E., Huang, K. C., & Gregerson, M. I. (1951) Effect of extracellular electrolyte depletion on water intake in dogs. *Amer. J. Physiol.* **164**, 415–422. [251]

Clark, J. W., & Bindra, D. (1956) Individual differences in pain threshold. *Canad. J. Psychol.* **10**, 69–76. [261]

Clark, R. A. (1952) The projective measurement of experimentally induced sexual motivation. *J. exp. Psychol.* **44**, 391–399. [727, 728]

Clark, R. A. (1955) The effects of sexual motivation on fantasy. In McClelland, D. C. (Ed.) *Studies in motivation.* New York: Appleton-Century-Crofts, pp. 44–57. [727, 728]

Clark, R. A., Teevan, R., & Ricciuti, H. N. (1956) Hope of success and fear of failure as aspects of need for achievement. *J. abn. soc. Psychol.* **53**, 182–186. [729]

Clayton, F. L. (1958) Light reinforcement as a function of water deprivation. *Psychol. Reports* **4**, 63–66. [541]

Cloche, Regine (1951) An introduction to the study of fatigue. *Arch. brasil. Psicotecnica* **3** (3) 69–76, **3** (4) 63–77. [143]

Cofer, C. N. (1954) *An evaluation of the concept of drive.* Paper presented in a symposium at annual convention, American Psychological Association, New York, Sept., 1954. [826]

Cofer, C. N. (1957) Reasoning as an associative process: III. The role of verbal responses in problem solving. *J. gen. Psychol.* **57**, 55–68. [48]

Cofer, C. N. (1959) Motivation, *Ann. rev. Psychol.* **10**, 173–202. [299]

Coghill, G. E. (1929) *Anatomy and the problem of behavior.* New York: Macmillan. [97]

Cohen, A. R. (1955) Social norms, arbitrariness of frustration, and status of the agent of frustration in the frustration-aggression hypothesis. *J. abn. soc. Psychol.* **51**, 222–226. [423, 758]

Cohen, B. D., Brown, G. W., & Brown, M. L. (1957) Avoidance learning motivated by hypothalamic stimulation. *J. exp. Psychol.* **53**, 228–233. [544]

Cohen, L. D., Kipnis, D., Kunkle, E. C., & Kubzansky, P. E. (1955) Observations of a person with congenital insensitivity to pain. *J. abn. soc. Psychol.* **51**, 333–338. [261]

Cohen, R. A., & Cohen, Mabel B. (1961) Research in psychotherapy: A preliminary report. *Psychiatry* **24**, 46–61. [646]

Colby, K. M. (1955) *Energy and structure in psychoanalysis.* New York: Ronald Press. [598, 643]

Cole, L. W. (1911) The relation of strength of stimulation to rate of learning in the chick. *J. anim. Behav.* **1**, 111–124. [521, 523]

Collias, N. E. (1951) Problems and principles of animal sociology. In Stone, C. P. (Ed.) *Comparative psychology* (3rd. ed.) New York: Prentice-Hall, pp. 388–422. [133, 748]

Conger, J. J. (1951) The effects of alcohol on conflict behavior in the albino rat. *Quart. J. Stud. Alcohol* **12**, 1–29. [584]

Cook, E. B., & Wherry, R. J. (1950) The urinary 17-ketosteroid output of Naval Submarine enlisted candidates during two stressful situations. *Human biol.* **22**, 104–124.   **[443]**

Cook, L., Davison, A., Davis, D. L., & Kelleher, R. T. (1960) Epinephrine, norepinephrine, and acetylcholine as conditioned stimuli for avoidance behavior. *Science* **131**, 990–991.   **[448]**

Coppock, H. W., & Chambers, R. M. (1954) Reinforcement of position preference by automatic intravenous injections of glucose. *J. comp. physiol. Psychol.* **47**, 355–357.   **[540]**

Cotton, J. W. (1953) Running time as a function of amount of food deprivation. *J. exp. Psychol.* **46**, 188–198.   **[270, 492, 527]**

Courts, F. A. (1939) Relations between experimentally induced muscular tension and memorization. *J. exp. Psychol.* **25**, 235–256.   **[393]**

Courts, F. A. (1942) Relations between muscular tension and performance. *Psychol. Bull.* **39**, 347–367.   **[332, 393, 397]**

Cowen, E. L., Heilizer, F., Axelrod, H. S., and Alexander, S. (1957) The correlates of manifest anxiety in perceptual reactivity, rigidity, and self-concept. *J. consult. Psychol.* **21**, 405–411.   **[708]**

Cowles, J. T. (1937) Food tokens as incentives for learning by chimpanzees. *Comp. Psychol. Monog.* **14**, No. 5, Whole No. 71.   **[474, 563, 572]**

Cox, E. N. (1952) Some effects of frustration: I. A methodological programme. *Austral. J. Psychol.* **4**, 94–106.   **[751]**

Craig, W. (1912) Observations on doves learning to drink. *J. anim. Behav.* **2**, 273–279.   **[258]**

Craig, W. (1918) Appetites and aversions as constituents of instincts. *Biol. Bull.* **34**, 91–107.   **[45]**

Cranston, R. E., Zubin, J., & Landis, C. (1952) The effect of small doses of thonzylamine, Dexedrine, and phenobarbital on test performance and self-ratings of subjective states. *J. Psychol.* **33**, 209–215.   **[145]**

Crawford, M. (1939) The social psychology of the vertebrates. *Psychol. Bull.* **36**, 407–446.   **[109, 195, 258, 748]**

Crespi, L. P. (1942) Quantitative variation of incentive and performance in the white rat. *Amer. J. Psychol.* **55**, 467–517.   **[489, 553, 554]**

Creutzfeldt, O., & Jung, R. (1960) Neuronal discharge in the cat's motor cortex during sleep and arousal. In Wolstenholme, G. E. W., & O'Connor, Maeve (Eds.) *Ciba Foundation symposium on the nature of sleep.* Boston: Little, Brown and Co., pp. 131–170.   **[168]**

Cronbach, L. J., and Meehl, P. E. (1955) Construct validity in psychological tests. *Psychol. Bull.* **52**, 281–302.   **[802]**

Crozier, W. J., & Hoagland, H. (1934) The study of living organisms. In Murchison, C. (Ed.) *A handbook of experimental psychology.* Worcester, Mass.: Clark University Press, pp. 3–108.   **[42]**

Dallenbach, K. M. (1939) Pain: History and present status. *Amer. J. Psychol.* **52**, 331–347.   **[260]**

Daniel, G. E. (1959) The idea of man's antiquity. *Sci. Amer.* **201**, 167–176.   **[32]**

Danziger, K., & Mainland, M. (1954) The habituation of exploratory behaviour. *Austral. J. Psychol.* **6**, 39–51.   **[292]**

Darchen, R. (1952) Sur l'activité exploratrice de *Blatella germanica*. *Z. Tierpsychol.* **9**, 362–372.   **[290]**

Darchen, R. (1954) Stimuli nouveau et tendance exploratrice chez *Blatella germanica*. *Z. Tierpsychol.* **11**, 1–11.   **[290]**

Darlington, C. D. (1959) The origins of Darwinism. *Sci. Amer.* **200**, 60–66.   **[32]**

Darrow, C. W., & Henry, C. E. (1949) Psychophysiology of stress. In Lindsley,

D. B., et al. (Eds.) *Human factors in undersea warfare.* Washington, D.C.: National Research Council, pp. 417–440.   [141, 142, 454, 459–460]

Darrow, D. C., & Yannett, H. (1935) The changes in the distribution of body water accompanying increase and decrease in extracellular electrolyte. *J. clin. Investig.* 14, 266–275.   [251]

Darwin, C. (1859) *Origin of species.* New York: Modern Library (1936 edition). [32, 590]

Darwin, C. (1872) *Expression of the emotions in man and animals.* London: Murray.   [35]

Dashiell, J. F. (1925) A quantitative demonstration of animal drive. *J. comp. Psychol.* 5, 205–208.   [271, 273, 288]

Dashiell, J. F. (1928) *Fundamentals of objective psychology.* Boston: Houghton-Mifflin.   [43, 45, 581]

Dashiell, J. F. (1930) An experimental analysis of some group effects. *J. abn. soc. Psychol.* 25, 190–199.   [776]

Dashiell, J. F. (1935) Experimental studies of the influence of social situations on the behavior of individual human adults. In Murchison, C. C. (Ed.) *Handbook of social psychology.* Worcester, Mass.: Clark University Press, pp. 1097–1158.   [769, 776, 777]

Davids, A. (1955) Relations among several objective measures of anxiety under different conditions of motivation. *J. consult. Psychol.* 19, 275–279.   [709]

Davis, D. M. (1928) Self-selection of diet by newly weaned infants. *Amer. J. dis. Child.* 36, 651–679.   [229]

Davis, D. R. (1947) Psychomotor effects of analeptics and their relation to "fatigue" phenomena in air-crew. *Brit. med. Bull.* 5, 43–45.   [145]

Davis, D. R. (1953) Satiation and frustration as determinants of fatigue. In Floyd, W. F., & Welford, A. T. (Eds.) *Symposium on fatigue.* London: H. K. Lewis & Co., pp. 179–182.   [140]

Davis, H. V., Sears, R. R., Miller, H. C., & Brodbeck, A. J. (1948) Effects of cup, bottle, and breast-feeding on oral activities of new-born infants. *Pediatrics* 3, 549–558.   [114, 651]

Davis, K. B. (1929) *Factors in the sex life of twenty-two hundred women.* New York: Harper & Bros.   [190]

Davis, L. E., & Josselyn, P. D. (1953) How fatigue affects productivity: A study of manual work patterns. *Personnel* 30, 54–59.   [139]

Davis, R. C. (1957) Response patterns. *Transac. N.Y. Acad. Sci.,* Ser. II 19, 731–739.   [800]

Davis, R. C. (1958) The domain of homeostasis. *Psychol. Rev.* 65, 8–13.   [302, 314, 320]

Davis, R. C. (1959) Somatic activity under reduced stimulation. *J. comp. physiol. Psychol.* 52, 309–314.   [300]

Davis, R. C., Garafalo, L., & Kveim, K. (1959) Conditions associated with gastrointestinal activity. *J. comp. physiol. Psychol.* 52, 466–475.   [207]

Davis, R. H. (1957) The effect of drive reversal on latency, amplitude, and activity level. *J. exp. Psychol.* 53, 310–315.   [527, 533]

Davis, S. W. (1955) Auditory and visual flicker-fusion as measures of fatigue. *Amer. J. Psychol.* 68, 654–657.   [143]

Davis, S. W., Elmadjian, N., et al. (1952) *A study of combat stress: Korea 1952.* Chevy Chase, Md.: Operations Research Office, Johns Hopkins University. [443, 462–463]

Davitz, J. R. (1952) The effects of previous training on post-frustration behavior *J. abn. soc. Psychol.* 47, 309–315.   [751, 758]

DeCharms, R. C., Morrison, H. W., Reitman, W. R., & McClelland, D. C. (1955) Behavioral correlates of directly and indirectly measured achievement motivation. In McClelland, D. C. (Ed.) *Studies in motivation.* New York: Appleton-Century-Crofts, pp. 414–423.   [724]

Deese, J. (1955) Some problems in the theory of vigilance. *Psychol. Rev.* **62**, 359–368. [410]

Deese, J., & Carpenter, J. A. (1951) Drive-level and reinforcement. *J. exp. Psychol.* **42**, 236–238. [521, 527, 533]

Deese, J., Lazarus, R. S., & Keenan, J. (1953) Anxiety, anxiety reduction, and stress in learning. *J. exp. Psychol.* **46**, 55–60. [709]

Deese, J., & Morgan, C. T. (1951) Comparative and physiological psychology. *Ann. rev. Psychol.* **2**, 193–216. [101]

Delafresnaye, J. F. (Ed.) (1954) *Brain mechanisms and consciousness.* Springfield, Ill.: Ch. E. Thomas. [150]

Delafresnaye, J. F. (Ed.) (1961) *Brain mechanisms and learning.* London: Blackwell. [150]

Delgado, J. M. R., & Anand, B. K. (1953) Increased food intake induced by electrical stimulation of the lateral hypothalamus. *Amer. J. Physiol.* **172**, 162–168. [219]

Delgado, J. M. R., Roberts, W. W., & Miller, N. E. (1954) Learning motivated by electrical stimulation of the brain. *Amer. J. Physiol.* **179**, 587–593. [544]

Delgado, J. M. R., Rosvold, H. E., & Looney, E. (1956) Evoking conditioned fear by electrical stimulation of subcortical structures in the monkey brain. *J. comp. physiol. Psychol.* **49**, 373–380. [544]

Dell, P. (1960) Discussion. In Wolstenholme, G. E. W., & O'Connor, Maeve (Eds.) *Ciba Foundation symposium on the nature of sleep.* Boston: Little, Brown and Co., p. 320. [169, 170]

Dell, P., Bonvallet, M., & Hugelin, A. (1960) Mechanisms of reticular deactivation. In Wolstenholme, G. E. W., & O'Connor, Maeve (Eds.) *Ciba Foundation symposium on the nature of sleep.* Boston: Little, Brown and Co., pp. 86–102. [159, 165, 166]

Dember, W. N., & Earl, R. W. (1957) Analysis of exploratory, manipulatory, and curiosity behaviors. *Psychol. Rev.* **64**, 91–96. [294, 299]

Dember, W. N., Earl, R. W., & Paradise, N. (1957) Response by rats to differential stimulus complexity. *J. comp. physiol. Psychol.* **50**, 514–518. [293]

Dement, W. (1958) The occurrence of low-voltage, fast electroencephalogram patterns during behavioural sleep in the cat. *Electroenceph. clin. Neurophysiol.* **10**, 291–296. [159, 168]

Dement, W. (1960) The effect of dream deprivation. *Science* **131**, 1705–1707. [172]

Dempsey, E. W. (1951) Homeostasis. In Stevens, S. S. (Ed.) *Handbook of experimental psychology.* New York: Wiley, pp. 209–235. [305, 306–307, 313]

Dennis, W. (1935) A comparison of the rat's first and second explorations of a maze unit. *Amer. J. Psychol.* **47**, 488–490. [290]

Dennis, W. (1938) Infant development under conditions of restricted practice and of minimum social stimulation. A preliminary report. *J. genet. Psychol.* **53**, 149–158. [688]

Dennis, W. (1939) Spontaneous alternation in rats as an indicator of the persistence of stimulus effects. *J. comp. Psychol.* **28**, 305–312. [290]

Dennis, W. (1941) Infant development under conditions of restricted practice and of minimum social stimulation. *Genet. psychol. Monog.* **23**, 143–189. [688]

Dennis, W. (1955) Early recognition of the manipulation drive in monkeys. *Brit. J. anim. Behav.* **3**, 71–72. [296]

Dennis, W., & Henneman, R. H. (1932) The non-random nature of initial maze behavior. *J. genet. Psychol.* **40**, 396–405. [290]

Dennis, W., & Najarian, P. (1957) Infant development under environmental handicap. *Psychol. Monog.* **71**, Whole No. 436. [688, 689]

Dennis, W., & Sollenberger, R. T. (1934) Negative adaptation in the maze exploration of rats. *J. comp. Psychol.* **18**, 197–205. [290]

Denny, M. R. (1957) Learning through stimulus satiation. *J. exp. Psychol.* 54, 62–64. [295]

Deutsch, J. A. (1954) A machine with insight. *Quart. J. exper. Psychol.* 6, 6–11. [354]

Deutsch, M. (1954) Field theory in social psychology. In Lindzey, G. (Ed.) *Handbook of social psychology.* Cambridge, Mass.: Addison-Wesley Press, pp. 181–222. [357, 362, 363]

Diamond, S., Balvin, R. S., & Diamond, Florence R. (1963) *Inhibition and choice.* New York: Harper and Row. [147, 148, 149, 151, 157]

Diggory, J. C. (1949) Responses to experimentally induced failure. *Amer. J. Psychol.* 62, 48–61. [772]

Dill, D. B., Bock, A. V., Edwards, H. T., & Kennedy, P. H. (1936) Industrial fatigue. *J. Indus. Hyg. and Toxicol.* 18, 417–431. [136]

Dinsmoor, J. A. (1950) A quantitative comparison of the discriminative and reinforcing functions of a stimulus. *J. exp. Psychol.* 40, 458–472. [564]

Dinsmoor, J. A. (1954) Punishment: I. The avoidance hypothesis. *Psychol. Rev.* 61, 34–46. [580]

Dinsmoor, J. A. (1955) Punishment: II. An interpretation of empirical findings. *Psychol. Rev.* 62, 96–105. [580]

Diserens, C. M., & Vaughn, J. (1931) The experimental psychology of motivation. *Psychol. Bull.* 28, 15–65. [769]

Dodson, J. D. (1915) The relation of strength of stimulus to rapidity of habit formation in the kitten. *J. anim. Behav.* 5, 330–336. [521, 523]

Dodson, J. D. (1917) Relative values of reward and punishment in habit formation. *Psychobiol.* 1, 231–276. [522, 523]

Dollard, J., Auld, F., & White, Alice (1953) *Steps in psychotherapy.* New York: Macmillan. [645]

Dollard, J., Doob, L. W., Miller, N. E., Mowrer, O. H., & Sears, R. R. (1939) *Frustration and aggression.* New Haven: Yale University Press. [74, 415, 423, 745, 749, 751, 759]

Dollard, J., & Miller, N. E. (1950) *Personality and psychotherapy: An analysis in terms of learning, thinking and culture.* New York: McGraw-Hill. [74, 378, 413, 436, 438, 494, 496, 497, 572, 582, 652, 745, 787]

Donhoffer, S., & Vonotzky, J. (1947) The effect of environmental temperature on food selection. *Amer. J. Physiol.* 150, 329–333. [242]

Doob, L. W., & Sears, R. R. (1939) Factors determining substitute behavior and the overt expression of aggression. *J. abn. soc. Psychol.* 34, 293–313. [750, 757]

Dorcus, R. M. (1956) *Hypnosis and its therapeutic applications.* New York: McGraw-Hill. [49]

Douvan, Elizabeth (1956) Social status and success strivings. *J. abn. soc. Psychol.* 52, 219–223. [570]

Dove, W. F. (1935) A study of individuality in the nutritive instincts and of the causes and effects of variations in the selection of food. *Amer. Nat.* 69, 469–544. [232]

Drever, J., II (1960) Perceptual learning. *Ann. rev. Psychol.* 11, 131–160. [104]

Dubois, Cora (1944) *The people of Alor.* Minneapolis: University of Minnesota Press. [569]

Ducharme, R., & Bélanger, D. (1961) Influence d'une stimulation electrique sur le niveau d'activation et la performance. [Influence of electrical stimulation on general activation and performance.] *Canad. J. Psychol.* 15, 61–68. [397]

Duffy, Elizabeth (1932) The relationship between muscular tension and quality of performance. *Amer. J. Psychol.* 44, 535–546. [394]

Duffy, Elizabeth (1934) Emotion: An example of the need for reorientation in psychology. *Psychol. Rev.* 41, 184–198. [368, 394]

Duffy, Elizabeth (1941a) An explanation of "emotional" phenomena without the use of the concept "emotion." *J. gen. Psychol.* 25, 283–293.   [369, 394]

Duffy, Elizabeth (1941b) The conceptual categories of psychology: A suggestion for revision. *Psychol. Rev.* 48, 177–203.   [369]

Duffy, Elizabeth (1948) Leeper's "Motivational theory of emotion . . ." *Psychol. Rev.* 55, 324–328.   [369]

Duffy, Elizabeth (1949) A systematic framework for the description of personality. *J. abn. soc. Psychol.* 44, 175–190.   [369]

Duffy, Elizabeth (1951) The concept of energy mobilization. *Psychol. Rev.* 58, 30–40.   [392, 394, 397, 398]

Duffy, Elizabeth (1957) The psychological significance of the concept of "arousal" or "activation." *Psychol. Rev.* 64, 265–275.   [394, 397, 398]

Duffy, Elizabeth (1962) *Activation and behavior.* New York: Wiley.   [832]

Duffy, Elizabeth, & Lacey, O. L. (1946) Adaptation in energy mobilization: Changes in general level of palmar skin conductance. *J. exp. Psychol.* 36, 437–452.   [396]

Dufort, R. H., & Kimble, G. A. (1956) Changes in response strength with changes in the amount of reinforcement. *J. exp. Psychol.* 51, 185–191.   [555]

Dukes, W. F. (1955) Psychological studies of values. *Psychol. Bull.* 52, 24–50.   [804]

Duncker, K. (1938) Experimental modification of children's food preferences through social suggestion. *J. abn. soc. Psychol.* 33, 489–507.   [243]

Duner, H. (1953) The influence of the blood glucose level on the secretion of adrenaline and noradrenaline from the suprarenal. *Acta. physiol. Scand.* 28, *Suppl. 102*, pp. 77.   [224]

Dunlap, K. (1919) Are there any instincts? *J. abn. Psychol.* 14, 35–50.   [43, 56]

Dunlap, K. (1922) *Elements of scientific psychology.* St. Louis: Mosby.   [43]

Earl, R. W. (1957) Motivation, performance, and extinction. *J. comp. physiol. Psychol.* 50, 248–251.   [535]

Easterbrook, J. A. (1959) The effect of emotion on cue utilization and the organization of behavior. *Psychol. Rev.* 66, 183–201.   [528]

Eayrs, J. T. (1954) Spontaneous activity in the rat. *Brit. J. anim. Behav.* 2, 25–30.   [271]

Eccles, J. C. (1953) *The neurophysiological basis of mind.* Oxford: Clarendon Press.   [148]

Eccles, J. C. (1959) Neurophysiology—introduction. In Magoun, H. W. (Ed.) *Handbook of physiology, Section 1: Neurophysiology.* Washington, D.C.: Amer. Physiol. Society, 3 vols., pp. 59–74.   [148]

Eccles, J. (1960) Chairman's opening remarks. In Wolstenholme, G. E. W., & O'Connor, Maeve (Eds.) *Ciba Foundation symposium on the nature of sleep.* Boston: Little, Brown and Co., pp. 1–3.   [158]

Economo, C. von (1930) Sleep as a problem of localization. *J. nerv. ment. Dis.* 71, 249–259.   [165]

Edwards, A. L. (1941) Political frames of reference as a factor influencing recognition. *J. abn. soc. Psychol.* 36, 34–50.   [785]

Edwards, W. (1950) Recent research on pain perception. *Psychol. Bull.* 47, 449–474.   [260]

Edwards, W. (1954) The theory of decision making. *Psychol. Bull.* 51, 380–417.   [773, 774]

Edwards, W. (1955) The prediction of decisions among bets. *J. exp. Psychol.* 50, 201–214.   [774]

Edwards, W. (1961) Behavioral decision theory. *Ann. rev. Psychol.* 12, 473–498.   [775]

Eggan, J. B. (1926) Is instinct an entity? *J. abn. soc. Psychol.* 21, 38–51.   [56]

Eglash, A. (1951) Perception, association, and reasoning in animal fixations. *Psychol. Rev.* 58, 424–434. [427]

Ehrenfreund, D., & Badia, P. (1962) Response strength as a function of drive level and pre- and postshift incentive magnitude. *J. exp. Psychol.* 63, 468–471. [554, 558]

Eibl-Eibesfeldt, I. (1955) Angeborenes und Erworbenes in Nestbauverhalten der Wanderratte. *Naturw.* 42, 633–634. [96]

Eibl-Eibesfeldt, I. (1956) Fortschritte der vergleichenden Verhaltenforschung. *Naturw.* 13, 86–90, 136–142. [96]

Eibl-Eibesfeldt, I. (1958) Das Verhalten der Nagetiere. In Helmake, J. G., Lenger-ken, H. von, & Starck, D. (Eds.) *Handbuch der Zoologie, Vol. 8*, Lief 12, Teil 10. Berlin: Walter de Gruyter. [97]

Eibl-Eibesfeldt, I., & Kramer, S. (1958) Ethology, the comparative study of animal behavior. *Quart. rev. Biol.* 33, 181–211. [99]

Eiseley, L. C. (1959a) Alfred Russell Wallace. *Sci. Amer.* 200, 70–84. [32]

Eiseley, L. C. (1959b) Charles Lyell. *Sci. Amer.* 201, 98–106. [32]

Eisner, E. (1960) The relationship of hormones to the reproductive behavior of birds, referring especially to parental behaviour: A review. *Anim. Behav.* 8, 155–179. [109]

Elithorn, A. (1960) Discussion. In Wolstenholme, G. E. W., & O'Connor, Maeve (Eds.) *Ciba Foundation symposium on the nature of sleep.* Boston: Little, Brown and Co., p. 385. [161]

Elizur, A. (1949) Content analysis of the Rorschach with regard to anxiety and hostility. *J. proj. Tech.* 13, 247–284. [753]

Ellen, P. (1956) The compulsive nature of abnormal fixations. *J. comp. physiol. Psychol.* 49, 309–317. [428]

Ellingson, R. J. (1956) Brain waves and problems of psychology. *Psychol. Bull.* 53, 1–34. [402]

Elliott, M. H. (1928) The effect of change of reward on the maze performance of rats. *Univ. Calif. Publ. Psychol.* 4, 19–30. [552]

Elliott, M. H. (1929a) The effect of change of "drive" on maze performance. *Univ. Calif. Publ. Psychol.* 4, 185–188. [523]

Elliott, M. H. (1929b) The effect of appropriateness of reward and of complex incentives on maze performance. *Univ. Calif. Publ. Psychol.* 4, 91–98. [552]

Elliott, M. H., & Bousfield, W. A. (1936) Two basic mechanisms in motivation. *Psychol. Rev.* 43, 94–99. [410]

Ellis, F. P. (1953) Tropical fatigue. In Floyd, W. F., & Welford, A. T. (Eds.) *Symposium on fatigue.* London: H. K. Lewis and Co., pp. 21–40. [142]

Ellis, N. R. (1957) The immediate effects of emotionality upon behavior strength. *J. exp. Psychol.* 54, 339–354. [535, 537]

Emerson, A. E. (1946) The biological basis of social cooperation. *Transac. Ill. Acad. Sci.* 39, 9–18. [328]

Emerson, A. E. (1954) Dynamic homeostasis: A unifying principle in organic, social and ethical evolution. *Sci. Month.* 77, 67–85. [323]

Emmons, W. H., & Simon, C. W. (1956) The non-recall of material presented during sleep. *Amer. J. Psychol.* 69, 76–81. [171]

Engel, R. (1928) Experimentelle Untersuchungen über die Anhängigkeit der Lust und Unlust von der Reizstärke beim Geschmacksinn. *Arch. Ges. Psychol.* 64, 1–36 (Cited by Woodworth, 1938). [377, 383]

Epstein, A. N. (1959) Suppression of eating and drinking by amphetamine and other drugs in normal and hyperphagic rats. *J. comp. physiol. Psychol.* 52, 37–45. [221]

Epstein, A. N. (1960) Water intake without the act of drinking. *Science*, 131, 497–498. [253]

Epstein, A. N., & Stellar, E. (1955) The control of salt preference in the adrena-lectomized rat. *J. comp. physiol. Psychol.* 48, 167–172. [234, 235]

Eriksen, C. W. (1954) Psychological defenses and "ego strength" in the recall of completed and incompleted tasks. *J. abn. soc. Psychol.* **49,** 45–50. [709, 786]

Eriksen, C. W., & Davids, A. (1955) The meaning and clinical validity of the Taylor Anxiety Scale and the Hysteria-Psychasthenia Scales from the MMPI. *J. abn. soc. Psychol.* **50,** 153–137. [709]

Erikson, E. H. (1950) *Childhood and society.* New York: W. W. Norton (rev. ed., 1963). [614, 616, 637, 638]

Erikson, E. H. (1953) On the sense of inner identity. In Knight, R., & Freedman, C. R. (Eds.) *Psychoanalytic psychiatry and psychology.* New York: International Universities Press (1954) pp. 351–364. [616]

Erikson, E. H. (1956) The problem of ego identity. *J. Amer. psychoanal. Ass.* **4,** 56–121. [637]

Erikson, E. H. (1959) Identity and the life cycle: Selected papers. *Psychol. Issues* **1,** No. 1. [637]

Escalona, Sybille K. (1945) Feeding disturbances in very young children. *Amer. J. Orthopsychiat.* **15,** 76–80. [686]

Escalona, Sybille K. (1948) An application of the level of aspiration experiment to the study of personality. *Teachers' College Contrib. Educ.* **937,** 1–132. [772]

Escalona, Sybille K. (1954) The influence of topological and vector psychology upon current research in child development: An addendum. In Carmichael, L. (Ed.) *Manual of child psychology.* (2nd ed.) New York: Wiley, pp. 971–983. [357]

Escalona, Sybille K., & Heider, G. M. (1959) *Prediction and outcome.* New York: Basic Books. [650]

Estes, W. K. (1943) Discriminative conditioning: I. A discriminative property of conditioned anticipation. *J. exp. Psychol.* **32,** 150–155. [564]

Estes, W. K. (1944) An experimental study of punishment. *Psychol. Monog.* **57,** Whole No. 263. [514, 580]

Estes, W. K. (1957) Current model. *Contemp. Psychol.* **2,** 153–155. [493]

Estes, W. K. (1958) Stimulus-response theory of drive. In Jones, M. R. (Ed.) *Nebraska symposium on motivation, 1958.* Lincoln: University of Nebraska Press, pp. 35–69. [538]

Estes, W. K. (1959) The statistical approach to learning theory. In Koch, S. (Ed.) *Psychology: A study of a science,* vol. 2. New York: McGraw-Hill, pp. 380–486. [512]

Estes, W. K., Koch, S., MacCorquodale, K., Meehl, P. E., Mueller, C. G., Jr., Schoenfeld, W. N., & Verplanck, W. S. (1954) *Modern learning theory: A critical analysis of five examples.* New York: Appleton-Century-Crofts. [467]

Estes, W. K., & Skinner, B. F. (1941) Some quantitative properties of anxiety. *J. exp. Psychol.* **29,** 390–400. [577]

Evarts, E. V. (1960) Effects of sleep and waking on activity of single units in the unrestrained cat. In Wolstenholme, G. E. W., & O'Connor, Maeve (Eds.) *Ciba Foundation symposium on the nature of sleep.* Boston: Little, Brown and Co., pp. 171–182. [168]

Eysenck, H. (1952) The effects of psychotherapy. *J. consult. Psychol.* **16,** 319–324. [683]

Eysenck, H. J. (1953) *The structure of personality.* New York: Wiley (out of print). [804]

Faigin, H. (1958) Case report: Social behavior of young children in the Kibbutz. *J. abn. soc. Psychol.* **56,** 117–129. [688]

Fantz, R. L. (1958a) Pattern vision in young infants. *Psychol. Rec.* **8,** 43–48. [287]

Fantz, R. L. (1958b) Visual discrimination in a neonote chimpanzee. *Percept. mot. Skills* 8, 59–66. [287]

Farber, I. E. (1948) Response fixation under anxiety and non-anxiety conditions. *J. exp. Psychol.* 38, 111–131. [428]

Farber, I. E. (1954) Anxiety as a drive state. In Jones, M. R. (Ed.) *Nebraska symposium on motivation, 1954.* Lincoln: University of Nebraska Press, pp. 1–46. [12, 13, 428, 479, 482, 800]

Farber, I. E. (1955) The role of motivation in verbal learning and performance. *Psychol. Bull.* 52, 311–327. [12, 13, 479, 482, 724, 800]

Farber, I. E., Harlow, H. F., & West, L. J. (1957) Brainwashing, conditioning, and DDD (debility, dependency, and dread). *Sociometry* 20, 271–285. [684]

Farner, D. S. (1961) Comparative physiology: Photoperiodicity. *Ann. rev. Physiol.* 23, 71–76. [128]

Feather, N. T. (1959) Subjective probability and decision under uncertainty. *Psychol. Rev.* 66, 150–164. [773, 774]

Feather, N. T. (1961) The relationship of persistence at a task to expectation of success and achievement-related motives. *J. abn. soc. Psychol.* 63, 552–561. [804]

Feather, N. T. (1962) The study of persistence. *Psychol. Bull.* 59, 94–115. [804]

Fechner, G. T. (1860) *Elemente der Psychophysik.* Leipzig: Breitkopf and Härtel. [590]

Fechner, G. T. (1873) *Einige Ideen zur Schöpfungs- und Entwicklungs- geschichte der Organismen.* Leipzig: Breitkopf and Härtel. [303, 314, 316]

Federn, P (1952) *Ego psychology and the psychoses.* New York: Basic Books. [604]

Fehrer, E. (1956a) The effects of hunger and familiarity of locale on exploration. *J. comp. physiol. Psychol.* 49, 549–552. [273, 291]

Fehrer, E. (1956b) Effects of amount of reinforcement and of pre- and postreinforcement delays on learning and extinction. *J. exp. Psychol.* 52, 167–176. [556]

Feigl, H., & Brodbeck, May (Eds.) (1953) *Readings in the philosophy of science.* New York: Appleton-Century-Crofts. [77]

Feigl, H., & Sellars, R. W. (Eds.) (1949) *Readings in philosophical analysis.* New York: Appleton-Century-Crofts. [77]

Felix, R. H. (1958) Statement concerning psychiatrically significant drugs. Presented to Subcommittee on Legal and Monetary Affairs, Committee on Government Operations, House of Representatives, Washington, D.C., February 24, 1958. [144]

Felsinger, J. M. von, Lasagna, L., & Beecher, H. K. (1953) The persistence of mental impairment following a hypnotic dose of a barbiturate. *J. pharmacol. exper. Ther.* 109, 284–291. [145]

Fenichel, O. (1945) *The psychoanalytic theory of neurosis.* New York: W. W. Norton. [317, 621, 622, 641]

Ferenczi, S. (1952) *Further contributions to the theory and technique of psychoanalysis.* New York: Basic Books. [629]

Ferster, C. B., & Skinner, B. F. (1957) *Schedules of reinforcement.* New York: Appleton-Century-Crofts. [514]

Feshbach, S. (1955) The drive-reducing function of fantasy behavior. *J. abn. soc. Psychol.* 50, 3–11. [728, 751, 755, 760]

Feshbach, S. (1961) The stimulating *versus* cathartic effects of a vicarious aggressive activity. *J. abn. soc. Psychol.* 63, 381–385. [760]

Festinger, L. (1943) Development of differential appetite in the rat. *J. exp. Psychol.* 32, 226–234. [265]

Festinger, L. (1950) Informal social communication. *Psychol. Rev.* 57, 271–282. [786–787]

Festinger, L. (1954a) A theory of social comparison processes. *Hum. Relations* 7, 117–140.   [787]

Festinger, L. (1954b) Motivations leading to social behavior. In Jones, M.R. (Ed.) *Nebraska symposium on motivation, 1954.* Lincoln: University of Nebraska Press, pp. 191–219.   [787]

Festinger, L. (1957) *A theory of cognitive dissonance.* Evanston, Ill.; Row, Peterson.   [788–789]

Festinger, L. (1958) The motivating effect of cognitive dissonance. In Lindzey, G. (Ed.) *Assessment of human motives.* New York: Rinehart, pp. 65–86. [788–789]

Festinger, L. (1961) The psychological effects of insufficient rewards. *Amer. Psychologist* 16, 1–11.   [788–789, 790]

Festinger, L., & Carlsmith, J. M. (1959) Cognitive consequences of forced compliance. *J. abn. soc. Psychol.* 58, 203–210.   [792]

Festinger, L., Gerard, H. B., Hymovitch, B., Kelley, H.H., & Raven, B. (1952) The influence process in the presence of extreme deviates. *Hum. Relations* 5, 327–346.   [788]

Field, W. F. (1951) The effects of thematic apperception upon certain experimentally aroused needs. Unpubl. doctoral dissert., University of Maryland. [722, 723, 724]

Fields, W. S. (Ed.) (1957) *Brain mechanisms and drug action.* Springfield, Ill.: Ch. E. Thomas.   [150, 402]

Finan, J. L. (1940) Quantitative studies in motivation: I. Strength of conditioning in rats under varying degrees of hunger. *J. comp. Psychol.* 29, 119–134. [525]

Finch, G. (1942) Chimpanzee frustration responses. *Psychosom. Med.* 4, 233–251. [421]

Finger, F. W. (1961a) Estrous activity as a function of measuring device. *J. comp. physiol. Psychol.* 54, 524–526.   [274]

Finger, F. W. (1961b) Activity and the measurement of drive. Presidential address, Division of General Psychology, American Psychological Association Convention, New York, Sept. 4, 1961.   [277]

Finger, F. W. (1962) Activity change under deprivation as a function of age. *J. comp. physiol. Psychol.* 55, 100–102.   [276]

Finger, F. W., Reid, L. S., & Weasner, M. H. (1957) The effect of reinforcement upon activity during cyclic food deprivation. *J. comp. physiol. Psychol.* 50, 495–498.   [277]

Fischer, Liselotte (1952) Hospitalism in six-month-old infants. *Amer. J. Orthopsychiat.* 22, 522–533.   [649]

Fischgold, H., & Schwartz, Betty A. (1960) A clinical, electroencephalographic and polygraphic study of sleep in the human adult. In Wolstenholme, G. E. W., & O'Connor, Maeve (Eds.) *Ciba Foundation symposium on the nature of sleep.* Boston: Little, Brown and Co., pp. 209–230.   [159]

Fisher, A. E. (1962) Effects of stimulus variation on sexual satiation in the male rat. *J. comp. physiol. Psychol.* 55, 614–620.   [193]

Fisher, K. C. (1950) The selected temperature of Atlantic salmon and speckled trout and the effect of temperature on the response to an electric stimulus. *Physiol. Zool.* 23, 27–34.   [133]

Fitzgerald, B. J. (1958) Some relationships among projective test, interview, and sociometric measures of dependent behavior. *J. abn. soc. Psychol.* 56, 199–203. [744]

Fletcher, J. M. (1938) The wisdom of the mind. *Sigma Xi Quart.* 26, 6–16. [314]

Fletcher, J. M. (1942) Homeostasis as an explanatory principle in psychology. *Psychol. Rev.* 49, 80–87.   [314, 315, 316, 604]

Fletcher, R. (1957) *Instinct in man: In the light of recent work in comparative psychology*. New York: International Universities Press.   [57, 71, 75, 83, 91, 92, 93, 95, 100, 598, 599, 601, 607]

Florey, E. (Ed.) (1961) *Nervous inhibition*. New York: Pergamon Press.   [150]

Flügel, J. C. (1949) The death instinct, homeostasis and allied concepts. In Flügel, J. *Studies in feeling and desire*. London: G. Duckworth, 1955.   [604]

Flügel, J. C. (1951) *A hundred years of psychology* (2nd ed.) London: G. Duckworth.   [47, 49]

Foerster, H. von (Ed.) (1951) *Cybernetics*. Trans. Eighth Conf. New York: Josiah Macy Jr. Found.   [342, 354]

Ford, C. S., & Beach, F. A. (1951) *Patterns of sexual behavior*. New York: Harper.   [175, 178, 179, 180, 181, 182, 183, 184, 185, 189, 190, 191, 192, 193, 195, 569]

Forgays, D. G., & Levin, H. (1958) Learning as a function of change of sensory stimulation in food-deprived and food-satiated rats. *J. comp. physiol. Psychol.* 51, 50–54.   [541]

Forssberg, A., & Larsson, S. (1954) On the hypothalamic organization of the nervous mechanism regulating food intake: II. Studies of isotope distribution and chemical composition in the hypothalamic region of hungry and fed rats. *Acta. physiol. Scand.* 32, Suppl. 115, 41–63.   [222]

Fortier, C. (1951) Dual control of adrenocorticotrophin release. *Endocrinology* 49, 782–788.   [313, 446]

Fortuin, G. J. (1958) Phiysieke arbeid en vermoeiheid (physical labor and fatigue). *Mens Onderneming* 12, 150–156 [*Abstr.*].   [143]

Fowler, H., & Whalen, R. E. (1961) Variation in incentive stimulus and sexual behavior in the male rat. *J. comp. physiol. Psychol.* 54, 68–71.   [193]

Fraisse, P. (1963) *The psychology of time* (transl. Jennifer Leith) New York: Harper and Row.   [169, 439]

Franks, C. M. (1956) Conditioning and personality: A study of normal and neurotic subjects. *J. abn. soc. Psychol.* 52, 143–150.   [709]

Franks, C. M. (1957) Effect of food, drink, and tobacco deprivation on the conditioning of the eyeblink response. *J. exp. Psychol.* 53, 117–120.   [537]

Fraser, D. C. (1956) *A study of fatigue in aircrew*. Farnborough, Engl.: Inst. Aviat. Med., RAF, Flying Personnel Research Committee Rep. FPRC984.   [142]

Freed, A., Chandler, P. J., Blake, R. R., & Mouton, Jane S. (1955) Stimulus and background factors in sign violation. *J. Pers.* 1955, 23, 499.   [340]

Freeden, R. C. (1948) Cup feeding of new-born infants. *Pediatrics* 3, 544–548.   [114]

Freedman, D. G., King, J. A., & Elliott, O. (1961) Critical period in the social development of dogs. *Science* 133, 1016–1017.   [88]

Freedman, S. J., & Held, R. (1960) Sensory deprivation and perceptual lag. *Percep. mot. Skills* 11, 277–280.   [282]

Freeman, G. L. (1931) Mental activity and the muscular processes. *Psychol. Rev.* 38, 428–447.   [394]

Freeman, G. L. (1933) The facilitative and inhibitory effects of muscular tension upon performance. *Amer. J. Psychol.* 45, 17–52.   [393, 394]

Freeman, G. L. (1938a) The effect of inhibited micturition upon interrupted and completed acts of unrelated origin. *J. gen. Psychol.* 19, 277–283.   [134]

Freeman, G. L. (1938b) Postural accompaniments of the voluntary inhibition of micturition. *J. exp. Psychol.* 23, 45–61.   [134]

Freeman, G. L. (1938c) The optimal muscular tensions for various performances. *Amer. J. Psychol.* 51, 146–150.   [393]

Freeman, G. L. (1940) The relationship between performance level and bodily activity level. *J. exp. Psychol.* 26, 602–608.   [396]

Freeman, G. L. (1948) *The energetics of human behavior*. Ithaca: Cornell University Press.   [316, 323, 330, 331, 332, 333, 334, 335, 394]

French, Elizabeth G. (1955) Some characteristics of achievement motivation. *J. exp. Psychol.* 50, 232–236.   [737]

French, Elizabeth G. (1956a) Motivation as a variable in work-partner selection. *J. abn. soc. Psychol.* **53,** 96–99.   [738]

French, Elizabeth G. (1956b) *Development of a measure of complex motivation.* Lackland Air Force Base, Texas: Res. Rep. AFPTRC-TN-56-48, Air Force Personnel and Training Research Center (April).   [725]

French, Elizabeth G. (1958) Effects of the interaction of motivation and feedback on task performance. In Atkinson, J. W. (Ed.) *Motives in fantasy, action, and society.* New York: Van Nostrand, pp. 400–408.   [725, 739]

French, Elizabeth G., & Thomas, F. H. (1958) The relation of achievement motivation to problem-solving effectiveness. *J. abn. soc. Psychol.* **56,** 45–48.   [731]

French, J. D., Hernandez-Peon, R., & Livingston, R. B. (1955) Projections from cortex to cephalic brain stem (reticular formation) in monkeys. *J. Neurophysiol.* **18,** 44–55.   [402]

Freud, Anna (1936) *The ego and the mechanisms of defense.* London: Hogarth, New York: International Universities Press, 1946.   [317, 621, 622, 641]

Freud, Anna (1945) Indications for child analysis. *Psychoanal. study Child.* **1,** 127–149.   [614]

Freud, Anna, & Burlingham, D. T. (1944) *Infants without families.* New York: International Universities Press.   [649]

Freud, Anna, et al. (1945 on) *The psychoanalytic study of the child* (Annual) New York: International Universities Press.   [638, 648]

Freud, S. (1895) A project for a scientific psychology. In Freud, S. *The origins of psychoanalysis: Letters to Wilhelm Fliess. Drafts and Notes, 1887–1902.* Bonaparte, Marie, Freud, Anna, & Kris, E. (Eds.) Mosbacher, E., & Strachey, J. (transl.) New York: Basic Books, 1954, pp. 347–445.   [608]

Freud, S. (1900) The interpretation of dreams. In Brill, A. A. (Ed. and transl.) *The basic writings of Sigmund Freud.* New York: Random House, 1938, pp. 179–549. Reprinted by permission of Gioia B. Bernheim and Edmund Brill. [594–595, 596]

Freud, S. (1901) The psychopathology of everyday life. In Brill, A. A. (Ed. and transl.) *The basic writings of Sigmund Freud.* New York: Random House, 1938, pp. 35–180. Reprinted by permission of Gioia B. Bernheim and Edmund Brill.   [596]

Freud, S. (1905) Three contributions to the theory of sex. In Brill, A. A. (Ed. and transl.) *The basic writings of Sigmund Freud.* New York: Random House, 1938, pp. 553–629. Reprinted by permission of Gioia B. Bernheim and Edmund Brill.   [603]

Freud, S. (1910) The origin and development of psychoanalysis. *Amer. J. Psychol.* **21,** 181–218.   [623]

Freud, S. (1911) Formulations regarding the two principles of mental functioning. In *Collected papers of Sigmund Freud,* vol. IV (Riviere, Joan, transl.) London: Hogarth Press, 1949, pp. 13–21.   [608]

Freud, S. (1914) On the history of the psychoanalytic movement. In *Collected papers of Sigmund Freud,* vol. I (Riviere, Joan, transl.) London: Hogarth Press, 1949, pp. 287–359.   [626]

Freud, S. (1915a) Instincts and their vicissitudes. In *Collected papers of Sigmund Freud,* vol. IV (Riviere, Joan, transl.) London: Hogarth Press, 1949, pp. 60–83.   [314, 598, 599, 600]

Freud, S. (1915b) The unconscious. In *Collected papers of Sigmund Freud,* vol. IV (Riviere, Joan, transl.) London: Hogarth Press, 1949, pp. 98–136.   [592]

Freud, S. (1920) *Beyond the pleasure principle* (Strachey, J., transl.) New York: International Psychoanalytic Press, 1922; Liveright Publication Corp., 1950. [317, 424, 606]

Freud, S. (1923) The ego and the id. In standard edition of *Complete psychological works of Sigmund Freud,* vol. XIX (Strachey, J., ed. and rev.) London: Hogarth Press, 1947.   [594, 595, 605, 612, 613]

Freud, S. (1924) The loss of reality in neurosis and psychosis. In *Collected papers of Sigmund Freud*, vol. II (Riviere, Joan, transl.) London: Hogarth Press, 1948, pp. 277–282.   **[423, 614]**

Freud, S. (1926) *The problem of anxiety*. New York: W. W. Norton, 1936. **[594, 618, 619, 641, 648]**

Freud, S. (1933) *New introductory lectures on psycho-analysis*. New York: W. W. Norton (Copyright renewed, 1961, by W. J. H. Sprott).   **[594, 595, 599, 600, 604, 606, 610, 612, 613, 619]**

Freud, S. (1939) *Moses and monotheism*, pt. III (Jones, Katherine, transl.) New York: Knopf, 1939.   **[594]**

Freud, S. (1940) *An outline of psychoanalysis* (Strachey, J., authorized transl.) New York: W. W. Norton, 1949.   **[594, 595, 598, 000, 605, 606, 607, 608, 609, 611, 614, 623]**

Freud, S. (1953 on) *The standard edition of the complete psychological works of Sigmund Freud*, 24 vols (Strachey, J., ed. and transl.) London: Hogarth Press and the Institute of Psycho-Analysis.   **[590]**

Friedlich, Olga (1962) A study of maternal behavior in the albino rat as a function of self-licking deprivation. Unpubl. master's thesis, Southern Illinois University.   **[97]**

Friedman, S. M. (1952) An empirical study of the castration and oedipus complex. *Genet. psychol. Monogr.* 46, 61–130.   **[653]**

Fries, M. E. (1946) The child's ego development and the training of adults in his development. *Psychoanal. study Child*. 2, 85–112.   **[686]**

Fromm, E. (1939) Selfishness and self-love. *Psychiatry* 2, 507–523.   **[668]**

Fromm, E. (1941) *Escape from freedom*. New York: Farrar and Rinehart.   **[649, 666, 667, 675]**

Fromm, E. (1947) *Man for himself*. New York: Rinehart.   **[667]**

Fromm, E. (1955) *The sane society*. New York: Rinehart.   **[632, 667, 668, 674, 675]**

Fromme, A. (1941) An experimental study of the factors of maturation and practice in the behavioral development of the embryo of the frog, *Rana pipiens*. *Genet. psychol. Monogr.* 24, 219–256.   **[79]**

Fromm-Reichmann, F. (1954) The academic lecture: Psychotherapy of schizophrenia. *Amer. J. Psychiat.* 111, 410–419.   **[690]**

Fromm-Reichmann, F. (1955) Intuitive processes in the psychotherapy of schizophrenics: Introduction. *J. Amer. psychoanal. Assoc.* 3, 5–6.   **[690]**

Fryer, J. H., Moore, N. S., Williams, H. H., & Young, C. M. (1955) A study of the interrelationships of the energy-yielding nutrients, blood glucose levels, and subjective appetite in man. *J. lab. clin. Med.* 45, 684–696.   **[225]**

Fuller, J. L. (1960) Behavior genetics. *Ann. rev. Psychol.* 11, 41–70.   **[104]**

Fuller, J. L., & Thompson, W. R. (1960) *Behavior genetics*. New York: Wiley. **[267, 271, 748]**

Fulton, J. F. (Ed.) (1955) *A textbook of physiology* (17th ed.) Philadelphia: Saunders.   **[133]**

Funkenstein, D. H., King, S. H., & Drolette, M. E. (1957) *Mastery of stress*. Cambridge: Harvard University Press.   **[449, 751]**

Fuster, J. M. (1958) Effects of stimulation of brain stem on tachistoscopic perception. *Science* 127, 150.   **[404]**

Ganong, W. F., & Forsham, P. H. (1960) Adenohypophysis and adrenal cortex. *Ann. rev. Physiol.* 22, 579–614.   **[442, 446]**

Gardiner, H. N., Metcalf, R. C., & Beebe-Center, J. G. (1937) *Feelings and emotions. A history of theories*. New York: American Book Co.   **[368, 382, 391]**

Garner, Ann M. (1954) Review of Klein, Melanie, Heimann, P., Isaacs, S., and

Riviere, J., *Developments in psychoanalysis*. (London: Hogarth Press, 1952). *Psychol. Bull.* 51, 191–193.   [650]

Garner, W. R. (1954) W. R. Ashby's *Design for a brain*. A review. *Psychometrika*, 19, 170–172.   [357]

Gates, E. (1895) The science of mentation and some new general methods of psychological research. *Monist.* 5, 574–597.   [551, 769]

Gaunt, R., Birnie, J. H., & Eversold, W. J. (1949) Adrenal cortex and water metabolism. *Physiol. Rev.* 29, 281–310.   [250]

Geldard, F. (1953) *The human senses*. New York: Wiley.   [260]

Gengerelli, J. A., & Cullen, J. W. (1955) Studies in the neurophysiology of learning: II. Effect of brain stimulation during black-white discrimination in learning behavior in the white rat. *J. comp. physiol. Psychol.* 48, 311–319.   [406]

George, C. E., & Bonney, W. C. (1956) *Consistency of personality in the framework of adaptation level theory*. Coll. Station, Tex.: Navy Technical (Final) Report, ONR Contract NR 174-054, Agric. and Mechan. Coll. of Texas, September 1956.   [341]

Gesell, A. (1946) The ontogenesis of infant behavior. In Carmichael, L. (Ed.) *Manual of Child psychology*. New York: Wiley, pp. 295–331.   [337]

Gewirtz, J. L. (1961) A learning analysis of the effects of normal stimulation, privation, and deprivation on the acquisition of social motivation and attachment. In Foss, B. M. *Determinants of infant behavior*. London: Methuen, pp. 213–290.   [763, 765]

Gewirtz, J. L., & Baer, D. M. (1958*a*) The effect of brief social deprivation on behaviors for a social reinforcer. *J. abn. soc. Psychol.* 56, 49–56.   [694]

Gewirtz, J. L., & Baer, D. M. (1958*b*) Deprivation and satiation of social reinforcers as drive conditions. *J. abn. soc. Psychol.* 57, 165–172.   [694, 695]

Gewirtz, J. L., Baer, D. M., & Roth, C. H. (1958) A note on the similar effects of low social availability of an adult and brief social deprivation on young children's behavior. *Child Develpm.* 29, 149–152.   [694]

Ghent, Lila (1951) The relation of experience to the development of hunger. *Canad. J. Psychol.* 5, 77–81.   [241]

Ghent, Lila (1957) Some effects of deprivation on eating and drinking behavior. *J. comp. physiol. Psychol.* 50, 172–176.   [241, 257]

Gilbert, G. J. (1956) The subcommissural organ. *Anat. Rec.* 126, 253–265.   [249]

Gilbert, T. F., & James, W. T. (1956) The dependency of cyclical feeding behavior on internal and external cues. *J. comp. physiol. Psychol.* 49, 342–344.   [243]

Gilbert, T. F., & Sturdivant, E. R. (1958) The effect of a food-associated stimulus on operant-level locomotor behavior. *J. comp. physiol. Psychol.* 51, 255–257.   [564]

Gilinsky, A. S., & Stewart, J. C. (1949) "Extinction" of a success aspiration following three conditions of reinforcement. *Amer. Psychologist* 4, 222–223.   [773]

Gill, M. M. (1959) The present state of psychoanalytic theory. *J. abn. soc. Psychol.* 58, 1–8.   [638]

Gillespie, J. (1961) Aggression in relation to frustration, attack, and inhibition. Unpubl. doctoral dissert. University of Pittsburgh.   [751]

Gilliard, E. T. (1958) *Living birds of the world*. Garden City, New York: Doubleday.   [109, 208]

Gilman, A. (1937) The relation between blood osmotic pressure, fluid distribution, and voluntary water intake. *Amer. J. Physiol.* 120, 323–328.   [251]

Ginsberg, A. (1952) A reconstructive analysis of the concept "instinct." *J. Psychol.* 33, 235–277.   [56, 99]

Glanzer, M. (1953) The role of stimulus satiation in spontaneous alternation. *J. exp. Psychol.* 45, 387–393.   [157, 289]

Glickman, S. E. (1958) Effects of peripheral blindness on exploratory behavior in the hooded rat. *Canad. J. Psychol.* **12**, 45–51. [294]

Glixman, A. F. (1948) An analysis of the use of the interruption-technique in experimental studies of "repression." *Psychol. Bull.* **45**, 491–506. [786]

Glixman, A. F. (1949) Recall of completed and incompleted activities under varying degrees of stress. *J. exp. Psychol.* **39**, 281–295. [786]

Glover, E. (1956) *On the early development of mind: Selected papers on psychoanalysis*, vol. I. New York: International Universities Press. [645, 647]

Gluck, M. R. (1955a) Rorschach content and hostile behavior. *J. consult. Psychol.* **19**, 475–478. [754]

Gluck, M. R. (1955b) The relationship between hostility in the TAT and behavioral hostility. *J. proj. Tech.* **10**, 21 26. [755]

Goldberger, L., & Holt, R. R. (1958) Experimental interference with reality contact (perceptual isolation): method and group results. *J. nerv. ment. Dis.* **127**, 99–112. [281, 282]

Goldberger, L., & Holt, R. R. (1961) Experimental interference with reality contact: individual differences. In Solomon, P., et al. (Eds.) *Sensory deprivation: A symposium at Harvard Medical School*. Cambridge: Harvard University Press. [283, 284]

Goldfarb, W. (1944) Effects of early institutional care on adolescent personality. Rorschach data. *Amer. J. Orthopsychiat.* **14**, 441–447. [649]

Goldstein, K. (1939) *The organism*. New York: American Book Co. [662, 666]

Goldstein, K. (1942) *After-effects of brain injuries in war*. New York: Grune & Stratton. [662, 684]

Gomberg, W. (1947) Measuring the fatigue factor. *Industr. labor relat. Rev.* **1**, 80–93. [143]

Gonzalez, R. C., & Diamond, L. (1960) A test of Spence's theory of incentive-motivation. *Amer. J. Psychol.* **73**, 396–403. [560]

Gooddy, W. (1958) Time and the nervous system. *Lancet,* Whole No. 7031, 1139–1144. [169]

Goodnow, R. E., Beecher, H. K., Brazier, Mary A. B., Mosteller, F., & Tagiuri, R. (1951) Physiological performance following a hypnotic dose of a barbiturate. *J. pharmacol. exper. Ther.* **102**, 55–61. [145]

Goodrich, K. P. (1959) Performance in different segments of an instrumental response chain as a function of reinforcement schedule. *J. exp. Psychol.* **57**, 57–63. [563]

Goy, R. W., & Young, W. C. (1957) Strain differences in the behavioral responses of female guinea pigs to alpha-estradiol benzoate and progesterone. *Behavior* **10**, 340–354. [189]

Graham, F. K., Charwat, W. A., Honig, A. S., & Weltz, P. C. (1951) Aggression as a function of the attack and the attacker. *J. abn. soc. Psychol.* **46**, 512–520. [758]

Grant, D. A., & Patel, A. S. (1957) Effect of an electric shock stimulus upon the conceptual behavior of "anxious" and "non-anxious" subjects. *J. gen. Psychol.* **57**, 247–256. [708]

Grassé, P. P. (Ed.) (1956) Foundation Singer-Polignac. *L'instinct dans le comportement des animaux et de l'homme*. Paris: Masson. [75, 91, 98]

Gray, J. (1950) The role of peripheral sense organs during locomotion in the vertebrates. In Society for Experimental Biology, Symposium No. 4: *Physiological mechanisms in behavior*. New York: Academic Press, pp. 112–126. [91]

Greenberg, I (1954) The acquisition of a thirst drive. Unpubl. doctoral dissert., University of Pennsylvania. [581–582]

Greer, M. A. (1955) Suggestive evidence of a primary "drinking center" in the hypothalamus of the rat. *Proc. Soc. exp. Biol. Med.* **89**, 59–62. [254]

Gregerson, M. I. (1932*a*) The physiological mechanism of thirst. *Amer. J. Physiol.* **101**, 44–45.   [**250**]

Gregerson, M. I. (1932*b*) Studies on the regulation of water intake: II. Conditions affecting the daily water intake of dogs as registered continuously by a potometer. *Amer. J. Physiol.* **102**, 344–349.   [**247**]

Gregerson, M. I., & Bullock, L. T. (1933) Observations on thirst in man in relation to changes in salivary flow and saliva volume. *Amer. J. Physiol.* **105**, 39–40.   [**250**]

Gregerson, M. I., & Cannon, W. B. (1932) Studies on the regulation of water intake: I. The effect of the extirpation of the salivary glands on the water intake of dogs while panting. *Amer. J. Physiol.* **102**, 336–343.   [**247**]

Grice, G. R. (1948) The relation of secondary reinforcement to delayed reward in visual discrimination learning. *J. exp. Psychol.* **38**, 1–16.   [**485**]

Grice, G. R., & Davis, J. D. (1957) Effect of irrelevant thirst motivation on a response learned with food reward. *J. exp. Psychol.* **53**, 347–352.   [**536**]

Griffin, D. R. (1958) *Listening in the dark: The acoustic orientation of bats and men.* New Haven: Yale University Press.   [**127, 130**]

Grindley, G. C. (1929) Experiments on the influence of the amount of reward on learning in young chickens. *Brit. J. Psychol.* **20**, 173–180.   [**553, 749**]

Grinker, R. R., Sabshin, M., Hamburg, D. A., Board, F. A., Basowitz, H., Korchin, S. J., Persky, H., & Chevalier, J. A. (1957) The use of an anxiety-producing interview and its meaning to the subject. *A.M.A. Arch. neurol. Psychiat.* **77**, 406–419.   [**457**]

Grinker, R. R., & Spiegel, J. (1945) *Men under stress.* Philadelphia: Blakiston.   [**461, 462**]

Grosslight, J. H., & Child, I. L. (1947) Persistence as a function of previous experience of failure followed by success. *Amer. J. Psychol.* **60**, 378–387.   [**783**]

Grossman, M. I. (1950) Gastrointestinal hormones. *Physiol. Rev.* **30**, 33–90.   [**211**]

Grossman, M. I. (1955) Integration of current views in the regulation of hunger and appetite. *Annals N.Y. Acad. Sci.* **63**, Art. 1, 76–89.   [**211, 212, 228**]

Grossman, M. I., Cummins, G. M., & Ivy, A. C. (1947) The effect of insulin on food intake after vagotomy and sympathectomy. *Amer. J. Physiol.* **149**, 100–102.   [**209**]

Grossman, M. I., & Stein, I. F., Jr. (1948) Vagotomy and the hunger-producing action of insulin in man. *J. appl. Physiol.* **1**, 263–269.   [**209**]

Grossman, S. P. (1960) Eating or drinking elicited by direct adrenergic or cholinergic stimulation of hypothalamus. *Science* **132**, 301–302.   [**222**]

Grundfest, H. (1960) Central inhibition and its mechanism. In Roberts, E. (Ed.) *Inhibition in the nervous system and gammaaminobutyric acid.* New York: Pergamon Press, pp. 47–65.   [**148**]

Grunt, J. A., & Young, W. C. (1952) Psychological modification of fatigue following orgasm (ejaculation) in the male guinea pig. *J. comp. physiol. Psychol.* **45**, 508–510.   [**193**]

Gugenheim, C. (1953) An experimental study of objective and subjective aspects of fatigue during monotonous work: I. A study on a group of students. *Travail Hum.* **16**, 219–240.   [**140–141**]

Guilford, J. P. (1959) *Personality.* New York: McGraw-Hill.   [**804**]

Guthrie, E. R. (1935) *The psychology of learning.* New York: Harper.   [**467, 512**]

Guthrie, E. R. (1938) *The psychology of human conflict.* New York: Harper.   [**314, 512, 513**]

Guthrie, E. R. (1940) Association and the law of effect. *Psychol. Rev.* **47**, 127–148.   [**512**]

Guthrie, E. R. (1942) Conditioning: A theory of learning in terms of stimulus, response, and association. *Yearbook Nat. Soc. Stud. Educ.* **41**, 17–60.   [**512**]

Guthrie, E. R. (1952) *The psychology of learning* (rev. ed.) New York: Harper. [512, 513]

Gutmann, E., & Jakoubek, B. (1960) Nervous regulation of conditioned hyperglycemia to nociceptive stimulation. *Science* 131, 1096–1098. [449]

Guttman, N. (1953) Operant conditioning, extinction, and periodic reinforcement in relation to concentration of sucrose used as reinforcing agent. *J. exp. Psychol.* 46, 213–224. [233, 542, 555, 556]

Guttman, N. (1954) Equal-reinforcement values for sucrose and glucose solutions compared with equal-sweetness values. *J. comp. physiol. Psychol.* 47, 358–361. [233, 555, 556]

Gwinn, G. T. (1951) Resistance to extinction of learned fear-drives. *J. exp. Psychol.* 42, 6–12. [577]

Haber, R. N. (1958) Discrepancy from adaptation level as a source of affect. *J. exp. Psychol.* 56, 370–375. [383, 384]

Haber, R. N., & Alpert, R. (1958) The role of situation and picture cues in projective measurement of the achievement motive. In Atkinson, J. W. (Ed.) *Motives in fantasy, action, and society.* New York: Van Nostrand, pp. 644–663. [723, 736]

Haggard, E. A. (1949) Psychological causes and results of stress. In Lindsley, D. B., et al. *Human factors in undersea warfare.* Washington, D.C.: National Research Council, pp. 441–461. [454, 459]

Haider, M. (1957) Experimental contribution to the reaction of the negative after-image in fatigue. *Z. exp. angewand. Psychol.* 4, 94–103. [144]

Halberg, F. (1961) Circadian rhythms: A basis of human engineering for aerospace. In Flaherty, B. E. (Ed.) *Psychophysiological aspects of space flight.* New York: Columbia University Press, pp. 166–194. [162, 163, 170]

Halberg, F. (1962) Physiological 24-hour rhythms: A determinant of response to environmental agents. In Schaefer, K. E. (Ed.) *International symposium on submarine and space medicine, Vol. I: Man's dependence on the earthly atmosphere.* New York: Macmillan, pp. 48–96. [162]

Hall, C. S. (1936) Emotional behavior in the rat: III. The relationship between emotionality and ambulatory activity. *J. comp. Psychol.* 22, 345–352. [271]

Hall, C. S. (1941) Temperament: A survey of animal studies. *Psychol. Bull.* 38, 909–943. [267, 273]

Hall, C. S. (1954) *A primer of Freudian psychology.* New York: World publishing Co. (and Mentor Books, 1955). [41, 589, 591, 597]

Hall, C., & Lindzey, G. (1954) Psychoanalytic theory and its applications in the social sciences. In Lindzey, G. (Ed.) *Handbook of social psychology,* vol. I. Cambridge, Mass.: Addison-Wesley Press. [580]

Hall, C. S., & Lindzey, G. (1957) *Theories of personality.* New York: Wiley. [4, 321, 589, 614, 628, 630, 662, 663, 664]

Hall, J. F. (1955) Activity as a function of a restricted drinking schedule. *J. comp. physiol. Psychol.* 48, 265–266. [274]

Hall, J. F. (1956) The relationship between external stimulation, food deprivation, and activity. *J. comp. physiol. Psychol.* 49, 339–341. [275]

Hall, J. F. (1958) The influence of learning on activity wheel behavior. *J. genet. Psychol.* 92, 121–125. [277]

Hall, J. F. (1961) *Psychology of motivation.* Philadelphia: J. B. Lippincott. [2, 266, 271, 272, 299, 414, 418, 424, 531, 654, 708, 751, 785]

Hall, J. F. & Cannon, H. E. (1957) Activity under low motivational levels as a function of manipulating the deprivation period. *J. genet. Psychol.* 91, 137–142. [274]

Hall, J. F., & Hanford, P. V. (1954) Activity as a function of a restricted feeding schedule. *J. comp. physiol. Psychol.* 47, 362–363. [274]

Hall, J. F., Hanford, P. V., & Low, L. (1960) The activity of hungry, thirsty, and satiated rats in the Dashiell checkerboard maze. *J. comp. physiol. Psychol.* **53**, 155–158.   **[275]**

Hall, J. F., Smith, K., Schnitzer, S. B., & Hanford, P. V. (1953) Elevation of the activity level in the rat following transition from *ad libitum* to restricted feeding. *J. comp. physiol. Psychol.* **46**, 429–433.   **[274]**

Hall, K. R. L. (1955) Relation of skin temperature to pain threshold. *Quart. J. exp. Psychol.* **7**, 74–81.   **[263]**

Hall, K. R. L., & Stride, E. (1954) The varying response to pain in psychiatric disorders: A study in abnormal psychology. *Brit. J. med. Psychol.* **27**, 48–60. **[261]**

Haller, A. O., & Sewell, W. H. (1957) Farm residence and levels of educational and occupational aspiration. *Amer. J. Sociol.* **62**, 407–412.   **[571]**

Halverson, H. M. (1938) Infant sucking and tensional behavior. *J. genet. Psychol.* **53**, 365–430.   **[651]**

Ham, A. W. (1957) *Histology* (3rd ed.), Philadelphia: J. B. Lippincott.   **[445]**

Hamilton, G. V. (1914) A study of sexual tendencies in monkeys and baboons. *J. anim. Behav.* **4**, 295–318.   **[183]**

Hamilton, G. V. (1929) *A research in marriage.* New York: Boni.   **[652]**

Hamilton, J. A., & Krechevsky, I. (1933) Studies in the effect of shock upor behavior plasticity in the rat. *J. compar. Psychol.* **16**, 237–253.   **[424]**

Hammes, J. A. (1956) Visual discrimination learning as a function of shock-fear and task difficulty. *J. comp. physiol. Psychol.* **49**, 481–484.   **[522, 523]**

Haner, C. F., & Brown, P. A. (1955) Clarification of the instigation to action concept in the frustration-aggression hypothesis. *J. abn. soc. Psychol.* **51**, 204–206.   **[750]**

Hardy, J. D., Wolff, H. G., & Goodell, H. (1952) *Pain sensations and reactions.* Baltimore: Williams and Wilkins.   **[260]**

Hardy, K. R. (1957) Determinants of conformity and attitude change. *J. abn. soc. Psychol.* **54**, 289–294.   **[739]**

Harker, J. E. (1958) Diurnal rhythms in the animal kingdom. *Biol. rev. Cambr. Philos. Soc.* **33**, 1–52.   **[92, 271]**

Harlow, H. F. (1932) Social facilitation of feeding in the albino rat. *J. genet. Psychol.* **41**, 211–221.   **[243]**

Harlow, H. F. (1950) Learning and satiation of response in intrinsically motivated complex puzzle performance by monkeys. *J. comp. physiol. Psychol.* **43**, 289–294.   **[296]**

Harlow, H. F. (1953*a*) Mice, monkeys, men and motives. *Psychol. Rev.* **60**, 23–32.   **[42, 44]**

Harlow, H. F. (1953*b*) Motivation as a factor in the acquisition of new responses. In Brown, J. S., et al. *Current theory and research in motivation: A symposium.* Lincoln: University of Nebraska Press, pp. 24–49.   **[284, 300, 685]**

Harlow, H. F. (1958) The nature of love. *Amer. Psychologist* **13**, 673–685. **[115]**

Harlow, H. F. (1959) Learning set and error factor theory. In Koch, S. (Ed.) *Psychology: A study of a science* (7 vols.), Vol. II. New York: McGraw-Hill, pp. 492–537.   **[157]**

Harlow, H. F. (1962) The heterosexual affectional system in monkeys. *Amer. Psychologist* **17**, 1–9.   **[116]**

Harlow, H. F., Blazek, N. C., & McClearn, G. E. (1956) Manipulatory motivation in the infant rhesus monkey. *J. comp. physiol. Psychol.* **49**, 444–448.   **[296]**

Harlow, H. F., & Harlow, Margaret K. (1962) Social deprivation in monkeys. *Sci. Amer.* **207**, 136–146.   **[116]**

Harlow, H. F., Harlow, Margaret K., & Meyer, D. R. (1950) Learning motivated by a manipulation drive. *J. exp. Psychol.* **40**, 228–234.   **[296]**

Harlow, H. F., & McClearn, G. E. (1954) Object discrimination learned by monkeys on the basis of manipulation motives. *J. comp. physiol. Psychol.* 47, 73–76. [296]

Harlow, H. F., & Yudin, H. C. (1933) Social behavior of primates: I. Social facilitation of feeding in the monkey and its relation to attitudes of ascendance and submission. *J. comp. Psychol.* 16, 171–188. [243]

Harlow, H. F., & Zimmermann, R. R. (1959) Affectional responses in the infant monkey. *Science* 130, 421–432. [115]

Harper, R. (1959) *Psychoanalysis and psychotherapy: 36 systems.* Englewood Cliffs, N.J.: Prentice-Hall. [589, 629, 630]

Harriman, A. E. (1955a) Provitamin A selection by Vitamin A depleted rats. *J. genet. Psychol.* 86, 45–50. [234]

Harriman, A. E. (1955b) The effect of a preoperative preference for sugar over salt upon compensatory salt selection by adrenalectomized rats. *J. Nutrit.* 57, 271–276. [232]

Harriman, A. E., & MacLeod, R. B. (1953) Discriminative thresholds for salt for normal and adrenalectomized rats. *Amer. J. Psychol.* 66, 465–471. [234]

Harris, G. W. (1955) *Neural control of the pituitary gland.* London: Arnold. [446]

Harris, L. J., Clay, J., Hargreaves, F. J., & Ward, A. (1933) Appetite and choice of diet: The ability of the vitamin B deficient rat to discriminate between diets containing and lacking the vitamin. *Proc. Roy. Soc., Lond., B* 113, 161–190. [230]

Harris, S. C. (1955) Clinically useful appetite depressants. *Annals N.Y. Acad. Sci.* 63, Art. 1, 121–131. [212]

Harsh, C. M. (1957) Mysticism resurgent. *Contemp. Psychol.* 2, 25. [667]

Hartmann, H. (1939) Psychoanalysis and the concept of health. *Int. J. Psychoanal.* 20, 308–321. [636]

Hartmann, H. (1950) Comments on the psychoanalytic theory of the ego. *Psychoanal. study Child* 5, 74–96. [636]

Hartmann, H. (1958) *Ego psychology and the problem of adaptation.* New York: International Universities Press. Also abridged in Rapaport, D. (Ed.) *Organization and pathology of thought.* New York: Columbia University Press, 1951, pp. 362–396. [610, 629, 630, 636]

Hartmann, H., Kris, E., & Loewenstein, R. M. (1946) Comments on the formation of psychic structure. *Psychoanal. study Child* 2, 11–38. [608, 636]

Hartmann, H., Kris, E., & Loewenstein, R. M. (1949) Notes on the theory of aggression. *Psychoanal. study Child* 3 and 4, 9–36. [598, 635, 636]

Hartup, H. W. (1958) Nurturance and nurturance-withdrawal in relation to the dependency behavior of pre-school children. *Child Develpm.* 29, 191–202. [742]

Hartup, W. W., & Himeno, Y. (1959) Social isolation vs. interaction with adults in relation to aggression in pre-school children. *J. abn. soc. Psychol.* 59, 17–22. [758]

Hastorf, A. H. (1950) Influence of suggestion on relationship between stimulus size and perceived distance. *J. Psychol.* 29, 195–217. [318]

Hattendorf, K. W. (1932) A study of the question of young children concerning sex: A phase of an experimental approach to parent education. *J. soc. Psychol.* 3, 37–65. [652]

Hausmann, M. F. (1932) The behavior of albino rats in choosing food and stimulants. *J. comp. Psychol.* 13, 279–309. [229]

Hauty, G. T., & Payne, R. B. (1956) Fatigue and the perceptual field of work. *J. appl. Psychol.* 40, 40–46. [138]

Havelka, J. (1956) Problem-seeking behavior in rats. *Canad. J. Psychol.* 10, 91–97. [293]

Hayes, K. J. (1960) Exploration and fear. *Psychol. Reports* 6, 91–93. [291]

Healy, W., Bronner, A., & Bowers, A. (1930) *The structure and meaning of psychoanalysis.* New York: Alfred Knopf. [606]

Heath, R. G. (1954) Behavioral changes following destructive lesions in the subcortical structure of the forebrain in cats. In Heath, R. G. (Ed.) *Studies in schizophrenia: A multidisciplinary approach to mid-brain relationships.* Cambridge, Mass.: Harvard University Press, pp. 83–84. [544]

Heathers, G. W. (1955a) Emotional dependence and independence in nursery school play. *J. genet. Psychol.* 87, 37–57. [744]

Heathers, G. W. (1955b) Acquiring dependence and independence: A theoretical orientation. *J. genet. Psychol.* 87, 277–291. [744]

Hebb, D. O. (1949) *The organization of behavior.* New York: Wiley. [8, 12, 318, 370, 376, 407, 408, 826]

Hebb, D. O. (1950) Animal and physiological psychology. *Ann. rev. Psychol.* 1, 173–188. [101]

Hebb, D. O. (1953) Heredity and environment in mammalian behaviour. *Brit. J. anim. Behav.* 1, 43–47. [94, 96, 102, 103]

Hebb, D. O. (1954) If man is a mammal why doan he act like a mammal? You tell me dat. *Amer. Psychologist* 9, 502 (title only). [103]

Hebb, D. O. (1955) Drives and C. N. S. (Conceptual nervous system). *Psychol. rev.* 62, 243–254. [8, 370, 393, 394, 404, 408, 409, 826]

Hebb, D. O. (1958) *A textbook of psychology.* Philadelphia: W. B. Saunders. [8, 370, 394, 404, 408, 409]

Heider, F. (1946) Attitudes and cognitive organization. *J. Psychol.* 21, 107–112. [788]

Heider, F. (1958) *The psychology of interpersonal relations.* New York: Wiley. [788]

Heider, F. (1960) The Gestalt theory of motivation. In Jones, M. R. (Ed.) *Nebraska symposium on motivation, 1960.* Lincoln: University of Nebraska Press, pp. 145–172. [782, 788]

Heineman, C. E. (1953) A forced-choice form of the Taylor Anxiety Scale. *J. consult. Psychol.* 17, 447–454. [702]

Held, R., & White, B. (1959) Sensory deprivation and visual speed: An analysis. *Science* 130, 860–861. [282]

Helson, H. (1938) Fundamental problems in color vision: I. The principle governing changes in hue, saturation, and lightness of non-selective samples in chromatic illumination. *J. exp. Psychol.* 26, 1–27. [338]

Helson, H. (1947) Adaptation level as a frame of reference for prediction of psychophysical data. *Amer. J. Psychol.* 60, 1–29. [316, 318, 336, 338]

Helson, H. (1948) Adaptation level as a basis for a quantitative theory of frames of reference. *Psychol. Rev.* 55, 297–313. [336]

Helson, H. (1951) Perception. In Helson, H. (Ed.) *Theoretical foundations of psychology.* New York: Van Nostrand, pp. 348–385. [336, 338]

Helson, H. (1953) *Perception and personality—A critique of recent experimental literature.* Randolph Field, Tex.: Proj. Rep. No. 1, Proj. 21-0202-0007, Air University, USAF, Sch. Aviat. Med. [316, 336, 337, 338, 339, 340]

Helson, H. (1959) Adaptation level theory. In Koch, S. (Ed.) *Psychology: A study of a science,* vol. I. New York: McGraw-Hill, pp. 565–621. [336, 338]

Helson, H., Blake, R. R., Mouton, Jane S., & Olmstead, J. A. (1956) The expression of attitudes as adjustments to stimulus, background and residual factors. *J. abn. soc. Psychol.* 52, 314–322. [340]

Hemingway, A. (1953) The physiological background of fatigue. In Floyd, W. F., & Welford, A. T. (Eds.) *Symposium on fatigue.* London: H. K. Lewis & Co., pp. 69–75. [136, 137]

Hempel, C. G. (1952) *Fundamentals of concept formation in empirical science.* Chicago: University of Chicago Press. [57]

Henderson, R. L. (1957) Stimulus-intensity dynamism and secondary reinforcement. *J. comp. physiol. Psychol.* **50**, 339–344. [541]

Henle, Mary (1942) An experimental investigation of dynamic and structural determinants of substitution. *Contr. psychol. Theor.* **2**, No. 3. [363]

Henry, J. (1955) Homeostasis, society, and evolution: A critique. *Sci. Month.* **81**, 300–309. [328, 329]

Hernandez-Peon, R., Scherrer, H., & Jouvet, M., (1956) Modification of electric activity in cochlear nucleus during "attention" in unanesthetized cats. *Science* **123**, 331–332. [405]

Heron, W. (1949) Internal stimuli and learning. *J. comp. physiol. Psychol.* **42**, 486–492. [265]

Heron, W. (1961) Cognitive and physiological effects of perceptual isolation. In Solomon, P., et al. (Eds.) *Sensory deprivation.* Cambridge, Mass.: Harvard University Press, pp. 6–33. [280]

Heron, W., Doane, B. K., & Scott, T. H. (1956) Visual disturbances after prolonged perceptual isolation. *Canad. J. Psychol.* **10**, 13–18. [279, 281, 283]

Herrick, C. J. (1922) *An introduction to neurology.* (3rd ed.) Philadelphia: W. B. Saunders. [314]

Hervey, G. R. (1959) The effects of lesions in the hypothalamus in parabiotic rats. *J. Physiol. Lond.* **145**, 336–352. [227]

Herzberg, F., Mausner, B., Peterson, R., & Capwell, D. (1957) *Job attitudes: Research and opinion.* Pittsburgh: Psychological Services of Pittsburgh. [771, 775]

Herzberg, F., Mausner, B., & Snyderman, B. B. (1959) *The motivation to work.* (2nd ed.) New York: Wiley. [771, 775]

Hess, E. H. (1953a) Comparative psychology. *Ann. rev. Psychol.* **4**, 239–254. [101]

Hess, E. H. (1953b) Shyness as a factor of hoarding in rats. *J. comp. physiol. Psychol.* **46**, 46–48. [125]

Hess, E. H. (1956) Comparative psychology. *Ann. rev. Psychol.* **7**, 305–322. [102]

Hess, E. H. (1957) Effects of meprobamate on imprinting in waterfowl. *Annals N.Y. Acad. Sci.* **67**, 724–732. [88]

Hess, E. H. (1959) The relationship between imprinting and motivation. In Jones, M. R. (Ed.) *Nebraska symposium on motivation, 1959.* Lincoln: University of Nebraska Press, pp. 44–77. [88, 89]

Hess, E. H. (1960) Effects of drugs on imprinting. In Uhr, L., & Miller, J. G. (Eds.) *Drugs and Behavior.* New York: Wiley, pp. 268–271. [89]

Hess, E. H. (1962) Ethology: An approach toward the complete analysis of behavior. In Brown, R., Galanter, E., Hess, E. H., & Mandler, G. *New directions in psychology.* New York: Holt, Rinehart & Winston, pp. 157–266. [57, 61, 65, 68, 69, 70, 73, 74, 75, 77, 79, 81, 86, 87, 88, 89, 90, 92, 97, 100]

Hess, E. H., Pott, J. M., & Goodwin, E. (1959) Effects of carisoprodol on early experience and learning. In Miller, J. G. (Ed.) *The pharmacology and clinical usefulness of carisoprodol.* Detroit: Wayne State University Press, pp. 51–85. [89]

Hess, W. R. (1954) The diencephalic sleep center. In Delafresnaye, J. F. (Ed.) *Brain mechanisms and consciousness.* Springfield, Ill.: Charles Thomas, pp. 117–125. [165]

Hess, W. R. (1957) *The functional organization of the diencephalon.* New York: Grune & Stratton. [165]

Hetherington, A. W., & Ranson, S. W. (1940) Hypothalamic lesions and adiposity in the rat. *Anat. Rec.* **78**, 149–172. [217]

Hightower, N. C., Jr. (1962) The digestive system. *Ann. rev. Physiol.* **24**, 109–138. [222]

Hilgard, E. R. (1948) *Theories of learning.* New York: Appleton-Century-Crofts (revised edition, 1956).   [**4, 266, 467, 474, 477, 482, 494, 505, 506, 508, 511, 512, 514, 552, 653, 654**]

Hilgard, E. R. (1952) Experimental approaches to psychoanalysis. In Pumpian-Mindlin, E. (Ed.) *Psychoanalysis as science.* Stanford: Stanford University Press, pp. 3–45.   [**652, 653, 654–655**]

Hilgard, E. R., Jones, L. V., & Kaplan, S. J. (1951) Conditioned discrimination as related to anxiety. *J. exp. Psychol.* **42**, 94–99.   [**704, 706**]

Hilgard, E. R., & Marquis, D. G. (1940) *Conditioning and learning.* New York: Appleton-Century-Crofts.   [**148, 374**]

Hill, D., Leo, P. St. J., Theobald, J., & Waddell, Marian, (1951) A central homeostatic mechanism in schizophrenia. *J. ment. Sci.* **97**, 111–131.   [**325**]

Hill, W. F. (1956) Activity as an autonomous drive. *J. comp. physiol. Psychol.* **49**, 15–19.   [**272**]

Hill, W. F. (1957) Comments on Taylor's "Drive theory and manifest anxiety." *Psychol. Bull.* **54**, 490–493.   [**707, 708, 803**]

Hill, W. F. (1958*a*) The effect of varying periods of confinement on activity in tilt cages. *J. comp. physiol. Psychol.* **51**, 570–574.   [**272**]

Hill, W. F. (1958*b*) The effect of long confinement on voluntary wheel-running by rats. *J. comp. physiol. Psychol.* **51**, 770–773.   [**272**]

Hill, W. F. (1960) Learning theory and the acquisition of values. *Psychol. Rev.* **67**, 317–331.   [**804**]

Hillman, Beverly, Hunter, W. S., & Kimble, G. A. (1953) The effect of drive level on the maze performance of the white rat. *J. comp. physiol. Psychol.* **46**, 87–89.   [**521, 527, 528, 533**]

Hinckley, E. D., & Rethlingshafer, Dorothy (1951) Value judgments of heights of men by college students. *J. Psychol.* **31**, 257–262.   [**339**]

Hinde, R. A. (1954) Changes in responsiveness to a constant stimulus. *Brit. J. anim. Behav.* **2**, 41–55.   [**94**]

Hinde, R. A. (1956) Ethological models and the concept of drive. *Brit. J. philos. Sci.* **6**, 321–331.   [**94**]

Hinde, R. A. (1959*a*) Unitary drives. *Animal Behaviour* **7**, 130–141.   [**94, 104**]

Hinde, R. A. (1959*b*) Some recent trends in ethology. In Koch, S. (Ed.) *Psychology: A study of a science,* vol. II. New York: McGraw-Hill, pp. 561–610. [**82, 86, 104**]

Hinde, R. A. (1959*c*) Motivation. *Ibis* **101**, 353–357.   [**94, 104**]

Hirsch, J., Lindley, R. H., & Tolman, E. C. (1955) An experimental test of an alleged innate sign stimulus. *J. comp. physiol. Psychol.* **48**, 278–280.   [**100**]

Hoagland, H. (Ed.) (1945 on) *Recent advances in hormone research.* New York: Academic Press.   [**313**]

Hochberg, J. E. (1962) Nativism and empiricism in perception. In Postman, L. (Ed.) *Psychology in the making.* New York: Alfred Knopf, pp. 255–330. [**316**]

Hochberg, J. E., Triebel, W., & Seaman, G. (1951) Color adaptation under conditions of homogeneous visual stimulation (Ganzfeld). *J. exp. Psychol.* **41**, 153–159.   [**283**]

Hoebel, B. G., & Teitelbaum, P. (1962) Hypothalamic control of feeding and self-stimulation. *Science* **135**, 375–377.   [**545**]

Hoelzel, F. (1927) Central factors in hunger. *Amer. J. Physiol.* **82**, 665–671. [**208**]

Höffding, H. (1955) *A history of modern philosophy,* 2 vols. (Meyer, B. E., transl.) London: Macmillan and St. Martin's Press, Inc. (reprinted by Dover Publications).   [**26, 27, 31**]

Hofstadter, R. (1959) *Social Darwinism in American thought.* (rev. ed.) New York: George Braziller.   [**34**]

Hokanson, J. E., & Shetler, S. (1961) The effect of overt aggression on physiological arousal level. *J. abn. soc. Psychol.* 63, 446–448. [760]

Holder, W., Marx, M. H., Holder, E., & Collier, G. (1957) Response strength as a function of delay of reward in a runway. *J. exp. Psychol.* 53, 316–323. [422]

Holland, J. G. (1954) The influence of previous experience and residual effects of deprivation on hoarding in the rat. *J. comp. physiol. Psychol.* 47, 244–247. [125]

Holland, J. G. (1958) Human vigilance. *Science* 128, 61–67. [278, 410]

Hollander, F., Sober, H. A., & Bandes, J. (1955) A study of hunger and appetite in a young man with esophogeal obstruction and jejunostomy. *Ann. N.Y. Acad. Sci.* 63, Art. 1, 107–120. [214]

Hollenberg, E., & Sperry, M. (1951) Some antecedents of aggression and effects of frustration in doll play. *Personality* 1, 32–43. [757]

Hollingshead, A. B. (1949) *Elmtown's youth: The impact of social classes on adolescents.* New York: Wiley. [570]

Holmes, J. H., & Cizek, L. J. (1951) Observations on sodium chloride depletion in the dog. *Amer. J. Physiol.* 164, 407–414. [251]

Holmes, J. H., & Gregerson, M. I. (1947) Relation of the salivary flow to the thirst produced in man by intravenous injection of hypertonic salt solution. *Amer. J. Physiol.* 151, 252–257. [251]

Holmes, J. H., & Gregerson, M. I. (1950) Role of sodium and chloride in thirst. *Amer. J. Physiol.* 162, 338–347. [251]

Holmes, J. H., & Montgomery, A. V. (1953) Thirst as a symptom. *Amer. J. med. Sci.* 225, 281–286. [253]

Holmes, T. H., & Ripley, H. S. (1955) Experimental studies on anxiety reactions. *Amer. J. Psychiat.* 111, 921–929. [324]

Holst, E. von (1936) Versuche zur Theorie der Relativen Koordination. *Pflug. Arch. ges. Physiol.* 237, 93–121 (cited by Thorpe, 1948). [74]

Holst, E. von, & St. Paul, U. von (1962) Electrically controlled behavior. *Sci. Amer.* 206, No. 3, 50–59. [86, 87, 92]

Holt, E. B. (1931) *Animal drive and the learning process: An essay toward radical empiricism, Vol. I.* New York: Holt. [56, 259]

Holt, R. R. (1960) Recent developments in psychoanalytic ego psychology and their implications for diagnostic testing. *J. proj. Tech.* 24, 254–266. [623, 636, 637]

Holtzman, W. H., & Bitterman, M. E. (1952) *Psychiatric screening of flying personnel: VI. Anxiety and reactions to stress.* Randolph Field, Texas: School of Aviat. Med. Proj. Rep., 1952. [454, 455]

Holtzman, W. H., & Bitterman, M. E. (1956) A factorial study of adjustment to stress. *J. abn. soc. Psychol.* 52, 179–185. [710]

Horenstein, Betty R. (1951) Performance of conditioned responses as a function of strength of hunger drive. *J. comp. physiol. Psychol.* 44, 210–224. [239, 530, 532, 535]

Horney, Karen (1937) *The neurotic personality of our time.* New York: W. W. Norton. [631]

Horney, Karen (1939) *New ways in psychoanalysis.* New York: W. W. Norton. [631, 649]

Horney, Karen (1945) *Our inner conflicts.* New York: W. W. Norton. [631, 745]

Horney, Karen (1950) *Neurosis and human growth.* New York: W. W. Norton. [631, 666]

Horwitz, M. (1954) The recall of interrupted group tasks: An experimental study of individual motivation in relation to group goals. *Hum. Rel.* 7, 3–38. [780]

Horwitz, M. (1956) Psychological needs as a function of social environments. In White, L. D. (Ed.) *The state of the social sciences.* Chicago: University of Chicago Press, pp. 162–183.   [781]

Horwitz, M., Exline, R. V., Goldman, M., & Lee, F. J. (1953) *Motivational effects of alternate decision-making processes in groups.* Urbana, Illinois: University of Illinois, ONR Tech. Rep., Contract N6ORI-07144.   [784]

Hoskins, R. G. (1946) *The biology of schizophrenia.* New York: W. W. Norton. [325]

Hovland, C. I. (1936) "Inhibition of reinforcement" and phenomena of experimental extinction. *Proc. Nat. Acad. Sci.* 22, 430–433.   [153]

Hovland, C. I., & Riesen, A. H. (1940) Magnitude of galvanic and vasomotor response as a function of stimulus intensity. *J. gen. Psychol.* 23, 103–121. [566]

Hovland, C. I., & Sears, R. R. (1938) Experiments on motor conflict: I. Types of conflict and their modes of resolution. *J. exp. Psychol.* 23, 477–493.   [430]

Hovland, C. I., & Sears, R. R. (1940) Minor studies of aggression: VI. Correlation of lynchings with economic indices. *J. Psychol.* 9, 301–310.   [750]

Howarth, C. I., & Deutsch, J. A. (1962) Drive decay: The cause of fast "extinction" of habits learned for brain stimulation. *Science* 137, 35–36.   [546]

Howells, T. H. (1947) Lamarckian-Darwinian reorientation. *Psychol. Rev.* 54, 24–40.   [306, 307]

Howells, T. H., & Vine, D. C. (1940) The innate differential in social learning. *J. abn. soc. Psychol.* 35, 537–548.   [98]

Hulicka, I. M. (1960a) Combination of drive and incentive. *Quart. J. exp. Psychol.* 12, 185–189.   [558]

Hulicka, I. M. (1960b) Additive versus multiplicative combination of drive and incentive. *Psychol. Rep.* 6, 403–409.   [558]

Hull, C. L. (1929) A functional interpretation of the conditioned reflex. *Psychol. Rev.* 36, 498–511.   [468, 483]

Hull, C. L. (1930) Knowledge and purpose as habit mechanisms. *Psychol. Rev.* 37, 511–525.   [486]

Hull, C. L. (1931) Goal attraction and directing ideas conceived as habit phenomena. *Psychol. Rev.* 38, 487–506.   [486]

Hull, C. L. (1932) The goal gradient hypothesis and maze learning. *Psychol. Rev.* 39, 25–43.   [484, 486]

Hull, C. L. (1933) Differential habituation to internal stimuli in the albino rat. *J. comp. Psychol.* 16, 255–273.   [265]

Hull, C. L. (1934a) The concept of the habit-family-hierarchy and maze learning: Part I. *Psychol. Rev.* 41, 33–54.   [486]

Hull, C. L. (1934b) The concept of the habit-family-hierarchy and maze learning: Part II. *Psychol. Rev.* 41, 134–152.   [486]

Hull, C. L. (1934c) The rat's speed-of-locomotion gradient in the approach to food. *J. comp. Psychol.* 7, 393–422.   [484]

Hull, C. L. (1936) The conflicting psychologies of learning—a way out. *Psychol. Rev.* 42, 491–516.   [467]

Hull, C. L. (1937) Mind, mechanism and adaptive behavior. *Psychol. Rev.* 44, 1–32.   [467]

Hull, C. L. (1943) *Principles of behavior.* New York: Appleton-Century-Crofts. [12, 148, 154, 155, 157, 288, 420, 422, 469, 470, 471, 472, 473, 475, 476, 477, 478, 479, 480, 481, 482, 483, 484, 485, 553, 703]

Hull, C. L. (1951) *Essentials of behavior.* New Haven: Yale University Press. [469, 471, 472, 473, 474, 475, 476, 477, 479, 480, 481, 486, 535]

Hull, C. L. (1952) *A behavior system: An introduction to behavior theory concerning the individual organism.* New Haven: Yale University Press.   [154, 157, 471, 472, 473, 474, 475, 476, 477, 479, 481, 485, 486, 561]

Hull, C. L., Livingston, J. R., Rouse, R. O., & Barker, O. N. (1951) True, sham, and esophogeal feeding as reinforcements. *J. comp. physiol. Psychol.* **44**, 236–245.   [216]

Humphrey, G. (1951) *An introduction to thinking: Its experimental psychology.* London: Methuen.   [48]

Hunt, H.. F., & Brady, J. V. (1951) Some effects of electroconvulsive shock on a conditioned emotional response ("anxiety"). *J. comp. physiol. Psychol.* **44**, 88–98.   [578]

Hunt, J. McV. (1941) The effect of infant feeding-frustration upon adult hoarding in the albino rat. *J. abn. soc. Psychol.* **36**, 338–360.   [122, 123, 124, 652, 685]

Hunt, J. McV. (1960) Experience and the development of motivation: Some reinterpretations. *Child Develpm.* **31**, 489–504.   [277, 819, 820]

Hunt, J. McV. (1963) Motivation inherent in information processing and action. In Harvey, O. J. (Ed.) *Cognitive factors in motivation and social organization.* New York: Ronald Press, pp. 35–94.   [825]

Hunt, J. McV., & Quay, H. C. (1961) Early vibratory experience and the question of innate reinforcement value of vibration and other stimuli: A limitation on the discrepancy (burnt soup) principle in motivation. *Psychol. Rev.* **68**, 149–156.   [542]

Hunt, J. McV., Schlosberg, H., Solomon, R. L., & Stellar, E. (1947) Studies of the effects of infantile experience on adult behavior in rats: I. Effects of infantile feeding frustration on adult hoarding. *J. comp. physiol. Psychol.* **40**, 291–304.   [124]

Hunt, J. McV., & Willoughby, R. R. (1939) The effect of frustration on hoarding in rats. *Psychosom. Med.* **1**, 309–310.   [122]

Hunt, W. A. (1939) A critical review of current approaches to affectivity. *Psychol. Bull.* **36**, 807–828.   [382]

Hunt, W. A. (1941) Recent developments in the field of emotion. *Psychol. Bull.* **38**, 249–276.   [382]

Hurley, J. R. (1955) The Iowa Picture Interpretation Test: A multiple-choice variation of the TAT. *J. consult. Psychol.* **19**, 372–376.   [724]

Hurlock, E. B. (1924) The value of praise and reproof as incentives for children. *Arch. Psychol.* **11**, No. 71.   [770]

Hurlock, E. B. (1925) An evaluation of certain incentives used in school work. *J. educ. Psychol.* **16**, 145–159.   [770]

Hurwitz, H. M. B. (1956) Conditioned responses in rats reinforced by light. *Brit. J. anim. Behav.* **4**, 31–33.   [541]

Hurwitz, H. M. B., & Appel, J. B. (1959) Light-onset reinforcement as a function of the light-dark maintenance schedule for the hooded rat. *J. comp. physiol. Psychol.* **52**, 710–712.   [541–542]

Hutt, P. J. (1954) Rate of bar pressing as a function of quality and quantity of food reward. *J. comp. physiol. Psychol.* **47**, 235–239.   [555]

Ingle, D. J., & Baker, B. L. (1953) A consideration of the relationship of experimentally produced and naturally occurring pathological changes in the rat to the adaptation diseases. In Pincus, G. (Ed.) *Recent progress in hormone research.* Proc. Laurentian Hormone Conf., vol. VIII. New York: Academic Press, pp. 143–169.   [447]

Inkeles, A., & Levinson, D. J. (1954) National character: The study of modal personality and socio-cultural systems. In Lindzey, G. (Ed.) *Handbook of social psychology,* 2 vols. Cambridge, Mass.: Addison-Wesley, vol. II, pp. 977–1016.   [568]

Irwin, F. W. (1958) An analysis of the concepts of *discrimination* and *preference.* *Amer. J. Psychol.* **71**, 152–163.   [12, 775, 801, 804, 830]

Irwin, O. C. (1932) The distribution of the amount of mobility in young infants between two nursing periods. *J. comp. Psychol.* **14**, 429–445.   [273]

882 BIBLIOGRAPHY—AUTHOR INDEX

Isch, M. J. (1952) Fantasied mother-child interaction in doll play. *J. genet. Psychol.* 81, 233–258.　**[756]**

Ishizuka, T. (1951) On the relation between the fatigue measured by flicker-test and the quantity of labour. Counted by step-counter. *Med. J. Osaka Univ.* 3, 217–222.　**[143]**

Iverson, M. A., & Reuder, M. E. (1956) Ego involvement as an experimental variable. *Psychol. Reports* 2, 147–181.　**[418, 784, 785]**

Jacobs, B., Jr. (1958) A method for investigating the cue characteristics of pictures. In Atkinson, J. W. (Ed.) *Motives in fantasy, action and society.* New York: Van Nostrand, pp. 617–629.　**[735]**

Jahoda, Marie (1958) *Current concepts of positive mental health.* New York: Basic Books.　**[683]**

Jakway, J. S. (1959) Inheritance of patterns of mating behavior in the male guinea pig. *Anim. Behav.* 7, 151–162.　**[188]**

James, W. (1884) What is emotion? *Mind* 9, 188–204.　**[391]**

James, W. (1890) *The principles of psychology,* 2 vols. New York: Henry Holt (reprinted in one volume by Dover Publications, Inc.).　**[37, 57]**

James, W. T. (1953) Social facilitation of eating behavior in puppies after satiation. *J. comp. physiol. Psychol.* 46, 427–428.　**[243]**

James, W. T. (1957) The effect of satiation on the sucking response in puppies. *J. comp. physiol. Psychol.* 50, 375–378.　**[113]**

James, W. T. (1959) A further analysis of the effect of satiation on the sucking response in puppies. *Psychol. Rec.* 9, 1–6.　**[113]**

James, W. T., & Gilbert, T. F. (1957) Elimination of eating behavior by food injection in weaned puppies. *Psychol. Reports* 3, 167–168.　**[114, 240]**

Janet, P. (1925) *Psychological healing: A historical and clinical study,* vol. I. New York: Macmillan.　**[49]**

Janis, I. L. (1951) *Air war and emotional stress.* New York: McGraw-Hill.　**[456]**

Janis, I. L. (1958) *Psychological stress.* New York: Wiley.　**[454, 461]**

Janowitz, H. D. (1958) Editorial: Hunger and appetite. *Amer. J. Med.* 25, 327.　**[228]**

Janowitz, H. D. (1961) Digestive system. *Ann. rev. Physiol.* 23, 153–182.　**[222, 227]**

Janowitz, H. D., & Grossman, M. I. (1949a) Some factors affecting the food intake of normal dogs and dogs with esophagostomy and gastric fistula. *Amer. J. Physiol.* 159, 143–148.　**[212–213, 215, 216]**

Janowitz, H. D., & Grossman, M. I. (1949b) Effect of variations in nutritive density on intake of foods of dogs and rats. *Amer. J. Physiol.* 158, 184–193.　**[214]**

Janowitz, H. D., Grossman, M. I., & Hanson, M. E. (1949c) Effect of intravenously administered glucose on food intake in the dog. *Amer. J. Physiol.* 156, 87–91.　**[214]**

Janowitz, H. D., & Grossman, M. I. (1951) Effect of prefeeding, alcohol and bitters on food intake of dogs. *Amer. J. Physiol.* 164, 182–186.　**[211]**

Janowitz, H. D., & Hollander, F. (1955) The time factor in the adjustment of food intake to varied caloric requirement in the dog: A study of the precision of appetite regulation. *Annals N.Y. Acad. Sci.* 63, Art. 1, 56–67.　**[213, 214, 215, 241]**

Jasper, H., et al. (Eds.) (1958) *Reticular formation of the brain.* Henry Ford Internat. Sympos. Boston: Little, Brown and Co.　**[150, 356, 601]**

Jastrow, J. (1928) The place of emotion in modern psychology. In Murchison, C. (Ed.) *Feelings and emotions: The Wittenberg symposium.* Worcester, Mass.: Clark University Press, pp. 24–38.　**[369]**

Jenkins, J. J., & Hanratty, Jacqueline A. (1949) Drive intensity discrimination in the albino rat. *J. comp. physiol. Psychol.* 42, 228–232.　**[265]**

Jenkins, M. (1928) The effect of segregation on the sex behavior of the white rat as measured by the obstruction method. *Genet. psychol. Monog.* 3, No. 6. [196]

Jenkins, W. L. (1951) Somesthesis. In Stevens, S. S. (Ed.) *Handbook of experimental psychology.* New York: Wiley, pp. 1172–1190. [260, 262]

Jenkins, W. O., & Stanley, J. S. (1950) Partial reinforcement: A review and critique. *Psychol. Bull.* 47, 193–234. [561]

Jennings, H. S. (1906) *The behavior of lower organisms.* New York: Columbia University Press. [42, 44, 814]

Jensen, A. R. (1958) Personality. *Ann. rev. Psychol.* 9, 295–322. [708]

Jensen, A. R. (1961) On the reformulation of inhibition in Hull's system. *Psychol. Bull.* 58, 274–298. [155]

Jensen, K. (1932) Differential reaction to taste and temperature stimuli in newborn infants. *Genet. psychol. Monog.* 12, 361–479. [651]

Jerome, E. A., Moody, J. A., Connor, T. J., & Fernandez, M. B. (1957) Learning in a multiple-door situation under various drive levels. *J. comp. physiol. Psychol.* 50, 588–591. [536]

Jessor, R., & Hammond, K. R. (1957) Construct validity and the Taylor Anxiety Scale, *Psychol. Bull.* 54, 161–170. [708, 803]

Johanson, A. M. (1922) The influence of incentive and punishment upon reaction-time. *Arch. Psychol.* 8, No. 54. [770]

Johnson, D. M. (1949) Learning function for a change in the scale of judgment. *J. exp. Psychol.* 39, 851–860. [338, 339]

Jones, E. (1953–1957) *The life and work of Sigmund Freud,* vols. I–III. New York: Basic Books. [593, 600, 604, 605, 606, 608, 626]

Jones, H. G. (1958) The status of inhibition in Hull's system: A theoretical revision. *Psychol. Rev.* 65, 179–182. [155]

Jones, M. R. (Ed.) (1954 on) *Nebraska symposium on motivation.* Lincoln: University of Nebraska Press. [2]

Jordan, N. (1953) Behavioral forces that are a function of attitudes and cognitive organization. *Human Relations* 6, 273–287. [788]

Jouvet, M. (1960) Telencephalic and rhombencephalic sleep in the cat. In Wolstenholme, G. E. W., & O'Connor, Maeve (Eds.) *Ciba Foundation symposium on the nature of sleep.* Boston: Little, Brown and Co., pp. 188–206. [159, 167]

Judson, A. J., & Cofer, C. N. (1956) Reasoning as an associative process: I. "Direction" in a single verbal problem. *Psychol. Reports* 2, 469–576. [48]

Judson, A. J., Cofer, C. N., & Gelfand, S. (1956) Reasoning as an associative process: II. "Direction" in problem solving as a function of prior reinforcement of relevant responses. *Psychol. Reports* 2, 501–507. [48]

Jung, C. G. (1933) *Modern man in search of a soul.* (Dill, W. S., & Baynes, Cary F., transl.) New York: Harcourt, Brace. [626]

Jung, C. G. (1938) *Psychology and religion.* New Haven: Yale University Press. [626]

Jung, C. G. (1939) *The integration of the personality.* (Dell, S. M., transl.) New York: Farrar and Rinehart. [626]

Jung, C. G. (1956) *Collected works, Vol. V. Symbols of transformation.* New York: Pantheon Press. [627]

Jung, C. G., & Kerenyi, C. (1949) *Essays on a science of mythology.* New York: Pantheon Press. [627]

Kagan, Eileen K. (1958) The effect of number and strength of electric shocks on running speed in a conflict situation. *Amer. Psychologist* 13, 389. (Abstr.). [436–437]

Kagan, J. (1955) Differential reward value of incomplete and complete sexual behavior. *J. comp. physiol. Psychol.* 48, 59–65. [187, 550]

Kagan, J. (1956) The measurement of overt aggression from fantasy. *J. abn. soc. Psychol.* 52, 390–393.   [755]

Kagan, J. (1959) The stability of TAT fantasy and stimulus ambiguity. *J. consult. Psychol.* 23, 266–271.   [755]

Kagan, J., & Berkun, M. M. (1954) The reward value of running activity. *J. comp. physiol. Psychol.* 47, 108.   [272, 550]

Kalish, H. I. (1954) Strength of fear as a function of the number of acquisition and extinction trials. *J. exp. Psychol.* 47, 1–9.   [577]

Kamin, L. J., & Clark, K. W. (1957) The Taylor Scale and reaction time. *J. abn. soc. Psychol.* 54, 262–263.   [705]

Kapp, R. (1931) Comment on Bernfeld and Feitelberg's "The Principles of Entropy and the Death Instinct." *Int. J. Psychoanal.* 12, 82–86.   [604]

Kardiner, A. (1939) *The individual and his society*. New York: Columbia University Press.   [629, 630]

Kardiner, A. (1945) *The psychological frontiers of society*. New York: Columbia University Press.   [569, 630, 748]

Karsten, A. (1928) Psychische Sättigung. *Psychol. Forsch.* 10, 142–254.   [279, 783]

Katz, D. (1937) *Animals and men*. New York: Longmans, Green.   [242]

Katz, D., & Stotland, E. (1959) A preliminary statement to a theory of attitude structure and change. In Koch, S. (Ed.) *Psychology: A study of a science*, Vol. III. New York: McGraw-Hill, pp. 423–475.   [805]

Kaufman, R. S. (1953) Effects of preventing intromission upon sexual behavior of rats. *J. comp. physiol. Psychol.* 46, 209–211.   [198]

Kausler, D. H., & Trapp, E. P. (1958) Relationship between achievement motivation scores and manifest anxiety scores. *J. consult. Psychol.* 22, 448–450.   [708, 740]

Kausler, D. H., & Trapp, E. P. (1959) Methodological considerations in the construct validation of drive-oriented scales. *Psychol. Bull.* 56, 152–157.   [803]

Keister, M. E., & Updegraff, R. (1937) A study of children's reactions to failure and an experimental attempt to modify them. *Child Develpm.* 8, 241–248.   [784]

Keller, F. S. (1937) *The definition of psychology*. New York: Appleton-Century-Crofts.   [467]

Keller, F. S., & Schoenfeld, W. N. (1950) *Principles of psychology*. New York: Appleton-Century-Crofts.   [514, 515, 516, 517]

Kelley, H. H., & Thibaut, J. W. (1954) Experimental studies of group problem solving and process. In Lindzey, G. (Ed.) *Handbook of social psychology*. Cambridge, Mass.: Addison-Wesley, pp. 735–785.   [777]

Kendeigh, S. C., West, G. C., & Cox, G. W. (1960) Annual stimulus for spring migration in birds. *Anim. Behav.* 8, 180–185.   [128]

Kendler, H. H. (1945a) Drive interaction: I. Learning as a function of the simultaneous presence of the hunger and thirst drives. *J. exp. Psychol.* 35, 96–109.   [524, 536]

Kendler, H. H. (1945b) Drive interaction: II. Experimental analysis of the role of drive in learning theory. *J. exp. Psychol.* 35, 188–198.   [527]

Kendler, H. H. (1946) The influence of simultaneous hunger and thirst drives upon the learning of two opposed spatial responses of the white rat. *J. exp. Psychol.* 36, 212–220.   [266]

Kendler, H. H. (1951) Reflections and confessions of a reinforcement theorist. *Psychol. Rev.* 58, 368–374.   [501]

Kendler, Tracy S. (1949) The effects of success and failure on the recall of tasks. *J. exp. Psychol.* 41, 79–87.   [785]

Kendrick, D. C. (1960) Inhibition: A symposium. III. Effects of drive and effort on inhibition and reinforcement. *Brit. J. Psychol.* 51, 215–227.   [155]

Kennedy, G. C. (1950) The hypothalamic control of food intake in rats. *Proc. Roy. Soc. Lond.,* B **137,** 535–549. **[221]**

Kennedy, G. C. (1952–1953) The role of depot fat in the hypothalamic control of food intake in the rat. *Proc. Roy. Soc., Lond.,* B **140,** 578–592. **[223, 225, 227]**

Kennedy, J. S. (1954) Is modern ethology objective? *Brit. J. anim. Behav.* **2,** 12–19. **[95, 102]**

Kety, S. S. (1960) Sleep and the energy metabolism of the brain. In Wolstenholme, G. E. W., & O'Connor, Maeve (Eds.) *Ciba Foundation symposium on the nature of sleep.* Boston: Little, Brown and Co., pp. 375–381. **[168, 170]**

Keys, A., Brožek, J., Henschel, A., Mickelsen, O., & Taylor, H. (1950) *The biology of human starvation* (2 vols.) Minneapolis: University of Minnesota Press. **[264, 684]**

Kilby, R. W. (1948) Psychoneurosis in times of trouble: Evidence for a hierarchy of motives. *J. abn. soc. Psychol.* **43,** 544–545. **[684]**

Kimble, G. A. (1949) An experimental test of a two-factor theory of inhibition. *J. exp. Psychol.* **39,** 15–23. **[155]**

Kimble, G. A. (1951) Behavior strength as a function of the intensity of the hunger drive. *J. exp. Psychol.* **41,** 341–348. **[530, 531, 535]**

Kimble, G. A. (1961) *Hilgard and Marquis' Conditioning and learning* (2nd ed.) New York: Appleton-Century-Crofts. **[151, 152, 153, 155, 156, 157, 506, 527, 528, 539, 552, 554, 561, 563, 566]**

Kimbrell, D., & Blake, R. R. (1958) Motivational factors in the violation of a prohibition. *J. abn. soc. Psychol.* **56,** 132–133. **[340]**

Kinder, Elaine F. (1927) A study of the nest-building activity of the albino rat. *J. exp. Zool.* **47,** 117–161. **[96, 109, 264, 311]**

King, R. A. (1959) The effects of training and motivation on the components of a learned instrumental response. Unpubl. doctoral dissert., Duke University. **[527]**

Kinsey, A. C., Pomeroy, W. B., & Martin, C. E. (1948) *Sexual behavior in the human male.* Philadelphia: W. B. Saunders. **[178, 185, 186, 193, 195]**

Kinsey, A. C., Pomeroy, W. B., Martin, C. E., & Gebhard, P. H. (1953) *Sexual behavior in the human female.* Philadelphia: W. B. Saunders. **[178, 185, 186, 191, 193, 195]**

Kintsch, W. (1962) Runway performance as a function of drive strength and magnitude of reinforcement. *J. comp. physiol. Psychol.* **55,** 882–887. **[558]**

Kish, G. B. (1955) Learning when the onset of illumination is used as reinforcing stimulus. *J. comp. physiol. Psychol.* **48,** 261–264. **[541]**

Klein, G. S. (1954) Need and regulation. In Jones, M. R. (Ed.) *Nebraska symposium on motivation, 1954.* Lincoln: University of Nebraska Press, pp. 224–274. **[805]**

Klein, Melanie (1932) *The psycho-analysis of children.* London: Hogarth Press. **[614]**

Klein, Melanie, Heimann, P., Isaacs, S., & Riviere, Joan (1952) *Development in psychoanalysis.* London: Hogarth Press. **[650]**

Kleitman, N. (1939) *Sleep and wakefulness.* Chicago: University of Chicago Press. **[159, 160, 161, 165, 170]**

Kleitman, N. (1949) The sleep-wakefulness cycle of submarine personnel. In Lindsley, D. B., et al. (Eds.) *A survey report of human factors in undersea warfare.* Baltimore: Williams & Wilkins, pp. 329–341. **[163, 164]**

Kleitman, N. (1957) Sleep, wakefulness and consciousness. *Psychol. Bull.* **54,** 354–359. **[158, 159, 161, 168]**

Kleitman, N. (1960a) The nature of dreaming. In Wolstenholme, G. E. W., & O'Connor, Maeve (Eds.) *Ciba Foundation symposium on the nature of sleep.* Boston: Little, Brown and Co., pp. 349–363. **[159, 172]**

Kleitman, N. (1960b) Discussion. In Wolstenholme, G. E. W., & O'Connor, Maeve

(Eds.) *Ciba Foundation symposium on the nature of sleep.* Boston: Little, Brown and Co., pp. 336–337.   **[161, 163, 172–173]**

Kleitman, N. (1961) Physiological cycling. In Flaherty, B. E. (Ed.) *Psychophysiological aspects of space flight.* New York: Columbia University Press, pp. 158–165.   **[163, 169, 170]**

Kleitman, N. (1963) *Sleep and wakefulness* (rev. and enlarged ed.) Chicago: University of Chicago Press.   **[162]**

Kleitman, N., & Engelmann, T. G. (1953) Sleep characteristics of infants. *J. appl. Physiol.* **6**, 269–282.   **[161]**

Kleitman, N., & Kleitman, E. (1953) Effect of non-24-hour routines of living on oral temperature and heart rate. *J. appl. Physiol.* **6**, 283–291.   **[163]**

Klineberg, O. (1940) *Social psychology.* New York: Holt.   **[568, 569]**

Kling, J. W. (1956) Speed of running as a function of goal-box behavior. *J. comp. physiol. Psychol.* **49**, 474–476.   **[556]**

Kling, J. W., Horowitz, L., & Delhagen, J. E. (1956) Light as a positive reinforcer for rat responding. *Psychol. Reports* **2**, 337–340.   **[541]**

Kling, J. W., & Matsumiya, Y. (1962) Relative reinforcement values of food and intracranial stimulation. *Science* **135**, 668–670.   **[546]**

Kluckhohn, C. (1953) Universal categories of culture. In Kroeber, A. L. (Ed.) *Anthropology today.* Chicago: University of Chicago Press, pp. 507–523. **[568]**

Kluckhohn, C. (1954) Culture and behavior. In Lindzey, G. (Ed.) *Handbook of social psychology,* 2 vols. Cambridge, Mass.: Addison-Wesley, vol. II, pp. 921–963.   **[568]**

Klüver, H., & Bucy, P. C. (1939) Preliminary analysis of functions of the temporal lobe in monkeys. *Arch. neurol. Psychiat., Chi.* **42**, 979–1000.   **[182]**

Knight, R. P., & Friedman, C. R. (Eds.) (1954) *Psychoanalytic psychiatry and psychology, clinical and theoretical papers.* Austen Riggs Center, vol. I, New York: International Universities Press.   **[638]**

Koch, S. (1954) Clark L. Hull. In Estes, W. K. et al. *Modern learning theory.* New York: Appleton-Century-Crofts, pp. 1–176.   **[156, 494]**

Koch, S. (Ed.) (1959) *Psychology: A study of a science. Study I: Conceptual and systematic. Vol. II. General systematic formulations, learning and special processes.* New York: McGraw-Hill.   **[467]**

Koch, S., & Daniel, W. J. (1945) The effect of satiation on the behavior mediated by a habit of maximum strength. *J. exp. Psychol.* **35**, 167–187.   **[530, 532, 535]**

Koehler, O, & Zagarus, A. (1937) Beiträge zum Brutverhalten des Halsbandregenpfeifers (*Charadrius h. hiaticula* L.) *Beitr. Fortpfl.-Biol. Vögel* **13**, 1–9 (cited by Hess, 1962).   **[70]**

Kohn, M. (1951) Satiation of hunger from food injected directly into the stomach versus food ingested by mouth. *J. comp. physiol. Psychol.* **44**, 412–422. **[215]**

Konorski, J. (1948) *Conditioned reflexes and neuron organization* (Garry, S., transl.) London: Cambridge University Press.   **[151]**

Korchin, S. J. (1962) Some psychological determinants of stress behavior. Prepared for a conference on "Self-control under stress situation." Washington, D.C., September.   **[454, 460, 462, 463]**

Kornetsky, C. (1958) Effects of meprobamate, phenobarbital and *dextro*-amphetamine. *J. pharmacol. exper. Ther.* **123**, 216–219.   **[145]**

Kornetsky, C., Humphries, O., & Evarts, E. V. (1957) Comparison of psychological effects of certain centrally acting drugs in man. *AMA Arch. neurol. Psychiat.* **77**, 318–324.   **[145]**

Kornetsky, C., & Humphries, O. (1958) Psychological effects of centrally acting drugs in man: Effects of chlorpromazine and secobarbital on visual and motor behavior. *J. ment. Sci.* **104**, 1093–1099.   **[145]**

Koster, R. (1943) Hormonal factors in male behavior of the female rat. *Endocrinology* 33, 337–348.   [182]

Kozlowski, S. (1952) Experiments on the physiological mechanism of "active rest." *Acta physiol. Polon.* 3, 85–92.   [137]

Kraeling, Doris (1961) Analysis of amount of reward as a variable in learning. *J. comp. physiol. Psychol.* 54, 560–565.   [557]

Kramer, G. (1959) Recent experiments on bird orientation. *Ibis* 101, 399–416. [130]

Krause, M. S. (1961) The measurement of transitory anxiety. *Psychol. Rev.* 68, 178–189.   [713]

Krebs, A. M. (1958) Two determinants of conformity: Age of independence training and nAchievement. *J. abn. soc. Psychol.* 50, 130–131.   [739, 779]

Krech, D. (1950) Dynamic systems as open neurological systems. *Psychol. Rev.* 57, 345–361.   [344]

Kroeber, A. L. (1917) The superorganic. *Amer. Anthrop.* 19, 163–213.   [328]

Kroeber, A. L. (Ed.) (1953) *Anthropology today: An encyclopedic inventory.* Chicago: University of Chicago Press.   [568]

Krumboltz, J. D., & Farquhar, W. W. (1957) Reliability and validity of nAchievement. *J. consult. Psychol.* 21, 226–231.   [723]

Kubic, L. S. (1952) Problems and techniques of psychoanalytic validation and progress. In Pumpian-Mindlin, E. (Ed.) *Psychoanalysis as science.* Stanford: Stanford University Press, pp. 46–124.   [654]

Kubie, L. S. (1956) Influence of symbolic processes on the role of instincts in human behavior. *Psychosom. Med.* 18, 189–208.   [100]

Kunst, M. S. (1948) A study of thumb- and finger-sucking in infants. *Psychol. Monog.* 62, 1–71.   [114]

Kuo, Z. Y. (1921) Giving up instincts in psychology. *J. Philos.* 18, 645–666.   [43]

Kuo, Z. Y. (1924) A psychology without heredity. *Psychol. Rev.* 31, 427–451. [56]

Kuo, Z. Y. (1932) Ontogeny of embryonic behavior in Aves. I: The chronology and general nature of the behavior of the chick embryo. II: The mechanical factors in the various stages leading to hatching. *J. exp. Zool.* 61, 395–430; 453–489. III: The structure and environmental factors in embryonic behavior. IV: The influence of embryonic movements upon the behavior after hatching. *J. comp. Psychol.* 13, 245–272; 14, 109–122.   [97]

Kurtz, P. W. (1956) Human nature, homeostasis, and value. *Phil. phenomenol. Res.* 17, 36–55.   [326]

Lacey, J. I. (1950) Individual differences in somatic response patterns. *J. comp. physiol. Psychol.* 43, 338–350.   [460]

Lacey, J. I., & Lacey, Beatrice C. (1958) The relationship of autonomic activity to motor impulsivity. *Res. Publ. Ass. nerv. ment. Dis.* 36, 144–209.   [398, 410, 800]

Lack, D. (1943) *The life of the robin.* London: Cambridge.   [69]

Lana, R. E. (1960) Manipulation-exploration drives and the drive reduction hypothesis. *J. gen. Psychol.* 63, 3–27.   [300, 831]

Lana, R. E. (1962) Exploration phenomena and the drive reduction hypothesis. *J. gen. Psychol.* 67, 101–104.   [300, 831]

Landis, C., Landis, A. T., Bolles, M. M., et al. (1940) *Sex in development.* New York: Haeber.   [652]

Landis, C., & Zubin, J. (1951) The effect of thonzylamine hydrochloride and phenobarbital sodium on certain psychological functions. *J. Psychol.* 31, 181–200.   [145]

Lange, C. (1885) *Om Leudsbeveegelser.* (original not available; see trans. by Haupt, I. A., for Dunlap, K. [ed.] *The emotions.* Baltimore: Williams & Wilkins, 1922).   [391]

Lanier, L. H. (1943) Variability in the pain threshold. *Science* 97, 49–50.   [260]

Lansing, R. W. (1957) Relation of brain and tremor rhythms to visual reaction time. *EEG clin. Neurophysiol.* 9, 497–504.   [406]

Lansing, R. W., Schwartz, E., & Lindsley, D. B. (1959) Reaction time and EEG activation under alerted and nonalerted conditions. *J. exp. Psychol.* 58, 1–7. [406]

Larber, S. H., Komarov, S. A., & Shay, H. (1950) Effect of sham feeding on gastric motor activity of the dog. *Amer. J. Physiol.* 162, 447–451.   [212]

Larsson, K. (1956) Conditioning and sexual behavior in the male albino rat. *Acta Psychol. Gothoburgensia* 1, 269.   [193]

Larsson, S. (1954) On the hypothalamic organisation of the nervous mechanism regulating food intake. *Acta physiol. Scand.* 32, suppl. 115, pp. 63.   [222]

Lashley, K. S. (1938a) Experimental analysis of instinctive behavior. *Psychol. Rev.* 45, 445–471.   [61, 823]

Lashley, K. S. (1938b) The thalamus and emotion. *Psychol. Rev.* 45, 42–61. [391]

Lawrence, D. H., & Mason, W. A. (1955a) Intake and weight adjustments in rats to changes in feeding schedule. *J. comp. physiol. Psychol.* 48, 43–46.   [241]

Lawrence, D. H., & Mason, W. A. (1955b) Food intake in the rat as a function of deprivation intervals and feeding rhythms. *J. comp. physiol. Psychol.* 48, 267–271.   [241]

Lawson, R. (1957) Brightness discrimination performance and secondary reward strength as a function of primary reward amount. *J. comp. physiol. Psychol.* 50, 35–39.   [555]

Lawson, R., & Marx, M. H. (1958) Frustration: Theory and experiment. *Genet. psychol. Monogr.* 57, 393–464.   [414, 423]

Lazarus, R. S., & Baker, R. W. (1956) Personality and psychological stress: A theoretical and methodological framework. *Psychol. Newsletter* 8, 21–32. [461, 806]

Lazarus, R. S., Baker, R. W., Broverman, D. M., & Mayer, J. (1957) Personality and psychological stress. *J. Person.* 25, 559–577.   [740, 806]

Lazarus, R. S., Deese, J., & Osler, S. F. (1952) The effects of psychological stress upon performance. *Psychol. Bull.* 49, 293–317.   [449, 450, 454, 713]

Leake, C. D. (1956) New mood-changing drugs. *Ohio State Med. J.* 52, 369–373. [144]

Leblond, C. P. (1940) Nervous and hormonal factors in the maternal behavior of the mouse. *J. genet. Psychol.* 57, 327–344.   [111]

Leblond, C. P., & Nelson, W. O. (1937) Maternal behavior in hypophysectomized male and female mice. *Amer. J. Physiol.* 120, 167–172.   [111]

Lecky, P. (1945) *Self-consistency: A theory of personality.* New York: Island Press.   [321, 666]

Lee, D. (1957) Cultural factors in dietary choice. *Amer. J. clin. Nutrit.* 5, 166–170. [241]

Leeper, R. (1935) The role of motivation in learning: A study of the phenomenon of differential motivational control of the utilization of habits. *J. genet. Psychol.* 46, 3–40.   [265]

Leeper, R. (1948) A motivational theory of emotion to replace "emotion as disorganized response." *Psychol. Rev.* 55, 5–21.   [369]

Leeper, R. N., & Madison, P. (1959) *Toward understanding personality.* New York: Appleton-Century-Crofts.   [2]

Leeper, R. W. (1943) *Lewin's topographical and vector psychology: A digest and a critique.* Eugene: University of Oregon Press.   [357, 433]

Lefkowitz, M., Blake, R. R., & Mouton, Jane S. (1955) Status factors in pedestrian violation of traffic signals. *J. abn. soc. Psychol.* 51, 704–705.   [340]

Lehmann, G. (1962) Effect of environmental factors on biological cycles and performance of work. In Schaefer, K. E. (Ed.) *International symposium on sub-*

marine and space medicine, Vol. I. Man's dependence on the earthly atmosphere. New York: Macmillan, pp. 381–388. [163]

Lehmann, H. E., & Czank, J. (1957) Differential screening of phrenotropic agents in man: Psychophysiological test data. *J. clin. exper. Psychopath.* 18, 222–235. [145]

Lehrman, D. S. (1953) A critique of Konrad Lorenz's theory of instinctive behavior. *Quart. rev. Biol.* 28, 337–363. [76, 96, 97, 98, 102]

Lehrman, D. S. (1955) The physiological basis of parental feeding behavior in the ring dove (*streptopelia risoria*). *Behaviour* 7 (4), 241–286. [98, 102, 118, 119]

Lehrman, D. S. (1956a) Comparative physiology (Behavior). *Ann. rev. Physiol.* 18, 527 542. [96, 130]

Lehrman, D. S. (1956b) On the organization of maternal behavior and the problem of instinct. In Grassé, P. P. (Ed.) Fondation Singer-Polignac. *L'instinct dans le comportement des animaux et de l'homme.* Paris: Masson, pp. 475–520. [96, 98, 109, 112]

Lehrman, D. S. (1958a) Induction of broodiness by participation in courtship and nest-building in the ring dove (*streptopelia risoria*). *J. comp. physiol. Psychol.* 51, 32–36. [98, 119, 120]

Lehrman, D. S. (1958b) Effect of female sex hormones on incubation behavior in the ring dove (*streptopelia risoria*). *J. comp. physiol. Psychol.* 51, 142–145. [98]

Lehrman, D. S. (1959a) On the origin of the reproductive behavior cycle in doves. *Transac. N.Y. Acad. Sci.*, Ser. II 21, 682–688. [118]

Lehrman, D. S. (1959b) Hormonal responses to external stimuli in birds. *Ibis* 101, 478–496. [121, 128]

Lehrman, D. S. (1961) Hormonal regulation of parental behavior in birds and infrahuman mammals. In Young, W. C. (Ed.) *Sex and internal secretion.* (3rd ed.) Baltimore: Williams & Wilkins, pp. 1268–1382. [97, 104, 109, 110, 111, 113, 117]

Lehrman, D. S., & Brody, P. (1957) Oviduct response to estrogen and progesterone in the ring dove (*streptopelia risoria*). *Proc. soc. exp. Biol. & Med.* 95, 373–375. [120]

Lehrman, D. S., & Brody, P. (1961) Does prolactin induce incubation in the ring dove? *J. endocrinol.* 22, 269–275. [120]

Lehrman, D. S., Brody, P., & Wortis, R. P. (1961) The presence of the mate and of nesting material as stimuli for the development of incubation behavior and for gonadotropin secretion in the ring dove (*streptopelia risoria*). *Endocrinology* 68, 507–516. [119, 121]

Lehrman, D. S., & Wortis, R. P. (1960) Previous breeding experience and hormone-induced incubation behavior in the ring dove. *Science* 132, 1667–1668. [120]

Lehrman, D. S., Wortis, R. P., & Brody, P. (1961) Gonadotropin secretion in response to external stimuli of varying duration in the ring dove (*streptopelia risoria*). *Proc. soc. exp. Biol. & Med.* 106, 298–300. [119–120]

Lerner, M. (1957) *America as a civilization: Life and thought in the United States today.* New York: Simon and Schuster. [34]

Leshan, L. L. (1952) Time orientation and social class. *J. abn. soc. Psychol.* 47, 589–592. [570]

Lesser, G. S. (1957) The relationship between overt and fantasy aggression as a function of maternal response to aggression. *J. abn. soc. Psychol.* 55, 218–221. [755]

Lesser, G. S. (1958a) Application of Guttman's scaling method to aggressive fantasy in children. *Educ. psychol. Meas.* 18, 543–551. [755]

Lesser, G. S. (1958b) Conflict analysis of fantasy aggression. *J. Person.* 26, 29–41. [758]

Levin, H., & Sears, R. R. (1956) Identification with parents as a determinant of doll play aggression. *Child Develpm.* **27**, 135–153.   [757]

Levin, H., & Turgeon, V. F. (1957) The influence of the mother's presence on children's doll play aggression. *J. abn. soc. Psychol.* **55**, 304–308.   [757]

Levin, H., & Wardwell, E. (1962) The research uses of doll play. *Psychol. Bull.* **59**, 27–56.   [756, 758]

Levine, S. (1953) The role of irrelevant drive stimuli in learning. *J. exp. Psychol.* **45**, 410–416.   [265]

Levy, D. M. (1928) Fingersucking and accessory movements in early infancy. *Amer. J. Psychiat.* **7**, 881–918.   [651]

Levy, D. M. (1934) Experiments on the sucking reflex and social behavior of dogs. *Amer. J. Orthopsychiat.* **4**, 203–224.   [113, 651]

Levy, D. M. (1937a) Studies in sibling rivalry. *Res. Monogr. Amer. Orthopsychiat. Assoc. Monog.* No. 2, pp. 96.   [686]

Levy, D. M. (1937b) Primary affect hunger. *Amer. J. Psychiat.* **94**, 643–652. [686]

Levy, D. M. (1943) *Maternal overprotection.* New York: Columbia University Press.   [686]

Levy, D. M. (1951) The deprived and indulged forms of psychopathic personality. *Amer. J. Orthopsychiat.* **21**, 250–254.   [686]

Levy, D. M. (1958) *Behavioral analyses: Analyses of clinical observations of behavior; as applied to mother-newborn relationships.* Springfield, Ill.: Charles C. Thomas.   [690]

Levy, E. Z., Thaler, V. H., & Ruff, G. E. (1958) New technique for recording skin resistance changes. *Science* **128**, 33–34.   [170]

Levy, N. (1958) A short form of the Children's Manifest Anxiety Scale. *Child Develpm.* **29**, 153–154.   [702]

Lewin, K. (1917) Der psychische Tätigkeit bei der Hemmung von Willensoorgängen und der Grundgesetz der assoziation. *Zeitschrift Psychol.* **77**, 212–247. [48]

Lewin, K. (1922) Das Problem der Willenmessung und das Grundgesetz der Assoziation. *Psychol. Forsch.* **1**, 191–302; **2**, 65–140.   [48]

Lewin, K. (1931) Environmental forces in child behavior and development. In Murchison, C. (Ed.) *A handbook of child psychology.* Worcester, Mass.: Clark University Press, pp. 94–127.   [433]

Lewin, K. (1935) *A dynamic theory of personality: Selected papers* (trans. by Adams, D. K., & Zener, K. E.) New York: McGraw-Hill.   [357, 387, 389, 433, 771–772]

Lewin, K. (1936) *Principles of topological psychology.* New York: McGraw-Hill. [357]

Lewin, K. (1938) *The conceptual representation and the measurement of psychological forces.* Durham, N.C.: Duke University Press.   [357, 361, 362, 433]

Lewin, K. (1948) *Resolving social conflicts.* New York: Harper.   [357]

Lewin, K. (1951) *Field theory in social science.* New York: Harper.   [357, 358, 363]

Lewin, K., Dembo, Tamara, Festinger, L., & Sears, Pauline S. (1944) Level of aspiration. In Hunt, J. McV. (Ed.) *Personality and the behavior disorders,* vol. I. New York: Ronald Press, pp. 333–378.   [316, 386, 388, 389, 772, 773, 774]

Lewis, D. J. (1960) Partial reinforcement: A selective review of the literature since 1950. *Psychol. Bull.* **57**, 1–28.   [561, 562]

Lewis, D. J., & Cotton, J. W. (1957) Learning and performance as a function of drive strength during acquisition and extinction. *J. comp. physiol. Psychol.* **50**, 189–194.   [521, 527, 533]

Lewis, H. (1954) *Deprived children.* New York: Oxford University Press. [688]

Lewis, H. E. (1960) Sleep patterns on polar expeditions. In Wolstenholme, G. E. W., & O'Connor, Maeve (Eds.) *Ciba Foundation symposium on the nature of sleep.* Boston: Little, Brown and Co., pp. 322–328. [162, 163]

Lewis, P. R., & Lobban, M. C. (1957) The effects of prolonged periods of life on abnormal time routines upon excretory rhythms in human subjects. Dissociation of diurnal rhythms in human subjects living on abnormal time routines. *Quart. J. exper. Physiol.* 42, 356–370; 371–386. [163, 169]

Licklider, L. C., & Licklider, J. C. R. (1950) Observations on the hoarding behavior of rats. *J. comp. physiol. Psychol.* 43, 129–134. [124, 126]

Liddell, H. S. (1925) The relation between maze learning and spontaneous activity in the sheep. *J. comp. Psychol.* 5, 475–483. [271]

Lilly, J. C. (1956) Mental effects of reduction of ordinary levels of physical stimuli on intact healthy persons. *Psychiat. Res. Reps.* 5, 1–9. [279, 280, 281]

Lilly, J. C. (1958) Learning motivated by subcortical stimulation: The "start" and "stop" patterns of behavior. In Jasper, H. H., et al. (Eds.) *Reticular formation of the brain.* Boston: Little, Brown and Co., pp. 705–721. [544]

Lilly, J. C. (1962) The effect of sensory deprivation on consciousness. In Schaefer, K. E. (Ed.) *International symposium on submarine and space medicine,* vol. II. *Environmental effects on consciousness.* New York: Macmillan Co., pp. 93–95. [164]

Lilly, J. C., & Miller, A. M. (1962) Operant conditioning of the bottlenose dolphin with electrical stimulation of the brain. *J. comp. physiol. Psychol.* 55, 73–79. [544]

Lindauer, M. (1962) Ethology, *Ann. rev. Psychol.* 13, 35–70. [104]

Lindner, R. M. (1945) Psychopathic personality and the concept of homeostasis. *J. clin. psychopath. and Psychother.* 6, 517–521. [314, 323]

Lindsley, D. B. (1950) Emotions and the electroencephalogram. In Reymert, M. L. (Ed.) *Feelings and emotions.* New York: McGraw-Hill, pp. 238–246. [398]

Lindsley, D. B. (1951) Emotion. In Stevens, S. S. (Ed.) *Handbook of experimental psychology.* New York: Wiley, pp. 473–516. [391, 394, 398, 399]

Lindsley, D. B. (1952) Psychological phenomena and the electroencephalogram. *EEG clin. Neurophysiol.* 4, 443–456. [398]

Lindsley, D. B. (1956) Physiological psychology. *Ann. rev. Psychol.* 7, 323–348. [402, 403]

Lindsley, D. B. (1957) Psychophysiology and motivation. In Jones, M. R. (Ed.) *Nebraska symposium on motivation, 1957.* Lincoln: University of Nebraska Press, pp. 44–105. [394, 400–401, 402, 404, 405, 406, 601]

Lindsley, D. B. (1958) Psychophysiology and perception. In Glazer, R., et al. *Current trends in the description and analysis of behavior.* Pittsburgh: University of Pittsburgh Press, pp. 48–91. [399, 400, 404, 405]

Lindsley, D. B. (1960) Attention, consciousness, sleep and wakefulness. In Field, J. (Ed.-in-chief) and Magoun, H. W. (2nd ed.) *Handbook of physiology. Section I. Neurophysiology.* vol. III. Washington, D.C.: Amer. Physiol. Society, pp. 1553–1593. [402]

Lindsley, D. B., Bowden, J., & Magoun, H. W. (1949) Effect upon the EEG of acute injury to the brain stem activating system. *EEG clin. Neurophysiol.* 1, 475–486. [399]

Lindzey, G. (Ed.) (1958) *Assessment of human motives.* New York: Rinehart. [2]

Lindzey, G., & Kalnins, D. (1958) Thematic Apperception Test: Some evidence bearing on the "hero assumption." *J. abn. soc. Psychol.* 57, 76–83. [754]

Lindzey, G., & Riecken, H. V. (1951) Inducing frustration in adult subjects. *J. consult. Psychol.* 15, 18–23. [749]

Lipps, T. (1897) Der Begriff des Unbewussten in der Psychologie. *Records of the Third Internat. Congr. Psychol., Munich 1897.* Cited by Freud (1900) p. 612. [594]

Lissner, K. (1933) Die Entspannung von Bedürfnissen durch Ersatzhandlungen. *Psychol. Forsch.* 18, 218–250.   [783]

Littman, R. A. (1958) Motives, history and causes. In Jones, M. R. (Ed.) *Nebraska symposium on motivation, 1958.* Lincoln: University of Nebraska Press, pp. 114–168.   [34, 47, 803]

Lockard, R. B. (1962) Self-regulated exposure to light by dark- or light-treated rats. *Science* 135, 377–378.   [542]

Logan, F. A. (1954) A note on stimulus intensity dynamism (*V*). *Psychol. Rev.* 61, 77–80.   [566]

Logan, F. A. (1959) The Hull-Spence approach. In Koch, S. (Ed.) *Psychology: A study of a science*, Vol. II. New York: McGraw-Hill, pp. 293–358.   [469, 481]

Logan, F. A. (1960) *Incentive: How the conditions of reinforcement affect the performance of rats.* New Haven: Yale University Press.   [489, 553, 555]

Loomis, A. L., Harvey, E. N., & Hobart, G. A. (1937) Cerebral states during sleep, as studied by human brain potentials. *J. exp. Psychol.* 21, 127–144.   [159]

Lorente de Nò, R. (1938) Analysis of the activity of the chains of internuncial neurons. *J. Neurophysiol.* 1, 207–244.   [355]

Lorenz, K. (1935) Der Kumpan in der Umwelt des Vögels. *J. Ornithol.* 83, 137–213; 289–413.   [88]

Lorenz, K. (1937) The conception of instinctive behavior. In Schiller, Claire H. (Ed.) *Instinctive behavior.* New York: International Universities Press, 1957, 129–175.   [69, 80]

Lorenz, K. (1939) Comparative study of behavior. In Schiller, Claire H. (Ed.) *Instinctive behavior.* New York: International Universities Press, 1957, pp. 239–263.   [66]

Lorenz, K. (1943) Die angeborenen Formen möglicher Erfahrung. *Zs. Tierpsychol.* 5, 235–409 (cited by Tinbergen, 1951).   [82]

Lorenz, K. (1950) The comparative method of studying innate behavior patterns. In Society for Experimental Biology, Symposium No. 4: *Physiological mechanisms in animal behaviour.* New York: Academic Press, pp. 221–268.   [60, 62, 65, 68, 70, 71, 82, 84, 86, 92, 95]

Lorenz, K. (1952a) The past twelve years in the comparative study of behavior. In Schiller, Claire H. (Ed.) *Instinctive behavior.* New York: International Universities Press, 1957, pp. 288–310.   [73, 77, 92]

Lorenz, K. (1952b) *King Solomon's ring.* New York: Thomas Y. Crowell. [75–76, 77, 78, 82, 85, 88]

Lorenz, K. (1955) Morphology and behavior patterns in closely allied species. In Schaffner, B. (Ed.) *Transactions of the first conference on group processes,* 1954. New York: Josiah Macy, Jr. Found., pp. 168–220.   [77]

Lorenz, K. (1958) The deprivation experiment; its limitations and its value as a means to separate learned and unlearned elements of behavior. Paper presented at the Downing State Hospital, Illinois (cited by Hess, 1962).   [74, 80, 97]

Lorenz, K. (1960) Prinzipien der vergleichenden Verhaltserforschung. *Fortschr. Zool.* 12, 265–294.   [74]

Lorenz, K. (1961) Phylogenetische Anpassung und adaptive Modifikation des Verhaltens. *Zeit. f. Tierpsychol.* 18, 139–187.   [74, 100]

Lorenz, K., & Tinbergen, N. (1938) Taxis and instinctive action in the egg-retrieving behavior of the greylag goose. In Schiller, Claire H. (Ed.) *Instinctive behavior.* New York: International Universities Press, 1957, pp. 176–208.   [61, 62, 78]

Lorge, I., Fox, D., Davitz, J., & Brenner, M. (1958) A survey of studies contrasting the quality of group performance and individual performance, 1920–1957. *Psychol. Bull.* 55, 337–372.   [777]

Lowell, E. L. (1952) The effect of need for achievement on learning and speed of performance. *J. Psychol.* **33,** 31–40. [730]

Lowenstein, O., & Loewenfeld, Irene E. (1951) Types of central autonomic innervation and fatigue: Pupillographic studies. *AMA Arch. neurol. Psychiat., Chi.* **66,** 580–599. [144]

Lowenstein, O., & Loewenfeld, Irene E. (1952) Disintegration of central autonomic regulation during fatigue and its reintegration by psychosensory controlling mechanisms. I: Disintegration. II: Reintegration. Pupillographic studies. *J. nerv. ment. Dis.* **115,** 1–21, 121–145. [144]

Lowrey, L. G. (1940) Personality distortion and early infant care. *Amer. J. Orthopsychiat.* **10,** 576–585. [649]

Luby, E. D., Frohman, C. E., Grisell, J. L., Lenzo, J. E., & Gottlieb, J. S. (1960) Sleep deprivation: Effects on behavior, thinking, motor performance, and biological energy transfer systems. *Psychosom. Med.* **22,** 182–192. [174]

Luckhardt, A. B., & Carlson, A. J. (1914) Contributions to the physiology of the stomach: XVII. On the chemical control of the gastric hunger mechanism. *Amer. J. Physiol.* **36,** 37–46. [210]

Luria, A. R. (1932) *The nature of human conflicts.* New York: Liveright. [332]

Lybrand, W. A., Andrews, T. G., & Ross, S. (1954) Systemic fatigue and perceptual organization. *Amer. J. Psychol.* **67,** 704–707. [144]

McCleary, R. A. (1953) Taste and post-ingestion factors in specific-hunger behavior. *J. comp. physiol. Psychol.* **46,** 411–421. [235]

McCleary, R. A., & Morgan, C. T. (1946) Food hoarding in rats as a function of environmental temperature. *J. comp. physiol. Psychol.* **39,** 371–378. [126]

McClelland, D. C. (1942) Functional autonomy of motives as an extinction phenomenon. *Psychol. Rev.* **49,** 272–283. [318, 572]

McClelland, D. C. (1950) Review of Maier's *Frustration. J. abn. soc. Psychol.* **45,** 564–566. [427]

McClelland, D. C. (1951) *Personality.* New York: William Sloane Associates (Dryden Press). [322, 374, 427]

McClelland, D. C. (Ed.) (1955a) *Studies in motivation.* New York: Appleton-Century-Crofts. [374]

McClelland, D. C. (1955b) Notes for a revised theory of motivation. In McClelland, D.C. (Ed.) *Studies in motivation.* New York: Appleton-Century-Crofts, pp. 226–234. [374]

McClelland, D. C. (1958a) Risk-taking in children with high and low need for achievement. In Atkinson, J. W. (Ed.) *Motives in fantasy, action and society.* New York: Van Nostrand, pp. 306–321. [740]

McClelland, D. C. (1958b) Methods of measuring human motivation. In Atkinson, J. W. (Ed.) *Motives in fantasy, action and society: A method of assessment and study.* New York: Van Nostrand, pp. 7–42. [800]

McClelland, D. C., & Apicella, F. S. (1945) A functional classification of verbal reactions to experimentally induced failure. *J. abn. soc. Psychol.* **40,** 376–390. [751]

McClelland, D. C., & Apicella, F. S. (1947) Reminiscence following experimentally induced failure. *J. exp. Psychol.* **37,** 159–169. [785]

McClelland, D. C., & Atkinson, J. W. (1948) The projective expression of needs. I: The effect of different intensities of the hunger drive on perception. *J. Psychol.* **25,** 205–222. [716]

McClelland, D. C., Atkinson, J. W., & Clark, R. A. (1949) The projective expression of needs. III: The effect of ego-involvement, success, and failure on perception. *J. Psychol.* **27,** 311–330. [716]

McClelland, D. C., Atkinson, J. W., Clark, R. A., & Lowell, E. L. (1953) *The achievement motive.* New York: Appleton-Century-Crofts. [12, 374, 376,

378, 379, 380, 381, 470, 715–716, 717, 718, 719, 720, 721, 722, 723, 724, 730, 731, 732, 733, 734, 735, 763, 764, 826]

McClelland, D. C., Baldwin, A. L., Bronfenbrenner, U., & Strodtbeck, F. L. (1958) *Talent and society*. New York: Van Nostrand.   [571]

McClelland, D. C., Clark, R. A., Roby, T. B., & Atkinson, J. W. (1949) The projective expression of needs. IV. The effect of the need for achievement on thematic apperception. *J. exp. Psychol.* 39, 242–255.   [716, 717, 718, 719, 722]

McClelland, D. C., & Friedman, G. A. (1952) A cross-cultural study of the relationship between child-training practices and achievement motivation appearing in folk tales. In Swanson, G. E., Newcomb, T. M., & Hartley, E. L. (Eds.) *Readings in social psychology*. New York: Holt, pp. 243–249.   [764]

McClelland, D. C., & Liberman, A. M. (1949) The effect of need for achievement on recognition of need-related words. *J. Person.* 18, 236–251.   [732]

McClelland, D. C., Rindlisbacher, A., & DeCharms, R. (1955) Religious and other sources of parental attitudes toward independence training. In McClelland, D. C. (Ed.) *Studies in motivation*. New York: Appleton-Century-Crofts, pp. 389–397.   [764]

McCord, F. (1941) The effect of frustration on hoarding in rats. *J. comp. Psychol.* 32, 531–541.   [124]

MacCorquodale, K., & Meehl, P. E. (1948) On a distinction between hypothetical constructs and intervening variables. *Psychol. Rev.* 55, 95–107.   [598]

MacCorquodale, K., & Meehl, P. E. (1953) Preliminary suggestions as to a formalization of expectancy theory. *Psychol. Rev.* 60, 55–63.   [467, 510]

MacCorquodale, K., & Meehl, P. E. (1954) Edward C. Tolman. In Estes, W. K., et al. *Modern learning theory*. New York: Appleton-Century-Crofts, pp. 177–266.   [467, 505, 506, 510]

McDonald, M., McGuire, C., & Havighurst, R. J. (1949) Leisure activities and the socioeconomic status of children. *Amer. J. Sociol.* 54, 505–519.   [570]

McDonough, L. B. (1958) A developmental study of motivation and reactions to frustration. Unpubl. doctoral dissert., Michigan State University.   [750]

McDougall, W. (1908) *An introduction to social psychology* (30th ed., 1950) London: Methuen.   [30, 31, 38, 39, 40, 368, 390, 568]

McDougall, W. (1923) *Outline of psychology*. Boston: Scribner.   [57]

McDougall, W. (1926) *An introduction to social psychology*. Boston: Luce and Co.   [57]

McDougall, W. (1933) *The energies of men*. New York: Scribner.   [57]

Mace, C. A. (1953) Homeostasis, needs and values. *Brit. J. Psychol.* 44, 200–210.   [325]

McFarland, R. A. (1946) *Human factors in air transport design*. New York: McGraw-Hill.   [142]

McFarland, R. A. (1953) *Human factors in air transportation*. New York: McGraw-Hill.   [135, 136, 141, 142]

McFarland, R. A., & Seitz, C. P. (1938) A psycho-somatic inventory. *J. appl. Psychol.* 22, 327–329.   [709]

McFarland, R. L., Clark, R. K., Powers, W. T., Arbit, J., & Van Buskirk, C. (1958) *Application of a general feedback theory to complex learning, concept formation and personality assessment*. Symposium, American Psychological Association Meetings, Washington, D.C., August 30, 1958.   [365]

MacFarlane, Jean W. (1939) The guidance study. *Sociometry* 2, 1–23.   [651]

McGeoch, J. A. (1942) *The psychology of human learning*. New York: Longmans, Green.   [13]

McKee, J. P., & Honzik, M. P. (1962) The sucking behavior of mammals: An illustration of the nature-nurture question. In Postman, L. (Ed.) *Psychology in the making: Histories of selected research problems*. New York: Knopf, pp. 585–661.   [113, 114]

McKelvey, R. K., & Marx, M. H. (1951) Effects of infantile food and water deprivation on adult hoarding in the rat. *J. comp. physiol. Psychol.* 44, 423–430. [124]

MacKinnon, D. W. (1954) A topological analysis of anxiety. In Brand, H. (Ed.) *The study of personality.* New York: Wiley, pp. 135–147. [359]

MacLeod, R. (1947) The phenomenological approach to social psychology. *Psychol. Rev.* 54, 193 210. [662]

MacLeod, R. B. (1957) Impact of diet on behavior. *Amer. J. clin. Nutrition* 5, 107–108. [19]

McMurray, G. A. (1950) Experimental study of a case of insensitivity to pain. *AMA Arch. neurol. Psychiat.* 64, 650–667. [261]

McMurray, G. A. (1955) Congenital insensitivity to pain and its implications for motivational theory. *Canad. J. Psychol.* 9, 121–131. [261]

McNeil, E. B. (1959) Psychology and aggression. *J. Conflict Resolution* 3, 195–293. [746]

McNiven, M. A. (1954) Responses of the chicken, duck, and pheasant to a hawk and goose silhouette—a controlled replication of Tinbergen's study. (Unpublished paper cited by Schneirla, 1956). [100]

McReynolds, P. (1956) A restricted conceptualization of human anxiety and motivation. *Psychol. Reports* 2, 293–312. [386]

Madsen, K. B. (1959) *Theories of motivation.* Copenhagen: Munksgaard. [2]

Magoun, H. W. (1952) The ascending reticular activating system. *Res. Publ. Ass. nerv. ment. Dis.* 30, 480–492. [325]

Magoun, H. W. (1958) *The waking brain.* Springfield, Ill.: Charles Thomas. [165, 356, 402, 601]

Magoun, H. W. (Ed.) (1959–1960) *Handbook of physiology. Section I. Neurophysiology.* Washington, D.C.: Amer. Physiol. Society, 3 vols. [150]

Mahl, G. F. (1949) Anxiety, HCl excretion, and peptic ulcer etiology. *Psychosom. Med.* 11, 30–44. [457]

Mahler, W. (1933) Ersatzhandlungen verschiedener Realitätgrades. *Psychol. Forsch.* 18, 27–89. [783]

Mahut, H. (1958) Breed differences in the dog's emotional behavior. *Canad. J. Psychol.* 12, 35–44. [410]

Maier, N. R. F. (1949) *Frustration: The study of behavior without a goal.* New York: McGraw-Hill. [8, 425]

Maier, N. R. F. (1956) Frustration theory: Restatement and extension. *Psychol. Rev.* 63, 370–388. [425, 428, 429]

Maier, N. R. F., & Ellen, P. (1951) Can the anxiety-reduction theory explain abnormal fixations? *Psychol. Rev.* 58, 435 445. [428]

Maier, N. R. F., & Ellen, P. (1954) Reinforcement vs. consistency of effect in habit modification. *J. comp. physiol. Psychol.* 47, 361 369. [428]

Malinowski, B. (1927) *Sex and repression in savage society.* New York: Harcourt, Brace. [652]

Malinowski, B. (1939) The group and the individual in functional analysis. *Amer. J. Sociol.* 44, 938–964. [326]

Malmo, R. B. (1957) Anxiety and behavioral arousal. *Psychol. Rev.* 64, 276–287. [394, 397, 398]

Malmo, R. B. (1958) Measurement of drive: An unsolved problem. In Jones, M. R. (Ed.) *Nebraska symposium on motivation, 1958.* Lincoln: University of Nebraska Press, pp. 229–265. [394, 396, 397]

Malmo, R. B. (1959) Activation: A neurophysiological dimension. *Psychol. Rev.* 66, 367–386. [397, 460]

Malmo, R. B., & Surwillo, W. W. (1960) Sleep deprivation: Changes in performance and physiological indicants of activation. *Psychol. Monogr.* 74, No. 15. [173]

Maltzman, I. (1952) The process need. *Psychol. Rev.* 59, 40–48. [553]

Maltzman, I., Fox, J., & Morrissett, L., Jr. (1953) Some effects of manifest anxiety on mental set. *J. exp. Psychol.* **46**, 50–54.   **[708]**

Mandler, G. (1962) Emotion. In Brown, R. N., Galanter, E., Hess, E. H., & Mandler, G. *New directions in psychology*. New York: Holt, Rinehart and Winston, pp. 267–343.   **[390, 391, 392]**

Mandler, G., & Kremen, I. (1958) Autonomic feedback: A correlational study. *J. Personal.* **26**, 388–399.   **[714]**

Mandler, G., Mandler, J. M., Kremen, I., & Sholiton, R. D. (1961) The response to threat: Relations among verbal and physiological indices. *Psychol. Monog.* **75**, Whole No. 513.   **[714]**

Mandler, G., Mandler, Jean M., & Uviller, Ellen T. (1958) Autonomic feedback: The perception of autonomic activity. *J. abn. soc. Psychol.* **56**, 367–373.   **[460, 714]**

Mandler, G., & Sarason, S. B. (1952) A study of anxiety and learning. *J. abn. soc. Psychol.* **47**, 166–173.   **[710, 711]**

Mangold, R., Sokoloff, L., Conner, E., Kleinerman, J., Therman, P. G., & Kety, S. S. (1955) The effects of sleep and lack of sleep on the cerebral circulation and metabolism of normal young men. *J. clin. Invest.* **34**, 1092–1100.   **[170]**

Mann, R. D. (1959) A review of the relationships between personality and performance in small groups. *Psychol. Bull.* **56**, 241–270.   **[777]**

Manning, H. M. (1956) The effect of varying conditions of hunger and thirst on two responses learned to hunger or thirst alone. *J. comp. physiol. Psychol.* **49**, 249–253.   **[264, 266]**

Margolin, J. B. (1954) The effect of perceived cooperation or competition on the transfer of hostility. Unpubl. doctoral dissert. New York University.   **[751]**

Margules, D. L., & Olds, J. (1962) Identical "feeding" and "rewarding" systems in the lateral hypothalamus of rats. *Science* **135**, 374–375.   **[545]**

Marina, A. (1915) Die Relationen des Palae-encephalons (Edinger) sind nicht fix. *Neurol. Centralbl.* **34**, 338 (cited by Ashby, W. R., The cerebral mechanisms of intelligent action. In Richter, D. [Ed.] *Perspectives in neuropsychiatry*. London: Lewis, 1950, pp. 79–94).   **[355]**

Marks, E. S. (1943) Skin color judgments of Negro college students. *J. abn. soc. Psychol.* **38**, 370–376.   **[339]**

Marler, P. (1957) Studies of fighting in chaffinches. IV: Appetitive and consummatory behavior. *Brit. J. anim. Behav.* **5**, 29–37.   **[748]**

Marshall, N. B., Barrnett, R. J., & Mayer, J. (1955) Hypothalamic lesions in goldthioglucose-injected mice. *Proc. Soc. exp. Biol. Med.* **90**, 240–244.   **[224]**

Martin, B. (1958) A factor analytic study of anxiety. *J. clin. Psychol.* **14**, 133–138.   **[710]**

Martin, B. (1959) The measurement of anxiety. *J. gen. Psychol.* **61**, 189–203.   **[710]**

Martin, B. (1961) The assessment of anxiety by physiological behavioral measures. *Psychol. Bull.* **58**, 234–255.   **[708, 713]**

Martin, W. W. (1945) Some basic implications of a concept of organism for psychology. *Psychol. Rev.* **52**, 333–343.   **[322, 323]**

Marx, M. H. (1950) A stimulus-response analysis of the hoarding habit in the rat. *Psychol. Rev.* **57**, 80–93.   **[123, 125]**

Marx, M. H. (1951) Experimental analysis of the hoarding habit in the rat. II: Terminal reinforcement. *J. comp. physiol. Psychol.* **44**, 168–177.   **[125]**

Marx, M. H. (1952) Infantile deprivation and adult behavior in the rat: Retention of increased rate of eating. *J. comp. physiol. Psychol.* **45**, 43–49.   **[124]**

Marx, M. H. (1956) Some relations between frustration and drive. In Jones, M. R. (Ed.) *Nebraska symposium on motivation, 1956*. Lincoln: University of Nebraska Press, pp. 92–130.   **[415, 419, 421, 422]**

Marx, M. H. (1957) Experimental analysis of the hoarding habit in the rat. III:

Terminal reinforcement under low drive. *J. comp. physiol. Psychol.* **50**, 168–171.   [125]

Marx, M. H., & Brownstein, A. J. (1957) Experimental analysis of the hoarding habit in the rat. IV: Terminal reinforcement followed by high drive at test. *J. comp. physiol. Psychol.* **50**, 617–620.   [125]

Marx, M. H., Henderson, R. L., & Roberts, C. L. (1955) Positive reinforcement of the bar-pressing response by a light stimulus following dark operant pretests with no aftereffect. *J. comp. physiol. Psychol.* **48**, 73–76.   [541]

Marx, M. H., Iwahara, S., & Brownstein, A. J. (1957) Hoarding behavior in the hooded rat as a function of varied alley illumination. *J. genet. Psychol.* **90**, 213–218.   [126]

Marx, M. H., & Murphy, W. W. (1961) Resistance to extinction as a function of the presentation of a motivating cue in the startbox. *J. comp. physiol. Psychol.* **54**, 207–210.   [564]

Maslow, A. H. (1936) The role of dominance in the social and sexual behavior of infra-human primates. III: A theory of sexual behavior of infra-human primates. *J. genet. Psychol.* **48**, 310–338.   [747]

Maslow, A. H. (1941) Deprivation, threat and frustration. *Psychol. Rev.* **48**, 364–366.   [751]

Maslow, A. H. (1943) Conflict, frustration and the theory of threat. *J. abn. soc. Psychol.* **38**, 81–86.   [415, 418]

Maslow, A. H. (1954) *Motivation and personality*. New York: Harper.   [2, 8, 666, 668, 669, 670, 676, 677, 678, 679, 680, 682, 684, 747]

Maslow, A. H. (1955) Deficiency motivation and growth motivation. In Jones, M. R. (Ed.) *Nebraska symposium on motivation, 1955*. Lincoln. University of Nebraska Press, pp. 1–30.   [670, 671, 678, 680]

Maslow, A. H. (1957) Two kinds of cognition and their integration. *Gen. Semant. Bull.* Nos. **20, 21**, 17–22.   [671]

Maslow, A. H. (1958*a*) Emotional blocks to creativity. *J. Indiv. Psychol.* **14**, 51–56.   [671]

Maslow, A. H. (1958*b*) *Creativity in self-actualizing people*. Lecture given in Creativity Symposium, Michigan State University, East Lansing, Michigan.   [671]

Maslow, A. H. (1959*a*) Cognition of being in the peak experiences. *J. genet. Psychol.* **94**, 43–66.   [672]

Maslow, A. H. (1959*b*) Critique of self-actualization. I: Some dangers of being-cognition. *J. Indiv. Psychol.* **15**, 24–32.   [671, 672]

Maslow, A. H. (1959*c*) Psychological data and value theory. In Maslow, A. H. (Ed.) *New knowledge in human values*. New York: Harper.   [678, 679, 682]

Mason, J. W. (1958) The central nervous system regulation of ACTH secretion. In Jasper, H., et al. (Eds.) *Reticular formation of the brain*. Boston: Little, Brown and Co., pp. 645–662.   [313, 460]

Mason, J. W. (1959) Psychological influence on the pituitary-adrenal cortical system. In Pincus, G. (Ed.) *Recent progress in hormone research*. Proceedings of the Laurentian Hormone Conference, vol. XV. New York: Academic Press, pp. 345–389.   [313, 443, 460]

Mason, W. A., Harlow, H. F., & Rueping, R. R. (1959) The development of manipulatory responsiveness in the infant rhesus monkey. *J. comp. physiol. Psychol.* **52**, 555–558.   [296]

Masserman, J. H. (1943) *Behavior and neurosis*. Chicago: University of Chicago Press.   [262]

Masserman, J. H. (1946) *Principles of dynamic psychiatry*. Philadelphia: Saunders.   [317, 323, 584]

Masserman, J. H., & Yum, K. (1946) An analysis of the influence of alcohol on experimental neuroses in cats. *Psychosom. Med.* **8**, 36–52.   [583]

Matarazzo, J. D. (1954) An experimental study of aggression in the hypertensive patient. *J. Personal.* **22**, 423–447.   [755]

Mathers, B. L. (1957) The effect of certain parameters on the acquisition of fear. *J. comp. physiol. Psychol.* **50**, 329–333.   [575]

Matthews, G. V. T. (1955) *Bird navigation.* Cambridge: Cambridge University Press.   [127, 128, 129, 130]

Matthews, H. L. (1939) Visual stimulation and ovulation in pigeons. *Proc. Roy. Soc., B.* **126**, 557–560.   [191]

Maxwell, J. C. (1868) On Governors. *Proc. Roy. Soc.* **16**, 270.   [343]

May, M. A. (1948) Experimentally acquired drives. *J. exp. Psychol.* **38**, 66–77.   [576]

May, R. (1950) *The meaning of anxiety.* New York: Ronald Press.   [713]

May, R. (1953) *Man's search for himself.* New York: W. W. Norton.   [666]

May, R., Angel, E., & Ellenberger, H. F. (Eds.) (1958) *Existence: A new dimension in psychiatry and psychology.* New York: Basic Books.   [659, 660, 667]

Mayer, J. (1953a) Glucostatic mechanism of regulation of food intake. *New Engl. J. Med.* **249**, 13–16.   [223]

Mayer, J. (1953b) Genetic, traumatic and environmental factors in the etiology of obesity. *Physiol. Rev.* **33**, 472–508.   [223, 224]

Mayer, J. (1955) Regulation of energy intake and the body weight: The glucostatic theory and the lipostatic hypothesis. *Annals N.Y. Acad. Sci.* **63**, Art. 1, 15–43.   [223, 225]

Mayer, J., & Greenberg, R. M. (1953) Hyperthermia in hypothalamic hyperphagia. *Amer. J. Physiol.* **173**, 523–525.   [227]

Maze, J. R. (1953) On some corruptions of the doctrine of homeostasis. *Psychol. Rev.* **60**, 405–412.   [329]

Mead, Margaret (1935) *Sex and temperament in three primitive societies.* New York: Morrow.   [652]

Mednick, M. T. (1957) Mediated generalization and the incubation effect as a function of manifest anxiety. *J. abn. soc. Psychol.* **55**, 315–321.   [706]

Mednick, S. A. (1957) Generalization as a function of manifest anxiety and adaptation to psychological experiments. *J. consult. Psychol.* **21**, 491–494.   [706]

Meehl, P. E. (1950) On the circularity of the law of effect. *Psychol. Bull.* **47**, 52–75.   [496]

Meehl, P. E. (1954) *Clinical vs. statistical prediction: A theoretical analysis and a review of the evidence.* Minneapolis: University of Minnesota Press.   [662]

Meier, G. W., Foshee, D. P., Wittrig, J. J., Peeler, D. F., & Huff, F. W. (1960) Helson's residual factor versus innate S-R relations. *Psychol. Reports,* **6**, 61–62.   [542]

Mellinkoff, S. (1957) Digestive system. *Ann. rev. Physiol.* **19**, 175–204.   [226]

Melton, A. W. (1941) Learning. In Monroe, W. S. (Ed.) *Encyclopedia of educational research.* New York: Macmillan.   [13, 416]

Melzack, R., & Scott, T. H. (1957) The effects of early experience on the response to pain. *J. comp. physiol. Psychol.* **50**, 155–161.   [262]

Menninger, K. A. (1954) Psychological aspects of the organism under stress. I: The homeostatic regulatory function of the ego. *J. Amer. Psychoanalyt. A.* **2**, 67–106.   [317, 322, 323]

Merlan, P. (1945) Brentano and Freud. *J. hist. Ideas* **6**, 375–377.   [48]

Merlan, P. (1949) Brentano and Freud—a sequel. *J. hist. Ideas* **10**, 451.   [48]

Merton, P. A., & Pampiglione, G. (1950) Strength and fatigue. *Nature, Lond.* **166**, 527.   [137, 140]

Merton, R. K. (1949) *Social theory and social structure.* Glencoe, Ill.: Free Press.   [326]

Meryman, J. J. (1952) Magnitude of startle response as a function of hunger and fear. Unpubl. master's thesis, State University of Iowa. [577]

Meryman, J. J. (1953) The magnitude of an unconditioned GSR as a function of fear conditioned at a long CS–UCS interval. Unpubl. doctoral dissert., State University of Iowa. [577]

Metzger, R., Cotton, J. W., & Lewis, D. J. (1957) Effect of reinforcement magnitude and order of presentation of different magnitudes on runway behavior. J. comp. physiol. Psychol. 50, 184–188. [554]

Meyer, D. R. (1951) Food deprivation and discrimination reversal learning by monkeys. J. exp. Psychol. 41, 10–16. [521]

Meyer, D. R. (1955) Comparative psychology. Ann. rev. Psychol. 6, 251–266. [102]

Meyer, M. F. (1933) That whale among the fishes—the theory of emotions. Psychol. Rev. 40, 292–300. [368]

Michels, W. C., & Helson, H. (1949) A reformulation of the Fechner Law in terms of adaptation-level applied to rating-scale data. Amer. J. Psychol. 62, 355–368. [338]

Miles, R. C. (1958) Learning in kittens with manipulatory, exploratory and food incentives. J. comp. physiol. Psychol. 51, 39–42. [295]

Miles, R. C. (1959) Discrimination in the squirrel monkey as a function of deprivation and problem difficulty. J. exp. Psychol. 57, 15–19. [521]

Miles, R. C., & Wickens, D. D. (1953) Effect of a secondary reinforcer on the primary hunger drive. J. comp. physiol. Psychol. 46, 77–79. [540]

Miles, W. R. (1919) The sex expression of men living on a lowered nutritional level. J. nerv. ment. Dis. 49, 208–224. [264]

Miller, D. R., & Swanson, G. E. (1958) The changing American parent. New York: Wiley. [571]

Miller, G. A., & Postman, L. J. (1946) Individual and group hoarding in rats. Amer. J. Psychol. 59, 652–668. [126]

Miller, G. A., & Viek, P. (1944) An analysis of the rat's response to unfamiliar aspects of the hoarding situation. J. comp. Psychol. 37, 221–231. [126]

Miller, J. G. (1942) Unconsciousness. New York: Wiley (out of print). [159, 594]

Miller, J. G. (1953) The development of experimental stress—sensitive tests for predicting performance in military tasks. PRB Tech. Rep. 1079. Washington, D.C.: Psychological Research Associates. [449, 450]

Miller, J. G. (1961) Sensory overloading. In Flaherty, B. E. (Ed.) Psychophysiological aspects of space flight. New York: Columbia University Press, pp. 215–224. [456]

Miller, N. E. (1941) The frustration-aggression hypothesis. Psychol. Rev. 38, 337–342. [424, 572, 573, 745, 751]

Miller, N. E. (1944) Experimental studies of conflict. In Hunt, J. McV. (Ed.) Personality and the behavior disorders. New York: Ronald Press, pp. 431–465. [430, 431, 432, 433, 435, 436, 758]

Miller, N. E. (1948a) Studies of fear as an acquirable drive. I: Fear as motivation and fear-reduction as reinforcement in the learning of new responses. J. exp. Psychol. 38, 89–101. [497, 573, 575]

Miller, N. E. (1948b) Theory and experiment relating psychoanalytic displacement to stimulus-response generalization. J. abn. soc. Psychol. 43, 155–178. [423, 438, 497, 652, 748, 759]

Miller, N. E. (1951a) Learnable drives and rewards. In Stevens, S. S. (Ed.) Handbook of experimental psychology. New York: Wiley, pp. 435–472. [13, 98, 496, 497, 573, 574, 575, 586, 742]

Miller, N. E. (1951b) Comments on multiple-process conceptions of learning. Psychol. Rev. 58, 375–381. [496, 501, 586]

Miller, N. E. (1951c) Comments on theoretical models illustrated by the development of a theory of conflict behavior. *J. Pers.* 20, 82–100.   [436, 437, 438]

Miller, N. E. (1955) Shortcomings of food consumption as a measure of hunger; results from other behavioral techniques. *Annals N.Y. Acad. Sci.* 63, Art 1, 141–143.   [216]

Miller, N.F. (1956) Effects of drugs on motivation: The value of using a variety of measures. *Annals N.Y. Acad. Sci.* 65, Art 4, 318–333.   [238, 239, 255, 256]

Miller, N. E. (1957) Experiments on motivation: Studies combining psychological, physiological and pharmacological techniques. *Science* 126, 1271–1278.   [215, 216, 254, 313, 540]

Miller, N. E. (1958) Central stimulation and other new approaches to motivation and reward. *Amer. Psychologist* 13, 100–108.   [221, 436]

Miller, N. E. (1959) Liberalization of basic S-R concepts: Extensions to conflict behavior, motivation and social learning. In Koch, S. (Ed.) *Psychology: A study of a science,* Vol. II. New York: McGraw-Hill, pp. 196–292.   [436, 494, 495, 496]

Miller, N. E. (1960) Some motivational effects of brain stimulation and drugs. *Federation Proc.* 19, 846–854.   [431]

Miller, N. E., Bailey, C. J., & Stevenson, J. A. F. (1950) Decreased "hunger" but increased food intake resulting from hypothalamic lesions. *Science* 112, 256–259.   [221]

Miller, N. E., & Bugelski, R. (1948) Minor studies of aggression. II: The influence of frustrations imposed by the in-group on attitudes expressed toward outgroups. *J. Psychol.* 25, 437–442.   [759]

Miller, N. E., & Dollard, J. (1941) *Social learning and imitation.* New Haven: Yale University Press.   [44, 58, 494, 495, 496, 572, 745, 746]

Miller, N. E., & Kessen, M. L. (1952) Reward effects of food via stomach fistula compared with those of food via mouth. *J. comp. physiol. Psychol.* 45, 555–564.   [216, 540]

Miller, N. E., & Lawrence, D. H. (1950) Studies of fear as an acquirable drive. III: Effect of strength of electric shock as a primary drive and of number of trials with the primary drive on the strength of fear. (unpublished paper cited in Miller, 1951a).   [263]

Miller, N. E., Sampliner, R. I., & Woodrow, P. (1957) Thirst-reducing effects of water by stomach fistula vs. water by mouth measured by both a consummatory and an instrumental response. *J. comp. physiol. Psychol.* 50, 1–5. [253]

Miller, R. Mirsky, I. A., & Stein, M. (1953) Relation of adrenocortical activity and adaptive behavior. *Psychosom. Med.* 15, 574–583.   [313]

Miller, R. E., & Ogawa, N. (1962) The effect of adrenocorticotrophic hormone (ACTH) on avoidance conditioning in the adrenalectomized rat. *J. comp. physiol. Psychol.* 55, 211–214.   [313]

Minnick, R. S., Warden, C. J., & Arieti, S. (1946) The effects of sex hormones on the copulatory behavior of senile white rats. *Science* 103, 749–750.   [181]

Minor, C. A., & Neel, R. G. (1958) The relationship between achievement motive and occupational preference. *J. couns. Psychol.* 5, 39–43.   [740]

Mintz, A. (1946) A re-examination of correlations between lynchings and economic indices. *J. abn. soc. Psychol.* 41, 159–160.   [750]

Moede, W. (1920) Experimentelle Massenpsychologie. Leipzig: Hirzel.   [776]

Moeller, G., & Applezweig, M. H. (1957) A motivational factor in conformity. *J. abn. soc. Psychol.* 55, 114–120.   [778]

Moltz, H. (1960) Imprinting: Empirical basis and theoretical significance. *Psychol. Bull.* 57, 291–314.   [90]

Moltz, H., & Rosenblum, L. A. (1958) Imprinting and associative learning: The stability of the following response in Peking ducks (*Anas Platyrhynchous*). *J. comp. physiol. Psychol.* 51, 580–583.   [90]

Moltz, H., Rosenblum, L., & Halikas, N. (1959) Imprinting and level of anxiety. *J. comp. physiol. Psychol.* 52, 240–244.   [90]

Money, J. (1961) Sex hormones and other variables in human eroticism. In Young, W. C. (Ed.) *Sex and internal secretions,* 2 vols. (3rd ed.) Baltimore: Williams & Wilkins, pp. 1383–1400.   [177]

Monjauze, R., Plas, F., Verdeaux, G., Verdeaux, J., Bourdinaud, J., Missenard, A., & Le Febvre, R. (1953) Clinical research on the subject of a test on aviator's fatigue. *J. aviat. Med.* 24, 143–145.   [144]

Montemurro, D. G., & Stevenson, J. A. F. (1957) Adipsia produced by hypothalamic lesions in the rat. *Canad. J. Biochem. Physiol.* 35, 31–37.   [219]

Montgomery, A. V., & Holmes, J. H. (1951) Role of the gastrointestinal tract in the satisfaction of thirst. *Amer. J. Physiol.* 167, 811 (Abstr.).   [253]

Montgomery, A. V., & Holmes, J. H. (1955) Gastric inhibition of the drinking response. *Amer. J. Physiol.* 182, 227–231.   [253]

Montgomery, K. C. (1951a) "Spontaneous alternation" as a function of time between trials and amount of work. *J. exp. Psychol.* 42, 82–93.   [288]

Montgomery, K. C. (1951b) The relation between exploratory behavior and spontaneous alternation in the white rat. *J. comp. physiol. Psychol.* 44, 582–589.   [288, 291]

Montgomery, K. C. (1952a) Exploratory behavior and its relation to spontaneous alternation in a series of maze exposures. *J. comp. physiol. Psychol.* 45, 50–57.   [289, 291]

Montgomery, K. C. (1952b) A test of two explanations of spontaneous alternation. *J. comp. physiol. Psychol.* 45, 287–293.   [289]

Montgomery, K. C. (1953a) Exploratory behavior as a function of "similarity" of stimulus situations. *J. comp. physiol. Psychol.* 46, 129–133.   [292]

Montgomery, K. C. (1953b) The effect of activity deprivation upon exploratory behavior. *J. comp. physiol. Psychol.* 46, 438–441.   [272, 290, 299]

Montgomery, K. C. (1953c) The effect of the hunger and thirst drives upon exploratory behavior. *J. comp. physiol. Psychol.* 46, 315–319.   [290]

Montgomery, K. C. (1954) The role of the exploratory drive in learning. *J. comp. physiol. Psychol.* 47, 60–64.   [294, 541]

Montgomery, K. C. (1955) The relations between fear induced by novel stimulation and exploratory behavior. *J. comp. physiol. Psychol.* 48, 254–260.   [291]

Montgomery, K. C., & Monkman, J. A. (1955) The relations between fear and exploratory behavior. *J. comp. physiol. Psychol.* 48, 132–136.   [291]

Montgomery, K. C., & Segall, M. (1955) Discrimination learning based upon the exploratory drive. *J. comp. physiol. Psychol.* 48, 225–228.   [294, 541]

Montgomery, K. C., & Zimbardo, P. G. (1957) Effect of sensory and behavioral deprivation upon exploratory behavior in the rat. *Percept. mot. Skills* 7, 223–229.   [294]

Montgomery, M. F. (1931a) The role of the salivary glands in the thirst mechanism. *Amer. J. Physiol.* 96, 221–227.   [247]

Montgomery, M. F. (1931b) The influence of atropin and pilocarpin on thirst (voluntary ingestion of water). *Amer. J. Physiol.* 98, 35–41.   [247]

Moore, K. (1944) Controlled temperatures and preliminary measures of motivation of the white rat. *J. exp. Psychol.* 34, 516–524.   [133]

Moreno, J. L. (1946) *Psychodrama.* New York: Beacon Press.   [629]

Morgan, C. D., & Murray, H. (1935) Method for investigating fantasies—the thematic apperception test. *Arch. neurol. Psychiat.* 34, 289–306.   [720]

Morgan, C. T. (1943) *Physiological psychology.* New York: McGraw-Hill.   [109, 222, 266, 271, 323, 391, 392]

Morgan, C. T. (1947) The hoarding instinct. *Psychol. Rev.* 54, 335–341.   [123, 126, 652]

Morgan, C. T. (1956) *Introduction to psychology.* New York: McGraw-Hill. [57]

Morgan, C. T. (1957) Physiological mechanisms of motivation. In Jones, M. R. (Ed.) *Nebraska symposium on motivation, 1957.* Lincoln: University of Nebraska Press, pp. 1–35. [222, 313]

Morgan, C. T. (1959) Physiological theory of drive. In Koch, S. (Ed.) *Psychology: A study of a science.* Vol. I. New York: McGraw-Hill, pp. 644–671. [234, 266]

Morgan, C. T., & Fields, P. E. (1938) The effect of variable preliminary feeding upon the rat's speed of locomotion. *J. comp. Psychol.* 26, 331–348. [552]

Morgan, C. T., & Morgan, J. T. (1940) Studies in hunger. II: The relation of gastric denervation and dietary sugar to the effect of insulin upon food-intake in the rat. *J. genet. Psychol.* 57, 153–163. [209]

Morgan, C. T., & Stellar, E. (1950) *Physiological psychology* (2nd ed.) New York: McGraw-Hill. [122, 159, 165, 170, 217, 222, 229, 230, 249, 260, 271, 305]

Morgan, C. T., Stellar, E., & Johnson, O. (1943) Food deprivation and hoarding in rats. *J. comp. Psychol.* 35, 275–295. [123]

Morgane, P. J. (1961) Distinct "feeding" and "hunger motivating" systems in the lateral hypothalamus of the rat. *Science* 133, 887–888. [222]

Moruzzi, G., & Magoun, H. W. (1949) Brain stem reticular formation and activation of the EEG. *EEG and clin. Neurophysiol.* 1, 455–473. [165, 399]

Moskowitz, M. J. (1959) Running-wheel activity in the white rat as a function of combined food and water deprivation. *J. comp. physiol. Psychol.* 52, 621–625. [275]

Moss, F. A. (1924) Study of animal drives. *J. exp. Psychol.* 7, 165–185. [132, 264]

Mote, F. A., Jr., & Finger, F. W. (1942) Exploratory drive and secondary reinforcement in the acquisition and extinction of a simple running response. *J. exp. Psychol.* 31, 57–68. [288]

Moulton, R. W. (1958) Notes for a projective measure of fear of failure. In Atkinson, J. W. (Ed.) *Motives in fantasy, action and society.* New York: Van Nostrand, pp. 563–571. [729]

Moulton, R. W., Raphelson, A. C., Kristofferson, A. B., & Atkinson, J. W. (1958) The achievement motive and perceptual sensitivity under two conditions of motive-arousal. In Atkinson, J. W. (Ed.) *Motives in fantasy, action and society.* New York: Van Nostrand, pp. 350–366. [732]

Moustakas, C. E. (Ed.) (1956) *The self: Explorations in personal growth.* New York: Harper. [667]

Mowrer, O. H. (1938) Some research implications of the frustration concept as related to social and educational problems. *Character and Pers.* 7, 129–135. [419]

Mowrer, O. H. (1939) A stimulus-response analysis of anxiety and its role as a reinforcing agent. *Psychol. Rev.* 46, 553–565. [499]

Mowrer, O. H. (1940) An experimental analogue of "regression" with incidental observations on "reaction formation." *J. abn. soc. Psychol.* 35, 56–87. [424, 652]

Mowrer, O. H. (1947) On the dual nature of learning: A reinterpretation of "conditioning" and "problem solving." *Harvard educ. Rev.* 17, 102–148 (reprinted in Mowrer, 1950a). [467, 500]

Mowrer, O. H. (1950a) *Learning theory and personality dynamics: Selected papers.* New York: Ronald Press. [499, 500, 572, 641, 693]

Mowrer, O. H. (1950b) Review of N.R.F. Maier. *Frustration—The study of behavior without a goal. Science* 111, 434. [427]

Mowrer, O. H. (1950c) Comment on Estes' study: "Generalization of secondary reinforcement from the primary drive." *J. comp. physiol. Psychol.* 43, 148–151. [685]

Mowrer, O. H. (1951) Two-factor learning theory: Summary and comment. *Psychol. Rev.* **58**, 350–354.   [501]

Mowrer, O. H. (1952) Motivation. *Ann. rev. Psychol.* **3**, 419–438.   [52, 500]

Mowrer, O. H. (1954) Ego psychology, cybernetics, and learning theory. In the *Kentucky symposium on learning theory, personality theory, and clinical research.* New York: Wiley, pp. 81–90.   [502]

Mowrer, O. H. (1956) Two-factor learning theory reconsidered, with special reference to secondary reinforcement and the concept of habit. *Psychol. Rev.* **63**, 114–128.   [467, 499, 501, 502]

Mowrer, O. H. (1960) *Learning theory and behavior.* New York: Wiley.   [427, 428, 439, 452, 467, 501, 502]

Mowrer, O. H., & Jones, Helen M. (1943) Extinction and behavior variability as functions of effortfulness of task. *J. exp. Psychol.* **33**, 369–386.   [155]

Mowrer, O. H., & Kluckhohn, C. (1944) Dynamic theory of personality. In Hunt, J. McV. (Ed.) *Personality and the behavior disorders* (2 vols.) New York: Ronald Press, pp. 69–135.   [500]

Moyer, K. E. (1957) The effect of shock on anxiety-motivated behavior in the rat. *J. genet. Psychol.* **91**, 197–203.   [537]

Mueller, C. G., Jr., & Schoenfeld, W. N. (1954) Edwin R. Guthrie. In Estes, W. K., et al. *Modern learning theory.* New York: Appleton-Century-Crofts, pp. 345–379.   [512]

Muenzinger, K. F. (1934a) Motivation in learning. I: Electric shock for correct response in the visual discrimination habit. *J. comp. Psychol.* **17**, 267–277.   [523]

Muenzinger, K. F. (1934b) Motivation in learning. II: The function of electric shock for right and wrong responses in human subjects. *J. exp. Psychol.* **17**, 439–448.   [523]

Muenzinger, K. F. (1942) *Psychology: The science of behavior.* New York: Harper.   [13]

Muenzinger, K. F., & Mize, R. H. (1933) The sensitivity of the white rat to electric shock: Threshold and skin resistance. *J. comp. Psychol.* **20**, 85–93.   [261]

Müller-Freienfels, R. (1935) *The evolution of modern psychology.* New Haven: Yale University Press.   [38, 42, 49]

Mullahy, P. (1945) A theory of interpersonal relations and the evolution of personality. *Psychiatry* **8**, 119–147.   [634]

Mullahy, P. (1948) *Oedipus: Myth and complex.* New York: Hermitage Press.   [589, 663, 664]

Munn, N. L. (1950) *Handbook of psychological research on the rat: An introduction to animal psychology.* Boston: Houghton-Mifflin.   [110, 122, 133, 185, 187, 238, 258, 271, 541, 748]

Munroe, R. (1955) *Schools of psychoanalytic thought.* New York: Dryden.   [589, 663, 664]

Murphy, G. (1932) *An historical introduction to modern psychology.* New York: Harcourt, Brace.   [594]

Murphy, G. (1947) *Personality: A biosocial approach to origins and structure.* New York: Harper.   [8, 272, 316, 329, 572, 617, 636–637, 826]

Murphy, G. (1950) *Historical introduction to modern psychology* (rev. ed.) New York: Harcourt, Brace.   [20, 26, 49]

Murphy, G. (1954) Social motivation. In Lindzey, G. (Ed.) *Handbook of social psychology* (2 vols.) Cambridge, Mass.: Addison-Wesley Press, Vol. II, pp. 601–633.   [44, 572]

Murphy, G., Murphy, L. B., & Newcomb, T. M. (1937) *Experimental social psychology: An interpretation of research upon the socialization of the individual.* New York: Harper.   [777]

Murray, E. J., Williams, H. L., & Lubin, A. (1958) Body temperature and psychological ratings during sleep deprivation. *J. exp. Psychol.* **56**, 271–273. [174]

Murray, H. A. (1933) The effect of fear upon estimates of the maliciousness of other personalities. *J. soc. Psychol.* **4**, 310–329. [727]

Murray, H. A. (1938) *Explorations in personality.* New York: Oxford University Press. [715, 719]

Murstein, B. I. (1956) The projection of hostility on the Rorschach and as a result of ego-threat. *J. proj. Tech.* **20**, 418–438. [753–754]

Mussen, P. H. (1953) Differences between the TAT responses of Negro and white boys. *J. consult. Psychol.* **17**, 373–376. [570]

Mussen, P. H., & Naylor, H. K. (1954) The relationships between overt and fantasy aggression. *J. abn. soc. Psychol.* **49**, 235–240. [755]

Mussen, P. H., & Scodel, A. (1955) The effect of sexual stimulation under varying conditions on TAT sexual responsiveness. *J. consult. Psychol.* **19**, 90. [728]

Myers, A. K., & Miller, N. E. (1954) Failure to find a learned drive based on hunger; evidence for learning motivated by "exploration." *J. comp. physiol. Psychol.* **47**, 428–436. [581]

Myers, J. L. (1958) Secondary reinforcement: A review of recent experimentation. *Psychol. Bull.* **55**, 284–301. [563]

Nagaty, M. O. (1951) The effect of reinforcement on closely following S–R connections. I: The effect of a backward conditioning procedure on the extinction of conditioned avoidance. *J. exp. Psychol.* **42**, 239–246. [537]

Nash, H. (1962) Psychologic effects of amphetamines and barbiturates. *J. nerv. ment. Dis.* **134**, 203–217. [145, 146]

Nash, Myrtle, C. (1950) An experimental test of the Michels-Helson theory of judgment. *Amer. J. Psychol.* **63**, 214–220. [338, 339]

Newcomb, T. M. (1953a) An approach to the study of communicative acts. *Psychol. Rev.* **60**, 393–404. [788]

Newcomb, T. M. (1953b) Motivation in social behavior. In Brown, J. S., et al. *Current theory and research in motivation: A symposium.* Lincoln: University of Nebraska Press, pp. 139–161. [788]

Newcomb, T. M. (1959) Individual systems of orientation. In Koch, S. (Ed.) *Psychology: A study of a science.* vol. III. New York: McGraw-Hill, pp. 384–422. [788]

Newman, W. J. (1961) *The futilitarian society.* New York: Braziller. [319]

Nicholls, E. E. (1922) A study of the spontaneous activity of the guinea pig. *J. comp. Psychol.* **2**, 303–330. [132]

Nissen, H. W. (1929) The effects of gonadectomy, vasotomy, and injections of placental and orchic extracts on the sex behavior of the white rat. *Genet. psychol. Monog.* **5**, 451–547. [176]

Nissen, H. W. (1930) A study of maternal behavior in the white rat by means of the obstruction method. *J. genet. Psychol.* **37**, 377–393. [112, 288]

Nissen, H. W. (1951) Social behavior in primates. In Stone, C. P. (Ed.) *Comparative psychology* (3rd ed.) New York: Prentice-Hall, pp. 423–457. [110, 111, 243, 748]

Nissen, H. W., Chow, K. L., & Semmes, Josephine (1951) Effects of restricted opportunity for tactual, kinesthetic, and manipulative experience on the behavior of a chimpanzee. *Amer. J. Psychol.* **64**, 485–507. [95]

Nissen, H. W., & Semmes, Josephine (1952) Comparative and physiological psychology. *Ann. rev. Psychol.* **3**, 233–260. [59, 101]

Noltie, H. R. (1953) A factor in postponing the onset of fatigue. In Floyd, W. F., & Welford, A. T. (Eds.) *Symposium on fatigue.* London: H. K. Lewis and Co., pp. 85–91. [136]

Novikoff, A. B. (1945) The concept of integrative levels and biology. *Science* **101**, 209–215. [322]

Novin, D., & Miller, N. E. (1962) Failure to condition thirst induced by feeding dry food to hungry rats. *J. comp. physiol. Psychol.* **55**, 373–374. [581]

Nowlis, Helen (1941) The influence of success and failure on the resumption of an interrupted task. *J. exp. Psychol.* **28**, 304–325. [783]

Nowlis, V. (1941) The relation of degree of hunger to competitive interaction in the chimpanzee. *J. comp. Psychol.* **32**, 91–115. [243]

Nowlis, V., & Nowlis, Helen (1956) The description and analysis of mood. *Annals N.Y. Acad. Sci.* **65**, 345–355. [145]

Nuttin, J. (1953) *Psychoanalysis and personality: A dynamic theory of normal personality.* New York: Sheed and Ward. [322, 323]

O'Connor, J., Lorr, M., & Stafford, J. W. (1956) Some patterns of manifest anxiety. *J. clin. Psychol.* **12**, 160–163. [710]

O'Connor, N., & Claridge, G. S. (1958) A 'Crespi effect' in male imbeciles. *Brit. J. Psychol.* **49**, 42–48. [554]

O'Kelley, L. I. (1940) An experimental study of regression. II: Some motivational determinants of regression and perseveration. *J. comp. Psychol.* **30**, 55–95. [424]

O'Kelley, L. I. (1954) The effect of preloads of water and sodium chloride on voluntary water intake of thirsty rats. *J. comp. physiol. Psychol.* **47**, 7–13. [250]

O'Kelley, L. I., & Falk, J. L. (1958) Water regulation in the rat. II: The effects of preloads of water and sodium chloride on the bar-pressing performance of thirsty rats. *J. comp. physiol. Psychol.* **51**, 22–25. [250]

O'Kelley, L. I., Falk, J. L., & Flint, D. (1958) Water regulation in the rat. I: Gastro-intestinal exchange rates of water and sodium chloride in thirsty animals. *J. comp. physiol. Psychol.* **51**, 16–21. [251]

Olds, J. (1955) Physiological mechanisms of reward. In Jones, M. R. (Ed.) *Nebraska symposium on motivation, 1955.* Lincoln: University of Nebraska Press, pp. 73–139. [373, 543, 544]

Olds, J. (1956a) A preliminary mapping of electrical reinforcing effects in the rat brain. *J. comp. physiol. Psychol.* **49**, 281–285. [544, 546]

Olds, J. (1956b) *The growth and structure of motives.* Glencoe, Ill.: Free Press. [2]

Olds, J. (1958a) Self-stimulation of the brain. *Science* **127**, 315–324. [543, 544, 546, 547, 548]

Olds, J. (1958b) Satiation effects in self-stimulation of the brain. *J. comp. physiol. Psychol.* **51**, 675–678. [544, 545]

Olds, J. (1959) High functions of the nervous system. *Ann. rev. Physiol.* **21**, 381–402. [544, 548]

Olds, J. (1962) Hypothalamic substrates of reward. *Physiol. Rev.* **42**, 554–604. [183, 544]

Olds, J., & Milner, P. (1954) Positive reinforcement produced by electrical stimulation of septal area and other regions of rat brain. *J. comp. physiol. Psychol.* **47**, 419–427. [543, 544]

Orlansky, H. (1949) Infant care and personality. *Psychol. Bull.* **46**, 1–48. [649, 687, 688]

Osgood, C. E. (1953) *Method and theory in experimental psychology.* New York: Oxford University Press. [475]

Osgood, C. E. (1957) Motivational dynamics of language behavior. In Jones, M. R. (Ed.) *Nebraska symposium on motivation, 1957.* Lincoln: University of Nebraska Press, pp. 348–424. [788]

Osgood, C. E. (1960) Cognitive dynamics in the conduct of human affairs. *Publ opin. Quart.* **24**, 341–365. [788]

Osgood, C. E., Suci, G. J., & Tannenbaum, P. H. (1957) *The measurement of meaning.* Urbana: University of Illinois Press. [788]

Osgood, C. E., & Tannenbaum, P. H. (1955) The principle of congruity in the prediction of attitude change. *Psychol. Rev.* 62, 42–55.   [788]

OSS Assessment Staff (1948) *Assessment of men.* New York: Rinehart.   [454, 749]

Oswald, I. (1962) *Sleeping and waking.* Amsterdam: Elsevier.   [159, 160, 161, 164, 167, 170, 171, 172, 173]

Oswald, I., Taylor, Anne M., & Treisman, M. (1960) Cortical function during human sleep. In Wolstenholme, G. E. W., & O'Connor, Maeve (Eds.) *Ciba Foundation symposium on the nature of sleep.* Boston: Little, Brown and Co., pp. 343–348.   [158]

Otani, T. (1953) Fatigue as a failure of nervous regularity. *Scientia* 88, 272–276. [137]

Otis, N. B., & McCandless, B. (1955) Responses to repeated frustrations of young children differentiated according to need area. *J. abn. soc. Psychol.* 50, 349–353.   [751]

Ovsiankina, Maria (1928) Die Wiederaufnahme von unterbrochener Handlungen. *Psychol. Forsch.* 11, 302–379.   [363, 783]

Pack, G. T. (1923) New experiments on the nature of the sensation of thirst. *Amer. J. Physiol.* 65, 346–349.   [247]

Paintal, A. S. (1954) A study of gastric stretch receptors. Their role in the peripheral mechanism of satiation of hunger and thirst. *J. Physiol.* 126, 255–270.   [215]

Palermo, D. S. (1957) Proactive interference and facilitation as a function of amount of training and stress. *J. exp. Psychol.* 53, 293–296.   [538]

Parkes, E. H. (1958) *Establishment of a conditioned drive based on hunger.* Unpubl. master's thesis, University of Maryland.   [581]

Parsons, T. (1949) *Essays in sociological theory.* Glencoe, Ill.: Free Press.   [326]

Pascal, G. R. (1951) Psychological deficit as a function of stress and constitution. *J. Personal.* 20, 175–187.   [450]

Passey, G. E. (1948) The influence of intensity of unconditioned stimulus upon acquisition of a conditioned response. *J. exp. Psychol.* 38, pp. 420–428.   [524]

Pastore, N. (1950) A neglected factor in the frustration-aggression hypothesis: A comment. *J. Psychol.* 29, 271–279.   [751]

Pastore, N. (1952) The role of arbitrariness in the frustration-aggression hypothesis. *J. abn. soc. Psychol.* 47, 728–731.   [423, 751]

Patterson, T. L. (1933) Comparative physiology of the gastric hunger mechanism. *Annals N.Y. Acad. Sci.* 34, 55–272.   [207]

Pavlov, I. P. (1927) *Conditioned reflexes* (transl. by G. V. Anrep). Oxford: Clarendon Press.   [148, 151, 153, 157, 262]

Pavlov, I. P. (1928) *Lectures on conditioned reflexes* (transl. by W. H. Gantt). New York: International Publishers.   [148, 151]

Pavlov, I. P. (1930) A brief outline of the higher nervous activity. In Murchison, C. (Ed.) *Psychologies of 1930.* Worcester, Mass.: Clark University Press, pp. 207–220.   [151]

Pavlov, I. P. (1941) *Conditioned reflexes and psychiatry* (transl. by W. H. Gantt). New York: International Publishers.   [151, 154]

Peak, Helen (1955) Attitude and motivation. In Jones, M. R. (Ed.) *Nebraska symposium on motivation, 1955.* Lincoln: University of Nebraska Press, pp. 149–189.   [386, 387, 388]

Peak, Helen (1958a) Psychological structure and psychological activity. *Psychol. Rev.* 65, 325–347.   [386]

Peak, Helen (1958b) Psychological structure and person perception. In Tagiuri, R., & Petrullo, L. (Eds.) *Person perception and interpersonal behavior.* Stanford, Calif.: Stanford University Press, pp. 337–352.   [386]

Peiper, A. (1951) Instinkt und angeborenes Schema bei Säugling. Z. *Tierpsychol.* 8, 449–456 (cited by Hess, E. H., 1953). [101]

Peirce, J. T., & Nuttall, R. L. (1961) Self-paced sexual behavior in the female rat. *J. comp. physiol. Psychol.* 54, 310–313. [193]

Pelc, S. R. (1959) Influence of sexual stimulation on the metabolic activity of deoxyribonucleic acid in the seminal vesicle. *Nature, London* 184, 1414. [192]

Penfield, W., & Rasmussen, T. (1950) *The cerebral cortex of man.* New York: Macmillan. [325]

Penrose, L. S. (1931) Freud's theory of instinct and other psychobiological theory. *Int. J. Psychoanaly.*, XII 87–97. [604]

Pereboom, A. C. (1957) A note on the Crespi effect. *Psychol. Rev.* 64, 263–264. [554]

Pereboom, A. C., & Crawford, B. M. (1958) Instrumental and competing behavior as a function of trials and reward magnitude. *J. exp. Psychol.* 56, 82–85. [554]

Perin, C. T. (1942) Behavior potentiality as a joint function of the amount of training and the degree of hunger at the time of extinction. *J. exp. Psychol.* 30, 93–113. [530]

Perin, C. T. (1943a) A quantitative investigation of the delay-of-reinforcement gradient. *J. exp. Psychol.* 32, 37–51. [485]

Perin, C. T. (1943b) The effect of delayed reinforcement upon the differentiation of bar responses in white rats. *J. exp. Psychol.* 32, 95–109. [485]

Perkins, C. C., Jr. (1947) The relation of secondary rewards to gradients of reinforcement. *J. exp. Psychol.* 37, 377–392. [485]

Perkins, C. C., Jr. (1953) The relation between conditioned stimulus intensity and response strength. *J. exp. Psychol.* 46, 225–231. [566]

Perkins, C. C., Jr., & Tilton, J. R. (1954) Change in stimulus conditions as a determiner of "regression" in the rat. *J. comp. physiol. Psychol.* 47, 341–343. [424]

Peters, H. N. (1942) The experimental study of affective judgments. *Psychol. Bull.* 39, 273–305. [382]

Peters, R. S. (Ed.) (1953) *Brett's history of psychology.* London: George Allen and Unwin. [27, 35, 40, 47]

Peters, R. S. (1958) *The concept of motivation.* London: Routledge and Kegan Paul. [2, 596]

Pfaffmann, C. (1955) Gustatory nerve impulses in rat, cat and rabbit. *J. Neurophysiol.* 18, 429–440. [233]

Pfaffmann, C., & Bare, J. K. (1950) Gustatory nerve discharges in normal and adrenalectomized rats. *J. comp. physiol. Psychol.* 43, 320–324. [234, 312]

Philip, B. R. (1951) The effect of general and specific labelling on judgmental scales. *Canad. J. Psychol.* 5, 18–28. [338]

Phillips, R. (1945) Doll play as a function of the realism of the materials and the length of the experimental session. *Child Develpm.* 16, 123–143. [758]

Piaget, J. (1936) *La Naissance de l'intelligence chez l'enfant.* Paris: Delachaux and Niestlé. [297]

Pick, J. (1954) The evolution of homeostasis: The phylogenetic development of the regulation of bodily and mental activities by the autonomic nervous system. *Proc. Amer. Phil. Soc.* 98, 298–303. [306]

Piéron, H. (1952) A test of mental fatigue based on visual fusion frequency. *BINOP* 8, 166. [146]

Pilgrim, F. J., & Patton, R. A. (1947) Patterns of self-selection of purified dietary components by the rat. *J. comp. physiol. Psychol.* 40, 343–348. [230, 232]

Pilkington, G. W., & McKellar, P. (1960) Inhibition: A symposium. I: Inhibition as a concept in psychology. *Brit. J. Psychol.* 51, 194–201. [147]

Pilz, G. F., & Ross, R. R. (1961) Imprinting as a function of arousal. *J. comp. physiol. Psychol.* 54, 602–604. [90]

Pincus, G., & Hoagland, H. (1950) Adrenal cortical responses to stress in normal men and in those with personality disorders. I: Some stress responses in normal and psychotic subjects. II: Analysis of pituitary-adrenal mechanism in man. *Amer. J. Psychiat.* 106, 641–659. [325]

Pinneau, S. R. (1950) A critique on the articles by Margaret Ribble. *Child Develpm.* 21, 203–228. [649, 687]

Pinneau, S. R. (1955a) The infantile disorders of hospitalism and anaclitic depression. *Psychol. Bull.* 52, 429–452. [649, 650, 687]

Pinneau, S. R. (1955b) Reply to Dr. Spitz. *Psychol. Bull.* 52, 459–462. [649, 650, 687]

Pintler, M. H. (1945) Doll play as a function of experimenter-child interaction and initial organization of materials. *Child Develpm.* 16, 145–166. [758]

Pittendrigh, C. S., & Bruce, V. G. (1957) An oscillator model for biological clocks. In Rudnick, D. (Ed.) *Rhythmic and synthetic processes in growth.* Princeton, N.J.: Princeton University Press, pp. 75–109. [92]

Pittendrigh, C. S., & Bruce, V. G. (1959) Daily rhythms as coupled oscillator systems and their relation to thermo-periodism and photo-periodism. In A.A.A.S. Symposium, *Photo-periodism and related phenomena in plants and animals.* Washington, D.C.: A.A.A.S., pp. 475–505. [92]

Poffenberger, A. T. (1938) Some unsolved problems of human adjustment. *Science* 87, 124–129. [314, 323]

Poffenberger, A. T. (1942) *Principles of applied psychology.* New York: Appleton-Century. [139]

Porter, J. H., Webster, F. A., & Licklider, J. C. R. (1951) The influence of age and food deprivation upon the hoarding behavior of rats. *J. comp. physiol. Psychol.* 44, 300–309. [126]

Porter, R. W., Conrad, D. G., & Brady, J. V. (1959) Some neural and behavioral correlates of electrical self-stimulation of the limbic system. *J. exp. anal. Behav.* 2, 43–55. [548]

Postman, L. (1947) The history and present status of the law of effect. *Psychol. Bull.* 44, 489–563. [52, 769]

Powelson, M. H. (1925) Gastric transplantation. *Science* 62, 247–248. [273]

Pratt, K. C., Nelson, A. K., & Sun, K. H. (1930) *The behavior of the newborn infant.* Columbus: The Ohio State University Press. [651]

Premack, D. (1959) Toward empirical behavior laws. I: Positive reinforcement. *Psychol. Rev.* 66, 219–233. [550]

Progoff, I. (1953) *Jung's psychology and its social meaning.* New York: Julian Press. [627]

Progoff, I. (1956) *The death and rebirth of psychology: An integrative evaluation of Freud, Adler, Jung, and Rank and the impact of their culminating insights on modern man.* New York: Julian Press. [663]

Prokasy, W. F., Jr., Grant, D. A., & Myers, N. A. (1958) Eyelid conditioning as a function of unconditioned stimulus intensity and intertrial interval. *J. exp. Psychol.* 55, 242–246. [524, 533]

Prokasy, W. F., Jr., & Truax, C. B. (1959) Reflex and conditioned responses as a function of manifest anxiety. *Amer. J. Psychol.* 72, 262–264. [706]

Pronko, N. H., & Leith, W. R. (1956) Behavior under stress: A study of its disintegration. *Psychol. Reports* 2, 205–222. [449]

Pubols, B. H., Jr. (1960) Incentive magnitude, learning and performance in animals. *Psychol. Bull.* 57, 89–115. [555]

Pumpian-Mindlin, E. (Ed.) (1952a) *Psychoanalysis as science.* Stanford, Calif.: Stanford University Press. [589, 638, 654]

Pumpian-Mindlin, E. (1952b) The position of psychoanalysis in relation to the biological and social sciences. In Pumpian-Mindlin, E. (Ed.) *Psychoanalysis as science.* Stanford, Calif.: Stanford University Press, pp. 125-158. [638, 649]

Quastler, H. (1953) (Ed.) *Essays on the use of information theory in biology.* Urbana: University of Illinois Press. [342]

Quigley, J. P. (1955) The role of the digestive tract in regulating the ingestion of food. *Annals N. Y. Acad. Sci.* 63, Art. 1, 6-14. [207, 211]

Quigley, J. P., & Lindquist, J. L. (1930) Action of phlorhizin on hunger contractions in the normal or vagotomized dog. *Amer. J. Physiol.* 92, 690-694. [212]

Räber, H. (1949) Das Verhalten gefangener Waldohreulen (*Asio otus otus*) und Wäldkäuze (*Strix aluco aluco*) zur Beute. *Behaviour* 2, 1-95. (English summary). (Cited by Tinbergen, N., 1951.) [69]

Rabin, A. I. (1957) Personality maturity of Kibbutz (Israeli collective settlement) and non-Kibbutz children as reflected in Rorschach. *J. proj. Tech.* 21, 148-153. [688]

Rabin, A. I. (1959) Attitudes of Kibbutz children to family and parents. *Amer. J. Orthopsychiat.* 29, 172-179. [688]

Ramond, C. K. (1953) Anxiety and task as determiners of verbal performance. *J. exp. Psychol.* 46, 120-124. [707]

Ramond, C. K. (1954a) Performance in instrumental learning as a joint function of delay of reinforcement and time of deprivation. *J. exp. Psychol.* 47, 248-250. [521]

Ramond, C. K. (1954b) Performance in selective learning as a function of hunger. *J. exp. Psychol.* 48, 265-270. [521]

Ramsay, A. O. (1951) Familial recognition in domestic birds. *Auk* 68, 1-16. [88]

Rank, O. (1929) *The trauma of birth.* New York: Harcourt, Brace. [628]

Rank, O. (1945) *Will therapy and truth and reality* (Taft, Julia, transl.) New York: Knopf. [628]

Rapaport, D. (Ed.) (1951a) *Organization and pathology of thought.* New York: Columbia University Press. [589, 654]

Rapaport, D. (1951b) The conceptual model of psychoanalysis. *J. Personal.* 20, 56-81. Also in Knight, R. P. & Friedman, C. R. (Eds.) *Psychoanalytic psychiatry and psychology: Clinical and theoretical papers.* Austen Riggs Center, vol. 1. New York: International Universities Press, 1954, pp. 221-247. [589, 636, 638]

Rapaport, D. (1953) On the psycho-analytic theory of affects. *Internat. J. Psycho-Anal.* 34, 177-198. Also in Knight, R. P. & Friedman, C. R. (1954) (Eds.), *Psychoanalytic psychiatry and psychology: Clinical and theoretical papers.* Austen Riggs Center, vol. 1. New York: International Universities Press, pp. 274-310, 1954. [642]

Rapaport, D. (1958) The theory of ego autonomy: A generalization. *Bull. Menn. Clinic* 22, 13-35. [598, 636, 638]

Rapaport, D. (1959) The structure of psychoanalytic theory: A systematizing attempt. In Koch, S. (Ed.) *Psychology: A study of a science,* vol. 3. New York: McGraw-Hill, pp. 55-183. [589, 592, 593, 607, 637, 638, 640, 641, 653, 655]

Rapaport, D. (1960) On the psychoanalytic theory of motivation. In Jones, M. R. (Ed.) *Nebraska symposium on motivation, 1960.* Lincoln: University of Nebraska Press, pp. 173-247. [589, 615, 616, 637, 638, 655]

Rapaport, D., & Gill, M. M. (1959) The points of view and assumptions of metapsychology. *Internat. J. Psycho-Anal.* 40, 153-162. [624, 638, 655]

Raphelson, A. C. (1957) The relationships among imaginative direct verbal and physiological measures of anxiety in an achievement situation. *J. abn. soc. Psychol.* **54**, 13–18.   [709, 740]

Raphelson, A. C., & Moulton, R. W. (1958) The relationship between imaginative and direct verbal measurements of test anxiety under two conditions of uncertainty. *J. Personal.* **26**, 556–567.   [740]

Rasmussen, J. E. (1963) Group behavior in isolation—Antarctica. Unpublished report. Bethesda, Md.: USN Med. Res. Inst.   [164]

Raup, R. B. (1925) *Complacency: The foundation of human behavior.* New York: Macmillan.   [303, 314]

Ray, J. T., Martin, O. E., Jr., & Alluisi, E. A. (1961) *Human performance as a function of the work-rest cycle. A review of selected studies.* Publ. No. 882. Washington, D.C.: National Academy of Sciences-National Research Council. [163]

Razran, G. (1961) The observable unconscious and the inferable conscious in current Soviet psychophysiology: Introceptive conditioning, semantic conditioning, and the orienting reflex. *Psychol. Rev.* **68**, 81–147.   [265]

Reed, J. D. (1947) Spontaneous activity of animals. *Psychol. Bull.* **44**, 393–412. [271]

Reich, W. (1933) *Character-analysis.* Los Angeles: Orgone Institute Press (2nd ed., 1945).   [629, 641]

Reid, L. S., & Finger, F. W. (1955) The rat's adjustment to 23-hour food-deprivation cycles. *J. comp. physiol. Psychol.* **48**, 110–113.   [241, 274]

Reid, L. S., & Finger, F. W. (1957) The effect of activity restriction upon adjustment to cyclic food deprivation. *J. comp. physiol. Psychol.* **50**, 491–494. [241, 274]

Reid, R. L. (1960) Inhibition: A symposium: V. Inhibition—Pavlov, Hull, Eysenck. *Brit. J. Psychol.* **51**, 226–232.   [151, 156]

Reiser, M. F., Reeves, R. B., & Armington, J. (1955) Effect of variations in laboratory procedure and experiments on ballistocardiogram, blood pressure, and heart rate in healthy young men. *Psychosom. Med.* **17**, 185–199.   [757]

Reitan, R. M. (1957) The comparative effects of placebo, Ultran, and meprobamate on psychologic test performances. *Antihistic Med. and clin. Ther.* **4**, 158–165. [145]

Reitman, W. R., & Atkinson, J. W. (1958) Some methodological problems in the use of thematic apperceptive measures of human motives. In Atkinson, J. W. (Ed.), *Motives in fantasy, action and society.* New York: Van Nostrand, pp. 664–683.   [723, 737]

Remane, A. (1956) *Die Grundlagen des natürlichen Systems der vergleichenden Anatomie und der Phylogenetik.* Leipzig: Akad. Verlag.   [81]

Rethlingshafer, Dorothy (1943) Experimental evidence for functional autonomy of motives. *Psychol. Rev.* **50**, 397–407.   [572]

Reynolds, B., Marx, M. H., & Henderson, R. L. (1952) Resistance to extinction as a function of drive-reward interaction. *J. comp. physiol. Psychol.* **45**, 36–42. [558]

Reynolds, R. W. (1958) The relationship between stimulation voltage and rate of hypothalamic self-stimulation in the rat. *J. comp. physiol. Psychol.* **51**, 193–198.   [548]

Reynolds, W. F., & Pavlik, W. B. (1958) Running speed as a function of deprivation period and reward magnitude. *J. comp. physiol. Psychol.* **53**, 615–618. [558]

Rheingold, H. L. (1956) The modification of social responsiveness in institutional babies. *Monog. Soc. Res. Child. Develpm.* **21**, No. 2, Ser. No. 63. [689]

Rheingold, H. L., Gewirtz, J. L., & Ross, H. W. (1959) Social conditioning of vocalizations in the infant. *J. comp. physiol. Psychol.* **52**, 68–73.   [690]

Rheingold, H. L., & Hess, E. H. (1957) The chick's "preference" for some visual properties of water. *J. comp. physiol. Psychol.* 50, 417–421. [258]

Ribble, Margaret A. (1939) The significance of infantile sucking for the psychic development of the individual. *J. nerv. ment. Dis.* 90, 455–463. [687]

Ribble, Margaret A. (1941) Disorganizing factors in infant personality. *Amer. J. Psychiat.* 98, 459–463. [687]

Ribble, Margaret A. (1943) *The rights of infants.* New York: Columbia University Press. [649, 687]

Ribble, Margaret A. (1944) Infantile experience in relation to personality development. In Hunt, J. McV. (Ed.) *Personality and the behavior disorders*, vol. 2., New York: Ronald Press, pp. 621–651. [643–644, 649, 687]

Ricciuti, H. N. (1951) *A review of procedural variations in level of aspiration studies.* Lackland, A. F. Base, Texas: U.S.A.F. Human Resources Research Center, Research Bulletin, 51-24. [772]

Ricciuti, H. N. (1954) *The prediction of academic grades with a projective test of achievement motivation: I. Initial validation studies.* Princeton, N.J.: Educational Testing Service. Tech. Rep. No. 1, Contract NONR-694, NR 151-113. [731]

Ricciuti, H. N., & Sadacca, R. (1955) *The prediction of academic grades with a projective test of achievement motivation: II. Cross-validation at the high school level.* Princeton, N.J.: Educational Testing Service, Contract NONR-694, NR 151-113. [731]

Ricciuti, H. N., & Schultz, D. G. (1958) *Level of aspiration measures and self-estimates of personality in relation to achievement motivation.* Princeton, N.J.: Educational Testing Service, Contract NONR-694, NR 151-113. [734]

Richards, D. W. (1953) Homeostasis vs. hyperexis: or Saint George and the dragon. *Sci. Month.* 77, 289–294. [314]

Richter, C. P. (1922) A behavioristic study of the activity of the rat. *Comp. psychol. Monog.* 1, 1–55. [134, 273, 276]

Richter, C. P. (1927) Animal behavior and internal drives. *Quart. rev. Biol.* 2, 307–343. [240, 273]

Richter, C. P. (1937) Hypophyseal control of behavior. *Cold Sprg. Harbor Symp. Quant. Biol.* 5, 258–268. [109, 311]

Richter, C. P. (1939) Salt taste thresholds of normal and adrenalectomized rats. *Endocrinol.* 24, 367–371. [234]

Richter, C. P. (1941) The internal environment and behavior: Part V. Internal secretions. *Amer. J. Psychiat.* 97, 878–893. [233]

Richter, C. P. (1942–1943) Total self-regulatory functions in animals and human beings. *Harvey Lectures* 38, 63–103. [306, 310, 311, 312, 313]

Richter, C. P. (1947) Biology of drives. *J. comp. physiol. Psychol.* 40, 129–134. [306, 323]

Richter, C. P., Holt, L. E., & Barelare, B. (1938) Nutritional requirements for normal growth and reproduction in rats studied by the self-selection method. *Amer. J. Physiol.* 122, 734–744. [229]

Riddle, O. (1924–1925) Birds without gonads: Their origin, behaviour and bearing on the theory of the internal secretion of the testis. *Brit. J. exp. Biol.* 2, 221–246. [177]

Riddle, O., Lahr, E. L., & Bates, R. W. (1942) The role of hormones in the initiation of maternal behavior in rats. *Amer. J. Physiol.* 137, 299–317. [117]

Riesen, A. H. (1940) Delayed reward in discrimination learning by chimpanzees. *Comp. psychol. Monog.* 15, 1–53. [485]

Riesman, D., Glazer, N., & Denny, R. (1950) *The lonely crowd.* New Haven: Yale University Press. [666]

Riess, B. F. (1950) The isolation of factors of learning and native behavior in field and laboratory studies. *Annals N.Y. Acad. Sci.* 51, 1093–1103. [96, 97]

Rigby, W. K. (1954) Approach and avoidance gradients and conflict behavior in a predominantly temporal situation. *J. comp. physiol. Psychol.* 47, 83–89. [438]

Roberts, C. L., Marx, M. H., & Collier, G. (1958) Light onset and light offset as reinforcers for the albino rat. *J. comp. physiol. Psychol.* 51, 575–579. [541]

Roberts, E. (Ed.) (1960) *Inhibition in the nervous system and gammaaminobutyric acid.* New York: Pergamon Press.   [150]

Roberts, W. W. (1958a) Rapid escape learning without avoidance learning motivated by hypothalamic stimulation in cats. *J. comp. physiol. Psychol.* 51, 391–399.   [548]

Roberts, W. W. (1958b) Both rewarding and punishing effects from stimulation of posterior hypothalamus of cats with same electrode at same intensity. *J. comp. physiol. Psychol.* 51, 400–407.   [544, 548]

Robinson, E. S. (1934) Work of the integrated organism. In Murchison, C. (Ed.) *Handbook of general experimental psychology.* Worcester: Clark University Press, pp. 571–650.   [308, 316, 393, 394]

Rockett, F. C. (1955) A note on 'An experimental test of an alleged innate sign stimulus' by Hirsch, Lindley, and Tolman. *Percept. mot. Skills* 5, 155–156. [100]

Roe, Anne (1953) *The making of a scientist.* New York: Dodd, Mead.   [671]

Roe, Anne, & Simpson, G. G. (Eds.) (1958) *Behavior and evolution.* New Haven: Yale University Press.   [33]

Roehl, A. C. (1959) The effects of frustration on the amplitude of a simple motor response. Unpubl. doctoral dissert., University of Minnesota.   [750]

Rogers, C. R. (1951) *Client-centered therapy: Its current practice, implications, and theory.* Boston: Houghton-Mifflin.   [666]

Rogers, C. R. (1955a) Persons or science? A philosophical question. *Amer. Psychologist.* 10, 267–278.   [660]

Rogers, C. R. (1955b) The concept of the fully functioning person. Mimeographed paper. Quoted by permission. (Later published in *Psychotherapy,* 1963, 1, 17–26.)   [666–667, 673, 679]

Rogers, C. R., & Dymond, Rosalind, F. (Eds.) (1954) *Psychotherapy and personality change: Co-ordinated studies in the client-centered approach.* Chicago: University of Chicago Press.   [645, 683]

Rogoff, J. M. (1945) A critique on the theory of emergency function of the adrenal glands: Implications for psychology. *J. gen. Psychol.* 32, 249–268. [314, 392]

Rohrer, J. H. (1959) Human adjustment to Antarctic isolation. *Nav. Res. Rev. ONR,* June, pp. 1–5.   [278]

Root, W. S., & Bard, P. (1947) The mediation of feline erection through sympathetic pathways with some remarks on sexual behavior after deafferentation of the genitalia. *Amer. J. Physiol.* 151, 80–90.   [177]

Rosenbaum, G. (1953) Stimulus generalization as a function of experimentally induced anxiety. *J. exp. Psychol.* 45, 35–43.   [705]

Rosenbaum, G., Dobie, S. I., & Cohen, B. D. (1959) Visual recognition thresholds following sensory deprivation. *Amer. J. Psychol.* 72, 429–433.   [283]

Rosenbaum, M. E. (1956) The effect of stimulus and background factors on the volunteering response. *J. abn. soc. Psychol.* 53, 118–121.   [340]

Rosenbaum, M. E., & Blake, R. R. (1955) Volunteering as a function of field structure. *J. abn. soc. Psychol.* 50, 193–196.   [340]

Rosenblatt, J. S., & Aronson, L. R. (1958) The influence of experience on the behavioral effects of androgen in prepuberally castrated male cats. *Animal Behav.* 6, 171–182.   [177]

Rosenbleuth, A., Wiener, N., & Bigelow, J. H. (1943) Behavior, purpose and teleology. *Philos. Sci.* 10, 18–24.   [345]

Rosenthal, B. G. (1944) Hypnotic recall of material learned under anxiety and nonanxiety producing conditions. *J. exp. Psychol.* 34, 369–389.   [785]

Rosenzweig, M. R. (1962) The mechanisms of hunger and thirst. In Postman, L. (Ed.), *Psychology in the making: Histories of selected research problems.* New York: Knopf, pp. 73–143.   [205, 206, 216, 218, 245, 255]

Rosenzweig, N. (1955) A mechanism in schizophrenia: A theoretical formulation. *AMA Arch. neurol. Psychiat.* 74, 544–555.   [324, 325]

Rosenzweig, S. (1943) An experimental study of "repression" with special reference to need-persistive and ego-defensive reactions to frustration. *J. exp. Psychol.* 32, 64–74.   [425, 786]

Rosenzweig, S. (1944) Frustration theory. In Hunt, J. McV. (Ed.) *Personality and the behavior disorders.* Vol. I. New York: Ronald Press, pp. 379–388.   [415, 416, 418, 423, 455]

Rosenzweig, S., & Mason, G. (1934) An experimental study of memory in relation to the theory of repression. *Brit. J. Psychol.* 24, 247–265.   [786]

Ross, S. (1951a) Sucking behavior in neonate dogs. *J. abn. soc. Psychol.* 46, 142–149.   [113]

Ross, S. (1951b) Effects of early weaning on sucking behavior in cocker spaniel puppies. *Anat. Rec.* 111, 492.   [113]

Ross, S. (1952) *Report on "symposium on fatigue" of the Ergonomics Research Society,* March, 1952. Tech. Rep. No. 9, AMRDB Proj. DA-49-007-MD-222(O.I. 19–52), *Indicators of behavior decrement.* College Park: University of Maryland.   [138]

Ross, S., Denenberg, V. H., Sawin, P. B., & Meyer, P. (1956) Changes in nest building behavior in multiparous rabbits. *Brit. J. anim. Behav.* 4, 69–74.   [109]

Ross, S., Fisher, A. E., & King, D. (1957) Sucking behavior: A review of the literature. *J. genet. Psychol.* 91, 63–81.   [113]

Ross, S., Hussmann, T. A., & Andrews, T. G. (1954) Effects of fatigue and anxiety on certain psychomotor and visual functions. *J. appl. Psychol.* 38, 119–125.   [143, 144]

Ross, S., & Ross, J. G. (1949a) Social facilitation of feeding behavior in dogs: I. Group and solitary feeding. *J. genet. Psychol.* 74, 97–108.   [243]

Ross, S., & Ross, J. G. (1949b) Social facilitation of feeding behavior in dogs: II. Feeding after satiation. *J. genet. Psychol.* 74, 293–304.   [243]

Ross, S., & Smith W. I. (1953) The hoarding behavior of the mouse: II. The role of deprivation, satiation and stress. *J. genet. Psychol.* 82, 299–307.   [124, 126]

Ross, S., Smith, W. I., & Denenberg, V. H. (1950) A preliminary study of individual and group hoarding in rats. *J. genet. Psychol.* 77, 123–127.   [126]

Ross, S., Smith, W. I., & Woessner, B. L. (1955) Hoarding. An analysis of experiments and trends. *J. genet. Psychol.* 52, 307–326.   [122, 123, 124, 126]

Rotter, J. B. (1954) *Social learning and clinical psychology.* New York: Prentice-Hall.   [774]

Rotter, J. B. (1960) Some implications of a social learning theory for the prediction of goal directed behavior from testing procedures. *Psychol. Rev.* 67, 301–316.   [800]

Royce, J. R. (1959) The search for meaning. *Amer. Scientist* 47, 515–535.   [660]

Ruch, F. L. (1930) Food-reward vs. escape-from-water as conditions motivating learning in the white rat. *J. genet. Psychol.* 38, 127–145.   [132]

Ruch, T. C., & Shenkin, H. A. (1943) The relation of area 13 of the orbital surface of the frontal lobe to hyperactivity and hyperphagia in monkeys. *J. Neurophysiol.* 6, 349–360.   [354]

Ruckmick, C. A. (1936) *The psychology of feeling and emotion.* New York: McGraw-Hill.   [368, 382, 391]

Rundquist, E. A. (1933) Inheritance of spontaneous activity in rats. *J. comp. physiol. Psychol.* 16, 415–438.   [273]

Runquist, W. N., & Ross, L. E. (1959) The relation between physiological measures of emotionality and performance in eyelid conditioning. *J. exp. Psychol.* 57, 329–332.   [706, 708]

Runquist, W. N., & Spence, K. W. (1959) Performance in eyelid conditioning related to changes in muscular tension and physiological measures of emotionality. *J. exp. Psychol.* 58, 417–422.   [706]

Runquist, W. N., Spence, K. W., & Stubbs, D. W. (1958) Differential conditioning and intensity of the UCS. *J. exp. Psychol.* 55, 51–55.   [705]

Russell, B. (1945) *A history of western philosophy.* New York: Simon and Schuster.   [20, 21, 27, 29]

Russell, R. W. (1954) Comparative psychology. *Ann. rev. Psychol.* 5, 229–246.   [101–102]

Russell, W. A. (1952) Retention of verbal material as a function of motivating instructions and experimentally-induced failure. *J. exp. Psychol.* 43, 207–216.   [785]

Ryan, T. A. (1947) *Work and effort, the psychology of production.* New York: Ronald Press.   [136]

Ryans, D. G. (1939) The measurement of persistence: An historical review. *Psychol. Bull.* 36, 715–739.   [804]

Sachs, H. (1944) *Freud: Master and friend.* Cambridge: Harvard University Press.   [593]

Sackler, M. D., Sackler, R. R., LaBurt, H. A., CoTui, C., & Sackler, A. M. (1951) A psychobiologic viewpoint on schizophrenias of childhood. *Nerv. Child* 10, 43–59.   [325]

Sadacca, R., Ricciuti, H. N., & Swanson, E. O. (1956) *Content analysis of achievement motivation protocols: A study of scorer agreement.* Princeton, N.J.: Educational Testing Service. Report under Contract NONR-694, NR 115–113, May.   [723]

Saltzman, I., & Koch, S. (1948) The effect of low intensities of hunger on the behavior mediated by a habit of maximum strength. *J. exp. Psychol.* 38, 347–370.   [530]

Samelson, F. (1957) Conforming behavior under two conditions of conflict in the cognitive field. *J. abn. soc. Psychol.* 55, 181–187.   [779]

Samelson, F. (1958) The relation of achievement and affiliation motives to conforming behavior in two conditions of conflict with a majority. In Atkinson, J. W. (Ed.) *Motives in fantasy, action and society.* New York: Van Nostrand, pp. 421–433.   [739, 779]

Sanders, F. K., & Young, J. Z. (1940) Learning and other functions of the higher nervous centers of *Sepia. J. Neurophysiol.* 3, 501–526.   [354]

Sanders, R., & Cleveland, S. E. (1953) The relationship between certain examiner personality variables and subject's Rorschach scores. *J. proj. Tech.* 17, 34–50.   [754]

Sanford, R. N. (1936) The effects of abstinence from food upon imaginal processes: A preliminary experiment. *J. Psychol.* 2, 129–136.   [716]

Sangster, W., Grossman, M. I., & Ivy, A. C. (1948) Effect of d-amphetamine in gastric hunger contractions and food intake in the dog. *Amer. J. Physiol.* 153, 259–263.   [212]

Sarason, I. G. (1960) Empirical findings and theoretical problems in the use of anxiety scales. *Psychol. Bull.* 57, 403–415.   [708, 709, 713]

Sarason, S. B., Davidson, K. S., Lighthall, F. F., & Waite, R. R. (1958) A test anxiety scale for children. *Child Develpm.* 29, 105–113.   [702]

Sarason, S. B., Davidson, K. S., Lighthall, F. F., Waite, R. R., & Ruebush, B. K.

(1960) *Anxiety in elementary school children: A report of research.* New York: Wiley.   [713]

Sarason, S. B., & Mandler, G. (1952) Some correlates of test anxiety. *J. abn. soc. Psychol.* 47, 810–817.   [711]

Sarason, S. B., Mandler, G., & Craighill, P. C. (1952) The effect of differential instructions on anxiety and learning. *J. abn. soc. Psychol.* 47, 561–565. [712]

Sargent, Helen D. (1961) Intrapsychic change: Methodological problems in psychotherapy research. *Psychiatry* 24, 93–108.   [646]

Sargent, S. S. (1948) Reaction to frustration—a critique and hypothesis. *Psychol. Rev.* 55, 108–114.   [418, 419, 751]

Sarnoff, I., & Zimbardo, P. G. (1961) Anxiety, fear and social affiliation. *J. abn. soc. Psychol.* 62, 356–363.   [700]

Sauer, E. G. F. (1958) Celestial navigation by birds. *Sci. Amer.* 199, 42–47. [130, 131]

Saul, L. J. (1956) *The hostile mind.* New York: Random House.   [745]

Scarborough, B. B. (1957) Lasting effects of alcohol on the reduction of anxiety in rats. *J. genet. Psychol.* 91, 173–179.   [584]

Scarborough, B. B., & Goodson, F. E. (1957) Properties of stimuli associated with strong and weak hunger drive in the rat. *J. genet. Psychol.* 91, 257–261. [581]

Schachter, S. (1959) *The psychology of affiliation: Experimental studies of the sources of gregariousness.* Stanford, Calif.: Stanford University Press.   [284, 695, 698, 699]

Schachter, S., & Singer, J. E. (1962) Cognitive, social and physiological determinants of emotional state. *Psychol. Rev.* 69, 379–399.   [368, 391]

Schafer, R. (1960) The loving and beloved superego in Freud's structual theory. *Psychoanal. Stud. Child* 15, 163–188.   [611]

Schaffer, H. R. (1954) Behavior under stress: A neurophysiological hypothesis. *Psychol. Rev.* 61, 323–333.   [450]

Schiller, Claire H. (Ed.) (1957) *Instinctive behavior: The development of a modern concept.* New York: International Universities Press.   [75, 86]

Schiller, P. H. (1949) Manipulative patterns in the chimpanzee. In Schiller, Claire H. (Ed.) *Instinctive behavior.* New York: International Universities Press, 1957, pp. 264–287.   [78]

Schlosberg, H. (1954a) Three dimensions of emotion. *Psychol. Rev.* 61, 81–88. [394–395, 396]

Schlosberg, H. (1954b) *Fatigue, effort and work output.* Presidential address, Eastern Psychological Association, April 9, 1954, New York City.   [394]

Schlosberg, H., & Kling, J. W. (1959) The relationship between "tension" and efficiency. *Percept. mot. Skills* 9, 395–397.   [396]

Schlosberg, H., & Stanley, W. C. (1953) A simple test of the normality of twenty-four distributions of electrical skin conductance. *Science* 117, 35–37.   [396]

Schmidt, H., Jr., Moak, S. J., & Van Meter, W. G. (1958) Atropine depression of food and water intake in the rat. *Amer. J. Physiol.* 192, 543–545.   [247]

Schmidt, H. O. (1941) The effect of praise and blame as incentives to learning. *Psychol. Monog.* 53, Whole No. 240.   [771]

Schneider, L. S., & Lysgaard, S. (1953) The deferred gratification pattern: A preliminary study. *Amer. sociol. Rev.* 18, 142–149.   [570]

Schneirla, T. C. (1947) Herbert Spencer Jennings: 1868–1947. *Amer. J. Psychol.* 60, 447–450.   [44]

Schneirla, T. C. (1949) Levels in the psychological capacities of animals. In Sellars, R. W., et al. (Eds.) *Philosophy for the future.* New York: Macmillan, pp. 243–286.   [96]

Schneirla, T. C. (1952) A consideration of some conceptual trends in comparative psychology. *Psychol. Bull.* 49, 559–597.   [96]

Schneirla, T. C. (1956) Interrelationships of the "innate" and the "acquired" in instinctive behavior. In Grassé, P. P. (Ed.) Fondation Singer-Polignac, *L'instinct dans le comportement des animaux et de l'homme.* Paris: Masson, pp. 387–452.   [96, 98, 99, 100]

Schneirla, T. C. (1957) The concept of development in comparative psychology. In Harris, D. B. (Ed.) *The concept of development. An issue in the study of human behavior.* Minneapolis: University of Minnesota Press, pp. 78–108. [96, 98]

Schneirla, T. C. (1959a) An evolutionary and developmental theory of biphasic processes underlying approach and withdrawal. In Jones, M. R. (Ed.) *Nebraska symposium on motivation, 1959.* Lincoln: University of Nebraska Press, pp. 1–42.   [99, 149, 827]

Schneirla, T. C. (1959b) Comments on Dr. Hess's paper. In Jones, M. R. (Ed.) *Nebraska symposium on motivation, 1959.* Lincoln: University of Nebraska Press, pp. 78–81.   [91]

Schoenfeld, W. N. (1950) An experimental approach to anxiety, escape and avoidance behavior. In Hoch, P. H., & Zubin, J. (Eds.) *Anxiety.* New York: Grune and Stratton, pp. 70–99.   [579, 580]

Schoenfeld, W. N., Antonitis, J. J., & Bersh, P. J. (1950) A preliminary study of training conditions necessary for secondary reinforcement. *J. exp. Psychol.* 40, 40–45.   [290]

Schooland, J. B. (1942) Are there any innate behavior tendencies? *Genet. psychol. Monog.* 25, 219–287.   [98]

Schumacher, G. A., Goodell, H., Hardy, J. D., & Wolff, H. G. (1940) Uniformity of the pain threshold in man. *Science* 110, 92.   [261]

Schütz, F. (1944) Induction of sleep by simultaneous administration of posterior pituitary extracts and water. *Nature, Lond.* 153, 432–433.   [170]

Schwab, R. S. (1949) Psychiatry attacks fatigue. *Naval Res. Rev.* (ONR) 2, (6), 17–22.   [137]

Schwab, R. S., & Prichard, J. S. (1951) Neurologic aspects of fatigue. *Neurology* 1, 133–135.   [140]

Schwartz, M. (1956) Instrumental and consummatory measures of sexual capacity in the male rat. *J. comp. physiol. psychol.* 49, 328–333.   [187]

Scott, E. M., & Quint, E. (1946) Self-selection of diet: IV. Appetite for protein. *J. Nutrit.* 32, 293–302.   [232]

Scott, E. M., & Verney, Ethel, L. (1947) Self-selection of diet: V. Appetite for carbohydrates. *J. Nutrit.* 34, 401–407.   [232]

Scott, E. M., & Verney, Ethel, L. (1948) Self-selection of diet: VIII. Appetite for fats. *J. Nutrit.* 36, 91–98.   [232]

Scott, E. M., & Verney, Ethel L. (1949) Self-selection of diet: IX. The appetite for thiamine. *J. Nutrit.* 37, 81–91.   [230]

Scott, J. H. (1955) Some effects at maturity of gentling, ignoring, or shocking rats during infancy. *J. abn. soc. Psychol.* 51, 412–414.   [103]

Scott, J. P. (1958) *Aggression.* Chicago: University of Chicago Press.   [652, 748]

Scott, W. C., Scott, C. C., & Luckhardt, A. B. (1938) Observations in the blood sugar level before, during and after hunger periods in humans. *Amer. J. Physiol.* 123, 243–247.   [211]

Sears, Pauline S. (1940) Levels of aspiration in academically successful and unsuccessful children. *J. abn. soc. Psychol.* 35, 498–536.   [772]

Sears, Pauline S. (1941) Level of aspiration in relation to some variables of personality: Clinical studies. *J. abn. soc. Psychol.* 14, 311–336.   [772]

Sears, Pauline S. (1951) Doll-play aggression in normal young children: Influence of sex, age, sibling status, father's absence. *Psychol. Monog.* 65, Whole No. 323.   [758]

Sears, Pauline S., & Levin, H. (1957) Levels of aspiration in school children. *Child Develpm.* **28**, 317–326. [772]

Sears, R. R. (1937) Initiation of the repression sequence by experienced failure. *J. exp. Psychol.* **20**, 570–580. [785]

Sears, R. R. (1943) *Survey of objective studies of psychoanalytic concepts.* New York: Soc. Sci. Res. Council, Bull. No. 51. [651]

Sears, R. R. (1944) Experimental analysis of psychoanalytic phenomena. In Hunt, J. McV. (Ed.) *Personality and the behavior disorders.* Vol. I. New York: Ronald Press, pp. 306–332. [651]

Sears, R. R., & Hovland, C. I. (1941) Experiments on motor conflict: II. Determination of mode of resolution of conflict by comparative strengths of conflicting responses. *J. exp. Psychol.* **28**, 280–286. [131]

Sears, R. R., Hovland, C. I., & Miller, N. E. (1940) Minor studies of aggression: I. Measurement of aggressive behavior. *J. Psychol.* **9**, 275–295. [749]

Sears, R. R., Maccoby, Eleanor E., & Levin, H. (1957) *Patterns of child rearing.* Evanston, Ill.: Row, Peterson. [650, 752]

Sears, R. R., & Sears, Pauline S. (1940) Minor studies of aggression: V. Strength of frustration-reaction as a function of strength of drive. *J. Psychol.* **9**, 297–300. [750]

Sears, R. R., Whiting, J. W. M., Nowlis, V., & Sears, Pauline S. (1953) Some child-rearing antecedents of aggression and dependency in young children. *Genet. Psychol. Monog.* **47**, 135–234. [741, 742, 743, 746, 752, 753, 758]

Sears, R. R., & Wise, G. W. (1950) Relation of cup feeding in infancy to thumb-sucking and the oral drive. *Amer. J. Orthopsychiat.* **20**, 123–138. [114]

Seashore, R. H. (1951) Work and motor performance. In Stevens, S. S. (Ed.) *Handbook of experimental psychology.* New York: Wiley, pp. 1341–1362. [316]

Seashore, R. H., & Ivy, A. C. (1953) The effects of analeptic drugs in relieving fatigue. *Psychol. Monog.* **67**, No. 15, Whole No. 365. [145]

Seeman, W., & Williams, H. (1952) An experimental note on a Hull-Leeper difference. *J. exp. Psychol.* **44**, 40–45. [265]

Seidman, D., Bensen, S. B., Miller, I., & Meeland, T. (1957) Influence of a partner on tolerance for a self-administered electric shock. *J. abn. soc. Psychol.* **54**, 210–212. [262]

Selye, H. (1936) A syndrome produced by diverse nocuous agents. *Nature* **138**, 32. [442]

Selye, H. (1937) Studies on adaptation. *Endocrinology* **21**, 169–188. [308, 313]

Selye, H. (1946) The general adaptation syndrome and the diseases of adaptation. *J. clin. endocrinol. Metab.* **2**, 117–130. [308]

Selye, H. (1950) *The physiology and pathology of exposure to stress.* Montreal: Acta, Inc. [308, 313, 346, 442, 445]

Selye, H. (1951–1956) *Annual report on stress.* Montreal: Acta, Inc., 1951; Selye & Horava, A. 1952, 1953; Selye & Heuser, G. 1954, M.D. Public (New York), 1955–1956. [308, 313, 442, 447]

Selye, H. (1952) *The story of the adaptation syndrome.* Montreal: Acta, Inc. [444, 445]

Selye, H. (1956a) *The stress of life.* New York: McGraw-Hill. [442, 454]

Selye, H. (1958) *The chemical prevention of cardiac damage.* New York: Ronald Press. [448]

Selye, H. (1959) Perspectives in stress research. *Perspect. Biol. Med.* **2**, 403–416. [442, 445, 447]

Selye, H. (1961) Nonspecific resistance. *Ergebnisse der Allgemeinen Pathologie und Pathologischen Anatomie.* Sonderdruck Aus Band 41. Berlin: Springer-Verlag, pp. 207–241. [448]

Sem-Jacobsen, C. W. (1958) Comment. In Jasper, H. H., et al. (Eds.) *Reticular formation of the brain.* Boston: Little, Brown and Co., pp. 725–726.   [356, 544]

Seward, G. H. (1940) Studies on the reproductive activities of the guinea pig: II. The role of hunger in filial behavior. *J. comp. physiol. Psychol.* 29, 25–41. [112]

Seward, J. P. (1950) Secondary reinforcement as tertiary motivation: A revision of Hull's revision. *Psychol. Rev.* 57, 362–374.   [489, 563]

Seward, J. P. (1951) Experimental evidence for the motivating function of reward. *Psychol. Bull.* 48, 130–149.   [422, 489, 555]

Seward, J. P. (1952) Introduction to a theory of motivation in learning. *Psychol. Rev.* 59, 405–413.   [489]

Seward, J. P. (1953) How are motives learned? *Psychol. Rev.* 46, 99–110.   [489]

Seward, J. P. (1956a) Drive, incentive and reinforcement. *Psychol. Rev.* 63, 195–203.   [489]

Seward, J. P. (1956b) Comments on Professor Marx's paper. In Jones, M. R. (Ed.) *Nebraska symposium on motivation, 1956.* Lincoln: University of Nebraska Press, pp. 131–136.   [421, 422]

Seward, J. P., & Pereboom, A. C. (1955a) A note on the learning of "spontaneous" activity. *Amer. J. Psychol.* 68, 139–142.   [276]

Seward, J. P., & Pereboom, A. C. (1955b) Does the activity wheel measure goal-striving? *J. comp. physiol. Psychol.* 48, 272–277.   [276]

Seward, J. P., Pereboom, A. C., Butler, B., & Jones, R. B. (1957) The role of prefeeding in an apparent frustration effect. *J. exp. Psychol.* 54, 445–450. [421]

Seward, J. P., & Procter, D. M. (1960) Performance as a function of drive, reward and habit strength. *Amer. J. Psychol.* 73, 448–453.   [558]

Seward, J. P., & Seward, G. H. (1940a) Studies on the reproductive activities of the guinea pig: I. Factors in maternal behavior. *J. comp. physiol. Psychol.* 29, 1–24.   [112]

Seward, J. P., & Seward, G. H. (1940b) Studies on reproductive activities in the guinea pig: IV. A comparison of sex drive in males and females. *J. genet. Psychol.* 57, 429–440.   [187]

Seward, J. P., Shea, R. A., & Davenport, R. H. (1960) Further evidence for the interaction of drive and reward. *Amer. J. Psychol.* 73, 370–379.   [558]

Seward, J. P., Shea, R. A., & Elkind, D. (1958) Evidence for the interaction of drive and reward. *Amer. J. Psychol.* 71, 404–407.   [558]

Seward, J. P., Uyeda, A., & Olds, J. (1959) Resistance to extinction following cranial self-stimulation. *J. comp. physiol. Psychol.* 52, 294–299.   [546]

Shakow, D. (1960) The recorded psychoanalytic interview as an objective approach to research in psychoanalysis. *Psychoanal. Quart.* 29, 82–97.   [646]

Shands, H. C., & Finesinger, J. E. (1952) A note on the significance of fatigue. *Psychosom. Med.* 14, 309–314.   [140]

Shannon, C. E. (1951) Presentation of a maze-solving machine. In Foerster, H. von (Ed.) *Cybernetics. Circular causal and feedback mechanisms in biological and social systems.* Trans. Eighth Conf. New York: Josiah Macy, Jr. Found., 1952. [354]

Share, I., & Grossman, M. I. (1950) Regulation of food intake in dogs. *Amer. J. Physiol.* 163, 749–750.   [214]

Share, I., Martyniuk, E., & Grossman, M. I. (1952) Effect of prolonged intragastric feeding on oral food intake in dogs. *Amer. J. Physiol.* 169, 229–235.   [214, 215]

Sharpless, S., & Jasper, H. (1956) Habituation of the arousal reaction. *Brain* 79, 655–680.   [157, 171, 403]

Shaw, W. A. (1956) Facilitating effects of induced tension upon the perception span for digits. *J. exp. Psychol.* 51, 113–117.   [406]

Sheer, D. E. (1957) Psychology. In Speigel, E. A. (Ed.) *Progress in neurology and psychiatry*. Vol. XII. New York: Grune and Stratton, pp. 399–432.   [402]

Sheer, D. E. (Ed.) (1961) *Electrical stimulation of the brain*. Austin: University of Texas Press.   [150]

Sheffield, F. D. (1948) Avoidance training and the contiguity principle. *J. comp. physiol. Psychol.* **41**, 165–177.   [579]

Sheffield, F. D. (1951) The contiguity principle in learning theory. *Psychol. Rev.* **58**, 362–367.   [501]

Sheffield, F. D., & Campbell, B. A. (1954) The role of experience in the "spontaneous" activity of hungry rats. *J. comp. physiol. Psychol.* **47**, 97–100.   [276, 290, 421]

Sheffield, F. D., & Roby, T. B. (1950) Reward value of a non-nutritive sweet taste. *J. comp. physiol. Psychol.* **43**, 471–481.   [319, 542, 557]

Sheffield, F. D., Roby, T. B., & Campbell, B. A. (1954) Drive reduction versus consummatory behavior as determinants of reinforcement. *J. comp. physiol. Psychol.* **47**, 349–354.   [490, 542, 550, 557]

Sheffield, F. D., Wulff, J. J., & Backer, R. (1951) Reward value of copulation without sex drive reduction. *J. comp. physiol. Psychol.* **44**, 3–8.   [549, 557]

Sherif, M. (1935) A study of some social factors in perception. *Arch. Psychol.*, No. 187.   [778]

Sherif, M., & Cantril, H. (1947) *The psychology of ego-involvements: Social attitudes and identification*. New York: Wiley (out of print).   [387, 389, 684, 784]

Sherif, M., & Sherif, C. W. (1956) *An outline of social psychology* (rev. ed.) New York: Harper.   [776, 777, 784]

Sherman, M. (1941) *Basic problems of behavior*. New York: Longmans, Green.   [418]

Sherriffs, A. C. (1948) The intuition questionnaire: A new projective test. *J. abn. soc. Psychol.* **43**, 326–337.   [725]

Sherrington, C. S. (1906) *The integrative action of the nervous system*. New Haven: Yale University Press.   [148]

Sherrington, C. S. (1924) Problems of muscular receptivity. *Nature* **113**, 732; 892–894; 924–932.   [157]

Shipley, T. E., Jr., & Veroff, J. (1952) A projective measure of need for affiliation. *J. exp. Psychol.* **43**, 349–356.   [725]

Shirley, M. (1928a) Studies of activity: I. Consistency of the revolving drum method of measuring the activity of the rat. *J. comp. physiol. Psychol.* **8**, 23–38.   [276]

Shirley, M. (1928b) Studies in activity: II. Activity rhythms; age and activity; activity after rest. *J. comp. physiol. Psychol.* **8**, 159–186.   [271]

Shirley, M. (1929) Spontaneous activity. *Psychol. Bull.* **26**, 341 365.   [271]

Shore, M. F. (1958) Perceptual efficiency as related to induced muscular effort and manifest anxiety. *J. exp. Psychol.* **55**, 179–183.   [538]

Sidman, M., Brady, J. V., Boren, J. J., Conrad, D. G., & Schulman, A. (1955) Reward schedules and behavior maintained by intracranial self-stimulation. *Science* **122**, 830–831.   [544, 546]

Siegel, A. E., & Kohn, L. G. (1959) Permissiveness, permission and aggression: The effect of adult presence or absence on aggression in children's play. *Child Develpm.* **30**, 131–141.   [758]

Siegel, P. S. (1943) Drive shift, a conceptual and experimental analysis. *J. comp. physiol. Psychol.* **35**, 139–148.   [581]

Siegel, P. S. (1946a) Activity level as a function of physically enforced inaction. *J. Psychol.* **21**, 285–291.   [272]

Siegel, P. S. (1946b) Alien drive, habit strength and resistance to extinction. *J. comp. physiol. Psychol.* **39**, 307–317.   [536]

Siegel, P. S. (1947) The relationship between voluntary water intake, body weight loss, and number of hours of water privation in the rat. *J. comp. physiol. Psychol.* **40**, 231–238.   [257]

Siegel, P. S. (1957a) The completion compulsion in human eating. *Psychol. Reports* **3**, 15–16.   [241]

Siegel, P. S. (1957b) The repetitive element in the diet. *Amer. J. clin. Nutrit.* **5**, 162–164.   [242]

Siegel, P. S., & Brantley, J. J. (1951) The relationship of emotionality to the consummatory response of eating. *J. exp. Psychol.* **42**, 304–306.   [537]

Siegel, P. S. & Dorman, L. B. (1954) Food intake of the rat following the intragastric administration of "hungry" and "satiated" blood. *J. comp. physiol. Psychol.* **47**, 227–229.   [210]

Siegel, P. S., & MacDonnell, M. F. (1954) A repetition of the Calvin-Bicknell-Sperling study of conditioned drive. *J. comp. physiol. Psychol.* **47**, 250–252. [581]

Siegel, P. S., & Siegel, H. S. (1949) The effect of emotionality on the water intake of the rat. *J. comp. physiol. Psychol.* **42**, 12–16.   [537]

Siegel, P. S., & Steinberg, M. (1949) Activity level as a function of hunger. *J. comp. physiol. Psychol.* **42**, 413–416.   [273]

Siegel, P. S., & Stuckey, H. L. (1947a) An examination of some factors relating to the voluntary water intake of the rat. *J. comp. physiol. Psychol.* **40**, 271–274. [257]

Siegel, P. S., & Stuckey, H. L. (1947b) The diurnal course of water and food intake in the normal mature rat. *J. comp. physiol. Psychol.* **40**, 365–370. [257]

Siegel, P. S., & Taub, D. V. (1952) A "hunger hormone"? *J. comp. physiol. Psychol.* **45**, 250–253.   [210]

Siegel, S. (1957) Level of aspiration and decision making. *Psychol. Rev.* **64**, 253–262.   [773, 775]

Silverman, R. E. (1957) The manifest anxiety scale as a measure of drive. *J. abn. soc. Psychol.* **55**, 94–97.   [709]

Simmons, R. (1924) The relative effectiveness of certain incentives in animal learning. *Comp. Psychol. Monog.* **2**, No. 7.   [112, 551]

Simon, C. W., & Emmons, W. H. (1955) Learning during sleep? *Psychol. Bull.* **52**, 328–342.   [171]

Simon, C. W., Wickens, D. D., Brown, U., & Pennock, L. (1951) Effect of the secondary reinforcing agents on the primary thirst drive. *J. comp. physiol. Psychol.* **44**, 67–70.   [540]

Simpson, G. G. (1953) *The major features of evolution.* New York: Columbia University Press.   [33]

Sims, V. M. (1928) The relative influence of two types of motivation on improvement. *J. educ. Psychol.* **19**, 480–484.   [777]

Skard, A. G. (1936) Studies in the psychology of needs: Observations and experiments on the sexual needs in hens. *Acta Psychol. The Hague* **2**, 175–232. [193]

Skinner, B. F. (1933) The measurement of "spontaneous activity." *J. gen. Psychol.* **9**, 3–23.   [276]

Skinner, B. F. (1936) Thirst as an arbitrary drive. *J. gen Psychol.* **15**, 205–210. [257]

Skinner, B. F. (1938) *The behavior of organisms: An experimental approach.* New York: Appleton-Century.   [239, 467, 514, 515–516, 517]

Skinner, B. F. (1948) *Walden II.* New York: Macmillan.   [514, 517]

Skinner, B. F. (1950) Are theories of learning necessary? *Psychol. Rev.* **57**, 193–216.   [514]

Skinner, B. F. (1953) *Science and human behavior.* New York: Macmillan. [514, 515, 516, 517]

Skinner, B. F. (1957) *Verbal behavior.* New York: Appleton-Century-Crofts. [58, 514]

Skinner, B. F. (1959) A case history in scientific method. In Koch, S. (Ed.) *Psychology: A study of a science,* Vol. 2. New York: McGraw-Hill, pp. 359–379. [514, 517]

Slonaker, J. R. (1912) The normal activity of the albino rat from birth to natural death, its rate of growth, and the duration of life. *J. anim. Behav.* **2**, 20–42. [276]

Sluckin, W. (1954) *Minds and machines.* London: Pelican (Penguin Books), No. 308. [342, 354]

Smith, E. A. (1935) Salivary secretion during thirst. *Amer. J. Physiol.* **113**, 123 (Abstr.). [250]

Smith, M. F., & Smith, K. U. (1939) Thirst-motivated activity and its extinction in the cat. *J. gen. Psychol.* **21**, 89–98. [257]

Smith, M. P., & Capretta, P. J. (1956) Effects of drive level and experience on the reward value of saccharine solutions. *J. comp. physiol. Psychol.* **49**, 553–557. [542]

Smith, M. P., & Duffy, M. (1957a) Evidence for a dual reinforcing effect of sugar. *J. comp. physiol. Psychol.* **50**, 242–247. [542]

Smith, M. P., & Duffy, M. (1957b) Some physiological factors that regulate eating behavior. *J. comp. physiol. Psychol.* **50**, 601–608. [215]

Smith, O. A. (1956) Stimulation of lateral and medial hypothalamus and food intake in the rat. *Anat. Rec.* **124**, 363–364. [219]

Smith, P. E. (1954) Continuation of pregnancy in rhesus monkey following hypophesectomy. *Endocrinology* **55**, 655–664. [111]

Smith, S., & Guthrie, E. R. (1921) *General psychology in terms of behavior.* New York: Appleton-Century-Crofts. [431, 434]

Smith, W. I., & Powell, E. K. (1955) The role of emotionality in hoarding. *Behaviour* **8**, 57–62. [125]

Smith, W. I., Powell, E. K., & Ross, S. (1955) Food aversions: Some additional personality correlates. *J. consult. Psychol.* **19**, 145–149. [242]

Smith, W. I., & Ross, S. (1950) Hoarding behavior in the hamster. *J. genet. Psychol.* **77**, 211–215. [126]

Smith, W. I., & Ross, S. (1952) The social behavior of vertebrates: A review of the literature (1939–1950). *Psychol. Bull.* **49**, 598–627. [109, 258, 748]

Smith, W. I., & Ross, S. (1953) The hoarding behavior of the mouse: I. The role of previous feeding experience. *J. genet. Psychol.* **82**, 279–297. [122, 125]

Snapper, I. (1955) Food preferences in man: Special cravings and aversions. *Annals N.Y. Acad. Sci.* **63**, Art 1, 92–106. [228]

Snygg, D., & Combs, A. W. (1949) *Individual behavior.* New York: Harper. [666]

Society for Experimental Biology (1950) Symposium No. 4. *Physiological mechanisms in animal behavior.* New York: Academic Press. [75]

Solarz, A. K. (1958) Effects of hydration on the running and drinking performance of thirsty rats. *J. comp. physiol. Psychol.* **51**, 146–151. [248]

Solomon, P. (1958) Sensory deprivation and the human mind. *Nav. Res. Rev.* (ONR), April, 9–11. [281, 283]

Solomon, P., Kubzansky, P. E., Leiderman, P. H., Mendelson, J. H., Trumbull, R., & Wexler, D. (Eds.) (1961) *Sensory deprivation: A symposium at Harvard Medical School.* Cambridge: Harvard University Press. [278, 280, 455–456, 601]

Solomon, P., Leiderman, P. H., Mendelson, J., & Wexler, D. (1957) Perceptual and sensory deprivation—a review. *Amer. J. Psychiat.* **114**, 357–363. [278]

Solomon, R. L. (1948) The influence of work on behavior. *Psychol. Bull.* **45**, 1–40. [155]

Solomon, R. L., & Brush, Elinor S. (1956) Experimentally derived conceptions of anxiety and aversion. In Jones, M. R. (Ed.) *Nebraska symposium on motivation, 1956.* Lincoln: University of Nebraska Press, pp. 212–305.   [579, 586]

Solomon, R. L., & Coles, M. R. (1954) A case of failure of generalization of imitation across drives and across situations. *J. abn. soc. Psychol.* 49, 7–13. [538]

Solomon, R. L., & Wynne, L. C. (1950) Avoidance conditioning in normal dogs and in dogs deprived of normal autonomic functioning. *Amer. Psychologist* 5, 264 (Abstr.).   [313]

Solomon, R. L., & Wynne, L. C. (1954) Traumatic avoidance learning: The principles of anxiety conservation and partial irreversibility. *Psychol. Rev.* 61, 353–385.   [579, 587]

Sommerhoff, G. (1950) *Analytical biology.* London: Oxford University Press. [345]

Spence, K. W. (1944) Types of constructs in psychology. *Pschol. Rev.* 51, 47–68.   [363]

Spence, K. W. (1947) The role of secondary reinforcement in delayed reward learning. *Psychol. Rev.* 54, 1–8.   [484, 485, 491, 561]

Spence, K. W. (1951a) Theoretical interpretations of learning. In Stone, C. P. (Ed.) *Comparative psychology* (3rd ed.) New York: Prentice-Hall, pp. 239–291.   [467]

Spence, K. W. (1951b) Theoretical interpretations of learning. In Stevens, S. S. (Ed.) *Handbook of experimental psychology.* New York: Wiley, pp. 690–729. [467]

Spence, K. W. (1953) Learning and performance in eyelid conditioning as a function of the intensity of the UCS. *J. exp. Psychol.* 45, 57–63.   [528, 529, 533]

Spence, K. W. (1956) *Behavior theory and conditioning.* New Haven, Conn.: Yale University Press.   [12, 373, 467, 485, 487, 488, 489, 490, 491, 492, 493, 523, 534, 554, 555, 556, 558, 561, 563, 704, 707]

Spence, K. W. (1958) A theory of emotionally based drive (D) and its relation to performance in simple learning situations. *Amer. Psychologist* 13, 131–141.   [492, 702, 703, 704, 705, 707, 713, 803]

Spence, K. W. (1960) *Behavior theory and learning: Selected papers.* Englewood Cliffs, N.J.: Prentice-Hall.   [373, 467, 487, 488, 493, 562, 563]

Spence, K. W., & Beecroft, R. S. (1954) Differential conditioning and level of anxiety. *J. exp. Psychol.* 48, 399–403.   [705]

Spence, K. W., & Farber, I. E. (1953) Conditioning and extinction as a function of anxiety. *J. exp. Psychol.* 45, 116–119.   [705]

Spence, K. W., & Farber, I. E. (1954) The relation of anxiety to differential eyelid conditioning. *J. exp. Psychol.* 47, 127–134.   [705]

Spence, K. W., Farber, I. E., & McFann, H. H. (1956) The relation of anxiety (drive) level to performance in competitional and noncompetitional paired-associates learning. *J. exp. Psychol.* 52, 296–305.   [707]

Spence, K. W., & Norris, Eugenia B. (1950) Eyelid conditioning as a function of inter-trial interval. *J. exp. Psychol.* 40, 716–720.   [155]

Spence, K. W., & Ross, L. E. (1957) *Experimental evidence on the relation between performance level in eyelid conditioning and anxiety (drive) level.* Iowa City, Iowa: Department of Psychology, Tech. Rep. No. 5, Contract N9 ONR 93802, Project NR154-107, Office of Naval Research.   [704]

Spence, K. W., Taylor, Janet A., & Ketchel, Rhoda (1956) Anxiety (drive) level and degree of competition in paired-associates learning. *J. exp. Psychol.* 52, 306–310.   [707]

Spencer, H. (1855) *Principles of psychology.* London: Williams and Norgate. [303, 306]

Spencer, H. (1862) *First principles.* London: Williams and Norgate.   [303]

Sperry, R. W. (1947) Effect of crossing nerves to antagonistic limb muscles in the monkey. *Arch. neurol. Psychiat., Chi.* **58**, 452–473.   [355]

Sperry, R. W. (1958) Physiological plasticity and brain circuit theory. In Harlow, H. F., & Woolsey, C. N. (Eds.) *Biological and biochemical bases of behavior.* Madison: University of Wisconsin Press, pp. 401–424.   [354, 355]

Spinoza, B. (1675) *Ethics, Part III* (Engl. transl. and ed., Gutmann, J.) New York: Hafner Publishing Co., 1957.   [303]

Spiro, M. E. (1958) *Children of the Kibbutz.* Cambridge, Mass.: Harvard University Press.   [688]

Spitz, R. A. (1945) Hospitalism: An inquiry into the genesis of psychiatric conditions in early childhood. *Psychoanal. Stud. Child* **1**, 53–74.   [649, 687]

Spitz, R. A. (1946a) Anaclitic depression. *Psychoanal. study Child* **2**, 313–342.   [649, 687]

Spitz, R. A. (1946b) Hospitalism: A follow-up report on investigation described in Volume I, 1945. *Psychoanal. Stud. Child* **2**, 113–117.   [649, 687]

Spitz, R. A. (1950) Anxiety in infancy: A study of its manifestations in the first year of life. *Intern. J. Psychoanal.* **31**, 138–143.   [642, 649]

Spitz, R. A. (1951) The psychogenic diseases in infancy: An attempt at their etiological classification. *Psychoanal. Stud. Child* **6**, 255–275.   [687]

Spitz, R. A. (1955) Reply to Dr. Pinneau. *Psychol. Bull.* **52**, 453–459.   [650, 688]

Spitzer, M. E. (1958) Level of aspiration as an extinction phenomenon. Unpubl. master's thesis, North Carolina State College.   [772, 773]

Spragg, S. D. S. (1940) Morphine addiction in chimpanzees. *Comp. Psychol. Monog.* **15**, No. 7.   [584]

Sprague, J. M., Chambers, W. W., & Stellar, E. (1961) Attentive, affective and adaptive behavior in the cat. *Science* **133**, 165–173.   [406]

Stacey, C. L., & DeMartino, M. F. (Eds.) (1958) *Understanding human motivation.* Cleveland, Ohio: Howard Allen.   [2]

Stagner, R. (1948) *The psychology of personality* (2nd ed.) New York: McGraw-Hill (see 1961b).   [686]

Stagner, R. (1951) Homeostasis as a unifying concept in personality theory. *Psychol. Rev.* **58**, 5–17.   [316, 317, 319, 323]

Stagner, R. (1954) Homeostasis: Corruptions or misconceptions? A reply. *Psychol. Rev.* **61**, 205–208.   [317]

Stagner, R. (1961a) Homeostasis, need reduction, and motivation. *Merrill-Palmer Quart.* **7**, 49–68.   [320]

Stagner, R. (1961b) *Psychology of personality* (3rd ed.) New York: McGraw-Hill.   [323, 423, 424]

Stagner, R., & Karwoski, T. F. (1952) *Psychology.* New York: McGraw-Hill.   [316, 317, 321, 323]

Stamm, J. S. (1954a) Control of hoarding activity in rats by the median cerebral cortex. *J. comp. physiol. Psychol.* **47**, 21–27.   [126]

Stamm, J. S. (1954b) Genetics of hoarding: I. Hoarding differences between homozygous strains of rats. *J. comp. physiol. Psychol.* **47**, 157–161.   [126]

Stamm, J. S. (1955) Hoarding and aggressive behavior in rats. *J. comp. physiol. Psychol.* **48**, 324–326.   [125]

Stamm, J. S. (1956) Genetics of hoarding: II. Hoarding behavior of hybrid and backcrossed strains of rats. *J. comp. physiol. Psychol.* **49**, 349–352.   [126]

Stauffacher, J. C. (1937) The effect of induced muscular tension upon various phases of the learning process. *J. exp. Psychol.* **21**, 26–46.   [393]

Stein, L. (1957) The classical conditioning of the consummatory response as a determinant of instrumental performance. *J. comp. physiol. Psychol.* **50**, 269–278.   [559]

Stein, L. (1958) Secondary reinforcement established with subcortical stimulation. *Science* **127**, 466–467.   [546]

Stein, L., & Ray, O. S. (1959) Self-regulation of brain-stimulating current intensity in the rat. *Science* 130, 570–572.   **[547–548]**

Stekel, W. (1949) *Disorders of the instincts and emotions.* (10 vols.) (ed. and transl., Gutheil, E. A.) New York: Liveright.   **[629]**

Stekel, W. (1950) *The autobiography of Wilhelm Stekel.* New York: Liveright. **[629]**

Stellar, E. (1954) The physiology of motivation. *Psychol. Rev.* 61, 5–22.   **[222, 228, 248, 266]**

Stellar, E. (1957) Physiological psychology. *Ann. rev. Psychol.* 8, 415–436.   **[404]**

Stellar, E., & Hill, J. H. (1952) The rat's rate of drinking as a function of water deprivation. *J. comp. physiol. Psychol.* 45, 96–102.   **[257]**

Stellar, E., & Morgan, C. T. (1943) The roles of experience and deprivation on the onset of hoarding behavior in the rat. *J. comp. Psychol.* 36, 47–55. **[124]**

Stendler, C. B. (1952) Critical periods in socialization and over-dependency. *Child Develpm.* 23, 3–12.   **[744]**

Stendler, C. B. (1954) Possible causes of overdependency in young children. *Child Develpm.* 25, 125–146.   **[744]**

Stennett, R. G. (1957) The relationship of performance level to level of arousal. *J. exp. Psychol.* 54, 54–61.   **[398]**

Sterling, T. D., & Cooper, G. P. (1957) Effect of irrelevant drive on extinction of barpressing. *Psychol. Reports* 3, 615–618.   **[537]**

Sternberg, Rae, S., Chapman, Jean, & Shakow, D. (1958) Psychotherapy research and the problem of intrusions on privacy. *Psychiatry* 21, 195–203.   **[647]**

Stevenson, H. W., & Iscoe, I. (1956) Anxiety and discriminative learning. *Amer. J. Psychol.* 69, 113–114.   **[708]**

Stevenson, I. (1957) Is the human personality more plastic in infancy and childhood? *Amer. J. Psychiat.* 114, 152–161.   **[688]**

Stevenson, J. A. F., & Rixon, R. H. (1957) Environmental temperature and deprivation of food and water on the spontaneous activity of rats. *Yale J. Biol. Med.* 29, 575–584.   **[819]**

Stevenson, J. A. F., Welt, L. G., & Orloff, J. (1950) Abnormalities of water and electrolyte metabolism in rats with hypothalamic lesions. *Amer. J. Physiol.* 161, 35–39.   **[255]**

Stewart, J., & Hurwitz, H. M. B. (1958) Studies in light reinforced behavior: III. The effect of continuous, zero and fixed-ratio reinforcement. *Quart. J. exp. Psychol.* 10, 56–61.   **[541]**

Stone, C. P. (1922) Congenital sexual behavior of young male albino rats. *J. comp. physiol. Psychol.* 2, 95–153.   **[196]**

Stone, C. P. (1924a) Delay in the awakening of copulatory ability in the male albino rat incurred by defective diets: I. Quantitative deficiency. *J. comp. physiol. Psychol.* 4, 195–224.   **[194]**

Stone, C. P. (1924b) The awakening of copulatory ability in male albino rats. *Amer. J. Physiol.* 68, 407–424.   **[194]**

Stone, C. P. (1925) Delay in the awakening of copulatory ability in the male albino rat incurred by defective diets: II. Qualitative deficiency. *J. comp. physiol. Psychol.* 5, 177–203.   **[194]**

Stone, C. P. (1926) The initial copulatory response of female rats reared in isolation from the age of 20 days to puberty. *J. comp. physiol. Psychol.* 6, 73–83.   **[196]**

Stone, C. P. (1927) The retention of copulatory ability in male rats following castration. *J. comp. physiol. Psychol.* 7, 369–387.   **[182]**

Stone, C. P. (1938) Activation of impotent male rats by injection of testosterone propionate. *J. comp. physiol. Psychol.* 25, 445–450.   **[181]**

Stone, C. P. (1951) Maturation and "instinctive" functions. In Stone, C. P. (Ed.) *Comparative psychology* (3rd ed.) New York: Prentice-Hall, pp. 30–61. **[122]**

Stone, C. P., Barker, R. G., & Tomilin, M. I. (1935) Sexual drive in potent and impotent male rats as measured by the Columbia Obstruction Apparatus. *J. genet. Psychol.* 47, 33–48. [189]

Stone, C. P., & Ferguson, L. (1938) Preferential responses of male albino rats to food and to receptive females. *J. comp. physiol. Psychol.* 26, 237–253. [194]

Stone, L. J. (1954) A critique of studies of infantile isolation. *Child Develpm.* 25, 9–20. [687]

Stone, L. J., & Jenkins, W. L. (1940) Recent research in cutaneous sensitivity: I. Pain and temperature. *Psychol. Bull.* 37, 285–311. [260]

Strassburger, R. C. (1950) Resistance to extinction of a conditioned operant as related to drive level at reinforcement. *J. exp. Psychol.* 40, 473–487. [525]

Stretch, R. G. A. (1960) Inhibition: A symposium: II. The investigation of inhibitory phenomena from the standpoint of comparative psychology. *Brit. J. Psychol.* 51, 202–215. [157]

Strong, P. N., Jr. (1957) Activity in the white rat as a function of apparatus and hunger. *J. comp. physiol. Psychol.* 50, 596–600. [275]

Stunkard, A. J. (1957) Studies in the physiology of hunger: II. The effects of the intravenous administration of various nutrients on the gastric hunger contractions of a man with severe brain damage. *Amer. J. clin. Nutrit.* 5, 203–211. [225, 227]

Stunkard, A. J., Van Itallie, T. B., & Reis, B. B. (1955) The mechanism of satiety: Effect of glucagon on gastric hunger contractions in man. *Proc. Soc. exp. Biol. Med.* 89, 258–261. [225]

Sturman-Hulbe, M., & Stone, C. P. (1929) Maternal behavior in the albino rat. *J. comp. physiol. Psychol.* 9, 203–237. [109, 110]

Sullivan, H. S. (1947) *Conceptions of modern psychiatry.* (2nd printing) Washington, D.C.: Wm. Alanson White Psychiatric Foundation. [633, 665]

Sullivan, J. J. (1950) Some factors affecting the conditioning of the galvanic skin response. Unpubl. doctoral dissert., State University of Iowa. [501]

Sumner, F. C., & Johnson, E. E. (1949) Sex differences in level of aspiration and in self-estimates of performance in a classroom situation. *J. Psychol.* 27, 483–490. [772]

Surwillo, W. W. (1956) Psychological factors in muscle-action potentials: EMG gradients. *J. exp. Psychol.* 52, 263–272. [397]

Sutcliffe, J. P. (1955) Task variability and the level of aspiration. *Australian J. Psychol., Monog. Suppl.,* No. 2. [772]

Sutherland, N. S. (1957) Spontaneous alternation and stimulus avoidance. *J. comp. physiol. Psychol.* 50, 358–362. [293]

Swift, C. F., & Wike, E. L. (1958) A test of Spence's theory of incentive motivation. *Psychol. Rec.* 8, 21–25. [559]

Symmes, D., & Leaton, R. N. (1962) Failure to observe reinforcing properties of sound onset in rats. *Psychol. Reports* 10, 458. [541]

Symonds, P. M. (1946) *The dynamics of human adjustment.* New York: Appleton-Century. [417]

Tatum, A. L., & Seevers, M. H. (1929) Experimental cocaine addiction. *J. Pharmacol. exp. Therap.* 36, 401–410. [585]

Taylor, A. E. (1919) *Aristotle* (rev. ed.) New York: Dover (1955 reprint). [23]

Taylor, A. E. (1933) *Socrates.* New York: Doubleday Anchor Books (1956 edition). [21]

Taylor, Janet A. (1951) The relationship of anxiety to the conditioned eyelid response. *J. exp. Psychol.* 41, 81–92. [701, 704]

Taylor, Janet A. (1953) A personality scale of manifest anxiety. *J. abn. soc. Psychol.* 48, 285–290. [701, 702, 703, 709]

Taylor, Janet A. (1956) Drive theory and manifest anxiety. *Psychol. Bull.* 53, 303–320. [702, 703, 704, 707, 708, 709, 713]

Taylor, Janet A., & Chapman J. P. (1955) Anxiety and the learning of paired associates. *Amer. J. Psychol.* 68, 671.   [707]
Taylor, Janet A., & Spence, K. W. (1954) Conditioning level in behavior disorders. *J. abn. soc. Psychol.* 49, 497–502.   [709]
Teel, K. S. (1952) Habit strength as a function of motivation during learning. *J. comp. physiol. Psychol.* 45, 188–191.   [521, 527, 532]
Teel, K. S., & Webb, W. B. (1951) Response evocation on satiated trials in the T-Maze. *J. exp. Psychol.* 41, 148–152.   [532, 535]
Teitelbaum, H. A. (1956) Homeostasis and personality. *AMA Arch. neurol. Psychiat.* 76, 317–324.   [322]
Teitelbaum, P. (1955) Sensory control of hypothalamic hyperphagia. *J. comp. physiol. Psychol.* 48, 156–163.   [221]
Teitelbaum, P. (1957) Random and food-directed activity in hyperphagic and normal rats. *J. comp. physiol. Psychol.* 50, 486–490.   [221, 273]
Teitelbaum, P., & Epstein, A. N. (1962) The lateral hypothalamic syndrome: Recovery of feeding and drinking after lateral hypothalamic lesions. *Psychol. Rev.* 69, 74–90.   [219, 220, 255]
Teitelbaum, P., & Stellar, E. (1954) Recovery from the failure to eat produced by hypothalamic lesions. *Science* 120, 894–895.   [219]
Terman, L. M. (1938) *Psychological factors in marital happiness.* New York: McGraw-Hill.   [190]
Terry, R. A. (1953) Autonomic balance and temperament. *J. comp. physiol. Psychol.* 46, 454–460.   [800]
Thetford, W. (1951) An organismic approach to frustration. *J. Personal.* 1, 1–19.   [419]
Thibaut, J., & Coules, J. (1952) The role of communication in the reduction of interpersonal hostility. *J. abn. soc. Psychol.* 47, 770–777.   [751]
Thistlethwaite, D. L. (1951) A critical review of latent learning and related experiments. *Psychol. Bull.* 48, 97–129.   [266, 506, 552]
Thompson, Clara (1950) *Psychoanalysis: Its evolution and development.* New York: Hermitage Press.   [589, 626, 628, 629, 630, 665]
Thompson, Clara, Mazer, M., & Witenberg, E. (Eds.) (1955) *Outline of psychoanalysis.* New York: Modern Library.   [589, 590, 643]
Thompson, M. E. (1960) A two-factor theory of inhibition. *Psychol. Rev.* 67, 200–206.   [157]
Thompson, W. R. (1953) Exploratory behavior as a function of hunger in "bright" and "dull" rats. *J. comp. physiol. Psychol.* 46, 323–326.   [290]
Thompson, W. R. (1955) Early environment—its importance for later behavior. In Hoch, P., & Zubin, J. (Eds.) *Psychopathology of children.* Philadelphia: Grune and Stratton, pp. 120–139.   [643]
Thompson, W. R., & Heron W. (1954) The effects of early restriction on activity in dogs. *J. comp. physiol. Psychol.* 47, 77–82.   [272, 294]
Thompson, W. R., & Schaefer, T., Jr. (1961) Early environmental stimulation. In Fiske, D., & Maddi, S., et al. *Functions of varied experience.* Homeward, Ill.: Dorsey Press, pp. 81–106.   [643]
Thompson, W. R., & Solomon, L. M. (1954) Spontaneous pattern discrimination in the rat. *J. comp. physiol. Psychol.* 47, 104–107.   [293]
Thorndike, E. L. (1927) The law of effect. *Amer. J. Psychol.* 29, 212–222.   [580]
Thorndike, E. L., et al. (1932) *The fundamentals of learning.* New York: Teachers College, Columbia University Press.   [580]
Thorndike, E. L. (1935) *The psychology of wants, interests and attitudes.* New York: Appleton-Century.   [580]
Thorpe, W. H. (1948) The modern concept of instinctive behavior. *Bull. anim. Behav.* 1 (7), 1–12.   [60, 65, 66, 68, 70, 74, 92]
Thorpe, W. H. (1950) The concepts of learning and their relation to those of instinct. In Society for Experimental Biology, Symposium No. 4: *Physiological*

mechanisms in animal behaviour. New York: Academic Press, pp. 387–408. [60]

Thorpe, W. H. (1956) *Learning and instinct in animals.* Cambridge, Mass.: Harvard University Press. [60, 74, 75, 77, 91, 92, 93]

Thorpe, W. H. (1961) Comparative psychology. *Ann. rev. Psychol.* 12, 27–50. [92, 104, 129]

Thorpe, W. H., & Jones, F. G. W. (1937) Olfactory conditioning and its relation to the problem of host selection. *Proc. Roy. Soc., B.* 124, 56–81. [97]

Tidwell, J., & Sutton, J. H. (1954) *Fatigue: An introduction to a concept.* Contr. NONR-126801, San Diego State College, Calif. [135, 136, 141]

Tinbergen, N. (1936) Eenvoudige proeven over de zintuigfuncties van larve en imago van de geelgerande watertor. *De Levende Natuur* 41, 225–236 (cited by Tinbergen, 1951). [67]

Tinbergen, N. (1948) Social releasers and the experimental method required for their study. *Wilson Bull.* 60, 6–52. [99]

Tinbergen, N. (1951) *The study of instinct.* Oxford: Oxford University Press. [57, 59, 60, 61, 63, 64, 67, 68, 69, 71, 72, 75, 78, 79, 80, 81, 82, 83, 92, 95, 376]

Tinbergen, N. (1952) "Derived" activities: Their causation, biological significance, origin, and emancipation during evolution. *Quart. rev. Biol.* 27, 1–32. [71, 72, 73, 76, 77, 92]

Tinbergen, N. (1953a) *Social behaviour in animals.* New York: Wiley. [77, 82]

Tinbergen, N. (1953b) *The herring gull's world.* London: Collins. [82]

Tinbergen, N., & Kuenen, D. J. (1939) Releasing and directing stimulation situations in feeding behavior in young thrushes. In Schiller, Claire, H. (Ed.) *Instinctive behavior.* New York: International Universities Press, 1957, pp. 209–238. [69, 78]

Tinklepaugh, O. L. (1928) An experimental study of representative factors in monkeys. *J. comp. physiol. Psychol.* 8, 197–236. [552]

Tinklepaugh, O. L. (1942) Social behavior of animals. In Moss, F. A. (Ed.) *Comparative psychology* (rev. ed.) New York: Prentice-Hall, pp. 366–393. [111, 112]

Titchener, E. B. (1908) *Lectures on the elementary psychology of feeling and attention.* New York: Macmillan. [47]

Toch, H. H., & Hastorf, A. H. (1955) Homeostasis in psychology. *Psychiatry* 18, 81–92. [314]

Tolman, E. C. (1932) *Purposive behavior in animals and men.* New York: Appleton-Century. [45, 59, 62, 467, 505, 506, 507, 508]

Tolman, E. C. (1938) The determiners of behavior at a choice point. *Psychol. Rev.* 45, 1–41. [505]

Tolman, E. C. (1942) *Drives toward war.* New York: Appleton-Century. [508]

Tolman, E. C. (1943) A drive-conversion diagram. *Psychol. Rev.* 50, 503–513. [508]

Tolman, E. C. (1945) A stimulus-expectancy need-cathexis psychology. *Science* 101, 160–166. [508]

Tolman, E. C. (1948) Cognitive maps in rats and men. *Psychol. Rev.* 55, 189–208. [506]

Tolman, E. C. (1949a) There is more than one kind of learning. *Psychol. Rev.* 56, 144–155. [505]

Tolman, E. C. (1949b) The nature and functioning of wants. *Psychol. Rev.* 56, 357–369. [505, 508]

Tolman, E. C. (1951) A psychological model. In Parsons, T., & Shils, E. (Eds.) *Toward a general theory of action.* Cambridge, Mass.: Harvard University Press, pp. 279–361. [505, 508, 509, 510]

Tolman, E. C. (1952) A cognition motivation model. *Psychol. Rev.* 59, 389–400. [505, 508]

Tolman, E. C. (1955) Principles of performance. *Psychol. Rev.* **62**, 315–326. [774]

Tolman, E. C. (1959) Principles of purposive behavior. In Koch, S. (Ed.) *Psychology: A study of a science.* Vol. 2. New York: McGraw-Hill, 1959, pp. 92–157. [505, 508]

Tolman, E. C., Hall, C. S., & Bretnall, E. P. (1932) A disproof of the law of effect and a substitution of the laws of emphasis, motivation and disruption. *J. exp. Psychol.* **15**, 601–614. [523]

Tolman, E. C., & Honzik, C. H. (1930) Introduction and removal of reward and maze performance in rats. *Univ. Calif. Publ. Psychol.* **4**, 257–275. [552]

Toman, W. (1960) *An introduction to the psychoanalytic theory of motivation.* New York: Pergamon Press. [2, 589, 655]

Towbin, E. J. (1949) Gastric distension as a factor in the satiation of thirst in esophagastomized dogs. *Amer. J. Physiol.* **159**, 533–541. [248, 252]

Towbin, E. J. (1955) Thirst and hunger behavior in normal dogs and the effects of vagotomy and sympathectomy. *Amer. J. Physiol.* **182**, 277–282. [253]

Troland, L. T. (1928) *The fundamentals of human motivation.* New York: Van Nostrand. [24, 29, 36, 41, 376, 390]

Tsai, C. (1925) The relative strength of sex and hunger motives in the albino rat. *J. comp. physiol. Psychol.* **5**, 407–416. [194]

Tsang, Y. C. (1938) Hunger motivation in gastrectomized rats. *J. comp. physiol. Psychol.* **26**, 1–17. [208]

Turner, W. D., & Carl, G. P. (1939) Temporary changes in affect and attitude following ingestion of various amounts of Benzedrine sulfate (amphetamine sulfate). *J. Psychol.* **8**, 415–482. [145]

Tyler, D. B. (1947) The effect of amphetamine sufate and some barbiturates on fatigue produced by long wakefulness. *Amer. J. Physiol.* **150**, 253–262. [145]

Uhr, L., & Miller, J. G. (Eds.) (1960) *Drugs and behavior.* New York: Wiley. [150]

Ulrich, R. E., & Azrin, N. H. (1962) Reflexive fighting in response to aversive stimulation. *J. exp. anal. Behav.* **5**, 511–520. [748]

Underwood, B. J. (1949) *Experimental psychology.* New York: Appleton-Century-Crofts. [12]

Utterback, R., & Ludwig, G. (1949) *A comparative study of schedules for standing watches aboard submarines, based on body temperature cycles.* Bethesda, Md.: USN Med. Res. Inst. Rep., Proj. NM 004003, No. 1. [164]

Valenstein, E. S., Riss, W., & Young, W. C. (1955) Experiential and genetic factors in the organization of sexual behavior in male guinea pigs. *J. comp. physiol. Psychol.* **48**, 397–403. [196]

Van Itallie, T. B. (1959) Physiologic aspects of hunger and satiety. *Diabetes, J. Amer. Diabetes Assoc.* **8**, 226–231. [222]

Van Vorst, R. (1947) Some responses of the psychopath as interpreted in light of Lindner's suggested application of the concept of homeostasis. *J. clin. Psychopath.* **8**, 827–830. [323]

Verney, E. B. (1947) The antidiuretic hormone and the factors which determine its release. *Proc. Roy. Soc., Lond., B.* **135**, 25–106. [249, 250, 255]

Vernon, J. A., & Hoffman, J. (1956) Effect of sensory deprivation on learning rate in human beings. *Science* **123**, 1074–1075. [282]

Vernon, J. A., & McGill, T. E. (1957) The effect of sensory deprivation on rote learning. *Amer. J. Psychol.* **70**, 637–639. [282]

Vernon, J. A., McGill, T. E., Gulick, W. L., & Candland, D. R. (1959) Effect of sensory deprivation on some perceptual and motor skills. *Percep. mot. Skills* **9**, 91–97. [281, 282]

Vernon, J. A., McGill, T. E., & Schiffman, H. (1958) Visual hallucinations during perceptual isolation. *Canad. J. Psychol.* 12, 31–34. [281]

Veroff, J. (1957) Development and validation of a projective measure of power motivation. *J. abn. soc. Psychol.* 54, 1–8. [726]

Verplanck, W. S. (1954) Burrhus F. Skinner. In Estes, W. K., et al., *Modern learning theory.* New York: Appleton-Century-Crofts, pp. 267–316. [514, 517]

Verplanck, W. S. (1957) A glossary of some terms used in the objective science of behavior. *Psychol. Rev.* 64, No. 6, Part 2, pp. 1–42. [58, 61]

Verplanck, W. S. (1958) Comparative psychology. *Ann. rev. Psychol.* 9, 99–108. [103–104]

Verplanck, W. S., & Hayes, J. R. (1953) Eating and drinking as a function of maintenance schedule. *J. comp. physiol. Psychol.* 46, 327–333. [264, 483]

Viek, P., & Miller, G. A. (1944) The cage as a factor in hoarding. *J. comp. physiol. Psychol.* 37, 203–210. [126]

Viteles, M. S. (1953) *Motivation and morale in industry.* New York: W. W. Norton. [771]

Vogt, Martha (1954) The role of the adrenal gland in homeostasis. *Quart. J. exp. Physiol.* 39, 245–252. [314]

Voigt, Johannes (1956) Handwriting as an indicator of fatigue. *Z. exp. angewand. Psychol.* 3, 458–471. [144]

Wada, T. (1922) An experimental study of hunger in its relation to activity. *Arch. Psychol. N.Y.* 8, No. 57, 1–65. [273, 536]

Wagner, A. R. (1959) The role of reinforcement and nonreinforcement in an "apparent frustration effect." *J. exp. Psychol.* 57, 130–136. [421]

Walder, L. O. (1961) Application of role and learning theories to the study of the development of aggression in children. III: An attempt at an empirical test of a theory. *Psychol. Reports* 9, 306–312. [752]

Walker, E. L. (1958) Action decrement and its relation to learning. *Psychol. Rev.* 65, 129–142. [157]

Walker, E. L., & Atkinson, J. W. (1958) The expression of fear-related motivation in thematic apperception as a function of proximity to an atomic explosion. In Atkinson, J. W. (Ed.), *Motives in fantasy, action and society.* New York: Van Nostrand, pp. 143–159. [727]

Walker, K. C. (1942) Effect of a discriminative stimulus transferred to a previously unassociated response. *J. exp. Psychol.* 31, 312–321. [564]

Wallerstein, H. (1954) An electromyographic study of attentive listening. *Canad. J. Psychol.* 8, 228–238. [397]

Wallerstein, R. S. (1961) Report of the Psychotherapy Research Project of the Menninger Foundation: January 1954—July 1961. *Internat. Ment. Hlth. Res. Newsletter* 3, Nos. 3 and 4; 12–15. [646]

Wallerstein, R. S., & Robbins, L. L. (1956) The Psychotherapy Research Project of the Menninger Foundation: IV. Concepts. *Bull. Menn. Clinic* 20, 239–262. [646]

Walter, W. G. (1953) *The living brain.* New York: W. W. Norton. [342, 353, 354]

Walters, R. H., & Karal, P. (1960) Social deprivation and verbal behavior. *J. Person.* 28, 89–107. [695]

Walters, R. H., Marshall, W. E., & Shooter, J. R. (1960) Anxiety, isolation, and susceptibility to social influence. *J. Personal.* 28, 518–529. [695]

Walters, R. H., & Ray, E. (1960) Anxiety, social isolation and reinforcer effectiveness. *J. Person.* 28, 358–367. [695]

Walters, R. H., & Zaks, M. S. (1959) Validation studies of an aggression scale. *J. Psychol.* 47, 209–218. [756]

Wang, G. H. (1923) The relation between "spontaneous" activity and oestrus cycle in the white rat. *Comp. Psychol. Monog.* **2**, No. 6.   [264, 274]

Warden, C. J. (1931) *Animal motivation: Experimental studies on the albino rat.* New York: Columbia University Press.   [238]

Warden, C. J., Jenkins, T. N., & Warner, L. (1935) *Comparative psychology: A comprehensive treatise.* 3 vols., New York: Ronald Press.   [36, 37, 314]

Warner, L. H. (1927) A study of sex behavior in the white rat by means of the obstruction method. *Comp. Psychol. Monog.* **4.**   [187, 189, 190]

Warner, L. H. (1928a) A study of hunger behavior in the white rat by means of the obstruction method. *J. comp. physiol. Psychol.* **8**, 273–299.   [240]

Warner, L. H. (1928b) A study of thirst behavior in the white rat by means of the obstruction method. *J. genet. Psychol.* **25**, 178–192.   [256, 264]

Warren, H. C. (1934) *Dictionary of psychology.* Boston: Houghton-Mifflin.   [66]

Warren, J. M., & Hall, J. F. (1956) Discrimination of visual patterns as a function of motivation and frequency of reinforcement. *J. genet. Psychol.* **88**, 245–250.   [521]

Warren, R. P., & Pfaffmann, C. (1959) Early experience and taste aversion. *J. comp. physiol. Psychol.* **52**, 263–266.   [542]

Waterhouse, I. K., & Child, I. (1953) Frustration and the quality of performance. *J. Person.* **21**, 298–311.   [425]

Waters, R. H., & Blackwood, D. F. (1949) The applicability of motivational criteria to emotions. *Psychol. Rev.* **56**, 351–356.   [369]

Watson, J. B. (1924) *Behaviorism.* New York: W. W. Norton.   [567]

Watson, J. B. (1930) *Behaviorism* (rev. ed.) New York: W. W. Norton (reprinted, University of Chicago Press).   [42]

Watson, J. B., & Morgan, J. J. B. (1917) Emotional reactions and psychological experimentation. *Amer. J. Psychol.* **28**, 163–174.   [42, 567]

Watson, J. B., & Rayner, Rosalie (1920) Conditioned emotional reactions. *J. exp. Psychol.* **3**, 1–14.   [567]

Waxler, S. H., & Brecher, G. (1950) Obesity and food requirements in albino mice following administration of gold-thioglucose. *Amer. J. Physiol.* **162**, 428–433.   [224]

Wayner, W. J., Jr., & Reimanis, G. (1958) Drinking in the rat induced by hypertonic saline. *J. comp. physiol. Psychol.* **51**, 11–15.   [250]

Weasner, M. H., Finger, F. W., & Reid, L. S. (1960) Activity changes under food deprivation as a function of recording device. *J. comp. physiol. Psychol.* **53**, 470–474.   [275]

Webb, W. B. (1948) "A motivational theory of emotions . . ." *Psychol. Rev.* **55**, 329–335.   [369]

Webb, W. B. (1949) The motivational aspect of an irrelevant drive in the behavior of the white rat. *J. exp. Psychol.* **39**, 1–14.   [535]

Webb, W. B. (1952) Response in the absence of the acquisition drive. *Psychol. Rev.* **59**, 54–61.   [535]

Webb, W. B. (1955) Drive stimuli as cues. *Psychol. Reports* **1**, 287–298.   [266]

Webb, W. B. (1956) An experimental analysis of the antecedents of sleep. Pensacola, Fla.: *USN Sch. Aviat. Med. Res. Rep.*, Proj. NM001 109 113 Rep. No. 1, 12 pp.   [174]

Webb, W. B., & Goodman, I. J. (1958) Activating role of an irrelevant drive in absence of the relevant drive. *Psychol. Reports* **4**, 235–238.   [536]

Weber, C. O. (1949) Homeostasis and servo-mechanisms for what? *Psychol. Rev.* **56**, 234–239.   [318]

Weber, M. (1930) *The Protestant ethic.* (Parsons, T., trans.) New York: Scribner.   [764]

Weiss, B. (1957) Thermal behavior of the subnourished and pantothenic-acid-deprived rat. *J. comp. physiol. Psychol.* **50**, 481–485.   [133]

Weiss, B. (1958) Effects of brief exposure to cold on performance and food intake. *Science* 127, 467–468. [133, 242]

Weiss, B., & Danford, M. B. (1956) *Reward values of heat at low temperatures during inanition and pantothenic acid deprivation.* Randolph Field, Texas: School of Aviation Medicine, USAF, Tech. Rep. No. 56-72. [133]

Weiss, P. (1941) Self-differentiation of the basic patterns of coordination. *Comp. Psychol. Monog.* 17, 1–96. [65]

Weiss, R. F. (1960) Deprivation and reward magnitude effects on speed throughout the goal gradient. *J. exp. Psychol.* 60, 384–390. [558]

Weiss, W., & Fine, B. J. (1956) The effect of induced aggressiveness on opinion change. *J. abn. soc. Psychol.* 52, 109–114. [751]

Welch, L., & Kubis, J. (1947a) The effect of anxiety on the conditioning rate and stability of the PGR. *J. Psychol.* 23, 831–891. [706]

Welch, L., & Kubis, J. (1947b) Conditioned PGR (psychogalvanic response) in states of pathological anxiety. *J. nerv. ment. Dis.* 105, 372–381. [706]

Welker, W. I. (1956a) Some determinants of play and exploration in chimpanzees. *J. comp. physiol. Psychol.* 49, 84–89. [296]

Welker, W. I. (1956b) Variability of play and exploratory behavior in chimpanzees. *J. comp. physiol. Psychol.* 49, 181–185. [296]

Welker, W. I. (1957) "Free" versus "forced" exploration of a novel situation by rats. *Psychol. Reports* 3, 95–108. [291, 293]

Welker, W. I. (1959) Escape, exploratory and food-seeking responses of rats in a novel situation. *J. comp. physiol. Psychol.* 52, 106–111. [291]

Welty, J. C. (1934) Experiments in group behavior of fishes. *Physiol. Zool.* 7, 85–128. [243]

Wenar, C. (1954) Reaction time as a function of manifest anxiety and stimulus intensity. *J. abn. soc. Psychol.* 49, 335–340. [705]

Wenger, M. A. (1948) Studies of autonomic balance in Army Air Force personnel. *Comp. psychol. Monogr.* 19, 1–110. [460, 800]

Wenger, M. A., Jones, F. N., & Jones, M. H. (1956) *Physiological psychology.* New York: Holt. [140]

Werner, H. (1948) *Comparative psychology of mental development* (rev. ed.) New York: International Universities Press. [20, 23]

Wertheim, J., & Mednick, S. A. (1958) The achievement motive and field independence. *J. consult. Psychol.* 22, 38. [740]

West, J. (pseud.) (1945) *Plainville, U.S.A.* New York: Columbia University Press. [569]

Wettendorff, H. (1901) Modification du sang sans l'influence de la privation d'eau. Contribution a l'étude de la soif. Travaux du laboratoire de physiologie, *Instituts Solvoy Bruxelles* 4, 353–484. [250]

Wever, E. G. (1932) Water temperature as an incentive to swimming activity in the rat. *J. comp. physiol. Psychol.* 14, 219–224. [132]

Whalen, R. W., Beach, F. A., & Kuehn, R. E. (1961) Effects of exogenous androgen on sexually responsive and unresponsive male rats. *Endocrinology* 69, 373–380. [188]

White, J., & Sweet, W. H. (1955) *Pain: Its mechanisms and neurosurgical control.* Springfield, Ill.: Charles C. Thomas. [260]

White, R. W. (1957) Is Alfred Adler alive today? *Contemp. Psychol.* 2, 1–4. [663]

White, R. W. (1959) Motivation reconsidered: The concept of competence. *Psychol. Rev.* 66, 297–333. [277, 615, 819, 826]

White, R. W. (1960) Competence and the psychosexual stages of development. In Jones, M. R. (Ed.) *Nebraska symposium on motivation, 1960.* Lincoln: University of Nebraska Press, pp. 97–140. [615]

Whitehorn, J. C., et al. (1953) National Research Council (Div. of Med. Sciences) and Army Medical Service Graduate School (Walter Reed Army Medical

Center) *Symposium on stress*. Washington, D.C.: Army Med. Serv. Gr. Sch., 1953. [461]

Whiting, J. W. M., & Child, I. (1953) *Child training and personality*. New Haven: Yale University Press.   [643, 742, 744]

Whiting, J. W. M., & Sears, R. R. (1949) Projection and displacement in doll play. Cambridge, Mass.: Harvard University Laboratory of Human Development (mimeographed).   [438]

Whitrow, G. J. (1961) *The natural philosophy of time*. London: Thomas Nelson. [169]

Wiener, N. (1948) *Cybernetics*. New York: Wiley.   [342, 343]

Wiener, N. (1954) *The human use of human beings: Cybernetics and society*. New York: Doubleday.   [342, 347, 356]

Wiener, N. (1958) Time and the science of organization. *Scientia* 93, 199–205; 225–230.   [169]

Wiesner, B. P., & Sheard, N. M. (1933) *Maternal behavior in the rat*. London: Oliver and Boyd.   [110, 111, 112, 117]

Wilcoxon, H. C. (1952) "Abnormal fixation" and learning. *J. exp. Psychol.* 44, 324–333.   [428]

Wilder, C. E. (1937) Selection of rachitic and antirachitic diets in the rat. *J. comp. physiol. Psychol.* 24, 547–577.   [229]

Wilkinson, R. T. (1960) Effects of sleep-deprivation on performance and muscle tension. In Wolstenholme, G. E. W., & O'Connor, Maeve (Eds.) *Ciba Foundation symposium on the nature of sleep*. Boston: Little, Brown and Co., pp. 329–336.   [172, 173]

Williams, C. D., & Kuchta, J. C. (1957) Exploratory behavior in two mazes with dissimilar alternatives. *J. comp. physiol. Psychol.* 50, 509–513.   [291, 293]

Williams, H. L., Lubin, A., & Goodnow, J. J. (1959) Impaired performance with acute sleep loss. *Psychol. Monog.* 73, No. 14.   [171, 173]

Williams, S. B. (1938) Resistance to extinction as a function of the number of reinforcements. *J. exp. Psychol.* 23, 506–522.   [530]

Wilm, E. C. (1925) *The theories of instinct. A study in the history of psychology*. New Haven: Yale University Press.   [24]

Windelband, W. (1956) *History of ancient philosophy* (trans. from 2nd German ed. [1893] by Cushman, H. E.). New York: Dover.   [21, 23, 28, 32]

Winnick, Wilma A. (1950) The discriminative function of drive-stimuli independent of the action of the drive as motivation. *Amer. J. Psychol.* 63, 196–205.   [265]

Winsor, A. L. (1930) The effect of dehydration on parotid secretion. *Amer. J Psychol.* 42, 602–607.   [248]

Winterbottom, M. R. (1958) The relation of need for achievement to learning experiences in independence and mastery. In Atkinson, J. W. (Ed.), *Motives in fantasy, action and society*. New York: Van Nostrand, pp. 453–478.   [764]

Wisdom, J. O. (1951) The hypothesis of cybernetics. *Brit. J. Phil. Sci.* 2, 1–24. [342, 344]

Wittels, F. (1924) *Sigmund Freud: His personality, his teaching and his school*. New York: Dodd, Mead.   [593]

Wittels, F. (1931) *Freud and his time*. New York: Liveright.   [593]

Wolf, A. V. (1958) *Thirst: Physiology of the urge to drink and problems of water lack*. Springfield, Ill.: Charles C. Thomas.   [245, 246, 247, 248, 249, 250, 251, 252, 253, 255, 256, 257, 258, 684]

Wolfe, J. B. (1936) Effectiveness of token rewards for chimpanzees. *Comp. psychol. Monogr.* 12, No. 5, Whole No. 60.   [474, 563, 564, 572]

Wolfe, J. B. (1939) An exploratory study of foodstoring in rats. *J. comp. physiol. Psychol.* 28, 97–108.   [122, 124]

Wolfe, J. B., & Kaplon, M. D. (1941) Effect of amount of reward and consummative activity on learning in chickens. *J. comp. physiol. Psychol.* 31, 353–361. [553, 554]

Wolff, H. G. (1953) Life situations, emotions and bodily disease. In Whitehorn, J. C., et al. *Symposium on stress.* Army Med. Serv. Grad. Sch. Washington, D.C.: Walter Reed Army Med. Cent., pp. 132–136. [447]

Wolff, H. G., & Wolf, S. (1958) *Pain* (2nd ed.) Springfield, Ill.: Charles C. Thomas. [260]

Wolfle, D., Buxton, C. E, Cofer, C N., Gustad, J. W., McKeachie, W. J., & Mac-Leod, R. B. (1952) *Improving undergraduate instruction in psychology.* New York: Macmillan. [2]

Wolpe, J. (1958) *Psychotherapy by reciprocal inhibition.* Stanford, Calif.: Stanford University Press. [157]

Wolstenholme, G. E. W., & O'Connor, Maeve (Eds.) (1960) *Ciba Foundation symposium on the nature of sleep.* Boston: Little, Brown and Co. [165]

Wood-Gush, D. G. M. (1960) A study of sex drive of two strains of cockerels through three generations. *Anim. Behav.* 8, 43–53. [188]

Woodworth, R. S. (1918) *Dynamic psychology.* New York: Columbia University Press. [40, 43, 44, 571, 581, 598]

Woodworth, R. S. (1938) *Experimental psychology.* New York: Holt. [377, 382]

Woodworth, R. S. (1958) *Dynamics of behavior.* New York: Holt. [2, 271]

Woodworth, R. S., & Marquis, D. G. (1947) *Psychology* (5th ed.) New York: Holt. [286]

Woodworth, R. S., & Schlosberg, H. (1954) *Experimental psychology* (rev. ed.) New York: Holt. [140, 152, 153, 286]

Worchel, P. (1957) Catharsis and the relief of hostility. *J. abn. soc. Psychol.* 55, 238–243. [757]

Wright, J. H. (1963) A test for acquired appetitive drive. *Amer. Psychologist* 18, 417 (Abstr.). [834]

Wrightsman, L. (1959) The effects of small-group membership on level of concern. Unpubl. doctoral dissert., University of Minnesota. [699]

Wundt, W. (1897) *Outlines of psychology* (trans. by Judd, C. H.). Leipzig: W. Engelmann; New York: G. E. Stechert. [47]

Wundt, W. (1902) *Grundzüge der physiologischen Psychologie* (5th ed.) Vol. II. Leipzig: W. Engelmann. [382]

Wyckoff, L. B., Sidowski, J., & Chambliss, D. J. (1958) An experimental study of the relationship between secondary reinforcing and cue effects of a stimulus. *J. comp. physiol. Psychol.* 51, 103–109. [565]

Yacorzynski, G. K. (1942) Degree of effort: III. Relationship to the level of aspiration. *J. exp. Psychol.* 30, 407–413. [773]

Yamaguchi, H. G. (1951) Drive (D) as a function of hours of hunger (h). *J. exp. Psychol.* 42, 108–117. [531]

Yarrow, L. J. (1948) The effect of antecedent frustration on projective play. *Psychol. Monog.* 62, Whole No. 293. [756]

Yarrow, L. J. (1954) The relationship between nutritive sucking experiences in infancy and non-nutritive sucking in childhood. *J. genet. Psychol.* 84, 149–162. [114]

Yerkes, R. M. (1934) Suggestibility in chimpanzee. *J. abn. soc. Psychol.* 5, 271–282. [243]

Yerkes, R. M., & Dodson, J. D. (1908) The relation of strength of stimulus to rapidity of habit-formation. *J. comp. neurol. Psychol.* 18, 459–482. [521, 523]

Yerkes, R. M., & Elder, J. H. (1936) Oestrus, receptivity and mating in the chimpanzee. *Comp. psychol. Monog.* 13, 1–39. [190, 196]

Yerkes, R. M., & Yerkes, A. W. (1929) *The great apes.* New Haven: Yale University Press.   [290]

Yoakum, C. S. (1909) Some experiments upon the behavior of squirrels. *J. comp. neurol. Psychol.* 19, 541–568.   [132]

Young, P. T. (1936) *Motivation of behavior: The fundamental determinants of human and animal activity.* New York: Wiley.   [56, 117, 238, 264, 776]

Young, P. T. (1941) The experimental analysis of appetite. *Psychol. Bull.* 38, 129–164.   [229, 230, 234, 370]

Young, P. T. (1943) *Emotion in man and animal.* New York: Wiley.   [367, 391]

Young, P. T. (1947) Studies of food preference, appetite and dietary habit: VII. Palatability in relation to learning and performance. *J. comp. physiol. Psychol.* 40, 37–72.   [552]

Young, P. T. (1948a) Appetite, palatability and feeding habit: A critical review. *Psychol. Bull.* 45, 289–320.   [230, 243, 370]

Young, P. T. (1948b) Studies of food preference, appetite and dietary preference: VIII. Food-seeking drives, palatability and the law of effect. *J. comp. physiol. Psychol.* 41, 269–300.   [229, 552]

Young, P. T. (1949a) Emotion as disorganized response—A reply to Professor Leeper. *Psychol. Rev.* 56, 184–191.   [369]

Young, P. T. (1949b) Food-seeking drive, affective process and learning. *Psychol. Rev.* 56, 98–121.   [234, 319, 329, 370, 371–372, 373]

Young, P. T. (1952) The role of hedonic processes in the organization of behavior. *Psychol. Rev.* 59, 249–262.   [370, 373]

Young, P. T. (1954) The place of hedonic processes in the theory of drive. Paper presented in Symposium on Drive, American Psychological Association meetings, New York, September 1954.   [370, 372]

Young, P. T. (1955) The role of hedonic processes in motivation. In Jones, M. R. (Ed.) *Nebraska symposium on motivation, 1955.* Lincoln: University of Nebraska Press, pp. 193–238.   [232, 233, 234, 258, 370, 373]

Young, P. T. (1959) The role of affective processes in learning and motivation. *Psychol. Rev.* 66, 104–125.   [234, 370]

Young, P. T. (1961) *Motivation and emotion. A survey of the determinants of human and animal activity.* New York: Wiley.   [2, 7, 12, 229, 230, 295, 305, 319, 335, 370, 391, 417]

Young, P. T., & Chaplin, J. P. (1945) Studies of food preference, appetite and dietary habit: III. Palatability and appetite in relation to bodily need. *Comp. psychol. Monog.* 18, No. 3, 1–45.   [232, 319]

Young, P. T., & Greene, J. T. (1953) Quantity of food ingested as a measure of relative acceptability. *J. comp. physiol. Psychol.* 46, 288–294.   [233]

Young, P. T., Heyer, A. W., & Richey, H. W. (1952) Drinking patterns in the rat following water deprivation and subcutaneous injections of sodium chloride. *J. comp. physiol. Psychol.* 45, 90–95.   [250]

Young, P. T., & Richey, H. W. (1952) Diurnal drinking patterns in the rat. *J. comp. physiol. Psychol.* 45, 80–89.   [257]

Young, P. T., & Shuford, E. H. (1954) Intensity, duration and repetition of hedonic processes as related to acquisition of motives. *J. comp. physiol. Psychol.* 47, 298–305.   [555]

Young, P. T., & Shuford, E. H. (1955) Quantitative control of motivation through sucrose solutions of different concentrations. *J. comp. physiol. Psychol.* 48, 114–118.   [555]

Young, W. C. (Ed.) (1961a) *Sex and internal secretions* (3rd ed.) 2 vols. Baltimore: Williams and Wilkins.   [175]

Young, W. C. (1961b) The hormones and mating behavior. In Young, W. C. (Ed.) *Sex and internal secretions* (3rd ed.) 2 vols. Baltimore: Williams and Wilkins, pp. 1173–1289.   [177, 178, 179, 185, 197]

Young, W. C., Boling, J. L., & Blandau, R. J. (1941) The vaginal smear picture, sexual receptivity and the time of ovulation in the albino rat. *Anat. Rec.* **80,** 37–45. [189]

Zanchetti, A. (1962) Somatic functions of the nervous system. *Ann. rev. Physiol.* **24,** 287–324. [402]

Zander, A. F. (1944) A study of experimental frustration. *Psychol. Monog.* **56,** No. 3. Whole No. 256. [418, 751]

Zeaman, D. (1949) Response latency as a function of the amount of reinforcement. *J. exp. Psychol.* **39,** 466–483. [385, 489, 553, 554]

Zeaman, D., & House, Betty J. (1950) Response latency at zero drive after varying numbers of reinforcements *J. exp. Psychol.* **40,** 570–583. [531, 535]

Zeigarnik, Bluma (1927) Über das Behalten von erledigten und unerledigten Handlungen. *Psychol. Forsch.* **9,** 1–85. [317, 362, 737, 782, 783]

Zeigler, H. P. (1957) Electrical stimulation of the brain and the psychophysiology of learning and motivation. *Psychol. Bull.* **54,** 363–382. [544]

Zeller, A. F. (1950a) An experimental analogue of repression: I. Historical summary. *Psychol. Bull.* **47,** 39–51. [363, 654, 785]

Zeller, A. F. (1950b) An experimental analogue of repression. II: The effect of individual failure and success on memory measured by relearning. *J. exp. Psychol.* **40,** 411–422. [363, 785]

Zeller, A. F. (1951) An experimental analogue of repression. III: The effect of induced failure and success on memory measured by recall. *J. exp. Psychol.* **42,** 32–38. [363, 785]

Zilboorg, G., & Henry, G. W. (1941) *A history of medical psychology.* New York: W. W. Norton. [28, 49, 50]

Zimbardo, P. G. (1958) The effects of early avoidance training and rearing conditions upon the sexual behavior of the male rat. *J. comp. physiol. Psychol.* **51,** 764–769. [196]

Zimbardo, P. G., & Miller, N. E. (1958) Facilitation of exploration by hunger in rats. *J. comp. physiol. Psychol.* **51,** 43–46. [291]

Zimbardo, P. G., & Montgomery, K. C. (1957a) Effects of "free-environment" rearing upon exploratory behavior. *Psychol. Reports* **3,** 589–594. [292, 294]

Zimbardo, P. G., & Montgomery, K. C. (1957b) The relative strengths of consummatory responses in hunger, thirst, and exploratory drive. *J. comp. physiol. Psychol.* **50,** 504–508. [257, 290, 291]

Zubek, J. P. (1951) Effects of cortical lesions upon the hoarding behavior in rats. *J. comp. physiol. Psychol.* **44,** 310–319. [126]

Zubek, J. P., Sansom, Wilma, & Prysiaznuik, A. (1960) Intellectual changes during prolonged perceptual isolation (darkness and silence). *Canad. J. Psychol.* **14,** 233–243. [281, 282, 283]

Zuckerman, M. (1955) The effect of frustration on the perception of neutral and aggressive words. *J. Person.* **23,** 407–422. [751]

Subject Index

(*Note:* Major treatments, section headings, and extensive discussions of a topic are indicated by use of italicized numbers)

938

anger, 369, 395, 423, 429, 449, 493, 497, 639, 745–747, 749, 751–756, 759
animism, 20
anorexia, 220
anticipation, 261, 300, 316–318, 381–382, 427, 443, 476, 499, 513, 585, 619, 819–825, 831, 833, 834, 836, 837–838
anticipation-arousal mechanism (see anticipation-invigoration mechanism)
anticipation-invigoration mechanism (AIM) 822, 824, 829, 830, 832, 833, 834, 835, 836, 837–838
anticipatory goal reaction, 374, 420–422, 475–476, 562
antidepressant drugs (see drugs)
anxiety, 134, 135, 196, 300, 316, 318, 324, 328, 375, 388, 390, 393, 398, 412, 436, 440, 443, 449–452, 459–463, 499–500, 514, 524–525, 534, 537–538, 567, 578–580, 583–587, 610, 615, 617, 618–624, 630, 633–635, 639, 641–642, 647, 653, 660, 664, 675, 693, 701–714, 728, 743–745, 758, 763, 768, 777, 784, 786, 797, 799, 816, 835
 physiological measures of (see autonomic responses)
anxiety reduction, 90, 427, 432–433, 700, 710
aortic arch, 170
apathy, 143
aphagia, 219–221
aphasia, 355, 593
appetite, 66, 204–206, 212, 221, 319, 375, 507, 513
 sex as, 175, 197–198
 perverted, 312
 vs. drive, 175
appetitive behavior, 62, 64, 65, 68–69, 74, 488, 599
appetitive drives, 523–524, 580
approach-avoidance (see conflict, approach-avoidance)
approach behavior, 238, 375, 382, 549, 601, 831
approval, 516
Aquinas, Thomas, 22–24
Arapesh, 569
arbitrariness, 781
archetypes, 626
Aristippus of Cyrene, 28–29
Aristotle, 21–25, 40, 52, 55, 205, 357, 659
arousal, 8, 90, 140, 157, 159, 172–173, 263, 300–301, 331–332, 334, 354, 364, 370, 376, 393, 396, 399, 407–410, 419, 451, 453, 455, 508, 534, 538, 641, 712, 714,

811, 822–825, 828, 831–832, 834–835, 837–838 (see also activation excitement)
affective, 371, 373, 528, 831–832
differential, 800
emotional, 578, 641, 703, 831, 836
experimental, 715–762, 786, 791, 797, 798–801
physiological, 369, 397–398
sexual, 177, 180, 187, 190, 196–200, 208, 823 (see also sexual arousal mechanism)
situational, 801–802
arousal function, inverted U-shaped, 393–394, 396, 453
arousal index (AI), 331
arousal-inhibitory processes, central, 146, 150, 167
arterial anoxemia, 168
ascending reticular activation system (ARAS) 400–404, 408–409
aspiration, 5, 308, 797 (see also level of aspiration)
assimilation, 388
association, in learning and thinking, 48, 52, 380–381, 483, 506, 512
association disturbances, 325
associations, emotional, 325
ataxia, 355
atmospheric pressure, 170
atropine, 246–247
attention, 139, 141–142, 145, 286, 299, 387, 398, 404, 511, 783
attitude, 5, 386–387, 458, 499, 502, 650, 771, 785, 787, 803, 805, 836
auditory fatigue, 135
auditory flutter, 143
Augustine, 22, 23, 25, 659
authority, 423
autoeroticism, 178, 417, 687 (see also masturbation)
autokinetic phenomenon, 695
autonomic nervous system, 305, 306, 330, 376, 394, 396, 399, 445–446, 453, 460, 501 (see also nervous system, sympathetic and parasympathetic)
autonomic responses, 708–709, 714, 838 (see also measurement, physiological)
autonomy, 669, 670, 675
autonomy apparatus, primary and secondary (see ego apparatus)
autophagia, 312
aversions, 219, 228, 242, 280, 488, 491, 507
aversive stimulation, 416, 448–449, 525, 537, 548, 573, 578–580